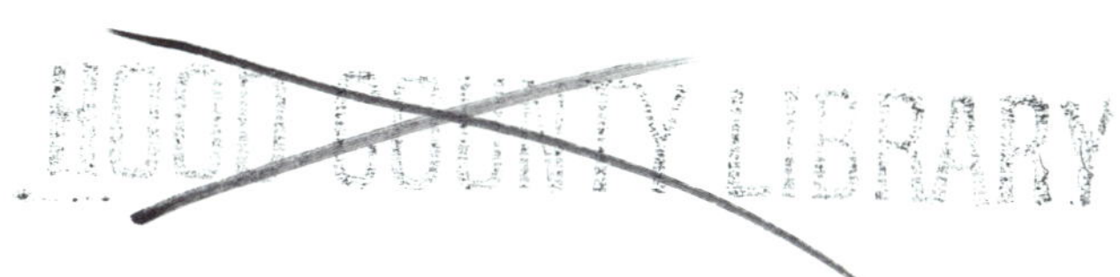

"Knowledge is of two kinds. We know a subject ourselves, or we know where we can find information upon it."

JAMES BOSWELL
THE LIFE OF SAMUEL JOHNSON, 1791

The Complete Small Truck Cost Guide

1993 Edition

Credits

Publisher
Peter Levy

Editor
Steve Gross

Text Editor
Peter Bohr

Editorial Staff
Vibha Bansal
Cheryl Ford Smith
Jamison J. Redding

Information Director
Charles A. Donaldson

Database Manager
Donald J. Oates

Database Supervisor
Deborah L. Eldridge

Database/Analysis
Jennifer Chu
Joannie M. Donaldson
Gary Grunwald
Dean Mello
Larry Montalvo
Anh Nguyen
Timothy Nugent
Timothy William Oates
Kristina A. Olson
Luiz Payne

Production
William Analla
Anna-Marie S. Herreria
Victoria Liou
Martha Flint Topor

Programming Manager
Timothy H. Denney

Programming
Stephen Smith

Art Director
Vincent Paul Mendolia

Photo Scanning
Gary Eldridge

Cover Photography
Jamie Krueger

Public Relations
Benton McMillian-Gordon

Thanks

A special thank you to:

Mr. Bryce Benjamin
Mr. Jonathan Bulkeley, Money Magazine
Mr. Walter Burns
Mr. Louis R. Cooper, Automotive Alliance LTD.
Mr. John Dinkel
Mr. Christopher L. Ford, Western National Warranty Corporation
Ms. Carol Jaech, Santa Clara County Library System
Mr. Tom Kempner
Mr. Wayne Oler
Mr. Ron Raymond
Mr. Steve Wood, GE Capital Fleet Services

Thanks to the public relations and marketing departments of all the manufacturers whose vehicles are represented in this book for their willingness to provide information and answer questions.

Thanks to the people of the United States Government, Department of Commerce, Department of Energy, and Department of Transportation for their information and support.

Thanks to Linotext.

Thanks to the technical support staff at ACI US for their technical information.

Finally, a special thanks to all of our customers for making this book a success.

Ordering Information

Are you in the market for a subcompact, compact, midsize, large, sport, or luxury car? If so, pick up a copy of *The Complete Car Cost Guide.*

Copies of *The Complete Small Truck Cost Guide* and *The Complete Car Cost Guide* may be ordered directly from the publisher.

Orders should be sent to IntelliChoice, Inc., 1135 So. Saratoga/Sunnyvale Rd., San Jose, CA 95129.

Phone orders may be placed toll-free at 1-800-CAR-BOOK (1-800-227-2665). Call (408) 554-8711 for current information on pricing and availability of these books.

The Complete Small Truck Cost Guide
(ISBN 0-941443-16-7)

The Complete Car Cost Guide
(ISBN 0-941443-15-9)

Are you interested in a custom report comparing any two vehicles of your choice?
See the advertisement in the center of this book for details.

Notice

This book was compiled solely by IntelliChoice, Inc. IntelliChoice is an independent information research firm not sponsored by or associated with any automobile manufacturer. IntelliChoice has conducted research to obtain the information contained in *The Complete Small Truck Cost Guide* in the manner IntelliChoice considers to be commercially reasonable from sources IntelliChoice considers to be reliable. IntelliChoice has made no independent verification of the accuracy of the information it has received. *The Complete Small Truck Cost Guide* contains and is based upon the information actually known by IntelliChoice at the time the book was compiled. IntelliChoice makes no guaranty, warranty or representation with respect to the completeness, adequacy or accuracy of the information contained in *The Complete Small Truck Cost Guide* other than as expressly set forth herein. All prices and specifications are subject to change without notice.

Restrictions

Copyrights

Production

This book was derived from IntelliCar™, a comprehensive automotive database developed with 4th Dimension® version 3.0 from ACI US Inc. 4th Dimension 3.0 is the most advanced relational database available for Macintosh computers. For information about 4th Dimension, contact ACI US at 408-252-4444.

This book was designed and produced using Macintosh® Quadra computer systems. Every page was printed directly onto film negatives. Photos were scanned using Adobe Photoshop® on a Microtek® scanning system.

Library of Congress Catalog Card Number: 88-83220

IntelliChoice, Inc.
1135 South Saratoga/Sunnyvale Road
San Jose, California 95129-3660
Phone (408) 554-8711
Fax (408) 253-4822

Printed and bound in the United States of America

To Our Continuing Readers

We have made a few changes to our cost calculations that may interest our continuing readers. The changes are as follows:

Engines

Engine size is now also considered when determining which engine is used on a particular model for ownership cost calculations. In previous editions, horsepower was the only criterion.

See page 53A for a more complete explanation.

Repairs

The figures used for the "Repair" cost category are now based on service contract pricing. This allows more vehicles to have complete repair profiles, but results in slightly higher repair costs than in prior editions of this book.

For further explanation of this approach, please see page 61A.

From the Publisher

Welcome to the fifth annual edition of *The Complete Small Truck Cost Guide*, the only publication that helps you evaluate how much a pickup truck, van, wagon, or utility vehicle really "costs."

The fundamental principle of this book—that it's not the purchase price, but the amount it takes to own and operate a new vehicle that determines its true value—is more relevant than ever in 1993.

From a price perspective, 1992 was a buyer's dream. The economy was weak and fewer people were buying new vehicles. Manufacturers, anxious to move inventory, responded by making great deals easily available to the fortunate few who were ready to buy.

This year, the economy is showing sparks of life, and more people are buying new vehicles. Consequently, manufacturers are making more profitable deals. They can now afford to promote features other than price, and are equipping more models with newer safety and convenience features. While it's definitely a step in the right direction, it makes selecting a vehicle more difficult. With more to choose from, it's harder to choose.

What this means is, buyers who want to strike a great bargain in 1993 must be more than just lucky. They must be prepared.

That's where *The Complete Small Truck Cost Guide* can help.

This book is designed to prepare shoppers like you to choose and buy a new vehicle. To get you started, we've divided the book into three distinct areas. The first, AutoExplorer™, will help you select vehicles that fit your taste and budget. The second area guides you through selecting and purchasing a new truck. Finally, the third section presents a comprehensive analysis of each vehicle, helping you evaluate and compare all your potential choices.

While it may not be easy to find the vehicle that's exactly right for you, I'm confident this book will help inform and prepare you to make an intelligent decision.

Good luck with your search!

And thank you for your ongoing and enthusiastic support of this book. We will always work hard to earn your respect.

Sincerely,

Peter S. Levy
Publisher

Short Cuts

Figures

1993 AutoExplorer™

All prices listed below are based on the manufacturer's suggested retail price and do not include factory or dealer installed options. Actual prices may vary due to rebates and local dealer markups.

Pickups	Under $12,500	$12,501-$15,000	$15,001-$17,500	Over $17,500
Chevrolet	C1500 Work Truck S-10 S-10 EL S-10 Maxi Cab (Ext.)	C1500 C2500 K1500 Work Truck (4) S-10 4WD (4) S-10 EL 4WD (4)	C1500 (Ext.) C2500 (Ext.) C3500 K1500 (4) K1500 (Ext.,4) K2500 (4) S-10 Maxi Cab 4WD (Ext.,4)	C1500 454 SS C3500 (Ext.) C3500 Crew Cab (Ext.) K2500 (Ext.,4) K3500 (4) K3500 (Ext.,4) K3500 Crew Cab (Ext.,4)
Dodge	Dakota Dakota S Dakota Sport Power Ram 50 (4) Ram 50 Ram 50 SE	Dakota Club Cab (Ext.) Dakota Sport 4WD (4) Ram D150 Ram D250	Dakota 4WD (4) Dakota Club Cab 4WD (Ext.,4) Ram D150 Club Cab (Ext.) Ram D250 Club Cab (Ext.) Ram D350 Ram W150 (4)	Ram D350 Club Cab (Ext.) Ram W150 Club Cab (Ext.,4) Ram W250 (4) Ram W250 Club Cab (Ext.,4) Ram W350 (4) Ram W350 Club Cab (Ext.,4)
Ford	F150 Styleside S Ranger STX Ranger XL Ranger XL SuperCab (Ext.) Ranger XLT Ranger XLT SuperCab (Ext.)	F150 Flareside XL F150 Styleside S 4WD (4) F150 Styleside XL F150 Styleside XL SC (Ext.) F250 Styleside XL Ranger STX 4WD (4) Ranger STX SuperCab (Ext.) Ranger XL 4WD (4) Ranger XLT 4WD (4)	F150 Flareside XL 4WD (4) F150 Flareside XL SC (Ext.) F150 Flareside XL SC 4WD (Ext.,4) F150 Styleside XL 4WD (4) F150 Styleside XL SC 4WD (Ext.,4) F250 Styleside XL SC (Ext.) F350 Styleside XL Ranger STX SuperCab 4WD (Ext.,4) Ranger XL SuperCab 4WD (Ext.,4) Ranger XLT SuperCab 4WD (Ext.,4)	F250 Styleside XL 4WD (4) F250 Styleside XL SC 4WD (Ext.,4) F350 Styleside XL 4WD (4) F350 Styleside XL Crew Cab (Ext.) F350 Styleside XL Crew Cab 4WD (Ext.,4) F350 Styleside XL SuperCab (Ext.)
GMC	Sierra C1500 Special Sonoma Sonoma Club Coupe (Ext.) Sonoma Special	Sierra C1500 Sierra C2500 Sierra K1500 Special (4) Sonoma 4WD (4) Sonoma Special 4WD (4)	Sierra C1500 (Ext.) Sierra C2500 (Ext.) Sierra C3500 Sierra K1500 (4) Sierra K2500 (4) Sonoma Club Coupe 4WD (Ext.,4)	Sierra C3500 (Ext.) Sierra C3500 Crew Cab (Ext.) Sierra K1500 (Ext.,4) Sierra K2500 (Ext.,4) Sierra K3500 (4) Sierra K3500 (Ext.,4) Sierra K3500 Crew Cab (Ext.,4)
Mazda	B2200 B2200 Cab Plus (Ext.) B2600i 4WD (4) B2600i Cab Plus (Ext.)	B2600i Cab Plus 4WD (Ext.,4)		
Mitsubishi	Mighty Max Mighty Max Macrocab (Ext.)	Mighty Max 4WD (4)		
Nissan	King Cab (Ext.) Pickup Pickup V6	King Cab 4WD (Ext.,4) King Cab SEV6 (Ext.) Pickup 4WD (4)	King Cab SEV6 4WD (Ext.,4)	
Toyota	Pickup Pickup DX Xtracab DX (Ext.)	Pickup DX 4WD (4) Pickup DX V6 4WD (4) T100 T100 One Ton Xtracab DX 4WD (Ext.,4) Xtracab DX V6 (Ext.) Xtracab SR5 V6 (Ext.)	T100 4WD (4) T100 SR5 Xtracab DX V6 4WD (Ext.,4)	T100 SR5 4WD (4) Xtracab SR5 V6 4WD (Ext.,4)

W—Wagon   Ext — Extended Cab   4—4-Wheel Drive

All prices listed below are based on the manufacturer's suggested retail price and do not include factory or dealer installed options. Actual prices may vary due to rebates and local dealer markups.

Full-Size Vans	Under $16,000	$16,001-$18,000	$18,001-$20,000	Over $20,000
Chevrolet	G10 Cargo Van G20 Cargo Van G30 Cargo Van	G10 Sportvan G20 Sportvan G30 Cargo Van Heavy Duty	G30 Sportvan G30 Sportvan Heavy Duty	
Dodge	Ram Van B150 Ram Van B250	Ram Van B250 Maxivan Ram Van B350 Ram Wagon B150 Ram Wagon B250	Ram Van B350 Maxivan Ram Wagon B250 Maxiwagon Ram Wagon B350 Ram Wagon B350 Maxiwagon	
Ford	Econoline E150 Econoline E250	Club Wagon Custom Econoline E250 Super Econoline E350 Econoline E350 Super	Club Wagon Custom Heavy Duty	Club Wagon Chateau Club Wagon Chateau Heavy Duty Club Wagon Custom Super Club Wagon XLT Club Wagon XLT Heavy Duty Club Wagon XLT Super
GMC	G1500 Vandura G2500 Vandura G3500 Vandura	G1500 Rally Wagon G2500 Rally Wagon G3500 Vandura Heavy Duty	G3500 Rally Wagon G3500 Rally Wagon Heavy Duty	

Mini-Vans	Under $16,000	$16,001-$18,000	$18,001-$21,000	Over $21,000
Chevrolet	Astro Astro Cargo Van Astro Cargo Van Extended Lumina APV	Astro AWD (4) Astro Cargo Van AWD (4) Astro Cargo Van Ext. AWD (4) Astro Extended Lumina APV LS	Astro Extended AWD (4)	
Chrysler				Town & Country Town & Country AWD (4)
Dodge	Caravan Caravan Cargo Van	Caravan Cargo Van Extended Caravan SE Grand Caravan Grand Caravan SE	Caravan LE Caravan SE AWD Grand Caravan SE AWD (4)	Caravan LE AWD (4) Grand Caravan LE Grand Caravan LE AWD (4)
Ford	Aerostar Cargo Van Aerostar Cargo Van Extended Aerostar XL Aerostar XL Extended	Aerostar Cargo Van 4WD (4) Aerostar Cargo Van Ext. 4WD (4) Aerostar XL 4WD (4)	Aerostar XL Ext. 4WD (4) Aerostar XLT Aerostar XLT Extended	Aerostar Eddie Bauer Aerostar Eddie Bauer 4WD (4) Aerostar Eddie Bauer Ext. Aerostar Eddie Bauer Ext. 4WD (4) Aerostar XLT 4WD (4) Aerostar XLT Ext. 4WD (4)
GMC	Safari Cargo Van Safari Cargo Van XT Safari SLX	Safari Cargo Van AWD (4) Safari Cargo Van XT AWD (4) Safari SLX XT	Safari SLX AWD (4) Safari SLX XT AWD (4)	
Mazda		MPV Wagon MPV Wagon Van		MPV Wagon 4WD (4)
Mercury		Villager GS		Villager LS
Nissan		Quest Cargo Van Quest XE		Quest GXE
Oldsmobile			Silhouette	

W—Wagon Ext — Extended Cab 4—4-Wheel Drive

All prices listed below are based on the manufacturer's suggested retail price and do not include factory or dealer installed options. Actual prices may vary due to rebates and local dealer markups.

Mini-Vans (Cont'd)	Under $16,000	$16,001-$18,000	$18,001-$21,000	Over $21,000
Plymouth	Voyager	Grand Voyager Grand Voyager SE Voyager SE	Grand Voyager SE AWD (4) Voyager LE Voyager SE AWD (4)	Grand Voyager LE Grand Voyager LE AWD (4) Voyager LE AWD (4)
Pontiac		Trans Sport SE		
Toyota			Previa DX	Previa All-Trac DX (4) Previa All-Trac LE (4) Previa LE
Volkswagen		Eurovan CL	Eurovan GL	Eurovan MV

Utility	Under $15,000	$15,001-$19,000	$19,001-$22,000	Over $22,000
Chevrolet		S-10 Blazer S-10 Blazer 4WD (4)	Blazer (4) Suburban C1500 Suburban C2500 Suburban K1500 (4)	Suburban K2500 (4)
Dodge		Ramcharger AD150 S	Ramcharger AD150 Ramcharger AW150 (4) Ramcharger AW150 S (4)	
Ford		Explorer Sport Explorer XL	Bronco Custom (4) Explorer Sport 4WD (4) Explorer XL 4WD (4) Explorer XLT Explorer XLT 4WD (4)	Bronco Eddie Bauer (4) Bronco XLT (4) Explorer Eddie Bauer Explorer Eddie Bauer 4WD (4)
Geo	Tracker Hardtop 4WD (4) Tracker LSi Hardtop 4WD (4) Tracker LSI Soft Top 4WD (4) Tracker Soft Top Tracker Soft Top 4WD (4)			
GMC		Jimmy Jimmy 4WD (4)	Suburban C1500 Suburban C2500 Suburban K1500 (4) Yukon (4)	Jimmy Typhoon 4WD (4) Suburban K2500 (4)
Jeep	Cherokee Cherokee 4WD (4) Wrangler (4) Wrangler S (4)	Cherokee Country Cherokee Country 4WD (4) Cherokee Sport Cherokee Sport 4WD (4) Wrangler Renegade (4) Wrangler Sahara (4)	Grand Cherokee 4WD (4) Grand Cherokee Laredo 4WD (4)	Grand Cherokee Limited 4WD (4) Grand Wagoneer 4WD (4)
Land Rover				Land Rover Defender 110 (4) Range Rover County (4) Range Rover County LWB (4)
Mazda		Navajo DX Navajo DX 4WD (4) Navajo LX	Navajo LX 4WD (4)	
Mitsubishi		Montero (4)	Montero RS (4)	Montero LS (4) Montero SR (4)
Nissan		Pathfinder XE-V6	Pathfinder XE-V6 4WD (4)	Pathfinder SE-V6 4WD (4)
Oldsmobile				Bravada (4)

W—Wagon Ext — Extended Cab 4—4-Wheel Drive

All prices listed below are based on the manufacturer's suggested retail price and do not include factory or dealer installed options. Actual prices may vary due to rebates and local dealer markups.

Utility (Cont'd)	*Under $15,000*	*$15,001-$18,000*	*$19,001-$22,000*	*Over $22,000*
Suzuki	Samurai JA Soft Top Samurai JL Soft Top (4) Sidekick JLX Hardtop (4) Sidekick JS Hardtop Sidekick JS Soft Top Sidekick JX Hardtop (4) Sidekick JX Soft Top (4)			
Toyota		4Runner SR5 4WD (4)	4Runner SR5 V6 4Runner SR5 V6 4WD (4)	Land Cruiser (4)

Wagons	*Under $12,000*	*$12,001-$15,000*	*$15,001-$19,000*	*Over $19,000*
Audi				100 CS Quattro (W,4)
BMW				525 i Touring (W)
Buick		Century Special (W)	Century Custom (W)	Roadmaster Estate Wagon (W)
Chevrolet	Cavalier RS (W) Cavalier VL (W)			Caprice Classic (W)
Eagle	Summit DL (W)	Summit AWD (W,4) Summit LX (W)		
Ford	Escort LX (W)		Taurus GL (W)	Taurus LX (W)
Honda			Accord LX (W)	Accord EX (W)
Mercedes Benz				300 TE (W) 300 TE 4Matic (W,4)
Mercury	Tracer (W)		Sable GS (W)	Sable LS (W)
Mitsubishi	Expo LRV (W)	Expo (W) Expo AWD (W,4) Expo LRV AWD (W,4) Expo LRV Sport (W)	Expo SP (W) Expo SP AWD (W,4)	
Oldsmobile		Cutlass Ciera Cruiser S (W)	Cutlass Ciera Cruiser SL (W)	
Plymouth	Colt Vista (W)	Colt Vista AWD (W,4) Colt Vista SE (W)		
Saturn	SW1 (W)	SW2 (W)		
Subaru	Loyale (W)	Loyale 4WD (W,4)	Legacy L (W) Legacy L AWD (W,4)	Legacy LS (W) Legacy LS AWD (W,4) Legacy LSi AWD (W,4) Legacy Touring Wagon AWD (W,4)
Toyota		Corolla DX (W)	Camry DX (W)	Camry LE (W) Camry LE V6 (W)
Volkswagen	Passat GL (W)			Passat GLX (W)
Volvo				240 (W) 940 (W) 940 Turbo (W) 960 (W)

W—Wagon   Ext — Extended Cab   4—4-Wheel Drive

Introduction

An inexpensive truck to buy could be expensive to own.

Do you want to get a good value the next time you buy a new truck? Of course. Why else would you be reading this book?

What does "good value" mean anyway? Most people think it means choosing a nice-looking, reliable truck, and negotiating the lowest possible price for it. So they trek through dealerships comparing truck features and prices.

This may be a reasonable sounding approach, but it doesn't have much to do with getting a good value. That's because ultimately a truck's value has less to do with its initial price than it does with its cost to own and operate.

You don't believe it? Let's take a closer look. The price you pay to buy a truck is not a cost. "Price" and "cost" are related, but there's a distinct difference between them. A truck's price is simply an amount of your hard-earned cash that you must exchange to own the vehicle. There's no expense involved at the time of the purchase because, at this point, the truck is still worth exactly what you just paid for it. If you paid the dealer $10,000, he or she will have the money, but you will have something of equal value — the truck.

Ah, but as soon as you slip behind the wheel, turn on the stereo, drive home, and park your new truck in the driveway hoping to attract envious glances from the neighbors, you'll start to run up a tab. The truck will begin to depreciate. It will use fuel. You'll have to pay insurance premiums, state fees and taxes, finance charges, and at some point down the road, repair bills. These are the vehicle's ownership costs. When you want the best value, it's more prudent to consider these costs than just the purchase price.

By the time the typical truck is five years old, the cost to own and operate it will exceed its original purchase price. Even more important, similarly priced trucks can have very different ownership costs over a five-year period *(See Figure 1)*. An inexpensive truck to buy could be expensive to own.

That's why it's important to understand ownership costs when you search for the truck that will truly be the best value.

The Complete Small Truck Cost Guide is unlike any other reference source. It's the only one that gives you a complete financial profile of today's new vehicles and detailed cost projections for five years into the future.

Figure 1

Ownership Cost Comparison

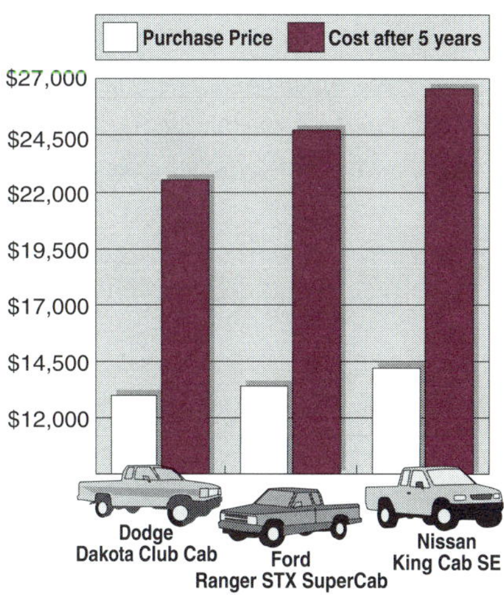

This graph illustrates how vehicles with a similar purchase price can have different ownership costs over time. In this example, the Nissan King Cab owner will spend about $1,500 more than the Ford Ranger owner and over $3,000 more than the Dodge Dakota owner in the first five years. (Prices are based on "Total Target Price" listed in the vehicle charts, beginning on page 1.)

Sources:

IntelliChoice, Inc. is not associated with any automobile manufacturer or supplier. We strive to be completely impartial in our analyses and conclusions. Our primary responsibility is to assist the new vehicle shopper.

The research used to compile the vehicle data and ratings in this book has been done in entirety by IntelliChoice, Inc. Where appropriate, we make use of information supplied by the United States Government, by automobile manufacturers, and by a variety of industry sources. If you have technical questions about any area of this book, please write to the Director of Research, IntelliChoice, Inc., 1135 S. Saratoga/Sunnyvale Road, San Jose, CA 95129.

Specifically, this book provides you with:

Detailed ownership costs. Allows you to compare the costs of owning different makes and models so you can choose the best value.

Expected annual costs for five years. Helps you budget your annual expenses.

Expected resale value for five years. Allows you to negotiate a favorable agreement if you plan to lease a truck.

Dealer cost and list price. Helps you to negotiate the best possible deal for your new truck.

Warranty information. Lets you see how well your truck is protected by the manufacturer.

Advice. Gives you tips on selecting options, on choosing a dealer, on maintaining your truck's resale value, on financing or leasing your new truck, and on selling your old vehicle.

Ratings. Lets you see at a glance which vehicles deliver the best overall value.

The Complete Small Truck Cost Guide is an economic guide. It doesn't offer subjective reviews of a vehicle's comfort, handling, or style. It doesn't list braking or zero-to-sixty miles-per-hour performance figures. Nor does it provide the results of government crash tests.

Of course performance, comfort, handling, style, and safety are important factors in buying a new vehicle. But then, if you can't afford to buy and operate the truck you want, nothing else really matters, does it?

Section One
Ownership Costs

Ownership Costs

Understanding ownership costs can save you money. Regardless of what you may read in new truck reviews or hear ads, it's not possible to know whether a vehicle is a good or a poor value until you learn about all the major ownership costs: depreciation, insurance, financing costs, maintenance, repairs, and more.

For example, a higher-priced vehicle that holds its value over the years may be a bargain compared to a lower-priced vehicle that plunges in value like Christmas tree ornaments on December 26th. In just one year, depreciation could eliminate the apparent initial advantage of the vehicle with the lower purchase price. However, even if the lower-priced vehicle holds its value well, it may still cost a fortune to insure. So which is the better value?

Here's a more specific example. You may be told that a particular vehicle, such as a Mitsubishi Mighty Max, is very reliable because it does not have frequent repair problems. Beware! Even though a Mitsubishi Mighty Max has a low expected repair cost, it only has average or below average costs in all other ownership cost areas. You cannot determine the overall value of a truck, or any savings you may realize in selecting one truck over another, without considering all the ownership costs. Information on overall economy is what this book provides.

All the major ownership costs can be divided into two categories: standing costs and running costs. Standing costs, also called fixed costs, are what you pay to own the vehicle whether you ever take it out of the driveway or not. Running costs, also called variable costs, are the expenses you incur as you use the vehicle.

Standing Costs

Standing costs include depreciation, insurance, financing, and various government fees. (We do not factor into our analysis the cost of garaging your truck, but if you live in Manhattan or downtown San Francisco, you should keep in mind that this expense can add substantially to your vehicle's standing costs.)

The good news about standing costs is that they usually decrease with time. Depreciation is less each year, insurance premiums may decline as the value of the truck decreases, state fees usually decrease on older trucks, and finance charges will be eliminated once you pay off the loan.

The seven major ownership categories:

- *Depreciation*
- *Insurance*
- *Financing*
- *State fees*
- *Fuel*
- *Repairs*
- *Maintenance*

Depreciation Tips

Before You Buy

• Choose a vehicle with low expected depreciation. Let the vehicle charts beginning on page 1 in this book be your guide.

• Select a popular, highly regarded model, or a vehicle from a prestigious automaker. Avoid offbeat or less well-known makes and models.

• Choose a vehicle from an automaker that doesn't frequently change body styles. If you are set on buying a vehicle that does have frequent style changes, make sure to buy soon after a change.

• Select a larger engine if it's an option offered on the vehicle you want. A larger engine generally adds to a vehicle's resale value.

• Select appropriate features and options for your geographic area. Vehicles in southern California or Florida are expected to have air conditioning, for instance. High-quality stereo sound systems almost always increase a vehicle's value. And keep in mind that pink trucks don't sell well anywhere.

• If a manufacturer is guaranteeing the resale value of a vehicle you are considering, make sure you understand exactly what's being guaranteed. For instance, how is the "guaranteed" resale value determined? How long is the guarantee? Do you have to buy the same vehicle in order to receive your guaranteed resale value?

• Find out if the vehicle you're considering has a "sister" model, a near-identical vehicle sold as a different brand or model. If possible, choose the one that holds its value better. For instance, the 1991 Mazda Navajo 4WD sold for more than its sister, the Ford Explorer 4WD, but the Explorer is worth more today.

Depreciation

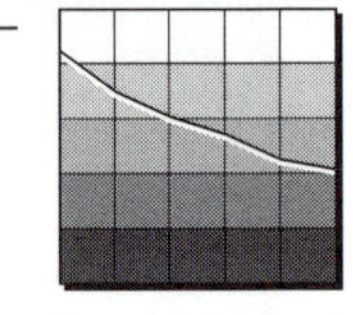

This is the big one — at least for most vehicles during the first few years they're on the road. In fact, some vehicles depreciate as much as 20 percent or more during the first year alone.

Depreciation is the amount something decreases in value over time. Although it's a very real cost, depreciation is tricky because you don't get a monthly bill for it. You don't continually dole out money from your pocket to pay depreciation as you do, for example, every time you visit your mechanic.

But, make no mistake about it; you will pay for depreciation when the time comes to sell your vehicle and buy another one. For instance, let's assume you purchase a truck in 1992 for $15,000. If you get tired of the old heap and unload it five years later for $5,000, you'll have spent $10,000 in depreciation to own the truck.

The cost of depreciation should be a primary factor in your choice of which vehicle to buy. If you expect to keep the vehicle five years or less, it may be the most important factor.

Not all vehicles depreciate as much or at the same rate. Often there's even a difference between two- and four-wheel drive versions of the same model. And why is this? It's one of life's little mysteries, but here are some likely reasons:

Vehicles that capture the public's fancy tend to hold their value. Many people would like to own a new Mercedes-Benz or Volvo, but few can afford to. So there's strong demand for used vehicles of these brands, which keeps resale values up.

When the price of a popular model increases, the price of used versions of the same vehicle may also rise. The price of a used vehicle is based, in part, upon the price of its new model. Therefore, when the price of a new model has a significant increase relative to other new vehicles, used versions of the same model tend to hold their value. However, this is not always true when all prices are rising. According to the *Wall Street Journal*, while new vehicle prices have risen an average of $3,000 since 1987, used vehicle prices rose from 1987 to 1991 an average of just $400.

Some manufacturers actively intervene in the used vehicle market to support the resale value of their vehicles. For example, some manufacturers have programs that guarantee the resale value of selected models. Also, most manufacturers have made changes to the ways they market their late-model fleet vehicles in an attempt to support resale values.

Quotas often result in higher prices for popular new vehicles, and eventually for used vehicles as well. Due to export quotas, many Japanese models are in perennial short supply. Basic supply and demand suggests that this will increase the prices of these vehicles, both in the new and used markets.

A model change can lower resale value. When a model is dropped or completely restyled by a manufacturer, trucks of that model already on the road are likely to decrease in value more than they would otherwise. For example, Dodge redesigned the Ram 50 Pickup for the 1988 model year. According to *Kelley Blue Book*, in December of 1988, a 1987 Ram 50 was only worth 79% of its original value. On the other hand, in December of 1989, a 1988 Ram 50 had retained 84% of its original value. The redesigned 1988 model held its value much better than the 1987 model.

A truck's depreciation will vary depending on whether the truck accumulates either very high or very low mileage for its age. The "normal" annual mileage range is generally considered to be between 10,000 and 15,000 miles.

The "base" model in a line-up usually holds its value better than the higher priced models. A "XLT" edition may cost several thousand dollars more than the base edition when new, but may have a resale value of just a few hundred dollars more after two or more years.

Figure 2

Depreciation Comparison

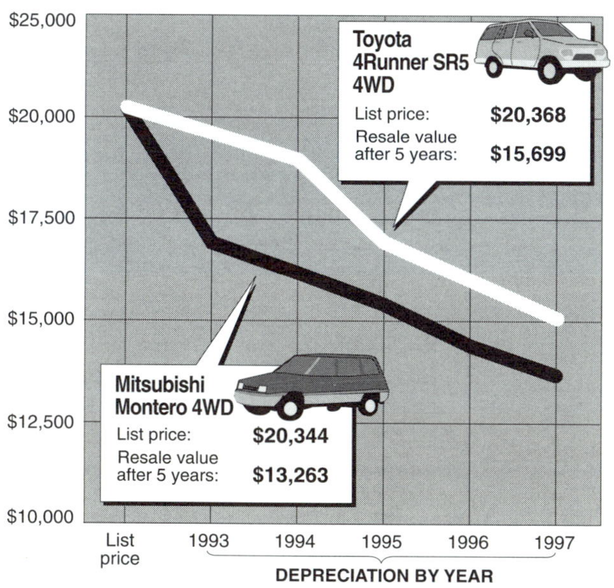

This graph illustrates how two vehicles with a similar purchase price have vastly different depreciation rates and, therefore, have substantially different resale values after 5 years. However, even though one van appears to be a better value than the other, you should not draw that conclusion until you have examined all of the major cost areas.

Depreciation Tips

Before You Buy *continued*

• Consider buying a one or two-year-old model, rather than brand new. Odd advice coming from a new truck book, but it could be worth the price of this book a hundred times over. Since depreciation expense is greatest in a vehicle's first year, you can save thousands of dollars by waiting a year. The best vehicles to purchase after a year are those that depreciate most in that first year. For instance, you may only save about $500 by buying a one-year-old Chevrolet Suburban, whereas you may save more than $3,000 by buying a one-year-old Dodge Ram Charger. The charts in this book show which models are best suited for this strategy.

• Maybe you shouldn't buy a new vehicle at all (See section "Keeping Your Old Truck vs. Buying a New One" on page 45A.)

After You've Bought

• Keep your truck longer. Vehicles typically depreciate the most during the first three years; after five years, depreciation will be minimal.

• When it comes time to sell your vehicle, don't trade it in to a dealer. You'll almost always get a higher price — and minimize depreciation — by selling it yourself to a private party.

• Perhaps most importantly, keep up the mechanical condition and appearance of your truck and save all receipts for maintenance work that you've done on your truck. Low mileage "cream puffs," no matter what make or model, will always have plenty of buyers and will command the highest resale value. (See maintenance tips on page 21A.)

Insurance Tips

Before You Buy

• *Make a package deal. When you insure more than one vehicle with the same company, you will usually qualify for a 10-25 percent discount off the total premium for each vehicle. And if you insure your home with the same company, you may get a discount of up to 15 percent off the total.*

• *Compare insurance costs before you buy. Use the charts in this book to compare different models.*

• *Ask your state insurance regulator for consumer information on auto insurance companies, particularly if you're considering purchasing insurance from an unfamiliar company. You can check with your local Better Business Bureau to see if any complaints have been filed against companies you are considering. (Appendix F on page 88A lists Better Business Bureau locations.) About 30 states provide price or complaint information on auto insurers, according to Consumer Insurance Interest Group. You can find the phone number of your insurance regulator by calling your state's Department of Motor Vehicles, listed in the white pages.*

Insurance

Ugh — insurance! The only thing worse than paying for it is not having it when you need it.

Insurance is the price you pay to protect yourself, your passengers, and your vehicle against unexpected losses. It's required by law and, if you've ever insured a vehicle, you know it makes up a formidable portion of your total ownership expense. In fact, the typical automobile insurance premium increased at almost twice the rate of other consumer prices during the last decade. Unlike depreciation, insurance is a very visible expense — your insurance bill is a regular visitor to your mailbox.

Although you pay a single auto insurance premium, you're actually protecting several entities: your vehicle (that's the collision and comprehensive part of your bill), and yourself and others (the bodily injury and property damage parts).

In most cases, where you live and the type of vehicle you own will determine the price of your collision and comprehensive coverage. The price of your bodily injury and property damage coverage (also known as "liability" coverage) depends on your driving record, as well as on who you are, where you live, and how frequently you drive your vehicle.

Figure 3

Insurance Coverages

Type of coverage	What it covers
Collision	Pays for damages to your vehicle that result from a collision with another vehicle or object.
Comprehensive	Pays for damages to your vehicle other than those caused in a collision (e.g. flood, fire, hail, theft, or vandalism).
Personal Liability	Pays claims against you, and covers the cost of legal defense if your vehicle damages property or injures or kills someone in an accident.
Property Damage	Pays for legal defense and claims if your vehicle damages someone else's property.
Medical Payments	Pays for medical expenses of the driver and passengers of your vehicle in an accident.
Un/Underinsured Motorist	Pays for injuries caused by an uninsured or hit-and-run driver.

Though the price of auto insurance is high, by shopping around, by eliminating coverage you don't need, and by taking no more than necessary on the rest, you may be able to trim your bill by hundreds of dollars.

Liability Coverage

(about 60% of your premium)

When it comes to insuring yourself against damage or harm to others, you certainly don't want to skimp, leaving yourself vulnerable to a lawsuit that could take away your assets. Most states require you to buy bodily injury and property damage liability coverage. While you may be able to satisfy the law with bodily injury coverage that pays $20,000 for each person you injure, up to $40,000 per accident, and property damage coverage that pays $5,000, these are minimum figures.

Most insurance advisors recommend bodily-injury coverage of at least $100,000 a person up to $300,000 an accident, and property damage coverage of $50,000. If your net worth is more than $300,000, you should carry coverage of $200,000 a person and $500,000 an accident, and perhaps an "umbrella" policy that will bolster coverage even further. A $1 million umbrella policy will typically add $120-$150 to your yearly bill.

You won't want to skimp on uninsured or underinsured motorist coverage. This pays for injuries to your passengers and for expenses health plans don't cover if you are involved in an accident with an uninsured driver. Keep in mind that one in ten drivers across the country doesn't have any auto insurance.

On the other hand, don't buy more coverage than your net worth requires. If you don't own a home and you've wiped out your bank account to put a down payment on a new Hyundai, you may not need that $1 million umbrella policy.

Collision and Comprehensive Coverage

(about 40% of your premium)

Many people can also save on other parts of their policy. Collision coverage pays for damages to your vehicle caused by an accident, while comprehensive coverage pays for damages to your vehicle caused by other risks, such as theft or fire. Unlike liability coverage, collision and comprehensive coverage is often subject to a deductible — an amount you must pay before you can collect.

Having a high deductible can save you substantial sums on the collision and comprehensive portion of your total insurance bill. For example, one insurer charges $99 a year more for a policy with a $300 deductible than for one with a $500 deductible. This means you'd pay almost $100 per year to save, at most, $200 if you have an accident. But if you instead take that $100 and put it in the bank each year, you'd soon have enough to pay the full deductible in the event of a collision.

Because you don't want to collect on minor mishaps and risk raising your premiums, you'll want a high deductible anyway. Collecting $50 beyond a $250 deductible to replace a $300 cracked windshield could raise your total premium by several hundred dollars.

Insurance Tips

After You've Bought

• Stay clean. No single factor is more important than your motor vehicle report (MVR) in determining the premiums for your liability coverage. Each time you receive a traffic ticket, you risk increasing your future premiums. In general, you will pay substantially higher premiums if you receive more than one or two tickets during a three-year period. If your state allows you to attend traffic school in exchange for removing a violation from your MVR, take advantage of the option.

• Stay a stranger to your insurance company. Claims, as well as tickets, upset insurers. Don't involve your insurance company in repairing door dings or annoyances like cracked windshields even if you could collect a little something beyond your deductible. Pay for these repairs out of your own pocket. If someone damages your vehicle and you don't live in a no-fault insurance state, try to collect from the other person's insurance company before you involve your own insurer. Obtain a police report that indicates you were not at fault in the accident.

• If you own a business, put your vehicle in your company's name. You may be able to persuade the insurer who writes your business policy to cover the truck as a company vehicle at a lower rate than you would receive on a personal policy.

• Get married. Insurers prefer drivers between the ages of 30 and 65. Some insurers give discounts to drivers aged 55-65. But once you're over 70, you are considered risky, as you are if you're under 30. However, insurers generally treat a married guy or gal under 30 years old as they would someone in the lower risk 30-65 age group. Marriage, they figure, puts an end to your partying days and keeps you off the streets at night.

Figure 4

Insurance Symbols

Approximate Original Sticker Price	Insurance Symbol*
0 — $6,500	1
$6,501 — $8,000	2
$8,001 — $9,000	3
$9,001— $10,000	4
$10,001— $11,250	5
$11,251— $12,500	6
$12,501— $13,750	7
$13,751— $15,000	8
$15,001— $16,250	10
$16,251— $17,500	11
$17,501— $18,750	12
$18,751— $20,000	13
$20,001— $22,000	14
$22,001— $24,000	15
$24,001— $26,000	16
$26,001— $28,000	17
$28,001— $30,000	18
$30,001— $33,000	19
$33,001— $36,000	20
$36,001— $40,000	21
$40,001— $45,000	22
$45,001— $50,000	23
$50,001— $60,000	24
$60,001— $70,000	25
$70,001— $80,000	26
$80,001and above	27

**The higher the symbol, the more costly to insure.*

Other Coverages

Medical coverage pays hospital and doctor fees for the driver and passengers. But if your health insurance already covers these things, you may not need medical coverage included with your auto insurance.

However, if you live in a state with no-fault insurance, you may be required to buy personal-injury protection that covers your medical bills. But again, you may be able to cut some of the costs for this coverage if your heath plan covers you in an auto accident.

There are a number of other minor types of auto insurance, like towing coverage. If you're a member of an auto club, you may not need towing coverage, for instance.

Insurance Symbols

Insurers use a vehicle rating system to determine the premium price for collision and comprehensive coverage. For many insurers, the symbols are compiled by Insurance Services Office in New York, NY.

Every vehicle is given a rating symbol between 1 and 27; the higher the rating number, the more costly the premium. All things being equal, two identically priced vehicles will have the same insurance rating.

However, insurance companies often loathe the vehicles most of us love — luxury and exciting high-performance vehicles — and these vehicles may be subject to surcharges. In addition, some vehicles are often more expensive to repair, incur more extensive damage in collisions, and are more likely to be stolen than others. So ratings are adjusted to account for these risk factors.

Insurance rating figures used in this book are based on "Insurance Symbols," *(See Figure 4)* with the rating for a particular vehicle adjusted for any special risk factors.

Shop Around

The insurance business is essentially a gigantic book-making operation that bets premiums against the probabilities of having to pay out on an accident or injury claim. Except in a handful of states where bureaucrats set the rates, it's up to each insurer to develop its own probabilities and set its rates accordingly. Rates and underwriting guidelines will reflect what market segments an insurer wishes to target and how efficiently the company is managed.

All of which is to say, rates for the same driver and vehicle can vary dramatically from company to company. If you live in a state with competitive insurance rates, start shopping by obtaining a quote from one of the major firms in the industry — State Farm, Allstate, Farmers, Nationwide, USAA, AAA, and Aetna are among the largest. (See Appendix D for the addresses and phone numbers of the ten largest insurance companies.) Then contact an independent agent who can query other companies for you. Compare them all. Use the worksheet on the following page to compare rates. You'll find that premium prices can differ by as much as 50 percent for the same coverage.

Figure 5 Insurance Worksheet

Insurance Comparison Worksheet

	Write desired coverage here	Write premium quotes here Company name 1:______	2:______
Level of coverage you desire for:			
Bodily injury liability:	______	______	______
Property-damage liability:	______	______	______
Medical payments:	______	______	______
Personal-injury protection (no-fault states):	______	______	______
Collision			
a. $100 deductible:	______	______	______
b. $250 deductible:	______	______	______
c. $500 deductible:	______	______	______
Comprehensive:			
a. $50 deductible:	______	______	______
b. $250 deductible:	______	______	______
c. $500 deductible:	______	______	______
Uninsured motorist:	______	______	______
Underinsured motorist:	______	______	______
	SUBTOTAL A:		
Other coverages you might consider			
Towing and labor:	______	______	______
Rental-car reimbursement:	______	______	______
	+ SUBTOTAL B:		
Do any other charges apply?			
Membership fee:		______	______
Surcharges:		______	______
	+ SUBTOTAL C:		
Do you qualify for any discounts?			
Theft Deterrent System:		______	______
Passive Restraint System:		______	______
Accident free driving record:		______	______
Multi-car (if adding a vehicle):		______	______
	− SUBTOTAL D:		
	= TOTAL PREMIUM: (Subtotals A, plus B, plus C, minus subtotal D)		

Finance Tips

• Consider buying the truck with a home equity loan. First, interest rates on home equity loans are often a little lower than on a truck loan. Second, payment schedules are often more flexible; that is, some home equity loans allow you to pay interest only. Third, and perhaps most significant, interest on home equity loans may be tax deductible— a big savings if you are able to itemize your deductions on your tax return. But be aware that securing a home equity loan just to buy a truck might cost you more. That's because there are often significant up-front fees to set up a home equity loan.

• You might also consider borrowing against a cash-value life insurance policy. The interest rate will often be lower than on a loan, and you never have to pay back the loan if you don't want to. Of course if you die or cash-in the policy, the proceeds will be reduced by the outstanding balance.

• Consider all discount financing offers on your dream truck. Dealers and manufacturers are making some terrific offers — 1.9% through 7.9% 48-month loan offers aren't unusual.

• Compare discount financing to a cash rebate if both are offered. "Buy now and we'll give you $500 cash, or provide a 4.8% loan for four years." Which should you choose? It depends on a lot of factors. Appendix J lets you easily determine which option is more advantageous for you.

• If you can afford to buy the truck out-right, do so — it's usually the least expensive way to buy a truck.

• If you take out a loan, put as large a down payment on the truck as you can manage. And pay as much per month as you can possibly budget to keep the length of the loan to a minimum.

• Be aware that there are several ways to lower monthly payments, but only a lower interest rate or a lower amount borrowed will lower your total interest expense.

Finance Costs

It is now time for a *very* brief accounting lesson. When we talk about finance costs, it is important to distinguish between what is actually a cost and what is not. Let's say you bought a new truck for $12,000. You no longer have the money, but you do have a truck of equal value — an asset. If a bank loaned you $12,000 to buy the truck, you owe the bank that money but it still hasn't cost you anything. However, when you borrow money from any lending institution, not only will the lender ask you to pay back the money they loaned you, but they will also charge you interest. The money that they loan you is not a cost — the interest charge is. End of lesson.

Pay Cash or Take Out A Loan?

For most truck buyers, the answer to that question is easy: Let me sign those loan docs! Most people don't have $16,000 (the average price of a new vehicle these days) lying around in their bank accounts. So if they want a new truck, they'll have to borrow to the hilt to get it.

But, what if a buyer has a choice: to pay cash or to take out a loan. Let's say that Debbie Debtor and Chris Cash each buy a $16,000 truck, and each has exactly $16,000 in the bank. Chris pays cash for her truck. Debbie puts 10% down, finances the $14,400 difference with a 48-month, 11% loan, and puts her $14,400 in a bank earning 6% interest. She withdraws $338.18 from the bank each month to pay her truck payment, which leaves her with a bank balance of $0 after 48 months. Who comes out ahead?

Chris doesn't earn any interest on her money, but didn't pay any either, so she has a net cost of zero. Debbie must pay $372.18 each month in truck payments, but she can only take out $338.18 each month from her bank account (or else she would deplete her bank account before 48 months). She has to pay an additional $34 per month for 48 months, or a total of $1,632 more than Chris.

Another way to look at it is that Debbie will pay $3,464 in interest over the 48 months, but will earn only $1,832 on her money in the bank, a difference of $1,632. To make matters worse, Debbie will probably pay income tax on the $1,832 that her money earned in the bank.

It used to be that Debbie could deduct her interest payments from her income taxes, which could have made her come out ahead of Chris, but interest deductions are no longer allowed.

The bottom line: as long as the after-tax interest rate on the truck loan is more than the after-tax interest rate that you could earn on your money, paying cash is less expensive than taking a loan.

Striking a Balance: Monthly Payments vs. Interest Expense

Determining the cost of a loan is inherently complex. There are a myriad of terms that affect the final cost of the loan. Through it all, a few simple truths exist:

- The higher the interest rate, the higher the monthly payment.
- The more you borrow, the higher the monthly payment.
- The longer the period of your loan, the lower the monthly payment.

In each of these cases, the cost of the loan will be higher.

While the first two points are fairly intuitive, the third point catches a lot of people off guard. A truck salesperson will frequently attempt to lower your monthly payment, sometimes quite substantially, by stretching out the loan period. But, buyer beware, this will ultimately cost you more. For example, the monthly payment on a $10,000 loan at 12% for five years is $40 less than the same loan over a four-year period. However, the total interest expense is $700 more for the five-year loan versus the four-year loan. This is the cost you pay for the privilege of stretching out your payments for one more year *(See Figure 6).*

Finding Yourself "Upside Down"

Nowadays, it seems you have to pay as much for a new truck as you did a few years ago for a house. But as new-truck prices rose dramatically in recent years, lenders found a clever way to allow people to continue to buy new vehicles — they simply extended the length of loans, thus keeping monthly payments affordable.

In the past, 24-month or 36-month truck loans were the norm. But today, 60- and even 72-month loans are common. With the longer loans, however, it takes longer to reach a positive equity position in a truck and owe less on it than it's worth. As soon as you drive that shiny new truck off the dealer's lot, the truck plunges in value — thanks to that ol' devil depreciation. But with a shorter length loan, after a year or so of making payments, your truck's value will begin to be worth more than you owe on it. Until then, you're "upside-down," as they say in the auto business.

With longer loans however, you could be upside down for two, three, or four years. And therein lies the rub: If during that time you want to trade in your vehicle on another one, you'll be in the frustrating situation of owing more on your old vehicle than it's worth, thus making it all the more expensive for you to buy the newer vehicle.

So if you must take a longer loan in order to lower the monthly payments on the truck you really want, plan on keeping the vehicle for nearly the life of the loan or more. But if you can't keep it that long, be sure you choose a vehicle that holds its resale value well *(See vehicle charts)* because that will reduce the time it takes you to reach a positive equity position.

Figure 6

Interest Expense

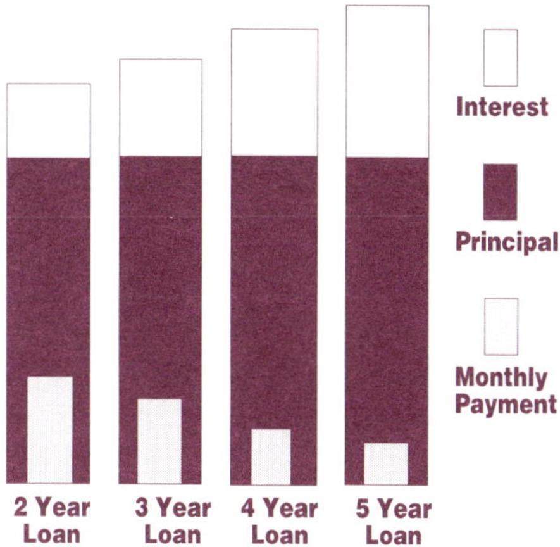

As the length of the loan increases, the interest cost also increases, yet the monthly payment decreases. The principal, however, remains the same regardless of the length of the payment period. The total interest that you pay can be computed by adding up the monthly payments and subtracting the amount that you initially borrowed (loan amount). You can convert the loan amount into a monthly payment using Appendix I.

Finance Tips

• If you take out a lengthy loan on a truck, refer to the vehicle charts in this book and buy one that will retain a high proportion of its value. This will shorten the time you are "upside down."

• When is an interest rate not an interest rate? When it doesn't include the "hidden" costs of a loan. All interest rates are not comparable. One rate may include a loan origination fee, and expensive "simple" interest, while another may have no loan fee and cheaper "compound" interest. APR (Annual Percentage Rate) is a very specific term that factors in any hidden fees and tells you the rate you will actually pay when all fees are taken into account. It is the "apples-to-apples" comparable rate. Lenders are required by law to tell you the APR of your loan. You should use this rate, and only this rate, in your comparisons.

• Shop around at different banks, savings and loans, thrifts, and credit unions to compare loan interest rates. Then compare those to ones offered by the truck dealer and his financing partners, such as GMAC.

• Your auto insurance company may also offer financing, sometimes on very favorable terms. Ask your agent.

Leasing

In the past few years, leasing has exploded in popularity. Automakers from General Motors to Mercedes-Benz are offering attractive lease programs and inundating their dealers with sales brochures touting all the charms of leasing. As a result, leasing now accounts for about one quarter of all new-car sales to individuals. Some predict that by the middle of the decade half of new-car sales will be leases.

The Allure of Leasing

No question about it, leasing has its advantages over buying:

- You don't have to come up with a big down payment. With the price of the typical new vehicle these days hovering around $16,000, the usual 20 percent down payment can amount to a hefty sum.

  Besides the difficulty for some people in just coming up with such substantial sums of cash, others don't want to pull their cash resources out of particularly lucrative investments to buy a vehicle.

- Your monthly payments on the truck you want will often be lower if you lease. Here's why: When you buy a $20,000 truck for instance, you make payments based on that price, minus the down payment. But when you lease, the payments are lower because the truck isn't yours when the lease is up; that means you don't have to pay for the whole truck. The truck that cost $20,000 might still be worth $10,000 after a 36-month lease, so the leasing company would base your payments on $10,000, not $20,000.

- Or, for a given monthly payment you can lease a more expensive truck than you could afford if you bought it with a loan. Again, the same reasoning holds — you're not paying for the entire truck because you won't own it at the end of the lease.

- You can drive a more expensive vehicle and trade it in more frequently. Many people can only afford to buy new vehicles by taking out long-term loans lasting five or even six years in order to get the monthly payment down to a manageable level. But because lease payments are often lower than loan payments, you may be able to take a shorter-term lease and still have an affordable monthly payment.

- You can walk away from the leased vehicle at the end of the contract and let the leasing company have the headache of reselling it.

The Catch

No down payment, lower monthly payments, no resale hassles — these are nice advantages, all right. But unfortunately, they don't come free.

Make no mistake, in the end leasing is almost always more expensive than buying a vehicle out-right with cash. (However, if you have some surefire investment that will pay a very high return for your cash, leasing may be less costly. But in these days of four- and five-percent money-market rates, few of us have such high-paying, risk-free investment opportunities).

Moreover, leasing a vehicle is often more expensive than buying it with a loan. At the end of the lease, you have nothing to show for all those monthly payments except memories and the wad of gasoline-credit receipts jammed in the glove compartment.

A New Wrinkle

In general, leasing may be the most expensive way to put a new vehicle in your garage. But now there's an added wrinkle in the lease game — factory subsidized leasing programs. These programs not only provide all the usual advantages of leasing, but can actually save you money compared to buying the vehicle with a loan — and possibly even compared to paying cash.

Figure 7

Leasing Comparison

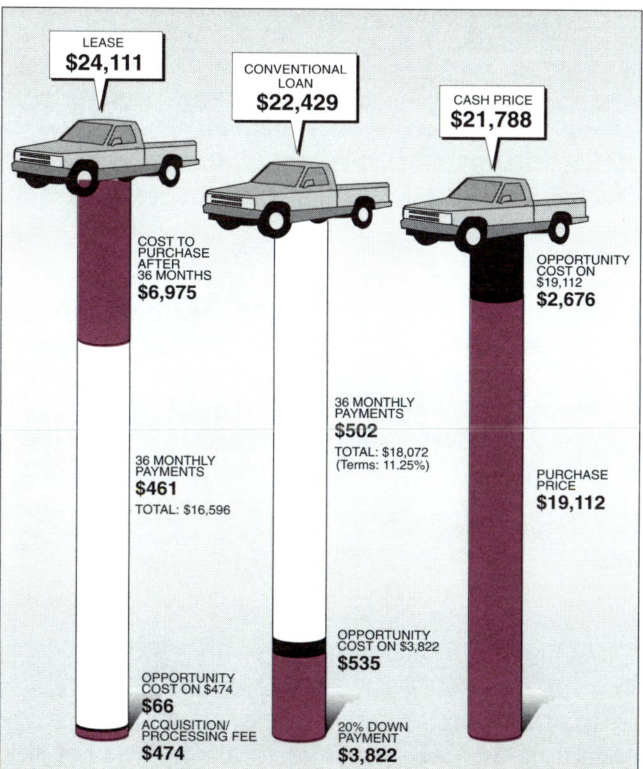

The leasing example above describes a typical lease arrangement for a 1993 pickup truck. The example shows if you pay cash for the truck, you will end up paying less than if you finance the truck or lease it for 36 months. This is true even after taking into account any investment income — or "opportunity cost"— that you may earn if you instead lease the truck and invest the cash (or finance the truck and invest the down payment) in a bank certificate of deposit.

In this example we assume the bank certificate of deposit has an after-tax annual yield of 4.5%. We also assume that the lessee will purchase the vehicle at the end of the lease for $6,975—the vehicle's resale value. To determine resale value, we use a residual rate of 37%.

To Lease or Not to Lease

Leasing may be right for you if:

- *The manufacturer is subsidizing the lease.*
- *You prefer to use your cash in investments other than a vehicle.*
- *You would like to drive a more expensive vehicle for a lower initial cash outlay.*
- *You like to trade in your vehicle every two, three, or four years on a new model.*
- *You want to avoid the hassle of disposing of a used vehicle.*

Leasing may not be right for you if:

- *Saving money is a major consideration.*
- *You usually drive your vehicle more than 15,000 miles a year.*
- *You are not inclined to take care of your vehicle.*
- *You object to paying penalties that will be imposed if you terminate a lease early for any reason.*
- *You want to significantly modify your vehicle.*

Comparing Lease Interest Rates

The interest rate used to calculate a lease is the one true measure of the cost of a lease. Unfortunately, this rate is very difficult to obtain from a lessor. To determine the lessor's interest rate, so you can compare leases on an apples-to-apples basis, use Appendix H on page 99A.

The Fine Print Of Leasing

Unfortunately, the details of leasing make new-vehicle shopping all the more painfully complex. And the savvy lessee must learn a new vocabulary.

The Residual. This is the predetermined/projected value of the vehicle at the end of the lease — and it's the key to the monthly payments, as well as the ultimate total cost of the deal.

The higher the residual value of the vehicle, the lower your monthly payments. Residual value is essentially a measure of the vehicle's expected depreciation. The lessee pays for the depreciation while he or she drives the vehicle. So if you select a vehicle that depreciates very little, your monthly payment will be lower.

Furthermore, the residual will determine the total cost of the lease deal and whether or not you should purchase the vehicle when the lease is up. In Figure 7, each comparison assumed the vehicle would actually have a market value at the end of the lease equal to the predetermined sales price or residual.

But if a vehicle were to actually have a market value less than the residual at the end of the lease, the lessee armed with this knowledge would be prudent to walk away from the deal. On the other hand, if the actual market value were greater than the residual, then the lessee should buy the vehicle at the predetermined residual, sell it, and pocket the difference.

How does the leasing company determine a residual? Like anything that involves projecting future values — be it stocks or used-vehicle prices — there's a certain amount of guesswork required. Leasing companies may offer widely varying residuals for the same make and model; a factory/dealer lease plan may offer a 50 percent residual, while a bank may be willing to go only 40 percent.

Regardless of whether you may want to buy the vehicle at the end of the lease, it's in your best interest to negotiate the highest possible residual.

The vehicle charts in this book are an excellent guide to the expected depreciation/resale value of any particular vehicle you may be considering leasing.

Open and Closed End Leases. Most leases today are closed-end leases, meaning that the residual value is fixed at the beginning of the lease.

With an open-end lease there is still a residual value set at the beginning of the lease. But if the vehicle is worth less than the residual value at the lease's end, the lessee must pay the difference. In other words, the lessee is assuming the risk for depreciation with an open-end lease, which negates one of the big advantages of leasing.

Purchase Option. In our examples, we've assumed that the lessee has the right to purchase the vehicle at the end of the lease for the vehicle's residual value set at the beginning of the lease. But unfortunately, not all leases allow this..

The Money Factor. This is the phrase used for the finance rate upon which the lease payments are based. The lower the rate, the lower the monthly payments. Automakers are subsidizing their lease plans by offering special low money factors. Obviously, you'll want the lowest rate you can find.

Capital Cost Reduction. This is a fancy name for a cash down payment. A large down payment will, of course, reduce the monthly payments, but it will also negate one of the big advantages of leasing. However, if you own your present vehicle, you may be able to use it as the down payment to start the lease.

Early Termination. Because a vehicle's depreciation is the highest in the first few months after it leaves the dealer's lot, and because the depreciation is spread out over the life of the lease in equal amounts, lessees who break a lease early have almost always used up more of a vehicle's value than they've paid for.

So lease plans generally carry steep penalties for early termination. Be aware of what those penalties are before you sign the lease.

Deficiency Liability Waiver or Gap Protection. Even if you had no intention of terminating the lease early, it will automatically happen if the vehicle is "totaled" in an accident or stolen. Your own auto insur-

The Fine Print Of Leasing continued

ance will cover the actual cash value of the vehicle at the time of its loss. But that may not be enough to cover the lease payoff balance and early-termination penalties.

Some manufacturers, General Motors for instance, have lease plans that include valuable gap insurance to cover any difference owed in case of an accidental loss.

Mileage Allowance. Here's another potential trap for the lessee. The typical lease requires that the lessee drive no more than an average of 15,000 miles per year over the term of the lease. If the total mileage is greater, there is a charge of anywhere between 8 cents and 25 cents per mile over the limit, depending upon the lease.

Some lease plans allow you to pay the penalty for excess mileage ahead of time at a lower rate. With GMAC's plans, if you know you'll be driving more than an average of 15,000 miles per year, the prepayment is 8 cents a mile. Otherwise, GMAC charges 10 cents a mile over the 15,000-mile limit if at the end of the lease you discover you've driven more than the limit.

Wear and Tear. It's your responsibility to keep the vehicle in good condition. Return it with a dented fender, bald tires, or a ruined engine because of lack of routine maintenance, and you'll be charged for the repairs. Some wear and tear is allowed, of course. But if you aren't inclined to take reasonable care of your vehicles, then a leased truck may not be for you.

Miscellaneous Fees. Expect a number of assorted fees with any lease. A security deposit, equal to one month's payment and refundable at the end of the lease, is usually required. There is often an "acquisition" fee — a sort of processing fee. And there may be a "disposition" fee of $150-$250 at the end of the lease for getting the vehicle ready to be sold.

A New Wrinkle continued

The automakers subsidize their plans by boosting the predetermined sales price at the end of the agreement (thus reducing the cost on which the monthly lease payments are based) and perhaps more significantly, offering reduced lease financing costs. These lease financing costs work out to as little as half — or even less — than the going rate for conventional auto loans.

The advantages of subsidized lease programs to the automakers are several when compared to other marketing schemes. For one, turned-in lease vehicles mean a steady supply of good used vehicles for their dealers. For another, the programs give the dealers a further opportunity to pitch the customer's business when the lease expires; dealers may wave a security deposit or month's payment for a repeat customer.

At the beginning of the 1993 model year, GMAC was offering a "Smartlease" on a 1993 Sonoma for $200 a month. With GMAC's subsidized lease, the customer may save money compared to either taking out a conventional loan or paying cash.

The Best Lease Deal

Always keep in mind that most everything is negotiable when leasing a truck. One of the biggest mistakes you can make is walking

State Fees Tips

• If you have a choice, register your vehicle as a passenger vehicle. State fees are usually lower on passenger vehicles than on commercial vehicles.

• If your county allows you to bring your personal vehicle into the county tax-free, and if you live near a county with a lower sales tax rate, consider buying your vehicle in the other county. A 1% reduction on your tax rate, on a $20,000 vehicle, will save you $200.

• Pay your state taxes and fees on time to avoid costly penalties.

into a dealership and announcing that you can pay so much a month to lease a truck.

Instead, start by negotiating the price of the truck, just as you would if you were buying it outright. Then negotiate the residual value and any other provisions in the lease, such as excess mileage fees and the purchase-option price.

Choosing a truck with a history of low depreciation and then negotiating the most favorable sales price for the truck will equal the lowest monthly lease payments.

Leasing and Taxes

Some folks are under the impression that there are special income tax advantages to leasing a vehicle, especially now that you can no longer write off interest on consumer loans.

The fact is, whether you buy or lease a vehicle, you can write off associated expenses if the vehicle is a legitimate business expense.

But, for those who can't write off a vehicle as a business expense, tax reform did not necessarily make leasing more attractive. Instead, it made buying a vehicle with a loan less attractive.

You may save on sales taxes by leasing a vehicle if you turn it in at the end of the lease. When you buy a vehicle, you pay sales tax on the full purchase price. But when you lease, you don't pay tax on the vehicle's residual value, unless of course, you buy the vehicle at the end of the lease.

State Fees

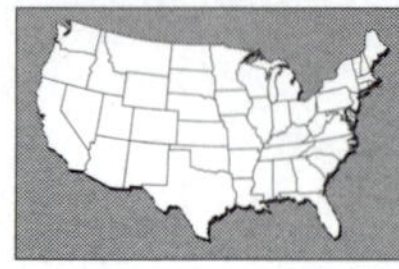

The government will have its paw out as soon as you buy your new truck. You'll have to pay tax and license, and registration fees. Furthermore, you'll be required to pay taxes and/or fees every year for as long as you own the truck.

Some states base their fees on the original price of the truck and/or on its age. Others base the fees on the truck's weight. Still others have fixed fees.

Running Costs

Running costs, or variable costs, are the costs you bear every time you take your truck out of your garage. They include fuel, maintenance, and repairs. (Bridge tolls, occasional parking fees, and when you're naughty, traffic tickets are running costs, too. However, they vary too greatly to be considered in this book.)

Running costs tend to increase as a vehicle gets older. But remember that standing costs usually decrease over time. Usually the increase in running costs is outweighed by the decrease in standing costs, so overall, the vehicle is less costly to own and operate when it becomes an old crock — a good reason to hang on to your truck for several years after you buy it. For example, after age five or so, the truck may require more repairs, but depreciation costs fall to practically nothing.

Fuel Costs

Fuel is the one expense truck owners face almost on a daily basis. Of course you can reduce your fuel costs by driving less, though that's often easier said than done.

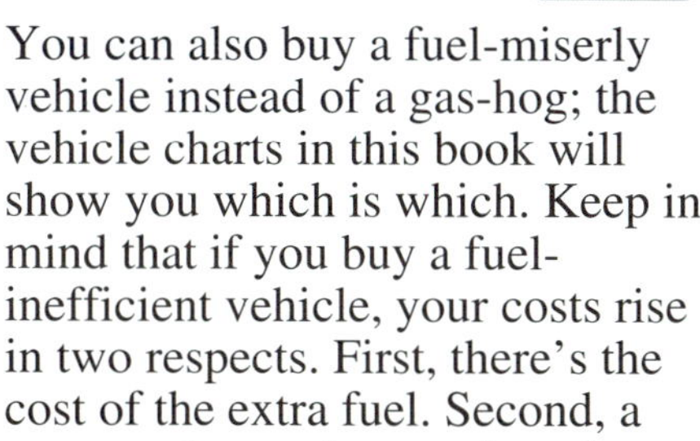

You can also buy a fuel-miserly vehicle instead of a gas-hog; the vehicle charts in this book will show you which is which. Keep in mind that if you buy a fuel-inefficient vehicle, your costs rise in two respects. First, there's the cost of the extra fuel. Second, a gas-guzzler tax imposed on the automaker by the federal government (the tax doubled in 1991) may also be included in the vehicles's purchase price — so you'll end up paying it.

But beyond the type of vehicle you buy, there are many other considerations in reducing fuel costs.

Is all gas alike?

Advertising hype about "Lead-Free Super," "Ultra-High Test Unleaded," "Extra-Mile Regular," "Irregular Regular," etc., can make buying gasoline a little confusing. You may begin to feel like a recent cartoon character; faced with all the choices, he tells the gas station attendant, "Just surprise me!"

It's an amusing approach, but not wise. It can even be illegal. Since the mid-1970s, most new vehicles must use unleaded gas or their emission-controlling catalytic converters will be damaged.

But you still must make the choice between regular unleaded or the more expensive premium "high-octane" unleaded. A truck's engine develops power because a mixture of gasoline and air is burned in the engine's combustion chambers. If this mixture burns too rapidly, there's an explosion in the combustion chambers. The engine won't fly apart, but the explosion will set up a vibration that you will hear as a ringing or "knocking" sound, especially when you accelerate briskly. Inside the engine, the effect is not unlike a hammer blow to the top of the piston. If the blows are severe enough, they can damage the engine.

By matching the engine's octane requirements to a gasoline's octane rating, you'll get a nice,

Fuel Tips

Before You Buy

• Buy a fuel-efficient vehicle. Refer to the vehicle charts in this book for fuel-economy ratings.

• Be aware that buying a truck that requires premium fuel will cost you considerably at the pump. If you drive a vehicle that gets 20 mpg 15,000 miles per year, you will pay an additional $112 per year if premium fuel costs 15 cents per gallon more than regular fuel. The charts in this book indicate which vehicles require premium fuel.

After You've Bought

• Buy gas with the proper octane rating for your vehicle.

• If you own a vehicle with fuel injection, buy a name-brand gasoline with a detergent additive that helps prevent clogged fuel injectors.

• Keep your vehicle's engine tuned, and its tires properly inflated and aligned.

• Avoid putting the pedal to the metal; accelerate smoothly instead.

• At highway speeds, it's more fuel-efficient to close the windows and turn on the air conditioner. At speeds over 40 mph, open windows create wind resistance that increases fuel consumption.

• The most fuel-efficient speed range is 35 to 55 mph.

• After starting a cold engine, don't let it idle for more than 30 seconds; instead drive slowly for several miles until the engine temperature warms up.

• If you think you'll be waiting for more than a minute — at a railroad crossing, for instance — turn off the engine.

• If you have a vehicle with a manual transmission, learn the proper shift points.

Consider these facts:

• Misaligned front wheels can increase fuel consumption by 2 percent.

• Underinflated tires can increase fuel consumption by 5 percent.

• A malfunctioning thermostat in the cooling system can increase fuel consumption by 7 percent.

• Worn spark plugs and other ignition components, as well as clogged air filters, can increase fuel consumption by 11 percent

• Altogether, these maladies could increase your fuel costs by a whopping 25 percent. The point here is obvious — a well-tuned vehicle uses less fuel.

even burn of the gas/air mixture. You can get an idea of your vehicle's octane requirements by looking in your vehicle's owner's manual. Unfortunately, finding the optimum choice of fuel for your vehicle is not quite that simple. An engine's octane requirements can vary according to its age, the outside air temperature, humidity, and altitude. All this means you have to experiment with different grades and brands until you find one that eliminates knocking in your vehicle.

Several years ago there really wasn't much difference between brands of gasoline, despite the big advertising bucks the oil companies spent trying to make motorists believe there was. But now the situation has changed. Today, with the near elimination of lead that was used to boost gasoline octane ratings, and with the popularity of fuel-injected vehicles, oil companies are paying more attention to the way they refine their gas and to the additives they use.

You'll not only find that octane ratings — even for premium grades of gas — will differ between brands, but that vehicles with fuel-injected engines will run better on certain brands. Most new vehicles have fuel injection, and the injectors are very sensitive to fuel contamination. The annoying symptoms of clogged fuel injectors include lack of power, stumbling, and even stalling.

The major oil companies are now promoting gasoline with additives that clean fuel injectors. The stuff — like Chevron's patented Techroline additive — really works.

Maintenance

Automakers do sometimes build vehicles that should simply have "headache" written on the side. But happily, most modern vehicles, no matter the make or model, are darned impressive machines — especially if they're given periodic care.

Regular maintenance includes all services required by the manufacturer to maintain the vehicle's warranty, services suggested by the manufacturer to ensure trouble-free operation, and other regular service, such as tune-ups and replacing brake pads, exhaust systems, tires, belts, fluids, and filters.

Some Thoughts on Extended Service Intervals

In the old days — the really old days — vehicles required routine service every few hundred miles. During the 1960s and 1970s, 3,000-mile oil and lubrication service intervals were the norm. Today, automakers have stretched recommended oil changes to 7,500 miles or more, while chassis components are sealed so they never need lubrication.

A program of routine maintenance, including oil changes, tune-ups, radiator flushes, tire pressure checks, and so on, can save you big money in several ways:

It will prevent premature break-downs and budget-busting repairs.

It will make your vehicle last longer, so you won't need to buy a new one as often. That means you avoid the costs of depreciation, taxes, and finance charges that go with a new vehicle.

When the time comes to sell your vehicle, you'll get a higher price for it.

Routine maintenance is required in order to keep your new-vehicle warranty in effect.

Routine maintenance may even improve your vehicle's fuel economy.

There's no question that technology has eliminated or reduced the need for several routine service chores. Electronic ignitions, for instance, have greatly prolonged the life of spark plugs. But when it comes to oil, many mechanics question the whole business of extended service intervals. They still prefer to see the oil changed every 3,000 miles or so; after all, oil is an engine's life blood.

Automaker recommendations can be tricky. In the fine print of the owner's manual, some automakers specify extended intervals for vehicles used in "normal driving," which they define as high-speed, highway driving. They classify puttering around town or getting stuck in commuter traffic as "severe driving," to which the extended changes don't apply.

Extended service intervals have one drawback: If your mechanic sees your truck less often, he has fewer opportunities to spot potential problems, which makes it all the more important for you to inspect your truck frequently. But if you're serious about giving your truck a long, trouble-free life, change the oil and filter every 3,000 to 5,000 miles. It's worth a few extra dollars in the long run.

Keep On Shining

Many a love affair with a vehicle is based on appearances. Today, thanks to automobile "detailers," the affair doesn't necessarily have to dim with age. With a combination of skill, elbow grease, and the right products, a professional detailer can keep a vehicle looking like new almost indefinitely. Treating your vehicle to the attentions of a detailer isn't merely an extravagance; it's protection for your investment. An old vehicle that looks new will have the highest resale value.

A complete detail job is far more than just a car wash. Every area where grease clings and dirt collects receives the detailer's attention — including vent louvers, door jambs, the trunk and the engine. The vehicle's paint is washed, rubbed out with polish, and then waxed. The carpets and upholstery are vacuumed and shampooed. Emblems, badges, chrome and plastic trim, and the wheels are all cleaned — with toothbrushes if necessary.

Having your vehicle detailed once or twice a year should be part of your routine maintenance program. It's far cheaper than buying a new vehicle, or even a new paint job.

Maintenance Warranties

Maintenance warranties cover the services required to maintain a new vehicle's overall warranty — typically tune-ups, oil changes, and minor adjustments — and may be offered for between one year and four years.

The actual dollar value of a maintenance warranty ranges from nothing (if you don't take advantage of it) to several hundred or a thousand dollars for three years of maintenance. Most of the really costly maintenance services occur after three years, e.g., tire replacement, exhaust system work, etc. That's one of the reasons you'll rarely see maintenance warranties extend much beyond three years.

Maintenance Tips

Before You Buy

• Many new trucks are designed and built to minimize maintenance costs. For instance, many GM trucks now feature long-lasting stainless steel mufflers, and distributor-less ignition systems. Use the charts to compare vehicles' overall maintenance costs, as well as costs for tune-ups and brake service.

• Take advantage of any maintenance warranty offered on your truck, but don't choose a vehicle just because it comes with a maintenance warranty. Use the charts to see which vehicles feature this type of warranty.

After You've Bought

• The most important tip of all: read your owner's manual.

• Don't skimp on routine maintenance. A regular maintenance program will protect your warranty, save you from costly, unexpected repairs, and will extend the life of your vehicle.

• Make a quick inspection of your vehicle every two weeks for problems in the making. (See "The Ten-Minute Technical Inspection" on the next page.)

• Be wary of extended service intervals; at minimum, have your vehicle's oil and filter changed every 3,000 to 5,000 miles.

• Keep all your service receipts; a complete set can increase your vehicle's resale value if it proves your vehicle was well maintained.

The Ten-Minute Technical Inspection

Your mechanic may deftly tune your truck's engine, but that won't matter a bit if the engine fries itself because you failed to notice that the radiator ran out of coolant. So roll up your sleeves, because now you're going to learn your way around your truck. And in the process, you may thwart a costly, irritating, and possibly dangerous breakdown in the making. Here goes:

✔ First, pop open the hood. Do you see the engine? Good. Actually that's quite an accomplishment, what with engines mounted sideways and all the complicated paraphernalia automakers hang on them these days.

✔ Now find the engine dipstick; it's sticking up somewhere along the side of the engine. (If you can't find it, look in your truck's owner's manual for the location.) Pull it out, wipe it off, stick it back in, and pull it out again. Does the oil level reach somewhere between the hatch marks on the dipstick? If not, add some. If it needs more than a quart, take the truck to your mechanic and find out why it is losing oil.

✔ Now find the radiator or the radiator overflow tank. Take off the cap and look inside. Do you see some greenish liquid that looks like lime Kool-Aid? If not, add water. Again, if it takes more than a quart, you'd better have your mechanic take a look. And if it's not green, you'll need to have the radiator drained and refilled with a 50/50 mixture of coolant and water.

✔ While you're at the radiator, examine all the rubber hoses running from the radiator to the engine. Look at any other hoses in the engine compartment for that matter. Are they cracked, or do they look so brittle that they should be? Are there any bulges, or are they squishy soft? If so, have them replaced. Chances are you'll not find the right size in a provincial gas station when a hose bursts on your next trip out of town.

✔ If your vehicle isn't quite as up to date as today's news, look for a distributor. It's a round thing with thick wires running out of the top. Follow each of the wires to the engine. Are they firmly attached to the distributor at one end, and to the spark plugs at the other? Are the little rubber booties that cover the ends in place? But if your vehicle is a new or nearly new model, the distributor and plug wires probably won't be visible, so you can skip this step. Indeed, some of the newest vehicles don't even have traditional distributors or plug wires.

✔ Next, find the belt (or belts) that run the alternator, air conditioning compressor, and perhaps the radiator cooling fan or other accessories. Make sure it isn't frayed or cracked. Find a spot where it's suspended between two pulleys and push down with your finger; if it gives more than a half inch, it needs tightening.

✔ Now find the battery. If it's a refillable type, take off the caps and check all six cells to see that there's water. If the terminals look like they've grown moss, scrub them with a little baking soda and water. And if you see signs of battery acid on the pan where the battery resides, wash the pan thoroughly and check the battery case for leaks. Acid will eventually eat right through metal.

✔ Now start the engine. Look back under the hood. Do you see the fan whirring? Does the engine settle into a smooth idle, or does it jerk around while it runs? Do you see any leaks from any hoses? Do you hear any ominous sounds? Once the novelty of all this has worn off, stop the engine and shut the hood.

✔ Glance under the truck. Your truck can hold up to 11 different fluids of one kind or another, and all of them should be in the truck, not on the driveway. Examine the exhaust system for rusty holes.

✔ Get up, turn on all the lights and walk around the truck to see that they work. Don't forget to check the turn signals. Look at the windshield wipers; make sure they're not shredding or you'll have a scratched windshield after the next rain.

✔ Now look at all four tires. Is there plenty of tread? Are the sidewalls cracking? Look especially closely at the front tires for signs of uneven wear. If they're scalloped or worn excessively on one side, either the suspension is tired or there's an alignment problem. Buy a tire gauge for a couple of bucks, and check the pressures. Don't forget the spare tire, too. Correct pressures are listed in your owner's manual.

That's it. You've just learned where all the more important fallible things are. Make this inspection a ritual every other week, and you'll forestall many expensive repairs.

Repairs

One of the blessings of a new truck is a warranty. If something goes kerplunk in the night, at least you won't have to pay to fix it.

But as your vehicle gets older you won't have the assurance of a warranty. However, follow the maintenance advice in the preceding section, and you will keep repair costs — even on an old truck — to a minimum. Preventive maintenance will prevent costly breakdowns.

Warranties

That old one-year/12,000 miles, whichever came first, warranty seems to have gone the way of necker knobs and eight-track stereos.

Now the standard fare with most automakers, American or foreign, is a three-year/36,000-mile plan. They usually provide "complete" or "bumper-to-bumper" protection for all parts of the vehicle during the warranty period — except for normal wear 'n tear on things like tires or brake linings.

The two years or 24,000 miles of added coverage is certainly good news for buyers. And there's even more good news: some automakers — mostly those who build luxury cars — are offering even longer coverage for 1993. At Mercedes, you'll be covered for four years and 50,000 miles, for instance.

Some automakers distinguish between complete, bumper-to-bumper coverage and powertrain-only warranties (the powertrain includes the engine, transmission, and other parts of the drivetrain). Chrysler offers buyers of its 1993 products a choice of a one-year/12,000-mile basic warranty PLUS a seven-year/70,000-mile powertrain warranty, or a three-year/36,000-mile bumper-to-bumper warranty. Toyota gives its customers a three-year/36,000-mile warranty PLUS an additional two years of coverage on the powertrain.

Almost all automakers are also throwing in five-, six-, or seven-year warranties that cover the vehicle against rusting.

Audi adds yet another twist to its bumper-to-bumper three-year/50,000-mile plan. Not only does it cover unexpected failures of components, but it includes routine maintenance, such as oil changes and tune-ups. The Audi buyer pays only for gasoline and new tires, if needed.

Keep in mind too, that no matter what the vehicle, federal law says that emissions-control related parts must be covered by its maker for five years or 50,000 miles. And that other items, including tires, batteries or sound systems, have their own warranties.

Service Bulletins

Manufacturers sometimes issue "service bulletins" for certain problems. A service bulletin can be an authorization to dealers to fix a particular problem on a truck for free — even if it is no longer covered by the warranty. Manufacturers do this when a large number of vehicles experience the same problem. Service bulletins are generally not publicized, and are often overlooked. Before you pay for any repairs, you should first check with your dealer's service manager to see if the

Warranties

Basic warranty: *Comes with the truck. If it is a three-year/36,000-mile warranty, the coverage ends at three years or 36,000 miles, whichever comes first.*

Powertrain warranty: *Covers the engine, transmission, and other parts of the drivetrain.*

Bumper-to-bumper warranty: *More extensive than a base warranty. Covers everything except the tires and items that normally wear out, such as windshield wipers and light bulbs.*

Safety Restraint Warranty: *Covers seat belts and air bags, although the warranty terms for each of these may differ. This coverage is usually equal to or longer than the powertrain warranty.*

Corrosion warranty: *Covers rust and deterioration caused by natural elements. Terms vary widely but often are six to seven years.*

Optional extended warranty (a.k.a. Mechanical Breakdown Insurance, Service Contracts): *Longer and more extensive coverage than the basic warranty, available for an extra charge.*

Emissions warranty: *Covers exhaust-related parts such as catalytic converters. By law, the coverage applies to all vehicles for five years or 50,000 miles.*

Service Contract Caution

Many independent service contract companies have gone out of business over the past several years, making it difficult or impossible for claims to be paid. If you are considering an independent service contract, be sure to ask who the underwriter is. If you aren't certain of the underwriter's financial strength, it may be wiser to choose a factory-backed plan.

repair costs are covered by a service bulletin.

Service Contracts (Mechanical Breakdown Insurance)

Dealers offer extended service contracts as a protection plan to truck buyers when the basic warranty expires. Even though the dealers sell contracts to their customers, they are often backed up by either the auto manufacturer, an insurance company, or some other independent contractor. If you are buying a service contract for the extra coverage, make sure you're not duplicating coverage on the basic warranty. Many factory warranties are much longer today than they were just a few years ago.

Just like the price of the vehicle itself, the price of the service contract is negotiable. In fact, the dealer markup on a service contract is far higher than the markup on the vehicle and other options. You should be able to negotiate a significant discount on the price of the service contract.

With certain brands, you may have a choice between a manufacturer's service contract and an independent service contract. If this is the case, compare each contract on the components covered, the term of the contract, the deductibles on each repair, the overall cost of the contract, and the convenience it offers. Independent contracts will usually allow repairs at your choice of repair facilities, whereas manufacturer programs require that you return your car to a franchised dealer (except for emergencies).

One thing to consider when you evaluate a service contract is that the peace of mind it offers may well exceed its price. A service contract offers comfort and security — the knowledge that you are covered in the event of a major problem. To some people, this is well worth the price.

Numbing the Pain of Repairs

For many truck owners, a visit to a repair shop is accompanied by all the joy and excitement of going to the dentist's chair. There are ways to make the visit less painful, however.

If your truck is under warranty, you're pretty much married to an authorized dealer for repairs. But if you receive lousy service from say, the Nissan dealer who sold you your Pickup, there's no reason why you can't high-tail it across town to another authorized Nissan dealer for service. All dealers must honor a manufacturer's warranty whether or not they originally sold the truck.

Once your truck is out of warranty *(See the previous section on warranties),* you have a couple of other choices. You can take your truck to an independent mechanic, or to a specialist who only works on specific components: radiators, brakes, mufflers, and so on.

Independent mechanics and specialists will often charge less than a dealer. But make sure they have a working knowledge of your kind of truck, can obtain the correct parts, and have the diagnostic equipment necessary to repair complex electronic gadgets found in so many vehicles today.

How do you find a competent, trustworthy mechanic? There's a certain amount of trial and error involved. But recommendations from friends or owners of vehicles like yours are usually your best bet. In addition, mechanics usually know the scoop on other mechanics in town; if you buy a Chevy and know a good Toyota mechanic, ask him or her to recommend someone who works on Chevys.

Whether you take your truck to a dealer, independent, or specialist, be polite. It's a great American pastime to bad-mouth auto mechanics — and unfortunately, some deserve it. But in the long run, a truck is only as good as the mechanic who takes care of it. Here are some pointers to help the two of you have a long and happy relationship:

- A good mechanic may have grease on his overalls, but don't treat him as if he's not intelligent. You can't be a dummy and properly repair complex, modern vehicles.

- Follow a trusted mechanic's repair recommendations. A good mechanic will spot potential problems before they occur.

- Look for ASE (Automotive Service Excellence) certification. ASE certified mechanics have passed rigorous industry tests and continually update their technical know-how.

- If you're not sure whether to trust a mechanic, ask to watch while he works on your truck. If that's not possible, you should at least expect him to explain the problem in simple language and to show you the defective part while it's still on the truck. If he's a good mechanic, he'll appreciate your interest.

- It's proper business practice for you to receive a written estimate before any work is performed. In some states it's the law. And if you authorize a repair and the mechanic later finds more is involved, he should get your permission to raise the estimate before he proceeds with the repair.

- If you don't trust your mechanic and if a quote seems too high, be sure you understand what's involved with the repair. Then before you agree to the repair, telephone one or two other mechanics for quotes so you can compare.

- When talking to your mechanic, be as specific as possible. "There's a high-pitched squeal that seems to come from the right rear wheel between 50 and 60 mph," is a lot more helpful than, "The wheel makes funny noises."

- If you're unhappy about warranty work, don't hesitate to complain to the manufacturer's regional service representative. Your truck's owner's manual will usually give an address. If you're unhappy about work you paid for, contact your state's bureau of automotive repair. As a last resort, small claims courts are generally sympathetic to truck owners who can present a well-documented case of an auto repair rip-off.

Repair Tips

Before You Buy

- *Don't reject a vehicle just because the charts show a high expected repair cost. The cost of repair is often the smallest of the seven major ownership costs, since most vehicles today are very reliable.*

After You've Bought

- *Keep receipts and document all the services performed on your vehicle. If you can't prove that you've followed the manufacturer's recommended service program, you could invalidate your warranty.*

- *Before you pay for a repair, see if the automaker has issued a service bulletin for the problem. Even if your vehicle is no longer under warranty, the repairs may be covered.*

- *Cultivate a good relationship with a mechanic. Interview mechanics in your area before you desperately need one.*

- *Don't be afraid to switch dealers if your vehicle is under warranty and you're dissatisfied with the service you are getting.*

- *Don't be afraid to try an independent mechanic for routine service or, if your vehicle is out of warranty, for repair. They're often less expensive than a dealer's service department.*

- *Expect full explanations and estimates of cost before you authorize your mechanic to perform any work.*

Reading Your Garage Floor

Have you ever looked at the garage floor underneath your truck and noticed a veritable palette of pretty colors? There may be rich browns, pale yellows, electric greens, or deep reds.

Unfortunately, they shouldn't be there. Your vehicle contains more varieties of fluids than the local tavern — well, nearly a dozen anyway. And sooner or later, one or more of them is going to leak, leaving a tell-tale puddle.

Once every week or two, bend down and take a peek. Some leaks are benign. But others could indicate your truck is about to give you grief.

In addition to the color, the smell and feel of the fluid, as well as its location on the floor, will give you clues as to which fuel is which.

Brown or black. Probably engine oil, especially if you find it underneath the front half of the truck where the engine resides (in most vehicles, anyway). If your vehicle has a manual transmission, it could be coming from there as well. In either instance, it will of course feel oily when you touch it. Engine oil leaks are especially noticeable after the truck has run hard at highway speeds.

Your engine contains several quarts of oil and won't miss the amount in a drip the size of a quarter. Older engines and transmissions are especially prone to dribble a little oil.

But if the leaks are substantial, you might find the engine running dangerously low on oil. Have the leak checked by a mechanic. It could be coming from a faulty seal or gasket that's costly to repair. Or it may be something easily fixed, like a loose oil filter.

Brownish or blackish oil dripping from your truck's aft end could indicate a leaking differential. It may just be a loose drain plug. Again, the danger is running out of oil, in which case the differential gears will grind themselves into oblivion.

Red or pink. You'll probably find this hue under the automatic transmission, beneath the center of a rear-wheel-drive vehicle, and towards the front of a front-wheel-drive truck. A small leak is no cause for immediate worry; once again, the danger is running out completely if the leak worsens, or if you fail to check the transmission fluid level regularly.

Red, amber, or clear fluid, oily to the touch. This could be coming from the power steering, if your truck has such a gadget. The power steering unit is usually located near the front of the truck, to one side of the engine. If the fluid level is too low, the power steering pump may be damaged.

Green, with a distinctive sweet odor. This is radiator coolant, and it will leak from the front half of the truck where the radiator, overflow tank, water pump, and various hoses reside.

Coolant should never leak. A coolant leak may either indicate something quite serious like a bad water pump, or something simple to repair like a loose hose clamp. But a coolant leak will usually lead to an overheated — and perhaps ruined — engine.

Reddish brown fluid that evaporates quickly means gasoline. A usual clue for a gas leak is a vague smell, perhaps in the trunk or engine compartment.

Gas leaks are dangerous. If you see a puddle, and a dab of the stuff on your finger smells of gas, don't drive the truck. Call the auto club immediately; otherwise, your vehicle may become a Molotov cocktail.

Clear fluid with a medicinal smell. This may come from the hydraulic clutch system (if your truck has a manual transmission). Or it may come from the braking system; both the clutch and brakes use the same kind of fluid.

The reservoirs for both are located in the engine compartment; if one reservoir is low, you'll know which system is leaking. If the clutch system becomes too low on fluid, you won't be able to engage the clutch. Even worse, if the brake system is too low, you won't be able to stop the truck. So in either case, have a mechanic check out the leak right away.

Clear water on the floor? No problem with this one. It means the air conditioner is doing its job of removing excess humidity from the truck's interior.

Section Two
Choosing and Buying a Truck

Choosing and Buying a Truck

It's inevitable. It happens to every truck driver. Sooner or later, you'll have fantasies. Fantasies of buying a brand-new truck. Fantasies of gazing into the deep, lustrous, unblemished paint of a brand-new truck. Fantasies of how you'll look — a sneer on your aristocratic lips, perhaps — as you sit behind the wheel of a brand-new truck. Fantasies of not having to worry about repairs and breakdowns of a brand-new truck. Freedom and power — a brand-new truck can provide it all.

...pop! Hold on. Back to reality for a moment. All this fantasizing can make you forget mundane matters like budget-busting monthly payments or how you're going to get rid of the old clunker you're currently driving.

Checking Out A New Truck

Chances are, when you walk in to the showroom door of your local truck dealer, a beaming salesperson will pounce on you. Hold him or her at bay for a few minutes while you contemplate the truck alone. Stand back and take a long look. View it from all angles. Even if you're just buying a pickup truck to haul furniture, it's nice to own a truck you like to look at every day.

Now get a little closer and look for indications of quality construction. Are the gaps between the fenders and hood even? Do the doors hang straight? Is the paint truly smooth, or is it thick and crinkly like orange peel? Open the hood. Run your hand around the inside edges; you won't find spurs or jagged edges on a well-made vehicle. Is the engine a rat's maze, or does the wiring seem neatly bundled, and are the components accessible for service?

Now slide behind the wheel, and make sure the seat gives you support at the small of your back and under your thighs. After several hours of driving, firm-feeling seats, by the way, can actually be less fatiguing than soft seats. Make sure you can comfortably reach all the controls. Look out all the windows and notice if there are any large blind spots that might make lane changes exciting events.

The salesperson will probably want to ride with you on the test drive. Once again, ask him or her to can the sales chatter. Concentrate on the truck. Try a variety of roads and speeds; some vehicles ride fine on smooth roads but lose their aplomb on rough ones. Note the vehicle's noise level with the windows open. A noisy vehicle can be tiresome on the highway. If the vehicle has a manual transmission, be sure you're comfortable with both the position and the operation of the gearshift lever.

Before you completely surrender yourself, resist temptation for a few moments and ask yourself some prudent questions:

• How much can I afford to spend each month? (Appendix I will show you how to convert a monthly payment into a truck price.) What's really more important, the kids' college tuition or my truck?

• How long do I expect to own the vehicle? If these buying-a-new-truck fantasies come infrequently, say once every eight or ten years, then depreciation is less of a factor and you can consider vehicles with a higher rate of depreciation.

• How well do I tend to maintain a vehicle? If you're the kind to drive 'em and leave 'em, you'd better steer clear of high-maintenance trucks.

• How many miles a year will I drive? If you pile on the miles, a truck with poor fuel economy and high maintenance costs could bankrupt you.

Test Drive Tip

If you fall in love with a vehicle during the test drive, don't let the salesperson know it. It will be easier to negotiate later if the salesperson does not sense that you have become emotionally attached to the vehicle.

Don't let the dealer salesperson talk you into options you don't need or want. Rustproofing is rarely needed on today's vehicles, which already come with lengthy rust-through warranties. Nor are dealer fabric treatments.

Front-wheel drive vehicles in particular often have balky transmissions that can make shifting a chore.

Take plenty of time on the test drive; really get to know the vehicle. After all, it may become your daily companion for several years. If the vehicle passes muster, you'll probably be eager to sign on the dotted line. But control the urge, because there are several other matters to consider first.

Options and Special Features

Options can be a mother lode of profit for dealers and automakers alike. But do you really want a vehicle "loaded" with options, or even one with advanced technical features that come as standard equipment? Some options and features are truly useful and add to a vehicle's resale value. Others end up being expensive maintenance headaches. *(Refer to Figure 8 on page 32A-33A to help make your choices a little easier.)*

Option Packages

Manufacturers often group options together in packages, sometimes providing a discount on the package over the price of the individual options. Option packages reduce the manufacturer's production cost, since they have to make fewer variations of each vehicle. It can also save you money if you want those options anyway. On the other hand, you can waste money on these packages if they mean you pay for options you don't want.

To properly evaluate an option package, first determine the options you really want, then add the prices of the individual options and compare them to the total price of the option package.

It's also not uncommon for a dealer to put vehicles on the lot with accessories and options already installed. "Sorry, you have to buy it as is," the salesperson will tell you. However, if you don't want this vehicle, try another dealership, or try to custom order, if you don't mind waiting. On the other hand, if you're willing to purchase a vehicle that is already on the dealer's lot, you may be able to negotiate a better deal than if you have the vehicle custom ordered.

What Price Should You Pay?

Wouldn't it be a relief if new-truck prices were no more negotiable than a can of tuna at the supermarket? Unfortunately, that's not the nature of the game.

And in many ways it is a game. Unless you've been trained, don't expect to beat the dealer — he or she is a pro, after all. But if you do a little homework, you can arrive at a fair deal for both yourself and the dealer.

Sometimes a dealer can purchase a truck for less than the figure shown as dealer cost. This is because manufacturers frequently allow volume discounts, and often provide other dollar incentives, such as rebates, for dealers to "move" trucks. Since there are many ways for dealers to hide their true costs, be wary of any numbers they quote you.

Knowing the dealer cost does not automatically guarantee that you will get the deal of the century. But, it is an effective weapon to have as part of your negotiating arsenal. Not only will it give you a good indication of how much profit a dealer is trying to make on each sale, but it will also serve as an excellent point from which to begin negotiating. Realistically, you should set your goal on purchasing a new truck at the "target price" listed in the vehicle charts starting on page 1. This figure is calculated using the dealer cost as a base, and factoring in current market conditions to arrive at a price that represents a good deal to you and a fair profit for the dealer.

Once upon a time, the manufacturer's suggested list price was the price at which the dealer was willing to start negotiating. These days the situation can be quite different; this truth becomes apparent when you discover that a particular model is priced hundreds, sometimes thousands, of dollars above the manufacturer's list price. This is simply a function of supply and demand. If a particular vehicle is in great demand, a dealer can sell it for whatever the market will bear. You may be able to bargain some money off the inflated price, but you will find it close to impossible to buy a truck at or below list. In this instance, check dealers outside your local market area. They may offer better pricing on your model.

On the other hand, it will be much easier to negotiate a better deal on overstocked vehicles or models that are not selling well. Dealers who are carrying less popular models that have been sitting on their lots for a long time are stuck with a double-edged liability. Not only are they losing profit on potential sales, but they are paying finance charges and other expenses while they keep the vehicles. They may be happy to get them off the lot at a bargain price.

Beware...

Frequently, a dealer will try to tack on an extra charge called an "advertising allowance," or, in industry parlance, a "pack." The dealer will argue that this figure is a legitimate business expense that he has to recover in addition to any profit on each vehicle sold. However, this is just accounting hocus-pocus. Like any other business, the dealer will cover his costs through the profit from the sale of his merchandise, and not by adding a special fee. The profit range suggested in the "target price" should reasonably compensate the dealer.

Figure 8

A Handy Guide To Options And Technical Features

Any option or feature you add will raise the sticker price of a new vehicle but may not increase the price when it comes time for resale. Just like trucks, options vary in how rapidly they depreciate. For example, $500 spent on air conditioning may add $400 to the vehicle price when it's time to resell, but $500 spent on a leather interior may add little or nothing to the resale price. Some options (e.g., anti-lock brakes) that are clearly beneficial may not be available on a particular model, or might not fit into your budget. When selecting your options, it is important to weigh emotional, safety, and practical aspects along with the economic ones. A vehicle with wisely chosen options will prove to be a better value.

Options	Benefits	Drawbacks
Active Suspension: Electronically controlled hydraulic actuators that respond to changing road surfaces and driver input to keep the vehicle level at all times.	Allows for comfortable ride and excellent emergency handling.	Expensive, with a lot of mechanical complexity. Unnecessary on most vehicles.
Adjustable Shock Absorbers: Shock absorbers that can be adjusted by either the driver or an on-board computer.	Allows you to adjust the ride according to different driving conditions. Sport handling means a firm, more controlled ride, and Touring means a softer, more comfortable ride.	Expensive to buy; expensive to replace when they wear out.
Air Bags: Hidden in the steering wheel, and on some vehicles, in the passenger side of the dashboard, they inflate during a collision to protect driver and/or passenger. They are not substitutes for seatbelts.	Have been proven to significantly reduce injuries in cases of head-on collision.	They only provide protection in a frontal collision, and are expensive to replace after use.
Air Conditioning	Reduces fatigue in hot weather. Adds considerably to resale value of truck.	Expensive to buy. Somewhat expensive to maintain, and will become more so as ban on Freon takes effect in the near future. Increases fuel consumption.
Anti-Lock Brakes or ABS: Electronic sensors and computer control prevent the brakes from locking up.	Prevents the vehicle from skidding uncontrollably during a panic stop. Shortens stopping distances.	Expensive to buy. May require some additional maintenance.
Automatic Transmission	Makes driving easier in stop-and-go traffic and on mountain or hilly roads. Adds to resale value if appropriate for vehicle.	May decrease fuel economy, though not as much as in years past. May decrease acceleration. May decrease resale value if on inappropriate vehicle.
Continuously Variable Transmission: An automatic transmission that, instead of using three or four separate gears, uses compressive belts to produce continuously changing speed ratios.	Better fuel economy than with a manual transmission, because it lets the engine work in its most efficient range.	It's a complex technology whose reliability hasn't been proven. May be very expensive to maintain.
Cruise Control	Reduces driver fatigue on long trips, and may help increase fuel economy.	May require some maintenance.
Digital Instrumentation	Amusing—if you're into video games.	Can be confusing and distracting; also very expensive to repair.
Diesel Engine	Fuel economy.	Slow acceleration, difficult to start in extremely cold weather, unpleasant fumes, fuel sometimes hard to find.
Four-Wheel Disc Brakes: Vehicles often have "disc" brakes on the front wheels and "drum" brakes on the rear wheels. However, under hard use, disc brakes remain cooler than drum brakes, which means they retain stopping power longer. Disc brakes on all four wheels are preferable.	Retain stopping power longer; disc brake pads cheaper to replace.	Disc brake pads wear more quickly than drum brake pads.
Four-Wheel or All-Wheel Drive	Increases traction; particularly useful in snow, rain, and in off-road driving.	Adds complexity and weight, which raises vehicle's price and lowers its fuel economy.
Four-Wheel Steering: At low speeds, the rear wheels turn in the opposite direction to the front wheels; at higher speeds, all four wheels turn in the same direction.	Makes the vehicle generally easier to steer, particularly during parking.	Added initial cost, and possibly added maintenance and repair cost.
Fuel Injection: Replaces the carburetor as the device that sends fuel and air to the engine's combustion chambers.	Improves engine response and fuel economy. Reduces exhaust pollutants.	Fuel injectors are sensitive to impurities in gas; may require detergent gas or additives to prevent clogging.

Options	Benefits	Drawbacks
Head-up Instrument Display: Projects a vehicle's speedometer reading or other instrument displays onto the front windshield.	Lets drivers read instrument displays without taking their eyes from the road.	Unnecessary gizmo. Only essential for fighter pilots.
Heavy Duty Cooling System	Necessary for hauling heavy loads in hot weather, especially on a vehicle with air conditioning.	No disadvantages except extra initial cost.
Heavy Duty Suspension	Necessary for hauling heavy loads.	Rougher ride when not hauling a load.
Keyless Entry: A keypad mounted on the front doors that unlocks them when you enter a five digit code.	Entry is possible, even if the keys are locked in the vehicle. Also, allows a third party access to the vehicle without giving him the keys.	You have to remember a five-digit code in order to use the system.
Larger Engine: Engine size is noted by the number of cylinders, and by "displacement." Displacement can be measured in liters, cubic centimeters or cubic inches. The more cylinders and the greater the displacement, the larger the engine. Larger engines generally provide more torque and more horsepower.	Quieter and smoother during highway cruising; added power for passing, for mountain travel, and for hauling a trailer.	Slightly higher maintenance costs; possibly higher costs for fuel, insurance, and state registration.
Multiple Valves: All engines have at least two valves for each cylinder. But some have three or four valves for each cylinder. The additional valves allow a more efficient movement of the air/fuel mixture in the combustion chambers so the engine develops more power.	Better acceleration without sacrificing fuel economy.	Added complication; possibly higher repair costs.
Overhead Cam: Some engines have single or double overhead camshafts instead of pushrods to open and close the valves as the engine operates.	Better engine response at high speeds.	Nothing really, except slightly higher manufacturing costs.
Power Seats	Impresses those who like gadgets.	Something else to go wrong.
Power Steering, and Power Steering with Variable Assist: At higher speeds, simple power steering can make the steering feel too light. Variable-assist or speed-sensitive steering is a type of power steering that automatically boosts the power assist at low speeds and reduces it at high speeds.	Makes it easier to turn the steering wheel, especially when parking. Necessary for large, heavy vehicles; can increase resale value for those vehicles.	Added initial cost; added maintenance cost.
Power Windows/Locks	Convenient; a safety feature when children are in vehicle.	Higher initial cost; increased repair costs.
Rear Window Defogger	Increases outward vision in icy or humid conditions.	Can crack window if left on in hot weather.
Rustproofing/Undercoating	No benefit, unless vehicle isn't rustproofed/undercoated by the factory.	Unnecessary because almost all new vehicles have rustproofing and undercoating.
Stereo Sound System	Improves resale value of vehicle. (Tip: Aftermarket products are often superior in price and sound to factory or dealer-installed units.)	Makes vehicle a target for theft.
Sunroof/T-Top/Moonroof	Fun. Can increase resale value substantially.	Added wind noise; may reduce interior headroom, and may leak or squeak if moldings deteriorate.
Tinted Windows	Keeps vehicle cooler in sunny weather, thus reducing sun-caused damage to upholstery, and dashboard. Reduces load on air conditioner.	Slightly higher initial cost.
Turbocharger/Supercharger: A turbocharger is operated by hot exhaust gases that continually rush out of the engine as it runs. A supercharger is driven by a belt or a shaft from the engine. Both devices force extra air and fuel into the engine's combustion chambers for more power.	Provides the acceleration of a larger engine, but without higher fuel consumption.	History of repair problems; requires extra maintenance; often more costly to insure.
Traction Control: Uses sensors to determine when wheels begin to slip and reduces engine speed/applies brakes to maintain optimum traction.	Allows for smooth acceleration on slippery roads. Worth having if you regularly drive wet, muddy, or icy roads.	Expensive, with a lot of mechanical complexity. No benefit under normal driving conditions.

Choosing Safety

Ponder this for a moment: According to the National Highway Traffic Safety Administration (NHTSA), two out of three motorists are involved in an accident at some time that injures someone in the car.

Other statistics show that every motorist can expect to be in a crash once every 10 years. And for about one out of 20, it will cause serious injury.

With numbers like this, it's no wonder that more and more motorists have gotten the safety religion. Today, safety ranks right up there with price, quality and reliability on most buyers' shopping lists.

Anatomy of a Crash

NHTSA research shows that the major causes of injury inside a vehicle during a collision are, in descending order, the steering wheel, the instrument panel, the doors, the windshield, the front roof pillar, the glove box area, the roof edges, and the roof itself. It's not surprising then, that front-seat passengers are more likely to be injured than rear-seat passengers who are protected by the padding of the front seat backs.

NHTSA data also shows that 51 percent of deaths occur in head-on impacts, 27 percent in side impacts and only 4 percent in rear impacts. Rollovers, however, are particularly lethal because they are more likely to eject unrestrained passengers from the vehicle than other types of collisions. And fatality rates are 25 times higher for ejected passengers than for those who remain in the vehicle.

The objectives of safety features are 1) to keep the occupants inside the vehicle; 2) to keep them from banging around inside; 3) to absorb some of the forces of impact rather than transfer it to the occupants; or 4) to help prevent a collision from happening in the first place.

Choosing a Safe Truck

NHTSA's book of *Federal Motor Vehicle Safety Standards And Regulations* is chock-a-block with mandated safety features — for cars, that is.

When it comes to 1993-model light trucks — all those pickups, vans and sport utility vehicles — many of the mandated safety features are missing. Light trucks have their own schedule for meeting federal safety standards, one that lags the passenger-car time table. Light trucks don't have to have many of the features now required in cars until 1998.

Nevertheless, automakers are in some cases equipping their light trucks with safety features not yet required by the law. Here are some important safety features that you should hope to find on a light truck:

Seat belts

A three-point seat belt is a belt with three attachment points: one on the side pillar or on the door, and one on each side of the driver's or passenger's hips.

The three-point belt is superior to the older lap-only seat belt for a couple of reasons. Not only do three-point belts reduce the likelihood of the wearer hitting the steering wheel, windshield or other interior surfaces, but they spread the crash forces over more of the body and reduce the strain of the lap belt on the lower body.

In 1993, light trucks are required to have some form of three-point seat belts for both front- AND rear-seat occupants.

Beginning in 1990, NHTSA began requiring some form of "passive" or automatic restraint system in passenger cars for the driver.

And what is a "passive system?" Either an air bag or some form of automatic seat belt, of which there are three. The first uses a motorized shoulder belt that positions itself around the occupant when the door is closed and the ignition is switched on. The second is also connected to the door, but is not motorized. With either of these, the lap belt must still be manually fastened by the driver or passenger.

A third type of automatic belt has both lap and shoulder belts attached to the door, and forces the driver or passenger to slide under this web as they enter the vehicle.

There are several drawbacks to these automatic belt systems. In some accidents, the door is torn off the vehicle; if the seat belts are attached to the door, the seat belts will obviously go with it. Many people also find the automatic belts an obstacle to getting in and out of the vehicle, and find ways to defeat them. Automatic belts also may not fit as well as manual belts. And finally, some of the automatic belts still require the user to manually fasten the lap belt portion; if they forget to fasten it, they risk "submarining" under the shoulder harness in an accident.

Air bags or automatic seat belts won't be required in light trucks until the 1995 model year. But some light trucks, particularly minivans, have them in 1993. Mercury's new Villager minivan and Nissan's new Quest minivan, for example, have motorized shoulder belts with manual lap belts in the front seats.

Look for the shoulder belt portion of a three-point belt that's attached to a pillar of the cab, not to the door. And the lap belt should ride across your pelvis, not across your stomach.

Above all, a seat belt must be comfortable when it's snug against the body. If it's not comfortable, it's tempting not to wear it. And if it's not snug, it may not provide the protection it should. In fact, slackened seat belts may INCREASE the risk of injury.

For these reasons, some 1993 light trucks have belt adjusters. It's a simple slide device that allows the shoulder belt anchor on the truck's pillar to be moved up and down to accommodate occupants of various heights and bodybuilds. It's not rocket-science, and it's a wonder all cars and trucks don't have them.

Air bags

Pundits once called them "automotive whoopee cushions." But air bags have proven important safety features since 1990, when automakers first began installing them in relatively large numbers on their cars. Costs have come down, doubts about reliability have been laid to rest, and buyers are eager to have them.

Yet, despite their acceptance, air bags are still a rarity in light trucks. Not until 1999 will all light trucks be required to have them for both drivers and passengers.

Safety Tips

• When you choose a vehicle, make sure that you will be able to see and recognize safety hazards approaching from all directions. Any part of the vehicle that obstructs your view, such as headrests, front or back roof pillars, large areas of reflection, or poorly placed rear-deck brake lights, poses a potential danger. And don't forget to consider the placement of passengers and cargo.

• When you're sitting in the dealer show room checking out the truck of your dreams, don't forget to try out the seatbelt system. Can you easily reach the belt from your driving position, pull it across your body in one motion, and snap it in place without having to search for the buckle? Does the lap belt fit snugly across your pelvis (not your stomach), and does the shoulder belt fit snugly across your torso and over your collar bone without riding up on your neck? Check to see if the shoulder mounting is adjustable, to provide you with the most comfortable fit. Reach down and see if the seatbelt release is easy to find and operate, and that the belt retracts smoothly to its original position. If the seatbelt system fails any of these tests, you may not use it consistently, and because seatbelts are so important, you're better off looking at another truck.

Don't Forget the Kids

If you have a family, there are several additional safety features you will want to look for when choosing a vehicle.

• *First, you want seatbelts designed to properly hold a child restraint in place, with an automatic locking retractor. This means that once the seatbelt is fastened, it will remain firmly in place without loosening so the child restraint stays put.*

• *You also want the driver to be able to lock automatic windows so children can't play with them. For the same reason, you want child-proof door locks, so small children cannot open rear doors from the inside.*

• *Also, small, wide-angle "child-view" mirrors are available that snap on to the regular rear-view mirror, and allow you to keep tabs on the kids in the back seat without taking your eyes far from the road.*

• ***Built-in Child Seats —*** *Chrysler pioneered the idea of built-in child restraint seat in its vans. The seat folds out from the regular, adult's seat, and comes complete with its own seat belts. It's recommended for kids weighing 20 to 45 pounds.*

Ford and GM both expect to offer the seats in some of their mini-vans later in 1993. Chrysler will also have them in the rear seats of its Eagle Vision, Concorde, and Intrepid.

There isn't a single 1993 pickup truck available with an air bag. Only one sports utility, the Jeep Grand Cherokee, has an air bag — for the driver only. But several 1993 minivans, including Chrysler's Caravan and Voyager, and Ford's Aerostar have driver's-side air bags.

It should be common knowledge why it's vital to wear a seat belt even in a vehicle with air bags. That is, because air bags don't protect in side impacts, rear impacts or rollovers — accidents that account for nearly half of all highway fatalities.

But if you're a dedicated seat-belt user, you may wonder why you need an air bag. A pamphlet entitled "Shopping For A Safer Car" from the Insurance Institute for Highway Safety (IIHS), an insurance industry research group, explains: "Because (even) the best belts — those with tensioners — allow some occupant movement in a crash as the belt pulls tightly around the reel. Plus, there's stretch designed into safety belts to keep people from stopping as abruptly in a crash as the car does. This combination of looseness and stretch means front-seat occupants wearing belts can still move forward enough in a serious crash to hit the steering wheel, dashboard or windshield...Serving as a pillow between car occupants and the vehicle interior, airbags cushion people's heads and faces."

Make sure to check the charts in this guide to see which vehicles come with air bags.

Crumple zones

Besides the choices each automaker has regarding seat belts and automatic restraint systems, automakers can choose various structural features that make their light trucks more crashworthy.

Automakers build two important structures into a truck to protect the occupants. The first is a collapsible energy-absorbing structure designed to crush in a controlled manner, absorbing the energy of the crash and increasing the time it takes for the truck to come to a stop.

The second structure is a reinforced, protective cabin that surrounds the occupants and protects them from injury by keeping the exterior impact from reaching them.

Each year NHTSA crash tests popular models into a fixed barrier at 35 mph. The tests measure the crash's impact on the driver and passenger dummies' heads, chests and thighbones, using all the vehicle's standard safety equipment. And the results, even among different models in the same size class, do indeed vary greatly. You can obtain information on NHTSA's crash tests by calling 1-800-424-9393.

The IIHS also publishes periodic reports, assembled from claims data collected from the institute's sponsoring insurance companies, that show injury frequencies for popular models. For further information, write IIHS, 1005 North Glebe Road, Arlington, VA 22201.

Side Impact Protection

Automakers add stronger steel beams beneath the body panels on the sides and doors and interior padding in an effort to keep the passenger compartment from being crushed when the vehicle takes a hit on the side. Side impacts are second only to head-on collisions as the most serious traffic accidents.

For light trucks, side-impact protection isn't required until the 1994 model year. But some already have it, like Mercury's Villager, Nissan's Quest and Volkswagen's EuroVan.

Roll-over Protection

A roof crush standard — designed to prevent injuries caused by a collapsed roof should the vehicle roll over — isn't slated to go into effect for light trucks until the 1994 model year.

Head Restraints

Of course, these are popularly known as "head rests," a terrible misnomer. Their purpose is not to give your head a place to rest, but to prevent it from snapping back sharply in a rear-end collision.

Light trucks must have front-seat head restraints; though they're not mandatory, look for them on other seats as well.

If a head restraint is adjustable, it should be adjusted high enough (about ear level) and far enough forward to hit the occupant's head, not his or her neck.

Crash Avoidance Features

Automakers actually build safety into their vehicles in two different ways. There are the crash survival features already discussed — from seat belts to head restraints. But of equal importance are features that help you avoid a crash in the first place.

In this respect, almost anything that gives you better control over your vehicle is a safety feature — from good acceleration that allows you to merge safely with the flow of traffic, to good ventilation that keeps you alert during long spells behind the wheel.

But here are a few particularly important crash-avoidance features you'll want to consider for your 1993 dream truck:

Anti-lock Brakes (ABS). Slam on the brakes during an emergency, and chances are your car will become Mr. Toad's wild ride as it skids down the road, especially if it's rain-slicked or icy. Locking up the wheels — or skidding — is dangerous because it not only increases the distance before the vehicle stops, but because the driver loses the ability to steer.

ABS on light trucks is often been available for the rear wheels only. But in 1993, more light trucks will be available with four-wheel ABS. Four-wheel ABS is a definite advantage over rear-wheel-only ABS when the truck is lightly loaded.

Check the charts in this guide to see which vehicles have ABS.

Proper Ergonomics. A truck's sound system may reproduce music that's the next best thing to a live performance, but if the system's controls are so tiny that you need your bifocals to find them, they're a detriment to safety.

Convenient placement and logical arrangement of controls in a truck's cabin is an important, yet often overlooked, safety feature.

Good Visibility. Clear vision from inside the vehicle would seem to be an obvious given in the design. Yet all too often window size and placement is dictated more by style than by function.

Crash Avoidance Safety Features Every Vehicle Should Have

- *Anti-lock brakes*
- *Legible instruments*
- *Easily operated controls and switches*
- *Clear field of vision to all sides*
- *Day/night rear-view mirror*
- *Dual side mirrors*
- *Center high-mounted brake light*
- *Windshield wiper/washer system*
- *Adequate heat/defrost system*
- *Electric rear-window defroster*
- *Comfortable but firmly-padded seats with driver's seat height adjustment*
- *Light, bright exterior color*

Optional Crash Avoidance Active Safety Features

- *Rear window wiper*
- *Headlight washing system*
- *All-wheel drive*
- *Traction control*
- *Active suspension*
- *Halogen headlights*
- *Power mirrors and locks*
- *Full-size spare tire*
- *Rear light bulb, tire pressure, brake system sensors*

Crash Survival Features

- *Deformable crash structure*
- *Collapsible steering column*
- *Easy to fasten and release, 3-point seat belts*
- *Automatic seat-belt tensioners*
- *Seat belt buckle that moves forward or back along with the seat*
- *Adjustable seat belt shoulder mount*
- *Driver's side airbag*
- *Front passenger's side airbag*
- *Adjustable or fixed head restraint properly positioned to prevent whiplash*
- *Jam-resistant door latches*
- *Safety glass side door anti-intrusion beams*
- *Roll bar (convertible vehicles)*

Rebate Tips

• Don't rely on the dealer to inform you of available rebates and incentives. Each issue of Automotive News, *available at many public libraries, lists consumer and dealer incentives. If you would like a complete report on a particular vehicle, including current consumer and dealer incentives, you can order the* ArmChair Compare® Report, *as advertised in this book.*

Sometimes, rebates are offered only in certain sales regions — and sometimes a regional rebate is less than the rebate available in the rest of the nation.

• Don't buy a truck just because it comes with a large rebate. A rebate tacked on a poor value doesn't automatically make it a good value. Use the charts in this book to determine the good values, then see which of those have a rebate.

Rebate: *Cash given by the auto manufacturer in return for a sale.*

Incentive: *The bait a manufacturer uses to fish for sales. An incentive may be a cash rebate, discount options packages, low-interest financing, and much more.*

Customer incentive: *An automaker's financial or non-financial offer intended to entice the customer to buy.*

Dealer incentive: *A financial offer by the manufacturer to the dealer for making a sale. The dealer may or may not pass on the incentive to the customer. If it is passed on, it may take one of many forms, such as a price discount, a rebate, free options, or free maintenance.*

Rebates and Sales Incentives

Cash-back rebates have become as much a part of the new-car sales routine as tire-kicking and test drives.

In recent years, manufacturers have added a number of other items to their sales-incentive menu as well. Automakers may offer a choice of discount financing or a cash rebate, for instance. (See Appendix J on page 108A)

Now there are discount leases, with automakers subsidizing some of the leasing costs the buyer would otherwise incur. (See "Leasing," page 14A.)

In addition to these monetary incentives, there are some new and intriguing non-monetary sales incentives.

Automakers and dealers alike are pushing customer service as a reason to buy their particular products. Virtually every automaker offers free towing in the event of a breakdown that's covered under warranty, and a growing number of automakers are providing roadside assistance. Pontiac, for example, is expanding its roadside assistance program in 1993 to include free help when the owner is out of fuel, locked out, or has a dead battery. If you're 150 miles or more from home and your new car breaks down, Oldsmobile covers food and lodging expense up to $500.

Several automakers are offering their customers courtesy transportation or loaner cars when their cars are taken to the dealer for service or repairs.

Oldsmobile and Saturn permit new-car buyers to return their cars to their dealers within a certain period for a full-credit exchange on another Olds or Saturn if they're unhappy with their car.

When is the Best Time to Buy a New Truck?

Best Time of Year

The winter months usually present good bargain opportunities. With increased cash outlays for clothing, utility bills, and holiday expenses, auto sales are slow and salespeople are eager to make a sale. The summer months can also be a good time to shop. This is when sales of the current-year model have slowed down and consumers are waiting for the new model year vehicles to be introduced. But be cautious during springtime! That's when consumers come out of their winter doldrums and vehicle sales increase. Dealers are less inclined to make price concessions while sales are up.

Best Time of Month

The end of the month is the best time to buy a new vehicle. A salesperson prospers by consistently meeting or exceeding his or her monthly quota. To increase a salesperson's incentive, dealers often have contests and offer bonuses for exceeding monthly quotas. As a result, salespeople are more likely to sacrifice a small part of their commission at the end of the month if it will help them meet or exceed a quota.

Buying, Financing, and Selling Your Old Truck

There is one golden rule when it comes to negotiating a new truck: Buying a new truck, financing it, and trading in your old truck may all occur at the same time, but these are three separate transactions and should be negotiated separately.

Imagine this scenario. A salesman is negotiating with a customer about the price of a new truck. Negotiations have come to a standstill because the customer says he can not afford a penny more than $13,000 for a particular truck that is priced at $13,200. The dialogue might sound like this:

"Well, what are your current monthly payments?" asks the salesman.

"$275 a month," the customer replies, "and I only have two payments left."

"How about this," says the salesman, "if I can get you into that new truck for $275 a month, have we got a deal?"

"That sounds reasonable," answers the customer.

The salesman smiles, "Do you want to trade your truck in? I could probably get your monthly payments even lower."

"Well, sure. I'll trade my truck in if you can give me a good deal," says the customer.

The salesman checks out the customer's truck and says, "How about this, I will buy out the balance of your loan, give you a $2,000 check on top of that to use as a down payment for a new truck, and then I'll finance the rest for 60 months at a monthly payment of only $250 — $25

When negotiating price, keep in mind that the following three prices are very different:

1) The dealer's cost or price (a.k.a. factory invoice) — the maximum price the dealer paid the factory for the truck.

2) The manufacturer's suggested list price.

3) The vehicle's sticker price, includes special equipment, options, preparation charges, and other fees.

lower than you're currently paying. Now, doesn't that sound terrific?"

"It certainly does!"

But, it isn't so terrific. In fact, the customer is going to pay more for his new truck than he initially wanted to. The salesman has confused him. $250 a month has the illusion of a good deal because it is less than the customer's current payments. However, upon closer examination we can see what is really happening. First of all, the salesman offered the customer $2,000 in addition to "buying out" his current loan on the old truck. That means the customer receives a total value of $2,550 for his truck. $550 will be paid to the title holder of the old truck (for the last two payments) and the $2,000 will be applied as a down payment for the new truck. If we then calculate the present value of $250 dollars per month over a 60-month term at 11% interest, it works out to be about $11,600. Combining all this together, we find that the customer has agreed to pay the equivalent of $13,600 for his truck: $2,000 from the trade-in and $11,600 from the loan. This is $600 more than the customer originally said he'd pay. To add insult to injury, the customer is without a doubt going to get less on his trade-in than if he sells the truck himself.

Even though this example is contrived, situations like this happen every day. Salespeople are experts at this tactic and employ it every chance they get. Even if you know all your facts, it is still easy to get confused. It can be difficult enough trying to negotiate a single transaction with a salesman, but when you try to do all three at once, you are stacking the deck in his favor. Don't even try; keep these three transactions separate.

Finance & Insurance Manager

Whew, you did it! It took hours of haggling. But you and the dealer have finally come to terms on your new truck.

You bargained hard to get what you consider a fair price for the car and its optional equipment. You even managed to get the dealer to give you a reasonable price in trade for that old jalopy you're now driving. And the salesman has quoted you a competitive interest rate on dealer-arranged financing.

Why, you can practically feel the keys to your new dream machine dropping into the palm of your hand. All that's left to do is a quick trip to the dealer's finance and insurance (F&I) office to wrap up a little paperwork. Time to relax, right?

Wrong, not unless you want to risk spending more than you had planned.

The dealer's F&I person is often one of his most adept salespersons. In a few strokes of the pen, he or she can turn a good deal for the customer into a bonanza for the dealer.

For instance, the F&I person can write the contract with a higher interest rate than the salesman had quoted. He or she can add on an overpriced extended warranty. ("It'll only cost you a couple of dollars a month," the F&I person will say.)

F&I folks also love to tack on life and accident insurance designed to pay off the auto loan should you die or become disabled. It's often expensive, and most people already have disability and life insurance, and don't need the additional coverage anyway.

Then there's the "Rule of 78," a clever accounting method that can only benefit the dealer. Few car buyers understand the Rule of 78. Yet those who take dealer-arranged financing are often asked to initial a little box on the loan agreement that states interest on the loan will be calculated using the Rule of 78.

Compared to a simple-interest loan, a Rule-of-78 loan increases the portion of each monthly payment that goes to the lender as interest in the early part of the loan. It decreases the portion of each monthly payment that goes to the lender as interest in the last part of the loan.

In other words, the lender gets his interest sooner while the amount you owe gets paid off later.

For example, on a $10,000 loan for 24 months at 12 percent interest, the monthly payment will be $470.80. If it is a simple-interest loan, $100 of the first month's payment will go to the lender as interest. The balance, $370.80, will be used to pay off the principal, $10,000. Under the Rule of 78, nearly $104 of the first month's payment will go as interest, leaving a smaller amount to payoff the principal. By the 24th month, $4.64 will go as interest, if the lender uses simple-interest calculations. Under the Rule of 78, $4.33 will go to the lender as interest.

Now these may seem like insignificant differences. But on larger loans for longer terms, the differences are more profound. On a 60-month, $16,500 loan at 10.5 percent interest, a little more than half the total interest will be paid just 18 months into the loan, but only 24 percent of the principal.

Using the Rule of 78 does not change the amount of the loan's monthly payment. And it doesn't change the total amount of interest you'll pay on the loan — IF you keep the loan (and the vehicle) for the entire length of the loan.

And that's the rub. What if you want to trade in the vehicle long before the end of the loan's term? It means that you'll owe more on the vehicle than you'd otherwise owe if it had been a simple-interest loan.

Or what if the vehicle is stolen or wrecked early in the loan's term? Your insurancc company will reimburse you for the value of the lost vehicle, not for what you owe on your loan. If you owe more than the vehicle was worth — and the possibility of that is greater under the Rule of 78 — you'll be stuck with paying the difference out of your pocket.

While many dealers and finance companies use the Rule of 78, banks and credit unions are more likely to offer simple-interest loans.

The point should be clear: Don't sign any contract unless you completely understand it. And until those keys actually drop into your hand, pay close attention to every transaction between you and the dealer.

No Dicker Stickers

Take-it-or-leave-it price tags have suddenly become all the rage in the auto industry. A handful of enlightened individual dealers across the country, as well as all the dealers of one automaker, have decided to face head-on the traditional notion that the new-car showroom should take on the atmosphere of a third-world bazaar.

General Motors' newest division, Saturn Corporation, took the lead in eliminating the haggling over a car's price at its dealerships. Instead of a commission, Saturn salespeople are paid salaries, which helps remove some of the incentive to use high-pressure sales tactics new-car shoppers detest. And most important, the sticker prices on new Saturns aren't negotiable.

Individual dealers for other automakers, after noting Saturn's success, are trying no-haggle policies in their own showrooms. And surveys have shown that most customers love it.

Instead of boosting the window sticker prices by thousands with the expectation of knocking them down during the grueling negotiating process, the dealers tack on a reasonable profit to the manufacturer's invoice price and refuse to bargain down the price with the customer.

Though no-dicker-stickers eliminate part of the shopping hassle, they are not however, a panacea for haggle-phobic customers. Even no-dicker-sticker dealers have other ways to line their pockets with your money.

Buyers who wish to trade in their used vehicle to the dealer must still negotiate a price for it.

Dealer "F&I" (finance and insurance) managers can still pad dealer-provided loan or lease agreements with high or unnecessary extra charges if the customer lets his or her guard down.

And because dealer overhead can vary depending upon a dealer's location, the no-dicker prices will vary. Buyers still need to shop around for the best price, even among one-price dealerships.

Moreover, salespersons may still pressure you to buy a vehicle the dealer has in stock rather than trade with another dealer so you can have the vehicle outfitted exactly the way you want.

Finally, if you really think you can beat the dealer at his own game (few people actually can), if you enjoy the challenge of a good haggle, and if you have the time and patience to try, there's still no substitute for hard, astute bargaining at a traditional dealer.

For dealers other than Saturn, no-dicker sticker prices tend to be well below the manufacturer's suggested retail prices, but they still tend to be $500 to $1,000 over the dealer's cost. A hard-bargaining customer at a traditional dealership should be able to pay as little as $200 to $500 over the dealer's cost.

Brokers

It's an odd thing, this business of buying a new vehicle.

Next to a home, an automobile is the second most expensive purchase most of us ever make. Yet when we buy a home, we can count on the counsel of our real estate agent, escrow officers, title company personnel, loan officers and perhaps even our attorney. Moreover, there's usually a lengthy waiting period until the close of escrow, during which time we can find a way to back out of the deal.

Yet when we face an auto dealer and his agents — salespersons, sales managers, finance and insurance managers — we face them alone. And we're expected to close the deal in less than a day.

No wonder then, auto brokers around the country have stepped forward to help the beleaguered new-car shopper. Like a real estate agent, an auto broker's mission is to negotiate the purchase for the buyer. An auto broker can be the answer for buyers who fear they can't beat the dealer at his own game — or don't wish to take the time to try.

Most brokers bypass dealer salespersons. Instead, they deal only with dealer sales managers or fleet managers. Successful brokers have good working relationships with their local dealers, and can avoid much of the time-consuming sales games the individual buyer faces in the showroom.

Brokers are also familiar with their local dealers' inventories. They keep on top of which models are hot and which are not. When a broker can locate a dealer with three of the exact vehicles you want, chances are good the broker can negotiate a more favorable deal on one of the vehicles than if the dealer has to order or trade with another dealer to obtain the vehicle of your dreams.

Of course, a competent auto broker knows the tricks of the trade and isn't likely to fall for them.

Auto brokers usually charge an up-front fee of $200 to $400 for their service. But a good broker may be able to arrange a better deal on the truck you want than you could by yourself, even including his fee.

Broker Varieties

Not all brokers are the same, however. Some brokers are like a shopping friend; they'll accompany you to dealerships and do the negotiating for you in your presence once you've found the truck you want. At the end of the process, you'll pay the dealer and take delivery of the truck from him.

Other brokers take your order, and then operating over the phone, find the truck you want at a dealer that may be close by or several hundred miles away. The broker will take delivery of the truck, and you will then purchase it from him.

Finally, other brokers act as a referral service by putting you in touch with a dealer who promises to sell you the truck at a favorable price. Auto clubs and credit unions often work with these referral brokers. It's up to you, however, to do the final negotiating.

Regardless of which type you use, you're relying on the broker to make you a truly good deal — one better than you could cut yourself.

How Much Can a Broker Save You?

If you're a good negotiator, you can almost always negotiate a better deal than what a broker offers. A broker has to make money, which means the price you pay the broker will always be more than the price the broker paid the dealer — a price you could probably get on your own. However, if you're not comfortable negotiating, a broker can get you a real bargain.

Six Steps To A Good Deal

Haggling, horse-trading, bartering. Call it what you will. Though some buyers may consider it great sport to try and beat the last penny of profit out of an auto dealer, most consumers hate the hassle.

Consider the sad saga of Mr. B. Innocently enough, he went to a showroom and announced that he had $10,000 to spend on a modest new truck for his new business. A salesman showed him a nice truck, and eventually they came to an agreement. Or so Mr. B thought.

Mr. B returned to the dealership the next day, ready to buy. "I'm sorry," said the salesman, "but my sales manager won't let me sell the truck for less than $12,000." Yep, it was the old bait and switch — and Mr. B was furious. "How can they get away with this?," he growled.

They can and they do. But in today's highly competitive auto market, dealers and automakers are beginning to realize that many auto buyers would just as soon face a firing squad as go through the tribulations of negotiating for a new vehicle. Thank goodness the system is beginning to change.

But until then, here are six steps to help you deal with the dealer:

1) Know the truck you want and how much you can afford to pay. Experts say your annual income should be at least twice the price of the new truck you buy. Check the "AutoExplorer" section in the front pages of this book. This will give you an idea of all the models offered by each manufacturer in several price ranges. Don't waste everyone's time test-driving and negotiating for a vehicle you can't possibly afford.

2) Be prepared. Review the charts in this book for vehicles you're interested in. Study the suggested retail prices and dealer's cost for the model and options you want. Knowing these gives you a vital negotiating advantage.

Find out about rebates *(see page 38A)*, and if a choice between a cash rebate and discount financing is given, use Appendix J to determine which is best for you.

3) Qualify the dealer. Call several dealers within a reasonable driving distance and ask each if they have the vehicle on their lot with the options you want. You'll nearly always get a better deal if the dealer doesn't have to trade with another dealer for the vehicle you want. Ask for a price quote on the phone, but understand that it may be a teaser price just to get you into the dealership.

4) Remember the golden rule of truck-buying: First negotiate the price of the truck. Then discuss financing. Then discuss the value of your trade-in. Always keep the three transactions separate; salespeople are adept at giving away with one hand and taking a lot more with the other.

For instance, they may talk about monthly payments instead of the truck's price; by stretching out the length of a loan — with correspondingly lower monthly payments — they can make an overpriced truck seem affordable.

5) Keep cool. The salesperson may try to pressure you — "Are you ready to buy today?" The salesperson may play on your sympathy — "I'll lose my job if I agree to ..." The salesperson may intimidate you — "The dealer cost figures you have are all wrong." Or the salesperson may indicate you have a deal and then turn you over to the sales manager who nixes it; together, they'll work on you to sweeten the deal in their favor.

Through it all, stay confident of your research and remember the Scout's motto: Be prepared. Be prepared to put down a deposit as soon as you've arrived a fair price, and if you feel mistreated, be prepared to walk out of the dealership.

6) Let the dealer make a buck. Bear in mind that "profit" is not a dirty word, and that no dealer is going to sell you a $10 bill for a buck and remain in business.

Keeping Your Old Truck vs. Buying a New One

Ok, you've done your homework. You've studied the charts in this book, compared your choices, and now you are ready to buy a new truck. All you need to do is get rid of your old clunker and purchase the truck of your dreams. Hold on for just a minute.

You probably have a list of reasons to buy a new vehicle. Reasons that might include the newest safety features, modern styling, or perhaps you need a larger vehicle to fit your growing family. These are just a few; the list goes on and on. Still, with all the good reasons to buy a new truck, there is a very compelling one to consider holding on to the old one. Cost!

Taking a purely left-brain, economic approach, keeping your old truck could save you thousands of dollars.

It is true that older vehicles generally cost more to maintain, and are more likely to break down, resulting in an expensive and aggravating repair. But before you push the panic button, look at the economics.

For example: Let's assume you own a 1988 Chevrolet S-10 Blazer and you are faced with the decision of buying a new one or keeping the old one. How do the numbers stack up? Figure 9 shows a comparison of the projected five-year ownership costs for your 1988 Chevrolet S-10 Blazer to a new 1993 model. (The example is based on the assumption that you drive the national average of 14,000 miles per year.)

Why is there such a large difference in expected ownership costs? For one thing, your used truck will depreciate at a rate much slower than the new one. Trucks depreciate the fastest in the first few years. Therefore, your 1988 Blazer has already been through its highest depreciation. You can see from the example that the 1993 truck will depreciate $3,200 more than the 1988 edition over the next five years.

More good news: Your insurance rates are likely to be lower on a used model. The example shows a $2,953 cost advantage for the used truck. You may even consider raising the deductible on the collision portion of your premium, or dropping collision entirely, lowering your insurance payments even more.

And then there are finance charges. Chances are you have paid back your loan or are close to making that last payment. The prospect of four or five years of paying loan interest may put a dent in your budget planning.

As for various annual taxes and license fees, again the used truck will cost approximately $261 less over five years, depending on the state you live in.

Fuel costs are likely to be slightly higher for the 1988 model. It is common for vehicles to drop off in fuel performance as they get older. Additionally, technological improvements for newer models often result in higher mileage per gallon.

After tallying up these costs, if you decide to keep your old truck for another five years you will save $14,212 ($27,419 minus $13,207), right?

Figure 9

Projected Five-year Comparison:

1993 S-10 Blazer vs.1988 S-10 Blazer

Cost areas	1993 Model	1988 Model
Depreciation	$6,700	$3,500
Financing	$2,736	$0
Insurance	$8,271	$5,318
State Fees	$653	$392
Fuel	$4,213	$3,997
Maintenance	$4,106	??
Repair	$740	??
Total	$27,419	$13,207
Difference	$14,212	

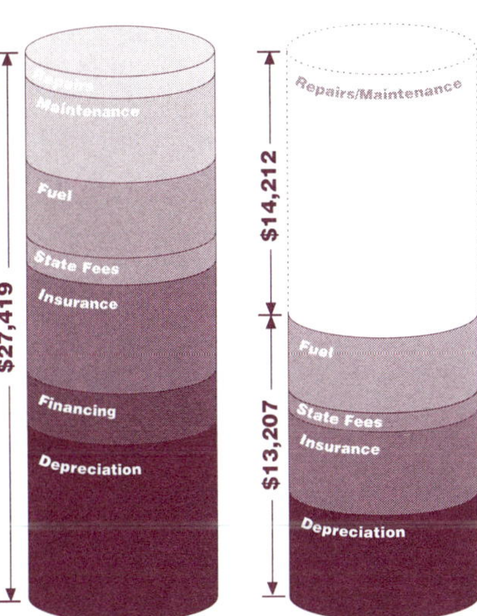

The 1988 S-10 Blazer could have 5 year maintenance/repair costs up to $14,212 - and still have lower overall costs than a new S-10 Blazer.

Well, not quite. What about maintenance and repair costs for the used vehicle? There is no reliable data that will show how much you will have to spend on maintenance and repairs over the next five years, but we can assume that it will be more than you'll spend on the new truck— particularly when you consider that the old truck is out of warranty. However, this example does show how much you can budget each year for maintenance and repairs. If you spread the $14,212 over five years, you can pay about $2,800 per year before it would be more cost effective to buy a new Blazer.

The old heap doesn't look so bad now, does it?

To Fix or Not to Fix

There may come a time when you're faced with the decision of whether to repair your truck or sell it and buy a new one. Barring any sentimental reasons you may have for holding on to that loveable old heap, you'll want to make your decision based on objective financial criteria. As illustrated in Figure 9, it probably makes sense to repair your truck and keep it.

However, even if you decide to get rid of the truck and buy a new one, you still have to decide whether to repair it.

Unless you've got money to burn, if it costs as much to repair the truck as it would to buy another one, it makes sense to skip the repairs and sell it for its scrap value. (And that's if your lucky. More often, you have to pay someone to tow away the old work horse!)

It's more likely, however, that the cost of repairs will be substantially less than the cost of replacing your current truck. In this case, the decision of whether or not to fix your truck is not so straightforward. It all depends on what the truck would be worth with the repairs vs. what you could sell it for without the repairs.

So, should you fix it before selling it, or sell it as it is? In most cases, you will be better off fixing it. By spending a few hundred dollars to repair your truck before selling it, you can increase its value by thousands of dollars. A truck in good condition will be easier to sell and it will command a much higher price.

For example, let's say you have a 1986 Ford Ranger S Pickup, which, if it were in good condition, would be worth $3,500. But, let's assume this truck requires $500 in repairs.

If you decide not to repair it, you'll have your choice of selling it to a buyer who is looking for a fixer-upper or trading it to a dealer. In either case, because the truck is not in good condition, you will be selling at a substantial discount, usually the wholesale price. In our example, the Ranger, without the repairs, would be worth about $2000. In addition, the buyer will probably take into consideration the cost of the needed repairs and deduct the $500 repair from the trade-in figure and pay you a net $1,500.

If, however, you opt to fix the truck before selling it, the truck can command its $3,500 full retail value. So, although you're out the $500 in repairs, you'll still net $3,000--$1,500 more than if you sold it without repairing it.

Unloading Your Old Truck

Finally, you've considered all of the advantages and disadvantages of keeping your old truck, and you have concluded that your best option is to buy a new one. So what should you do about that old lump you're now driving? The easiest solution would be to trade it in on the new truck — no ads to write, no waiting by the phone for replies, and no worries about smog or safety certificates (in many states, the seller's responsibility). Of course, you pay for the convenience. The dealer has to make a fair profit on any transaction, and if he takes your old truck in trade, he's got to be able to turn around and sell it for more than he or she paid you. So the dealer will probably offer you the "wholesale price," or even less if the truck needs fixing. But, if you sold the truck yourself, you could probably get a figure between the dealer wholesale price and the dealer's full retail price.

Selling it yourself needn't be an ordeal. It just takes a little marketing. As anyone on Madison Avenue will tell you, a successful sale involves the right packaging, the right price, and the right advertising. First, make an honest assessment of the old heap. If relatively inexpensive items aren't working, fix them — things like mufflers, the radio, or the speedometer. But if the truck needs major mechanical or cosmetic repairs, think twice.

It's amazing, but the vast majority of buyers will overlook mechanical ills, sometimes major ones, if the paint shines and the interior seems fresh. And conversely, a truck in good mechanical shape but with a ratty appearance will turn off most buyers. So by all means, have your truck detailed before you try to sell it yourself, or even before you trade it in to the dealer. It will be worth the extra cost because a good-looking truck will not only fetch a higher price, it'll sell faster.

Once you've transformed the old heap into a "meticulously maintained, fine machine," attach a price to it. Look in your local newspaper's classifieds or in any used vehicle pricing guide such as *Kelley Blue Book* or *NADA Used Truck Guide,* and see how similar trucks are priced. Then write your own ad: include the brand name, the year, the model, and any important features such as automatic transmission or air conditioning. Mention the condition of the truck. And always list a price even if you're willing to bargain. (However, never use phrases like "asking $7,000" with the price. You don't want to broadcast your willingness to negotiate.) If you have space in the ad, mention the vehicle's color.

Now just sit back and let the calls come in. When someone makes you an acceptable offer, always ask for cash or a bank check. Never take a personal check.

Here's an example of a good ad:

Jeep Cherokee'83, Blue,
A/C, stereo, 4-wheel drive.
Perfect cond. $6,500. (219) 689-0000

Section Three
Annotated Vehicle Charts

Annotated Vehicle Charts

This section will give you an in-depth explanation of every aspect of the vehicle charts in this book. On pages 52A–55A you will find a sample vehicle chart divided into distinct sections: vehicle description; purchase price; warranty, maintenance and repair frequency; and ownership costs.

The text on pages 57A–61A explains the formulas we used and the assumptions made to calculate the ownership costs for every vehicle included in this book.

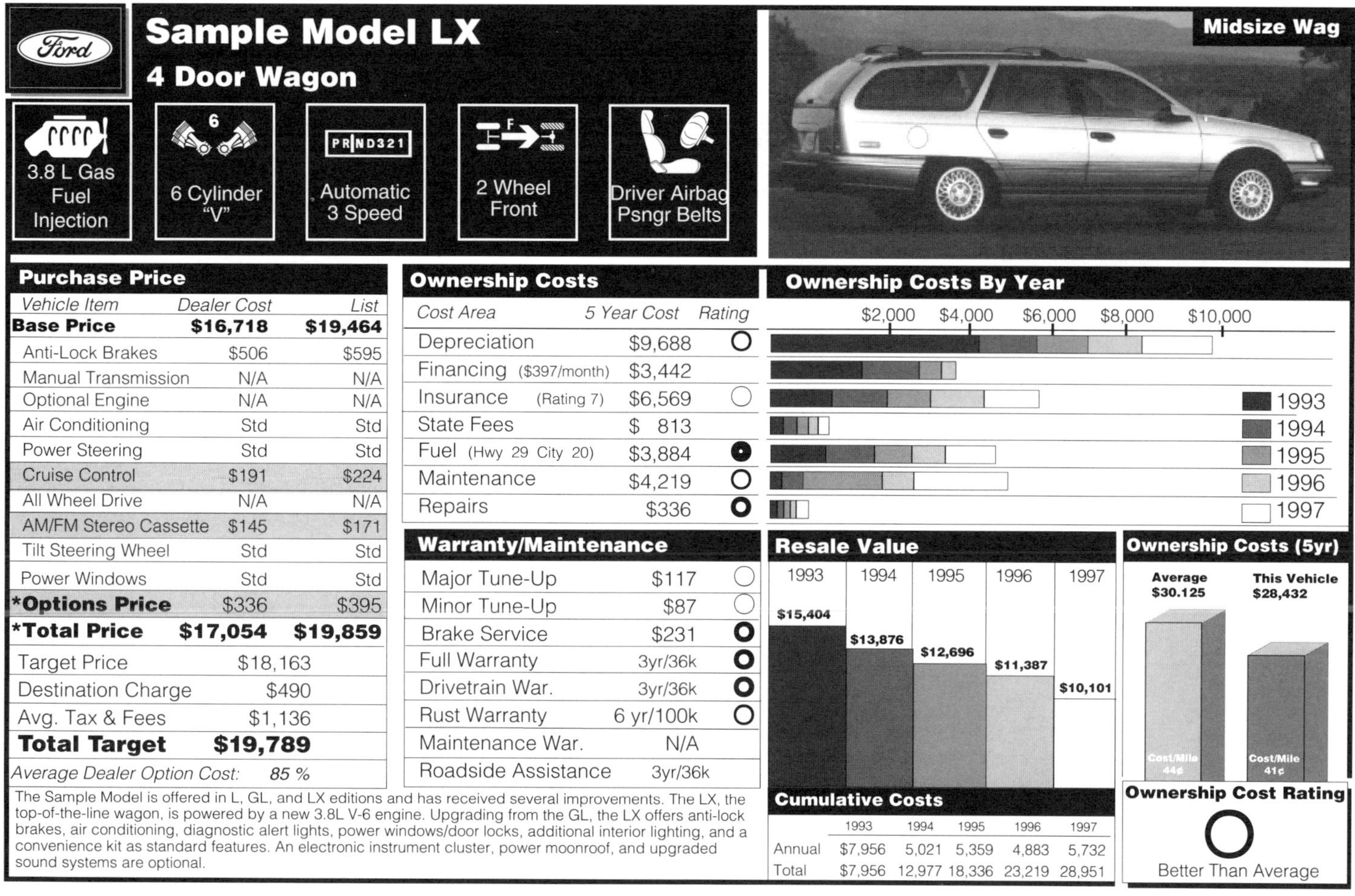

It is very important for a new truck buyer to distinguish between *price* and *cost*. The consumer who compares vehicles based only on purchase price is using a set of criteria that can be misleading. The true cost of owning a vehicle is not the money you exchange for the "pink slip," the true cost is what you pay after you drive your new truck off the dealer's lot. This cost includes depreciation, interest payments, insurance, state fees, fuel, maintenance, and repairs. Therefore, when you shop and compare new trucks, use the purchase price to find the trucks that fit your budget, and use the expected ownership costs to determine the vehicle that is the best value.

Vehicle Description

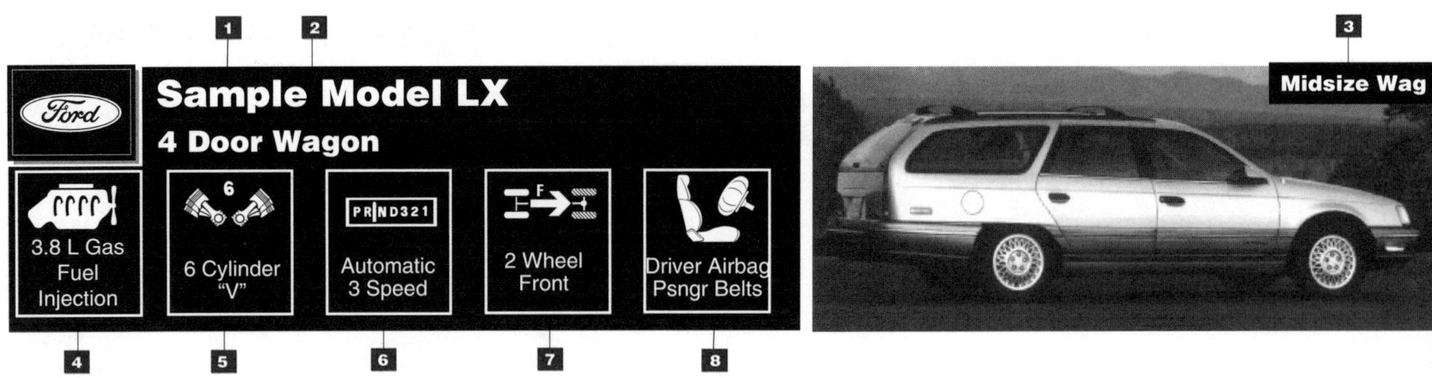

1 The brand and model name of the vehicle.

2 The number of doors and body style of the vehicle, defined as follows:

Convertible	An open-topped vehicle.
Extended cab	A pickup truck design with a large space behind the seats, sometimes including a rear seat.
Regular cab	A truck with a single bench seat or two bucket seats for passengers and a rectangular bed for cargo.
Wagon	Usually square-looking rear end with rear cargo door that provides for expanded cargo area behind the seats.
Passenger Van	A 3-door vehicle capable of transporting 5 to 12 passengers with an integrated space for cargo in the rear and a liftgate or single/double door for cargo access.
Passenger Ext Van	A passenger van in every respect but having at least 10 inches additional exterior length over the passenger van version and a possible 15-passenger capacity.
Cargo Van	A 3-door vehicle with room for one to two passengers whose primary purpose is to transport cargo. The rear consists of a liftgate or single/double door for cargo access.
Cargo Ext Van	A cargo van in every respect but having at least 10 inches additional exterior length over the cargo van version.
Sport Utility	A square-looking vehicle with a relatively high center of gravity and an integrated rear cargo area with liftgate for cargo access.

3 The vehicle class, defined as follows:

Small Pickup	A pickup truck under 3,500 pounds.
Large Pickup	A pickup truck over 3,500 pounds.
Subcompact Wagon	A wagon with a wheelbase under 98.9 inches.
Compact Wagon	A wagon with a wheelbase over 98.9 and under 104.9 inches.
Midsize Wagon	A wagon with a wheelbase over 104.9 and under 109.9 inches.
Large Wagon	A wagon with a wheelbase over 110 inches.
Mini Van	A van with height under 77.9 inches and cargo volume under 203.8 cu. ft.
Full-Size Van	A van with height over 77.8 inches and cargo volume over 203.7 cu.ft.
Utility	Utility vehicles are built on heavy-duty chassis capable of off-road use.

4 The engine type/engine aspiration, defined as follows:

Gas	Standard piston powered engine.
Turbo	Turbo charged piston engine.
Diesel	Diesel piston engine requiring diesel fuel.
Turbodiesel	Turbo charged diesel design piston engine.
Rotary	Wankel engine (no pistons).
Carburetor	Mechanical air/fuel mixing device.
Fuel Injection	A pump/injector method of metering fuel.

5 Cylinders

In a rotary engine, this number refers to the number of chambers.

In-line	Cylinders are in a straight line.
Opposing	Cylinders are in two rows facing each other.
V-shaped	Cylinders are in two rows that form a V.

6 Transmission

Manual 3-speed, Manual 4-speed, Manual 5-speed, Manual 6-speed, Automatic 3-speed, Automatic 4-speed, Automatic 5-speed, Continuosly Variable Automatic.

7 Drive

Front Wheel Drive	Front wheels deliver power.
Rear Wheel Drive	Rear wheels deliver power.
4 WD On-Demand (a.k.a. Part-time)	All-wheel drive that the driver manually engages and disengages.
4 WD Full-Time (a.k.a. AWD)	All-wheel drive that automatically delivers power to wheels as needed.

8 Restraint system

Dual Airbags	Driver and passenger airbags are standard.
Driver Airbag Psngr Opt	Driver airbag is standard—passenger airbag is optional.
Driver Airbag Psngr Belts	Driver airbag is standard—passenger airbag is not available.
Belts Standard Airbag Opt	Automatic seatbelts are standard for driver and passenger—airbags are optional for driver and passenger.
Belts Standard Driver Air Opt	Automatic seatbelts are standard for driver and passenger—airbags are optional for driver only.
Automatic Seatbelts	Automatic seatbelts are standard for driver—airbags are not available.
Manual Seatbelts	Manual seatbelts are standard for driver—automatic seatbelts are optional.
Manual Seatbelts Only	Manual seatbelts are standard for driver—automatic seatbelts are not available.

Purchase Price

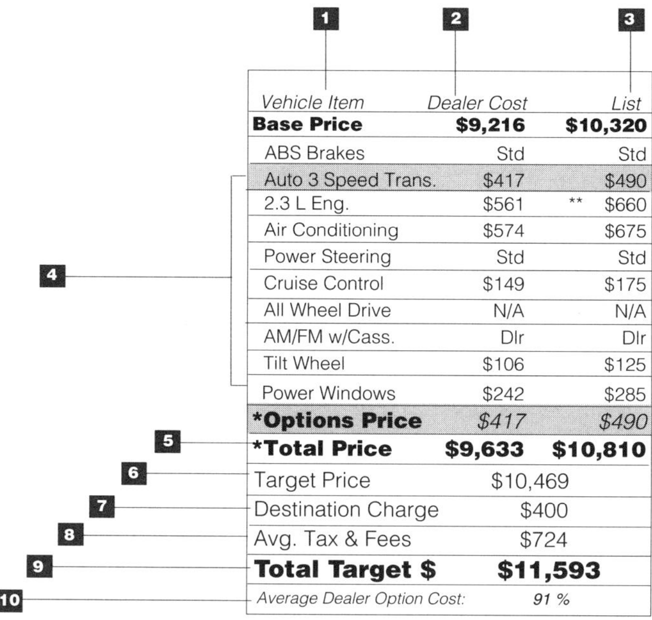

Vehicle Item	Dealer Cost		List
Base Price	**$9,216**		**$10,320**
ABS Brakes	Std		Std
Auto 3 Speed Trans.	$417		$490
2.3 L Eng.	$561	**	$660
Air Conditioning	$574		$675
Power Steering	Std		Std
Cruise Control	$149		$175
All Wheel Drive	N/A		N/A
AM/FM w/Cass.	Dlr		Dlr
Tilt Wheel	$106		$125
Power Windows	$242		$285
***Options Price**	*$417*		*$490*
***Total Price**	**$9,633**		**$10,810**
Target Price	$10,469		
Destination Charge	$400		
Avg. Tax & Fees	$724		
Total Target $	**$11,593**		
Average Dealer Option Cost:	*91 %*		

* Only the shaded options are included in the Options Price and Total Price figures. They are also included in ownership cost calculations. Other options are listed for your convenience.

Shading- All shaded options are included in the total price of the vehicle, as well as in all ownership cost calculations. In an effort to make true "apples-to-apples" comparisons, we attempt to include the same equipment on similar vehicles. (It would not be fair for one compact wagon to be evaluated with a manual transmission while another is evaluated with an automatic transmission.)

The options that we include/shade differ by class, as shown in the chart below. Generally, we include/shade options that are equipped in two-thirds or more of the vehicles sold in that class.

Additionally, the only options that can be included/shaded are those with a price, or those marked "N/C" (No Charge). Items that are standard equipment, items marked "**" (restrictions), items marked "Dlr" (Dealer Installed), and items marked "Pkg" or "Grp" (available only as part of a package of options) are not included/shaded.

Optional engines are shaded and included in the analysis based on horsepower and engine size. For each class of vehicle, we establish a "target" horsepower and engine size based on the average horsepower and the average size of all standard engines on all models in the class. If the standard engine of a particular model meets the size and horsepower targets, it is used in the analysis. If the standard engine is too small or has insufficient horsepower, then we choose the least expensive engine available without purchase restrictions that does meet the size and horsepower targets. If no engine meets the requirements, the largest engine is used.

1 The-left hand column identifies specific vehicle items. Each line represents a different item, such as the Base Price and various options.

2 Dealer Cost is the dealer's factory invoiced cost for each item. It is the price paid by the dealer, not including any manufacturer's incentive or holdback.

3 List price. This is the manufacturer's suggested retail price for the particular vehicle item.

4 The feature list. The list includes the most popular major features/options in use today. If a feature does not have a price listed next to it, it will have one of the following designations:

Dlr	Dealer Installed Equipment
N/A	Not available on this model
N/C	No Charge
Pkg	Available as part of a package of options
Std	Standard equipment for this model
N/R	Not reported at time of printing
Grp	Available only with another option

Some features have a double asterisk ("**") next to the price. This indicates that the particular feature can only be purchased at that price if certain other requirements are met. If there is a choice, we show the option price that can be purchased without restrictions. We only list options with restrictions if there is no unrestricted way to purchase the item.

5 Total Price is the sum of the base vehicle price plus the options price.

6 The Target Price is the price that you can reasonably expect to negotiate for the vehicle as configured; however, it is not necessarily the lowest price you may find. It includes an average acceptable mark-up for the dealer, which varies from model to model based on market conditions. Recent market conditions have been included in the Target Prices shown.

7 The destination charge is usually the same anywhere in the country, but may vary in some locations.

8 Forty seven out of fifty states have a sales tax on vehicles, which ranges from 1.5% to 8%. We have used an average tax rate of 5%, based on the price of the specific vehicle shown. Furthermore, most states have annual registration fees, which are often paid to the dealer at the time of delivery. An average figure is used here based on the price of the specific vehicle. You can refer to Figure 13 on page 64A to determine the applicable fees for your state.

9 The Total Target is the grand total price that you can reasonably expect to pay for the vehicle as configured. It is the sum of the Target Price, plus all taxes, destination fees, and registration fees.

10 The Average Dealer Option Cost is the average percent of list price that the dealer pays for options. You can use this to estimate the dealer's cost for any option not specifically shown in the chart. For example, if the Average Dealer Option Cost shown is 91%, and the suggested retail price of leather seats is $400, then the dealer's cost for the leather seats is about .91 x $400, or $364. This is shown as "N/A" on vehicles that have no available manufacturer-installed options.

This table shows features that are either shaded or not shaded for each vehicle class.
Yes-Shaded
No-Not Shaded

Shaded Features By Vehicle Class

	Cruise Control	Air Cond.	Auto Trans.	Power Steer	4 Wheel Drive	AM/FM Cassette	Tilt Wheel	Power Windows	Optional Bed	ABS Brakes	Gas Guzzler Tax
Small Pickup	No	No	No	Yes	No	Yes	No	No	No	No	No
Large Pickup	No	Yes	No	Yes	No	Yes	No	No	No	No	No
Subcmpct Wag.	No	No	No	Yes	No	No	No	No	N/A	No	Yes
Compact Wagon	No	Yes	Yes	Yes	No	Yes	No	No	N/A	No	Yes
Midsize Wagon	Yes	Yes	Yes	Yes	No	Yes	No	No	N/A	No	Yes
Large Wagon	Yes	Yes	Yes	Yes	No	Yes	No	Yes	N/A	No	Yes
Mini Van	Yes	Yes	Yes	Yes	No	Yes	No	No	N/A	No	No
Full-Size Van	No	Yes	Yes	Yes	No	No	No	No	N/A	No	No
Utility	No	Yes	No	Yes	No	Yes	No	No	N/A	No	No

Warranty and Maintenance

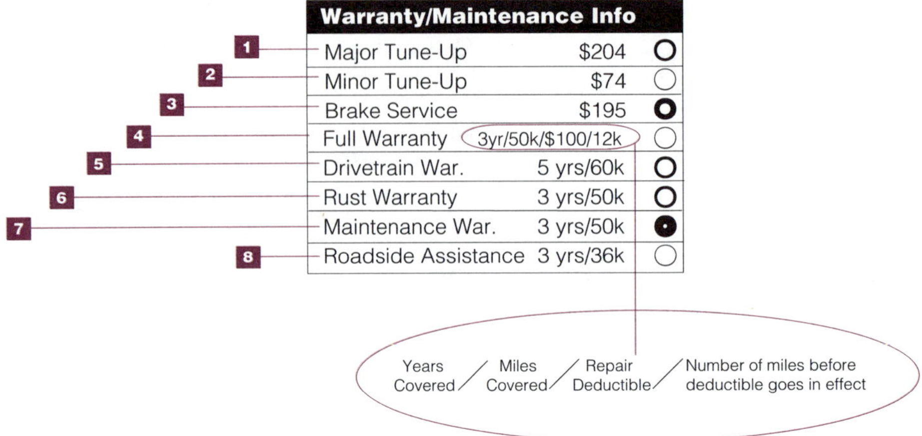

NOTE: For all items in this section, the rating symbol compares the expected dollar expense for the specific vehicle against the average expected dollar expense for vehicles of the same category. Parts prices are manufacturer labeled, while labor rates are the national average for the brand.

1 The average cost of a major tune-up (minor tune-up, distributor cap and rotor replacement, fuel filter and PCV valve replacement, and ignition system inspection).

2 The average cost of a minor tune-up (replacing the air cleaner and spark plugs, inspecting the distributor cap, rotor, and ignition wires, checking compression, and adjusting the ignition timing and idle speed).

3 The average cost of brake service (replacing the pads on disk brakes, or shoes on drum brakes, on all four wheels, and checking, bleeding, and adjusting the brake system).

4 The full warranty on the vehicle. The full warranty typically covers parts and labor for any factory-installed part that is defective in material or workmanship under normal use. This typically excludes tires, emission system parts (covered by a separate warranty), expendable maintenance items, glass breakage, and air conditioning lubricant. Some manufacturers, Saab for example, include a deductible on each repair after a specific number of miles.

5 Coverage on the engine, transaxle, transmission, and axle and drive components. For some manufacturers, this warranty applies to the original purchaser only. In other cases, the coverage changes if the vehicle is sold. Also, some manufacturers require a fixed payment for any repair covered under this warranty.

6 Rust-through coverage. This applies to perforation only, generally meaning complete rust-through in a sheet metal panel. Surface corrosion resulting from stone chips or paint scratches are typically not covered.

7 Maintenance Warranty. With this coverage, all routine services and oil changes will be paid for when the work is performed at an authorized dealer (includes wiper blades, brake pads, light bulbs, wheel alignments, and other wear items).

8 Roadside Assistance. The length of time and mileage for which the manufacturer will provide a toll-free 800 number and free towing in the event of a breakdown. Many manufacturers provide additional services as part of their roadside assistance plan. To determine all the components of a roadside assistance plan for a particular vehicle, ask your dealer.

Ownership Costs

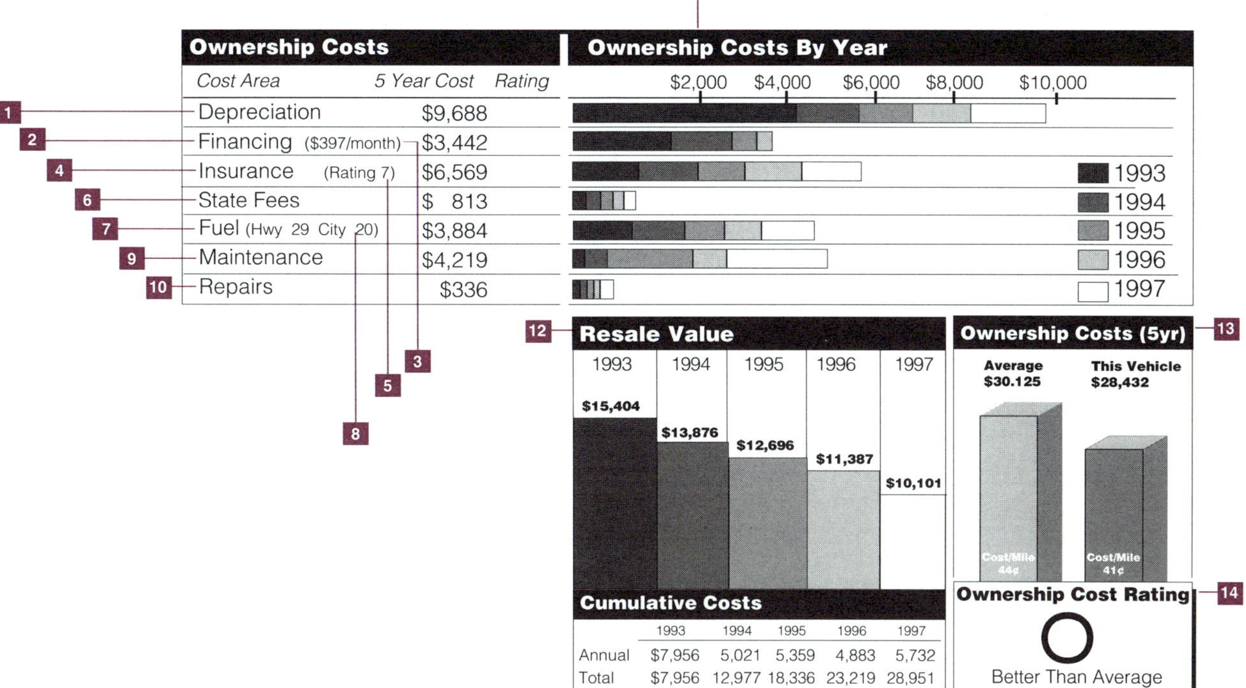

NOTE: For all rating symbols other than "overall rating," the symbol compares the expected figure for the specific vehicle against the average expected figure for vehicles of the same category and price range. The overall rating symbol considers all vehicles in addition to vehicles of the same category and price range.

1 The total cost of depreciation over five years. (See page 57A)

2 The total cost of financing over five years. Financing cost includes the interest on a loan, but not the principal. (See Page 59A)

3 The monthly payment. (See page 59A)

4 The total cost of insurance over five years. (See page 58A)

5 The insurance rating for this vehicle. If a surcharge applies, the rating is followed by "+," "++," "sport," or "sport+," depending on the degree of the surcharge. The charge is also reflected in the premium. If a rating is estimated, it is followed by "[Est]."

6 The total cost of state fees over five years. (See page 59A)

7 The total cost of fuel over five years. (See page 59A)

8 The EPA reported miles per gallon figures for the specific vehicle. "Hwy" refers to highway driving. If a figure is estimated, it is indicated by "[Est]." If premium gasoline is required, it is indicated by "Prem."

9 The total cost of maintenance over five years. (See page 60A)

10 The total cost of repair insurance over five years. (See page 61A)

11 **Ownership Costs By Year**. In this graph, each cost area is represented by a horizontal bar that shows the total of that cost over a five-year period. The bar is broken up into different shaded sections, with each section representing one year between 1993 and 1997. For example, look at the depreciation bar in the sample chart. The bar consists of five shaded segments that extend to $9,688. This is the total amount of depreciation for this vehicle over the next five years However, if you want to be more specific, you can measure the distance of a shaded segment to find out the depreciation for a single year. For instance, note that the shade representing 1994 ▇ extends from about $4,200 to $5,800. The difference between these two figures, $1,600, is the amount of depreciation for 1994. (In some cost areas, most often "Repairs," it can be difficult to distinguish where one shade ends and the next begins. However, since shorter bars always mean less cost compared to longer ones, it is a positive sign when shaded segments are extremely close together.)

12 **Resale value.** The bar graph illustrates the vehicle's expected resale value over time. This graph allows you to determine what this vehicle is likely to be worth at annual intervals during the five-year period.

13 **Ownership Costs (5yr).** This graph illustrates the vehicle's total expected ownership costs after a five-year period and how it compares to the average cost of vehicles in its class and price range. Additionally, the cost per mile is shown on the bottom of each bar.

14 **Ownership Cost Rating.** The ownership cost rating is a summary of a vehicle's economic value, considering its purchase price and overall ownership costs. This rating compares a vehicle's economic value to that of other vehicles of similar price and style.

> Why are there no rating symbols for "Financing" and "State Fees?" Because these two costs are *mathematically derived* from the purchase price of the vehicle, using our economic assumptions. If two vehicles have the same purchase price, they will have the same finance charge and state fees, so there is no point in comparing these areas. On the other hand, these two vehicles could have very different depreciation, insurance, fuel, repair, and maintenance costs.

Figure 10

Ownership Costs (Assumptions)

Ownership Period	5 years
Annual Inflation	4.0%
Annual Mileage	14,000 miles
Dealer Cost/Manufacturer Suggested List Price/Destination Fees	As reported by manufacturers. Actual dealer cost may be somewhat lower than listed dealer cost due to manufacturer allowances.
Target Purchase Price	Based on dealer cost of an individual model with options shown and shaded. Varies by market condition, by class, and by individual model. Target price is always more than dealer cost, usually below list price, but sometimes higher.
Luxury/Gas Guzzler taxes:	Rates that went into effect on January 1, 1991.
State Sales/Use tax/ State Registration fees	5% sales tax is used as a nationwide average; 1% initial state registration fee based on MSRP. Refer to Figure 13 on page 64A to determine the exact figure for your state.
Resale Value	There is a large range in used vehicle prices, ranging from a low "wholesale auction" price, to a high "private party" transaction price. Prices here are assumed to be close to the private party price. Each individual vehicle will follow a pattern set by earlier models, by brand, by country of origin, by vehicle class, by vehicle price range, and by area of the country.
Insurance	Principal operator is under age 65; all drivers have more than six years experience with no chargeable accidents; personal use; lives in a suburban/urban community, with: Collision — $500 Deductible Comprehensive — $500 Deductible Personal liability — $100,000/$300,000 Medical — $25,000 Property — $50,000 Uninsured driver — $25,000/$50,000
Finance Costs	20% down payment on a 48 month loan. Annual interest rate of 9.5%.
State Fees	1% of MSRP in the first year, reduced by .1% in each succesive year. Refer to Figure 11 on page 56A to determine the exact figure for your state.
Fuel	U.S. Government EPA mileage figures. Mileage is 60% highway, 40% city. Fuel cost per gallon is $1.15 for unleaded regular, $1.27 for premium, and $1.30 for diesel (subject to inflation).
Repairs	Cost of a $0 deductible extended service contract that will pay for repairs for 5 years or 70,000 miles. Figures used are actual prices averaged from two nationally available service contract providers.
Maintenance	Services performed generally at manufacturer's suggested intervals where stated. Other services done at selected intervals. (See page 60A) Cost per service is based upon industry-standard service times and national labor rate averages by brand. Parts prices are based on manufacturers suggested list price where available.

Ownership Cost Derivation

The following pages describe the methods used, as well as the basic assumptions made for each ownership cost area shown in the vehicle charts.

Depreciation

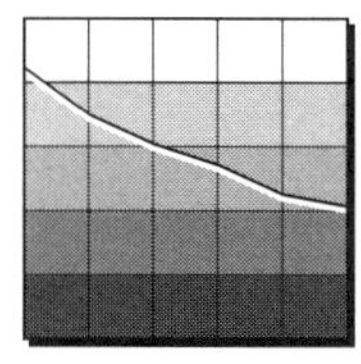

The vehicle charts show, for each new vehicle, the projected annual and cumulative amount of depreciation over five years. A rating symbol gives you an easy way to compare one vehicle's depreciation to all other vehicles of a similar class and price. Additionally, the charts have a resale section that shows the expected resale value of the vehicle each year over the next five years.

Depreciation and resale value are two measures of the same element. A vehicle's purchase price less depreciation equals a its resale value. By the same token, a vehicle's purchase price less its resale value equals its depreciation.

We project the future resale value of a vehicle on the basis of several factors. We assume that the vehicle will be purchased at the Total Target Price, which is the total "out-the-door" price that the buyer can expect to pay. This price includes state and local taxes, destination fees, and luxury and/or Gas Guzzler taxes if applicable. We then factor in the historical depreciation for that specific model. We also consider depreciation trends by brand, vehicle category, price, and country of origin. For example, to forecast the expected resale value of a 1993 Ford Ranger XL 2-Door Regular Cab, we consider the resale value history of previous Rangers, of other Ford models, of pickup trucks as a class, of American-built trucks, and of pickups in the $8,000 to $10,000 price range. When actual history is lacking for the exact model, we rely more on these other areas. To this statistical method, we add our own economic, industry, and model-specific expectations to determine the expected resale value for that particular vehicle.

Depreciation is determined by a vehicle's resale value, and can vary somewhat depending on where you're selling the vehicle, who you're selling it to, optional equipment, and the condition and mileage of the vehicle. We assume values for the Western United States (East coast values are a few percentage points higher), and that your vehicle is sold to a private buyer. Furthermore, in our resale value/depreciation calculations, we include the cost of optional equipment (the shaded options in the vehicle charts). Additionally, we assume that the vehicle is in good, but not mint, condition, and that you've driven it approximately 14,000 miles per year.

Depreciation is determined by a vehicle's resale value, and can vary somewhat depending on where you're selling the vehicle, who you're selling it to, optional equipment, and the condition and mileage of the vehicle.

It's almost always true that an older vehicle will cost less to insure than a newer vehicle of the same model. However, over time, inflation makes the insurance premium increase faster than the age of the vehicle makes it decrease, so the overall cost goes up.

Insurance

The vehicle charts show the insurance industry symbol (see Figure 4 on page 10A) of each vehicle, courtesy of Insurance Services Office. The lower the symbol, the less expensive collision and comprehensive insurance will be. Additionally, the charts show, based on the assumed coverages and deductibles, how much you can expect to spend on insurance over five years. Our rating symbol lets you easily compare the cost of insuring different vehicles in the same class and price range.

Many personal, geographic, and political factors determine your exact insurance premium. We assume that you're under age 65. You have a good driving record, drive about 14,000 miles per year, and have no inexperienced drivers in your household.

Insurance rates vary tremendously depending on where you live. We assume that you live in a suburban area in a state with average insurance rates. You can refer to Figure 11 on page 62A to adjust the insurance figures to match your state's figures.

You may be wondering why the annual insurance premium shown in the vehicle charts goes up every year, especially since you may know that it generally costs less to insure a used vehicle than a new one. It's almost always true that an older vehicle will cost less to insure than a newer vehicle of the same model. However, over time, inflation makes the premium increase faster than the age of the vehicle makes it decrease, so the overall cost goes up.

Of all costs, insurance is the most variable. Your actual rates will probably differ somewhat from those found in *The Complete Small Truck Cost Guide.* However, when comparing vehicles, the difference between our projections and your actual rates will be consistent from vehicle to vehicle. If you need more precise information, we recommend that you call a local insurance agent to determine the actual insurance costs for each vehicle that you consider.

Finance Costs

The vehicle charts show the total interest charges you can expect to pay for the vehicle over five years. They also show your monthly payment if you purchase the vehicle at the "target purchase price."

There is no rating symbol for finance costs. This is because these costs do not depend on the vehicle you buy, but are related to the purchase price. If two different vehicles are purchased for the same amount, they will have the same finance cost.

Our financial projections are based on the latest economic information. We assume that you will put down 20% immediately and take a 48 month, 9.5% loan.

If you're considering a loan with terms other than these, you can use Appendix I to determine your monthly payment.

Even if you pay cash for your vehicle instead of borrowing money to pay for it, you should factor a finance cost into the cost of ownership. The reason for this is that if you didn't invest the money in the vehicle, it could be in the bank earning interest.

State Fees

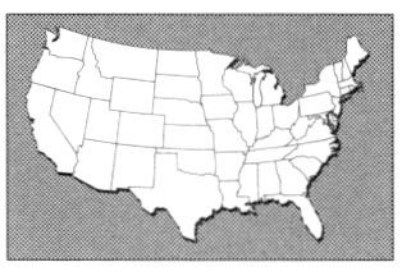

The charts show the amount you can expect to pay in state taxes and registration fees over five years. Our state fee calculations assume initial state fees of 1% of the current MSRP of the vehicle, reduced by .1% in each successive year.

Registration fees and taxes vary by state. You can use Figure 13 (see Page 64A) to determine the exact fee structure for your state.

Fuel

The vehicle charts show EPA (U.S. Environmental Protection Agency) fuel mileage figures for both "highway" and "city" driving. If automatic transmission is standard or is a shaded option, the fuel figures are for automatic transmission; otherwise, the figures are based on manual transmission. The charts also show the amount you can expect to pay in fuel expenses over a five-year period. A rating symbol gives you an easy way to compare this vehicle's fuel expense against all other vehicles of a similar class and price.

To determine actual fuel costs, we assume that vehicles will perform closer to the "highway" mileage figure. We assume that fuel will cost $1.15 per gallon for unleaded regular, $1.27 per gallon for unleaded premium, and $1.30 for diesel. Additionally, we assume that fuel costs will increase by the rate of inflation and that you will drive 14,000 miles per year.

Maintenance

The vehicle charts show the amount you can expect to pay for routine maintenance expenses over five years. A rating symbol gives you an easy way to compare a particular vehicle's maintenance costs against all other vehicles of a similar class and price. The charts also show average costs to perform the standard maintenance services of a major tune-up, a minor tune-up, and a standard brake service.

We include the following services in determining our maintenance cost figures:

- Oil changes
- Major tune-ups
- Minor tune-ups
- Basic brake service
- Basic clutch service
- Basic automatic transmission service
- Alignments
- Front bearing service
- Cooling system maintenance
- Shock absorber service
- Muffler replacement
- Hoses and belts (including timing belt)
- Fluids and filters
- Tires
- Batteries
- Headlamp replacement
- Regular inspections

We assume that services take place at an authorized dealer location, using standard flat labor times, an average hourly labor rate for each individual brand, and manufacturer's suggested retail prices for parts, where available. You can often get better prices than these. (We use them for consistency from vehicle to vehicle.)

We generally factor in a manufacturer suggested mileage or time interval to perform a particular service. If the manufacturer does not specify, we apply our own intervals for particular services. We assume that most trips are longer than 5 miles ("normal" driving conditions).

Repairs

The vehicle charts project the amount you can expect to pay for repair expenses over five years or 70,000 miles. A rating symbol helps you easily compare one vehicle's expected repair costs against all other vehicles in the same class. The charts also show manufacturers' warranties for full coverage, power train coverage, corrosion coverage, maintenance coverage, and roadside assistance coverage. Repair costs in the charts take into account all of these manufacturer warranties.

To determine the cost projection, we take advantage of service contract pricing. Conceptually, a service contract is an insurance policy protecting against repair costs. In exchange for your "premium," the service contract provider agrees to pay for any needed repairs. (See page 24A for a more detailed description of service contracts.) To provide this service profitably, the service contract provider has to make sure that, on average, the actual cost of repairs on the vehicle is less than the premium price. Service contract providers take great pains in pricing their products low enough to stay competitive, yet high enough to make a profit.

Therefore, we can expect that the service contract price is an excellent estimate of likely repair costs (in fact, their price is somewhat higher than the likely repair costs, allowing for a reasonable profit).

Whether or not you purchase a service contract, you can use the service contract price to estimate the cost of repairs.

We utilize pricing from two separate service contract providers to determine the repair costs shown in this book. The plans used from both providers are for five years or 70,000 miles, and are $0 deductible plans, meaning you pay nothing during the plan period other than the initial premium. The price shown is what you can reasonably expect to pay. It allows for a reasonable profit for the service contract provider, as well as for the dealer who sells the contract.

It's important to separate hype from reality when considering how a truck's expected repair incidence will influence your decision on which truck to buy.

At one time, there were vast differences in relative reliability among vehicles. Today, most any new vehicle you purchase is likely to be highly reliable. Other than minor state fees, the expected cost of repairs in the first five years will be less than any other cost associated with your new truck! That's right, and it's true even for the vehicles with the highest expected repair cost. The cost of depreciation, insurance, interest, fuel, and maintenance will all be considerably higher than the cost of repairs.

Therefore, you are likely to jump to the wrong economic conclusion if you purchase a truck because you heard it's "very reliable," or avoid a truck because you heard it's a "lemon." In fact, the difference in repair cost between the vehicle with the highest expected repair cost and the one with the lowest expected cost is only $435.

Figure 11

Insurance Factors

	1990 Rank	1990 Index
Alabama	31	0.87
Alaska	7	1.29
Arizona	20	1.1
Arkansas	40	0.79
California	4	1.47
Colorado	21	1.05
Connecticut	2	1.51
DC	9	1.28
Delaware	8	1.29
Florida	19	1.11
Georgia	13	1.18
Hawaii	14	1.16
Idaho	45	0.72
Illinois	25	0.95
Indiana	41	0.78
Iowa	51	0.55
Kansas	47	0.71
Kentucky	48	0.7
Louisiana	17	1.11
Maine	29	0.89
Maryland	12	1.24
Massachusetts	11	1.27
Michigan	15	1.15
Minnesota	36	0.84
Mississippi	34	0.85
Missouri	32	0.87
Montana	44	0.73
Nebraska	46	0.71
Nevada	18	1.11
New Hampshire	6	1.3
New Jersey	1	1.71
New Mexico	30	0.89
New York	5	1.31
North Carolina	33	0.86
North Dakota	50	0.64
Ohio	28	0.9
Oklahoma	26	0.91
Oregon	23	0.99
Pennsylvania	10	1.27
Rhode Island	3	1.49
South Carolina	27	0.9
South Dakota	49	0.66
Tennessee	39	0.82
Texas	16	1.13
Utah	38	0.82
Vermont	35	0.84
Virginia	24	0.95
Washington	22	1.03
West Virginia	37	0.84
Wisconsin	43	0.73
Wyoming	42	0.75
NATIONAL AVG		1

Insurance Adjustment Table

To calculate the total five-year insurance cost for each vehicle listed in the "Vehicle Charts," we use a national average. To be more precise, the Insurance Factors table (Figure 11) will allow you to adjust the total insurance cost listed in the vehicle charts for the state in which you live. To make this adjustment, simply find your state on the chart and then multiply its Index by the total insurance cost shown in the vehicle charts. The figures in the left column (Rank) shows the highest insurance rate (1- New Jersey) to the lowest (51-Iowa).

Remember that insurance rates can vary greatly, even within a state. For an exact insurance rate, you should contact an insurance agent. We recommend that you get quotes from several different agents before you actually buy your insurance.

Mileage Adjustment Table

To calculate the total five-year fuel cost for each vehicle listed in the charts, we assume that the vehicle is driven 14,000 miles per year, and that the price of gasoline is $1.15 per gallon. If your annual mileage differs from our assumptions, or if you expect to pay more (or less) for gas, then this table allows you to adjust the total fuel cost for any vehicle in which you are interested. To make this adjustment, first find your annual mileage in the left-hand column. Then, find the column that corresponds with the price you pay for a gallon of gasoline. Finally, multiply the number (factor) shown in this column by the total fuel cost shown in the vehicle charts.

Figure 12

Annual Mileage	Fuel Price Per Gallon								
	$0.90	$1.00	$1.05	$1.10	$1.15	$1.20	$1.25	$1.35	$1.50
4,000	0.22	0.25	0.26	0.27	0.29	0.3	0.31	0.34	0.37
6,000	0.34	0.37	0.39	0.41	0.43	0.45	0.47	0.5	0.56
8,000	0.45	0.5	0.52	0.55	0.57	0.6	0.62	0.67	0.75
10,000	0.56	0.62	0.65	0.68	0.71	0.75	0.78	0.84	0.93
12,000	0.67	0.75	0.78	0.82	0.86	0.89	0.93	1.01	1.12
14,000	0.78	0.87	0.91	0.96	1	1.04	1.09	1.17	1.3
16,000	0.89	0.99	1.04	1.09	1.14	1.19	1.24	1.34	1.49
18,000	1.01	1.12	1.17	1.23	1.29	1.34	1.4	1.51	1.68
20,000	1.12	1.24	1.3	1.37	1.43	1.49	1.55	1.68	1.86
22,000	1.23	1.37	1.43	1.5	1.57	1.64	1.71	1.84	2.05
24,000	1.34	1.49	1.57	1.64	1.71	1.79	1.86	2.01	2.24
26,000	1.45	1.61	1.7	1.78	1.86	1.94	2.02	2.18	2.42
28,000	1.57	1.74	1.83	1.91	2	2.09	2.17	2.35	2.61
30,000	1.68	1.86	1.96	2.05	2.14	2.24	2.33	2.52	2.8
35,000	1.96	2.17	2.28	2.39	2.5	2.61	2.72	2.93	3.26
40,000	2.24	2.48	2.61	2.73	2.86	2.98	3.11	3.35	3.73
45,000	2.52	2.8	2.93	3.07	3.21	3.35	3.49	3.77	4.19
50,000	2.8	3.11	3.26	3.42	3.57	3.73	3.88	4.19	4.66
55,000	3.07	3.42	3.59	3.76	3.93	4.1	4.27	4.61	5.12
60,000	3.35	3.73	3.91	4.1	4.29	4.47	4.66	5.03	5.59
65,000	3.63	4.04	4.24	4.44	4.64	4.84	5.05	5.45	6.06
70,000	3.91	4.35	4.57	4.78	5	5.22	5.43	5.87	6.52
75,000	4.19	4.66	4.89	5.12	5.36	5.59	5.82	6.29	6.99
80,000	4.47	4.97	5.22	5.47	5.71	5.96	6.21	6.71	7.45
85,000	4.75	5.28	5.54	5.81	6.07	6.34	6.6	7.13	7.92
90,000	5.03	5.59	5.87	6.15	6.43	6.71	6.99	7.55	8.39
95,000	5.31	5.9	6.2	6.49	6.79	7.08	7.38	7.97	8.85
100,000	5.59	6.21	6.52	6.83	7.14	7.45	7.76	8.39	9.32

Figure 13

State Fees, Regulations, and Insurance Information

State	Taxes: Sales/Use Tax Rate	Taxes: Based on	Taxes: Additional Local Tax	Registration Fees: Fixed Fee	Registration Fees: By Value[1]	Registration Fees: By Weight[2]	Insurance: Competitive	Insurance: No Fault	Insurance: Minimum Financial Responsibility
Alabama	2.00%	Net of trade	Yes	$15.00	$14.70	$0.00	Somewhat	No	20/40/10
Alaska	0.00%		Yes	$5.00	$40.00	$0.00	Somewhat	No	50/100/25
Arizona	5.00%	Net of trade	Yes	$4.00	$360.00	$0.00	Yes	No	15/30/10
Arkansas	4.50%	Full Value	Yes	$5.00	$0.00	$21.00	Yes	Yes	25/50/15
California	7.25%	Full Value	Yes	$10.00	$308.00	$0.00	Somewhat	No	15/30/5
Colorado	3.00%	Net of trade	Yes	$5.50	$0.00	$15.00	Yes	Yes	25/50/15
Connecticut	6.00%	Net of trade	Yes	$16.00	$0.00	$0.00	Somewhat	Yes	20/40/10
DC	6.00%	Full Value	No	$10.00	$0.00	$45.00	Somewhat	Yes	10/20/05
Delaware	2.00%	Net of trade	No	$15.00	$0.00	$0.00	Somewhat	Yes	15/30/10
Florida	6.00%	Net of trade	No	$31.25	$0.00	$40.60	Yes	Yes	10/20/10
Georgia	3.00%	Net of trade	Yes	$5.00	$0.00	$0.00	Somewhat	No	10/20/05
Hawaii	4.00%	Net of trade	Yes	$0.00	$0.00	$52.50	Somewhat	Yes	25/25/10
Idaho	5.00%	Net of trade	No	$8.00	$0.00	$0.00	Yes	No	25/50/15
Illinois	6.25%	Net of trade	Yes	$5.00	$0.00	$0.00	Yes	No	20/40/15
Indiana	5.00%	Net of trade	No	$5.00	$0.00	$20.75	Somewhat	No	25/50/10
Iowa	4.00%	Net of trade	No	$15.00	$150.00	$12.00	Somewhat	No	20/40/15
Kansas	4.90%	Net of trade	Yes	$3.50	$0.00	$37.25	Somewhat	Yes	25/50/10
Kentucky	6.00%	Full Value	Yes	$6.00	$0.00	$0.00	Yes	Yes	25/50/10
Louisiana	4.00%	Net of trade	Yes	$24.50	$10.00	$0.00	Somewhat	No	10/20/10
Maine	6.00%	Net of trade	Yes	$10.00	$0.00	$20.00	Yes	No	20/40/10
Maryland	5.00%	Full Value	No	$12.00	$0.00	$35.00	Somewhat	Yes	20/40/10
Massachusetts	5.00%	Net of trade	Yes	$50.00	$0.00	$36.00	No	Yes	10/20/10
Michigan	4.00%	Full Value	No	$11.00	$81.00	$0.00	Somewhat	Yes	20/40/10
Minnesota	6.50%	Net of trade	No	$2.00	$192.50	$0.00	Yes	Yes	30/60/10
Mississippi	3.00%	Net of trade	Yes	$4.00	$0.00	$0.00	Somewhat	No	10/20/05
Missouri	4.23%	Net of trade	Yes	$7.50	$0.00	$18.00	Yes	No	25/50/10
Montana	1.50%	Full Value	Yes	$5.00	$300.00	$15.00	Yes	No	25/50/10
Nebraska	5.00%	Net of trade	Yes	$6.00	$0.00	$0.00	Somewhat	No	25/50/25
Nevada	7.00%	Unique trade	Yes	$20.00	$210.00	$0.00	Yes	No	15/30/10
New Hampshire	0.00%		No	$20.00	$27.00	$31.20	Somewhat	Yes	25/50/25
New Jersey	6.00%	Net of trade	No	$0.00	$0.00	$106.40	Somewhat	Yes	15/30/5
New Mexico	3.00%	Net of trade	No	$5.45	$0.00	$42.00	Somewhat	No	25/50/10
New York	4.00%	Full Value	Yes	$5.00	$0.00	$15.00	Somewhat	Yes	10/20/05
North Carolina	3.00%	Net of trade	Yes	$35.00	$0.00	$0.00	Somewhat	No	25/50/10
North Dakota	5.00%	Net of trade	No	$7.00	$0.00	$48.00	Somewhat	Yes	25/50/25
Ohio	5.00%	Net of trade	Yes	$3.00	$36.50	$0.00	Yes	No	12.5/25/7.5
Oklahoma	3.25%	Full Value	No	$11.00	$187.50	$0.00	Somewhat	No	10/20/10
Oregon	0.00%		No	$14.00	$0.00	$15.00	Yes	Yes	25/50/10
Pennsylvania	6.00%	Net of trade	No	$15.00	$0.00	$39.00	Yes	Yes	15/30/5
Rhode Island	7.00%	Net of trade	Yes	$0.00	$0.00	$34.00	Yes	No	25/50/10
South Carolina	5.00%	Net of trade	Yes	$5.00	$0.00	$0.00	Somewhat	Yes	15/30/5
South Dakota	3.00%	Net of trade	No	$5.00	$0.00	$30.00	Yes	Yes	25/50/25
Tennessee	5.50%	Net of trade	Yes	$6.50	$0.00	$38.25	Somewhat	No	15/30/10
Texas	6.25%	Net of trade	Yes	$13.00	$0.00	$38.20	No	Yes	10/20/05
Utah	5.88%	Net of trade	Yes	$6.00	$0.00	$14.50	Yes	Yes	15/30/5
Vermont	5.00%	Net of trade	No	$10.00	$0.00	$32.10	Yes	No	20/40/10
Virginia	3.00%	Full Value	Yes	$10.00	$0.00	$30.00	Yes	Yes	25/50/20
Washington	7.50%	Full Value	Yes	$4.25	$368.10	$37.00	Somewhat	Yes	25/50/10
West Virginia	5.00%	Net of trade	Yes	$5.00	$0.00	$26.50	Somewhat	No	20/40/10
Wisconsin	5.00%	Net of trade	Yes	$5.00	$0.00	$0.00	Yes	Yes	25/50/10
Wyoming	3.00%	Net of trade	Yes	$5.00	$270.00	$0.00	Yes	No	25/50/20

[1]Fee based on a $15,000 vehicle.
[2]Fee based on 3,000 pound vehicle weight.

Section Four
Vehicle Charts

Audi 100 CS Quattro
4 Door Wagon

2.8L 172 hp Gas Fuel Inject.

6 Cylinder "V"

Automatic 4 Speed

4 Wheel Full-Time

Driver/Psngr Airbags Std

Luxury

Purchase Price

Car Item	Dealer Cost	List
Base Price	**$36,973**	**$44,250**
Anti-Lock Brakes	Std	Std
Manual Transmission	N/A	N/A
Optional Engine	N/A	N/A
Auto Climate Control	Std	Std
Power Steering	Std	Std
Cruise Control	Std	Std
4 Wheel Full-Time Drive	Std	Std
AM/FM Stereo Cassette	Std	Std
Steering Wheel, Scope	Std	Std
Power Windows	Std	Std
***Options Price**	$0	$0
***Total Price**	**$36,973**	**$44,250**
Target Price	$40,301	
Destination Charge	$445	
Avg. Tax & Fees	$2,484	
Luxury Tax	$1,075	
Total Target $	**$44,305**	

Ownership Costs

Cost Area	5 Year Cost	Rate
Depreciation	$26,285	Worse Than Average
Financing ($890/month)	$7,298	
Insurance (Rating 18)	$9,058	Better Than Average
State Fees	$1,788	
Fuel (Hwy 22 City 18 -Prem.)	$4,766	Worse Than Average
Maintenance	$3,754	Better Than Average
Repairs	$1,425	Worse Than Average

Ownership Cost By Year

Warranty/Maintenance Info

Item		Rate
Major Tune-Up	$166	Better Than Average
Minor Tune-Up	$121	Average
Brake Service	$319	Poor
Overall Warranty	3 yr/50k	Average
Drivetrain Warranty	3 yr/50k	Average
Rust Warranty	10 yr/unlim. mi	Better Than Average
Maintenance Warranty	3 yr/50k	Better Than Average
Roadside Assistance	3 yr/50k	

Resale Value

1993	1994	1995	1996	1997
$29,761	$26,442	$23,569	$20,457	$18,020

Ownership Costs (5yr)

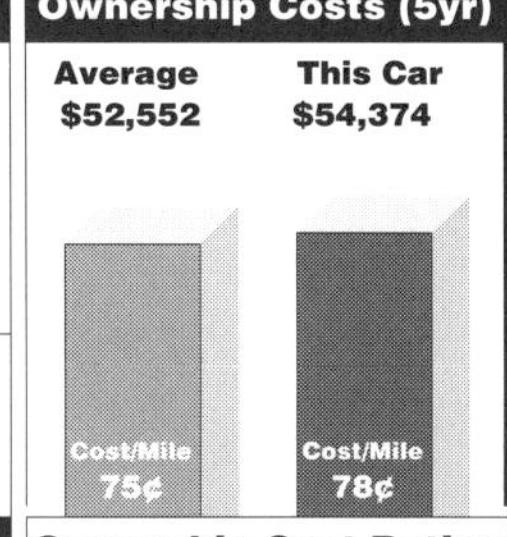

Average	This Car
$52,552	$54,374
Cost/Mile 75¢	Cost/Mile 78¢

The Audi 100 is available in five models-(Base) 100, S and CS Quattro sedan and wagon. New for 1993, the 100 CS Quattro wagon features a driver and passenger airbag to complement such existing standard equipment as anti-lock brakes, a front seat belt tensioning system and permanent all-wheel-drive. In addition to the automatic transmission, the Wagon features as standard eequipment leather seat upholstery and a Cold Weather Package which includes heated front seats with individual temperature controls.

Cumulative Costs

	1993	1994	1995	1996	1997
Annual	$20,583	$8,656	$7,439	$8,564	$9,132
Total	$20,583	$29,239	$36,678	$45,242	$54,374

Ownership Cost Rating

Average

BMW 525 i Touring
4 Door Wagon

2.5L 189 hp Gas Fuel Inject.

6 Cylinder In-Line

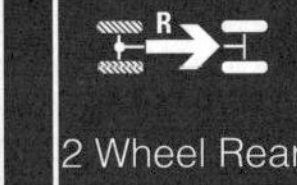
Automatic 4 Speed

2 Wheel Rear

Driver Airbag Psngr Belts

Luxury

Purchase Price

Car Item	Dealer Cost	List
Base Price	**$33,355**	**$39,800**
Anti-Lock Brakes	Std	Std
Manual Transmission	N/A	N/A
Optional Engine	N/A	N/A
Air Conditioning	Std	Std
Power Steering	Std	Std
Cruise Control	Std	Std
All Wheel Drive	N/A	N/A
AM/FM Stereo Cassette	Std	Std
Steering Wheel, Scope	Std	Std
Power Windows	Std	Std
***Options Price**	$0	$0
***Total Price**	**$33,355**	**$39,800**
Target Price	$37,191	
Destination Charge	$405	
Avg. Tax & Fees	$2,282	
Luxury Tax	$760	
Total Target $	**$40,638**	

Ownership Costs

Cost Area	5 Year Cost	Rate
Depreciation	$19,954	Average
Financing ($817/month)	$6,693	
Insurance (Rating 20 [Est.])	$10,244	Average
State Fees	$1,608	
Fuel (Hwy 25 City 18 -Prem.)	$4,451	Average
Maintenance	$4,308	Better Than Average
Repairs	$1,055	Average

Ownership Cost By Year

Warranty/Maintenance Info

Item		Rate
Major Tune-Up	$299	Poor
Minor Tune-Up	$207	Poor
Brake Service	$209	Average
Overall Warranty	4 yr/50k	Average
Drivetrain Warranty	4 yr/50k	Average
Rust Warranty	6 yr/unlim. mi	Average
Maintenance Warranty	N/A	
Roadside Assistance	4 yr/50k	

Resale Value

1993	1994	1995	1996	1997
$31,163	$28,774	$26,072	$23,348	$20,684

Ownership Costs (5yr)

Average	This Car
$49,221	$48,313
Cost/Mile 70¢	Cost/Mile 69¢

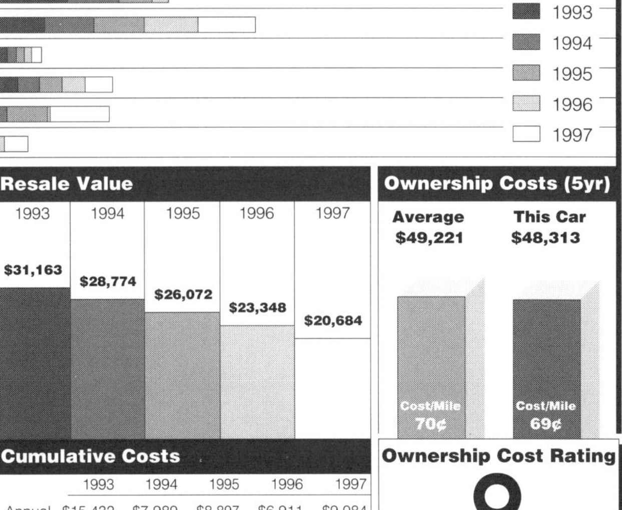

The BMW 5-Series is available in four models-525i sedan and Touring wagon, and 535i and M5 sedans. New for 1993, the 525i Touring features wood interior trim and automatic front seatbelt tensioners. Standard features include multi-function tailgate, roof-rack system and split fold-down seatbacks. Other features include a twin-panel sunroof, heated outside mirrors and optional Inclement Weather Package. The 525i Touring is the first BMW sports-wagon model to be offered in North America.

Cumulative Costs

	1993	1994	1995	1996	1997
Annual	$15,432	$7,989	$8,897	$6,911	$9,084
Total	$15,432	$23,421	$32,318	$39,229	$48,313

Ownership Cost Rating

Average

* Includes shaded options

** Other purchase requirements apply

Poor | Worse Than Average | Average | Better Than Average | Excellent | Insufficient Information

Refer to *Section 3: Annotated Vehicle Charts* for an explanation of these charts.

Buick Century Special
4 Door Wagon

2.2L 110 hp Gas Fuel Inject.	4 Cylinder In-Line	Automatic 3 Speed	2 Wheel Front	Belts Std, Driv Air Opt

Midsize Wagon

Purchase Price

Car Item	Dealer Cost	List
Base Price	**$13,389**	**$14,960**
Anti-Lock Brakes	N/A	N/A
4 Spd Auto	$172	$200
3.3L 160 hp Gas	$568	$660
Air Conditioning	Std	Std
Power Steering	Std	Std
Cruise Control	Pkg	** Pkg
All Wheel Drive	N/A	N/A
AM/FM Stereo Cassette	$120	$140
Steering Wheel, Tilt	Pkg	Pkg
Power Windows	Pkg	Pkg
***Options Price**	$688	$800
***Total Price**	**$14,077**	**$15,760**
Target Price	$15,383	
Destination Charge	$500	
Avg. Tax & Fees	$957	
Total Target $	**$16,840**	
Average Dealer Option Cost:	***86%***	

Ownership Costs

Cost Area	5 Year Cost	Rate
Depreciation	$9,462	Worse Than Average
Financing ($338/month)	$2,774	
Insurance (Rating 5)	$6,786	Excellent
State Fees	$651	
Fuel (Hwy 26 City 19)	$3,847	Average
Maintenance	$4,611	Average
Repairs	$709	Better Than Average

Ownership Cost By Year

Warranty/Maintenance Info

Item		Rate
Major Tune-Up	$196	Average
Minor Tune-Up	$138	Worse Than Average
Brake Service	$213	Average
Overall Warranty	3 yr/36k	Average
Drivetrain Warranty	3 yr/36k	Average
Rust Warranty	6 yr/100k	Better Than Average
Maintenance Warranty	N/A	
Roadside Assistance	3 yr/36k	

Resale Value

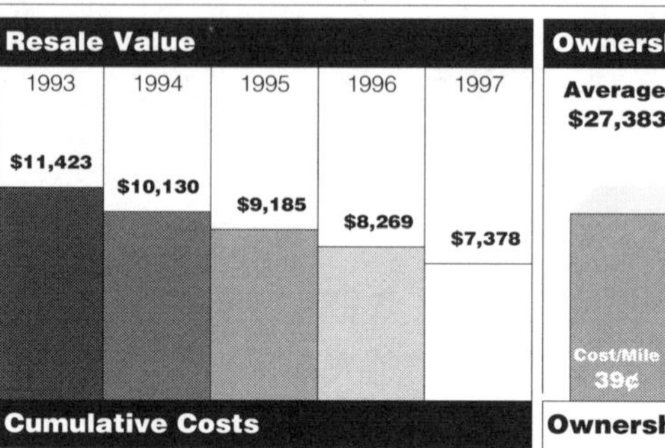

1993	1994	1995	1996	1997
$11,423	$10,130	$9,185	$8,269	$7,378

Ownership Costs (5yr)

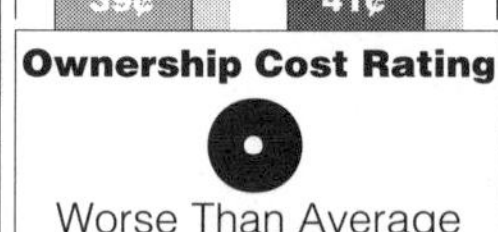

Average	This Car
$27,383	$28,840
Cost/Mile 39¢	Cost/Mile 41¢

Cumulative Costs

	1993	1994	1995	1996	1997
Annual	$8,750	$4,641	$4,992	$4,804	$5,653
Total	$8,750	$13,391	$18,383	$23,187	$28,840

Ownership Cost Rating

Worse Than Average

The 1993 Century is available in six models - Special, Custom, and Limited sedans; Special and Custom wagons; and the Custom coupe. New for 1993, the Special wagon features four new colors (Light Driftwood Metallic, Bright White, Ruby Red Metallic, and Dark Cherry Metallic). Other features include deluxe wheel covers, all-season tires, cloth notchback seat covering, 55/45 seats with a front-seat armrest, and a new trim level has been added.

Buick Century Custom
4 Door Wagon

2.2L 110 hp Gas Fuel Inject.	4 Cylinder In-Line	Automatic 3 Speed	2 Wheel Front	Driver Airbag Psngr Belts

Midsize Wagon

Purchase Price

Car Item	Dealer Cost	List
Base Price	**$15,094**	**$17,250**
Anti-Lock Brakes	N/A	N/A
4 Spd Auto	$172	$200
3.3L 160 hp Gas	$568	$660
Air Conditioning	Std	Std
Power Steering	Std	Std
Cruise Control	Pkg	** Pkg
All Wheel Drive	N/A	N/A
AM/FM Stereo Cassette	$120	$140
Steering Wheel, Tilt	Std	Std
Power Windows	Pkg	Pkg
***Options Price**	$688	$800
***Total Price**	**$15,782**	**$18,050**
Target Price	$17,320	
Destination Charge	$500	
Avg. Tax & Fees	$1,077	
Total Target $	**$18,897**	
Average Dealer Option Cost:	***86%***	

Ownership Costs

Cost Area	5 Year Cost	Rate
Depreciation	$10,633	Worse Than Average
Financing ($380/month)	$3,113	
Insurance (Rating 7)	$7,035	Excellent
State Fees	$742	
Fuel (Hwy 26 City 19)	$3,847	Average
Maintenance	$4,611	Average
Repairs	$709	Better Than Average

Ownership Cost By Year

Warranty/Maintenance Info

Item		Rate
Major Tune-Up	$196	Average
Minor Tune-Up	$138	Worse Than Average
Brake Service	$213	Average
Overall Warranty	3 yr/36k	Average
Drivetrain Warranty	3 yr/36k	Average
Rust Warranty	6 yr/100k	Better Than Average
Maintenance Warranty	N/A	
Roadside Assistance	3 yr/36k	

Resale Value

1993	1994	1995	1996	1997
$12,961	$11,471	$10,354	$9,290	$8,264

Ownership Costs (5yr)

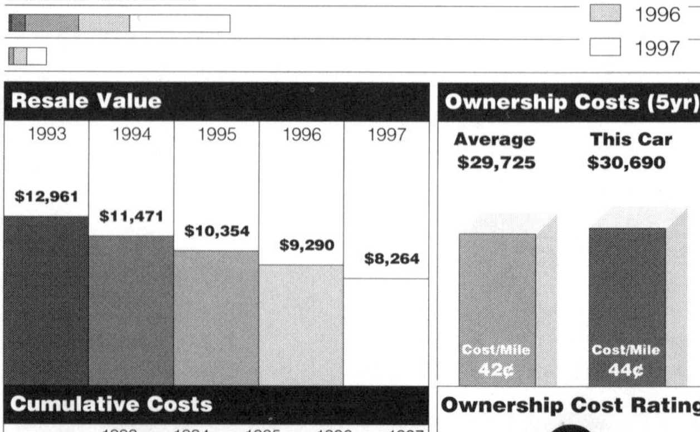

Average	This Car
$29,725	$30,690
Cost/Mile 42¢	Cost/Mile 44¢

Cumulative Costs

	1993	1994	1995	1996	1997
Annual	$9,480	$5,013	$5,299	$5,044	$5,854
Total	$9,480	$14,493	$19,792	$24,836	$30,690

Ownership Cost Rating

Average

The 1993 Century is available in six models - Special, Custom, and Limited sedans; Special and Custom wagons; and the Custom coupe. New for 1993, the Custom wagon features four new colors (Light Driftwood Metallic, Bright White, Ruby Red Metallic, and Dark Cherry Metallic). Other features include door edge guards, temperature and voltmeter guages, reading/map lights, trip odometer, and split folding rear seat.

* Includes shaded options

** Other purchase requirements apply

Poor  Worse Than Average  Average  Better Than Average  Excellent 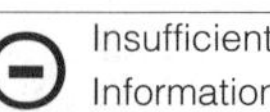 Insufficient Information

Refer to *Section 3: Annotated Vehicle Charts* for an explanation of these charts.

Buick Roadmaster Estate Wagon
4 Door Wagon

5.7L 180 hp Gas Fuel Inject. | 8 Cylinder "V" | Automatic 4 Speed | 2 Wheel Rear | Driver Airbag Psngr Belts

Large Wagon

Purchase Price

Car Item	Dealer Cost	List
Base Price	**$20,869**	**$23,850**
Anti-Lock Brakes	Std	Std
Manual Transmission	N/A	N/A
Optional Engine	N/A	N/A
Air Conditioning	Std	Std
Power Steering	Std	Std
Cruise Control	Pkg	Pkg
All Wheel Drive	N/A	N/A
AM/FM Stereo Cassette	$159	** $185
Steering Wheel, Tilt	Std	Std
Power Windows	Std	Std
***Options Price**	$0	$0
***Total Price**	**$20,869**	**$23,850**
Target Price	$22,618	
Destination Charge	$555	
Avg. Tax & Fees	$1,403	
Total Target $	**$24,576**	
Average Dealer Option Cost:	***86%***	

Ownership Costs

Cost Area	5 Year Cost	Rate
Depreciation	$14,566	Poor
Financing ($494/month)	$4,048	
Insurance (Rating 12)	$7,898	Excellent
State Fees	$976	
Fuel (Hwy 25 City 16)	$4,272	Average
Maintenance	$4,307	Worse Than Average
Repairs	$709	Better Than Average

Warranty/Maintenance Info

Item		Rate
Major Tune-Up	$198	Average
Minor Tune-Up	$133	Average
Brake Service	$230	Average
Overall Warranty	3 yr/36k	Average
Drivetrain Warranty	3 yr/36k	Average
Rust Warranty	6 yr/100k	Better Than Average
Maintenance Warranty	N/A	
Roadside Assistance	3 yr/36k	

The 1993 Roadmaster is available in three models - (Base) Roadmaster and Limited sedans and the Estate wagon. New for 1993, the Estate wagon features a locking system for power windows which allows the driver to control operation of the windows and two new exterior colors. The Estate wagon continues to have the vista roof, a dark-tinted glass panel in the roof. A vista cover for the roof glass is optional. A two-way tailgate provides instant access to the rear cargo or seating area.

Ownership Cost By Year

$5,000 | $10,000 | $15,000

1993 | 1994 | 1995 | 1996 | 1997

Resale Value

1993	1994	1995	1996	1997
$16,451	$14,727	$13,068	$11,571	$10,010

Cumulative Costs

	1993	1994	1995	1996	1997
Annual	$12,358	$5,840	$6,567	$5,559	$6,452
Total	$12,358	$18,198	$24,765	$30,324	$36,776

Ownership Costs (5yr)

Average	This Car
$36,123	$36,776
Cost/Mile 52¢	Cost/Mile 53¢

Ownership Cost Rating

Worse Than Average

Chevrolet Astro
3 Door Pass Van

4.3L 165 hp Gas Fuel Inject. | 6 Cylinder "V" | Automatic 4 Speed | 2 Wheel Rear | Manual Seatbelts Only

Mini Van

Purchase Price

Car Item	Dealer Cost	List
Base Price	**$14,123**	**$15,605**
Anti-Lock Brakes	Std	Std
Manual Transmission	N/A	N/A
4.3L 200 hp Gas	$430	$500
Air Conditioning	$727	$845
Power Steering	Std	Std
Cruise Control	Pkg	Pkg
All Wheel Drive	N/A	N/A
AM/FM Stereo Cassette	$235	$273
Steering Wheel, Tilt	Pkg	Pkg
Power Windows	Pkg	Pkg
***Options Price**	$962	$1,118
***Total Price**	**$15,085**	**$16,723**
Target Price	$16,038	
Destination Charge	$545	
Avg. Tax & Fees	$1,002	
Total Target $	**$17,585**	
Average Dealer Option Cost:	***86%***	

Ownership Costs

Cost Area	5 Year Cost	Rate
Depreciation	$5,160	Excellent
Financing ($353/month)	$2,896	
Insurance (Rating 2)	$6,542	Excellent
State Fees	$691	
Fuel (Hwy 21 City 16)	$4,672	Worse Than Average
Maintenance	$4,405	Average
Repairs	$700	Better Than Average

Warranty/Maintenance Info

Item		Rate
Major Tune-Up	$221	Worse Than Average
Minor Tune-Up	$138	Worse Than Average
Brake Service	$236	Average
Overall Warranty	3 yr/36k	Average
Drivetrain Warranty	3 yr/36k	Average
Rust Warranty	6 yr/100k	Better Than Average
Maintenance Warranty	N/A	
Roadside Assistance	3 yr/36k	

The 1993 Astro is available in four models - Regular and Extended passenger vans with two-wheel-drive (2WD) or all-wheel-drive (AWD) configurations. New for 1993, the Regular model is powered by a 4.3-liter V6 engine with Elecronic Fuel Injection and new four-speed electronically controlled automatic transmission with overdrive. It features a new brake-transmission shift interlock, ABS brakes, and a more readable instrument cluster.

Ownership Cost By Year

$2,000 | $4,000 | $6,000 | $8,000

1993 | 1994 | 1995 | 1996 | 1997

Resale Value

1993	1994	1995	1996	1997
$15,673	$14,931	$14,308	$13,446	$12,425

Cumulative Costs

	1993	1994	1995	1996	1997
Annual	$5,422	$4,258	$5,010	$4,586	$5,790
Total	$5,422	$9,680	$14,690	$19,276	$25,066

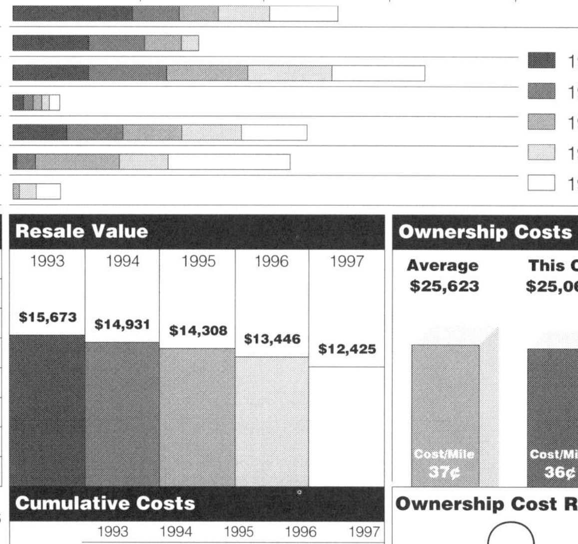

Ownership Costs (5yr)

Average	This Car
$25,623	$25,066
Cost/Mile 37¢	Cost/Mile 36¢

Ownership Cost Rating

Excellent

* Includes shaded options

** Other purchase requirements apply

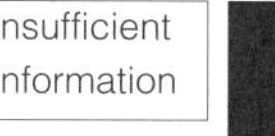

Poor | Worse Than Average | Average | Better Than Average | Excellent | Insufficient Information

Refer to *Section 3: Annotated Vehicle Charts* for an explanation of these charts.

Chevrolet Astro Extended

3 Door Pass Ext Van

CHEVROLET

Mini Van

Purchase Price

Car Item	Dealer Cost	List
Base Price	**$14,747**	**$16,295**
Anti-Lock Brakes	Std	Std
Manual Transmission	N/A	N/A
4.3L 200 hp Gas	$430	$500
Air Conditioning	$727	$845
Power Steering	Std	Std
Cruise Control	Pkg	Pkg
All Wheel Drive	N/A	N/A
AM/FM Stereo Cassette	$235	$273
Steering Wheel, Tilt	Pkg	Pkg
Power Windows	Pkg	Pkg
***Options Price**	$962	$1,118
***Total Price**	**$15,709**	**$17,413**
Target Price	$16,719	
Destination Charge	$545	
Avg. Tax & Fees	$1,043	
Total Target $	**$18,307**	
Average Dealer Option Cost:	***86%***	

Ownership Costs

Cost Area	5 Year Cost	Rate
Depreciation	$5,501	Better Than Average
Financing ($368/month)	$3,016	
Insurance (Rating 4)	$6,867	Excellent
State Fees	$720	
Fuel (Hwy 21 City 16)	$4,672	Worse Than Average
Maintenance	$4,434	Average
Repairs	$700	Better Than Average

Ownership Cost By Year

$2,000 $4,000 $6,000 $8,000

1993 1994 1995 1996 1997

Warranty/Maintenance Info

Item		Rate
Major Tune-Up	$221	Worse Than Average
Minor Tune-Up	$138	Worse Than Average
Brake Service	$236	Average
Overall Warranty	3 yr/36k	Average
Drivetrain Warranty	3 yr/36k	Average
Rust Warranty	6 yr/100k	Better Than Average
Maintenance Warranty	N/A	
Roadside Assistance	3 yr/36k	

Resale Value

1993	1994	1995	1996	1997
$16,110	$15,363	$14,732	$13,859	$12,806

Ownership Costs (5yr)

Average	This Car
$26,198	$25,910

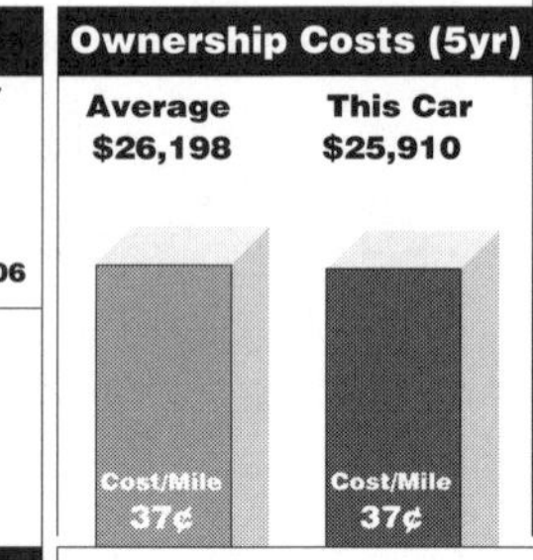

The 1993 Astro is available in four models - Regular and Extended passenger vans with two-wheel-drive (2WD) or all-wheel-drive (AWD) configurations. New for 1993, the Extended model features four-wheel anti-lock brakes and 10 inches more depth than the Regular-Body Astro, for a total cargo area of 41.3 cu. ft. The option list includes "Dutch doors", Heavy-Duty Cooling Package, air conditioning, electric defogger and seating for up to eight.

Cumulative Costs

	1993	1994	1995	1996	1997
Annual	$5,823	$4,371	$5,127	$4,678	$5,911
Total	$5,823	$10,194	$15,321	$19,999	$25,910

Ownership Cost Rating

Better Than Average

Chevrolet Astro Cargo Van

3 Door Cargo Van

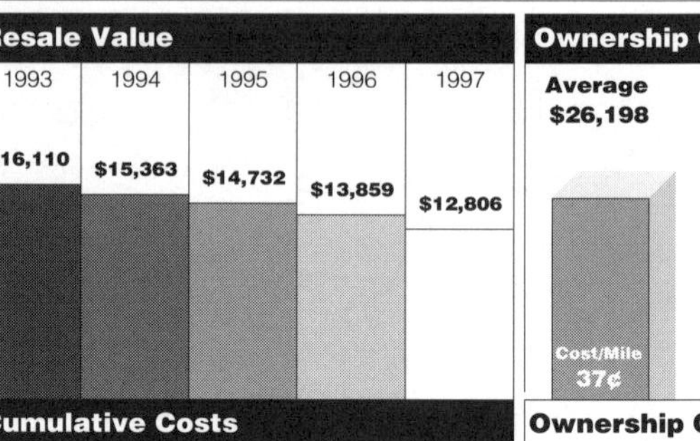

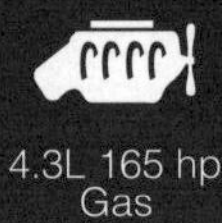

Mini Van

Passenger van Shown

Purchase Price

Car Item	Dealer Cost	List
Base Price	**$13,299**	**$14,695**
Anti-Lock Brakes	Std	Std
Manual Transmission	N/A	N/A
4.3L 200 hp Gas	$430	$500
Air Conditioning	$727	$845
Power Steering	Std	Std
Cruise Control	Pkg	Pkg
All Wheel Drive	N/A	N/A
AM/FM Stereo Cassette	$187	$218
Steering Wheel, Tilt	Pkg	Pkg
Power Windows	Pkg	Pkg
***Options Price**	$914	$1,063
***Total Price**	**$14,213**	**$15,758**
Target Price	$15,090	
Destination Charge	$545	
Avg. Tax & Fees	$945	
Total Target $	**$16,580**	
Average Dealer Option Cost:	***86%***	

Ownership Costs

Cost Area	5 Year Cost	Rate
Depreciation	$7,159	Excellent
Financing ($333/month)	$2,732	
Insurance (Rating 2)	$6,542	Excellent
State Fees	$652	
Fuel (Hwy 21 City 17)	$4,543	Worse Than Average
Maintenance	$4,405	Average
Repairs	$700	Better Than Average

Ownership Cost By Year

$2,000 $4,000 $6,000 $8,000

1993 1994 1995 1996 1997

Warranty/Maintenance Info

Item		Rate
Major Tune-Up	$221	Worse Than Average
Minor Tune-Up	$138	Worse Than Average
Brake Service	$236	Average
Overall Warranty	3 yr/36k	Average
Drivetrain Warranty	3 yr/36k	Average
Rust Warranty	6 yr/100k	Better Than Average
Maintenance Warranty	N/A	
Roadside Assistance	3 yr/36k	

Resale Value

1993	1994	1995	1996	1997
$12,903	$12,049	$11,370	$10,452	$9,421

Ownership Costs (5yr)

Average	This Car
$24,819	$26,733

Cost/Mile 35¢ Cost/Mile 38¢

The 1993 Astro Cargo Van is available in four models - Regular and Extended passenger vans with two-wheel-drive (2WD) or all-wheel-drive (AWD) configurations. New for 1993, the Regular model features a four-wheel anti-lock brake system and a brake-transmission shift interlock. It offers 5,750-lb. towing capacity and features its 4.3-liter V6 engine with Electronic Fuel Injection and new 4-speed electronically controlled automatic transmission . It is equipped with a driver's seat only.

Cumulative Costs

	1993	1994	1995	1996	1997
Annual	$7,084	$4,286	$5,000	$4,597	$5,766
Total	$7,084	$11,370	$16,370	$20,967	$26,733

Ownership Cost Rating

Worse Than Average

* Includes shaded options

** Other purchase requirements apply

Poor

Worse Than Average — Average — Better Than Average — Excellent — Insufficient Information

Refer to *Section 3: Annotated Vehicle Charts* for an explanation of these charts.

Chevrolet Astro Cargo Van Extended
3 Door Cargo Ext Van

4.3L 165 hp Gas Fuel Inject.

6 Cylinder "V"

Automatic 4 Speed

2 Wheel Rear

Manual Seatbelts Only

Mini Van

Passenger van Shown

Purchase Price

Car Item	Dealer Cost	List
Base Price	**$13,905**	**$15,365**
Anti-Lock Brakes	Std	Std
Manual Transmission	N/A	N/A
4.3L 200 hp Gas	$430	$500
Air Conditioning	$727	$845
Power Steering	Std	Std
Cruise Control	Pkg	Pkg
All Wheel Drive	N/A	N/A
AM/FM Stereo Cassette	$187	$218
Steering Wheel, Tilt	Pkg	Pkg
Power Windows	Pkg	Pkg
***Options Price**	$914	$1,063
***Total Price**	**$14,819**	**$16,428**
Target Price	$15,749	
Destination Charge	$545	
Avg. Tax & Fees	$985	
Total Target $	**$17,279**	
Average Dealer Option Cost:	***86%***	

Ownership Costs

Cost Area	5 Year Cost	Rate
Depreciation	$7,439	Excellent
Financing ($347/month)	$2,847	
Insurance (Rating 2)	$6,542	Excellent
State Fees	$680	
Fuel (Hwy 21 City 17)	$4,543	Worse Than Average
Maintenance	$4,434	Average
Repairs	$700	Better Than Average

Ownership Cost By Year

(Bar chart: $2,000 / $4,000 / $6,000 / $8,000; legend 1993, 1994, 1995, 1996, 1997)

Warranty/Maintenance Info

Item		Rate
Major Tune-Up	$221	Worse Than Average
Minor Tune-Up	$138	Worse Than Average
Brake Service	$236	Average
Overall Warranty	3 yr/36k	Average
Drivetrain Warranty	3 yr/36k	Average
Rust Warranty	6 yr/100k	Better Than Average
Maintenance Warranty	N/A	
Roadside Assistance	3 yr/36k	

Resale Value

1993	1994	1995	1996	1997
$13,453	$12,568	$11,859	$10,908	$9,840

Ownership Costs (5yr)

Average	This Car
$25,377	$27,185
Cost/Mile 36¢	Cost/Mile 39¢

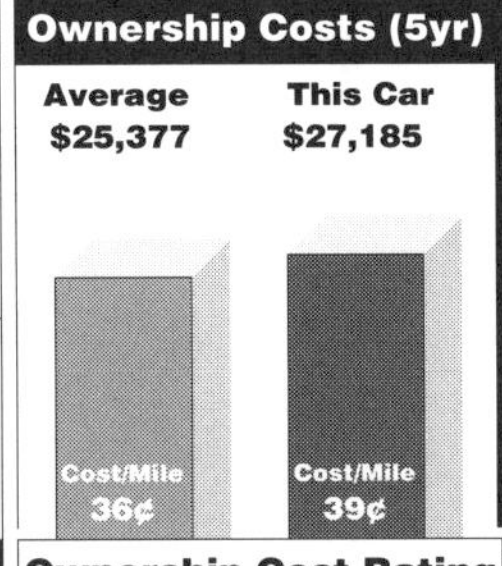

Cumulative Costs

	1993	1994	1995	1996	1997
Annual	$7,288	$4,359	$5,072	$4,644	$5,822
Total	$7,288	$11,647	$16,719	$21,363	$27,185

Ownership Cost Rating

Worse Than Average

The 1993 Astro Cargo Van is available in four models - Regular and Extended passenger vans with two-wheel-drive (2WD) or all-wheel-drive (AWD) configurations. New for 1993, the Extended model provides 10 inches more depth in cargo space, for a total cargo capacity of up to 200.1 cu. ft. The four-wheel anti-lock brake system is now standard for 1993. Other features include a new 4-speed electronically controlled automatic transmission with overdrive. It is equipped with a driver's seat only.

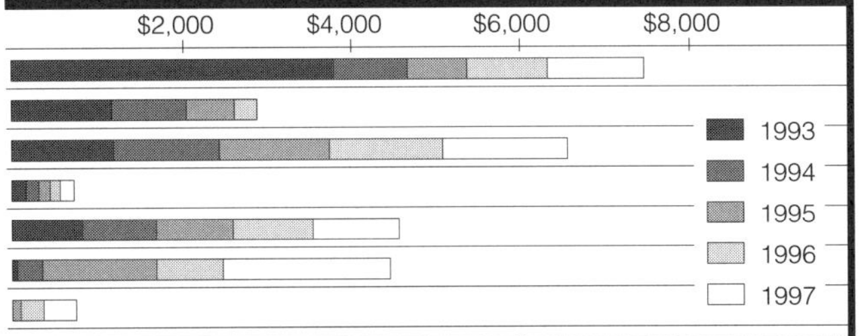

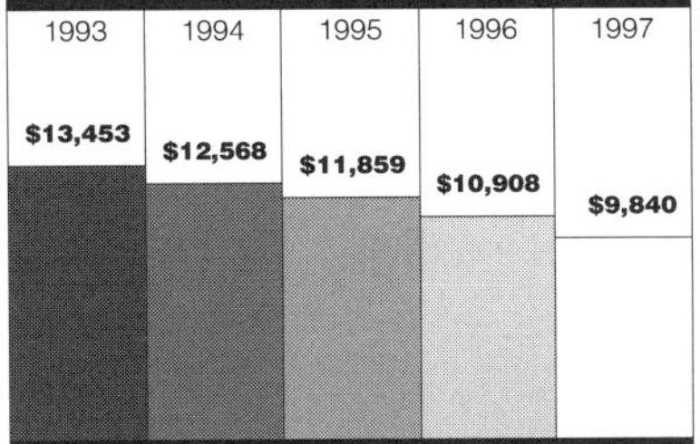

Chevrolet Astro AWD
3 Door Pass Van

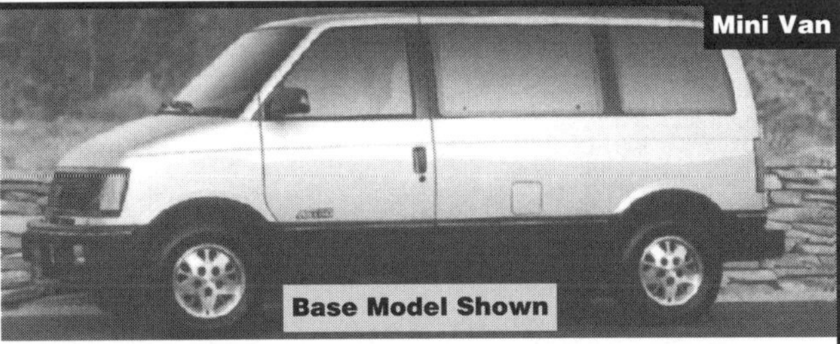

4.3L 200 hp Gas Fuel Inject.

6 Cylinder "V"

Automatic 4 Speed

4 Wheel Full-Time

Manual Seatbelts Only

Mini Van

Base Model Shown

Purchase Price

Car Item	Dealer Cost	List
Base Price	**$16,222**	**$17,925**
Anti-Lock Brakes	Std	Std
Manual Transmission	N/A	N/A
Optional Engine	N/A	N/A
Air Conditioning	$727	$845
Power Steering	Std	Std
Cruise Control	Pkg	Pkg
4 Wheel Full-Time Drive	Std	Std
AM/FM Stereo Cassette	$235	$273
Steering Wheel, Tilt	Pkg	Pkg
Power Windows	Pkg	Pkg
***Options Price**	$962	$1,118
***Total Price**	**$17,184**	**$19,043**
Target Price	$18,335	
Destination Charge	$545	
Avg. Tax & Fees	$1,140	
Total Target $	**$20,020**	
Average Dealer Option Cost:	***86%***	

Ownership Costs

Cost Area	5 Year Cost	Rate
Depreciation	$5,972	Better Than Average
Financing ($402/month)	$3,299	
Insurance (Rating 4)	$6,867	Excellent
State Fees	$784	
Fuel (Hwy 20 City 15 -Prem.)	$5,458	Poor
Maintenance	$5,034	Worse Than Average
Repairs	$791	Average

Ownership Cost By Year

(Bar chart: $2,000 / $4,000 / $6,000 / $8,000; legend 1993, 1994, 1995, 1996, 1997)

Warranty/Maintenance Info

Item		Rate
Major Tune-Up	$221	Worse Than Average
Minor Tune-Up	$138	Worse Than Average
Brake Service	$239	Average
Overall Warranty	3 yr/36k	Average
Drivetrain Warranty	3 yr/36k	Average
Rust Warranty	6 yr/100k	Better Than Average
Maintenance Warranty	N/A	
Roadside Assistance	3 yr/36k	

Resale Value

1993	1994	1995	1996	1997
$18,257	$17,201	$16,374	$15,317	$14,048

Ownership Costs (5yr)

Average	This Car
$27,555	$28,205
Cost/Mile 39¢	Cost/Mile 40¢

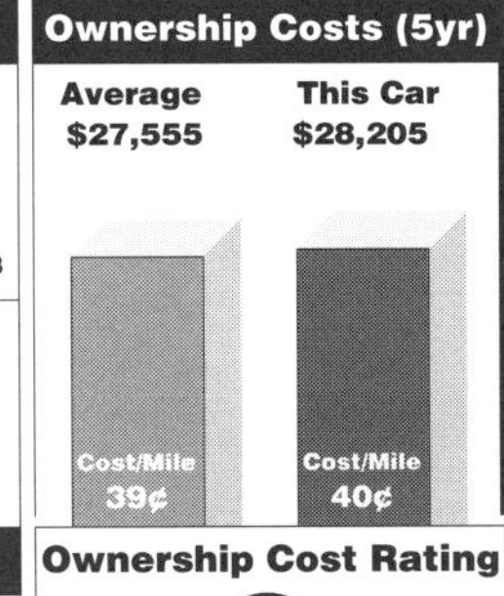

Cumulative Costs

	1993	1994	1995	1996	1997
Annual	$5,668	$4,933	$5,452	$5,131	$7,021
Total	$5,668	$10,601	$16,053	$21,184	$28,205

Ownership Cost Rating

Average

The 1993 Astro is available in four models - Regular and Extended passenger vans with two-wheel-drive (2WD) or all-wheel-drive (AWD) configurations. New for 1993, the Astro AWD features a new electronic four-speed automatic transmission--the Hydra-matic 4L60-E. It is powered by a 4.3-liter V6 engine with electronic fuel injection. Other features include four-wheel anti-lock brakes , new optional brushed aluminum wheels and air conditioning.

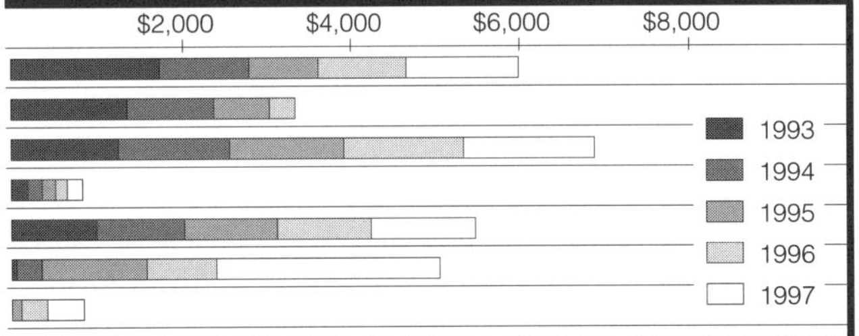

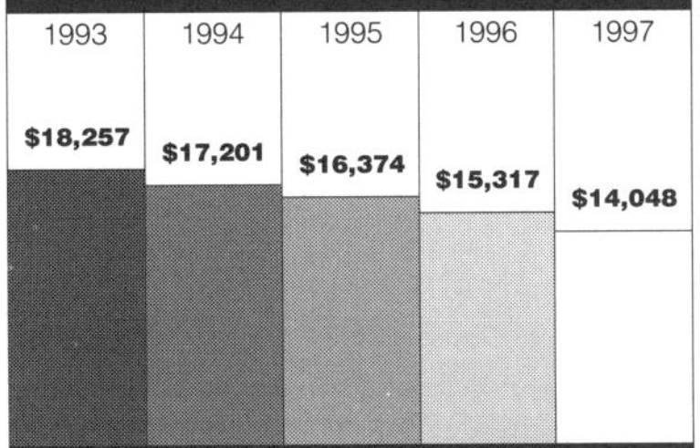

* Includes shaded options

** Other purchase requirements apply

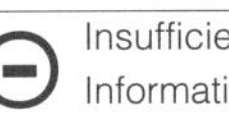

 Poor  Worse Than Average Average Better Than Average  Excellent  Insufficient Information

Refer to *Section 3: Annotated Vehicle Charts* for an explanation of these charts.

Chevrolet Astro Extended AWD
3 Door Pass Ext Van

4.3L 200 hp Gas Fuel Inject.

6 Cylinder "V"

Automatic 4 Speed

4 Wheel Full-Time

Manual Seatbelts Only

Mini Van

Purchase Price

Car Item	Dealer Cost	List
Base Price	**$16,801**	**$18,565**
Anti-Lock Brakes	Std	Std
Manual Transmission	N/A	N/A
Optional Engine	N/A	N/A
Air Conditioning	$727	$845
Power Steering	Std	Std
Cruise Control	Pkg	Pkg
4 Wheel Full-Time Drive	Std	Std
AM/FM Stereo Cassette	$235	$273
Steering Wheel, Tilt	Pkg	Pkg
Power Windows	Pkg	Pkg
***Options Price**	$962	$1,118
***Total Price**	**$17,763**	**$19,683**
Target Price	$18,972	
Destination Charge	$545	
Avg. Tax & Fees	$1,178	
Total Target $	**$20,695**	
Average Dealer Option Cost:	***86%***	

Ownership Costs

Cost Area	5 Year Cost	Rate
Depreciation	$6,525	Better Than Average
Financing ($416/month)	$3,410	
Insurance (Rating 6)	$7,129	Excellent
State Fees	$809	
Fuel (Hwy 20 City 15 -Prem.)	$5,458	Poor
Maintenance	$5,034	Worse Than Average
Repairs	$791	Average

Warranty/Maintenance Info

Item		Rate
Major Tune-Up	$221	Worse Than Average
Minor Tune-Up	$138	Worse Than Average
Brake Service	$239	Average
Overall Warranty	3 yr/36k	Average
Drivetrain Warranty	3 yr/36k	Average
Rust Warranty	6 yr/100k	Better Than Average
Maintenance Warranty	N/A	
Roadside Assistance	3 yr/36k	

The 1993 Astro is available in four models - Regular and Extended passenger vans with two-wheel-drive (2WD) or all-wheel-drive (AWD) configurations. New for 1993, the AWD Extended model provides 10 inches more depth and up to 170.4 cu. ft. of cargo space with center-row and rear-row seats removed than the Regular-Body Astro. Other new features include a brake-transmission shift interlock, Dutch doors", and three new exterior colors for 1993.

Ownership Cost By Year

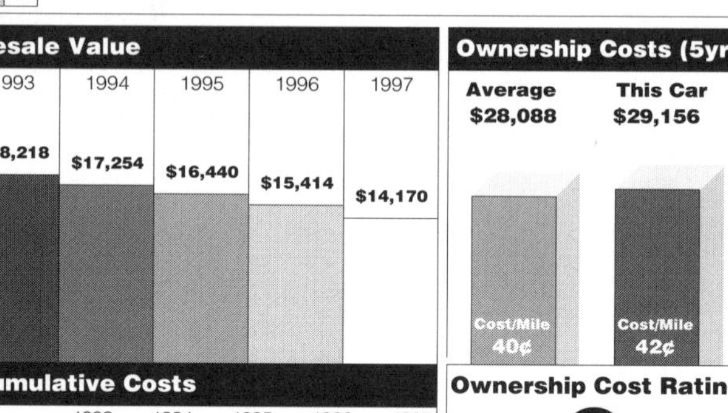

Resale Value

1993	1994	1995	1996	1997
$18,218	$17,254	$16,440	$15,414	$14,170

Ownership Costs (5yr)

Average	This Car
$28,088	$29,156
Cost/Mile 40¢	Cost/Mile 42¢

Cumulative Costs

	1993	1994	1995	1996	1997
Annual	$6,482	$4,932	$5,519	$5,167	$7,056
Total	$6,482	$11,414	$16,933	$22,100	$29,156

Ownership Cost Rating

Average

Chevrolet Astro Cargo Van AWD
3 Door Cargo Van

4.3L 200 hp Gas Fuel Inject.

6 Cylinder "V"

Automatic 4 Speed

4 Wheel Full-Time

Manual Seatbelts Only

Mini Van

Passenger 2WD Shown

Purchase Price

Car Item	Dealer Cost	List
Base Price	**$15,390**	**$17,005**
Anti-Lock Brakes	Std	Std
Manual Transmission	N/A	N/A
Optional Engine	N/A	N/A
Air Conditioning	$727	$845
Power Steering	Std	Std
Cruise Control	Pkg	Pkg
4 Wheel Full-Time Drive	Std	Std
AM/FM Stereo Cassette	$187	$218
Steering Wheel, Tilt	Pkg	Pkg
Power Windows	Pkg	Pkg
***Options Price**	$914	$1,063
***Total Price**	**$16,304**	**$18,068**
Target Price	$17,372	
Destination Charge	$545	
Avg. Tax & Fees	$1,082	
Total Target $	**$18,999**	
Average Dealer Option Cost:	***86%***	

Ownership Costs

Cost Area	5 Year Cost	Rate
Depreciation	$7,990	Excellent
Financing ($382/month)	$3,130	
Insurance (Rating 4)	$6,867	Excellent
State Fees	$745	
Fuel (Hwy 21 City 16 -Prem.)	$5,159	Worse Than Average
Maintenance	$5,034	Worse Than Average
Repairs	$791	Average

Warranty/Maintenance Info

Item		Rate
Major Tune-Up	$221	Worse Than Average
Minor Tune-Up	$138	Worse Than Average
Brake Service	$239	Average
Overall Warranty	3 yr/36k	Average
Drivetrain Warranty	3 yr/36k	Average
Rust Warranty	6 yr/100k	Better Than Average
Maintenance Warranty	N/A	
Roadside Assistance	3 yr/36k	

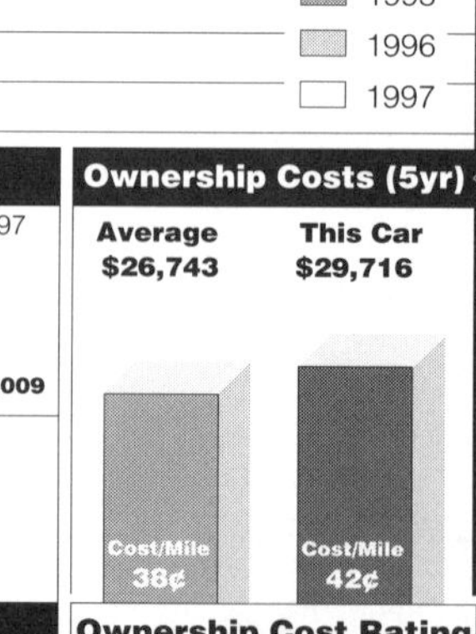

The 1993 Astro Cargo Van is available in four models - Regular and Extended passenger vans with two-wheel-drive (2WD) or all-wheel-drive (AWD) configurations. New for 1993, the Astro AWD features a 4.3-liter V6 engine with Electronic Fuel injection and new 4-speed electronically controlled automatic transmission with overdrive. Other new features include ABS brakes and a brake-transmission shift interlock. The option list includes "Dutch doors", seating for two, and air conditioning.

Ownership Cost By Year

$2,000 · $4,000 · $6,000 · $8,000 — 1993, 1994, 1995, 1996, 1997

Resale Value

1993	1994	1995	1996	1997
$14,902	$13,940	$13,168	$12,153	$11,009

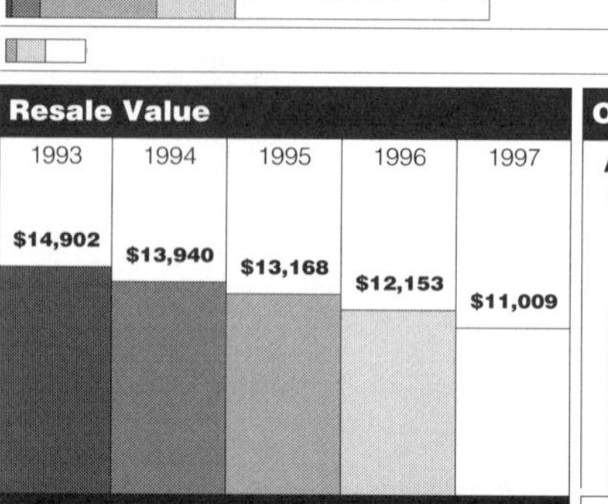

Ownership Costs (5yr)

Average	This Car
$26,743	$29,716
Cost/Mile 38¢	Cost/Mile 42¢

Cumulative Costs

	1993	1994	1995	1996	1997
Annual	$7,867	$4,721	$5,296	$5,007	$6,825
Total	$7,867	$12,588	$17,884	$22,891	$29,716

Ownership Cost Rating

Poor

* Includes shaded options

** Other purchase requirements apply

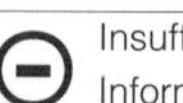

 Poor  Worse Than Average · Average · Better Than Average · Excellent  Insufficient Information

Refer to *Section 3: Annotated Vehicle Charts* for an explanation of these charts.

Chevrolet Astro Cargo Van Extended AWD
3 Door Cargo Ext Van

Mini Van

4.3L 200 hp Gas Fuel Inject.

6 Cylinder "V"

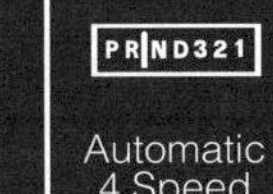
Automatic 4 Speed

4 Wheel Full-Time

Manual Seatbelts Only

Passenger van Shown

Purchase Price

Car Item	Dealer Cost	List
Base Price	**$15,969**	**$17,645**
Anti-Lock Brakes	Std	Std
Manual Transmission	N/A	N/A
Optional Engine	N/A	N/A
Air Conditioning	$727	$845
Power Steering	Std	Std
Cruise Control	Pkg	Pkg
4 Wheel Full-Time Drive	Std	Std
AM/FM Stereo Cassette	$187	$218
Steering Wheel, Tilt	Pkg	Pkg
Power Windows	Pkg	Pkg
***Options Price**	$914	$1,063
***Total Price**	**$16,883**	**$18,708**
Target Price	$18,006	
Destination Charge	$545	
Avg. Tax & Fees	$1,121	
Total Target $	**$19,672**	
Average Dealer Option Cost:	***86%***	

Ownership Costs

Cost Area	5 Year Cost	Rate
Depreciation	$8,120	Excellent
Financing ($395/month)	$3,241	
Insurance (Rating 4)	$6,867	Excellent
State Fees	$771	
Fuel (Hwy 21 City 16 -Prem.)	$5,159	Worse Than Average
Maintenance	$5,034	Worse Than Average
Repairs	$791	Average

Ownership Cost By Year

$2,000 $4,000 $6,000 $8,000 $10,000

1993 1994 1995 1996 1997

Warranty/Maintenance Info

Major Tune-Up	$221	Worse Than Average
Minor Tune-Up	$138	Worse Than Average
Brake Service	$239	Average
Overall Warranty	3 yr/36k	Average
Drivetrain Warranty	3 yr/36k	Average
Rust Warranty	6 yr/100k	Better Than Average
Maintenance Warranty	N/A	
Roadside Assistance	3 yr/36k	

Resale Value

1993	1994	1995	1996	1997
$15,457	$14,529	$13,739	$12,726	$11,552

Ownership Costs (5yr)

Average	This Car
$27,276	$29,983
Cost/Mile 39¢	Cost/Mile 43¢

The 1993 Astro Cargo Van is available in four models - Regular and Extended passenger vans with two-wheel-drive (2WD) or all-wheel-drive (AWD) configurations. New for 1993, the Extended AWD offers 5,570 lb. towing capacity and the performance of its 4.3-liter V6 engine with Electronic Fuel Injection. It provides 10 inches more depth in cargo space, for a total cargo capacity of up to 200.1 cu. ft. Other features include a new 4-speed electronically controlled automatic transmission.

Cumulative Costs

	1993	1994	1995	1996	1997
Annual	$8,038	$4,727	$5,341	$5,018	$6,859
Total	$8,038	$12,765	$18,106	$23,124	$29,983

Ownership Cost Rating

Poor

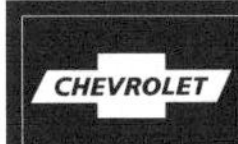

Chevrolet Blazer
2 Door Sport Utility

Utility

5.7L 210 hp Gas Fuel Inject.

8 Cylinder "V"

Manual 5 Speed

4 Wheel On-Demand

Manual Seatbelts Only

Purchase Price

Car Item	Dealer Cost	List
Base Price	**$17,504**	**$20,005**
Anti-Lock Brakes	Std	Std
Automatic 4 Speed	$765	$890
Optional Engine	N/A	N/A
Air Conditioning	$727	$845
Power Steering	Std	Std
Cruise Control	Pkg	Pkg
4 Whl On-Demand Dr.	Std	Std
AM/FM Stereo Cassette	$251	$292
Steering Wheel, Tilt	Pkg	Pkg
Power Windows	Pkg	Pkg
***Options Price**	$978	$1,137
***Total Price**	**$18,482**	**$21,142**
Target Price	$20,119	
Destination Charge	$595	
Avg. Tax & Fees	$1,253	
Total Target $	**$21,967**	
Average Dealer Option Cost:	***86%***	

Ownership Costs

Cost Area	5 Year Cost	Rate
Depreciation	$7,396	Better Than Average
Financing ($442/month)	$3,618	
Insurance (Rating 16)	$8,995	Average
State Fees	$869	
Fuel (Hwy 17 City 13)	$5,760	Poor
Maintenance	$4,446	Average
Repairs	$945	Worse Than Average

Ownership Cost By Year

$2,000 $4,000 $6,000 $8,000 $10,000

1993 1994 1995 1996 1997

Warranty/Maintenance Info

Major Tune-Up	$184	Average
Minor Tune-Up	$112	Worse Than Average
Brake Service	$268	Worse Than Average
Overall Warranty	3 yr/36k	Average
Drivetrain Warranty	3 yr/36k	Average
Rust Warranty	6 yr/100k	Better Than Average
Maintenance Warranty	N/A	
Roadside Assistance	3 yr/36k	

Resale Value

1993	1994	1995	1996	1997
$17,821	$17,057	$16,421	$15,545	$14,571

Ownership Costs (5yr)

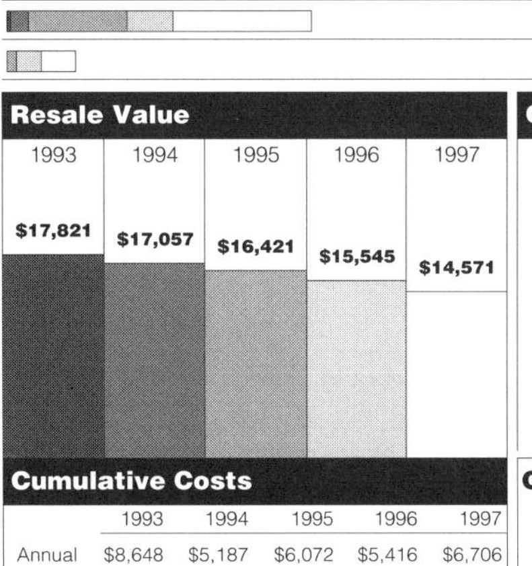

Average	This Car
$31,084	$32,029
Cost/Mile 44¢	Cost/Mile 46¢

The 1993 Blazer is available in one model edition with three optional trim levels - Cheyenne (standard), Silverado and Sport (both optional). New for 1993, the Blazer features an electronic 4-speed automatic optional transmission--the Hydra-matic 4L60-E. Another new feature includes a single-rail shift control that improves reliability and durability. Other standard features include 4-wheel anti-lock brakes and Chevrolet's patented Insta-Trac system for "shift-on-the-fly" convenience.

Cumulative Costs

	1993	1994	1995	1996	1997
Annual	$8,648	$5,187	$6,072	$5,416	$6,706
Total	$8,648	$13,835	$19,907	$25,323	$32,029

Ownership Cost Rating

Average

* Includes shaded options

** Other purchase requirements apply

   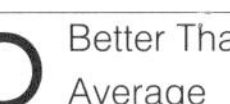 

Poor | Worse Than Average | Average | Better Than Average | Excellent | Insufficient Information

Refer to ***Section 3: Annotated Vehicle Charts*** for an explanation of these charts.

Chevrolet C1500 Work Truck
2 Door Regular Cab

CHEVROLET

Large Pickup

4.3L 165 hp Gas Fuel Inject.

6 Cylinder "V"

1 3 5 / 2 4 R
Manual 5 Speed

2 Wheel Rear

Manual Seatbelts Only

K1500 Model Shown

Purchase Price

Car Item	Dealer Cost	List
Base Price	**$10,186**	**$11,255**
Anti-Lock Brakes	Std	Std
Automatic 4 Speed	$765	$890
Optional Engine	N/A	N/A
Air Conditioning	$692	$805
Power Steering	Std	Std
Cruise Control	N/A	N/A
All Wheel Drive	N/A	N/A
AM/FM Stereo Cassette	$390	$454
Steering Wheel, Tilt	N/A	N/A
Power Windows	N/A	N/A
***Options Price**	$1,082	$1,259
***Total Price**	**$11,268**	**$12,514**
Target Price	$11,970	
Destination Charge	$595	
Avg. Tax & Fees	$759	
Total Target $	**$13,324**	
Average Dealer Option Cost:	***86%***	

Ownership Costs

Cost Area	5 Year Cost	Rate
Depreciation	$3,347	Excellent
Financing ($268/month)	$2,194	
Insurance (Rating 5)	$6,996	Better Than Average
State Fees	$525	
Fuel (Hwy 21 City 15)	$4,816	Excellent
Maintenance	$4,166	Average
Repairs	$700	Excellent

Ownership Cost By Year

$2,000 $4,000 $6,000 $8,000

1993 1994 1995 1996 1997

Warranty/Maintenance Info

Major Tune-Up	$171	Average
Minor Tune-Up	$98	Better Than Average
Brake Service	$268	Better Than Average
Overall Warranty	3 yr/36k	Average
Drivetrain Warranty	3 yr/36k	Average
Rust Warranty	6 yr/100k	Better Than Average
Maintenance Warranty	N/A	
Roadside Assistance	3 yr/36k	

Resale Value

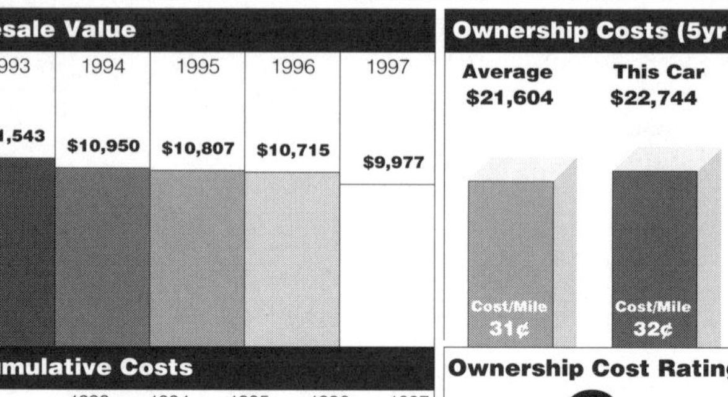

1993	1994	1995	1996	1997
$11,543	$10,950	$10,807	$10,715	$9,977

Ownership Costs (5yr)

Average	This Car
$21,604	$22,744
Cost/Mile 31¢	Cost/Mile 32¢

The 1993 C1500 Pickup is available in four models - (Base) C1500, 454 SS and Work Truck two-wheel drive Regular Cabs and the Base C1500 two-wheel drive Extended Cab. New for 1993, the Work Truck uses an anti-chip coating on leading edges of the hood, roof and entire "A" pillars, which helps prevent stone chips, and the RPO MXO 4-speed automatic transmission now has electronic controls. Four new exterior colors are available (Quasar Blue, Teal Green, Indigo Blue and Dark Garnet Red - all metallic).

Cumulative Costs

	1993	1994	1995	1996	1997
Annual	$5,066	$3,927	$4,452	$3,807	$5,492
Total	$5,066	$8,993	$13,445	$17,252	$22,744

Ownership Cost Rating

Average

Chevrolet C1500
2 Door Regular Cab

CHEVROLET

Large Pickup

4.3L 165 hp Gas Fuel Inject.

6 Cylinder "V"

1 3 5 / 2 4 R
Manual 5 Speed

2 Wheel Rear

Manual Seatbelts Only

Sport Package Shown

Purchase Price

Car Item	Dealer Cost	List
Base Price	**$11,887**	**$13,585**
Anti-Lock Brakes	Std	Std
Automatic 4 Speed	$765	$890
5.0L 175 hp Gas	$495	$575
Air Conditioning	$692	$805
Power Steering	Std	Std
Cruise Control	Pkg	Pkg
All Wheel Drive	N/A	N/A
AM/FM Stereo Cassette	$251	$292
Steering Wheel, Tilt	Pkg	Pkg
8 Foot Bed	$263	$300
***Options Price**	$1,438	$1,672
***Total Price**	**$13,325**	**$15,257**
Target Price	$14,200	
Destination Charge	$595	
Avg. Tax & Fees	$899	
Total Target $	**$15,694**	
Average Dealer Option Cost:	***86%***	

Ownership Costs

Cost Area	5 Year Cost	Rate
Depreciation	$4,784	Better Than Average
Financing ($315/month)	$2,586	
Insurance (Rating 7)	$7,244	Better Than Average
State Fees	$635	
Fuel (Hwy 19 City 14)	$5,244	Better Than Average
Maintenance	$4,290	Average
Repairs	$700	Excellent

Ownership Cost By Year

$2,000 $4,000 $6,000 $8,000

1993 1994 1995 1996 1997

Warranty/Maintenance Info

Major Tune-Up	$187	Worse Than Average
Minor Tune-Up	$116	Worse Than Average
Brake Service	$268	Better Than Average
Overall Warranty	3 yr/36k	Average
Drivetrain Warranty	3 yr/36k	Average
Rust Warranty	6 yr/100k	Better Than Average
Maintenance Warranty	N/A	
Roadside Assistance	3 yr/36k	

Resale Value

1993	1994	1995	1996	1997
$13,230	$12,790	$12,401	$11,772	$10,910

Ownership Costs (5yr)

Average	This Car
$24,972	$25,483
Cost/Mile 36¢	Cost/Mile 36¢

The 1993 C1500 Pickup is available in four models - (Base) C1500, 454 SS and Work Truck two-wheel drive Regular Cabs and the Base C1500 two-wheel drive Extended Cab. New for 1993, the Base C1500 uses an anti-chip coating on leading edges of the hood, roof and entire "A" pillars. A new Sportside Sport Pickup is offered that includes Silverado trim, "Sport" decals, body-color Duragrille, Sportside box and cast aluminum wheels. This package is available in Summit White, Onyx Black or Victory Red.

Cumulative Costs

	1993	1994	1995	1996	1997
Annual	$6,067	$4,075	$4,957	$4,558	$5,826
Total	$6,067	$10,142	$15,099	$19,657	$25,483

Ownership Cost Rating

Average

* Includes shaded options

** Other purchase requirements apply

Poor

Worse Than Average

Average

Better Than Average

Excellent
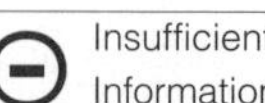
Insufficient Information

Refer to *Section 3: Annotated Vehicle Charts* for an explanation of these charts.

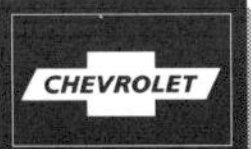

Chevrolet C2500
2 Door Regular Cab

4.3L 165 hp Gas Fuel Inject.

6 Cylinder "V"

Manual 5 Speed

2 Wheel Rear

Manual Seatbelts Only

Purchase Price

Car Item	Dealer Cost	List
Base Price	**$12,622**	**$14,425**
Anti-Lock Brakes	Std	Std
Automatic 4 Speed	$765	$890
5.0L 175 hp Gas	$495	$575
Air Conditioning	$692	$805
Power Steering	Std	Std
Cruise Control	Pkg	Pkg
All Wheel Drive	N/A	N/A
AM/FM Stereo Cassette	$251	$292
Steering Wheel, Tilt	Pkg	Pkg
Power Windows	Pkg	Pkg
***Options Price**	$1,438	$1,672
***Total Price**	**$14,060**	**$16,097**
Target Price	$15,005	
Destination Charge	$595	
Avg. Tax & Fees	$947	
Total Target $	**$16,547**	
Average Dealer Option Cost:	***86%***	

Ownership Costs

Cost Area	5 Year Cost	Rate
Depreciation	$4,675	Excellent
Financing ($333/month)	$2,725	
Insurance (Rating 8)	$7,432	Better Than Average
State Fees	$668	
Fuel (Hwy 19 City 14)	$5,244	Better Than Average
Maintenance	$4,835	Worse Than Average
Repairs	$700	Excellent

Ownership Cost By Year

$2,000 $4,000 $6,000 $8,000

1993 1994 1995 1996 1997

Warranty/Maintenance Info

Item		Rate
Major Tune-Up	$187	Worse Than Average
Minor Tune-Up	$116	Worse Than Average
Brake Service	$285	Average
Overall Warranty	3 yr/36k	Average
Drivetrain Warranty	3 yr/36k	Average
Rust Warranty	6 yr/100k	Better Than Average
Maintenance Warranty	N/A	
Roadside Assistance	3 yr/36k	

Resale Value

1993	1994	1995	1996	1997
$15,001	$14,380	$13,822	$12,965	$11,872

Ownership Costs (5yr)

Average	This Car
$26,003	$26,279
Cost/Mile 37¢	Cost/Mile 38¢

The 1993 C Pickup is available in three models - 1500, 2500 and 3500. C2500 Pickups are available in 2-wheel drive, Fleetside and Sportside styling, regular and extended cabs, and two trim levels-Cheyenne (standard) and Silverado. New for 1993, the C2500 Regular cab features the new electronic 4-speed transmission--the Hydra-matic 4L60-E. Standard features include an all-welded frame and cargo box and an independent front suspension with anti-roll bar.

Cumulative Costs

	1993	1994	1995	1996	1997
Annual	$5,250	$4,343	$5,381	$4,945	$6,360
Total	$5,250	$9,593	$14,974	$19,919	$26,279

Ownership Cost Rating

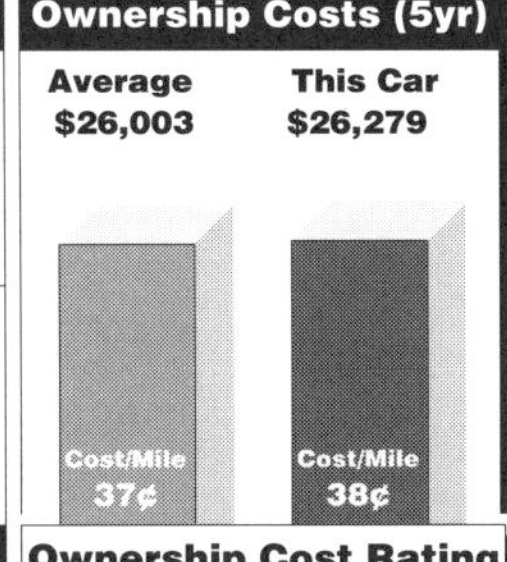
Average

Chevrolet C3500
2 Door Regular Cab

5.7L 190 hp Gas Fuel Inject.

8 Cylinder "V"

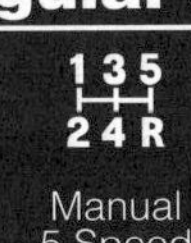
Manual 5 Speed

2 Wheel Rear

Manual Seatbelts Only

Large Pickup

C2500 Model Shown

Purchase Price

Car Item	Dealer Cost	List
Base Price	**$14,140**	**$16,164**
Anti-Lock Brakes	Std	Std
Automatic 4 Speed	$765	$890
7.4L 230 hp Gas	$404	$470
Air Conditioning	$692	$805
Power Steering	Std	Std
Cruise Control	Pkg	Pkg
All Wheel Drive	N/A	N/A
AM/FM Stereo Cassette	$251	$292
Steering Wheel, Tilt	Pkg	Pkg
Power Windows	Pkg	Pkg
***Options Price**	$943	$1,097
***Total Price**	**$15,083**	**$17,261**
Target Price	$16,142	
Destination Charge	$595	
Avg. Tax & Fees	$1,016	
Total Target $	**$17,753**	
Average Dealer Option Cost:	***86%***	

Ownership Costs

Cost Area	5 Year Cost	Rate
Depreciation	$6,389	Average
Financing ($357/month)	$2,924	
Insurance (Rating 7)	$7,244	Better Than Average
State Fees	$715	
Fuel (Hwy 17 City 13 [Est.])	$5,760	Average
Maintenance	$5,265	Poor
Repairs	$700	Excellent

Ownership Cost By Year

$2,000 $4,000 $6,000 $8,000

1993 1994 1995 1996 1997

Warranty/Maintenance Info

Item		Rate
Major Tune-Up	$187	Worse Than Average
Minor Tune-Up	$116	Worse Than Average
Brake Service	$477	Poor
Overall Warranty	3 yr/36k	Average
Drivetrain Warranty	3 yr/36k	Average
Rust Warranty	6 yr/100k	Better Than Average
Maintenance Warranty	N/A	
Roadside Assistance	3 yr/36k	

Resale Value

1993	1994	1995	1996	1997
$14,026	$13,536	$13,101	$12,388	$11,364

Ownership Costs (5yr)

Average	This Car
$27,433	$28,997
Cost/Mile 39¢	Cost/Mile 41¢

The 1993 C3500 two-wheel drive pickup is available in two models - Regular and Extended Cabs. Three trim levels are offered - Cheyenne, Scottsdale and Silverado. New for the 1993 lineup, the C3500 Regular Cab features a new electronic 4-speed automatic, a modified 5.7L V8 available for conversion to gaseous fuel and expanded availability of the 6.5L turbo diesel. Corrosion and anti-paint chipping protection have been improved.

Cumulative Costs

	1993	1994	1995	1996	1997
Annual	$7,587	$4,348	$5,614	$4,828	$6,620
Total	$7,587	$11,935	$17,549	$22,377	$28,997

Ownership Cost Rating

Average

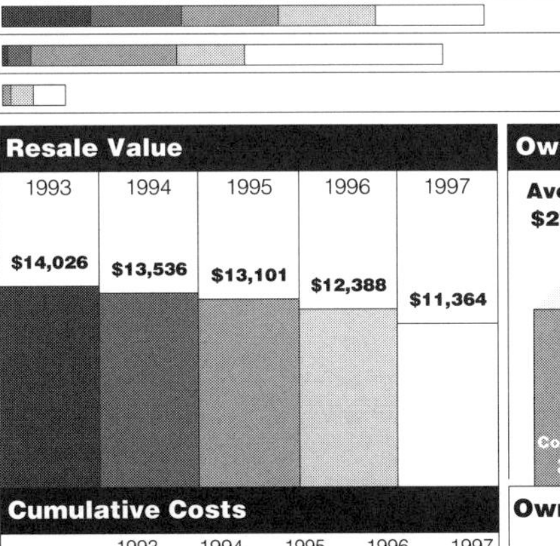

* Includes shaded options

** Other purchase requirements apply

Poor · Worse Than Average · Average · Better Than Average · Excellent · Insufficient Information

Refer to *Section 3: Annotated Vehicle Charts* for an explanation of these charts.

Chevrolet C1500 454 SS
2 Door Regular Cab

7.4L 255 hp Gas Fuel Inject.

8 Cylinder "V"

Automatic 4 Speed

2 Wheel Rear

Manual Seatbelts Only

Purchase Price

Car Item	Dealer Cost	List
Base Price	**$18,585**	**$21,240**
Anti-Lock Brakes	Std	Std
Manual Transmission	N/A	N/A
Optional Engine	N/A	N/A
Air Conditioning	Std	Std
Power Steering	Std	Std
Cruise Control	Std	Std
All Wheel Drive	N/A	N/A
AM/FM Stereo Cassette	Std	Std
Steering Wheel, Tilt	Std	Std
Power Windows	Std	Std
***Options Price**	$0	$0
***Total Price**	**$18,585**	**$21,240**
Target Price	$20,057	
Destination Charge	$595	
Avg. Tax & Fees	$1,251	
Total Target $	**$21,903**	
Average Dealer Option Cost:	***86%***	

Ownership Costs

Cost Area	5 Year Cost	Rate
Depreciation	$8,329	Average
Financing ($440/month)	$3,608	
Insurance (Rating 12)	$8,108	Better Than Average
State Fees	$874	
Fuel (Hwy 12 City 10)	$7,848	Poor
Maintenance	$4,695	Worse Than Average
Repairs	$700	Excellent

Warranty/Maintenance Info

Item		Rate
Major Tune-Up	$187	Worse Than Average
Minor Tune-Up	$116	Worse Than Average
Brake Service	$285	Average
Overall Warranty	3 yr/36k	Average
Drivetrain Warranty	3 yr/36k	Average
Rust Warranty	6 yr/100k	Better Than Average
Maintenance Warranty	N/A	
Roadside Assistance	3 yr/36k	

The 1993 C1500 Pickup is available in four models - (Base) C1500, 454 SS and Work Truck two-wheel drive Regular Cabs and the Base C1500 two-wheel drive Extended Cab. New for 1993, the 454 SS uses an anti-chip coating on leading edges of hood, roof and entire "A" pillars and a steel sleeve steering column (w/comfortilt only) has been designed for improved security. The 454 SS also features 15-inch wheels, a heavy-duty electronic transmission and an upgraded tachometer-equipped gauge cluster.

Ownership Cost By Year

$2,000 $4,000 $6,000 $8,000 $10,000

Legend: 1993, 1994, 1995, 1996, 1997

Resale Value

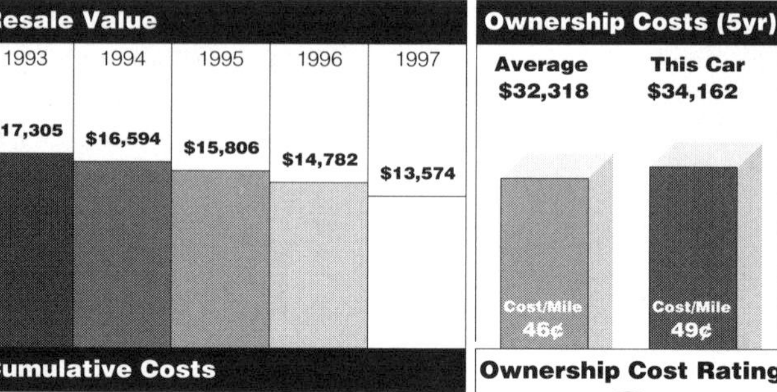

1993	1994	1995	1996	1997
$17,305	$16,594	$15,806	$14,782	$13,574

Ownership Costs (5yr)

Average	This Car
$32,318	$34,162
Cost/Mile 46¢	Cost/Mile 49¢

Cumulative Costs

	1993	1994	1995	1996	1997
Annual	$9,327	$5,386	$6,404	$5,952	$7,093
Total	$9,327	$14,713	$21,117	$27,069	$34,162

Ownership Cost Rating

Average

Chevrolet C1500
2 Door Extended Cab

4.3L 165 hp Gas Fuel Inject.

6 Cylinder "V"

Manual 5 Speed

2 Wheel Rear

Manual Seatbelts Only

Large Pickup

Purchase Price

Car Item	Dealer Cost	List
Base Price	**$13,239**	**$15,130**
Anti-Lock Brakes	Std	Std
Automatic 4 Speed	$765	$890
5.0L 175 hp Gas	$495	$575
Air Conditioning	$692	$805
Power Steering	Std	Std
Cruise Control	Pkg	Pkg
All Wheel Drive	N/A	N/A
AM/FM Stereo Cassette	$251	$292
Steering Wheel, Tilt	Pkg	Pkg
8 Foot Bed	$228	$260
***Options Price**	$1,438	$1,672
***Total Price**	**$14,677**	**$16,802**
Target Price	$15,681	
Destination Charge	$595	
Avg. Tax & Fees	$988	
Total Target $	**$17,264**	
Average Dealer Option Cost:	***86%***	

Ownership Costs

Cost Area	5 Year Cost	Rate
Depreciation	$4,130	Excellent
Financing ($347/month)	$2,845	
Insurance (Rating 10)	$7,689	Better Than Average
State Fees	$696	
Fuel (Hwy 19 City 14)	$5,244	Better Than Average
Maintenance	$4,367	Average
Repairs	$700	Excellent

Warranty/Maintenance Info

Item		Rate
Major Tune-Up	$187	Worse Than Average
Minor Tune-Up	$116	Worse Than Average
Brake Service	$268	Better Than Average
Overall Warranty	3 yr/36k	Average
Drivetrain Warranty	3 yr/36k	Average
Rust Warranty	6 yr/100k	Better Than Average
Maintenance Warranty	N/A	
Roadside Assistance	3 yr/36k	

The 1993 C1500 Pickup is available in four models - (Base) C1500, 454 SS and Work Truck two-wheel drive Regular Cabs and the Base C1500 two-wheel drive Extended Cab. New for 1993, the C1500 Extended Cab uses an anti-chip coating which helps prevent stone chips on leading edges of the hood, roof and entire "A" pillars. The RPO MXO 4-speed automatic transmission now has electronic controls and there are four new colors (Quasar Blue, Teal Green, Indigo Blue and Dark Garnet Red - all metallic).

Ownership Cost By Year

$2,000 $4,000 $6,000 $8,000

Legend: 1993, 1994, 1995, 1996, 1997

Resale Value

1993	1994	1995	1996	1997
$15,309	$14,913	$14,541	$14,000	$13,134

Ownership Costs (5yr)

Average	This Car
$26,869	$25,671
Cost/Mile 38¢	Cost/Mile 37¢

Cumulative Costs

	1993	1994	1995	1996	1997
Annual	$5,764	$4,211	$5,110	$4,631	$5,955
Total	$5,764	$9,975	$15,085	$19,716	$25,671

Ownership Cost Rating

Excellent

* Includes shaded options

** Other purchase requirements apply

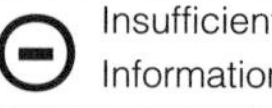

 Poor  Worse Than Average  Average 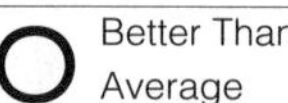 Better Than Average  Excellent ⊖ Insufficient Information

Refer to *Section 3: Annotated Vehicle Charts* for an explanation of these charts.

Chevrolet C2500
2 Door Extended Cab

4.3L 165 hp Gas Fuel Inject.

6 Cylinder "V"

Manual 5 Speed

2 Wheel Rear

Manual Seatbelts Only

C1500 Model Shown

Purchase Price

Car Item	Dealer Cost	List
Base Price	**$14,210**	**$16,240**
Anti-Lock Brakes	Std	Std
Automatic 4 Speed	$765	$890
5.0L 175 hp Gas	$495	$575
Air Conditioning	$692	$805
Power Steering	Std	Std
Cruise Control	Pkg	Pkg
All Wheel Drive	N/A	N/A
AM/FM Stereo Cassette	$251	$292
Steering Wheel, Tilt	Pkg	Pkg
8 Foot Bed	$245	$280
***Options Price**	$1,438	$1,672
***Total Price**	**$15,648**	**$17,912**
Target Price	$16,749	
Destination Charge	$595	
Avg. Tax & Fees	$1,052	
Total Target $	**$18,396**	
Average Dealer Option Cost:	***86%***	

Ownership Costs

Cost Area	5 Year Cost	Rate
Depreciation	$4,811	Excellent
Financing ($370/month)	$3,030	
Insurance (Rating 10)	$7,689	Better Than Average
State Fees	$741	
Fuel (Hwy 19 City 14)	$5,244	Better Than Average
Maintenance	$4,770	Worse Than Average
Repairs	$700	Excellent

Ownership Cost By Year

$2,000 $4,000 $6,000 $8,000

1993 1994 1995 1996 1997

Warranty/Maintenance Info

Major Tune-Up	$187	Worse Than Average
Minor Tune-Up	$116	Worse Than Average
Brake Service	$285	Average
Overall Warranty	3 yr/36k	Average
Drivetrain Warranty	3 yr/36k	Average
Rust Warranty	6 yr/100k	Better Than Average
Maintenance Warranty	N/A	
Roadside Assistance	3 yr/36k	

Resale Value

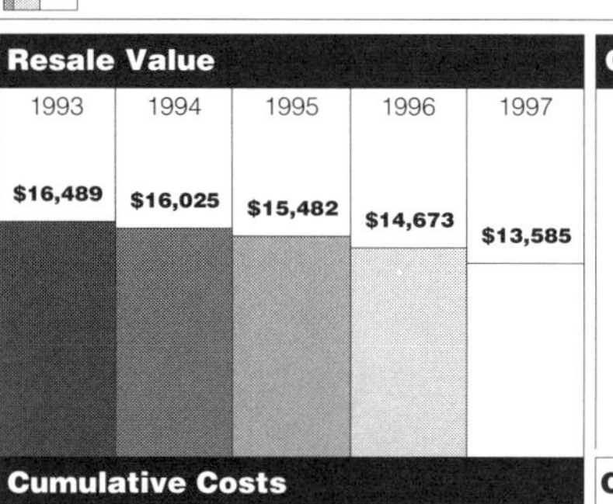

Ownership Costs (5yr)

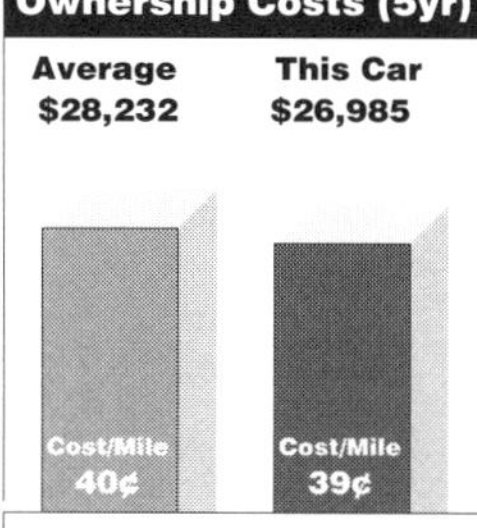

The 1993 C Pickup is available in three models - 1500, 2500 and 3500. C2500 Pickups are available in 2-wheel drive, Fleetside and Sportside styling, regular and extended cabs, and two trim levels-Cheyenne (standard) and Silveraldo. New for 1993, the C2500 Extended cab is now available with 2-passenger seating with optional folding rear seat. Standard features include integral head restraints, and a steel sleeve steering column. Other features include four new exterior colors for 1993.

Cumulative Costs

	1993	1994	1995	1996	1997
Annual	$5,804	$4,347	$5,492	$4,920	$6,422
Total	$5,804	$10,151	$15,643	$20,563	$26,985

Ownership Cost Rating

Excellent

Chevrolet C3500
2 Door Extended Cab

5.7L 190 hp Gas Fuel Inject.

8 Cylinder "V"

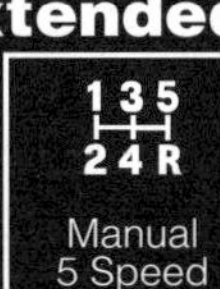
Manual 5 Speed

2 Wheel Rear

Manual Seatbelts Only

Large Pickup

C1500 Model Shown

Purchase Price

Car Item	Dealer Cost	List
Base Price	**$15,593**	**$17,824**
Anti-Lock Brakes	Std	Std
Automatic 4 Speed	$765	$890
7.4L 230 hp Gas	$404	$470
Air Conditioning	$692	$805
Power Steering	Std	Std
Cruise Control	Pkg	Pkg
All Wheel Drive	N/A	N/A
AM/FM Stereo Cassette	$251	$292
Steering Wheel, Tilt	Pkg	Pkg
Power Windows	Pkg	Pkg
***Options Price**	$943	$1,097
***Total Price**	**$16,536**	**$18,921**
Target Price	$17,746	
Destination Charge	$595	
Avg. Tax & Fees	$1,112	
Total Target $	**$19,453**	
Average Dealer Option Cost:	***86%***	

Ownership Costs

Cost Area	5 Year Cost	Rate
Depreciation	$6,457	Average
Financing ($391/month)	$3,205	
Insurance (Rating 10)	$7,689	Better Than Average
State Fees	$781	
Fuel (Hwy 17 City 13 [Est.])	$5,760	Average
Maintenance	$5,265	Poor
Repairs	$700	Excellent

Ownership Cost By Year

$2,000 $4,000 $6,000 $8,000

1993 1994 1995 1996 1997

Warranty/Maintenance Info

Major Tune-Up	$187	Worse Than Average
Minor Tune-Up	$116	Worse Than Average
Brake Service	$477	Poor
Overall Warranty	3 yr/36k	Average
Drivetrain Warranty	3 yr/36k	Average
Rust Warranty	6 yr/100k	Better Than Average
Maintenance Warranty	N/A	
Roadside Assistance	3 yr/36k	

Resale Value

1993	1994	1995	1996	1997
$16,025	$15,487	$14,936	$14,127	$12,996

Ownership Costs (5yr)

Average	This Car
$29,471	$29,857
Cost/Mile 42¢	Cost/Mile 43¢

The 1993 C3500 two-wheel drive pickup is available in two models - Regular and Extended Cabs. Three trim levels are offered - Cheyenne, Scottsdale and Silverado. New for the 1993 lineup, the C3500 Extended Cab features a new electronic 4-speed automatic, a modified 5.7L V8 available for conversion to gaseous fuel and expanded availability of the 6.5L turbo diesel. The Extended Cab is now available with two-passenger seating.

Cumulative Costs

	1993	1994	1995	1996	1997
Annual	$7,504	$4,584	$5,886	$5,050	$6,833
Total	$7,504	$12,088	$17,974	$23,024	$29,857

Ownership Cost Rating

Average

* Includes shaded options

** Other purchase requirements apply

 Poor 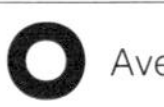 Worse Than Average  Average  Better Than Average ◯ Excellent ⊖ Insufficient Information

Refer to *Section 3: Annotated Vehicle Charts* for an explanation of these charts.

Chevrolet C3500 Crew Cab

4 Door Extended Cab

Large Pickup

5.7L 190 hp Gas Fuel Inject.	8 Cylinder "V"	Manual 5 Speed	2 Wheel Rear	Manual Seatbelts Only

Purchase Price

Car Item	Dealer Cost	List
Base Price	**$15,873**	**$18,144**
Anti-Lock Brakes	Std	Std
Automatic 4 Speed	$765	$890
7.4L 230 hp Gas	$404	$470
Air Conditioning	$692	$805
Power Steering	Std	Std
Cruise Control	Pkg	Pkg
All Wheel Drive	N/A	N/A
AM/FM Stereo Cassette	$251	$292
Steering Wheel, Tilt	Pkg	Pkg
Power Windows	Pkg	Pkg
***Options Price**	$943	$1,097
***Total Price**	**$16,816**	**$19,241**
Target Price	$18,056	
Destination Charge	$595	
Avg. Tax & Fees	$1,131	
Total Target $	**$19,782**	
Average Dealer Option Cost:	***86%***	

Ownership Costs

Cost Area	5 Year Cost	Rate
Depreciation	$6,567	Average
Financing ($398/month)	$3,259	
Insurance (Rating 10)	$7,689	Better Than Average
State Fees	$794	
Fuel (Hwy 16 City 12 [Est.])	$6,176	Worse Than Average
Maintenance	$5,265	Poor
Repairs	$750	Excellent

Warranty/Maintenance Info

Item		Rate
Major Tune-Up	$187	Worse Than Average
Minor Tune-Up	$116	Worse Than Average
Brake Service	$477	Poor
Overall Warranty	3 yr/36k	Average
Drivetrain Warranty	3 yr/36k	Average
Rust Warranty	6 yr/100k	Better Than Average
Maintenance Warranty	N/A	
Roadside Assistance	3 yr/36k	

Ownership Cost By Year

$2,000 $4,000 $6,000 $8,000

1993 1994 1995 1996 1997

Resale Value

1993	1994	1995	1996	1997
$16,283	$15,739	$15,180	$14,359	$13,215

Ownership Costs (5yr)

Average	This Car
$29,864	$30,500
Cost/Mile 43¢	Cost/Mile 44¢

Cumulative Costs

	1993	1994	1995	1996	1997
Annual	$7,676	$4,690	$5,998	$5,175	$6,961
Total	$7,676	$12,366	$18,364	$23,539	$30,500

Ownership Cost Rating

Average

The 1993 Chevrolet Crew Cab Pickup is available in two models - two- wheel drive and four-wheel drive. Three trim levels are offered - Cheyenne, Scottsdale and Silverado. New for the 1993 lineup, the C3500 Crew Cab features a new electronic four-speed automatic, a modified 5.7L V8 available for conversion to gaseous fuel and expanded availability of the 6.5L turbo diesel. Corrosion protection has been improved and four new exterior colors have been added.

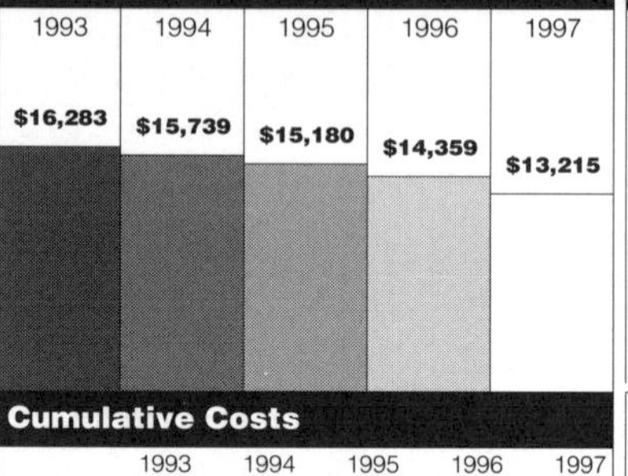

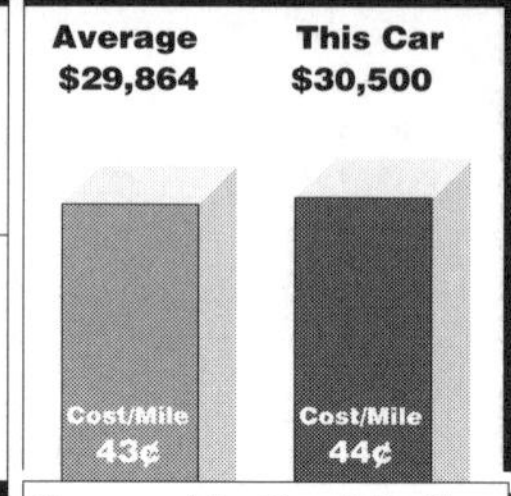

Chevrolet K1500 Work Truck

2 Door Regular Cab

Large Pickup

4.3L 165 hp Gas Fuel Inject.	6 Cylinder "V"	Manual 5 Speed	4 Wheel On-Demand	Manual Seatbelts Only

Purchase Price

Car Item	Dealer Cost	List
Base Price	**$13,109**	**$14,485**
Anti-Lock Brakes	Std	Std
Automatic 4 Speed	$765	$890
Optional Engine	N/A	N/A
Air Conditioning	$692	$805
Power Steering	Std	Std
Cruise Control	N/A	N/A
4 Whl On-Demand Dr.	Std	Std
AM/FM Stereo Cassette	$390	$454
Steering Wheel, Tilt	N/A	N/A
Power Windows	N/A	N/A
***Options Price**	$1,082	$1,259
***Total Price**	**$14,191**	**$15,744**
Target Price	$15,158	
Destination Charge	$595	
Avg. Tax & Fees	$951	
Total Target $	**$16,704**	
Average Dealer Option Cost:	***86%***	

Ownership Costs

Cost Area	5 Year Cost	Rate
Depreciation	$4,208	Excellent
Financing ($336/month)	$2,752	
Insurance (Rating 8)	$7,432	Better Than Average
State Fees	$653	
Fuel (Hwy 19 City 15)	$5,079	Better Than Average
Maintenance	$4,606	Average
Repairs	$791	Better Than Average

Warranty/Maintenance Info

Item		Rate
Major Tune-Up	$171	Average
Minor Tune-Up	$98	Better Than Average
Brake Service	$268	Better Than Average
Overall Warranty	3 yr/36k	Average
Drivetrain Warranty	3 yr/36k	Average
Rust Warranty	6 yr/100k	Better Than Average
Maintenance Warranty	N/A	
Roadside Assistance	3 yr/36k	

Ownership Cost By Year

$2,000 $4,000 $6,000 $8,000

1993 1994 1995 1996 1997

Resale Value

1993	1994	1995	1996	1997
$14,788	$13,915	$13,695	$13,442	$12,496

Ownership Costs (5yr)

Average	This Car
$25,570	$25,521
Cost/Mile 37¢	Cost/Mile 36¢

Cumulative Costs

	1993	1994	1995	1996	1997
Annual	$5,594	$4,544	$4,973	$4,264	$6,146
Total	$5,594	$10,138	$15,111	$19,375	$25,521

Ownership Cost Rating

Better Than Average

The 1993 K1500 Pickup is available in three models - (Base) K1500 and Work Truck four-wheel drive Regular Cabs, and the Base K1500 four-wheel drive Extended Cab. New for 1993, the Work Truck four-wheel drive uses an anti-chip coating which helps prevent stone chips on leading edges of the hood, roof, and entire "A" pillars, and the RPO MXO 4-speed automatic transmission now has electronic controls. Four new exterior colors are available.

* Includes shaded options

** Other purchase requirements apply

Poor

Worse Than Average

Average

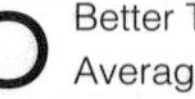
Better Than Average

Excellent

Insufficient Information

Refer to *Section 3: Annotated Vehicle Charts* for an explanation of these charts.

Chevrolet K1500
2 Door Regular Cab

4.3L 165 hp Gas Fuel Inject.

6 Cylinder "V"

Manual 5 Speed

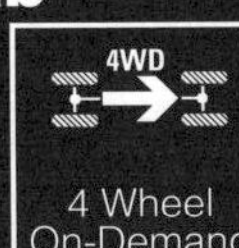

4 Wheel On-Demand

Manual Seatbelts Only

Large Pickup

Purchase Price

Car Item	Dealer Cost	List
Base Price	**$13,856**	**$15,835**
Anti-Lock Brakes	Std	Std
Automatic 4 Speed	$765	$890
5.0L 175 hp Gas	$495	$575
Air Conditioning	$692	$805
Power Steering	Std	Std
Cruise Control	Pkg	Pkg
4 Whl On-Demand Dr.	Std	Std
AM/FM Stereo Cassette	$251	$292
Steering Wheel, Tilt	Pkg	Pkg
8 Foot Bed	$254	$290
***Options Price**	$1,438	$1,672
***Total Price**	**$15,294**	**$17,507**
Target Price	$16,359	
Destination Charge	$595	
Avg. Tax & Fees	$1,029	
Total Target $	**$17,983**	
Average Dealer Option Cost:	***86%***	

Ownership Costs

Cost Area	5 Year Cost	Rate
Depreciation	$5,444	Better Than Average
Financing ($361/month)	$2,962	
Insurance (Rating 10)	$7,689	Better Than Average
State Fees	$725	
Fuel (Hwy 17 City 13)	$5,760	Average
Maintenance	$4,717	Worse Than Average
Repairs	$791	Better Than Average

Warranty/Maintenance Info

Item		Rate
Major Tune-Up	$184	Worse Than Average
Minor Tune-Up	$112	Worse Than Average
Brake Service	$268	Better Than Average
Overall Warranty	3 yr/36k	Average
Drivetrain Warranty	3 yr/36k	Average
Rust Warranty	6 yr/100k	Better Than Average
Maintenance Warranty	N/A	
Roadside Assistance	3 yr/36k	

The 1993 K1500 Pickup is available in three models - (Base) K1500 and Work Truck four-wheel drive Regular Cabs, and the Base K1500 four-wheel drive Extended Cab. New for 1993, the Base K1500 uses an anti-chip coating which helps prevent stone chips on leading edges of the hood, roof, and entire "A" pillars, and the RPO MXO 4-speed automatic transmission now has electronic controls. Four new exterior colors are available (Quasar Blue, Teal Green, Indigo Blue and Dark Garnet Red - all metallic).

Ownership Cost By Year

$2,000 $4,000 $6,000 $8,000

1993 1994 1995 1996 1997

Resale Value

1993	1994	1995	1996	1997
$14,958	$14,518	$14,150	$13,464	$12,539

Cumulative Costs

	1993	1994	1995	1996	1997
Annual	$6,986	$4,394	$5,383	$4,942	$6,383
Total	$6,986	$11,380	$16,763	$21,705	$28,088

Ownership Costs (5yr)

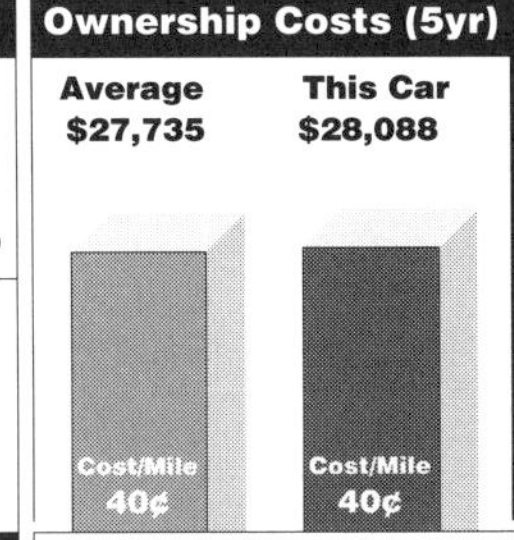

Ownership Cost Rating

Average

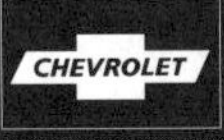

Chevrolet K2500
2 Door Regular Cab

4.3L 165 hp Gas Fuel Inject.

6 Cylinder "V"

Manual 5 Speed

4 Wheel On-Demand

Manual Seatbelts Only

Large Pickup

K1500 Model Shown

Purchase Price

Car Item	Dealer Cost	List
Base Price	**$14,258**	**$16,295**
Anti-Lock Brakes	Std	Std
Automatic 4 Speed	$765	$890
5.0L 175 hp Gas	$495	$575
Air Conditioning	$692	$805
Power Steering	Std	Std
Cruise Control	Pkg	Pkg
4 Whl On-Demand Dr.	Std	Std
AM/FM Stereo Cassette	$251	$292
Steering Wheel, Tilt	Pkg	Pkg
Power Windows	Pkg	Pkg
***Options Price**	$1,438	$1,672
***Total Price**	**$15,696**	**$17,967**
Target Price	$16,802	
Destination Charge	$595	
Avg. Tax & Fees	$1,056	
Total Target $	**$18,453**	
Average Dealer Option Cost:	***86%***	

Ownership Costs

Cost Area	5 Year Cost	Rate
Depreciation	$4,307	Excellent
Financing ($371/month)	$3,040	
Insurance (Rating 10)	$7,689	Better Than Average
State Fees	$742	
Fuel (Hwy 17 City 13)	$5,760	Average
Maintenance	$4,801	Worse Than Average
Repairs	$791	Better Than Average

Warranty/Maintenance Info

Item		Rate
Major Tune-Up	$184	Worse Than Average
Minor Tune-Up	$112	Worse Than Average
Brake Service	$285	Average
Overall Warranty	3 yr/36k	Average
Drivetrain Warranty	3 yr/36k	Average
Rust Warranty	6 yr/100k	Better Than Average
Maintenance Warranty	N/A	
Roadside Assistance	3 yr/36k	

The 1993 K Pickup is available in three models-1500, 2500 and 3500. K2500 Pickups are available with 4WD, Fleetside and Sportside styling, regular and extended cabs, and two trim levels-Cheyene (standard) and Silverado. New for 1993, the K2500 Regular cab features the new electronic 4-speed transmission--the Hydra-matic 4L60-E. Standard features include an all-welded frame and cargo box and an independent front suspension with anti-roll bar.

Ownership Cost By Year

$2,000 $4,000 $6,000 $8,000

1993 1994 1995 1996 1997

Resale Value

1993	1994	1995	1996	1997
$17,224	$16,684	$16,140	$15,255	$14,146

Cumulative Costs

	1993	1994	1995	1996	1997
Annual	$5,227	$4,522	$5,619	$5,150	$6,612
Total	$5,227	$9,749	$15,368	$20,518	$27,130

Ownership Costs (5yr)

Average $28,300 — This Car $27,130

Cost/Mile 40¢ — Cost/Mile 39¢

Ownership Cost Rating

Excellent

* Includes shaded options

** Other purchase requirements apply

 Poor  Worse Than Average  Average  Better Than Average  Excellent 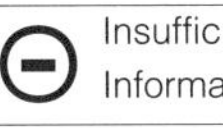 Insufficient Information

Refer to *Section 3: Annotated Vehicle Charts* for an explanation of these charts.

Chevrolet K3500
2 Door Regular Cab

5.7L 190 hp Gas Fuel Inject.	8 Cylinder "V"	Manual 5 Speed	4 Wheel On-Demand	Manual Seatbelts Only

Large Pickup

K1500 Model Shown

Purchase Price

Car Item	Dealer Cost	List
Base Price	**$16,100**	**$18,404**
Anti-Lock Brakes	Std	Std
Automatic 4 Speed	$765	$890
7.4L 230 hp Gas	$404	$470
Air Conditioning	$692	$805
Power Steering	Std	Std
Cruise Control	Pkg	Pkg
4 Whl On-Demand Dr.	Std	Std
AM/FM Stereo Cassette	$251	$292
Steering Wheel, Tilt	Pkg	Pkg
Power Windows	Pkg	Pkg
***Options Price**	$943	$1,097
***Total Price**	**$17,043**	**$19,501**
Target Price	$18,307	
Destination Charge	$595	
Avg. Tax & Fees	$1,146	
Total Target $	**$20,048**	
Average Dealer Option Cost:	***86%***	

Ownership Costs

Cost Area	5 Year Cost	Rate
Depreciation	$6,917	Average
Financing ($403/month)	$3,303	
Insurance (Rating 10)	$7,689	Better Than Average
State Fees	$805	
Fuel (Hwy 14 City 11 [Est.])	$6,908	Poor
Maintenance	$5,261	Poor
Repairs	$791	Better Than Average

Warranty/Maintenance Info

Major Tune-Up	$184	Worse Than Average
Minor Tune-Up	$112	Worse Than Average
Brake Service	$477	Poor
Overall Warranty	3 yr/36k	Average
Drivetrain Warranty	3 yr/36k	Average
Rust Warranty	6 yr/100k	Better Than Average
Maintenance Warranty	N/A	
Roadside Assistance	3 yr/36k	

The 1993 K3500 four-wheel drive pickup is available in two models - Regular and Extended Cabs. Three trim levels are offered - Cheyenne, Scottsdale and Silverado. New for the 1993 lineup, the K3500 Regular Cab features a new electronic four-speed automatic, a modified 5.7L V8 available for conversion to gaseous fuel and expanded availability of the 6.5L turbo diesel. Four new exterior colors have been added and tinted glass is standard.

Ownership Cost By Year

$2,000 $4,000 $6,000 $8,000

1993 1994 1995 1996 1997

Resale Value

1993	1994	1995	1996	1997
$15,648	$15,241	$14,855	$14,146	$13,131

Ownership Costs (5yr)

Average	This Car
$30,183	$31,674
Cost/Mile 43¢	Cost/Mile 45¢

Cumulative Costs

	1993	1994	1995	1996	1997
Annual	$8,734	$4,705	$5,997	$5,192	$7,046
Total	$8,734	$13,439	$19,436	$24,628	$31,674

Ownership Cost Rating

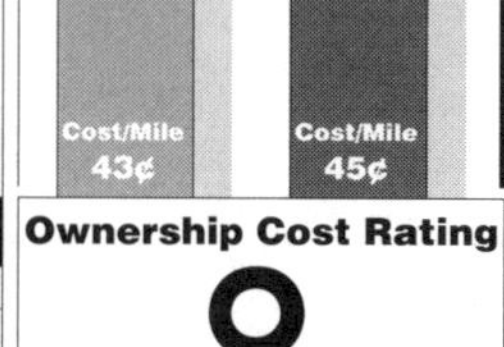

Average

Chevrolet K1500
2 Door Extended Cab

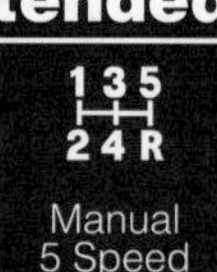

4.3L 165 hp Gas Fuel Inject.	6 Cylinder "V"	Manual 5 Speed	4 Wheel On-Demand	Manual Seatbelts Only

Large Pickup

Regular Cab Shown

Purchase Price

Car Item	Dealer Cost	List
Base Price	**$15,208**	**$17,383**
Anti-Lock Brakes	Std	Std
Automatic 4 Speed	$765	$890
5.0L 175 hp Gas	$495	$575
Air Conditioning	$692	$805
Power Steering	Std	Std
Cruise Control	Pkg	Pkg
4 Whl On-Demand Dr.	Std	Std
AM/FM Stereo Cassette	$251	$292
Steering Wheel, Tilt	Pkg	Pkg
8 Foot Bed	$254	$290
***Options Price**	$1,438	$1,672
***Total Price**	**$16,646**	**$19,055**
Target Price	$17,851	
Destination Charge	$595	
Avg. Tax & Fees	$1,119	
Total Target $	**$19,565**	
Average Dealer Option Cost:	***86%***	

Ownership Costs

Cost Area	5 Year Cost	Rate
Depreciation	$4,434	Excellent
Financing ($393/month)	$3,222	
Insurance (Rating 12)	$8,108	Better Than Average
State Fees	$787	
Fuel (Hwy 17 City 13)	$5,760	Average
Maintenance	$4,835	Worse Than Average
Repairs	$791	Better Than Average

Warranty/Maintenance Info

Major Tune-Up	$184	Worse Than Average
Minor Tune-Up	$112	Worse Than Average
Brake Service	$268	Better Than Average
Overall Warranty	3 yr/36k	Average
Drivetrain Warranty	3 yr/36k	Average
Rust Warranty	6 yr/100k	Better Than Average
Maintenance Warranty	N/A	
Roadside Assistance	3 yr/36k	

The 1993 K1500 Pickup is available in three models - (Base) K1500 and Work Truck four-wheel drive Regular Cabs, and the Base K1500 four-wheel drive Extended Cab. New for 1993, the K1500 Extended Cab uses an anti-chip coating which helps prevent stone chips on leading edges of the hood, roof, and entire "A" pillars, and the RPO MXO 4-speed automatic transmission now has electronic controls. Four new exterior colors are available (Quasar Blue, Teal Green, Indigo Blue and Dark Garnet Red - all metallic).

Ownership Cost By Year

$2,000 $4,000 $6,000 $8,000 $10,000

1993 1994 1995 1996 1997

Resale Value

1993	1994	1995	1996	1997
$17,076	$16,791	$16,512	$15,993	$15,131

Ownership Costs (5yr)

Average	This Car
$29,636	$27,937
Cost/Mile 42¢	Cost/Mile 40¢

Cumulative Costs

	1993	1994	1995	1996	1997
Annual	$6,651	$4,415	$5,499	$4,892	$6,480
Total	$6,651	$11,066	$16,565	$21,457	$27,937

Ownership Cost Rating

Excellent

* Includes shaded options

** Other purchase requirements apply

 Poor  Worse Than Average  Average  Better Than Average 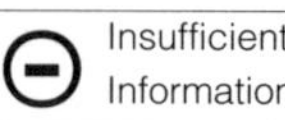 Excellent — Insufficient Information

Refer to *Section 3: Annotated Vehicle Charts* for an explanation of these charts.

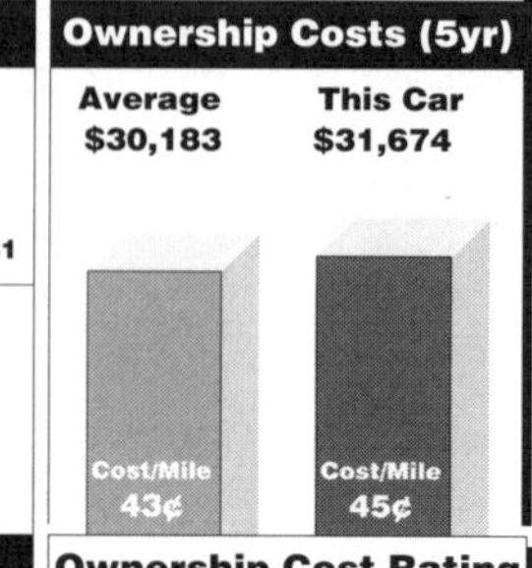

Chevrolet K2500
2 Door Extended Cab

4.3L 165 hp Gas Fuel Inject.

6 Cylinder "V"

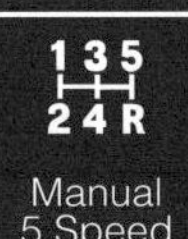
Manual 5 Speed

4 Wheel On-Demand

Manual Seatbelts Only

Large Pickup

K1500 Regular Cab Shown

Purchase Price

Car Item	Dealer Cost	List
Base Price	**$15,706**	**$17,952**
Anti-Lock Brakes	Std	Std
Automatic 4 Speed	$765	$890
5.0L 175 hp Gas	$495	$575
Air Conditioning	$692	$805
Power Steering	Std	Std
Cruise Control	Pkg	Pkg
4 Whl On-Demand Dr.	Std	Std
AM/FM Stereo Cassette	$251	$292
Steering Wheel, Tilt	Pkg	Pkg
8 Foot Bed	$263	$300
***Options Price**	$1,438	$1,672
***Total Price**	**$17,144**	**$19,624**
Target Price	$18,402	
Destination Charge	$595	
Avg. Tax & Fees	$1,152	
Total Target $	**$20,149**	
Average Dealer Option Cost:	***86%***	

Ownership Costs

Cost Area	5 Year Cost	Rate
Depreciation	$4,934	Excellent
Financing ($405/month)	$3,318	
Insurance (Rating 12)	$8,108	Better Than Average
State Fees	$809	
Fuel (Hwy 17 City 13)	$5,760	Average
Maintenance	$4,907	Worse Than Average
Repairs	$791	Better Than Average

Warranty/Maintenance Info

Item		Rate
Major Tune-Up	$184	Worse Than Average
Minor Tune-Up	$112	Worse Than Average
Brake Service	$285	Average
Overall Warranty	3 yr/36k	Average
Drivetrain Warranty	3 yr/36k	Average
Rust Warranty	6 yr/100k	Better Than Average
Maintenance Warranty	N/A	
Roadside Assistance	3 yr/36k	

The 1993 K Pickup is available in three models-1500, 2500, and 3500. K2500 Pickups are available with 4WD, Fleetside and Sportside styling, regular and extended cabs, and two trim levels-Cheyene (standard) and Silverado. New for 1993, the K2500 Extended cab features the new electronic 4-speed transmission--the Hydra-matic 4L60-E. Standard features include an all-welded frame and cargo box and an independent front suspension with anti-roll bar.

Ownership Cost By Year

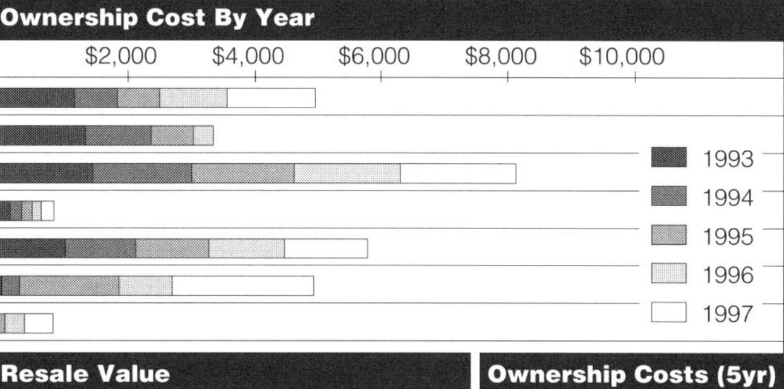

Resale Value

1993	1994	1995	1996	1997
$18,937	$18,265	$17,594	$16,538	$15,215

Ownership Costs (5yr)

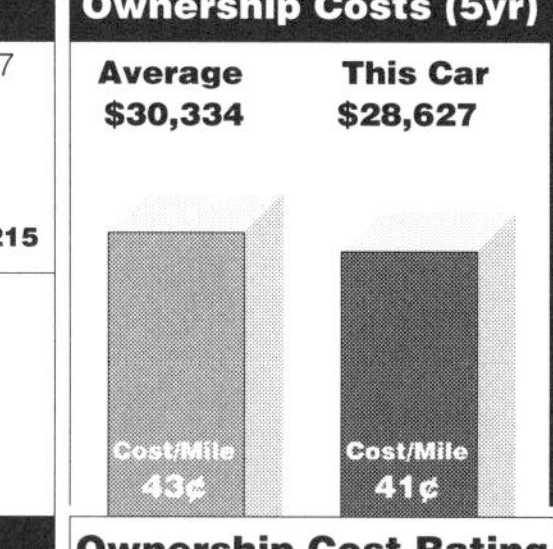

Average	This Car
$30,334	$28,627
Cost/Mile 43¢	Cost/Mile 41¢

Cumulative Costs

	1993	1994	1995	1996	1997
Annual	$5,419	$4,837	$5,933	$5,474	$6,964
Total	$5,419	$10,256	$16,189	$21,663	$28,627

Ownership Cost Rating

Excellent

Chevrolet K3500
2 Door Extended Cab

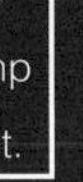
5.7L 190 hp Gas Fuel Inject.

8 Cylinder "V"

Manual 5 Speed

4 Wheel On-Demand

Manual Seatbelts Only

Large Pickup

K1500 Regular Cab Shown

Purchase Price

Car Item	Dealer Cost	List
Base Price	**$17,596**	**$20,114**
Anti-Lock Brakes	Std	Std
Automatic 4 Speed	$765	$890
7.4L 230 hp Gas	$404	$470
Air Conditioning	$692	$805
Power Steering	Std	Std
Cruise Control	Pkg	Pkg
4 Whl On-Demand Dr.	Std	Std
AM/FM Stereo Cassette	$251	$292
Steering Wheel, Tilt	Pkg	Pkg
Power Windows	Pkg	Pkg
***Options Price**	$943	$1,097
***Total Price**	**$18,539**	**$21,211**
Target Price	$19,970	
Destination Charge	$595	
Avg. Tax & Fees	$1,246	
Total Target $	**$21,811**	
Average Dealer Option Cost:	***86%***	

Ownership Costs

Cost Area	5 Year Cost	Rate
Depreciation	$6,860	Better Than Average
Financing ($438/month)	$3,593	
Insurance (Rating 12)	$8,108	Better Than Average
State Fees	$872	
Fuel (Hwy 14 City 11 [Est.])	$6,908	Poor
Maintenance	$5,296	Poor
Repairs	$791	Better Than Average

Warranty/Maintenance Info

Item		Rate
Major Tune-Up	$184	Worse Than Average
Minor Tune-Up	$112	Worse Than Average
Brake Service	$477	Poor
Overall Warranty	3 yr/36k	Average
Drivetrain Warranty	3 yr/36k	Average
Rust Warranty	6 yr/100k	Better Than Average
Maintenance Warranty	N/A	
Roadside Assistance	3 yr/36k	

The 1993 K3500 four-wheel drive pickup is available in two models - Regular and Extended Cabs. Three trim levels are offered - Cheyenne, Scottsdale and Silverado. New for the 1993 lineup, the K3500 Extended Cab features a new electronic four-speed automatic, a modified 5.7L V8 available for conversion to gaseous fuel and expanded availability of the 6.5L turbo diesel. The Extended Cab is now available with two-passenger seating.

Ownership Cost By Year

$2,000 · $4,000 · $6,000 · $8,000 · $10,000

1993 · 1994 · 1995 · 1996 · 1997

Resale Value

1993	1994	1995	1996	1997
$17,718	$17,292	$16,875	$16,093	$14,951

Ownership Costs (5yr)

Average	This Car
$32,283	$32,428
Cost/Mile 46¢	Cost/Mile 46¢

Cumulative Costs

	1993	1994	1995	1996	1997
Annual	$8,642	$4,911	$6,182	$5,420	$7,273
Total	$8,642	$13,553	$19,735	$25,155	$32,428

Ownership Cost Rating

Average

* Includes shaded options

** Other purchase requirements apply

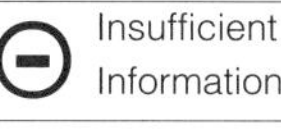

Poor · Worse Than Average · Average · Better Than Average · Excellent · Insufficient Information

Refer to *Section 3: Annotated Vehicle Charts* for an explanation of these charts.

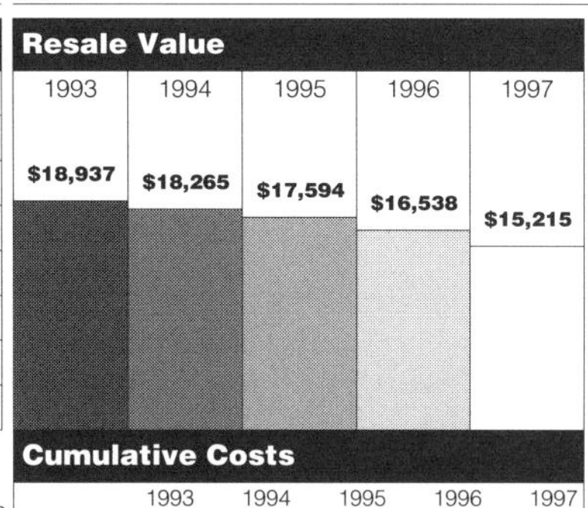

Chevrolet K3500 Crew Cab
4 Door Extended Cab

Large Pickup

5.7L 190 hp Gas Fuel Inject. | 8 Cylinder "V" | Manual 5 Speed | 4 Wheel On-Demand | Manual Seatbelts Only

Purchase Price

Car Item	Dealer Cost	List
Base Price	**$18,498**	**$21,144**
Anti-Lock Brakes	Std	Std
Automatic 4 Speed	$765	$890
7.4L 230 hp Gas	$404	$470
Air Conditioning	$692	$805
Power Steering	Std	Std
Cruise Control	Pkg	Pkg
4 Whl On-Demand Dr.	Std	Std
AM/FM Stereo Cassette	$251	$292
Steering Wheel, Tilt	Pkg	Pkg
Power Windows	Pkg	Pkg
***Options Price**	$943	$1,097
***Total Price**	**$19,441**	**$22,241**
Target Price	$20,977	
Destination Charge	$595	
Avg. Tax & Fees	$1,307	
Total Target $	**$22,879**	
Average Dealer Option Cost:	***86%***	

Ownership Costs

Cost Area	5 Year Cost	Rate
Depreciation	$7,207	Excellent
Financing ($460/month)	$3,769	
Insurance (Rating 12)	$8,108	Better Than Average
State Fees	$914	
Fuel (Hwy 16 City 12 [Est.])	$6,176	Worse Than Average
Maintenance	$5,296	Poor
Repairs	$750	Excellent

Ownership Cost By Year

$2,000 $4,000 $6,000 $8,000 $10,000

1993 1994 1995 1996 1997

Warranty/Maintenance Info

Item		Rate
Major Tune-Up	$184	Worse Than Average
Minor Tune-Up	$112	Worse Than Average
Brake Service	$477	Poor
Overall Warranty	3 yr/36k	Average
Drivetrain Warranty	3 yr/36k	Average
Rust Warranty	6 yr/100k	Better Than Average
Maintenance Warranty	N/A	
Roadside Assistance	3 yr/36k	

Resale Value

1993	1994	1995	1996	1997
$18,541	$18,103	$17,668	$16,854	$15,672

Ownership Costs (5yr)

Average	This Car
$33,548	$32,220
Cost/Mile 48¢	Cost/Mile 46¢

The 1993 Chevrolet Crew Cab Pickup is available in two models - two- wheel drive and four-wheel drive. Three trim levels are offered - Cheyenne, Scottsdale and Silverado. New for the 1993 lineup, the K3500 four-wheel drive Crew Cab features a new electronic four-speed automatic, a modified 5.7L V8 available for conversion to gaseous fuel and expanded availability of the 6.5L turbo diesel. Corrosion protection has been improved and four new exterior colors have been added.

Cumulative Costs

	1993	1994	1995	1996	1997
Annual	$8,835	$4,848	$6,091	$5,304	$7,142
Total	$8,835	$13,683	$19,774	$25,078	$32,220

Ownership Cost Rating

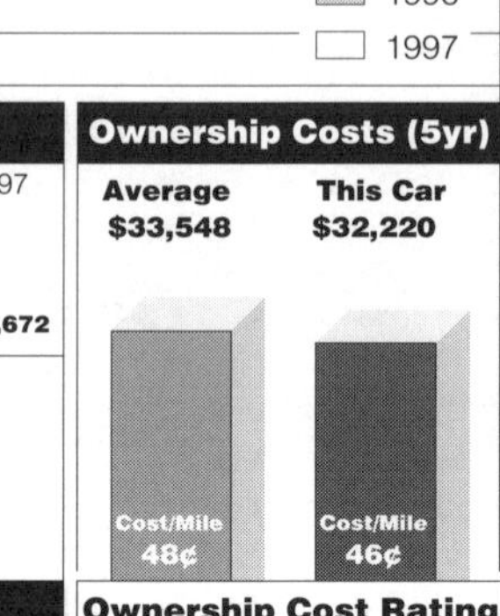

Excellent

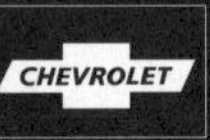

Chevrolet Caprice Classic
4 Door Wagon

Large Wagon

5.0L 170 hp Gas Fuel Inject. | 8 Cylinder "V" | Automatic 4 Speed | 2 Wheel Rear | Driver Airbag Psngr Belts

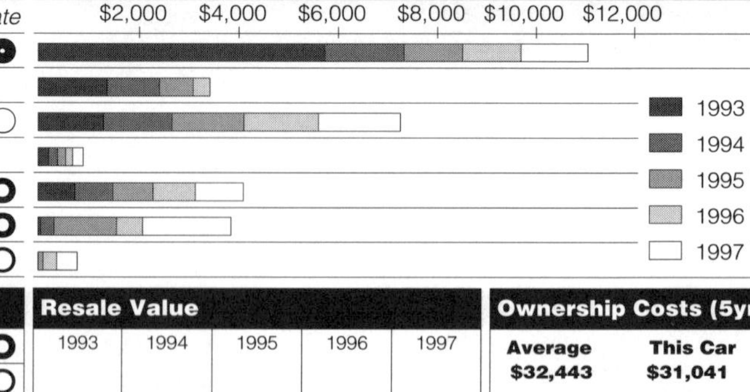

Purchase Price

Car Item	Dealer Cost	List
Base Price	**$17,128**	**$19,575**
Anti-Lock Brakes	Std	Std
Manual Transmission	N/A	N/A
5.7L 180 hp Gas	$215	$250
Air Conditioning	Std	Std
Power Steering	Std	Std
Cruise Control	$194	$225
All Wheel Drive	N/A	N/A
AM/FM Stereo Cassette	$151	** $175
Steering Wheel, Tilt	Std	Std
Power Windows	$292	$340
***Options Price**	$486	$565
***Total Price**	**$17,614**	**$20,140**
Target Price	$18,823	
Destination Charge	$555	
Avg. Tax & Fees	$1,176	
Total Target $	**$20,554**	
Average Dealer Option Cost:	***86%***	

Ownership Costs

Cost Area	5 Year Cost	Rate
Depreciation	$11,017	Worse Than Average
Financing ($413/month)	$3,385	
Insurance (Rating 8)	$7,223	Excellent
State Fees	$828	
Fuel (Hwy 26 City 17)	$4,064	Average
Maintenance	$3,815	Average
Repairs	$709	Better Than Average

Ownership Cost By Year

$2,000 $4,000 $6,000 $8,000 $10,000 $12,000

1993 1994 1995 1996 1997

Warranty/Maintenance Info

Item		Rate
Major Tune-Up	$173	Average
Minor Tune-Up	$124	Better Than Average
Brake Service	$222	Average
Overall Warranty	3 yr/36k	Average
Drivetrain Warranty	3 yr/36k	Average
Rust Warranty	6 yr/100k	Better Than Average
Maintenance Warranty	N/A	
Roadside Assistance	3 yr/36k	

Resale Value

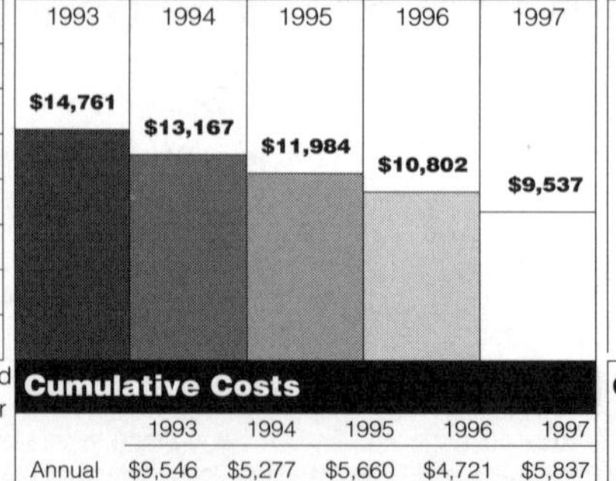

1993	1994	1995	1996	1997
$14,761	$13,167	$11,984	$10,802	$9,537

Ownership Costs (5yr)

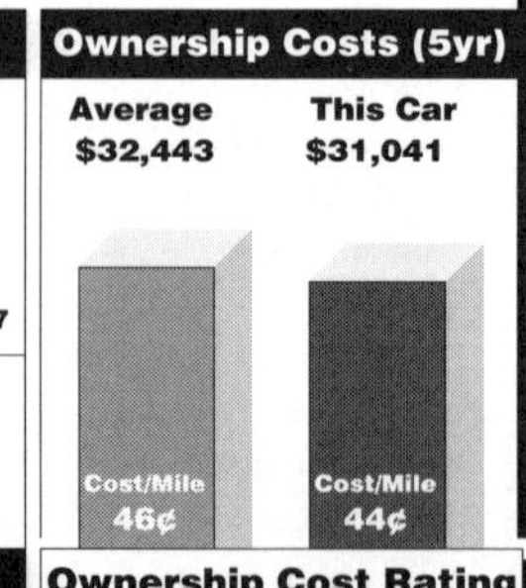

Average	This Car
$32,443	$31,041
Cost/Mile 46¢	Cost/Mile 44¢

The 1993 Chevrolet Caprice Classic is available in three models - (Base) Caprice Classic and LS sedans, and (Base) Classic wagon. New for 1993, the Base Caprice Classic wagon adds several new interior and exterior colors, redesigned wheel covers, and newly optional rear reading lamps and door edge guards. Among the standard equipment is a stainless steel exhaust system, pull-down center arm rest, child security rear door locks, and dual body-color aero sport mirrors. The 5.7L V-8 engine is optional.

Cumulative Costs

	1993	1994	1995	1996	1997
Annual	$9,546	$5,277	$5,660	$4,721	$5,837
Total	$9,546	$14,823	$20,483	$25,204	$31,041

Ownership Cost Rating

Better Than Average

* Includes shaded options

** Other purchase requirements apply

 Poor  Worse Than Average  Average 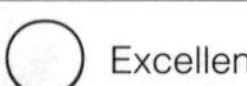 Better Than Average Excellent 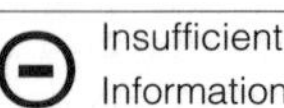 Insufficient Information

Refer to *Section 3: Annotated Vehicle Charts* for an explanation of these charts.

Chevrolet Cavalier VL
4 Door Wagon

2.2L 110 hp Gas Fuel Inject.	4 Cylinder In-Line	Automatic 3 Speed	2 Wheel Front	Automatic Seatbelts

Purchase Price

Car Item	Dealer Cost	List
Base Price	**$9,200**	**$9,735**
Anti-Lock Brakes	Std	Std
Manual Transmission	N/A	N/A
Optional Engine	N/A	N/A
Air Conditioning	$641	$745
Power Steering	Std	Std
Cruise Control	Pkg	Pkg
All Wheel Drive	N/A	N/A
AM/FM Stereo Cassette	$406	$472
Steering Wheel, Tilt	$125	$145
Power Windows	N/A	N/A
***Options Price**	$1,047	$1,217
***Total Price**	**$10,247**	**$10,952**
Target Price	$10,926	
Destination Charge	$475	
Avg. Tax & Fees	$684	
Total Target $	**$12,085**	
Average Dealer Option Cost:	***86%***	

Ownership Costs

Cost Area	5 Year Cost	Rate
Depreciation	$7,295	Worse Than Average
Financing ($243/month)	$1,991	
Insurance (Rating 4)	$6,658	Average
State Fees	$457	
Fuel (Hwy 32 City 23)	$3,152	Excellent
Maintenance	$4,060	Better Than Average
Repairs	$651	Better Than Average

Ownership Cost By Year

$2,000 $4,000 $6,000 $8,000

1993 1994 1995 1996 1997

Warranty/Maintenance Info

Item		Rate
Major Tune-Up	$128	Excellent
Minor Tune-Up	$84	Excellent
Brake Service	$216	Average
Overall Warranty	3 yr/36k	Average
Drivetrain Warranty	3 yr/36k	Average
Rust Warranty	6 yr/100k	Better Than Average
Maintenance Warranty	N/A	
Roadside Assistance	3 yr/36k	

Resale Value

1993	1994	1995	1996	1997
$8,476	$7,388	$6,537	$5,671	$4,790

Ownership Costs (5yr)

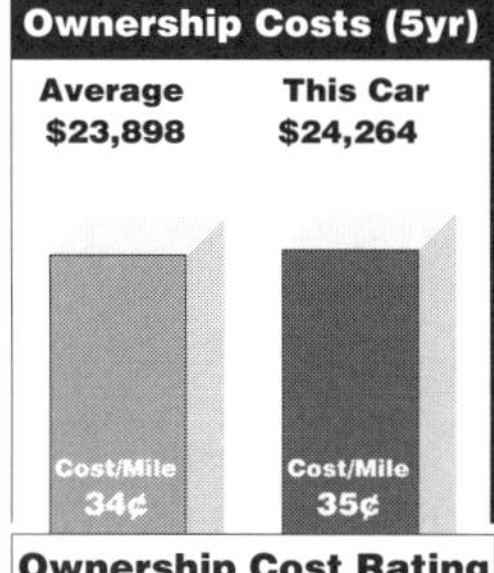

Cumulative Costs

	1993	1994	1995	1996	1997
Annual	$6,409	$3,911	$4,419	$3,640	$5,885
Total	$6,409	$10,320	$14,739	$18,379	$24,264

Ownership Cost Rating

Average

The 1993 Chevrolet Cavalier is available in nine models - Z24 coupe, RS and Z24 convertibles, and VL and RS wagons, coupes and sedans. New for 1993, the VL wagon features wind noise improvements, three new exterior colors, and dual visor vanity mirrors as an option. Standard features include a self-aligning steering wheel, 14 inch steel wheels with bolt-on full wheel covers, bucket seats and a stainless steel exhaust system. Optional features include a roof rack and bodyside moldings.

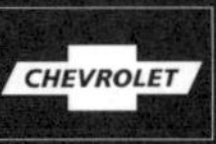

Chevrolet Cavalier RS
4 Door Wagon

	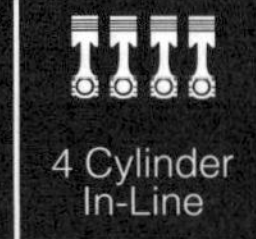			
2.2L 110 hp Gas Fuel Inject.	4 Cylinder In-Line	Automatic 3 Speed	2 Wheel Front	Automatic Seatbelts

Purchase Price

Car Item	Dealer Cost	List
Base Price	**$10,084**	**$10,785**
Anti-Lock Brakes	Std	Std
Manual Transmission	N/A	N/A
3.1L 140 hp Gas	$525	$610
Air Conditioning	$641	$745
Power Steering	Std	Std
Cruise Control	$194	$225
All Wheel Drive	N/A	N/A
AM/FM Stereo Cassette	$120	$140
Steering Wheel, Tilt	$125	$145
Power Windows	$284	$330
***Options Price**	$1,286	$1,495
***Total Price**	**$11,370**	**$12,280**
Target Price	$12,146	
Destination Charge	$475	
Avg. Tax & Fees	$759	
Total Target $	**$13,380**	
Average Dealer Option Cost:	***86%***	

Ownership Costs

Cost Area	5 Year Cost	Rate
Depreciation	$8,199	Poor
Financing ($269/month)	$2,204	
Insurance (Rating 5)	$6,786	Average
State Fees	$511	
Fuel (Hwy 28 City 20)	$3,612	Average
Maintenance	$4,232	Better Than Average
Repairs	$651	Better Than Average

Ownership Cost By Year

$2,000 $4,000 $6,000 $8,000 $10,000

1993 1994 1995 1996 1997

Warranty/Maintenance Info

Item		Rate
Major Tune-Up	$157	Better Than Average
Minor Tune-Up	$109	Average
Brake Service	$216	Average
Overall Warranty	3 yr/36k	Average
Drivetrain Warranty	3 yr/36k	Average
Rust Warranty	6 yr/100k	Better Than Average
Maintenance Warranty	N/A	
Roadside Assistance	3 yr/36k	

Resale Value

1993	1994	1995	1996	1997
$9,354	$8,099	$7,123	$6,156	$5,181

Ownership Costs (5yr)

Average
$25,038

This Car
$26,195

Cost/Mile 36¢ — Cost/Mile 37¢

Cumulative Costs

	1993	1994	1995	1996	1997
Annual	$7,041	$4,302	$4,751	$3,920	$6,181
Total	$7,041	$11,343	$16,094	$20,014	$26,195

Ownership Cost Rating

Worse Than Average

The 1993 Chevrolet Cavalier is available in nine models - Z24 coupe, RS and Z24 convertibles, and VL and RS wagons, coupes and sedans. New for 1993, the RS wagon features a standard split-folding rear seat, Z24 Sport cloth trim with seat-back storage pockets, dual visor vanity mirrors and a manual right hand outside rearview mirror. The RS upgrades the VL wagon with standard bodyside moldings, tinted glass, and the optional Performance Handling Package with includes a faster steering ratio.

* Includes shaded options

** Other purchase requirements apply

 Poor  Worse Than Average  Average  Better Than Average ○ Excellent ⊖ Insufficient Information

Refer to *Section 3: Annotated Vehicle Charts* for an explanation of these charts.

Chevrolet G10 Cargo Van
3 Door Cargo Van

4.3L 155 hp Gas Fuel Inject.

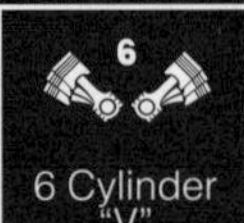
6 Cylinder "V"

Automatic 4 Speed

2 Wheel Rear

Manual Seatbelts Only

G20 Sportvan Model Shown

Purchase Price

Car Item	Dealer Cost	List
Base Price	**$12,775**	**$14,600**
Anti-Lock Brakes	Std	Std
Manual Transmission	N/A	N/A
5.0L 170 hp Gas	$495	$575
Air Conditioning	$839	$975
Power Steering	Std	Std
Cruise Control	Pkg	Pkg
All Wheel Drive	N/A	N/A
AM/FM Stereo Cassette	$187	$218
Steering Wheel, Tilt	Pkg	Pkg
Power Windows	Pkg	Pkg
***Options Price**	$1,334	$1,550
***Total Price**	**$14,109**	**$16,150**
Target Price	$14,918	
Destination Charge	$580	
Avg. Tax & Fees	$942	
Total Target $	**$16,440**	
Average Dealer Option Cost:	***86%***	

Ownership Costs

Cost Area	5 Year Cost	Rate
Depreciation	$7,686	Average
Financing ($330/month)	$2,708	
Insurance (Rating 4)	$6,867	Excellent
State Fees	$669	
Fuel (Hwy 18 City 14)	$5,399	Better Than Average
Maintenance	$4,543	Average
Repairs	$740	Excellent

Ownership Cost By Year

Warranty/Maintenance Info

Major Tune-Up	$214	Poor
Minor Tune-Up	$132	Worse Than Average
Brake Service	$265	Average
Overall Warranty	3 yr/36k	Average
Drivetrain Warranty	3 yr/36k	Average
Rust Warranty	6 yr/100k	Better Than Average
Maintenance Warranty	N/A	
Roadside Assistance	3 yr/36k	

Resale Value

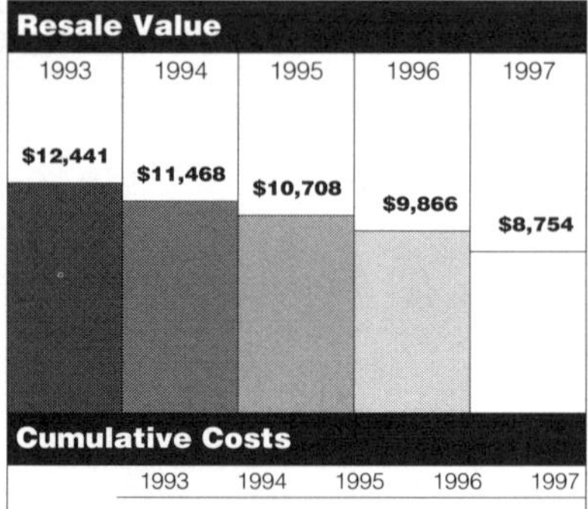

Ownership Costs (5yr)

Average	This Car
$28,332	$28,612
Cost/Mile 40¢	Cost/Mile 41¢

Cumulative Costs

	1993	1994	1995	1996	1997
Annual	$7,621	$4,630	$5,425	$4,784	$6,152
Total	$7,621	$12,251	$17,676	$22,460	$28,612

Ownership Cost Rating

Average

The 1993 Chevrolet Cargo Van is available in four models - G10, G20, G30, and G30 Heavy Duty full-size cargo vans. New for 1993 the G10 Cargo Van features a standard four-wheel anti-lock braking system and an optional air conditioning system which operates with 134-A refrigerant, instead of freon. The new electronic four-speed, the Hydra-matic 4L60-E, is General Motors' first rear-wheel drive electronic transmission to interface with the cruise control.

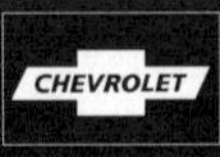

Chevrolet G20 Cargo Van
3 Door Cargo Van

4.3L 155 hp Gas Fuel Inject.

6 Cylinder "V"

Automatic 4 Speed

2 Wheel Rear

Manual Seatbelts Only

Full-Size Van

Sportvan Model Shown

Purchase Price

Car Item	Dealer Cost	List
Base Price	**$12,880**	**$14,720**
Anti-Lock Brakes	Std	Std
Manual Transmission	N/A	N/A
5.0L 170 hp Gas	$495	$575
Air Conditioning	$839	$975
Power Steering	Std	Std
Cruise Control	Pkg	Pkg
All Wheel Drive	N/A	N/A
AM/FM Stereo Cassette	$187	$218
Steering Wheel, Tilt	Pkg	Pkg
Power Windows	Pkg	Pkg
***Options Price**	$1,334	$1,550
***Total Price**	**$14,214**	**$16,270**
Target Price	$15,032	
Destination Charge	$580	
Avg. Tax & Fees	$950	
Total Target $	**$16,562**	
Average Dealer Option Cost:	***86%***	

Ownership Costs

Cost Area	5 Year Cost	Rate
Depreciation	$7,760	Average
Financing ($333/month)	$2,728	
Insurance (Rating 5)	$6,996	Excellent
State Fees	$675	
Fuel (Hwy 18 City 14)	$5,399	Better Than Average
Maintenance	$4,590	Average
Repairs	$740	Excellent

Ownership Cost By Year

$2,000 · $4,000 · $6,000 · $8,000

1993 · 1994 · 1995 · 1996 · 1997

Warranty/Maintenance Info

Major Tune-Up	$214	Poor
Minor Tune-Up	$112	Average
Brake Service	$282	Average
Overall Warranty	3 yr/36k	Average
Drivetrain Warranty	3 yr/36k	Average
Rust Warranty	6 yr/100k	Better Than Average
Maintenance Warranty	N/A	
Roadside Assistance	3 yr/36k	

Resale Value

1993	1994	1995	1996	1997
$12,545	$11,567	$10,784	$9,937	$8,802

Ownership Costs (5yr)

Average	This Car
$28,474	$28,888
Cost/Mile 41¢	Cost/Mile 41¢

Cumulative Costs

	1993	1994	1995	1996	1997
Annual	$7,673	$4,646	$5,522	$4,796	$6,251
Total	$7,673	$12,319	$17,841	$22,637	$28,888

Ownership Cost Rating

Average

The 1993 Cargo Van is available in four models - G10, G20, G30, and G30 Heavy Duty full-size cargo vans. New for 1993 the G20 Cargo Van features a standard four-wheel anti-lock braking system, an optional air conditioning system which operates with environment-friendly 134-A refrigerant (instead of freon), and a new electronic four-speed automatic transmission which interfaces with the cruise control. Other features include an enhanced V6 and three new exterior colors (khaki, Mojave Beige, and Summit White).

* Includes shaded options

** Other purchase requirements apply

 Poor  Worse Than Average  Average 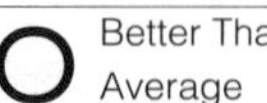 Better Than Average  Excellent 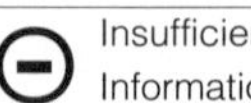 Insufficient Information

Refer to *Section 3: Annotated Vehicle Charts* for an explanation of these charts.

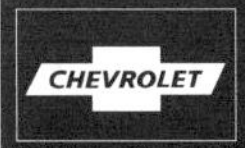

Chevrolet G30 Cargo Van
3 Door Cargo Ext Van

4.3L 155 hp Gas Fuel Inject.

6 Cylinder "V"

Automatic 4 Speed

2 Wheel Rear

Manual Seatbelts Only

Full-Size Van

Sportvan Model Shown

Purchase Price

Car Item	Dealer Cost	List
Base Price	**$13,160**	**$15,040**
Anti-Lock Brakes	Std	Std
Manual Transmission	N/A	N/A
5.7L 195 hp Gas	Grp	Grp
Air Conditioning	$839	$975
Power Steering	Std	Std
Cruise Control	Pkg	Pkg
All Wheel Drive	N/A	N/A
AM/FM Stereo Cassette	$187	$218
Steering Wheel, Tilt	Pkg	Pkg
Power Windows	Pkg	Pkg
***Options Price**	$839	$975
***Total Price**	**$13,999**	**$16,015**
Target Price	$14,811	
Destination Charge	$580	
Avg. Tax & Fees	$936	
Total Target $	**$16,327**	
Average Dealer Option Cost:	***86%***	

Ownership Costs

Cost Area	5 Year Cost	Rate
Depreciation	$8,094	Average
Financing ($328/month)	$2,689	
Insurance (Rating 6)	$7,129	Excellent
State Fees	$664	
Fuel (Hwy 19 City 14)	$5,244	Excellent
Maintenance	$5,182	Worse Than Average
Repairs	$740	Excellent

Ownership Cost By Year

$2,000 $4,000 $6,000 $8,000 $10,000

1993 1994 1995 1996 1997

Warranty/Maintenance Info

Item		Rate
Major Tune-Up	$214	Poor
Minor Tune-Up	$132	Worse Than Average
Brake Service	$477	Poor
Overall Warranty	3 yr/36k	Average
Drivetrain Warranty	3 yr/36k	Average
Rust Warranty	6 yr/100k	Better Than Average
Maintenance Warranty	N/A	
Roadside Assistance	3 yr/36k	

Resale Value

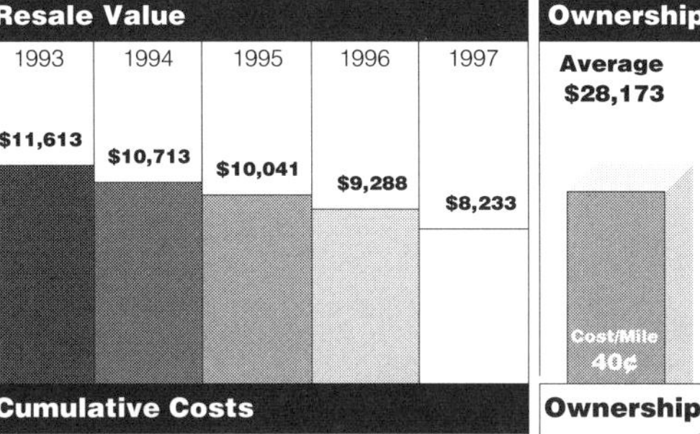

Ownership Costs (5yr)

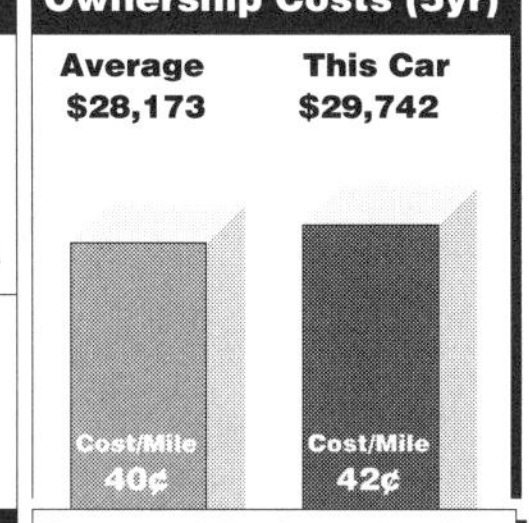

The 1993 Chevrolet Cargo Van is available in four models - G10, G20, G30, and G30 Heavy Duty full-size cargo vans. New for 1993 the G30 Cargo Van features a standard four-wheel anti-lock braking system and an optional air conditioning system which operates with 134-A refrigerant. The new electronic four-speed, the Hydra-matic 4L60-E, is General Motors' first rear-wheel drive electronic transmission to interface with the cruise control.

Cumulative Costs

	1993	1994	1995	1996	1997
Annual	$8,346	$4,570	$5,656	$4,664	$6,506
Total	$8,346	$12,916	$18,572	$23,236	$29,742

Ownership Cost Rating

Poor

Chevrolet G30 Cargo Van Heavy Duty
3 Door Cargo Ext Van

5.7L 195 hp Gas Fuel Inject.

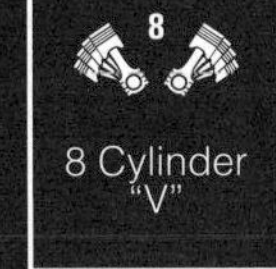
8 Cylinder "V"

Automatic 4 Speed

2 Wheel Rear

Manual Seatbelts Only

Full-Size Van

Sportvan Model Shown

Purchase Price

Car Item	Dealer Cost	List
Base Price	**$14,420**	**$16,480**
Anti-Lock Brakes	Std	Std
Manual Transmission	N/A	N/A
4.3L 155 hp Gas	($727)	($845)
Air Conditioning	$839	$975
Power Steering	Std	Std
Cruise Control	Pkg	Pkg
All Wheel Drive	N/A	N/A
AM/FM Stereo Cassette	$187	$218
Steering Wheel, Tilt	Pkg	Pkg
Power Windows	Pkg	Pkg
***Options Price**	$839	$975
***Total Price**	**$15,259**	**$17,455**
Target Price	$16,177	
Destination Charge	$580	
Avg. Tax & Fees	$1,018	
Total Target $	**$17,775**	
Average Dealer Option Cost:	***86%***	

Ownership Costs

Cost Area	5 Year Cost	Rate
Depreciation		Insufficient Information
Financing ($357/month)	$2,929	
Insurance (Rating 6)	$7,129	Excellent
State Fees	$720	
Fuel (Hwy 19 City 14)	$5,244	Excellent
Maintenance	$5,182	Worse Than Average
Repairs	$740	Excellent

Ownership Cost By Year

$2,000 $4,000 $6,000 $8,000

Insufficient Depreciation Information

1993 1994 1995 1996 1997

Warranty/Maintenance Info

Item		Rate
Major Tune-Up	$214	Poor
Minor Tune-Up	$132	Worse Than Average
Brake Service	$477	Poor
Overall Warranty	3 yr/36k	Average
Drivetrain Warranty	3 yr/36k	Average
Rust Warranty	6 yr/100k	Better Than Average
Maintenance Warranty	N/A	
Roadside Assistance	3 yr/36k	

Resale Value

Insufficient Information

Ownership Costs (5yr)

Insufficient Information

The 1993 Chevrolet Cargo Van is available in four models - G10, G20, G30, and G30 Heavy Duty full-size cargo vans. New for 1993 the G30 Heavy Duty Cargo Van features a standard four-wheel anti-lock braking system and an optional air conditioning system which operates with 134-A refrigerant. Also standard is a 33-gallon fuel tank; heavy duty: chassis, front/rear axles, and front and rear springs; and a maximum gross vehicle weight of 9200 lbs.

Cumulative Costs

	1993	1994	1995	1996	1997
Annual	*Insufficient Information*				
Total	*Insufficient Information*				

Ownership Cost Rating

Insufficient Information

* Includes shaded options

** Other purchase requirements apply

 Poor  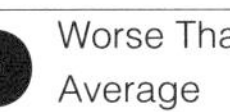 Worse Than Average  Average   Better Than Average  Excellent 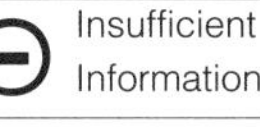 Insufficient Information

Refer to ***Section 3: Annotated Vehicle Charts*** for an explanation of these charts.

Chevrolet G10 Sportvan
3 Door Pass Van

4.3L 155 hp Gas Fuel Inject.

6 Cylinder "V"

Automatic 4 Speed

2 Wheel Rear

Manual Seatbelts Only

Full-Size Van
G20 Model Shown

Purchase Price

Car Item	Dealer Cost	List
Base Price	**$14,315**	**$16,360**
Anti-Lock Brakes	Std	Std
Manual Transmission	N/A	N/A
5.0L 170 hp Gas	$495	$575
Air Conditioning	$839	$975
Power Steering	Std	Std
Cruise Control	Pkg	Pkg
All Wheel Drive	N/A	N/A
AM/FM Stereo Cassette	$226	$263
Steering Wheel, Tilt	Pkg	Pkg
Power Windows	Pkg	Pkg
***Options Price**	$1,334	$1,550
***Total Price**	**$15,649**	**$17,910**
Target Price	$16,754	
Destination Charge	$580	
Avg. Tax & Fees	$1,052	
Total Target $	**$18,386**	
Average Dealer Option Cost:	***86%***	

Ownership Costs

Cost Area	5 Year Cost	Rate
Depreciation	$8,678	Average
Financing ($370/month)	$3,030	
Insurance (Rating 6)	$7,129	Excellent
State Fees	$739	
Fuel (Hwy 18 City 14)	$5,399	Better Than Average
Maintenance	$4,543	Average
Repairs	$740	Excellent

Ownership Cost By Year

$2,000 $4,000 $6,000 $8,000 $10,000

1993 1994 1995 1996 1997

Warranty/Maintenance Info

Item		Rate
Major Tune-Up	$214	Poor
Minor Tune-Up	$132	Worse Than Average
Brake Service	$265	Average
Overall Warranty	3 yr/36k	Average
Drivetrain Warranty	3 yr/36k	Average
Rust Warranty	6 yr/100k	Better Than Average
Maintenance Warranty	N/A	
Roadside Assistance	3 yr/36k	

Resale Value

1993	1994	1995	1996	1997
$13,719	$12,663	$11,825	$10,906	$9,708

Ownership Costs (5yr)

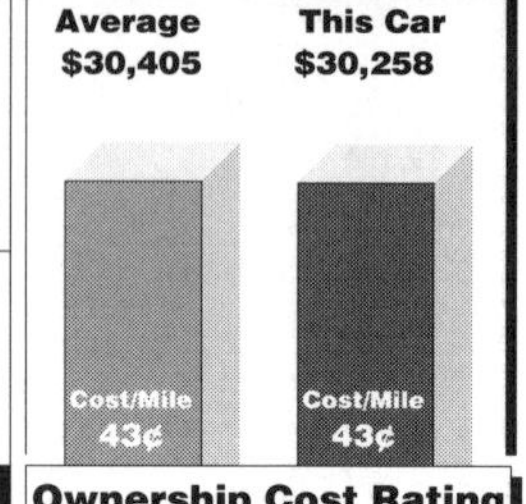

Average	This Car
$30,405	$30,258
Cost/Mile 43¢	Cost/Mile 43¢

The 1992 Chevrolet Sportvan is available in four models - G10, G20, G30 and G30 Heavy Duty full-size passenger vans. New for 1993, the G10 Sportvan features a four-wheel anti-lock braking system, and an optional air conditioning system which operates with 134-A refrigerant, instead of freon. The new electronic four-speed, the Hydra-matic 4L60-E, is General Motors' first rear-wheel electronic transmission to interface with the cruise control.

Cumulative Costs

	1993	1994	1995	1996	1997
Annual	$8,489	$4,879	$5,634	$4,950	$6,306
Total	$8,489	$13,368	$19,002	$23,952	$30,258

Ownership Cost Rating

Average

Chevrolet G20 Sportvan
3 Door Pass Ext Van

4.3L 155 hp Gas Fuel Inject.

6 Cylinder "V"
Automatic 4 Speed

2 Wheel Rear

Manual Seatbelts Only

Full-Size Van

Purchase Price

Car Item	Dealer Cost	List
Base Price	**$15,094**	**$17,250**
Anti-Lock Brakes	Std	Std
Manual Transmission	N/A	N/A
5.0L 170 hp Gas	$495	$575
Air Conditioning	$839	$975
Power Steering	Std	Std
Cruise Control	Pkg	Pkg
All Wheel Drive	N/A	N/A
AM/FM Stereo Cassette	$226	$263
Steering Wheel, Tilt	Pkg	Pkg
Power Windows	Pkg	Pkg
***Options Price**	$1,334	$1,550
***Total Price**	**$16,428**	**$18,800**
Target Price	$17,613	
Destination Charge	$580	
Avg. Tax & Fees	$1,104	
Total Target $	**$19,297**	
Average Dealer Option Cost:	***86%***	

Ownership Costs

Cost Area	5 Year Cost	Rate
Depreciation	$9,126	Average
Financing ($388/month)	$3,179	
Insurance (Rating 7)	$7,244	Excellent
State Fees	$775	
Fuel (Hwy 17 City 13)	$5,760	Average
Maintenance	$4,590	Average
Repairs	$740	Excellent

Ownership Cost By Year

$2,000 $4,000 $6,000 $8,000 $10,000

1993 1994 1995 1996 1997

Warranty/Maintenance Info

Item		Rate
Major Tune-Up	$214	Poor
Minor Tune-Up	$112	Average
Brake Service	$282	Average
Overall Warranty	3 yr/36k	Average
Drivetrain Warranty	3 yr/36k	Average
Rust Warranty	6 yr/100k	Better Than Average
Maintenance Warranty	N/A	
Roadside Assistance	3 yr/36k	

Resale Value

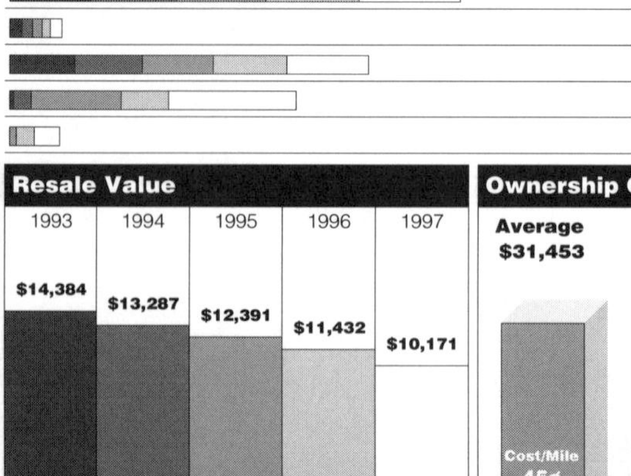

1993	1994	1995	1996	1997
$14,384	$13,287	$12,391	$11,432	$10,171

Ownership Costs (5yr)

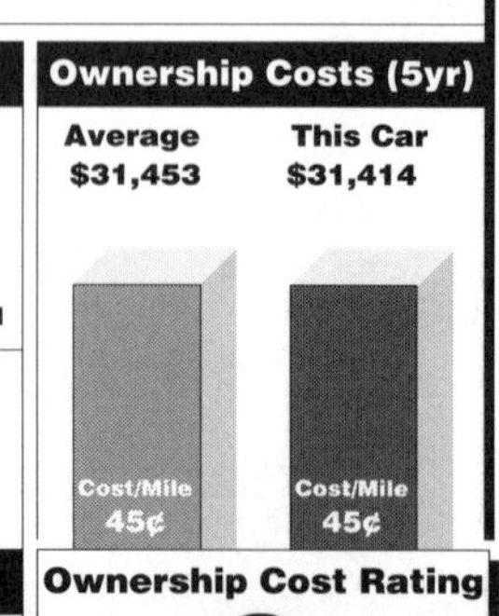

Average	This Car
$31,453	$31,414
Cost/Mile 45¢	Cost/Mile 45¢

The 1992 Chevrolet Sportvan is available in four models - G10, G20, G30 and G30 Heavy Duty full-size passenger vans. New for 1993, the G20 Sportvan features a four-wheel anti-lock braking system, and an optional air conditioning system which operates with environment-friendly 134-A refrigerant and a new electronic four-speed automatic transmission which interfaces with the cruise control. Other features include an enhanced V6 and three new exterior colors (khaki, Mojave Beige and Summit White).

Cumulative Costs

	1993	1994	1995	1996	1997
Annual	$8,894	$5,045	$5,866	$5,085	$6,524
Total	$8,894	$13,939	$19,805	$24,890	$31,414

Ownership Cost Rating

Average

* Includes shaded options

** Other purchase requirements apply

 Poor  Worse Than Average 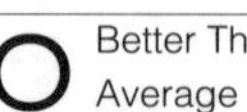 Average  Better Than Average Excellent 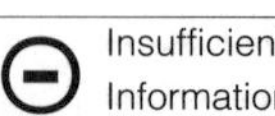 Insufficient Information

Refer to *Section 3: Annotated Vehicle Charts* for an explanation of these charts.

Chevrolet G30 Sportvan Heavy Duty 3 Door Pass Ext Van

5.7L 195 hp Gas Fuel Inject.

8 Cylinder "V"

Automatic 4 Speed

2 Wheel Rear

Manual Seatbelts Only

Purchase Price

Car Item	Dealer Cost	List
Base Price	**$16,520**	**$18,880**
Anti-Lock Brakes	Std	Std
Manual Transmission	N/A	N/A
7.4L 230 hp Gas	$520	$605
Air Conditioning	$839	$975
Power Steering	Std	Std
Cruise Control	Pkg	Pkg
All Wheel Drive	N/A	N/A
AM/FM Stereo Cassette	$226	$263
Steering Wheel, Tilt	Pkg	Pkg
Power Windows	Pkg	Pkg
***Options Price**	$839	$975
***Total Price**	**$17,359**	**$19,855**
Target Price	$18,662	
Destination Charge	$580	
Avg. Tax & Fees	$1,166	
Total Target $	**$20,408**	
Average Dealer Option Cost:	***86%***	

Ownership Costs

Cost Area	5 Year Cost	Rate
Depreciation		Insufficient Information
Financing ($410/month)	$3,362	
Insurance (Rating 8)	$7,432	Excellent
State Fees	$817	
Fuel (Hwy 17 City 13)	$5,760	Average
Maintenance	$5,182	Worse Than Average
Repairs	$740	Excellent

Ownership Cost By Year

$2,000 $4,000 $6,000 $8,000

Insufficient Depreciation Information

1993 1994 1995 1996 1997

Warranty/Maintenance Info

Item		Rate
Major Tune-Up	$214	Poor
Minor Tune-Up	$132	Worse Than Average
Brake Service	$477	Poor
Overall Warranty	3 yr/36k	Average
Drivetrain Warranty	3 yr/36k	Average
Rust Warranty	6 yr/100k	Better Than Average
Maintenance Warranty	N/A	
Roadside Assistance	3 yr/36k	

Resale Value

Insufficient Information

Ownership Costs (5yr)

Insufficient Information

The 1992 Chevrolet Sportvan is available in four models - G10, G20, G30 and G30 Heavy Duty full-size passenger vans. New for 1993, the G30 Heavy Duty Sportvan features a four-wheel anti-lock braking system, and an optional air conditioning system which operates with 134-A refrigerant. Features include heavy duty chassis, 6000 lb. capacity rear axle and larger gross vehicle weight and optional long wheelbase.

Cumulative Costs

	1993	1994	1995	1996	1997
Annual	*Insufficient Information*				
Total	*Insufficient Information*				

Ownership Cost Rating

Insufficient Information

Chevrolet G30 Sportvan 3 Door Pass Ext Van

5.7L 195 hp Gas Fuel Inject.

8 Cylinder "V"

Automatic 4 Speed

2 Wheel Rear

Manual Seatbelts Only

Purchase Price

Car Item	Dealer Cost	List
Base Price	**$16,625**	**$19,000**
Anti-Lock Brakes	Std	Std
Manual Transmission	N/A	N/A
Optional Engine	N/A	N/A
Air Conditioning	$839	$975
Power Steering	Std	Std
Cruise Control	Pkg	Pkg
All Wheel Drive	N/A	N/A
AM/FM Stereo Cassette	$226	$263
Steering Wheel, Tilt	Pkg	Pkg
Power Windows	Pkg	Pkg
***Options Price**	$839	$975
***Total Price**	**$17,464**	**$19,975**
Target Price	$18,778	
Destination Charge	$580	
Avg. Tax & Fees	$1,174	
Total Target $	**$20,532**	
Average Dealer Option Cost:	***86%***	

Ownership Costs

Cost Area	5 Year Cost	Rate
Depreciation	$10,260	Average
Financing ($413/month)	$3,383	
Insurance (Rating 7)	$7,244	Excellent
State Fees	$822	
Fuel (Hwy 17 City 13)	$5,760	Average
Maintenance	$5,182	Worse Than Average
Repairs	$740	Excellent

Ownership Cost By Year

$2,000 $4,000 $6,000 $8,000 $10,000 $12,000

1993 1994 1995 1996 1997

Warranty/Maintenance Info

Item		Rate
Major Tune-Up	$214	Poor
Minor Tune-Up	$132	Worse Than Average
Brake Service	$477	Poor
Overall Warranty	3 yr/36k	Average
Drivetrain Warranty	3 yr/36k	Average
Rust Warranty	6 yr/100k	Better Than Average
Maintenance Warranty	N/A	
Roadside Assistance	3 yr/36k	

Resale Value

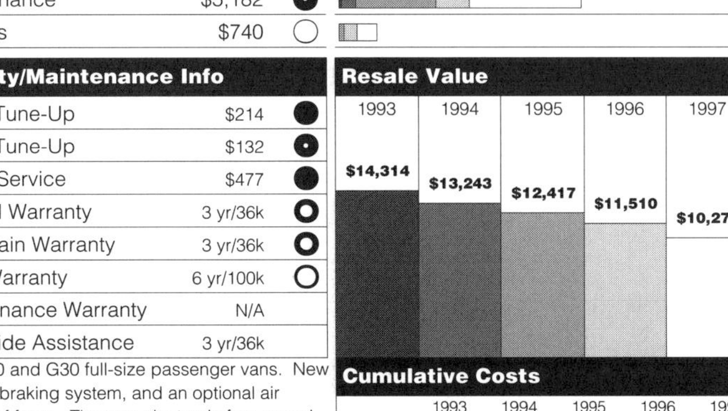

1993	1994	1995	1996	1997
$14,314	$13,243	$12,417	$11,510	$10,272

Ownership Costs (5yr)

Average	This Car
$32,837	$33,391
Cost/Mile 47¢	Cost/Mile 48¢

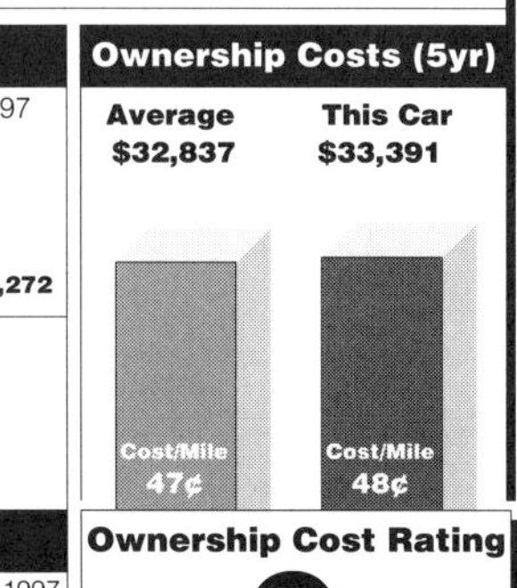

The 1993 Chevrolet Sportvan is available in three models - G10, G20 and G30 full-size passenger vans. New for 1993, the G30 Sportvan features a standard four-wheel anti-lock braking system, and an optional air conditioning system which operates with 134-A refrigerant, instead of freon. The new electronic four-speed, the Hydra-matic 4L60-E, is General Motors' first rear-wheel electronic transmission to interface with the cruise control which has the strongest torque-to-mass weight ratio in its class.

Cumulative Costs

	1993	1994	1995	1996	1997
Annual	$10,296	$5,114	$6,105	$5,028	$6,848
Total	$10,296	$15,410	$21,515	$26,543	$33,391

Ownership Cost Rating

Average

* Includes shaded options

** Other purchase requirements apply

 Poor  Worse Than Average  Average  Better Than Average  Excellent  Insufficient Information

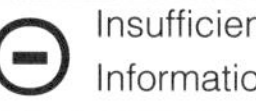

Refer to *Section 3: Annotated Vehicle Charts* for an explanation of these charts.

Chevrolet Lumina APV

3 Door Pass Van

 3.1L 120 hp Gas Fuel Inject.

 6 Cylinder "V"

Automatic 3 Speed

 2 Wheel Front

 Manual Seatbelts Only

Mini Van

LS Model Shown

Purchase Price

Car Item	Dealer Cost	List
Base Price	**$14,385**	**$15,895**
Anti-Lock Brakes	Std	Std
4 Spd Auto	$172	$200
3.8L 170 hp Gas	$532	$619
Air Conditioning	$714	$830
Power Steering	Std	Std
Cruise Control	$194	$225
All Wheel Drive	N/A	N/A
AM/FM Stereo Cassette	$120	$140
Steering Wheel, Tilt	$125	$145
Power Windows	$237	$275
***Options Price**	$1,560	$1,814
***Total Price**	**$15,945**	**$17,709**
Target Price	$17,242	
Destination Charge	$530	
Avg. Tax & Fees	$1,071	
Total Target $	**$18,843**	
Average Dealer Option Cost:	***86%***	

Ownership Costs

Cost Area	5 Year Cost	Rate
Depreciation	$6,855	Average
Financing ($379/month)	$3,103	
Insurance (Rating 7)	$7,244	Excellent
State Fees	$729	
Fuel (Hwy 25 City 17)	$4,145	Better Than Average
Maintenance	$4,305	Average
Repairs	$659	Excellent

Ownership Cost By Year

$2,000 $4,000 $6,000 $8,000

1993 1994 1995 1996 1997

Warranty/Maintenance Info

Item		Rate
Major Tune-Up	$157	Better Than Average
Minor Tune-Up	$105	Better Than Average
Brake Service	$207	Better Than Average
Overall Warranty	3 yr/36k	Average
Drivetrain Warranty	3 yr/36k	Average
Rust Warranty	6 yr/100k	Better Than Average
Maintenance Warranty	N/A	
Roadside Assistance	3 yr/36k	

Resale Value

1993	1994	1995	1996	1997
$15,611	$14,745	$14,067	$13,074	$11,988

Ownership Costs (5yr)

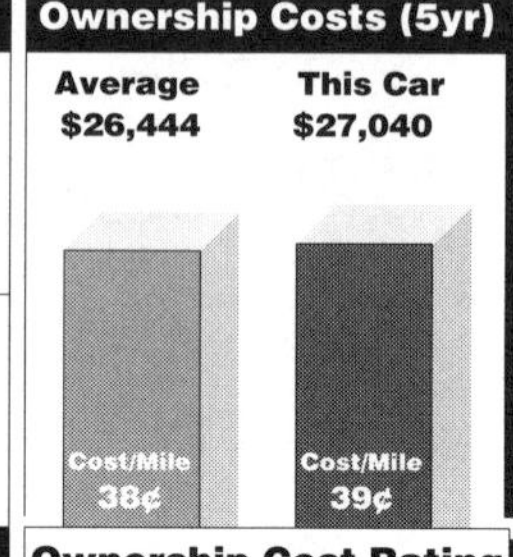

Average	This Car
$26,444	$27,040
Cost/Mile 38¢	Cost/Mile 39¢

The 1993 Lumina APV is available in two models-(Base) Lumina APV and LS. New for 1993, the Lumina APV features optional power-sliding side door and non-removable pop-up sunroof (both scheduled for interim '93 release). The APV features five-passenger seating with center-row bench and a newly designed center console with a lockable storage bin. It also features a maximum cargo capacity of 112.6 cu. ft. New Purple Metallic and seven other exterior colors are available for 1993.

Cumulative Costs

	1993	1994	1995	1996	1997
Annual	$6,858	$4,435	$4,933	$4,892	$5,922
Total	$6,858	$11,293	$16,226	$21,118	$27,040

Ownership Cost Rating

Average

Chevrolet Lumina APV LS

3 Door Pass Van

 3.1L 120 hp Gas Fuel Inject.

 6 Cylinder "V"

 Automatic 3 Speed

 2 Wheel Front

 Manual Seatbelts Only

Mini Van

Purchase Price

Car Item	Dealer Cost	List
Base Price	**$16,285**	**$17,995**
Anti-Lock Brakes	Std	Std
4 Spd Auto	$172	$200
3.8L 170 hp Gas	$532	$619
Air Conditioning	Std	Std
Power Steering	Std	Std
Cruise Control	$194	$225
All Wheel Drive	N/A	N/A
AM/FM Stereo Cassette	$120	$140
Steering Wheel, Tilt	Std	Std
Power Windows	$237	$275
***Options Price**	$846	$984
***Total Price**	**$17,131**	**$18,979**
Target Price	$18,600	
Destination Charge	$530	
Avg. Tax & Fees	$1,152	
Total Target $	**$20,282**	
Average Dealer Option Cost:	***86%***	

Ownership Costs

Cost Area	5 Year Cost	Rate
Depreciation	$7,775	Average
Financing ($408/month)	$3,341	
Insurance (Rating 7)	$7,244	Excellent
State Fees	$781	
Fuel (Hwy 25 City 17)	$4,145	Better Than Average
Maintenance	$4,305	Average
Repairs	$659	Excellent

Ownership Cost By Year

$2,000 $4,000 $6,000 $8,000

1993 1994 1995 1996 1997

Warranty/Maintenance Info

Item		Rate
Major Tune-Up	$157	Better Than Average
Minor Tune-Up	$105	Better Than Average
Brake Service	$207	Better Than Average
Overall Warranty	3 yr/36k	Average
Drivetrain Warranty	3 yr/36k	Average
Rust Warranty	6 yr/100k	Better Than Average
Maintenance Warranty	N/A	
Roadside Assistance	3 yr/36k	

Resale Value

1993	1994	1995	1996	1997
$16,233	$15,454	$14,689	$13,655	$12,507

Ownership Costs (5yr)

Average	This Car
$27,502	$28,250
Cost/Mile 39¢	Cost/Mile 40¢

The 1993 Lumina APV is available in two models-(Base) Lumina APV and LS. New for 1993, the Lumina APV LS features optional power-sliding side door and a non-removable pop-up sunroof (both scheduled for interim '93 release). The LS features a new acoustic package that reduces engine, road and wind noise. Other features include six-passenger bucket seats with optional seating for seven and a maximum cargo capacity of 115. 4 cu. ft. One new exterior color is available for 1993: Purple Metallic.

Cumulative Costs

	1993	1994	1995	1996	1997
Annual	$7,787	$4,434	$5,077	$4,960	$5,992
Total	$7,787	$12,221	$17,298	$22,258	$28,250

Ownership Cost Rating

Average

* Includes shaded options

** Other purchase requirements apply

 Poor  Worse Than Average  Average  Better Than Average  Excellent 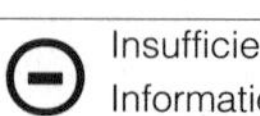 Insufficient Information

Refer to *Section 3: Annotated Vehicle Charts* for an explanation of these charts.

Chevrolet S-10 EL
2 Door Regular Cab

 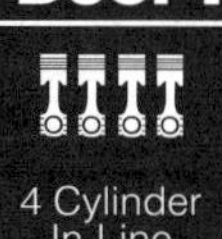   

2.5L 105 hp Gas Fuel Inject. | 4 Cylinder In-Line | Manual 5 Speed | 2 Wheel Rear | Manual Seatbelts Only

Small Pickup

Purchase Price

Car Item	Dealer Cost	List
Base Price	**$8,264**	**$8,745**
Anti-Lock Brakes	Std	Std
Automatic 4 Speed	$765	$890
Optional Engine	N/A	N/A
Air Conditioning	$649	$755
Power Steering	$237	$275
Cruise Control	N/A	N/A
All Wheel Drive	N/A	N/A
AM/FM Stereo Cassette	$390	$454
Steering Wheel, Tilt	N/A	N/A
Power Windows	N/A	N/A
***Options Price**	$627	$729
***Total Price**	**$8,891**	**$9,474**
Target Price	$9,358	
Destination Charge	$470	
Avg. Tax & Fees	$590	
Total Target $	**$10,418**	
Average Dealer Option Cost:	***86%***	

Ownership Costs

Cost Area	5 Year Cost	Rate
Depreciation	$4,857	Average
Financing ($209/month)	$1,716	
Insurance (Rating 4)	$6,867	Average
State Fees	$398	
Fuel (Hwy 27 City 23)	$3,454	Excellent
Maintenance	$3,947	Average
Repairs	$700	Better Than Average

Ownership Cost By Year

$2,000 $4,000 $6,000 $8,000

1993 1994 1995 1996 1997

Warranty/Maintenance Info

Item		Rate
Major Tune-Up	$182	Worse Than Average
Minor Tune-Up	$94	Average
Brake Service	$218	Average
Overall Warranty	3 yr/36k	Average
Drivetrain Warranty	3 yr/36k	Average
Rust Warranty	6 yr/100k	Better Than Average
Maintenance Warranty	N/A	
Roadside Assistance	3 yr/36k	

Resale Value

1993	1994	1995	1996	1997
$8,112	$7,442	$6,970	$6,314	$5,561

Ownership Costs (5yr)

	Average	This Car
	$21,587	$21,939
Cost/Mile	31¢	31¢

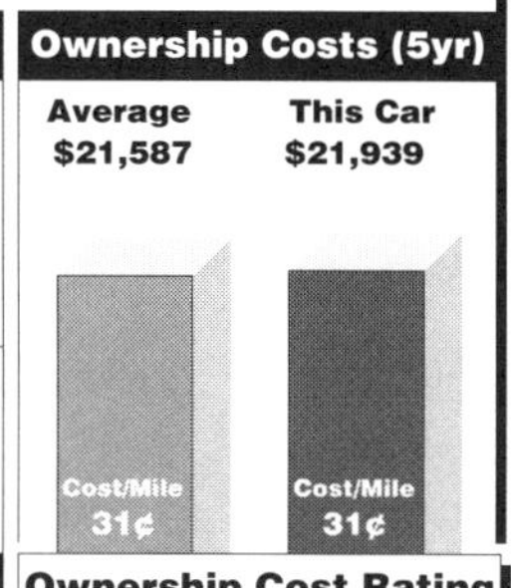

Cumulative Costs

	1993	1994	1995	1996	1997
Annual	$5,073	$3,508	$4,268	$3,966	$5,124
Total	$5,073	$8,581	$12,849	$16,815	$21,939

Ownership Cost Rating

Average

The 1993 S-10 Pickup is available in both regular and extended cab versions with 2-wheel-drive (2WD) or 4-wheel-drive (4WD) configurations. New for 1993, the S-10 EL Regular cab features a redesigned interior which offers bucket seats, a floor console with a 12-volt power outlet and new sun visors with illuminated mirrors. Standard features include a 3-passenger folding bench seat with integral head restaints. New colors for 1993 are beige for the interior and Dove Gray and khaki for the exterior.

Chevrolet S-10
2 Door Regular Cab

2.5L 105 hp Gas Fuel Inject. | 4 Cylinder In-Line | Manual 5 Speed | 2 Wheel Rear | Manual Seatbelts Only

Small Pickup

Purchase Price

Car Item	Dealer Cost	List
Base Price	**$9,168**	**$10,130**
Anti-Lock Brakes	Std	Std
Automatic 4 Speed	$765	$890
4.3L 160 hp Gas	$533	** $620
Air Conditioning	$649	$755
Power Steering	$237	$275
Cruise Control	$205	** $238
All Wheel Drive	N/A	N/A
AM/FM Stereo Cassette	$218	$253
Steering Wheel, Tilt	Pkg	Pkg
7.3 Foot Bed	$271	$300
***Options Price**	$455	$528
***Total Price**	**$9,623**	**$10,658**
Target Price	$10,144	
Destination Charge	$470	
Avg. Tax & Fees	$642	
Total Target $	**$11,256**	
Average Dealer Option Cost:	***86%***	

Ownership Costs

Cost Area	5 Year Cost	Rate
Depreciation	$5,084	Average
Financing ($226/month)	$1,855	
Insurance (Rating 4)	$6,867	Average
State Fees	$445	
Fuel (Hwy 27 City 23)	$3,454	Excellent
Maintenance	$3,947	Average
Repairs	$700	Better Than Average

Ownership Cost By Year

$2,000 $4,000 $6,000 $8,000

1993 1994 1995 1996 1997

Warranty/Maintenance Info

Item		Rate
Major Tune-Up	$182	Worse Than Average
Minor Tune-Up	$94	Average
Brake Service	$218	Average
Overall Warranty	3 yr/36k	Average
Drivetrain Warranty	3 yr/36k	Average
Rust Warranty	6 yr/100k	Better Than Average
Maintenance Warranty	N/A	
Roadside Assistance	3 yr/36k	

Resale Value

1993	1994	1995	1996	1997
$8,759	$8,109	$7,636	$6,980	$6,172

Ownership Costs (5yr)

	Average	This Car
	$22,790	$22,352
Cost/Mile	33¢	32¢

Cumulative Costs

	1993	1994	1995	1996	1997
Annual	$5,333	$3,543	$4,306	$3,984	$5,186
Total	$5,333	$8,876	$13,182	$17,166	$22,352

Ownership Cost Rating

Better Than Average

The 1993 S-10 Pickup is available in both regular and extended cab versions with 2-wheel drive (2WD) or 4-wheel-drive (4WD) configurations. New for 1993, the S-10 Regular cab offers color-keyed door trim, radio bezels and 15-inch aluminum wheels. Other options include illuminated entry light under the rear view mirror, bucket seats, and a new mini-barbless antenna connector for improved reliability. New colors for 1993 are beige for the interior and Dove Gray and khaki for the exterior.

* Includes shaded options

** Other purchase requirements apply

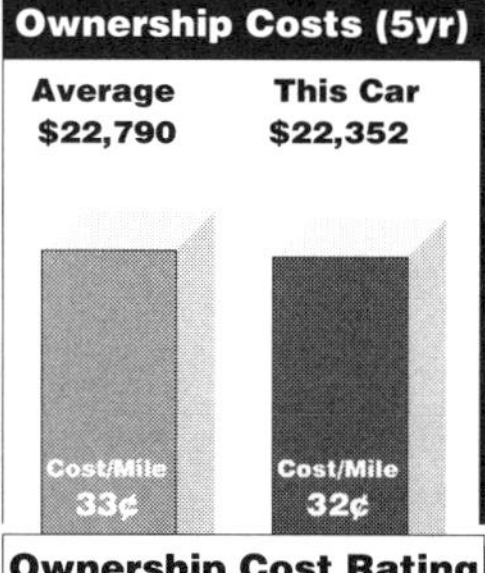

 Poor  Worse Than Average  Average  Better Than Average 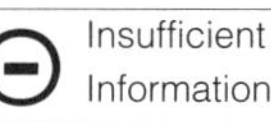 Excellent — Insufficient Information

Refer to *Section 3: Annotated Vehicle Charts* for an explanation of these charts.

Chevrolet S-10 Maxi Cab

2 Door Extended Cab

2.5L 105 hp Gas Fuel Inject.

4 Cylinder In-Line

Manual 5 Speed

2 Wheel Rear

Manual Seatbelts Only

Small Pickup

Purchase Price

Car Item	Dealer Cost	List
Base Price	**$10,525**	**$11,630**
Anti-Lock Brakes	Std	Std
Automatic 4 Speed	$765	** $890
2.8L 125 hp Gas	$335	$390
Air Conditioning	$649	$755
Power Steering	Std	Std
Cruise Control	$205	** $238
All Wheel Drive	N/A	N/A
AM/FM Stereo Cassette	$218	$253
Steering Wheel, Tilt	Pkg	Pkg
Power Windows	Pkg	Pkg
***Options Price**	$553	$643
***Total Price**	**$11,078**	**$12,273**
Target Price	$11,706	
Destination Charge	$470	
Avg. Tax & Fees	$736	
Total Target $	**$12,912**	
Average Dealer Option Cost:	***86%***	

Ownership Costs

Cost Area	5 Year Cost	Rate
Depreciation	$5,429	Better Than Average
Financing ($260/month)	$2,128	
Insurance (Rating 7)	$7,244	Average
State Fees	$509	
Fuel (Hwy 25 City 19)	$3,929	Better Than Average
Maintenance	$4,006	Average
Repairs	$700	Better Than Average

Ownership Cost By Year

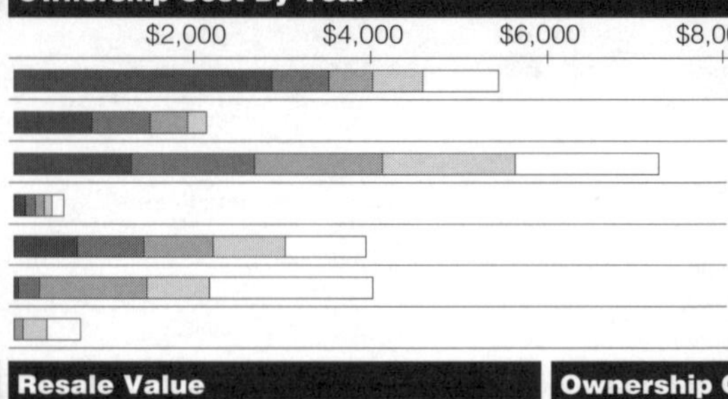

Warranty/Maintenance Info

Item		Rate
Major Tune-Up	$187	Worse Than Average
Minor Tune-Up	$99	Average
Brake Service	$218	Average
Overall Warranty	3 yr/36k	Average
Drivetrain Warranty	3 yr/36k	Average
Rust Warranty	6 yr/100k	Better Than Average
Maintenance Warranty	N/A	
Roadside Assistance	3 yr/36k	

Resale Value

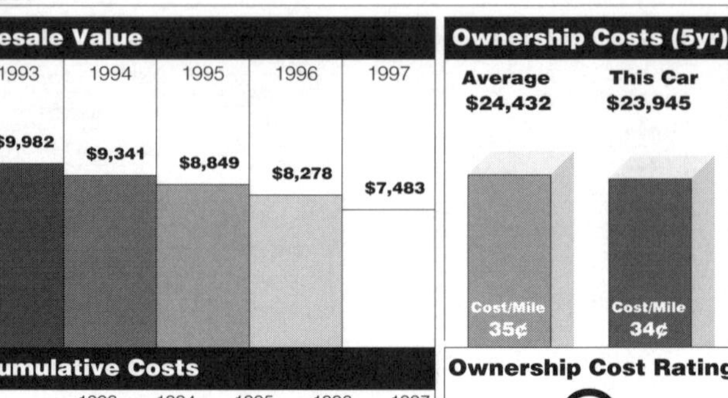

Ownership Costs (5yr)

Average	This Car
$24,432	$23,945
Cost/Mile 35¢	Cost/Mile 34¢

The 1993 S-10 Pickup is available in both regular and extended cab versions with 2 wheel drive (2WD) or 4-wheel-drive (4WD) configurations. New for 1993, the S-10 Maxi Cab offers a new electronic 4-speed automatic transmission--the Hydra-matic 4L60-E. This new "smart" transmission monitors every element of the driving experience several times a second, then determines the proper shift points and shift smoothness. Other features include two trim levels for 1993--Standard and optional Tahoe.

Cumulative Costs

	1993	1994	1995	1996	1997
Annual	$6,054	$3,807	$4,574	$4,118	$5,392
Total	$6,054	$9,861	$14,435	$18,553	$23,945

Ownership Cost Rating

Better Than Average

Chevrolet S-10 EL 4WD

2 Door Regular Cab

4.3L 160 hp Gas Fuel Inject.

6 Cylinder "V"

Manual 5 Speed

4 Wheel On-Demand

Manual Seatbelts Only

Small Pickup

2WD Model Shown

Purchase Price

Car Item	Dealer Cost	List
Base Price	**$11,855**	**$12,545**
Anti-Lock Brakes	Std	Std
Automatic 4 Speed	$765	$890
Optional Engine	N/A	N/A
Air Conditioning	$649	$755
Power Steering	Std	Std
Cruise Control	N/A	N/A
4 Whl On-Demand Dr.	Std	Std
AM/FM Stereo Cassette	$390	$454
Steering Wheel, Tilt	N/A	N/A
Power Windows	N/A	N/A
***Options Price**	$390	$454
***Total Price**	**$12,245**	**$12,999**
Target Price	$12,968	
Destination Charge	$470	
Avg. Tax & Fees	$807	
Total Target $	**$14,245**	
Average Dealer Option Cost:	***86%***	

Ownership Costs

Cost Area	5 Year Cost	Rate
Depreciation	$7,091	Average
Financing ($286/month)	$2,345	
Insurance (Rating 8)	$7,432	Average
State Fees	$539	
Fuel (Hwy 21 City 16)	$4,672	Worse Than Average
Maintenance	$4,584	Poor
Repairs	$791	Average

Ownership Cost By Year

$2,000 $4,000 $6,000 $8,000

1993 1994 1995 1996 1997

Warranty/Maintenance Info

Item		Rate
Major Tune-Up	$197	Worse Than Average
Minor Tune-Up	$114	Poor
Brake Service	$218	Average
Overall Warranty	3 yr/36k	Average
Drivetrain Warranty	3 yr/36k	Average
Rust Warranty	6 yr/100k	Better Than Average
Maintenance Warranty	N/A	
Roadside Assistance	3 yr/36k	

Resale Value

1993	1994	1995	1996	1997
$9,639	$9,007	$8,555	$7,916	$7,154

Ownership Costs (5yr)

Average	This Car
$25,170	$27,454
Cost/Mile 36¢	Cost/Mile 39¢

The 1993 S-10 Pickup is available in both regular and extended cab versions with 2-wheel drive (2WD) or 4-wheel-drive (4WD) configurations. New for 1993, the S-10 EL 4WD Regular cab offers an electronic 4-speed automatic transmission--the Hydra-matic 4L60-E. An internal balance shaft has been added to the 4.3-liter V6 to provide a smoother engine performance. Standard equipment features include an energy absorbing steering column, four-wheel anti-lock brakes and a 3-passenger folding bench seat.

Cumulative Costs

	1993	1994	1995	1996	1997
Annual	$8,002	$4,067	$4,687	$4,453	$6,245
Total	$8,002	$12,069	$16,756	$21,209	$27,454

Ownership Cost Rating

Poor

* Includes shaded options

** Other purchase requirements apply

 Poor  Worse Than Average 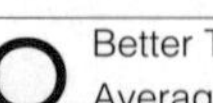 Average  Better Than Average · Excellent · Insufficient Information

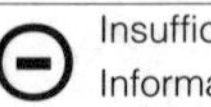

Refer to *Section 3: Annotated Vehicle Charts* for an explanation of these charts.

Chevrolet S-10 4WD
2 Door Regular Cab

4.3L 160 hp Gas Fuel Inject.

6 Cylinder "V"

Manual 5 Speed

4 Wheel On-Demand

Manual Seatbelts Only

Small Pickup

Purchase Price

Car Item	Dealer Cost	List
Base Price	**$12,395**	**$13,696**
Anti-Lock Brakes	Std	Std
Automatic 4 Speed	$765	$890
Optional Engine	N/A	N/A
Air Conditioning	$649	$755
Power Steering	Std	Std
Cruise Control	$205	** $238
4 Whl On-Demand Dr.	Std	Std
AM/FM Stereo Cassette	$218	$253
Steering Wheel, Tilt	Pkg	Pkg
7.3 Foot Bed	$271	$300
***Options Price**	$218	$253
***Total Price**	**$12,613**	**$13,949**
Target Price	$13,370	
Destination Charge	$470	
Avg. Tax & Fees	$836	
Total Target $	**$14,676**	
Average Dealer Option Cost:	***86%***	

Ownership Costs

Cost Area	5 Year Cost	Rate
Depreciation	$7,261	Worse Than Average
Financing ($295/month)	$2,418	
Insurance (Rating 8)	$7,432	Average
State Fees	$577	
Fuel (Hwy 21 City 16)	$4,672	Worse Than Average
Maintenance	$4,584	Poor
Repairs	$791	Average

Warranty/Maintenance Info

Item		Rate
Major Tune-Up	$197	Worse Than Average
Minor Tune-Up	$114	Poor
Brake Service	$218	Average
Overall Warranty	3 yr/36k	Average
Drivetrain Warranty	3 yr/36k	Average
Rust Warranty	6 yr/100k	Better Than Average
Maintenance Warranty	N/A	
Roadside Assistance	3 yr/36k	

The 1993 S-10 Pickup is available in both regular and extended cab versions with 2-wheel drive (2WD) or 4-wheel-drive (4WD) configurations. New for 1993, the S-10 4WD Regular cab features the addition of a balance shaft to the 4.3 Liter V6 to provide a smoother engine performance. Other features include the 4-speed automatic transmission--the Hydra-matic 4L60-E. Standard features include 15-inch steel wheels and a 3-passenger folding bench seat with integral head restraints.

Ownership Cost By Year

$2,000 $4,000 $6,000 $8,000

1993 1994 1995 1996 1997

Resale Value

1993	1994	1995	1996	1997
$10,164	$9,465	$8,937	$8,246	$7,415

Ownership Costs (5yr)

Cumulative Costs

	1993	1994	1995	1996	1997
Annual	$7,947	$4,166	$4,784	$4,518	$6,320
Total	$7,947	$12,113	$16,897	$21,415	$27,735

Ownership Cost Rating

Worse Than Average

Chevrolet S-10 Maxi Cab 4WD
2 Door Extended Cab

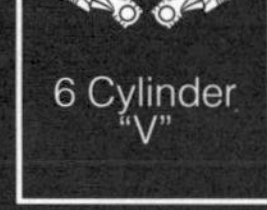
4.3L 160 hp Gas Fuel Inject.

6 Cylinder "V"

Manual 5 Speed

4 Wheel On-Demand

Manual Seatbelts Only

Small Pickup

2WD Model Shown

Purchase Price

Car Item	Dealer Cost	List
Base Price	**$13,752**	**$15,196**
Anti-Lock Brakes	Std	Std
Automatic 4 Speed	$765	$890
Optional Engine	N/A	N/A
Air Conditioning	$649	$755
Power Steering	Std	Std
Cruise Control	$205	** $238
4 Whl On-Demand Dr.	Std	Std
AM/FM Stereo Cassette	$218	$253
Steering Wheel, Tilt	Pkg	Pkg
Power Windows	Pkg	Pkg
***Options Price**	$218	$253
***Total Price**	**$13,970**	**$15,449**
Target Price	$14,843	
Destination Charge	$470	
Avg. Tax & Fees	$925	
Total Target $	**$16,238**	
Average Dealer Option Cost:	***86%***	

Ownership Costs

Cost Area	5 Year Cost	Rate
Depreciation	$7,232	Average
Financing ($326/month)	$2,674	
Insurance (Rating 11)	$7,902	Average
State Fees	$636	
Fuel (Hwy 20 City 16 [Est.])	$4,797	Poor
Maintenance	$4,584	Poor
Repairs	$791	Average

Warranty/Maintenance Info

Item		Rate
Major Tune-Up	$197	Worse Than Average
Minor Tune-Up	$114	Poor
Brake Service	$218	Average
Overall Warranty	3 yr/36k	Average
Drivetrain Warranty	3 yr/36k	Average
Rust Warranty	6 yr/100k	Better Than Average
Maintenance Warranty	N/A	
Roadside Assistance	3 yr/36k	

The 1993 S-10 Pickup is available in both regular and extended cab versions with 2-wheel drive (2WD) or 4-wheel-drive (4WD) configurations. New for 1993, the S-10 Maxi-Cab 4WD features a redesigned interior with an illuminated entry light under the rear view mirror, a convenience net, a new 60/40 reclining front bench seat with center armrest and bucket seats. Other features include the Hydra-matic 4L60-E and an internal balance shaft to provide a smoother V6 engine performance.

Ownership Cost By Year

$2,000 $4,000 $6,000 $8,000

1993 1994 1995 1996 1997

Resale Value

1993	1994	1995	1996	1997
$11,683	$10,968	$10,464	$9,791	$9,006

Ownership Costs (5yr)

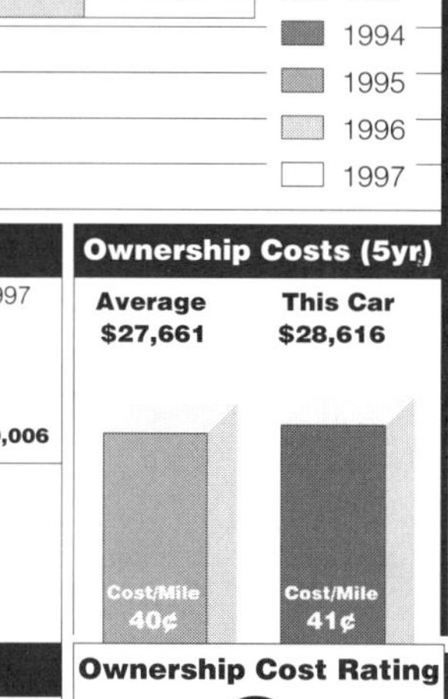

Cumulative Costs

	1993	1994	1995	1996	1997
Annual	$8,222	$4,389	$4,942	$4,651	$6,412
Total	$8,222	$12,611	$17,553	$22,204	$28,616

Ownership Cost Rating

Worse Than Average

* Includes shaded options

** Other purchase requirements apply

Poor  Worse Than Average · Average  Better Than Average · Excellent · Insufficient Information

Refer to *Section 3: Annotated Vehicle Charts* for an explanation of these charts.

Chevrolet S-10 Blazer
2 Door Sport Utility

4.3L 165 hp Gas Fuel Inject.

6 Cylinder "V"

Manual 5 Speed

2 Wheel Rear

Manual Seatbelts Only

Purchase Price

Car Item	Dealer Cost	List
Base Price	**$13,415**	**$14,823**
Anti-Lock Brakes	Std	Std
Automatic 4 Speed	Pkg	Pkg
4.3L 200 hp Gas	Pkg	Pkg
Air Conditioning	$671	$780
Power Steering	Std	Std
Cruise Control	$205	** $238
All Wheel Drive	N/A	N/A
AM/FM Stereo Cassette	$218	$253
Steering Wheel, Tilt	Pkg	Pkg
Power Windows	Pkg	Pkg
***Options Price**	$889	$1,033
***Total Price**	**$14,304**	**$15,856**
Target Price	$15,189	
Destination Charge	$475	
Avg. Tax & Fees	$946	
Total Target $	**$16,610**	
Average Dealer Option Cost:	***86%***	

Ownership Costs

Cost Area	5 Year Cost	Rate
Depreciation	$6,700	Average
Financing ($334/month)	$2,736	
Insurance (Rating 13)	$8,271	Worse Than Average
State Fees	$653	
Fuel (Hwy 23 City 18)	$4,213	Average
Maintenance	$4,106	Average
Repairs	$740	Better Than Average

Ownership Cost By Year

$2,000 $4,000 $6,000 $8,000 $10,000

1993 1994 1995 1996 1997

Warranty/Maintenance Info

Major Tune-Up	$197	Worse Than Average
Minor Tune-Up	$114	Worse Than Average
Brake Service	$218	Better Than Average
Overall Warranty	3 yr/36k	Average
Drivetrain Warranty	3 yr/36k	Average
Rust Warranty	6 yr/100k	Better Than Average
Maintenance Warranty	N/A	
Roadside Assistance	3 yr/36k	

Resale Value

1993	1994	1995	1996	1997
$13,464	$12,590	$11,887	$10,901	$9,910

Ownership Costs (5yr)

Average	This Car
$26,638	$27,419
Cost/Mile 38¢	Cost/Mile 39¢

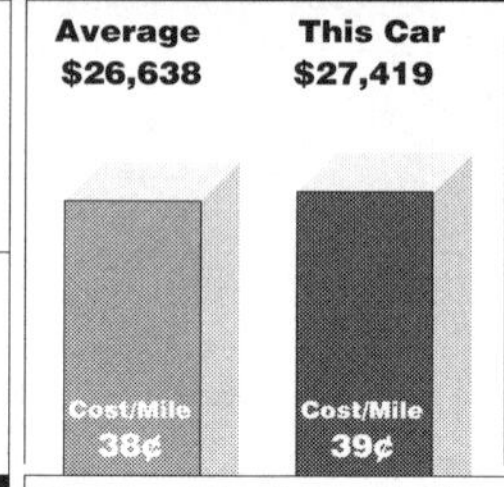

Cumulative Costs

	1993	1994	1995	1996	1997
Annual	$6,803	$4,530	$5,239	$4,908	$5,939
Total	$6,803	$11,333	$16,572	$21,480	$27,419

Ownership Cost Rating

Average

The 1993 S-10 Blazer is available in both 2-door and 4-door models with either 2-wheel-drive or 4-wheel-drive. New for 1993, the 2-door Blazers are available in three trim levels- Standard and Tahoe, plus the-top-of-the-line Tahoe LT. The S-10 Blazer's standard 4.3L EFI V6 engine is refined and offers less noise, less vibration, smoother performance and a five-horsepower increase. Other features include reclining high-back bucket seats and four-wheel anti-lock brakes as standard equipment.

Chevrolet S-10 Blazer
4 Door Sport Utility

4.3L 165 hp Gas Fuel Inject.

6 Cylinder "V"

Manual 5 Speed

2 Wheel Rear

Manual Seatbelts Only

Utility

Purchase Price

Car Item	Dealer Cost	List
Base Price	**$14,284**	**$15,783**
Anti-Lock Brakes	Std	Std
Automatic 4 Speed	Pkg	Pkg
4.3L 200 hp Gas	Pkg	Pkg
Air Conditioning	$671	$780
Power Steering	Std	Std
Cruise Control	$205	** $238
All Wheel Drive	N/A	N/A
AM/FM Stereo Cassette	$218	$253
Steering Wheel, Tilt	Pkg	Pkg
Power Windows	Pkg	Pkg
***Options Price**	$889	$1,033
***Total Price**	**$15,173**	**$16,816**
Target Price	$16,136	
Destination Charge	$475	
Avg. Tax & Fees	$1,004	
Total Target $	**$17,615**	
Average Dealer Option Cost:	***86%***	

Ownership Costs

Cost Area	5 Year Cost	Rate
Depreciation	$7,196	Average
Financing ($354/month)	$2,902	
Insurance (Rating 14)	$8,446	Worse Than Average
State Fees	$692	
Fuel (Hwy 23 City 18)	$4,213	Average
Maintenance	$4,106	Average
Repairs	$740	Better Than Average

Ownership Cost By Year

$2,000 $4,000 $6,000 $8,000 $10,000

1993 1994 1995 1996 1997

Warranty/Maintenance Info

Major Tune-Up	$197	Worse Than Average
Minor Tune-Up	$114	Worse Than Average
Brake Service	$218	Better Than Average
Overall Warranty	3 yr/36k	Average
Drivetrain Warranty	3 yr/36k	Average
Rust Warranty	6 yr/100k	Better Than Average
Maintenance Warranty	N/A	
Roadside Assistance	3 yr/36k	

Resale Value

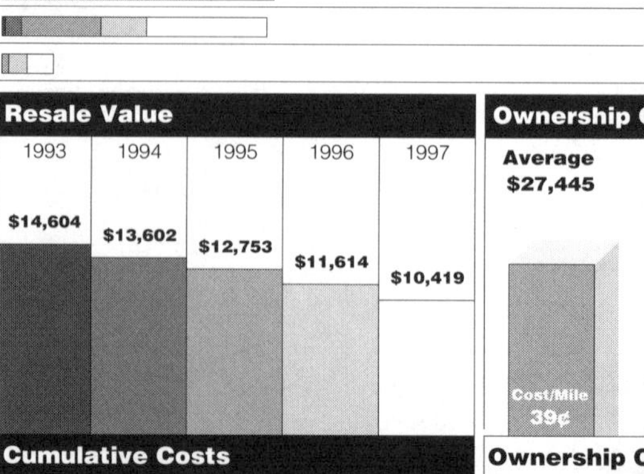

1993	1994	1995	1996	1997
$14,604	$13,602	$12,753	$11,614	$10,419

Ownership Costs (5yr)

Average	This Car
$27,445	$28,295
Cost/Mile 39¢	Cost/Mile 40¢

Cumulative Costs

	1993	1994	1995	1996	1997
Annual	$6,779	$4,753	$5,460	$5,116	$6,187
Total	$6,779	$11,532	$16,992	$22,108	$28,295

Ownership Cost Rating

Average

The 1993 S-10 Blazer is available in both 2-door and 4-door models with either 2-wheel-drive or 4-wheel drive. New for 1993, the 4-door Blazers are available in two trim levels-Tahoe (standard) and Tahoe LT. It features seating for six passengers with the optional rear seat folded down, the 4-door model has 74.3 cu. ft. of cargo space. Convenience features include illuminated entry lights, keyless entry, a floor console with a 12-volt power outlet (on some models) and an overhead console with lights and storage areas.

* Includes shaded options

** Other purchase requirements apply

Poor
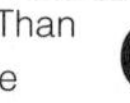
Worse Than Average

Average
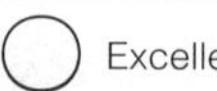
Better Than Average
Excellent
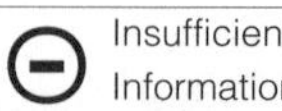
Insufficient Information

Refer to *Section 3: Annotated Vehicle Charts* for an explanation of these charts.

Chevrolet S-10 Blazer 4WD
2 Door Sport Utility

4.3L 165 hp Gas Fuel Inject.

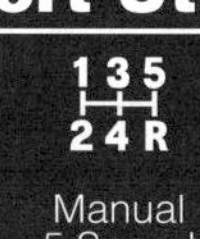

6 Cylinder "V"

Manual 5 Speed

4 Wheel On-Demand

Manual Seatbelts Only

Utility

Purchase Price

Car Item	Dealer Cost	List
Base Price	**$15,008**	**$16,583**
Anti-Lock Brakes	Std	Std
Automatic 4 Speed	Pkg	Pkg
4.3L 200 hp Gas	Pkg	Pkg
Air Conditioning	$671	$780
Power Steering	Std	Std
Cruise Control	$205	** $238
4 Whl On-Demand Dr.	Std	Std
AM/FM Stereo Cassette	$218	$253
Steering Wheel, Tilt	Pkg	Pkg
Power Windows	Pkg	Pkg
***Options Price**	$889	$1,033
***Total Price**	**$15,897**	**$17,616**
Target Price	$16,927	
Destination Charge	$475	
Avg. Tax & Fees	$1,051	
Total Target $	**$18,453**	
Average Dealer Option Cost:	***86%***	

Ownership Costs

Cost Area	5 Year Cost	Rate
Depreciation	$7,450	Average
Financing ($371/month)	$3,040	
Insurance (Rating 14)	$8,446	Worse Than Average
State Fees	$725	
Fuel (Hwy 21 City 16)	$4,672	Average
Maintenance	$4,584	Worse Than Average
Repairs	$791	Average

Ownership Cost By Year

$2,000 $4,000 $6,000 $8,000 $10,000

1993 1994 1995 1996 1997

Warranty/Maintenance Info

Item		Rate
Major Tune-Up	$197	Worse Than Average
Minor Tune-Up	$114	Worse Than Average
Brake Service	$218	Better Than Average
Overall Warranty	3 yr/36k	Average
Drivetrain Warranty	3 yr/36k	Average
Rust Warranty	6 yr/100k	Better Than Average
Maintenance Warranty	N/A	
Roadside Assistance	3 yr/36k	

Resale Value

1993	1994	1995	1996	1997
$14,853	$13,939	$13,140	$12,081	$11,003

Ownership Costs (5yr)

Average	This Car
$28,118	$29,708
Cost/Mile 40¢	Cost/Mile 42¢

The 1993 S-10 Blazer is available in both 2-door and 4-door models with either 2-wheel drive or 4-wheel drive. New for 1993, the 2-door 4WD has a maximum trailer-towing capacity of 5500-lbs when properly equipped. With the optional rear seat folded down, it has 67.3 cu. ft. of cargo space. An internal balance shaft has been added to the 4.3-liter V6 engine to provide a smoother engine performance reducing vibration in higher RPM ranges. Other features include air conditioning and reclining bucket seats.

Cumulative Costs

	1993	1994	1995	1996	1997
Annual	$7,518	$4,803	$5,412	$5,167	$6,808
Total	$7,518	$12,321	$17,733	$22,900	$29,708

Ownership Cost Rating

Worse Than Average

Chevrolet S-10 Blazer 4WD
4 Door Sport Utility

4.3L 165 hp Gas Fuel Inject.

6 Cylinder "V"

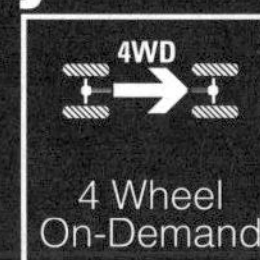

Manual 5 Speed

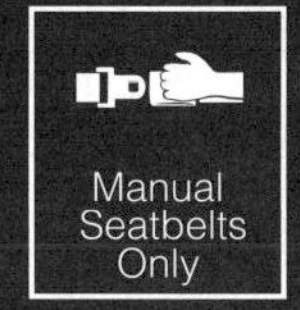

4 Wheel On-Demand

Manual Seatbelts Only

Utility

2WD Model Shown

Purchase Price

Car Item	Dealer Cost	List
Base Price	**$16,247**	**$17,953**
Anti-Lock Brakes	Std	Std
Automatic 4 Speed	Pkg	Pkg
4.3L 200 hp Gas	Pkg	Pkg
Air Conditioning	$671	$780
Power Steering	Std	Std
Cruise Control	$205	** $238
4 Whl On-Demand Dr.	Std	Std
AM/FM Stereo Cassette	$218	$253
Steering Wheel, Tilt	Pkg	Pkg
Power Windows	Pkg	Pkg
***Options Price**	$889	$1,033
***Total Price**	**$17,136**	**$18,986**
Target Price	$18,285	
Destination Charge	$475	
Avg. Tax & Fees	$1,133	
Total Target $	**$19,893**	
Average Dealer Option Cost:	***86%***	

Ownership Costs

Cost Area	5 Year Cost	Rate
Depreciation	$8,293	Average
Financing ($400/month)	$3,277	
Insurance (Rating 15)	$8,717	Worse Than Average
State Fees	$779	
Fuel (Hwy 21 City 16)	$4,672	Average
Maintenance	$4,584	Worse Than Average
Repairs	$791	Average

Ownership Cost By Year

$2,000 $4,000 $6,000 $8,000 $10,000

1993 1994 1995 1996 1997

Warranty/Maintenance Info

Item		Rate
Major Tune-Up	$197	Worse Than Average
Minor Tune-Up	$114	Worse Than Average
Brake Service	$218	Better Than Average
Overall Warranty	3 yr/36k	Average
Drivetrain Warranty	3 yr/36k	Average
Rust Warranty	6 yr/100k	Better Than Average
Maintenance Warranty	N/A	
Roadside Assistance	3 yr/36k	

Resale Value

1993	1994	1995	1996	1997
$16,233	$15,144	$14,186	$12,940	$11,600

Ownership Costs (5yr)

Average	This Car
$29,271	$31,113
Cost/Mile 42¢	Cost/Mile 44¢

The 1993 S-10 Blazer is available in both 2-door and 4-door models with either 2-wheel drive or 4-wheel drive. New for 1993, the 4-door 4-WD is powered by a 4.3L V6 engine with EFI in all models with 5-speed manual transmission. It features a rugged ladder-type all-steel frame and self aligning steering wheel, and a redesigned black grille with body-color front and rear bumpers. Other features include ABS brakes, seating for six, reclining bucket seats and a floor console with a 12-volt power outlet.

Cumulative Costs

	1993	1994	1995	1996	1997
Annual	$7,741	$5,116	$5,683	$5,436	$7,137
Total	$7,741	$12,857	$18,540	$23,976	$31,113

Ownership Cost Rating

Worse Than Average

* Includes shaded options

** Other purchase requirements apply

 Poor  Worse Than Average  Average  Better Than Average  Excellent 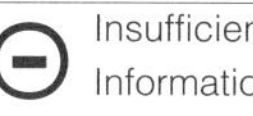 Insufficient Information

Refer to ***Section 3: Annotated Vehicle Charts*** for an explanation of these charts.

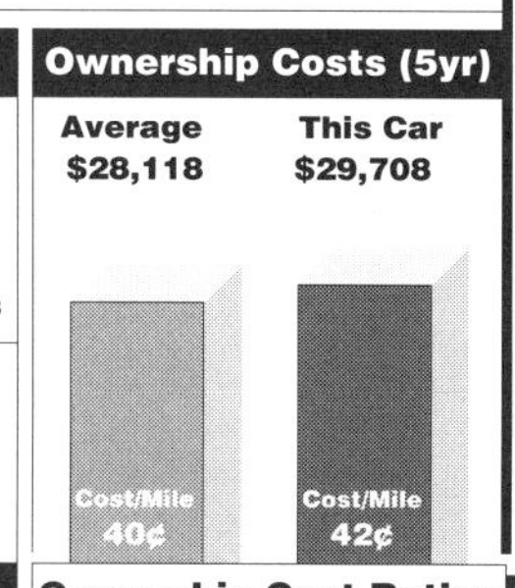

Chevrolet Suburban C1500
5 Door Sport Utility

Utility

5.7L 210 hp Gas Fuel Inject.

8 Cylinder "V"

Automatic 4 Speed

2 Wheel Rear

Manual Seatbelts Only

Purchase Price

Car Item	Dealer Cost	List
Base Price	**$16,695**	**$19,080**
Anti-Lock Brakes	Std	Std
Manual Transmission	N/A	N/A
Optional Engine	N/A	N/A
Air Conditioning	$727	$845
Power Steering	Std	Std
Cruise Control	Pkg	Pkg
All Wheel Drive	N/A	N/A
AM/FM Stereo Cassette	$251	$292
Steering Wheel, Tilt	Pkg	Pkg
Power Windows	Pkg	Pkg
***Options Price**	$978	$1,137
***Total Price**	**$17,673**	**$20,217**
Target Price	$19,472	
Destination Charge	$640	
Avg. Tax & Fees	$1,215	
Total Target $	**$21,327**	
Average Dealer Option Cost:	***86%***	

Ownership Costs

Cost Area	5 Year Cost	Rate
Depreciation	$5,541	Excellent
Financing ($429/month)	$3,513	
Insurance (Rating 15)	$8,717	Average
State Fees	$835	
Fuel (Hwy 17 City 13)	$5,760	Worse Than Average
Maintenance	$4,654	Worse Than Average
Repairs	$740	Better Than Average

Ownership Cost By Year

$2,000 $4,000 $6,000 $8,000 $10,000

1993 1994 1995 1996 1997

Warranty/Maintenance Info

Major Tune-Up	$184	Average
Minor Tune-Up	$112	Worse Than Average
Brake Service	$268	Worse Than Average
Overall Warranty	3 yr/36k	Average
Drivetrain Warranty	3 yr/36k	Average
Rust Warranty	6 yr/100k	Excellent
Maintenance Warranty	N/A	
Roadside Assistance	3 yr/36k	

Resale Value

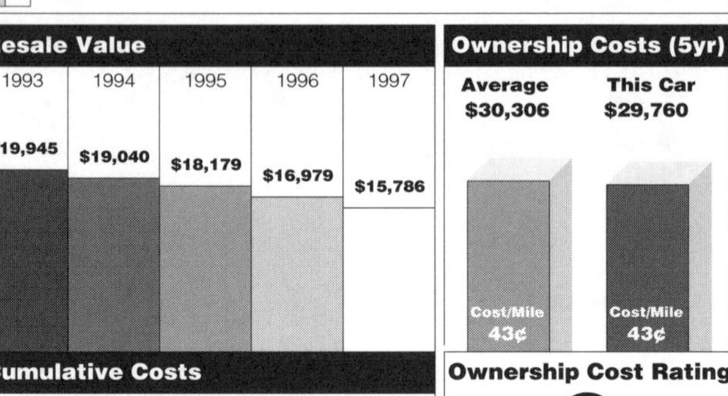

1993	1994	1995	1996	1997
$19,945	$19,040	$18,179	$16,979	$15,786

Ownership Costs (5yr)

Average	This Car
$30,306	$29,760

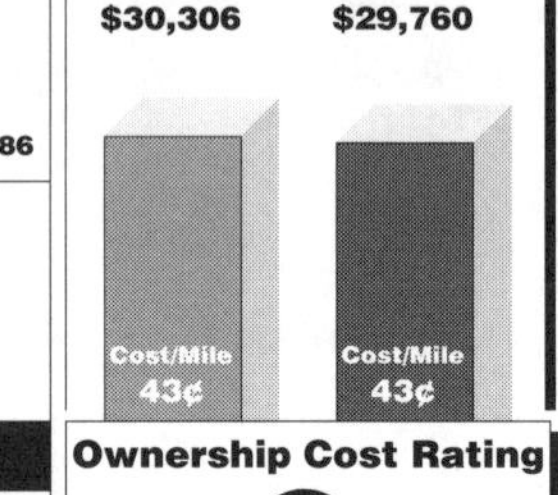

The 1993 Suburban is available in four models - C (2WD) and K (4WD) 1500 and 2500 full-size sport utility wagons. New for 1993, the C1500 features two trim levels - Cheyenne (standard) and Silverado (uplevel). An anti-chip coating is now applied on leading edges of the hood, roof, and "A" pillars to help prevent stone chips. A new tinted glass is used which blocks out 60 percent of the sun's energy to reduce interior heat buildup. One new exterior color has been added, Indigo Blue Metallic.

Cumulative Costs

	1993	1994	1995	1996	1997
Annual	$5,780	$5,234	$6,278	$5,588	$6,880
Total	$5,780	$11,014	$17,292	$22,880	$29,760

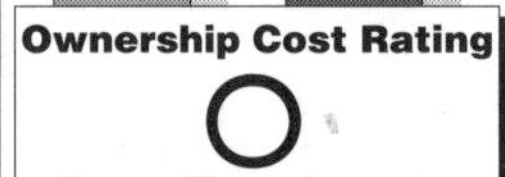

Ownership Cost Rating

Better Than Average

Chevrolet Suburban C2500
5 Door Sport Utility

Utility

5.7L 190 hp Gas Fuel Inject.

8 Cylinder "V"

Automatic 4 Speed

2 Wheel Rear

Manual Seatbelts Only

Purchase Price

Car Item	Dealer Cost	List
Base Price	**$17,745**	**$20,285**
Anti-Lock Brakes	Std	Std
Manual Transmission	N/A	N/A
7.4L 230 hp Gas	$520	** $605
Air Conditioning	$727	$845
Power Steering	Std	Std
Cruise Control	Pkg	Pkg
All Wheel Drive	N/A	N/A
AM/FM Stereo Cassette	$251	$292
Steering Wheel, Tilt	Pkg	Pkg
Power Windows	Pkg	Pkg
***Options Price**	$978	$1,137
***Total Price**	**$18,723**	**$21,422**
Target Price	$20,682	
Destination Charge	$640	
Avg. Tax & Fees	$1,287	
Total Target $	**$22,609**	
Average Dealer Option Cost:	***86%***	

Ownership Costs

Cost Area	5 Year Cost	Rate
Depreciation	$5,941	Excellent
Financing ($454/month)	$3,724	
Insurance (Rating 16)	$8,995	Average
State Fees	$882	
Fuel (Hwy 17 City 13 [Est.])	$5,760	Worse Than Average
Maintenance	$4,836	Worse Than Average
Repairs	$740	Better Than Average

Ownership Cost By Year

$2,000 $4,000 $6,000 $8,000 $10,000

1993 1994 1995 1996 1997

Warranty/Maintenance Info

Major Tune-Up	$184	Average
Minor Tune-Up	$112	Worse Than Average
Brake Service	$285	Poor
Overall Warranty	3 yr/36k	Average
Drivetrain Warranty	3 yr/36k	Average
Rust Warranty	6 yr/100k	Excellent
Maintenance Warranty	N/A	
Roadside Assistance	3 yr/36k	

Resale Value

1993	1994	1995	1996	1997
$20,864	$20,003	$19,202	$17,984	$16,668

Ownership Costs (5yr)

Average	This Car
$31,320	$30,878

Cost/Mile 45¢

Cost/Mile 44¢

The 1993 Suburban is available in four models - C (2WD) and K (4WD) 1500 and 2500 full-size sport utility wagons. New for 1993, the C2500 features two trim levels - Cheyenne (standard) and Silverado (uplevel). An anti-chip coating is now applied on leading edges of the hood, roof, and "A" pillars to help prevent stone chips. A new tinted glass is used which blocks out 60 percent of the sun's energy to reduce interior heat buildup. One new exterior color has been added, Indigo Blue Metallic.

Cumulative Costs

	1993	1994	1995	1996	1997
Annual	$6,295	$5,320	$6,410	$5,688	$7,165
Total	$6,295	$11,615	$18,025	$23,713	$30,878

Ownership Cost Rating

Better Than Average

* Includes shaded options

** Other purchase requirements apply

Poor

Worse Than Average
Average

Better Than Average
Excellent

Insufficient Information

Refer to ***Section 3: Annotated Vehicle Charts*** for an explanation of these charts.

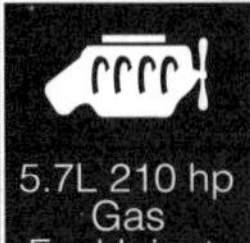

Chevrolet Suburban K1500
5 Door Sport Utility

5.7L 210 hp Gas Fuel Inject.

8 Cylinder "V"

Automatic 4 Speed

4 Wheel On-Demand

Manual Seatbelts Only

Utility

Purchase Price

Car Item	Dealer Cost	List
Base Price	**$18,620**	**$21,280**
Anti-Lock Brakes	Std	Std
Manual Transmission	N/A	N/A
Optional Engine	N/A	N/A
Air Conditioning	$727	$845
Power Steering	Std	Std
Cruise Control	Pkg	Pkg
4 Whl On-Demand Dr.	Std	Std
AM/FM Stereo Cassette	$251	$292
Steering Wheel, Tilt	Pkg	Pkg
Power Windows	Pkg	Pkg
***Options Price**	$978	$1,137
***Total Price**	**$19,598**	**$22,417**
Target Price	$21,695	
Destination Charge	$640	
Avg. Tax & Fees	$1,348	
Total Target $	**$23,683**	
Average Dealer Option Cost:	***86%***	

Ownership Costs

Cost Area	5 Year Cost	Rate
Depreciation	$5,631	Excellent
Financing ($476/month)	$3,900	
Insurance (Rating 16)	$8,995	Average
State Fees	$922	
Fuel (Hwy 17 City 13 [Est.])	$5,760	Worse Than Average
Maintenance	$4,726	Worse Than Average
Repairs	$945	Worse Than Average

Ownership Cost By Year

$2,000 $4,000 $6,000 $8,000 $10,000

1993 1994 1995 1996 1997

Warranty/Maintenance Info

Item		Rate
Major Tune-Up	$184	Average
Minor Tune-Up	$112	Worse Than Average
Brake Service	$268	Worse Than Average
Overall Warranty	3 yr/36k	Average
Drivetrain Warranty	3 yr/36k	Average
Rust Warranty	6 yr/100k	Better Than Average
Maintenance Warranty	N/A	
Roadside Assistance	3 yr/36k	

Resale Value

1993	1994	1995	1996	1997
$22,340	$20,925	$19,908	$18,932	$18,052

Ownership Costs (5yr)

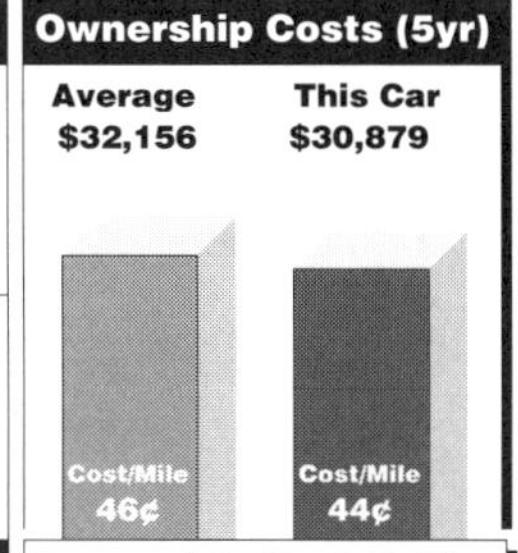

Average	This Car
$32,156	$30,879
Cost/Mile 46¢	Cost/Mile 44¢

The 1993 Suburban is available in four models - C (2WD) and K (4WD) 1500 and 2500 full-size sport utility wagons. New for 1993, the K1500 features two trim levels - Cheyenne (standard) and Silverado (uplevel). An anti-chip coating is applied on leading edges of the hood, roof, and "A" pillars to help prevent stone chips. Refinements include a larger radiator to reduce engine wear and minimize overheating, an air cleaner w/improved sealing and increased underhood and underbody corrosion protection.

Cumulative Costs

	1993	1994	1995	1996	1997
Annual	$5,977	$5,938	$6,645	$5,545	$6,774
Total	$5,977	$11,915	$18,560	$24,105	$30,879

Ownership Cost Rating

Excellent

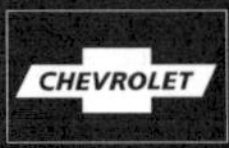

Chevrolet Suburban K2500
5 Door Sport Utility

5.7L 190 hp Gas Fuel Inject.

8 Cylinder "V"

Automatic 4 Speed

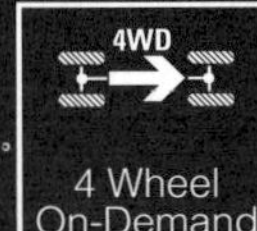
4 Wheel On-Demand

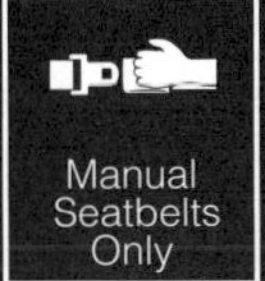
Manual Seatbelts Only

Utility

K1500 Model Shown

Purchase Price

Car Item	Dealer Cost	List
Base Price	**$19,670**	**$22,485**
Anti-Lock Brakes	Std	Std
Manual Transmission	N/A	N/A
7.4L 230 hp Gas	$520	** $605
Air Conditioning	$727	$845
Power Steering	Std	Std
Cruise Control	Pkg	Pkg
4 Whl On-Demand Dr.	Std	Std
AM/FM Stereo Cassette	$251	$292
Steering Wheel, Tilt	Pkg	Pkg
Power Windows	Pkg	Pkg
***Options Price**	$978	$1,137
***Total Price**	**$20,648**	**$23,622**
Target Price	$22,917	
Destination Charge	$640	
Avg. Tax & Fees	$1,421	
Total Target $	**$24,978**	
Average Dealer Option Cost:	***86%***	

Ownership Costs

Cost Area	5 Year Cost	Rate
Depreciation	$6,140	Excellent
Financing ($502/month)	$4,115	
Insurance (Rating 17)	$9,294	Average
State Fees	$971	
Fuel (Hwy 17 City 13 [Est.])	$5,760	Worse Than Average
Maintenance	$4,836	Worse Than Average
Repairs	$945	Worse Than Average

Ownership Cost By Year

$2,000 $4,000 $6,000 $8,000 $10,000

1993 1994 1995 1996 1997

Warranty/Maintenance Info

Item		Rate
Major Tune-Up	$184	Average
Minor Tune-Up	$112	Worse Than Average
Brake Service	$285	Poor
Overall Warranty	3 yr/36k	Average
Drivetrain Warranty	3 yr/36k	Average
Rust Warranty	6 yr/100k	Better Than Average
Maintenance Warranty	N/A	
Roadside Assistance	3 yr/36k	

Resale Value

1993	1994	1995	1996	1997
$23,018	$22,208	$21,422	$20,194	$18,838

Ownership Costs (5yr)

Average	This Car
$33,170	$32,061
Cost/Mile 47¢	Cost/Mile 46¢

The 1993 Suburban is available in four models - C (2WD) and K (4WD) 1500 and 2500 full-size sport utility wagons. New for 1993, the K2500 features two trim levels - Cheyenne (standard) and Silverado (uplevel). An anti-chip coating is applied on leading edges of the hood, roof, and "A" pillars to help prevent stone chips. Refinements include a larger radiator to reduce engine wear and minimize overheating, an air cleaner w/improved sealing and increased underhood and underbody corrosion protection.

Cumulative Costs

	1993	1994	1995	1996	1997
Annual	$6,750	$5,468	$6,580	$5,884	$7,379
Total	$6,750	$12,218	$18,798	$24,682	$32,061

Ownership Cost Rating

Better Than Average

* Includes shaded options

** Other purchase requirements apply

Poor  Worse Than Average  Average  Better Than Average  Excellent 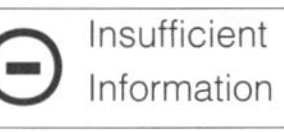 Insufficient Information

Refer to *Section 3: Annotated Vehicle Charts* for an explanation of these charts.

Chrysler Town & Country

3 Door Pass Ext Van

Mini Van

3.3L 150 hp Gas Fuel Inject.

6 Cylinder "V"

Automatic 4 Speed

2 Wheel Front

Driver Airbag Psngr Belts

Purchase Price

Car Item	Dealer Cost	List
Base Price	**$23,153**	**$25,538**
Anti-Lock Brakes	Std	Std
Manual Transmission	N/A	N/A
Optional Engine	N/A	N/A
Air Conditioning	Std	Std
Power Steering	Std	Std
Cruise Control	Std	Std
All Wheel Drive	N/A	N/A
AM/FM Stereo Cassette	Std	Std
Steering Wheel, Tilt	Std	Std
Power Windows	Std	Std
***Options Price**	$0	$0
***Total Price**	**$23,153**	**$25,538**
Target Price	$25,446	
Destination Charge	$540	
Avg. Tax & Fees	$1,560	
Total Target $	**$27,546**	
Average Dealer Option Cost:	***85%***	

Ownership Costs

Cost Area	5 Year Cost	Rate
Depreciation	$11,114	Average
Financing ($554/month)	$4,538	
Insurance (Rating 8)	$7,223	Excellent
State Fees	$1,044	
Fuel (Hwy 23 City 17)	$4,328	Better Than Average
Maintenance	$4,218	Average
Repairs	$731	Average

Ownership Cost By Year

$2,000 $4,000 $6,000 $8,000 $10,000 $12,000

1993 1994 1995 1996 1997

Warranty/Maintenance Info

Item		Rate
Major Tune-Up	$153	Better Than Average
Minor Tune-Up	$97	Better Than Average
Brake Service	$265	Worse Than Average
Overall Warranty	1 yr/12k	Poor
Drivetrain Warranty	7 yr/70k	Excellent
Rust Warranty	7 yr/100k	Excellent
Maintenance Warranty	N/A	
Roadside Assistance	N/A	

Resale Value

1993	1994	1995	1996	1997
$21,098	$19,431	$18,611	$17,562	$16,432

Ownership Costs (5yr)

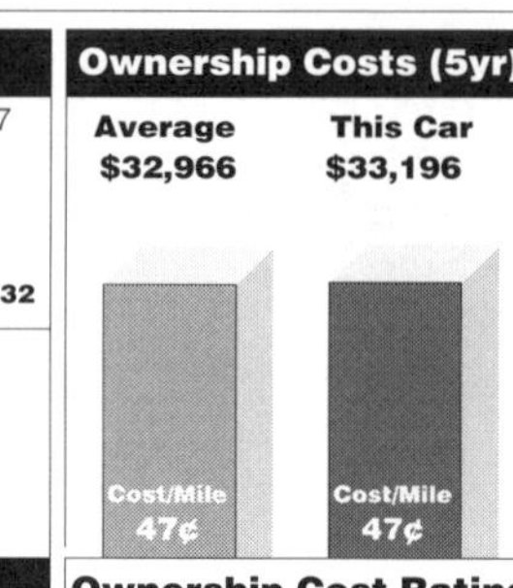

Cumulative Costs

	1993	1994	1995	1996	1997
Annual	$10,801	$5,930	$5,623	$4,837	$6,005
Total	$10,801	$16,731	$22,354	$27,191	$33,196

Ownership Cost Rating

Average

The 1993 Town & Country is available in two models-FWD and AWD. New for 1993, the FWD model features cloth and leather "Quad Command" seating with tilt feature. Standard features include a driver's-side air bag, air conditioning, power anti-lock brakes, electric rear window defroster and power window and door locks. The option list includes all leather 7-passenger bench seats and cast aluminum wheels. New colors for 1993 includes Wildberry (exterior) and Light and Dark Quartz (interior).

Chrysler Town & Country AWD

3 Door Pass Ext Van

Mini Van

3.3L 150 hp Gas Fuel Inject.

6 Cylinder "V"

Automatic 4 Speed

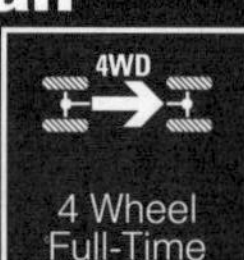
4 Wheel Full-Time

Driver Airbag Psngr Belts

Purchase Price

Car Item	Dealer Cost	List
Base Price	**$24,906**	**$27,529**
Anti-Lock Brakes	Std	Std
Manual Transmission	N/A	N/A
Optional Engine	N/A	N/A
Air Conditioning	Std	Std
Power Steering	Std	Std
Cruise Control	Std	Std
4 Wheel Full-Time Drive	Std	Std
AM/FM Stereo Cassette	Std	Std
Steering Wheel, Tilt	Std	Std
Power Windows	Std	Std
***Options Price**	$0	$0
***Total Price**	**$24,906**	**$27,529**
Target Price	$27,471	
Destination Charge	$540	
Avg. Tax & Fees	$1,682	
Total Target $	**$29,693**	
Average Dealer Option Cost:	***85%***	

Ownership Costs

Cost Area	5 Year Cost	Rate
Depreciation	$11,849	Average
Financing ($597/month)	$4,891	
Insurance (Rating 10)	$7,479	Excellent
State Fees	$1,123	
Fuel (Hwy 20 City 15)	$4,941	Poor
Maintenance	$4,290	Average
Repairs	$731	Average

Ownership Cost By Year

$2,000 $4,000 $6,000 $8,000 $10,000 $12,000

1993 1994 1995 1996 1997

Warranty/Maintenance Info

Item		Rate
Major Tune-Up	$153	Better Than Average
Minor Tune-Up	$97	Better Than Average
Brake Service	$296	Poor
Overall Warranty	1 yr/12k	Poor
Drivetrain Warranty	7 yr/70k	Excellent
Rust Warranty	7 yr/100k	Excellent
Maintenance Warranty	N/A	
Roadside Assistance	N/A	

Resale Value

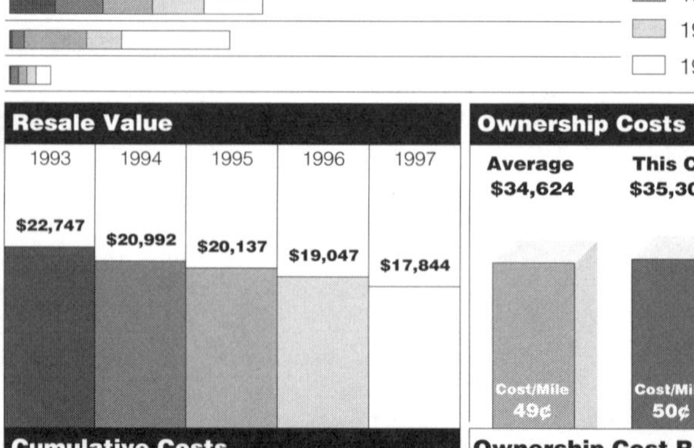

Ownership Costs (5yr)

Average $34,624

This Car $35,304

Cost/Mile 49¢

Cost/Mile 50¢

Cumulative Costs

	1993	1994	1995	1996	1997
Annual	$11,626	$6,314	$5,952	$5,100	$6,312
Total	$11,626	$17,940	$23,892	$28,992	$35,304

Ownership Cost Rating

Average

The 1993 Town & Country is available in two models-FWD and AWD. New for 1993, the AWD model features two new colors: Wildberry (exterior) and Light and Dark Quartz (interior). Other features for 1993 include "Quad Command" reclining bucket seats and air conditioning with non CFC refrigerant. Standard features include a driver's-side air bag, a full stainless steel exhaust system, 15-inch "Cathedral" aluminum wheels, power anti-lock brakes and electric rear window defroster.

* Includes shaded options

** Other purchase requirements apply

 Poor  Worse Than Average  Average Better Than Average Excellent Insufficient Information

Refer to *Section 3: Annotated Vehicle Charts* for an explanation of these charts.

Dodge Caravan
3 Door Pass Van

2.5L 100 hp Gas Fuel Inject.

4 Cylinder In-Line

Manual 5 Speed

2 Wheel Front

Driver Airbag Psngr Belts

Purchase Price

Car Item	Dealer Cost	List
Base Price	**$12,869**	**$14,073**
Anti-Lock Brakes	N/A	N/A
Automatic 3 Speed	$511	$601
3.0L 142 hp Gas	$590	** $694
Air Conditioning	$728	$857
Power Steering	Std	Std
Cruise Control	Pkg	Pkg
All Wheel Drive	N/A	N/A
AM/FM Stereo Cassette	$140	$165
Steering Wheel, Tilt	Pkg	Pkg
Power Windows	N/A	N/A
***Options Price**	$1,379	$1,623
***Total Price**	**$14,248**	**$15,696**
Target Price	$15,357	
Destination Charge	$540	
Avg. Tax & Fees	$957	
Total Target $	**$16,854**	
Average Dealer Option Cost:	***85%***	

Ownership Costs

Cost Area	5 Year Cost	Rate
Depreciation	$5,185	Excellent
Financing ($339/month)	$2,776	
Insurance (Rating 1 [Est.])	$6,191	Excellent
State Fees	$649	
Fuel (Hwy 26 City 20)	$3,756	Excellent
Maintenance	$3,869	Better Than Average
Repairs	$731	Average

Ownership Cost By Year

$2,000 $4,000 $6,000 $8,000

1993 1994 1995 1996 1997

Warranty/Maintenance Info

Item		Rate
Major Tune-Up	$126	Excellent
Minor Tune-Up	$66	Excellent
Brake Service	$252	Average
Overall Warranty	1 yr/12k	Poor
Drivetrain Warranty	7 yr/70k	Excellent
Rust Warranty	7 yr/100k	Excellent
Maintenance Warranty	N/A	
Roadside Assistance	N/A	

Resale Value

1993	1994	1995	1996	1997
$15,416	$14,498	$13,718	$12,770	$11,669

Ownership Costs (5yr)

Average	This Car
$24,767	$23,157
Cost/Mile 35¢	Cost/Mile 33¢

The 1993 Caravan is available in five models - (Base) Caravan, SE, SE AWD, LE, LE AWD passenger vans. For 1993, the Base Caravan has a higher-performance torque converter and modular clutch on the 2.5L I-4 engine, full stainless steel exhaust system, air conditioning with non-CFC refrigerant, quieter, higher capacity heater-air conditioner fan, and available sport suspension package. Also new are vertically-adjustable front shoulder belts and more comfortable rear shoulder belts.

Cumulative Costs

	1993	1994	1995	1996	1997
Annual	$4,656	$4,185	$4,673	$4,121	$5,522
Total	$4,656	$8,841	$13,514	$17,635	$23,157

Ownership Cost Rating

Excellent

Dodge Caravan SE
3 Door Pass Van

2.5L 100 hp Gas Fuel Inject.

4 Cylinder In-Line

Automatic 3 Speed

2 Wheel Front

Driver Airbag Psngr Belts

Mini Van

Purchase Price

Car Item	Dealer Cost	List
Base Price	**$14,654**	**$16,101**
Anti-Lock Brakes	$584	** $687
4 Spd Auto Electronic	$168	$198
3.3L 150 hp Gas	$677	$796
Air Conditioning	Pkg	Pkg
Power Steering	Std	Std
Cruise Control	Pkg	Pkg
All Wheel Drive	N/A	N/A
AM/FM Stereo Cassette	$140	$165
Steering Wheel, Tilt	Pkg	Pkg
Power Windows	Pkg	Pkg
***Options Price**	$817	$961
***Total Price**	**$15,471**	**$17,062**
Target Price	$16,739	
Destination Charge	$540	
Avg. Tax & Fees	$1,040	
Total Target $	**$18,319**	
Average Dealer Option Cost:	***85%***	

Ownership Costs

Cost Area	5 Year Cost	Rate
Depreciation	$6,142	Better Than Average
Financing ($368/month)	$3,017	
Insurance (Rating 2 [Est.])	$6,333	Excellent
State Fees	$704	
Fuel (Hwy 23 City 18)	$4,213	Better Than Average
Maintenance	$3,835	Better Than Average
Repairs	$731	Average

Ownership Cost By Year

$2,000 $4,000 $6,000 $8,000

1993 1994 1995 1996 1997

Warranty/Maintenance Info

Item		Rate
Major Tune-Up	$141	Excellent
Minor Tune-Up	$88	Excellent
Brake Service	$252	Average
Overall Warranty	1 yr/12k	Poor
Drivetrain Warranty	7 yr/70k	Excellent
Rust Warranty	7 yr/100k	Excellent
Maintenance Warranty	N/A	
Roadside Assistance	N/A	

Resale Value

1993	1994	1995	1996	1997
$16,218	$15,219	$14,354	$13,337	$12,177

Ownership Costs (5yr)

Average	This Car
$25,905	$24,975
Cost/Mile 37¢	Cost/Mile 36¢

The 1993 Caravan is available in five models - (Base) Caravan, SE, SE AWD, LE, LE AWD passenger vans. For 1993, the SE Caravan has a higher-performance torque converter and modular clutch on the 2.5L I-4 engine, full stainless steel exhaust system, air conditioning with non-CFC refrigerant, quieter, higher capacity heater-air conditioner fan, and available sport suspension package. Also new are vertically-adjustable front shoulder belts and more comfortable rear shoulder belts.

Cumulative Costs

	1993	1994	1995	1996	1997
Annual	$5,547	$4,496	$4,959	$4,371	$5,602
Total	$5,547	$10,043	$15,002	$19,373	$24,975

Ownership Cost Rating

Excellent

* Includes shaded options

** Other purchase requirements apply

 Poor 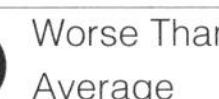 Worse Than Average  Average  Better Than Average  Excellent  Insufficient Information

Refer to *Section 3: Annotated Vehicle Charts* for an explanation of these charts.

Dodge Caravan LE

3 Door Pass Van

3.0L 142 hp Gas Fuel Inject.

6 Cylinder "V"

Automatic 3 Speed

2 Wheel Front

Driver Airbag Psngr Belts

Mini Van

Purchase Price

Car Item	Dealer Cost	List
Base Price	**$18,825**	**$20,841**
Anti-Lock Brakes	$509	** $599
4 Spd Auto Electronic	$168	$198
3.3L 150 hp Gas	$87	$102
Air Conditioning	Std	Std
Power Steering	Std	Std
Cruise Control	Std	Std
All Wheel Drive	N/A	N/A
AM/FM Stereo Cassette	$140	** $165
Steering Wheel, Tilt	Std	Std
Power Windows	Pkg	Pkg
***Options Price**	$87	$102
***Total Price**	**$18,912**	**$20,943**
Target Price	$20,645	
Destination Charge	$540	
Avg. Tax & Fees	$1,274	
Total Target $	**$22,459**	
Average Dealer Option Cost:	***85%***	

Ownership Costs

Cost Area	5 Year Cost	Rate
Depreciation	$8,920	Average
Financing ($451/month)	$3,700	
Insurance (Rating 5 [Est.])	$6,786	Excellent
State Fees	$859	
Fuel (Hwy 23 City 18)	$4,213	Better Than Average
Maintenance	$3,923	Better Than Average
Repairs	$731	Average

Ownership Cost By Year

$2,000 $4,000 $6,000 $8,000 $10,000

1993 1994 1995 1996 1997

Warranty/Maintenance Info

Major Tune-Up	$141	Excellent
Minor Tune-Up	$88	Excellent
Brake Service	$252	Average
Overall Warranty	1 yr/12k	Poor
Drivetrain Warranty	7 yr/70k	Excellent
Rust Warranty	7 yr/100k	Excellent
Maintenance Warranty	N/A	
Roadside Assistance	N/A	

Resale Value

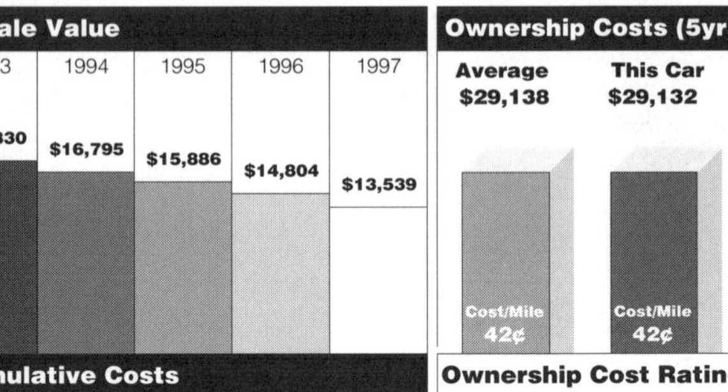

1993	1994	1995	1996	1997
$17,830	$16,795	$15,886	$14,804	$13,539

Ownership Costs (5yr)

Average	This Car
$29,138	$29,132
Cost/Mile 42¢	Cost/Mile 42¢

The 1993 Caravan is available in five models - (Base) Caravan, SE, SE AWD, LE, LE AWD passenger vans. For 1993, the LE Caravan is available in four new exterior colors (Wildberry, Light Driftwood, Sky Blue, and Flame Red) and has two new interior colors (Slate Blue and Crimson Red) with new fabrics. Other new features include a full stainless steel exhaust system, air conditioning with non-CFC refrigerant, and vertically adjustable front shoulder belts. Caravans are built in Windsor, Ontario, Canada.

Cumulative Costs

	1993	1994	1995	1996	1997
Annual	$8,482	$4,867	$5,302	$4,607	$5,874
Total	$8,482	$13,349	$18,651	$23,258	$29,132

Ownership Cost Rating

Average

Dodge Grand Caravan

3 Door Pass Ext Van

3.0L 142 hp Gas Fuel Inject.

6 Cylinder "V"

Automatic 3 Speed

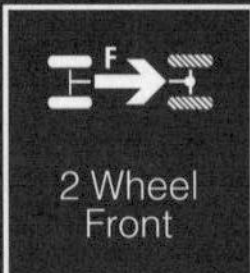
2 Wheel Front

Driver Airbag Psngr Belts

Mini Van

LE Model Shown

Purchase Price

Car Item	Dealer Cost	List
Base Price	**$15,958**	**$17,555**
Anti-Lock Brakes	N/A	N/A
Manual Transmission	N/A	N/A
Optional Engine	N/A	N/A
Air Conditioning	Pkg	** Pkg
Power Steering	Std	Std
Cruise Control	Pkg	Pkg
All Wheel Drive	N/A	N/A
AM/FM Stereo Cassette	$140	$165
Steering Wheel, Tilt	Pkg	Pkg
Power Windows	N/A	N/A
***Options Price**	$140	$165
***Total Price**	**$16,098**	**$17,720**
Target Price	$17,466	
Destination Charge	$540	
Avg. Tax & Fees	$1,083	
Total Target $	**$19,089**	
Average Dealer Option Cost:	***85%***	

Ownership Costs

Cost Area	5 Year Cost	Rate
Depreciation	$5,991	Better Than Average
Financing ($384/month)	$3,144	
Insurance (Rating 3 [Est.])	$6,520	Excellent
State Fees	$731	
Fuel (Hwy 24 City 19)	$4,015	Better Than Average
Maintenance	$4,179	Average
Repairs	$731	Average

Ownership Cost By Year

$2,000 $4,000 $6,000 $8,000

1993 1994 1995 1996 1997

Warranty/Maintenance Info

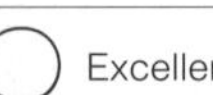

Major Tune-Up	$160	Better Than Average
Minor Tune-Up	$91	Excellent
Brake Service	$252	Average
Overall Warranty	1 yr/12k	Poor
Drivetrain Warranty	7 yr/70k	Excellent
Rust Warranty	7 yr/100k	Excellent
Maintenance Warranty	N/A	
Roadside Assistance	N/A	

Resale Value

1993	1994	1995	1996	1997
$16,304	$15,602	$14,978	$14,148	$13,098

Ownership Costs (5yr)

Average	This Car
$26,453	$25,311
Cost/Mile 38¢	Cost/Mile 36¢

The 1993 Grand Caravan is available in five models - (Base) Grand Caravan, SE, LE, SE AWD, LE AWD passenger vans. New for 1993, the Base Grand Caravan is available in four new exterior colors (Wildberry, Light Driftwood, Sky Blue, and Flame Red). New features include a full stainless steel exhaust system, air conditioning with non-CFC refrigerant, a quieter, higher capacity heater-air conditioner, vertically-adjustable front shoulder belt, and quad command seating with tilt feature.

Cumulative Costs

	1993	1994	1995	1996	1997
Annual	$6,289	$4,246	$4,808	$4,206	$5,762
Total	$6,289	$10,535	$15,343	$19,549	$25,311

Ownership Cost Rating

Excellent

* Includes shaded options

** Other purchase requirements apply

Poor

Worse Than Average

Average

Better Than Average

Excellent

Insufficient Information

Refer to *Section 3: Annotated Vehicle Charts* for an explanation of these charts.

Dodge Grand Caravan SE
3 Door Pass Ext Van

3.3L 150 hp Gas Fuel Inject.	6 Cylinder "V"	Automatic 4 Speed	2 Wheel Front	Driver Airbag Psngr Belts

Mini Van

Purchase Price

Car Item	Dealer Cost	List
Base Price	**$16,293**	**$17,935**
Anti-Lock Brakes	$509	** $599
Manual Transmission	N/A	N/A
Optional Engine	N/A	N/A
Air Conditioning	Pkg	Pkg
Power Steering	Std	Std
Cruise Control	Pkg	Pkg
All Wheel Drive	N/A	N/A
AM/FM Stereo Cassette	$140	$165
Steering Wheel, Tilt	Pkg	Pkg
Power Windows	Pkg	Pkg
***Options Price**	$140	$165
***Total Price**	**$16,433**	**$18,100**
Target Price	$17,842	
Destination Charge	$540	
Avg. Tax & Fees	$1,105	
Total Target $	**$19,487**	
Average Dealer Option Cost:	***85%***	

Ownership Costs

Cost Area	5 Year Cost	Rate
Depreciation	$5,664	
Financing ($392/month)	$3,209	
Insurance (Rating 3 [Est.])	$6,520	
State Fees	$745	
Fuel (Hwy 23 City 18)	$4,213	
Maintenance	$3,938	
Repairs	$731	

Ownership Cost By Year

$2,000 $4,000 $6,000 $8,000

1993 1994 1995 1996 1997

Warranty/Maintenance Info

Item		
Major Tune-Up	$141	
Minor Tune-Up	$88	
Brake Service	$252	
Overall Warranty	1 yr/12k	
Drivetrain Warranty	7 yr/70k	
Rust Warranty	7 yr/100k	
Maintenance Warranty	N/A	
Roadside Assistance	N/A	

Resale Value

1993	1994	1995	1996	1997
$17,720	$16,838	$16,015	$15,021	$13,823

Ownership Costs (5yr)

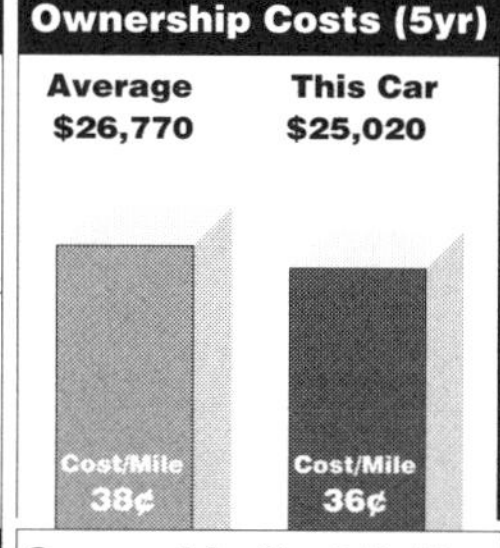

Cumulative Costs

	1993	1994	1995	1996	1997
Annual	$5,338	$4,485	$5,046	$4,415	$5,736
Total	$5,338	$9,823	$14,869	$19,284	$25,020

Ownership Cost Rating

Excellent

The 1993 Grand Caravan is available in five models - (Base) Grand Caravan, SE, LE, SE AWD, LE AWD passenger vans. New for 1993, the SE Grand Caravan is available in four new exterior colors (Wildberry, Light Driftwood, Sky Blue, and Flame Red). New features include a full stainless steel exhaust system, more comfortable rear shoulder belts, air conditioning w/non-CFC refrigerant, an optional sport suspension package, new interior fabrics, and an optional decor package.

Dodge Grand Caravan LE
3 Door Pass Ext Van

3.3L 150 hp Gas Fuel Inject.	6 Cylinder "V"	Automatic 4 Speed	2 Wheel Front	Driver Airbag Psngr Belts

Mini Van

Purchase Price

Car Item	Dealer Cost	List
Base Price	**$19,680**	**$21,784**
Anti-Lock Brakes	$509	$599
Manual Transmission	N/A	N/A
Optional Engine	N/A	N/A
Air Conditioning	Std	Std
Power Steering	Std	Std
Cruise Control	Std	Std
All Wheel Drive	N/A	N/A
AM/FM Stereo CD	$145	$170
Steering Wheel, Tilt	Std	Std
Power Windows	Pkg	Pkg
***Options Price**	$145	$170
***Total Price**	**$19,825**	**$21,954**
Target Price	$21,681	
Destination Charge	$540	
Avg. Tax & Fees	$1,336	
Total Target $	**$23,557**	
Average Dealer Option Cost:	***85%***	

Ownership Costs

Cost Area	5 Year Cost	Rate
Depreciation	$8,538	
Financing ($473/month)	$3,880	
Insurance (Rating 5 [Est.])	$6,786	
State Fees	$899	
Fuel (Hwy 23 City 18)	$4,213	
Maintenance	$3,865	
Repairs	$731	

Ownership Cost By Year

$2,000 $4,000 $6,000 $8,000 $10,000

1993 1994 1995 1996 1997

Warranty/Maintenance Info

Item		
Major Tune-Up	$141	
Minor Tune-Up	$88	
Brake Service	$252	
Overall Warranty	1 yr/12k	
Drivetrain Warranty	7 yr/70k	
Rust Warranty	7 yr/100k	
Maintenance Warranty	N/A	
Roadside Assistance	N/A	

Resale Value

1993	1994	1995	1996	1997
$19,356	$18,391	$17,484	$16,380	$15,019

Ownership Costs (5yr)

Average	This Car
$29,980	$28,912
Cost/Mile 43¢	Cost/Mile 41¢

Cumulative Costs

	1993	1994	1995	1996	1997
Annual	$8,139	$4,863	$5,312	$4,656	$5,942
Total	$8,139	$13,002	$18,314	$22,970	$28,912

Ownership Cost Rating

Excellent

The 1993 Grand Caravan is available in five models - (Base) Grand Caravan, SE, LE, SE AWD, LE AWD passenger vans. New for 1993, the LE Grand Caravan is available in four new exterior colors (Wildberry, Light Driftwood, Sky Blue, and Flame Red). New features include a stainless steel exhaust system, air conditioning with non-CFC refrigerant, a quieter, higher capacity heater-air conditioner, vertically-adjustable front shoulder belts, new interior colors and fabrics, and an optional suspension package.

* Includes shaded options

** Other purchase requirements apply

 Poor — Worse Than Average — Average — 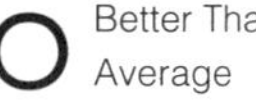 Better Than Average —  Excellent — Insufficient Information

Refer to ***Section 3: Annotated Vehicle Charts*** for an explanation of these charts.

Dodge Caravan Cargo Van

3 Door Cargo Van

2.5L 100 hp Gas Fuel Inject.	4 Cylinder In-Line	Manual 5 Speed	2 Wheel Front	Driver Airbag Psngr Belts

Mini Van

Purchase Price

Car Item	Dealer Cost	List
Base Price	**$12,353**	**$13,566**
Anti-Lock Brakes	N/A	N/A
Automatic 3 Speed	$511	$601
3.0L 142 hp Gas	$590	** $694
Air Conditioning	$728	** $857
Power Steering	Std	Std
Cruise Control	Pkg	Pkg
All Wheel Drive	N/A	N/A
AM/FM Stereo Cassette	$183	$215
Steering Wheel, Tilt	$126	$148
Power Windows	Pkg	Pkg
***Options Price**	$694	$816
***Total Price**	**$13,047**	**$14,382**
Target Price	$14,221	
Destination Charge	$540	
Avg. Tax & Fees	$887	
Total Target $	**$15,648**	
Average Dealer Option Cost:	***85%***	

Ownership Costs

Cost Area	5 Year Cost	Rate
Depreciation		Insufficient Information
Financing ($314/month)	$2,578	
Insurance (Rating 1 [Est.])	$6,191	Excellent
State Fees	$596	
Fuel (Hwy 26 City 20)	$3,756	Excellent
Maintenance	$3,869	Better Than Average
Repairs	$771	Average

Ownership Cost By Year

$2,000 $4,000 $6,000 $8,000

Insufficient Depreciation Information

1993 1994 1995 1996 1997

Warranty/Maintenance Info

Major Tune-Up	$126	Excellent
Minor Tune-Up	$66	Excellent
Brake Service	$252	Average
Overall Warranty	1 yr/12k	Poor
Drivetrain Warranty	7 yr/70k	Excellent
Rust Warranty	7 yr/100k	Excellent
Maintenance Warranty	N/A	
Roadside Assistance	N/A	

Resale Value

Insufficient

Information

Ownership Costs (5yr)

Insufficient

Information

The 1993 Caravan Cargo Van is available in two models, (Base) Caravan C/V and Extended C/V. New for 1993, the Base C/V offers a higher performance torque converter with the 2.5 liter engine, a full stainless steel exhaust system, vertically-adjustable shoulder belt, and an added commercial-use option package. Three new exterior colors have been added, Wildberry, Flame Red, and Sky Blue. The C/V has the highest optional payload rating and the lowest overall vehicle height of any vehicle in its class.

Cumulative Costs

	1993	1994	1995	1996	1997
Annual	*Insufficient Information*				
Total	*Insufficient Information*				

Ownership Cost Rating

Insufficient Information

Dodge Caravan Cargo Van Extended

3 Door Cargo Ext Van

3.3L 150 hp Gas Fuel Inject.	6 Cylinder "V"	Automatic 4 Speed	2 Wheel Front	Driver Airbag Psngr Belts

Mini Van

Base Model Shown

Purchase Price

Car Item	Dealer Cost	List
Base Price	**$14,513**	**$16,020**
Anti-Lock Brakes	$509	$599
Manual Transmission	N/A	N/A
Optional Engine	N/A	N/A
Air Conditioning	$728	** $857
Power Steering	Std	Std
Cruise Control	Pkg	Pkg
All Wheel Drive	N/A	N/A
AM/FM Stereo Cassette	$183	$215
Steering Wheel, Tilt	$126	$148
Power Windows	Pkg	Pkg
***Options Price**	$183	$215
***Total Price**	**$14,696**	**$16,235**
Target Price	$16,104	
Destination Charge	$540	
Avg. Tax & Fees	$1,000	
Total Target $	**$17,644**	
Average Dealer Option Cost:	***85%***	

Ownership Costs

Cost Area	5 Year Cost	Rate
Depreciation		Insufficient Information
Financing ($355/month)	$2,906	
Insurance (Rating 1 [Est.])	$6,191	Excellent
State Fees	$671	
Fuel (Hwy 23 City 18)	$4,213	Better Than Average
Maintenance	$3,695	Better Than Average
Repairs	$771	Average

Ownership Cost By Year

$2,000 $4,000 $6,000 $8,000

Insufficient Depreciation Information

1993 1994 1995 1996 1997

Warranty/Maintenance Info

Major Tune-Up	$141	Excellent
Minor Tune-Up	$88	Excellent
Brake Service	$252	Average
Overall Warranty	1 yr/12k	Poor
Drivetrain Warranty	7 yr/70k	Excellent
Rust Warranty	7 yr/100k	Excellent
Maintenance Warranty	N/A	
Roadside Assistance	N/A	

Resale Value

Insufficient

Information

Ownership Costs (5yr)

Insufficient

Information

The 1993 Caravan Cargo Van is available in two models, (Base) Caravan C/V and Extended C/V. New for 1993, the Extended C/V offers a higher performance torque converter with the 2.5 liter engine, a full stainless steel exhaust system, vertically-adjustable shoulder belt, and an added commercial-use option package. Three new exterior colors have been added, Wildberry, Flame Red, and Sky Blue. The C/V has the highest optional payload rating and the lowest overall vehicle height of any vehicle in its class.

Cumulative Costs

	1993	1994	1995	1996	1997
Annual	*Insufficient Information*				
Total	*Insufficient Information*				

Ownership Cost Rating

Insufficient Information

* Includes shaded options

** Other purchase requirements apply

Poor | Worse Than Average | Average | Better Than Average | Excellent | Insufficient Information

Refer to *Section 3: Annotated Vehicle Charts* for an explanation of these charts.

Dodge Caravan SE AWD
3 Door Pass Van

3.3L 150 hp Gas Fuel Inject. | 6 Cylinder "V" | Automatic 4 Speed | 4 Wheel Full-Time | Driver Airbag Psngr Belts

Purchase Price

Car Item	Dealer Cost	List
Base Price	**$17,481**	**$19,285**
Anti-Lock Brakes	$509	** $599
Manual Transmission	N/A	N/A
Optional Engine	N/A	N/A
Air Conditioning	Pkg	Pkg
Power Steering	Std	Std
Cruise Control	Pkg	Pkg
4 Wheel Full-Time Drive	Std	Std
AM/FM Stereo Cassette	$140	$165
Steering Wheel, Tilt	Pkg	Pkg
Power Windows	Pkg	Pkg
***Options Price**	$140	$165
***Total Price**	**$17,621**	**$19,450**
Target Price	$19,181	
Destination Charge	$540	
Avg. Tax & Fees	$1,186	
Total Target $	**$20,907**	
Average Dealer Option Cost:	***85%***	

Ownership Costs

Cost Area	5 Year Cost	Rate
Depreciation	$7,166	Excellent
Financing ($420/month)	$3,444	
Insurance (Rating 4 [Est.])	$6,658	Excellent
State Fees	$800	
Fuel (Hwy 22 City 17)	$4,431	Average
Maintenance	$4,098	Average
Repairs	$731	Average

Ownership Cost By Year

Warranty/Maintenance Info

Major Tune-Up	$141	Excellent
Minor Tune-Up	$88	Excellent
Brake Service	$282	Worse Than Average
Overall Warranty	1 yr/12k	Poor
Drivetrain Warranty	7 yr/70k	Excellent
Rust Warranty	7 yr/100k	Excellent
Maintenance Warranty	N/A	
Roadside Assistance	N/A	

Resale Value

1993	1994	1995	1996	1997
$18,227	$17,132	$16,168	$15,032	$13,741

Ownership Costs (5yr)

Average	This Car
$27,894	$27,328
Cost/Mile 40¢	Cost/Mile 39¢

Cumulative Costs

	1993	1994	1995	1996	1997
Annual	$6,428	$4,851	$5,350	$4,749	$5,950
Total	$6,428	$11,279	$16,629	$21,378	$27,328

Ownership Cost Rating

Excellent

The 1993 Caravan is available in five models - (Base) Caravan, SE, SE AWD, LE, LE AWD passenger vans. For 1993, the SE AWD Caravan has a higher-performance torque converter and modular clutch on the 2.5L I-4 engine, full stainless steel exhaust system, air conditioning with non-CFC refrigerant, quieter, higher capacity heater-air conditioner fan, and available sport suspension package. Also new is an optional decor package featuring aluminum wheels and the gold package adopts blk/gld nerf inserts.

Dodge Caravan LE AWD
3 Door Pass Van

3.3L 150 hp Gas Fuel Inject. | 6 Cylinder "V" | Automatic 4 Speed | 4 Wheel Full-Time | Driver Airbag Psngr Belts

Mini Van

Purchase Price

Car Item	Dealer Cost	List
Base Price	**$20,963**	**$23,242**
Anti-Lock Brakes	$509	$599
Manual Transmission	N/A	N/A
Optional Engine	N/A	N/A
Air Conditioning	Std	Std
Power Steering	Std	Std
Cruise Control	Std	Std
4 Wheel Full-Time Drive	Std	Std
AM/FM Stereo Cassette	$140	** $165
Steering Wheel, Tilt	Std	Std
Power Windows	Pkg	Pkg
***Options Price**	$0	$0
***Total Price**	**$20,963**	**$23,242**
Target Price	$22,988	
Destination Charge	$540	
Avg. Tax & Fees	$1,414	
Total Target $	**$24,942**	
Average Dealer Option Cost:	***86%***	

Ownership Costs

Cost Area	5 Year Cost	Rate
Depreciation	$9,454	Average
Financing ($501/month)	$4,108	
Insurance (Rating 6 [Est.])	$6,919	Excellent
State Fees	$951	
Fuel (Hwy 22 City 17)	$4,431	Average
Maintenance	$4,098	Average
Repairs	$731	Average

Ownership Cost By Year

Warranty/Maintenance Info

Major Tune-Up	$141	Excellent
Minor Tune-Up	$88	Excellent
Brake Service	$282	Worse Than Average
Overall Warranty	1 yr/12k	Poor
Drivetrain Warranty	7 yr/70k	Excellent
Rust Warranty	7 yr/100k	Excellent
Maintenance Warranty	N/A	
Roadside Assistance	N/A	

Resale Value

1993	1994	1995	1996	1997
$19,975	$18,916	$17,980	$16,845	$15,488

Ownership Costs (5yr)

Average	This Car
$31,053	$30,692
Cost/Mile 44¢	Cost/Mile 44¢

Cumulative Costs

	1993	1994	1995	1996	1997
Annual	$9,077	$5,108	$5,536	$4,876	$6,095
Total	$9,077	$14,185	$19,721	$24,597	$30,692

Ownership Cost Rating

Better Than Average

The 1993 Caravan is available in five models - (Base) Caravan, SE, SE AWD, LE, LE AWD passenger vans. For 1993, the LE AWD Caravan is available in four new exterior colors (Wildberry, Light Driftwood, Sky Blue, and Flame Red) and has two new interior colors (Slate Blue and Crimson Red) with new fabrics. Other new features include a full stainless steel exhaust system, air conditioning with non-CFC refrigerant, and an optional decor package featuring five-spoke (15-inch) aluminum wheels.

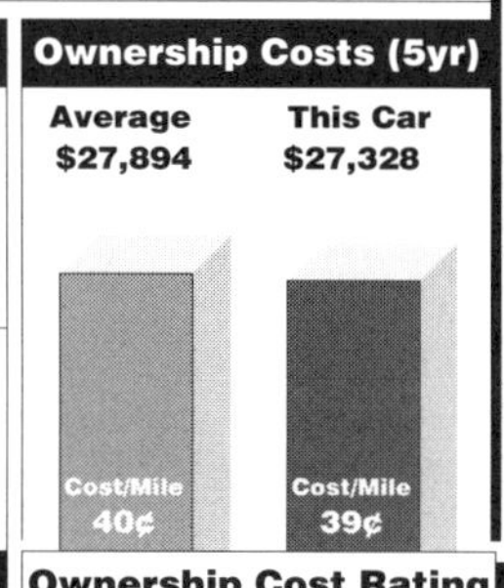

* Includes shaded options

** Other purchase requirements apply

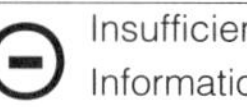

Poor | Worse Than Average | Average | Better Than Average | Excellent | Insufficient Information

Refer to *Section 3: Annotated Vehicle Charts* for an explanation of these charts.

Dodge Grand Caravan SE AWD
3 Door Pass Ext Van

Mini Van

3.3L 150 hp Gas Fuel Inject.

6 Cylinder "V"

Automatic 4 Speed

4 Wheel Full-Time

Driver Airbag Psngr Belts

Base Model Shown

Purchase Price

Car Item	Dealer Cost	List
Base Price	**$18,141**	**$20,035**
Anti-Lock Brakes	$509	** $599
Manual Transmission	N/A	N/A
Optional Engine	N/A	N/A
Air Conditioning	Pkg	Pkg
Power Steering	Std	Std
Cruise Control	Pkg	Pkg
4 Wheel Full-Time Drive	Std	Std
AM/FM Stereo Cassette	$140	$165
Steering Wheel, Tilt	Pkg	Pkg
Power Windows	Pkg	Pkg
***Options Price**	$140	$165
***Total Price**	**$18,281**	**$20,200**
Target Price	$19,927	
Destination Charge	$540	
Avg. Tax & Fees	$1,230	
Total Target $	**$21,697**	
Average Dealer Option Cost:	***85%***	

Ownership Costs

Cost Area	5 Year Cost	Rate
Depreciation	$5,648	Excellent
Financing ($436/month)	$3,575	
Insurance (Rating 5 [Est.])	$6,786	Excellent
State Fees	$829	
Fuel (Hwy 22 City 17)	$4,431	Average
Maintenance	$4,092	Average
Repairs	$731	Average

Ownership Cost By Year

$2,000 $4,000 $6,000 $8,000

1993 1994 1995 1996 1997

Warranty/Maintenance Info

Major Tune-Up	$141	Excellent
Minor Tune-Up	$88	Excellent
Brake Service	$282	Worse Than Average
Overall Warranty	1 yr/12k	Poor
Drivetrain Warranty	7 yr/70k	Excellent
Rust Warranty	7 yr/100k	Excellent
Maintenance Warranty	N/A	
Roadside Assistance	N/A	

Resale Value

1993	1994	1995	1996	1997
$20,084	$19,182	$18,347	$17,340	$16,049

Ownership Costs (5yr)

Average	This Car
$28,519	$26,092

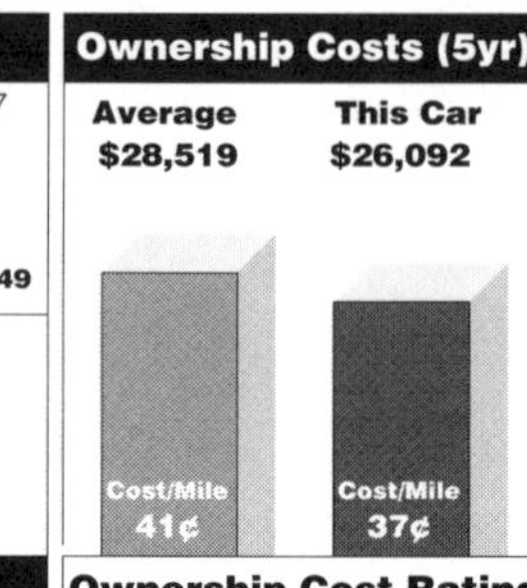

Cumulative Costs

	1993	1994	1995	1996	1997
Annual	$5,446	$4,731	$5,278	$4,656	$5,981
Total	$5,446	$10,177	$15,455	$20,111	$26,092

Ownership Cost Rating

Excellent

The 1993 Grand Caravan is available in five models - (Base) Grand Caravan, SE, LE, SE AWD, LE AWD passenger vans. New for 1993, the SE AWD Grand Caravan is available in four new exterior colors (Wildberry, Light Driftwood, Sky Blue, and Flame Red). New features include a full stainless steel exhaust system, air conditioning w/non-CFC refrigerant, quad command seating, an optional sport suspension package, and a quieter, higher capacity heater-air conditioner fan. A new decor package is also offered.

Dodge Grand Caravan LE AWD
3 Door Pass Ext Van

Mini Van

3.3L 150 hp Gas Fuel Inject.

6 Cylinder "V"

Automatic 4 Speed

4 Wheel Full-Time

Driver Airbag Psngr Belts

Base Model Shown

Purchase Price

Car Item	Dealer Cost	List
Base Price	**$21,528**	**$23,884**
Anti-Lock Brakes	$509	$599
Manual Transmission	N/A	N/A
Optional Engine	N/A	N/A
Air Conditioning	Std	Std
Power Steering	Std	Std
Cruise Control	Std	Std
4 Wheel Full-Time Drive	Std	Std
AM/FM Stereo Cassette	$140	** $165
Steering Wheel, Tilt	Std	Std
Power Windows	Pkg	Pkg
***Options Price**	$0	$0
***Total Price**	**$21,528**	**$23,884**
Target Price	$23,636	
Destination Charge	$540	
Avg. Tax & Fees	$1,453	
Total Target $	**$25,629**	
Average Dealer Option Cost:	***85%***	

Ownership Costs

Cost Area	5 Year Cost	Rate
Depreciation	$8,496	Better Than Average
Financing ($515/month)	$4,223	
Insurance (Rating 6 [Est.])	$6,919	Excellent
State Fees	$977	
Fuel (Hwy 22 City 17)	$4,431	Average
Maintenance	$4,092	Average
Repairs	$731	Average

Ownership Cost By Year

$2,000 $4,000 $6,000 $8,000 $10,000

1993 1994 1995 1996 1997

Warranty/Maintenance Info

Major Tune-Up	$141	Excellent
Minor Tune-Up	$88	Excellent
Brake Service	$282	Worse Than Average
Overall Warranty	1 yr/12k	Poor
Drivetrain Warranty	7 yr/70k	Excellent
Rust Warranty	7 yr/100k	Excellent
Maintenance Warranty	N/A	
Roadside Assistance	N/A	

Resale Value

1993	1994	1995	1996	1997
$21,582	$20,597	$19,660	$18,546	$17,133

Ownership Costs (5yr)

Average	This Car
$31,588	$29,869

Cost/Mile 45¢ — Cost/Mile 43¢

Cumulative Costs

	1993	1994	1995	1996	1997
Annual	$8,211	$5,076	$5,564	$4,864	$6,154
Total	$8,211	$13,287	$18,851	$23,715	$29,869

Ownership Cost Rating

Excellent

The 1993 Grand Caravan is available in five models - (Base) Grand Caravan, SE, LE, SE AWD, LE AWD passenger vans. New for 1993, the LE AWD Grand Caravan is available in four new exterior colors (Wildberry, Light Driftwood, Sky Blue, and Flame Red). New features include a full stainless steel exhaust system, more comfortable rear shoulder belts, air conditioning w/non-CFC refrigerant, an optional sport suspension package, new interior fabrics, and an optional decor package.

* Includes shaded options
** Other purchase requirements apply

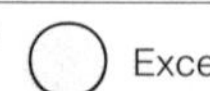

 Poor  Worse Than Average  Average 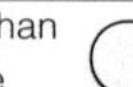 Better Than Average Excellent 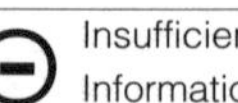 Insufficient Information

Refer to *Section 3: Annotated Vehicle Charts* for an explanation of these charts.

Dodge Dakota S
2 Door Regular Cab

2.5L 99 hp Gas Fuel Inject.

4 Cylinder In-Line

Manual 5 Speed

2 Wheel Rear

Manual Seatbelts Only

Small Pickup
Base Model Shown

Purchase Price

Car Item	Dealer Cost	List
Base Price	**$8,777**	**$9,154**
Anti-Lock Brakes	Std	Std
Automatic Transmission	N/A	N/A
Optional Engine	N/A	N/A
Air Conditioning	$677	** $797
Power Steering	$239	$281
Cruise Control	N/A	N/A
All Wheel Drive	N/A	N/A
AM/FM Stereo Cassette	N/A	N/A
Steering Wheel, Tilt	N/A	N/A
Power Windows	N/A	N/A
***Options Price**	$239	$281
***Total Price**	**$9,016**	**$9,435**
Target Price	$9,393	
Destination Charge	$470	
Avg. Tax & Fees	$592	
Total Target $	**$10,455**	
Average Dealer Option Cost:	***85%***	

Ownership Costs

Cost Area	5 Year Cost	Rate
Depreciation	$5,353	Average
Financing ($210/month)	$1,721	
Insurance (Rating 2 [Est.])	$6,542	Better Than Average
State Fees	$395	
Fuel (Hwy 27 City 22)	$3,525	Excellent
Maintenance	$3,281	Better Than Average
Repairs	$779	Average

Ownership Cost By Year

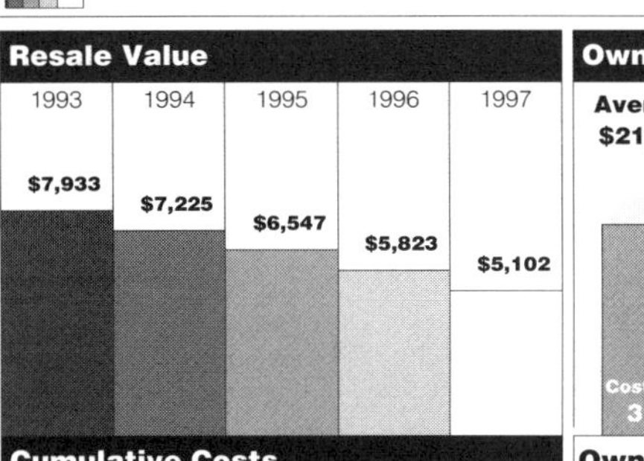

Warranty/Maintenance Info

Major Tune-Up	$124	Excellent
Minor Tune-Up	$62	Excellent
Brake Service	$285	Poor
Overall Warranty	1 yr/12k	Poor
Drivetrain Warranty	7 yr/70k	Excellent
Rust Warranty	7 yr/100k	Excellent
Maintenance Warranty	N/A	
Roadside Assistance	N/A	

Resale Value

1993	1994	1995	1996	1997
$7,933	$7,225	$6,547	$5,823	$5,102

Ownership Costs (5yr)

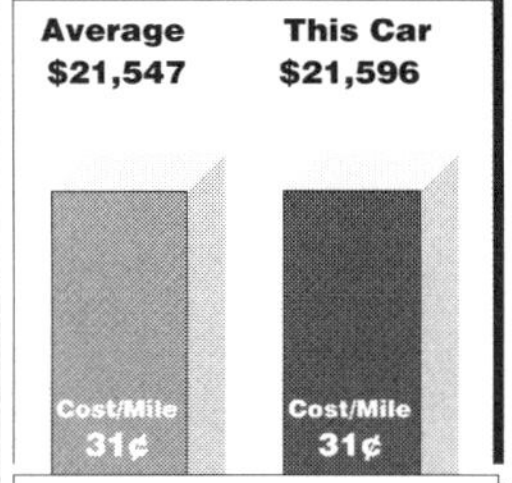

Average	This Car
$21,547	$21,596
Cost/Mile 31¢	Cost/Mile 31¢

The 1993 Dodge Dakota is available in five models - (Base) Dakota, S, Sport, (Base) Dakota 4WD, and Sport 4WD. New 1993 standard equipment includes stainless steel exhaust system, and two more exterior colors. New options include four-wheel anti-lock brakes, and AM/FM/cassette radio. Other options on the S model include air conditioning, sliding rear window, power steering, Trailer Towing Package, and six two tone color combinations. The Dodge Dakota is also available in an extended cab version.

Cumulative Costs

	1993	1994	1995	1996	1997
Annual	$5,262	$3,612	$4,312	$3,652	$4,758
Total	$5,262	$8,874	$13,186	$16,838	$21,596

Ownership Cost Rating

Average

Dodge Dakota Sport
2 Door Regular Cab

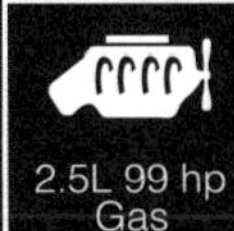
2.5L 99 hp Gas Fuel Inject.

4 Cylinder In-Line

Manual 5 Speed

2 Wheel Rear

Manual Seatbelts Only

Small Pickup

Purchase Price

Car Item	Dealer Cost	List
Base Price	**$9,304**	**$9,943**
Anti-Lock Brakes	Std	Std
Automatic 4 Speed	$754	$887
3.9L 180 hp Gas	$451	$531
Air Conditioning	$677	$797
Power Steering	Std	Std
Cruise Control	Pkg	Pkg
All Wheel Drive	N/A	N/A
AM/FM Stereo Cassette	Std	Std
Steering Wheel, Tilt	$114	$134
Power Windows	Pkg	Pkg
***Options Price**	$451	$531
***Total Price**	**$9,755**	**$10,474**
Target Price	$10,286	
Destination Charge	$470	
Avg. Tax & Fees	$647	
Total Target $	**$11,403**	
Average Dealer Option Cost:	***85%***	

Ownership Costs

Cost Area	5 Year Cost	Rate
Depreciation	$5,917	Worse Than Average
Financing ($229/month)	$1,877	
Insurance (Rating 3 [Est.])	$6,731	Better Than Average
State Fees	$438	
Fuel (Hwy 22 City 16)	$4,559	Worse Than Average
Maintenance	$3,366	Better Than Average
Repairs	$779	Average

Ownership Cost By Year

$2,000 $4,000 $6,000 $8,000

1993 1994 1995 1996 1997

Warranty/Maintenance Info

Major Tune-Up	$131	Excellent
Minor Tune-Up	$77	Better Than Average
Brake Service	$285	Poor
Overall Warranty	1 yr/12k	Poor
Drivetrain Warranty	7 yr/70k	Excellent
Rust Warranty	7 yr/100k	Excellent
Maintenance Warranty	N/A	
Roadside Assistance	N/A	

Resale Value

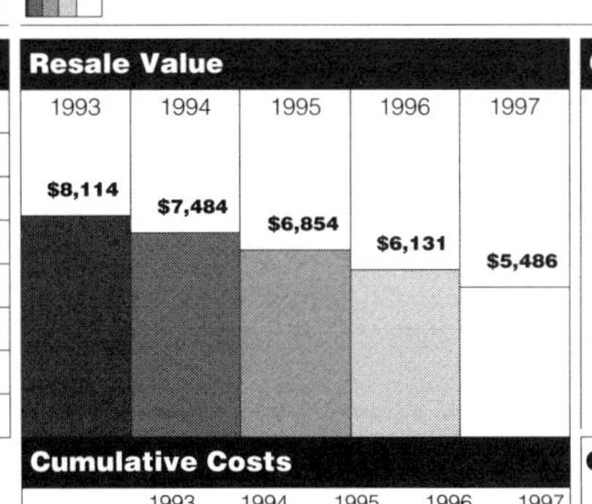

1993	1994	1995	1996	1997
$8,114	$7,484	$6,854	$6,131	$5,486

Ownership Costs (5yr)

Average	This Car
$22,603	$23,667
Cost/Mile 32¢	Cost/Mile 34¢

The 1993 Dodge Dakota is available in five models - (Base) Dakota, S, Sport, (Base) 4WD, and Sport 4WD. New standard equipment includes stainless steel exhaust system, and two additional exterior colors. New options include four-wheel anti-lock brakes. The Sport upgrades the Base model by including in the list of options an AM/FM/ cassette equalizer radio, Bright Package and Off-Road packages, power door locks and windows, and cruise control. The Dodge Dakota is also available in an extended cab version.

Cumulative Costs

	1993	1994	1995	1996	1997
Annual	$6,333	$3,848	$4,632	$3,948	$4,906
Total	$6,333	$10,181	$14,813	$18,761	$23,667

Ownership Cost Rating

Worse Than Average

* Includes shaded options

** Other purchase requirements apply

 Poor  Worse Than Average  Average  Better Than Average  Excellent 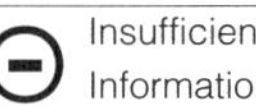 Insufficient Information

Refer to *Section 3: Annotated Vehicle Charts* for an explanation of these charts.

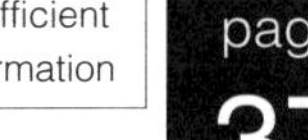

Dodge Dakota
2 Door Regular Cab

2.5L 99 hp Gas Fuel Inject.	4 Cylinder In-Line	Manual 5 Speed	2 Wheel Rear	Manual Seatbelts Only

Purchase Price

Car Item	Dealer Cost	List
Base Price	**$10,364**	**$11,674**
Anti-Lock Brakes	Std	Std
Automatic 4 Speed	$754	$887
3.9L 180 hp Gas	$451	$531
Air Conditioning	$677	** $797
Power Steering	$239	$281
Cruise Control	Pkg	Pkg
All Wheel Drive	N/A	N/A
AM/FM Stereo Cassette	$174	$205
Steering Wheel, Tilt	$173	$204
8 Foot Bed	$161	$183
***Options Price**	$864	$1,017
***Total Price**	**$11,228**	**$12,691**
Target Price	$11,861	
Destination Charge	$470	
Avg. Tax & Fees	$749	
Total Target $	**$13,080**	
Average Dealer Option Cost:	***85%***	

Ownership Costs

Cost Area	5 Year Cost	Rate
Depreciation	$6,687	Poor
Financing ($263/month)	$2,154	
Insurance (Rating 5 [Est.])	$6,996	Better Than Average
State Fees	$526	
Fuel (Hwy 22 City 16)	$4,559	Worse Than Average
Maintenance	$3,221	Better Than Average
Repairs	$779	Average

Ownership Cost By Year

Scale: $2,000 · $4,000 · $6,000 · $8,000 — Legend: 1993, 1994, 1995, 1996, 1997

Warranty/Maintenance Info

Major Tune-Up	$131	Excellent
Minor Tune-Up	$77	Better Than Average
Brake Service	$285	Poor
Overall Warranty	1 yr/12k	Poor
Drivetrain Warranty	7 yr/70k	Excellent
Rust Warranty	7 yr/100k	Excellent
Maintenance Warranty	N/A	
Roadside Assistance	N/A	

Resale Value

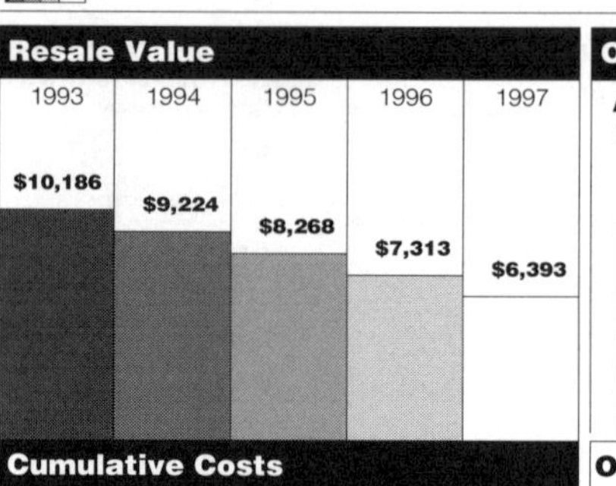

1993	1994	1995	1996	1997
$10,186	$9,224	$8,268	$7,313	$6,393

Ownership Costs (5yr)

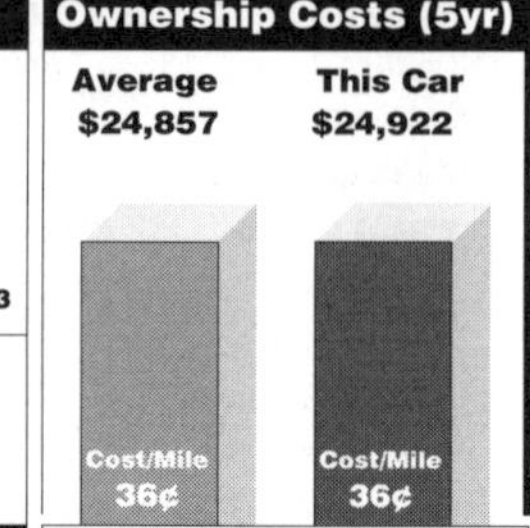

Average	This Car
$24,857	$24,922
Cost/Mile 36¢	Cost/Mile 36¢

The 1993 Dodge Dakota is available in five models - (Base) Dakota, S, Sport, (Base) Dakota 4WD, and Sport 4WD. New 1993 standard equipment includes stainless steel exhaust system, and two additional exterior colors. New options include four-wheel anti-lock brakes, and AM/FM cassette radio. The Base upgrades the S model by including in the list of options a heavy duty suspension, Light and Snow packages, tilt steering column, and 4WD. The Dodge Dakota is also available in an extended cab version.

Cumulative Costs

	1993	1994	1995	1996	1997
Annual	$6,125	$4,337	$5,013	$4,271	$5,176
Total	$6,125	$10,462	$15,475	$19,746	$24,922

Ownership Cost Rating

Average

Dodge Dakota Club Cab
2 Door Extended Cab

2.5L 99 hp Gas Fuel Inject.	4 Cylinder In-Line	Manual 5 Speed	2 Wheel Rear	Manual Seatbelts Only

Small Pickup

4WD Model Shown

Purchase Price

Car Item	Dealer Cost	List
Base Price	**$11,466**	**$12,626**
Anti-Lock Brakes	Std	Std
Automatic 4 Speed	$754	** $887
5.2L 230 hp Gas	$950	** $1,118
Air Conditioning	$677	** $797
Power Steering	$239	$281
Cruise Control	Pkg	Pkg
All Wheel Drive	N/A	N/A
AM/FM Stereo Cassette	$174	$205
Steering Wheel, Tilt	$173	$204
Power Windows	Pkg	Pkg
***Options Price**	$413	$486
***Total Price**	**$11,879**	**$13,112**
Target Price	$12,572	
Destination Charge	$470	
Avg. Tax & Fees	$788	
Total Target $	**$13,830**	
Average Dealer Option Cost:	***85%***	

Ownership Costs

Cost Area	5 Year Cost	Rate
Depreciation	$6,016	Average
Financing ($278/month)	$2,278	
Insurance (Rating 4 [Est.])	$6,867	Better Than Average
State Fees	$543	
Fuel (Hwy 27 City 22)	$3,525	Excellent
Maintenance	$3,281	Better Than Average
Repairs	$779	Average

Ownership Cost By Year

Scale: $2,000 · $4,000 · $6,000 · $8,000 — Legend: 1993, 1994, 1995, 1996, 1997

Warranty/Maintenance Info

Major Tune-Up	$124	Excellent
Minor Tune-Up	$62	Excellent
Brake Service	$285	Poor
Overall Warranty	1 yr/12k	Poor
Drivetrain Warranty	7 yr/70k	Excellent
Rust Warranty	7 yr/100k	Excellent
Maintenance Warranty	N/A	
Roadside Assistance	N/A	

Resale Value

1993	1994	1995	1996	1997
$9,991	$9,462	$9,074	$8,485	$7,814

Ownership Costs (5yr)

Average	This Car
$25,285	$23,289
Cost/Mile 36¢	Cost/Mile 33¢

The 1993 Dodge Dakota Club Cab is available in two models - (Base) Dakota, and 4WD. New 1993 standard equipment includes stainless steel exhaust system, rear folding seat, and two additional exterior colors. New optional equipment includes four-wheel anti-lock brakes. Other options include a Trailer Towing Package, heavy duty suspension, rear black step bumper, Light and Snow Packages, tilt steering column, cruise control, power door locks and windows, AM/FM cassette radio, and tilt steering wheel.

Cumulative Costs

	1993	1994	1995	1996	1997
Annual	$6,908	$3,703	$4,228	$3,650	$4,800
Total	$6,908	$10,611	$14,839	$18,489	$23,289

Ownership Cost Rating

Excellent

* Includes shaded options

** Other purchase requirements apply

Poor · Worse Than Average · Average · Better Than Average · Excellent · Insufficient Information

Refer to *Section 3: Annotated Vehicle Charts* for an explanation of these charts.

Dodge Dakota Sport 4WD
2 Door Regular Cab

3.9L 180 hp Gas Fuel Inject.

6 Cylinder "V"

Manual 5 Speed

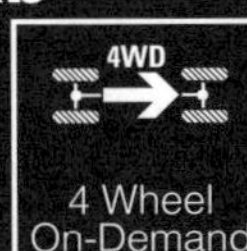
4 Wheel On-Demand

Manual Seatbelts Only

Small Pickup
2WD Model Shown

Purchase Price

Car Item	Dealer Cost	List
Base Price	**$13,118**	**$14,137**
Anti-Lock Brakes	Std	Std
Automatic 4 Speed	$754	$887
5.2L 230 hp Gas	$499	** $587
Air Conditioning	$677	$797
Power Steering	Std	Std
Cruise Control	Pkg	Pkg
4 Whl On-Demand Dr.	Std	Std
AM/FM Stereo Cassette	Std	Std
Steering Wheel, Tilt	$114	$134
Power Windows	Pkg	Pkg
***Options Price**	$0	$0
***Total Price**	**$13,118**	**$14,137**
Target Price	$13,923	
Destination Charge	$470	
Avg. Tax & Fees	$866	
Total Target $	**$15,259**	
Average Dealer Option Cost:	***85%***	

Ownership Costs

Cost Area	5 Year Cost	Rate
Depreciation	$8,284	Poor
Financing ($307/month)	$2,514	
Insurance (Rating 6 [Est.])	$7,129	Better Than Average
State Fees	$584	
Fuel (Hwy 19 City 15)	$5,079	Poor
Maintenance	$3,850	Average
Repairs	$935	Worse Than Average

Warranty/Maintenance Info

Item		Rate
Major Tune-Up	$131	Excellent
Minor Tune-Up	$77	Average
Brake Service	$285	Poor
Overall Warranty	1 yr/12k	Poor
Drivetrain Warranty	7 yr/70k	Excellent
Rust Warranty	7 yr/100k	Excellent
Maintenance Warranty	N/A	
Roadside Assistance	N/A	

Ownership Cost By Year

$2,000 $4,000 $6,000 $8,000 $10,000
1993 1994 1995 1996 1997

Resale Value

1993	1994	1995	1996	1997
$10,353	$9,544	$8,673	$7,784	$6,975

Ownership Costs (5yr)

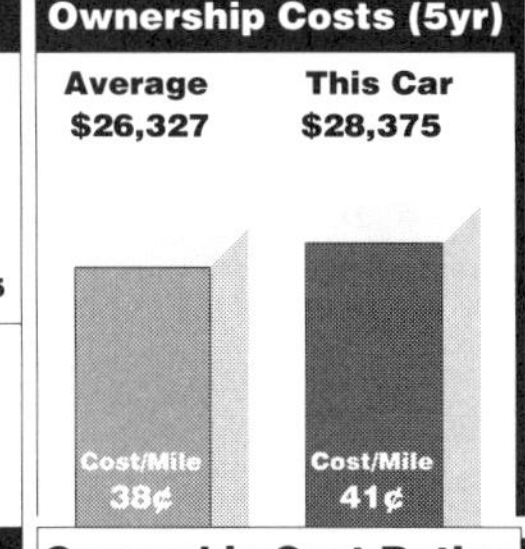

Average	This Car
$26,327	$28,375
Cost/Mile 38¢	Cost/Mile 41¢

Cumulative Costs

	1993	1994	1995	1996	1997
Annual	$8,426	$4,468	$5,369	$4,465	$5,647
Total	$8,426	$12,894	$18,263	$22,728	$28,375

Ownership Cost Rating

Poor

The 1993 Dodge Dakota is available in five models - (Base) Dakota, S, Sport, (Base) 4WD, and Sport 4WD. New for 1993, the Dakota Sport 4WD features a stainless steel exhaust system, and two additional exterior colors. Standard equipment includes a cloth and vinyl 3-man bench seat, tachometer and aluminum wheels. Options include power remote outside mirrors, power door locks and windows, two-tone paint and several equipment packages. The Dakota Sport 4WD is available in an extended cab version.

Dodge Dakota 4WD
2 Door Regular Cab

3.9L 180 hp Gas Fuel Inject.

6 Cylinder "V"

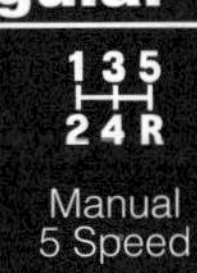
Manual 5 Speed

4 Wheel On-Demand

Manual Seatbelts Only

Small Pickup
2WD Model Shown

Purchase Price

Car Item	Dealer Cost	List
Base Price	**$13,684**	**$15,101**
Anti-Lock Brakes	Std	Std
Automatic 4 Speed	$754	$887
5.2L 230 hp Gas	$551	** $648
Air Conditioning	$677	$797
Power Steering	Std	Std
Cruise Control	Pkg	Pkg
4 Whl On-Demand Dr.	Std	Std
AM/FM Stereo Cassette	$174	$205
Steering Wheel, Tilt	$173	$204
8 Foot Bed	$100	$114
***Options Price**	$174	$205
***Total Price**	**$13,858**	**$15,306**
Target Price	$14,723	
Destination Charge	$470	
Avg. Tax & Fees	$918	
Total Target $	**$16,111**	
Average Dealer Option Cost:	***85%***	

Ownership Costs

Cost Area	5 Year Cost	Rate
Depreciation	$8,465	Poor
Financing ($324/month)	$2,654	
Insurance (Rating 8 [Est.])	$7,432	Better Than Average
State Fees	$631	
Fuel (Hwy 19 City 15)	$5,079	Poor
Maintenance	$3,409	Better Than Average
Repairs	$935	Worse Than Average

Warranty/Maintenance Info

Item		Rate
Major Tune-Up	$131	Excellent
Minor Tune-Up	$77	Average
Brake Service	$285	Poor
Overall Warranty	1 yr/12k	Poor
Drivetrain Warranty	7 yr/70k	Excellent
Rust Warranty	7 yr/100k	Excellent
Maintenance Warranty	N/A	
Roadside Assistance	N/A	

Ownership Cost By Year

$2,000 $4,000 $6,000 $8,000 $10,000
1993 1994 1995 1996 1997

Resale Value

1993	1994	1995	1996	1997
$11,374	$10,413	$9,503	$8,536	$7,646

Ownership Costs (5yr)

Average	This Car
$27,516	$28,605
Cost/Mile 39¢	Cost/Mile 41¢

Cumulative Costs

	1993	1994	1995	1996	1997
Annual	$8,383	$4,733	$5,293	$4,625	$5,571
Total	$8,383	$13,116	$18,409	$23,034	$28,605

Ownership Cost Rating

Worse Than Average

The 1993 Dodge Dakota is available in five models - (Base) Dakota, S, Sport, (Base) 4WD, and Sport 4WD. New for 1993, the Dakota 4WD features a stainless steel exhaust system, and two additional exterior colors. Features include a serpentine belt accessory drive and two new exterior colors. Options include air conditioning, power remote outside mirrors, power door locks and windows, two-tone paint and several equipment packages. The Dakota 4WD is also available in an extended cab version.

* Includes shaded options

** Other purchase requirements apply

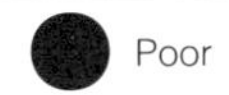 Poor  Worse Than Average  Average  Better Than Average  Excellent  Insufficient Information

Refer to *Section 3: Annotated Vehicle Charts* for an explanation of these charts.

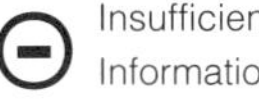

Dodge Dakota Club Cab 4WD
2 Door Extended Cab

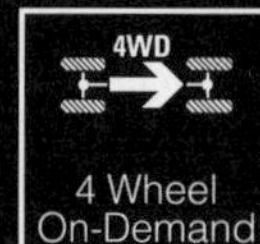

3.9L 180 hp Gas Fuel Inject. | 6 Cylinder "V" | Manual 5 Speed | 4 Wheel On-Demand | Manual Seatbelts Only

Small Pickup

Purchase Price

Car Item	Dealer Cost	List
Base Price	**$14,686**	**$16,240**
Anti-Lock Brakes	Std	Std
Automatic 4 Speed	$754	$887
5.2L 230 hp Gas	$499	** $587
Air Conditioning	$677	$797
Power Steering	Std	Std
Cruise Control	Pkg	Pkg
4 Whl On-Demand Dr.	Std	Std
AM/FM Stereo Cassette	$174	$205
Steering Wheel, Tilt	$173	$204
Power Windows	Pkg	Pkg
***Options Price**	$174	$205
***Total Price**	**$14,860**	**$16,445**
Target Price	$15,814	
Destination Charge	$470	
Avg. Tax & Fees	$983	
Total Target $	**$17,267**	
Average Dealer Option Cost:	***85%***	

Ownership Costs

Cost Area	5 Year Cost	Rate
Depreciation	$8,495	Worse Than Average
Financing ($347/month)	$2,845	
Insurance (Rating 7 [Est.])	$7,244	Better Than Average
State Fees	$675	
Fuel (Hwy 19 City 15)	$5,079	Poor
Maintenance	$3,553	Better Than Average
Repairs	$935	Worse Than Average

Ownership Cost By Year

$2,000 $4,000 $6,000 $8,000 $10,000

1993 1994 1995 1996 1997

Warranty/Maintenance Info

Major Tune-Up	$131	Excellent
Minor Tune-Up	$77	Better Than Average
Brake Service	$285	Poor
Overall Warranty	1 yr/12k	Poor
Drivetrain Warranty	7 yr/70k	Excellent
Rust Warranty	7 yr/100k	Excellent
Maintenance Warranty	N/A	
Roadside Assistance	N/A	

Resale Value

1993	1994	1995	1996	1997
$12,674	$11,650	$10,692	$9,679	$8,772

Ownership Costs (5yr)

Average	This Car
$28,673	$28,826
Cost/Mile 41¢	Cost/Mile 41¢

Cumulative Costs

	1993	1994	1995	1996	1997
Annual	$8,295	$4,829	$5,420	$4,653	$5,629
Total	$8,295	$13,124	$18,544	$23,197	$28,826

Ownership Cost Rating

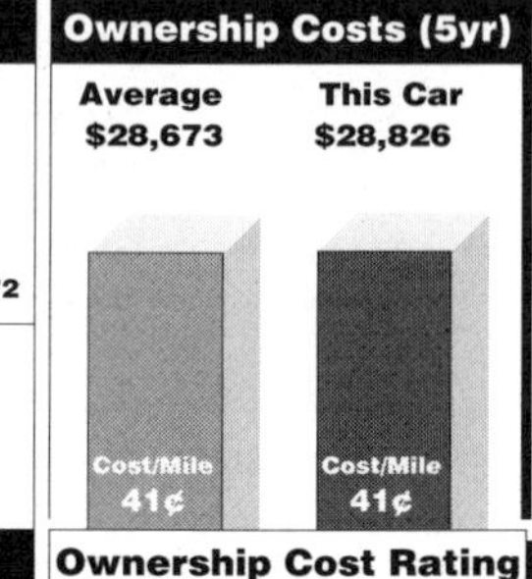

Average

The 1993 Dodge Dakota Club Cab is available in two models - (Base) Dakota, and 4WD. New 1993 standard equipment includes stainless steel exhaust system, rear folding seat, and two additional exterior colors. New options include four-wheel anti-lock brakes. The 4WD upgrades the Base model by adding as standard equipment an air conditioning, cruise control, tilt steering column, and cast aluminum wheels. Power locks and windows, heavy duty suspension, and a Trailer Towing Package are optional.

Dodge Ram 50
2 Door Regular Cab

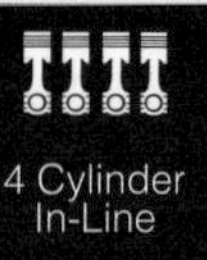

2.4L 116 hp Gas Fuel Inject. | 4 Cylinder In-Line | Manual 5 Speed | 2 Wheel Rear | Manual Seatbelts Only

Small Pickup

Purchase Price

Car Item	Dealer Cost	List
Base Price	**$8,475**	**$8,865**
Anti-Lock Brakes	Std	Std
Automatic 4 Speed	$603	$701
Optional Engine	N/A	N/A
Air Conditioning	$648	$753
Power Steering	Pkg	Pkg
Cruise Control	N/A	N/A
All Wheel Drive	N/A	N/A
AM/FM Stereo Cassette	N/A	N/A
Steering Wheel, Tilt	Std	Std
Long Bed	$524	$567
***Options Price**	$0	$0
***Total Price**	**$8,475**	**$8,865**
Target Price	$8,826	
Destination Charge	$400	
Avg. Tax & Fees	$554	
Total Target $	**$9,780**	
Average Dealer Option Cost:	***86%***	

Ownership Costs

Cost Area	5 Year Cost	Rate
Depreciation	$4,411	Better Than Average
Financing ($197/month)	$1,611	
Insurance (Rating 7 [Est.])	$7,244	Worse Than Average
State Fees	$371	
Fuel (Hwy 24 City 19)	$4,015	Average
Maintenance	$3,605	Average
Repairs	$731	Better Than Average

Ownership Cost By Year

$2,000 $4,000 $6,000 $8,000

1993 1994 1995 1996 1997

Warranty/Maintenance Info

Major Tune-Up	$156	Better Than Average
Minor Tune-Up	$81	Better Than Average
Brake Service	$202	Average
Overall Warranty	1 yr/12k	Poor
Drivetrain Warranty	7 yr/70k	Excellent
Rust Warranty	5 yr/unlim. mi	Better Than Average
Maintenance Warranty	N/A	
Roadside Assistance	N/A	

Resale Value

1993	1994	1995	1996	1997
$7,699	$7,049	$6,573	$6,010	$5,369

Ownership Costs (5yr)

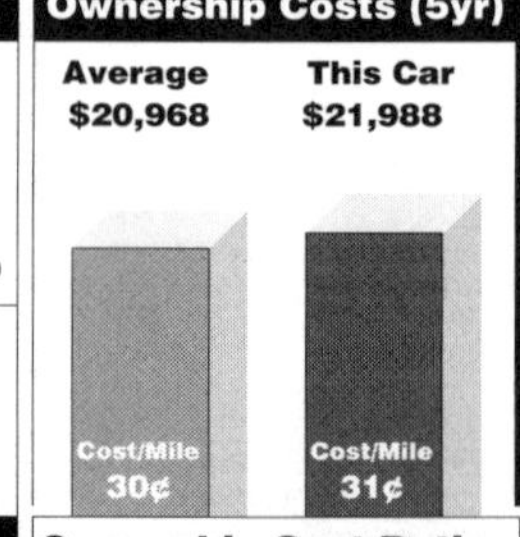

Average	This Car
$20,968	$21,988
Cost/Mile 30¢	Cost/Mile 31¢

Cumulative Costs

	1993	1994	1995	1996	1997
Annual	$4,986	$3,757	$4,346	$3,933	$4,966
Total	$4,986	$8,743	$13,089	$17,022	$21,988

Ownership Cost Rating

Worse Than Average

The 1993 Ram 50 is available in three models-(Base) Ram 50 and SE 2WD, and the Power Ram 50 4WD. New for 1993, the Ram 50 features rear wheel anti-lock brakes as standard equipment. Standard equipment include passenger assist grip, power front disc brakes, carpeting, electronic ignition, tinted glass, dual outside mirrors and adjustable steering column. Key options include air conditioning, speed control, power steering, sliding rear window, sound systems, and argent or chrome wheels.

* Includes shaded options

** Other purchase requirements apply

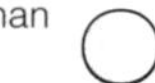
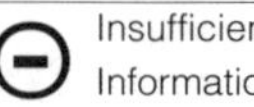

Poor | Worse Than Average | Average | Better Than Average | Excellent | Insufficient Information

Refer to *Section 3: Annotated Vehicle Charts* for an explanation of these charts.

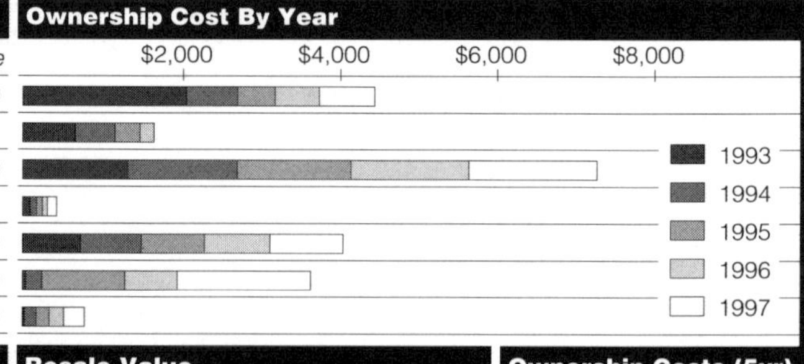

Dodge Ram 50 SE
2 Door Regular Cab

2.4L 116 hp Gas Fuel Inject.

4 Cylinder In-Line

Manual 5 Speed

2 Wheel Rear

Manual Seatbelts Only

Small Pickup

Base Model Shown

Purchase Price

Car Item	Dealer Cost	List
Base Price	**$9,467**	**$10,035**
Anti-Lock Brakes	Std	Std
Automatic 4 Speed	$603	$701
Optional Engine	N/A	N/A
Air Conditioning	$648	$753
Power Steering	Std	Std
Cruise Control	Pkg	Pkg
All Wheel Drive	N/A	N/A
AM/FM Stereo Cassette	N/A	N/A
Steering Wheel, Tilt	Std	Std
Power Windows	Pkg	Pkg
***Options Price**	$0	$0
***Total Price**	**$9,467**	**$10,035**
Target Price	$9,985	
Destination Charge	$400	
Avg. Tax & Fees	$623	
Total Target $	**$11,008**	
Average Dealer Option Cost:	***86%***	

Ownership Costs

Cost Area	5 Year Cost	Rate
Depreciation	$5,235	Average
Financing ($221/month)	$1,814	
Insurance (Rating 10 [Est.])	$7,689	Poor
State Fees	$417	
Fuel (Hwy 24 City 19)	$4,015	Average
Maintenance	$3,605	Average
Repairs	$731	Better Than Average

Ownership Cost By Year

Warranty/Maintenance Info

Major Tune-Up	$156	Better Than Average
Minor Tune-Up	$81	Better Than Average
Brake Service	$202	Average
Overall Warranty	1 yr/12k	Poor
Drivetrain Warranty	7 yr/70k	Excellent
Rust Warranty	5 yr/unlim. mi	Better Than Average
Maintenance Warranty	N/A	
Roadside Assistance	N/A	

Resale Value

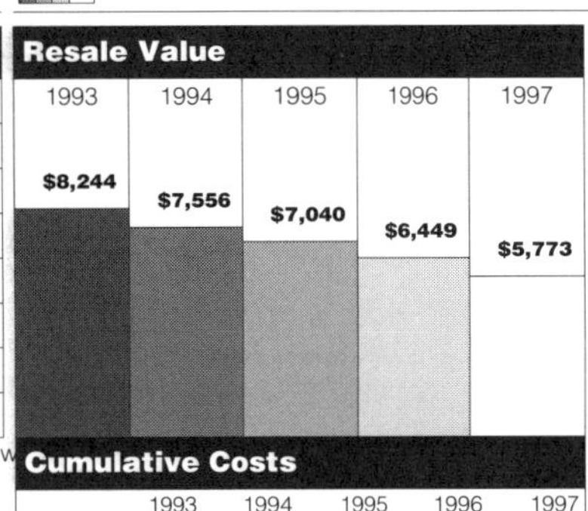

Ownership Costs (5yr)

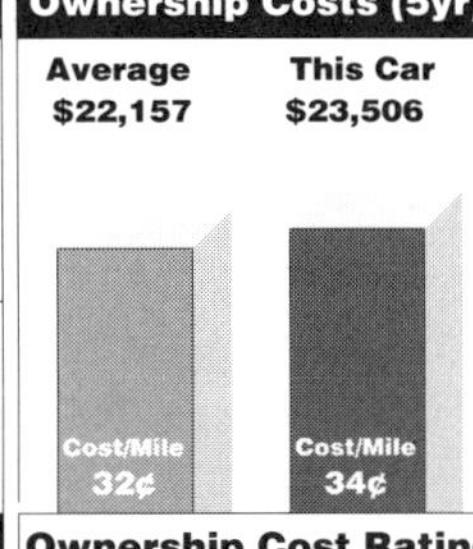

The 1993 Ram 50 is available in three models-(Base) Ram 50 and SE 2WD, and the Power Ram 50 4WD. New for 1993, the Ram 50 SE features rear wheel anti-lock brakes as standard eqiupment. Standard equipment include cloth and vinyl bench seat, tilt steering wheel, cargo box and power steering. Key options include power steering, sliding rear window, and argent or chrome wheels. Other features include three new exterior colors for 1993: Blue Pearl-Coat, Dark Silver Metallic and Blue Green.

Cumulative Costs

	1993	1994	1995	1996	1997
Annual	$5,847	$3,954	$4,524	$4,077	$5,104
Total	$5,847	$9,801	$14,325	$18,402	$23,506

Ownership Cost Rating

Worse Than Average

Dodge Power Ram 50
2 Door Regular Cab

2.4L 116 hp Gas Fuel Inject.

4 Cylinder In-Line

Manual 5 Speed

4 Wheel On-Demand

Manual Seatbelts Only

Small Pickup

Purchase Price

Car Item	Dealer Cost	List
Base Price	**$11,149**	**$11,956**
Anti-Lock Brakes	Std	Std
Automatic 4 Speed	$608	$707
Optional Engine	N/A	N/A
Air Conditioning	$648	$753
Power Steering	Std	Std
Cruise Control	N/A	N/A
4 Whl On-Demand Dr.	Std	Std
AM/FM Stereo Cassette	N/A	N/A
Steering Wheel, Tilt	Std	Std
Power Windows	N/A	N/A
***Options Price**	$0	$0
***Total Price**	**$11,149**	**$11,956**
Target Price	$11,793	
Destination Charge	$400	
Avg. Tax & Fees	$734	
Total Target $	**$12,927**	
Average Dealer Option Cost:	***86%***	

Ownership Costs

Cost Area	5 Year Cost	Rate
Depreciation	$5,061	Excellent
Financing ($260/month)	$2,130	
Insurance (Rating 11 [Est.])	$7,902	Poor
State Fees	$494	
Fuel (Hwy 22 City 19)	$4,214	Worse Than Average
Maintenance	$3,710	Average
Repairs	$820	Average

Ownership Cost By Year

Warranty/Maintenance Info

Major Tune-Up	$150	Better Than Average
Minor Tune-Up	$81	Better Than Average
Brake Service	$202	Average
Overall Warranty	1 yr/12k	Poor
Drivetrain Warranty	7 yr/70k	Excellent
Rust Warranty	5 yr/unlim. mi	Better Than Average
Maintenance Warranty	N/A	
Roadside Assistance	N/A	

Resale Value

Ownership Costs (5yr)

The 193 Ram 50 is available in three models-(Base) Ram 50 and SE 2WD, and the Power Ram 50 4WD. New for 1993, the Power Ram 50 4WD features rear wheel anti-lock brakes as standard equipment. Standard equipment also includes a full stainless steel exhaust system, power steering, tilt steering wheel and cargo box. Key options include sliding rear window, and argent or chrome wheels. Also available are three new colors for 1993: Blue Pearl-Coat, Dark Silver Metallic and Blue Green.

Cumulative Costs

	1993	1994	1995	1996	1997
Annual	$5,865	$4,178	$4,687	$4,334	$5,267
Total	$5,865	$10,043	$14,730	$19,064	$24,331

Ownership Cost Rating

Average

* Includes shaded options

** Other purchase requirements apply

Poor

Worse Than Average

Average

Better Than Average
Excellent
Insufficient Information

Refer to *Section 3: Annotated Vehicle Charts* for an explanation of these charts.

Dodge Ram D150

2 Door Regular Cab

3.9L 180 hp Gas Fuel Inject.	6 Cylinder "V"	Manual 5 Speed	2 Wheel Rear	Manual Seatbelts Only

Large Pickup

Purchase Price

Car Item	Dealer Cost	List
Base Price	**$12,118**	**$13,733**
Anti-Lock Brakes	Std	Std
Automatic 4 Speed	$754	$887
5.2L 230 hp Gas	$499	$587
Air Conditioning	$677	$797
Power Steering	Std	Std
Cruise Control	Pkg	Pkg
All Wheel Drive	N/A	N/A
AM/FM Stereo Cassette	$304	** $358
Steering Wheel, Tilt	$114	** $134
8 Foot Bed	$184	$217
***Options Price**	$1,176	$1,384
***Total Price**	**$13,294**	**$15,117**
Target Price	$14,174	
Destination Charge	$595	
Avg. Tax & Fees	$895	
Total Target $	**$15,664**	
Average Dealer Option Cost:	***82%***	

Ownership Costs

Cost Area	5 Year Cost	Rate
Depreciation	$7,289	Poor
Financing ($315/month)	$2,580	
Insurance (Rating 7 [Est.])	$7,244	Better Than Average
State Fees	$628	
Fuel (Hwy 17 City 13)	$5,760	Average
Maintenance	$3,452	Better Than Average
Repairs	$779	Better Than Average

Ownership Cost By Year

$2,000 $4,000 $6,000 $8,000

1993 1994 1995 1996 1997

Warranty/Maintenance Info

Item		Rate
Major Tune-Up	$153	Better Than Average
Minor Tune-Up	$90	Better Than Average
Brake Service	$246	Better Than Average
Overall Warranty	1 yr/12k	Poor
Drivetrain Warranty	7 yr/70k	Excellent
Rust Warranty	7 yr/100k	Excellent
Maintenance Warranty	N/A	
Roadside Assistance	N/A	

Resale Value

1993	1994	1995	1996	1997
$11,121	$10,494	$9,983	$9,296	$8,375

Ownership Costs (5yr)

Average	This Car
$24,800	$27,732
Cost/Mile 35¢	Cost/Mile 40¢

Cumulative Costs

	1993	1994	1995	1996	1997
Annual	$8,247	$4,456	$5,040	$4,440	$5,549
Total	$8,247	$12,703	$17,743	$22,183	$27,732

Ownership Cost Rating

Poor

The 1993 Ram 150 is available in four models - (Base) Ram 150 Regular and Club Cabs in two (D150)- and four (W150)-wheel drive. New for 1993, the Ram D150 offers a new "Magnum" 5.9L (360 cubic inch) engine that produces 230-horsepower, has sequential multi-point injection, returnless fuel system and a serpentine belt accessory drive. Two new exterior colors have been added (Flame Red and Emerald Green Pearl) along with three new two-tone color combos. An engine block heater is also available.

Dodge Ram D250

2 Door Regular Cab

3.9L 180 hp Gas Fuel Inject.	6 Cylinder "V"	Manual 5 Speed	2 Wheel Rear	Manual Seatbelts Only

Large Pickup

D150 Model Shown

Purchase Price

Car Item	Dealer Cost	List
Base Price	**$13,204**	**$15,010**
Anti-Lock Brakes	Std	Std
Automatic 4 Speed	$754	$887
5.2L 230 hp Gas	$499	$587
Air Conditioning	$677	$797
Power Steering	Std	Std
Cruise Control	Pkg	Pkg
All Wheel Drive	N/A	N/A
AM/FM Stereo Cassette	$304	$358
Steering Wheel, Tilt	$114	** $134
Power Windows	Pkg	Pkg
***Options Price**	$1,480	$1,742
***Total Price**	**$14,684**	**$16,752**
Target Price	$15,688	
Destination Charge	$595	
Avg. Tax & Fees	$987	
Total Target $	**$17,270**	
Average Dealer Option Cost:	***85%***	

Ownership Costs

Cost Area	5 Year Cost	Rate
Depreciation	$7,366	Worse Than Average
Financing ($347/month)	$2,845	
Insurance (Rating 7 [Est.])	$7,244	Better Than Average
State Fees	$693	
Fuel (Hwy 17 City 13)	$5,760	Average
Maintenance	$3,639	Better Than Average
Repairs	$779	Better Than Average

Ownership Cost By Year

$2,000 $4,000 $6,000 $8,000

1993 1994 1995 1996 1997

Warranty/Maintenance Info

Item		Rate
Major Tune-Up	$153	Better Than Average
Minor Tune-Up	$90	Better Than Average
Brake Service	$297	Average
Overall Warranty	1 yr/12k	Poor
Drivetrain Warranty	7 yr/70k	Excellent
Rust Warranty	7 yr/100k	Excellent
Maintenance Warranty	N/A	
Roadside Assistance	N/A	

Resale Value

1993	1994	1995	1996	1997
$13,427	$12,633	$11,950	$11,028	$9,904

Ownership Costs (5yr)

Average	This Car
$26,808	$28,326
Cost/Mile 38¢	Cost/Mile 40¢

Cumulative Costs

	1993	1994	1995	1996	1997
Annual	$7,673	$4,721	$5,367	$4,706	$5,859
Total	$7,673	$12,394	$17,761	$22,467	$28,326

Ownership Cost Rating

Average

The 1993 Dodge Ram 250 pickup is available in four models - the D250, D250 Club Cab, W250, and W250 Club Cab. The Dodge Ram D250 pickup truck can be modified with options from three packages -- Base, Work, and/or Super LE. The choices include a 75-amp alternator, power brakes, a front stabilizer bar, and power window and door locks. The Super LE package includes lower body side moldings, cloth bench with head rests (split-back on club Cabs), and electronic speed control.

* Includes shaded options

** Other purchase requirements apply

Poor  Worse Than Average  Average  Better Than Average  Excellent Insufficient Information

Refer to *Section 3: Annotated Vehicle Charts* for an explanation of these charts.

Dodge Ram D350
2 Door Regular Cab

5.9L 230 hp Gas Fuel Inject.

8 Cylinder "V"

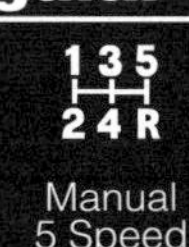
Manual 5 Speed

2 Wheel Rear

Manual Seatbelts Only

Large Pickup

D150 Model Shown

Purchase Price

Car Item	Dealer Cost	List
Base Price	**$13,940**	**$15,876**
Anti-Lock Brakes	Std	Std
Automatic 4 Speed	$754	$887
Turb Dsl 5.9L 160 hp	$3,207	$3,773
Air Conditioning	$677	$797
Power Steering	Std	Std
Cruise Control	Pkg	Pkg
All Wheel Drive	N/A	N/A
AM/FM Stereo Cassette	$174	$205
Steering Wheel, Tilt	$114	** $134
Power Windows	Pkg	Pkg
***Options Price**	$851	$1,002
***Total Price**	**$14,791**	**$16,878**
Target Price	$15,824	
Destination Charge	$595	
Avg. Tax & Fees	$996	
Total Target $	**$17,415**	
Average Dealer Option Cost:	***85%***	

Ownership Costs

Cost Area	5 Year Cost	Rate
Depreciation	$8,328	Poor
Financing ($350/month)	$2,869	
Insurance (Rating 8 [Est.])	$7,432	Better Than Average
State Fees	$699	
Fuel (Hwy 14 City 10 [Est.])	$7,226	Poor
Maintenance	$4,013	Better Than Average
Repairs	$820	Average

Ownership Cost By Year

Warranty/Maintenance Info

Item		Rate
Major Tune-Up	$153	Better Than Average
Minor Tune-Up	$90	Better Than Average
Brake Service	$297	Average
Overall Warranty	1 yr/12k	Poor
Drivetrain Warranty	7 yr/70k	Excellent
Rust Warranty	7 yr/100k	Excellent
Maintenance Warranty	N/A	
Roadside Assistance	N/A	

Resale Value

1993	1994	1995	1996	1997
$12,142	$11,466	$10,883	$10,078	$9,087

Ownership Costs (5yr)

Average	This Car
$26,962	$31,387
Cost/Mile 39¢	Cost/Mile 45¢

The 1993 Ram 350 is available in both two-wheel-drive and four-wheel-drive in either regular or Club Cab configurations. New for 1993, the D350 features a multi-port, fuel-injected Magnum 5.9-liter V-8 engine. Standard features include dual low mount mirrors, vinyl bucket seats, power steering and cloth headliner. Among the available options on the D350 pickups are air conditioning, GVW packages, power windows and door locks, tilt steering, speed control and sliding rear window.

Cumulative Costs

	1993	1994	1995	1996	1997
Annual	$9,421	$4,937	$5,776	$4,957	$6,296
Total	$9,421	$14,358	$20,134	$25,091	$31,387

Ownership Cost Rating

Poor

Dodge Ram D150 Club Cab
2 Door Extended Cab

5.2L 230 hp Gas Fuel Inject.

8 Cylinder "V"

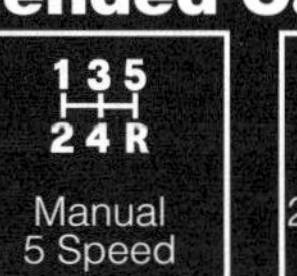
Manual 5 Speed

2 Wheel Rear

Manual Seatbelts Only

Large Pickup

D350 Model Shown

Purchase Price

Car Item	Dealer Cost	List
Base Price	**$14,058**	**$16,015**
Anti-Lock Brakes	Std	Std
Automatic 4 Speed	$754	$887
5.9L 230 hp Gas	$230	$270
Air Conditioning	$677	$797
Power Steering	Std	Std
Cruise Control	Pkg	Pkg
All Wheel Drive	N/A	N/A
AM/FM Stereo Cassette	$132	$155
Steering Wheel, Tilt	$114	** $134
8 Foot Bed	$186	$219
***Options Price**	$809	$952
***Total Price**	**$14,867**	**$16,967**
Target Price	$15,909	
Destination Charge	$595	
Avg. Tax & Fees	$1,001	
Total Target $	**$17,505**	
Average Dealer Option Cost:	***85%***	

Ownership Costs

Cost Area	5 Year Cost	Rate
Depreciation	$7,685	Worse Than Average
Financing ($352/month)	$2,883	
Insurance (Rating 10 [Est.])	$7,689	Average
State Fees	$702	
Fuel (Hwy 17 City 13)	$5,760	Average
Maintenance	$3,770	Better Than Average
Repairs	$779	Better Than Average

Ownership Cost By Year

Warranty/Maintenance Info

Item		Rate
Major Tune-Up	$153	Better Than Average
Minor Tune-Up	$90	Better Than Average
Brake Service	$246	Better Than Average
Overall Warranty	1 yr/12k	Poor
Drivetrain Warranty	7 yr/70k	Excellent
Rust Warranty	7 yr/100k	Excellent
Maintenance Warranty	N/A	
Roadside Assistance	N/A	

Resale Value

1993	1994	1995	1996	1997
$12,834	$12,156	$11,570	$10,814	$9,820

Ownership Costs (5yr)

Average	This Car
$27,072	$29,268
Cost/Mile 39¢	Cost/Mile 42¢

The 1993 Ram 150 is available in four models - (Base) Ram 150 Regular and Club Cabs in two (D150)- and four (W150)-wheel drive. New for 1993, the Ram D150 Club Cab offers a new "Magnum" 5.9L (360 cubic inch) engine that produces 230-horsepower, has sequential multi-point injection, returnless fuel system and a serpentine belt accessory drive. Two new colors have been added (Flame Red and Emerald Green Pearl) along with three new two-tone color combos. An engine block heater is also available.

Cumulative Costs

	1993	1994	1995	1996	1997
Annual	$8,603	$4,704	$5,430	$4,637	$5,894
Total	$8,603	$13,307	$18,737	$23,374	$29,268

Ownership Cost Rating

Worse Than Average

* Includes shaded options

** Other purchase requirements apply

Poor  Worse Than Average  Average  Better Than Average  Excellent — Insufficient Information

Refer to *Section 3: Annotated Vehicle Charts* for an explanation of these charts.

Dodge Ram D250 Club Cab

2 Door Extended Cab

3.9L 180 hp Gas Fuel Inject. | 6 Cylinder "V" | Manual 5 Speed

2 Wheel Rear

Manual Seatbelts Only

Purchase Price

Car Item	Dealer Cost	List
Base Price	**$15,044**	**$17,175**
Anti-Lock Brakes	Std	Std
Automatic 4 Speed	$754	$887
5.2L 230 hp Gas	$499	$587
Air Conditioning	$677	$797
Power Steering	Std	Std
Cruise Control	Pkg	Pkg
All Wheel Drive	N/A	N/A
AM/FM Stereo Cassette	$304	$358
Steering Wheel, Tilt	$114	** $134
Power Windows	Pkg	Pkg
***Options Price**	$1,480	$1,742
***Total Price**	**$16,524**	**$18,917**
Target Price	$17,715	
Destination Charge	$595	
Avg. Tax & Fees	$1,111	
Total Target $	**$19,421**	
Average Dealer Option Cost:	***85%***	

Ownership Costs

Cost Area	5 Year Cost	Rate
Depreciation	$8,301	Worse Than Average
Financing ($390/month)	$3,199	
Insurance (Rating 12 [Est.])	$8,108	Average
State Fees	$781	
Fuel (Hwy 17 City 13)	$5,760	Average
Maintenance	$3,639	Better Than Average
Repairs	$779	Better Than Average

Ownership Cost By Year

$2,000 $4,000 $6,000 $8,000 $10,000

1993 1994 1995 1996 1997

Warranty/Maintenance Info

Major Tune-Up	$153	Better Than Average
Minor Tune-Up	$90	Better Than Average
Brake Service	$297	Average
Overall Warranty	1 yr/12k	Poor
Drivetrain Warranty	7 yr/70k	Excellent
Rust Warranty	7 yr/100k	Excellent
Maintenance Warranty	N/A	
Roadside Assistance	N/A	

Resale Value

1993	1994	1995	1996	1997
$14,793	$13,982	$13,294	$12,329	$11,120

Ownership Costs (5yr)

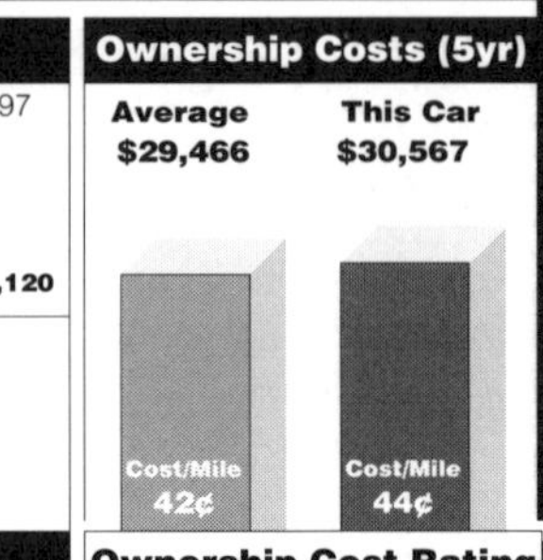

The 1993 Dodge Ram 250 pickup is available in four models - the D250, D250 Club Cab, W250, and W250 Club Cab. The Dodge Ram D250 Club Cab can be upgraded with options from three packages -- Base, Work, and/or Super LE. Choices include a power steering, heavy-duty vinyl bench with head rest, a front stabilizer bar, and power window and door locks. The Super LE package includes lower body side moldings, cloth bench with head rests (split-back on this model), and electronic speed control.

Cumulative Costs

	1993	1994	1995	1996	1997
Annual	$8,788	$5,035	$5,631	$4,970	$6,143
Total	$8,788	$13,823	$19,454	$24,424	$30,567

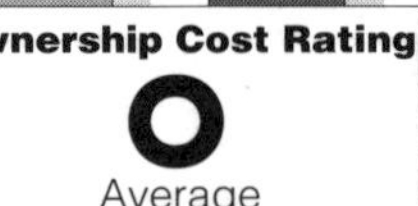

Ownership Cost Rating

Average

Dodge Ram D350 Club Cab

2 Door Extended Cab

5.9L 160 hp Turbo Dsl Fuel Inject.

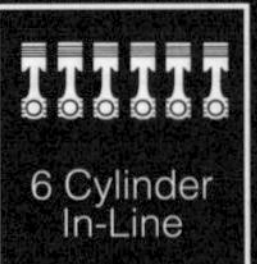

6 Cylinder In-Line

Manual 5 Speed

2 Wheel Rear

Manual Seatbelts Only

Large Pickup

Purchase Price

Car Item	Dealer Cost	List
Base Price	**$19,196**	**$22,060**
Anti-Lock Brakes	Std	Std
Automatic 4 Speed	$754	$887
Optional Engine	N/A	N/A
Air Conditioning	$677	$797
Power Steering	Std	Std
Cruise Control	Pkg	Pkg
All Wheel Drive	N/A	N/A
AM/FM Stereo Cassette	$174	$205
Steering Wheel, Tilt	$114	** $134
Power Windows	Pkg	Pkg
***Options Price**	$851	$1,002
***Total Price**	**$20,047**	**$23,062**
Target Price	$21,660	
Destination Charge	$595	
Avg. Tax & Fees	$1,350	
Total Target $	**$23,605**	
Average Dealer Option Cost:	***85%***	

Ownership Costs

Cost Area	5 Year Cost	Rate
Depreciation	$12,303	Poor
Financing ($474/month)	$3,888	
Insurance (Rating 14 [Est.])	$8,446	Average
State Fees	$947	
Fuel (Hwy 13 City 10 [Est.])	$8,493	Poor
Maintenance	$3,973	Better Than Average
Repairs	$820	Average

Ownership Cost By Year

$2,000 $4,000 $6,000 $8,000 $10,000 $12,000 $14,000

1993 1994 1995 1996 1997

Warranty/Maintenance Info

Major Tune-Up	$125	Excellent
Minor Tune-Up	$96	Better Than Average
Brake Service	$297	Average
Overall Warranty	1 yr/12k	Poor
Drivetrain Warranty	7 yr/70k	Excellent
Rust Warranty	7 yr/100k	Excellent
Maintenance Warranty	N/A	
Roadside Assistance	N/A	

Resale Value

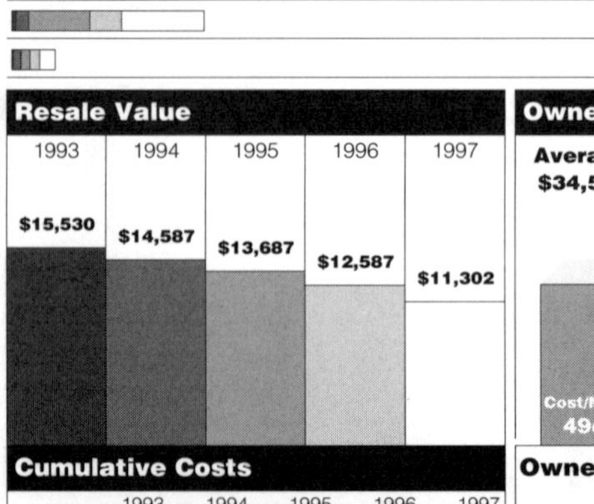

1993	1994	1995	1996	1997
$15,530	$14,587	$13,687	$12,587	$11,302

Ownership Costs (5yr)

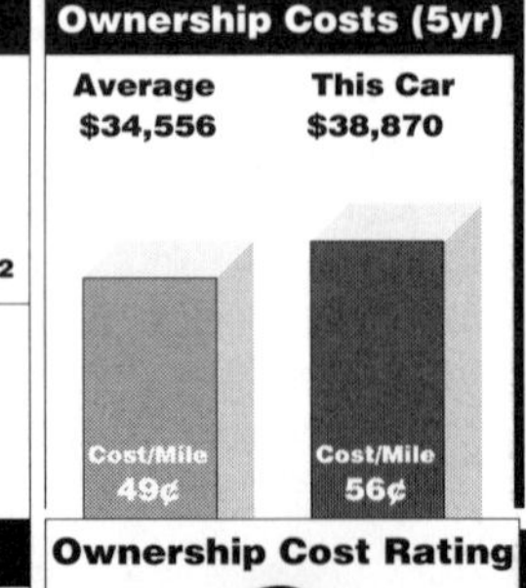

The 1993 Ram 350 is available in both two-wheel-drive and four-wheel-drive in either regular or Club Cab configurations. New for 1993, the D350 Club Cab features the availability of a 30-gallon fuel tank; dual rear wheels and a heavy-duty snow plow prep package with the Cummins 5.9-liter Turbo Diesel engine. Among the available options on the D350 pickups are air conditioning, GVW packages, power windows and door locks, tilt steering, speed control and sliding rear window.

Cumulative Costs

	1993	1994	1995	1996	1997
Annual	$13,171	$6,062	$6,741	$5,938	$6,958
Total	$13,171	$19,233	$25,974	$31,912	$38,870

Ownership Cost Rating

Poor

* Includes shaded options

** Other purchase requirements apply

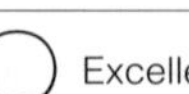

Poor 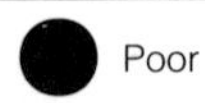 Worse Than Average  Average Better Than Average  Excellent Insufficient Information

Refer to *Section 3: Annotated Vehicle Charts* for an explanation of these charts.

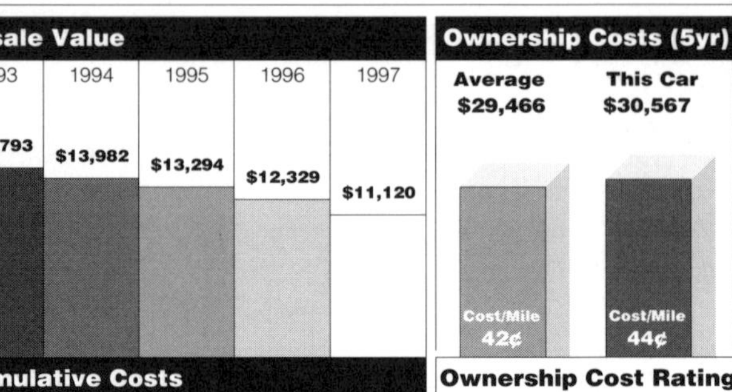

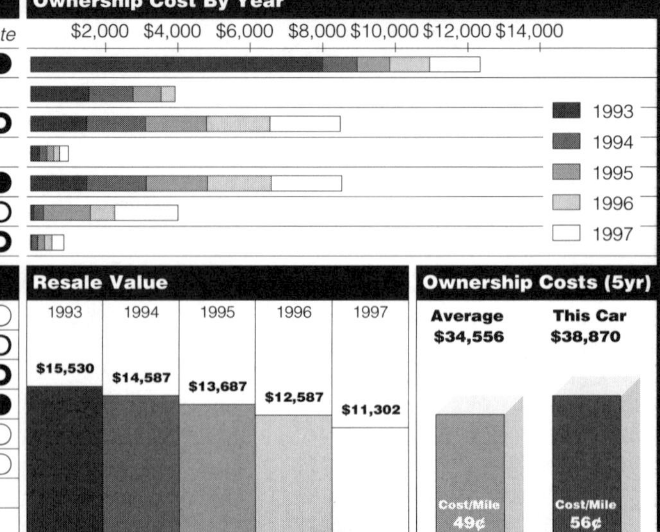

Dodge Ram W150
2 Door Regular Cab

3.9L 180 hp Gas Fuel Inject.

6 Cylinder "V"

Manual 5 Speed

4 Wheel On-Demand

Manual Seatbelts Only

Large Pickup

Purchase Price

Car Item	*Dealer Cost*	*List*
Base Price	**$14,316**	**$16,289**
Anti-Lock Brakes	Std	Std
Automatic 4 Speed	$754	$887
5.2L 230 hp Gas	$499	$587
Air Conditioning	$677	$797
Power Steering	Std	Std
Cruise Control	Pkg	Pkg
4 Whl On-Demand Dr.	Std	Std
AM/FM Stereo Cassette	$132	$155
Steering Wheel, Tilt	$114	** $134
8 Foot Bed	$187	$220
***Options Price**	$1,308	$1,539
***Total Price**	**$15,624**	**$17,828**
Target Price	$16,727	
Destination Charge	$595	
Avg. Tax & Fees	$1,050	
Total Target $	**$18,372**	
Average Dealer Option Cost:	***85%***	

Ownership Costs

Cost Area	*5 Year Cost*	*Rate*
Depreciation	$7,890	Worse Than Average
Financing ($369/month)	$3,027	
Insurance (Rating 10 [Est.])	$7,689	Average
State Fees	$737	
Fuel (Hwy 16 City 13)	$5,953	Worse Than Average
Maintenance	$3,831	Better Than Average
Repairs	$935	Worse Than Average

Ownership Cost By Year

$2,000 $4,000 $6,000 $8,000

1993 1994 1995 1996 1997

Warranty/Maintenance Info

Major Tune-Up	$153	Better Than Average
Minor Tune-Up	$90	Better Than Average
Brake Service	$246	Better Than Average
Overall Warranty	1 yr/12k	Poor
Drivetrain Warranty	7 yr/70k	Excellent
Rust Warranty	7 yr/100k	Excellent
Maintenance Warranty	N/A	
Roadside Assistance	N/A	

Resale Value

1993	1994	1995	1996	1997
$13,320	$12,710	$12,115	$11,456	$10,482

Ownership Costs (5yr)

Average	This Car
$28,129	$30,062
Cost/Mile 40¢	Cost/Mile 43¢

Cumulative Costs

	1993	1994	1995	1996	1997
Annual	$9,092	$4,758	$5,566	$4,617	$6,029
Total	$9,092	$13,850	$19,416	$24,033	$30,062

Ownership Cost Rating

Worse Than Average

The 1993 Ram 150 is available in four models - (Base) Ram 150 Regular and Club Cabs in two (D150)- and four (W150)-wheel drive. New for 1993, the Ram W150 offers a new "Magnum" 5.9L (360 cubic inch) engine that produces 230-horsepower, has sequential multi-point injection, tuned intake, returnless fuel system and a serpentine belt accessory drive. Other features include an optional 30-gallon fuel tank, modified styled wheels, an available engine block heater and heavy-duty snow plow prep package.

Dodge Ram W250
2 Door Regular Cab

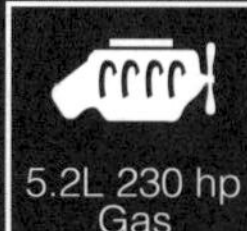
5.2L 230 hp Gas Fuel Inject.

8 Cylinder "V"

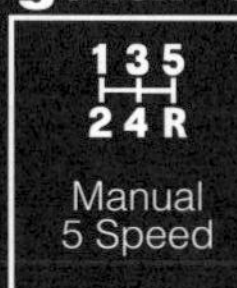
Manual 5 Speed

4 Wheel Full-Time

Manual Seatbelts Only

Large Pickup

Purchase Price

Car Item	*Dealer Cost*	*List*
Base Price	**$15,422**	**$17,591**
Anti-Lock Brakes	Std	Std
Automatic 4 Speed	$754	$887
5.9L 230 hp Gas	$230	$270
Air Conditioning	$677	$797
Power Steering	Std	Std
Cruise Control	Pkg	Pkg
4 Wheel Full-Time Drive	Std	Std
AM/FM Stereo Cassette	$304	$358
Steering Wheel, Tilt	$114	** $134
Power Windows	Pkg	Pkg
***Options Price**	$981	$1,155
***Total Price**	**$16,403**	**$18,746**
Target Price	$17,598	
Destination Charge	$595	
Avg. Tax & Fees	$1,103	
Total Target $	**$19,296**	
Average Dealer Option Cost:	***85%***	

Ownership Costs

Cost Area	*5 Year Cost*	*Rate*
Depreciation	$7,405	Average
Financing ($388/month)	$3,179	
Insurance (Rating 11 [Est.])	$7,902	Average
State Fees	$773	
Fuel (Hwy 16 City 13)	$5,953	Worse Than Average
Maintenance	$3,722	Better Than Average
Repairs	$935	Worse Than Average

Ownership Cost By Year

$2,000 $4,000 $6,000 $8,000

1993 1994 1995 1996 1997

Warranty/Maintenance Info

Major Tune-Up	$153	Better Than Average
Minor Tune-Up	$90	Better Than Average
Brake Service	$297	Average
Overall Warranty	1 yr/12k	Poor
Drivetrain Warranty	7 yr/70k	Excellent
Rust Warranty	7 yr/100k	Excellent
Maintenance Warranty	N/A	
Roadside Assistance	N/A	

Resale Value

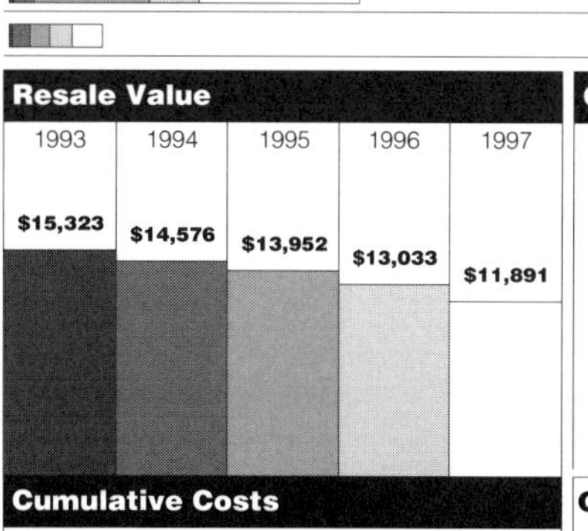

1993	1994	1995	1996	1997
$15,323	$14,576	$13,952	$13,033	$11,891

Ownership Costs (5yr)

Average	This Car
$29,256	$29,869
Cost/Mile 42¢	Cost/Mile 43¢

Cumulative Costs

	1993	1994	1995	1996	1997
Annual	$8,124	$4,992	$5,624	$4,938	$6,191
Total	$8,124	$13,116	$18,740	$23,678	$29,869

Ownership Cost Rating

Average

The 1993 Dodge Ram 250 pickup is available in four models - the D250, D250 Club Cab, W250, and W250 Club Cab. The Dodge Ram W250 is a 4WD pickup truck that has the options of any of the three packages -- Base, Work, and/or Super LE. Choices include power steering, heavy-duty vinyl bench with head rest, a front stabilizer bar, and power window and door locks. The Super LE package includes lower body side moldings, cloth bench with head rests, and electronic speed control.

* Includes shaded options

** Other purchase requirements apply

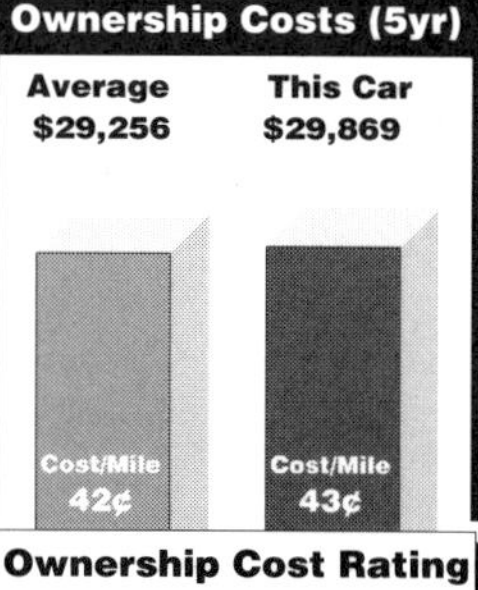

 Poor  Worse Than Average  Average  Better Than Average  Excellent  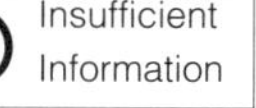 Insufficient Information

Refer to *Section 3: Annotated Vehicle Charts* for an explanation of these charts.

Dodge Ram W350

2 Door Regular Cab

5.9L 230 hp Gas Fuel Inject.

8 Cylinder "V"

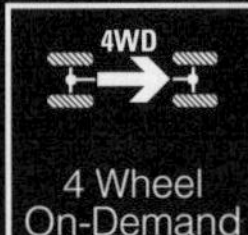
Manual 5 Speed

4 Wheel On-Demand

Manual Seatbelts Only

Large Pickup

W250 Model Shown

Purchase Price

Car Item	Dealer Cost	List
Base Price	**$16,188**	**$18,492**
Anti-Lock Brakes	Std	Std
Automatic 4 Speed	$754	$887
Turb Dsl 5.9L 160 hp	$3,207	$3,773
Air Conditioning	$677	$797
Power Steering	Std	Std
Cruise Control	Pkg	Pkg
4 Whl On-Demand Dr.	Std	Std
AM/FM Stereo Cassette	$174	$205
Steering Wheel, Tilt	$114	** $134
Power Windows	Pkg	Pkg
***Options Price**	$851	$1,002
***Total Price**	**$17,039**	**$19,494**
Target Price	$18,306	
Destination Charge	$595	
Avg. Tax & Fees	$1,146	
Total Target $	**$20,047**	
Average Dealer Option Cost:	***85%***	

Ownership Costs

Cost Area	5 Year Cost	Rate
Depreciation	$8,870	Worse Than Average
Financing ($403/month)	$3,303	
Insurance (Rating 11 [Est.])	$7,902	Average
State Fees	$805	
Fuel (Hwy 13 City 10 [Est.])	$7,513	Poor
Maintenance	$4,081	Better Than Average
Repairs	$965	Worse Than Average

Ownership Cost By Year

$2,000 $4,000 $6,000 $8,000 $10,000

1993 1994 1995 1996 1997

Warranty/Maintenance Info

Major Tune-Up	$153	Better Than Average
Minor Tune-Up	$90	Better Than Average
Brake Service	$297	Average
Overall Warranty	1 yr/12k	Poor
Drivetrain Warranty	7 yr/70k	Excellent
Rust Warranty	7 yr/100k	Excellent
Maintenance Warranty	N/A	
Roadside Assistance	N/A	

Resale Value

1993	1994	1995	1996	1997
$14,699	$13,990	$13,263	$12,333	$11,177

Ownership Costs (5yr)

Average	This Car
$30,175	$33,439
Cost/Mile 43¢	Cost/Mile 48¢

The 1993 Ram 350 is available in both two-wheel-drive and four -wheel-drive in either regular or Club Cab configurations. New for 1993, the W350 features a multi-port, fuel-injected Magnum 5.9-liter V-8 engine. Interior features include split back vinyl bench front seat with folding seatback and adjustable headrest. Other features include dual low mount mirrors, power steering and cloth headliner. Among the available options on Ram 350 pickups are power windows and door locks and sliding rear window.

Cumulative Costs

	1993	1994	1995	1996	1997
Annual	$9,848	$5,305	$6,226	$5,276	$6,784
Total	$9,848	$15,153	$21,379	$26,655	$33,439

Ownership Cost Rating

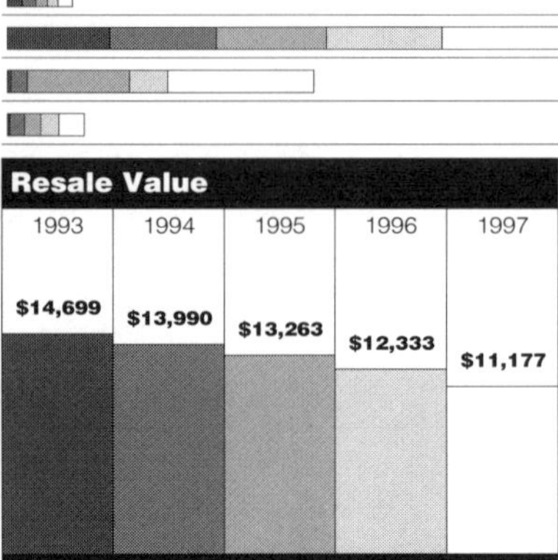
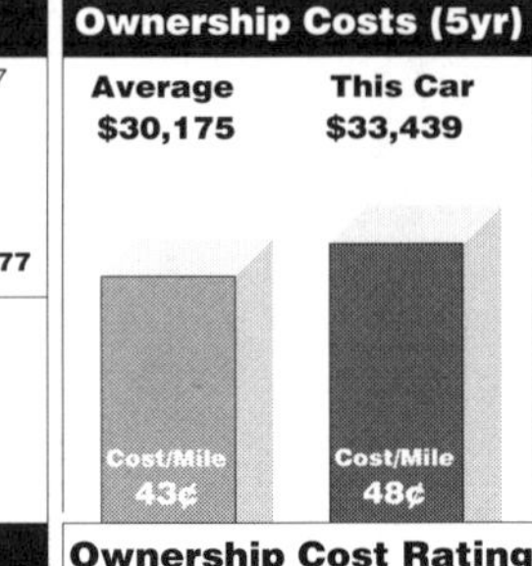

Worse Than Average

Dodge Ram W150 Club Cab

2 Door Extended Cab

5.2L 230 hp Gas Fuel Inject.

8 Cylinder "V"

Manual 5 Speed

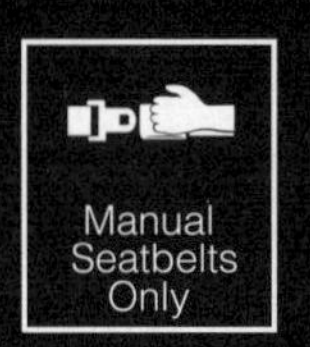
4 Wheel On-Demand

Manual Seatbelts Only

Large Pickup

D350 Model Shown

Purchase Price

Car Item	Dealer Cost	List
Base Price	**$16,629**	**$19,010**
Anti-Lock Brakes	Std	Std
Automatic 4 Speed	$754	$887
5.9L 230 hp Gas	$230	$270
Air Conditioning	$677	$797
Power Steering	Std	Std
Cruise Control	Pkg	Pkg
4 Whl On-Demand Dr.	Std	Std
AM/FM Stereo Cassette	$132	$155
Steering Wheel, Tilt	$114	** $134
Power Windows	Pkg	Pkg
***Options Price**	$809	$952
***Total Price**	**$17,438**	**$19,962**
Target Price	$18,750	
Destination Charge	$595	
Avg. Tax & Fees	$1,173	
Total Target $	**$20,518**	
Average Dealer Option Cost:	***85%***	

Ownership Costs

Cost Area	5 Year Cost	Rate
Depreciation	$8,004	Average
Financing ($412/month)	$3,380	
Insurance (Rating 12 [Est.])	$8,108	Average
State Fees	$822	
Fuel (Hwy 16 City 13)	$5,953	Worse Than Average
Maintenance	$3,851	Better Than Average
Repairs	$935	Worse Than Average

Ownership Cost By Year

$2,000 $4,000 $6,000 $8,000 $10,000

1993 1994 1995 1996 1997

Warranty/Maintenance Info

Major Tune-Up	$153	Better Than Average
Minor Tune-Up	$90	Better Than Average
Brake Service	$246	Better Than Average
Overall Warranty	1 yr/12k	Poor
Drivetrain Warranty	7 yr/70k	Excellent
Rust Warranty	7 yr/100k	Excellent
Maintenance Warranty	N/A	
Roadside Assistance	N/A	

Resale Value

1993	1994	1995	1996	1997
$14,438	$14,067	$13,734	$13,320	$12,514

Ownership Costs (5yr)

Average	This Car
$30,749	$31,053
Cost/Mile 44¢	Cost/Mile 44¢

The 1993 Ram 150 is available in four models - (Base) Ram 150 Regular and Club Cabs in two (D150)- and four (W150)-wheel drive. New for 1993, the Ram W150 Club Cab offers a new "Magnum" 5.9L (360 cubic inch) engine that produces 230-horsepower, has sequential multi-point injection, returnless fuel system and serpentine belt accessory drive. Other features include an optional 30-gallon fuel tank, modified styled wheels, an available engine block heater and heavy-duty snow plow prep package.

Cumulative Costs

	1993	1994	1995	1996	1997
Annual	$10,366	$4,729	$5,485	$4,500	$5,973
Total	$10,366	$15,095	$20,580	$25,080	$31,053

Ownership Cost Rating

Average

* Includes shaded options

** Other purchase requirements apply

Refer to *Section 3: Annotated Vehicle Charts* for an explanation of these charts.

Dodge Ram W250 Club Cab
2 Door Extended Cab

5.2L 230 hp Gas Fuel Inject.

8 Cylinder "V"

Manual 5 Speed

4 Wheel On-Demand

Manual Seatbelts Only

Large Pickup
D350 Model Shown

Purchase Price

Car Item	Dealer Cost	List
Base Price	**$16,918**	**$19,350**
Anti-Lock Brakes	Std	Std
Automatic 4 Speed	$754	$887
5.9L 230 hp Gas	$230	$270
Air Conditioning	$677	$797
Power Steering	Std	Std
Cruise Control	Pkg	Pkg
4 Whl On-Demand Dr.	Std	Std
AM/FM Stereo Cassette	$304	$358
Steering Wheel, Tilt	$114	** $134
Power Windows	Pkg	Pkg
***Options Price**	$981	$1,155
***Total Price**	**$17,899**	**$20,505**
Target Price	$19,257	
Destination Charge	$595	
Avg. Tax & Fees	$1,204	
Total Target $	**$21,056**	
Average Dealer Option Cost:	***85%***	

Ownership Costs

Cost Area	5 Year Cost	Rate
Depreciation	$8,055	Average
Financing ($423/month)	$3,469	
Insurance (Rating 12 [Est.])	$8,108	Average
State Fees	$845	
Fuel (Hwy 16 City 13)	$5,953	Worse Than Average
Maintenance	$3,722	Better Than Average
Repairs	$935	Worse Than Average

Ownership Cost By Year

$2,000 $4,000 $6,000 $8,000 $10,000
1993 1994 1995 1996 1997

Warranty/Maintenance Info

Item		Rate
Major Tune-Up	$153	Better Than Average
Minor Tune-Up	$90	Better Than Average
Brake Service	$297	Average
Overall Warranty	1 yr/12k	Poor
Drivetrain Warranty	7 yr/70k	Excellent
Rust Warranty	7 yr/100k	Excellent
Maintenance Warranty	N/A	
Roadside Assistance	N/A	

Resale Value

1993	1994	1995	1996	1997
$16,500	$15,786	$15,129	$14,179	$13,001

Ownership Costs (5yr)

Average	This Car
$31,416	$31,087
Cost/Mile 45¢	Cost/Mile 44¢

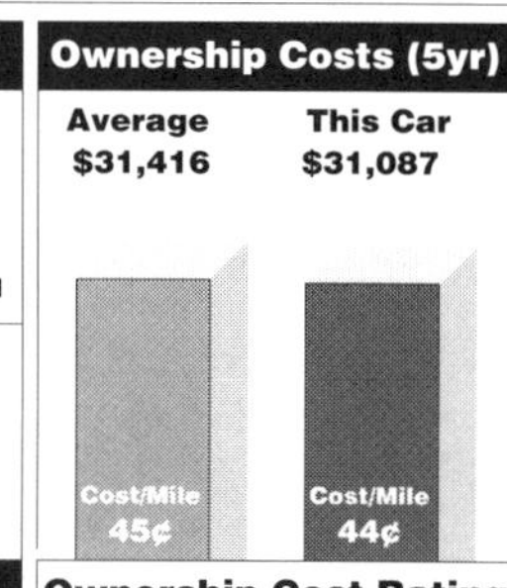

The 1993 Dodge Ram 250 pickup is available in four models - the D250, D250 Club Cab, W250, and W250 Club Cab. The Dodge Ram W250 Club Cab is a 4WD pickup truck that can be upgraded with options from three packages -- Base, Work, and/or Super LE. Choices include a 30-gallon fuel tank, heavy-duty vinyl bench with head rest, a front stabilizer bar, and power window and door locks. The Super LE package includes lower body side moldings, cloth bench with head rests, and electronic speed control.

Cumulative Costs

	1993	1994	1995	1996	1997
Annual	$8,884	$5,105	$5,770	$5,046	$6,282
Total	$8,884	$13,989	$19,759	$24,805	$31,087

Ownership Cost Rating

Better Than Average

Dodge Ram W350 Club Cab
2 Door Extended Cab

5.9L 160 hp Turbo Dsl Fuel Inject.

6 Cylinder In-Line

Manual 5 Speed

4 Wheel On-Demand

Manual Seatbelts Only

Large Pickup
D350 Model Shown

Purchase Price

Car Item	Dealer Cost	List
Base Price	**$21,258**	**$24,457**
Anti-Lock Brakes	Std	Std
Automatic 4 Speed	$754	$887
Optional Engine	N/A	N/A
Air Conditioning	$677	$797
Power Steering	Std	Std
Cruise Control	Pkg	Pkg
4 Whl On-Demand Dr.	Std	Std
AM/FM Stereo Cassette	$174	$205
Steering Wheel, Tilt	$114	** $134
Power Windows	Pkg	Pkg
***Options Price**	$851	$1,002
***Total Price**	**$22,109**	**$25,459**
Target Price	$23,979	
Destination Charge	$595	
Avg. Tax & Fees	$1,490	
Total Target $	**$26,064**	
Average Dealer Option Cost:	***85%***	

Ownership Costs

Cost Area	5 Year Cost	Rate
Depreciation	$13,298	Poor
Financing ($524/month)	$4,293	
Insurance (Rating 15 [Est.])	$8,717	Average
State Fees	$1,041	
Fuel (Hwy 12 City 9 [Est.])	$9,311	Poor
Maintenance	$3,901	Better Than Average
Repairs	$965	Worse Than Average

Ownership Cost By Year

$2,000 $4,000 $6,000 $8,000 $10,000 $12,000 $14,000
1993 1994 1995 1996 1997

Warranty/Maintenance Info

Item		Rate
Major Tune-Up	$125	Excellent
Minor Tune-Up	$96	Better Than Average
Brake Service	$297	Average
Overall Warranty	1 yr/12k	Poor
Drivetrain Warranty	7 yr/70k	Excellent
Rust Warranty	7 yr/100k	Excellent
Maintenance Warranty	N/A	
Roadside Assistance	N/A	

Resale Value

1993	1994	1995	1996	1997
$18,038	$16,887	$15,717	$14,334	$12,766

Ownership Costs (5yr)

Average	This Car
$37,499	$41,526
Cost/Mile 54¢	Cost/Mile 59¢

The 1993 Ram 350 is available in both two-wheel-drive and four-wheel-drive in either regular or Club Cab configurations. New for 1993, the W350 Club Cab features a multi-port, fuel injected Magnum 5.9-liter V-8 engine. Standard features include dual low mount mirrors, vinyl bucket seats, power steering and cloth headliner. Among the available options on Ram 350 pickups are air conditioning, GVW packages, power windows and door locks, tilt steering, speed control and sliding rear window.

Cumulative Costs

	1993	1994	1995	1996	1997
Annual	$13,520	$6,657	$7,308	$6,480	$7,561
Total	$13,520	$20,177	$27,485	$33,965	$41,526

Ownership Cost Rating

Worse Than Average

* Includes shaded options

** Other purchase requirements apply

 Poor  Worse Than Average  Average  Better Than Average  Excellent — Insufficient Information

Refer to *Section 3: Annotated Vehicle Charts* for an explanation of these charts.

Dodge Ram Van B150

3 Door Cargo Van

3.9L 180 hp Gas Fuel Inject.

6 Cylinder "V"

Manual 5 Speed

2 Wheel Rear

Manual Seatbelts Only

B350 Maxivan Shown

Purchase Price

Car Item	Dealer Cost	List
Base Price	**$12,819**	**$14,564**
Anti-Lock Brakes	Std	Std
Automatic 3 Speed	$277	$326
5.2L 235 hp Gas	$499	$587
Air Conditioning	$825	$970
Power Steering	Std	Std
Cruise Control	Pkg	Pkg
All Wheel Drive	N/A	N/A
AM/FM Stereo Cassette	$174	** $205
Steering Wheel, Tilt	$114	** $134
Power Windows	N/A	N/A
***Options Price**	$1,601	$1,883
***Total Price**	**$14,420**	**$16,447**
Target Price	$15,248	
Destination Charge	$570	
Avg. Tax & Fees	$961	
Total Target $	**$16,779**	
Average Dealer Option Cost:	***85%***	

Ownership Costs

Cost Area	5 Year Cost	Rate
Depreciation	$6,746	Better Than Average
Financing ($337/month)	$2,764	
Insurance (Rating 3 [Est.])	$6,731	Better Than Average
State Fees	$680	
Fuel (Hwy 14 City 12)	$6,645	Worse Than Average
Maintenance	$3,483	Better Than Average
Repairs	$820	Average

Ownership Cost By Year

$2,000 $4,000 $6,000 $8,000

1993 1994 1995 1996 1997

Warranty/Maintenance Info

Major Tune-Up	$151	Average
Minor Tune-Up	$90	Average
Brake Service	$246	Average
Overall Warranty	1 yr/12k	Poor
Drivetrain Warranty	7 yr/70k	Excellent
Rust Warranty	7 yr/100k	Excellent
Maintenance Warranty	N/A	
Roadside Assistance	N/A	

Resale Value

1993	1994	1995	1996	1997
$13,585	$12,650	$11,996	$11,073	$10,033

Ownership Costs (5yr)

Average	This Car
$28,682	$27,869
Cost/Mile 41¢	Cost/Mile 40¢

The 1993 Dodge Ram Van is available in five models - B150, B250, B350, Maxivan B250, and Maxivan B350. The B150 features standard electronic ignition system and exhaust emission control system. Color-keyed arm rests on front door panels, 15" color-keyed steering wheel, and 22 gallon fuel tank are all standard. Options must be selected in packages. Available equipment includes 35-gallon fuel tank, engine block heater, and heavy duty suspension and springs.

Cumulative Costs

	1993	1994	1995	1996	1997
Annual	$7,057	$4,913	$5,343	$4,749	$5,807
Total	$7,057	$11,970	$17,313	$22,062	$27,869

Ownership Cost Rating

Better Than Average

Dodge Ram Van B250

3 Door Cargo Van

3.9L 180 hp Gas Fuel Inject.

6 Cylinder "V"

Manual 5 Speed

2 Wheel Rear

Manual Seatbelts Only

Full-Size Van

B350 Maxivan Shown

Purchase Price

Car Item	Dealer Cost	List
Base Price	**$13,285**	**$15,112**
Anti-Lock Brakes	Std	Std
Automatic 4 Speed	$213	$250
5.2L 235 hp Gas	$499	$587
Air Conditioning	$825	$970
Power Steering	Std	Std
Cruise Control	Pkg	Pkg
All Wheel Drive	N/A	N/A
AM/FM Stereo Cassette	$174	** $205
Steering Wheel, Tilt	$114	** $134
Power Windows	Pkg	Pkg
***Options Price**	$1,537	$1,807
***Total Price**	**$14,822**	**$16,919**
Target Price	$15,685	
Destination Charge	$570	
Avg. Tax & Fees	$988	
Total Target $	**$17,243**	
Average Dealer Option Cost:	***85%***	

Ownership Costs

Cost Area	5 Year Cost	Rate
Depreciation	$7,273	Average
Financing ($347/month)	$2,840	
Insurance (Rating 6 [Est.])	$7,129	Excellent
State Fees	$699	
Fuel (Hwy 14 City 12)	$6,645	Worse Than Average
Maintenance	$3,766	Average
Repairs	$820	Average

Ownership Cost By Year

$2,000 $4,000 $6,000 $8,000

1993 1994 1995 1996 1997

Warranty/Maintenance Info

Major Tune-Up	$151	Average
Minor Tune-Up	$90	Average
Brake Service	$297	Average
Overall Warranty	1 yr/12k	Poor
Drivetrain Warranty	7 yr/70k	Excellent
Rust Warranty	7 yr/100k	Excellent
Maintenance Warranty	N/A	
Roadside Assistance	N/A	

Resale Value

1993	1994	1995	1996	1997
$13,482	$12,596	$12,012	$11,119	$9,970

Ownership Costs (5yr)

Average	This Car
$29,238	$29,172
Cost/Mile 42¢	Cost/Mile 42¢

The 1993 Dodge Ram Van is available in five models - B150, B250, B350, Maxivan B250, and Maxivan B350. The B250 features standard front door panel armrests, and highback non-reclining buckets seas and rear bench with vinyl trim. Options must be selected in packages. They include 35-gallon fuel tank, engine block heater, heavy duty suspension and springs, rear window electric defroster, and glass sunscreen.

Cumulative Costs

	1993	1994	1995	1996	1997
Annual	$7,734	$4,969	$5,508	$4,809	$6,152
Total	$7,734	$12,703	$18,211	$23,020	$29,172

Ownership Cost Rating

Average

* Includes shaded options

** Other purchase requirements apply

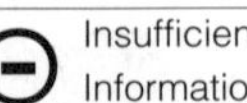

Poor  Worse Than Average  Average 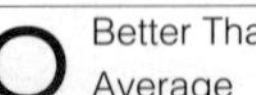 Better Than Average  Excellent Insufficient Information

Refer to *Section 3: Annotated Vehicle Charts* for an explanation of these charts.

Dodge Ram Van B250 Maxivan
3 Door Cargo Ext Van

3.9L 180 hp Gas Fuel Inject.

6 Cylinder "V"

Automatic 3 Speed

2 Wheel Rear

Manual Seatbelts Only

B350 Model Shown

Purchase Price

Car Item	Dealer Cost	List
Base Price	**$14,714**	**$16,793**
Anti-Lock Brakes	Std	Std
4 Spd Auto	$213	$250
5.2L 235 hp Gas	$499	$587
Air Conditioning	$825	$970
Power Steering	Std	Std
Cruise Control	Pkg	Pkg
All Wheel Drive	N/A	N/A
AM/FM Stereo Cassette	$174	$205
Steering Wheel, Tilt	$114	** $134
Power Windows	Pkg	Pkg
***Options Price**	$1,324	$1,557
***Total Price**	**$16,038**	**$18,350**
Target Price	$17,011	
Destination Charge	$570	
Avg. Tax & Fees	$1,068	
Total Target $	**$18,649**	
Average Dealer Option Cost:	***85%***	

Ownership Costs

Cost Area	5 Year Cost	Rate
Depreciation	$7,838	Better Than Average
Financing ($375/month)	$3,072	
Insurance (Rating 7 [Est.])	$7,244	Excellent
State Fees	$756	
Fuel (Hwy 14 City 13)	$6,420	Worse Than Average
Maintenance	$4,057	Better Than Average
Repairs	$820	Average

Ownership Cost By Year

$2,000 $4,000 $6,000 $8,000

1993 1994 1995 1996 1997

Warranty/Maintenance Info

Item		Rate
Major Tune-Up	$151	Better Than Average
Minor Tune-Up	$90	Better Than Average
Brake Service	$297	Average
Overall Warranty	1 yr/12k	Poor
Drivetrain Warranty	7 yr/70k	Excellent
Rust Warranty	7 yr/100k	Excellent
Maintenance Warranty	N/A	
Roadside Assistance	N/A	

Resale Value

1993	1994	1995	1996	1997
$14,561	$13,617	$12,988	$12,030	$10,811

Ownership Costs (5yr)

Average	This Car
$30,923	$30,207

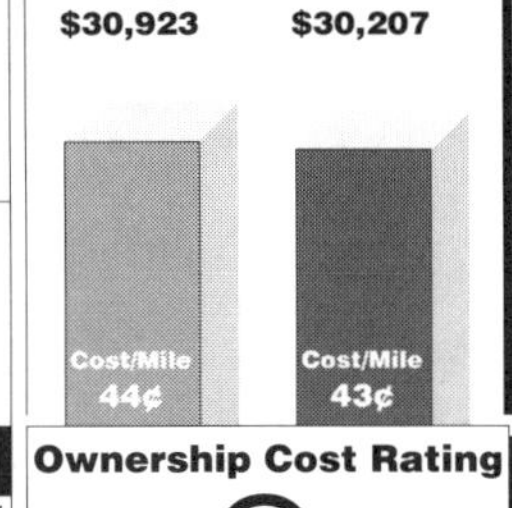

Cumulative Costs

	1993	1994	1995	1996	1997
Annual	$8,151	$5,091	$5,719	$4,896	$6,350
Total	$8,151	$13,242	$18,961	$23,857	$30,207

Ownership Cost Rating

Better Than Average

The 1993 Dodge Ram Van is available in five models - B150, B250, B350, Maxivan B250, and Maxivan B350. The Maxivan B250 is longer than the Base van, and features 304 cubic feet of cargo volume. Standard features on this model include dual bright outside mirrors, front and side door scuff pads,, and wipers with intermittent timing. Options for the vans must be bought in packages. They include 35-gallon fuel tank, vented glass with dual rear and right cargo doors and cast aluminum wheels.

Dodge Ram Van B350
3 Door Cargo Ext Van

5.2L 235 hp Gas Fuel Inject.

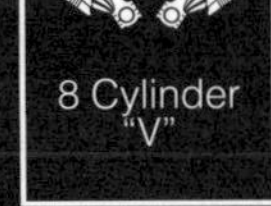

8 Cylinder "V"

Automatic 4 Speed

2 Wheel Rear

Manual Seatbelts Only

Full-Size Van

Maxivan Model Shown

Purchase Price

Car Item	Dealer Cost	List
Base Price	**$14,963**	**$17,086**
Anti-Lock Brakes	Std	Std
Manual Transmission	N/A	N/A
5.9L 230 hp Gas	$230	** $270
Air Conditioning	$825	$970
Power Steering	Std	Std
Cruise Control	Pkg	Pkg
All Wheel Drive	N/A	N/A
AM/FM Stereo Cassette	$174	** $205
Steering Wheel, Tilt	$114	** $134
Power Windows	Pkg	Pkg
***Options Price**	$825	$970
***Total Price**	**$15,788**	**$18,056**
Target Price	$16,753	
Destination Charge	$570	
Avg. Tax & Fees	$1,052	
Total Target $	**$18,375**	
Average Dealer Option Cost:	***85%***	

Ownership Costs

Cost Area	5 Year Cost	Rate
Depreciation	$7,401	Excellent
Financing ($369/month)	$3,027	
Insurance (Rating 5 [Est.])	$6,996	Excellent
State Fees	$745	
Fuel (Hwy 17 City 13)	$5,760	Average
Maintenance	$4,161	Average
Repairs	$820	Average

Ownership Cost By Year

$2,000 $4,000 $6,000 $8,000

1993 1994 1995 1996 1997

Warranty/Maintenance Info

Item		Rate
Major Tune-Up	$151	Better Than Average
Minor Tune-Up	$90	Better Than Average
Brake Service	$297	Average
Overall Warranty	1 yr/12k	Poor
Drivetrain Warranty	7 yr/70k	Excellent
Rust Warranty	7 yr/100k	Excellent
Maintenance Warranty	N/A	
Roadside Assistance	N/A	

Resale Value

1993	1994	1995	1996	1997
$13,724	$13,035	$12,620	$11,862	$10,974

Ownership Costs (5yr)

Average	This Car
$30,577	$28,910

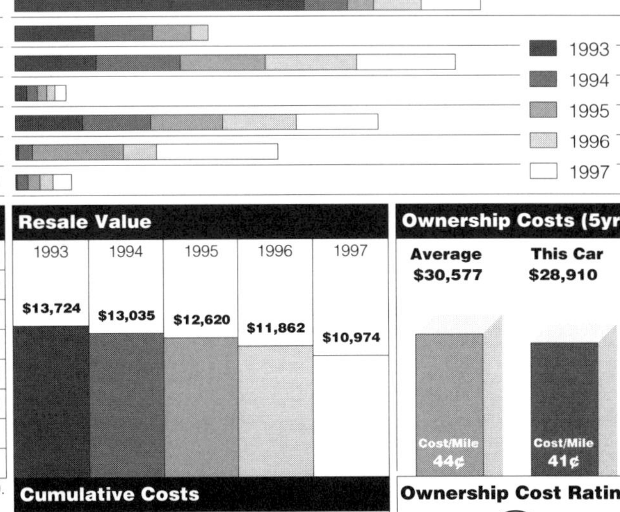

Cumulative Costs

	1993	1994	1995	1996	1997
Annual	$8,526	$4,645	$5,351	$4,503	$5,885
Total	$8,526	$13,171	$18,522	$23,025	$28,910

Ownership Cost Rating

Excellent

The 1993 Dodge Ram Van is available in five models - B150, B250, B350, Maxivan B250, and Maxivan B350. The B350 features standard dual bright outside mirrors, front and side door scuff pads,, and wipers with intermittent timing. Options for the vans must be bought in packages. They include 35-gallon fuel tank, vented glass with dual rear and right cargo doors, cast aluminum wheels, and bumper guards with nerf strips.

* Includes shaded options

** Other purchase requirements apply

 Poor  Worse Than Average  Average  Better Than Average 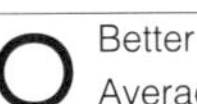 Excellent  Insufficient Information

Refer to *Section 3: Annotated Vehicle Charts* for an explanation of these charts.

Dodge Ram Van B350 Maxivan
3 Door Cargo Ext Van

5.2L 235 hp Gas Fuel Inject.

8 Cylinder "V"

Automatic 4 Speed

2 Wheel Rear

Manual Seatbelts Only

Full-Size Van

Purchase Price

Car Item	Dealer Cost	List
Base Price	**$15,783**	**$18,051**
Anti-Lock Brakes	Std	Std
Manual Transmission	N/A	N/A
5.9L 230 hp Gas	$230	$270
Air Conditioning	$825	$970
Power Steering	Std	Std
Cruise Control	Pkg	Pkg
All Wheel Drive	N/A	N/A
AM/FM Stereo Cassette	$174	$205
Steering Wheel, Tilt	$114	** $134
Power Windows	Pkg	Pkg
***Options Price**	$825	$970
***Total Price**	**$16,608**	**$19,021**
Target Price	$17,646	
Destination Charge	$570	
Avg. Tax & Fees	$1,107	
Total Target $	**$19,323**	
Average Dealer Option Cost:	***85%***	

Ownership Costs

Cost Area	5 Year Cost	Rate
Depreciation	$7,764	Excellent
Financing ($388/month)	$3,183	
Insurance (Rating 6 [Est.])	$7,129	Excellent
State Fees	$784	
Fuel (Hwy 17 City 13)	$5,760	Average
Maintenance	$4,197	Average
Repairs	$820	Average

Warranty/Maintenance Info

Major Tune-Up	$151	Better Than Average
Minor Tune-Up	$90	Better Than Average
Brake Service	$297	Average
Overall Warranty	1 yr/12k	Poor
Drivetrain Warranty	7 yr/70k	Excellent
Rust Warranty	7 yr/100k	Excellent
Maintenance Warranty	N/A	
Roadside Assistance	N/A	

Ownership Cost By Year

Resale Value

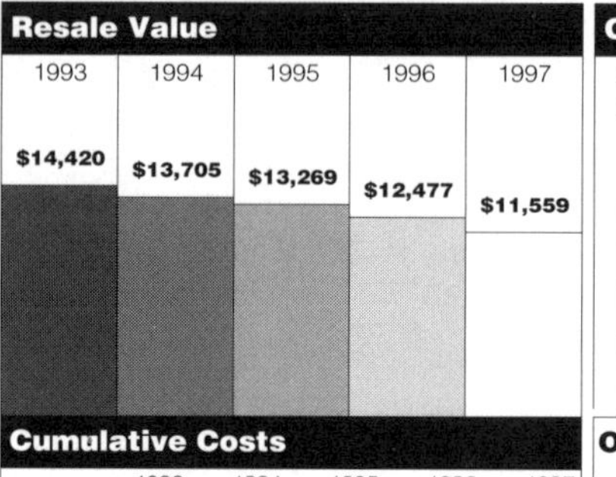

Ownership Costs (5yr)

Average	This Car
$31,713	$29,637

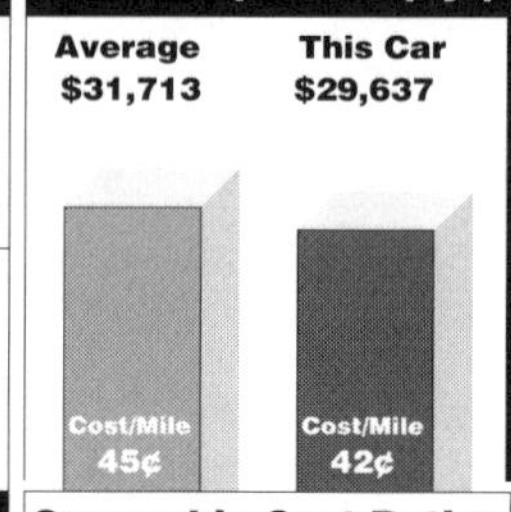

Cumulative Costs

	1993	1994	1995	1996	1997
Annual	$8,877	$4,754	$5,455	$4,582	$5,969
Total	$8,877	$13,631	$19,086	$23,668	$29,637

Ownership Cost Rating

Excellent

The 1993 Dodge Ram Van is available in five models - B150, B250, B350, Maxivan B250, and Maxivan B350. The Maxivan B350 is longer than the Base van, and features 304 cubic feet of cargo volume. Standard features on this model include dual bright outside mirrors, front and side door scuff pads,, and wipers with intermittent timing. Options for the vans must be bought in packages. They include 35-gallon fuel tank and vented glass with dual rear and right cargo doors.

Dodge Ram Wagon B150
3 Door Pass Van

3.9L 180 hp Gas Fuel Inject.

6 Cylinder "V"

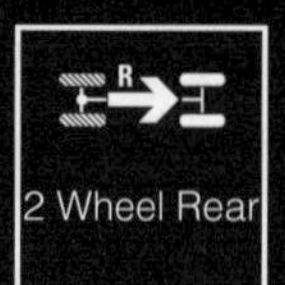
Manual 5 Speed

2 Wheel Rear

Manual Seatbelts Only

Full-Size Van

B250 Model Shown

Purchase Price

Car Item	Dealer Cost	List
Base Price	**$14,226**	**$16,160**
Anti-Lock Brakes	Std	Std
Automatic 3 Speed	$277	$326
5.2L 235 hp Gas	$499	$587
Air Conditioning	$825	$970
Power Steering	Std	Std
Cruise Control	Pkg	Pkg
All Wheel Drive	N/A	N/A
AM/FM Stereo Cassette	$132	** $155
Steering Wheel, Tilt	$114	$134
Power Windows	Pkg	Pkg
***Options Price**	$1,601	$1,883
***Total Price**	**$15,827**	**$18,043**
Target Price	$17,220	
Destination Charge	$570	
Avg. Tax & Fees	$1,076	
Total Target $	**$18,866**	
Average Dealer Option Cost:	***85%***	

Ownership Costs

Cost Area	5 Year Cost	Rate
Depreciation	$8,645	Average
Financing ($379/month)	$3,107	
Insurance (Rating 4 [Est.])	$6,867	Excellent
State Fees	$745	
Fuel (Hwy 14 City 12)	$6,645	Worse Than Average
Maintenance	$3,592	Better Than Average
Repairs	$820	Average

Warranty/Maintenance Info

Major Tune-Up	$151	Better Than Average
Minor Tune-Up	$90	Better Than Average
Brake Service	$246	Better Than Average
Overall Warranty	1 yr/12k	Poor
Drivetrain Warranty	7 yr/70k	Excellent
Rust Warranty	7 yr/100k	Excellent
Maintenance Warranty	N/A	
Roadside Assistance	N/A	

Ownership Cost By Year

Resale Value

Ownership Costs (5yr)

Average	This Car
$30,562	$30,421

Cumulative Costs

	1993	1994	1995	1996	1997
Annual	$8,751	$5,170	$5,677	$4,777	$6,046
Total	$8,751	$13,921	$19,598	$24,375	$30,421

Ownership Cost Rating

Average

The Dodge Ram Wagon is available in five models - B150, B250, B350, Maxiwagon B250, and Maxiwagon B350. The Ram Wagon B150 features new door trim panel. The model also offers standard power steering, power front disc/rear drum brakes with rear anti-lock system, and front and rear gas shock absorbers. Options include front and rear carpeting, 35 gallon fuel tank (22 gallon is standard), dual bright manual mirrors, spare tire cover, and eight-passenger seating group.

* Includes shaded options
** Other purchase requirements apply

 Poor  Worse Than Average — Average —  Better Than Average — Excellent 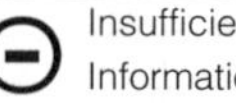 Insufficient Information

Refer to *Section 3: Annotated Vehicle Charts* for an explanation of these charts.

Dodge Ram Wagon B250
3 Door Pass Van

3.9L 180 hp Gas Fuel Inject.

6 Cylinder "V"

Automatic 3 Speed

2 Wheel Rear

Manual Seatbelts Only

Full-Size Van

Purchase Price

Car Item	Dealer Cost	List
Base Price	**$15,503**	**$17,662**
Anti-Lock Brakes	Std	Std
4 Spd Auto	$213	$250
5.2L 235 hp Gas	$499	$587
Air Conditioning	$825	$970
Power Steering	Std	Std
Cruise Control	Pkg	Pkg
All Wheel Drive	N/A	N/A
AM/FM Stereo Cassette	$132	** $155
Steering Wheel, Tilt	$114	$134
Power Windows	Pkg	Pkg
***Options Price**	$1,324	$1,557
***Total Price**	**$16,827**	**$19,219**
Target Price	$18,362	
Destination Charge	$570	
Avg. Tax & Fees	$1,145	
Total Target $	**$20,077**	
Average Dealer Option Cost:	***85%***	

Ownership Costs

Cost Area	5 Year Cost	Rate
Depreciation	$9,526	Average
Financing ($404/month)	$3,308	
Insurance (Rating 6 [Est.])	$7,129	Excellent
State Fees	$792	
Fuel (Hwy 14 City 12)	$6,645	Worse Than Average
Maintenance	$3,760	Better Than Average
Repairs	$820	Average

Ownership Cost By Year

$2,000 $4,000 $6,000 $8,000 $10,000

1993 1994 1995 1996 1997

Warranty/Maintenance Info

Item		Rate
Major Tune-Up	$151	Better Than Average
Minor Tune-Up	$90	Better Than Average
Brake Service	$297	Average
Overall Warranty	1 yr/12k	Poor
Drivetrain Warranty	7 yr/70k	Excellent
Rust Warranty	7 yr/100k	Excellent
Maintenance Warranty	N/A	
Roadside Assistance	N/A	

Resale Value

1993	1994	1995	1996	1997
$14,385	$13,367	$12,551	$11,674	$10,551

Ownership Costs (5yr)

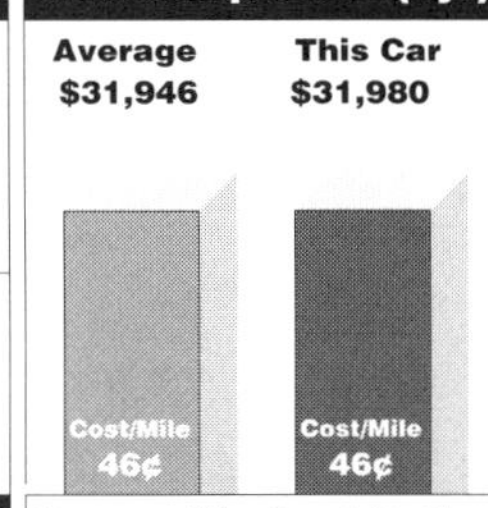

Average	This Car
$31,946	$31,980
Cost/Mile 46¢	Cost/Mile 46¢

The Dodge Ram Wagon is available in five models - B150, B250, B350, Maxiwagon B250, and Maxiwagon B350. The Wagon B250 offers standard power steering, power front disc/rear drum brakes with rear anti-lock system, and front and rear gas shock absorbers. Options include 35 gallon fuel tank, dual bright power mirrors, power locks and windows, eight-passenger seating, spare tire cover, and conventional wheels.

Cumulative Costs

	1993	1994	1995	1996	1997
Annual	$9,883	$5,268	$5,851	$4,844	$6,134
Total	$9,883	$15,151	$21,002	$25,846	$31,980

Ownership Cost Rating

Average

Dodge Ram Wagon B350
3 Door Pass Van

5.2L 235 hp Gas Fuel Inject.

8 Cylinder "V"

Automatic 4 Speed

2 Wheel Rear

Manual Seatbelts Only

Full-Size Van

B250 Model Shown

Purchase Price

Car Item	Dealer Cost	List
Base Price	**$16,598**	**$18,950**
Anti-Lock Brakes	Std	Std
Manual Transmission	N/A	N/A
5.9L 230 hp Gas	$230	** $270
Air Conditioning	$825	$970
Power Steering	Std	Std
Cruise Control	Pkg	Pkg
All Wheel Drive	N/A	N/A
AM/FM Stereo Cassette	$132	** $155
Steering Wheel, Tilt	$114	$134
Power Windows	Pkg	Pkg
***Options Price**	$825	$970
***Total Price**	**$17,423**	**$19,920**
Target Price	$19,061	
Destination Charge	$570	
Avg. Tax & Fees	$1,187	
Total Target $	**$20,818**	
Average Dealer Option Cost:	***85%***	

Ownership Costs

Cost Area	5 Year Cost	Rate
Depreciation	$9,985	Average
Financing ($418/month)	$3,429	
Insurance (Rating 7 [Est.])	$7,244	Excellent
State Fees	$819	
Fuel (Hwy 15 City 12)	$6,395	Worse Than Average
Maintenance	$4,155	Average
Repairs	$820	Average

Ownership Cost By Year

$2,000 $4,000 $6,000 $8,000 $10,000

1993 1994 1995 1996 1997

Warranty/Maintenance Info

Item		Rate
Major Tune-Up	$151	Better Than Average
Minor Tune-Up	$90	Better Than Average
Brake Service	$297	Average
Overall Warranty	1 yr/12k	Poor
Drivetrain Warranty	7 yr/70k	Excellent
Rust Warranty	7 yr/100k	Excellent
Maintenance Warranty	N/A	
Roadside Assistance	N/A	

Resale Value

1993	1994	1995	1996	1997
$14,904	$13,837	$12,952	$12,026	$10,833

Ownership Costs (5yr)

Average	This Car
$32,772	$32,847
Cost/Mile 47¢	Cost/Mile 47¢

The Dodge Ram Wagon is available in five models - B150, B250, B350, Maxiwagon B250, and Maxiwagon B350. Wagon B350 features standard color-keyed sun visors, tinted glass on all windows, and high back vinyl front command bucket seats with unibelt restraint system. A stainless steel exhaust system is also standard. Options include 35 gallon fuel tank, dual bright power mirrors, power locks and windows, eight-passenger seating, spare tire cover, and conventional wheels.

Cumulative Costs

	1993	1994	1995	1996	1997
Annual	$10,137	$5,335	$6,093	$4,896	$6,386
Total	$10,137	$15,472	$21,565	$26,461	$32,847

Ownership Cost Rating

Average

* Includes shaded options

** Other purchase requirements apply

Poor

Worse Than Average

Average

Better Than Average

Excellent
Insufficient Information

Refer to *Section 3: Annotated Vehicle Charts* for an explanation of these charts.

Dodge Ram Wagon B250 Maxiwagon 3 Door Pass Ext Van

5.2L 235 hp Gas Fuel Inject.

8 Cylinder "V"

PR|ND21
Automatic 3 Speed

2 Wheel Rear

Manual Seatbelts Only

Full-Size Van

Base Model Shown

Purchase Price

Car Item	Dealer Cost	List
Base Price	**$16,596**	**$18,948**
Anti-Lock Brakes	Std	Std
4 Spd Auto	$213	$250
5.9L 230 hp Gas	$230	** $270
Air Conditioning	$825	$970
Power Steering	Std	Std
Cruise Control	Pkg	Pkg
All Wheel Drive	N/A	N/A
AM/FM Stereo Cassette	N/A	N/A
Steering Wheel, Tilt	$114	$134
Power Windows	N/A	N/A
***Options Price**	$825	$970
***Total Price**	**$17,421**	**$19,918**
Target Price	$19,058	
Destination Charge	$570	
Avg. Tax & Fees	$1,186	
Total Target $	**$20,814**	
Average Dealer Option Cost:	***85%***	

Ownership Costs

Cost Area	5 Year Cost	Rate
Depreciation	$9,490	Average
Financing ($418/month)	$3,429	
Insurance (Rating 7 [Est.])	$7,244	Excellent
State Fees	$819	
Fuel (Hwy 14 City 12)	$6,645	Worse Than Average
Maintenance	$4,051	Better Than Average
Repairs	$820	Average

Warranty/Maintenance Info

Item		Rate
Major Tune-Up	$151	Better Than Average
Minor Tune-Up	$90	Better Than Average
Brake Service	$297	Average
Overall Warranty	1 yr/12k	Poor
Drivetrain Warranty	7 yr/70k	Excellent
Rust Warranty	7 yr/100k	Excellent
Maintenance Warranty	N/A	
Roadside Assistance	N/A	

Ownership Cost By Year

$2,000 $4,000 $6,000 $8,000 $10,000

1993 1994 1995 1996 1997

Resale Value

1993	1994	1995	1996	1997
$15,251	$14,327	$13,504	$12,599	$11,324

Ownership Costs (5yr)

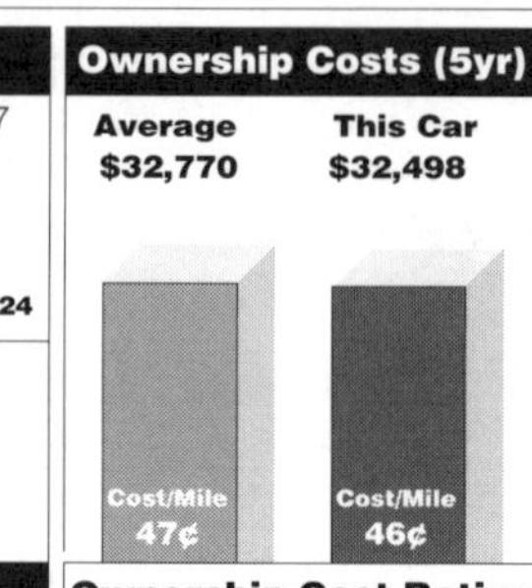

Average	This Car
$32,770	$32,498
Cost/Mile 47¢	Cost/Mile 46¢

Cumulative Costs

	1993	1994	1995	1996	1997
Annual	$9,832	$5,240	$6,042	$4,927	$6,457
Total	$9,832	$15,072	$21,114	$26,041	$32,498

Ownership Cost Rating

Average

The Dodge Ram Wagon is available in five models - B150, B250, B350, Maxiwagon B250, and Maxiwagon B350. The Maxiwagon B250 is longer than the non-maxi models, and can seat up to 15 passengers. A stainless steel exhaust system is standard. Option packages on this model include a single rear door with vented glass, 35 gallon fuel tank, bright grille, dual bright manual mirrors, radio speakers, 15 passenger seating, and spare tire cover.

Dodge Ram Wagon B350 Maxiwagon 3 Door Pass Ext Van

5.2L 235 hp Gas Fuel Inject.

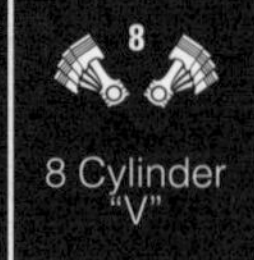
8 Cylinder "V"

Automatic 4 Speed

2 Wheel Rear

Manual Seatbelts Only

Full-Size Van

B250 Base Model Shown

Purchase Price

Car Item	Dealer Cost	List
Base Price	**$17,462**	**$19,967**
Anti-Lock Brakes	Std	Std
Manual Transmission	N/A	N/A
5.9L 230 hp Gas	$230	** $270
Air Conditioning	$825	$970
Power Steering	Std	Std
Cruise Control	Pkg	Pkg
All Wheel Drive	N/A	N/A
AM/FM Stereo Cassette	$132	** $155
Steering Wheel, Tilt	$114	$134
Power Windows	Pkg	Pkg
***Options Price**	$825	$970
***Total Price**	**$18,287**	**$20,937**
Target Price	$20,046	
Destination Charge	$570	
Avg. Tax & Fees	$1,246	
Total Target $	**$21,862**	
Average Dealer Option Cost:	***85%***	

Ownership Costs

Cost Area	5 Year Cost	Rate
Depreciation	$10,153	Average
Financing ($439/month)	$3,602	
Insurance (Rating 7 [Est.])	$7,244	Excellent
State Fees	$861	
Fuel (Hwy 15 City 12)	$6,395	Worse Than Average
Maintenance	$4,155	Average
Repairs	$820	Average

Warranty/Maintenance Info

Item		Rate
Major Tune-Up	$151	Better Than Average
Minor Tune-Up	$90	Better Than Average
Brake Service	$297	Average
Overall Warranty	1 yr/12k	Poor
Drivetrain Warranty	7 yr/70k	Excellent
Rust Warranty	7 yr/100k	Excellent
Maintenance Warranty	N/A	
Roadside Assistance	N/A	

Ownership Cost By Year

$2,000 $4,000 $6,000 $8,000 $10,000 $12,000

1993 1994 1995 1996 1997

Resale Value

1993	1994	1995	1996	1997
$15,737	$14,798	$13,956	$13,012	$11,709

Ownership Costs (5yr)

Average	This Car
$33,970	$33,230
Cost/Mile 49¢	Cost/Mile 47¢

Cumulative Costs

	1993	1994	1995	1996	1997
Annual	$10,430	$5,271	$6,092	$4,935	$6,502
Total	$10,430	$15,701	$21,793	$26,728	$33,230

Ownership Cost Rating

Better Than Average

The Dodge Ram Wagon is available in five models - B150, B250, B350, Maxiwagon B250, and Maxiwagon B350. The Maxiwagon B350 is longer than the non-maxi models, and can seat up to 15 passengers. Color-keyed sun visors, tinted glass on all windows, and high back vinyl front command bucket seats with unibelt restraint system are all standard equipment. Options on this model include 15 passenger seating, bumper guards with nerf strips, power door locks and windows, and 35 gallon fuel tank.

* Includes shaded options

** Other purchase requirements apply

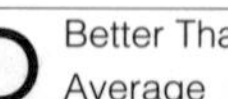

Poor 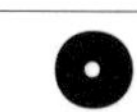 Worse Than Average  Average | Better Than Average | Excellent | Insufficient Information

Refer to *Section 3: Annotated Vehicle Charts* for an explanation of these charts.

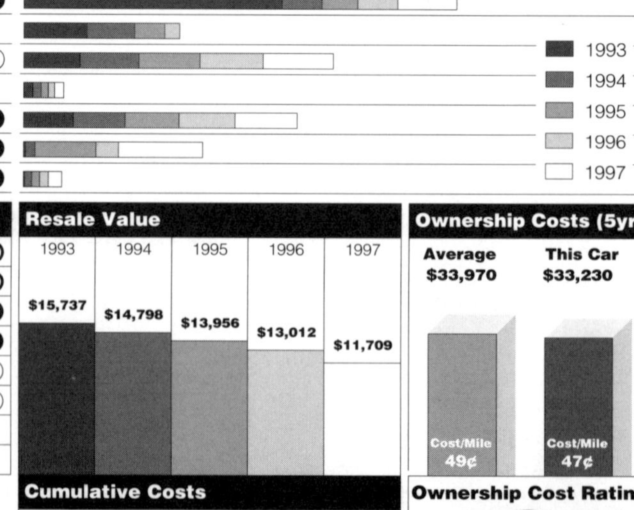

Dodge Ramcharger AD150 S

2 Door Sport Utility

Utility

5.2L 230 hp Gas Fuel Inject.

8 Cylinder "V"

Automatic 4 Speed

2 Wheel Rear

Manual Seatbelts Only

4WD Model Shown

Purchase Price

Car Item	Dealer Cost	List
Base Price	**$16,549**	**$17,636**
Anti-Lock Brakes	Std	Std
Manual Transmission	N/A	N/A
Optional Engine	N/A	N/A
Air Conditioning	$711	$836
Power Steering	Std	Std
Cruise Control	Pkg	Pkg
All Wheel Drive	N/A	N/A
AM/FM Stereo Cassette	$339	$399
Steering Wheel, Tilt	Pkg	Pkg
Power Windows	N/A	N/A
***Options Price**	$1,050	$1,235
***Total Price**	**$17,599**	**$18,871**
Target Price	$18,722	
Destination Charge	$595	
Avg. Tax & Fees	$1,161	
Total Target $	**$20,478**	
Average Dealer Option Cost:	***85%***	

Ownership Costs

Cost Area	5 Year Cost	Rate
Depreciation	$10,296	Worse Than Average
Financing ($412/month)	$3,373	
Insurance (Rating 11 [Est.])	$7,902	Average
State Fees	$779	
Fuel (Hwy 16 City 12)	$6,176	Poor
Maintenance	$3,935	Better Than Average
Repairs	$955	Worse Than Average

Ownership Cost By Year

$2,000 $4,000 $6,000 $8,000 $10,000 $12,000

1993 1994 1995 1996 1997

Warranty/Maintenance Info

Item		Rate
Major Tune-Up	$153	Better Than Average
Minor Tune-Up	$90	Better Than Average
Brake Service	$246	Average
Overall Warranty	1 yr/12k	Poor
Drivetrain Warranty	7 yr/70k	Excellent
Rust Warranty	7 yr/100k	Excellent
Maintenance Warranty	N/A	
Roadside Assistance	N/A	

Resale Value

1993	1994	1995	1996	1997
$13,258	$12,422	$11,659	$10,919	$10,182

Ownership Costs (5yr)

	Average	This Car
	$29,174	$33,416
Cost/Mile	42¢	48¢

Cumulative Costs

	1993	1994	1995	1996	1997
Annual	$11,496	$5,189	$5,965	$4,846	$5,920
Total	$11,496	$16,685	$22,650	$27,496	$33,416

Ownership Cost Rating

Poor

The 1993 Ramcharger is available as a two-door full-size sport utility wagon in either 2WD(AD) or 4WD(AW) with five optional trim levels - S, S Plus, Base, LE and Canyon Sport. New for 1993, the AD150 S Ramcharger features two new colors (Flame Red and Emerald Green). Also new are modified styled steel wheels, a standard heavy-duty automatic transmission and a premium AM/FM stereo radio w/graphic equalizer and available cassette player.

Dodge Ramcharger AD150

2 Door Sport Utility

Utility

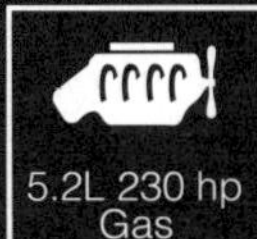
5.2L 230 hp Gas Fuel Inject.

8 Cylinder "V"

Automatic 4 Speed

2 Wheel Rear

Manual Seatbelts Only

4WD Model Shown

Purchase Price

Car Item	Dealer Cost	List
Base Price	**$17,437**	**$19,926**
Anti-Lock Brakes	Std	Std
Manual Transmission	N/A	N/A
5.9L 230 hp Gas	$339	$399
Air Conditioning	$711	$836
Power Steering	Std	Std
Cruise Control	Pkg	Pkg
All Wheel Drive	N/A	N/A
AM/FM Stereo Cassette	$174	$205
Steering Wheel, Tilt	$114	** $134
Power Windows	Pkg	Pkg
***Options Price**	$885	$1,041
***Total Price**	**$18,322**	**$20,967**
Target Price	$19,519	
Destination Charge	$595	
Avg. Tax & Fees	$1,222	
Total Target $	**$21,336**	
Average Dealer Option Cost:	***85%***	

Ownership Costs

Cost Area	5 Year Cost	Rate
Depreciation	$10,442	Poor
Financing ($429/month)	$3,515	
Insurance (Rating 12 [Est.])	$8,108	Average
State Fees	$862	
Fuel (Hwy 16 City 12)	$6,176	Poor
Maintenance	$3,935	Better Than Average
Repairs	$955	Worse Than Average

Ownership Cost By Year

$2,000 $4,000 $6,000 $8,000 $10,000 $12,000

1993 1994 1995 1996 1997

Warranty/Maintenance Info

Item		Rate
Major Tune-Up	$153	Better Than Average
Minor Tune-Up	$90	Better Than Average
Brake Service	$246	Average
Overall Warranty	1 yr/12k	Poor
Drivetrain Warranty	7 yr/70k	Excellent
Rust Warranty	7 yr/100k	Excellent
Maintenance Warranty	N/A	
Roadside Assistance	N/A	

Resale Value

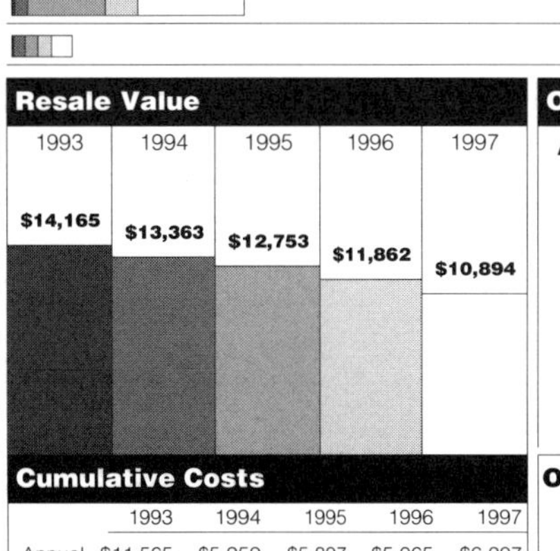

1993	1994	1995	1996	1997
$14,165	$13,363	$12,753	$11,862	$10,894

Ownership Costs (5yr)

	Average	This Car
	$30,937	$33,993
Cost/Mile	44¢	49¢

Cumulative Costs

	1993	1994	1995	1996	1997
Annual	$11,565	$5,259	$5,897	$5,065	$6,207
Total	$11,565	$16,824	$22,721	$27,786	$33,993

Ownership Cost Rating

Poor

The 1993 Dodge Ramcharger is available as a two-door full-size sport utility wagon in either 2WD(AD) or 4WD(AW) with five optional trim levels - S, S Plus, Base, LE and Canyon Sport. New for 1993, the AD150 Ramcharger features two new exterior colors (Flame Red and Emerald Green). Also new are styled steel wheels, a standard four-speed heavy-duty automatic transmission and, sequential multi-point fuel injection, tuned intake manifold and serpentine belt accessory drive on Magnum 5.9L V-8 engine.

* Includes shaded options

** Other purchase requirements apply

 Poor  Worse Than Average 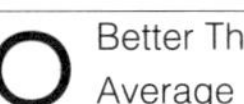 Average  Better Than Average 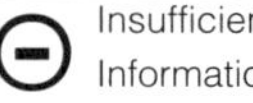 Excellent 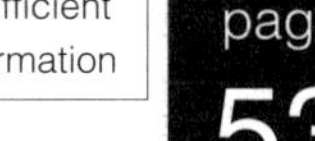 Insufficient Information

Refer to *Section 3: Annotated Vehicle Charts* for an explanation of these charts.

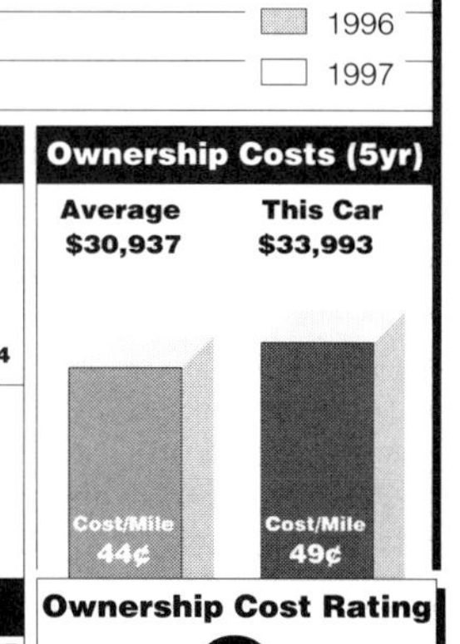

Dodge Ramcharger AW150 S

2 Door Sport Utility

5.2L 230 hp Gas Fuel Inject.

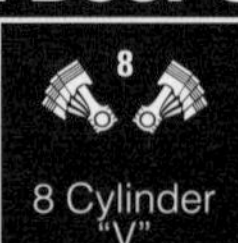

8 Cylinder "V"

Automatic 4 Speed

4 Wheel On-Demand

Manual Seatbelts Only

Utility

Purchase Price

Car Item	Dealer Cost	List
Base Price	**$18,686**	**$19,985**
Anti-Lock Brakes	Std	Std
Manual Transmission	N/A	N/A
Optional Engine	N/A	N/A
Air Conditioning	$711	$836
Power Steering	Std	Std
Cruise Control	Pkg	Pkg
4 Whl On-Demand Dr.	Std	Std
AM/FM Stereo Cassette	$339	$399
Steering Wheel, Tilt	Pkg	Pkg
Power Windows	N/A	N/A
***Options Price**	$1,050	$1,235
***Total Price**	**$19,736**	**$21,220**
Target Price	$21,068	
Destination Charge	$595	
Avg. Tax & Fees	$1,301	
Total Target $	**$22,964**	
Average Dealer Option Cost:	***85%***	

Ownership Costs

Cost Area	5 Year Cost	Rate
Depreciation	$11,220	Worse Than Average
Financing ($462/month)	$3,783	
Insurance (Rating 12 [Est.])	$8,108	Average
State Fees	$873	
Fuel (Hwy 16 City 12)	$6,176	Poor
Maintenance	$4,016	Average
Repairs	$820	Average

Ownership Cost By Year

$2,000 $4,000 $6,000 $8,000 $10,000 $12,000

1993 1994 1995 1996 1997

Warranty/Maintenance Info

Item		Rate
Major Tune-Up	$153	Better Than Average
Minor Tune-Up	$90	Better Than Average
Brake Service	$246	Average
Overall Warranty	1 yr/12k	Poor
Drivetrain Warranty	7 yr/70k	Excellent
Rust Warranty	7 yr/100k	Excellent
Maintenance Warranty	N/A	
Roadside Assistance	N/A	

Resale Value

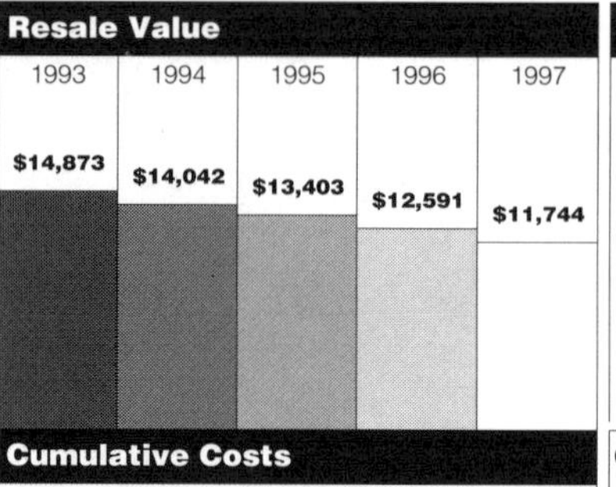

1993	1994	1995	1996	1997
$14,873	$14,042	$13,403	$12,591	$11,744

Ownership Costs (5yr)

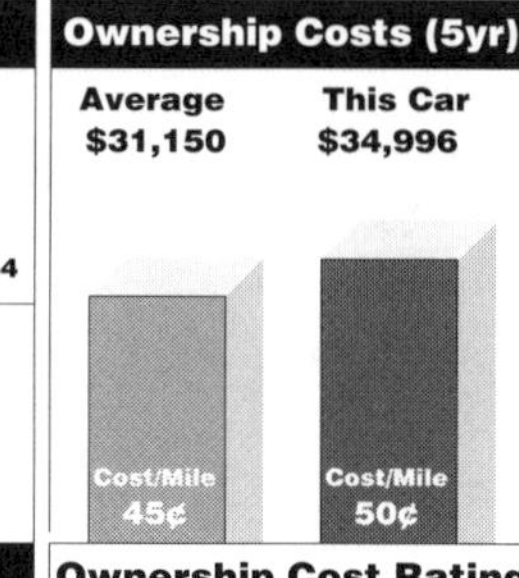

Average	This Car
$31,150	$34,996
Cost/Mile 45¢	Cost/Mile 50¢

Cumulative Costs

	1993	1994	1995	1996	1997
Annual	$12,594	$5,345	$5,978	$4,954	$6,125
Total	$12,594	$17,939	$23,917	$28,871	$34,996

Ownership Cost Rating

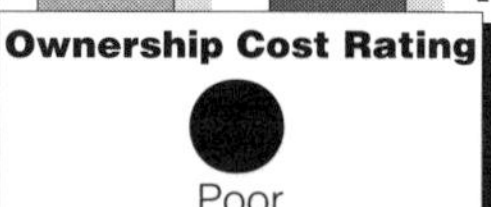

Poor

The 1993 Dodge Ramcharger is available as a two-door full-size sport utility wagon in either 2WD(AD) or 4WD(AW) with five optional trim levels - S, S Plus, Base, LE and Canyon Sport. New for 1993, the AW150 S Ramcharger features two new exterior colors (Flame Red and Emerald Green). Also new are modified styled steel wheels and a standard heavy-duty automatic transmission. Standard features include electric rear window defroster, clear coat paint finish w/anti-chip coating and power steering.

Dodge Ramcharger AW150

2 Door Sport Utility

5.2L 230 hp Gas Fuel Inject.

8 Cylinder "V"

Automatic 4 Speed

4 Wheel On-Demand

Manual Seatbelts Only

Utility

Purchase Price

Car Item	Dealer Cost	List
Base Price	**$18,942**	**$21,696**
Anti-Lock Brakes	Std	Std
Manual Transmission	N/A	N/A
5.9L 230 hp Gas	$339	$399
Air Conditioning	$711	$836
Power Steering	Std	Std
Cruise Control	Pkg	Pkg
4 Whl On-Demand Dr.	Std	Std
AM/FM Stereo Cassette	$174	$205
Steering Wheel, Tilt	$114	** $134
Power Windows	Pkg	Pkg
***Options Price**	$885	$1,041
***Total Price**	**$19,827**	**$22,737**
Target Price	$21,174	
Destination Charge	$595	
Avg. Tax & Fees	$1,321	
Total Target $	**$23,090**	
Average Dealer Option Cost:	***85%***	

Ownership Costs

Cost Area	5 Year Cost	Rate
Depreciation	$10,326	Worse Than Average
Financing ($464/month)	$3,803	
Insurance (Rating 13 [Est.])	$8,271	Average
State Fees	$933	
Fuel (Hwy 16 City 12)	$6,176	Poor
Maintenance	$4,016	Average
Repairs	$820	Average

Ownership Cost By Year

$2,000 $4,000 $6,000 $8,000 $10,000 $12,000

1993 1994 1995 1996 1997

Warranty/Maintenance Info

Item		Rate
Major Tune-Up	$153	Better Than Average
Minor Tune-Up	$90	Better Than Average
Brake Service	$246	Average
Overall Warranty	1 yr/12k	Poor
Drivetrain Warranty	7 yr/70k	Excellent
Rust Warranty	7 yr/100k	Excellent
Maintenance Warranty	N/A	
Roadside Assistance	N/A	

Resale Value

1993	1994	1995	1996	1997
$16,451	$15,550	$14,842	$13,842	$12,764

Ownership Costs (5yr)

Average	This Car
$32,426	$34,345
Cost/Mile 46¢	Cost/Mile 49¢

Cumulative Costs

	1993	1994	1995	1996	1997
Annual	$11,195	$5,467	$6,096	$5,187	$6,400
Total	$11,195	$16,662	$22,758	$27,945	$34,345

Ownership Cost Rating

Worse Than Average

The 1993 Dodge Ramcharger is available as a two-door full-size sport utility wagon in either 2WD(AD) or 4WD(AW) with five optional trim levels - S, S Plus, Base, LE and Canyon Sport. New for 1993, the AW150 Ramcharger features two new exterior colors (Flame Red and Emerald Green). Also new are modified styled steel wheels, a standard heavy-duty automatic transmission, sequential multi-point fuel injection, tuned intake manifold and serpentine belt accessory drive on Magnum 5.9L V-8 engine.

* Includes shaded options

** Other purchase requirements apply

Poor
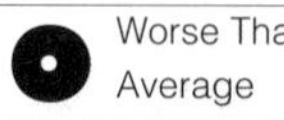
Worse Than Average

Average

Better Than Average

Excellent
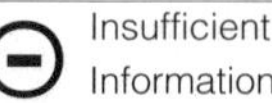
Insufficient Information

Refer to *Section 3: Annotated Vehicle Charts* for an explanation of these charts.

Eagle Summit DL

3 Door Wagon

1.8L 113 hp Gas Fuel Inject.

4 Cylinder In-Line

Manual 5 Speed

2 Wheel Front

Automatic Seatbelts

Purchase Price

Car Item	Dealer Cost	List
Base Price	**$10,660**	**$11,455**
Anti-Lock Brakes	$829	** $964
Automatic 4 Speed	$622	$723
2.4L 136 hp Gas	$156	$181
Air Conditioning	$673	$783
Power Steering	Std	Std
Cruise Control	Pkg	Pkg
All Wheel Drive	N/A	N/A
AM/FM Stereo Cassette	$156	$181
Steering Wheel, Tilt	N/A	N/A
Power Windows	N/A	N/A
***Options Price**	$1,607	$1,868
***Total Price**	**$12,267**	**$13,323**
Target Price	$13,043	
Destination Charge	$400	
Avg. Tax & Fees	$809	
Total Target $	**$14,252**	
Average Dealer Option Cost:	***86%***	

Ownership Costs

Cost Area	5 Year Cost	Rate
Depreciation	$8,427	Worse Than Average
Financing ($286/month)	$2,348	
Insurance (Rating 6 [Est.])	$6,919	Average
State Fees	$549	
Fuel (Hwy 26 City 20)	$3,756	Worse Than Average
Maintenance		Insufficient Information
Repairs	$789	Worse Than Average

Ownership Cost By Year

$2,000 $4,000 $6,000 $8,000 $10,000

Insufficient Maintenance Information

1993 1994 1995 1996 1997

Warranty/Maintenance Info

Item		Rate
Major Tune-Up		Insufficient Information
Minor Tune-Up		Insufficient Information
Brake Service	$177	Better Than Average
Overall Warranty	1 yr/12k	Poor
Drivetrain Warranty	7 yr/70k	Excellent
Rust Warranty	7 yr/100k	Excellent
Maintenance Warranty	N/A	
Roadside Assistance	N/A	

Resale Value

1993	1994	1995	1996	1997
$9,503	$8,421	$7,576	$6,666	$5,825

Ownership Costs (5yr)

Insufficient Information

The 1993 Eagle Summit Wagon is available in three models - DL, LX, and AWD. The 1993 Eagle Summit Wagon DL offers for the first time, a cargo security cover on the outside. Other changes from the previous model include the addition of bodyside moldings, halogen headlamps, variable, intermittent windshield wipers, full wheel covers, and an optional luggage rack. Other options include anti-lock brakes, rear-window defroster, tinted glass, and rear wiper and washer.

Cumulative Costs

	1993	1994	1995	1996	1997
Annual	*Insufficient Information*				
Total	*Insufficient Information*				

Ownership Cost Rating

Insufficient Information

Eagle Summit LX

3 Door Wagon

2.4L 136 hp Gas Fuel Inject.

4 Cylinder In-Line

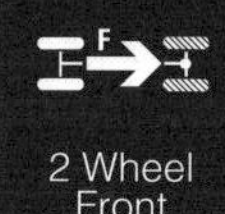

Manual 5 Speed

2 Wheel Front

Automatic Seatbelts

Purchase Price

Car Item	Dealer Cost	List
Base Price	**$11,481**	**$12,368**
Anti-Lock Brakes	$829	$964
Automatic 4 Speed	$622	$723
Optional Engine	N/A	N/A
Air Conditioning	Pkg	Pkg
Power Steering	Std	Std
Cruise Control	Pkg	Pkg
All Wheel Drive	N/A	N/A
AM/FM Stereo Cassette	Pkg	Pkg
Steering Wheel, Tilt	Std	Std
Power Windows	Pkg	Pkg
***Options Price**	$622	$723
***Total Price**	**$12,103**	**$13,091**
Target Price	$12,888	
Destination Charge	$400	
Avg. Tax & Fees	$799	
Total Target $	**$14,087**	
Average Dealer Option Cost:	***86%***	

Ownership Costs

Cost Area	5 Year Cost	Rate
Depreciation	$8,405	Worse Than Average
Financing ($283/month)	$2,321	
Insurance (Rating 6 [Est.])	$6,919	Average
State Fees	$539	
Fuel (Hwy 26 City 20)	$3,756	Worse Than Average
Maintenance		Insufficient Information
Repairs	$789	Worse Than Average

Ownership Cost By Year

$2,000 $4,000 $6,000 $8,000 $10,000

Insufficient Maintenance Information

1993 1994 1995 1996 1997

Warranty/Maintenance Info

Item		Rate
Major Tune-Up		Insufficient Information
Minor Tune-Up		Insufficient Information
Brake Service	$177	Better Than Average
Overall Warranty	1 yr/12k	Poor
Drivetrain Warranty	7 yr/70k	Excellent
Rust Warranty	7 yr/100k	Excellent
Maintenance Warranty	N/A	
Roadside Assistance	N/A	

Resale Value

1993	1994	1995	1996	1997
$9,318	$8,253	$7,422	$6,512	$5,682

Ownership Costs (5yr)

Insufficient Information

The 1993 Eagle Summit Wagon is available in three models - DL, LX, and AWD. The 1993 Eagle Summit Wagon LX features a new, full-cloth velour fabric. This model offers a standard child safety lock for the rear sliding door, power lock tailgate, dual electric mirrors, and rear, left side shelf for storage. The reclining, split-back bench in the rear can fold, tumble, and is removable. Options include remote keyless entry, luggage rack, electronic speed control, and rear window defroster.

Cumulative Costs

	1993	1994	1995	1996	1997
Annual	*Insufficient Information*				
Total	*Insufficient Information*				

Ownership Cost Rating

Insufficient Information

* Includes shaded options

** Other purchase requirements apply

 Poor  Worse Than Average  Average  Better Than Average — Excellent — Insufficient Information

Refer to *Section 3: Annotated Vehicle Charts* for an explanation of these charts.

Eagle Summit AWD
3 Door Wagon

1.8L 113 hp Gas Fuel Inject.

4 Cylinder In-Line

Manual 5 Speed

4 Wheel Full-Time

Automatic Seatbelts

Compact Wagon

Purchase Price

Car Item	Dealer Cost	List
Base Price	**$12,535**	**$13,539**
Anti-Lock Brakes	$829	** $964
Automatic 4 Speed	$622	$723
2.4L 136 hp Gas	$156	$181
Air Conditioning	$673	$783
Power Steering	Std	Std
Cruise Control	Pkg	Pkg
4 Wheel Full-Time Drive	Std	Std
AM/FM Stereo Cassette	$156	$181
Steering Wheel, Tilt	Std	Std
Power Windows	Pkg	Pkg
***Options Price**	$1,607	$1,868
***Total Price**	**$14,142**	**$15,407**
Target Price	$15,090	
Destination Charge	$400	
Avg. Tax & Fees	$933	
Total Target $	**$16,423**	
Average Dealer Option Cost:	***86%***	

Ownership Costs

Cost Area	5 Year Cost	Rate
Depreciation	$9,584	Worse Than Average
Financing ($330/month)	$2,706	
Insurance (Rating 7 [Est.])	$7,035	Average
State Fees	$632	
Fuel (Hwy 23 City 19)	$4,111	Poor
Maintenance		Insufficient Information
Repairs	$789	Worse Than Average

Ownership Cost By Year

$2,000 $4,000 $6,000 $8,000 $10,000

Insufficient Maintenance Information

1993 1994 1995 1996 1997

Warranty/Maintenance Info

Item		Rate
Major Tune-Up		Insufficient Information
Minor Tune-Up		Insufficient Information
Brake Service	$185	Better Than Average
Overall Warranty	1 yr/12k	Poor
Drivetrain Warranty	7 yr/70k	Excellent
Rust Warranty	7 yr/100k	Excellent
Maintenance Warranty	N/A	
Roadside Assistance	N/A	

Resale Value

1993	1994	1995	1996	1997
$10,890	$9,706	$8,779	$7,762	$6,839

Ownership Costs (5yr)

Insufficient Information

Cumulative Costs

	1993	1994	1995	1996	1997
Annual	Insufficient Information				
Total	Insufficient Information				

Ownership Cost Rating

Insufficient Information

The 1993 Eagle Summit Wagon is available in three models - DL, LX, and AWD. The 1993 Eagle Summit Wagon AWD. The AWD model features a standard stainless steel exhaust system, leather-wrapped sport steering wheel, bodyside moldings, front and rear body color fascias, and full tinted glass with windshield sun shaded band. Leather front seats, sunroof, anti-lock brakes, rear lift gate wiper/washer, and power windows and door locks are optional.

Ford Aerostar XL
3 Door Pass Van

3.0L 135 hp Gas Fuel Inject.

6 Cylinder "V"

Manual 5 Speed

2 Wheel Rear

Driver Airbag Psngr Belts

Mini Van

Purchase Price

Car Item	Dealer Cost	List
Base Price	**$12,787**	**$14,360**
Anti-Lock Brakes	Std	Std
Automatic 4 Speed	$638	$750
Optional Engine	N/A	N/A
Air Conditioning	Pkg	Pkg
Power Steering	Std	Std
Cruise Control	$315	$371
All Wheel Drive	N/A	N/A
AM/FM Stereo Cassette	$166	$195
Steering Wheel, Tilt	Grp	Grp
Power Windows	Pkg	Pkg
***Options Price**	$1,119	$1,316
***Total Price**	**$13,906**	**$15,676**
Target Price	$14,986	
Destination Charge	$535	
Avg. Tax & Fees	$938	
Total Target $	**$16,459**	
Average Dealer Option Cost:	***86%***	

Ownership Costs

Cost Area	5 Year Cost	Rate
Depreciation	$5,359	Better Than Average
Financing ($331/month)	$2,711	
Insurance (Rating 5)	$6,786	Excellent
State Fees	$648	
Fuel (Hwy 23 City 17)	$4,328	Better Than Average
Maintenance	$3,932	Better Than Average
Repairs	$840	Worse Than Average

Ownership Cost By Year

$2,000 $4,000 $6,000 $8,000

1993 1994 1995 1996 1997

Warranty/Maintenance Info

Item		Rate
Major Tune-Up	$213	Worse Than Average
Minor Tune-Up	$150	Poor
Brake Service	$210	Better Than Average
Overall Warranty	3 yr/36k	Average
Drivetrain Warranty	3 yr/36k	Average
Rust Warranty	6 yr/100k	Better Than Average
Maintenance Warranty	N/A	
Roadside Assistance	N/A	

Resale Value

1993	1994	1995	1996	1997
$14,680	$13,795	$13,227	$12,167	$11,100

Ownership Costs (5yr)

Average	This Car
$24,751	$24,604
Cost/Mile 35¢	Cost/Mile 35¢

Cumulative Costs

	1993	1994	1995	1996	1997
Annual	$5,168	$4,285	$4,827	$4,729	$5,595
Total	$5,168	$9,453	$14,280	$19,009	$24,604

Ownership Cost Rating

Better Than Average

The Ford Aerostar is available in twelve model editions - Eddie Bauer, XL, and XLT passenger vans with standard or extended lengths and two- or four-wheel drive. New for 1993, the XL two-wheel drive model features black body side moldings, three new exterior colors (Cayman Green, Ruby Red and Bimini Blue), a new 90-mph mechanical analog speedometer, new Euro-perforation treatment for leather interior, Ruby Red interior trim replaces currant red, and integrated second row bench child safety seats.

* Includes shaded options
** Other purchase requirements apply

Poor ·  Worse Than Average · Average ·  Better Than Average · Excellent · Insufficient Information

Refer to *Section 3: Annotated Vehicle Charts* for an explanation of these charts.

Ford Aerostar XLT
3 Door Pass Van

3.0L 135 hp Gas Fuel Inject.

6 Cylinder "V"

Automatic 4 Speed

2 Wheel Rear

Driver Airbag Psngr Belts

Mini Van

Extended Model Shown

Purchase Price

Car Item	Dealer Cost	List
Base Price	**$17,385**	**$19,585**
Anti-Lock Brakes	Std	Std
Manual Transmission	N/A	N/A
Optional Engine	N/A	N/A
Air Conditioning	Std	Std
Power Steering	Std	Std
Cruise Control	Std	Std
All Wheel Drive	N/A	N/A
AM/FM Stereo Cassette	Pkg	Pkg
Steering Wheel, Tilt	Std	Std
Power Windows	Pkg	Pkg
***Options Price**	$0	$0
***Total Price**	**$17,385**	**$19,585**
Target Price	$18,920	
Destination Charge	$535	
Avg. Tax & Fees	$1,174	
Total Target $	**$20,629**	
Average Dealer Option Cost:	***85%***	

Ownership Costs

Cost Area	5 Year Cost	Rate
Depreciation	$7,984	Average
Financing ($415/month)	$3,398	
Insurance (Rating 4)	$6,658	Excellent
State Fees	$805	
Fuel (Hwy 23 City 17)	$4,328	Better Than Average
Maintenance	$3,932	Better Than Average
Repairs	$840	Worse Than Average

Ownership Cost By Year

$2,000 $4,000 $6,000 $8,000

1993 1994 1995 1996 1997

Warranty/Maintenance Info

Item	Cost/Term	Rate
Major Tune-Up	$213	Worse Than Average
Minor Tune-Up	$150	Poor
Brake Service	$210	Better Than Average
Overall Warranty	3 yr/36k	Average
Drivetrain Warranty	3 yr/36k	Average
Rust Warranty	6 yr/100k	Better Than Average
Maintenance Warranty	N/A	
Roadside Assistance	N/A	

Resale Value

1993	1994	1995	1996	1997
$17,418	$16,217	$15,367	$13,983	$12,645

Ownership Costs (5yr)

Average	This Car
$28,007	$27,945
Cost/Mile 40¢	Cost/Mile 40¢

The Ford Aerostar is available in twelve model editions - Eddie Bauer, XL, and XLT passenger vans with standard or extended lengths and two- or four-wheel drive. New for 1993, the XLT two-wheel drive model features black body side moldings, three new exterior colors (Cayman Green, Ruby Red and Bimini Blue), a new 90-mph mechanical analog speedometer, new Euro-perforation treatment for leather interior, ruby red interior trim replaces currant red, and integrated second row bench child safety seats.

Cumulative Costs

	1993	1994	1995	1996	1997
Annual	$6,901	$4,826	$5,251	$5,105	$5,862
Total	$6,901	$11,727	$16,978	$22,083	$27,945

Ownership Cost Rating

Average

Ford Aerostar Eddie Bauer
3 Door Pass Van

3.0L 135 hp Gas Fuel Inject.

6 Cylinder "V"

Automatic 4 Speed

2 Wheel Rear

Driver Airbag Psngr Belts

Mini Van

Base Extended Model Shown

Purchase Price

Car Item	Dealer Cost	List
Base Price	**$19,917**	**$22,462**
Anti-Lock Brakes	Std	Std
Manual Transmission	N/A	N/A
Optional Engine	N/A	N/A
Air Cond., High Capacity	Std	Std
Power Steering	Std	Std
Cruise Control	Std	Std
All Wheel Drive	N/A	N/A
AM/FM Stereo Cassette	Std	Std
Steering Wheel, Tilt	Std	Std
Power Windows	Std	Std
***Options Price**	$0	$0
***Total Price**	**$19,917**	**$22,462**
Target Price	$21,793	
Destination Charge	$535	
Avg. Tax & Fees	$1,346	
Total Target $	**$23,674**	
Average Dealer Option Cost:	***85%***	

Ownership Costs

Cost Area	5 Year Cost	Rate
Depreciation	$9,740	Average
Financing ($476/month)	$3,899	
Insurance (Rating 4)	$6,658	Excellent
State Fees	$920	
Fuel (Hwy 23 City 17)	$4,328	Better Than Average
Maintenance	$3,932	Better Than Average
Repairs	$840	Worse Than Average

Ownership Cost By Year

$2,000 $4,000 $6,000 $8,000 $10,000

1993 1994 1995 1996 1997

Warranty/Maintenance Info

Item	Cost/Term	Rate
Major Tune-Up	$213	Worse Than Average
Minor Tune-Up	$150	Poor
Brake Service	$210	Better Than Average
Overall Warranty	3 yr/36k	Average
Drivetrain Warranty	3 yr/36k	Average
Rust Warranty	6 yr/100k	Better Than Average
Maintenance Warranty	N/A	
Roadside Assistance	N/A	

Resale Value

1993	1994	1995	1996	1997
$18,357	$17,214	$16,263	$15,138	$13,934

Ownership Costs (5yr)

Average	This Car
$30,403	$30,317
Cost/Mile 43¢	Cost/Mile 43¢

The Ford Aerostar is available in twelve model editions - Eddie Bauer, XL, and XLT passenger vans with standard or extended lengths and two- or four-wheel drive. New for 1993, the Eddie Bauer two-wheel drive model features mocha body side moldings, three new exterior colors (Cayman Green, Ruby Red and Bimini Blue), a new 90-mph mechanical analog speedometer, new Euro-perforation treatment for leather interior, ruby red interior trim replaces currant red, and integrated second row bench child safety seats.

Cumulative Costs

	1993	1994	1995	1996	1997
Annual	$9,245	$4,951	$5,474	$4,902	$5,745
Total	$9,245	$14,196	$19,670	$24,572	$30,317

Ownership Cost Rating

Average

* Includes shaded options

** Other purchase requirements apply

 Poor  Worse Than Average  Average  Better Than Average ◯ Excellent ⊖ Insufficient Information

Refer to *Section 3: Annotated Vehicle Charts* for an explanation of these charts.

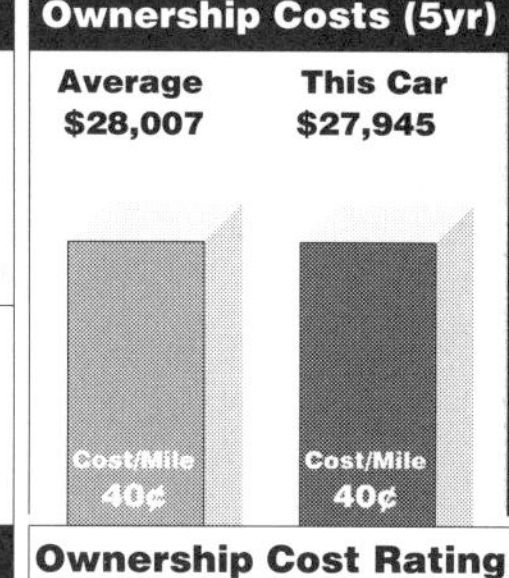

Ford Aerostar XL Extended
3 Door Pass Ext Van

3.0L 135 hp Gas Fuel Inject.

6 Cylinder "V"

Manual 5 Speed

2 Wheel Rear

Driver Airbag Psngr Belts

Mini Van

Regular-length Plus Model Shown

Purchase Price

Car Item	Dealer Cost	List
Base Price	**$14,018**	**$15,759**
Anti-Lock Brakes	Std	Std
Automatic 4 Speed	$638	$750
4.0L 155 hp Gas	$255	$300
Air Conditioning	Pkg	Pkg
Power Steering	Std	Std
Cruise Control	$315	$371
All Wheel Drive	N/A	N/A
AM/FM Stereo Cassette	$166	$195
Steering Wheel, Tilt	Grp	Grp
Power Windows	Pkg	Pkg
***Options Price**	$1,374	$1,616
***Total Price**	**$15,392**	**$17,375**
Target Price	$16,631	
Destination Charge	$535	
Avg. Tax & Fees	$1,037	
Total Target $	**$18,203**	
Average Dealer Option Cost:	***85%***	

Ownership Costs

Cost Area	5 Year Cost	Rate
Depreciation	$6,507	Average
Financing ($366/month)	$2,999	
Insurance (Rating 5)	$6,786	Excellent
State Fees	$715	
Fuel (Hwy 22 City 16)	$4,559	Average
Maintenance	$3,707	Better Than Average
Repairs	$840	Worse Than Average

Ownership Cost By Year

$2,000 $4,000 $6,000 $8,000

1993 1994 1995 1996 1997

Warranty/Maintenance Info

Major Tune-Up	$161	Better Than Average
Minor Tune-Up	$116	Average
Brake Service	$210	Better Than Average
Overall Warranty	3 yr/36k	Average
Drivetrain Warranty	3 yr/36k	Average
Rust Warranty	6 yr/100k	Better Than Average
Maintenance Warranty	N/A	
Roadside Assistance	N/A	

Resale Value

1993	1994	1995	1996	1997
$15,817	$14,821	$14,102	$12,891	$11,696

Ownership Costs (5yr)

Average	This Car
$26,166	$26,113
Cost/Mile 37¢	Cost/Mile 37¢

Cumulative Costs

	1993	1994	1995	1996	1997
Annual	$5,954	$4,509	$5,037	$4,923	$5,690
Total	$5,954	$10,463	$15,500	$20,423	$26,113

Ownership Cost Rating

Average

The Ford Aerostar is available in twelve model editions - Eddie Bauer, XL, and XLT passenger vans with standard or extended lengths and two- or four-wheel drive. New for 1993, the XL Extended features a new Euro-perforation treatment for leather interior, black body side moldings, three new exterior colors (Cayman Green, Ruby Red and Bimini Blue), a 90-mph mechanical analog speedometer, and integrated second row bench child safety seats. Aerostars are built in St. Louis, Missouri.

Ford Aerostar XLT Extended
3 Door Pass Ext Van

3.0L 135 hp Gas Fuel Inject.

6 Cylinder "V"

Automatic 4 Speed

2 Wheel Rear

Driver Airbag Psngr Belts

Mini Van

Purchase Price

Car Item	Dealer Cost	List
Base Price	**$17,825**	**$20,085**
Anti-Lock Brakes	Std	Std
Manual Transmission	N/A	N/A
4.0L 155 hp Gas	$255	$300
Air Conditioning	Std	Std
Power Steering	Std	Std
Cruise Control	Std	Std
All Wheel Drive	N/A	N/A
AM/FM Stereo Cassette	Pkg	Pkg
Steering Wheel, Tilt	Std	Std
Power Windows	Pkg	Pkg
***Options Price**	$255	$300
***Total Price**	**$18,080**	**$20,385**
Target Price	$19,695	
Destination Charge	$535	
Avg. Tax & Fees	$1,221	
Total Target $	**$21,451**	
Average Dealer Option Cost:	***85%***	

Ownership Costs

Cost Area	5 Year Cost	Rate
Depreciation	$8,190	Average
Financing ($431/month)	$3,534	
Insurance (Rating 5)	$6,786	Excellent
State Fees	$836	
Fuel (Hwy 22 City 16)	$4,559	Average
Maintenance	$3,707	Better Than Average
Repairs	$840	Worse Than Average

Ownership Cost By Year

$2,000 $4,000 $6,000 $8,000 $10,000

1993 1994 1995 1996 1997

Warranty/Maintenance Info

Major Tune-Up	$161	Better Than Average
Minor Tune-Up	$116	Average
Brake Service	$210	Better Than Average
Overall Warranty	3 yr/36k	Average
Drivetrain Warranty	3 yr/36k	Average
Rust Warranty	6 yr/100k	Better Than Average
Maintenance Warranty	N/A	
Roadside Assistance	N/A	

Resale Value

1993	1994	1995	1996	1997
$18,122	$16,963	$16,079	$14,666	$13,261

Ownership Costs (5yr)

Average	This Car
$28,673	$28,452
Cost/Mile 41¢	Cost/Mile 41¢

Cumulative Costs

	1993	1994	1995	1996	1997
Annual	$7,150	$4,866	$5,332	$5,185	$5,919
Total	$7,150	$12,016	$17,348	$22,533	$28,452

Ownership Cost Rating

Better Than Average

The Ford Aerostar is available in twelve model editions - Eddie Bauer, XL, and XLT passenger vans with standard or extended lengths and two- or four-wheel drive. New for 1993, the XLT Extended features a new Euro-perforation treatment for leather interior, black body side moldings, three new exterior colors (Cayman Green, Ruby Red and Bimini Blue), a 90-mph mechanical analog speedometer, and integrated second row bench child safety seats. Aerostars are built in St. Louis, Missouri.

* Includes shaded options

** Other purchase requirements apply

 Poor  Worse Than Average  Average  Better Than Average — Excellent — Insufficient Information

Refer to *Section 3: Annotated Vehicle Charts* for an explanation of these charts.

Ford Aerostar Eddie Bauer Extended
3 Door Pass Ext Van

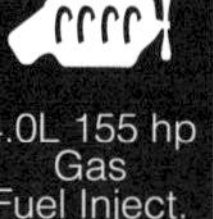
4.0L 155 hp Gas Fuel Inject.

6 Cylinder "V"

Automatic 4 Speed

2 Wheel Rear

Driver Airbag Psngr Belts

Mini Van

Purchase Price

Car Item	Dealer Cost	List
Base Price	**$20,640**	**$23,284**
Anti-Lock Brakes	Std	Std
Manual Transmission	N/A	N/A
Optional Engine	N/A	N/A
Air Cond., High Capacity	Std	Std
Power Steering	Std	Std
Cruise Control	Std	Std
All Wheel Drive	N/A	N/A
AM/FM Stereo Cassette	Std	Std
Steering Wheel, Tilt	Std	Std
Power Windows	Std	Std
***Options Price**	$0	$0
***Total Price**	**$20,640**	**$23,284**
Target Price	$22,618	
Destination Charge	$535	
Avg. Tax & Fees	$1,396	
Total Target $	**$24,549**	
Average Dealer Option Cost:	***85%***	

Ownership Costs

Cost Area	5 Year Cost	Rate
Depreciation	$9,632	Average
Financing ($493/month)	$4,044	
Insurance (Rating 4)	$6,658	Excellent
State Fees	$953	
Fuel (Hwy 22 City 16)	$4,559	Average
Maintenance	$3,703	Better Than Average
Repairs	$840	Worse Than Average

Ownership Cost By Year

$2,000 $4,000 $6,000 $8,000 $10,000

1993 1994 1995 1996 1997

Warranty/Maintenance Info

Major Tune-Up	$161	Better Than Average
Minor Tune-Up	$116	Average
Brake Service	$210	Better Than Average
Overall Warranty	3 yr/36k	Average
Drivetrain Warranty	3 yr/36k	Average
Rust Warranty	6 yr/100k	Better Than Average
Maintenance Warranty	N/A	
Roadside Assistance	N/A	

Resale Value

1993	1994	1995	1996	1997
$19,100	$18,017	$17,174	$16,109	$14,917

Ownership Costs (5yr)

Average	This Car
$31,088	$30,389
Cost/Mile 44¢	Cost/Mile 43¢

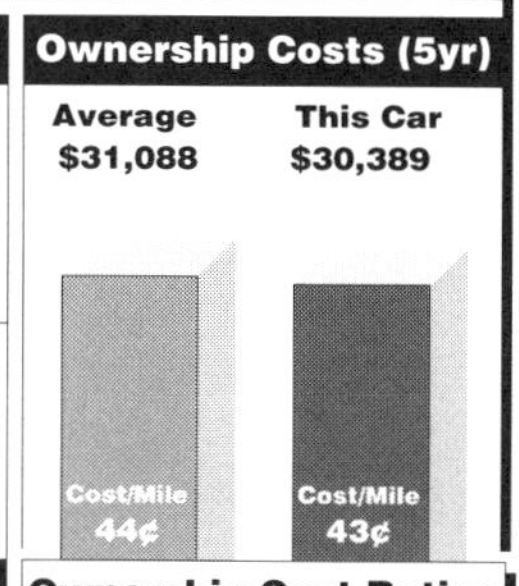

Cumulative Costs

	1993	1994	1995	1996	1997
Annual	$9,487	$4,951	$5,389	$4,869	$5,693
Total	$9,487	$14,438	$19,827	$24,696	$30,389

Ownership Cost Rating

Excellent

The Ford Aerostar is available in twelve model editions - Eddie Bauer, XL, and XLT passenger vans with standard or extended lengths and two- or four-wheel drive. New for 1993, the Eddie Bauer Extended features a new Euro-perforation treatment for leather interior, mocha body side moldings, three new exterior colors (Cayman Green, Ruby Red and Bimini Blue), a 90-mph mechanical analog speedometer, and integrated second row bench child safety seats. Aerostars are built in St. Louis, Missouri.

Ford Aerostar Cargo Van
3 Door Cargo Van

3.0L 135 hp Gas Fuel Inject.

6 Cylinder "V"

Manual 5 Speed

2 Wheel Rear

Driver Airbag Psngr Belts

Mini Van

Purchase Price

Car Item	Dealer Cost	List
Base Price	**$12,640**	**$14,221**
Anti-Lock Brakes	Std	Std
Automatic 4 Speed	$638	$750
Optional Engine	N/A	N/A
Air Conditioning	$738	$868
Power Steering	Std	Std
Cruise Control	$315	$371
All Wheel Drive	N/A	N/A
AM/FM Stereo Cassette	$291	** $343
Steering Wheel, Tilt	Grp	Grp
Power Windows	Pkg	Pkg
***Options Price**	$1,691	$1,989
***Total Price**	**$14,331**	**$16,210**
Target Price	$15,439	
Destination Charge	$535	
Avg. Tax & Fees	$966	
Total Target $	**$16,940**	
Average Dealer Option Cost:	***85%***	

Ownership Costs

Cost Area	5 Year Cost	Rate
Depreciation	$7,242	Worse Than Average
Financing ($340/month)	$2,790	
Insurance (Rating 4)	$6,658	Excellent
State Fees	$669	
Fuel (Hwy 24 City 18)	$4,117	Better Than Average
Maintenance	$3,932	Better Than Average
Repairs	$954	Worse Than Average

Ownership Cost By Year

$2,000 $4,000 $6,000 $8,000

1993 1994 1995 1996 1997

Warranty/Maintenance Info

Major Tune-Up	$213	Worse Than Average
Minor Tune-Up	$150	Poor
Brake Service	$210	Better Than Average
Overall Warranty	3 yr/36k	Average
Drivetrain Warranty	3 yr/36k	Average
Rust Warranty	6 yr/100k	Better Than Average
Maintenance Warranty	N/A	
Roadside Assistance	N/A	

Resale Value

1993	1994	1995	1996	1997
$13,213	$12,355	$11,600	$10,760	$9,698

Ownership Costs (5yr)

Average	This Car
$25,195	$26,362
Cost/Mile 36¢	Cost/Mile 38¢

Cumulative Costs

	1993	1994	1995	1996	1997
Annual	$7,091	$4,223	$4,982	$4,494	$5,572
Total	$7,091	$11,314	$16,296	$20,790	$26,362

Ownership Cost Rating

Average

The Ford Aerostar Cargo Van is available in four models - (Base) Aerostar Cargo Van, Extended Cargo Van, (Base) 4WD, and Extended 4WD. New for 1993, the (Base) Cargo Van features black body side moldings, three new exterior colors (Cayman Green, Ruby Red and Bimini Blue), and a 90-mph mechanical analog speedometer. Standard features include black aero, fold-away LH and RH mirrors, color-keyed front carpeting, front, black aero spoiler, V-6 EFI engine, overdrive transmission and 21-gal. fuel tank.

* Includes shaded options

** Other purchase requirements apply

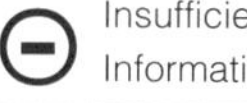

 Poor  Worse Than Average  Average 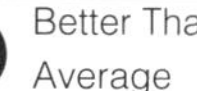 Better Than Average  Excellent ⊖ Insufficient Information

Refer to *Section 3: Annotated Vehicle Charts* for an explanation of these charts.

Ford Aerostar Cargo Van Extended
3 Door Cargo Ext Van

 3.0L 135 hp Gas Fuel Inject.	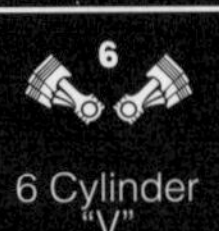 6 Cylinder "V"	1 3 5 / 2 4 R Manual 5 Speed	 2 Wheel Rear	 Driver Airbag Psngr Belts

Base Model Shown

Purchase Price

Car Item	Dealer Cost	List
Base Price	**$13,297**	**$14,968**
Anti-Lock Brakes	Std	Std
Automatic 4 Speed	$638	$750
4.0L 155 hp Gas	$268	$316
Air Conditioning	$738	$868
Power Steering	Std	Std
Cruise Control	$315	$371
All Wheel Drive	N/A	N/A
AM/FM Stereo Cassette	$291	** $343
Steering Wheel, Tilt	Grp	Grp
Power Windows	Pkg	Pkg
***Options Price**	$1,959	$2,305
***Total Price**	**$15,256**	**$17,273**
Target Price	$16,458	
Destination Charge	$535	
Avg. Tax & Fees	$1,028	
Total Target $	**$18,021**	
Average Dealer Option Cost:	***85%***	

Ownership Costs

Cost Area	5 Year Cost	Rate
Depreciation	$8,209	Poor
Financing ($362/month)	$2,970	
Insurance (Rating 4)	$6,658	Excellent
State Fees	$712	
Fuel (Hwy 22 City 16)	$4,559	Average
Maintenance	$3,707	Better Than Average
Repairs	$954	Worse Than Average

Ownership Cost By Year

$2,000 $4,000 $6,000 $8,000 $10,000

1993 1994 1995 1996 1997

Warranty/Maintenance Info

Major Tune-Up	$161	Better Than Average
Minor Tune-Up	$116	Average
Brake Service	$210	Better Than Average
Overall Warranty	3 yr/36k	Average
Drivetrain Warranty	3 yr/36k	Average
Rust Warranty	6 yr/100k	Better Than Average
Maintenance Warranty	N/A	
Roadside Assistance	N/A	

Resale Value

1993	1994	1995	1996	1997
$13,360	$12,511	$11,742	$10,894	$9,812

Ownership Costs (5yr)

Average	This Car
$26,081	$27,769
Cost/Mile 37¢	Cost/Mile 40¢

The Ford Aerostar Cargo Van is available in four models - (Base) Aerostar Cargo Van, Extended Cargo Van, (Base) 4WD, and Extended 4WD. New for 1993, the Extended Cargo Van features black body side moldings, three new exterior colors (Cayman Green, Ruby Red and Bimini Blue), and a 90-mph mechanical analog speedometer. Standard features include black aero, fold-away LH and RH mirrors, color-keyed front carpeting, front, black aero spoiler, V-6 EFI engine, overdrive transmission and 21-gal. fuel tank.

Cumulative Costs

	1993	1994	1995	1996	1997
Annual	$8,192	$4,327	$5,071	$4,577	$5,602
Total	$8,192	$12,519	$17,590	$22,167	$27,769

Ownership Cost Rating

Worse Than Average

Ford Aerostar XL 4WD
3 Door Pass Van

 4.0L 155 hp Gas Fuel Inject.	 6 Cylinder "V"	 Automatic 4 Speed	 4 Wheel Full-Time	 Driver Airbag Psngr Belts

2WD Model Shown

Purchase Price

Car Item	Dealer Cost	List
Base Price	**$15,840**	**$17,829**
Anti-Lock Brakes	Std	Std
Manual Transmission	N/A	N/A
Optional Engine	N/A	N/A
Air Conditioning	Pkg	Pkg
Power Steering	Std	Std
Cruise Control	$315	$371
4 Wheel Full-Time Drive	Std	Std
AM/FM Stereo Cassette	$166	$195
Steering Wheel, Tilt	Grp	Grp
Power Windows	Pkg	Pkg
***Options Price**	$481	$566
***Total Price**	**$16,321**	**$18,395**
Target Price	$17,704	
Destination Charge	$535	
Avg. Tax & Fees	$1,101	
Total Target $	**$19,340**	
Average Dealer Option Cost:	***86%***	

Ownership Costs

Cost Area	5 Year Cost	Rate
Depreciation	$6,605	Average
Financing ($389/month)	$3,186	
Insurance (Rating 7)	$7,035	Excellent
State Fees	$757	
Fuel (Hwy 20 City 15)	$4,941	Poor
Maintenance	$3,964	Better Than Average
Repairs	$954	Worse Than Average

Ownership Cost By Year

$2,000 $4,000 $6,000 $8,000

1993 1994 1995 1996 1997

Warranty/Maintenance Info

Major Tune-Up	$161	Better Than Average
Minor Tune-Up	$116	Average
Brake Service	$210	Better Than Average
Overall Warranty	3 yr/36k	Average
Drivetrain Warranty	3 yr/36k	Average
Rust Warranty	6 yr/100k	Better Than Average
Maintenance Warranty	N/A	
Roadside Assistance	N/A	

Resale Value

1993	1994	1995	1996	1997
$17,197	$16,115	$15,297	$14,025	$12,735

Ownership Costs (5yr)

Average	This Car
$27,016	$27,442
Cost/Mile 39¢	Cost/Mile 39¢

The Ford Aerostar is available in twelve model editions - Eddie Bauer, XL, and XLT passenger vans with standard or extended lengths and two- or four-wheel drive. New for 1993, the XL four-wheel drive model features black body side moldings, three new exterior colors (Cayman Green, Ruby Red and Bimini Blue), new Euro-perforation treatment for leather interior, a 90-mph mechanical analog speedometer, and integrated second row bench child safety seats. Aerostars are built in St. Louis, Missouri.

Cumulative Costs

	1993	1994	1995	1996	1997
Annual	$5,915	$4,785	$5,239	$5,181	$6,322
Total	$5,915	$10,700	$15,939	$21,120	$27,442

Ownership Cost Rating

Average

* Includes shaded options

** Other purchase requirements apply

 Poor  Worse Than Average Average 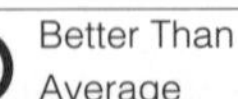 Better Than Average  Excellent Insufficient Information

Refer to *Section 3: Annotated Vehicle Charts* for an explanation of these charts.

Ford Aerostar XLT 4WD

3 Door Pass Van

4.0L 155 hp Gas Fuel Inject.

6 Cylinder "V"

Automatic 4 Speed

4 Wheel Full-Time

Driver Airbag Psngr Belts

Mini Van

Extended 2WD Model Shown

Purchase Price

Car Item	Dealer Cost	List
Base Price	**$18,749**	**$21,135**
Anti-Lock Brakes	Std	Std
Manual Transmission	N/A	N/A
Optional Engine	N/A	N/A
Air Conditioning	Std	Std
Power Steering	Std	Std
Cruise Control	Std	Std
4 Wheel Full-Time Drive	Std	Std
AM/FM Stereo Cassette	Pkg	Pkg
Steering Wheel, Tilt	Std	Std
Power Windows	Pkg	Pkg
***Options Price**	$0	$0
***Total Price**	**$18,749**	**$21,135**
Target Price	$20,464	
Destination Charge	$535	
Avg. Tax & Fees	$1,267	
Total Target $	**$22,266**	
Average Dealer Option Cost:	***86%***	

Ownership Costs

Cost Area	5 Year Cost	Rate
Depreciation	$8,261	Average
Financing ($448/month)	$3,667	
Insurance (Rating 5)	$6,786	Excellent
State Fees	$867	
Fuel (Hwy 20 City 15)	$4,941	Poor
Maintenance	$3,969	Better Than Average
Repairs	$954	Worse Than Average

Ownership Cost By Year

$2,000 $4,000 $6,000 $8,000 $10,000

1993 1994 1995 1996 1997

Warranty/Maintenance Info

Item		Rate
Major Tune-Up	$161	Better Than Average
Minor Tune-Up	$116	Average
Brake Service	$210	Better Than Average
Overall Warranty	3 yr/36k	Average
Drivetrain Warranty	3 yr/36k	Average
Rust Warranty	6 yr/100k	Better Than Average
Maintenance Warranty	N/A	
Roadside Assistance	N/A	

Resale Value

1993	1994	1995	1996	1997
$19,219	$17,980	$16,977	$15,475	$14,005

Ownership Costs (5yr)

Average	This Car
$29,298	$29,445
Cost/Mile 42¢	Cost/Mile 42¢

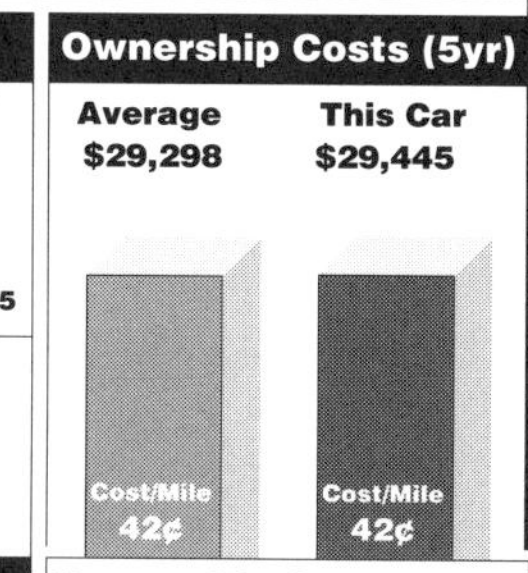

Cumulative Costs

	1993	1994	1995	1996	1997
Annual	$7,002	$5,069	$5,491	$5,413	$6,470
Total	$7,002	$12,071	$17,562	$22,975	$29,445

Ownership Cost Rating

Average

The Ford Aerostar is available in twelve model editions - Eddie Bauer, XL, and XLT passenger vans with standard or extended lengths and two- or four-wheel drive. New for 1993, the XLT four-wheel drive model features black body side moldings, three new exterior colors (Cayman Green, Ruby Red and Bimini Blue), new Euro-perforation treatment for leather interior, a 90-mph mechanical analog speedometer, and integrated second row bench child safety seats. Aerostars are built in St. Louis, Missouri.

Ford Aerostar Eddie Bauer 4WD

3 Door Pass Van

4.0L 155 hp Gas Fuel Inject.

6 Cylinder "V"

Automatic 4 Speed

4 Wheel Full-Time

Driver Airbag Psngr Belts

Mini Van

Base Extended Model Shown

Purchase Price

Car Item	Dealer Cost	List
Base Price	**$21,596**	**$24,371**
Anti-Lock Brakes	Std	Std
Manual Transmission	N/A	N/A
Optional Engine	N/A	N/A
Air Cond., High Capacity	Std	Std
Power Steering	Std	Std
Cruise Control	Std	Std
4 Wheel Full-Time Drive	Std	Std
AM/FM Stereo Cassette	Std	Std
Steering Wheel, Tilt	Std	Std
Power Windows	Std	Std
***Options Price**	$0	$0
***Total Price**	**$21,596**	**$24,371**
Target Price	$23,714	
Destination Charge	$535	
Avg. Tax & Fees	$1,461	
Total Target $	**$25,710**	
Average Dealer Option Cost:	***85%***	

Ownership Costs

Cost Area	5 Year Cost	Rate
Depreciation	$9,927	Average
Financing ($517/month)	$4,236	
Insurance (Rating 6)	$6,919	Excellent
State Fees	$995	
Fuel (Hwy 20 City 15)	$4,941	Poor
Maintenance	$3,960	Better Than Average
Repairs	$954	Worse Than Average

Ownership Cost By Year

$2,000 $4,000 $6,000 $8,000 $10,000

1993 1994 1995 1996 1997

Warranty/Maintenance Info

Item		Rate
Major Tune-Up	$161	Better Than Average
Minor Tune-Up	$116	Average
Brake Service	$210	Better Than Average
Overall Warranty	3 yr/36k	Average
Drivetrain Warranty	3 yr/36k	Average
Rust Warranty	6 yr/100k	Better Than Average
Maintenance Warranty	N/A	
Roadside Assistance	N/A	

Resale Value

1993	1994	1995	1996	1997
$20,260	$19,109	$18,153	$17,020	$15,783

Ownership Costs (5yr)

Average	This Car
$31,994	$31,932
Cost/Mile 46¢	Cost/Mile 46¢

Cumulative Costs

	1993	1994	1995	1996	1997
Annual	$9,697	$5,214	$5,610	$5,136	$6,275
Total	$9,697	$14,911	$20,521	$25,657	$31,932

Ownership Cost Rating

Average

The Ford Aerostar is available in twelve model editions - Eddie Bauer, XL, and XLT passenger vans with standard or extended lengths and two- or four-wheel drive. New for 1993, the Eddie Bauer four-wheel drive model features mocha body side moldings, three new exterior colors (Cayman Green, Ruby Red and Bimini Blue), new Euro-perforation treatment for leather interior, a 90-mph mechanical analog speedometer, and integrated second row bench child safety seats. Aerostars are built in St. Louis, Missouri.

* Includes shaded options

** Other purchase requirements apply

Poor  Worse Than Average  Average Better Than Average 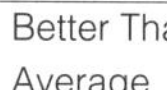 Excellent  Insufficient Information

Refer to *Section 3: Annotated Vehicle Charts* for an explanation of these charts.

Ford Aerostar XL Extended 4WD 3 Door Pass Ext Van

4.0L 155 hp Gas Fuel Inject.

6 Cylinder "V"

Automatic 4 Speed

4 Wheel Full-Time

Driver Airbag Psngr Belts

Base Model Shown

Purchase Price

Car Item	Dealer Cost	List
Base Price	**$16,408**	**$18,475**
Anti-Lock Brakes	Std	Std
Manual Transmission	N/A	N/A
Optional Engine	N/A	N/A
Air Conditioning	Pkg	Pkg
Power Steering	Std	Std
Cruise Control	$315	$371
4 Wheel Full-Time Drive	Std	Std
AM/FM Stereo Cassette	$166	$195
Steering Wheel, Tilt	Grp	Grp
Power Windows	Pkg	Pkg
***Options Price**	$481	$566
***Total Price**	**$16,889**	**$19,041**
Target Price	$18,342	
Destination Charge	$535	
Avg. Tax & Fees	$1,140	
Total Target $	**$20,017**	
Average Dealer Option Cost:	***86%***	

Ownership Costs

Cost Area	5 Year Cost	Rate
Depreciation	$6,996	Average
Financing ($402/month)	$3,298	
Insurance (Rating 6)	$6,919	Excellent
State Fees	$783	
Fuel (Hwy 20 City 15)	$4,941	Poor
Maintenance	$3,967	Better Than Average
Repairs	$954	Worse Than Average

Ownership Cost By Year

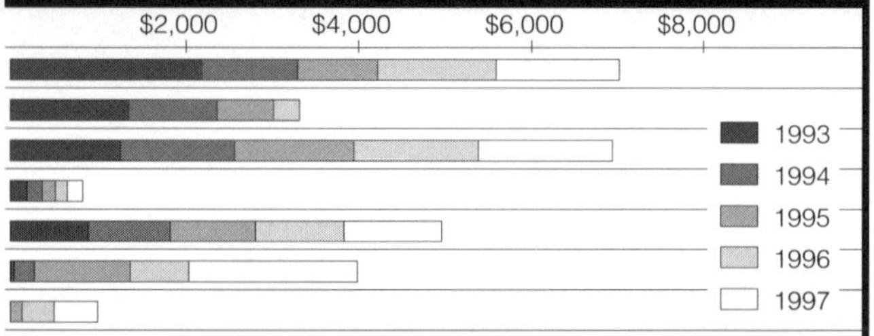

(Chart scale: $2,000, $4,000, $6,000, $8,000; legend: 1993, 1994, 1995, 1996, 1997)

Warranty/Maintenance Info

Item		Rate
Major Tune-Up	$161	Better Than Average
Minor Tune-Up	$116	Average
Brake Service	$210	Better Than Average
Overall Warranty	3 yr/36k	Average
Drivetrain Warranty	3 yr/36k	Average
Rust Warranty	6 yr/100k	Better Than Average
Maintenance Warranty	N/A	
Roadside Assistance	N/A	

Resale Value

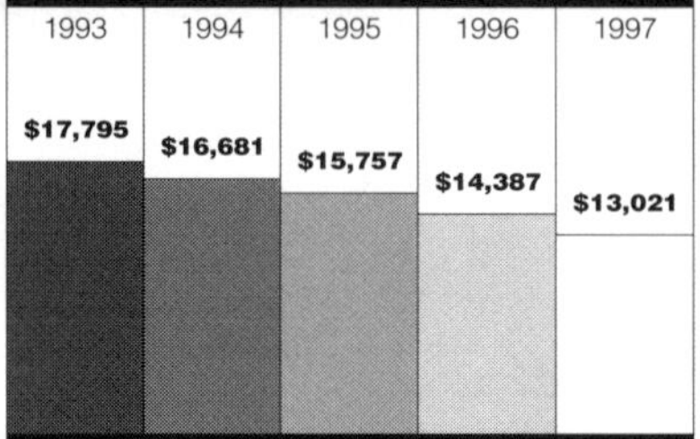

1993	1994	1995	1996	1997
$17,795	$16,681	$15,757	$14,387	$13,021

Ownership Costs (5yr)

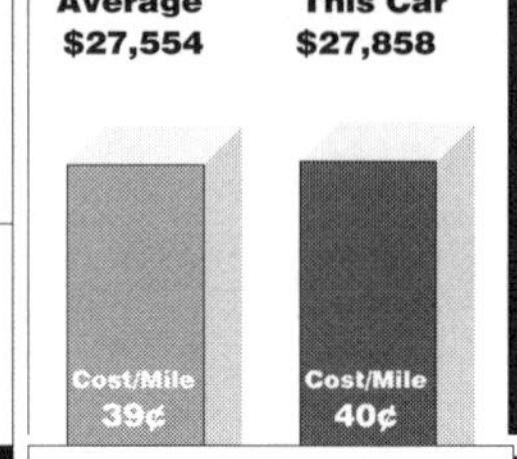

Cumulative Costs

	1993	1994	1995	1996	1997
Annual	$6,025	$4,836	$5,350	$5,268	$6,379
Total	$6,025	$10,861	$16,211	$21,479	$27,858

Ownership Cost Rating

Average

The Ford Aerostar is available in twelve model editions - Eddie Bauer, XL, and XLT passenger vans with standard or extended lengths and two- or four-wheel drive. New for 1993, the XL 4WD Extended features a new Euro-perforation treatment for leather interior, black body side moldings, three new exterior colors (Cayman Green, Ruby Red and Bimini Blue), a 90-mph mechanical analog speedometer, and integrated second row bench child safety seats. Aerostars are built in St. Louis, Missouri.

Ford Aerostar XLT Extended 4WD 3 Door Pass Ext Van

4.0L 155 hp Gas Fuel Inject.

6 Cylinder "V"

Automatic 4 Speed

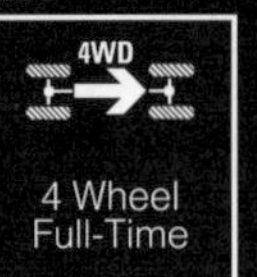

4 Wheel Full-Time

Driver Airbag Psngr Belts

Mini Van

2WD Model Shown

Purchase Price

Car Item	Dealer Cost	List
Base Price	**$19,409**	**$21,885**
Anti-Lock Brakes	Std	Std
Manual Transmission	N/A	N/A
Optional Engine	N/A	N/A
Air Conditioning	Std	Std
Power Steering	Std	Std
Cruise Control	Std	Std
4 Wheel Full-Time Drive	Std	Std
AM/FM Stereo Cassette	Pkg	Pkg
Steering Wheel, Tilt	Std	Std
Power Windows	Pkg	Pkg
***Options Price**	$0	$0
***Total Price**	**$19,409**	**$21,885**
Target Price	$21,214	
Destination Charge	$535	
Avg. Tax & Fees	$1,311	
Total Target $	**$23,060**	
Average Dealer Option Cost:	***85%***	

Ownership Costs

Cost Area	5 Year Cost	Rate
Depreciation	$8,629	Average
Financing ($463/month)	$3,798	
Insurance (Rating 6)	$6,919	Excellent
State Fees	$897	
Fuel (Hwy 20 City 15)	$4,941	Poor
Maintenance	$3,971	Better Than Average
Repairs	$954	Worse Than Average

Ownership Cost By Year

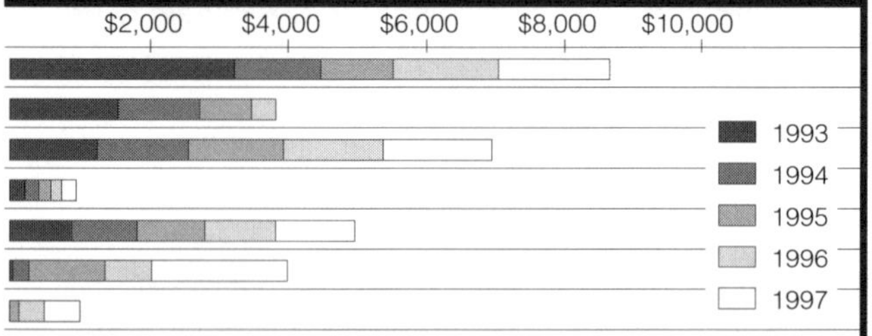

(Chart scale: $2,000, $4,000, $6,000, $8,000, $10,000; legend: 1993, 1994, 1995, 1996, 1997)

Warranty/Maintenance Info

Item		Rate
Major Tune-Up	$161	Better Than Average
Minor Tune-Up	$116	Average
Brake Service	$210	Better Than Average
Overall Warranty	3 yr/36k	Average
Drivetrain Warranty	3 yr/36k	Average
Rust Warranty	6 yr/100k	Better Than Average
Maintenance Warranty	N/A	
Roadside Assistance	N/A	

Resale Value

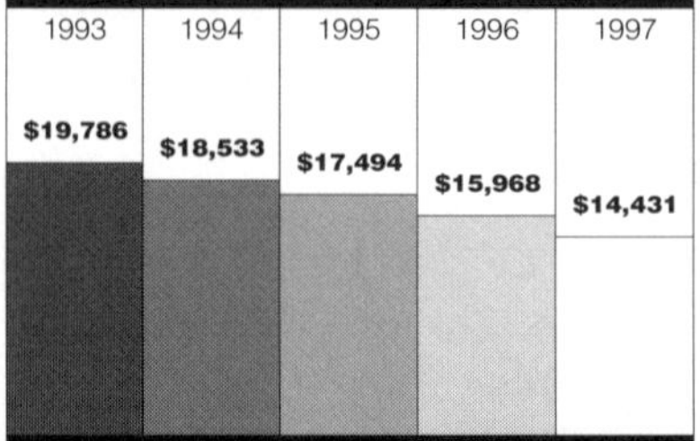

1993	1994	1995	1996	1997
$19,786	$18,533	$17,494	$15,968	$14,431

Ownership Costs (5yr)

	Average	This Car
	$29,923	$30,109
Cost/Mile	43¢	43¢

Cumulative Costs

	1993	1994	1995	1996	1997
Annual	$7,314	$5,157	$5,586	$5,480	$6,572
Total	$7,314	$12,471	$18,057	$23,537	$30,109

Ownership Cost Rating

Average

The Ford Aerostar is available in twelve model editions - Eddie Bauer, XL, and XLT passenger vans with standard or extended lengths and two- or four-wheel drive. New for 1993, the XLT 4WD Extended features a new Euro-perforation treatment for leather interior, black body side moldings, three new exterior colors (Cayman Green, Ruby Red and Bimini Blue), a 90-mph mechanical analog speedometer, and integrated second row bench child safety seats. Aerostars are built in St. Louis, Missouri.

* Includes shaded options

** Other purchase requirements apply

Poor

Worse Than Average

Average

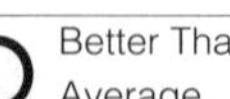
Better Than Average

Excellent

Insufficient Information

Refer to *Section 3: Annotated Vehicle Charts* for an explanation of these charts.

Ford Aerostar Eddie Bauer Extended 4WD
3 Door Pass Ext Van

Mini Van

4.0L 155 hp Gas Fuel Inject.	6 Cylinder "V"	Automatic 4 Speed	4 Wheel Full-Time	Driver Airbag Psngr Belts

Base Model Shown

Purchase Price

Car Item	Dealer Cost	List
Base Price	**$22,292**	**$25,161**
Anti-Lock Brakes	Std	Std
Manual Transmission	N/A	N/A
Optional Engine	N/A	N/A
Air Cond., High Capacity	Std	Std
Power Steering	Std	Std
Cruise Control	Std	Std
4 Wheel Full-Time Drive	Std	Std
AM/FM Stereo Cassette	Std	Std
Steering Wheel, Tilt	Std	Std
Power Windows	Std	Std
***Options Price**	$0	$0
***Total Price**	**$22,292**	**$25,161**
Target Price	$24,514	
Destination Charge	$535	
Avg. Tax & Fees	$1,509	
Total Target $	**$26,558**	
Average Dealer Option Cost:	***85%***	

Ownership Costs

Cost Area	5 Year Cost	Rate
Depreciation	$9,908	Average
Financing ($534/month)	$4,374	
Insurance (Rating 6)	$6,919	Excellent
State Fees	$1,028	
Fuel (Hwy 20 City 15)	$4,941	Poor
Maintenance	$3,962	Better Than Average
Repairs	$954	Worse Than Average

Ownership Cost By Year

$2,000 $4,000 $6,000 $8,000 $10,000

1993 1994 1995 1996 1997

Warranty/Maintenance Info

Major Tune-Up	$161	Better Than Average
Minor Tune-Up	$116	Average
Brake Service	$210	Better Than Average
Overall Warranty	3 yr/36k	Average
Drivetrain Warranty	3 yr/36k	Average
Rust Warranty	6 yr/100k	Better Than Average
Maintenance Warranty	N/A	
Roadside Assistance	N/A	

Resale Value

1993	1994	1995	1996	1997
$21,152	$19,995	$19,060	$17,896	$16,650

Ownership Costs (5yr)

Average	This Car
$32,652	$32,086
Cost/Mile 47¢	Cost/Mile 46¢

Cumulative Costs

	1993	1994	1995	1996	1997
Annual	$9,719	$5,270	$5,623	$5,183	$6,291
Total	$9,719	$14,989	$20,612	$25,795	$32,086

Ownership Cost Rating

Excellent

The Ford Aerostar is available in twelve model editions - Eddie Bauer, XL, and XLT passenger vans with standard or extended lengths and two- or four-wheel drive. New for 1993, the Eddie Bauer 4WD Extended features a Euro-perforation treatment for leather interior, black body side moldings, three new exterior colors (Cayman Green, Ruby Red and Bimini Blue), a 90-mph mechanical analog speedometer, and integrated second row bench child safety seats. Aerostars are built in St. Louis, Missouri.

Ford Aerostar Cargo Van 4WD
3 Door Cargo Van

Mini Van

4.0L 155 hp Gas Fuel Inject.	6 Cylinder "V"	Automatic 4 Speed	4 Wheel Full-Time	Driver Airbag Psngr Belts

Base Model Shown

Purchase Price

Car Item	Dealer Cost	List
Base Price	**$14,825**	**$16,705**
Anti-Lock Brakes	Std	Std
Manual Transmission	N/A	N/A
Optional Engine	N/A	N/A
Air Conditioning	$738	$868
Power Steering	Std	Std
Cruise Control	$315	$371
4 Wheel Full-Time Drive	Std	Std
AM/FM Stereo Cassette	$291	** $343
Steering Wheel, Tilt	Grp	Grp
Power Windows	Pkg	Pkg
***Options Price**	$1,053	$1,239
***Total Price**	**$15,878**	**$17,944**
Target Price	$17,186	
Destination Charge	$535	
Avg. Tax & Fees	$1,071	
Total Target $	**$18,792**	
Average Dealer Option Cost:	***85%***	

Ownership Costs

Cost Area	5 Year Cost	Rate
Depreciation	$8,047	Worse Than Average
Financing ($378/month)	$3,096	
Insurance (Rating 5)	$6,786	Excellent
State Fees	$739	
Fuel (Hwy 21 City 16)	$4,672	Worse Than Average
Maintenance	$3,974	Better Than Average
Repairs	$954	Worse Than Average

Ownership Cost By Year

$2,000 $4,000 $6,000 $8,000 $10,000

1993 1994 1995 1996 1997

Warranty/Maintenance Info

Major Tune-Up	$161	Better Than Average
Minor Tune-Up	$116	Average
Brake Service	$210	Better Than Average
Overall Warranty	3 yr/36k	Average
Drivetrain Warranty	3 yr/36k	Average
Rust Warranty	6 yr/100k	Better Than Average
Maintenance Warranty	N/A	
Roadside Assistance	N/A	

Resale Value

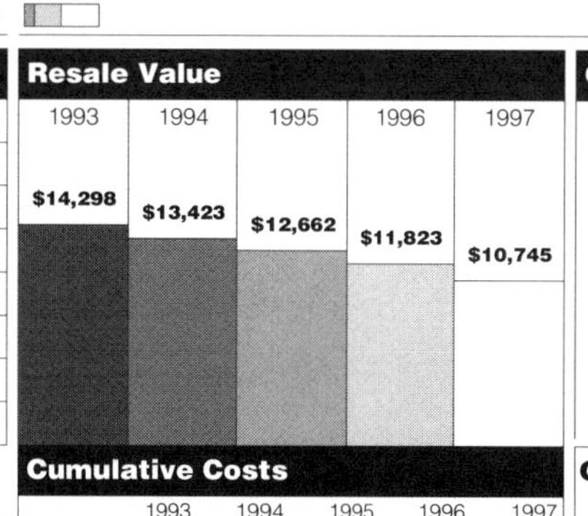

1993	1994	1995	1996	1997
$14,298	$13,423	$12,662	$11,823	$10,745

Ownership Costs (5yr)

Average	This Car
$26,640	$28,268
Cost/Mile 38¢	Cost/Mile 40¢

Cumulative Costs

	1993	1994	1995	1996	1997
Annual	$8,129	$4,446	$5,057	$4,630	$6,006
Total	$8,129	$12,575	$17,632	$22,262	$28,268

Ownership Cost Rating

Worse Than Average

The Ford Aerostar Cargo Van is available in four models - (Base) Aerostar Cargo Van, Extended Cargo Van, (Base) 4WD, and Extended 4WD. New for 1993, the Base 4WD Cargo Van features black body side moldings, three new colors (Cayman Green, Ruby Red and Bimini Blue), and a 90-mph mechanical analog speedometer. Standard features include black aero, fold-away LH and RH mirrors, color-keyed front carpeting, front, black aero spoiler, V-6 EFI engine, overdrive transmission, and 21-gal. fuel tank.

* Includes shaded options

** Other purchase requirements apply

 Poor 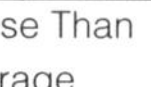 Worse Than Average  Average  Better Than Average  Excellent  Insufficient Information

Refer to *Section 3: Annotated Vehicle Charts* for an explanation of these charts.

Ford Aerostar Cargo Van Extended 4WD
3 Door Cargo Ext Van

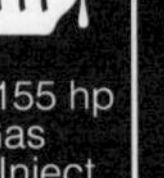
4.0L 155 hp Gas Fuel Inject.

6 Cylinder "V"

Automatic 4 Speed

4 Wheel Full-Time

Driver Airbag Psngr Belts

Mini Van

Base Model Shown

Purchase Price

Car Item	Dealer Cost	List
Base Price	**$15,501**	**$17,473**
Anti-Lock Brakes	Std	Std
Manual Transmission	N/A	N/A
Optional Engine	N/A	N/A
Air Conditioning	$738	$868
Power Steering	Std	Std
Cruise Control	$315	$371
4 Wheel Full-Time Drive	Std	Std
AM/FM Stereo Cassette	$291	** $343
Steering Wheel, Tilt	Grp	Grp
Power Windows	Pkg	Pkg
***Options Price**	$1,053	$1,239
***Total Price**	**$16,554**	**$18,712**
Target Price	$17,943	
Destination Charge	$535	
Avg. Tax & Fees	$1,116	
Total Target $	**$19,594**	
Average Dealer Option Cost:	***85%***	

Ownership Costs

Cost Area	5 Year Cost	Rate
Depreciation	$8,374	Worse Than Average
Financing ($394/month)	$3,227	
Insurance (Rating 6)	$6,919	Excellent
State Fees	$769	
Fuel (Hwy 21 City 16)	$4,672	Worse Than Average
Maintenance	$3,957	Better Than Average
Repairs	$954	Worse Than Average

Ownership Cost By Year

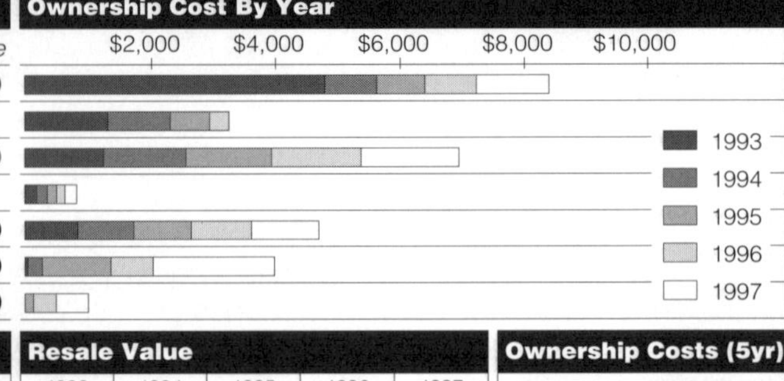

Warranty/Maintenance Info

Major Tune-Up	$161	Better Than Average
Minor Tune-Up	$116	Average
Brake Service	$210	Better Than Average
Overall Warranty	3 yr/36k	Average
Drivetrain Warranty	3 yr/36k	Average
Rust Warranty	6 yr/100k	Better Than Average
Maintenance Warranty	N/A	
Roadside Assistance	N/A	

Resale Value

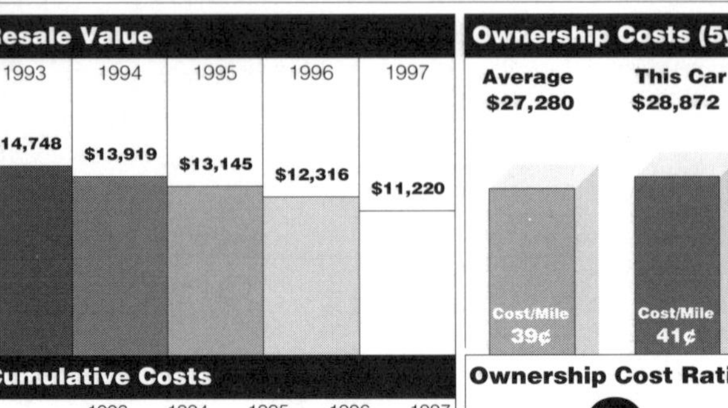

Ownership Costs (5yr)

Average	This Car
$27,280	$28,872
Cost/Mile 39¢	Cost/Mile 41¢

Cumulative Costs

	1993	1994	1995	1996	1997
Annual	$8,567	$4,474	$5,129	$4,663	$6,039
Total	$8,567	$13,041	$18,170	$22,833	$28,872

Ownership Cost Rating

Worse Than Average

The Ford Aerostar Cargo Van is available in four models - (Base) Aerostar Cargo Van, Extended Cargo Van, (Base) 4WD, and Extended 4WD. New for 1993, the Extended 4WD Cargo Van features black body side moldings, three new colors (Cayman Green, Ruby Red and Bimini Blue), and a 90-mph mechanical analog speedometer. Standard features include black aero, fold-away LH and RH mirrors, color-keyed front carpeting, front, black aero spoiler, V-6 EFI engine, overdrive transmission, and 21-gal. fuel tank.

Ford Bronco Custom
2 Door Sport Utility

5.0L 185 hp Gas Fuel Inject.

8 Cylinder "V"

1 3 5 / 2 4 R
Manual 5 Speed

4 Wheel On-Demand

Manual Seatbelts Only

Utility

XLT Model Shown

Purchase Price

Car Item	Dealer Cost	List
Base Price	**$17,257**	**$20,084**
Anti-Lock Brakes	Std	Std
Automatic 4 Speed	$786	$924
Optional Engine	N/A	N/A
Air Conditioning	Pkg	Pkg
Power Steering	Std	Std
Cruise Control	N/A	N/A
4 Whl On-Demand Dr.	Std	Std
AM/FM Stereo Cassette	N/A	N/A
Steering Wheel, Tilt	N/A	N/A
Power Windows	N/A	N/A
***Options Price**	$0	$0
***Total Price**	**$17,257**	**$20,084**
Target Price	$18,512	
Destination Charge	$585	
Avg. Tax & Fees	$1,162	
Total Target $	**$20,259**	
Average Dealer Option Cost:	***85%***	

Ownership Costs

Cost Area	5 Year Cost	Rate
Depreciation	$7,015	Average
Financing ($407/month)	$3,337	
Insurance (Rating 10)	$7,689	Excellent
State Fees	$827	
Fuel (Hwy 17 City 13)	$5,760	Poor
Maintenance	$4,063	Average
Repairs	$1,035	Worse Than Average

Ownership Cost By Year

$2,000	$4,000	$6,000	$8,000

1993 / 1994 / 1995 / 1996 / 1997

Warranty/Maintenance Info

Major Tune-Up	$145	Better Than Average
Minor Tune-Up	$100	Better Than Average
Brake Service	$241	Average
Overall Warranty	3 yr/36k	Average
Drivetrain Warranty	3 yr/36k	Average
Rust Warranty	6 yr/100k	Better Than Average
Maintenance Warranty	N/A	
Roadside Assistance	N/A	

Resale Value

1993	1994	1995	1996	1997
$16,378	$15,645	$15,040	$14,180	$13,244

Ownership Costs (5yr)

Average	This Car
$30,194	$29,726
Cost/Mile 43¢	Cost/Mile 42¢

Cumulative Costs

	1993	1994	1995	1996	1997
Annual	$8,010	$4,770	$5,519	$5,215	$6,212
Total	$8,010	$12,780	$18,299	$23,514	$29,726

Ownership Cost Rating

Better Than Average

The 1993 Ford Bronco is available in three model editions - Custom, XLT and Eddie Bauer full-size sport utility vehicles. New for 1993, the Custom Bronco offers a four-wheel anti-lock brake system for improved stopping and Ford's "next generation" speed control system which responds faster to driver commands. Other features include chromed, aerodynamic side mirrors, styled steel wheels, chrome front bumper, swing-down tailgate with power window, wraparound taillights and interval wipers.

* Includes shaded options

** Other purchase requirements apply

Poor  Worse Than Average  Average · Better Than Average · Excellent  Insufficient Information

Refer to *Section 3: Annotated Vehicle Charts* for an explanation of these charts.

Ford Bronco XLT
2 Door Sport Utility

5.0L 185 hp Gas Fuel Inject.

8 Cylinder "V"

Manual 5 Speed

4 Wheel On-Demand

Manual Seatbelts Only

Purchase Price

Car Item	*Dealer Cost*	*List*
Base Price	**$19,116**	**$22,272**
Anti-Lock Brakes	Std	Std
Automatic 4 Speed	$786	$924
5.8L 200 hp Gas	$188	** $221
Air Conditioning	Pkg	Pkg
Power Steering	Std	Std
Cruise Control	Std	Std
4 Whl On-Demand Dr.	Std	Std
AM/FM Stereo Cassette	Pkg	Pkg
Steering Wheel, Tilt	Std	Std
Power Windows	Pkg	Pkg
***Options Price**	$0	$0
***Total Price**	**$19,116**	**$22,272**
Target Price	$20,574	
Destination Charge	$585	
Avg. Tax & Fees	$1,287	
Total Target $	**$22,446**	
Average Dealer Option Cost:	***85%***	

Ownership Costs

Cost Area	*5 Year Cost*	*Rate*
Depreciation	$8,987	Average
Financing ($451/month)	$3,698	
Insurance (Rating 10)	$7,689	Excellent
State Fees	$915	
Fuel (Hwy 17 City 13)	$5,760	Poor
Maintenance	$4,063	Average
Repairs	$1,035	Worse Than Average

Ownership Cost By Year

$2,000 $4,000 $6,000 $8,000 $10,000

1993 1994 1995 1996 1997

Warranty/Maintenance Info

Major Tune-Up	$145	Better Than Average
Minor Tune-Up	$100	Better Than Average
Brake Service	$241	Average
Overall Warranty	3 yr/36k	Average
Drivetrain Warranty	3 yr/36k	Average
Rust Warranty	6 yr/100k	Better Than Average
Maintenance Warranty	N/A	
Roadside Assistance	N/A	

Resale Value

1993	1994	1995	1996	1997
$17,173	$16,332	$15,570	$14,542	$13,459

Ownership Costs (5yr)

Average	This Car
$32,034	$32,147
Cost/Mile 46¢	Cost/Mile 46¢

The 1993 Ford Bronco is available in three model editions - Custom, XLT and Eddie Bauer full-size sport utility vehicles. New for 1993, the XLT Bronco offers a four-wheel anti-lock brake system for improved stopping and Ford's "next generation" speed control system which responds faster to driver commands. Other features include chromed, aerodynamic side mirrors, styled steel wheels, lower bodyside protection moldings, swing-down tailgate with power window, color-keyed carpet and wraparound taillights.

Cumulative Costs

	1993	1994	1995	1996	1997
Annual	$9,574	$5,011	$5,765	$5,425	$6,372
Total	$9,574	$14,585	$20,350	$25,775	$32,147

Ownership Cost Rating

Average

Ford Bronco Eddie Bauer
2 Door Sport Utility

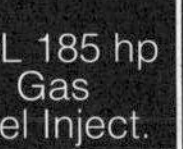
5.0L 185 hp Gas Fuel Inject.

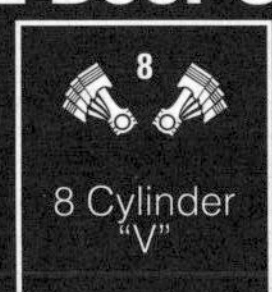
8 Cylinder "V"

Automatic 4 Speed

4 Wheel On-Demand

Manual Seatbelts Only

Utility

Purchase Price

Car Item	*Dealer Cost*	*List*
Base Price	**$21,198**	**$24,721**
Anti-Lock Brakes	Std	Std
Manual Transmission	N/A	N/A
5.8L 200 hp Gas	$188	$221
Air Conditioning	Std	Std
Power Steering	Std	Std
Cruise Control	Std	Std
4 Whl On-Demand Dr.	Std	Std
AM/FM Stereo Cassette	Pkg	Pkg
Steering Wheel, Tilt	Std	Std
Power Windows	Pkg	Pkg
***Options Price**	$0	$0
***Total Price**	**$21,198**	**$24,721**
Target Price	$22,899	
Destination Charge	$585	
Avg. Tax & Fees	$1,427	
Total Target $	**$24,911**	
Average Dealer Option Cost:	***85%***	

Ownership Costs

Cost Area	*5 Year Cost*	*Rate*
Depreciation	$10,187	Average
Financing ($501/month)	$4,104	
Insurance (Rating 10)	$7,689	Excellent
State Fees	$1,012	
Fuel (Hwy 18 City 14)	$5,399	Worse Than Average
Maintenance	$4,281	Average
Repairs	$1,035	Worse Than Average

Ownership Cost By Year

$2,000 $4,000 $6,000 $8,000 $10,000 $12,000

1993 1994 1995 1996 1997

Warranty/Maintenance Info

Major Tune-Up	$145	Better Than Average
Minor Tune-Up	$100	Better Than Average
Brake Service	$241	Average
Overall Warranty	3 yr/36k	Average
Drivetrain Warranty	3 yr/36k	Average
Rust Warranty	6 yr/100k	Better Than Average
Maintenance Warranty	N/A	
Roadside Assistance	N/A	

Resale Value

1993	1994	1995	1996	1997
$18,911	$17,972	$17,102	$15,928	$14,724

Ownership Costs (5yr)

Average	This Car
$34,094	$33,707
Cost/Mile 49¢	Cost/Mile 48¢

The 1993 Ford Bronco is available in three model editions - Custom, XLT and Eddie Bauer full-size sport utility vehicles. New for 1993, the Eddie Bauer Bronco offers a four-wheel anti-lock brake system for improved stopping and Ford's "next generation" speed control system which responds faster to driver commands. Other features include privacy glass, cloth captain's chairs, swing-down tailgate with power window, standard air conditioning, color-keyed carpet and carpeted floor mats.

Cumulative Costs

	1993	1994	1995	1996	1997
Annual	$10,427	$5,189	$6,006	$5,542	$6,543
Total	$10,427	$15,616	$21,622	$27,164	$33,707

Ownership Cost Rating

Better Than Average

* Includes shaded options

** Other purchase requirements apply

Poor

Worse Than Average

Average

Better Than Average
Excellent
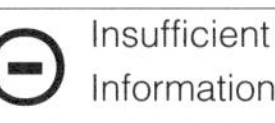
Insufficient Information

Refer to *Section 3: Annotated Vehicle Charts* for an explanation of these charts.

Ford Club Wagon Custom
3 Door Pass Van

4.9L 150 hp Gas Fuel Inject.

6 Cylinder In-Line

Automatic 4 Speed

2 Wheel Rear

Driver Airbag Psngr Belts

Purchase Price

Car Item	Dealer Cost	List
Base Price	**$14,811**	**$17,249**
Anti-Lock Brakes	Std	Std
4 Spd Auto O/D	N/C	N/C
5.0L 185 hp Gas	$608	$716
Air Conditioning	$827	** $973
Power Steering	Std	Std
Cruise Control	$325	$383
All Wheel Drive	N/A	N/A
AM/FM Stereo Cassette	$238	$280
Steering Wheel, Tilt	Grp	Grp
Power Windows	$555	$652
***Options Price**	$608	$716
***Total Price**	**$15,419**	**$17,965**
Target Price	$16,909	
Destination Charge	$560	
Avg. Tax & Fees	$1,058	
Total Target $	**$18,527**	
Average Dealer Option Cost:	***85%***	

Ownership Costs

Cost Area	5 Year Cost	Rate
Depreciation	$8,911	Average
Financing ($372/month)	$3,052	
Insurance (Rating 7)	$7,035	Excellent
State Fees	$741	
Fuel (Hwy 17 City 13)	$5,760	Average
Maintenance	$4,147	Average
Repairs	$799	Better Than Average

Ownership Cost By Year

$2,000 $4,000 $6,000 $8,000 $10,000

1993 1994 1995 1996 1997

Warranty/Maintenance Info

Major Tune-Up	$152	Better Than Average
Minor Tune-Up	$108	Better Than Average
Brake Service	$185	Excellent
Overall Warranty	3 yr/36k	Average
Drivetrain Warranty	3 yr/36k	Average
Rust Warranty	6 yr/100k	Better Than Average
Maintenance Warranty	N/A	
Roadside Assistance	N/A	

Resale Value

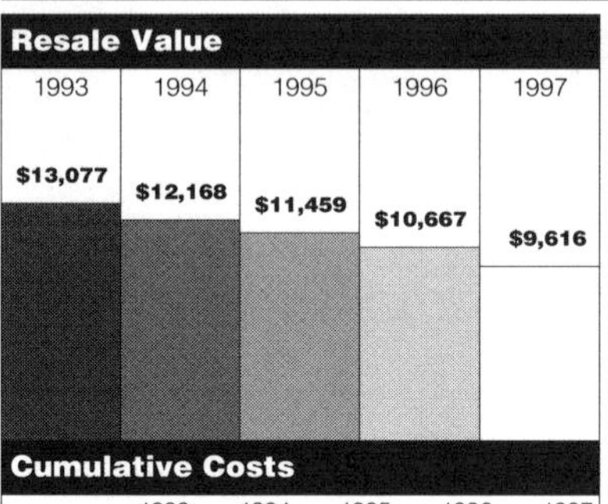

1993	1994	1995	1996	1997
$13,077	$12,168	$11,459	$10,667	$9,616

Ownership Costs (5yr)

Average	This Car
$30,470	$30,445
Cost/Mile 44¢	Cost/Mile 43¢

Cumulative Costs

	1993	1994	1995	1996	1997
Annual	$9,317	$4,722	$5,414	$4,948	$6,044
Total	$9,317	$14,039	$19,453	$24,401	$30,445

Ownership Cost Rating

Average

The 1993 Ford Club Wagon is available in two model editions - Regular and Heavy Duty and has three trim levels - Custom, XLT and Chateau vans. New for 1993, the Custom Club Wagon has optional black protective bodyside moldings and an improved automatic overdrive electronic wide-ratio (AODE-W) transmission standard with the 5.0L V-8 engine. Standard features include color-keyed door trim panels, all-season radial tires, halogen sealed beam headlights and color-keyed dual bucket seats and rear bench.

Ford Club Wagon Custom Heavy Duty
3 Door Pass Van

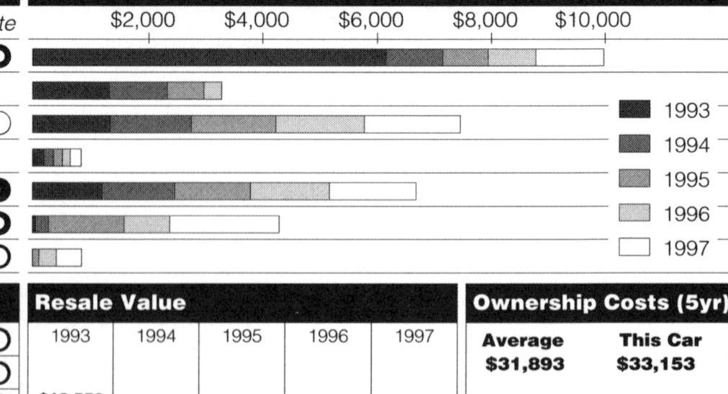

4.9L 150 hp Gas Fuel Inject.

6 Cylinder In-Line

Automatic 3 Speed

2 Wheel Rear

Manual Seatbelts Only

Full-Size Van

Base Model Shown

Purchase Price

Car Item	Dealer Cost	List
Base Price	**$15,651**	**$18,237**
Anti-Lock Brakes	Std	Std
4 Spd Electronic Auto	$254	$299
5.8L 200 hp Gas	$796	$937
Air Conditioning	$827	** $973
Power Steering	Std	Std
Cruise Control	$325	$383
All Wheel Drive	N/A	N/A
AM/FM Stereo Cassette	$238	$280
Steering Wheel, Tilt	Grp	Grp
Power Windows	$555	$652
***Options Price**	$796	$937
***Total Price**	**$16,447**	**$19,174**
Target Price	$18,074	
Destination Charge	$560	
Avg. Tax & Fees	$1,129	
Total Target $	**$19,763**	
Average Dealer Option Cost:	***85%***	

Ownership Costs

Cost Area	5 Year Cost	Rate
Depreciation	$9,953	Average
Financing ($397/month)	$3,255	
Insurance (Rating 8)	$7,432	Excellent
State Fees	$789	
Fuel (Hwy 15 City 11)	$6,659	Worse Than Average
Maintenance	$4,266	Average
Repairs	$799	Better Than Average

Ownership Cost By Year

$2,000 $4,000 $6,000 $8,000 $10,000

1993 1994 1995 1996 1997

Warranty/Maintenance Info

Major Tune-Up	$152	Better Than Average
Minor Tune-Up	$108	Better Than Average
Brake Service	$185	Excellent
Overall Warranty	3 yr/36k	Average
Drivetrain Warranty	3 yr/36k	Average
Rust Warranty	6 yr/100k	Better Than Average
Maintenance Warranty	N/A	
Roadside Assistance	N/A	

Resale Value

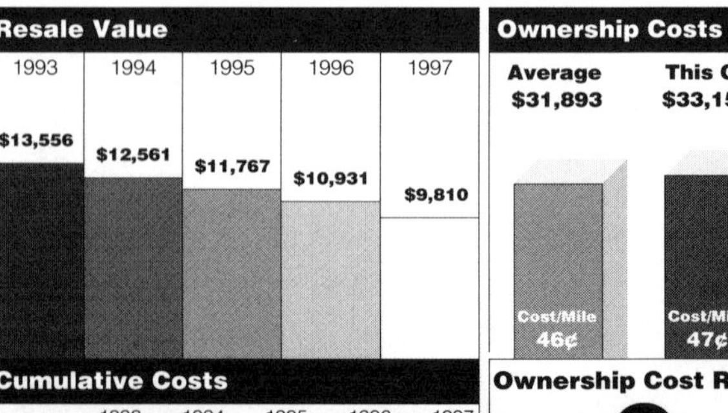

1993	1994	1995	1996	1997
$13,556	$12,561	$11,767	$10,931	$9,810

Ownership Costs (5yr)

Average	This Car
$31,893	$33,153
Cost/Mile 46¢	Cost/Mile 47¢

Cumulative Costs

	1993	1994	1995	1996	1997
Annual	$10,409	$5,132	$5,860	$5,255	$6,497
Total	$10,409	$15,541	$21,401	$26,656	$33,153

Ownership Cost Rating

Worse Than Average

The 1993 Ford Club Wagon is available in two model editions - Regular and Heavy Duty and has three trim levels - Custom, XLT and Chateau vans. New for 1993, the Custom Heavy Duty Club Wagon has optional black protective bodyside moldings and an improved automatic overdrive electronic wide-ratio (AODE-W) transmission standard with the 5.0L V-8 engine. Standard features include color-keyed front door trim panels, 22.0 gallon fuel tank, halogen headlights and color-keyed dual bucket seats and rear bench.

* Includes shaded options

** Other purchase requirements apply

 Poor 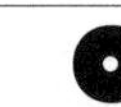 Worse Than Average  Average  Better Than Average 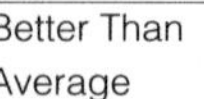 Excellent  Insufficient Information

Refer to *Section 3: Annotated Vehicle Charts* for an explanation of these charts.

Ford Club Wagon XLT
3 Door Pass Van

4.9L 150 hp Gas Fuel Inject.

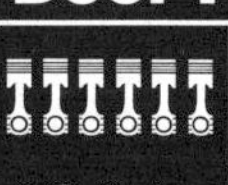
6 Cylinder In-Line

Automatic 4 Speed

2 Wheel Rear

Driver Airbag Psngr Belts

Full-Size Van

Purchase Price

Car Item	Dealer Cost	List
Base Price	**$17,396**	**$20,289**
Anti-Lock Brakes	Std	Std
4 Spd Auto O/D	N/C	N/C
5.0L 185 hp Gas	$608	$716
Air Conditioning	Std	Std
Power Steering	Std	Std
Cruise Control	$325	$383
All Wheel Drive	N/A	N/A
AM/FM Stereo Cassette	$175	$206
Steering Wheel, Tilt	Grp	Grp
Power Windows	Std	Std
***Options Price**	$608	$716
***Total Price**	**$18,004**	**$21,005**
Target Price	$19,871	
Destination Charge	$560	
Avg. Tax & Fees	$1,238	
Total Target $	**$21,669**	
Average Dealer Option Cost:	***85%***	

Ownership Costs

Cost Area	5 Year Cost	Rate
Depreciation	$11,286	Worse Than Average
Financing ($436/month)	$3,570	
Insurance (Rating 7)	$7,035	Excellent
State Fees	$863	
Fuel (Hwy 17 City 13)	$5,760	Average
Maintenance	$4,147	Average
Repairs	$799	Better Than Average

Ownership Cost By Year

$2,000 $4,000 $6,000 $8,000 $10,000 $12,000

1993 1994 1995 1996 1997

Warranty/Maintenance Info

Item		Rate
Major Tune-Up	$152	Better Than Average
Minor Tune-Up	$108	Better Than Average
Brake Service	$185	Excellent
Overall Warranty	3 yr/36k	Average
Drivetrain Warranty	3 yr/36k	Average
Rust Warranty	6 yr/100k	Better Than Average
Maintenance Warranty	N/A	
Roadside Assistance	N/A	

Resale Value

1993	1994	1995	1996	1997
$15,002	$13,802	$12,808	$11,731	$10,383

Ownership Costs (5yr)

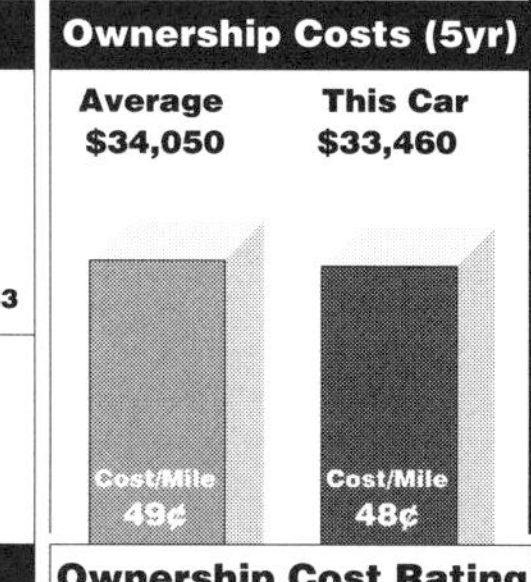

Average	This Car
$34,050	$33,460
Cost/Mile 49¢	Cost/Mile 48¢

Cumulative Costs

	1993	1994	1995	1996	1997
Annual	$10,781	$5,202	$5,827	$5,291	$6,359
Total	$10,781	$15,983	$21,810	$27,101	$33,460

Ownership Cost Rating

Better Than Average

The 1993 Ford Club Wagon is available in two model editions - Regular and Heavy Duty and has three trim levels - Custom, XLT and Chateau vans. New for 1993, the XLT Club Wagon has optional black protective bodyside moldings and an improved automatic overdrive electronic wide-ratio (AODE-W) transmission standard with the 5.0L V-8 engine. Standard features include color-keyed front door trim panels, 22.0 gallon fuel tank, aero, halogen headlights and color-keyed dual bucket seats and rear bench seat.

Ford Club Wagon XLT Heavy Duty
3 Door Pass Van

4.9L 150 hp Gas Fuel Inject.

6 Cylinder In-Line

Automatic 3 Speed

2 Wheel Rear

Manual Seatbelts Only

Full-Size Van

Base Model Shown

Purchase Price

Car Item	Dealer Cost	List
Base Price	**$18,424**	**$21,499**
Anti-Lock Brakes	Std	Std
4 Spd Electronic Auto	$254	$299
5.8L 200 hp Gas	$796	$937
Air Conditioning	Std	Std
Power Steering	Std	Std
Cruise Control	$325	$383
All Wheel Drive	N/A	N/A
AM/FM Stereo Cassette	$175	$206
Steering Wheel, Tilt	Grp	Grp
Power Windows	Std	Std
***Options Price**	$796	$937
***Total Price**	**$19,220**	**$22,436**
Target Price	$21,267	
Destination Charge	$560	
Avg. Tax & Fees	$1,321	
Total Target $	**$23,148**	
Average Dealer Option Cost:	***85%***	

Ownership Costs

Cost Area	5 Year Cost	Rate
Depreciation	$12,584	Worse Than Average
Financing ($465/month)	$3,813	
Insurance (Rating 8)	$7,432	Excellent
State Fees	$920	
Fuel (Hwy 15 City 11)	$6,659	Worse Than Average
Maintenance	$4,266	Average
Repairs	$799	Better Than Average

Ownership Cost By Year

$2,000 $4,000 $6,000 $8,000 $10,000 $12,000 $14,000

1993 1994 1995 1996 1997

Warranty/Maintenance Info

Item		Rate
Major Tune-Up	$152	Better Than Average
Minor Tune-Up	$108	Better Than Average
Brake Service	$185	Excellent
Overall Warranty	3 yr/36k	Average
Drivetrain Warranty	3 yr/36k	Average
Rust Warranty	6 yr/100k	Better Than Average
Maintenance Warranty	N/A	
Roadside Assistance	N/A	

Resale Value

1993	1994	1995	1996	1997
$15,564	$14,251	$13,146	$12,005	$10,564

Ownership Costs (5yr)

Average	This Car
$35,735	$36,473
Cost/Mile 51¢	Cost/Mile 52¢

Cumulative Costs

	1993	1994	1995	1996	1997
Annual	$12,051	$5,653	$6,308	$5,624	$6,837
Total	$12,051	$17,704	$24,012	$29,636	$36,473

Ownership Cost Rating

Average

The 1993 Ford Club Wagon is available in two model editions - Regular and Heavy Duty and has three trim levels - Custom, XLT and Chateau vans. New for 1993, the XLT Heavy Duty Club Wagon has optional black protective bodyside moldings and an improved automatic overdrive electronic wide-ratio (AODE-W) transmission standard with the 5.0L V-8 engine. Standard features include color-keyed front door trim panels, 22.0 gallon fuel tank, halogen headlights and color-keyed dual bucket seats and rear bench.

* Includes shaded options

** Other purchase requirements apply

Poor | Worse Than Average |  Average | Better Than Average | Excellent | Insufficient Information

Refer to *Section 3: Annotated Vehicle Charts* for an explanation of these charts.

Ford Club Wagon Chateau
3 Door Pass Van

4.9L 150 hp Gas Fuel Inject.

6 Cylinder In-Line

Automatic 4 Speed

2 Wheel Rear

Driver Airbag Psngr Belts

Full-Size Van

Purchase Price

Car Item	Dealer Cost	List
Base Price	**$20,858**	**$24,362**
Anti-Lock Brakes	Std	Std
4 Spd Auto O/D	N/C	N/C
5.0L 185 hp Gas	$608	$716
Air Conditioning	N/A	N/A
Power Steering	Std	Std
Cruise Control	Std	Std
All Wheel Drive	N/A	N/A
AM/FM Stereo Cassette	Std	Std
Steering Wheel, Tilt	Std	Std
Power Windows	Std	Std
***Options Price**	$608	$716
***Total Price**	**$21,466**	**$25,078**
Target Price	$23,894	
Destination Charge	$560	
Avg. Tax & Fees	$1,479	
Total Target $	**$25,933**	
Average Dealer Option Cost:	***85%***	

Ownership Costs

Cost Area	5 Year Cost	Rate
Depreciation	$14,556	Poor
Financing ($521/month)	$4,271	
Insurance (Rating 7)	$6,869	Excellent
State Fees	$1,025	
Fuel (Hwy 17 City 13)	$5,760	Average
Maintenance	$4,147	Average
Repairs	$799	Better Than Average

Ownership Cost By Year

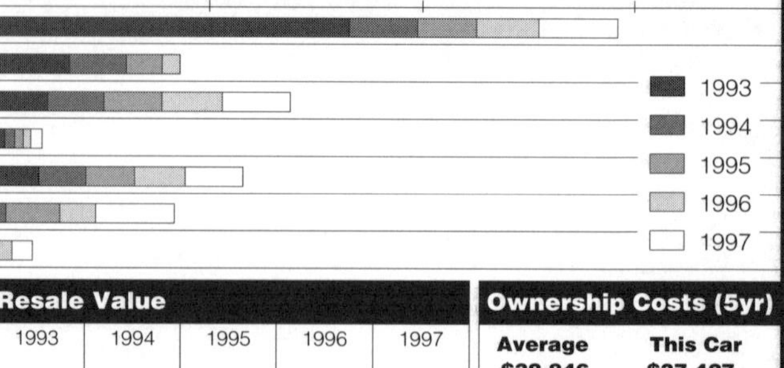

Warranty/Maintenance Info

Item	Value	Rate
Major Tune-Up	$152	Better Than Average
Minor Tune-Up	$108	Better Than Average
Brake Service	$185	Excellent
Overall Warranty	3 yr/36k	Average
Drivetrain Warranty	3 yr/36k	Average
Rust Warranty	6 yr/100k	Better Than Average
Maintenance Warranty	N/A	
Roadside Assistance	N/A	

Resale Value

1993	1994	1995	1996	1997
$17,575	$15,978	$14,595	$13,131	$11,377

Ownership Costs (5yr)

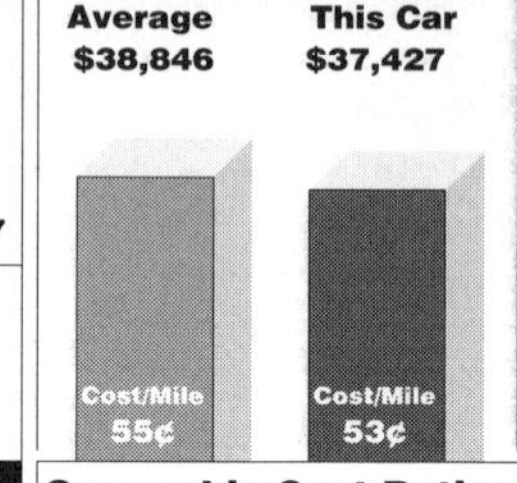

The 1993 Ford Club Wagon is available in two model editions - Regular and Heavy Duty and has three trim levels - Custom, XLT and Chateau vans. New for 1993, the Chateau Club Wagon has optional black protective bodyside moldings and an improved automatic overdrive electronic wide-ratio (AODE-W) transmission standard with the 5.0L V-8 engine. Standard features include color-keyed full-length carpeting, anti-theft system, six-speaker stereo system, high capacity air conditioning and forged aluminum wheels.

Cumulative Costs

	1993	1994	1995	1996	1997
Annual	$12,773	$5,823	$6,354	$5,722	$6,755
Total	$12,773	$18,596	$24,950	$30,672	$37,427

Ownership Cost Rating

Excellent

Ford Club Wagon Chateau Heavy Duty
3 Door Pass Van

4.9L 150 hp Gas Fuel Inject.

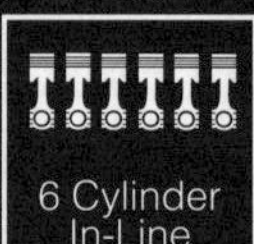
6 Cylinder In-Line

Automatic 3 Speed

2 Wheel Rear

Manual Seatbelts Only

Full-Size Van

Base Model Shown

Purchase Price

Car Item	Dealer Cost	List
Base Price	**$21,501**	**$25,118**
Anti-Lock Brakes	Std	Std
4 Spd Electronic Auto	$254	$299
5.8L 200 hp Gas	$796	$937
Air Conditioning	N/A	N/A
Power Steering	Std	Std
Cruise Control	Std	Std
All Wheel Drive	N/A	N/A
AM/FM Stereo Cassette	Std	Std
Steering Wheel, Tilt	Std	Std
Power Windows	Std	Std
***Options Price**	$796	$937
***Total Price**	**$22,297**	**$26,055**
Target Price	$24,858	
Destination Charge	$560	
Avg. Tax & Fees	$1,537	
Total Target $	**$26,955**	
Average Dealer Option Cost:	***85%***	

Ownership Costs

Cost Area	5 Year Cost	Rate
Depreciation	$15,744	Poor
Financing ($542/month)	$4,441	
Insurance (Rating 8)	$7,250	Excellent
State Fees	$1,065	
Fuel (Hwy 15 City 11)	$6,659	Worse Than Average
Maintenance	$4,266	Average
Repairs	$799	Better Than Average

Ownership Cost By Year

$5,000 | $10,000 | $15,000 | $20,000

1993 · 1994 · 1995 · 1996 · 1997

Warranty/Maintenance Info

Item	Value	Rate
Major Tune-Up	$152	Better Than Average
Minor Tune-Up	$108	Better Than Average
Brake Service	$185	Excellent
Overall Warranty	3 yr/36k	Average
Drivetrain Warranty	3 yr/36k	Average
Rust Warranty	6 yr/100k	Better Than Average
Maintenance Warranty	N/A	
Roadside Assistance	N/A	

Resale Value

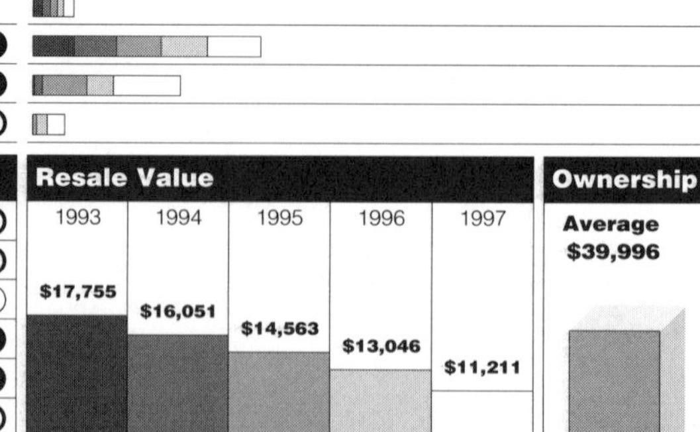

1993	1994	1995	1996	1997
$17,755	$16,051	$14,563	$13,046	$11,211

Ownership Costs (5yr)

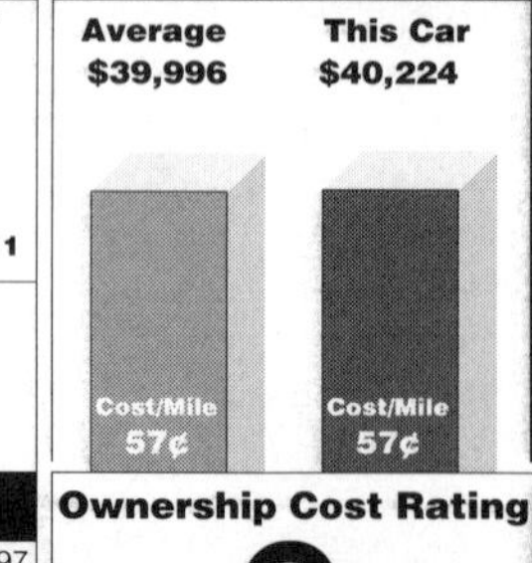

The 1993 Ford Club Wagon is available in two model editions - Regular and Heavy Duty and has three trim levels - Custom, XLT and Chateau vans. New for 1993, the Chateau Heavy Duty Club Wagon has optional black protective bodyside molding and an improved automatic overdrive electronic wide-ratio (AODE-W) transmission standard with the 5.0L engine. Standard features include color-keyed full-length carpeting, anti-theft system, six-speaker stereo system, high capacity air conditioning and sport wheels.

Cumulative Costs

	1993	1994	1995	1996	1997
Annual	$13,931	$6,238	$6,808	$6,033	$7,214
Total	$13,931	$20,169	$26,977	$33,010	$40,224

Ownership Cost Rating

Average

* Includes shaded options

** Other purchase requirements apply

 Poor  Worse Than Average  Average Better Than Average  Excellent  Insufficient Information

Refer to *Section 3: Annotated Vehicle Charts* for an explanation of these charts.

Ford Club Wagon Custom Super
3 Door Pass Ext Van

4.9L 150 hp Gas Fuel Inject.	6 Cylinder In-Line	Automatic 3 Speed	2 Wheel Rear	Manual Seatbelts Only

Purchase Price

Car Item	Dealer Cost	List
Base Price	**$17,394**	**$20,287**
Anti-Lock Brakes	Std	Std
4 Spd Electronic Auto	$254	$299
5.8L 200 hp Gas	$796	$937
Air Conditioning	Pkg	** Pkg
Power Steering	Std	Std
Cruise Control	$325	$383
All Wheel Drive	N/A	N/A
AM/FM Stereo Cassette	$238	$280
Steering Wheel, Tilt	Grp	Grp
Power Windows	$555	$652
***Options Price**	$796	$937
***Total Price**	**$18,190**	**$21,224**
Target Price	$20,076	
Destination Charge	$560	
Avg. Tax & Fees	$1,250	
Total Target $	**$21,886**	
Average Dealer Option Cost:	***85%***	

Ownership Costs

Cost Area	5 Year Cost	Rate
Depreciation	$11,199	Average
Financing ($440/month)	$3,606	
Insurance (Rating 10)	$7,689	Excellent
State Fees	$871	
Fuel (Hwy 15 City 11)	$6,659	Worse Than Average
Maintenance	$4,302	Average
Repairs	$799	Better Than Average

Ownership Cost By Year

$2,000 $4,000 $6,000 $8,000 $10,000 $12,000

1993 1994 1995 1996 1997

Warranty/Maintenance Info

Item	Value	Rate
Major Tune-Up	$152	Better Than Average
Minor Tune-Up	$108	Better Than Average
Brake Service	$185	Excellent
Overall Warranty	3 yr/36k	Average
Drivetrain Warranty	3 yr/36k	Average
Rust Warranty	6 yr/100k	Better Than Average
Maintenance Warranty	N/A	
Roadside Assistance	N/A	

Resale Value

1993	1994	1995	1996	1997
$14,237	$13,331	$12,588	$11,785	$10,687

Ownership Costs (5yr)

Average	This Car
$34,307	$35,125
Cost/Mile 49¢	Cost/Mile 50¢

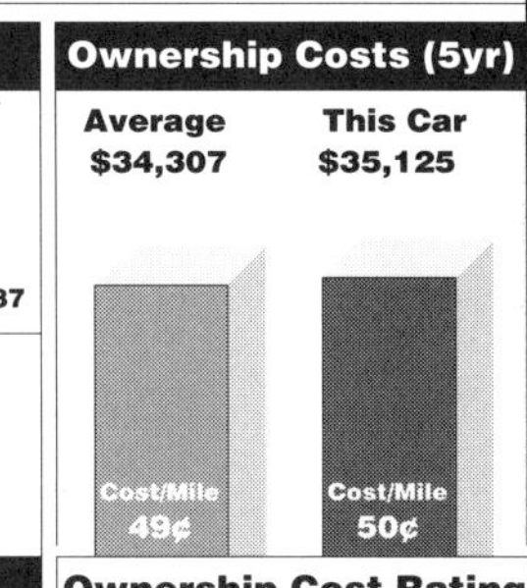

The 1993 Ford Super Club Wagon is available in one model edition, and has two trim levels - Custom and XLT vans. New for 1993, the Custom Super Club Wagon has optional black protective bodyside molding and an improved automatic overdrive electronic wide-ratio (AODE-W) transmission standard with the 5.0 liter V-8 engine. Standard features include color-keyed front door trim panels, 22.0 gallon fuel tank, aero halogen headlights and cloth color-keyed dual captain's chairs and rear bench seat.

Cumulative Costs

	1993	1994	1995	1996	1997
Annual	$12,066	$5,219	$5,963	$5,315	$6,562
Total	$12,066	$17,285	$23,248	$28,563	$35,125

Ownership Cost Rating

Worse Than Average

Ford Club Wagon XLT Super
3 Door Pass Ext Van

4.9L 150 hp Gas Fuel Inject.	6 Cylinder In-Line	Automatic 3 Speed	2 Wheel Rear	Manual Seatbelts Only

Purchase Price

Car Item	Dealer Cost	List
Base Price	**$18,985**	**$22,158**
Anti-Lock Brakes	Std	Std
4 Spd Electronic Auto	$254	$299
5.8L 200 hp Gas	$796	$937
Air Conditioning	Grp	** Grp
Power Steering	Std	Std
Cruise Control	$325	$383
All Wheel Drive	N/A	N/A
AM/FM Stereo Cassette	$175	$206
Steering Wheel, Tilt	Grp	Grp
Power Windows	Std	Std
***Options Price**	$796	$937
***Total Price**	**$19,781**	**$23,095**
Target Price	$21,918	
Destination Charge	$560	
Avg. Tax & Fees	$1,361	
Total Target $	**$23,839**	
Average Dealer Option Cost:	***85%***	

Ownership Costs

Cost Area	5 Year Cost	Rate
Depreciation	$12,680	Worse Than Average
Financing ($479/month)	$3,927	
Insurance (Rating 10)	$7,689	Excellent
State Fees	$947	
Fuel (Hwy 15 City 11)	$6,659	Worse Than Average
Maintenance	$4,302	Average
Repairs	$799	Better Than Average

Ownership Cost By Year

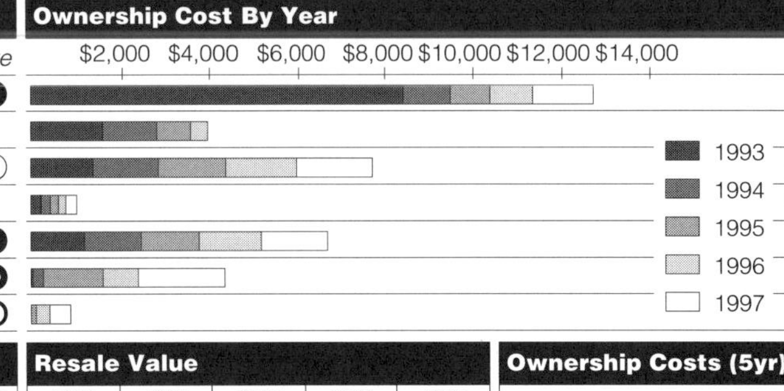

Warranty/Maintenance Info

Item	Value	Rate
Major Tune-Up	$152	Better Than Average
Minor Tune-Up	$108	Better Than Average
Brake Service	$185	Excellent
Overall Warranty	3 yr/36k	Average
Drivetrain Warranty	3 yr/36k	Average
Rust Warranty	6 yr/100k	Better Than Average
Maintenance Warranty	N/A	
Roadside Assistance	N/A	

Resale Value

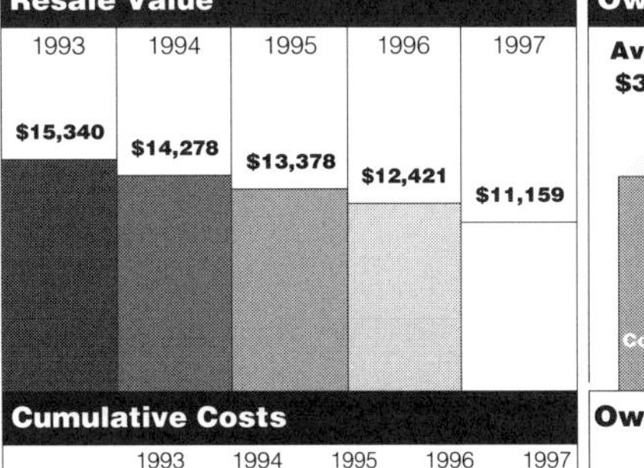

1993	1994	1995	1996	1997
$15,340	$14,278	$13,378	$12,421	$11,159

Ownership Costs (5yr)

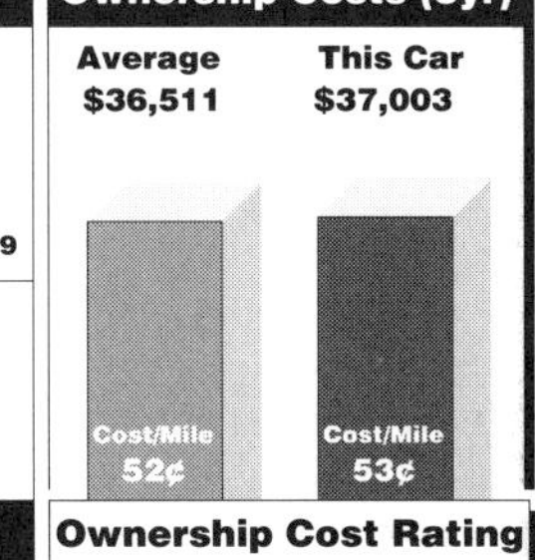

Average	This Car
$36,511	$37,003
Cost/Mile 52¢	Cost/Mile 53¢

The 1993 Ford Super Club Wagon is available in one model edition, and has two trim levels - Custom and XLT vans. New for 1993, the XLT Super Club Wagon has optional black protective bodyside moldings and an improved automatic overdrive electronic wide-ratio (AODE-W) transmission standard with the 5.0 liter V-8 engine. Standard features include color-keyed front door trim panels, 22.0 gallon fuel tank, aero, halogen headlights and cloth color-keyed dual captain's chairs and rear bench seat.

Cumulative Costs

	1993	1994	1995	1996	1997
Annual	$13,069	$5,492	$6,199	$5,506	$6,737
Total	$13,069	$18,561	$24,760	$30,266	$37,003

Ownership Cost Rating

Average

* Includes shaded options

** Other purchase requirements apply

 Poor  Worse Than Average  Average  Better Than Average ◯ Excellent ⊖ Insufficient Information

Refer to *Section 3: Annotated Vehicle Charts* for an explanation of these charts.

Ford Econoline E150

3 Door Cargo Van

4.9L 145 hp Gas Fuel Inject.

6 Cylinder In-Line

Automatic 3 Speed

2 Wheel Rear

Driver Airbag Psngr Belts

Full-Size Van

Purchase Price

Car Item	Dealer Cost	List
Base Price	**$13,194**	**$15,346**
Anti-Lock Brakes	Std	Std
4 Spd Auto O/D	$207	$244
5.0L 185 hp Gas	$608	$716
Air Conditioning	$827	$973
Power Steering	Std	Std
Cruise Control	$325	$383
All Wheel Drive	N/A	N/A
AM/FM Stereo Cassette	$238	$280
Steering Wheel, Tilt	Pkg	Pkg
Power Windows	$555	$652
***Options Price**	$1,435	$1,689
***Total Price**	**$14,629**	**$17,035**
Target Price	$15,529	
Destination Charge	$560	
Avg. Tax & Fees	$980	
Total Target $	**$17,069**	
Average Dealer Option Cost:	***85%***	

Ownership Costs

Cost Area	5 Year Cost	Rate
Depreciation	$6,773	Excellent
Financing ($343/month)	$2,811	
Insurance (Rating 5)	$6,786	Excellent
State Fees	$704	
Fuel (Hwy 18 City 14)	$5,399	Better Than Average
Maintenance	$3,850	Better Than Average
Repairs	$799	Better Than Average

Ownership Cost By Year

$2,000 $4,000 $6,000 $8,000

1993 1994 1995 1996 1997

Warranty/Maintenance Info

Item		Rate
Major Tune-Up	$152	Better Than Average
Minor Tune-Up	$108	Better Than Average
Brake Service	$185	Excellent
Overall Warranty	3 yr/36k	Average
Drivetrain Warranty	3 yr/36k	Average
Rust Warranty	6 yr/100k	Better Than Average
Maintenance Warranty	N/A	
Roadside Assistance	N/A	

Resale Value

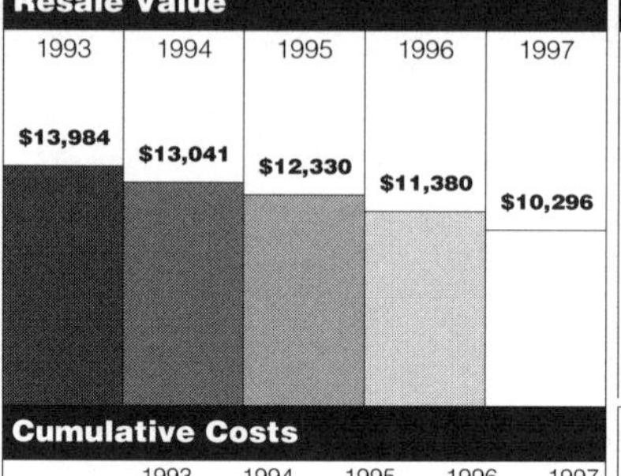

Ownership Costs (5yr)

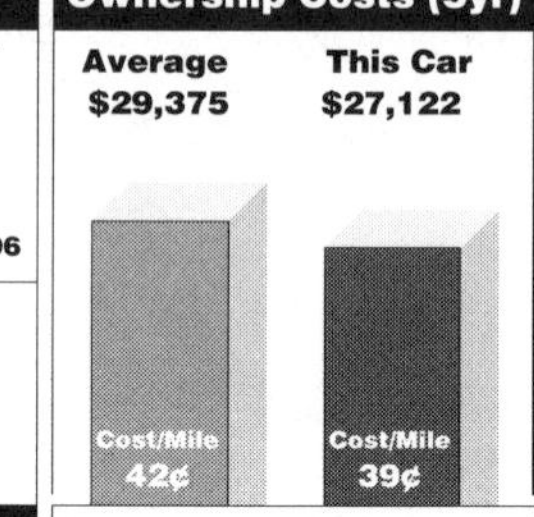

The 1993 Econoline Cargo Van is available in five models: E-150, E-250, E-350, E-250 Super and E-350 Super. New for 1993, the Econoline E-150 features an improved automatic electronic wide-ratio transmission with the 5.0L engine. Standard features for the E-150 includes aero headlamps and grille, chrome accents, chrome bumpers and plastic facia. The Econoline is the first full-sized van in the industry to include a driver's-side airbag as standard equipment to supplement safety belts.

Cumulative Costs

	1993	1994	1995	1996	1997
Annual	$6,730	$4,555	$5,096	$4,954	$5,787
Total	$6,730	$11,285	$16,381	$21,335	$27,122

Ownership Cost Rating

Excellent

Ford Econoline E250

3 Door Cargo Van

4.9L 145 hp Gas Fuel Inject.

6 Cylinder In-Line

Automatic 3 Speed

2 Wheel Rear

Driver Airbag Psngr Belts

Full-Size Van

E150 Model Shown

Purchase Price

Car Item	Dealer Cost	List
Base Price	**$13,547**	**$15,761**
Anti-Lock Brakes	Std	Std
4 Spd Electronic Auto	$254	$299
5.8L 200 hp Gas	$796	$937
Air Conditioning	$827	$973
Power Steering	Std	Std
Cruise Control	$325	$383
All Wheel Drive	N/A	N/A
AM/FM Stereo Cassette	$238	$280
Steering Wheel, Tilt	Pkg	Pkg
Power Windows	$555	$652
***Options Price**	$1,623	$1,910
***Total Price**	**$15,170**	**$17,671**
Target Price	$16,113	
Destination Charge	$560	
Avg. Tax & Fees	$1,016	
Total Target $	**$17,689**	
Average Dealer Option Cost:	***85%***	

Ownership Costs

Cost Area	5 Year Cost	Rate
Depreciation	$7,447	Average
Financing ($356/month)	$2,915	
Insurance (Rating 5)	$6,786	Excellent
State Fees	$729	
Fuel (Hwy 15 City 11)	$6,659	Worse Than Average
Maintenance	$4,230	Average
Repairs	$799	Better Than Average

Ownership Cost By Year

$2,000 $4,000 $6,000 $8,000

1993 1994 1995 1996 1997

Warranty/Maintenance Info

Item		Rate
Major Tune-Up	$152	Better Than Average
Minor Tune-Up	$108	Better Than Average
Brake Service	$185	Excellent
Overall Warranty	3 yr/36k	Average
Drivetrain Warranty	3 yr/36k	Average
Rust Warranty	6 yr/100k	Better Than Average
Maintenance Warranty	N/A	
Roadside Assistance	N/A	

Resale Value

1993	1994	1995	1996	1997
$13,768	$12,852	$12,171	$11,282	$10,242

Ownership Costs (5yr)

Average $30,123 — This Car $29,565

Cost/Mile 43¢ — Cost/Mile 42¢

The 1993 Econolime Cargo Van is available in five-models: E-150, E-250, E-350, E-250 Super and E-350 Super. New for 1993 the Econoline E-250 offers black bodyside molding and a 35 gallon fuel tank. Features include driver's-side airbag, color-keyed carpeting, power window and door locks and the Deluxe Insulation Package. Other features include sliding side cargo door, light and convenience group, new trailer tow harness features and a clamp-on hitch that is compatible with the rear bumper.

Cumulative Costs

	1993	1994	1995	1996	1997
Annual	$7,847	$4,808	$5,522	$5,139	$6,249
Total	$7,847	$12,655	$18,177	$23,316	$29,565

Ownership Cost Rating

Better Than Average

* Includes shaded options

** Other purchase requirements apply

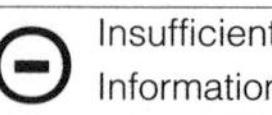

Poor  Worse Than Average  Average  Better Than Average  Excellent — Insufficient Information

Refer to *Section 3: Annotated Vehicle Charts* for an explanation of these charts.

Ford Econoline E350
3 Door Cargo Van

4.9L 145 hp Gas Fuel Inject.

6 Cylinder In-Line

Automatic 3 Speed

2 Wheel Rear

Manual Seatbelts Only

Full-Size Van

Super Van Shown

Purchase Price

Car Item	Dealer Cost	List
Base Price	**$14,482**	**$16,860**
Anti-Lock Brakes	Std	Std
4 Spd Electronic Auto	N/C	N/C
7.5L 230 hp Gas	$1,208	$1,421
Air Conditioning	$827	$973
Power Steering	Std	Std
Cruise Control	$325	$383
All Wheel Drive	N/A	N/A
AM/FM Stereo Cassette	$238	$280
Steering Wheel, Tilt	Pkg	Pkg
Power Windows	$555	$652
***Options Price**	$2,035	$2,394
***Total Price**	**$16,517**	**$19,254**
Target Price	$17,571	
Destination Charge	$560	
Avg. Tax & Fees	$1,105	
Total Target $	**$19,236**	
Average Dealer Option Cost:	***85%***	

Ownership Costs

Cost Area	5 Year Cost	Rate
Depreciation	$8,711	Average
Financing ($387/month)	$3,168	
Insurance (Rating 6)	$7,129	Excellent
State Fees	$793	
Fuel (Hwy 10 City 8 [Est.])	$9,593	Poor
Maintenance	$4,220	Average
Repairs	$799	Better Than Average

Ownership Cost By Year

$2,000 $4,000 $6,000 $8,000 $10,000

1993 1994 1995 1996 1997

Warranty/Maintenance Info

Major Tune-Up	$149	Better Than Average
Minor Tune-Up	$94	Better Than Average
Brake Service	$185	Excellent
Overall Warranty	3 yr/36k	Average
Drivetrain Warranty	3 yr/36k	Average
Rust Warranty	6 yr/100k	Better Than Average
Maintenance Warranty	N/A	
Roadside Assistance	N/A	

Resale Value

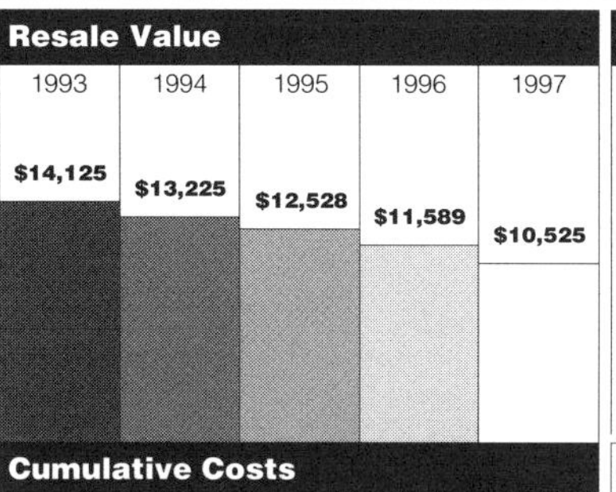

1993	1994	1995	1996	1997
$14,125	$13,225	$12,528	$11,589	$10,525

Ownership Costs (5yr)

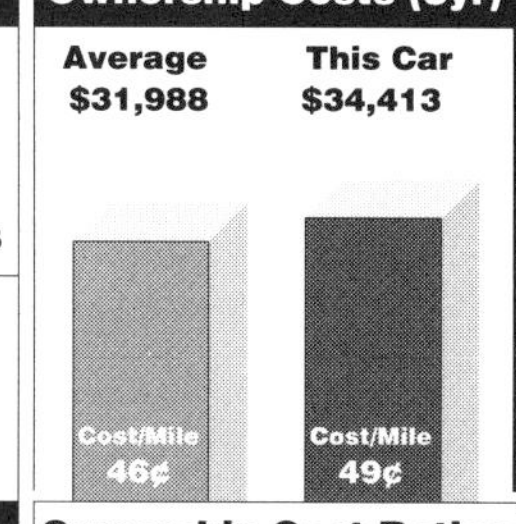

Average	This Car
$31,988	$34,413
Cost/Mile 46¢	Cost/Mile 49¢

Cumulative Costs

	1993	1994	1995	1996	1997
Annual	$9,764	$5,499	$6,270	$5,882	$6,998
Total	$9,764	$15,263	$21,533	$27,415	$34,413

Ownership Cost Rating

Poor

The 1993 Econoline Cargo Van is available in five-models: E-150, E-250, E-350, E-250 Super and E-350 Super. New for 1993, the Econoline E-350 features all-new sheet metal. New front end styling includes aero headlamps and grille, chrome accents, chrome bumpers and plastic facia. Other features include an instrument panel with new guages. The Econoline is the first full-sized van in the industry to offer driver-side airbags to supplement safety belts and optional electronically operated mirrors.

Ford Econoline E250 Super
3 Door Cargo Ext Van

4.9L 145 hp Gas Fuel Inject.

6 Cylinder In-Line

Automatic 3 Speed

2 Wheel Rear

Driver Airbag Psngr Belts

Full-Size Van

Purchase Price

Car Item	Dealer Cost	List
Base Price	**$14,099**	**$16,411**
Anti-Lock Brakes	Std	Std
4 Spd Electronic Auto	$254	$299
5.8L 200 hp Gas	$796	$937
Air Conditioning	$827	$973
Power Steering	Std	Std
Cruise Control	$325	$383
All Wheel Drive	N/A	N/A
AM/FM Stereo Cassette	$238	$280
Steering Wheel, Tilt	Pkg	Pkg
Power Windows	$555	$652
***Options Price**	$1,623	$1,910
***Total Price**	**$15,722**	**$18,321**
Target Price	$16,715	
Destination Charge	$560	
Avg. Tax & Fees	$1,053	
Total Target $	**$18,328**	
Average Dealer Option Cost:	***85%***	

Ownership Costs

Cost Area	5 Year Cost	Rate
Depreciation	$7,785	Average
Financing ($368/month)	$3,020	
Insurance (Rating 6)	$6,919	Excellent
State Fees	$755	
Fuel (Hwy 15 City 11)	$6,659	Worse Than Average
Maintenance	$4,230	Average
Repairs	$799	Better Than Average

Ownership Cost By Year

$2,000 $4,000 $6,000 $8,000

1993 1994 1995 1996 1997

Warranty/Maintenance Info

Major Tune-Up	$152	Better Than Average
Minor Tune-Up	$108	Better Than Average
Brake Service	$185	Excellent
Overall Warranty	3 yr/36k	Average
Drivetrain Warranty	3 yr/36k	Average
Rust Warranty	6 yr/100k	Better Than Average
Maintenance Warranty	N/A	
Roadside Assistance	N/A	

Resale Value

1993	1994	1995	1996	1997
$14,192	$13,250	$12,546	$11,609	$10,543

Ownership Costs (5yr)

Average	This Car
$30,889	$30,167
Cost/Mile 44¢	Cost/Mile 43¢

Cumulative Costs

	1993	1994	1995	1996	1997
Annual	$8,137	$4,899	$5,598	$5,226	$6,307
Total	$8,137	$13,036	$18,634	$23,860	$30,167

Ownership Cost Rating

Better Than Average

The 1993 Econoline Cargo Van is available in five-models: E-150, E-250, E-350, E-250 Super and E-350 Super. New for 1993, the E-250 Super features all-new front end styling. Features include aero headlamps and grille, chrome accents, chrome bumpers and plastic facia. Flush side glass and tri-colored wraparound tail lamps complete the design theme. The Econoline E-250 Super also features a driver's-side airbag to supplement safety belts, and optional electronically operated mirors.

* Includes shaded options

** Other purchase requirements apply

 Poor
 Worse Than Average
 Average
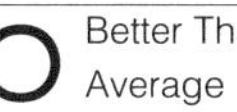 Better Than Average
 Excellent
Insufficient Information

Refer to *Section 3: Annotated Vehicle Charts* for an explanation of these charts.

Ford Econoline E350 Super
3 Door Cargo Ext Van

Full-Size Van

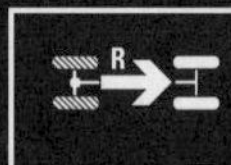

4.9L 145 hp Gas Fuel Inject.	6 Cylinder In-Line	Automatic 3 Speed	2 Wheel Rear	Manual Seatbelts Only

Purchase Price

Car Item	Dealer Cost	List
Base Price	**$15,256**	**$17,771**
Anti-Lock Brakes	Std	Std
4 Spd Electronic Auto	N/C	N/C
7.5L 230 hp Gas	$1,208	$1,421
Air Conditioning	$827	$973
Power Steering	Std	Std
Cruise Control	$325	$383
All Wheel Drive	N/A	N/A
AM/FM Stereo Cassette	$238	$280
Steering Wheel, Tilt	Pkg	Pkg
Power Windows	$555	$652
***Options Price**	$2,035	$2,394
***Total Price**	**$17,291**	**$20,165**
Target Price	$18,419	
Destination Charge	$560	
Avg. Tax & Fees	$1,156	
Total Target $	**$20,135**	
Average Dealer Option Cost:	***85%***	

Ownership Costs

Cost Area	5 Year Cost	Rate
Depreciation	$9,340	Average
Financing ($405/month)	$3,318	
Insurance (Rating 7)	$7,244	Excellent
State Fees	$829	
Fuel (Hwy 10 City 8 [Est.])	$9,593	Poor
Maintenance	$4,238	Average
Repairs	$799	Better Than Average

Ownership Cost By Year

$2,000 $4,000 $6,000 $8,000 $10,000

1993 1994 1995 1996 1997

Warranty/Maintenance Info

Item		Rate
Major Tune-Up	$149	Better Than Average
Minor Tune-Up	$94	Better Than Average
Brake Service	$185	Excellent
Overall Warranty	3 yr/36k	Average
Drivetrain Warranty	3 yr/36k	Average
Rust Warranty	6 yr/100k	Better Than Average
Maintenance Warranty	N/A	
Roadside Assistance	N/A	

Resale Value

1993	1994	1995	1996	1997
$14,720	$13,725	$12,955	$11,937	$10,795

Ownership Costs (5yr)

Average	This Car
$33,060	$35,361
Cost/Mile 47¢	Cost/Mile 51¢

The 1993 Econoline Cargo Van is available in five models: E-150, E-250, E-350, E-250 Super and E-350 Super. New for 1993, the Econoline E-350 Super offers an improved automatic overdrive electronic wide-ratio transmission standard with the 5.0-liter engine and optional black protective bodyside molding. Exterior features include new trailer tow harness features and a clamp-on hitch that is compatible with the rear bumper. Interior features include an instrument panel with new guages.

Cumulative Costs

	1993	1994	1995	1996	1997
Annual	$10,160	$5,672	$6,412	$6,002	$7,115
Total	$10,160	$15,832	$22,244	$28,246	$35,361

Ownership Cost Rating

Poor

Ford Escort LX
4 Door Wagon

Subcompact Wag

1.9L 88 hp Gas Fuel Inject.	4 Cylinder In-Line	Manual 5 Speed	2 Wheel Front	Automatic Seatbelts

Purchase Price

Car Item	Dealer Cost	List
Base Price	**$9,312**	**$10,367**
Anti-Lock Brakes	N/A	N/A
Automatic 4 Speed	$622	** $732
Optional Engine	N/A	N/A
Air Conditioning	$645	** $759
Power Steering	$222	$261
Cruise Control	Pkg	Pkg
All Wheel Drive	N/A	N/A
AM/FM Stereo Cassette	$132	$155
Steering Wheel, Tilt	Pkg	Pkg
Power Windows	Pkg	Pkg
***Options Price**	$0	$0
***Total Price**	**$9,312**	**$10,367**
Target Price	$9,819	
Destination Charge	$375	
Avg. Tax & Fees	$617	
Total Target $	**$10,811**	
Average Dealer Option Cost:	***85%***	

Ownership Costs

Cost Area	5 Year Cost	Rate
Depreciation	$6,161	Worse Than Average
Financing ($217/month)	$1,781	
Insurance (Rating 8)	$7,223	Worse Than Average
State Fees	$429	
Fuel (Hwy 36 City 29)	$2,656	Better Than Average
Maintenance	$3,417	Better Than Average
Repairs	$680	Average

Ownership Cost By Year

$2,000 $4,000 $6,000 $8,000

1993 1994 1995 1996 1997

Warranty/Maintenance Info

Item		Rate
Major Tune-Up	$120	Better Than Average
Minor Tune-Up	$68	Excellent
Brake Service	$206	Worse Than Average
Overall Warranty	3 yr/36k	Average
Drivetrain Warranty	3 yr/36k	Average
Rust Warranty	6 yr/100k	Better Than Average
Maintenance Warranty	N/A	
Roadside Assistance	N/A	

Resale Value

1993	1994	1995	1996	1997
$7,827	$6,896	$6,203	$5,416	$4,650

Ownership Costs (5yr)

Average	This Car
$23,242	$22,347
Cost/Mile 33¢	Cost/Mile 32¢

The 1993 Escort is available in seven models - Pony, LX and GT two-door hatchbacks; LX and LX-E sedans; and the LX four-door hatchback and wagon. New for 1993, the LX wagon offers a new grille, and several new exterior colors. Functional changes for the wagon include the addition of a liftgate lock to the power lock option. The LX features a tachometer, and dual visor vanity mirrors, and variable intermittent wipers. Ford will continue to market its "One-Price" LX Advantage for the 1993 model year.

Cumulative Costs

	1993	1994	1995	1996	1997
Annual	$5,700	$3,672	$4,150	$3,520	$5,305
Total	$5,700	$9,372	$13,522	$17,042	$22,347

Ownership Cost Rating

Excellent

* Includes shaded options

** Other purchase requirements apply

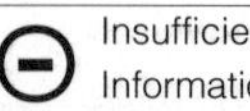

 Poor  Worse Than Average  Average 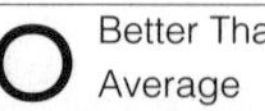 Better Than Average  Excellent ⊖ Insufficient Information

Refer to *Section 3: Annotated Vehicle Charts* for an explanation of these charts.

Ford Explorer XL

2 Door Sport Utility

4.0L 160 hp Gas Fuel Inject.

6 Cylinder "V"

Manual 5 Speed

2 Wheel Rear

Manual Seatbelts Only

Purchase Price

Car Item	Dealer Cost	List
Base Price	**$14,829**	**$16,652**
Anti-Lock Brakes	Std	Std
Automatic 4 Speed	$757	$890
Optional Engine	N/A	N/A
Air Conditioning	$663	$780
Power Steering	Std	Std
Cruise Control	$325	$383
All Wheel Drive	N/A	N/A
AM/FM Stereo Cassette	$117	$138
Steering Wheel, Tilt	Grp	Grp
Power Windows	Pkg	Pkg
***Options Price**	$780	$918
***Total Price**	**$15,609**	**$17,570**
Target Price	$17,118	
Destination Charge	$485	
Avg. Tax & Fees	$1,061	
Total Target $	**$18,664**	
Average Dealer Option Cost:	***85%***	

Ownership Costs

Cost Area	5 Year Cost	Rate
Depreciation	$5,896	Better Than Average
Financing ($375/month)	$3,075	
Insurance (Rating 8)	$7,432	Excellent
State Fees	$721	
Fuel (Hwy 23 City 18)	$4,213	Average
Maintenance	$3,431	Excellent
Repairs	$709	Excellent

Ownership Cost By Year

Warranty/Maintenance Info

Item		Rate
Major Tune-Up	$118	Excellent
Minor Tune-Up	$79	Excellent
Brake Service	$210	Better Than Average
Overall Warranty	3 yr/36k	Average
Drivetrain Warranty	3 yr/36k	Average
Rust Warranty	6 yr/100k	Better Than Average
Maintenance Warranty	N/A	
Roadside Assistance	N/A	

Resale Value

1993	1994	1995	1996	1997
$16,214	$15,518	$14,757	$13,772	$12,768

Ownership Costs (5yr)

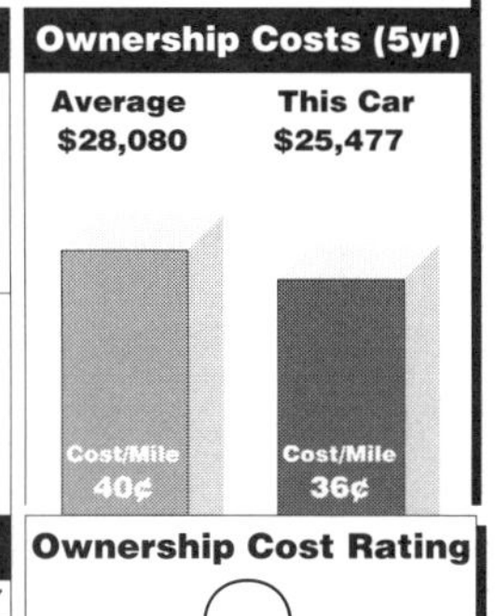

Cumulative Costs

	1993	1994	1995	1996	1997
Annual	$6,107	$4,253	$5,003	$4,758	$5,356
Total	$6,107	$10,360	$15,363	$20,121	$25,477

Ownership Cost Rating

Excellent

The 1993 Explorer is available in twelve models - XL, XLT, Sport, and Eddie Bauer with two- or four-wheel drive. New for 1993, the two-door XL 2WD offers new deep dish aluminum wheels, standard lower rocker panel moldings, freshened seat styles, 60/40 cloth split bench, steering wheel, instrument panel appliques, instrument cluster graphics, and 4-wheel ABS becomes standard. Six new exterior colors are also available (Electric Red, Dk. Cranberry, Vibrant Red, Dk. Blue, Dk. Forest Green, and Opal Grey).

Ford Explorer XL

4 Door Sport Utility

4.0L 160 hp Gas Fuel Inject.

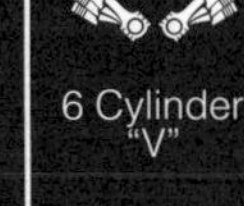
6 Cylinder "V"

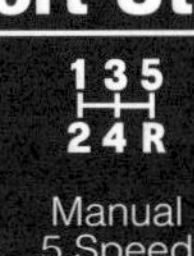
Manual 5 Speed

2 Wheel Rear

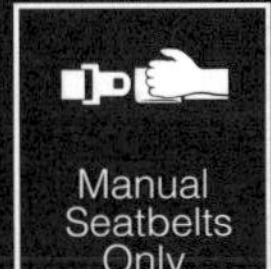
Manual Seatbelts Only

Utility

2 Door Model Shown

Purchase Price

Car Item	Dealer Cost	List
Base Price	**$15,501**	**$17,416**
Anti-Lock Brakes	Std	Std
Automatic 4 Speed	$757	$890
Optional Engine	N/A	N/A
Air Conditioning	$663	$780
Power Steering	Std	Std
Cruise Control	$352	$383
All Wheel Drive	N/A	N/A
AM/FM Stereo Cassette	$117	$138
Steering Wheel, Tilt	Grp	Grp
Power Windows	Pkg	Pkg
***Options Price**	$780	$918
***Total Price**	**$16,281**	**$18,334**
Target Price	$17,885	
Destination Charge	$485	
Avg. Tax & Fees	$1,107	
Total Target $	**$19,477**	
Average Dealer Option Cost:	***86%***	

Ownership Costs

Cost Area	5 Year Cost	Rate
Depreciation	$5,933	Excellent
Financing ($391/month)	$3,208	
Insurance (Rating 10)	$7,689	Excellent
State Fees	$753	
Fuel (Hwy 23 City 18)	$4,213	Average
Maintenance	$3,449	Excellent
Repairs	$709	Excellent

Ownership Cost By Year

$2,000 | $4,000 | $6,000 | $8,000

1993 | 1994 | 1995 | 1996 | 1997

Warranty/Maintenance Info

Item		Rate
Major Tune-Up	$118	Excellent
Minor Tune-Up	$79	Excellent
Brake Service	$210	Better Than Average
Overall Warranty	3 yr/36k	Average
Drivetrain Warranty	3 yr/36k	Average
Rust Warranty	6 yr/100k	Better Than Average
Maintenance Warranty	N/A	
Roadside Assistance	N/A	

Resale Value

1993	1994	1995	1996	1997
$17,116	$16,416	$15,622	$14,582	$13,544

Ownership Costs (5yr)

Average	This Car
$28,722	$25,954
Cost/Mile 41¢	Cost/Mile 37¢

Cumulative Costs

	1993	1994	1995	1996	1997
Annual	$6,128	$4,355	$5,120	$4,900	$5,451
Total	$6,128	$10,483	$15,603	$20,503	$25,954

Ownership Cost Rating

Excellent

The 1993 Explorer is available in twelve models - XL, XLT, Sport, and Eddie Bauer with two- or four-wheel drive. New for 1993, the four-door XL 2WD offers new deep dish aluminum wheels, standard lower rocker panel moldings, freshened seat styles, 60/40 cloth split bench, steering wheel, instrument panel appliques, instrument cluster graphics, and 4-wheel ABS becomes standard. Six new exterior colors are also available (Electric Red, Dk. Cranberry, Vibrant Red, Dk. Blue, Dk. Forest Green, and Opal Grey).

* Includes shaded options

** Other purchase requirements apply

Refer to *Section 3: Annotated Vehicle Charts* for an explanation of these charts.

Ford Explorer Sport

2 Door Sport Utility

 4.0L 160 hp Gas Fuel Inject.

 6 Cylinder "V"

 Manual 5 Speed

 2 Wheel Rear

Manual Seatbelts Only

Purchase Price

Car Item	Dealer Cost	List
Base Price	**$15,706**	**$17,649**
Anti-Lock Brakes	Std	Std
Automatic 4 Speed	$757	$890
Optional Engine	N/A	N/A
Air Conditioning	$663	$780
Power Steering	Std	Std
Cruise Control	$325	$383
All Wheel Drive	N/A	N/A
AM/FM Stereo Cassette	$117	$138
Steering Wheel, Tilt	Grp	Grp
Power Windows	Pkg	Pkg
***Options Price**	$780	$918
***Total Price**	**$16,486**	**$18,567**
Target Price	$18,120	
Destination Charge	$485	
Avg. Tax & Fees	$1,121	
Total Target $	**$19,726**	
Average Dealer Option Cost:	***85%***	

Ownership Costs

Cost Area	5 Year Cost	Rate
Depreciation	$6,755	Better Than Average
Financing ($396/month)	$3,250	
Insurance (Rating 8)	$7,432	Excellent
State Fees	$761	
Fuel (Hwy 23 City 18)	$4,213	Worse Than Average
Maintenance	$3,431	Excellent
Repairs	$709	Excellent

Ownership Cost By Year

Warranty/Maintenance Info

Major Tune-Up	$118	Excellent
Minor Tune-Up	$79	Excellent
Brake Service	$210	Better Than Average
Overall Warranty	3 yr/36k	Average
Drivetrain Warranty	3 yr/36k	Average
Rust Warranty	6 yr/100k	Better Than Average
Maintenance Warranty	N/A	
Roadside Assistance	N/A	

Resale Value

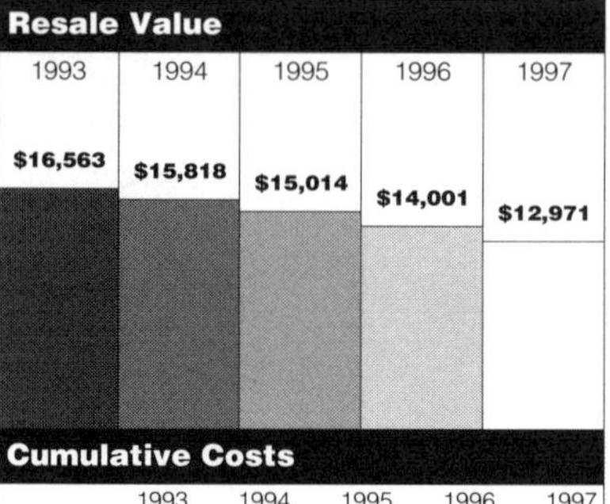

Ownership Costs (5yr)

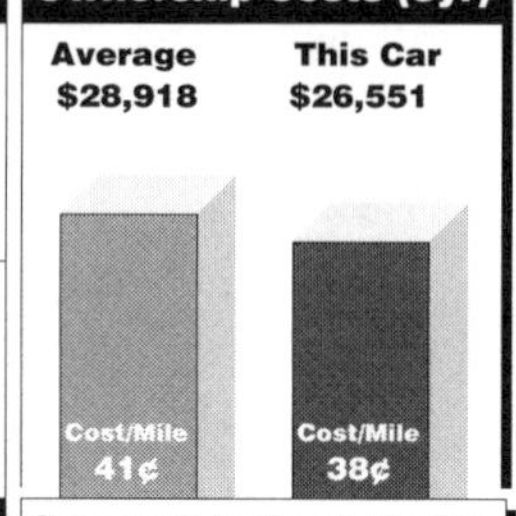

Average	This Car
$28,918	$26,551
Cost/Mile 41¢	Cost/Mile 38¢

Cumulative Costs

	1993	1994	1995	1996	1997
Annual	$6,903	$4,366	$5,088	$4,806	$5,388
Total	$6,903	$11,269	$16,357	$21,163	$26,551

Ownership Cost Rating

Excellent

The 1993 Explorer is available in twelve models - XL, XLT, Sport, and Eddie Bauer with two- or four-wheel drive. New for 1993, the two-door Sport 2WD offers new deep dish aluminum wheels, standard lower rocker panel moldings, freshened seat styles, 60/40 cloth split bench, steering wheel, instrument panel appliques, instrument cluster graphics, and 4-wheel ABS becomes standard. Six new exterior colors are also available (Electric Red, Dk. Cranberry, Vibrant Red, Dk. Blue, Dk. Forest Green, and Opal Grey).

Ford Explorer XLT

4 Door Sport Utility

 4.0L 160 hp Gas Fuel Inject.

 6 Cylinder "V"

 Manual 5 Speed

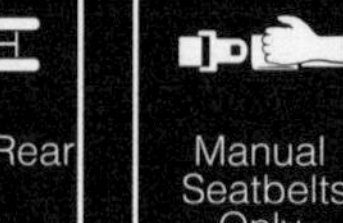 2 Wheel Rear

Manual Seatbelts Only

Purchase Price

Car Item	Dealer Cost	List
Base Price	**$17,391**	**$19,564**
Anti-Lock Brakes	Std	Std
Automatic 4 Speed	$757	$890
Optional Engine	N/A	N/A
Air Conditioning	$663	$780
Power Steering	Std	Std
Cruise Control	Std	Std
All Wheel Drive	N/A	N/A
AM/FM Stereo Cassette	$117	$138
Steering Wheel, Tilt	Std	Std
Power Windows	Std	Std
***Options Price**	$780	$918
***Total Price**	**$18,171**	**$20,482**
Target Price	$20,055	
Destination Charge	$485	
Avg. Tax & Fees	$1,237	
Total Target $	**$21,777**	
Average Dealer Option Cost:	***85%***	

Ownership Costs

Cost Area	5 Year Cost	Rate
Depreciation	$7,751	Better Than Average
Financing ($438/month)	$3,587	
Insurance (Rating 10)	$7,689	Excellent
State Fees	$840	
Fuel (Hwy 23 City 18)	$4,213	Worse Than Average
Maintenance	$3,449	Excellent
Repairs	$709	Excellent

Ownership Cost By Year

Warranty/Maintenance Info

Major Tune-Up	$118	Excellent
Minor Tune-Up	$79	Excellent
Brake Service	$210	Better Than Average
Overall Warranty	3 yr/36k	Average
Drivetrain Warranty	3 yr/36k	Average
Rust Warranty	6 yr/100k	Better Than Average
Maintenance Warranty	N/A	
Roadside Assistance	N/A	

Resale Value

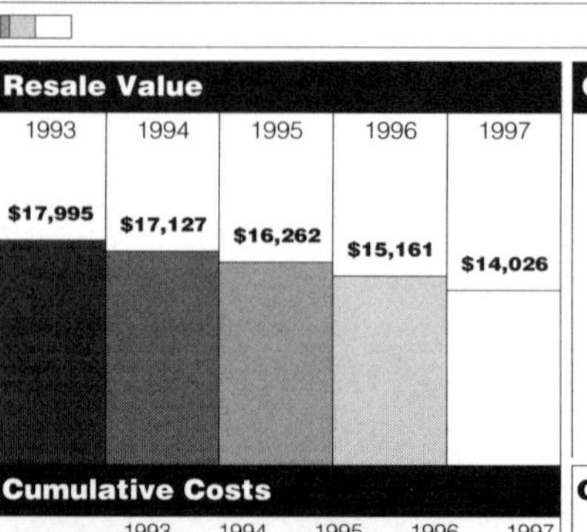

Ownership Costs (5yr)

Average	This Car
$30,529	$28,238
Cost/Mile 44¢	Cost/Mile 40¢

Cumulative Costs

	1993	1994	1995	1996	1997
Annual	$7,729	$4,661	$5,283	$5,004	$5,561
Total	$7,729	$12,390	$17,673	$22,677	$28,238

Ownership Cost Rating

Excellent

The 1993 Explorer is available in twelve models - XL, XLT, Sport, and Eddie Bauer with two- or four-wheel drive. New for 1993, the four-door XLT 2WD offers new deep dish aluminum wheels, standard lower rocker panel moldings, freshened seat styles, 60/40 cloth split bench, steering wheel, the two right-hand A/C registers and glove box latch are color-keyed, and 4-wheel ABS becomes standard. Six new exterior colors are available while there are three new interior colors (red, blue, and grey).

* Includes shaded options

** Other purchase requirements apply

 Poor  Worse Than Average 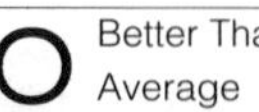 Average  Better Than Average — Excellent — Insufficient Information

Refer to *Section 3: Annotated Vehicle Charts* for an explanation of these charts.

Ford Explorer Eddie Bauer
2 Door Sport Utility

4.0L 160 hp Gas Fuel Inject.

6 Cylinder "V"

Manual 5 Speed

2 Wheel Rear

Manual Seatbelts Only

Utility

4 Door Model Shown

Purchase Price

Car Item	Dealer Cost	List
Base Price	**$18,621**	**$20,961**
Anti-Lock Brakes	Std	Std
Automatic 4 Speed	$757	$890
Optional Engine	N/A	N/A
Air Conditioning	$663	$780
Power Steering	Std	Std
Cruise Control	Std	Std
All Wheel Drive	N/A	N/A
AM/FM Stereo Cassette	$117	$138
Steering Wheel, Tilt	Std	Std
Power Windows	Std	Std
***Options Price**	$780	$918
***Total Price**	**$19,401**	**$21,879**
Target Price	$21,477	
Destination Charge	$485	
Avg. Tax & Fees	$1,322	
Total Target $	**$23,284**	
Average Dealer Option Cost:	***85%***	

Ownership Costs

Cost Area	5 Year Cost	Rate
Depreciation	$9,784	Average
Financing ($468/month)	$3,836	
Insurance (Rating 8)	$7,432	Excellent
State Fees	$895	
Fuel (Hwy 23 City 18)	$4,213	Average
Maintenance	$3,458	Excellent
Repairs	$709	Excellent

Ownership Cost By Year

$2,000 $4,000 $6,000 $8,000 $10,000

1993 1994 1995 1996 1997

Warranty/Maintenance Info

Item		Rate
Major Tune-Up	$118	Excellent
Minor Tune-Up	$79	Excellent
Brake Service	$210	Better Than Average
Overall Warranty	3 yr/36k	Average
Drivetrain Warranty	3 yr/36k	Average
Rust Warranty	6 yr/100k	Better Than Average
Maintenance Warranty	N/A	
Roadside Assistance	N/A	

Resale Value

1993	1994	1995	1996	1997
$17,009	$16,340	$15,550	$14,541	$13,500

Ownership Costs (5yr)

Average	This Car
$31,704	$30,327
Cost/Mile 45¢	Cost/Mile 43¢

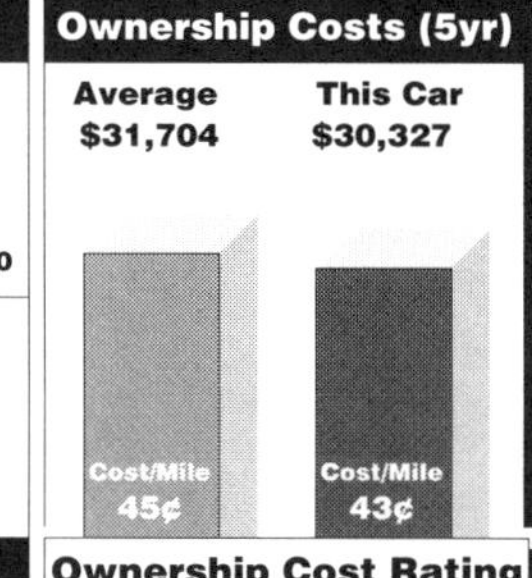

Cumulative Costs

	1993	1994	1995	1996	1997
Annual	$10,292	$4,503	$5,230	$4,869	$5,433
Total	$10,292	$14,795	$20,025	$24,894	$30,327

Ownership Cost Rating

Excellent

The 1993 Explorer is available in twelve models - XL, XLT, Sport, and Eddie Bauer with two- or four-wheel drive. New for 1993, the two-door Eddie Bauer 2WD offers new deep dish aluminum wheels, standard lower rocker panel moldings, freshened seat styles, 60/40 cloth split bench, steering wheel, the two right-hand A/C registers and glove box latch are color-keyed, and 4-wheel ABS becomes standard. Six new exterior colors are available while there are three new interior colors (red, blue, and grey).

Ford Explorer Eddie Bauer
4 Door Sport Utility

4.0L 160 hp Gas Fuel Inject.

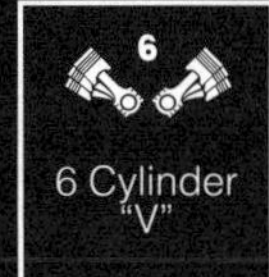
6 Cylinder "V"

Manual 5 Speed

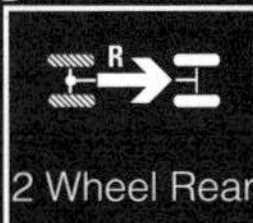
2 Wheel Rear

Manual Seatbelts Only

Utility

Purchase Price

Car Item	Dealer Cost	List
Base Price	**$19,808**	**$22,311**
Anti-Lock Brakes	Std	Std
Automatic 4 Speed	$757	$890
Optional Engine	N/A	N/A
Air Conditioning	$663	$780
Power Steering	Std	Std
Cruise Control	Std	Std
All Wheel Drive	N/A	N/A
AM/FM Stereo Cassette	$117	$138
Steering Wheel, Tilt	Std	Std
Power Windows	Std	Std
***Options Price**	$780	$918
***Total Price**	**$20,588**	**$23,229**
Target Price	$22,858	
Destination Charge	$485	
Avg. Tax & Fees	$1,404	
Total Target $	**$24,747**	
Average Dealer Option Cost:	***85%***	

Ownership Costs

Cost Area	5 Year Cost	Rate
Depreciation	$10,015	Average
Financing ($497/month)	$4,076	
Insurance (Rating 10)	$7,689	Excellent
State Fees	$948	
Fuel (Hwy 23 City 18)	$4,213	Average
Maintenance	$3,476	Better Than Average
Repairs	$709	Excellent

Ownership Cost By Year

$2,000 $4,000 $6,000 $8,000 $10,000 $12,000

1993 1994 1995 1996 1997

Warranty/Maintenance Info

Item		Rate
Major Tune-Up	$118	Excellent
Minor Tune-Up	$79	Excellent
Brake Service	$210	Better Than Average
Overall Warranty	3 yr/36k	Average
Drivetrain Warranty	3 yr/36k	Average
Rust Warranty	6 yr/100k	Better Than Average
Maintenance Warranty	N/A	
Roadside Assistance	N/A	

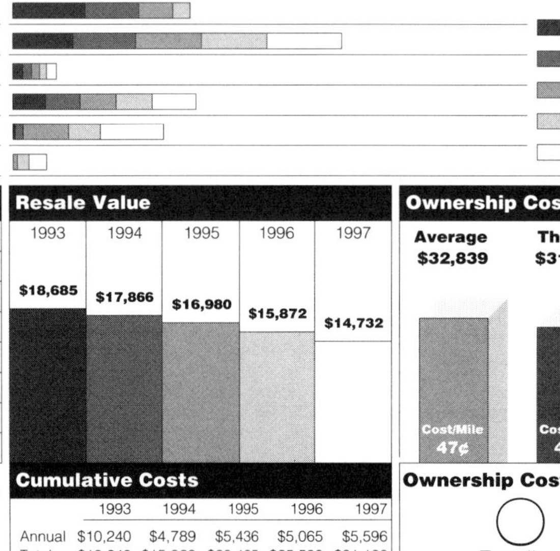

Resale Value

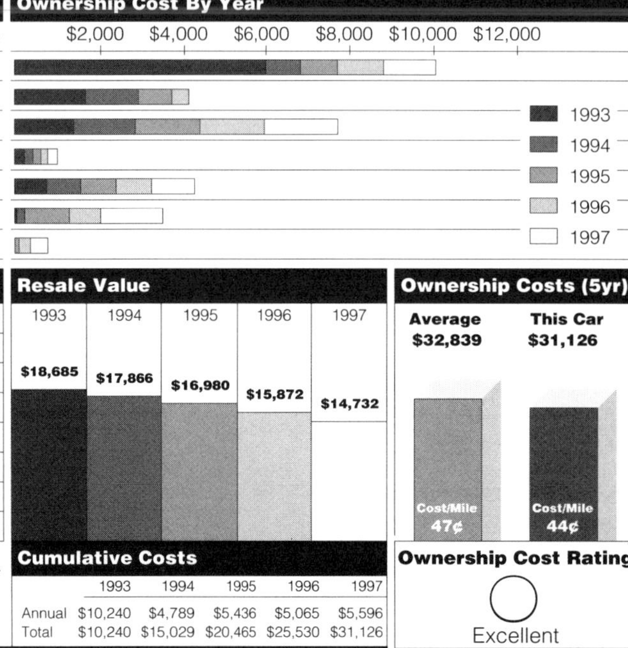

1993	1994	1995	1996	1997
$18,685	$17,866	$16,980	$15,872	$14,732

Ownership Costs (5yr)

Average	This Car
$32,839	$31,126
Cost/Mile 47¢	Cost/Mile 44¢

Cumulative Costs

	1993	1994	1995	1996	1997
Annual	$10,240	$4,789	$5,436	$5,065	$5,596
Total	$10,240	$15,029	$20,465	$25,530	$31,126

Ownership Cost Rating

Excellent

The 1993 Explorer is available in twelve models - XL, XLT, Sport, and Eddie Bauer with two- or four-wheel drive. New for 1993, the four-door Eddie Bauer 2WD offers new deep dish aluminum wheels, standard lower rocker panel moldings, freshened seat styles, 60/40 cloth split bench, steering wheel, the two right-hand A/C registers and glove box latch are color-keyed, and 4-wheel ABS becomes standard. Six new exterior colors are available while there are three new interior colors (red, blue, and grey).

* Includes shaded options

** Other purchase requirements apply

Poor

Worse Than Average

Average

Better Than Average

Excellent
Insufficient Information

Refer to *Section 3: Annotated Vehicle Charts* for an explanation of these charts.

Ford Explorer XL 4WD
2 Door Sport Utility

4.0L 160 hp Gas Fuel Inject.

6 Cylinder "V"

Manual 5 Speed

4 Wheel On-Demand

Manual Seatbelts Only

Utility

2WD Model Shown

Purchase Price

Car Item	Dealer Cost	List
Base Price	**$16,418**	**$18,458**
Anti-Lock Brakes	Std	Std
Automatic 4 Speed	$757	$890
Optional Engine	N/A	N/A
Air Conditioning	$663	$780
Power Steering	Std	Std
Cruise Control	$325	$383
4 Whl On-Demand Dr.	Std	Std
AM/FM Stereo Cassette	$117	$138
Steering Wheel, Tilt	Grp	Grp
Power Windows	Pkg	Pkg
***Options Price**	$780	$918
***Total Price**	**$17,198**	**$19,376**
Target Price	$18,935	
Destination Charge	$485	
Avg. Tax & Fees	$1,170	
Total Target $	**$20,590**	
Average Dealer Option Cost:	***85%***	

Ownership Costs

Cost Area	5 Year Cost	Rate
Depreciation	$6,681	Better Than Average
Financing ($414/month)	$3,391	
Insurance (Rating 10)	$7,689	Excellent
State Fees	$795	
Fuel (Hwy 22 City 17)	$4,431	Average
Maintenance	$3,470	Excellent
Repairs	$840	Average

Ownership Cost By Year

Warranty/Maintenance Info

Item		Rate
Major Tune-Up	$118	Excellent
Minor Tune-Up	$79	Excellent
Brake Service	$210	Better Than Average
Overall Warranty	3 yr/36k	Average
Drivetrain Warranty	3 yr/36k	Average
Rust Warranty	6 yr/100k	Better Than Average
Maintenance Warranty	N/A	
Roadside Assistance	N/A	

Resale Value

1993	1994	1995	1996	1997
$17,793	$16,983	$16,104	$15,034	$13,909

Ownership Costs (5yr)

Average	This Car
$29,599	$27,297
Cost/Mile 42¢	Cost/Mile 39¢

Cumulative Costs

	1993	1994	1995	1996	1997
Annual	$6,692	$4,574	$5,312	$5,038	$5,681
Total	$6,692	$11,266	$16,578	$21,616	$27,297

Ownership Cost Rating

Excellent

The 1993 Explorer is available in twelve models - XL, XLT, Sport, and Eddie Bauer with two- or four-wheel drive. New for 1993, the two-door XL 4WD offers new 15x7in. deep dish aluminum wheels, standard lower rocker panel moldings, freshened seat styles, 60/40 cloth split bench, steering wheel, and the two right-hand A/C registers and glove box latch are color-keyed. The new ABS helps provide better vehicle steering control during hard braking situations by helping to prevent wheel lockup.

Ford Explorer XL 4WD
4 Door Sport Utility

4.0L 160 hp Gas Fuel Inject.

6 Cylinder "V"

Manual 5 Speed

4 Wheel On-Demand

Manual Seatbelts Only

Utility

2 Door 2WD Shown

Purchase Price

Car Item	Dealer Cost	List
Base Price	**$17,111**	**$19,246**
Anti-Lock Brakes	Std	Std
Automatic 4 Speed	$757	$890
Optional Engine	N/A	N/A
Air Conditioning	$663	$780
Power Steering	Std	Std
Cruise Control	$352	$383
4 Whl On-Demand Dr.	Std	Std
AM/FM Stereo Cassette	$117	$138
Steering Wheel, Tilt	Grp	Grp
Power Windows	Pkg	Pkg
***Options Price**	$780	$918
***Total Price**	**$17,891**	**$20,164**
Target Price	$19,732	
Destination Charge	$485	
Avg. Tax & Fees	$1,217	
Total Target $	**$21,434**	
Average Dealer Option Cost:	***86%***	

Ownership Costs

Cost Area	5 Year Cost	Rate
Depreciation	$6,737	Better Than Average
Financing ($431/month)	$3,531	
Insurance (Rating 11)	$7,902	Excellent
State Fees	$826	
Fuel (Hwy 22 City 17)	$4,431	Average
Maintenance	$3,487	Better Than Average
Repairs	$840	Average

Ownership Cost By Year

Warranty/Maintenance Info

Item		Rate
Major Tune-Up	$118	Excellent
Minor Tune-Up	$79	Excellent
Brake Service	$210	Better Than Average
Overall Warranty	3 yr/36k	Average
Drivetrain Warranty	3 yr/36k	Average
Rust Warranty	6 yr/100k	Better Than Average
Maintenance Warranty	N/A	
Roadside Assistance	N/A	

Resale Value

1993	1994	1995	1996	1997
$18,716	$17,901	$16,987	$15,859	$14,697

Ownership Costs (5yr)

Average	This Car
$30,261	$27,754
Cost/Mile 43¢	Cost/Mile 40¢

Cumulative Costs

	1993	1994	1995	1996	1997
Annual	$6,717	$4,671	$5,424	$5,173	$5,769
Total	$6,717	$11,388	$16,812	$21,985	$27,754

Ownership Cost Rating

Excellent

The 1993 Explorer is available in twelve models - XL, XLT, Sport, and Eddie Bauer with two- or four-wheel drive. New for 1993, the four-door XL 4WD offers new 15x7in. deep dish aluminum wheels, standard lower rocker panel moldings, freshened seat styles, 60/40 cloth split bench, steering wheel, and the two right-hand A/C registers and glove box latch are color-keyed. The new ABS helps provide better vehicle steering control during hard braking situations by helping to prevent wheel lockup.

* Includes shaded options

** Other purchase requirements apply

 Poor  Worse Than Average  Average  Better Than Average Excellent 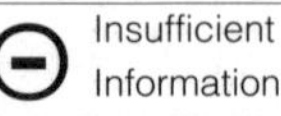 Insufficient Information

Refer to *Section 3: Annotated Vehicle Charts* for an explanation of these charts.

Ford Explorer Sport 4WD

2 Door Sport Utility

4.0L 160 hp Gas Fuel Inject.

6 Cylinder "V"

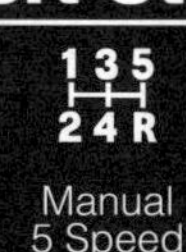

Manual 5 Speed

4 Wheel On-Demand

Manual Seatbelts Only

Purchase Price

Car Item	*Dealer Cost*	*List*
Base Price	**$17,229**	**$19,380**
Anti-Lock Brakes	Std	Std
Automatic 4 Speed	$757	$890
Optional Engine	N/A	N/A
Air Conditioning	$663	$780
Power Steering	Std	Std
Cruise Control	$325	$383
4 Whl On-Demand Dr.	Std	Std
AM/FM Stereo Cassette	$117	$138
Steering Wheel, Tilt	Grp	Grp
Power Windows	Pkg	Pkg
***Options Price**	$780	$918
***Total Price**	**$18,009**	**$20,298**
Target Price	$19,868	
Destination Charge	$485	
Avg. Tax & Fees	$1,226	
Total Target $	**$21,579**	
Average Dealer Option Cost:	***85%***	

Ownership Costs

Cost Area	*5 Year Cost*	*Rate*
Depreciation	$7,491	Average
Financing ($434/month)	$3,555	
Insurance (Rating 10)	$7,689	Excellent
State Fees	$831	
Fuel (Hwy 22 City 17)	$4,431	Worse Than Average
Maintenance	$3,470	Excellent
Repairs	$840	Worse Than Average

Ownership Cost By Year

$2,000 $4,000 $6,000 $8,000

1993 1994 1995 1996 1997

Warranty/Maintenance Info

Major Tune-Up	$118	Excellent
Minor Tune-Up	$79	Excellent
Brake Service	$210	Better Than Average
Overall Warranty	3 yr/36k	Average
Drivetrain Warranty	3 yr/36k	Average
Rust Warranty	6 yr/100k	Better Than Average
Maintenance Warranty	N/A	
Roadside Assistance	N/A	

Resale Value

1993	1994	1995	1996	1997
$18,109	$17,248	$16,348	$15,235	$14,088

Ownership Costs (5yr)

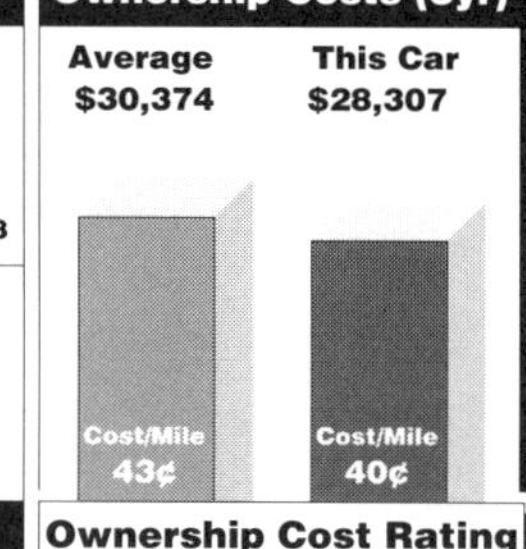

Average	This Car
$30,374	$28,307
Cost/Mile 43¢	Cost/Mile 40¢

The 1993 Explorer is available in twelve models - XL, XLT, Sport, and Eddie Bauer with two- or four-wheel drive. New for 1993, the two-door Sport 4WD offers new 15x7in. deep dish aluminum wheels, standard lower rocker panel moldings, freshened seat styles, 60/40 cloth split bench, steering wheel, and the two right-hand A/C registers and glove box latch are color-keyed. Six new exterior colors are offered while three new interior colors are available. An ABS braking system is now standard.

Cumulative Costs

	1993	1994	1995	1996	1997
Annual	$7,442	$4,684	$5,373	$5,099	$5,709
Total	$7,442	$12,126	$17,499	$22,598	$28,307

Ownership Cost Rating

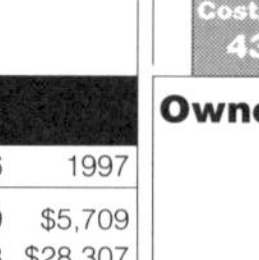

Excellent

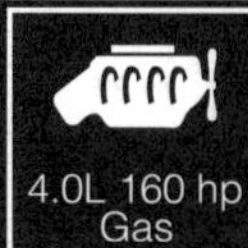

Ford Explorer XLT 4WD

4 Door Sport Utility

4.0L 160 hp Gas Fuel Inject.

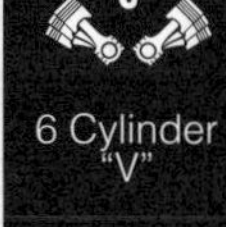

6 Cylinder "V"

Manual 5 Speed

4 Wheel On-Demand

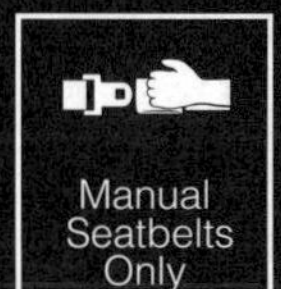

Manual Seatbelts Only

Utility

2WD Model Shown

Purchase Price

Car Item	*Dealer Cost*	*List*
Base Price	**$18,935**	**$21,318**
Anti-Lock Brakes	Std	Std
Automatic 4 Speed	$757	$890
Optional Engine	N/A	N/A
Air Conditioning	$663	$780
Power Steering	Std	Std
Cruise Control	Std	Std
4 Whl On-Demand Dr.	Std	Std
AM/FM Stereo Cassette	$117	$138
Steering Wheel, Tilt	Std	Std
Power Windows	Std	Std
***Options Price**	$780	$918
***Total Price**	**$19,715**	**$22,236**
Target Price	$21,842	
Destination Charge	$485	
Avg. Tax & Fees	$1,343	
Total Target $	**$23,670**	
Average Dealer Option Cost:	***85%***	

Ownership Costs

Cost Area	*5 Year Cost*	*Rate*
Depreciation	$8,520	Better Than Average
Financing ($476/month)	$3,899	
Insurance (Rating 11)	$7,902	Excellent
State Fees	$908	
Fuel (Hwy 22 City 17)	$4,431	Worse Than Average
Maintenance	$3,487	Better Than Average
Repairs	$840	Worse Than Average

Ownership Cost By Year

$2,000 $4,000 $6,000 $8,000 $10,000

1993 1994 1995 1996 1997

Warranty/Maintenance Info

Major Tune-Up	$118	Excellent
Minor Tune-Up	$79	Excellent
Brake Service	$210	Better Than Average
Overall Warranty	3 yr/36k	Average
Drivetrain Warranty	3 yr/36k	Average
Rust Warranty	6 yr/100k	Better Than Average
Maintenance Warranty	N/A	
Roadside Assistance	N/A	

Resale Value

1993	1994	1995	1996	1997
$19,548	$18,576	$17,591	$16,387	$15,150

Ownership Costs (5yr)

Average	This Car
$32,004	$29,987

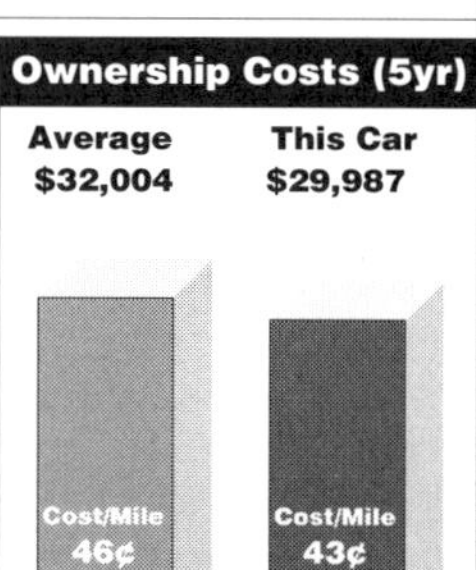

The 1993 Explorer is available in twelve models - XL, XLT, Sport, and Eddie Bauer with two- or four-wheel drive. New for 1993, the four-door XLT 4WD offers new 15x7in. deep dish aluminum wheels, standard lower rocker panel moldings, freshened seat styles, 60/40 cloth split bench, steering wheel, the two right-hand A/C registers and glove box latch are color-keyed, and a running board is now available. Ford's 4.0L EFI V-6 engine teams with a five-speed manual overdrive as the standard powertrain.

Cumulative Costs

	1993	1994	1995	1996	1997
Annual	$8,295	$4,961	$5,585	$5,290	$5,856
Total	$8,295	$13,256	$18,841	$24,131	$29,987

Ownership Cost Rating

Excellent

* Includes shaded options

** Other purchase requirements apply

 Poor  Worse Than Average  Average 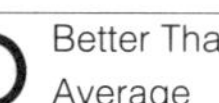 Better Than Average 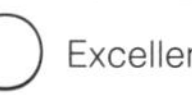 Excellent Insufficient Information

Refer to *Section 3: Annotated Vehicle Charts* for an explanation of these charts.

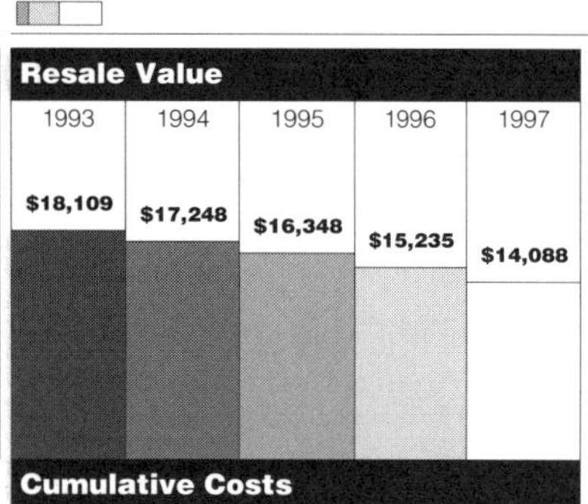

Ford Explorer Eddie Bauer 4WD 2 Door Sport Utility

Utility

4.0L 160 hp Gas Fuel Inject.

6 Cylinder "V"

Manual 5 Speed

4 Wheel On-Demand

Manual Seatbelts Only

4 Door Model Shown

Purchase Price

Car Item	Dealer Cost	List
Base Price	**$20,144**	**$22,692**
Anti-Lock Brakes	Std	Std
Automatic 4 Speed	$757	$890
Optional Engine	N/A	N/A
Air Conditioning	$663	$780
Power Steering	Std	Std
Cruise Control	Std	Std
4 Whl On-Demand Dr.	Std	Std
AM/FM Stereo Cassette	$117	$138
Steering Wheel, Tilt	Std	Std
Power Windows	Std	Std
***Options Price**	$780	$918
***Total Price**	**$20,924**	**$23,610**
Target Price	$23,250	
Destination Charge	$485	
Avg. Tax & Fees	$1,428	
Total Target $	**$25,163**	
Average Dealer Option Cost:	***85%***	

Ownership Costs

Cost Area	5 Year Cost	Rate
Depreciation	$10,673	Average
Financing ($506/month)	$4,146	
Insurance (Rating 10)	$7,689	Excellent
State Fees	$965	
Fuel (Hwy 22 City 17)	$4,431	Average
Maintenance	$3,497	Better Than Average
Repairs	$840	Average

Ownership Cost By Year

$2,000 $4,000 $6,000 $8,000 $10,000 $12,000

1993 1994 1995 1996 1997

Warranty/Maintenance Info

Major Tune-Up	$118	Excellent
Minor Tune-Up	$79	Excellent
Brake Service	$210	Better Than Average
Overall Warranty	3 yr/36k	Average
Drivetrain Warranty	3 yr/36k	Average
Rust Warranty	6 yr/100k	Better Than Average
Maintenance Warranty	N/A	
Roadside Assistance	N/A	

Resale Value

1993	1994	1995	1996	1997
$18,500	$17,694	$16,794	$15,646	$14,490

Ownership Costs (5yr)

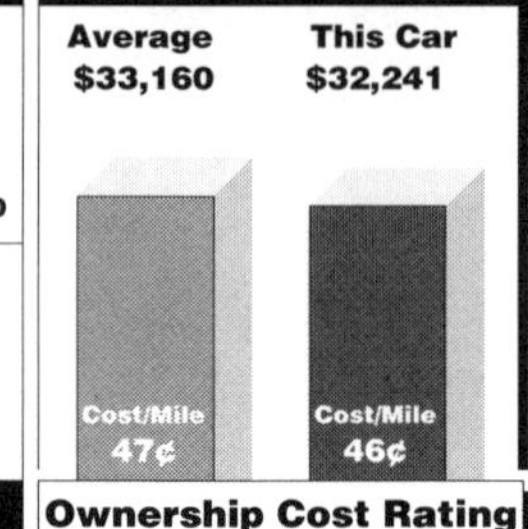

Average	This Car
$33,160	$32,241
Cost/Mile 47¢	Cost/Mile 46¢

Cumulative Costs

	1993	1994	1995	1996	1997
Annual	$10,914	$4,844	$5,530	$5,201	$5,752
Total	$10,914	$15,758	$21,288	$26,489	$32,241

Ownership Cost Rating

Better Than Average

The 1993 Explorer is available in twelve models - XL, XLT, Sport, and Eddie Bauer with two- or four-wheel drive. New for 1993, the two-door Eddie Bauer 4WD offers a new array of stereos (including CD), standard lower rocker panel moldings, freshened seat styles, 60/40 cloth split bench, steering wheel, the two right-hand A/C registers and glove box latch are color-keyed, and a running board is available. Ford's 4.0L EFI V-6 engine teams with a five-speed manual overdrive as standard powertrain.

Ford Explorer Eddie Bauer 4WD 4 Door Sport Utility

Utility

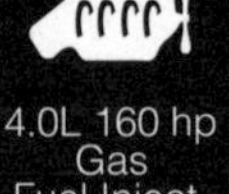
4.0L 160 hp Gas Fuel Inject.

6 Cylinder "V"

Manual 5 Speed

4 Wheel On-Demand

Manual Seatbelts Only

Purchase Price

Car Item	Dealer Cost	List
Base Price	**$21,353**	**$24,066**
Anti-Lock Brakes	Std	Std
Automatic 4 Speed	$757	$890
Optional Engine	N/A	N/A
Air Conditioning	$663	$780
Power Steering	Std	Std
Cruise Control	Std	Std
4 Whl On-Demand Dr.	Std	Std
AM/FM Stereo Cassette	$117	$138
Steering Wheel, Tilt	Std	Std
Power Windows	Std	Std
***Options Price**	$780	$918
***Total Price**	**$22,133**	**$24,984**
Target Price	$24,666	
Destination Charge	$485	
Avg. Tax & Fees	$1,513	
Total Target $	**$26,664**	
Average Dealer Option Cost:	***85%***	

Ownership Costs

Cost Area	5 Year Cost	Rate
Depreciation	$11,029	Average
Financing ($536/month)	$4,393	
Insurance (Rating 11)	$7,902	Excellent
State Fees	$1,019	
Fuel (Hwy 22 City 17)	$4,431	Average
Maintenance	$3,514	Better Than Average
Repairs	$840	Average

Ownership Cost By Year

$2,000 $4,000 $6,000 $8,000 $10,000 $12,000

1993 1994 1995 1996 1997

Warranty/Maintenance Info

Major Tune-Up	$118	Excellent
Minor Tune-Up	$79	Excellent
Brake Service	$210	Better Than Average
Overall Warranty	3 yr/36k	Average
Drivetrain Warranty	3 yr/36k	Average
Rust Warranty	6 yr/100k	Better Than Average
Maintenance Warranty	N/A	
Roadside Assistance	N/A	

Resale Value

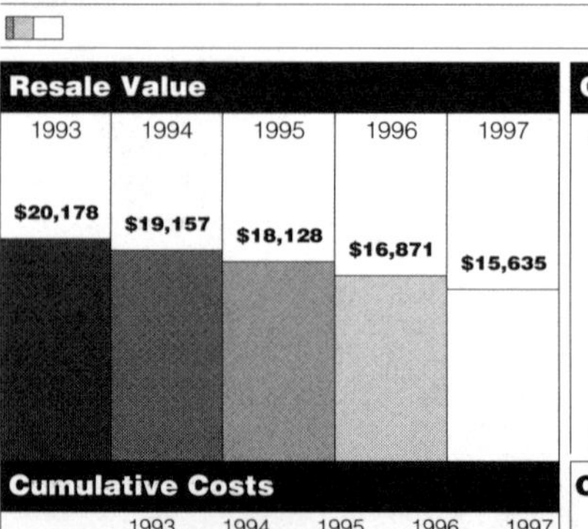

1993	1994	1995	1996	1997
$20,178	$19,157	$18,128	$16,871	$15,635

Ownership Costs (5yr)

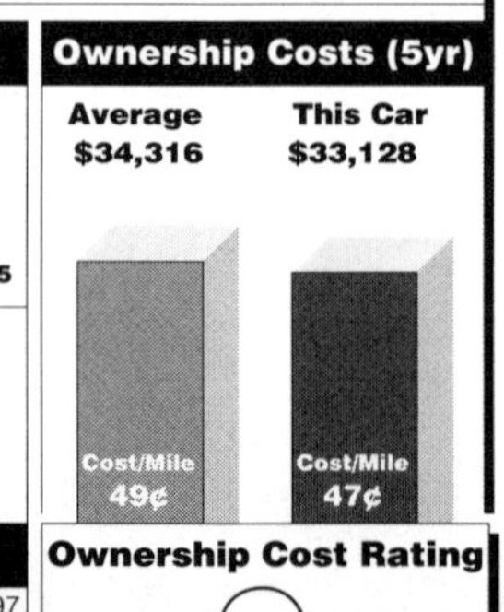

Average	This Car
$34,316	$33,128
Cost/Mile 49¢	Cost/Mile 47¢

Cumulative Costs

	1993	1994	1995	1996	1997
Annual	$10,893	$5,189	$5,762	$5,398	$5,886
Total	$10,893	$16,082	$21,844	$27,242	$33,128

Ownership Cost Rating

Excellent

The 1993 Explorer is available in twelve models - XL, XLT, Sport, and Eddie Bauer with two- or four-wheel drive. New for 1993, the four-door Eddie Bauer 4WD offers a new array of stereos (including CD), standard lower rocker panel moldings, freshened seat styles, 60/40 cloth split bench, steering wheel, the two right-hand A/C registers and glove box latch are color-keyed, and a running board is available. Ford's 4.0L EFI V-6 engine teams with a five-speed manual overdrive as standard powertrain.

* Includes shaded options

** Other purchase requirements apply

 Poor  Worse Than Average  Average 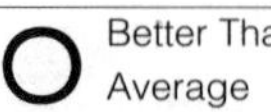 Better Than Average  Excellent 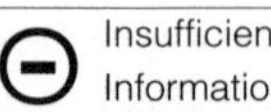 Insufficient Information

Refer to *Section 3: Annotated Vehicle Charts* for an explanation of these charts.

Ford F150 Styleside S
2 Door Regular Cab

4.9L 145 hp Gas Fuel Inject.

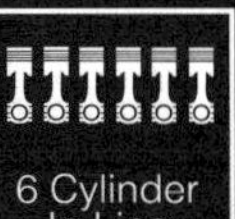
6 Cylinder In-Line

Manual 5 Speed

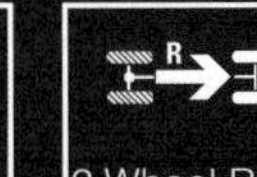
2 Wheel Rear

Manual Seatbelts Only

Large Pickup

XL Model Shown

Purchase Price

Car Item	Dealer Cost	List
Base Price	**$9,849**	**$11,033**
Anti-Lock Brakes	Std	Std
Automatic 4 Speed	$786	** $924
Optional Engine	N/A	N/A
Air Conditioning	$685	$806
Power Steering	Std	Std
Cruise Control	$325	** $383
All Wheel Drive	N/A	N/A
AM/FM Stereo Cassette	$205	** $241
Steering Wheel, Tilt	Grp	Grp
8 Foot Bed	$207	$235
***Options Price**	$685	$806
***Total Price**	**$10,534**	**$11,839**
Target Price	$11,183	
Destination Charge	$585	
Avg. Tax & Fees	$712	
Total Target $	**$12,480**	
Average Dealer Option Cost:	***85%***	

The F150 is available in ten models - (Base) S 2WD and 4WD Styleside Regular Cabs and XL 2WD and 4WD Styleside and Flareside in Regular or Super Cab versions. New for 1993, the S 2WD Styleside Regular Cab has a new electronic speed control which provides faster response, better speed-holding capacity, and tap-up/tap-down feature. Standard on the S 2WD Styleside Regular Cab is tinted window glass, door courtesy lights, locking glove box, trip odometer and argent steel wheels with wheel trim.

Ownership Costs

Cost Area	5 Year Cost	Rate
Depreciation	$3,649	Excellent
Financing ($251/month)	$2,056	
Insurance (Rating 2)	$6,542	Excellent
State Fees	$497	
Fuel (Hwy 20 City 15)	$4,941	Excellent
Maintenance	$3,647	Better Than Average
Repairs	$761	Excellent

Ownership Cost By Year

$2,000 $4,000 $6,000 $8,000

1993 1994 1995 1996 1997

Warranty/Maintenance Info

Major Tune-Up	$148	Better Than Average
Minor Tune-Up	$95	Better Than Average
Brake Service	$241	Excellent
Overall Warranty	3 yr/36k	Average
Drivetrain Warranty	3 yr/36k	Average
Rust Warranty	6 yr/100k	Better Than Average
Maintenance Warranty	N/A	
Roadside Assistance	N/A	

Resale Value

1993	1994	1995	1996	1997
$11,079	$10,557	$10,110	$9,570	$8,831

Ownership Costs (5yr)

Average	This Car
$20,775	$22,093
Cost/Mile 30¢	Cost/Mile 32¢

Cumulative Costs

	1993	1994	1995	1996	1997
Annual	$4,546	$3,697	$4,448	$4,269	$5,133
Total	$4,546	$8,243	$12,691	$16,960	$22,093

Ownership Cost Rating

Worse Than Average

Ford F150 Styleside XL
2 Door Regular Cab

4.9L 145 hp Gas Fuel Inject.

6 Cylinder In-Line

Manual 5 Speed

2 Wheel Rear

Manual Seatbelts Only

Large Pickup

Purchase Price

Car Item	Dealer Cost	List
Base Price	**$11,246**	**$13,066**
Anti-Lock Brakes	Std	Std
Automatic 4 Speed	$594	$699
5.0L 185 hp Gas	$541	$637
Air Conditioning	$685	$806
Power Steering	Std	Std
Cruise Control	$325	$383
All Wheel Drive	N/A	N/A
AM/FM Stereo Cassette	$205	** $241
Steering Wheel, Tilt	Grp	Grp
8 Foot Bed	$207	$235
***Options Price**	$1,226	$1,443
***Total Price**	**$12,472**	**$14,509**
Target Price	$13,275	
Destination Charge	$585	
Avg. Tax & Fees	$844	
Total Target $	**$14,704**	
Average Dealer Option Cost:	***85%***	

The F150 is available in ten models - (Base) S 2WD and 4WD Styleside Regular Cabs and XL 2WD and 4WD Styleside and Flareside in Regular or Super Cab versions. New for 1993, the XL 2WD Styleside Regular Cab has an electronic speed control which provides faster response, better speed-holding capacity, and tap-up/tap-down feature in 1-mph increments. The XL 2WD Styleside Regular Cab comes standard with chrome bumpers and electronic AM radio. The XLT Trim Preferred Equipment Packages are optional.

Ownership Costs

Cost Area	5 Year Cost	Rate
Depreciation	$4,346	Better Than Average
Financing ($296/month)	$2,422	
Insurance (Rating 3)	$6,731	Excellent
State Fees	$605	
Fuel (Hwy 19 City 15)	$5,079	Better Than Average
Maintenance	$3,717	Better Than Average
Repairs	$761	Excellent

Ownership Cost By Year

$2,000 $4,000 $6,000 $8,000

1993 1994 1995 1996 1997

Warranty/Maintenance Info

Major Tune-Up	$145	Better Than Average
Minor Tune-Up	$100	Better Than Average
Brake Service	$241	Excellent
Overall Warranty	3 yr/36k	Average
Drivetrain Warranty	3 yr/36k	Average
Rust Warranty	6 yr/100k	Better Than Average
Maintenance Warranty	N/A	
Roadside Assistance	N/A	

Resale Value

1993	1994	1995	1996	1997
$12,763	$12,274	$11,888	$11,299	$10,358

Ownership Costs (5yr)

Average	This Car
$24,054	$23,661
Cost/Mile 34¢	Cost/Mile 34¢

Cumulative Costs

	1993	1994	1995	1996	1997
Annual	$5,330	$3,875	$4,549	$4,444	$5,463
Total	$5,330	$9,205	$13,754	$18,198	$23,661

Ownership Cost Rating

Better Than Average

* Includes shaded options

** Other purchase requirements apply

Poor

Worse Than Average

Average

Better Than Average

Excellent

Insufficient Information

Refer to *Section 3: Annotated Vehicle Charts* for an explanation of these charts.

Ford F150 Flareside XL

2 Door Regular Cab

4.9L 145 hp Gas Fuel Inject.

6 Cylinder In-Line

1 3 5 / 2 4 R

Manual 5 Speed

2 Wheel Rear

Manual Seatbelts Only

Large Pickup

4WD Model Shown

Purchase Price

Car Item	Dealer Cost	List
Base Price	**$11,968**	**$13,916**
Anti-Lock Brakes	Std	Std
Automatic 4 Speed	$594	$699
5.0L 185 hp Gas	$541	$637
Air Conditioning	$685	$806
Power Steering	Std	Std
Cruise Control	$325	$383
All Wheel Drive	N/A	N/A
AM/FM Stereo Cassette	$205	** $241
Steering Wheel, Tilt	Grp	Grp
Power Windows	$312	** $367
***Options Price**	$1,226	$1,443
***Total Price**	**$13,194**	**$15,359**
Target Price	$14,063	
Destination Charge	$585	
Avg. Tax & Fees	$891	
Total Target $	**$15,539**	
Average Dealer Option Cost:	***87%***	

Ownership Costs

Cost Area	5 Year Cost	Rate
Depreciation	$4,580	Better Than Average
Financing ($312/month)	$2,560	
Insurance (Rating 3)	$6,731	Excellent
State Fees	$638	
Fuel (Hwy 19 City 15)	$5,079	Better Than Average
Maintenance	$3,717	Better Than Average
Repairs	$761	Excellent

Ownership Cost By Year

Warranty/Maintenance Info

Item		Rate
Major Tune-Up	$145	Better Than Average
Minor Tune-Up	$100	Better Than Average
Brake Service	$241	Excellent
Overall Warranty	3 yr/36k	Average
Drivetrain Warranty	3 yr/36k	Average
Rust Warranty	6 yr/100k	Better Than Average
Maintenance Warranty	N/A	
Roadside Assistance	N/A	

Resale Value

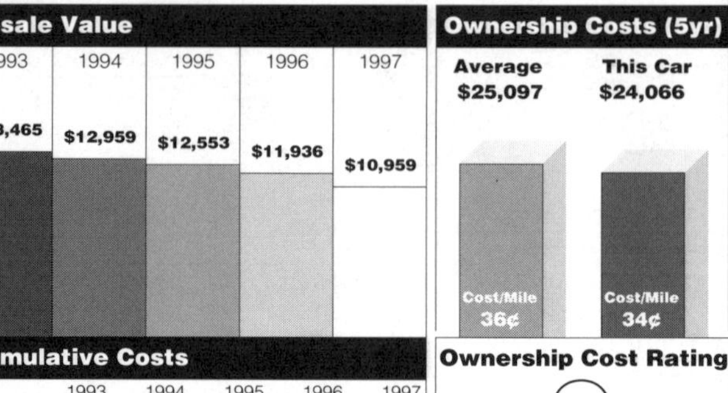

1993	1994	1995	1996	1997
$13,465	$12,959	$12,553	$11,936	$10,959

Ownership Costs (5yr)

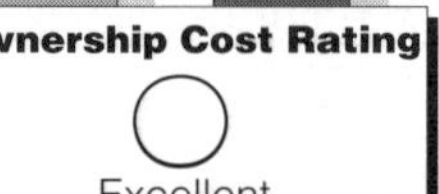

Average	This Car
$25,097	$24,066
Cost/Mile 36¢	Cost/Mile 34¢

The F150 is available in ten models - (Base) S 2WD and 4WD Styleside Regular Cabs and XL 2WD and 4WD Styleside and Flareside in Regular or Super Cab versions. New for 1993, the XL 2WD Flareside Regular Cab features an electronic speed control which provides faster response, better speed-holding capacity, a rear bench seat w/improved comfort from a raised height and an added seatback bolster (late availability) and eight new colors. The XLT Trim Preferred Equipment Packages are optional.

Cumulative Costs

	1993	1994	1995	1996	1997
Annual	$5,528	$3,942	$4,604	$4,488	$5,504
Total	$5,528	$9,470	$14,074	$18,562	$24,066

Ownership Cost Rating

Excellent

Ford F150 Styleside XL SuperCab

2 Door Extended Cab

4.9L 145 hp Gas Fuel Inject.

6 Cylinder In-Line

1 3 5 / 2 4 R

Manual 5 Speed

2 Wheel Rear

Manual Seatbelts Only

Large Pickup

Purchase Price

Car Item	Dealer Cost	List
Base Price	**$12,469**	**$14,505**
Anti-Lock Brakes	Std	Std
Automatic 4 Speed	$594	$699
5.0L 185 hp Gas	$541	$637
Air Conditioning	$685	$806
Power Steering	Std	Std
Cruise Control	$325	$383
All Wheel Drive	N/A	N/A
AM/FM Stereo Cassette	$205	$241
Steering Wheel, Tilt	Grp	Grp
8 Foot Bed	$198	$233
***Options Price**	$1,431	$1,684
***Total Price**	**$13,900**	**$16,189**
Target Price	$14,829	
Destination Charge	$585	
Avg. Tax & Fees	$939	
Total Target $	**$16,353**	
Average Dealer Option Cost:	***85%***	

Ownership Costs

Cost Area	5 Year Cost	Rate
Depreciation	$4,589	Better Than Average
Financing ($329/month)	$2,694	
Insurance (Rating 6)	$7,129	Excellent
State Fees	$671	
Fuel (Hwy 19 City 15)	$5,079	Better Than Average
Maintenance	$3,780	Better Than Average
Repairs	$761	Excellent

Ownership Cost By Year

Warranty/Maintenance Info

Item		Rate
Major Tune-Up	$145	Better Than Average
Minor Tune-Up	$100	Better Than Average
Brake Service	$241	Excellent
Overall Warranty	3 yr/36k	Average
Drivetrain Warranty	3 yr/36k	Average
Rust Warranty	6 yr/100k	Better Than Average
Maintenance Warranty	N/A	
Roadside Assistance	N/A	

Resale Value

1993	1994	1995	1996	1997
$14,587	$14,014	$13,504	$12,760	$11,764

Ownership Costs (5yr)

Average	This Car
$26,116	$24,703
Cost/Mile 37¢	Cost/Mile 35¢

The F150 is available in ten models - (Base) S 2WD and 4WD Styleside Regular Cab and XL 2WD and 4WD Styleside and Flareside in Regular or Super Cab versions. New for 1993, the XL 2WD Styleside Super Cab features an electronic speed control which provides faster response, better speed-holding capacity and tap-up/tap-down feature in 1-mph increments. The XL 4WD Styleside Super Cab comes standard with chrome bumpers and electronic AM radio. The XLT Trim Preferred Equipment Packages are optional.

Cumulative Costs

	1993	1994	1995	1996	1997
Annual	$5,358	$4,136	$4,850	$4,712	$5,647
Total	$5,358	$9,494	$14,344	$19,056	$24,703

Ownership Cost Rating

Excellent

* Includes shaded options

** Other purchase requirements apply

Poor  Worse Than Average  Average · Better Than Average · Excellent 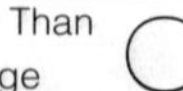 Insufficient Information

Refer to *Section 3: Annotated Vehicle Charts* for an explanation of these charts.

Ford F150 Flareside XL SuperCab
2 Door Extended Cab

4.9L 145 hp Gas Fuel Inject.

6 Cylinder In-Line

135 24R
Manual 5 Speed

2 Wheel Rear

Manual Seatbelts Only

Large Pickup

Purchase Price

Car Item	Dealer Cost	List
Base Price	**$13,072**	**$15,215**
Anti-Lock Brakes	Std	Std
Automatic 4 Speed	$594	$699
5.0L 185 hp Gas	$541	$637
Air Conditioning	$685	$806
Power Steering	Std	Std
Cruise Control	$325	$383
All Wheel Drive	N/A	N/A
AM/FM Stereo Cassette	$205	$241
Steering Wheel, Tilt	Grp	Grp
Power Windows	$312	** $367
***Options Price**	$1,431	$1,684
***Total Price**	**$14,503**	**$16,899**
Target Price	$15,490	
Destination Charge	$585	
Avg. Tax & Fees	$979	
Total Target $	**$17,054**	
Average Dealer Option Cost:	***85%***	

Ownership Costs

Cost Area	5 Year Cost	Rate
Depreciation	$4,779	Average
Financing ($343/month)	$2,809	
Insurance (Rating 6)	$7,129	Excellent
State Fees	$699	
Fuel (Hwy 19 City 15)	$5,079	Average
Maintenance	$3,780	Average
Repairs	$761	Excellent

Ownership Cost By Year

$2,000 $4,000 $6,000 $8,000
1993 1994 1995 1996 1997

Warranty/Maintenance Info

Item	Cost/Term	Rate
Major Tune-Up	$145	Average
Minor Tune-Up	$100	Average
Brake Service	$241	Excellent
Overall Warranty	3 yr/36k	Worse Than Average
Drivetrain Warranty	3 yr/36k	Worse Than Average
Rust Warranty	6 yr/100k	Average
Maintenance Warranty	N/A	
Roadside Assistance	N/A	

Resale Value

1993	1994	1995	1996	1997
$15,191	$14,603	$14,072	$13,301	$12,275

Ownership Costs (5yr)

Average	This Car
$26,988	$25,036
Cost/Mile 39¢	Cost/Mile 36¢

The F150 is available in ten models - (Base) S 2WD and 4WD Styleside Regular Cabs and XL 2WD and 4WD Styleside and Flareside in Regular or Super Cab versions. New for 1993, the XL 2WD Flareside Super Cab features an electronic speed control which provides faster response, better speed-holding capacity, a rear bench seat w/improved comfort from a raised height and an added seatback bolster (late availability) and eight new colors. The XLT Trim Preferred Equipment Packages are optional.

Cumulative Costs

	1993	1994	1995	1996	1997
Annual	$5,510	$4,193	$4,900	$4,752	$5,681
Total	$5,510	$9,703	$14,603	$19,355	$25,036

Ownership Cost Rating

Excellent

Ford F150 Styleside S 4WD
2 Door Regular Cab

4.9L 145 hp Gas Fuel Inject.

6 Cylinder In-Line

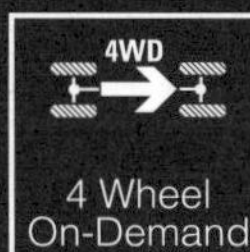
Manual 5 Speed

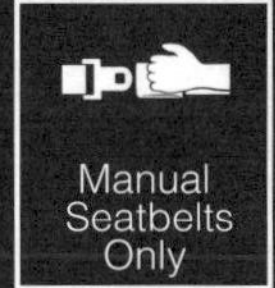
4 Wheel On-Demand

Manual Seatbelts Only

Large Pickup

XL Model Shown

Purchase Price

Car Item	Dealer Cost	List
Base Price	**$12,695**	**$14,267**
Anti-Lock Brakes	Std	Std
Automatic 4 Speed	$786	** $924
Optional Engine	N/A	N/A
Air Conditioning	$685	$806
Power Steering	Std	Std
Cruise Control	$325	** $383
4 Whl On-Demand Dr.	Std	Std
AM/FM Stereo Cassette	$205	** $241
Steering Wheel, Tilt	Grp	Grp
8 Foot Bed	$289	$328
***Options Price**	$685	$806
***Total Price**	**$13,380**	**$15,073**
Target Price	$14,281	
Destination Charge	$585	
Avg. Tax & Fees	$900	
Total Target $	**$15,766**	
Average Dealer Option Cost:	***85%***	

Ownership Costs

Cost Area	5 Year Cost	Rate
Depreciation	$4,430	Excellent
Financing ($317/month)	$2,598	
Insurance (Rating 5)	$6,996	Excellent
State Fees	$627	
Fuel (Hwy 18 City 15)	$5,233	Worse Than Average
Maintenance	$3,726	Average
Repairs	$840	Worse Than Average

Ownership Cost By Year

$2,000 $4,000 $6,000 $8,000
1993 1994 1995 1996 1997

Warranty/Maintenance Info

Item	Cost/Term	Rate
Major Tune-Up	$148	Average
Minor Tune-Up	$95	Average
Brake Service	$241	Excellent
Overall Warranty	3 yr/36k	Worse Than Average
Drivetrain Warranty	3 yr/36k	Worse Than Average
Rust Warranty	6 yr/100k	Average
Maintenance Warranty	N/A	
Roadside Assistance	N/A	

Resale Value

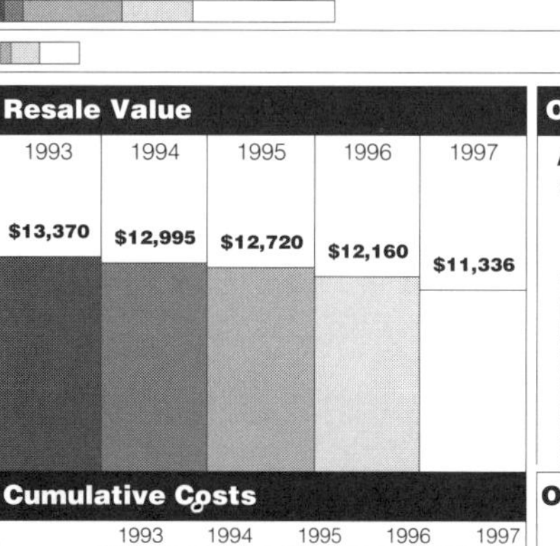

1993	1994	1995	1996	1997
$13,370	$12,995	$12,720	$12,160	$11,336

Ownership Costs (5yr)

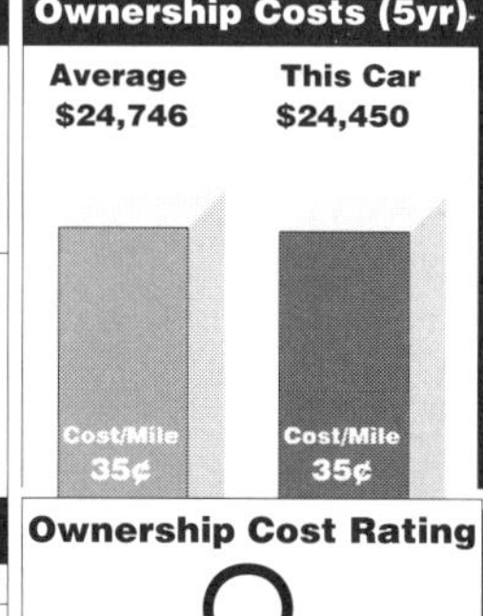

Average	This Car
$24,746	$24,450
Cost/Mile 35¢	Cost/Mile 35¢

The F150 is available in ten models - (Base) S 2WD and 4WD Styleside Regular Cabs and XL 2WD and 4WD Styleside and Flareside in Regular or Super Cab versions. New for 1993, the S 4WD Styleside Regular Cab features an electronic speed control which provides faster response and better speed-holding capacity. Standard items include tinted window glass, door courtesy lights, locking glove box, trip odometer and argent steel wheels with wheel trim. An optional off-road package is also offered.

Cumulative Costs

	1993	1994	1995	1996	1997
Annual	$5,938	$3,891	$4,600	$4,531	$5,490
Total	$5,938	$9,829	$14,429	$18,960	$24,450

Ownership Cost Rating

Better Than Average

* Includes shaded options

** Other purchase requirements apply

 Poor  Worse Than Average · Average  Better Than Average · Excellent · Insufficient Information

Refer to *Section 3: Annotated Vehicle Charts* for an explanation of these charts.

Ford F150 Styleside XL 4WD

2 Door Regular Cab

4.9L 145 hp Gas Fuel Inject.

6 Cylinder In-Line

Manual 5 Speed

4 Wheel On-Demand

Manual Seatbelts Only

Large Pickup

Purchase Price

Car Item	Dealer Cost	List
Base Price	**$13,127**	**$15,279**
Anti-Lock Brakes	Std	Std
Automatic 4 Speed	$594	$699
5.0L 185 hp Gas	$541	$637
Air Conditioning	$685	$806
Power Steering	Std	Std
Cruise Control	$325	$383
4 Whl On-Demand Dr.	Std	Std
AM/FM Stereo Cassette	$205	** $241
Steering Wheel, Tilt	Grp	Grp
8 Foot Bed	$207	$235
***Options Price**	$1,226	$1,443
***Total Price**	**$14,353**	**$16,722**
Target Price	$15,332	
Destination Charge	$585	
Avg. Tax & Fees	$969	
Total Target $	**$16,886**	
Average Dealer Option Cost:	***85%***	

Ownership Costs

Cost Area	5 Year Cost	Rate
Depreciation	$4,167	Excellent
Financing ($339/month)	$2,782	
Insurance (Rating 5)	$6,996	Excellent
State Fees	$692	
Fuel (Hwy 17 City 13)	$5,760	Average
Maintenance	$3,796	Better Than Average
Repairs	$840	Average

Warranty/Maintenance Info

Item		Rate
Major Tune-Up	$145	Better Than Average
Minor Tune-Up	$100	Better Than Average
Brake Service	$241	Excellent
Overall Warranty	3 yr/36k	Average
Drivetrain Warranty	3 yr/36k	Average
Rust Warranty	6 yr/100k	Better Than Average
Maintenance Warranty	N/A	
Roadside Assistance	N/A	

Ownership Cost By Year

$2,000 $4,000 $6,000 $8,000

1993 1994 1995 1996 1997

Resale Value

1993	1994	1995	1996	1997
$14,781	$14,421	$14,138	$13,564	$12,719

Ownership Costs (5yr)

Average	This Car
$26,771	$25,033
Cost/Mile 38¢	Cost/Mile 36¢

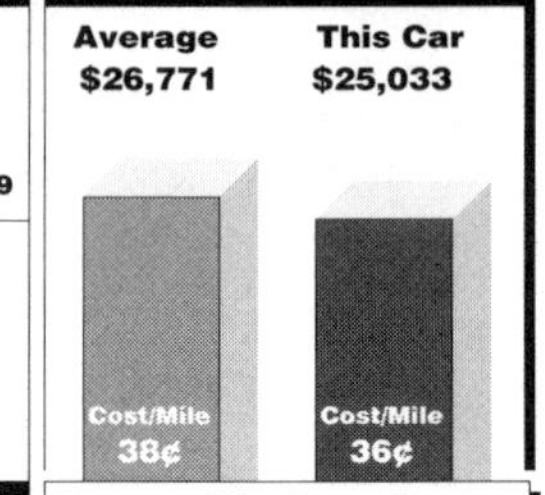

The F150 is available in ten models - (Base) S 2WD and 4WD Styleside Regular Cabs and XL 2WD and 4WD Styleside and Flareside in Regular or Super Cab versions. New for 1993, the XL 4WD Styleside Regular Cab has an electronic speed control which provides faster response, better speed-holding capacity, and tap-up/tap-down feature in 1-mph increments. The XL 4WD Styleside Regular Cab comes standard with chrome bumpers and electronic AM radio. The XLT Trim Preferred Equipment Packages are optional.

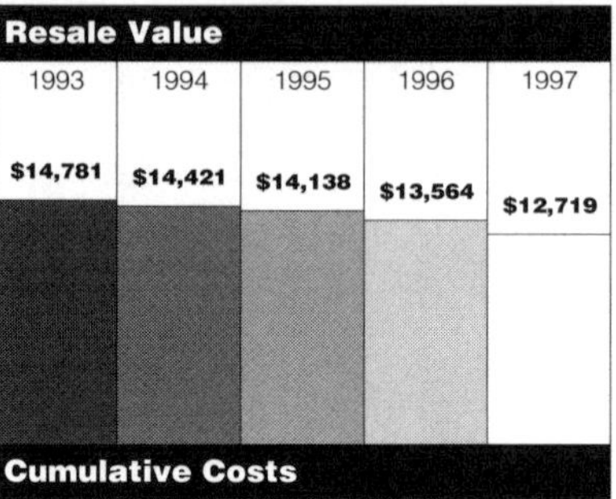

Cumulative Costs

	1993	1994	1995	1996	1997
Annual	$5,841	$4,060	$4,765	$4,690	$5,677
Total	$5,841	$9,901	$14,666	$19,356	$25,033

Ownership Cost Rating

Excellent

Ford F150 Flareside XL 4WD

2 Door Regular Cab

4.9L 145 hp Gas Fuel Inject.

6 Cylinder In-Line

Manual 5 Speed

4 Wheel On-Demand

Manual Seatbelts Only

Large Pickup

Purchase Price

Car Item	Dealer Cost	List
Base Price	**$13,858**	**$16,139**
Anti-Lock Brakes	Std	Std
Automatic 4 Speed	$594	$699
5.0L 185 hp Gas	$541	$637
Air Conditioning	$685	$806
Power Steering	Std	Std
Cruise Control	$325	$383
4 Whl On-Demand Dr.	Std	Std
AM/FM Stereo Cassette	$205	** $241
Steering Wheel, Tilt	Grp	Grp
Power Windows	$312	** $367
***Options Price**	$1,226	$1,443
***Total Price**	**$15,084**	**$17,582**
Target Price	$16,135	
Destination Charge	$585	
Avg. Tax & Fees	$1,018	
Total Target $	**$17,738**	
Average Dealer Option Cost:	***85%***	

Ownership Costs

Cost Area	5 Year Cost	Rate
Depreciation	$4,372	Excellent
Financing ($356/month)	$2,921	
Insurance (Rating 5)	$6,996	Excellent
State Fees	$727	
Fuel (Hwy 17 City 13)	$5,760	Average
Maintenance	$3,796	Better Than Average
Repairs	$840	Average

Warranty/Maintenance Info

Item		Rate
Major Tune-Up	$145	Better Than Average
Minor Tune-Up	$100	Better Than Average
Brake Service	$241	Excellent
Overall Warranty	3 yr/36k	Average
Drivetrain Warranty	3 yr/36k	Average
Rust Warranty	6 yr/100k	Better Than Average
Maintenance Warranty	N/A	
Roadside Assistance	N/A	

Ownership Cost By Year

$2,000 $4,000 $6,000 $8,000

1993 1994 1995 1996 1997

Resale Value

1993	1994	1995	1996	1997
$15,501	$15,133	$14,836	$14,239	$13,366

Ownership Costs (5yr)

Average	This Car
$27,827	$25,412
Cost/Mile 40¢	Cost/Mile 36¢

The F150 is available in ten models - (Base) S 2WD and 4WD Styleside Regular Cabs and XL 2WD and 4WD Styleside and Flareside in Regular or Super Cab versions. New for 1993, the XL 4WD Flareside Regular Cab features an electronic speed control which provides faster response, better speed-holding capacity, a rear bench seat w/improved comfort from a raised height and an added seatback bolster (late availability) and eight new colors. The XLT Trim Preferred Equipment Packages are optional.

Cumulative Costs

	1993	1994	1995	1996	1997
Annual	$6,040	$4,120	$4,813	$4,729	$5,710
Total	$6,040	$10,160	$14,973	$19,702	$25,412

Ownership Cost Rating

Excellent

* Includes shaded options

** Other purchase requirements apply

 Poor · Worse Than Average ·  Average · Better Than Average · Excellent · Insufficient Information

Refer to *Section 3: Annotated Vehicle Charts* for an explanation of these charts.

Ford F150 Styleside XL SuperCab 4WD
2 Door Extended Cab

4.9L 145 hp Gas Fuel Inject. | 6 Cylinder In-Line | Manual 5 Speed | 4 Wheel On-Demand | Manual Seatbelts Only

Large Pickup

2WD Model Shown

Purchase Price

Car Item	Dealer Cost	List
Base Price	**$14,265**	**$16,617**
Anti-Lock Brakes	Std	Std
Automatic 4 Speed	$594	$699
5.0L 185 hp Gas	$541	$637
Air Conditioning	$685	$806
Power Steering	Std	Std
Cruise Control	$325	$383
4 Whl On-Demand Dr.	Std	Std
AM/FM Stereo Cassette	$205	$241
Steering Wheel, Tilt	Grp	Grp
8 Foot Bed	$198	$233
***Options Price**	$1,431	$1,684
***Total Price**	**$15,696**	**$18,301**
Target Price	$16,802	
Destination Charge	$585	
Avg. Tax & Fees	$1,058	
Total Target $	**$18,445**	
Average Dealer Option Cost:	***85%***	

Ownership Costs

Cost Area	5 Year Cost	Rate
Depreciation	$4,518	Better Than Average
Financing ($371/month)	$3,039	
Insurance (Rating 7)	$7,244	Better Than Average
State Fees	$755	
Fuel (Hwy 17 City 13)	$5,760	Worse Than Average
Maintenance	$3,796	Average
Repairs	$840	Worse Than Average

Ownership Cost By Year

$2,000 $4,000 $6,000 $8,000

1993 1994 1995 1996 1997

Warranty/Maintenance Info

Item		Rate
Major Tune-Up	$145	Average
Minor Tune-Up	$100	Average
Brake Service	$241	Better Than Average
Overall Warranty	3 yr/36k	Worse Than Average
Drivetrain Warranty	3 yr/36k	Worse Than Average
Rust Warranty	6 yr/100k	Average
Maintenance Warranty	N/A	
Roadside Assistance	N/A	

Resale Value

1993	1994	1995	1996	1997
$16,575	$16,105	$15,930	$15,030	$13,927

Ownership Costs (5yr)

Average	This Car
$28,710	$25,952
Cost/Mile 41¢	Cost/Mile 37¢

The F150 is available in ten models - (Base) S 2WD and 4WD Styleside Regular Cabs and XL 2WD and 4WD Styleside and Flareside in Regular or Super Cab versions. New for 1993, the XL 4WD Styleside Super Cab offers a new electronic speed control which provides faster response, better speed-holding capacity and tap-up/tap-down feature, and a rear bench seat w/improved comfort. Standard features include chrome bumpers and electronic AM radio. An optional off-road package with skid plates is offered.

Cumulative Costs

	1993	1994	1995	1996	1997
Annual	$5,774	$4,313	$4,770	$5,097	$5,998
Total	$5,774	$10,087	$14,857	$19,954	$25,952

Ownership Cost Rating

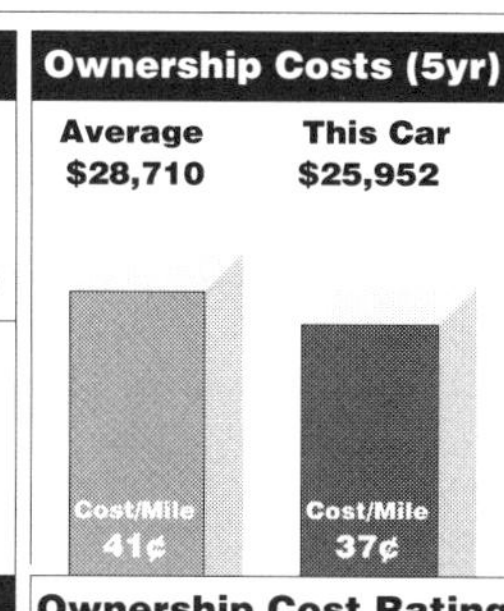
Excellent

Ford F150 Flareside XL SuperCab 4WD
2 Door Extended Cab

4.9L 145 hp Gas Fuel Inject. | 6 Cylinder In-Line | Manual 5 Speed | 4 Wheel On-Demand | Manual Seatbelts Only

Large Pickup

2WD Model Shown

Purchase Price

Car Item	Dealer Cost	List
Base Price	**$14,868**	**$17,327**
Anti-Lock Brakes	Std	Std
Automatic 4 Speed	$594	$699
5.0L 185 hp Gas	$541	$637
Air Conditioning	$685	$806
Power Steering	Std	Std
Cruise Control	$325	$383
4 Whl On-Demand Dr.	Std	Std
AM/FM Stereo Cassette	$205	$241
Steering Wheel, Tilt	Grp	Grp
Power Windows	$312	** $367
***Options Price**	$1,431	$1,684
***Total Price**	**$16,299**	**$19,011**
Target Price	$17,468	
Destination Charge	$585	
Avg. Tax & Fees	$1,099	
Total Target $	**$19,152**	
Average Dealer Option Cost:	***85%***	

Ownership Costs

Cost Area	5 Year Cost	Rate
Depreciation	$4,729	Better Than Average
Financing ($385/month)	$3,155	
Insurance (Rating 7)	$7,244	Better Than Average
State Fees	$784	
Fuel (Hwy 17 City 13)	$5,760	Worse Than Average
Maintenance	$3,796	Average
Repairs	$840	Worse Than Average

Ownership Cost By Year

$2,000 $4,000 $6,000 $8,000

1993 1994 1995 1996 1997

Warranty/Maintenance Info

Item		Rate
Major Tune-Up	$145	Average
Minor Tune-Up	$100	Average
Brake Service	$241	Better Than Average
Overall Warranty	3 yr/36k	Worse Than Average
Drivetrain Warranty	3 yr/36k	Worse Than Average
Rust Warranty	6 yr/100k	Average
Maintenance Warranty	N/A	
Roadside Assistance	N/A	

Resale Value

1993	1994	1995	1996	1997
$17,226	$16,706	$16,231	$15,459	$14,423

Ownership Costs (5yr)

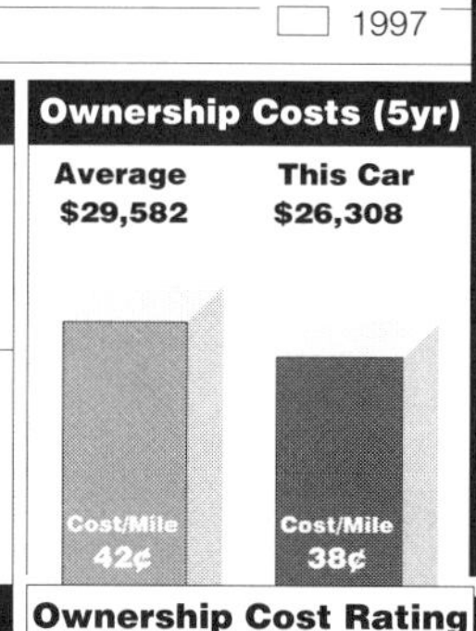

Average	This Car
$29,582	$26,308
Cost/Mile 42¢	Cost/Mile 38¢

The F150 is available in ten models - (Base) S 2WD and 4WD Styleside Regular Cabs and XL 2WD and 4WD Styleside and Flareside in Regular or Super Cab versions. New for 1993, the XL 4WD Flareside Super Cab features an electronic speed control which provides faster response, better speed-holding capacity, a rear bench seat w/improved comfort from a raised height and an added seatback bolster (late availability) and eight new colors. The XLT Trim Preferred Equipment Packages are optional.

Cumulative Costs

	1993	1994	1995	1996	1997
Annual	$5,885	$4,405	$5,100	$4,982	$5,936
Total	$5,885	$10,290	$15,390	$20,372	$26,308

Ownership Cost Rating

Excellent

* Includes shaded options

** Other purchase requirements apply

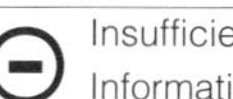

 Poor  Worse Than Average  Average  Better Than Average  Excellent — Insufficient Information

Refer to *Section 3: Annotated Vehicle Charts* for an explanation of these charts.

Ford F250 Styleside XL
2 Door Regular Cab

4.9L 150 hp Gas Fuel Inject.

6 Cylinder In-Line

1 3 5 / 2 4 R
Manual 5 Speed

2 Wheel Rear

Manual Seatbelts Only

Purchase Price

Car Item	Dealer Cost	List
Base Price	**$12,061**	**$14,024**
Anti-Lock Brakes	Std	Std
Automatic 4 Speed	$786	$924
5.0L 185 hp Gas	$541	$637
Air Conditioning	$685	$806
Power Steering	Std	Std
Cruise Control	$325	$383
All Wheel Drive	N/A	N/A
AM/FM Stereo Cassette	$205	** $241
Steering Wheel, Tilt	Grp	Grp
Power Windows	Pkg	Pkg
***Options Price**	$1,226	$1,443
***Total Price**	**$13,287**	**$15,467**
Target Price	$14,165	
Destination Charge	$585	
Avg. Tax & Fees	$899	
Total Target $	**$15,649**	
Average Dealer Option Cost:	***85%***	

Ownership Costs

Cost Area	5 Year Cost	Rate
Depreciation	$4,373	
Financing ($315/month)	$2,578	
Insurance (Rating 5)	$6,996	
State Fees	$641	
Fuel (Hwy 19 City 15)	$5,079	
Maintenance	$3,901	
Repairs	$761	

Ownership Cost By Year

$2,000 $4,000 $6,000 $8,000

1993 1994 1995 1996 1997

Warranty/Maintenance Info

Major Tune-Up	$145	
Minor Tune-Up	$100	
Brake Service	$281	
Overall Warranty	3 yr/36k	
Drivetrain Warranty	3 yr/36k	
Rust Warranty	6 yr/100k	
Maintenance Warranty	N/A	
Roadside Assistance	N/A	

Resale Value

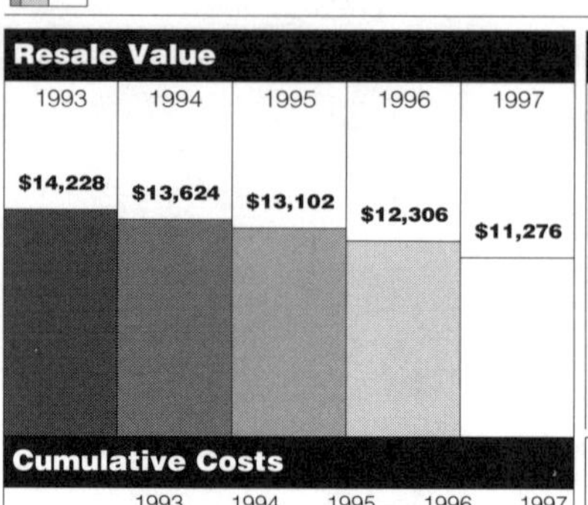

Ownership Costs (5yr)

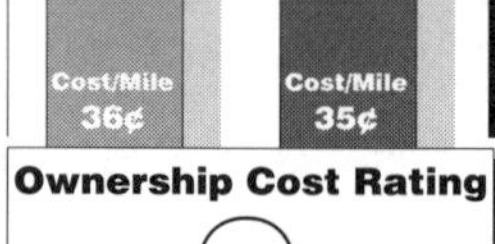

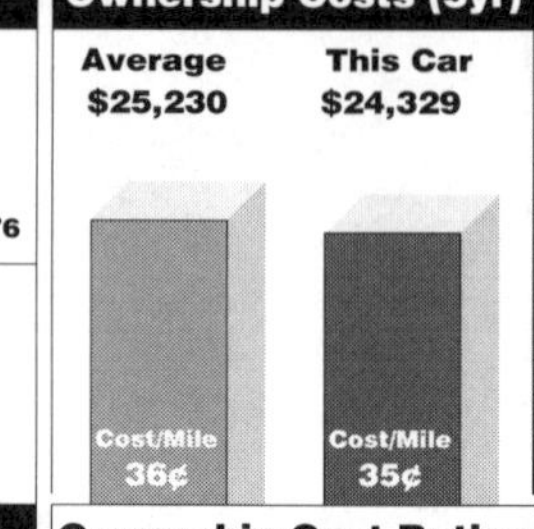

The 1993 F250 is available in four models - Regular Cab two- and four-wheel drive and Extended Cab two- and four-wheel drive pickups. New for 1993, the F250 Styleside XL offers a "Preferred Care" program which offers roadside assistance 24hrs a day, seven days a week. Also new is a "next-generation" electronic speed-control which has greater speed-holding capabilities and responds better to driver commands, three new exterior colors and (later in the year) a more powerful 7.5L V-8 engine.

Cumulative Costs

	1993	1994	1995	1996	1997
Annual	$4,934	$4,098	$4,853	$4,723	$5,721
Total	$4,934	$9,032	$13,885	$18,608	$24,329

Ownership Cost Rating

Excellent

Ford F250 Styleside XL Supercab
2 Door Extended Cab

5.8L 200 hp Gas Fuel Inject.

8 Cylinder "V"

Manual 5 Speed

2 Wheel Rear

Manual Seatbelts Only

Large Pickup

Purchase Price

Car Item	Dealer Cost	List
Base Price	**$14,914**	**$17,381**
Anti-Lock Brakes	Std	Std
Automatic 3 Speed	$592	$696
7.5L 230 hp Gas	$412	$484
Air Conditioning	$685	$806
Power Steering	Std	Std
Cruise Control	$325	$383
All Wheel Drive	N/A	N/A
AM/FM Stereo Cassette	$205	$241
Steering Wheel, Tilt	Grp	Grp
Power Windows	Pkg	Pkg
***Options Price**	$890	$1,047
***Total Price**	**$15,804**	**$18,428**
Target Price	$16,939	
Destination Charge	$585	
Avg. Tax & Fees	$1,066	
Total Target $	**$18,590**	
Average Dealer Option Cost:	***85%***	

Ownership Costs

Cost Area	5 Year Cost	Rate
Depreciation	$6,336	
Financing ($374/month)	$3,062	
Insurance (Rating 7)	$7,244	
State Fees	$760	
Fuel (Hwy 16 City 11)	$6,441	
Maintenance	$4,178	
Repairs	$761	

Ownership Cost By Year

$2,000 $4,000 $6,000 $8,000

1993 1994 1995 1996 1997

Warranty/Maintenance Info

Major Tune-Up	$145	
Minor Tune-Up	$100	
Brake Service	$281	
Overall Warranty	3 yr/36k	
Drivetrain Warranty	3 yr/36k	
Rust Warranty	6 yr/100k	
Maintenance Warranty	N/A	
Roadside Assistance	N/A	

Resale Value

1993	1994	1995	1996	1997
$14,992	$14,444	$13,964	$13,249	$12,254

Ownership Costs (5yr)

Average $28,866 — Cost/Mile 41¢

This Car $28,782 — Cost/Mile 41¢

The 1993 F250 is available in four models - Regular Cab two- and four-wheel drive and Extended Cab two- and four-wheel drive pickups. New for 1993, the F250 Styleside XL Supercab offers a "Preferred Care" program which offers roadside assistance 24hrs a day, seven days a week. Also new is a "next-generation" electronic speed-control which has greater speed-holding capabilities and responds better to driver commands, three new exterior colors and (later in the year) a more powerful 7.5L V-8 engine.

Cumulative Costs

	1993	1994	1995	1996	1997
Annual	$7,638	$4,530	$5,391	$5,032	$6,191
Total	$7,638	$12,168	$17,559	$22,591	$28,782

Ownership Cost Rating

Better Than Average

* Includes shaded options

** Other purchase requirements apply

Poor  Worse Than Average  Average Better Than Average Excellent  Insufficient Information

Refer to *Section 3: Annotated Vehicle Charts* for an explanation of these charts.

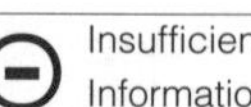

Ford F250 Styleside XL 4WD
2 Door Regular Cab

5.8L 200 hp Gas Fuel Inject.

8 Cylinder "V"

Manual 5 Speed

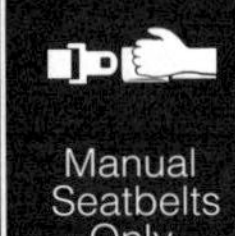
4 Wheel On-Demand

Manual Seatbelts Only

Large Pickup

F150 Model Shown

Purchase Price

Car Item	Dealer Cost	List
Base Price	**$15,563**	**$18,145**
Anti-Lock Brakes	Std	Std
Automatic 3 Speed	$592	$696
7.5L 230 hp Gas	$412	$484
Air Conditioning	$685	$806
Power Steering	Std	Std
Cruise Control	$325	$383
4 Whl On-Demand Dr.	Std	Std
AM/FM Stereo Cassette	$205	** $241
Steering Wheel, Tilt	Grp	Grp
Power Windows	Pkg	Pkg
***Options Price**	$685	$806
***Total Price**	**$16,248**	**$18,951**
Target Price	$17,436	
Destination Charge	$585	
Avg. Tax & Fees	$1,096	
Total Target $	**$19,117**	
Average Dealer Option Cost:	***85%***	

Ownership Costs

Cost Area	5 Year Cost	Rate
Depreciation	$4,876	Excellent
Financing ($384/month)	$3,149	
Insurance (Rating 8)	$7,432	Excellent
State Fees	$781	
Fuel (Hwy 15 City 10 [Est.])	$6,977	Worse Than Average
Maintenance	$4,170	Average
Repairs	$840	Average

Ownership Cost By Year

$2,000 $4,000 $6,000 $8,000 — 1993, 1994, 1995, 1996, 1997

Warranty/Maintenance Info

Item		Rate
Major Tune-Up	$145	Better Than Average
Minor Tune-Up	$100	Better Than Average
Brake Service	$281	Average
Overall Warranty	3 yr/36k	Average
Drivetrain Warranty	3 yr/36k	Average
Rust Warranty	6 yr/100k	Better Than Average
Maintenance Warranty	N/A	
Roadside Assistance	N/A	

Resale Value

1993	1994	1995	1996	1997
$17,155	$16,597	$16,260	$15,490	$14,241

Ownership Costs (5yr)

Average	This Car
$29,508	$28,225
Cost/Mile 42¢	Cost/Mile 40¢

The 1993 F250 is available in four models - Regular Cab two- and four-wheel drive and Extended Cab two- and four-wheel drive pickups. New for 1993, the F250 Styleside XL 4WD offers a "Preferred Care" program which offers roadside assistance 24hrs a day, seven days a week. Also new is a "next-generation" electronic speed-control, an optional off-road package (skid plates, handling package and manual locking hubs), three new colors and (later in the year) a more powerful 7.5L V-8.

Cumulative Costs

	1993	1994	1995	1996	1997
Annual	$6,177	$4,711	$5,424	$5,273	$6,640
Total	$6,177	$10,888	$16,312	$21,585	$28,225

Ownership Cost Rating

Excellent

Ford F250 Styleside XL Supercab 4WD
2 Door Extended Cab

5.8L 200 hp Gas Fuel Inject.

8 Cylinder "V"

Manual 5 Speed

4 Wheel On-Demand

Manual Seatbelts Only

Large Pickup

2WD Model Shown

Purchase Price

Car Item	Dealer Cost	List
Base Price	**$16,822**	**$19,625**
Anti-Lock Brakes	Std	Std
Automatic 3 Speed	$592	$696
7.5L 230 hp Gas	$412	$484
Air Conditioning	$685	$806
Power Steering	Std	Std
Cruise Control	$325	$383
4 Whl On-Demand Dr.	Std	Std
AM/FM Stereo Cassette	$205	$241
Steering Wheel, Tilt	Grp	Grp
Power Windows	Pkg	Pkg
***Options Price**	$890	$1,047
***Total Price**	**$17,712**	**$20,672**
Target Price	$19,052	
Destination Charge	$585	
Avg. Tax & Fees	$1,195	
Total Target $	**$20,832**	
Average Dealer Option Cost:	***85%***	

Ownership Costs

Cost Area	5 Year Cost	Rate
Depreciation	$6,584	Average
Financing ($419/month)	$3,431	
Insurance (Rating 10)	$7,689	Excellent
State Fees	$851	
Fuel (Hwy 14 City 9 [Est.])	$7,613	Poor
Maintenance	$4,170	Average
Repairs	$840	Average

Ownership Cost By Year

$2,000 $4,000 $6,000 $8,000 — 1993, 1994, 1995, 1996, 1997

Warranty/Maintenance Info

Item		Rate
Major Tune-Up	$145	Better Than Average
Minor Tune-Up	$100	Better Than Average
Brake Service	$281	Average
Overall Warranty	3 yr/36k	Average
Drivetrain Warranty	3 yr/36k	Average
Rust Warranty	6 yr/100k	Better Than Average
Maintenance Warranty	N/A	
Roadside Assistance	N/A	

Resale Value

1993	1994	1995	1996	1997
$16,663	$16,243	$15,857	$15,198	$14,248

Ownership Costs (5yr)

Average	This Car
$31,621	$31,178
Cost/Mile 45¢	Cost/Mile 45¢

The 1993 F250 is available in four models - Regular Cab two- and four-wheel drive and Extended Cab two- and four-wheel drive pickups. New for 1993, the F250 Styleside XL Supercab 4WD offers a "Preferred Care" program which offers roadside assistance 24hrs a day, seven days a week. Also new is a "next-generation" electronic speed-control, an optional off-road package (skid plates, handling package and manual locking hubs), three new colors and (later in the year) a more powerful 7.5L V-8.

Cumulative Costs

	1993	1994	1995	1996	1997
Annual	$8,685	$4,848	$5,721	$5,379	$6,545
Total	$8,685	$13,533	$19,254	$24,633	$31,178

Ownership Cost Rating

Better Than Average

* Includes shaded options

** Other purchase requirements apply

 Poor  Worse Than Average  Average 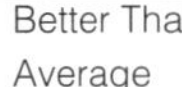 Better Than Average  Excellent  Insufficient Information

Refer to *Section 3: Annotated Vehicle Charts* for an explanation of these charts.

Ford F350 Styleside XL
2 Door Regular Cab

5.8L 200 hp Gas Fuel Inject.

8 Cylinder "V"

Manual 5 Speed

2 Wheel Rear

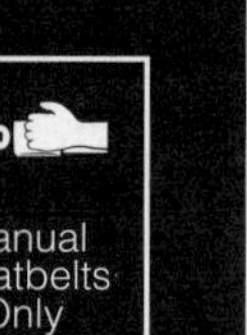
Manual Seatbelts Only

Large Pickup

F150 Model Shown

Purchase Price

Car Item	Dealer Cost	List
Base Price	**$14,722**	**$17,155**
Anti-Lock Brakes	Std	Std
Automatic 3 Speed	$592	$696
7.5L 230 hp Gas	$412	$484
Air Conditioning	$685	$806
Power Steering	Std	Std
Cruise Control	$325	$383
All Wheel Drive	N/A	N/A
AM/FM Stereo Cassette	$205	** $241
Steering Wheel, Tilt	Grp	Grp
Power Windows	Grp	Grp
***Options Price**	$685	$806
***Total Price**	**$15,407**	**$17,961**
Target Price	$16,507	
Destination Charge	$585	
Avg. Tax & Fees	$1,040	
Total Target $	**$18,132**	
Average Dealer Option Cost:	***85%***	

Ownership Costs

Cost Area	5 Year Cost	Rate
Depreciation	$6,298	Average
Financing ($364/month)	$2,987	
Insurance (Rating 6)	$7,129	Excellent
State Fees	$741	
Fuel (Hwy 15 City 11 [Est.])	$6,659	Worse Than Average
Maintenance	$3,918	Better Than Average
Repairs	$840	Average

Ownership Cost By Year

Warranty/Maintenance Info

Item		Rate
Major Tune-Up	$145	Better Than Average
Minor Tune-Up	$100	Better Than Average
Brake Service	$281	Average
Overall Warranty	3 yr/36k	Average
Drivetrain Warranty	3 yr/36k	Average
Rust Warranty	6 yr/100k	Better Than Average
Maintenance Warranty	N/A	
Roadside Assistance	N/A	

Resale Value

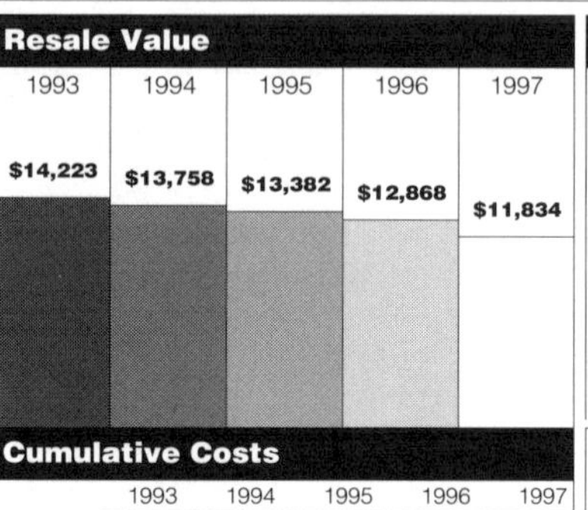

Ownership Costs (5yr)

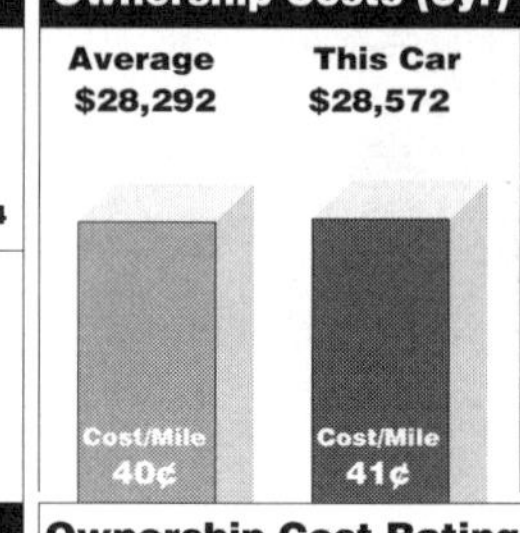

The 1993 F350 is available in three models-Regular Cab Styleside in either two- or four-wheel drive and Supercab Styleside with two-wheel drive. New for 1993, the F350 Styleside XL features a palette of new colors. Standard features include chrome front bumpers and aero halogen headlights with impact-resistant lenses and color-keyed door trim. Functional changes include optional in-box spare tire carrier and "Off-Road" Package including skid plates, handling package and manual locking hubs.

Cumulative Costs

	1993	1994	1995	1996	1997
Annual	$7,931	$4,440	$5,175	$4,875	$6,151
Total	$7,931	$12,371	$17,546	$22,421	$28,572

Ownership Cost Rating

Average

Ford F350 Styleside XL Crew Cab
4 Door Extended Cab

Large Pickup

5.8L 200 hp Gas Fuel Inject.

8 Cylinder "V"

Manual 5 Speed

2 Wheel Rear

Manual Seatbelts Only

Purchase Price

Car Item	Dealer Cost	List
Base Price	**$15,785**	**$18,406**
Anti-Lock Brakes	Std	Std
Automatic 3 Speed	$592	$696
7.5L 230 hp Gas	$412	$484
Air Conditioning	$685	$806
Power Steering	Std	Std
Cruise Control	$325	$383
All Wheel Drive	N/A	N/A
AM/FM Stereo Cassette	$205	$241
Steering Wheel, Tilt	Grp	Grp
Power Windows	Grp	Grp
***Options Price**	$890	$1,047
***Total Price**	**$16,675**	**$19,453**
Target Price	$17,902	
Destination Charge	$585	
Avg. Tax & Fees	$1,124	
Total Target $	**$19,611**	
Average Dealer Option Cost:	***85%***	

Ownership Costs

Cost Area	5 Year Cost	Rate
Depreciation	$7,220	Average
Financing ($394/month)	$3,232	
Insurance (Rating 7)	$7,244	Excellent
State Fees	$800	
Fuel (Hwy 15 City 11 [Est.])	$6,659	Worse Than Average
Maintenance	$4,178	Average
Repairs	$840	Average

Ownership Cost By Year

Warranty/Maintenance Info

Item		Rate
Major Tune-Up	$145	Better Than Average
Minor Tune-Up	$100	Better Than Average
Brake Service	$281	Average
Overall Warranty	3 yr/36k	Average
Drivetrain Warranty	3 yr/36k	Average
Rust Warranty	6 yr/100k	Better Than Average
Maintenance Warranty	N/A	
Roadside Assistance	N/A	

Resale Value

1993	1994	1995	1996	1997
$15,704	$14,977	$14,271	$13,544	$12,391

Ownership Costs (5yr)

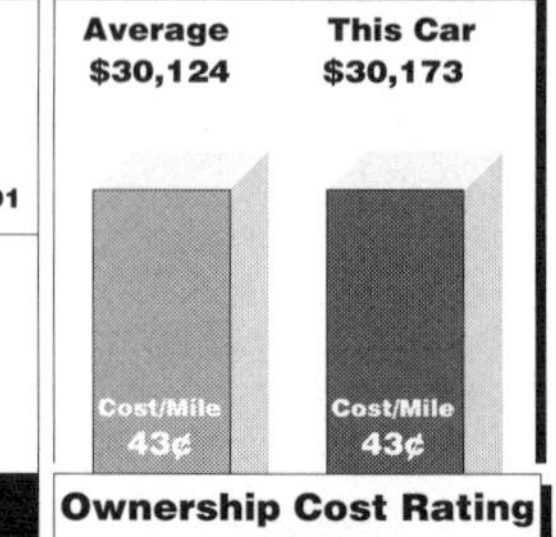

Average $30,124 — This Car $30,173

Cost/Mile 43¢ — Cost/Mile 43¢

The Crew Cab is available in two-wheel-drive with single and dual rear wheels, and also in four-wheel-drive with single rear wheels. Two trim levels are available on the 1993 Crew Cab-XL and XLT. New for 1993, the F350 Styleside XL Crew Cab features new exterior styling. It is more aerodynamic, with a new front end, bodyside moldings, flush headlamps, and restyled tailgate. Other features include improved exterior badging and graphics. The interior features new styling and bench seats.

Cumulative Costs

	1993	1994	1995	1996	1997
Annual	$8,067	$4,813	$5,714	$5,140	$6,439
Total	$8,067	$12,880	$18,594	$23,734	$30,173

Ownership Cost Rating

Better Than Average

* Includes shaded options

** Other purchase requirements apply

 Poor 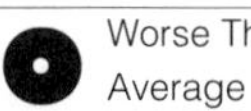 Worse Than Average  Average 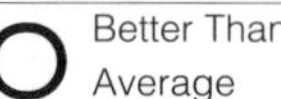 Better Than Average  Excellent 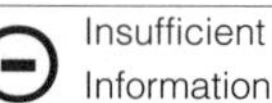 Insufficient Information

Refer to *Section 3: Annotated Vehicle Charts* for an explanation of these charts.

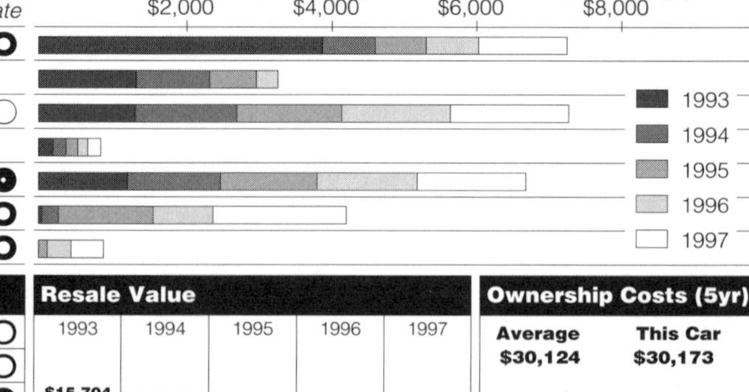

Ford F350 Styleside XL SuperCab
2 Door Extended Cab

7.5L 230 hp Gas Fuel Inject.

8 Cylinder "V"

Manual 5 Speed

2 Wheel Rear

Manual Seatbelts Only

Large Pickup

F250 Model Shown

Purchase Price

Car Item	Dealer Cost	List
Base Price	**$16,382**	**$19,109**
Anti-Lock Brakes	Std	Std
Automatic 4 Speed	$786	$924
7.3L 185 hp Diesel	$1,471	$1,730
Air Conditioning	$685	$806
Power Steering	Std	Std
Cruise Control	$325	$383
All Wheel Drive	N/A	N/A
AM/FM Stereo Cassette	$205	$241
Steering Wheel, Tilt	Grp	Grp
Power Windows	Grp	Grp
***Options Price**	$890	$1,047
***Total Price**	**$17,272**	**$20,156**
Target Price	$18,563	
Destination Charge	$585	
Avg. Tax & Fees	$1,164	
Total Target $	**$20,312**	
Average Dealer Option Cost:	***85%***	

Ownership Costs

Cost Area	5 Year Cost	Rate
Depreciation	$7,019	Average
Financing ($408/month)	$3,346	
Insurance (Rating 8)	$7,432	Excellent
State Fees	$829	
Fuel (Hwy 14 City 10 [Est.])	$7,226	Poor
Maintenance	$3,893	Better Than Average
Repairs	$840	Average

Ownership Cost By Year

$2,000 $4,000 $6,000 $8,000

1993 1994 1995 1996 1997

Warranty/Maintenance Info

Item	Cost/Term	Rate
Major Tune-Up	$145	Better Than Average
Minor Tune-Up	$100	Better Than Average
Brake Service	$281	Average
Overall Warranty	3 yr/36k	Average
Drivetrain Warranty	3 yr/36k	Average
Rust Warranty	6 yr/100k	Better Than Average
Maintenance Warranty	N/A	
Roadside Assistance	N/A	

Resale Value

1993	1994	1995	1996	1997
$15,623	$15,146	$14,748	$14,144	$13,293

Ownership Costs (5yr)

Average	This Car
$30,987	$30,585
Cost/Mile 44¢	Cost/Mile 44¢

Cumulative Costs

	1993	1994	1995	1996	1997
Annual	$9,044	$4,750	$5,446	$5,188	$6,157
Total	$9,044	$13,794	$19,240	$24,428	$30,585

Ownership Cost Rating

Better Than Average

The 1993 F350 is available in three models-Regular Cab Styleside in either two- or four-wheel drive and Supercab Styleside with two-wheel drive. New for 1993, the F350 Styleside XL Supercab features optional in-box spare tire carrier and "Off-road" Package including skid plates, handling package and manual locking hubs. Other features include front chrome bumpers, argent grille, cowl side trim panel, black leather steering wheel, audible alert and front bench with split/folding seatback.

Ford F350 Styleside XL 4WD
2 Door Regular Cab

5.8L 200 hp Gas Fuel Inject.

8 Cylinder "V"

Manual 5 Speed

4 Wheel On-Demand

Manual Seatbelts Only

Large Pickup

F150 Model Shown

Purchase Price

Car Item	Dealer Cost	List
Base Price	**$15,905**	**$18,547**
Anti-Lock Brakes	Std	Std
Automatic 3 Speed	$592	$696
7.5L 230 hp Gas	$412	$484
Air Conditioning	$685	$806
Power Steering	Std	Std
Cruise Control	$325	$383
4 Whl On-Demand Dr.	Std	Std
AM/FM Stereo Cassette	$205	** $241
Steering Wheel, Tilt	Grp	Grp
Power Windows	Grp	Grp
***Options Price**	$685	$806
***Total Price**	**$16,590**	**$19,353**
Target Price	$17,814	
Destination Charge	$585	
Avg. Tax & Fees	$1,119	
Total Target $	**$19,518**	
Average Dealer Option Cost:	***85%***	

Ownership Costs

Cost Area	5 Year Cost	Rate
Depreciation	$5,895	Better Than Average
Financing ($392/month)	$3,215	
Insurance (Rating 8)	$7,432	Excellent
State Fees	$798	
Fuel (Hwy 15 City 11 [Est.])	$6,659	Worse Than Average
Maintenance	$4,210	Average
Repairs	$985	Worse Than Average

Ownership Cost By Year

$2,000 $4,000 $6,000 $8,000

1993 1994 1995 1996 1997

Warranty/Maintenance Info

Item	Cost/Term	Rate
Major Tune-Up	$145	Better Than Average
Minor Tune-Up	$100	Better Than Average
Brake Service	$281	Average
Overall Warranty	3 yr/36k	Average
Drivetrain Warranty	3 yr/36k	Average
Rust Warranty	6 yr/100k	Better Than Average
Maintenance Warranty	N/A	
Roadside Assistance	N/A	

Resale Value

1993	1994	1995	1996	1997
$15,368	$15,182	$14,958	$14,413	$13,623

Ownership Costs (5yr)

Average	This Car
$30,001	$29,194
Cost/Mile 43¢	Cost/Mile 42¢

Cumulative Costs

	1993	1994	1995	1996	1997
Annual	$8,337	$4,302	$5,286	$5,047	$6,222
Total	$8,337	$12,639	$17,925	$22,972	$29,194

Ownership Cost Rating

Excellent

The 1993 F350 is available in three models-Regular Cab Styleside in either two- or four-wheel drive and Supercab Styleside with two-wheel drive. New for 1993, the F350 Styleside XL 4WD features a palette of new colors. Standard features include front chrome bumpers, aero-style headlights with impact resistant lenses and color-keyed door trim. Functional changes include optional in-box spare tire carrier and "Off-road" Package including skid plates, handling package and manual locking hubs.

* Includes shaded options

** Other purchase requirements apply

Poor  Worse Than Average  Average 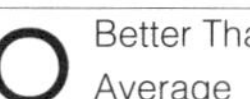 Better Than Average 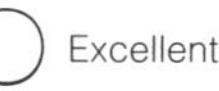 Excellent — Insufficient Information

Refer to *Section 3: Annotated Vehicle Charts* for an explanation of these charts.

Ford F350 Styleside XL Crew Cab 4WD
4 Door Extended Cab

5.8L 200 hp Gas Fuel Inject.

8 Cylinder "V"

Manual 5 Speed

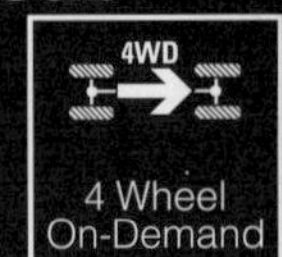
4 Wheel On-Demand

Manual Seatbelts Only

Large Pickup

2WD Model Shown

Purchase Price

Car Item	Dealer Cost	List
Base Price	**$18,276**	**$21,336**
Anti-Lock Brakes	Std	Std
Automatic 3 Speed	$592	$696
7.5L 230 hp Gas	$412	$484
Air Conditioning	$685	$806
Power Steering	Std	Std
Cruise Control	$325	$383
4 Whl On-Demand Dr.	Std	Std
AM/FM Stereo Cassette	$205	$241
Steering Wheel, Tilt	Grp	Grp
Power Windows	Grp	Grp
***Options Price**	$890	$1,047
***Total Price**	**$19,166**	**$22,383**
Target Price	$20,672	
Destination Charge	$585	
Avg. Tax & Fees	$1,293	
Total Target $	**$22,550**	
Average Dealer Option Cost:	***85%***	

Ownership Costs

Cost Area	5 Year Cost	Rate
Depreciation	$7,751	Average
Financing ($453/month)	$3,715	
Insurance (Rating 10)	$7,689	Excellent
State Fees	$920	
Fuel (Hwy 15 City 11 [Est.])	$6,659	Worse Than Average
Maintenance	$4,210	Average
Repairs	$985	Worse Than Average

Ownership Cost By Year

$2,000 · $4,000 · $6,000 · $8,000

Legend: 1993 · 1994 · 1995 · 1996 · 1997

Warranty/Maintenance Info

Item		Rate
Major Tune-Up	$145	Better Than Average
Minor Tune-Up	$100	Better Than Average
Brake Service	$281	Average
Overall Warranty	3 yr/36k	Average
Drivetrain Warranty	3 yr/36k	Average
Rust Warranty	6 yr/100k	Better Than Average
Maintenance Warranty	N/A	
Roadside Assistance	N/A	

Resale Value

1993	1994	1995	1996	1997
$18,784	$18,437	$17,150	$17,089	$14,799

Ownership Costs (5yr)

	Average	This Car
	$33,722	$31,929
Cost/Mile	48¢	46¢

Cumulative Costs

	1993	1994	1995	1996	1997
Annual	$8,240	$4,696	$6,524	$4,673	$7,796
Total	$8,240	$12,936	$19,460	$24,133	$31,929

Ownership Cost Rating

Excellent

The Crew Cab is available in two-wheel-drive with single and dual rear wheels, and also in four-wheel-drive with single rear wheels. Two trim levels are available on the 1993 Crew Cab-XL and XLT. New for 1993, the F350 Stlyeside XL Crew Cab 4WD features new exterior styling. It is more aerodynamic, with a new front end, bodyside moldings, flush headlamps, and restlyed tailgate. Also new are improved exterior badging and graphics. The interior features an improved instrument panel and bench seats.

Ford Ranger XL
2 Door Regular Cab

2.3L 98 hp Gas Fuel Inject.

4 Cylinder In-Line

Manual 5 Speed

2 Wheel Rear

Manual Seatbelts Only

Small Pickup

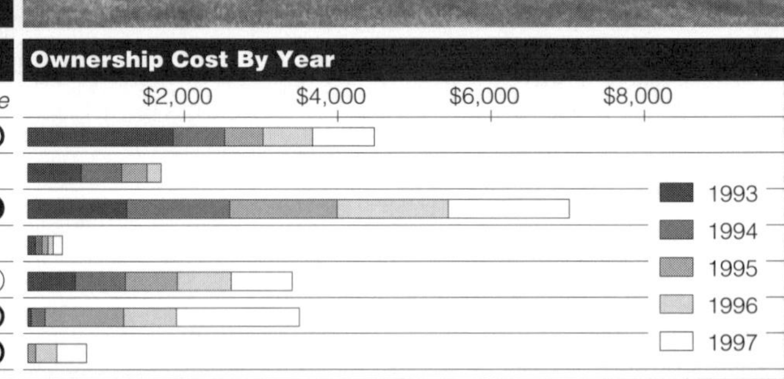

Purchase Price

Car Item	Dealer Cost	List
Base Price	**$8,158**	**$8,753**
Anti-Lock Brakes	Std	Std
Automatic 4 Speed	$842	$990
4.0L 160 hp Gas	$568	** $668
Air Conditioning	$663	** $780
Power Steering	$233	$274
Cruise Control	$325	** $383
All Wheel Drive	N/A	N/A
AM/FM Stereo Cassette	$267	$315
Steering Wheel, Tilt	Grp	Grp
7 Foot Bed	$656	$713
***Options Price**	$500	$589
***Total Price**	**$8,658**	**$9,342**
Target Price	$9,162	
Destination Charge	$460	
Avg. Tax & Fees	$579	
Total Target $	**$10,201**	
Average Dealer Option Cost:	***85%***	

Ownership Costs

Cost Area	5 Year Cost	Rate
Depreciation	$4,458	Better Than Average
Financing ($205/month)	$1,680	
Insurance (Rating 5)	$6,996	Average
State Fees	$392	
Fuel (Hwy 28 City 23)	$3,385	Excellent
Maintenance	$3,480	Better Than Average
Repairs	$709	Better Than Average

Ownership Cost By Year

$2,000 · $4,000 · $6,000 · $8,000

Legend: 1993 · 1994 · 1995 · 1996 · 1997

Warranty/Maintenance Info

Item		Rate
Major Tune-Up	$110	Excellent
Minor Tune-Up	$70	Excellent
Brake Service	$210	Average
Overall Warranty	3 yr/36k	Average
Drivetrain Warranty	3 yr/36k	Average
Rust Warranty	6 yr/100k	Better Than Average
Maintenance Warranty	N/A	
Roadside Assistance	N/A	

Resale Value

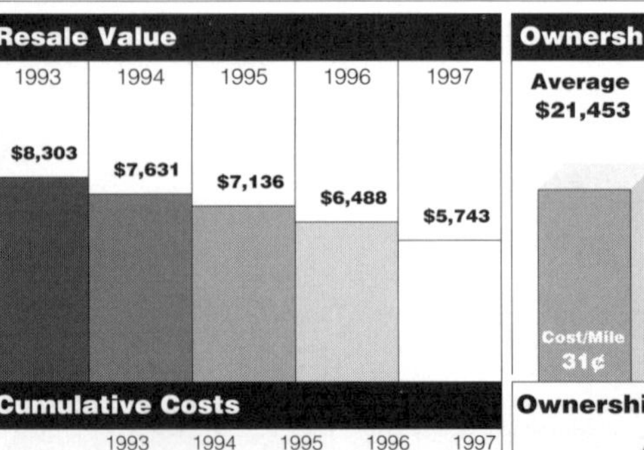

1993	1994	1995	1996	1997
$8,303	$7,631	$7,136	$6,488	$5,743

Ownership Costs (5yr)

	Average	This Car
	$21,453	$21,100
Cost/Mile	31¢	30¢

Cumulative Costs

	1993	1994	1995	1996	1997
Annual	$4,655	$3,461	$4,107	$3,962	$4,915
Total	$4,655	$8,116	$12,223	$16,185	$21,100

Ownership Cost Rating

Better Than Average

The 1993 Ranger is available in six models - XL, XLT, STX, and in either 2WD or 4WD pickups. New for 1993, the XL 2WD has new exterior sheet metal that sports a more aerodynamic look, a greater and flusher windshield and side-window glass, and limousine-style doors which blend into the roof and have concealed drip rails. Other refinements include a new power steering gear, an easier-to-use tailgate, single-key locks, corrosion protection upgrades, an increased payload, and a restyled interior.

* Includes shaded options

** Other purchase requirements apply

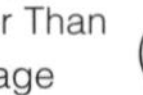

 Poor  Worse Than Average  Average  Better Than Average  Excellent · Insufficient Information

Refer to *Section 3: Annotated Vehicle Charts* for an explanation of these charts.

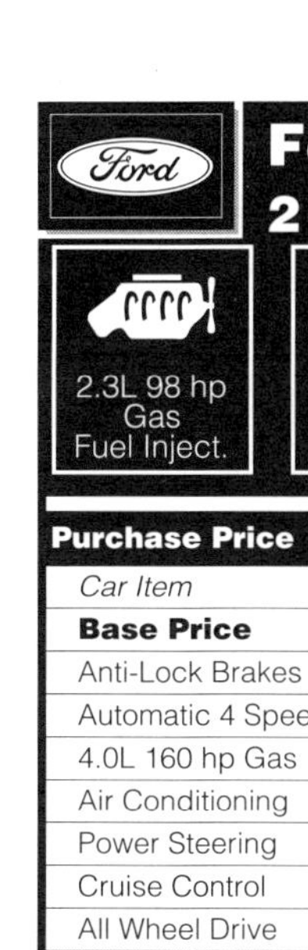

Ford Ranger XLT

2 Door Regular Cab

2.3L 98 hp Gas Fuel Inject.

4 Cylinder In-Line

Manual 5 Speed

2 Wheel Rear

Manual Seatbelts Only

Small Pickup

4WD SuperCab Shown

Purchase Price

Car Item	Dealer Cost	List
Base Price	**$9,289**	**$10,436**
Anti-Lock Brakes	Std	Std
Automatic 4 Speed	$842	$990
4.0L 160 hp Gas	$598	** $668
Air Conditioning	$663	** $780
Power Steering	Pkg	Pkg
Cruise Control	$325	** $383
All Wheel Drive	N/A	N/A
AM/FM Stereo Cassette	$117	$138
Steering Wheel, Tilt	Grp	Grp
7 Foot Bed	$282	$320
***Options Price**	$117	$138
***Total Price**	**$9,406**	**$10,574**
Target Price	$9,975	
Destination Charge	$460	
Avg. Tax & Fees	$632	
Total Target $	**$11,067**	
Average Dealer Option Cost:	***86%***	

Ownership Costs

Cost Area	5 Year Cost	Rate
Depreciation	$4,353	Better Than Average
Financing ($222/month)	$1,822	
Insurance (Rating 5)	$6,996	Average
State Fees	$440	
Fuel (Hwy 28 City 23)	$3,385	Excellent
Maintenance	$3,480	Better Than Average
Repairs	$709	Better Than Average

Ownership Cost By Year

$2,000 $4,000 $6,000 $8,000

1993 1994 1995 1996 1997

Warranty/Maintenance Info

Item		Rate
Major Tune-Up	$110	Excellent
Minor Tune-Up	$70	Excellent
Brake Service	$210	Average
Overall Warranty	3 yr/36k	Average
Drivetrain Warranty	3 yr/36k	Average
Rust Warranty	6 yr/100k	Better Than Average
Maintenance Warranty	N/A	
Roadside Assistance	N/A	

Resale Value

1993	1994	1995	1996	1997
$8,863	$8,317	$7,881	$7,384	$6,714

Ownership Costs (5yr)

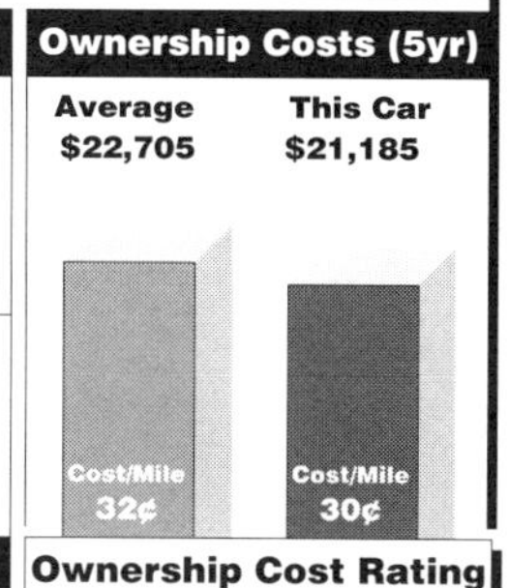

Average	This Car
$22,705	$21,185
Cost/Mile 32¢	Cost/Mile 30¢

Cumulative Costs

	1993	1994	1995	1996	1997
Annual	$5,032	$3,391	$4,086	$3,829	$4,847
Total	$5,032	$8,423	$12,509	$16,338	$21,185

Ownership Cost Rating

Excellent

The 1993 Ranger is available in six models - XL, XLT, STX, and in either two- or four-wheel drive pickups. New for 1993, the XLT two-wheel drive has all-new exterior sheet metal with modern, aerodynamic styling, including limo-style doors and flusher glass. The interior is freshened with new seat and door trims, steering wheel, instrument panel appliques, and new graphics. Functional improvements include a wider tread, improved steering on-center feel, a payload increase, and reduced wind noise.

Ford Ranger STX

2 Door Regular Cab

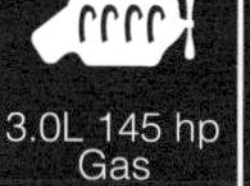

3.0L 145 hp Gas Fuel Inject.

6 Cylinder "V"

Manual 5 Speed

2 Wheel Rear

Manual Seatbelts Only

Small Pickup

4WD Model Shown

Purchase Price

Car Item	Dealer Cost	List
Base Price	**$10,043**	**$11,293**
Anti-Lock Brakes	Std	Std
Automatic 4 Speed	$842	$990
4.0L 160 hp Gas	$152	$179
Air Conditioning	$663	$780
Power Steering	Std	Std
Cruise Control	$325	$383
All Wheel Drive	N/A	N/A
AM/FM Stereo Cassette	$117	$138
Steering Wheel, Tilt	Grp	Grp
7 Foot Bed	$281	$320
***Options Price**	$117	$138
***Total Price**	**$10,160**	**$11,431**
Target Price	$10,790	
Destination Charge	$460	
Avg. Tax & Fees	$682	
Total Target $	**$11,932**	
Average Dealer Option Cost:	***85%***	

Ownership Costs

Cost Area	5 Year Cost	Rate
Depreciation	$5,309	Average
Financing ($240/month)	$1,966	
Insurance (Rating 6)	$7,129	Average
State Fees	$475	
Fuel (Hwy 25 City 19)	$3,929	Better Than Average
Maintenance	$3,562	Better Than Average
Repairs	$709	Better Than Average

Ownership Cost By Year

$2,000 $4,000 $6,000 $8,000

1993 1994 1995 1996 1997

Warranty/Maintenance Info

Item		Rate
Major Tune-Up	$124	Excellent
Minor Tune-Up	$79	Better Than Average
Brake Service	$210	Average
Overall Warranty	3 yr/36k	Average
Drivetrain Warranty	3 yr/36k	Average
Rust Warranty	6 yr/100k	Better Than Average
Maintenance Warranty	N/A	
Roadside Assistance	N/A	

Resale Value

1993	1994	1995	1996	1997
$9,052	$8,435	$8,000	$7,377	$6,623

Ownership Costs (5yr)

Average	This Car
$23,576	$23,079
Cost/Mile 34¢	Cost/Mile 33¢

Cumulative Costs

	1993	1994	1995	1996	1997
Annual	$5,904	$3,659	$4,350	$4,133	$5,033
Total	$5,904	$9,563	$13,913	$18,046	$23,079

Ownership Cost Rating

Better Than Average

The 1993 Ranger is available in six models - XL, XLT, STX, and in either two- or four-wheel drive pickups. New for 1993, the STX two-wheel drive has all-new exterior sheet metal with modern, aerodynamic styling, including limo-style doors and flusher glass. The interior is freshened with new seat and door trims, steering wheel, instrument panel appliques, and new graphics. Functional improvements include a wider tread, improved steering on-center feel, a payload increase, and reduced wind noise.

* Includes shaded options

** Other purchase requirements apply

Poor · Worse Than Average · Average · Better Than Average · Excellent · Insufficient Information

Refer to *Section 3: Annotated Vehicle Charts* for an explanation of these charts.

Need More Facts? - All the Facts?

When you've decided on a model line, but need to know
— all feature and option pricing for each model in the line
— how the models in the line differ

Order:

Just the Facts™

Model & Competitor Pricing — Just the Facts™

1993 Ford Explorer 2WD

The 1993 Explorer 2WD is available in four different model editions with two- or four-door applications. The two-door Explorer is available with XL, Sport, and Eddie Bauer trim packages. The four-door Explorer is available with XL, XLT, and Eddie Bauer trim packages. New for 1993, the Explorer offers both deep dish cast aluminum wheels and spoke design steel wheels, standard lower rocker panel moldings, six new exterior colors, freshened seat designs and three new interior colors (Ruby Red, Royal Blue, and Opal Grey). The standard Explorer powertrain consists of Ford's 160-horsepower 4.0L EFI V-6 engine and 5-speed manual overdrive transmission. For information on the 4WD model, order Report #324006.

Standard features: (unless otherwise indicated)

Prices

	XL Sport Utility 2 Door	XL Sport Utility 4 Door	Sport Sport Utility 2 Door	XLT Sport Utility 4 Door	Eddie Bauer Sport Utility 2 Door	Eddie Bauer Sport Utility 4 Door
Invoice	$14,829	$15,501	$15,706	$17,391	$18,621	$19,808
Retail	$16,652	$17,416	$17,649	$19,564	$20,961	$22,311
Destination	$485	$485	$485	$485	$485	$485
Gas Guzzler	$0	$0	$0	$0	$0	$0
Luxury Tax	$0	$0	$0	$0	$0	$0
TOTAL INVOICE	$15,314	$15,986	$16,191	$17,876	$19,106	$20,293
TOTAL RETAIL	$17,137	$17,901	$18,134	$20,049	$21,446	$22,796
Consumer Rebate	None	None	None	None	None	None
dealer Incentive	None	None	None	None	None	None

Comparable Models

	Invoice	Retail
Chevrolet S-10 Blazer 4 Door Wagon	$13,471	$15,085
Jeep Cherokee Laredo 4Door Wagon	$14,145	$15,810
Toyota 4Runner SR5 V6 4Door Wagon	$15,394	$18,218
Nissan Pathfinder XE-V6 4Door Wagon	$14,847	$16,635
GMC S-15 Jimmy 2 Door Wagon	$12,556	$14,060

Note: All comparable models belong to the same class as the vehicle in this report. Individual **Just the Facts®** reports are available for these models and additional comparable vehicles not listed here.

All manufacturer and product names and logos are trademarks or registered trademarks of their respective holders. This report was compiled solely by IntelliChoice, Inc.. IntelliChoice, Inc. is an independent information research firm not sponsered by or associated with any automobile manufacturer. We have carefully researched and compiled the information contained herein. However, IntelliChoice, Inc. assumes no responsibilty for errors or omissions. All prices and specificationre subject to change without notice.

Pg. 1

Includes:

- Latest dealer and consumer rebates
- Information provided for each car in the line, not just for one specific model!!
- Complete pricing and feature information, selected safety and specification information
- Competitor model prices also included
- Latest information - updated daily
- Easy to read and understand
- Shipped 1st class within 24 hours, or faxed immediately

To order your copy of the Just the Facts™ report

call 1-800-227-2665 ext 1, or complete the request form in back of the book.

Just the Facts™

Up to 6 vehicles

All information in the report is provided for the model line (up to 6 vehicles), not just on a single vehicle.

Complete Price Breakout

Dealer Cost (factory invoice), retail price, fees, gas and/or luxury car tax clearly shown for each car.

Rebates, Incentives, Discount Financing

The latest factory-to-consumer and factory-to-dealer incentive programs.

Competitor Model Pricing

Provided for up to 6 competitor vehicles. For instance, a Ford Taurus report also shows pricing for Buick Century Custom, Honda Accord LX, Mercury Sable GS, Chevrolet Euro Lumina, and 2 other models.

All Available Equipment

Standard equipment is shown, plus availability, order code, dealer cost, and list price for all factory installed, and some dealer installed, optional equipment. Option package content is shown, as well as dealer cost and list price.

Safety Information

Availability of anti-lock brakes, driver airbag, passenger airbag, and automatic seatbelts, plus U.S. Government and insurance industry results for crash tests, stopping distance, and injury ratings.

Plus

U.S. Government complaint file, industry theft rating, collision cost rating, interior and exterior dimensions, warranty information, and where each vehicle is built.

Designed to be Easy and Useful

Every element of the report has been designed to be simple to use, clear, understandable, and friendly.

$14.95

(VISA, Mastercard, Personal Check)

Delivery Choices

Shipping	Price		Delivery
1st class mail	$14.95		Included
Instant Fax	$14.95	+	$6.00
Next-Day Air	$14.95	+	$12.50
2nd-Day Air	$14.95	+	$7.50

***To order call:* 1-800-227-2655**

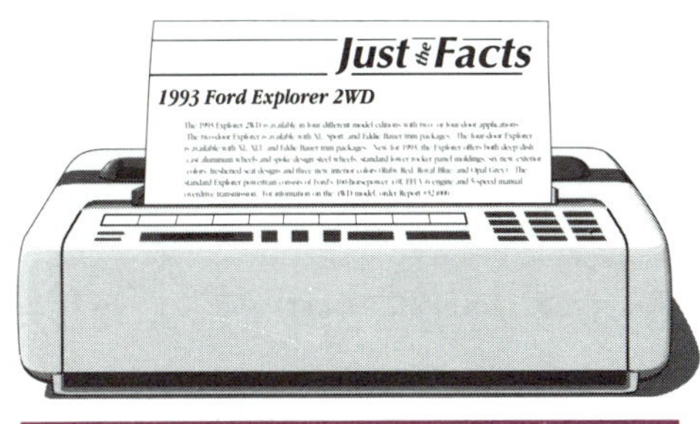

Immediate Faxing Available

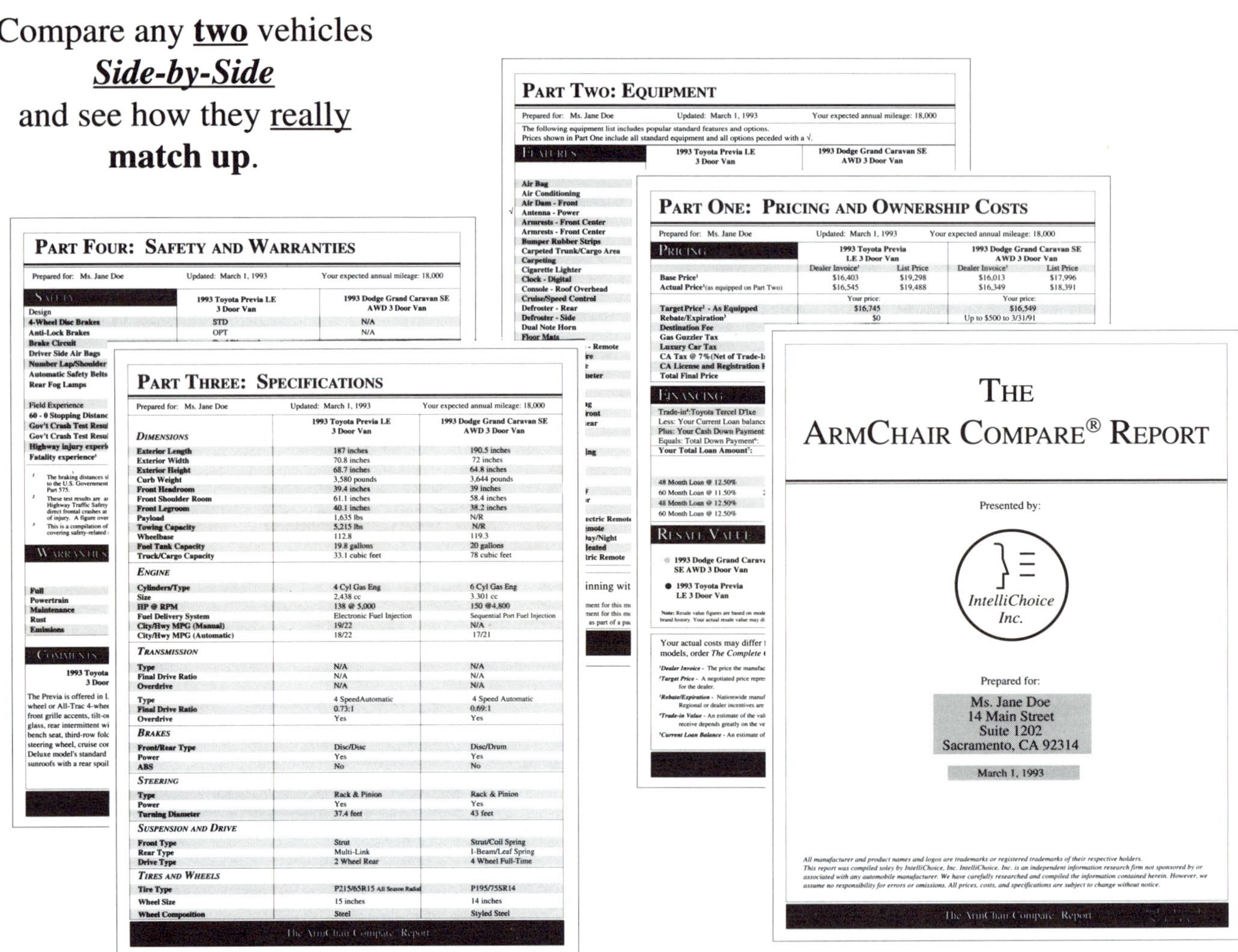

The ArmChair Compare® Report

Includes everything from the Just-the-Facts report shown on the previous pages, PLUS:

Direct Comparison

This report shows any two competitive models of your choice in a side-by-side comparison. Use it to see just how the cars "stack up" in features, prices, safety, ownership costs, and specifications.

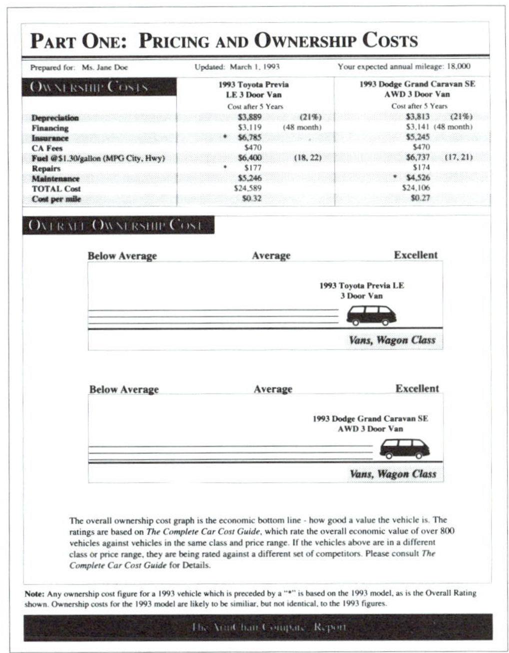

PART ONE: PRICING AND OWNERSHIP COSTS

Prepared for: Ms. Jane Doe | Updated: March 1, 1993 | Your expected annual mileage: 18,000

OWNERSHIP COSTS	1993 Toyota Previa LE 3 Door Van — Cost after 5 Years		1993 Dodge Grand Caravan SE AWD 3 Door Van — Cost after 5 Years	
Depreciation	$3,889	(21%)	$3,813	(21%)
Financing	$3,119	(48 month)	$3,141	(48 month)
Insurance	* $6,785		$5,245	
CA Fees	$470		$470	
Fuel @$1.30/gallon (MPG City, Hwy)	$6,400	(18, 22)	$6,737	(17, 21)
Repairs	* $177		$174	
Maintenance	$5,246		* $4,526	
TOTAL Cost	$24,589		$24,106	
Cost per mile	$0.32		$0.27	

OVERALL OWNERSHIP COST

The overall ownership cost graph is the economic bottom line - how good a value the vehicle is. The ratings are based on *The Complete Car Cost Guide*, which rate the overall economic value of over 800 vehicles against vehicles in the same class and price range. If the vehicles above are in a different class or price range, they are being rated against a different set of competitors. Please consult *The Complete Car Cost Guide* for Details.

Note: Any ownership cost figure for a 1993 vehicle which is preceded by a "*" is based on the 1993 model, as is the Overall Rating shown. Ownership costs for the 1993 model are likely to be similiar, but not identical, to the 1993 figures.

The ArmChair Compare Report

Personalized Ownership Costs

The information in this report is customized to your state and how many miles per year you drive.

Trade-In Value

The current value of your existing car.

Financing Costs

Monthly payments based on latest rates, and your personal down payment, and your trade-in value.

Expected Resale Value

The value of your new car in 5 years.

Additional Dimensions and Specifications

See how the two vehicles compare on horsepower, brakes, turning diameter, and much more.

IntelliChoice Inc.

$19.95

(VISA, Mastercard, Personal Check)

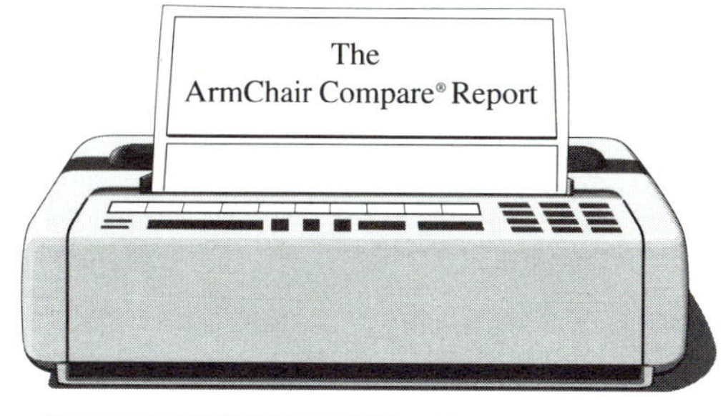

Immediate Faxing Available

Delivery Choices

Shipping	Price		Delivery
1st class mail	$19.95		Included
Instant Fax	$19.95	+	$6.00
Next-Day Air	$19.95	+	$12.50
2nd-Day Air	$19.95	+	$7.50

***To order call:* 1-800-227-2655**

The ArmChair Compare® Report

Ford Ranger XL SuperCab
2 Door Extended Cab

 2.3L 98 hp Gas Fuel Inject.

 4 Cylinder In-Line

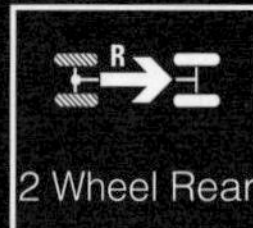 Manual 5 Speed

 2 Wheel Rear

Manual Seatbelts Only

Small Pickup

Purchase Price

Car Item	Dealer Cost	List
Base Price	**$10,409**	**$11,709**
Anti-Lock Brakes	Std	Std
Automatic 4 Speed	$842	$990
3.0L 145 hp Gas	$416	$489
Air Conditioning	$663	$780
Power Steering	Std	Std
Cruise Control	$325	$383
All Wheel Drive	N/A	N/A
AM/FM Stereo Cassette	$267	$315
Steering Wheel, Tilt	Grp	Grp
Power Windows	N/A	N/A
***Options Price**	$683	$804
***Total Price**	**$11,092**	**$12,513**
Target Price	$11,788	
Destination Charge	$460	
Avg. Tax & Fees	$742	
Total Target $	**$12,990**	
Average Dealer Option Cost:	***85%***	

Ownership Costs

Cost Area	5 Year Cost	Rate
Depreciation	$5,744	Worse Than Average
Financing ($261/month)	$2,139	
Insurance (Rating 8)	$7,432	Worse Than Average
State Fees	$520	
Fuel (Hwy 25 City 19)	$3,929	Better Than Average
Maintenance	$3,409	Better Than Average
Repairs	$709	Better Than Average

Ownership Cost By Year

$2,000 $4,000 $6,000 $8,000

1993 1994 1995 1996 1997

Warranty/Maintenance Info

Item		Rate
Major Tune-Up	$124	Excellent
Minor Tune-Up	$79	Better Than Average
Brake Service	$210	Average
Overall Warranty	3 yr/36k	Average
Drivetrain Warranty	3 yr/36k	Average
Rust Warranty	6 yr/100k	Better Than Average
Maintenance Warranty	N/A	
Roadside Assistance	N/A	

Resale Value

1993	1994	1995	1996	1997
$9,199	$8,704	$8,398	$7,870	$7,246

Ownership Costs (5yr)

Average	This Car
$24,676	$23,882
Cost/Mile 35¢	Cost/Mile 34¢

Cumulative Costs

	1993	1994	1995	1996	1997
Annual	$6,954	$3,660	$4,253	$4,117	$4,898
Total	$6,954	$10,614	$14,867	$18,984	$23,882

Ownership Cost Rating

Excellent

The 1993 Ranger Supercab is available in six models - XL, XLT, STX, and in either two- or four-wheel drive pickups. New for 1993, the XL two-wheel drive has all-new sheet metal with modern, aerodynamic styling, including limo-style doors and flusher glass. The interior is restyled with new seat trim and sew styles, steering wheel, and instrument panel appliques. Six new exterior colors are offered, as well as an optional payload package. Corrosion protection upgrades have also been made.

Ford Ranger XLT SuperCab
2 Door Extended Cab

 2.3L 98 hp Gas Fuel Inject.

 4 Cylinder In-Line

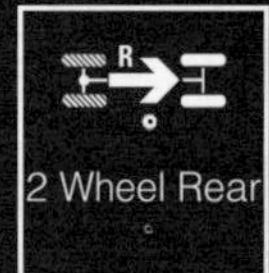 Manual 5 Speed

 2 Wheel Rear

Manual Seatbelts Only

Small Pickup

4WD Model Shown

Purchase Price

Car Item	Dealer Cost	List
Base Price	**$10,794**	**$12,147**
Anti-Lock Brakes	Std	Std
Automatic 4 Speed	$842	$990
3.0L 145 hp Gas	$416	$489
Air Conditioning	$663	$780
Power Steering	Std	Std
Cruise Control	$325	$383
All Wheel Drive	N/A	N/A
AM/FM Stereo Cassette	$117	$138
Steering Wheel, Tilt	Grp	Grp
Power Windows	$312	** $367
***Options Price**	$533	$627
***Total Price**	**$11,327**	**$12,774**
Target Price	$12,046	
Destination Charge	$460	
Avg. Tax & Fees	$757	
Total Target $	**$13,263**	
Average Dealer Option Cost:	***85%***	

Ownership Costs

Cost Area	5 Year Cost	Rate
Depreciation	$5,999	Worse Than Average
Financing ($267/month)	$2,185	
Insurance (Rating 8)	$7,432	Worse Than Average
State Fees	$529	
Fuel (Hwy 25 City 19)	$3,929	Better Than Average
Maintenance	$3,409	Better Than Average
Repairs	$709	Better Than Average

Ownership Cost By Year

$2,000 $4,000 $6,000 $8,000

1993 1994 1995 1996 1997

Warranty/Maintenance Info

Item		Rate
Major Tune-Up	$124	Excellent
Minor Tune-Up	$79	Better Than Average
Brake Service	$210	Average
Overall Warranty	3 yr/36k	Average
Drivetrain Warranty	3 yr/36k	Average
Rust Warranty	6 yr/100k	Better Than Average
Maintenance Warranty	N/A	
Roadside Assistance	N/A	

Resale Value

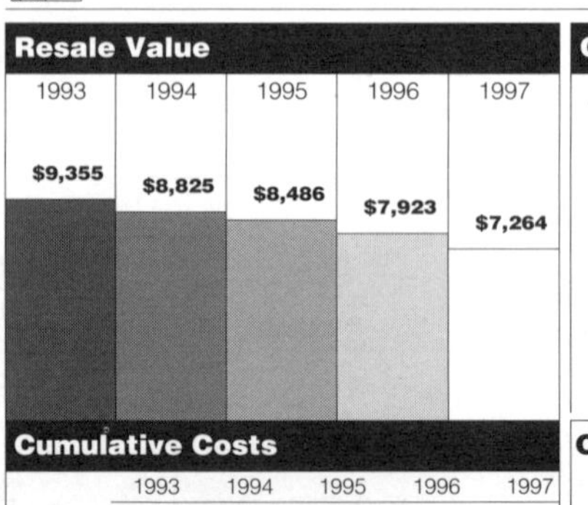

1993	1994	1995	1996	1997
$9,355	$8,825	$8,486	$7,923	$7,264

Ownership Costs (5yr)

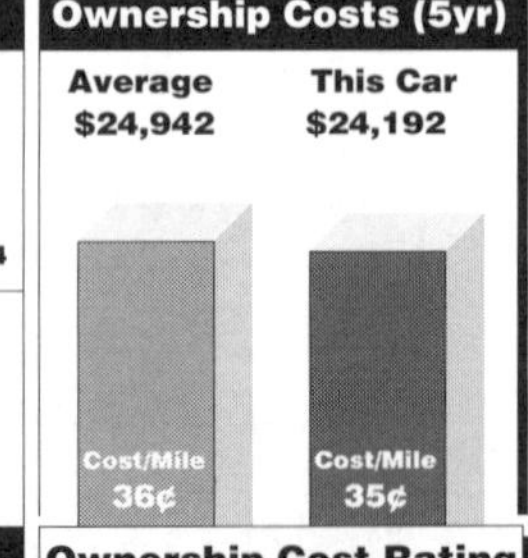

Average	This Car
$24,942	$24,192
Cost/Mile 36¢	Cost/Mile 35¢

Cumulative Costs

	1993	1994	1995	1996	1997
Annual	$7,092	$3,711	$4,297	$4,158	$4,934
Total	$7,092	$10,803	$15,100	$19,258	$24,192

Ownership Cost Rating

Better Than Average

The 1993 Ranger Supercab is available in six models - XL, XLT, STX, and in either two- or four-wheel drive pickups. New for 1993, the XLT two-wheel drive has all-new sheet metal with modern, aerodynamic styling, including limo-style doors and flusher glass. The interior is restyled with new seat trim and sew styles, steering wheel, and instrument panel appliques. Other new features include single key locks, tailgate latch improvements, corrosion protection upgrades, and an optional payload increase.

* Includes shaded options

** Other purchase requirements apply

Poor | Worse Than Average | Average | Better Than Average | Excellent | Insufficient Information

Refer to *Section 3: Annotated Vehicle Charts* for an explanation of these charts.

Ford Ranger STX SuperCab

2 Door Extended Cab

3.0L 145 hp Gas Fuel Inject.	6 Cylinder "V"	Manual 5 Speed	2 Wheel Rear	Manual Seatbelts Only

Small Pickup

4WD Regular Cab Shown

Purchase Price

Car Item	Dealer Cost	List
Base Price	**$11,513**	**$12,964**
Anti-Lock Brakes	Std	Std
Automatic 4 Speed	$842	$990
4.0L 160 hp Gas	$152	$179
Air Conditioning	$663	$780
Power Steering	Std	Std
Cruise Control	Pkg	Pkg
All Wheel Drive	N/A	N/A
AM/FM Stereo Cassette	$117	$138
Steering Wheel, Tilt	Grp	Grp
Power Windows	$312	** $367
***Options Price**	$117	$138
***Total Price**	**$11,630**	**$13,102**
Target Price	$12,385	
Destination Charge	$460	
Avg. Tax & Fees	$778	
Total Target $	**$13,623**	
Average Dealer Option Cost:	***85%***	

Ownership Costs

Cost Area	5 Year Cost	Rate
Depreciation	$6,852	Worse Than Average
Financing ($274/month)	$2,244	
Insurance (Rating 8)	$7,432	Average
State Fees	$542	
Fuel (Hwy 25 City 19)	$3,929	Better Than Average
Maintenance	$3,562	Better Than Average
Repairs	$709	Better Than Average

Warranty/Maintenance Info

Item		Rate
Major Tune-Up	$124	Excellent
Minor Tune-Up	$79	Better Than Average
Brake Service	$210	Average
Overall Warranty	3 yr/36k	Average
Drivetrain Warranty	3 yr/36k	Average
Rust Warranty	6 yr/100k	Better Than Average
Maintenance Warranty	N/A	
Roadside Assistance	N/A	

The 1993 Ranger Supercab is available in six models - XL, XLT, STX, and in either two- or four-wheel drive pickups. New for 1993, the STX two-wheel drive has all-new sheet metal with modern, aerodynamic styling, including limo-style doors and flusher glass. The interior is restyled with new seat trim and sew styles, steering wheel, and instrument panel appliques. Other new features include single key locks, tailgate latch improvements, corrosion protection upgrades, and an optional payload increase.

Ownership Cost By Year

Resale Value

1993	1994	1995	1996	1997
$9,447	$8,770	$8,288	$7,578	$6,771

Ownership Costs (5yr)

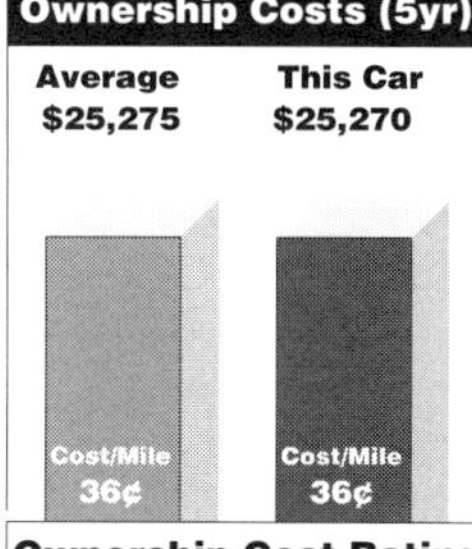

Cumulative Costs

	1993	1994	1995	1996	1997
Annual	$7,389	$3,879	$4,525	$4,316	$5,161
Total	$7,389	$11,268	$15,793	$20,109	$25,270

Ownership Cost Rating

Average

Ford Ranger XL 4WD

2 Door Regular Cab

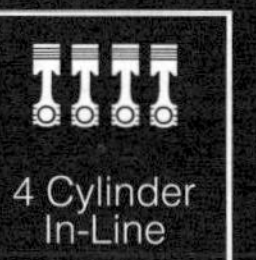

2.3L 98 hp Gas Fuel Inject.	4 Cylinder In-Line	Manual 5 Speed	4 Wheel On-Demand	Manual Seatbelts Only

Small Pickup

2WD Model Shown

Purchase Price

Car Item	Dealer Cost	List
Base Price	**$11,737**	**$12,644**
Anti-Lock Brakes	Std	Std
Automatic 4 Speed	$842	$990
3.0L 145 hp Gas	$514	$605
Air Conditioning	$663	$780
Power Steering	Std	Std
Cruise Control	$325	** $383
4 Whl On-Demand Dr.	Std	Std
AM/FM Stereo Cassette	$267	$315
Steering Wheel, Tilt	Grp	Grp
Power Windows	N/A	N/A
***Options Price**	$781	$920
***Total Price**	**$12,518**	**$13,564**
Target Price	$13,337	
Destination Charge	$460	
Avg. Tax & Fees	$830	
Total Target $	**$14,627**	
Average Dealer Option Cost:	***85%***	

Ownership Costs

Cost Area	5 Year Cost	Rate
Depreciation	$7,281	Average
Financing ($294/month)	$2,410	
Insurance (Rating 10)	$7,689	Worse Than Average
State Fees	$560	
Fuel (Hwy 24 City 18)	$4,117	Average
Maintenance	$3,339	Better Than Average
Repairs	$840	Average

Warranty/Maintenance Info

Item		Rate
Major Tune-Up	$124	Excellent
Minor Tune-Up	$79	Better Than Average
Brake Service	$210	Average
Overall Warranty	3 yr/36k	Average
Drivetrain Warranty	3 yr/36k	Average
Rust Warranty	6 yr/100k	Better Than Average
Maintenance Warranty	N/A	
Roadside Assistance	N/A	

The 1993 Ranger is available in six models - XL, XLT, STX, and in either two- or four-wheel drive pickups. New for 1993, the XL four-wheel drive has all-new exterior sheet metal with modern aerodynamic styling, including limo-style doors and flusher glass. Other new features include an increased differentiation, redesigned wheels, an integral fog lamp valance panel, and a 3.0L V-6 replaces the 2.9L. Also new are seven exterior colors, corrosion protection upgrades, and a payload increase.

Ownership Cost By Year

Resale Value

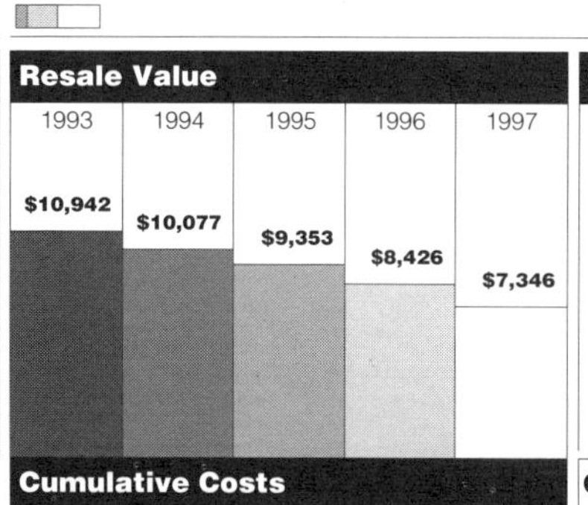

1993	1994	1995	1996	1997
$10,942	$10,077	$9,353	$8,426	$7,346

Ownership Costs (5yr)

Cumulative Costs

	1993	1994	1995	1996	1997
Annual	$7,054	$4,209	$4,815	$4,668	$5,490
Total	$7,054	$11,263	$16,078	$20,746	$26,236

Ownership Cost Rating

Average

* Includes shaded options

** Other purchase requirements apply

 Poor  Worse Than Average  Average 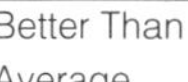 Better Than Average  Excellent 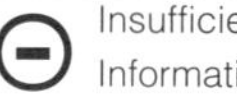 Insufficient Information

Refer to *Section 3: Annotated Vehicle Charts* for an explanation of these charts.

Ford Ranger XLT 4WD

2 Door Regular Cab

2.3L 98 hp Gas Fuel Inject.	4 Cylinder In-Line	Manual 5 Speed	4 Wheel On-Demand	Manual Seatbelts Only

Purchase Price

Car Item	Dealer Cost	List
Base Price	**$12,526**	**$14,115**
Anti-Lock Brakes	Std	Std
Automatic 4 Speed	$842	$990
3.0L 145 hp Gas	$514	$605
Air Conditioning	$663	$780
Power Steering	Std	Std
Cruise Control	$325	** $383
4 Whl On-Demand Dr.	Std	Std
AM/FM Stereo Cassette	$117	$138
Steering Wheel, Tilt	Grp	Grp
Power Windows	$312	** $367
***Options Price**	$631	$743
***Total Price**	**$13,157**	**$14,858**
Target Price	$14,038	
Destination Charge	$460	
Avg. Tax & Fees	$878	
Total Target $	**$15,376**	
Average Dealer Option Cost:	***85%***	

Ownership Costs

Cost Area	5 Year Cost	Rate
Depreciation	$7,454	Worse Than Average
Financing ($309/month)	$2,533	
Insurance (Rating 10)	$7,689	Worse Than Average
State Fees	$613	
Fuel (Hwy 24 City 18)	$4,117	Average
Maintenance	$3,339	Better Than Average
Repairs	$840	Average

Ownership Cost By Year

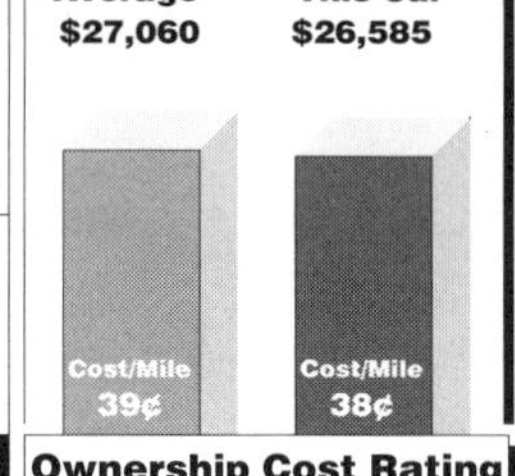

Warranty/Maintenance Info

Major Tune-Up	$124	Excellent
Minor Tune-Up	$79	Better Than Average
Brake Service	$210	Average
Overall Warranty	3 yr/36k	Average
Drivetrain Warranty	3 yr/36k	Average
Rust Warranty	6 yr/100k	Better Than Average
Maintenance Warranty	N/A	
Roadside Assistance	N/A	

Resale Value

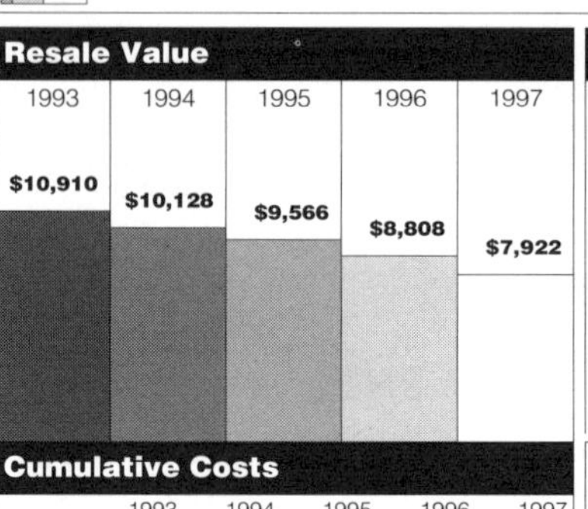

1993	1994	1995	1996	1997
$10,910	$10,128	$9,566	$8,808	$7,922

Ownership Costs (5yr)

	Average	This Car
Total	$27,060	$26,585
Cost/Mile	39¢	38¢

Cumulative Costs

	1993	1994	1995	1996	1997
Annual	$7,899	$4,177	$4,688	$4,517	$5,304
Total	$7,899	$12,076	$16,764	$21,281	$26,585

Ownership Cost Rating

Better Than Average

The 1993 Ranger is available in six models - XL, XLT, STX, and in either two- or four-wheel drive pickups. New for 1993, the XLT four-wheel drive has all-new exterior sheet metal with modern, aerodynamic styling, including limo-style doors and flusher glass. The interior is freshened with all-new seat and door trims, instrument panel appliques, and cluster graphics. Other new features include larger tires, increased differentiation, an integral fog lamp valance panel, and alloy wheels.

Ford Ranger STX 4WD

2 Door Regular Cab

3.0L 145 hp Gas Fuel Inject.	6 Cylinder "V"	Manual 5 Speed	4 Wheel On-Demand	Manual Seatbelts Only

Small Pickup

Purchase Price

Car Item	Dealer Cost	List
Base Price	**$13,183**	**$14,861**
Anti-Lock Brakes	Std	Std
Automatic 4 Speed	$842	$990
4.0L 160 hp Gas	$152	$179
Air Conditioning	$663	$780
Power Steering	Std	Std
Cruise Control	$325	$383
4 Whl On-Demand Dr.	Std	Std
AM/FM Stereo Cassette	$117	$138
Steering Wheel, Tilt	Grp	Grp
7 Foot Bed	$186	$212
***Options Price**	$117	$138
***Total Price**	**$13,300**	**$14,999**
Target Price	$14,209	
Destination Charge	$460	
Avg. Tax & Fees	$888	
Total Target $	**$15,557**	
Average Dealer Option Cost:	***85%***	

Ownership Costs

Cost Area	5 Year Cost	Rate
Depreciation	$8,255	Poor
Financing ($313/month)	$2,562	
Insurance (Rating 10)	$7,689	Worse Than Average
State Fees	$619	
Fuel (Hwy 24 City 18)	$4,117	Average
Maintenance	$3,391	Better Than Average
Repairs	$840	Average

Ownership Cost By Year

$2,000 · $4,000 · $6,000 · $8,000 · $10,000

1993 · 1994 · 1995 · 1996 · 1997

Warranty/Maintenance Info

Major Tune-Up	$124	Excellent
Minor Tune-Up	$79	Better Than Average
Brake Service	$210	Average
Overall Warranty	3 yr/36k	Average
Drivetrain Warranty	3 yr/36k	Average
Rust Warranty	6 yr/100k	Better Than Average
Maintenance Warranty	N/A	
Roadside Assistance	N/A	

Resale Value

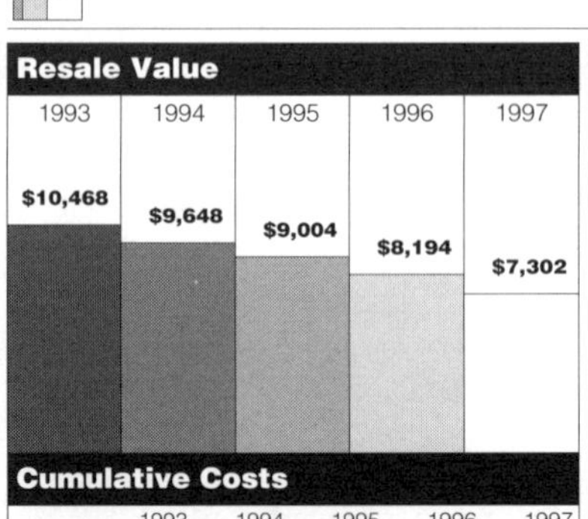

1993	1994	1995	1996	1997
$10,468	$9,648	$9,004	$8,194	$7,302

Ownership Costs (5yr)

	Average	This Car
Total	$27,203	$27,473
Cost/Mile	39¢	39¢

Cumulative Costs

	1993	1994	1995	1996	1997
Annual	$8,536	$4,225	$4,800	$4,577	$5,335
Total	$8,536	$12,761	$17,561	$22,138	$27,473

Ownership Cost Rating

Average

The 1993 Ranger is available in six models - XL, XLT, STX, and in either two- or four-wheel drive pickups. New for 1993, the STX four-wheel drive sports all-new exterior sheet metal with modern, aerodynamic styling, including limo-style doors and flusher glass. The interior is freshened with all-new seat and door trims, instrument panel appliques, and cluster graphics. Other new features include larger diameter tires (P235 and P265), increased differentiation, alloy wheels, and a payload increase.

* Includes shaded options

** Other purchase requirements apply

Poor · Worse Than Average · Average · Better Than Average · Excellent · Insufficient Information

Refer to *Section 3: Annotated Vehicle Charts* for an explanation of these charts.

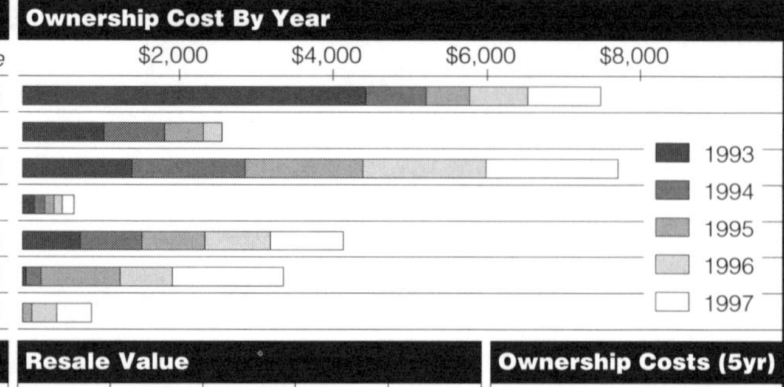

Ford Ranger XL SuperCab 4WD
2 Door Extended Cab

3.0L 145 hp Gas Fuel Inject.

6 Cylinder "V"

Manual 5 Speed

4 Wheel On-Demand

Manual Seatbelts Only

Purchase Price

Car Item	Dealer Cost	List
Base Price	**$13,450**	**$15,165**
Anti-Lock Brakes	Std	Std
Automatic 4 Speed	$842	$990
4.0L 160 hp Gas	$667	$784
Air Conditioning	$663	$780
Power Steering	Std	Std
Cruise Control	$325	$383
4 Whl On-Demand Dr.	Std	Std
AM/FM Stereo Cassette	$267	$315
Steering Wheel, Tilt	Grp	Grp
Power Windows	N/A	N/A
***Options Price**	$267	$315
***Total Price**	**$13,717**	**$15,480**
Target Price	$14,661	
Destination Charge	$460	
Avg. Tax & Fees	$915	
Total Target $	**$16,036**	
Average Dealer Option Cost:	***85%***	

Ownership Costs

Cost Area	5 Year Cost	Rate
Depreciation	$7,257	Average
Financing ($322/month)	$2,642	
Insurance (Rating 11)	$7,902	Average
State Fees	$638	
Fuel (Hwy 24 City 18)	$4,117	Average
Maintenance	$3,339	Better Than Average
Repairs	$840	Average

Ownership Cost By Year

$2,000 $4,000 $6,000 $8,000 — 1993, 1994, 1995, 1996, 1997

Warranty/Maintenance Info

Major Tune-Up	$124	Excellent
Minor Tune-Up	$79	Better Than Average
Brake Service	$210	Average
Overall Warranty	3 yr/36k	Average
Drivetrain Warranty	3 yr/36k	Average
Rust Warranty	6 yr/100k	Better Than Average
Maintenance Warranty	N/A	
Roadside Assistance	N/A	

Resale Value

1993	1994	1995	1996	1997
$10,662	$10,186	$9,872	$9,390	$8,779

Ownership Costs (5yr)

Average	This Car
$27,692	$26,735
Cost/Mile 40¢	Cost/Mile 38¢

The 1993 Ranger Supercab is available in six models - XL, XLT, STX, and in either two- or four-wheel drive pickups. New for 1993, the XL four-wheel drive has all-new sheet metal with modern, aerodynamic styling, including limo-style doors and flusher glass. The interior is restyled with new seat trim and sew styles, steering wheel, and instrument panel appliques. Other new features include larger diameter tires (P235 and P265), 3.0L V-6 replaces the 2.9L, optional alloy wheels, and wheel flares.

Cumulative Costs

	1993	1994	1995	1996	1997
Annual	$8,897	$3,951	$4,510	$4,298	$5,079
Total	$8,897	$12,848	$17,358	$21,656	$26,735

Ownership Cost Rating

Excellent

Ford Ranger XLT SuperCab 4WD
2 Door Extended Cab

3.0L 145 hp Gas Fuel Inject.
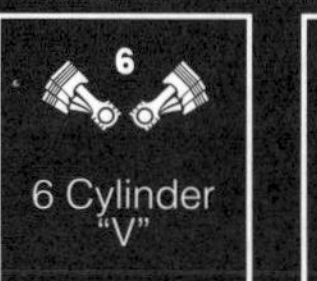
6 Cylinder "V"
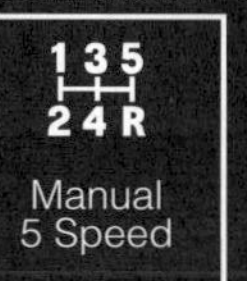
Manual 5 Speed
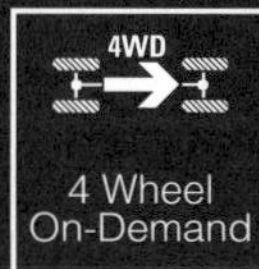
4 Wheel On-Demand

Manual Seatbelts Only

Small Pickup

Purchase Price

Car Item	Dealer Cost	List
Base Price	**$14,138**	**$15,947**
Anti-Lock Brakes	Std	Std
Automatic 4 Speed	$842	$990
4.0L 160 hp Gas	$568	$668
Air Conditioning	$663	$780
Power Steering	Std	Std
Cruise Control	$325	$383
4 Whl On-Demand Dr.	Std	Std
AM/FM Stereo Cassette	$117	$138
Steering Wheel, Tilt	Grp	Grp
Power Windows	$312	** $367
***Options Price**	$117	$138
***Total Price**	**$14,255**	**$16,085**
Target Price	$15,256	
Destination Charge	$460	
Avg. Tax & Fees	$951	
Total Target $	**$16,667**	
Average Dealer Option Cost:	***85%***	

Ownership Costs

Cost Area	5 Year Cost	Rate
Depreciation	$7,877	Average
Financing ($335/month)	$2,745	
Insurance (Rating 11)	$7,902	Average
State Fees	$661	
Fuel (Hwy 24 City 18)	$4,117	Average
Maintenance	$3,339	Better Than Average
Repairs	$840	Average

Ownership Cost By Year

$2,000 $4,000 $6,000 $8,000 — 1993, 1994, 1995, 1996, 1997

Warranty/Maintenance Info

Major Tune-Up	$124	Excellent
Minor Tune-Up	$79	Better Than Average
Brake Service	$210	Average
Overall Warranty	3 yr/36k	Average
Drivetrain Warranty	3 yr/36k	Average
Rust Warranty	6 yr/100k	Better Than Average
Maintenance Warranty	N/A	
Roadside Assistance	N/A	

Resale Value

1993	1994	1995	1996	1997
$10,994	$10,437	$10,046	$9,483	$8,790

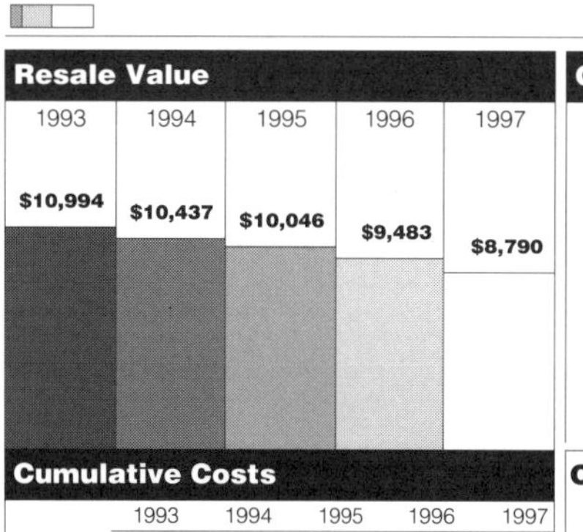

Ownership Costs (5yr)

Average	This Car
$28,308	$27,481
Cost/Mile 40¢	Cost/Mile 39¢

The 1993 Ranger Supercab is available in six models - XL, XLT, STX, and in either two- or four-wheel drive pickups. New for 1993, the XLT four-wheel drive has all-new sheet metal with modern, aerodynamic styling, including limo-style doors and flusher glass. The interior is restyled with new seat trim , steering wheel, and instrument panel appliques. Other new features include improved steering on-center feel, larger diameter tires, corrosion protection upgrades, and optional alloy wheels.

Cumulative Costs

	1993	1994	1995	1996	1997
Annual	$9,246	$4,070	$4,611	$4,390	$5,164
Total	$9,246	$13,316	$17,927	$22,317	$27,481

Ownership Cost Rating

Better Than Average

* Includes shaded options

** Other purchase requirements apply

 Poor  Worse Than Average  Average 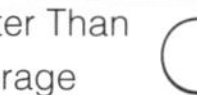 Better Than Average  Excellent 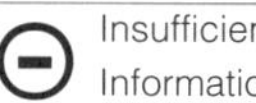 Insufficient Information

Refer to *Section 3: Annotated Vehicle Charts* for an explanation of these charts.

Ford Ranger STX SuperCab 4WD
2 Door Extended Cab

3.0L 145 hp Gas Fuel Inject.

6 Cylinder "V"

Manual 5 Speed

4 Wheel On-Demand

Manual Seatbelts Only

Regular Cab Shown

Purchase Price

Car Item	Dealer Cost	List
Base Price	**$14,656**	**$16,535**
Anti-Lock Brakes	Std	Std
Automatic 4 Speed	$842	$990
4.0L 160 hp Gas	$152	$179
Air Conditioning	$663	$780
Power Steering	Std	Std
Cruise Control	Pkg	Pkg
4 Whl On-Demand Dr.	Std	Std
AM/FM Stereo Cassette	$117	$138
Steering Wheel, Tilt	Grp	Grp
Power Windows	$315	** $367
***Options Price**	$117	$138
***Total Price**	**$14,773**	**$16,673**
Target Price	$15,826	
Destination Charge	$460	
Avg. Tax & Fees	$985	
Total Target $	**$17,271**	
Average Dealer Option Cost:	***85%***	

Ownership Costs

Cost Area	5 Year Cost	Rate
Depreciation	$8,846	Poor
Financing ($347/month)	$2,845	
Insurance (Rating 11)	$7,902	Average
State Fees	$685	
Fuel (Hwy 24 City 18)	$4,117	Average
Maintenance	$3,391	Better Than Average
Repairs	$840	Average

Ownership Cost By Year

$2,000 $4,000 $6,000 $8,000 $10,000

1993 1994 1995 1996 1997

Warranty/Maintenance Info

Major Tune-Up	$124	Excellent
Minor Tune-Up	$79	Better Than Average
Brake Service	$210	Average
Overall Warranty	3 yr/36k	Average
Drivetrain Warranty	3 yr/36k	Average
Rust Warranty	6 yr/100k	Better Than Average
Maintenance Warranty	N/A	
Roadside Assistance	N/A	

Resale Value

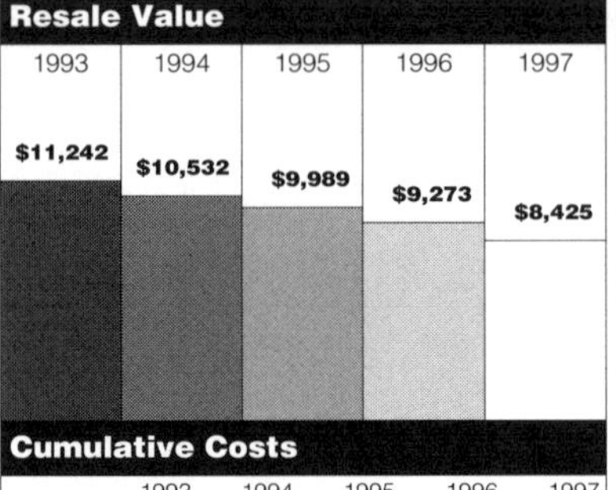

1993	1994	1995	1996	1997
$11,242	$10,532	$9,989	$9,273	$8,425

Ownership Costs (5yr)

Average	This Car
$28,905	$28,626
Cost/Mile 41¢	Cost/Mile 41¢

The 1993 Ranger Supercab is available in six models - XL, XLT, STX, and in either two- or four-wheel drive pickups. New for 1993, the STX four-wheel drive has all-new sheet metal with modern, aerodynamic styling, including limo-style doors and flusher glass. The interior is restyled with new seat trim , steering wheel, and instrument panel appliques. Other new features include available payload increase, larger diameter tires, corrosion protection upgrades, and optional 15-in. alloy wheels.

Cumulative Costs

	1993	1994	1995	1996	1997
Annual	$9,649	$4,259	$4,811	$4,560	$5,347
Total	$9,649	$13,908	$18,719	$23,279	$28,626

Ownership Cost Rating

Average

Ford Taurus GL
4 Door Wagon

3.0L 140 hp Gas Fuel Inject.

6 Cylinder "V"

Automatic 4 Speed

2 Wheel Front

Driver Airbag Psngr Opt

Midsize Wagon

Purchase Price

Car Item	Dealer Cost	List
Base Price	**$14,298**	**$16,656**
Anti-Lock Brakes	$506	$595
Manual Transmission	N/A	N/A
3.8L 140 hp Gas	$472	** $555
Air Conditioning	Pkg	Pkg
Power Steering	Std	Std
Cruise Control	$191	$224
All Wheel Drive	N/A	N/A
AM/FM Stereo Cassette	$145	$171
Steering Wheel, Tilt	Std	Std
Power Windows	$303	$356
***Options Price**	$639	$751
***Total Price**	**$14,937**	**$17,407**
Target Price	$16,202	
Destination Charge	$490	
Avg. Tax & Fees	$1,014	
Total Target $	**$17,706**	
Average Dealer Option Cost:	***85%***	

Ownership Costs

Cost Area	5 Year Cost	Rate
Depreciation	$8,148	Better Than Average
Financing ($356/month)	$2,917	
Insurance (Rating 4)	$6,658	Excellent
State Fees	$715	
Fuel (Hwy 30 City 21)	$3,405	Excellent
Maintenance	$4,173	Average
Repairs	$709	Average

Ownership Cost By Year

$2,000 $4,000 $6,000 $8,000 $10,000

1993 1994 1995 1996 1997

Warranty/Maintenance Info

Major Tune-Up	$137	Excellent
Minor Tune-Up	$87	Excellent
Brake Service	$271	Worse Than Average
Overall Warranty	3 yr/36k	Average
Drivetrain Warranty	3 yr/36k	Average
Rust Warranty	6 yr/100k	Better Than Average
Maintenance Warranty	N/A	
Roadside Assistance	N/A	

Resale Value

1993	1994	1995	1996	1997
$14,768	$13,253	$12,087	$10,805	$9,558

Ownership Costs (5yr)

Average	This Car
$29,067	$26,725
Cost/Mile 42¢	Cost/Mile 38¢

The 1993 Ford Taurus wagon is available in two models - GL and LX. New for 1993, the GL wagon features body-colored bumpers, all new seat trim, and a variety of new colors. Standard features include an exterior accent group, luggage rack, dual electric remote control mirrors, door trim panels, split bench seat with dual recliners and tinted glass. Optional features include a GL decor/equipment group, a light group, cellular phone, Luxury Convenience group and power moonroof.

Cumulative Costs

	1993	1994	1995	1996	1997
Annual	$6,236	$4,727	$5,350	$4,803	$5,609
Total	$6,236	$10,963	$16,313	$21,116	$26,725

Ownership Cost Rating

Better Than Average

* Includes shaded options

** Other purchase requirements apply

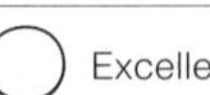

 Poor  Worse Than Average  Average — Better Than Average — Excellent — Insufficient Information

Refer to *Section 3: Annotated Vehicle Charts* for an explanation of these charts.

Ford Taurus LX
4 Door Wagon

3.8L 140 hp Gas Fuel Inject.

6 Cylinder "V"

Automatic 4 Speed

2 Wheel Front

Driver Airbag Psngr Opt

Midsize Wagon

Purchase Price

Car Item	Dealer Cost	List
Base Price	**$17,131**	**$19,989**
Anti-Lock Brakes	$506	$595
Manual Transmission	N/A	N/A
Optional Engine	N/A	N/A
Air Conditioning	Std	Std
Power Steering	Std	Std
Cruise Control	Pkg	Pkg
All Wheel Drive	N/A	N/A
AM/FM Stereo Cassette	$282	$332
Steering Wheel, Tilt	Std	Std
Power Windows	Std	Std
***Options Price**	$282	$332
***Total Price**	**$17,413**	**$20,321**
Target Price	$19,007	
Destination Charge	$490	
Avg. Tax & Fees	$1,183	
Total Target $	**$20,680**	
Average Dealer Option Cost:	***85%***	

Ownership Costs

Cost Area	5 Year Cost	Rate
Depreciation	$9,903	Average
Financing ($416/month)	$3,406	
Insurance (Rating 6)	$6,919	Excellent
State Fees	$832	
Fuel (Hwy 27 City 19)	$3,775	Average
Maintenance	$4,225	Average
Repairs	$709	Better Than Average

Warranty/Maintenance Info

Item	Cost/Coverage	Rate
Major Tune-Up	$138	Excellent
Minor Tune-Up	$87	Excellent
Brake Service	$271	Worse Than Average
Overall Warranty	3 yr/36k	Average
Drivetrain Warranty	3 yr/36k	Average
Rust Warranty	6 yr/100k	Better Than Average
Maintenance Warranty	N/A	
Roadside Assistance	N/A	

Ownership Cost By Year

$2,000 $4,000 $6,000 $8,000 $10,000

1993 1994 1995 1996 1997

Resale Value

1993	1994	1995	1996	1997
$16,094	$14,607	$13,394	$12,093	$10,777

Ownership Costs (5yr)

	Average	This Car
Total	$32,047	$29,769
Cost/Mile	46¢	43¢

Cumulative Costs

	1993	1994	1995	1996	1997
Annual	$8,233	$5,000	$5,657	$5,009	$5,870
Total	$8,233	$13,233	$18,890	$23,899	$29,769

Ownership Cost Rating

Better Than Average

The 1993 Ford Taurus wagon is available in two models - GL and LX. New for 1993, the LX wagon features a new floor console and a variety of new exterior colors. The LX wagon upgrades the GL with a console floor shift, convenience kit, cast aluminum wheels, leather seat trim, and a light group. Other standard features include an exterior accent group, luggage rack, and dual electric remote control mirrors. Optional features include a cellular phone, power moonroof and a Luxury Convenience group.

Geo Tracker Soft Top
2 Door Sport Utility

1.6L 80 hp Gas Fuel Inject.

4 Cylinder In-Line

Manual 5 Speed

2 Wheel Rear

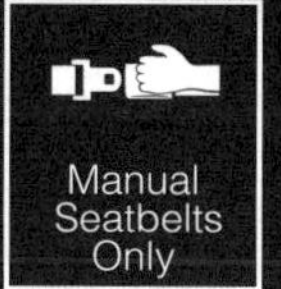
Manual Seatbelts Only

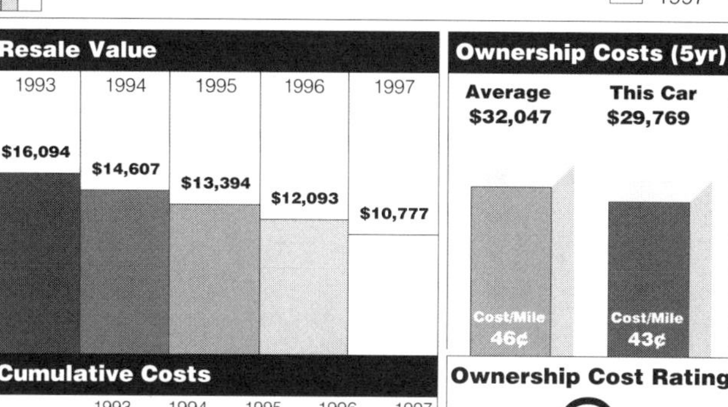

Utility

Purchase Price

Car Item	Dealer Cost	List
Base Price	**$9,834**	**$10,330**
Anti-Lock Brakes	Std	Std
Automatic 3 Speed	$530	$595
Optional Engine	N/A	N/A
Air Conditioning	$663	$745
Power Steering	Pkg	Pkg
Cruise Control	N/A	N/A
All Wheel Drive	N/A	N/A
AM/FM Stereo Cassette	$441	$496
Steering Wheel, Tilt	$102	$115
Power Windows	N/A	N/A
***Options Price**	$1,104	$1,241
***Total Price**	**$10,938**	**$11,571**
Target Price	$11,510	
Destination Charge	$300	
Avg. Tax & Fees	$710	
Total Target $	**$12,520**	
Average Dealer Option Cost:	***89%***	

Ownership Costs

Cost Area	5 Year Cost	Rate
Depreciation	$5,249	Average
Financing ($252/month)	$2,063	
Insurance (Rating 6)	$7,129	Worse Than Average
State Fees	$475	
Fuel (Hwy 27 City 25)	$3,333	Excellent
Maintenance	$4,752	Worse Than Average
Repairs	$651	Excellent

Warranty/Maintenance Info

Item	Cost/Coverage	Rate
Major Tune-Up	$249	Poor
Minor Tune-Up	$103	Average
Brake Service	$280	Worse Than Average
Overall Warranty	3 yr/36k	Average
Drivetrain Warranty	3 yr/36k	Average
Rust Warranty	6 yr/100k	Better Than Average
Maintenance Warranty	N/A	
Roadside Assistance	3 yr/36k	

Ownership Cost By Year

$2,000 $4,000 $6,000 $8,000

1993 1994 1995 1996 1997

Resale Value

1993	1994	1995	1996	1997
$10,278	$9,435	$8,786	$8,032	$7,271

Ownership Costs (5yr)

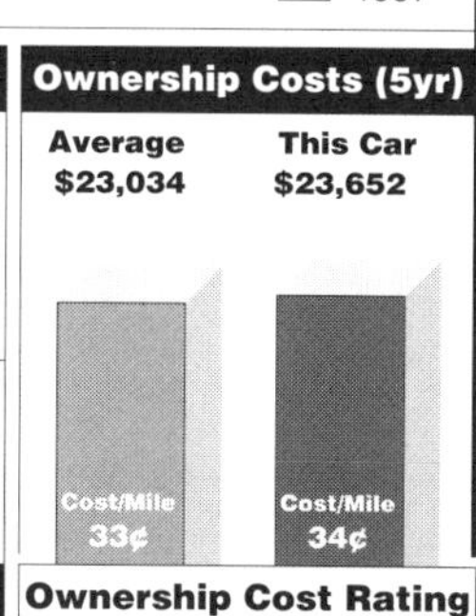

	Average	This Car
Total	$23,034	$23,652
Cost/Mile	33¢	34¢

Cumulative Costs

	1993	1994	1995	1996	1997
Annual	$5,198	$3,845	$4,477	$3,889	$6,243
Total	$5,198	$9,043	$13,520	$17,409	$23,652

Ownership Cost Rating

Average

The 1993 Geo Tracker is available in five models - (Base) 2WD and 4WD Soft Tops, 4WD Hardtop, and LSI 4WD Soft Top and Hardtop. New for 1993, the Tracker 2WD Soft Top features a new variety of exterior colors, magenta seat insert, and an upgraded sound system available as an option. Standard features include a full-size lockable spare tire, gauge cluster, front and rear tow hooks, and a canvas top with fold-and-stow feature. Fifteen inch alloy wheels are available as an option.

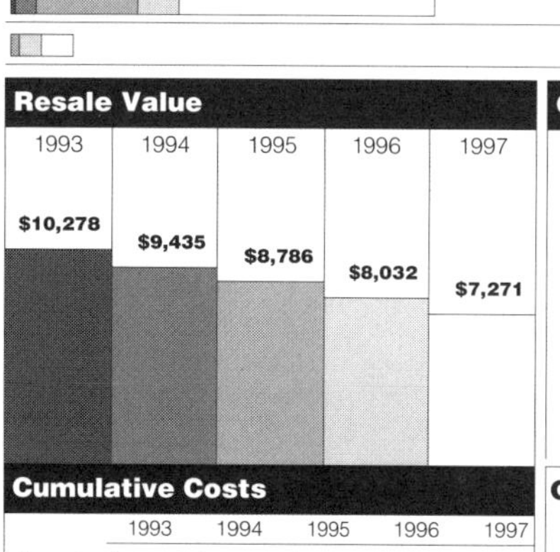

* Includes shaded options

** Other purchase requirements apply

Poor  Worse Than Average  Average  Better Than Average  Excellent  Insufficient Information

Refer to *Section 3: Annotated Vehicle Charts* for an explanation of these charts.

Geo Tracker Soft Top 4WD

2 Door Sport Utility

1.6L 80 hp Gas Fuel Inject.

4 Cylinder In-Line

Manual 5 Speed

4 Wheel On-Demand

Manual Seatbelts Only

Utility

Purchase Price

Car Item	Dealer Cost	List
Base Price	**$11,029**	**$11,585**
Anti-Lock Brakes	Std	Std
Automatic 3 Speed	$530	$595
Optional Engine	N/A	N/A
Air Conditioning	$663	$745
Power Steering	Pkg	Pkg
Cruise Control	N/A	N/A
4 Whl On-Demand Dr.	Std	Std
AM/FM Stereo Cassette	$441	$496
Steering Wheel, Tilt	$102	$115
Power Windows	N/A	N/A
***Options Price**	$1,104	$1,241
***Total Price**	**$12,133**	**$12,826**
Target Price	$12,793	
Destination Charge	$300	
Avg. Tax & Fees	$786	
Total Target $	**$13,879**	
Average Dealer Option Cost:	***89%***	

Ownership Costs

Cost Area	5 Year Cost	Rate
Depreciation	$5,592	Average
Financing ($279/month)	$2,286	
Insurance (Rating 12)	$8,108	Poor
State Fees	$525	
Fuel (Hwy 27 City 25)	$3,333	Excellent
Maintenance	$4,818	Worse Than Average
Repairs	$700	Excellent

Ownership Cost By Year

$2,000 $4,000 $6,000 $8,000 $10,000

1993 1994 1995 1996 1997

Warranty/Maintenance Info

Item		Rate
Major Tune-Up	$249	Poor
Minor Tune-Up	$103	Average
Brake Service	$280	Worse Than Average
Overall Warranty	3 yr/36k	Average
Drivetrain Warranty	3 yr/36k	Average
Rust Warranty	6 yr/100k	Excellent
Maintenance Warranty	N/A	
Roadside Assistance	3 yr/36k	

Resale Value

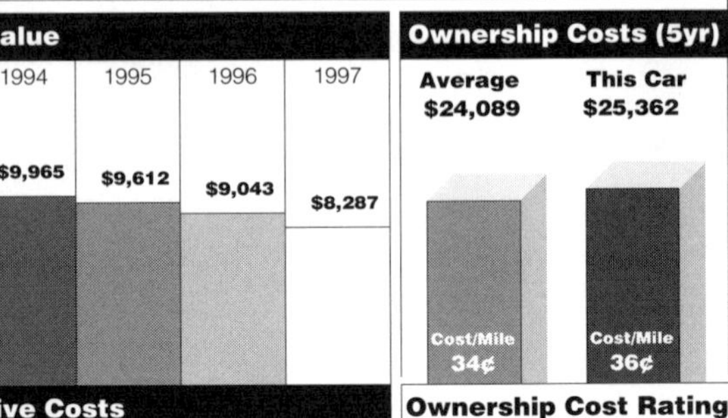

1993	1994	1995	1996	1997
$10,907	$9,965	$9,612	$9,043	$8,287

Ownership Costs (5yr)

Average	This Car
$24,089	$25,362
Cost/Mile 34¢	Cost/Mile 36¢

The 1993 Geo Tracker is available in five models - (Base) 2WD and 4WD Soft Tops, 4WD Hardtop, and LSi 4WD Soft Top and Hardtop. New for 1993, the Tracker 4WD Soft Top features a new variety of exterior colors, upgraded sound system available as an option, and a magenta seat insert. Standard features include manual locking hubs, full-size lockable spare tire, front and rear tow hooks and a canvas top with fold-and-stow feature. The LSi Apperance Package is available as an option.

Cumulative Costs

	1993	1994	1995	1996	1997
Annual	$6,214	$4,213	$4,639	$3,952	$6,344
Total	$6,214	$10,427	$15,066	$19,018	$25,362

Ownership Cost Rating

Average

Geo Tracker Hardtop 4WD

2 Door Sport Utility

1.6L 80 hp Gas Fuel Inject.

4 Cylinder In-Line

Manual 5 Speed

4 Wheel On-Demand

Manual Seatbelts Only

Utility

Soft Top Model Shown

Purchase Price

Car Item	Dealer Cost	List
Base Price	**$11,186**	**$11,750**
Anti-Lock Brakes	Std	Std
Automatic 3 Speed	$530	$595
Optional Engine	N/A	N/A
Air Conditioning	$663	$745
Power Steering	Pkg	Pkg
Cruise Control	N/A	N/A
4 Whl On-Demand Dr.	Std	Std
AM/FM Stereo Cassette	$441	$496
Steering Wheel, Tilt	$102	$115
Power Windows	N/A	N/A
***Options Price**	$1,104	$1,241
***Total Price**	**$12,290**	**$12,991**
Target Price	$12,962	
Destination Charge	$300	
Avg. Tax & Fees	$796	
Total Target $	**$14,058**	
Average Dealer Option Cost:	***89%***	

Ownership Costs

Cost Area	5 Year Cost	Rate
Depreciation	$5,744	Average
Financing ($283/month)	$2,316	
Insurance (Rating 12)	$8,108	Poor
State Fees	$532	
Fuel (Hwy 27 City 25)	$3,333	Excellent
Maintenance	$4,818	Worse Than Average
Repairs	$700	Excellent

Ownership Cost By Year

$2,000 $4,000 $6,000 $8,000 $10,000

1993 1994 1995 1996 1997

Warranty/Maintenance Info

Item		Rate
Major Tune-Up	$249	Poor
Minor Tune-Up	$103	Average
Brake Service	$280	Worse Than Average
Overall Warranty	3 yr/36k	Average
Drivetrain Warranty	3 yr/36k	Average
Rust Warranty	6 yr/100k	Excellent
Maintenance Warranty	N/A	
Roadside Assistance	3 yr/36k	

Resale Value

1993	1994	1995	1996	1997
$10,961	$10,049	$9,692	$9,091	$8,314

Ownership Costs (5yr)

Average	This Car
$24,228	$25,551
Cost/Mile 35¢	Cost/Mile 37¢

The 1993 Geo Tracker is available in five models - (Base) 2WD and 4WD Soft Tops, 4WD Hardtop, and LSi 4WD Soft Top and Hardtop. New for 1993, the Tracker 4WD Hardtop features a magenta seat insert, a new variety of exterior colors, and upgraded sound system available as an option. Standard features include manual locking hubs, gauge cluster with tachometer, front and rear tow hooks, off road tires, and composite halogen headlamps. The LSi Apperance Package is available as an option.

Cumulative Costs

	1993	1994	1995	1996	1997
Annual	$6,354	$4,194	$4,650	$3,987	$6,366
Total	$6,354	$10,548	$15,198	$19,185	$25,551

Ownership Cost Rating

Average

* Includes shaded options

** Other purchase requirements apply

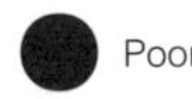 Poor  Worse Than Average 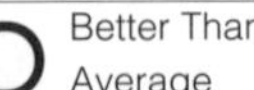 Average  Better Than Average — Excellent — Insufficient Information

Refer to *Section 3: Annotated Vehicle Charts* for an explanation of these charts.

Geo Tracker LSI Soft Top 4WD

2 Door Sport Utility

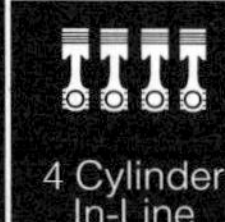

1.6L 80 hp Gas Fuel Inject.

4 Cylinder In-Line

Manual 5 Speed

4 Wheel On-Demand

Manual Seatbelts Only

Utility

Base Model Shown

Purchase Price

Car Item	Dealer Cost	List
Base Price	**$12,076**	**$12,685**
Anti-Lock Brakes	Std	Std
Automatic 3 Speed	$530	$595
Optional Engine	N/A	N/A
Air Conditioning	$663	$745
Power Steering	Pkg	Pkg
Cruise Control	N/A	N/A
4 Whl On-Demand Dr.	Std	Std
AM/FM Stereo Cassette	$174	$195
Steering Wheel, Tilt	$102	$115
Power Windows	N/A	N/A
***Options Price**	$837	$940
***Total Price**	**$12,913**	**$13,625**
Target Price	$13,554	
Destination Charge	$300	
Avg. Tax & Fees	$832	
Total Target $	**$14,686**	
Average Dealer Option Cost:	***89%***	

Ownership Costs

Cost Area	5 Year Cost	Rate
Depreciation	$5,978	Average
Financing ($295/month)	$2,420	
Insurance (Rating 12)	$8,108	Poor
State Fees	$556	
Fuel (Hwy 27 City 25)	$3,333	Better Than Average
Maintenance	$4,818	Worse Than Average
Repairs	$700	Better Than Average

Ownership Cost By Year

$2,000 $4,000 $6,000 $8,000 $10,000

1993 1994 1995 1996 1997

Warranty/Maintenance Info

Item		Rate
Major Tune-Up	$249	Poor
Minor Tune-Up	$103	Average
Brake Service	$280	Worse Than Average
Overall Warranty	3 yr/36k	Average
Drivetrain Warranty	3 yr/36k	Average
Rust Warranty	6 yr/100k	Better Than Average
Maintenance Warranty	N/A	
Roadside Assistance	3 yr/36k	

Resale Value

1993	1994	1995	1996	1997
$11,779	$10,873	$10,289	$9,498	$8,708

Ownership Costs (5yr)

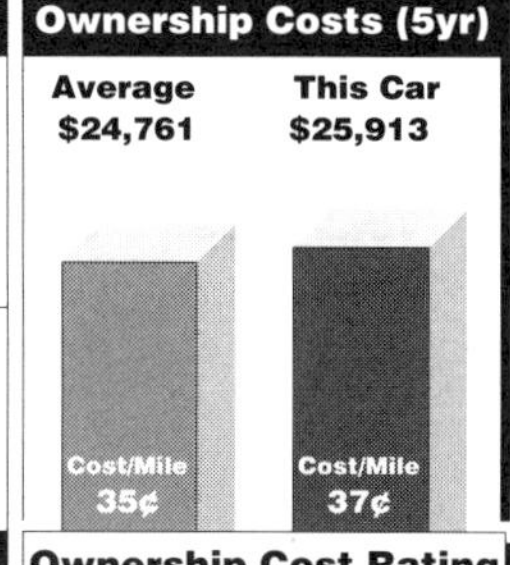

Average	This Car
$24,761	$25,913
Cost/Mile 35¢	Cost/Mile 37¢

Cumulative Costs

	1993	1994	1995	1996	1997
Annual	$6,213	$4,225	$4,903	$4,189	$6,383
Total	$6,213	$10,438	$15,341	$19,530	$25,913

Ownership Cost Rating

Average

The 1993 Geo Tracker is available in five models - (Base) 2WD and 4WD Soft Tops, 4WD Hardtop, and LSi 4WD Soft Top and Hardtop. New for 1993, the Tracker LSi 4WD Soft Top features a new variety of exterior colors, upgraded sound system available as an option, and a magenta seat insert. The LSi upgrades the base edition with automatic locking hubs, custom cloth seat facing trim, reclining high-back front bucket seats with see-through adjustable head rests, and styled steel wheels.

Geo Tracker LSi Hardtop 4WD

2 Door Sport Utility

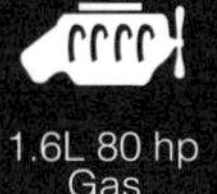

1.6L 80 hp Gas Fuel Inject.

4 Cylinder In-Line

Manual 5 Speed

4 Wheel On-Demand

Manual Seatbelts Only

Utility

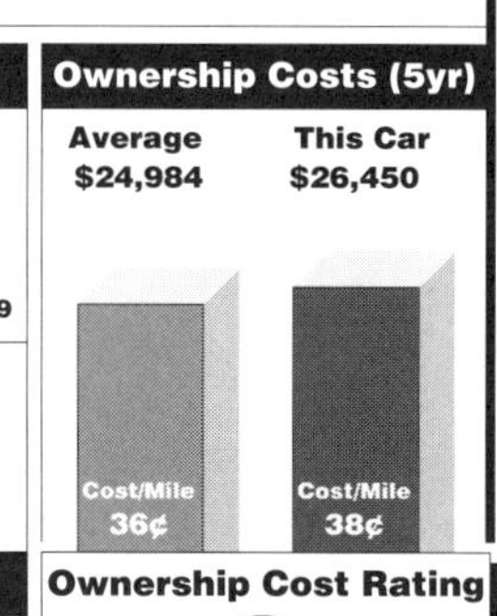

Soft Top Model Shown

Purchase Price

Car Item	Dealer Cost	List
Base Price	**$12,328**	**$12,950**
Anti-Lock Brakes	Std	Std
Automatic 3 Speed	$530	$595
Optional Engine	N/A	N/A
Air Conditioning	$663	$745
Power Steering	Pkg	Pkg
Cruise Control	N/A	N/A
4 Whl On-Demand Dr.	Std	Std
AM/FM Stereo Cassette	$174	$195
Steering Wheel, Tilt	$102	$115
Power Windows	N/A	N/A
***Options Price**	$837	$940
***Total Price**	**$13,165**	**$13,890**
Target Price	$13,818	
Destination Charge	$300	
Avg. Tax & Fees	$848	
Total Target $	**$14,966**	
Average Dealer Option Cost:	***89%***	

Ownership Costs

Cost Area	5 Year Cost	Rate
Depreciation	$6,457	Average
Financing ($301/month)	$2,466	
Insurance (Rating 12)	$8,108	Poor
State Fees	$568	
Fuel (Hwy 27 City 25)	$3,333	Better Than Average
Maintenance	$4,818	Worse Than Average
Repairs	$700	Better Than Average

Ownership Cost By Year

$2,000 $4,000 $6,000 $8,000 $10,000

1993 1994 1995 1996 1997

Warranty/Maintenance Info

Item		Rate
Major Tune-Up	$249	Poor
Minor Tune-Up	$103	Average
Brake Service	$280	Worse Than Average
Overall Warranty	3 yr/36k	Average
Drivetrain Warranty	3 yr/36k	Average
Rust Warranty	6 yr/100k	Better Than Average
Maintenance Warranty	N/A	
Roadside Assistance	3 yr/36k	

Resale Value

1993	1994	1995	1996	1997
$11,460	$10,468	$9,830	$9,254	$8,509

Ownership Costs (5yr)

Average	This Car
$24,984	$26,450
Cost/Mile 36¢	Cost/Mile 38¢

Cumulative Costs

	1993	1994	1995	1996	1997
Annual	$6,834	$4,329	$4,969	$3,979	$6,339
Total	$6,834	$11,163	$16,132	$20,111	$26,450

Ownership Cost Rating

Worse Than Average

The 1993 Geo Tracker is available in five models - (Base) 2WD and 4WD Soft Tops, 4WD Hardtop, and LSi 4WDSoft Top and Hardtop. New for 1993, the Tracker LSi 4WD Hardtop features an upgraded sound system available as an option, a new variety of exterior colors and a magenta seat insert. The LSi upgrades the base edition with styled steel wheels, reclining high-back front bucket seats with see-through adjustable head rests, automatic locking hubs and custom cloth seat facing trim.

* Includes shaded options

** Other purchase requirements apply

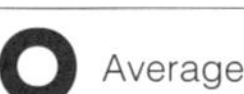

Poor  Worse Than Average  Average  Better Than Average  Excellent 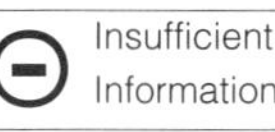 Insufficient Information

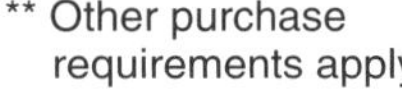

Refer to *Section 3: Annotated Vehicle Charts* for an explanation of these charts.

GMC G1500 Rally Wagon
3 Door Pass Van

Full-Size Van

4.3L 155 hp Gas Fuel Inject.

6 Cylinder "V"

Automatic 4 Speed

2 Wheel Rear

Manual Seatbelts Only

Purchase Price

Car Item	Dealer Cost	List
Base Price	**$14,464**	**$16,569**
Anti-Lock Brakes	Std	Std
Manual Transmission	N/A	N/A
5.0L 170 hp Gas	$495	$575
Air Conditioning	$839	$975
Power Steering	Std	Std
Cruise Control	Pkg	Pkg
All Wheel Drive	N/A	N/A
AM/FM Stereo Cassette	$66	$77
Steering Wheel, Tilt	Pkg	Pkg
Power Windows	Pkg	Pkg
***Options Price**	$1,334	$1,550
***Total Price**	**$15,798**	**$18,119**
Target Price	$16,750	
Destination Charge	$580	
Avg. Tax & Fees	$1,054	
Total Target $	**$18,384**	
Average Dealer Option Cost:	***86%***	

Ownership Costs

Cost Area	5 Year Cost	Rate
Depreciation	$8,563	Average
Financing ($369/month)	$3,028	
Insurance (Rating 6 [Est.])	$7,129	Excellent
State Fees	$748	
Fuel (Hwy 17 City 13)	$5,760	Average
Maintenance	$4,745	Worse Than Average
Repairs	$740	Excellent

Ownership Cost By Year

$2,000 $4,000 $6,000 $8,000 $10,000

1993 1994 1995 1996 1997

Warranty/Maintenance Info

Major Tune-Up	$219	Poor
Minor Tune-Up	$137	Poor
Brake Service	$270	Average
Overall Warranty	3 yr/36k	Average
Drivetrain Warranty	3 yr/36k	Average
Rust Warranty	6 yr/100k	Better Than Average
Maintenance Warranty	N/A	
Roadside Assistance	3 yr/36k	

Resale Value

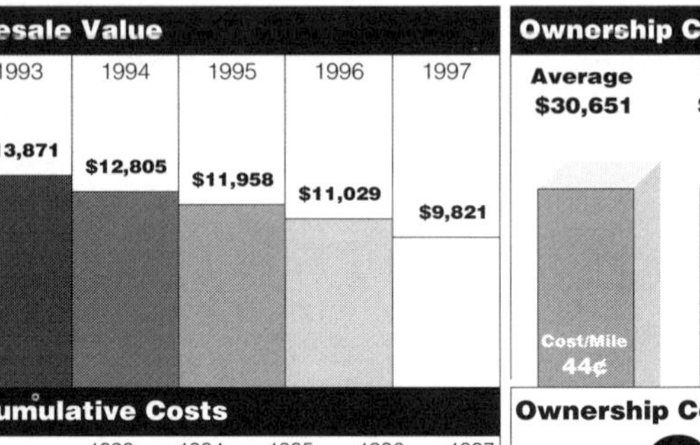

Ownership Costs (5yr)

Average	This Car
$30,651	$30,713
Cost/Mile 44¢	Cost/Mile 44¢

Cumulative Costs

	1993	1994	1995	1996	1997
Annual	$8,404	$4,968	$5,795	$5,075	$6,471
Total	$8,404	$13,372	$19,167	$24,242	$30,713

Ownership Cost Rating

Average

The 1993 GMC Rally Wagon is available in four models - G1500, G2500 and G3500, and G3500 Heavy Duty full-size passenger vans. New for 1993, the G1500 Rally Wagon offers a new electronically controlled four-speed automatic transmission designed for more reliable operation, smoother shifts, improved fuel efficiency and second-gear part-throttle starting for better slippery-road performance. All engines receive a new, quieter, fan clutch, lowering engine noise, especially during cold star

GMC G2500 Rally Wagon
3 Door Pass Ext Van

Full-Size Van

4.3L 155 hp Gas Fuel Inject.

6 Cylinder "V"

Automatic 4 Speed

2 Wheel Rear

Manual Seatbelts Only

Purchase Price

Car Item	Dealer Cost	List
Base Price	**$15,241**	**$17,459**
Anti-Lock Brakes	Std	Std
Manual Transmission	N/A	N/A
5.0L 170 hp Gas	$495	$575
Air Conditioning	$839	$975
Power Steering	Std	Std
Cruise Control	Pkg	Pkg
All Wheel Drive	N/A	N/A
AM/FM Stereo Cassette	$66	$77
Steering Wheel, Tilt	Pkg	Pkg
Power Windows	Pkg	Pkg
***Options Price**	$1,334	$1,550
***Total Price**	**$16,575**	**$19,009**
Target Price	$17,596	
Destination Charge	$580	
Avg. Tax & Fees	$1,105	
Total Target $	**$19,281**	
Average Dealer Option Cost:	***86%***	

Ownership Costs

Cost Area	5 Year Cost	Rate
Depreciation	$8,919	Average
Financing ($388/month)	$3,177	
Insurance (Rating 7 [Est.])	$7,244	Excellent
State Fees	$784	
Fuel (Hwy 17 City 13)	$5,760	Average
Maintenance	$4,797	Worse Than Average
Repairs	$740	Excellent

Ownership Cost By Year

$2,000 $4,000 $6,000 $8,000 $10,000

1993 1994 1995 1996 1997

Warranty/Maintenance Info

Major Tune-Up	$219	Poor
Minor Tune-Up	$137	Poor
Brake Service	$270	Average
Overall Warranty	3 yr/36k	Average
Drivetrain Warranty	3 yr/36k	Average
Rust Warranty	6 yr/100k	Better Than Average
Maintenance Warranty	N/A	
Roadside Assistance	3 yr/36k	

Resale Value

1993	1994	1995	1996	1997
$14,478	$13,409	$12,543	$11,614	$10,362

Ownership Costs (5yr)

Average	This Car
$31,699	$31,421
Cost/Mile 45¢	Cost/Mile 45¢

Cumulative Costs

	1993	1994	1995	1996	1997
Annual	$8,786	$5,047	$5,899	$5,116	$6,573
Total	$8,786	$13,833	$19,732	$24,848	$31,421

Ownership Cost Rating

Average

The 1993 GMC Rally Wagon is available in four models - G1500, G2500 and G3500, and G3500 Heavy Duty full-size passenger vans. New for 1993, the G2500 Rally Wagon offers a new electronically controlled four-speed automatic transmission designed for more reliable operation, smoother shifts, improved fuel efficiency and second-gear part-throttle starting for better slippery-road performance. All engines receive a new, quieter, fan clutch, lowering engine noise, especially during cold starts.

* Includes shaded options

** Other purchase requirements apply

Poor | Worse Than Average | Average | Better Than Average | Excellent | Insufficient Information

Refer to *Section 3: Annotated Vehicle Charts* for an explanation of these charts.

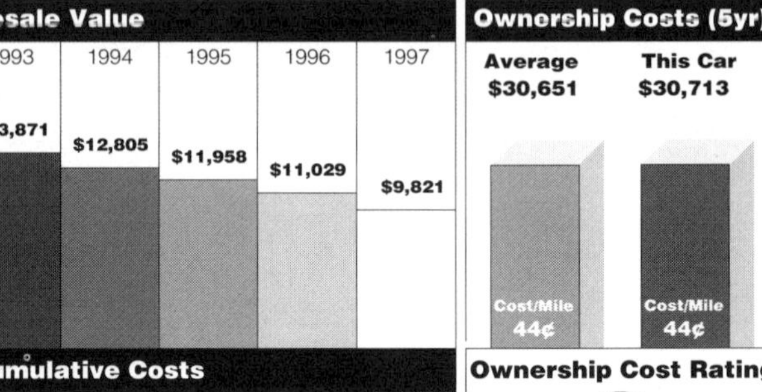

GMC G3500 Rally Wagon Heavy Duty 3 Door Pass Ext Van

5.7L 195 hp Gas Fuel Inject.

8 Cylinder "V"

Automatic 4 Speed

2 Wheel Rear

Manual Seatbelts Only

G150 Rally Wagon Shown

Purchase Price

Car Item	Dealer Cost	List
Base Price	**$16,607**	**$19,023**
Anti-Lock Brakes	Std	Std
Manual Transmission	N/A	N/A
7.4L 230 hp Gas	$520	$605
Air Conditioning	$839	$975
Power Steering	Std	Std
Cruise Control	Pkg	Pkg
All Wheel Drive	N/A	N/A
AM/FM Stereo Cassette	$66	$77
Steering Wheel, Tilt	Pkg	Pkg
Power Windows	Pkg	Pkg
***Options Price**	$839	$975
***Total Price**	**$17,446**	**$19,998**
Target Price	$18,561	
Destination Charge	$580	
Avg. Tax & Fees	$1,163	
Total Target $	**$20,304**	
Average Dealer Option Cost:	***86%***	

Ownership Costs

Cost Area	5 Year Cost	Rate
Depreciation	$9,999	Average
Financing ($408/month)	$3,344	
Insurance (Rating 7 [Est.])	$7,244	Excellent
State Fees	$823	
Fuel (Hwy 17 City 13)	$5,760	Average
Maintenance	$5,653	Poor
Repairs	$740	Excellent

Warranty/Maintenance Info

Item		Rate
Major Tune-Up	$219	Poor
Minor Tune-Up	$137	Poor
Brake Service	$482	Poor
Overall Warranty	3 yr/36k	Average
Drivetrain Warranty	3 yr/36k	Average
Rust Warranty	6 yr/100k	Excellent
Maintenance Warranty	N/A	
Roadside Assistance	3 yr/36k	

Ownership Cost By Year

$2,000 $4,000 $6,000 $8,000 $10,000

1993 1994 1995 1996 1997

Resale Value

1993	1994	1995	1996	1997
$14,247	$13,217	$12,390	$11,502	$10,305

Ownership Costs (5yr)

Average	This Car
$32,864	$33,563
Cost/Mile 47¢	Cost/Mile 48¢

Cumulative Costs

	1993	1994	1995	1996	1997
Annual	$10,120	$5,069	$6,312	$5,094	$6,968
Total	$10,120	$15,189	$21,501	$26,595	$33,563

Ownership Cost Rating

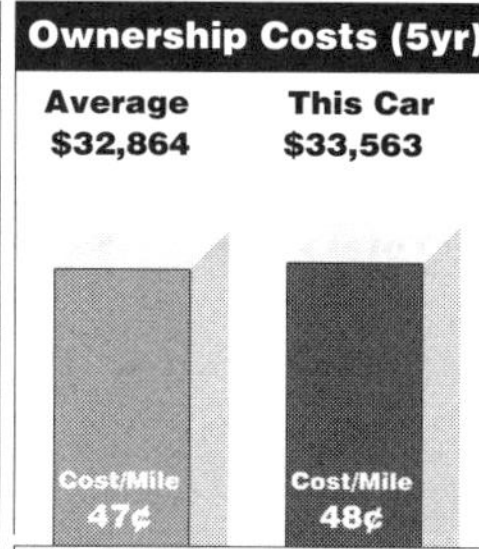
Worse Than Average

The 1993 Rally Wagon is available in four models - G1500, G2500 and G3500, and G3500 Heavy Duty full-size passenger vans. New for 1993, the G3500 HD Rally Wagon offers a new electronically controlled 4-speed automatic transmission designed for more reliable operation, smoother shifts, improved fuel efficiency and second-gear part-throttle starting for better slippery-road performance. To reduce the likelihood of theft, a new steel steering column sleeve helps protect the ignition lock cylinder.

GMC G3500 Rally Wagon 3 Door Pass Ext Van

5.7L 195 hp Gas Fuel Inject.

8 Cylinder "V"

Automatic 4 Speed

2 Wheel Rear

Manual Seatbelts Only

Full-Size Van

G150 Rally Wagon Shown

Purchase Price

Car Item	Dealer Cost	List
Base Price	**$16,712**	**$19,143**
Anti-Lock Brakes	Std	Std
Manual Transmission	N/A	N/A
7.4L 230 hp Gas	$520	$605
Air Conditioning	$839	$975
Power Steering	Std	Std
Cruise Control	Pkg	Pkg
All Wheel Drive	N/A	N/A
AM/FM Stereo Cassette	$66	$77
Steering Wheel, Tilt	Pkg	Pkg
Power Windows	Pkg	Pkg
***Options Price**	$839	$975
***Total Price**	**$17,551**	**$20,118**
Target Price	$18,676	
Destination Charge	$580	
Avg. Tax & Fees	$1,170	
Total Target $	**$20,426**	
Average Dealer Option Cost:	***86%***	

Ownership Costs

Cost Area	5 Year Cost	Rate
Depreciation	$9,956	Average
Financing ($411/month)	$3,365	
Insurance (Rating 7 [Est.])	$7,244	Excellent
State Fees	$828	
Fuel (Hwy 17 City 13)	$5,760	Average
Maintenance	$5,618	Poor
Repairs	$740	Excellent

Warranty/Maintenance Info

Item		Rate
Major Tune-Up	$219	Poor
Minor Tune-Up	$137	Poor
Brake Service	$482	Poor
Overall Warranty	3 yr/36k	Average
Drivetrain Warranty	3 yr/36k	Average
Rust Warranty	6 yr/100k	Excellent
Maintenance Warranty	N/A	
Roadside Assistance	3 yr/36k	

Ownership Cost By Year

$2,000 $4,000 $6,000 $8,000 $10,000

1993 1994 1995 1996 1997

Resale Value

1993	1994	1995	1996	1997
$14,308	$13,314	$12,524	$11,652	$10,470

Ownership Costs (5yr)

Average	This Car
$33,005	$33,511
Cost/Mile 47¢	Cost/Mile 48¢

Cumulative Costs

	1993	1994	1995	1996	1997
Annual	$10,191	$5,041	$6,263	$5,080	$6,936
Total	$10,191	$15,232	$21,495	$26,575	$33,511

Ownership Cost Rating

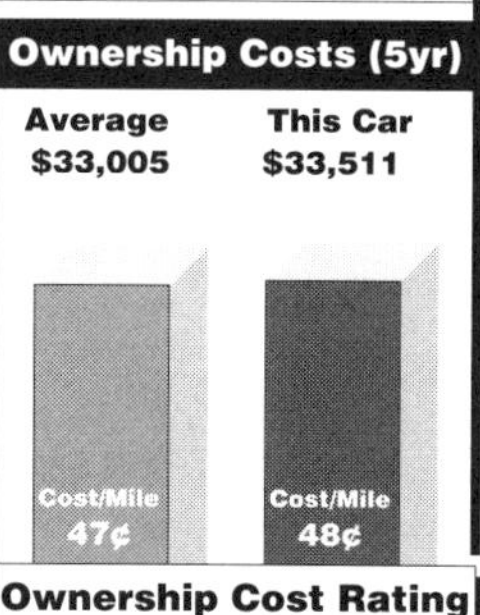
Average

The 1993 Rally Wagon is available in four models - G1500, G2500 and G3500, and G3500 Heavy Duty full-size passenger vans. New for 1993, the G3500 Rally Wagon offers a new electronically controlled 4-speed automatic transmission designed for more reliable operation, smoother shifts, improved fuel efficiency and second-gear part-throttle starting for better slippery-road performance. To reduce the likelihood of theft, a new steel steering column sleeve helps protect the ignition lock cylinder.

* Includes shaded options

** Other purchase requirements apply

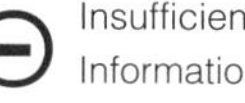
Poor · Worse Than Average · Average · Better Than Average · Excellent · Insufficient Information

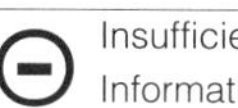

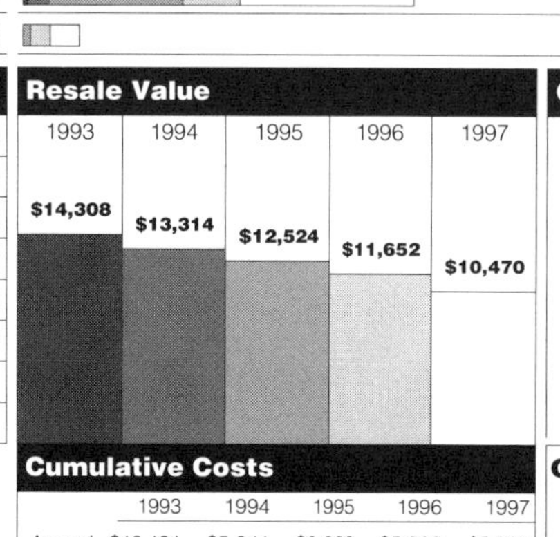

Refer to *Section 3: Annotated Vehicle Charts* for an explanation of these charts.

GMC G1500 Vandura
3 Door Cargo Van

4.3L 155 hp Gas Fuel Inject.

6 Cylinder "V"

Automatic 4 Speed

2 Wheel Rear

Manual Seatbelts Only

Full-Size Van

Rally Wagon Shown

Purchase Price

Car Item	Dealer Cost	List
Base Price	**$12,835**	**$14,668**
Anti-Lock Brakes	Std	Std
Manual Transmission	N/A	N/A
5.0L 170 hp Gas	$495	$575
Air Conditioning	$839	$975
Power Steering	Std	Std
Cruise Control	Pkg	Pkg
All Wheel Drive	N/A	N/A
AM/FM Stereo Cassette	$187	$218
Steering Wheel, Tilt	Pkg	Pkg
Power Windows	Pkg	Pkg
***Options Price**	$1,334	$1,550
***Total Price**	**$14,169**	**$16,218**
Target Price	$14,983	
Destination Charge	$580	
Avg. Tax & Fees	$946	
Total Target $	**$16,509**	
Average Dealer Option Cost:	***86%***	

Ownership Costs

Cost Area	5 Year Cost	Rate
Depreciation	$6,794	Better Than Average
Financing ($332/month)	$2,720	
Insurance (Rating 4 [Est.])	$6,867	Excellent
State Fees	$672	
Fuel (Hwy 18 City 14)	$5,399	Better Than Average
Maintenance	$4,745	Worse Than Average
Repairs	$740	Excellent

Ownership Cost By Year

$2,000 $4,000 $6,000 $8,000

1993 1994 1995 1996 1997

Warranty/Maintenance Info

Major Tune-Up	$219	Poor
Minor Tune-Up	$137	Poor
Brake Service	$270	Average
Overall Warranty	3 yr/36k	Average
Drivetrain Warranty	3 yr/36k	Average
Rust Warranty	6 yr/100k	Better Than Average
Maintenance Warranty	N/A	
Roadside Assistance	3 yr/36k	

Resale Value

1993	1994	1995	1996	1997
$12,944	$12,069	$11,725	$10,695	$9,715

Ownership Costs (5yr)

Average	This Car
$28,412	$27,937

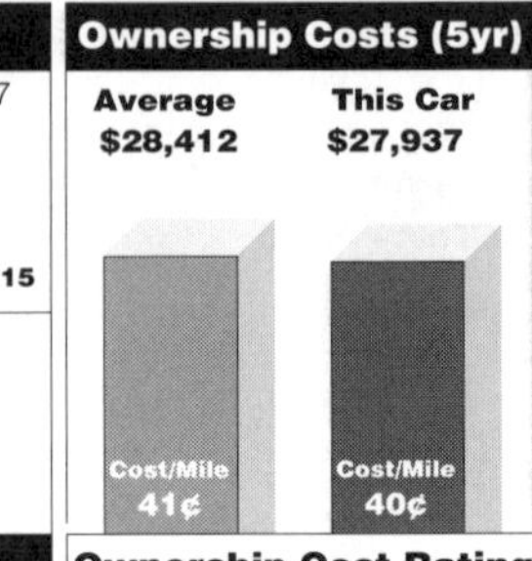

Cumulative Costs

	1993	1994	1995	1996	1997
Annual	$7,194	$4,544	$5,090	$5,012	$6,097
Total	$7,194	$11,738	$16,828	$21,840	$27,937

Ownership Cost Rating

Better Than Average

The 1993 Vandura Cargo Van is available in four models-G1500, G2500, G3500 and G3500 Heavy Duty. New for 1993, the G1500 features a new electronically controlled four-speed transmission-the Hydra-matic 4L60-E. Other features include a brake/transmission shift interlock and a four-wheel anti-lock braking system. To reduce the likelihood of vehicle theft, a new steel steering column sleeve helps protect the ignition lock cylinder.

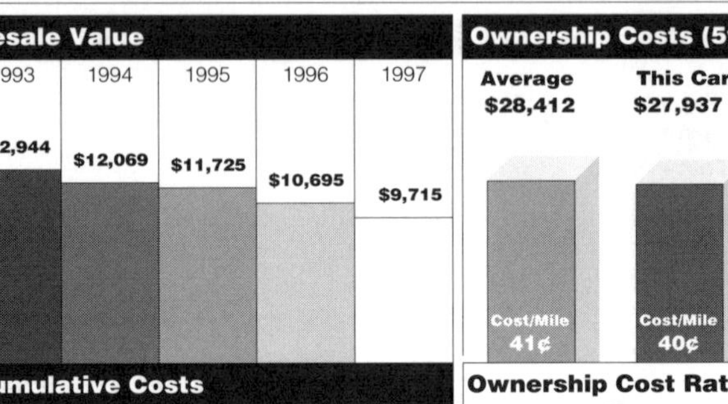

GMC G2500 Vandura
3 Door Cargo Van

4.3L 155 hp Gas Fuel Inject.

6 Cylinder "V"

Automatic 4 Speed

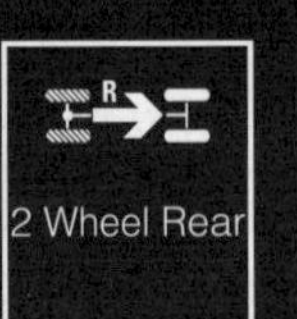
2 Wheel Rear

Manual Seatbelts Only

Full-Size Van

Rally Wagon Shown

Purchase Price

Car Item	Dealer Cost	List
Base Price	**$12,940**	**$14,788**
Anti-Lock Brakes	Std	Std
Manual Transmission	N/A	N/A
5.0L 170 hp Gas	$495	$575
Air Conditioning	$839	$975
Power Steering	Std	Std
Cruise Control	Pkg	Pkg
All Wheel Drive	N/A	N/A
AM/FM Stereo Cassette	$187	$218
Steering Wheel, Tilt	Pkg	Pkg
Power Windows	Pkg	Pkg
***Options Price**	$1,334	$1,550
***Total Price**	**$14,274**	**$16,338**
Target Price	$15,097	
Destination Charge	$580	
Avg. Tax & Fees	$953	
Total Target $	**$16,630**	
Average Dealer Option Cost:	***86%***	

Ownership Costs

Cost Area	5 Year Cost	Rate
Depreciation	$7,199	Average
Financing ($334/month)	$2,739	
Insurance (Rating 2 [Est.])	$6,542	Excellent
State Fees	$676	
Fuel (Hwy 18 City 14)	$5,399	Better Than Average
Maintenance	$4,797	Worse Than Average
Repairs	$740	Excellent

Ownership Cost By Year

$2,000 $4,000 $6,000 $8,000

1993 1994 1995 1996 1997

Warranty/Maintenance Info

Major Tune-Up	$219	Poor
Minor Tune-Up	$137	Poor
Brake Service	$270	Average
Overall Warranty	3 yr/36k	Average
Drivetrain Warranty	3 yr/36k	Average
Rust Warranty	6 yr/100k	Better Than Average
Maintenance Warranty	N/A	
Roadside Assistance	3 yr/36k	

Resale Value

1993	1994	1995	1996	1997
$12,933	$12,053	$11,605	$10,755	$9,431

Ownership Costs (5yr)

Average	This Car
$28,554	$28,092

Cost/Mile 41¢ | Cost/Mile 40¢

Cumulative Costs

	1993	1994	1995	1996	1997
Annual	$7,275	$4,493	$5,159	$4,766	$6,399
Total	$7,275	$11,768	$16,927	$21,693	$28,092

Ownership Cost Rating

Average

The 1993 Vandura Cargo Van is available in four models-G1500, G2500, G3500 and G3500 Heavy Duty. New for 1993, the G2500 features a new electronically controlled four-speed transmission-the Hydra-matic 4L60-E. Other features include a four-wheel anti-lock braking system that provides added steering control under braking. The G2500 also features a new quiet drive fan clutch, a device that quiets engine noise, especially during cold starts. A brake/transmission shift interlock is standard on the G2500.

* Includes shaded options

** Other purchase requirements apply

Poor | Worse Than Average |  Average | Better Than Average | Excellent | Insufficient Information

Refer to *Section 3: Annotated Vehicle Charts* for an explanation of these charts.

GMC G3500 Vandura
3 Door Cargo Ext Van

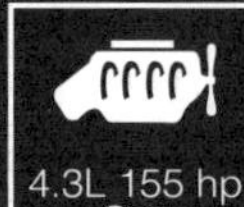
4.3L 155 hp Gas Fuel Inject.

6 Cylinder "V"

Automatic 4 Speed

2 Wheel Rear

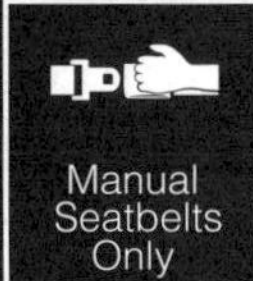
Manual Seatbelts Only

Full-Size Van

G250 Rally Wagon Shown

Purchase Price

Car Item	Dealer Cost	List
Base Price	**$13,162**	**$15,042**
Anti-Lock Brakes	Std	Std
4 Spd H.D. Elec.	N/C	N/C
5.7L 195 hp Gas	N/C	N/C
Air Conditioning	$839	$975
Power Steering	Std	Std
Cruise Control	Pkg	Pkg
All Wheel Drive	N/A	N/A
AM/FM Stereo Cassette	$187	$218
Steering Wheel, Tilt	Pkg	Pkg
Power Windows	Pkg	Pkg
***Options Price**	$839	$975
***Total Price**	**$14,001**	**$16,017**
Target Price	$14,813	
Destination Charge	$580	
Avg. Tax & Fees	$936	
Total Target $	**$16,329**	
Average Dealer Option Cost:	***86%***	

Ownership Costs

Cost Area	5 Year Cost	Rate
Depreciation	$7,747	Average
Financing ($328/month)	$2,689	
Insurance (Rating 5 [Est.])	$6,996	Excellent
State Fees	$664	
Fuel (Hwy 19 City 14)	$5,244	Excellent
Maintenance	$5,620	Poor
Repairs	$740	Excellent

Ownership Cost By Year

$2,000 $4,000 $6,000 $8,000

1993 1994 1995 1996 1997

Warranty/Maintenance Info

Item	Cost/Coverage	Rate
Major Tune-Up	$219	Poor
Minor Tune-Up	$137	Poor
Brake Service	$482	Poor
Overall Warranty	3 yr/36k	Average
Drivetrain Warranty	3 yr/36k	Average
Rust Warranty	6 yr/100k	Excellent
Maintenance Warranty	N/A	
Roadside Assistance	3 yr/36k	

Resale Value

1993	1994	1995	1996	1997
$12,892	$11,726	$11,238	$9,787	$8,582

Ownership Costs (5yr)

Average	This Car
$28,176	$29,700
Cost/Mile 40¢	Cost/Mile 42¢

The 1993 Vandura Cargo Van is available in four models-G1500, G2500, G3500 and G3500 Heavy Duty. New for 1993, the G3500 van features a new electronically controlled four-speed transmission-the Hydra-matic 4L60-E. Other features include a four-wheel anti-lock braking system that provides added steering control. It also features a new quiet drive fan clutch, a device that quiets engine noise, especially during cold starts. The G3500 Extended may also be ordered in cutaway configurations.

Cumulative Costs

	1993	1994	1995	1996	1997
Annual	$7,046	$4,818	$5,642	$5,423	$6,771
Total	$7,046	$11,864	$17,506	$22,929	$29,700

Ownership Cost Rating

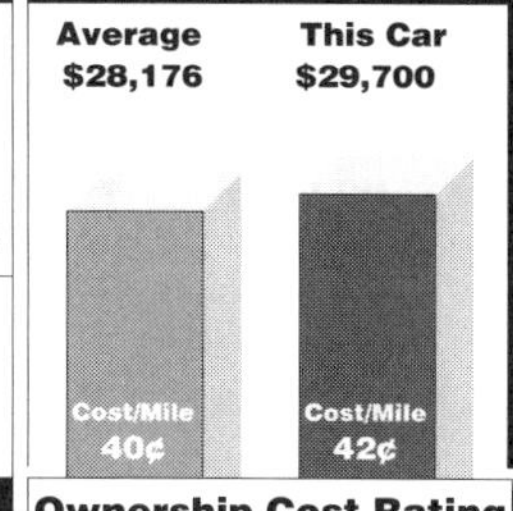
Worse Than Average

GMC G3500 Vandura Heavy Duty
3 Door Cargo Ext Van

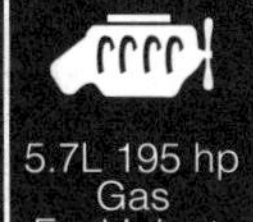
5.7L 195 hp Gas Fuel Inject.

8 Cylinder "V"

Automatic 4 Speed

2 Wheel Rear

Manual Seatbelts Only

Full-Size Van

G250 Rally Wagon Shown

Purchase Price

Car Item	Dealer Cost	List
Base Price	**$14,422**	**$16,482**
Anti-Lock Brakes	Std	Std
4 Spd H.D. Elec.	N/C	N/C
7.4L 230 hp Gas	$520	$605
Air Conditioning	$839	$975
Power Steering	Std	Std
Cruise Control	Pkg	Pkg
All Wheel Drive	N/A	N/A
AM/FM Stereo Cassette	$187	$218
Steering Wheel, Tilt	Pkg	Pkg
Power Windows	Pkg	Pkg
***Options Price**	$839	$975
***Total Price**	**$15,261**	**$17,457**
Target Price	$16,180	
Destination Charge	$580	
Avg. Tax & Fees	$1,018	
Total Target $	**$17,778**	
Average Dealer Option Cost:	***86%***	

Ownership Costs

Cost Area	5 Year Cost	Rate
Depreciation	$8,424	Average
Financing ($357/month)	$2,929	
Insurance (Rating 6 [Est.])	$7,129	Excellent
State Fees	$720	
Fuel (Hwy 19 City 14)	$5,244	Excellent
Maintenance	$5,657	Poor
Repairs	$740	Excellent

Ownership Cost By Year

$2,000 $4,000 $6,000 $8,000 $10,000

1993 1994 1995 1996 1997

Warranty/Maintenance Info

Item	Cost/Coverage	Rate
Major Tune-Up	$219	Poor
Minor Tune-Up	$137	Poor
Brake Service	$482	Poor
Overall Warranty	3 yr/36k	Average
Drivetrain Warranty	3 yr/36k	Average
Rust Warranty	6 yr/100k	Excellent
Maintenance Warranty	N/A	
Roadside Assistance	3 yr/36k	

Resale Value

1993	1994	1995	1996	1997
$13,985	$12,734	$12,205	$10,638	$9,354

Ownership Costs (5yr)

Average	This Car
$29,871	$30,843
Cost/Mile 43¢	Cost/Mile 44¢

The 1993 Vandura Cargo Van is available in four models-G1500, G2500, G3500 and G3500 Heavy Duty. New for 1993, the G3500 Heavy Duty van features a new electronically controlled four-speed transmission-the Hydra-matic 4L60-E. Other features include a four-wheel anti-lock braking system that provides added steering control, heavy duty springs, chassis and rear axle. It also features a new drive fan clutch that quiets engine noise during cold starts. An optional extended wheelbase is also available.

Cumulative Costs

	1993	1994	1995	1996	1997
Annual	$7,540	$5,016	$5,787	$5,594	$6,906
Total	$7,540	$12,556	$18,343	$23,937	$30,843

Ownership Cost Rating

Worse Than Average

* Includes shaded options

** Other purchase requirements apply

 Poor  Worse Than Average  Average  Better Than Average — Excellent — Insufficient Information

Refer to *Section 3: Annotated Vehicle Charts* for an explanation of these charts.

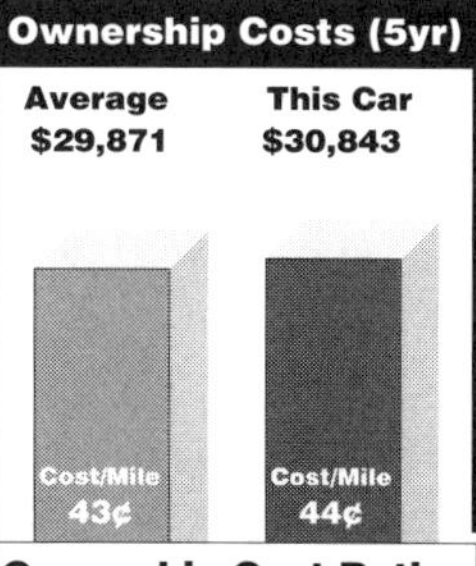

GMC Jimmy
2 Door Sport Utility

4.3L 165 hp Gas Fuel Inject.

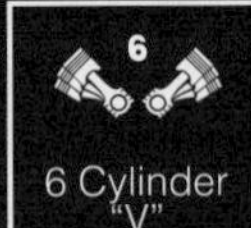
6 Cylinder "V"

Manual 5 Speed

2 Wheel Rear

Manual Seatbelts Only

Purchase Price

Car Item	Dealer Cost	List
Base Price	**$13,595**	**$15,022**
Anti-Lock Brakes	Std	Std
Automatic 4 Speed	Pkg	Pkg
4.3L 285 hp Gas	Pkg	Pkg
Air Conditioning	$671	$780
Power Steering	Std	Std
Cruise Control	$205	** $238
All Wheel Drive	N/A	N/A
AM/FM Stereo Cassette	$105	$122
Steering Wheel, Tilt	Pkg	Pkg
Power Windows	Pkg	Pkg
***Options Price**	$776	$902
***Total Price**	**$14,371**	**$15,924**
Target Price	$15,365	
Destination Charge	$475	
Avg. Tax & Fees	$956	
Total Target $	**$16,796**	
Average Dealer Option Cost:	***86%***	

Ownership Costs

Cost Area	5 Year Cost	Rate
Depreciation	$7,189	Better Than Average
Financing ($338/month)	$2,767	
Insurance (Rating 12 [Est.])	$8,108	Worse Than Average
State Fees	$656	
Fuel (Hwy 23 City 18)	$4,213	Better Than Average
Maintenance	$4,363	Better Than Average
Repairs	$820	Better Than Average

Ownership Cost By Year

Warranty/Maintenance Info

Major Tune-Up	$226	Poor
Minor Tune-Up	$141	Poor
Brake Service	$223	Better Than Average
Overall Warranty	3 yr/36k/$100/12k	Worse Than Average
Drivetrain Warranty	3 yr/36k/$100/12k	Worse Than Average
Rust Warranty	6 yr/100k	Excellent
Maintenance Warranty	N/A	
Roadside Assistance	3 yr/36k	

Resale Value

1993	1994	1995	1996	1997
$13,748	$12,675	$11,772	$10,685	$9,607

Ownership Costs (5yr)

Average	This Car
$26,695	$28,116
Cost/Mile 38¢	Cost/Mile 40¢

The 1993 GMC Jimmy is available in five models - the (Base), four-door, 2WD, 4WD, and the Jimmy Typhoon 4WD. The Base model is available with the optional SLT Touring Package this year. The package consists of leather trim interior with power driver's seat, standard overhead console, keyless entry, luggage rack, and all-season highway radials. The leather trim interiors are offered in charcoal, gray, and garnet.

Cumulative Costs

	1993	1994	1995	1996	1997
Annual	$6,699	$4,762	$5,469	$5,100	$6,086
Total	$6,699	$11,461	$16,930	$22,030	$28,116

Ownership Cost Rating

Average

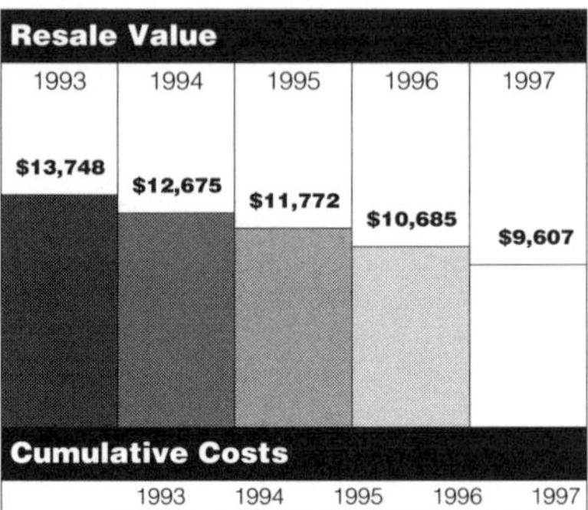

GMC Jimmy
4 Door Sport Utility

4.3L 165 hp Gas Fuel Inject.

6 Cylinder "V"

Manual 5 Speed

2 Wheel Rear

Manual Seatbelts Only

Utility

Purchase Price

Car Item	Dealer Cost	List
Base Price	**$14,475**	**$15,994**
Anti-Lock Brakes	Std	Std
Automatic 4 Speed	Pkg	Pkg
4.3L 285 hp Gas	Pkg	Pkg
Air Conditioning	$671	$780
Power Steering	Std	Std
Cruise Control	$205	** $238
All Wheel Drive	N/A	N/A
AM/FM Stereo Cassette	$105	$122
Steering Wheel, Tilt	Pkg	Pkg
Power Windows	Pkg	Pkg
***Options Price**	$776	$902
***Total Price**	**$15,251**	**$16,896**
Target Price	$16,333	
Destination Charge	$475	
Avg. Tax & Fees	$1,014	
Total Target $	**$17,822**	
Average Dealer Option Cost:	***86%***	

Ownership Costs

Cost Area	5 Year Cost	Rate
Depreciation	$7,319	Better Than Average
Financing ($358/month)	$2,936	
Insurance (Rating 13 [Est.])	$8,271	Worse Than Average
State Fees	$695	
Fuel (Hwy 23 City 18)	$4,213	Better Than Average
Maintenance	$4,363	Better Than Average
Repairs	$820	Better Than Average

Ownership Cost By Year

$2,000 $4,000 $6,000 $8,000 $10,000

1993 1994 1995 1996 1997

Warranty/Maintenance Info

Major Tune-Up	$226	Poor
Minor Tune-Up	$141	Poor
Brake Service	$223	Better Than Average
Overall Warranty	3 yr/36k/$100/12k	Worse Than Average
Drivetrain Warranty	3 yr/36k/$100/12k	Worse Than Average
Rust Warranty	6 yr/100k	Excellent
Maintenance Warranty	N/A	
Roadside Assistance	3 yr/36k	

Resale Value

1993	1994	1995	1996	1997
$14,827	$13,717	$12,777	$11,633	$10,503

Ownership Costs (5yr)

Average	This Car
$27,513	$28,617
Cost/Mile 39¢	Cost/Mile 41¢

The 1993 GMC Jimmy is available in five models - the (Base), four-door, 2WD, 4WD, and the Jimmy Typhoon 4WD. The Jimmy 2WD with four doors offers three option packages - SLS, SLE and SLT. The SLS package includes a full monochromatic look with a body-color grille, wheel-lip moldings, and color-keyed aluminum wheels. An overhead console that includes adjustable map lights and storage space for sunglasses and a garage door opener is standard.

Cumulative Costs

	1993	1994	1995	1996	1997
Annual	$6,757	$4,891	$5,580	$5,210	$6,179
Total	$6,757	$11,648	$17,228	$22,438	$28,617

Ownership Cost Rating

Average

* Includes shaded options

** Other purchase requirements apply

 Poor  Worse Than Average  Average 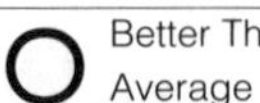 Better Than Average   Excellent 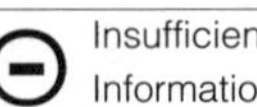 Insufficient Information

Refer to *Section 3: Annotated Vehicle Charts* for an explanation of these charts.

GMC Jimmy 4WD
2 Door Sport Utility

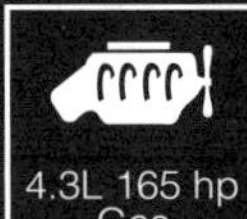
4.3L 165 hp Gas Fuel Inject.

6 Cylinder "V"

Manual 5 Speed

4 Wheel On-Demand

Manual Seatbelts Only

Utility

Base 2WD Model Shown

Purchase Price

Car Item	Dealer Cost	List
Base Price	**$15,299**	**$16,905**
Anti-Lock Brakes	Std	Std
Automatic 4 Speed	Pkg	Pkg
4.3L 285 hp Gas	Pkg	Pkg
Air Conditioning	$671	$780
Power Steering	Std	Std
Cruise Control	$205	** $238
4 Whl On-Demand Dr.	Std	Std
AM/FM Stereo Cassette	$105	$122
Steering Wheel, Tilt	Pkg	Pkg
Power Windows	Pkg	Pkg
***Options Price**	$776	$902
***Total Price**	**$16,075**	**$17,807**
Target Price	$17,242	
Destination Charge	$475	
Avg. Tax & Fees	$1,069	
Total Target $	**$18,786**	
Average Dealer Option Cost:	***86%***	

Ownership Costs

Cost Area	5 Year Cost	Rate
Depreciation	$7,756	Average
Financing ($378/month)	$3,095	
Insurance (Rating 13 [Est.])	$8,271	Worse Than Average
State Fees	$732	
Fuel (Hwy 21 City 16)	$4,672	Average
Maintenance	$5,078	Worse Than Average
Repairs	$791	Average

Ownership Cost By Year

$2,000 $4,000 $6,000 $8,000 $10,000

1993 1994 1995 1996 1997

Warranty/Maintenance Info

Item		Rate
Major Tune-Up	$226	Poor
Minor Tune-Up	$141	Poor
Brake Service	$223	Average
Overall Warranty	3 yr/36k/$100/12k	Worse Than Average
Drivetrain Warranty	3 yr/36k/$100/12k	Worse Than Average
Rust Warranty	6 yr/100k	Better Than Average
Maintenance Warranty	N/A	
Roadside Assistance	3 yr/36k	

Resale Value

1993	1994	1995	1996	1997
$15,117	$14,140	$13,259	$12,172	$11,030

Ownership Costs (5yr)

Average	This Car
$28,279	$30,395
Cost/Mile 40¢	Cost/Mile 43¢

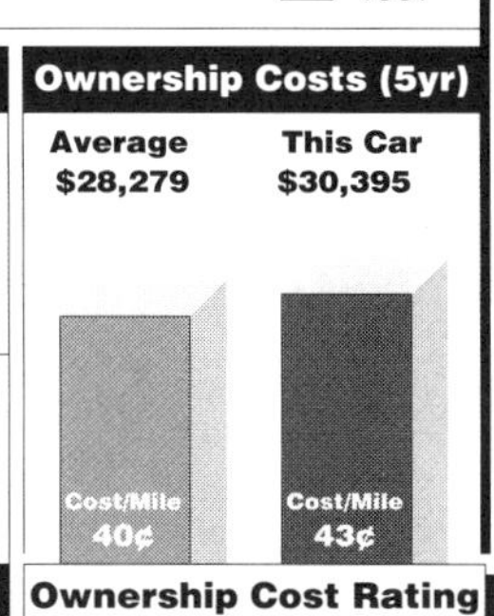

The 1993 GMC Jimmy is available in five models - the (Base), four-door, 2WD, 4WD, and the Jimmy Typhoon 4WD. The Jimmy 4WD with two doors has rear suspension that is designed for on-road and off-road duty. A Softride Suspension Package is optional. The package includes gas-charged shock absorbers and steel-belted all-season radials. An SL Trim Package is also optional. Anti-lock brakes, all-cloth bucket seats, and illuminated entry are standard.

Cumulative Costs

	1993	1994	1995	1996	1997
Annual	$7,591	$4,904	$5,530	$5,255	$7,115
Total	$7,591	$12,495	$18,025	$23,280	$30,395

Ownership Cost Rating

Poor

GMC Jimmy 4WD
4 Door Sport Utility

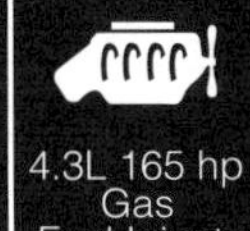
4.3L 165 hp Gas Fuel Inject.

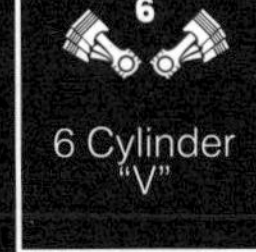
6 Cylinder "V"

Manual 5 Speed

4 Wheel On-Demand

Manual Seatbelts Only

Utility

Purchase Price

Car Item	Dealer Cost	List
Base Price	**$16,550**	**$18,287**
Anti-Lock Brakes	Std	Std
Automatic 4 Speed	Pkg	Pkg
4.3L 285 hp Gas	Pkg	Pkg
Air Conditioning	$671	$780
Power Steering	Std	Std
Cruise Control	$205	** $238
4 Whl On-Demand Dr.	Std	Std
AM/FM Stereo Cassette	$105	$122
Steering Wheel, Tilt	Pkg	Pkg
Power Windows	Pkg	Pkg
***Options Price**	$776	$902
***Total Price**	**$17,326**	**$19,189**
Target Price	$18,627	
Destination Charge	$475	
Avg. Tax & Fees	$1,152	
Total Target $	**$20,254**	
Average Dealer Option Cost:	***86%***	

Ownership Costs

Cost Area	5 Year Cost	Rate
Depreciation	$8,157	Average
Financing ($407/month)	$3,337	
Insurance (Rating 14 [Est.])	$8,446	Worse Than Average
State Fees	$787	
Fuel (Hwy 21 City 16)	$4,672	Average
Maintenance	$5,078	Worse Than Average
Repairs	$791	Average

Ownership Cost By Year

$2,000 $4,000 $6,000 $8,000 $10,000

1993 1994 1995 1996 1997

Warranty/Maintenance Info

Item		Rate
Major Tune-Up	$226	Poor
Minor Tune-Up	$141	Poor
Brake Service	$223	Average
Overall Warranty	3 yr/36k/$100/12k	Worse Than Average
Drivetrain Warranty	3 yr/36k/$100/12k	Worse Than Average
Rust Warranty	6 yr/100k	Better Than Average
Maintenance Warranty	N/A	
Roadside Assistance	3 yr/36k	

Resale Value

1993	1994	1995	1996	1997
$16,399	$15,379	$14,451	$13,292	$12,097

Ownership Costs (5yr)

Average	This Car
$29,441	$31,268
Cost/Mile 42¢	Cost/Mile 45¢

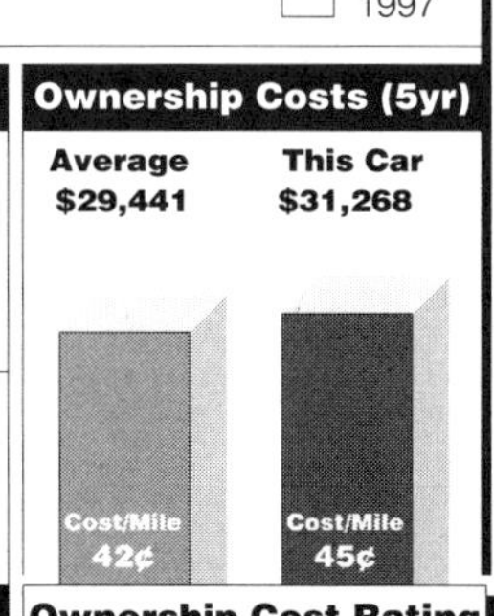

The 1993 GMC Jimmy is available in five models - the (Base), four-door, 2WD, 4WD, and the Jimmy Typhoon 4WD. The Jimmy 4WD with four doors is offered with optional SLS, SLE and SLT packages. The SLS Trim Package includes a full monochromatic look with a body-color grille, wheel-lip moldings, and color-keyed aluminum wheels. To reduce the likelihood of theft, an internal steel sleeve is used on steering columns to protect the ignition lock cylinder.

Cumulative Costs

	1993	1994	1995	1996	1997
Annual	$7,924	$5,069	$5,671	$5,390	$7,214
Total	$7,924	$12,993	$18,664	$24,054	$31,268

Ownership Cost Rating

Worse Than Average

* Includes shaded options

** Other purchase requirements apply

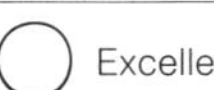

 Poor  Worse Than Average  Average  Better Than Average 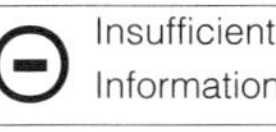 Excellent — Insufficient Information

Refer to *Section 3: Annotated Vehicle Charts* for an explanation of these charts.

GMC Jimmy Typhoon 4WD

2 Door Sport Utility

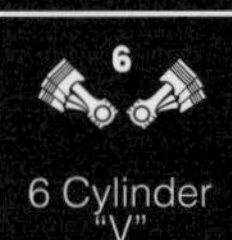
4.3L 285 hp Turbo Gas Fuel Inject.

6 Cylinder "V"

Automatic 4 Speed

4 Wheel On-Demand

Manual Seatbelts Only

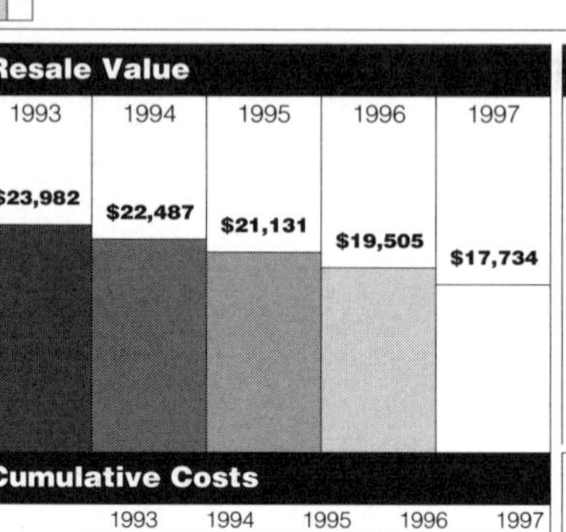

Utility

Purchase Price

Car Item	Dealer Cost	List
Base Price	**$25,596**	**$29,320**
Anti-Lock Brakes	Std	Std
Manual Transmission	N/A	N/A
Optional Engine	N/A	N/A
Air Conditioning	Std	Std
Power Steering	Std	Std
Cruise Control	Std	Std
4 Whl On-Demand Dr.	Std	Std
AM/FM Stereo Cassette	Std	Std
Steering Wheel, Tilt	Std	Std
Power Windows	Std	Std
***Options Price**	$0	$0
***Total Price**	**$25,596**	**$29,320**
Target Price	$27,985	
Destination Charge	$475	
Avg. Tax & Fees	$1,721	
Total Target $	**$30,181**	
Average Dealer Option Cost:	***86%***	

Ownership Costs

Cost Area	5 Year Cost	Rate
Depreciation	$12,447	Average
Financing ($607/month)	$4,972	
Insurance (Rating 20 [Est.])	$10,453	Worse Than Average
State Fees	$1,192	
Fuel (Hwy 19 City 15 [Est.])	$5,079	Average
Maintenance	$7,092	Poor
Repairs	$791	Average

Ownership Cost By Year

Warranty/Maintenance Info

Item		Rate
Major Tune-Up	$257	Poor
Minor Tune-Up	$172	Poor
Brake Service	$235	Average
Overall Warranty	3 yr/36k/$100/12k	Worse Than Average
Drivetrain Warranty	3 yr/36k/$100/12k	Worse Than Average
Rust Warranty	6 yr/100k	Better Than Average
Maintenance Warranty	N/A	
Roadside Assistance	3 yr/36k	

Resale Value

1993	1994	1995	1996	1997
$23,982	$22,487	$21,131	$19,505	$17,734

Ownership Costs (5yr)

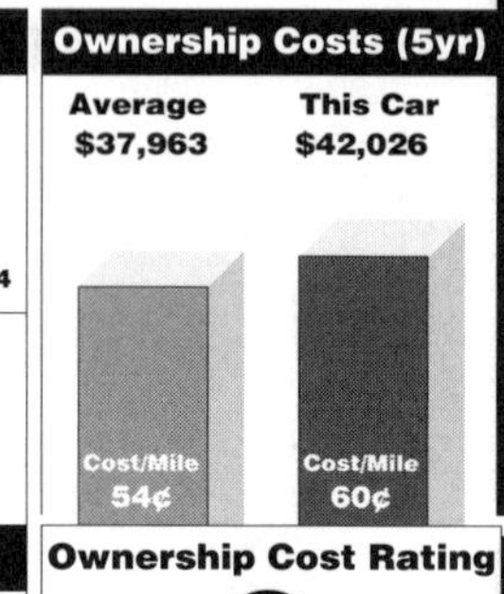

Average	This Car
$37,963	$42,026
Cost/Mile 54¢	Cost/Mile 60¢

Cumulative Costs

	1993	1994	1995	1996	1997
Annual	$11,565	$6,713	$7,800	$6,724	$9,224
Total	$11,565	$18,278	$26,078	$32,802	$42,026

Ownership Cost Rating

Poor

The 1993 GMC Jimmy is available in five models - the (Base), four-door, 2WD, 4WD, and the Jimmy Typhoon 4WD. The Jimmy Typhoon 4WD features standards like an overhead console with two reading lamps, a leather trim driver's seat with six-way power adjustments, and a front passenger seat with power lumbar support. Other standard items include a front fascia with integral fog lamps, rear fascia, and aero moldings on the front fenders, doors, rocker, and quarter panels.

GMC Safari SLX

3 Door Pass Van

4.3L 150 hp Gas Fuel Inject.

6 Cylinder "V"

Automatic 4 Speed

2 Wheel Rear

Manual Seatbelts Only

Mini Van

XT AWD Model Shown

Purchase Price

Car Item	Dealer Cost	List
Base Price	**$14,321**	**$15,824**
Anti-Lock Brakes	Std	Std
Manual Transmission	N/A	N/A
4.3L 200 hp Gas	$430	$500
Air Conditioning	$727	$845
Power Steering	Std	Std
Cruise Control	Pkg	Pkg
All Wheel Drive	N/A	N/A
AM/FM Stereo Cassette	$105	$122
Steering Wheel, Tilt	Pkg	Pkg
Power Windows	Pkg	Pkg
***Options Price**	$832	$967
***Total Price**	**$15,153**	**$16,791**
Target Price	$16,062	
Destination Charge	$545	
Avg. Tax & Fees	$1,003	
Total Target $	**$17,610**	
Average Dealer Option Cost:	***86%***	

Ownership Costs

Cost Area	5 Year Cost	Rate
Depreciation	$4,979	Excellent
Financing ($354/month)	$2,901	
Insurance (Rating 3 [Est.])	$6,731	Excellent
State Fees	$693	
Fuel (Hwy 21 City 16)	$4,672	Worse Than Average
Maintenance	$4,481	Average
Repairs	$700	Better Than Average

Ownership Cost By Year

Warranty/Maintenance Info

Item		Rate
Major Tune-Up	$226	Poor
Minor Tune-Up	$141	Poor
Brake Service	$241	Average
Overall Warranty	3 yr/36k	Average
Drivetrain Warranty	3 yr/36k	Average
Rust Warranty	6 yr/100k	Better Than Average
Maintenance Warranty	N/A	
Roadside Assistance	3 yr/36k	

Resale Value

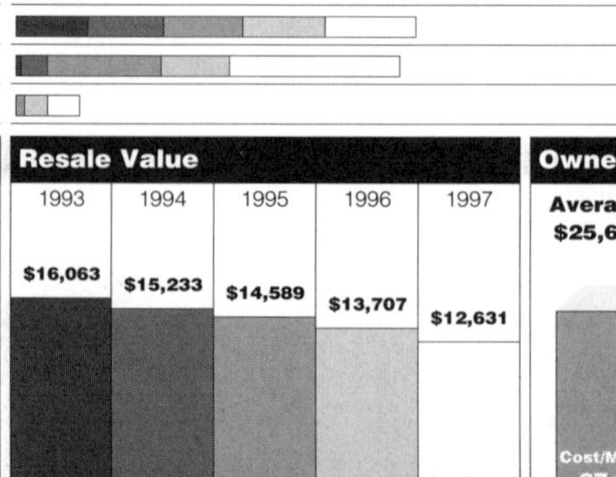

1993	1994	1995	1996	1997
$16,063	$15,233	$14,589	$13,707	$12,631

Ownership Costs (5yr)

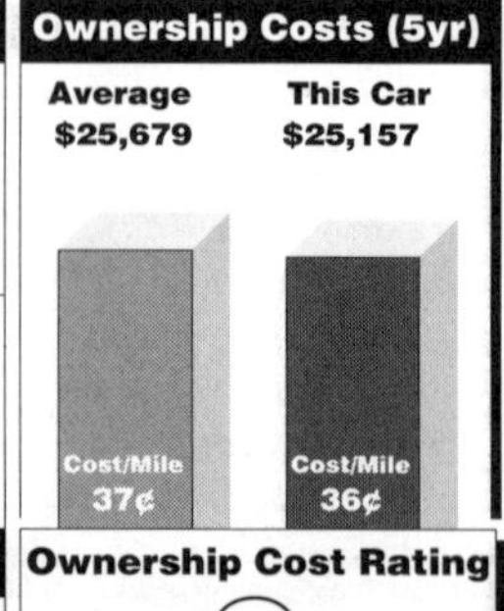

Average	This Car
$25,679	$25,157
Cost/Mile 37¢	Cost/Mile 36¢

Cumulative Costs

	1993	1994	1995	1996	1997
Annual	$5,094	$4,392	$5,097	$4,662	$5,912
Total	$5,094	$9,486	$14,583	$19,245	$25,157

Ownership Cost Rating

Excellent

The 1993 GMC Safari is available in four models - the SLX, SLX XT, SLX AWD and SLX XT AWD. The SLX is the shorter of the rear-wheel-drive Safaris. Dutch-type rear doors are optional. Other optional features include light, medium, and heavy-duty trailering packages with capacities up to 5,000 pounds, a choice of three wheels, and a variety of tire sizes ranging from the standard P205/75R15 to the P245/60R15. Standard seating is augmented by optional seating for seven and eight passengers.

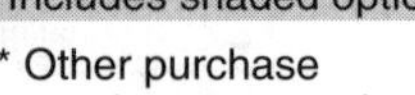

* Includes shaded options

** Other purchase requirements apply

Poor

Worse Than Average

Average

Better Than Average

Excellent
Insufficient Information

Refer to *Section 3: Annotated Vehicle Charts* for an explanation of these charts.

GMC Safari SLX XT

3 Door Pass Ext Van

4.3L 150 hp Gas Fuel Inject.	6 Cylinder "V"	Automatic 4 Speed	2 Wheel Rear	Manual Seatbelts Only

Mini Van

AWD Model Shown

Purchase Price

Car Item	Dealer Cost	List
Base Price	**$14,945**	**$16,514**
Anti-Lock Brakes	Std	Std
Manual Transmission	N/A	N/A
4.3L 200 hp Gas	$430	$500
Air Conditioning	$727	$845
Power Steering	Std	Std
Cruise Control	Pkg	Pkg
All Wheel Drive	N/A	N/A
AM/FM Stereo Cassette	$105	$122
Steering Wheel, Tilt	Pkg	Pkg
Power Windows	Pkg	Pkg
***Options Price**	$832	$967
***Total Price**	**$15,777**	**$17,481**
Target Price	$16,741	
Destination Charge	$545	
Avg. Tax & Fees	$1,044	
Total Target $	**$18,330**	
Average Dealer Option Cost:	***86%***	

Ownership Costs

Cost Area	5 Year Cost	Rate
Depreciation	$5,223	Excellent
Financing ($368/month)	$3,020	
Insurance (Rating 3 [Est.])	$6,731	Excellent
State Fees	$720	
Fuel (Hwy 21 City 16)	$4,672	Worse Than Average
Maintenance	$4,510	Average
Repairs	$700	Better Than Average

Warranty/Maintenance Info

Item		Rate
Major Tune-Up	$226	Poor
Minor Tune-Up	$141	Poor
Brake Service	$241	Average
Overall Warranty	3 yr/36k	Average
Drivetrain Warranty	3 yr/36k	Average
Rust Warranty	6 yr/100k	Better Than Average
Maintenance Warranty	N/A	
Roadside Assistance	3 yr/36k	

Ownership Cost By Year

$2,000 $4,000 $6,000 $8,000

1993 1994 1995 1996 1997

Resale Value

1993	1994	1995	1996	1997
$16,639	$15,782	$15,130	$14,200	$13,107

Ownership Costs (5yr)

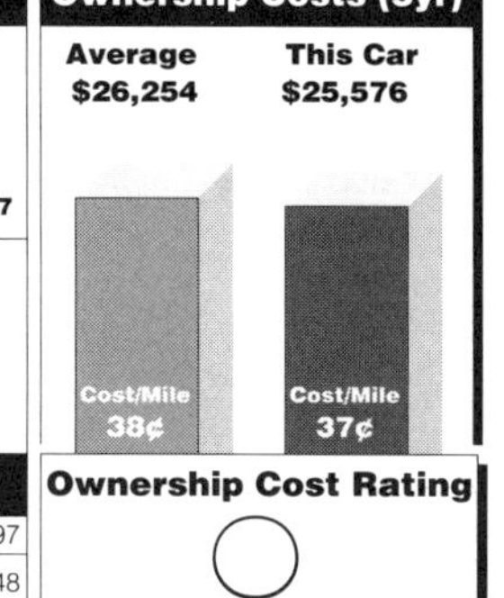

Average	This Car
$26,254	$25,576
Cost/Mile 38¢	Cost/Mile 37¢

The 1993 GMC Safari is available in four models - the SLX, SLX XT, SLX AWD and SLX XT AWD. The SLX XT has an extra added length of 10 inches. This model features standard a heavy-duty cooling system, a new analog instrument cluster, brushed aluminum wheels, three new exterior colors and five new decal colors. The steering column has a new internal steel sleeve to protect the ignition lock cylinder and reduce the likelihood of vehicle theft.

Cumulative Costs

	1993	1994	1995	1996	1997
Annual	$5,295	$4,462	$5,148	$4,723	$5,948
Total	$5,295	$9,757	$14,905	$19,628	$25,576

Ownership Cost Rating

Excellent

GMC Safari Cargo Van

3 Door Cargo Van

4.3L 150 hp Gas Fuel Inject.	6 Cylinder "V"	Automatic 4 Speed	2 Wheel Rear	Manual Seatbelts Only

Mini Van

SLX XT AWD Model Shown

Purchase Price

Car Item	Dealer Cost	List
Base Price	**$13,361**	**$14,763**
Anti-Lock Brakes	Std	Std
Manual Transmission	N/A	N/A
4.3L 200 hp Gas	$430	** $500
Air Conditioning	$727	$845
Power Steering	Std	Std
Cruise Control	Pkg	Pkg
All Wheel Drive	N/A	N/A
AM/FM Stereo Cassette	$187	$218
Steering Wheel, Tilt	Pkg	Pkg
Power Windows	Pkg	Pkg
***Options Price**	$914	$1,063
***Total Price**	**$14,275**	**$15,826**
Target Price	$15,108	
Destination Charge	$545	
Avg. Tax & Fees	$947	
Total Target $	**$16,600**	
Average Dealer Option Cost:	***86%***	

Ownership Costs

Cost Area	5 Year Cost	Rate
Depreciation	$6,977	Excellent
Financing ($334/month)	$2,735	
Insurance (Rating 1 [Est.])	$6,401	Excellent
State Fees	$655	
Fuel (Hwy 23 City 17)	$4,328	Better Than Average
Maintenance	$4,481	Average
Repairs	$700	Better Than Average

Warranty/Maintenance Info

Item		Rate
Major Tune-Up	$226	Poor
Minor Tune-Up	$141	Poor
Brake Service	$241	Average
Overall Warranty	3 yr/36k	Average
Drivetrain Warranty	3 yr/36k	Average
Rust Warranty	6 yr/100k	Better Than Average
Maintenance Warranty	N/A	
Roadside Assistance	3 yr/36k	

Ownership Cost By Year

$2,000 $4,000 $6,000 $8,000

1993 1994 1995 1996 1997

Resale Value

1993	1994	1995	1996	1997
$12,989	$12,163	$11,523	$10,634	$9,623

Ownership Costs (5yr)

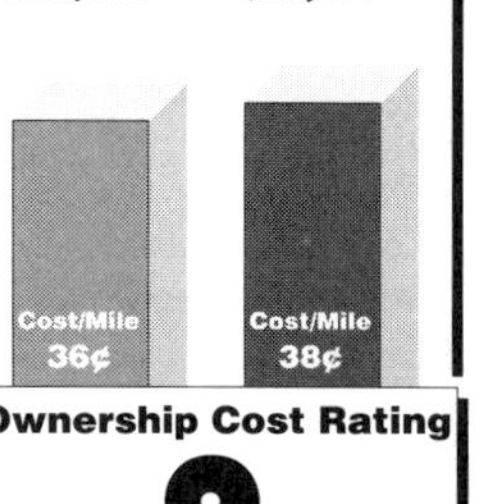

Average	This Car
$24,876	$26,277
Cost/Mile 36¢	Cost/Mile 38¢

The 1993 GMC Safari Cargo Van is available in four models - (Base) Cargo Van, Extended (XT), AWD, and Extended (XT) AWD. The Base model offers optional Dutch-type rear doors for access to the cargo. The rear window and frame lift skyward in lift-hatch style while the lower doors swing out to either side like full-size panel doors. Other options include light, medium, and heavy-duty trailering packages with capacities up to 5,000 pounds. Three wheels and several tire sizes are also available.

Cumulative Costs

	1993	1994	1995	1996	1997
Annual	$6,955	$4,198	$4,917	$4,511	$5,696
Total	$6,955	$11,153	$16,070	$20,581	$26,277

Ownership Cost Rating

Worse Than Average

* Includes shaded options

** Other purchase requirements apply

 Poor  Worse Than Average  Average  Better Than Average 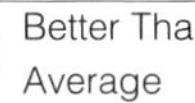 Excellent  Insufficient Information

Refer to *Section 3: Annotated Vehicle Charts* for an explanation of these charts.

GMC Safari Cargo Van XT

3 Door Cargo Ext Van

4.3L 150 hp Gas Fuel Inject.

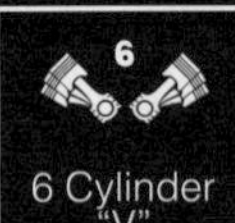
6 Cylinder "V"

Automatic 4 Speed

2 Wheel Rear

Manual Seatbelts Only

Mini Van

SLX AWD Model Shown

Purchase Price

Car Item	Dealer Cost	List
Base Price	**$13,967**	**$15,433**
Anti-Lock Brakes	Std	Std
Manual Transmission	N/A	N/A
4.3L 200 hp Gas	$430	** $500
Air Conditioning	$727	$845
Power Steering	Std	Std
Cruise Control	Pkg	Pkg
All Wheel Drive	N/A	N/A
AM/FM Stereo Cassette	$187	$218
Steering Wheel, Tilt	Pkg	Pkg
Power Windows	Pkg	Pkg
***Options Price**	$914	$1,063
***Total Price**	**$14,881**	**$16,496**
Target Price	$15,765	
Destination Charge	$545	
Avg. Tax & Fees	$986	
Total Target $	**$17,296**	
Average Dealer Option Cost:	***86%***	

Ownership Costs

Cost Area	5 Year Cost	Rate
Depreciation	$7,252	Excellent
Financing ($348/month)	$2,850	
Insurance (Rating 2 [Est.])	$6,542	Excellent
State Fees	$680	
Fuel (Hwy 23 City 17)	$4,328	Better Than Average
Maintenance	$4,510	Average
Repairs	$700	Better Than Average

Ownership Cost By Year

$2,000 $4,000 $6,000 $8,000

1993 1994 1995 1996 1997

Warranty/Maintenance Info

Major Tune-Up	$226	Poor
Minor Tune-Up	$141	Poor
Brake Service	$241	Average
Overall Warranty	3 yr/36k	Average
Drivetrain Warranty	3 yr/36k	Average
Rust Warranty	6 yr/100k	Better Than Average
Maintenance Warranty	N/A	
Roadside Assistance	3 yr/36k	

Resale Value

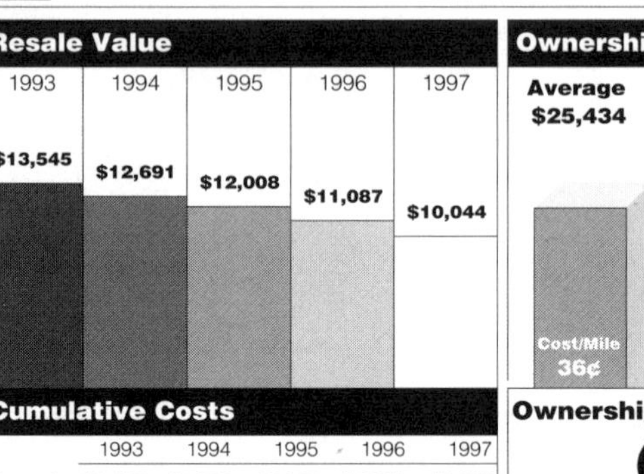

Ownership Costs (5yr)

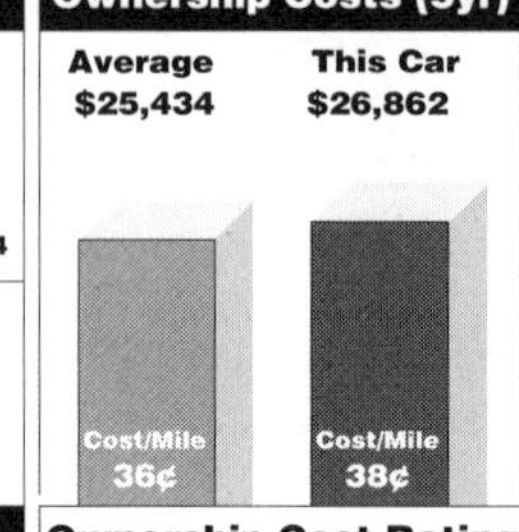

Average	This Car
$25,434	$26,862
Cost/Mile 36¢	Cost/Mile 38¢

Cumulative Costs

	1993	1994	1995	1996	1997
Annual	$7,175	$4,295	$5,030	$4,585	$5,777
Total	$7,175	$11,470	$16,500	$21,085	$26,862

Ownership Cost Rating

Worse Than Average

The 1993 GMC Safari Cargo Van is available in four models - (Base) Cargo Van, Extended (XT), AWD, and Extended (XT) AWD. The 1993 GMC Cargo Van Extended is 10 inches longer than the Base model and offers an additional 18.6 cubic feet of cargo space. This model offers optional Dutch-type rear doors for access to the cargo. The rear window and frame lift skyward in lift hatch style while the lower doors swing out to either side like full-size panel doors.

GMC Safari SLX AWD

3 Door Pass Van

4.3L 200 hp Gas Fuel Inject.

6 Cylinder "V"

Automatic 4 Speed

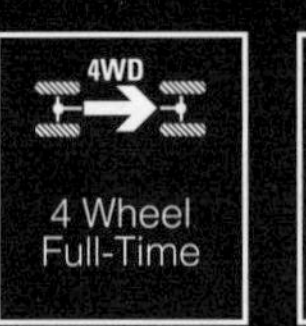
4 Wheel Full-Time

Manual Seatbelts Only

Mini Van

XT Model Shown

Purchase Price

Car Item	Dealer Cost	List
Base Price	**$16,420**	**$18,144**
Anti-Lock Brakes	Std	Std
Manual Transmission	N/A	N/A
Optional Engine	N/A	N/A
Air Conditioning	$727	$845
Power Steering	Std	Std
Cruise Control	Pkg	Pkg
4 Wheel Full-Time Drive	Std	Std
AM/FM Stereo Cassette	$105	$122
Steering Wheel, Tilt	Pkg	Pkg
Power Windows	Pkg	Pkg
***Options Price**	$832	$967
***Total Price**	**$17,252**	**$19,111**
Target Price	$18,349	
Destination Charge	$545	
Avg. Tax & Fees	$1,142	
Total Target $	**$20,036**	
Average Dealer Option Cost:	***86%***	

Ownership Costs

Cost Area	5 Year Cost	Rate
Depreciation	$5,251	Excellent
Financing ($403/month)	$3,301	
Insurance (Rating 4 [Est.])	$6,867	Excellent
State Fees	$787	
Fuel (Hwy 20 City 15 -Prem.)	$5,458	Poor
Maintenance	$5,109	Poor
Repairs	$700	Better Than Average

Ownership Cost By Year

$2,000 $4,000 $6,000 $8,000

1993 1994 1995 1996 1997

Warranty/Maintenance Info

Major Tune-Up	$226	Poor
Minor Tune-Up	$141	Poor
Brake Service	$245	Average
Overall Warranty	3 yr/36k	Average
Drivetrain Warranty	3 yr/36k	Average
Rust Warranty	6 yr/100k	Better Than Average
Maintenance Warranty	N/A	
Roadside Assistance	3 yr/36k	

Resale Value

1993	1994	1995	1996	1997
$19,046	$18,066	$17,177	$16,097	$14,785

Ownership Costs (5yr)

Average	This Car
$27,612	$27,473
Cost/Mile 39¢	Cost/Mile 39¢

Cumulative Costs

	1993	1994	1995	1996	1997
Annual	$4,898	$4,866	$5,522	$5,135	$7,052
Total	$4,898	$9,764	$15,286	$20,421	$27,473

Ownership Cost Rating

Better Than Average

The 1993 GMC Safari is available in four models - the SLX, SLX XT, SLX AWD and SLX XT AWD. The SLX AWD features four-wheel anti-lock front disc and rear drum brakes. Safety features include a collapsible steering column, self-aligning steering wheel, and brake/shift interlock system, which requires that brakes be applied before the transmission can be shifted out of "Park." Dutch-type rear doors, an AM/FM stereo with graphic equalizer or compact disc player are optional.

* Includes shaded options

** Other purchase requirements apply

 Poor 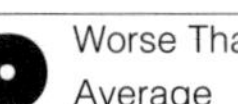 Worse Than Average  Average  Better Than Average 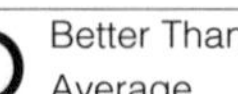 Excellent 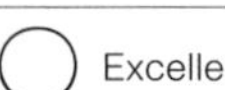 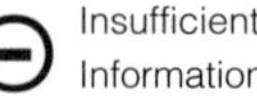 Insufficient Information

Refer to *Section 3: Annotated Vehicle Charts* for an explanation of these charts.

GMC Safari SLX XT AWD

3 Door Pass Ext Van

4.3L 200 hp Gas Fuel Inject.

6 Cylinder "V"

Automatic 4 Speed

4 Wheel Full-Time

Manual Seatbelts Only

Mini Van

Purchase Price

Car Item	Dealer Cost	List
Base Price	**$17,000**	**$18,784**
Anti-Lock Brakes	Std	Std
Manual Transmission	N/A	N/A
Optional Engine	N/A	N/A
Air Conditioning	$727	$845
Power Steering	Std	Std
Cruise Control	Pkg	Pkg
4 Wheel Full-Time Drive	Std	Std
AM/FM Stereo Cassette	$105	$122
Steering Wheel, Tilt	Pkg	Pkg
Power Windows	Pkg	Pkg
***Options Price**	$832	$967
***Total Price**	**$17,832**	**$19,751**
Target Price	$18,984	
Destination Charge	$545	
Avg. Tax & Fees	$1,179	
Total Target $	**$20,708**	
Average Dealer Option Cost:	***86%***	

Ownership Costs

Cost Area	5 Year Cost	Rate
Depreciation	$5,393	Excellent
Financing ($416/month)	$3,411	
Insurance (Rating 5 [Est.])	$6,996	Excellent
State Fees	$812	
Fuel (Hwy 20 City 15 -Prem.)	$5,458	Poor
Maintenance	$5,109	Poor
Repairs	$700	Better Than Average

Ownership Cost By Year

$2,000 $4,000 $6,000 $8,000

1993 1994 1995 1996 1997

Warranty/Maintenance Info

Item		Rate
Major Tune-Up	$226	Poor
Minor Tune-Up	$141	Poor
Brake Service	$245	Average
Overall Warranty	3 yr/36k	Average
Drivetrain Warranty	3 yr/36k	Average
Rust Warranty	6 yr/100k	Better Than Average
Maintenance Warranty	N/A	
Roadside Assistance	3 yr/36k	

Resale Value

1993	1994	1995	1996	1997
$19,334	$18,307	$17,571	$16,460	$15,315

Ownership Costs (5yr)

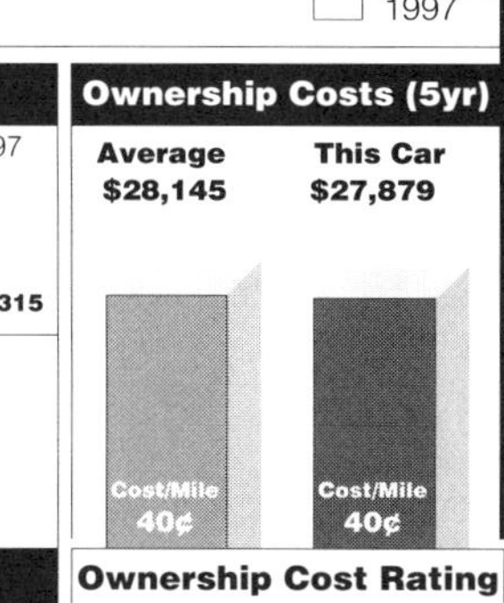

Average	This Car
$28,145	$27,879
Cost/Mile 40¢	Cost/Mile 40¢

The 1993 GMC Safari is available in four models - the SLX, SLX XT, SLX AWD and SLX XT AWD. The SLX XT AWD offers the options of three trim levels - the standard SLX, mid-level SLE, and SLT. Dutch-type rear doors are also optional. Standard safety features include four-wheel anti-lock brakes and a brake/transmission shift interlock system that requires that the brake be applied before the vehicle is shifted out of "Park".

Cumulative Costs

	1993	1994	1995	1996	1997
Annual	$5,358	$4,977	$5,422	$5,205	$6,917
Total	$5,358	$10,335	$15,757	$20,962	$27,879

Ownership Cost Rating

Better Than Average

GMC Safari Cargo Van AWD

3 Door Cargo Van

4.3L 200 hp Gas Fuel Inject.

6 Cylinder "V"

Automatic 4 Speed

4 Wheel Full-Time

Manual Seatbelts Only

Mini Van

SLX XT Model Shown

Purchase Price

Car Item	Dealer Cost	List
Base Price	**$15,451**	**$17,073**
Anti-Lock Brakes	Std	Std
Manual Transmission	N/A	N/A
Optional Engine	N/A	N/A
Air Conditioning	$727	$845
Power Steering	Std	Std
Cruise Control	Pkg	Pkg
4 Wheel Full-Time Drive	Std	Std
AM/FM Stereo Cassette	$187	$218
Steering Wheel, Tilt	Pkg	Pkg
Power Windows	Pkg	Pkg
***Options Price**	$914	$1,063
***Total Price**	**$16,365**	**$18,136**
Target Price	$17,379	
Destination Charge	$545	
Avg. Tax & Fees	$1,083	
Total Target $	**$19,007**	
Average Dealer Option Cost:	***86%***	

Ownership Costs

Cost Area	5 Year Cost	Rate
Depreciation	$7,769	Excellent
Financing ($382/month)	$3,131	
Insurance (Rating 3 [Est.])	$6,731	Excellent
State Fees	$747	
Fuel (Hwy 21 City 16 -Prem.)	$5,159	Worse Than Average
Maintenance	$5,109	Poor
Repairs	$700	Better Than Average

Ownership Cost By Year

$2,000 $4,000 $6,000 $8,000

1993 1994 1995 1996 1997

Warranty/Maintenance Info

Item		Rate
Major Tune-Up	$226	Poor
Minor Tune-Up	$141	Poor
Brake Service	$245	Average
Overall Warranty	3 yr/36k	Average
Drivetrain Warranty	3 yr/36k	Average
Rust Warranty	6 yr/100k	Better Than Average
Maintenance Warranty	N/A	
Roadside Assistance	3 yr/36k	

Resale Value

1993	1994	1995	1996	1997
$14,994	$14,073	$13,322	$12,345	$11,238

Ownership Costs (5yr)

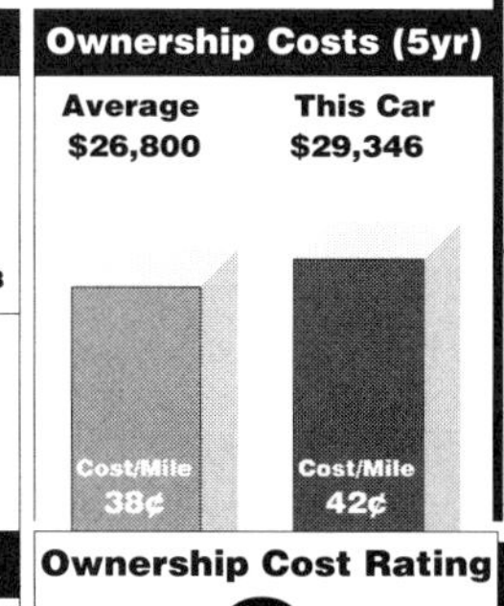

Average	This Car
$26,800	$29,346
Cost/Mile 38¢	Cost/Mile 42¢

The 1993 GMC Safari Cargo Van is available in four models - (Base) Cargo Van, Extended (XT), AWD, and Extended (XT) AWD. The Cargo Van AWD features standard four-wheel anti-lock brakes, which have so far been standard only on Safari passenger vans. This model offers optional Dutch-type rear doors for access to the cargo. Light, medium, and heavy-duty trailering packages with capacities up to 5,500 pounds are optional. Three wheels and several tire sizes are also available.

Cumulative Costs

	1993	1994	1995	1996	1997
Annual	$7,760	$4,661	$5,256	$4,922	$6,747
Total	$7,760	$12,421	$17,677	$22,599	$29,346

Ownership Cost Rating

Poor

* Includes shaded options

** Other purchase requirements apply

Poor  Worse Than Average  Average  Better Than Average  Excellent Insufficient Information

Refer to *Section 3: Annotated Vehicle Charts* for an explanation of these charts.

GMC Safari Cargo Van XT AWD

3 Door Cargo Ext Van

4.3L 200 hp Gas Fuel Inject.

6 Cylinder "V"

Automatic 4 Speed

4 Wheel Full-Time

Manual Seatbelts Only

Mini Van

SLX Model Shown

Purchase Price

Car Item	Dealer Cost	List
Base Price	**$16,030**	**$17,713**
Anti-Lock Brakes	Std	Std
Manual Transmission	N/A	N/A
Optional Engine	N/A	N/A
Air Conditioning	$727	$845
Power Steering	Std	Std
Cruise Control	Pkg	Pkg
4 Wheel Full-Time Drive	Std	Std
AM/FM Stereo Cassette	$187	$218
Steering Wheel, Tilt	Pkg	Pkg
Power Windows	Pkg	Pkg
***Options Price**	$914	$1,063
***Total Price**	**$16,944**	**$18,776**
Target Price	$18,011	
Destination Charge	$545	
Avg. Tax & Fees	$1,121	
Total Target $	**$19,677**	
Average Dealer Option Cost:	***86%***	

Ownership Costs

Cost Area	5 Year Cost	Rate
Depreciation	$7,891	Excellent
Financing ($395/month)	$3,241	
Insurance (Rating 4 [Est.])	$6,867	Excellent
State Fees	$773	
Fuel (Hwy 21 City 16 -Prem.)	$5,159	Worse Than Average
Maintenance	$5,109	Poor
Repairs	$700	Better Than Average

Warranty/Maintenance Info

Item		Rate
Major Tune-Up	$226	Poor
Minor Tune-Up	$141	Poor
Brake Service	$245	Average
Overall Warranty	3 yr/36k	Average
Drivetrain Warranty	3 yr/36k	Average
Rust Warranty	6 yr/100k	Better Than Average
Maintenance Warranty	N/A	
Roadside Assistance	3 yr/36k	

Ownership Cost By Year

$2,000 $4,000 $6,000 $8,000

1993 1994 1995 1996 1997

Resale Value

1993	1994	1995	1996	1997
$15,557	$14,649	$13,911	$12,924	$11,786

Ownership Costs (5yr)

Average	This Car
$27,333	$29,740
Cost/Mile 39¢	Cost/Mile 42¢

Cumulative Costs

	1993	1994	1995	1996	1997
Annual	$7,944	$4,715	$5,298	$4,972	$6,811
Total	$7,944	$12,659	$17,957	$22,929	$29,740

Ownership Cost Rating

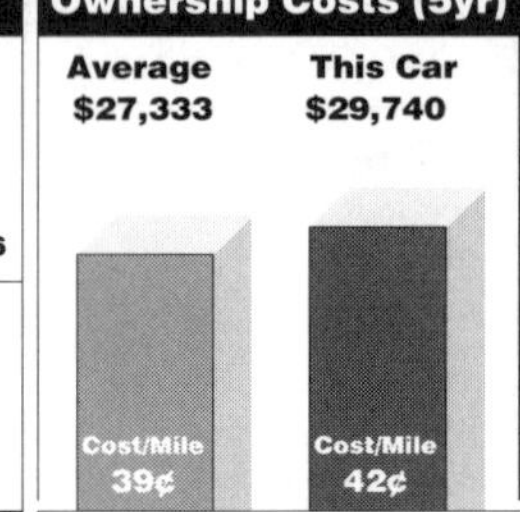
Poor

The 1993 GMC Safari Cargo Van is available in four models - (Base) Cargo Van, Extended (XT), AWD, and Extended (XT) AWD. The Cargo Van Extended AWD is 10 inches longer than the Base model and offers an additional 18.6 cubic feet of cargo space. This model features standard four-wheel anti-lock brakes, which have so far been standard only on Safari passenger vans. Dutch-type rear doors for access to the cargo are optional.

GMC Sierra C1500 Special

2 Door Regular Cab

4.3L 165 hp Gas Fuel Inject.

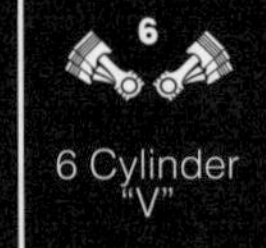
6 Cylinder "V"

Manual 5 Speed

2 Wheel Rear

Manual Seatbelts Only

Large Pickup

Base Stepside Model Shown

Purchase Price

Car Item	Dealer Cost	List
Base Price	**$10,188**	**$11,257**
Anti-Lock Brakes	Std	Std
Automatic 4 Speed	$765	$890
Optional Engine	N/A	N/A
Air Conditioning	$692	$805
Power Steering	Std	Std
Cruise Control	N/A	N/A
All Wheel Drive	N/A	N/A
AM/FM Stereo Cassette	$390	$454
Steering Wheel, Tilt	N/A	N/A
Power Windows	N/A	N/A
***Options Price**	$1,082	$1,259
***Total Price**	**$11,270**	**$12,516**
Target Price	$11,937	
Destination Charge	$595	
Avg. Tax & Fees	$758	
Total Target $	**$13,290**	
Average Dealer Option Cost:	***86%***	

Ownership Costs

Cost Area	5 Year Cost	Rate
Depreciation	$3,574	Excellent
Financing ($267/month)	$2,189	
Insurance (Rating 4 [Est.])	$6,867	Better Than Average
State Fees	$525	
Fuel (Hwy 21 City 15)	$4,816	Excellent
Maintenance	$4,413	Average
Repairs	$700	Excellent

Warranty/Maintenance Info

Item		Rate
Major Tune-Up	$175	Average
Minor Tune-Up	$101	Better Than Average
Brake Service	$273	Better Than Average
Overall Warranty	3 yr/36k	Average
Drivetrain Warranty	3 yr/36k	Average
Rust Warranty	6 yr/100k	Better Than Average
Maintenance Warranty	N/A	
Roadside Assistance	3 yr/36k	

Ownership Cost By Year

$2,000 $4,000 $6,000 $8,000

1993 1994 1995 1996 1997

Resale Value

1993	1994	1995	1996	1997
$10,994	$10,742	$10,573	$10,310	$9,716

Ownership Costs (5yr)

Average	This Car
$21,606	$23,084
Cost/Mile 31¢	Cost/Mile 33¢

Cumulative Costs

	1993	1994	1995	1996	1997
Annual	$5,556	$3,566	$4,408	$3,782	$5,772
Total	$5,556	$9,122	$13,530	$17,312	$23,084

Ownership Cost Rating

Worse Than Average

The 1993 GMC C1500 is available in three models - (Base) C1500 and Special Regular cab two-wheel drives and the Extended cab two-wheel drive. New for 1993, the Special C1500 offers a new electronically controlled four-speed automatic transmission. A new GT Sport Package that features a monochromatic look in either Fire Red or Bright Teal metallic. To reduce the likelihood of theft, a new internal steel steering-column sleeve helps protect the ignition lock cylinder.

* Includes shaded options

** Other purchase requirements apply

 Poor 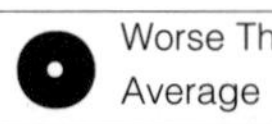 Worse Than Average  Average 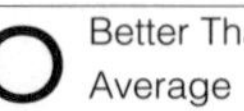 Better Than Average  Excellent 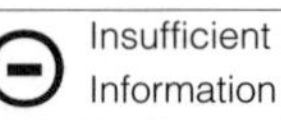 Insufficient Information

Refer to *Section 3: Annotated Vehicle Charts* for an explanation of these charts.

GMC Sierra C1500
2 Door Regular Cab

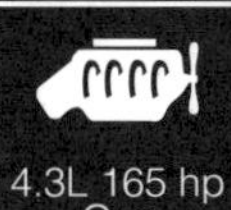		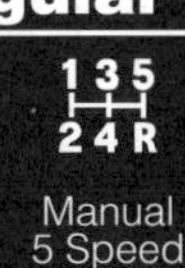		
4.3L 165 hp Gas Fuel Inject.	6 Cylinder "V"	Manual 5 Speed	2 Wheel Rear	Manual Seatbelts Only

Large Pickup

Stepside & GT Package Shown

Purchase Price

Car Item	Dealer Cost	List
Base Price	**$12,095**	**$13,823**
Anti-Lock Brakes	Std	Std
Automatic 4 Speed	$765	$890
5.0L 175 hp Gas	$495	$575
Air Conditioning	$692	$805
Power Steering	Std	Std
Cruise Control	Pkg	Pkg
All Wheel Drive	N/A	N/A
AM/FM Stereo Cassette	$105	$122
Steering Wheel, Tilt	Pkg	Pkg
8 Foot Bed	$263	$300
***Options Price**	$1,292	$1,502
***Total Price**	**$13,387**	**$15,325**
Target Price	$14,228	
Destination Charge	$595	
Avg. Tax & Fees	$900	
Total Target $	**$15,723**	
Average Dealer Option Cost:	***86%***	

Ownership Costs

Cost Area	5 Year Cost	Rate
Depreciation	$4,701	Better Than Average
Financing ($316/month)	$2,591	
Insurance (Rating 6 [Est.])	$7,129	Better Than Average
State Fees	$636	
Fuel (Hwy 19 City 14)	$5,244	Better Than Average
Maintenance	$4,539	Average
Repairs	$700	Excellent

Warranty/Maintenance Info

Item		Rate
Major Tune-Up	$191	Worse Than Average
Minor Tune-Up	$119	Worse Than Average
Brake Service	$273	Better Than Average
Overall Warranty	3 yr/36k	Average
Drivetrain Warranty	3 yr/36k	Average
Rust Warranty	6 yr/100k	Better Than Average
Maintenance Warranty	N/A	
Roadside Assistance	3 yr/36k	

Ownership Cost By Year

$2,000 $4,000 $6,000 $8,000

1993 1994 1995 1996 1997

Resale Value

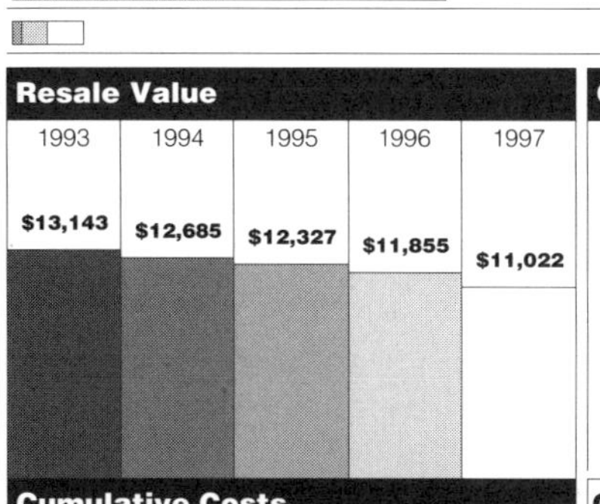

Ownership Costs (5yr)

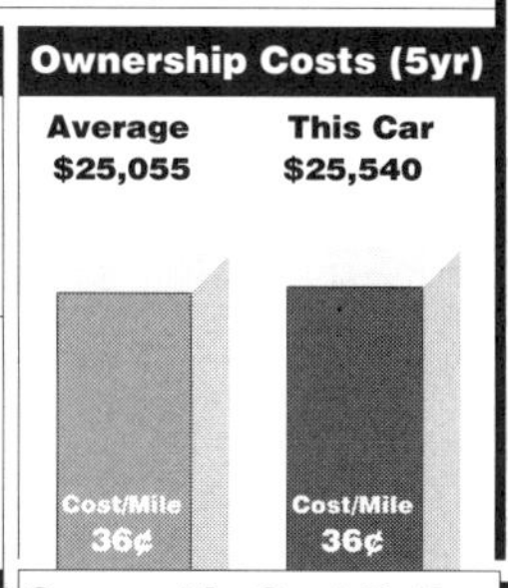

Cumulative Costs

	1993	1994	1995	1996	1997
Annual	$6,165	$4,080	$4,861	$4,209	$6,225
Total	$6,165	$10,245	$15,106	$19,315	$25,540

Ownership Cost Rating

Average

The 1993 GMC C1500 is available in three models - (Base) C1500 and Special Regular cab two-wheel drives and the Extended cab two-wheel drive. New for 1993, the Base C1500 offers a new GT Sport Package that features a monochromatic look in either Fire Red or Bright Teal metallic. The GT package includes aluminum wheels, sport handling suspension, and sport appearance with painted body-colored grille, wheel flare moldings and bumpers. The ventilation system has also been improved.

GMC Sierra C2500
2 Door Regular Cab

4.3L 165 hp Gas Fuel Inject.	6 Cylinder "V"	Manual 5 Speed	2 Wheel Rear	Manual Seatbelts Only

Large Pickup

Stepside C1500 Model Shown

Purchase Price

Car Item	Dealer Cost	List
Base Price	**$12,830**	**$14,663**
Anti-Lock Brakes	Std	Std
Automatic 4 Speed	$765	$890
5.0L 175 hp Gas	$495	$575
Air Conditioning	$692	$805
Power Steering	Std	Std
Cruise Control	Pkg	Pkg
All Wheel Drive	N/A	N/A
AM/FM Stereo Cassette	$105	$122
Steering Wheel, Tilt	Pkg	Pkg
Power Windows	Pkg	Pkg
***Options Price**	$1,292	$1,502
***Total Price**	**$14,122**	**$16,165**
Target Price	$15,029	
Destination Charge	$595	
Avg. Tax & Fees	$949	
Total Target $	**$16,573**	
Average Dealer Option Cost:	***86%***	

Ownership Costs

Cost Area	5 Year Cost	Rate
Depreciation	$4,568	Excellent
Financing ($333/month)	$2,729	
Insurance (Rating 5 [Est.])	$6,996	Better Than Average
State Fees	$671	
Fuel (Hwy 19 City 14)	$5,244	Better Than Average
Maintenance	$4,885	Worse Than Average
Repairs	$700	Excellent

Warranty/Maintenance Info

Item		Rate
Major Tune-Up	$191	Worse Than Average
Minor Tune-Up	$119	Worse Than Average
Brake Service	$273	Better Than Average
Overall Warranty	3 yr/36k	Average
Drivetrain Warranty	3 yr/36k	Average
Rust Warranty	6 yr/100k	Better Than Average
Maintenance Warranty	N/A	
Roadside Assistance	3 yr/36k	

Ownership Cost By Year

$2,000 $4,000 $6,000 $8,000

1993 1994 1995 1996 1997

Resale Value

1993	1994	1995	1996	1997
$14,876	$14,271	$13,744	$13,034	$12,005

Ownership Costs (5yr)

Average $26,087

This Car $25,793

Cost/Mile 37¢ — Cost/Mile 37¢

Cumulative Costs

	1993	1994	1995	1996	1997
Annual	$5,325	$4,252	$5,203	$4,436	$6,577
Total	$5,325	$9,577	$14,780	$19,216	$25,793

Ownership Cost Rating

Better Than Average

The 1993 Sierra C2500 Pickup is available in two models - Regular and Extended Cab. New for 1993, the Sierra C2500 Regular Cab offers a new electronically controlled four-speed automatic transmission. It is designed for reliable operation, smoother shifts, improved fuel efficiency and second-gear part-throttle starting for better slippery-road performance. The heating and cooling ventilation has also been improved. All driver side front seats have a seat-back recliner.

* Includes shaded options

** Other purchase requirements apply

 Poor  Worse Than Average  Average 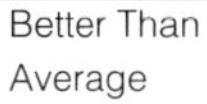 Better Than Average  Excellent — Insufficient Information

Refer to *Section 3: Annotated Vehicle Charts* for an explanation of these charts.

GMC Sierra C3500
2 Door Regular Cab

5.7L 190 hp Gas Fuel Inject.

8 Cylinder "V"

1 3 5 / 2 4 R
Manual 5 Speed

2 Wheel Rear

Manual Seatbelts Only

Large Pickup

Stepside C1500 Model Shown

Purchase Price

Car Item	Dealer Cost	List
Base Price	**$14,262**	**$16,336**
Anti-Lock Brakes	Std	Std
Automatic 4 Speed	$765	$890
7.4L 230 hp Gas	$404	$470
Air Conditioning	$692	$805
Power Steering	Std	Std
Cruise Control	Pkg	Pkg
All Wheel Drive	N/A	N/A
AM/FM Stereo Cassette	$105	$122
Steering Wheel, Tilt	Pkg	Pkg
Power Windows	Pkg	Pkg
***Options Price**	$797	$927
***Total Price**	**$15,059**	**$17,263**
Target Price	$16,067	
Destination Charge	$595	
Avg. Tax & Fees	$1,012	
Total Target $	**$17,674**	
Average Dealer Option Cost:	***86%***	

Ownership Costs

Cost Area	5 Year Cost	Rate
Depreciation	$5,969	Average
Financing ($355/month)	$2,911	
Insurance (Rating 8 [Est.])	$7,432	Better Than Average
State Fees	$715	
Fuel (Hwy 17 City 13 [Est.])	$5,760	Average
Maintenance	$5,158	Worse Than Average
Repairs	$750	Excellent

Warranty/Maintenance Info

Item		Rate
Major Tune-Up	$191	Worse Than Average
Minor Tune-Up	$119	Worse Than Average
Brake Service	$371	Poor
Overall Warranty	3 yr/36k	Average
Drivetrain Warranty	3 yr/36k	Average
Rust Warranty	6 yr/100k	Better Than Average
Maintenance Warranty	N/A	
Roadside Assistance	3 yr/36k	

The 1993 GMC C3500 is available in two models - (Base) Regular and Extended cab two-wheel drive. New for the 1993 lineup, the C3500 Regular Cab features a new electronic 4-speed automatic, a modified 5.7L V8 available for conversion to gaseous fuel and expanded availability of the 6.5L turbo diesel.

Ownership Cost By Year

$2,000 $4,000 $6,000 $8,000

1993 1994 1995 1996 1997

Resale Value

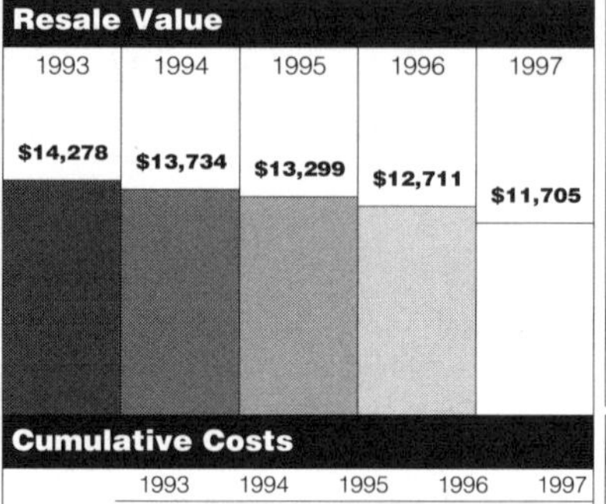

1993	1994	1995	1996	1997
$14,278	$13,734	$13,299	$12,711	$11,705

Ownership Costs (5yr)

Average	This Car
$27,435	$28,695
Cost/Mile 39¢	Cost/Mile 41¢

Cumulative Costs

	1993	1994	1995	1996	1997
Annual	$7,287	$4,441	$5,492	$4,983	$6,492
Total	$7,287	$11,728	$17,220	$22,203	$28,695

Ownership Cost Rating

Average

GMC Sierra C1500
2 Door Extended Cab

4.3L 165 hp Gas Fuel Inject.

6 Cylinder "V"

Manual 5 Speed

2 Wheel Rear

Manual Seatbelts Only

Large Pickup

Purchase Price

Car Item	Dealer Cost	List
Base Price	**$13,447**	**$15,368**
Anti-Lock Brakes	Std	Std
Automatic 4 Speed	$765	$890
5.0L 175 hp Gas	$495	$575
Air Conditioning	$692	$805
Power Steering	Std	Std
Cruise Control	Pkg	Pkg
All Wheel Drive	N/A	N/A
AM/FM Stereo Cassette	$105	$122
Steering Wheel, Tilt	Pkg	Pkg
8 Foot Bed	$228	$260
***Options Price**	$1,292	$1,502
***Total Price**	**$14,739**	**$16,870**
Target Price	$15,703	
Destination Charge	$595	
Avg. Tax & Fees	$990	
Total Target $	**$17,288**	
Average Dealer Option Cost:	***86%***	

Ownership Costs

Cost Area	5 Year Cost	Rate
Depreciation	$4,014	Excellent
Financing ($347/month)	$2,848	
Insurance (Rating 7 [Est.])	$7,244	Better Than Average
State Fees	$699	
Fuel (Hwy 19 City 14)	$5,244	Better Than Average
Maintenance	$4,579	Average
Repairs	$700	Excellent

Warranty/Maintenance Info

Item		Rate
Major Tune-Up	$191	Worse Than Average
Minor Tune-Up	$119	Worse Than Average
Brake Service	$273	Better Than Average
Overall Warranty	3 yr/36k	Average
Drivetrain Warranty	3 yr/36k	Average
Rust Warranty	6 yr/100k	Better Than Average
Maintenance Warranty	N/A	
Roadside Assistance	3 yr/36k	

The 1993 GMC C1500 is available in three models - (Base) C1500 and Special Regular cab two-wheel drives and the Extended cab two-wheel drive. New for 1993, the Extended C1500 offers a new GT Sport Package that features a monochromatic look in either Fire Red or Bright Teal metallic. The GT Sport Package includes aluminum wheels, sport handling suspension, and sport appearance with painted body-colored grille, wheel flare moldings and bumpers. The ventilation system has also been improved.

Ownership Cost By Year

$2,000 $4,000 $6,000 $8,000

1993 1994 1995 1996 1997

Resale Value

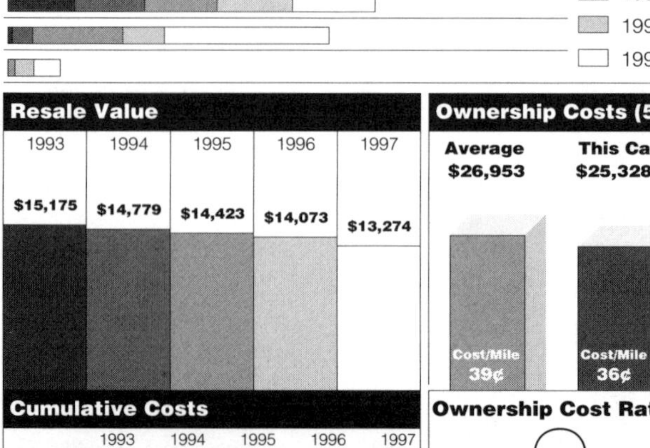

1993	1994	1995	1996	1997
$15,175	$14,779	$14,423	$14,073	$13,274

Ownership Costs (5yr)

Average	This Car
$26,953	$25,328
Cost/Mile 39¢	Cost/Mile 36¢

Cumulative Costs

	1993	1994	1995	1996	1997
Annual	$5,842	$4,134	$4,965	$4,141	$6,246
Total	$5,842	$9,976	$14,941	$19,082	$25,328

Ownership Cost Rating

Excellent

* Includes shaded options

** Other purchase requirements apply

 Poor  Worse Than Average  Average — Better Than Average — Excellent — Insufficient Information

Refer to *Section 3: Annotated Vehicle Charts* for an explanation of these charts.

GMC Sierra C2500
2 Door Extended Cab

Large Pickup

4.3L 165 hp Gas Fuel Inject.

6 Cylinder "V"

Manual 5 Speed

2 Wheel Rear

Manual Seatbelts Only

C1500 Model Shown

Purchase Price

Car Item	Dealer Cost	List
Base Price	**$14,418**	**$16,478**
Anti-Lock Brakes	Std	Std
Automatic 4 Speed	$765	$890
5.0L 175 hp Gas	$495	$575
Air Conditioning	$692	$805
Power Steering	Std	Std
Cruise Control	Pkg	Pkg
All Wheel Drive	N/A	N/A
AM/FM Stereo Cassette	$105	$122
Steering Wheel, Tilt	Pkg	Pkg
8 Foot Bed	$245	$280
***Options Price**	$1,292	$1,502
***Total Price**	**$15,710**	**$17,980**
Target Price	$16,767	
Destination Charge	$595	
Avg. Tax & Fees	$1,054	
Total Target $	**$18,416**	
Average Dealer Option Cost:	***86%***	

The 1993 Sierra C2500 Pickup is available in two models - Regular and Extended Cab. New for 1993, the Sierra C2500 Extended Cab offers a new electronically controlled four-speed automatic transmission. It is designed for reliable operation, smoother shifts, improved fuel efficiency and second-gear part-throttle starting for better slippery-road performance. Sierras equipped with the 7.5L V-8 engine receive a larger radiator designed to improve cooling and reduce engine wear.

Ownership Costs

Cost Area	5 Year Cost	Rate
Depreciation	$4,668	Excellent
Financing ($370/month)	$3,033	
Insurance (Rating 8 [Est.])	$7,432	Average
State Fees	$743	
Fuel (Hwy 19 City 14)	$5,244	Average
Maintenance	$4,885	Worse Than Average
Repairs	$700	Excellent

Ownership Cost By Year

$2,000 $4,000 $6,000 $8,000

1993 1994 1995 1996 1997

Warranty/Maintenance Info

Item		Rate
Major Tune-Up	$191	Worse Than Average
Minor Tune-Up	$119	Worse Than Average
Brake Service	$273	Better Than Average
Overall Warranty	3 yr/36k	Average
Drivetrain Warranty	3 yr/36k	Average
Rust Warranty	6 yr/100k	Better Than Average
Maintenance Warranty	N/A	
Roadside Assistance	3 yr/36k	

Resale Value

1993	1994	1995	1996	1997
$16,418	$15,897	$15,427	$14,783	$13,748

Ownership Costs (5yr)

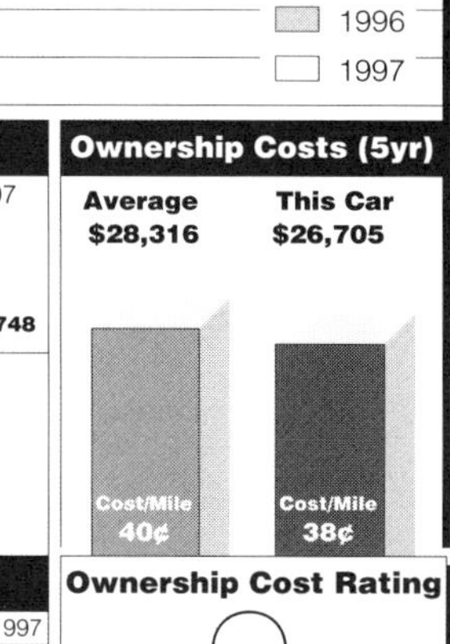

Cumulative Costs

	1993	1994	1995	1996	1997
Annual	$5,851	$4,363	$5,308	$4,496	$6,687
Total	$5,851	$10,214	$15,522	$20,018	$26,705

Ownership Cost Rating

Excellent

GMC Sierra C3500
2 Door Extended Cab

Large Pickup

5.7L 190 hp Gas Fuel Inject.

8 Cylinder "V"

Manual 5 Speed

2 Wheel Rear

Manual Seatbelts Only

C1500 Model Shown

Purchase Price

Car Item	Dealer Cost	List
Base Price	**$15,711**	**$17,996**
Anti-Lock Brakes	Std	Std
Automatic 4 Speed	$765	$890
7.4L 230 hp Gas	$404	$470
Air Conditioning	$692	$805
Power Steering	Std	Std
Cruise Control	Pkg	Pkg
All Wheel Drive	N/A	N/A
AM/FM Stereo Cassette	$105	$122
Steering Wheel, Tilt	Pkg	Pkg
Power Windows	Pkg	Pkg
***Options Price**	$797	$927
***Total Price**	**$16,508**	**$18,923**
Target Price	$17,659	
Destination Charge	$595	
Avg. Tax & Fees	$1,108	
Total Target $	**$19,362**	
Average Dealer Option Cost:	***86%***	

The 1993 GMC C3500 is available in two models - (Base) Regular and Extended cab two-wheel drive. New for the 1993 lineup, the C3500 Extended Cab features a new electronic 4-speed automatic, a modified 5.7L V8 available for conversion to gaseous fuel and expanded availability of the 6.5L turbo diesel. The Extended Cab is now available with two-passenger seating.

Ownership Costs

Cost Area	5 Year Cost	Rate
Depreciation	$5,837	Better Than Average
Financing ($389/month)	$3,190	
Insurance (Rating 10 [Est.])	$7,689	Average
State Fees	$781	
Fuel (Hwy 17 City 13 [Est.])	$5,760	Average
Maintenance	$5,158	Worse Than Average
Repairs	$750	Excellent

Ownership Cost By Year

$2,000 $4,000 $6,000 $8,000

1993 1994 1995 1996 1997

Warranty/Maintenance Info

Item		Rate
Major Tune-Up	$191	Worse Than Average
Minor Tune-Up	$119	Worse Than Average
Brake Service	$371	Poor
Overall Warranty	3 yr/36k	Average
Drivetrain Warranty	3 yr/36k	Average
Rust Warranty	6 yr/100k	Better Than Average
Maintenance Warranty	N/A	
Roadside Assistance	3 yr/36k	

Resale Value

1993	1994	1995	1996	1997
$15,870	$15,489	$15,113	$14,519	$13,525

Ownership Costs (5yr)

Average $29,473 — This Car $29,165

Cost/Mile 42¢ — Cost/Mile 42¢

Cumulative Costs

	1993	1994	1995	1996	1997
Annual	$7,563	$4,429	$5,552	$5,075	$6,546
Total	$7,563	$11,992	$17,544	$22,619	$29,165

Ownership Cost Rating

Better Than Average

* Includes shaded options

** Other purchase requirements apply

 Poor  Worse Than Average  Average  Better Than Average 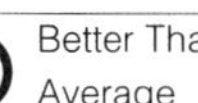  Excellent 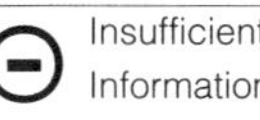 Insufficient Information

Refer to *Section 3: Annotated Vehicle Charts* for an explanation of these charts.

GMC Sierra K1500 Special
2 Door Regular Cab

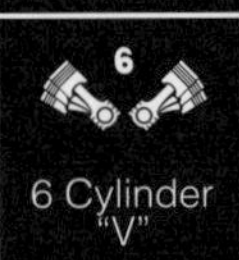

4.3L 165 hp Gas Fuel Inject. | 6 Cylinder "V" | Manual 5 Speed | 4 Wheel On-Demand | Manual Seatbelts Only

Purchase Price

Car Item	Dealer Cost	List
Base Price	**$13,111**	**$14,487**
Anti-Lock Brakes	Std	Std
Automatic 4 Speed	$765	$890
Optional Engine	N/A	N/A
Air Conditioning	$692	$805
Power Steering	Std	Std
Cruise Control	N/A	N/A
4 Whl On-Demand Dr.	Std	Std
AM/FM Stereo Cassette	$390	$454
Steering Wheel, Tilt	N/A	N/A
Power Windows	N/A	N/A
***Options Price**	$1,082	$1,259
***Total Price**	**$14,193**	**$15,746**
Target Price	$15,112	
Destination Charge	$595	
Avg. Tax & Fees	$948	
Total Target $	**$16,655**	
Average Dealer Option Cost:	***86%***	

Ownership Costs

Cost Area	5 Year Cost	Rate
Depreciation	$5,056	Better Than Average
Financing ($335/month)	$2,744	
Insurance (Rating 5 [Est.])	$6,996	Better Than Average
State Fees	$653	
Fuel (Hwy 19 City 15)	$5,079	Better Than Average
Maintenance	$4,966	Worse Than Average
Repairs	$791	Better Than Average

Warranty/Maintenance Info

Item		Rate
Major Tune-Up	$175	Average
Minor Tune-Up	$101	Better Than Average
Brake Service	$273	Better Than Average
Overall Warranty	3 yr/36k	Average
Drivetrain Warranty	3 yr/36k	Average
Rust Warranty	6 yr/100k	Better Than Average
Maintenance Warranty	N/A	
Roadside Assistance	3 yr/36k	

Ownership Cost By Year

$2,000 $4,000 $6,000 $8,000

1993 1994 1995 1996 1997

Resale Value

1993	1994	1995	1996	1997
$14,267	$13,753	$13,239	$12,561	$11,599

Ownership Costs (5yr)

Average	This Car
$25,572	$26,285
Cost/Mile 37¢	Cost/Mile 38¢

Cumulative Costs

	1993	1994	1995	1996	1997
Annual	$5,984	$4,105	$5,006	$4,372	$6,818
Total	$5,984	$10,089	$15,095	$19,467	$26,285

Ownership Cost Rating

Average

The 1993 GMC K1500 is available in three models - (Base) K1500 and Special Regular cab four-wheel drives and the Extended cab four-wheel drive. New for 1993, the Special K1500 offers a new electronically controlled four-speed automatic transmission. A new GT Sport Package that features a monochromatic look in either Fire Red or Bright Teal metallic. To reduce the likelihood of theft, a new internal steel steering-column sleeve helps protect the ignition lock cylinder.

GMC Sierra K1500
2 Door Regular Cab

4.3L 165 hp Gas Fuel Inject. | 6 Cylinder "V" | Manual 5 Speed | 4 Wheel On-Demand | Manual Seatbelts Only

Large Pickup

Purchase Price

Car Item	Dealer Cost	List
Base Price	**$14,064**	**$16,073**
Anti-Lock Brakes	Std	Std
Automatic 4 Speed	$765	$890
5.0L 175 hp Gas	$495	$575
Air Conditioning	$692	$805
Power Steering	Std	Std
Cruise Control	Pkg	Pkg
4 Whl On-Demand Dr.	Std	Std
AM/FM Stereo Cassette	$105	$122
Steering Wheel, Tilt	Pkg	Pkg
8 Foot Bed	$254	$290
***Options Price**	$1,292	$1,502
***Total Price**	**$15,356**	**$17,575**
Target Price	$16,378	
Destination Charge	$595	
Avg. Tax & Fees	$1,031	
Total Target $	**$18,004**	
Average Dealer Option Cost:	***86%***	

Ownership Costs

Cost Area	5 Year Cost	Rate
Depreciation	$5,072	Excellent
Financing ($362/month)	$2,965	
Insurance (Rating 8 [Est.])	$7,432	Better Than Average
State Fees	$727	
Fuel (Hwy 17 City 13)	$5,760	Average
Maintenance	$5,093	Worse Than Average
Repairs	$791	Better Than Average

Warranty/Maintenance Info

Item		Rate
Major Tune-Up	$191	Worse Than Average
Minor Tune-Up	$119	Worse Than Average
Brake Service	$273	Better Than Average
Overall Warranty	3 yr/36k	Average
Drivetrain Warranty	3 yr/36k	Average
Rust Warranty	6 yr/100k	Better Than Average
Maintenance Warranty	N/A	
Roadside Assistance	3 yr/36k	

Ownership Cost By Year

$2,000 $4,000 $6,000 $8,000

1993 1994 1995 1996 1997

Resale Value

1993	1994	1995	1996	1997
$15,867	$15,299	$14,711	$13,969	$12,932

Ownership Costs (5yr)

Average	This Car
$27,818	$27,840
Cost/Mile 40¢	Cost/Mile 40¢

Cumulative Costs

	1993	1994	1995	1996	1997
Annual	$6,053	$4,485	$5,385	$4,724	$7,193
Total	$6,053	$10,538	$15,923	$20,647	$27,840

Ownership Cost Rating

Better Than Average

The 1993 GMC K1500 is available in three models - (Base) K1500 and Special Regular cab four-wheel drives and the Extended cab four-wheel drive. New for 1993, the Base K1500 offers a new GT Sport Package that features a monochromatic look in either Fire Red or Bright Teal metallic. The GT package includes aluminum wheels, sport handling suspension, and sport appearance with painted body-colored grille, wheel flare moldings and bumpers. The ventilation system has also been improved.

* Includes shaded options

** Other purchase requirements apply

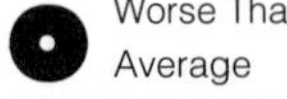

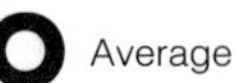

 Poor  Worse Than Average  Average  Better Than Average  Excellent — Insufficient Information

Refer to *Section 3: Annotated Vehicle Charts* for an explanation of these charts.

GMC Sierra K2500
2 Door Regular Cab

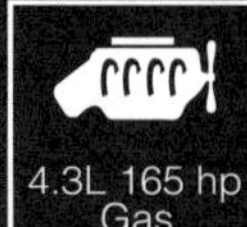
4.3L 165 hp Gas Fuel Inject.

6 Cylinder "V"

Manual 5 Speed

4 Wheel On-Demand

Manual Seatbelts Only

Purchase Price

Car Item	Dealer Cost	List
Base Price	**$14,466**	**$16,533**
Anti-Lock Brakes	Std	Std
Automatic 4 Speed	$765	$890
5.0L 175 hp Gas	$495	$575
Air Conditioning	$692	$805
Power Steering	Std	Std
Cruise Control	Pkg	Pkg
4 Whl On-Demand Dr.	Std	Std
AM/FM Stereo Cassette	$105	$122
Steering Wheel, Tilt	Pkg	Pkg
Power Windows	Pkg	Pkg
***Options Price**	$1,292	$1,502
***Total Price**	**$15,758**	**$18,035**
Target Price	$16,819	
Destination Charge	$595	
Avg. Tax & Fees	$1,057	
Total Target $	**$18,471**	
Average Dealer Option Cost:	***86%***	

Ownership Costs

Cost Area	5 Year Cost	Rate
Depreciation	$3,918	Excellent
Financing ($371/month)	$3,042	
Insurance (Rating 10 [Est.])	$7,689	Better Than Average
State Fees	$745	
Fuel (Hwy 17 City 13)	$5,760	Average
Maintenance	$5,053	Worse Than Average
Repairs	$791	Better Than Average

Ownership Cost By Year

$2,000 · $4,000 · $6,000 · $8,000

1993 · 1994 · 1995 · 1996 · 1997

Warranty/Maintenance Info

Item		Rate
Major Tune-Up	$191	Worse Than Average
Minor Tune-Up	$119	Worse Than Average
Brake Service	$273	Better Than Average
Overall Warranty	3 yr/36k	Average
Drivetrain Warranty	3 yr/36k	Average
Rust Warranty	6 yr/100k	Better Than Average
Maintenance Warranty	N/A	
Roadside Assistance	3 yr/36k	

Resale Value

1993	1994	1995	1996	1997
$17,640	$17,062	$16,479	$15,683	$14,553

Ownership Costs (5yr)

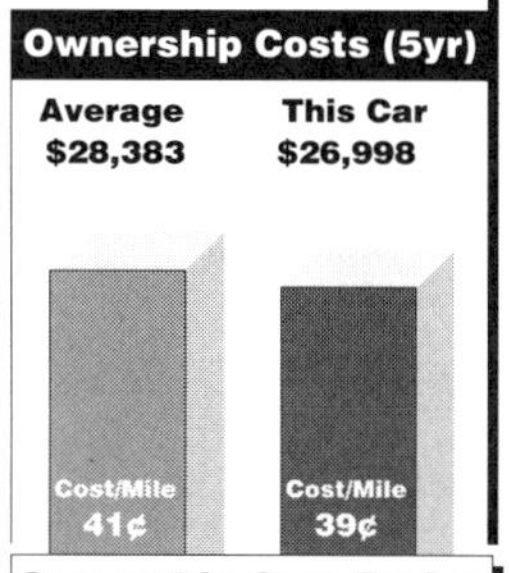

The 1993 GMC Sierra K2500 four-wheel drive pickup is available in two models - Regular and Extended Cab. New for 1993, the Sierra K2500 Regular Cab pickup offers a new electronically controlled four-speed automatic transmission. It is designed for reliable operation, smoother shifts, improved fuel efficiency and second-gear part-throttle starting for better slippery-road performance. The heating and cooling ventilation system has also been improved on the Sierra.

Cumulative Costs

	1993	1994	1995	1996	1997
Annual	$4,831	$4,572	$5,472	$5,266	$6,857
Total	$4,831	$9,403	$14,875	$20,141	$26,998

Ownership Cost Rating

Excellent

GMC Sierra K3500
2 Door Regular Cab

5.7L 190 hp Gas Fuel Inject.

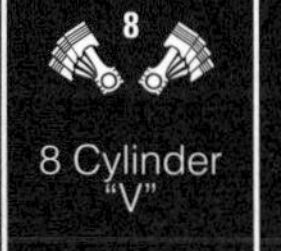
8 Cylinder "V"

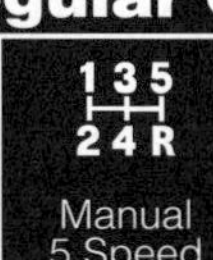
Manual 5 Speed

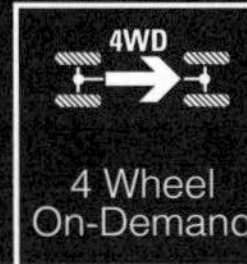
4 Wheel On-Demand

Manual Seatbelts Only

Large Pickup

K1500 Model Shown

Purchase Price

Car Item	Dealer Cost	List
Base Price	**$16,217**	**$18,576**
Anti-Lock Brakes	Std	Std
Automatic 4 Speed	$765	$890
7.4L 230 hp Gas	$404	$470
Air Conditioning	$692	$805
Power Steering	Std	Std
Cruise Control	Pkg	Pkg
4 Whl On-Demand Dr.	Std	Std
AM/FM Stereo Cassette	$105	$122
Steering Wheel, Tilt	Pkg	Pkg
Power Windows	Pkg	Pkg
***Options Price**	$797	$927
***Total Price**	**$17,014**	**$19,503**
Target Price	$18,217	
Destination Charge	$595	
Avg. Tax & Fees	$1,142	
Total Target $	**$19,954**	
Average Dealer Option Cost:	***86%***	

Ownership Costs

Cost Area	5 Year Cost	Rate
Depreciation	$5,958	Better Than Average
Financing ($401/month)	$3,287	
Insurance (Rating 10 [Est.])	$7,689	Better Than Average
State Fees	$805	
Fuel (Hwy 14 City 11 [Est.])	$6,908	Poor
Maintenance	$5,667	Poor
Repairs	$830	Average

Ownership Cost By Year

$2,000 · $4,000 · $6,000 · $8,000

1993 · 1994 · 1995 · 1996 · 1997

Warranty/Maintenance Info

Item		Rate
Major Tune-Up	$191	Worse Than Average
Minor Tune-Up	$119	Worse Than Average
Brake Service	$371	Poor
Overall Warranty	3 yr/36k	Average
Drivetrain Warranty	3 yr/36k	Average
Rust Warranty	6 yr/100k	Better Than Average
Maintenance Warranty	N/A	
Roadside Assistance	3 yr/36k	

Resale Value

1993	1994	1995	1996	1997
$17,479	$16,730	$16,062	$15,253	$13,996

Ownership Costs (5yr)

Average	This Car
$30,186	$31,144
Cost/Mile 43¢	Cost/Mile 44¢

The 1993 Sierra K3500 is available in two models - Regular and Extended Cabs with four-wheel drive. New for 1993, the Sierra K3500 Regular Cab offers a new electronically controlled four-speed automatic transmission. It is designed for reliable operation, smoother shifts, improved fuel efficiency and second-gear part-throttle starting for better slippery-road performance. Sierras with the 7.5L engine receive a larger radiator designed to improve cooling and reduce engine wear.

Cumulative Costs

	1993	1994	1995	1996	1997
Annual	$6,803	$5,052	$5,993	$5,531	$7,765
Total	$6,803	$11,855	$17,848	$23,379	$31,144

Ownership Cost Rating

Average

* Includes shaded options

** Other purchase requirements apply

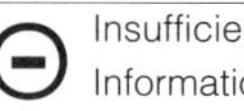

Poor ·  Worse Than Average ·  Average · Better Than Average ·  Excellent ·  Insufficient Information

Refer to *Section 3: Annotated Vehicle Charts* for an explanation of these charts.

GMC Sierra K1500

2 Door Extended Cab

4.3L 165 hp Gas Fuel Inject.

6 Cylinder "V"

Manual 5 Speed

4 Wheel On-Demand

Manual Seatbelts Only

Purchase Price

Car Item	Dealer Cost	List
Base Price	**$15,418**	**$17,621**
Anti-Lock Brakes	Std	Std
Automatic 4 Speed	$765	$890
5.0L 175 hp Gas	$495	$575
Air Conditioning	$692	$805
Power Steering	Std	Std
Cruise Control	Pkg	Pkg
4 Whl On-Demand Dr.	Std	Std
AM/FM Stereo Cassette	$105	$122
Steering Wheel, Tilt	Pkg	Pkg
8 Foot Bed	$254	$290
***Options Price**	$1,292	$1,502
***Total Price**	**$16,710**	**$19,123**
Target Price	$17,866	
Destination Charge	$595	
Avg. Tax & Fees	$1,120	
Total Target $	**$19,581**	
Average Dealer Option Cost:	***86%***	

Ownership Costs

Cost Area	5 Year Cost	Rate
Depreciation	$4,100	Excellent
Financing ($394/month)	$3,226	
Insurance (Rating 11 [Est.])	$7,902	Better Than Average
State Fees	$788	
Fuel (Hwy 17 City 13)	$5,760	Average
Maintenance	$5,210	Poor
Repairs	$791	Better Than Average

Ownership Cost By Year

$2,000 $4,000 $6,000 $8,000

1993 1994 1995 1996 1997

Warranty/Maintenance Info

Major Tune-Up	$191	Worse Than Average
Minor Tune-Up	$119	Worse Than Average
Brake Service	$273	Better Than Average
Overall Warranty	3 yr/36k	Average
Drivetrain Warranty	3 yr/36k	Average
Rust Warranty	6 yr/100k	Better Than Average
Maintenance Warranty	N/A	
Roadside Assistance	3 yr/36k	

Resale Value

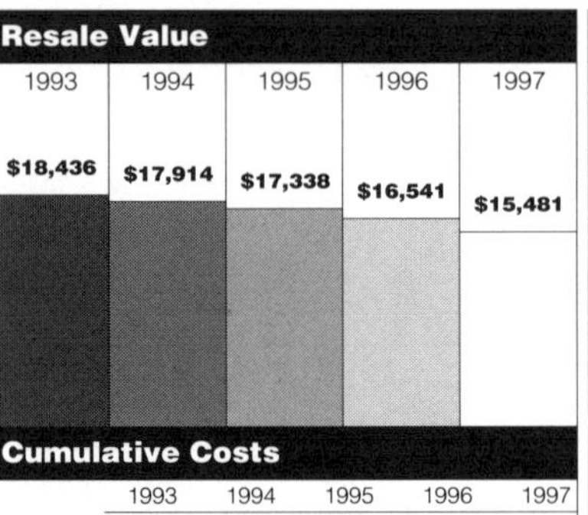

1993	1994	1995	1996	1997
$18,436	$17,914	$17,338	$16,541	$15,481

Ownership Costs (5yr)

Average	This Car
$29,719	$27,777
Cost/Mile 42¢	Cost/Mile 40¢

Cumulative Costs

	1993	1994	1995	1996	1997
Annual	$5,272	$4,623	$5,589	$4,906	$7,387
Total	$5,272	$9,895	$15,484	$20,390	$27,777

Ownership Cost Rating

Excellent

The 1993 GMC K1500 is available in three models - (Base) K1500 and Special Regular cab four-wheel drives and the Extended cab four-wheel drive. New for 1993, the Extended K1500 offers a new GT package that features a monochromatic look in either Fire Red or Bright Teal metallic. The GT Sport Package includes aluminum wheels, sport handling suspension, and sport appearance with painted body-colored grille, wheel flare moldings and bumpers. The ventilation system has also been improved.

GMC Sierra K2500

2 Door Extended Cab

4.3L 165 hp Gas Fuel Inject.

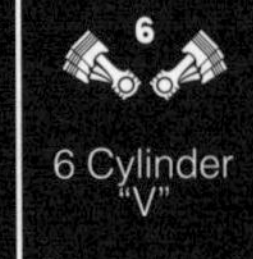
6 Cylinder "V"

Manual 5 Speed

4 Wheel On-Demand

Manual Seatbelts Only

Large Pickup

C1500 Model Shown

Purchase Price

Car Item	Dealer Cost	List
Base Price	**$15,916**	**$18,190**
Anti-Lock Brakes	Std	Std
Automatic 4 Speed	$765	$890
5.0L 175 hp Gas	$495	$575
Air Conditioning	$692	$805
Power Steering	Std	Std
Cruise Control	Pkg	Pkg
4 Whl On-Demand Dr.	Std	Std
AM/FM Stereo Cassette	$105	$122
Steering Wheel, Tilt	Pkg	Pkg
8 Foot Bed	$263	$300
***Options Price**	$1,292	$1,502
***Total Price**	**$17,208**	**$19,692**
Target Price	$18,415	
Destination Charge	$595	
Avg. Tax & Fees	$1,154	
Total Target $	**$20,164**	
Average Dealer Option Cost:	***86%***	

Ownership Costs

Cost Area	5 Year Cost	Rate
Depreciation	$4,471	Excellent
Financing ($405/month)	$3,322	
Insurance (Rating 10 [Est.])	$7,689	Better Than Average
State Fees	$812	
Fuel (Hwy 17 City 13)	$5,760	Average
Maintenance	$5,125	Worse Than Average
Repairs	$791	Better Than Average

Ownership Cost By Year

$2,000 $4,000 $6,000 $8,000

1993 1994 1995 1996 1997

Warranty/Maintenance Info

Major Tune-Up	$191	Worse Than Average
Minor Tune-Up	$119	Worse Than Average
Brake Service	$273	Better Than Average
Overall Warranty	3 yr/36k	Average
Drivetrain Warranty	3 yr/36k	Average
Rust Warranty	6 yr/100k	Better Than Average
Maintenance Warranty	N/A	
Roadside Assistance	3 yr/36k	

Resale Value

1993	1994	1995	1996	1997
$18,939	$18,407	$17,754	$16,898	$15,693

Ownership Costs (5yr)

Average	This Car
$30,418	$27,970
Cost/Mile 43¢	Cost/Mile 40¢

Cumulative Costs

	1993	1994	1995	1996	1997
Annual	$5,359	$4,628	$5,646	$5,358	$6,979
Total	$5,359	$9,987	$15,633	$20,991	$27,970

Ownership Cost Rating

Excellent

The 1993 GMC Sierra K2500 four-wheel drive pickup is available in two models - Regular and Extended Cab. New for 1993, the Sierra K2500 Extended Cab pickup offers a new four-speed automatic transmission. It is designed for reliable operation, smoother shifts, improved fuel efficiency and second-gear part-throttle starting for better slippery-road performance. Sierras equipped with the 7.5L engine receive a larger radiator designed to improve cooling and reduce engine wear.

* Includes shaded options

** Other purchase requirements apply

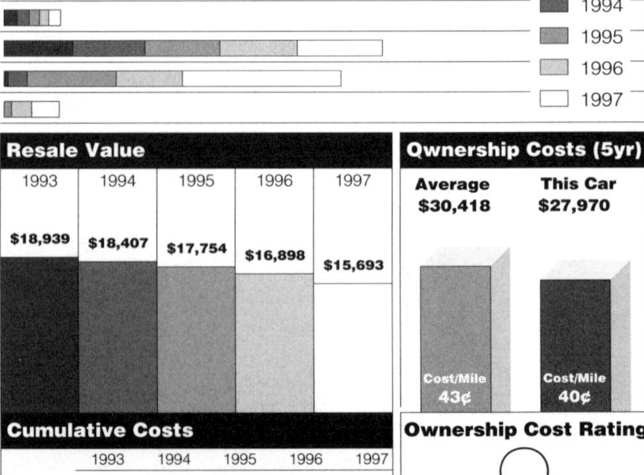

 Poor  Worse Than Average  Average 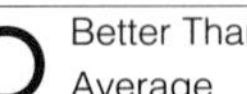 Better Than Average  Excellent — Insufficient Information

Refer to *Section 3: Annotated Vehicle Charts* for an explanation of these charts.

GMC TRUCK

GMC Sierra K3500
2 Door Extended Cab

5.7L 190 hp Gas Fuel Inject.

8 Cylinder "V"

Manual 5 Speed

4 Wheel On-Demand

Manual Seatbelts Only

C1500 Model Shown

Purchase Price

Car Item	Dealer Cost	List
Base Price	**$17,710**	**$20,286**
Anti-Lock Brakes	Std	Std
Automatic 4 Speed	$765	$890
7.4L 230 hp Gas	$404	$470
Air Conditioning	$692	$805
Power Steering	Std	Std
Cruise Control	Pkg	Pkg
4 Whl On-Demand Dr.	Std	Std
AM/FM Stereo Cassette	$105	$122
Steering Wheel, Tilt	Pkg	Pkg
Power Windows	Pkg	Pkg
***Options Price**	$797	$927
***Total Price**	**$18,507**	**$21,213**
Target Price	$19,869	
Destination Charge	$595	
Avg. Tax & Fees	$1,241	
Total Target $	**$21,705**	
Average Dealer Option Cost:	***86%***	

Ownership Costs

Cost Area	5 Year Cost	Rate
Depreciation	$6,033	Excellent
Financing ($436/month)	$3,576	
Insurance (Rating 12 [Est.])	$8,108	Better Than Average
State Fees	$872	
Fuel (Hwy 14 City 11 [Est.])	$6,908	Poor
Maintenance	$5,667	Poor
Repairs	$830	Average

Ownership Cost By Year

$2,000 $4,000 $6,000 $8,000 $10,000

1993 1994 1995 1996 1997

Warranty/Maintenance Info

Item		Rate
Major Tune-Up	$191	Worse Than Average
Minor Tune-Up	$119	Worse Than Average
Brake Service	$371	Poor
Overall Warranty	3 yr/36k	Average
Drivetrain Warranty	3 yr/36k	Average
Rust Warranty	6 yr/100k	Better Than Average
Maintenance Warranty	N/A	
Roadside Assistance	3 yr/36k	

Resale Value

1993	1994	1995	1996	1997
$19,726	$18,951	$18,141	$17,054	$15,672

Ownership Costs (5yr)

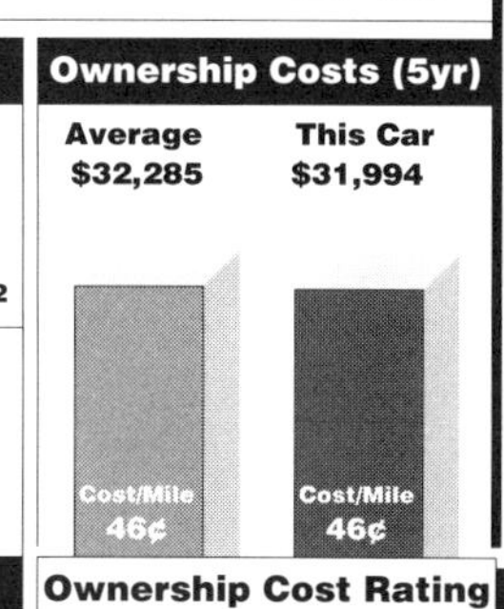

The 1993 Sierra K3500 is available in two models - Regular and Extended Cabs with four-wheel drive. New for 1993, the Sierra K3500 Extended Cab offers a new electronically controlled four-speed automatic transmission. It is designed for reliable operation, smoother shifts, improved fuel efficiency and second-gear part-throttle starting for better slippery-road performance. Sierras with the 7.5L engine receive a larger radiator designed to improve cooling and reduce engine wear.

Cumulative Costs

	1993	1994	1995	1996	1997
Annual	$6,521	$5,265	$6,289	$5,929	$7,990
Total	$6,521	$11,786	$18,075	$24,004	$31,994

Ownership Cost Rating

Better Than Average

GMC Sierra C3500 Crew Cab
4 Door Extended Cab

5.7L 210 hp Gas Fuel Inject.

8 Cylinder "V"

Manual 5 Speed

2 Wheel Rear

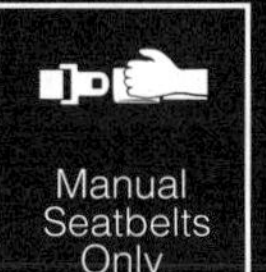
Manual Seatbelts Only

K3500 Model Shown

Purchase Price

Car Item	Dealer Cost	List
Base Price	**$16,027**	**$18,316**
Anti-Lock Brakes	Std	Std
Automatic 4 Speed	$765	$890
7.4L 230 hp Gas	$404	$470
Air Conditioning	$692	$805
Power Steering	Std	Std
Cruise Control	Pkg	Pkg
All Wheel Drive	N/A	N/A
AM/FM Stereo Cassette	$105	$122
Steering Wheel, Tilt	Pkg	Pkg
Power Windows	Pkg	Pkg
***Options Price**	$797	$927
***Total Price**	**$16,824**	**$19,243**
Target Price	$18,007	
Destination Charge	$595	
Avg. Tax & Fees	$1,128	
Total Target $	**$19,730**	
Average Dealer Option Cost:	***86%***	

Ownership Costs

Cost Area	5 Year Cost	Rate
Depreciation	$7,109	Average
Financing ($397/month)	$3,250	
Insurance (Rating 10 [Est.])	$7,689	Average
State Fees	$794	
Fuel (Hwy 19 City 14 [Est.])	$5,244	Better Than Average
Maintenance	$5,158	Worse Than Average
Repairs	$750	Excellent

Ownership Cost By Year

$2,000 $4,000 $6,000 $8,000

1993 1994 1995 1996 1997

Warranty/Maintenance Info

Item		Rate
Major Tune-Up	$191	Worse Than Average
Minor Tune-Up	$119	Worse Than Average
Brake Service	$371	Poor
Overall Warranty	3 yr/36k	Average
Drivetrain Warranty	3 yr/36k	Average
Rust Warranty	6 yr/100k	Better Than Average
Maintenance Warranty	N/A	
Roadside Assistance	3 yr/36k	

Resale Value

1993	1994	1995	1996	1997
$16,681	$15,463	$14,745	$13,786	$12,621

Ownership Costs (5yr)

Average	This Car
$29,866	$29,994
Cost/Mile 43¢	Cost/Mile 43¢

The 1993 GMC Crew Cab is available in two models - C (2WD) and K (4WD) 3500. New for 1993, the Sierra Crew Cab C3500 offers a new electronically controlled four-speed automatic transmission. Sierras equipped with the 7.5L V-8 engine receive a larger radiator designed to improve cooling and reduce engine wear. The heating and cooling ventilation has also been improved for 1993. To reduce the liklihood of theft, a new internal steel steering-column sleeve helps protect the ignition lock cylinder.

Cumulative Costs

	1993	1994	1995	1996	1997
Annual	$7,052	$5,189	$5,806	$5,339	$6,608
Total	$7,052	$12,241	$18,047	$23,386	$29,994

Ownership Cost Rating

Average

* Includes shaded options

** Other purchase requirements apply

Poor  Worse Than Average Average  Better Than Average Excellent  Insufficient Information

Refer to *Section 3: Annotated Vehicle Charts* for an explanation of these charts.

GMC Sierra K3500 Crew Cab

4 Door Extended Cab

5.7L 210 hp Gas Fuel Inject. | 8 Cylinder "V" | Manual 5 Speed | 4 Wheel On-Demand | Manual Seatbelts Only

Large Pickup

Purchase Price

Car Item	Dealer Cost	List
Base Price	**$18,652**	**$21,316**
Anti-Lock Brakes	Std	Std
Automatic 4 Speed	$765	$890
7.4L 230 hp Gas	$404	$470
Air Conditioning	$692	$805
Power Steering	Std	Std
Cruise Control	Pkg	Pkg
4 Whl On-Demand Dr.	Std	Std
AM/FM Stereo Cassette	$105	$122
Steering Wheel, Tilt	Pkg	Pkg
Power Windows	Pkg	Pkg
***Options Price**	$797	$927
***Total Price**	**$19,449**	**$22,243**
Target Price	$20,915	
Destination Charge	$595	
Avg. Tax & Fees	$1,304	
Total Target $	**$22,814**	
Average Dealer Option Cost:	***86%***	

Ownership Costs

Cost Area	5 Year Cost	Rate
Depreciation	$7,050	Better Than Average
Financing ($459/month)	$3,758	
Insurance (Rating 12 [Est.])	$8,108	Better Than Average
State Fees	$914	
Fuel (Hwy 18 City 14 [Est.])	$5,399	Average
Maintenance	$5,667	Poor
Repairs	$840	Average

Warranty/Maintenance Info

Major Tune-Up	$191	Worse Than Average
Minor Tune-Up	$119	Worse Than Average
Brake Service	$371	Poor
Overall Warranty	3 yr/36k	Average
Drivetrain Warranty	3 yr/36k	Average
Rust Warranty	6 yr/100k	Better Than Average
Maintenance Warranty	N/A	
Roadside Assistance	3 yr/36k	

Ownership Cost By Year

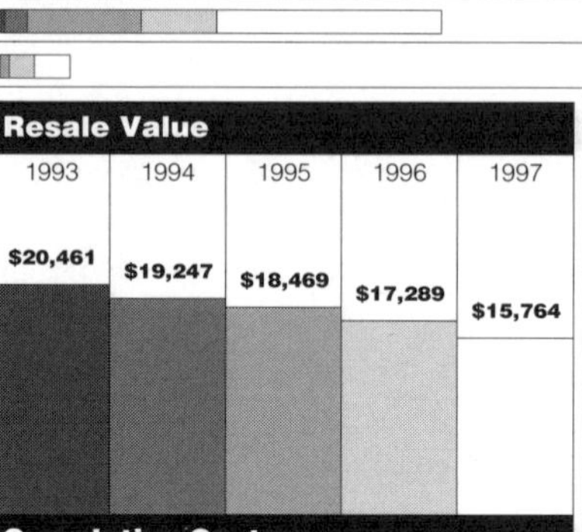

Resale Value

1993	1994	1995	1996	1997
$20,461	$19,247	$18,469	$17,289	$15,764

Ownership Costs (5yr)

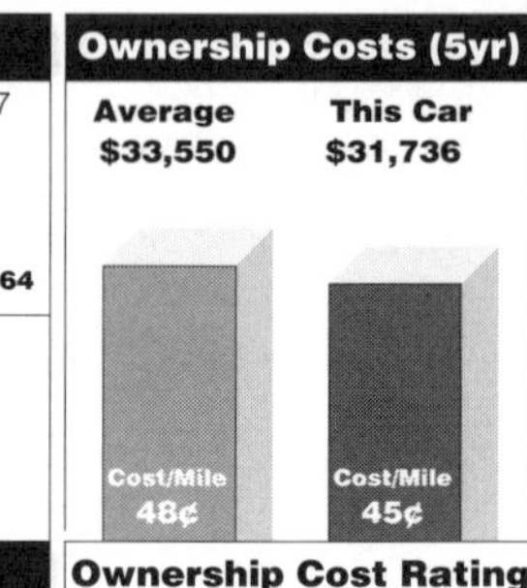

The 1993 GMC Crew Cab is available in two models - C (2WD) and K (4WD) 3500. New for 1993, the Sierra Crew Cab K3500 offers a new electronically controlled four-speed automatic transmission. Sierras equipped with the 7.5L V-8 engine receive a larger radiator designed to improve cooling and reduce engine wear. The heating and cooling ventilation has also been improved for 1993. To reduce the liklihood of theft, a new internal steel steering-column sleeve helps protect the ignition lock cylinder.

Cumulative Costs

	1993	1994	1995	1996	1997
Annual	$6,703	$5,482	$6,001	$5,732	$7,818
Total	$6,703	$12,185	$18,186	$23,918	$31,736

Ownership Cost Rating

Excellent

GMC Sonoma Special

2 Door Regular Cab

2.5L 105 hp Gas Fuel Inject. | 4 Cylinder In-Line | Manual 5 Speed | 2 Wheel Rear | Manual Seatbelts Only

Small Pickup

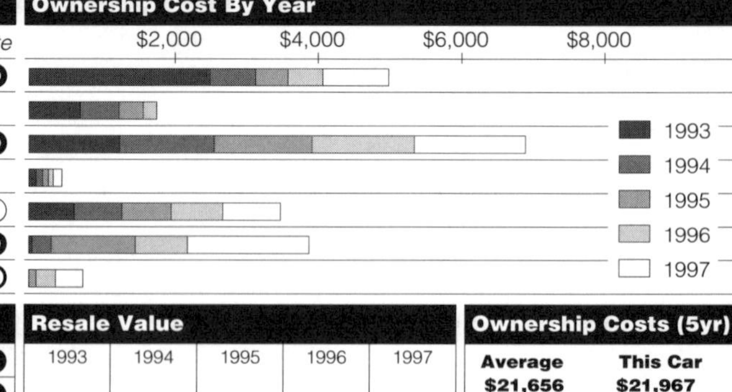

Purchase Price

Car Item	Dealer Cost	List
Base Price	**$8,328**	**$8,813**
Anti-Lock Brakes	Std	Std
Automatic 4 Speed	$765	$890
Optional Engine	N/A	N/A
Air Conditioning	$649	$755
Power Steering	$237	$275
Cruise Control	N/A	N/A
All Wheel Drive	N/A	N/A
AM/FM Stereo Cassette	$390	$454
Steering Wheel, Tilt	N/A	N/A
Power Windows	N/A	N/A
***Options Price**	$627	$729
***Total Price**	**$8,955**	**$9,542**
Target Price	$9,400	
Destination Charge	$470	
Avg. Tax & Fees	$594	
Total Target $	**$10,464**	
Average Dealer Option Cost:	***86%***	

Ownership Costs

Cost Area	5 Year Cost	Rate
Depreciation	$4,964	Average
Financing ($210/month)	$1,724	
Insurance (Rating 4 [Est.])	$6,867	Average
State Fees	$400	
Fuel (Hwy 27 City 23)	$3,454	Excellent
Maintenance	$3,858	Average
Repairs	$700	Better Than Average

Warranty/Maintenance Info

Major Tune-Up	$218	Poor
Minor Tune-Up	$121	Poor
Brake Service	$223	Average
Overall Warranty	3 yr/36k	Average
Drivetrain Warranty	3 yr/36k	Average
Rust Warranty	6 yr/100k	Better Than Average
Maintenance Warranty	N/A	
Roadside Assistance	3 yr/36k	

Ownership Cost By Year

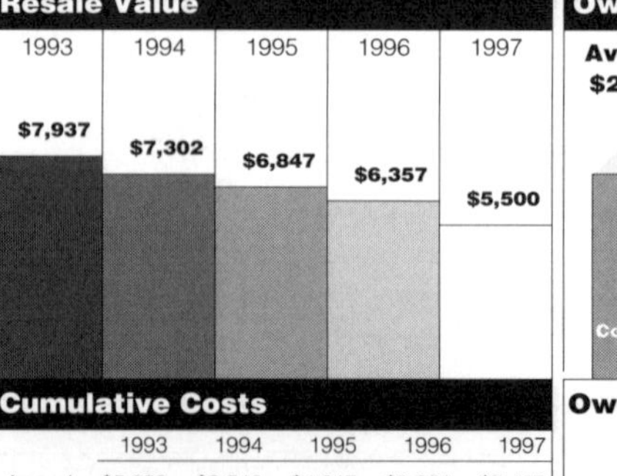

Resale Value

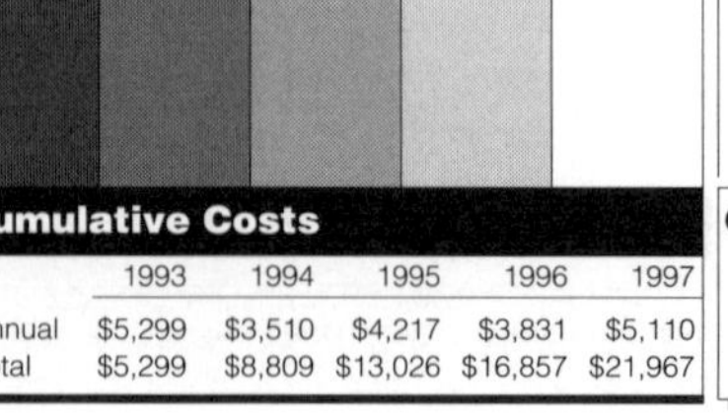

1993	1994	1995	1996	1997
$7,937	$7,302	$6,847	$6,357	$5,500

Ownership Costs (5yr)

The 1993 Sonoma is available in four models-(Base) Sonoma and Special 2WD and 4WD pickups. New for 1993, the Sonoma Special 2WD features the Hydra-matic 4L60-E to provide smoother shifts, improved fuel efficiency and second-gear part-throttle starting for better slippery-surface performance. The Special 2WD features extensive use of double-sided galvanized metal to protect against corrosion.

Cumulative Costs

	1993	1994	1995	1996	1997
Annual	$5,299	$3,510	$4,217	$3,831	$5,110
Total	$5,299	$8,809	$13,026	$16,857	$21,967

Ownership Cost Rating

Average

* Includes shaded options

** Other purchase requirements apply

 Poor  Worse Than Average  Average  Better Than Average  Excellent — Insufficient Information

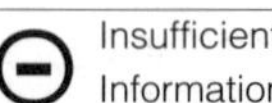

Refer to *Section 3: Annotated Vehicle Charts* for an explanation of these charts.

GMC Sonoma
2 Door Regular Cab

2.5L 105 hp Gas Carburetor	4 Cylinder In-Line	Manual 5 Speed	2 Wheel Rear	Manual Seatbelts Only

Purchase Price

Car Item	Dealer Cost	List
Base Price	**$9,348**	**$10,329**
Anti-Lock Brakes	Std	Std
Automatic 4 Speed	$765	$890
4.3L 195 hp Gas	$963	** $1,120
Air Conditioning	$649	$755
Power Steering	$237	$275
Cruise Control	$205	** $238
All Wheel Drive	N/A	N/A
AM/FM Stereo Cassette	$105	$122
Steering Wheel, Tilt	Pkg	Pkg
7.33 Foot Bed	$262	$300
***Options Price**	$342	$397
***Total Price**	**$9,690**	**$10,726**
Target Price	$10,189	
Destination Charge	$470	
Avg. Tax & Fees	$645	
Total Target $	**$11,304**	
Average Dealer Option Cost:	***86%***	

Ownership Costs

Cost Area	5 Year Cost	Rate
Depreciation	$5,194	Average
Financing ($227/month)	$1,862	
Insurance (Rating 6 [Est.])	$7,129	Average
State Fees	$448	
Fuel (Hwy 27 City 23)	$3,454	Excellent
Maintenance	$3,858	Average
Repairs	$700	Better Than Average

Ownership Cost By Year

$2,000 $4,000 $6,000 $8,000

1993 1994 1995 1996 1997

Warranty/Maintenance Info

Item		Rate
Major Tune-Up	$218	Poor
Minor Tune-Up	$121	Poor
Brake Service	$223	Average
Overall Warranty	3 yr/36k	Average
Drivetrain Warranty	3 yr/36k	Average
Rust Warranty	6 yr/100k	Better Than Average
Maintenance Warranty	N/A	
Roadside Assistance	3 yr/36k	

Resale Value

1993	1994	1995	1996	1997
$8,913	$8,192	$7,649	$7,090	$6,110

Ownership Costs (5yr)

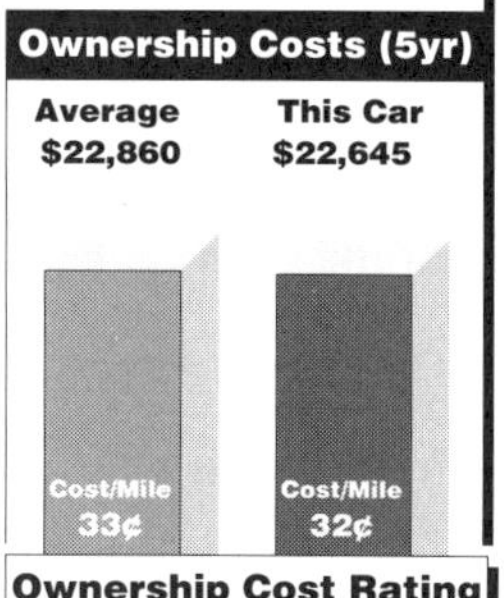

Average	This Car
$22,860	$22,645
Cost/Mile 33¢	Cost/Mile 32¢

The 1993 Sonoma is available in four models-(Base) Sonoma and Special 2WD and 4WD pickups. New for 1993, the Sonoma 2WD features the Hydra-matic 4L60-E to provide smoother shifts, improved fuel efficiency and second-gear part-throttle starting for better slippery-surface performance. Other features include reclining bucket seats, power outside rearview mirrors and an internal steel steering column sleeve.

Cumulative Costs

	1993	1994	1995	1996	1997
Annual	$5,281	$3,700	$4,395	$3,972	$5,297
Total	$5,281	$8,981	$13,376	$17,348	$22,645

Ownership Cost Rating

Average

GMC Sonoma Club Coupe
2 Door Extended Cab

2.5L 105 hp Gas Fuel Inject.	4 Cylinder In-Line	Manual 5 Speed	2 Wheel Rear	Manual Seatbelts Only

Purchase Price

Car Item	Dealer Cost	List
Base Price	**$10,705**	**$11,829**
Anti-Lock Brakes	Std	Std
Automatic 4 Speed	$765	$890
4.3L 165 hp Gas	$533	$620
Air Conditioning	$649	$755
Power Steering	Std	Std
Cruise Control	$205	** $238
All Wheel Drive	N/A	N/A
AM/FM Stereo Cassette	$105	$122
Steering Wheel, Tilt	Pkg	Pkg
Power Windows	Pkg	Pkg
***Options Price**	$638	$742
***Total Price**	**$11,343**	**$12,571**
Target Price	$11,953	
Destination Charge	$470	
Avg. Tax & Fees	$751	
Total Target $	**$13,174**	
Average Dealer Option Cost:	***86%***	

Ownership Costs

Cost Area	5 Year Cost	Rate
Depreciation	$5,772	Average
Financing ($265/month)	$2,170	
Insurance (Rating 7 [Est.])	$7,244	Average
State Fees	$520	
Fuel (Hwy 24 City 18)	$4,117	Average
Maintenance	$4,130	Worse Than Average
Repairs	$700	Better Than Average

Ownership Cost By Year

$2,000 $4,000 $6,000 $8,000

1993 1994 1995 1996 1997

Warranty/Maintenance Info

Item		Rate
Major Tune-Up	$226	Poor
Minor Tune-Up	$141	Poor
Brake Service	$223	Average
Overall Warranty	3 yr/36k	Average
Drivetrain Warranty	3 yr/36k	Average
Rust Warranty	6 yr/100k	Better Than Average
Maintenance Warranty	N/A	
Roadside Assistance	3 yr/36k	

Resale Value

1993	1994	1995	1996	1997
$10,421	$9,675	$9,133	$8,485	$7,402

Ownership Costs (5yr)

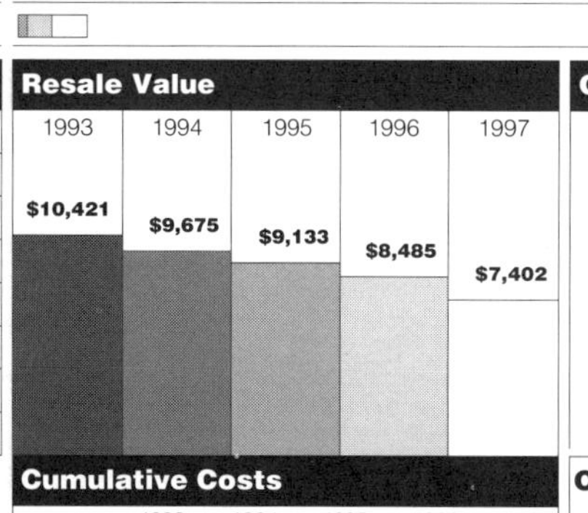

Average	This Car
$24,735	$24,653
Cost/Mile 35¢	Cost/Mile 35¢

The 1993 Sonoma Club Coupe is available in two extended cab versions-Base and 4WD. The Sonoma Club Coupe features the Hydra-matic 4L60-E to provide smoother shifts and second-gear part-throttle starting for better slippery-surface performance. For Club Coupe models with SLS Trim, carpeting has been added to the back panel of the cab and a convenience net is included with SLS and SLE Trim levels. Other features include reclining bucket seats, dual sunvisors and power outside rearview mirrors.

Cumulative Costs

	1993	1994	1995	1996	1997
Annual	$5,944	$4,033	$4,660	$4,310	$5,706
Total	$5,944	$9,977	$14,637	$18,947	$24,653

Ownership Cost Rating

Average

* Includes shaded options

** Other purchase requirements apply

 Poor  Worse Than Average  Average  Better Than Average  Excellent 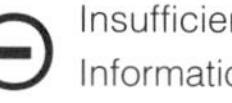 Insufficient Information

Refer to ***Section 3: Annotated Vehicle Charts*** **for an explanation of these charts.**

GMC Sonoma Special 4WD

2 Door Regular Cab

4.3L 165 hp Gas Fuel Inject.

6 Cylinder "V"

135 24R
Manual 5 Speed

4 Wheel On-Demand

Manual Seatbelts Only

Small Pickup

2WD Model Shown

Purchase Price

Car Item	Dealer Cost	List
Base Price	**$11,919**	**$12,613**
Anti-Lock Brakes	Std	Std
Automatic 4 Speed	$765	$890
Optional Engine	N/A	N/A
Air Conditioning	$649	$755
Power Steering	Std	Std
Cruise Control	N/A	N/A
4 Whl On-Demand Dr.	Std	Std
AM/FM Stereo Cassette	$390	$454
Steering Wheel, Tilt	N/A	N/A
Power Windows	N/A	N/A
***Options Price**	$390	$454
***Total Price**	**$12,309**	**$13,067**
Target Price	$12,997	
Destination Charge	$470	
Avg. Tax & Fees	$808	
Total Target $	**$14,275**	
Average Dealer Option Cost:	***86%***	

Ownership Costs

Cost Area	5 Year Cost	Rate
Depreciation	$7,259	Worse Than Average
Financing ($287/month)	$2,351	
Insurance (Rating 8 [Est.])	$7,432	Average
State Fees	$541	
Fuel (Hwy 21 City 16)	$4,672	Worse Than Average
Maintenance	$4,797	Poor
Repairs	$791	Average

Ownership Cost By Year

$2,000 $4,000 $6,000 $8,000

1993 1994 1995 1996 1997

Warranty/Maintenance Info

Item		Rate
Major Tune-Up	$226	Poor
Minor Tune-Up	$141	Poor
Brake Service	$223	Average
Overall Warranty	3 yr/36k	Average
Drivetrain Warranty	3 yr/36k	Average
Rust Warranty	6 yr/100k	Better Than Average
Maintenance Warranty	N/A	
Roadside Assistance	3 yr/36k	

Resale Value

1993	1994	1995	1996	1997
$10,432	$9,594	$8,922	$8,186	$7,016

Ownership Costs (5yr)

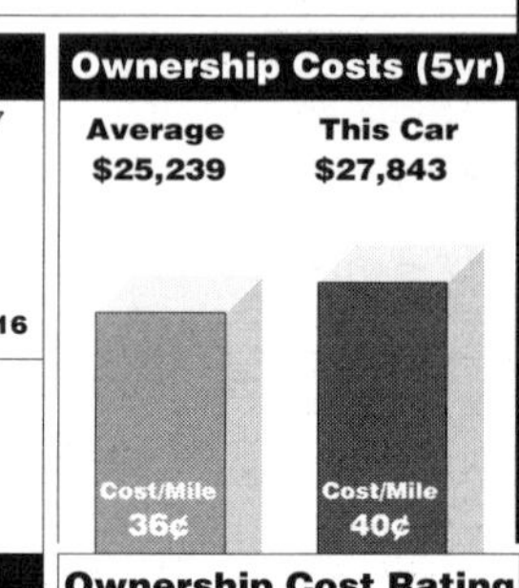

Cumulative Costs

	1993	1994	1995	1996	1997
Annual	$7,252	$4,329	$4,900	$4,641	$6,721
Total	$7,252	$11,581	$16,481	$21,122	$27,843

Ownership Cost Rating

Poor

The 1993 Sonoma is available in four models-(Base) Sonoma and Special 2WD and 4WD pickups. New for 1993, the Sonoma Special 4WD features the Hydra-matic 4L60-E to provide smoother shifts, improved fuel efficiency and second-gear part-throttle starting for better slippery-surface performance. The Special 4WD includes reclining bucket seats, a new internal steel steering column sleeve and an upgraded cooling system.

GMC TRUCK

GMC Sonoma 4WD

2 Door Regular Cab

4.3L 165 hp Gas Fuel Inject.

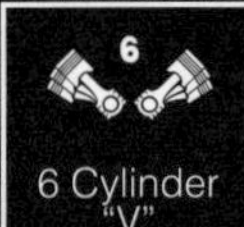
6 Cylinder "V"

135 24R
Manual 5 Speed

4 Wheel On-Demand

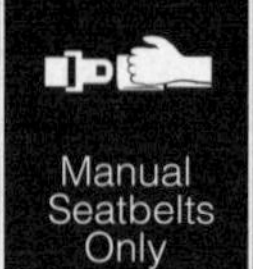
Manual Seatbelts Only

Small Pickup

Purchase Price

Car Item	Dealer Cost	List
Base Price	**$12,575**	**$13,895**
Anti-Lock Brakes	Std	Std
Automatic 4 Speed	$765	$890
4.3L 195 hp Gas	$430	** $500
Air Conditioning	$649	$755
Power Steering	Std	Std
Cruise Control	$205	** $238
4 Whl On-Demand Dr.	Std	Std
AM/FM Stereo Cassette	$105	$122
Steering Wheel, Tilt	Pkg	Pkg
7.33 Foot Bed	$262	$300
***Options Price**	$105	$122
***Total Price**	**$12,680**	**$14,017**
Target Price	$13,403	
Destination Charge	$470	
Avg. Tax & Fees	$839	
Total Target $	**$14,712**	
Average Dealer Option Cost:	***86%***	

Ownership Costs

Cost Area	5 Year Cost	Rate
Depreciation	$7,029	Average
Financing ($296/month)	$2,424	
Insurance (Rating 10 [Est.])	$7,689	Worse Than Average
State Fees	$579	
Fuel (Hwy 21 City 16)	$4,672	Worse Than Average
Maintenance	$4,797	Poor
Repairs	$791	Average

Ownership Cost By Year

$2,000 $4,000 $6,000 $8,000

1993 1994 1995 1996 1997

Warranty/Maintenance Info

Item		Rate
Major Tune-Up	$226	Poor
Minor Tune-Up	$141	Poor
Brake Service	$223	Average
Overall Warranty	3 yr/36k	Average
Drivetrain Warranty	3 yr/36k	Average
Rust Warranty	6 yr/100k	Better Than Average
Maintenance Warranty	N/A	
Roadside Assistance	3 yr/36k	

Resale Value

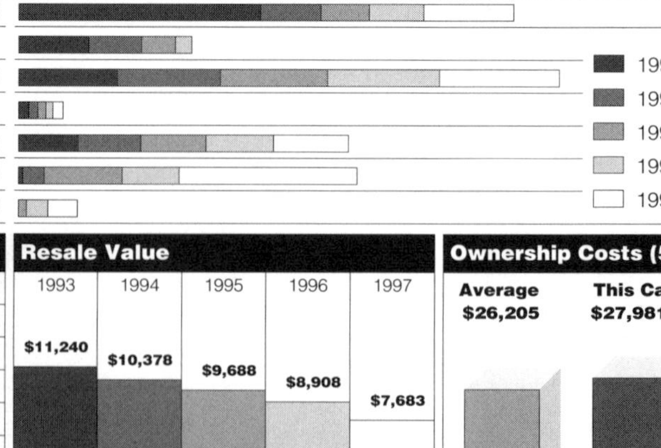

1993	1994	1995	1996	1997
$11,240	$10,378	$9,688	$8,908	$7,683

Ownership Costs (5yr)

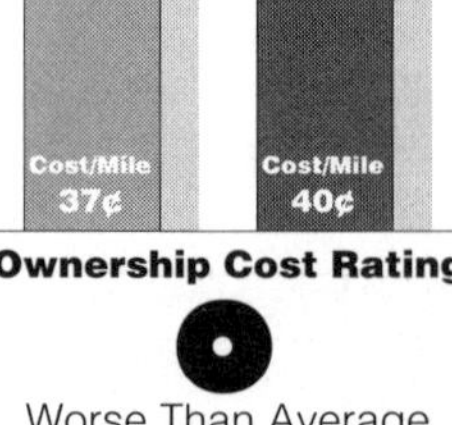

Cumulative Costs

	1993	1994	1995	1996	1997
Annual	$6,969	$4,433	$4,992	$4,749	$6,838
Total	$6,969	$11,402	$16,394	$21,143	$27,981

Ownership Cost Rating

Worse Than Average

The 1993 Sonoma is available in four models-(Base) Sonoma and Special 2WD and 4WD pickups. New for 1993, the Sonoma 4WD features the Hydra-matic 4L60-E to provide smoother shifts, improved fuel efficiency and second-gear part-throttle starting for better slippery-surface performance. The Sonoma 4WD features reclining bucket seats and a new internal steel steering column sleeve. It also features the use of double-sided galvanized metal to protect against corrosion.

* Includes shaded options
** Other purchase requirements apply

 Poor 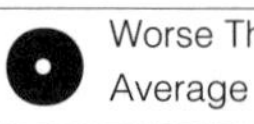 Worse Than Average  Average 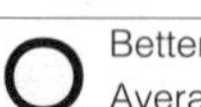 Better Than Average  Excellent  Insufficient Information

Refer to *Section 3: Annotated Vehicle Charts* for an explanation of these charts.

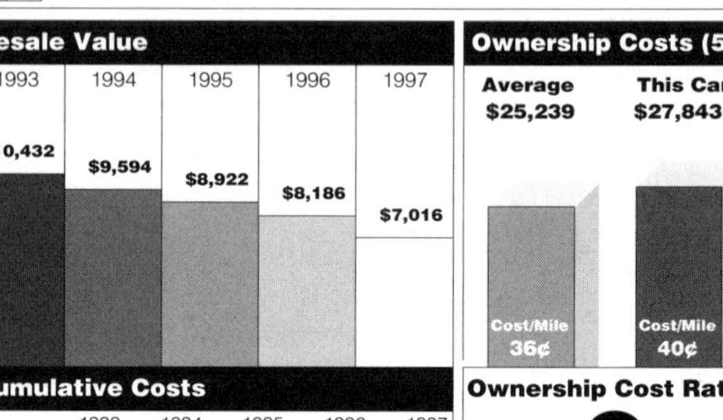

GMC Sonoma Club Coupe 4WD

2 Door Extended Cab

4.3L 165 hp Gas Carburetor | 6 Cylinder "V" | Manual 5 Speed | 4 Wheel On-Demand | Manual Seatbelts Only

Purchase Price

Car Item	Dealer Cost	List
Base Price	**$13,932**	**$15,395**
Anti-Lock Brakes	Std	Std
Automatic 4 Speed	$765	$890
4.3L 195 hp Gas	$430	** $500
Air Conditioning	$649	$755
Power Steering	Std	Std
Cruise Control	$205	** $238
4 Whl On-Demand Dr.	Std	Std
AM/FM Stereo Cassette	$105	$122
Steering Wheel, Tilt	Pkg	Pkg
Power Windows	Pkg	Pkg
***Options Price**	$105	$122
***Total Price**	**$14,037**	**$15,517**
Target Price	$14,870	
Destination Charge	$470	
Avg. Tax & Fees	$927	
Total Target $	**$16,267**	
Average Dealer Option Cost:	***86%***	

Ownership Costs

Cost Area	5 Year Cost	Rate
Depreciation	$7,877	Average
Financing ($327/month)	$2,680	
Insurance (Rating 11 [Est.])	$7,902	Average
State Fees	$640	
Fuel (Hwy 21 City 16)	$4,672	Worse Than Average
Maintenance	$4,797	Poor
Repairs	$791	Average

Warranty/Maintenance Info

Item		Rate
Major Tune-Up	$226	Poor
Minor Tune-Up	$141	Poor
Brake Service	$223	Average
Overall Warranty	3 yr/36k	Average
Drivetrain Warranty	3 yr/36k	Average
Rust Warranty	6 yr/100k	Excellent
Maintenance Warranty	N/A	
Roadside Assistance	3 yr/36k	

Ownership Cost By Year

$2,000 | $4,000 | $6,000 | $8,000

1993 | 1994 | 1995 | 1996 | 1997

Resale Value

1993	1994	1995	1996	1997
$12,547	$11,494	$10,700	$9,769	$8,390

Ownership Costs (5yr)

	Average	This Car
Total	$27,730	$29,359
Cost/Mile	40¢	42¢

Cumulative Costs

	1993	1994	1995	1996	1997
Annual	$7,378	$4,759	$5,201	$4,974	$7,047
Total	$7,378	$12,137	$17,338	$22,312	$29,359

Ownership Cost Rating

Worse Than Average

The 1993 Sonoma Club Coupe is available in two extended cab versions-Base and 4WD. The 4WD Sonoma Club Coupe features the Hydra-matic 4L60-E to provide smoother shifts and second-gear part-throttle starting for better slippery-surface performance. For Club Coupe models with SLS Trim, carpeting has been added to the back panel of the cab and a convenience net is included with SLS and SLE Trim levels. Other features include reclining bucket seats, dual sunvisors and power outside rearview mirrors.

GMC Suburban C1500

5 Door Sport Utility

5.7L 210 hp Gas Fuel Inject. | 8 Cylinder "V" | Automatic 4 Speed | 2 Wheel Rear | Manual Seatbelts Only

Purchase Price

Car Item	Dealer Cost	List
Base Price	**$16,903**	**$19,318**
Anti-Lock Brakes	Std	Std
Manual Transmission	N/A	N/A
Optional Engine	N/A	N/A
Air Conditioning	$727	$845
Power Steering	Std	Std
Cruise Control	Pkg	Pkg
All Wheel Drive	N/A	N/A
AM/FM Stereo Cassette	$105	$122
Steering Wheel, Tilt	Pkg	Pkg
Power Windows	Pkg	Pkg
***Options Price**	$832	$967
***Total Price**	**$17,735**	**$20,285**
Target Price	$19,685	
Destination Charge	$640	
Avg. Tax & Fees	$1,225	
Total Target $	**$21,550**	
Average Dealer Option Cost:	***86%***	

Ownership Costs

Cost Area	5 Year Cost	Rate
Depreciation	$5,753	Excellent
Financing ($433/month)	$3,551	
Insurance (Rating 13 [Est.])	$8,271	Average
State Fees	$836	
Fuel (Hwy 17 City 13)	$5,760	Worse Than Average
Maintenance	$4,841	Worse Than Average
Repairs	$791	Average

Warranty/Maintenance Info

Item		Rate
Major Tune-Up	$188	Average
Minor Tune-Up	$116	Worse Than Average
Brake Service	$273	Worse Than Average
Overall Warranty	3 yr/36k	Average
Drivetrain Warranty	3 yr/36k	Average
Rust Warranty	6 yr/100k	Excellent
Maintenance Warranty	N/A	
Roadside Assistance	3 yr/36k	

Ownership Cost By Year

$2,000 | $4,000 | $6,000 | $8,000 | $10,000

1993 | 1994 | 1995 | 1996 | 1997

Resale Value

1993	1994	1995	1996	1997
$19,926	$18,976	$18,112	$16,993	$15,797

Ownership Costs (5yr)

	Average	This Car
Total	$30,363	$29,803
Cost/Mile	43¢	43¢

Cumulative Costs

	1993	1994	1995	1996	1997
Annual	$5,966	$5,232	$6,181	$5,670	$6,754
Total	$5,966	$11,198	$17,379	$23,049	$29,803

Ownership Cost Rating

Better Than Average

The 1993 Sierra Suburban is available in four models - C1500 and C2500 two-wheel drive and K1500 and K2500 four-wheel drive utility vehicles. New for 1993, the C1500 Suburban features a new electronically controlled 4-speed automatic transmission standard. Other new features include an improved fan clutch designed to quiet engine operation on cold startups and there is new passenger-side seat-back recliners on the available 60/40 split-bench and high-back bucket seats add an additional adjustability.

* Includes shaded options

** Other purchase requirements apply

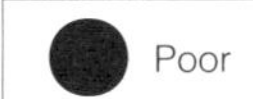

Poor | Worse Than Average | Average | Better Than Average | Excellent | Insufficient Information

Refer to ***Section 3: Annotated Vehicle Charts*** for an explanation of these charts.

GMC Suburban C2500

5 Door Sport Utility

5.7L 190 hp Gas Fuel Inject.

8 Cylinder "V"

Automatic 4 Speed

2 Wheel Rear

Manual Seatbelts Only

Utility

Purchase Price

Car Item	Dealer Cost	List
Base Price	**$17,958**	**$20,523**
Anti-Lock Brakes	Std	Std
Manual Transmission	N/A	N/A
7.4L 230 hp Gas	$520	** $605
Air Conditioning	$727	$845
Power Steering	Std	Std
Cruise Control	Pkg	Pkg
All Wheel Drive	N/A	N/A
AM/FM Stereo Cassette	$105	$122
Steering Wheel, Tilt	Pkg	Pkg
Power Windows	Pkg	Pkg
***Options Price**	$832	$967
***Total Price**	**$18,790**	**$21,490**
Target Price	$20,914	
Destination Charge	$640	
Avg. Tax & Fees	$1,299	
Total Target $	**$22,853**	
Average Dealer Option Cost:	***86%***	

Ownership Costs

Cost Area	5 Year Cost	Rate
Depreciation	$6,089	Excellent
Financing ($459/month)	$3,764	
Insurance (Rating 14 [Est.])	$8,446	Average
State Fees	$885	
Fuel (Hwy 17 City 13)	$5,760	Worse Than Average
Maintenance	$4,985	Worse Than Average
Repairs	$791	Average

Ownership Cost By Year

$2,000 $4,000 $6,000 $8,000 $10,000

1993 1994 1995 1996 1997

Warranty/Maintenance Info

Item		Rate
Major Tune-Up	$188	Average
Minor Tune-Up	$116	Worse Than Average
Brake Service	$273	Worse Than Average
Overall Warranty	3 yr/36k	Average
Drivetrain Warranty	3 yr/36k	Average
Rust Warranty	6 yr/100k	Excellent
Maintenance Warranty	N/A	
Roadside Assistance	3 yr/36k	

Resale Value

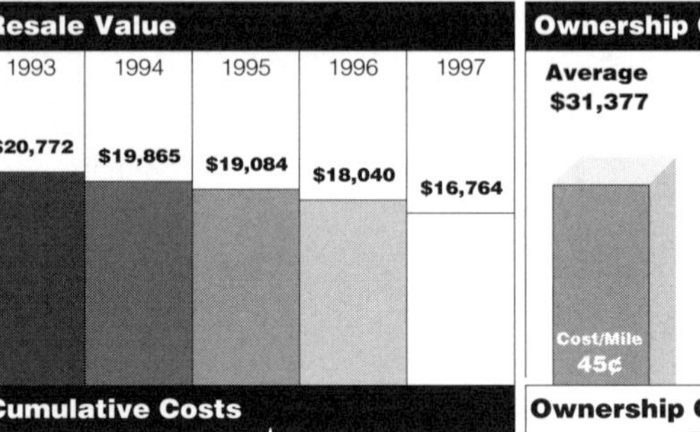

1993	1994	1995	1996	1997
$20,772	$19,865	$19,084	$18,040	$16,764

Ownership Costs (5yr)

Average	This Car
$31,377	$30,720
Cost/Mile 45¢	Cost/Mile 44¢

The 1993 Sierra Suburban is available in four models - C1500 and C2500 two-wheel drive and K1500 and K2500 four-wheel drive utility vehicles. New for 1993, the C2500 Suburban features a new electronically controlled 4-speed automatic transmission, the Hydra-matic 4L60-E, standard. On Suburbans with a Gross Vehicle Weight Rating over 8,500 pounds, a higher-capacity 4L80-E is standard. Also new is a larger radiator (with the 7.5L engine designed to improve cooling and reduce engine wear).

Cumulative Costs

	1993	1994	1995	1996	1997
Annual	$6,556	$5,301	$6,254	$5,655	$6,954
Total	$6,556	$11,857	$18,111	$23,766	$30,720

Ownership Cost Rating

Better Than Average

GMC Suburban K1500

5 Door Sport Utility

5.7L 210 hp Gas Fuel Inject.

8 Cylinder "V"

Automatic 4 Speed

4WD

4 Wheel On-Demand

Manual Seatbelts Only

Utility

C1500 Model Shown

Purchase Price

Car Item	Dealer Cost	List
Base Price	**$18,828**	**$21,518**
Anti-Lock Brakes	Std	Std
Manual Transmission	N/A	N/A
Optional Engine	N/A	N/A
Air Conditioning	$727	$845
Power Steering	Std	Std
Cruise Control	Pkg	Pkg
4 Whl On-Demand Dr.	Std	Std
AM/FM Stereo Cassette	$105	$122
Steering Wheel, Tilt	Pkg	Pkg
Power Windows	Pkg	Pkg
***Options Price**	$832	$967
***Total Price**	**$19,660**	**$22,485**
Target Price	$21,932	
Destination Charge	$640	
Avg. Tax & Fees	$1,360	
Total Target $	**$23,932**	
Average Dealer Option Cost:	***86%***	

Ownership Costs

Cost Area	5 Year Cost	Rate
Depreciation	$6,427	Excellent
Financing ($481/month)	$3,942	
Insurance (Rating 14 [Est.])	$8,446	Average
State Fees	$925	
Fuel (Hwy 16 City 12 [Est.])	$6,176	Poor
Maintenance	$5,177	Poor
Repairs	$945	Poor

Ownership Cost By Year

$2,000 $4,000 $6,000 $8,000 $10,000

1993 1994 1995 1996 1997

Warranty/Maintenance Info

Item		Rate
Major Tune-Up	$188	Average
Minor Tune-Up	$116	Worse Than Average
Brake Service	$273	Worse Than Average
Overall Warranty	3 yr/36k	Average
Drivetrain Warranty	3 yr/36k	Average
Rust Warranty	6 yr/100k	Excellent
Maintenance Warranty	N/A	
Roadside Assistance	3 yr/36k	

Resale Value

1993	1994	1995	1996	1997
$22,576	$20,902	$19,674	$18,525	$17,505

Ownership Costs (5yr)

Average	This Car
$32,214	$32,038
Cost/Mile 46¢	Cost/Mile 46¢

The 1993 Sierra Suburban is available in four models - C1500 and C2500 two-wheel drive and K1500 and K2500 four-wheel drive utility vehicles. New for 1993, the K1500 Suburban features a new electronically controlled four-speed automatic transmission, the Hydra-matic 4L60-E. On Suburbans with a Gross Vehicle Weight Rating over 8,500 pounds, a higher-capacity 4L80-E is standard. Other new features include a quieter fan clutch and passenger-side seat-back recliners on the available 60/40 split-bench.

Cumulative Costs

	1993	1994	1995	1996	1997
Annual	$5,991	$6,212	$6,698	$5,921	$7,216
Total	$5,991	$12,203	$18,901	$24,822	$32,038

Ownership Cost Rating

Better Than Average

* Includes shaded options

** Other purchase requirements apply

Poor

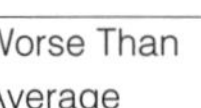

Worse Than Average

Average

Better Than Average

Excellent

Insufficient Information

Refer to *Section 3: Annotated Vehicle Charts* for an explanation of these charts.

GMC Suburban K2500

5 Door Sport Utility

5.7L 190 hp Gas Fuel Inject.

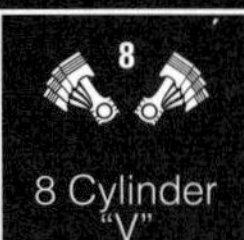

8 Cylinder "V"

Automatic 4 Speed

4 Wheel On-Demand

Manual Seatbelts Only

Purchase Price

Car Item	Dealer Cost	List
Base Price	**$19,926**	**$22,773**
Anti-Lock Brakes	Std	Std
Manual Transmission	N/A	N/A
7.4L 230 hp Gas	$520	** $605
Air Conditioning	$727	$845
Power Steering	Std	Std
Cruise Control	Pkg	Pkg
4 Whl On-Demand Dr.	Std	Std
AM/FM Stereo Cassette	$105	$122
Steering Wheel, Tilt	Pkg	Pkg
Power Windows	Pkg	Pkg
***Options Price**	$832	$967
***Total Price**	**$20,758**	**$23,740**
Target Price	$23,223	
Destination Charge	$640	
Avg. Tax & Fees	$1,437	
Total Target $	**$25,300**	
Average Dealer Option Cost:	***86%***	

Ownership Costs

Cost Area	5 Year Cost	Rate
Depreciation	$6,662	Better Than Average
Financing ($508/month)	$4,168	
Insurance (Rating 15 [Est.])	$8,717	Average
State Fees	$975	
Fuel (Hwy 16 City 12)	$6,176	Poor
Maintenance	$5,249	Poor
Repairs	$945	Worse Than Average

Warranty/Maintenance Info

Item		Rate
Major Tune-Up	$188	Average
Minor Tune-Up	$116	Worse Than Average
Brake Service	$273	Worse Than Average
Overall Warranty	3 yr/36k	Average
Drivetrain Warranty	3 yr/36k	Average
Rust Warranty	6 yr/100k	Better Than Average
Maintenance Warranty	N/A	
Roadside Assistance	3 yr/36k	

Ownership Cost By Year

$2,000 $4,000 $6,000 $8,000 $10,000

1993 1994 1995 1996 1997

Resale Value

1993	1994	1995	1996	1997
$23,811	$22,706	$21,550	$20,171	$18,638

Ownership Costs (5yr)

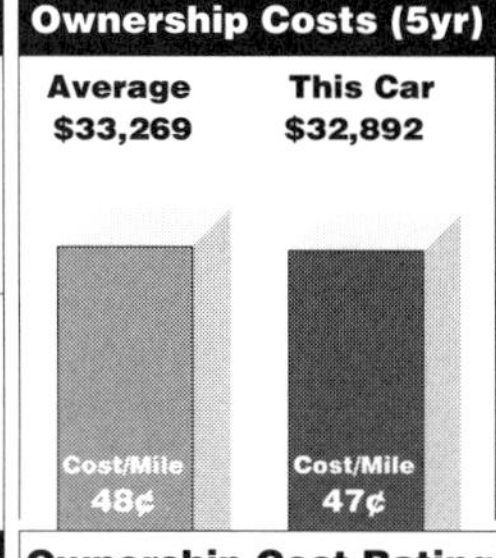

The 1993 GMC Sierra Suburban is available in four models - C1500 and C2500 two-wheel drive and K1500 and K2500 four-wheel drive utility vehicles. New for 1993, the K2500 Suburban features a new electronically controlled four-speed automatic transmission. Other new features include a larger radiator (with the 7.5L V-8 engine), an improved fan clutch designed to quiet engine operation on cold startups and there is new passenger-side seat-back recliners on the available 60/40 split-bench.

Cumulative Costs

	1993	1994	1995	1996	1997
Annual	$6,281	$5,777	$6,768	$6,233	$7,833
Total	$6,281	$12,058	$18,826	$25,059	$32,892

Ownership Cost Rating

Better Than Average

GMC Yukon

2 Door Sport Utility

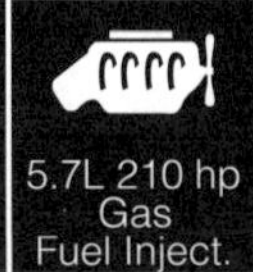

5.7L 210 hp Gas Fuel Inject.

8 Cylinder "V"

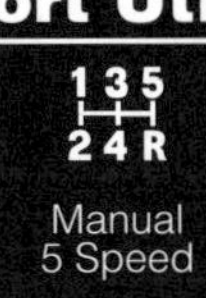

Manual 5 Speed

4 Wheel On-Demand

Manual Seatbelts Only

Purchase Price

Car Item	Dealer Cost	List
Base Price	**$17,713**	**$20,243**
Anti-Lock Brakes	Std	Std
Automatic 4 Speed	$765	$890
Optional Engine	N/A	N/A
Air Conditioning	$727	$845
Power Steering	Std	Std
Cruise Control	Pkg	Pkg
4 Whl On-Demand Dr.	Std	Std
AM/FM Stereo Cassette	$105	$122
Steering Wheel, Tilt	Pkg	Pkg
Power Windows	Pkg	Pkg
***Options Price**	$832	$967
***Total Price**	**$18,545**	**$21,210**
Target Price	$20,628	
Destination Charge	$595	
Avg. Tax & Fees	$1,279	
Total Target $	**$22,502**	
Average Dealer Option Cost:	***86%***	

Ownership Costs

Cost Area	5 Year Cost	Rate
Depreciation	$7,536	Better Than Average
Financing ($452/month)	$3,707	
Insurance (Rating 15 [Est.])	$8,717	Average
State Fees	$872	
Fuel (Hwy 17 City 13)	$5,760	Poor
Maintenance	$4,884	Worse Than Average
Repairs	$995	Worse Than Average

Warranty/Maintenance Info

Item		Rate
Major Tune-Up	$188	Average
Minor Tune-Up	$116	Worse Than Average
Brake Service	$273	Worse Than Average
Overall Warranty	3 yr/36k	Average
Drivetrain Warranty	3 yr/36k	Average
Rust Warranty	6 yr/100k	Better Than Average
Maintenance Warranty	N/A	
Roadside Assistance	3 yr/36k	

Ownership Cost By Year

$2,000 $4,000 $6,000 $8,000 $10,000

1993 1994 1995 1996 1997

Resale Value

1993	1994	1995	1996	1997
$17,549	$16,914	$16,537	$15,790	$14,966

Ownership Costs (5yr)

Average	This Car
$31,141	$32,471
Cost/Mile 44¢	Cost/Mile 46¢

The 1993 Yukon is available as one model edition. New for 1993, the Yukon features an electronically controlled four-speed automatic transmission--the Hydramatic 4L60-E. Also new is a GT Sport Appearance Package that features a monochromatic look, in either Black or Dark Garnet. Other features include an improved fan clutch, a revised air induction sytem, a new steel sleeve and an improved lock cylinder. New passenger seat-back recliners are standard on 40/60 split-bench and high-back bucket seats.

Cumulative Costs

	1993	1994	1995	1996	1997
Annual	$9,451	$5,060	$5,626	$5,482	$6,852
Total	$9,451	$14,511	$20,137	$25,619	$32,471

Ownership Cost Rating

Average

* Includes shaded options

** Other purchase requirements apply

 Poor  Worse Than Average  Average  Better Than Average Excellent Insufficient Information

Refer to ***Section 3: Annotated Vehicle Charts*** for an explanation of these charts.

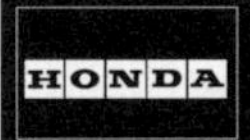

Honda Accord LX
4 Door Wagon

2.2L 125 hp Gas Fuel Inject.

4 Cylinder In-Line

Manual 5 Speed

2 Wheel Front

Driver Airbag Psngr Belts

Purchase Price

Car Item	Dealer Cost	List
Base Price	**$15,099**	**$17,975**
Anti-Lock Brakes	N/A	N/A
Automatic 4 Speed	$630	$750
Optional Engine	N/A	N/A
Air Conditioning	Std	Std
Power Steering	Std	Std
Cruise Control	Std	Std
All Wheel Drive	N/A	N/A
AM/FM Stereo Cassette	Std	Std
Steering Wheel, Tilt	Std	Std
Power Windows	Std	Std
***Options Price**	$630	$750
***Total Price**	**$15,729**	**$18,725**
Target Price	$16,978	
Destination Charge	$310	
Avg. Tax & Fees	$1,054	
Total Target $	**$18,342**	
Average Dealer Option Cost:	***84%***	

Ownership Costs

Cost Area	5 Year Cost	Rate
Depreciation	$6,411	Excellent
Financing ($369/month)	$3,021	
Insurance (Rating 10)	$7,479	Better Than Average
State Fees	$760	
Fuel (Hwy 27 City 21)	$3,598	Better Than Average
Maintenance	$4,921	Worse Than Average
Repairs	$570	Excellent

Ownership Cost By Year

$2,000 $4,000 $6,000 $8,000

1993 1994 1995 1996 1997

Warranty/Maintenance Info

Major Tune-Up	$254	Poor
Minor Tune-Up	$133	Worse Than Average
Brake Service	$217	Average
Overall Warranty	3 yr/36k	Average
Drivetrain Warranty	3 yr/36k	Average
Rust Warranty	3 yr/unlim. mi	Worse Than Average
Maintenance Warranty	N/A	
Roadside Assistance	N/A	

Resale Value

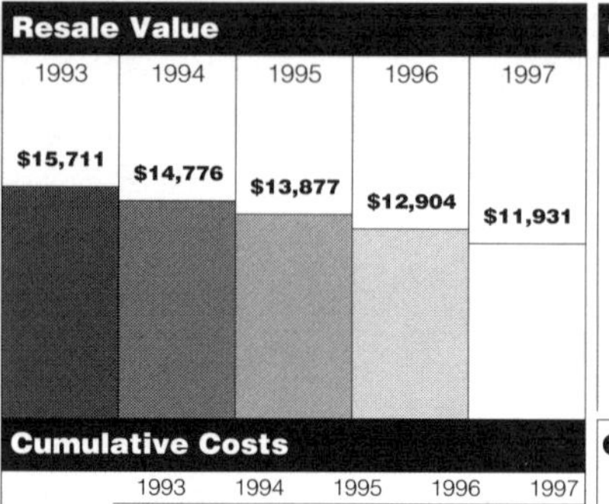

1993	1994	1995	1996	1997
$15,711	$14,776	$13,877	$12,904	$11,931

Ownership Costs (5yr)

Average	This Car
$30,415	$26,760
Cost/Mile 43¢	Cost/Mile 38¢

The 1993 Accord in available in ten models - LX and EX wagons; and DX, LX, EX and SE sedans and coupes. The LX wagon includes body side moldings, integrated rear bumper step, full-size spare tire, air conditioning, power door locks and tailgate lock, rear window defroster with timer, cruise control, fold-down rear seatback (split 60/40), and a choice of five exterior colors. The Honda Accord is built in Marysville, Ohio. All 1993 Honda Accords feature a 3-year/36,000-mile limited warranty.

Cumulative Costs

	1993	1994	1995	1996	1997
Annual	$6,170	$4,420	$5,362	$4,106	$6,702
Total	$6,170	$10,590	$15,952	$20,058	$26,760

Ownership Cost Rating

Excellent

Honda Accord EX
4 Door Wagon

2.2L 140 hp Gas Fuel Inject.

4 Cylinder In-Line

Manual 5 Speed

2 Wheel Front

Driver Airbag Psngr Belts

Purchase Price

Car Item	Dealer Cost	List
Base Price	**$17,157**	**$20,425**
Anti-Lock Brakes	Std	Std
Automatic 4 Speed	$630	$750
Optional Engine	N/A	N/A
Air Conditioning	Std	Std
Power Steering	Std	Std
Cruise Control	Std	Std
All Wheel Drive	N/A	N/A
AM/FM Stereo Cassette	Std	Std
Steering Wheel, Tilt	Std	Std
Power Windows	Std	Std
***Options Price**	$630	$750
***Total Price**	**$17,787**	**$21,175**
Target Price	$19,280	
Destination Charge	$310	
Avg. Tax & Fees	$1,195	
Total Target $	**$20,785**	
Average Dealer Option Cost:	***84%***	

Ownership Costs

Cost Area	5 Year Cost	Rate
Depreciation	$8,642	Better Than Average
Financing ($418/month)	$3,424	
Insurance (Rating 12)	$7,898	Better Than Average
State Fees	$859	
Fuel (Hwy 27 City 21)	$3,598	Better Than Average
Maintenance	$5,061	Worse Than Average
Repairs	$570	Excellent

Ownership Cost By Year

$2,000 $4,000 $6,000 $8,000 $10,000

1993 1994 1995 1996 1997

Warranty/Maintenance Info

Major Tune-Up	$254	Poor
Minor Tune-Up	$133	Worse Than Average
Brake Service	$280	Poor
Overall Warranty	3 yr/36k	Average
Drivetrain Warranty	3 yr/36k	Average
Rust Warranty	3 yr/unlim. mi	Worse Than Average
Maintenance Warranty	N/A	
Roadside Assistance	N/A	

Resale Value

1993	1994	1995	1996	1997
$16,371	$15,206	$14,212	$13,194	$12,143

Ownership Costs (5yr)

Average	This Car
$32,920	$30,052
Cost/Mile 47¢	Cost/Mile 43¢

The 1993 Accord in available in ten models - LX and EX wagons; and DX, LX, EX and SE sedans and coupes. The EX wagon includes body side moldings, integrated rear bumper step, full-size spare tire, air conditioning, power door locks and tailgate lock, power moonroof, a remote entry system, cruise control, fold-down rear seatback (split 60/40), and a choice of five exterior colors. The Honda Accord is built in Marysville, Ohio. All 1993 Honda Accords feature a 3-year/36,000-mile limited warranty.

Cumulative Costs

	1993	1994	1995	1996	1997
Annual	$8,222	$4,879	$5,707	$4,285	$6,959
Total	$8,222	$13,101	$18,808	$23,093	$30,052

Ownership Cost Rating

Excellent

* Includes shaded options

** Other purchase requirements apply

 Poor  Worse Than Average  Average  Better Than Average Excellent  Insufficient Information

Refer to *Section 3: Annotated Vehicle Charts* for an explanation of these charts.

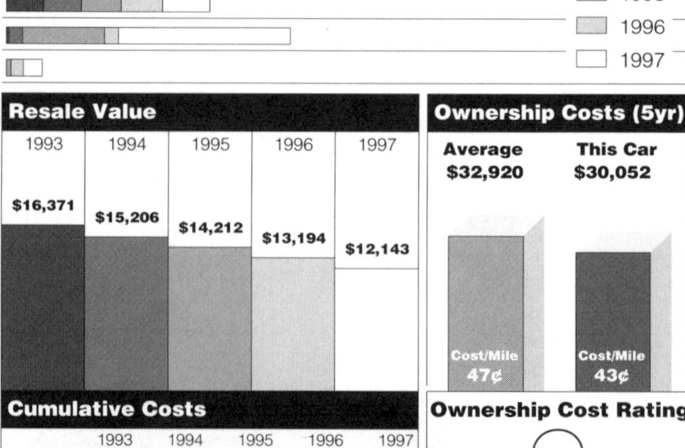

Jeep Cherokee

2 Door Sport Utility

2.5L 130 hp Gas Fuel Inject. | 4 Cylinder In-Line | Manual 5 Speed | 2 Wheel Rear | Manual Seatbelts Only

Utility

4 Door 4WD Shown

Purchase Price

Car Item	Dealer Cost	List
Base Price	**$11,490**	**$12,137**
Anti-Lock Brakes	$509	$599
Automatic 4 Speed	$745	$877
4.0L 190 hp Gas	$520	$612
Air Conditioning	$711	$836
Power Steering	Std	Std
Cruise Control	$196	** $230
All Wheel Drive	N/A	N/A
AM/FM Stereo Cassette	$171	$201
Steering Wheel, Tilt	$112	** $132
Power Windows	N/A	N/A
***Options Price**	$1,402	$1,649
***Total Price**	**$12,892**	**$13,786**
Target Price	$13,750	
Destination Charge	$485	
Avg. Tax & Fees	$855	
Total Target $	**$15,090**	
Average Dealer Option Cost:	***85%***	

Ownership Costs

Cost Area	5 Year Cost	Rate
Depreciation	$6,146	Average
Financing ($303/month)	$2,486	
Insurance (Rating 10)	$7,689	Average
State Fees	$571	
Fuel (Hwy 22 City 17)	$4,431	Average
Maintenance	$3,777	Better Than Average
Repairs	$840	Average

Ownership Cost By Year

$2,000 | $4,000 | $6,000 | $8,000

1993 | 1994 | 1995 | 1996 | 1997

Warranty/Maintenance Info

Item		Rate
Major Tune-Up	$166	Better Than Average
Minor Tune-Up	$113	Worse Than Average
Brake Service	$241	Average
Overall Warranty	1 yr/12k	Poor
Drivetrain Warranty	7 yr/70k	Excellent
Rust Warranty	7 yr/100k	Excellent
Maintenance Warranty	N/A	
Roadside Assistance	N/A	

Resale Value

1993	1994	1995	1996	1997
$11,938	$11,227	$10,699	$9,850	$8,944

Ownership Costs (5yr)

Average	This Car
$24,897	$25,940
Cost/Mile 36¢	Cost/Mile 37¢

Cumulative Costs

	1993	1994	1995	1996	1997
Annual	$6,646	$4,375	$4,930	$4,552	$5,437
Total	$6,646	$11,021	$15,951	$20,503	$25,940

Ownership Cost Rating

Average

The 1993 Cherokee is available in twelve models - (Base) Cherokee, Sport, and Country two- and four-door, and two- and four-wheel drive utility wagons. New for 1993, the Base Cherokee 2-door, 2WD model features a full stainless steel exhaust system, a trac-lock limited-slip differential available with the 2.5L engine, black lower bodyside scuff molding, outboard unibelt restraints w/free running cinching tips, and a visibility package. There are also six new exterior colors to choose from.

Jeep Cherokee

4 Door Sport Utility

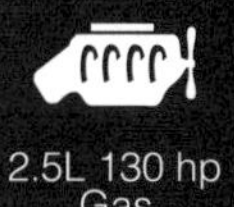

2.5L 130 hp Gas Fuel Inject. | 4 Cylinder In-Line | Manual 5 Speed | 2 Wheel Rear | Manual Seatbelts Only

Utility

4WD Model Shown

Purchase Price

Car Item	Dealer Cost	List
Base Price	**$12,419**	**$13,147**
Anti-Lock Brakes	$509	$599
Automatic 4 Speed	$745	$877
4.0L 190 hp Gas	$520	$612
Air Conditioning	$711	$836
Power Steering	Std	Std
Cruise Control	$196	** $230
All Wheel Drive	N/A	N/A
AM/FM Stereo Cassette	$171	$201
Steering Wheel, Tilt	$112	** $132
Power Windows	N/A	N/A
***Options Price**	$1,402	$1,649
***Total Price**	**$13,821**	**$14,796**
Target Price	$14,767	
Destination Charge	$485	
Avg. Tax & Fees	$916	
Total Target $	**$16,168**	
Average Dealer Option Cost:	***85%***	

Ownership Costs

Cost Area	5 Year Cost	Rate
Depreciation	$6,315	Average
Financing ($325/month)	$2,662	
Insurance (Rating 11)	$7,902	Average
State Fees	$612	
Fuel (Hwy 22 City 17)	$4,431	Average
Maintenance	$3,777	Better Than Average
Repairs	$840	Average

Ownership Cost By Year

$2,000 | $4,000 | $6,000 | $8,000

1993 | 1994 | 1995 | 1996 | 1997

Warranty/Maintenance Info

Item		Rate
Major Tune-Up	$166	Better Than Average
Minor Tune-Up	$113	Worse Than Average
Brake Service	$241	Average
Overall Warranty	1 yr/12k	Poor
Drivetrain Warranty	7 yr/70k	Excellent
Rust Warranty	7 yr/100k	Excellent
Maintenance Warranty	N/A	
Roadside Assistance	N/A	

Resale Value

1993	1994	1995	1996	1997
$12,506	$11,954	$11,496	$10,702	$9,853

Ownership Costs (5yr)

Average	This Car
$25,746	$26,539
Cost/Mile 37¢	Cost/Mile 38¢

Cumulative Costs

	1993	1994	1995	1996	1997
Annual	$7,279	$4,322	$4,946	$4,560	$5,432
Total	$7,279	$11,601	$16,547	$21,107	$26,539

Ownership Cost Rating

Average

The 1993 Cherokee is available in twelve models - (Base) Cherokee, Sport, and Country two- and four-door, and two- and four-wheel drive utility wagons. New for 1993, the Base Cherokee 4-door, 2WD model features a full stainless steel exhaust system, a trac-lock limited-slip differential available with the 2.5L engine, black lower bodyside scuff molding, outboard unibelt restraints w/free running cinching tips, and a visibility package. There are also six new exterior colors to choose from.

* Includes shaded options

** Other purchase requirements apply

Poor | Worse Than Average | 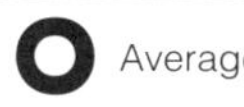 Average | 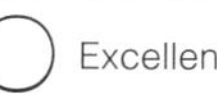 Better Than Average | Excellent | Insufficient Information

Refer to *Section 3: Annotated Vehicle Charts* for an explanation of these charts.

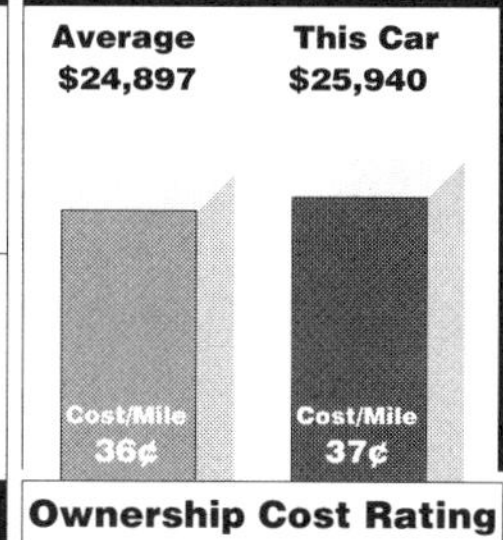

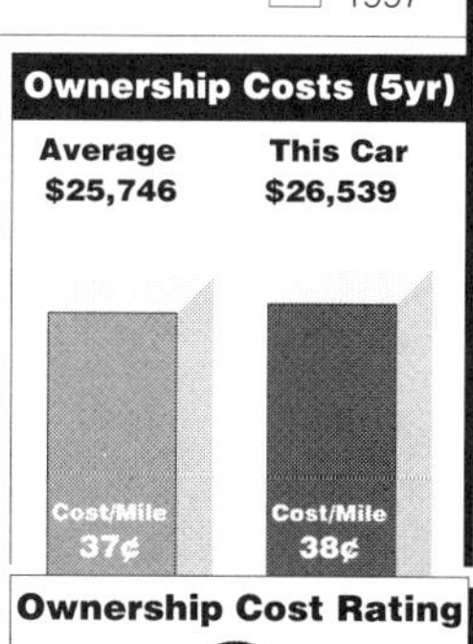

Jeep Cherokee Sport
2 Door Sport Utility

4.0L 190 hp Gas Fuel Inject.

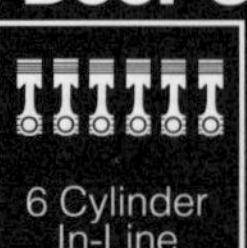
6 Cylinder In-Line

Manual 5 Speed

2 Wheel Rear

Manual Seatbelts Only

Utility

4WD Model Shown

Purchase Price

Car Item	Dealer Cost	List
Base Price	**$13,073**	**$14,350**
Anti-Lock Brakes	$509	$599
Automatic 4 Speed	$745	$877
Optional Engine	N/A	N/A
Air Conditioning	$711	$836
Power Steering	Std	Std
Cruise Control	$196	$230
All Wheel Drive	N/A	N/A
AM/FM Stereo Cassette	$171	$201
Steering Wheel, Tilt	$112	$132
Power Windows	Pkg	Pkg
***Options Price**	$882	$1,037
***Total Price**	**$13,955**	**$15,387**
Target Price	$14,929	
Destination Charge	$485	
Avg. Tax & Fees	$930	
Total Target $	**$16,344**	
Average Dealer Option Cost:	***85%***	

Ownership Costs

Cost Area	5 Year Cost	Rate
Depreciation	$6,291	Average
Financing ($328/month)	$2,692	
Insurance (Rating 11)	$7,902	Average
State Fees	$635	
Fuel (Hwy 22 City 17)	$4,431	Average
Maintenance	$3,897	Better Than Average
Repairs	$840	Average

Ownership Cost By Year

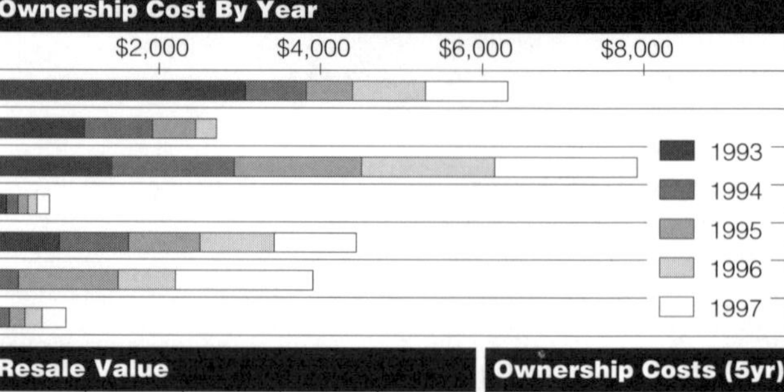

Warranty/Maintenance Info

Item	Value	Rate
Major Tune-Up	$166	Better Than Average
Minor Tune-Up	$113	Worse Than Average
Brake Service	$241	Average
Overall Warranty	1 yr/12k	Poor
Drivetrain Warranty	7 yr/70k	Excellent
Rust Warranty	7 yr/100k	Excellent
Maintenance Warranty	N/A	
Roadside Assistance	N/A	

Resale Value

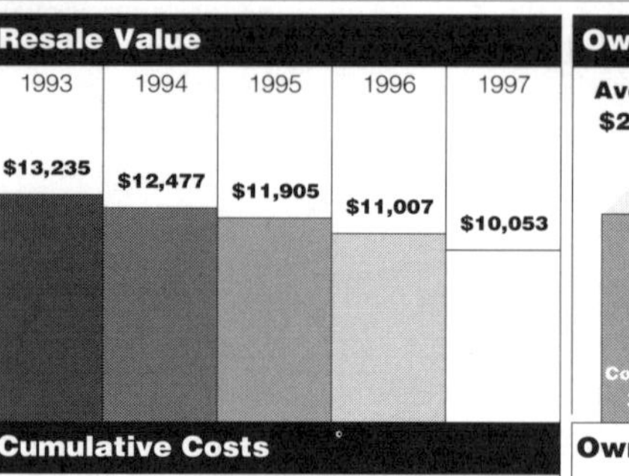

1993	1994	1995	1996	1997
$13,235	$12,477	$11,905	$11,007	$10,053

Ownership Costs (5yr)

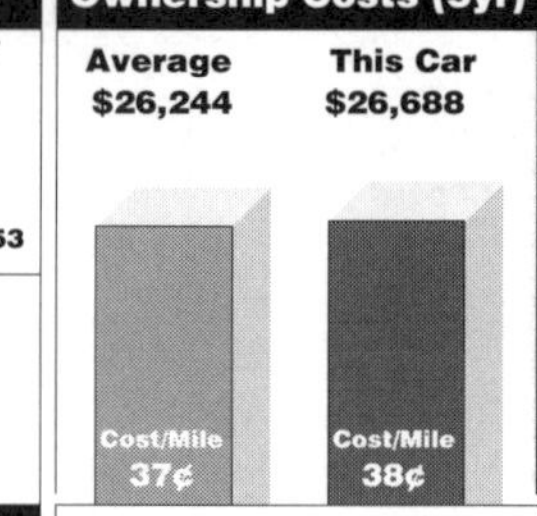

Average	This Car
$26,244	$26,688
Cost/Mile 37¢	Cost/Mile 38¢

The 1993 Cherokee is available in twelve models - (Base) Cherokee, Sport, and Country two- and four-door, and two- and four-wheel drive utility wagons. New for 1993, the Sport Cherokee 2-door, 2WD model features styled steel wheels, lower body side two-tone treatment (black), black w/red insert, lower body side scuff molding, and a stainless steel exhaust system. Cherokee also offers a protection plan - 3/36 full coverage warranty or 12/12 full coverage with a 7/70 powertrain warranty.

Cumulative Costs

	1993	1994	1995	1996	1997
Annual	$6,744	$4,542	$5,120	$4,689	$5,593
Total	$6,744	$11,286	$16,406	$21,095	$26,688

Ownership Cost Rating

Average

Jeep Cherokee Sport
4 Door Sport Utility

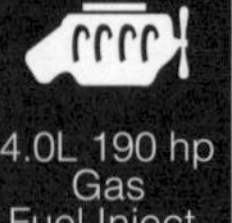
4.0L 190 hp Gas Fuel Inject.

6 Cylinder In-Line

Manual 5 Speed

2 Wheel Rear

Manual Seatbelts Only

Utility

4 Door 4WD Shown

Purchase Price

Car Item	Dealer Cost	List
Base Price	**$13,972**	**$15,360**
Anti-Lock Brakes	$509	$599
Automatic 4 Speed	$745	$877
Optional Engine	N/A	N/A
Air Conditioning	$711	$836
Power Steering	Std	Std
Cruise Control	$196	$230
All Wheel Drive	N/A	N/A
AM/FM Stereo Cassette	$171	$201
Steering Wheel, Tilt	$112	$132
Power Windows	Pkg	Pkg
***Options Price**	$882	$1,037
***Total Price**	**$14,854**	**$16,397**
Target Price	$15,918	
Destination Charge	$485	
Avg. Tax & Fees	$989	
Total Target $	**$17,392**	
Average Dealer Option Cost:	***85%***	

Ownership Costs

Cost Area	5 Year Cost	Rate
Depreciation	$6,921	Average
Financing ($350/month)	$2,864	
Insurance (Rating 12)	$8,108	Average
State Fees	$675	
Fuel (Hwy 22 City 17)	$4,431	Average
Maintenance	$3,897	Better Than Average
Repairs	$840	Average

Ownership Cost By Year

$2,000 · $4,000 · $6,000 · $8,000 · $10,000

1993 · 1994 · 1995 · 1996 · 1997

Warranty/Maintenance Info

Item	Value	Rate
Major Tune-Up	$166	Better Than Average
Minor Tune-Up	$113	Worse Than Average
Brake Service	$241	Average
Overall Warranty	1 yr/12k	Poor
Drivetrain Warranty	7 yr/70k	Excellent
Rust Warranty	7 yr/100k	Excellent
Maintenance Warranty	N/A	
Roadside Assistance	N/A	

Resale Value

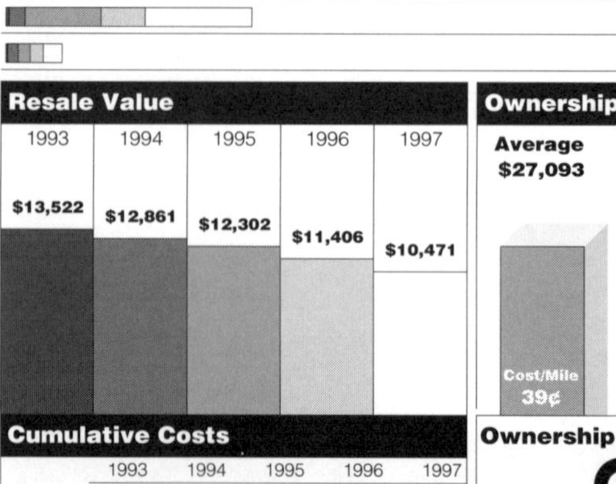

1993	1994	1995	1996	1997
$13,522	$12,861	$12,302	$11,406	$10,471

Ownership Costs (5yr)

Average	This Car
$27,093	$27,736
Cost/Mile 39¢	Cost/Mile 40¢

The 1993 Cherokee is available in twelve models - (Base) Cherokee, Sport, and Country two- and four-door, and two- and four-wheel drive utility wagons. New for 1993, the Sport Cherokee 4-door, 2WD model features styled steel wheels, lower body side two-tone treatment (black), black w/red insert, lower body side scuff molding, and a stainless steel exhaust system. ee also offers a protection plan - 3/36 full coverage warranty or 12/12 full coverage with a 7/70 powertrain warranty.

Cumulative Costs

	1993	1994	1995	1996	1997
Annual	$7,625	$4,548	$5,190	$4,749	$5,624
Total	$7,625	$12,173	$17,363	$22,112	$27,736

Ownership Cost Rating

Average

* Includes shaded options

** Other purchase requirements apply

Poor ·  Worse Than Average · Average · Better Than Average ·  Excellent · Insufficient Information

Refer to *Section 3: Annotated Vehicle Charts* for an explanation of these charts.

Jeep Cherokee Country
2 Door Sport Utility

Utility

4.0L 190 hp Gas Fuel Inject.

6 Cylinder In-Line

Manual 5 Speed

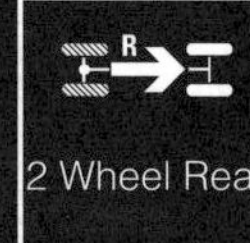
2 Wheel Rear

Manual Seatbelts Only

4 Door Model Shown

Purchase Price

Car Item	Dealer Cost	List
Base Price	**$14,558**	**$16,038**
Anti-Lock Brakes	$509	$599
Automatic 4 Speed	$745	$877
Optional Engine	N/A	N/A
Air Conditioning	$711	$836
Power Steering	Std	Std
Cruise Control	$196	$230
All Wheel Drive	N/A	N/A
AM/FM Stereo Cassette	$171	$201
Steering Wheel, Tilt	$112	$132
Power Windows	Pkg	Pkg
***Options Price**	$882	$1,037
***Total Price**	**$15,440**	**$17,075**
Target Price	$16,565	
Destination Charge	$485	
Avg. Tax & Fees	$1,029	
Total Target $	**$18,079**	
Average Dealer Option Cost:	***85%***	

Ownership Costs

Cost Area	5 Year Cost	Rate
Depreciation	$6,669	Average
Financing ($363/month)	$2,977	
Insurance (Rating 12)	$8,108	Average
State Fees	$702	
Fuel (Hwy 22 City 17)	$4,431	Average
Maintenance	$3,894	Better Than Average
Repairs	$840	Average

Warranty/Maintenance Info

Major Tune-Up	$166	Better Than Average
Minor Tune-Up	$113	Worse Than Average
Brake Service	$241	Average
Overall Warranty	1 yr/12k	Poor
Drivetrain Warranty	7 yr/70k	Excellent
Rust Warranty	7 yr/100k	Excellent
Maintenance Warranty	N/A	
Roadside Assistance	N/A	

Ownership Cost By Year

$2,000 $4,000 $6,000 $8,000 $10,000

1993 1994 1995 1996 1997

Resale Value

1993	1994	1995	1996	1997
$14,705	$13,936	$13,354	$12,410	$11,410

Ownership Costs (5yr)

	Average	This Car
5 Year Cost	$27,663	$27,621
Cost/Mile	40¢	39¢

Cumulative Costs

	1993	1994	1995	1996	1997
Annual	$7,183	$4,698	$5,239	$4,810	$5,691
Total	$7,183	$11,881	$17,120	$21,930	$27,621

Ownership Cost Rating

Better Than Average

The 1993 Cherokee is available in twelve models - (Base) Cherokee, Sport, and Country two- and four-door, and two- and four-wheel drive utility wagons. New for 1993, the Country Cherokee 2-door, 2WD model features champagne lower body side treatment w/cladding, fender flares, bumpers and endcaps, body color grille and headlamp bezels, and champagne body side and liftgate tape treatment. Other features include a stainless steel exhaust system, a new visibility pack, and five exterior colors.

Jeep Cherokee Country
4 Door Sport Utility

Utility

4.0L 190 hp Gas Fuel Inject.

6 Cylinder In-Line

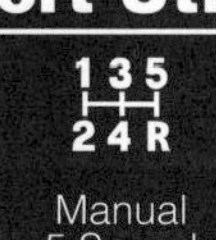
Manual 5 Speed

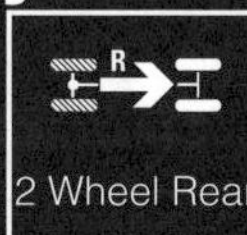
2 Wheel Rear

Manual Seatbelts Only

Purchase Price

Car Item	Dealer Cost	List
Base Price	**$15,457**	**$17,048**
Anti-Lock Brakes	$509	$599
Automatic 4 Speed	$745	$877
Optional Engine	N/A	N/A
Air Conditioning	$711	$836
Power Steering	Std	Std
Cruise Control	$196	$230
All Wheel Drive	N/A	N/A
AM/FM Stereo Cassette	$171	$201
Steering Wheel, Tilt	$112	$132
Power Windows	Pkg	Pkg
***Options Price**	$882	$1,037
***Total Price**	**$16,339**	**$18,085**
Target Price	$17,560	
Destination Charge	$485	
Avg. Tax & Fees	$1,088	
Total Target $	**$19,133**	
Average Dealer Option Cost:	***85%***	

Ownership Costs

Cost Area	5 Year Cost	Rate
Depreciation	$6,273	Better Than Average
Financing ($385/month)	$3,152	
Insurance (Rating 13)	$8,271	Average
State Fees	$743	
Fuel (Hwy 22 City 17)	$4,431	Average
Maintenance	$3,894	Better Than Average
Repairs	$840	Average

Warranty/Maintenance Info

Major Tune-Up	$166	Better Than Average
Minor Tune-Up	$113	Worse Than Average
Brake Service	$241	Average
Overall Warranty	1 yr/12k	Poor
Drivetrain Warranty	7 yr/70k	Excellent
Rust Warranty	7 yr/100k	Excellent
Maintenance Warranty	N/A	
Roadside Assistance	N/A	

Ownership Cost By Year

$2,000 $4,000 $6,000 $8,000 $10,000

1993 1994 1995 1996 1997

Resale Value

1993	1994	1995	1996	1997
$16,094	$15,401	$14,841	$13,869	$12,860

Ownership Costs (5yr)

	Average	This Car
5 Year Cost	$28,513	$27,604
Cost/Mile	41¢	39¢

Cumulative Costs

	1993	1994	1995	1996	1997
Annual	$6,961	$4,716	$5,294	$4,892	$5,741
Total	$6,961	$11,677	$16,971	$21,863	$27,604

Ownership Cost Rating

Better Than Average

The 1993 Cherokee is available in twelve models - (Base) Cherokee, Sport, and Country two- and four-door, and two- and four-wheel drive utility wagons. New for 1993, the Country Cherokee 4-door, 2WD model features champagne lower body side treatment w/cladding, fender flares, bumpers and endcaps, body color grille and headlamp bezels, and champagne body side and liftgate tape treatment. Other features include a stainless steel exhaust system, a new visibility pack, and five exterior colors.

* Includes shaded options

** Other purchase requirements apply

 Poor  Worse Than Average  Average  Better Than Average  Excellent — Insufficient Information

Refer to *Section 3: Annotated Vehicle Charts* for an explanation of these charts.

Jeep Cherokee 4WD
2 Door Sport Utility

2.5L 130 hp Gas Fuel Inject.

4 Cylinder In-Line

Manual 5 Speed

4 Wheel On-Demand

Manual Seatbelts Only

Purchase Price

Car Item	Dealer Cost	List
Base Price	**$12,856**	**$13,622**
Anti-Lock Brakes	$509	$599
Automatic 4 Speed	$745	$877
4.0L 190 hp Gas	$520	$612
Air Conditioning	$711	$836
Power Steering	Std	Std
Cruise Control	$196	** $230
Command-Trac 4WD	Std	Std
AM/FM Stereo Cassette	$171	$201
Steering Wheel, Tilt	$112	** $132
Power Windows	N/A	N/A
***Options Price**	$1,402	$1,640
***Total Price**	**$14,258**	**$15,271**
Target Price	$15,247	
Destination Charge	$485	
Avg. Tax & Fees	$945	
Total Target $	**$16,677**	
Average Dealer Option Cost:	***85%***	

Ownership Costs

Cost Area	5 Year Cost	Rate
Depreciation	$5,848	Better Than Average
Financing ($335/month)	$2,748	
Insurance (Rating 11)	$7,902	Average
State Fees	$631	
Fuel (Hwy 20 City 16)	$4,797	Worse Than Average
Maintenance	$4,152	Average
Repairs	$1,085	Worse Than Average

Ownership Cost By Year

Warranty/Maintenance Info

Item		Rate
Major Tune-Up	$166	Better Than Average
Minor Tune-Up	$113	Worse Than Average
Brake Service	$241	Average
Overall Warranty	1 yr/12k	Poor
Drivetrain Warranty	7 yr/70k	Excellent
Rust Warranty	7 yr/100k	Excellent
Maintenance Warranty	N/A	
Roadside Assistance	N/A	

Resale Value

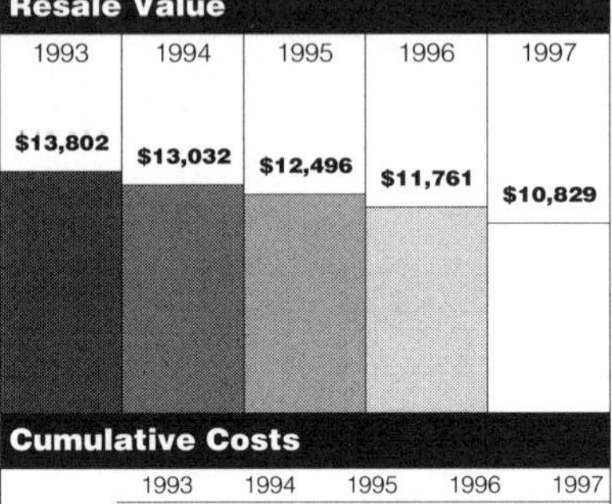

1993	1994	1995	1996	1997
$13,802	$13,032	$12,496	$11,761	$10,829

Ownership Costs (5yr)

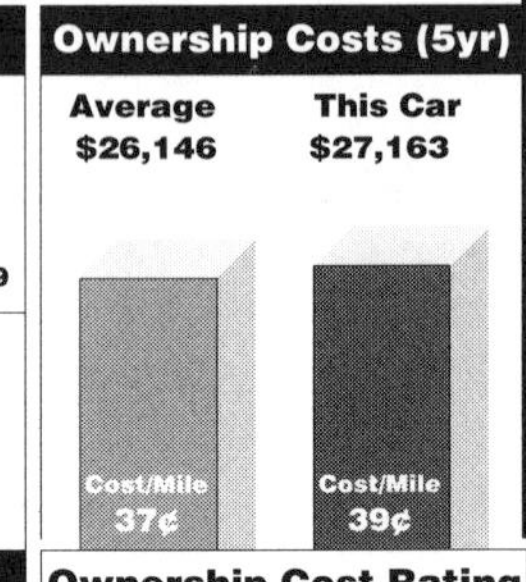

Cumulative Costs

	1993	1994	1995	1996	1997
Annual	$6,608	$4,692	$5,087	$4,656	$6,120
Total	$6,608	$11,300	$16,387	$21,043	$27,163

Ownership Cost Rating

Average

The 1993 Cherokee is available in twelve models - (Base) Cherokee, Sport, and Country two- and four-door, and two- and four-wheel drive utility wagons. New for 1993, the Base Cherokee 2-door, 4WD model features a full stainless steel exhaust system, a trac-lock limited-slip differential available with the 2.5L engine, black lower bodyside scuff molding, outboard unibelt restraints w/free running cinching tips, and five new colors (Light Champagne, Turquoise, Dark Blue, Canyon Blue, and Flame Red.)

Jeep Cherokee 4WD
4 Door Sport Utility

2.5L 130 hp Gas Fuel Inject.

4 Cylinder In-Line

Manual 5 Speed

4 Wheel On-Demand

Manual Seatbelts Only

Purchase Price

Car Item	Dealer Cost	List
Base Price	**$13,785**	**$14,632**
Anti-Lock Brakes	$509	$599
Automatic 4 Speed	$745	$877
4.0L 190 hp Gas	$520	$612
Air Conditioning	$711	$836
Power Steering	Std	Std
Cruise Control	$196	** $230
Command-Trac 4WD	Std	Std
AM/FM Stereo Cassette	$171	$201
Steering Wheel, Tilt	$112	** $132
Power Windows	N/A	N/A
***Options Price**	$1,402	$1,649
***Total Price**	**$15,187**	**$16,281**
Target Price	$16,269	
Destination Charge	$485	
Avg. Tax & Fees	$1,006	
Total Target $	**$17,760**	
Average Dealer Option Cost:	***85%***	

Ownership Costs

Cost Area	5 Year Cost	Rate
Depreciation	$5,820	Better Than Average
Financing ($357/month)	$2,926	
Insurance (Rating 12)	$8,108	Average
State Fees	$671	
Fuel (Hwy 20 City 16)	$4,797	Worse Than Average
Maintenance	$4,152	Average
Repairs	$1,085	Worse Than Average

Ownership Cost By Year

Warranty/Maintenance Info

Item		Rate
Major Tune-Up	$166	Better Than Average
Minor Tune-Up	$113	Worse Than Average
Brake Service	$241	Average
Overall Warranty	1 yr/12k	Poor
Drivetrain Warranty	7 yr/70k	Excellent
Rust Warranty	7 yr/100k	Excellent
Maintenance Warranty	N/A	
Roadside Assistance	N/A	

Resale Value

1993	1994	1995	1996	1997
$14,654	$13,980	$13,509	$12,819	$11,940

Ownership Costs (5yr)

Average	This Car
$26,995	$27,559
Cost/Mile 39¢	Cost/Mile 39¢

Cumulative Costs

	1993	1994	1995	1996	1997
Annual	$6,962	$4,700	$5,106	$4,674	$6,117
Total	$6,962	$11,662	$16,768	$21,442	$27,559

Ownership Cost Rating

Average

The 1993 Cherokee is available in twelve models - (Base) Cherokee, Sport, and Country two- and four-door, and two- and four-wheel drive utility wagons. New for 1993, the Base Cherokee 4-door, 4WD model features a full stainless steel exhaust system, a trac-lock limited-slip differential available with the 2.5L engine, black lower bodyside scuff molding, outboard unibelt restraints w/free running cinching tips, and five new colors (Light Champagne, Turquoise, Dark Blue, Canyon Blue, and Flame Red.)

* Includes shaded options

** Other purchase requirements apply

Poor

Worse Than Average

Average
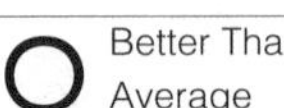
Better Than Average

Excellent
Insufficient Information

Refer to *Section 3: Annotated Vehicle Charts* for an explanation of these charts.

Jeep Cherokee Sport 4WD
2 Door Sport Utility

4.0L 190 hp Gas Fuel Inject.	6 Cylinder In-Line	Manual 5 Speed	 4 Wheel On-Demand	 Manual Seatbelts Only

Purchase Price

Car Item	Dealer Cost	List
Base Price	**$14,395**	**$15,835**
Anti-Lock Brakes	$509	$599
Automatic 4 Speed	$745	$877
Optional Engine	N/A	N/A
Air Conditioning	$711	$836
Power Steering	Std	Std
Cruise Control	$196	$230
Command-Trac 4WD	Std	Std
AM/FM Stereo Cassette	$171	$201
Steering Wheel, Tilt	$112	$132
Power Windows	Pkg	Pkg
***Options Price**	$882	$1,037
***Total Price**	**$15,277**	**$16,872**
Target Price	$16,385	
Destination Charge	$485	
Avg. Tax & Fees	$1,018	
Total Target $	**$17,888**	
Average Dealer Option Cost:	***85%***	

Ownership Costs

Cost Area	5 Year Cost	Rate
Depreciation	$5,432	Excellent
Financing ($360/month)	$2,946	
Insurance (Rating 12)	$8,108	Average
State Fees	$694	
Fuel (Hwy 20 City 16)	$4,797	Worse Than Average
Maintenance	$4,271	Average
Repairs	$1,085	Worse Than Average

Ownership Cost By Year

$2,000 $4,000 $6,000 $8,000 $10,000

1993 1994 1995 1996 1997

Warranty/Maintenance Info

Major Tune-Up	$166	Better Than Average
Minor Tune-Up	$113	Worse Than Average
Brake Service	$241	Average
Overall Warranty	1 yr/12k	Poor
Drivetrain Warranty	7 yr/70k	Excellent
Rust Warranty	7 yr/100k	Excellent
Maintenance Warranty	N/A	
Roadside Assistance	N/A	

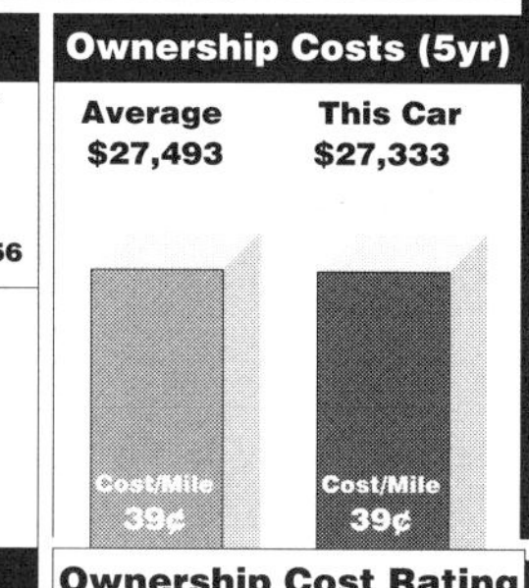

Resale Value

1993	1994	1995	1996	1997
$14,225	$13,793	$13,444	$12,960	$12,456

Ownership Costs (5yr)

Average	This Car
$27,493	$27,333
Cost/Mile 39¢	Cost/Mile 39¢

Cumulative Costs

	1993	1994	1995	1996	1997
Annual	$7,533	$4,470	$5,041	$4,491	$5,798
Total	$7,533	$12,003	$17,044	$21,535	$27,333

Ownership Cost Rating

Better Than Average

The 1993 Cherokee is available in twelve models - (Base) Cherokee, Sport, and Country two- and four-door, and two- and four-wheel drive utility wagons. New for 1993, the Sport Cherokee 2-door, 4WD model features styled steel wheels, a new visibility package, lower body side two-tone treatment (black), black w/red insert, lower body side scuff molding, and a stainless steel exhaust system. Cherokee is one of the best-selling vehicles in its class. Cherokees are built in Toledo, Ohio.

Jeep Cherokee Sport 4WD
4 Door Sport Utility

4.0L 190 hp Gas Fuel Inject.	6 Cylinder In-Line	Manual 5 Speed	4 Wheel On-Demand	 Manual Seatbelts Only

Purchase Price

Car Item	Dealer Cost	List
Base Price	**$15,294**	**$16,845**
Anti-Lock Brakes	$509	$599
Automatic 4 Speed	$745	$877
Optional Engine	N/A	N/A
Air Conditioning	$711	$836
Power Steering	Std	Std
Cruise Control	$196	$230
Command-Trac 4WD	Std	Std
AM/FM Stereo Cassette	$171	$201
Steering Wheel, Tilt	$112	$132
Power Windows	Pkg	Pkg
***Options Price**	$882	$1,037
***Total Price**	**$16,176**	**$17,882**
Target Price	$17,379	
Destination Charge	$485	
Avg. Tax & Fees	$1,077	
Total Target $	**$18,941**	
Average Dealer Option Cost:	***85%***	

Ownership Costs

Cost Area	5 Year Cost	Rate
Depreciation	$6,188	Excellent
Financing ($381/month)	$3,121	
Insurance (Rating 13)	$8,271	Average
State Fees	$735	
Fuel (Hwy 20 City 16)	$4,797	Worse Than Average
Maintenance	$4,271	Average
Repairs	$1,085	Worse Than Average

Ownership Cost By Year

$2,000 $4,000 $6,000 $8,000 $10,000

1993 1994 1995 1996 1997

Warranty/Maintenance Info

Major Tune-Up	$166	Better Than Average
Minor Tune-Up	$113	Worse Than Average
Brake Service	$241	Average
Overall Warranty	1 yr/12k	Poor
Drivetrain Warranty	7 yr/70k	Excellent
Rust Warranty	7 yr/100k	Excellent
Maintenance Warranty	N/A	
Roadside Assistance	N/A	

Resale Value

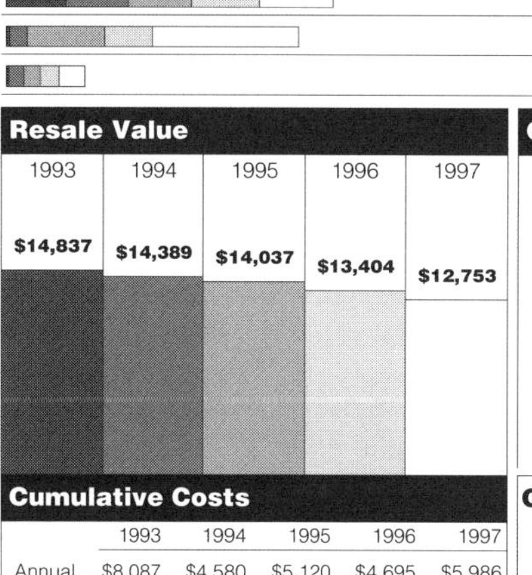

1993	1994	1995	1996	1997
$14,837	$14,389	$14,037	$13,404	$12,753

Ownership Costs (5yr)

Average	This Car
$28,342	$28,468
Cost/Mile 40¢	Cost/Mile 41¢

Cumulative Costs

	1993	1994	1995	1996	1997
Annual	$8,087	$4,580	$5,120	$4,695	$5,986
Total	$8,087	$12,667	$17,787	$22,482	$28,468

Ownership Cost Rating

Average

The 1993 Cherokee is available in twelve models - (Base) Cherokee, Sport, and Country two- and four-door, and two- and four-wheel drive utility wagons. New for 1993, the Sport Cherokee 4-door, 4WD model features styled steel wheels, a new visibility package, lower body side two-tone treatment (black), black w/red insert, lower body side scuff molding, and a stainless steel exhaust system. Cherokee is one of P-selling vehicles in its class. Cherokees are built in Toledo, Ohio.

* Includes shaded options

** Other purchase requirements apply

 Poor  Worse Than Average 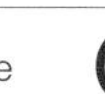 Average 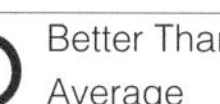 Better Than Average  Excellent 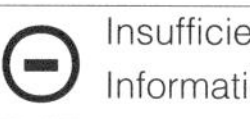 Insufficient Information

Refer to *Section 3: Annotated Vehicle Charts* for an explanation of these charts.

Jeep Cherokee Country 4WD
2 Door Sport Utility

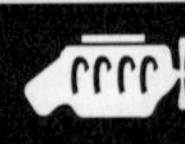

4.0L 190 hp Gas Fuel Inject.

6 Cylinder In-Line

Manual 5 Speed

4 Wheel On-Demand

Manual Seatbelts Only

Utility

4 Door 2WD Model Shown

Purchase Price

Car Item	Dealer Cost	List
Base Price	**$15,880**	**$17,523**
Anti-Lock Brakes	$509	$599
Automatic 4 Speed	$745	$877
Optional Engine	N/A	N/A
Air Conditioning	$711	$836
Power Steering	Std	Std
Cruise Control	$196	$230
Command-Trac 4WD	Std	Std
AM/FM Stereo Cassette	$171	$201
Steering Wheel, Tilt	$112	$132
Power Windows	Pkg	Pkg
***Options Price**	$882	$1,037
***Total Price**	**$16,762**	**$18,560**
Target Price	$18,029	
Destination Charge	$485	
Avg. Tax & Fees	$1,116	
Total Target $	**$19,630**	
Average Dealer Option Cost:	***85%***	

Ownership Costs

Cost Area	5 Year Cost	Rate
Depreciation	$6,131	Better Than Average
Financing ($395/month)	$3,234	
Insurance (Rating 13)	$8,271	Average
State Fees	$760	
Fuel (Hwy 20 City 16)	$4,797	Worse Than Average
Maintenance	$4,269	Average
Repairs	$1,085	Worse Than Average

Ownership Cost By Year

$2,000 $4,000 $6,000 $8,000 $10,000

1993 1994 1995 1996 1997

Warranty/Maintenance Info

Item		Rate
Major Tune-Up	$166	Better Than Average
Minor Tune-Up	$113	Worse Than Average
Brake Service	$241	Average
Overall Warranty	1 yr/12k	Poor
Drivetrain Warranty	7 yr/70k	Excellent
Rust Warranty	7 yr/100k	Excellent
Maintenance Warranty	N/A	
Roadside Assistance	N/A	

Resale Value

1993	1994	1995	1996	1997
$16,786	$15,964	$15,351	$14,529	$13,499

Ownership Costs (5yr)

Average	This Car
$28,912	$28,547
Cost/Mile 41¢	Cost/Mile 41¢

Cumulative Costs

	1993	1994	1995	1996	1997
Annual	$6,880	$4,996	$5,407	$4,896	$6,368
Total	$6,880	$11,876	$17,283	$22,179	$28,547

Ownership Cost Rating

Better Than Average

The 1993 Cherokee is available in twelve models - (Base) Cherokee, Sport, and Country two- and four-door, and two- and four-wheel drive utility wagons. New for 1993, the Country Cherokee 2-door, 4WD model features champagne lower body side treatment w/cladding, fender flares, bumpers and endcaps, body color grille and headlamp bezels, and champagne body side and liftgate tape treatment. Other features include a stainless steel exhaust system, a new visibility pack, and five exterior colors.

Jeep Cherokee Country 4WD
4 Door Sport Utility

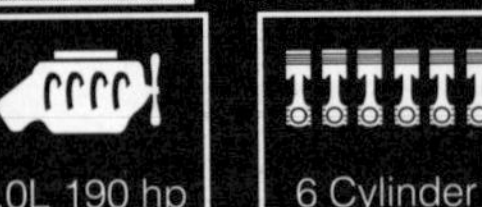

4.0L 190 hp Gas Fuel Inject.

6 Cylinder In-Line

Manual 5 Speed

4 Wheel On-Demand

Manual Seatbelts Only

Utility

2WD Model Shown

Purchase Price

Car Item	Dealer Cost	List
Base Price	**$16,779**	**$18,533**
Anti-Lock Brakes	$509	$599
Automatic 4 Speed	$745	$877
Optional Engine	N/A	N/A
Air Conditioning	$711	$836
Power Steering	Std	Std
Cruise Control	$196	$230
Command-Trac 4WD	Std	Std
AM/FM Stereo Cassette	$171	$201
Steering Wheel, Tilt	$112	$132
Power Windows	Pkg	Pkg
***Options Price**	$882	$1,037
***Total Price**	**$17,661**	**$19,570**
Target Price	$19,029	
Destination Charge	$485	
Avg. Tax & Fees	$1,177	
Total Target $	**$20,691**	
Average Dealer Option Cost:	***85%***	

Ownership Costs

Cost Area	5 Year Cost	Rate
Depreciation	$6,203	Excellent
Financing ($416/month)	$3,409	
Insurance (Rating 14)	$8,446	Average
State Fees	$801	
Fuel (Hwy 20 City 16)	$4,797	Worse Than Average
Maintenance	$4,269	Average
Repairs	$1,085	Worse Than Average

Ownership Cost By Year

$2,000 $4,000 $6,000 $8,000 $10,000

1993 1994 1995 1996 1997

Warranty/Maintenance Info

Item		Rate
Major Tune-Up	$166	Better Than Average
Minor Tune-Up	$113	Worse Than Average
Brake Service	$241	Average
Overall Warranty	1 yr/12k	Poor
Drivetrain Warranty	7 yr/70k	Excellent
Rust Warranty	7 yr/100k	Excellent
Maintenance Warranty	N/A	
Roadside Assistance	N/A	

Resale Value

1993	1994	1995	1996	1997
$17,683	$16,927	$16,341	$15,522	$14,488

Ownership Costs (5yr)

Average	This Car
$29,762	$29,010
Cost/Mile 43¢	Cost/Mile 41¢

Cumulative Costs

	1993	1994	1995	1996	1997
Annual	$7,160	$5,027	$5,458	$4,949	$6,416
Total	$7,160	$12,187	$17,645	$22,594	$29,010

Ownership Cost Rating

Better Than Average

The 1993 Cherokee is available in twelve models - (Base) Cherokee, Sport, and Country two- and four-door, and two- and four-wheel drive utility wagons. New for 1993, the Country Cherokee 4-door, 4WD model features champagne lower body side treatment w/cladding, fender flares, bumpers and endcaps, body color grille and headlamp bezels, and champagne body side and liftgate tape treatment. Other features include a stainless steel exhaust system, a new visibility pack, and five exterior colors.

* Includes shaded options

** Other purchase requirements apply

Poor  Worse Than Average  Average 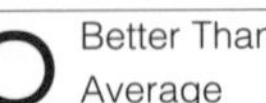 Better Than Average  Excellent Insufficient Information

Refer to *Section 3: Annotated Vehicle Charts* for an explanation of these charts.

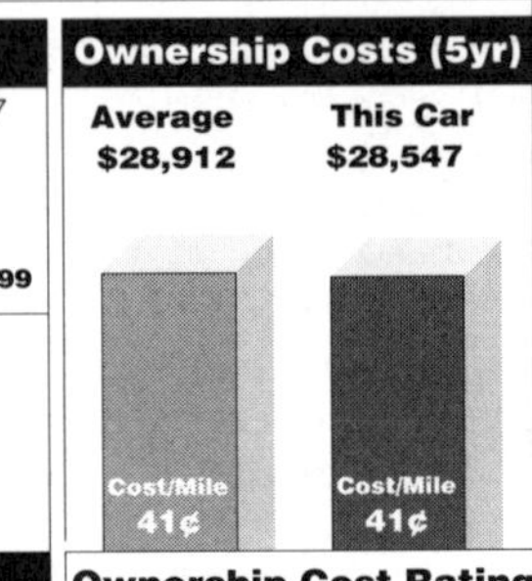

Jeep Grand Cherokee 4WD
4 Door Sport Utility

4.0L 190 hp Gas Fuel Inject.

6 Cylinder In-Line

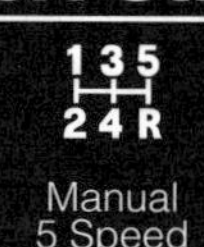

Manual 5 Speed

4 Wheel On-Demand

Driver Airbag Psngr Belts

Utility

Purchase Price

Car Item	Dealer Cost	List
Base Price	**$17,951**	**$19,700**
Anti-Lock Brakes	Std	Std
Automatic 4 Speed	$745	$877
5.2L 220 hp Gas	Pkg	Pkg
Air Conditioning	$711	$836
Power Steering	Std	Std
Cruise Control	Pkg	Pkg
Command-Trac 4WD	Std	Std
AM/FM Stereo Cassette	$132	$155
Steering Wheel, Tilt	Pkg	Pkg
Power Windows	Pkg	Pkg
***Options Price**	$843	$991
***Total Price**	**$18,794**	**$20,691**
Target Price	$20,537	
Destination Charge	$485	
Avg. Tax & Fees	$1,263	
Total Target $	**$22,285**	
Average Dealer Option Cost:	***85%***	

Ownership Costs

Cost Area	5 Year Cost	Rate
Depreciation		Insufficient Information
Financing ($448/month)	$3,671	
Insurance (Rating 15)	$8,507	Average
State Fees	$847	
Fuel (Hwy 21 City 16)	$4,672	Average
Maintenance	$4,202	Average
Repairs	$1,215	Poor

Ownership Cost By Year

$2,000 $4,000 $6,000 $8,000 $10,000

Insufficient Depreciation Information

1993 1994 1995 1996 1997

Warranty/Maintenance Info

Item		Rate
Major Tune-Up	$166	Better Than Average
Minor Tune-Up	$113	Worse Than Average
Brake Service	$223	Average
Overall Warranty	1 yr/12k	Poor
Drivetrain Warranty	7 yr/70k	Excellent
Rust Warranty	7 yr/100k	Excellent
Maintenance Warranty	N/A	
Roadside Assistance	N/A	

Resale Value

Insufficient Information

Ownership Costs (5yr)

Insufficient Information

The 1993 Grand Cherokee is available in three models - (Base) Grand Cherokee, Laredo and Limited. New to the Jeep lineup, the Grand Cherokee features a unibody construction, quieter and more rigid than body-on-frame vehicles. Interior refinements include more rear-seat hip room, front and rear-seat shoulder room and more cargo space than the Cherokee. The Grand Cherokee offers standard features such as anti-lock brakes, tinted glass, reclining high-back bucket seats and five-spoke steel wheels.

Cumulative Costs

	1993	1994	1995	1996	1997
Annual	*Insufficient Information*				
Total	*Insufficient Information*				

Ownership Cost Rating

Insufficient Information

Jeep Grand Cherokee Laredo 4WD
4 Door Sport Utility

4.0L 190 hp Gas Fuel Inject.

6 Cylinder In-Line

1 3 5
2 4 R
Manual 5 Speed

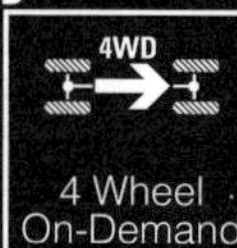

4 Wheel On-Demand

Driver Airbag Psngr Belts

Utility

Purchase Price

Car Item	Dealer Cost	List
Base Price	**$18,993**	**$20,884**
Anti-Lock Brakes	Std	Std
Automatic 4 Speed	$745	$877
5.2L 220 hp Gas	Pkg	Pkg
Air Conditioning	$711	$836
Power Steering	Std	Std
Cruise Control	Std	Std
Command-Trac 4WD	Std	Std
AM/FM Stereo Cassette	$132	$155
Steering Wheel, Tilt	Std	Std
Power Windows	Pkg	Pkg
***Options Price**	$843	$991
***Total Price**	**$19,836**	**$21,875**
Target Price	$21,725	
Destination Charge	$485	
Avg. Tax & Fees	$1,335	
Total Target $	**$23,545**	
Average Dealer Option Cost:	***85%***	

Ownership Costs

Cost Area	5 Year Cost	Rate
Depreciation		Insufficient Information
Financing ($473/month)	$3,879	
Insurance (Rating 15)	$8,507	Average
State Fees	$895	
Fuel (Hwy 21 City 16)	$4,672	Average
Maintenance	$4,202	Average
Repairs	$1,215	Poor

Ownership Cost By Year

$2,000 $4,000 $6,000 $8,000 $10,000

Insufficient Depreciation Information

1993 1994 1995 1996 1997

Warranty/Maintenance Info

Item		Rate
Major Tune-Up	$166	Better Than Average
Minor Tune-Up	$113	Worse Than Average
Brake Service	$223	Average
Overall Warranty	1 yr/12k	Poor
Drivetrain Warranty	7 yr/70k	Excellent
Rust Warranty	7 yr/100k	Excellent
Maintenance Warranty	N/A	
Roadside Assistance	N/A	

Resale Value

Insufficient Information

Ownership Costs (5yr)

Insufficient Information

The 1993 Grand Cherokee is available in three models - (Base) Grand Cherokee, Laredo and Limited. New to the Jeep lineup, the Grand Cherokee features unibody construction, quieter and more rigid than body-on-frame vehicles. Interior refinements include more rear seat hip room, front and rear seat shoulder room and more cargo space than the Cherokee. The Laredo upgrades the base model with cruise control, power remote mirrors, tilt steering wheel and the Convenience and Protection Groups.

Cumulative Costs

	1993	1994	1995	1996	1997
Annual	*Insufficient Information*				
Total	*Insufficient Information*				

Ownership Cost Rating

Insufficient Information

* Includes shaded options

** Other purchase requirements apply

 Poor  Worse Than Average  Average  Better Than Average  Excellent  Insufficient Information

Refer to *Section 3: Annotated Vehicle Charts* for an explanation of these charts.

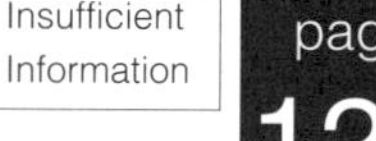

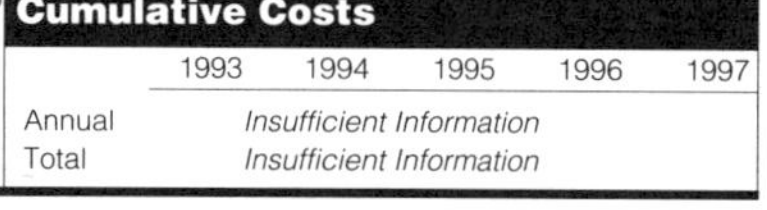

Jeep Grand Cherokee Limited 4WD
4 Door Sport Utility

4.0L 190 hp Gas Fuel Inject.

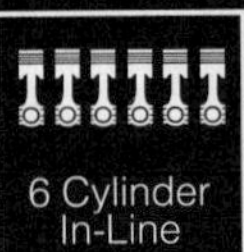

6 Cylinder In-Line

Automatic 4 Speed

4 Wheel Full-Time

Driver Airbag Psngr Belts

Purchase Price

Car Item	Dealer Cost	List
Base Price	**$25,642**	**$28,440**
Anti-Lock Brakes	Std	Std
Manual Transmission	N/A	N/A
5.2L 220 hp Gas	Pkg	Pkg
Auto Climate Control	Std	Std
Power Steering	Std	Std
Cruise Control	Std	Std
Quadra-Trac 4WD	Std	Std
AM/FM Stereo Cassette	Std	Std
Steering Wheel, Tilt	Std	Std
Power Windows	Std	Std
***Options Price**	$0	$0
***Total Price**	**$25,642**	**$28,440**
Target Price	$28,110	
Destination Charge	$485	
Avg. Tax & Fees	$1,719	
Total Target $	**$30,314**	
Average Dealer Option Cost: **85%**		

Ownership Costs

Cost Area	5 Year Cost	Rate
Depreciation		Insufficient Information
Financing ($609/month)	$4,994	
Insurance (Rating 18)	$9,058	Average
State Fees	$1,156	
Fuel (Hwy 20 City 15)	$4,941	Average
Maintenance	$4,456	Average
Repairs	$1,215	Poor

Ownership Cost By Year

$2,000 $4,000 $6,000 $8,000 $10,000

Insufficient Depreciation Information

1993 1994 1995 1996 1997

Warranty/Maintenance Info

Major Tune-Up	$166	Better Than Average
Minor Tune-Up	$113	Worse Than Average
Brake Service	$223	Average
Overall Warranty	1 yr/12k	Poor
Drivetrain Warranty	7 yr/70k	Excellent
Rust Warranty	7 yr/100k	Excellent
Maintenance Warranty	N/A	
Roadside Assistance	N/A	

Resale Value

Insufficient Information

Ownership Costs (5yr)

Insufficient Information

Cumulative Costs

	1993	1994	1995	1996	1997
Annual	*Insufficient Information*				
Total	*Insufficient Information*				

Ownership Cost Rating

Insufficient Information

The 1993 Grand Cherokee is available in three models -(Base) Grand Cherokee, Laredo and Limited. New to the Jeep lineup, the base Grand Cherokee features a unibody construction, quieter and more rigid than body-on-frame vehicles. Interior refinements include more rear-seat hip room, front and rear-seat shoulder room and more cargo space than the Cherokee. The Grand Cherokee Limited upgrades the Laredo with crosswire aluminum wheels, AM/FM Cassette stereo, and the Luxury, Power, and Security Groups.

Jeep Grand Wagoneer 4WD
4 Door Sport Utility

5.2L 220 hp Gas Fuel Inject.

8 Cylinder "V"

Automatic 4 Speed

4 Wheel Full-Time

Driver Airbag Psngr Belts

Utility

Purchase Price

Car Item	Dealer Cost	List
Base Price	**$26,435**	**$29,341**
Anti-Lock Brakes	Std	Std
Manual Transmission	N/A	N/A
Optional Engine	N/A	N/A
Auto Climate Control	Std	Std
Power Steering	Std	Std
Cruise Control	Std	Std
Quadra-Trac 4WD	Std	Std
AM/FM Stereo Cassette	Std	Std
Steering Wheel, Tilt	Std	Std
Power Windows	Std	Std
***Options Price**	$0	$0
***Total Price**	**$26,435**	**$29,341**
Target Price	$28,947	
Destination Charge	$485	
Avg. Tax & Fees	$1,770	
Total Target $	**$31,202**	
Average Dealer Option Cost: **85%**		

Ownership Costs

Cost Area	5 Year Cost	Rate
Depreciation		Insufficient Information
Financing ($627/month)	$5,140	
Insurance (Rating 18)	$9,058	Average
State Fees	$1,193	
Fuel (Hwy 18 City 14)	$5,399	Worse Than Average
Maintenance	$4,207	Average
Repairs	$1,163	Poor

Ownership Cost By Year

$2,000 $4,000 $6,000 $8,000 $10,000

Insufficient Depreciation Information

1993 1994 1995 1996 1997

Warranty/Maintenance Info

Major Tune-Up	$160	Better Than Average
Minor Tune-Up	$117	Worse Than Average
Brake Service	$223	Average
Overall Warranty	1 yr/12k	Poor
Drivetrain Warranty	7 yr/70k	Excellent
Rust Warranty	7 yr/100k	Excellent
Maintenance Warranty	N/A	
Roadside Assistance	N/A	

Resale Value

Insufficient Information

Ownership Costs (5yr)

Insufficient Information

Cumulative Costs

	1993	1994	1995	1996	1997
Annual	*Insufficient Information*				
Total	*Insufficient Information*				

Ownership Cost Rating

Insufficient Information

The 1993 Grand Wagoneer is a one model edition. New to the Jeep lineup, the Grand Wagoneer features a unibody construction, quieter and more rigid than body-on-frame vehicles. Interior refinements include more rear-seat hip room, front and rear-seat shoulder room and more cargo space than the Cherokee. The Grand Wagoneer offers standard features such as luxury aluminum wheels, reclining high-back bucket seats and exterior woodgrain decals and molding.

* Includes shaded options

** Other purchase requirements apply

 Poor  Worse Than Average 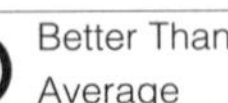 Average Better Than Average 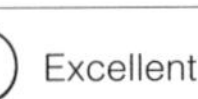 Excellent Insufficient Information

Refer to *Section 3: Annotated Vehicle Charts* for an explanation of these charts.

Jeep Wrangler S

2 Door Sport Utility

2.5L 123 hp Gas Fuel Inject.

4 Cylinder In-Line

Manual 5 Speed

4 Wheel On-Demand

Manual Seatbelts Only

Utility

Purchase Price

Car Item	*Dealer Cost*	*List*
Base Price	**$10,545**	**$10,925**
Anti-Lock Brakes	N/A	N/A
Automatic Transmission	N/A	N/A
Optional Engine	N/A	N/A
Air Conditioning	N/A	N/A
Power Steering	$255	$300
Cruise Control	N/A	N/A
Command-Trac 4WD	Std	Std
AM/FM Stereo Cassette	$454	$534
Steering Wheel, Tilt	$164	$193
Power Windows	N/A	N/A
***Options Price**	$709	$834
***Total Price**	**$11,254**	**$11,759**
Target Price	$11,708	
Destination Charge	$485	
Avg. Tax & Fees	$732	
Total Target $	**$12,925**	
Average Dealer Option Cost:	***84%***	

Ownership Costs

Cost Area	*5 Year Cost*	*Rate*
Depreciation	$3,692	Excellent
Financing ($260/month)	$2,129	
Insurance (Rating 7)	$7,244	Worse Than Average
State Fees	$489	
Fuel (Hwy 20 City 18)	$4,554	Worse Than Average
Maintenance	$3,942	Better Than Average
Repairs	$1,085	Worse Than Average

Ownership Cost By Year

$2,000 $4,000 $6,000 $8,000

1993 1994 1995 1996 1997

Warranty/Maintenance Info

Major Tune-Up	$146	Better Than Average
Minor Tune-Up	$91	Better Than Average
Brake Service	$241	Average
Overall Warranty	1 yr/12k	Poor
Drivetrain Warranty	7 yr/70k	Excellent
Rust Warranty	7 yr/100k	Excellent
Maintenance Warranty	N/A	
Roadside Assistance	N/A	

Resale Value

1993	1994	1995	1996	1997
$12,306	$11,291	$10,603	$9,893	$9,233

Ownership Costs (5yr)

Average	This Car
$23,192	$23,135
Cost/Mile 33¢	Cost/Mile 33¢

Cumulative Costs

	1993	1994	1995	1996	1997
Annual	$3,889	$4,509	$4,871	$4,269	$5,597
Total	$3,889	$8,398	$13,269	$17,538	$23,135

Ownership Cost Rating

Better Than Average

The 1993 Wrangler is available in four models - S, Base Wrangler, Sahara, and Renegade convertible sport utility vehicles. New for 1993, the S model has a stainless steel exhaust system, tamper resistant odometer, and blue/gray tinted quarter and rear windows on soft tops. Other new features include four new exterior colors, flame red, gray mist, light champagne, and deep blue. The S model offers 15"x6" steel wheels and high-back front bucket seats with an optional fold and tumble rear seat.

Jeep Wrangler

2 Door Sport Utility

2.5L 123 hp Gas Fuel Inject.

4 Cylinder In-Line

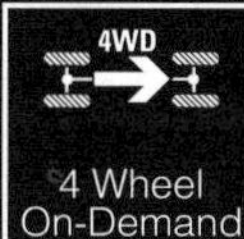

Manual 5 Speed

4 Wheel On-Demand

Manual Seatbelts Only

S Model Shown

Utility

Purchase Price

Car Item	*Dealer Cost*	*List*
Base Price	**$12,127**	**$13,343**
Anti-Lock Brakes	$509	$599
Automatic 3 Speed	Pkg	Pkg
4.0L 180 hp Gas	Pkg	Pkg
Air Conditioning	$746	$878
Power Steering	$255	$300
Cruise Control	N/A	N/A
Command-Trac 4WD	Std	Std
AM/FM Stereo Cassette	$224	$264
Steering Wheel, Tilt	$164	$193
Power Windows	N/A	N/A
***Options Price**	$1,225	$1,442
***Total Price**	**$13,352**	**$14,785**
Target Price	$14,191	
Destination Charge	$485	
Avg. Tax & Fees	$887	
Total Target $	**$15,563**	
Average Dealer Option Cost:	***85%***	

Ownership Costs

Cost Area	*5 Year Cost*	*Rate*
Depreciation	$5,427	Better Than Average
Financing ($313/month)	$2,563	
Insurance (Rating 11)	$7,902	Worse Than Average
State Fees	$611	
Fuel (Hwy 20 City 16)	$4,797	Worse Than Average
Maintenance	$4,061	Average
Repairs	$1,085	Worse Than Average

Ownership Cost By Year

$2,000 $4,000 $6,000 $8,000

1993 1994 1995 1996 1997

Warranty/Maintenance Info

Major Tune-Up	$166	Better Than Average
Minor Tune-Up	$113	Worse Than Average
Brake Service	$241	Average
Overall Warranty	1 yr/12k	Poor
Drivetrain Warranty	7 yr/70k	Excellent
Rust Warranty	7 yr/100k	Excellent
Maintenance Warranty	N/A	
Roadside Assistance	N/A	

Resale Value

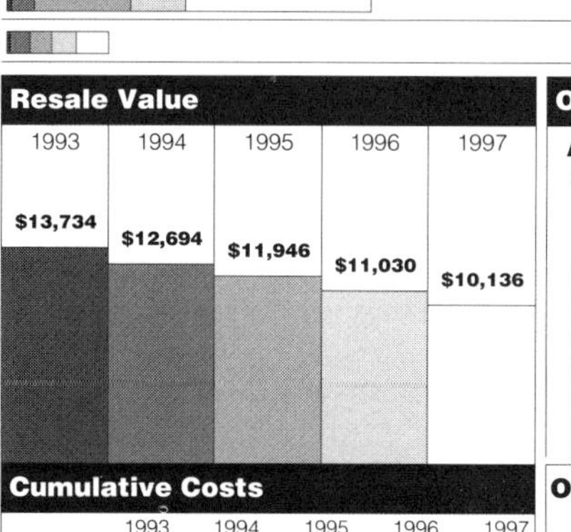

1993	1994	1995	1996	1997
$13,734	$12,694	$11,946	$11,030	$10,136

Ownership Costs (5yr)

Average	This Car
$25,737	$26,446
Cost/Mile 37¢	Cost/Mile 38¢

Cumulative Costs

	1993	1994	1995	1996	1997
Annual	$5,481	$4,899	$5,249	$4,746	$6,071
Total	$5,481	$10,380	$15,629	$20,375	$26,446

Ownership Cost Rating

Average

The 1993 Wrangler is available in four models - S, Base Wrangler, Sahara, and Renegade convertible sport utility vehicles. New for 1993, the Base Wrangler receives a stainless steel exhaust system and four-wheel anti-lock brake system (w/4.0L engine). Other new features include a tamper resistant odometer, blue/gray tinted quarter and rear windows on soft top models, and four new colors. An optional off-road package is offered, including H.D. gas shocks.

* Includes shaded options

** Other purchase requirements apply

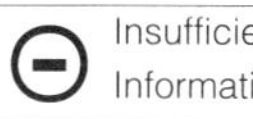

 Poor  Worse Than Average  Average  Better Than Average Excellent Insufficient Information

Refer to *Section 3: Annotated Vehicle Charts* for an explanation of these charts.

Jeep Wrangler Sahara
2 Door Sport Utility

4.0L 180 hp Gas Fuel Inject.

6 Cylinder In-Line

Manual 5 Speed

4 Wheel On-Demand

Manual Seatbelts Only

Purchase Price

Car Item	Dealer Cost	List
Base Price	**$14,251**	**$15,842**
Anti-Lock Brakes	$509	$599
Automatic 3 Speed	Pkg	Pkg
Optional Engine	N/A	N/A
Air Conditioning	$746	$878
Power Steering	Std	Std
Cruise Control	N/A	N/A
Command-Trac 4WD	Std	Std
AM/FM Stereo Cassette	$224	$264
Steering Wheel, Tilt	$111	$130
Power Windows	N/A	N/A
***Options Price**	$970	$1,142
***Total Price**	**$15,221**	**$16,984**
Target Price	$16,240	
Destination Charge	$485	
Avg. Tax & Fees	$1,011	
Total Target $	**$17,736**	
Average Dealer Option Cost:	***85%***	

Ownership Costs

Cost Area	5 Year Cost	Rate
Depreciation	$5,932	Better Than Average
Financing ($356/month)	$2,921	
Insurance (Rating 12)	$8,108	Worse Than Average
State Fees	$699	
Fuel (Hwy 20 City 16)	$4,797	Worse Than Average
Maintenance	$4,127	Average
Repairs	$1,085	Worse Than Average

Ownership Cost By Year

$2,000 $4,000 $6,000 $8,000 $10,000

1993 1994 1995 1996 1997

Warranty/Maintenance Info

Item		Rate
Major Tune-Up	$166	Better Than Average
Minor Tune-Up	$113	Worse Than Average
Brake Service	$241	Average
Overall Warranty	1 yr/12k	Poor
Drivetrain Warranty	7 yr/70k	Excellent
Rust Warranty	7 yr/100k	Excellent
Maintenance Warranty	N/A	
Roadside Assistance	N/A	

Resale Value

1993	1994	1995	1996	1997
$16,709	$15,331	$14,263	$12,992	$11,804

Ownership Costs (5yr)

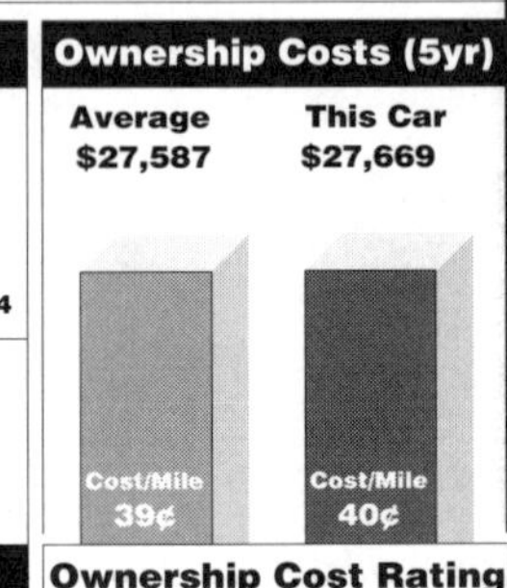

Cumulative Costs

	1993	1994	1995	1996	1997
Annual	$4,888	$5,409	$5,731	$5,185	$6,456
Total	$4,888	$10,297	$16,028	$21,213	$27,669

Ownership Cost Rating

Average

The 1993 Wrangler is available in four models - S, Base Wrangler, Sahara, and Renegade convertible sport utility vehicles. New for 1993, the Sahara model has a stainless steel exhaust system, a tamper resistant odometer, and a 4-wheel anti-lock braking system. Features include a low-lustre exterior paint and color coordinated wheels, bumper extensions with tow hooks, a center console, leather wrapped steering wheel, and trailcloth fabric seats. Also included are fog lamps and a conventional spare tire.

Jeep Wrangler Renegade
2 Door Sport Utility

4.0L 180 hp Gas Fuel Inject.

6 Cylinder In-Line

Manual 5 Speed

4 Wheel On-Demand

Manual Seatbelts Only

Utility

Purchase Price

Car Item	Dealer Cost	List
Base Price	**$15,753**	**$17,609**
Anti-Lock Brakes	$509	$599
Automatic 3 Speed	Pkg	Pkg
Optional Engine	N/A	N/A
Air Conditioning	$746	$878
Power Steering	Std	Std
Cruise Control	N/A	N/A
Command-Trac 4WD	Std	Std
AM/FM Stereo Cassette	$224	$264
Steering Wheel, Tilt	$111	$130
Power Windows	N/A	N/A
***Options Price**	$970	$1,142
***Total Price**	**$16,723**	**$18,751**
Target Price	$17,891	
Destination Charge	$485	
Avg. Tax & Fees	$1,111	
Total Target $	**$19,487**	
Average Dealer Option Cost:	***85%***	

Ownership Costs

Cost Area	5 Year Cost	Rate
Depreciation	$6,485	Better Than Average
Financing ($392/month)	$3,209	
Insurance (Rating 14)	$8,446	Worse Than Average
State Fees	$769	
Fuel (Hwy 20 City 16)	$4,797	Worse Than Average
Maintenance	$4,389	Average
Repairs	$1,085	Worse Than Average

Ownership Cost By Year

$2,000 $4,000 $6,000 $8,000 $10,000

1993 1994 1995 1996 1997

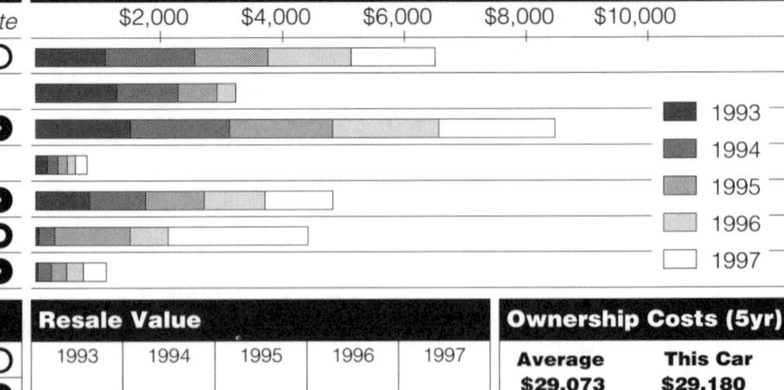

Warranty/Maintenance Info

Item		Rate
Major Tune-Up	$166	Better Than Average
Minor Tune-Up	$113	Worse Than Average
Brake Service	$241	Average
Overall Warranty	1 yr/12k	Poor
Drivetrain Warranty	7 yr/70k	Excellent
Rust Warranty	7 yr/100k	Excellent
Maintenance Warranty	N/A	
Roadside Assistance	N/A	

Resale Value

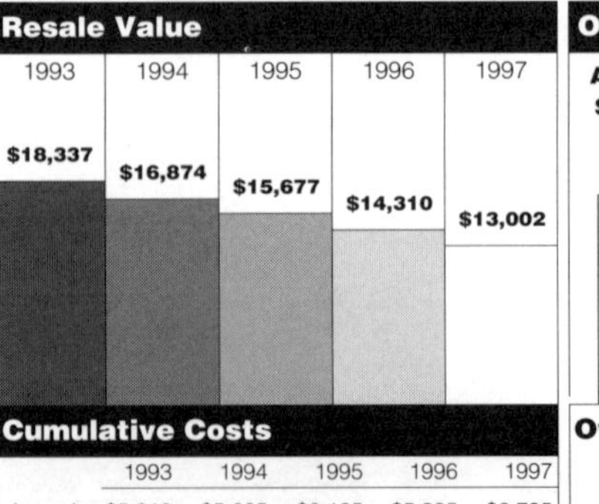

1993	1994	1995	1996	1997
$18,337	$16,874	$15,677	$14,310	$13,002

Ownership Costs (5yr)

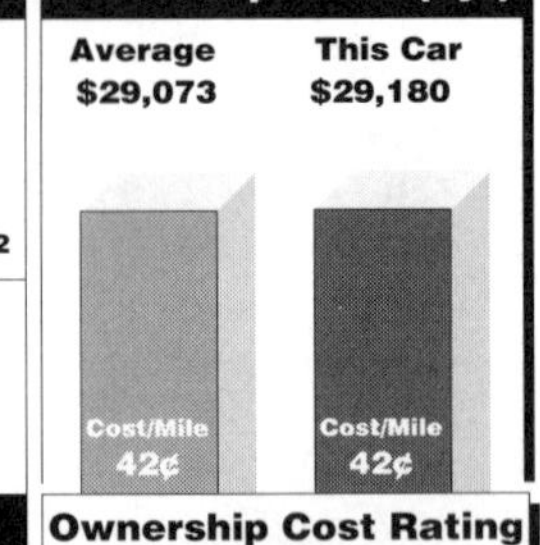

Cumulative Costs

	1993	1994	1995	1996	1997
Annual	$5,210	$5,665	$6,125	$5,385	$6,795
Total	$5,210	$10,875	$17,000	$22,385	$29,180

Ownership Cost Rating

Average

The 1993 Wrangler is available in four models - S, Base Wrangler, Sahara, and Renegade convertible sport utility vehicles. New for 1993, the Renegade now features a new stainless steel exhaust system, tamper resistant odometer, and 4-wheel anti-lock braking system. The Renegade model includes 15"x8" aluminum wheels, leather wrapped steering wheel, front bumpers and rear bumperettes in matching body color, as well as full carpeting, and sculptured lower body panels. Wranglers are built in Toledo, Ohio.

* Includes shaded options

** Other purchase requirements apply

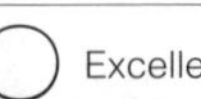

Poor  Worse Than Average  Average  Better Than Average | Excellent | Insufficient Information

Refer to *Section 3: Annotated Vehicle Charts* for an explanation of these charts.

Land Rover Defender 110
4 Door Sport Utility

Utility

3.9L 180 hp Gas Fuel Inject.

8 Cylinder "V"

Manual 5 Speed

4 Wheel Full-Time

Manual Seatbelts Only

Purchase Price

Car Item	Dealer Cost	List
Base Price	**$34,400**	**$39,900**
Anti-Lock Brakes	N/A	N/A
Automatic Transmission	N/A	N/A
Optional Engine	N/A	N/A
Air Conditioning	Std	Std
Power Steering	Std	Std
Cruise Control	N/A	N/A
4 Wheel Full-Time Drive	Std	Std
AM/FM Stereo Cassette	Std	Std
Steering Wheel, Tilt	N/A	N/A
Power Windows	N/A	N/A
***Options Price**	$0	$0
***Total Price**	**$34,400**	**$39,900**
Target Price	$37,840	
Destination Charge	$675	
Avg. Tax & Fees	$2,332	
Total Target $	**$40,847**	
Average Dealer Option Cost:	***80%***	

Ownership Costs

Cost Area	5 Year Cost	Rate
Depreciation		Insufficient Information
Financing ($821/month)	$6,729	
Insurance (Rating 21 [Est.])	$10,916	Average
State Fees	$1,623	
Fuel (Hwy 12 City 10 -Prem.)	$8,667	Poor
Maintenance		Insufficient Information
Repairs	$1,275	Poor

Ownership Cost By Year

$2,000 $4,000 $6,000 $8,000 $10,000 $12,000

Depreciation: *Insufficient Depreciation Information*

Maintenance: *Insufficient Maintenance Information*

1993 1994 1995 1996 1997

Warranty/Maintenance Info

Item		Rate
Major Tune-Up		Insufficient Information
Minor Tune-Up		Insufficient Information
Brake Service	$183	Better Than Average
Overall Warranty	3 yr/42k	Average
Drivetrain Warranty	3 yr/42k	Average
Rust Warranty	6 yr/unlim. mi	Better Than Average
Maintenance Warranty	N/A	
Roadside Assistance	3 yr/42k	

Resale Value

Insufficient Information

Ownership Costs (5yr)

Insufficient Information

The 1993 Defender 110 is offered as one model edition. All new for 1993, the Land Rover Defender 110 offers as standard equipment a 20.4-gallon fuel tank, self-leveling suspension, and Safari Cage with luggage bars. The Defender 110s are a limited production run of 500. With a five-door station wagon body, the Defender 110 also features front bucket seats, a rear bench and four folding jump seats in the cargo area, an electrically heated windshield, tachometer, auto-dimming rearview mirror and complete analog gauges.

Cumulative Costs

	1993	1994	1995	1996	1997
Annual	*Insufficient Information*				
Total	*Insufficient Information*				

Ownership Cost Rating

Insufficient Information

Land Rover Range Rover County
4 Door Sport Utility

Utility

3.9L 182 hp Gas Fuel Inject.

8 Cylinder "V"

Automatic 4 Speed

4 Wheel Full-Time

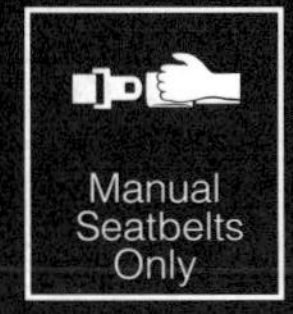
Manual Seatbelts Only

Purchase Price

Car Item	Dealer Cost	List
Base Price	**$38,000**	**$44,500**
Anti-Lock Brakes	Std	Std
Manual Transmission	N/A	N/A
Optional Engine	N/A	N/A
Air Conditioning	Std	Std
Power Steering	Std	Std
Cruise Control	Std	Std
4 Wheel Full-Time Drive	Std	Std
AM/FM Stereo CD	Std	Std
Steering Wheel, Tilt	N/A	N/A
Power Windows	Std	Std
***Options Price**	$0	$0
***Total Price**	**$38,000**	**$44,500**
Target Price	$41,800	
Destination Charge	$625	
Avg. Tax & Fees	$2,572	
Total Target $	**$44,997**	
Average Dealer Option Cost:	***N/A***	

Ownership Costs

Cost Area	5 Year Cost	Rate
Depreciation	$19,237	Worse Than Average
Financing ($904/month)	$7,412	
Insurance (Rating 25 [Est.])	$12,556	Worse Than Average
State Fees	$1,805	
Fuel (Hwy 15 City 12 -Prem.)	$7,062	Poor
Maintenance	$6,894	Poor
Repairs	$1,275	Poor

Ownership Cost By Year

$5,000 $10,000 $15,000 $20,000

1993 1994 1995 1996 1997

Warranty/Maintenance Info

Item		Rate
Major Tune-Up	$297	Poor
Minor Tune-Up	$133	Poor
Brake Service	$337	Poor
Overall Warranty	3 yr/42k	Average
Drivetrain Warranty	3 yr/42k	Average
Rust Warranty	6 yr/unlim. mi	Better Than Average
Maintenance Warranty	N/A	
Roadside Assistance	3 yr/42k	

Resale Value

1993	1994	1995	1996	1997
$35,343	$33,338	$30,330	$26,854	$25,760

Ownership Costs (5yr)

	Average	This Car
	$50,730	$56,241
Cost/Mile	72¢	80¢

The 1993 Range Rover sport utility is available in two models-County and County LWB. New for 1993, the Range Rover County features its permanent four-wheel-drive design and now becomes the world's first dual purpose vehicle to be fitted with an Electronic Traction Control System. Interior features include Burl walnut panels, Connolly leather upholstery and power slide and tilt glass sunroof. Other features include remote keyless entry, power window and door locks and six-disc CD changer.

Cumulative Costs

	1993	1994	1995	1996	1997
Annual	$16,873	$8,813	$10,903	$9,702	$9,950
Total	$16,873	$25,686	$36,589	$46,291	$56,241

Ownership Cost Rating

Poor

* Includes shaded options

** Other purchase requirements apply

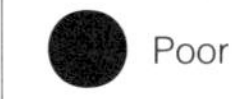

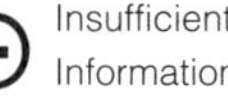

Poor | Worse Than Average | Average | Better Than Average | Excellent | Insufficient Information

Refer to *Section 3: Annotated Vehicle Charts* for an explanation of these charts.

Land Rover Range Rover County LWB
4 Door Sport Utility

4.3L 200 hp Gas Fuel Inject. | 8 Cylinder "V" | Automatic 4 Speed | 4 Wheel Full-Time | Manual Seatbelts Only

Utility

Base Model Shown

Purchase Price

Car Item	Dealer Cost	List
Base Price	**$41,900**	**$49,200**
Anti-Lock Brakes	Std	Std
Manual Transmission	N/A	N/A
Optional Engine	N/A	N/A
Air Conditioning	Std	Std
Power Steering	Std	Std
Cruise Control	Std	Std
4 Wheel Full-Time Drive	Std	Std
AM/FM Stereo CD	Std	Std
Steering Wheel, Tilt	N/A	N/A
Power Windows	Std	Std
***Options Price**	$0	$0
***Total Price**	**$41,900**	**$49,200**
Target Price	$46,090	
Destination Charge	$625	
Avg. Tax & Fees	$2,834	
Total Target $	**$49,549**	
Average Dealer Option Cost:	***82%***	

Ownership Costs

Cost Area	5 Year Cost	Rate
Depreciation	$20,334	Average
Financing ($996/month)	$8,162	
Insurance (Rating 26 [Est.])	$13,194	Worse Than Average
State Fees	$1,993	
Fuel (Hwy 15 City 12 -Prem.)	$7,062	Poor
Maintenance		Insufficient Information
Repairs	$1,275	Poor

Ownership Cost By Year

$5,000 $10,000 $15,000 $20,000 $25,000

Insufficient Maintenance Information

1993 1994 1995 1996 1997

Warranty/Maintenance Info

Item		Rate
Major Tune-Up		Insufficient Information
Minor Tune-Up		Insufficient Information
Brake Service		Insufficient Information
Overall Warranty	3 yr/42k	Average
Drivetrain Warranty	3 yr/42k	Average
Rust Warranty	6 yr/50k	Worse Than Average
Maintenance Warranty	N/A	
Roadside Assistance	3 yr/42k	

Resale Value

1993	1994	1995	1996	1997
$38,601	$36,503	$34,326	$31,599	$29,215

Ownership Costs (5yr)

Insufficient Information

Cumulative Costs

	1993	1994	1995	1996	1997
Annual	Insufficient Information				
Total	Insufficient Information				

Ownership Cost Rating

Insufficient Information

The 1993 Range Rover sport utility is available in two models-County and County LWB. New for 1993, the Range Rover County LWB features the unique electronically controlled air suspension. The County LWB features Connolly leather upholstery, eight-way power adjustable and heated seats and power slide and tilt glass sunroof. Other convenience features include power operated windows, heated door lock and front spoiler with fog lamps. The County LWB is available in six new exterior colors for 1993.

Mazda B2200
2 Door Regular Cab

2.2L 85 hp Gas Carburetor | 4 Cylinder In-Line | Manual 5 Speed | 2 Wheel Rear | Manual Seatbelts Only

Small Pickup

4WD Model Shown

Purchase Price

Car Item	Dealer Cost	List
Base Price	**$8,086**	**$8,775**
Anti-Lock Brakes	Std	Std
Automatic 4 Speed	$700	$795
Optional Engine	N/A	N/A
Air Conditioning	$635	$785
Power Steering	$234	$275
Cruise Control	N/A	N/A
All Wheel Drive	N/A	N/A
AM/FM Stereo Cassette	$227	** $295
Steering Wheel, Tilt	N/A	N/A
Long Bed	$650	$715
***Options Price**	$234	$275
***Total Price**	**$8,320**	**$9,050**
Target Price	$8,755	
Destination Charge	$350	
Avg. Tax & Fees	$549	
Total Target $	**$9,654**	
Average Dealer Option Cost:	***76%***	

Ownership Costs

Cost Area	5 Year Cost	Rate
Depreciation	$3,395	Excellent
Financing ($194/month)	$1,590	
Insurance (Rating 6)	$7,129	Worse Than Average
State Fees	$376	
Fuel (Hwy 26 City 21)	$3,673	Better Than Average
Maintenance	$3,702	Average
Repairs	$580	Excellent

Ownership Cost By Year

$2,000 $4,000 $6,000 $8,000

1993 1994 1995 1996 1997

Warranty/Maintenance Info

Item		Rate
Major Tune-Up	$184	Worse Than Average
Minor Tune-Up	$76	Better Than Average
Brake Service	$192	Better Than Average
Overall Warranty	3 yr/50k	Average
Drivetrain Warranty	3 yr/50k	Average
Rust Warranty	5 yr/unlim. mi	Better Than Average
Maintenance Warranty	N/A	
Roadside Assistance	1 yr/unlim. mi	

Resale Value

1993	1994	1995	1996	1997
$8,721	$8,072	$7,561	$6,944	$6,259

Ownership Costs (5yr)

Average	This Car
$21,156	$20,445
Cost/Mile 30¢	Cost/Mile 29¢

Cumulative Costs

	1993	1994	1995	1996	1997
Annual	$3,728	$3,488	$4,150	$3,750	$5,329
Total	$3,728	$7,216	$11,366	$15,116	$20,445

Ownership Cost Rating

Excellent

The 1993 Pickup is available in five models - B2200 two-wheel drive regular and extended cab; B2600i two-wheel drive extended cab, and B2600i four-wheel drive regular and extended cab. The regular cab model features a three passenger bench seat with reclining seatback and adjustable head restraints, vinyl upholstery, color keyed floor carpeting and a resetable trip odometer. Other features include styled steel wheels, steel belted radial tires and a double wall cargo bed.

* Includes shaded options

** Other purchase requirements apply

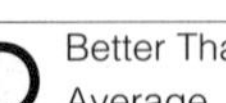

Poor | Worse Than Average | Average | Better Than Average | Excellent | Insufficient Information

Refer to *Section 3: Annotated Vehicle Charts* for an explanation of these charts.

Mazda B2200 Cab Plus
2 Door Extended Cab

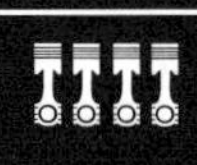

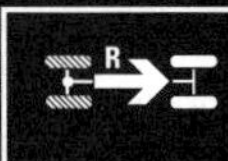

2.2L 85 hp Gas Carburetor | 4 Cylinder In-Line | Manual 5 Speed | 2 Wheel Rear | Manual Seatbelts Only

Purchase Price

Car Item	Dealer Cost	List
Base Price	**$9,509**	**$10,435**
Anti-Lock Brakes	Std	Std
Automatic Transmission	N/A	N/A
Optional Engine	N/A	N/A
Air Conditioning	$635	$785
Power Steering	Std	Std
Cruise Control	N/A	N/A
All Wheel Drive	N/A	N/A
AM/FM Stereo Cassette	$242	** $315
Steering Wheel, Tilt	N/A	N/A
Power Windows	N/A	N/A
***Options Price**	$0	$0
***Total Price**	**$9,509**	**$10,435**
Target Price	$10,030	
Destination Charge	$350	
Avg. Tax & Fees	$627	
Total Target $	**$11,007**	
Average Dealer Option Cost:	***72%***	

Ownership Costs

Cost Area	5 Year Cost	Rate
Depreciation	$3,307	Excellent
Financing ($221/month)	$1,814	
Insurance (Rating 8)	$7,432	Worse Than Average
State Fees	$431	
Fuel (Hwy 26 City 21)	$3,673	Better Than Average
Maintenance	$3,702	Average
Repairs	$580	Excellent

Warranty/Maintenance Info

Item		Rate
Major Tune-Up	$184	Worse Than Average
Minor Tune-Up	$76	Better Than Average
Brake Service	$192	Better Than Average
Overall Warranty	3 yr/50k	Average
Drivetrain Warranty	3 yr/50k	Average
Rust Warranty	5 yr/unlim. mi	Better Than Average
Maintenance Warranty	N/A	
Roadside Assistance	1 yr/unlim. mi	

Ownership Cost By Year

$2,000 $4,000 $6,000 $8,000

1993 1994 1995 1996 1997

Resale Value

1993	1994	1995	1996	1997
$9,670	$9,155	$8,783	$8,263	$7,700

Ownership Costs (5yr)

Average	This Car
$22,564	$20,939
Cost/Mile 32¢	Cost/Mile 30¢

Cumulative Costs

	1993	1994	1995	1996	1997
Annual	$4,295	$3,494	$4,127	$3,742	$5,281
Total	$4,295	$7,789	$11,916	$15,658	$20,939

Ownership Cost Rating

Excellent

The 1993 Pickup is available in five models - B2200 two-wheel drive regular and extended cab; B2600i two-wheel drive extended cab, and B2600i four-wheel drive regular and extended cab. The 1993 two-wheel drive extended cab model features styled steel wheels and a double-wall cargo bed with one-touch tailgate release. Other features include fold-down rear jump seats and swing-out rear side windows. Options include Sport and Luxury Trim packages.

Mazda B2600i Cab Plus
2 Door Extended Cab

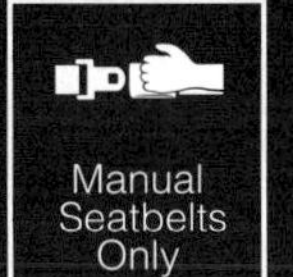

2.6L 121 hp Gas Fuel Inject. | 4 Cylinder In-Line | Manual 5 Speed | 2 Wheel Rear | Manual Seatbelts Only

Purchase Price

Car Item	Dealer Cost	List
Base Price	**$9,715**	**$10,785**
Anti-Lock Brakes	Std	Std
Automatic 4 Speed	$700	$795
Optional Engine	N/A	N/A
Air Conditioning	$635	$785
Power Steering	Std	Std
Cruise Control	N/A	N/A
All Wheel Drive	N/A	N/A
AM/FM Stereo Cassette	$242	** $315
Steering Wheel, Tilt	N/A	N/A
Power Windows	N/A	N/A
***Options Price**	$0	$0
***Total Price**	**$9,715**	**$10,785**
Target Price	$10,251	
Destination Charge	$350	
Avg. Tax & Fees	$641	
Total Target $	**$11,242**	
Average Dealer Option Cost:	***75%***	

Ownership Costs

Cost Area	5 Year Cost	Rate
Depreciation	$3,362	Excellent
Financing ($226/month)	$1,852	
Insurance (Rating 8)	$7,432	Worse Than Average
State Fees	$445	
Fuel (Hwy 23 City 19)	$4,111	Average
Maintenance	$3,837	Average
Repairs	$580	Excellent

Warranty/Maintenance Info

Item		Rate
Major Tune-Up	$217	Poor
Minor Tune-Up	$84	Better Than Average
Brake Service	$192	Better Than Average
Overall Warranty	3 yr/50k	Average
Drivetrain Warranty	3 yr/50k	Average
Rust Warranty	5 yr/unlim. mi	Better Than Average
Maintenance Warranty	N/A	
Roadside Assistance	1 yr/unlim. mi	

Ownership Cost By Year

$2,000 $4,000 $6,000 $8,000

1993 1994 1995 1996 1997

Resale Value

1993	1994	1995	1996	1997
$9,956	$9,417	$9,022	$8,499	$7,880

Ownership Costs (5yr)

Average	This Car
$22,920	$21,619
Cost/Mile 33¢	Cost/Mile 31¢

Cumulative Costs

	1993	1994	1995	1996	1997
Annual	$4,344	$3,626	$4,303	$3,852	$5,494
Total	$4,344	$7,970	$12,273	$16,125	$21,619

Ownership Cost Rating

Excellent

The 1993 Pickup is available in five models - B2200 two-wheel drive regular and extended cab; B2600i two-wheel drive extended cab, and B2600i four-wheel drive regular and extended cab. The 1993 two-wheel drive extended cab model features styled steel wheels and a double-wall cargo bed with one-touch tailgate release. Other features include fold-down rear jump seats and swing-out rear side windows. Options include Sport and Luxury Trim Packages. This vehicle requires purchase of either the SE-5 or LE-5 Packages.

* Includes shaded options

** Other purchase requirements apply

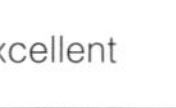

Poor | Worse Than Average | Average | Better Than Average | Excellent | Insufficient Information

Refer to *Section 3: Annotated Vehicle Charts* for an explanation of these charts.

Mazda B2600i 4WD

2 Door Regular Cab

2.6L 121 hp Gas Fuel Inject.

4 Cylinder In-Line

135 24R Manual 5 Speed

4 Wheel On-Demand

Manual Seatbelts Only

Purchase Price

Car Item	Dealer Cost	List
Base Price	**$10,906**	**$11,835**
Anti-Lock Brakes	Std	Std
Automatic 4 Speed	$700	** $795
Optional Engine	N/A	N/A
Air Conditioning	$635	$785
Power Steering	Std	Std
Cruise Control	N/A	N/A
4 Whl On-Demand Dr.	Std	Std
AM/FM Stereo Cassette	$227	** $295
Steering Wheel, Tilt	N/A	N/A
Power Windows	N/A	N/A
***Options Price**	$0	$0
***Total Price**	**$10,906**	**$11,835**
Target Price	$11,531	
Destination Charge	$400	
Avg. Tax & Fees	$719	
Total Target $	**$12,650**	
Average Dealer Option Cost:	***75%***	

Ownership Costs

Cost Area	5 Year Cost	Rate
Depreciation	$4,863	Excellent
Financing ($254/month)	$2,083	
Insurance (Rating 10)	$7,689	Worse Than Average
State Fees	$489	
Fuel (Hwy 20 City 18)	$4,554	Poor
Maintenance	$4,007	Average
Repairs	$700	Better Than Average

Ownership Cost By Year

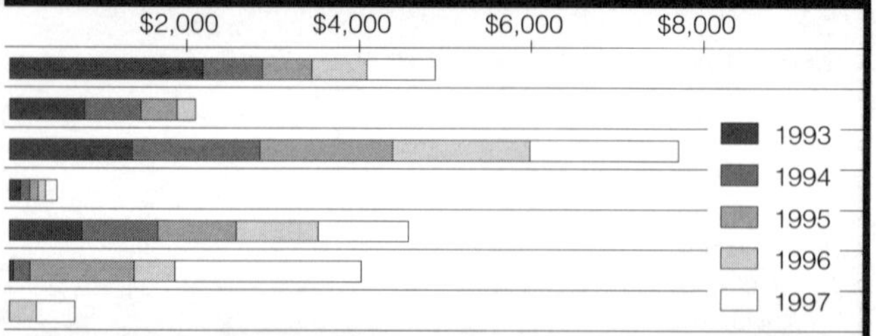

(Chart: $2,000 – $4,000 – $6,000 – $8,000; legend 1993, 1994, 1995, 1996, 1997)

Warranty/Maintenance Info

Item		Rate
Major Tune-Up	$217	Poor
Minor Tune-Up	$84	Better Than Average
Brake Service	$200	Average
Overall Warranty	3 yr/50k	Average
Drivetrain Warranty	3 yr/50k	Average
Rust Warranty	5 yr/unlim. mi	Better Than Average
Maintenance Warranty	N/A	
Roadside Assistance	1 yr/unlim. mi	

Resale Value

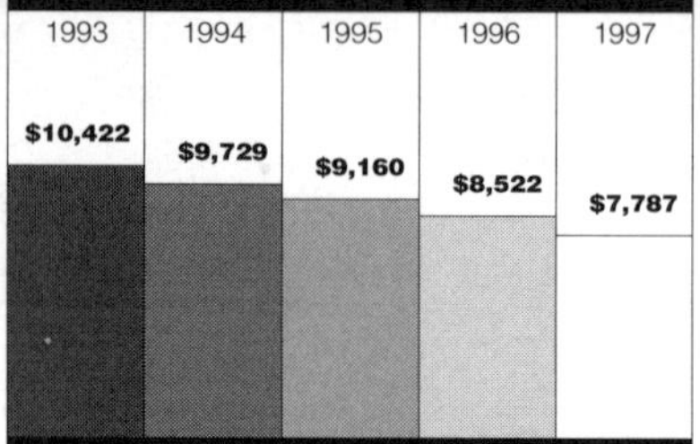

1993	1994	1995	1996	1997
$10,422	$9,729	$9,160	$8,522	$7,787

Ownership Costs (5yr)

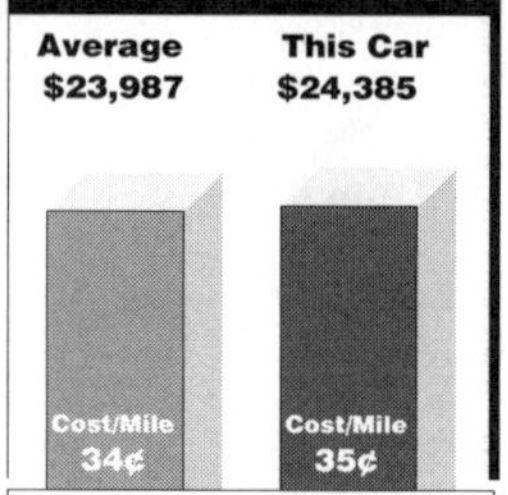

Average	This Car
$23,987	$24,385
Cost/Mile 34¢	Cost/Mile 35¢

The 1993 Pickup is available in five models - B2200 two-wheel drive regular and extended cab; B2600i two-wheel drive extended cab, and B2600i four-wheel drive regular and extended cab. The four-wheel drive regular cab model features a resetable trip odometer and a double wall cargo bed with one-touch tailgate release. Other features include a two speed transfer case, fender flares and rear stone guards. Options include Sport and Luxury Trim Packages.

Cumulative Costs

	1993	1994	1995	1996	1997
Annual	$5,524	$3,996	$4,731	$4,198	$5,936
Total	$5,524	$9,520	$14,251	$18,449	$24,385

Ownership Cost Rating

Average

Mazda B2600i Cab Plus 4WD

2 Door Extended Cab

2.6L 121 hp Gas Fuel Inject.

4 Cylinder In-Line

135 24R Manual 5 Speed

4 Wheel On-Demand

Manual Seatbelts Only

Purchase Price

Car Item	Dealer Cost	List
Base Price	**$12,013**	**$13,335**
Anti-Lock Brakes	Std	Std
Automatic 4 Speed	$700	** $795
Optional Engine	N/A	N/A
Air Conditioning	$635	$785
Power Steering	Std	Std
Cruise Control	N/A	N/A
4 Whl On-Demand Dr.	Std	Std
AM/FM Stereo Cassette	$242	** $315
Steering Wheel, Tilt	N/A	N/A
Power Windows	N/A	N/A
***Options Price**	$0	$0
***Total Price**	**$12,013**	**$13,335**
Target Price	$12,726	
Destination Charge	$400	
Avg. Tax & Fees	$793	
Total Target $	**$13,919**	
Average Dealer Option Cost:	***75%***	

Ownership Costs

Cost Area	5 Year Cost	Rate
Depreciation	$4,298	Excellent
Financing ($280/month)	$2,294	
Insurance (Rating 11)	$7,902	Worse Than Average
State Fees	$549	
Fuel (Hwy 20 City 18)	$4,554	Poor
Maintenance	$4,007	Average
Repairs	$700	Better Than Average

Ownership Cost By Year

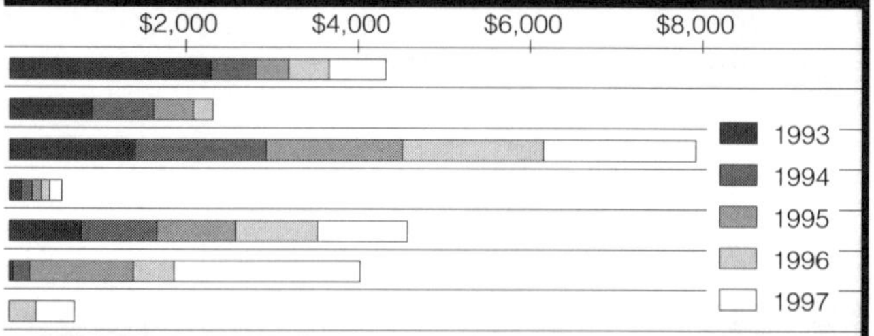

(Chart: $2,000 – $4,000 – $6,000 – $8,000; legend 1993, 1994, 1995, 1996, 1997)

Warranty/Maintenance Info

Item		Rate
Major Tune-Up	$217	Poor
Minor Tune-Up	$84	Better Than Average
Brake Service	$200	Average
Overall Warranty	3 yr/50k	Average
Drivetrain Warranty	3 yr/50k	Average
Rust Warranty	5 yr/unlim. mi	Better Than Average
Maintenance Warranty	N/A	
Roadside Assistance	1 yr/unlim. mi	

Resale Value

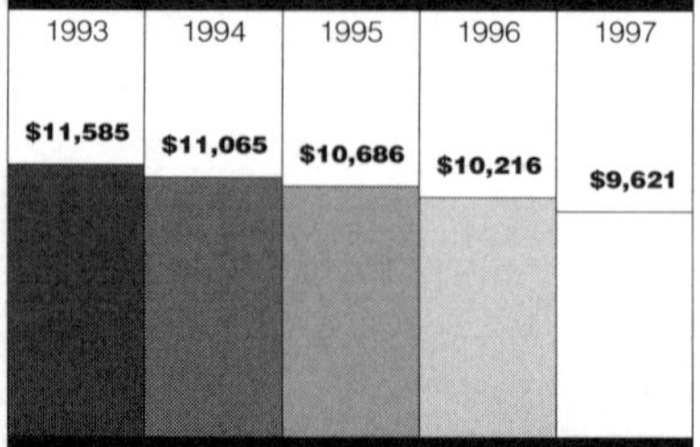

1993	1994	1995	1996	1997
$11,585	$11,065	$10,686	$10,216	$9,621

Ownership Costs (5yr)

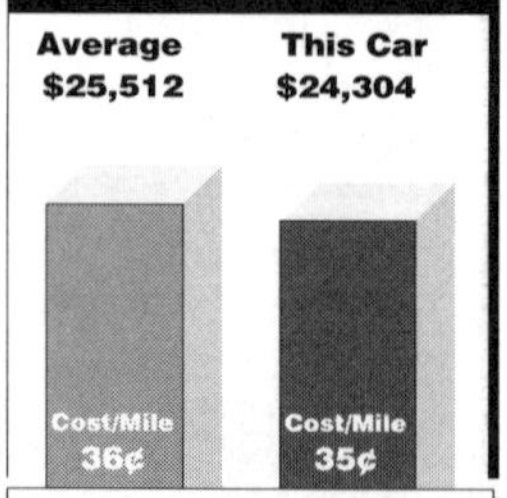

Average	This Car
$25,512	$24,304
Cost/Mile 36¢	Cost/Mile 35¢

The 1993 Pickup is available in five models - B2200 two-wheel drive regular and extended cab; B2600i two-wheel drive extended cab, and B2600i four-wheel drive regular and extended cab. The four-wheel drive extended cab model features a trip odometer and a double wall cargo bed with one-touch tailgate release. Other features include a two speed transfer case, fender flares and rear stone guards. Options include Sport and Luxury Trim Packages. This vehicle requires purchase of either the SE-5 or LE-5 Packages.

Cumulative Costs

	1993	1994	1995	1996	1997
Annual	$5,771	$3,944	$4,638	$4,100	$5,851
Total	$5,771	$9,715	$14,353	$18,453	$24,304

Ownership Cost Rating

Excellent

* Includes shaded options

** Other purchase requirements apply

 Poor · Worse Than Average  Average · Better Than Average  Excellent · Insufficient Information

Refer to *Section 3: Annotated Vehicle Charts* for an explanation of these charts.

Mazda MPV Wagon Van
3 Door Pass Van

2.6L 121 hp Gas Fuel Inject. | 4 Cylinder In-Line | Automatic 4 Speed | 2 Wheel Rear | Manual Seatbelts Only

Purchase Price

Car Item	Dealer Cost	List
Base Price	**$14,750**	**$16,555**
Anti-Lock Brakes	Std	Std
Manual Transmission	N/A	N/A
Optional Engine	N/A	N/A
Air Conditioning	$705	$860
Power Steering	Std	Std
Cruise Control	N/A	N/A
All Wheel Drive	N/A	N/A
AM/FM Stereo Cassette	Std	Std
Steering Wheel, Tilt	Std	Std
Power Windows	N/A	N/A
***Options Price**	$705	$860
***Total Price**	**$15,455**	**$17,415**
Target Price	$16,449	
Destination Charge	$400	
Avg. Tax & Fees	$1,020	
Total Target $	**$17,869**	
Average Dealer Option Cost:	***83%***	

Ownership Costs

Cost Area	5 Year Cost	Rate
Depreciation	$5,328	Better Than Average
Financing ($359/month)	$2,944	
Insurance (Rating 10)	$7,689	Better Than Average
State Fees	$713	
Fuel (Hwy 24 City 18)	$4,117	Better Than Average
Maintenance	$4,399	Average
Repairs	$580	Excellent

Ownership Cost By Year

$2,000 $4,000 $6,000 $8,000

1993 1994 1995 1996 1997

Warranty/Maintenance Info

Major Tune-Up	$249	Poor
Minor Tune-Up	$84	Excellent
Brake Service	$194	Excellent
Overall Warranty	3 yr/50k	Average
Drivetrain Warranty	3 yr/50k	Average
Rust Warranty	5 yr/unlim. mi	Better Than Average
Maintenance Warranty	N/A	
Roadside Assistance	1 yr/unlim. mi	

Resale Value

1993	1994	1995	1996	1997
$16,305	$15,366	$14,633	$13,766	$12,541

Ownership Costs (5yr)

Average	This Car
$26,199	$25,770
Cost/Mile 37¢	Cost/Mile 37¢

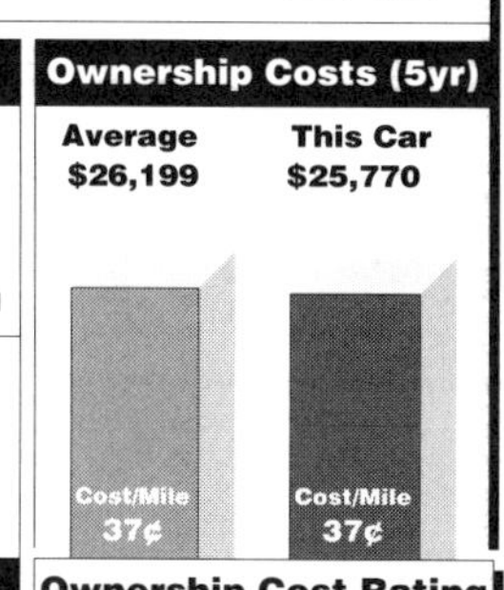

The 1993 MPV Van/Wagon is available in one five-passenger model, with much of the same standard equipment as the Base wagon. Interior features include AM/FM ETR cassette stereo, reclining front bucket seats, and tilt steering wheel. An optional dealer installed Towing Package-which increases the standard towing capacity to 4,600 pounds, includes engine oil cooler, self-leveling suspension, conventional spare tire, larger disc brakes, and heavy duty radiator.

Cumulative Costs

	1993	1994	1995	1996	1997
Annual	$5,193	$4,478	$4,996	$4,641	$6,462
Total	$5,193	$9,671	$14,667	$19,308	$25,770

Ownership Cost Rating

Better Than Average

Mazda MPV Wagon
3 Door Pass Van

2.6L 121 hp Gas Fuel Inject. | 4 Cylinder In-Line | Automatic 4 Speed | 2 Wheel Rear | Manual Seatbelts Only

Purchase Price

Car Item	Dealer Cost	List
Base Price	**$16,034**	**$17,995**
Anti-Lock Brakes	Std	Std
4 Spd Elec.	N/C	N/C
3.0L 155 hp Gas	$704	$790
Air Conditioning	$705	$860
Power Steering	Std	Std
Cruise Control	Pkg	Pkg
All Wheel Drive	N/A	N/A
AM/FM Stereo Cassette	Std	Std
Steering Wheel, Tilt	Std	Std
Power Windows	Pkg	Pkg
***Options Price**	$1,409	$1,650
***Total Price**	**$17,443**	**$19,645**
Target Price	$18,606	
Destination Charge	$400	
Avg. Tax & Fees	$1,150	
Total Target $	**$20,156**	
Average Dealer Option Cost:	***83%***	

Ownership Costs

Cost Area	5 Year Cost	Rate
Depreciation	$5,374	Excellent
Financing ($405/month)	$3,320	
Insurance (Rating 11)	$7,902	Better Than Average
State Fees	$800	
Fuel (Hwy 22 City 17)	$4,431	Average
Maintenance	$4,680	Worse Than Average
Repairs	$580	Excellent

Ownership Cost By Year

$2,000 $4,000 $6,000 $8,000

1993 1994 1995 1996 1997

Warranty/Maintenance Info

Major Tune-Up	$297	Poor
Minor Tune-Up	$109	Better Than Average
Brake Service	$194	Excellent
Overall Warranty	3 yr/50k	Average
Drivetrain Warranty	3 yr/50k	Average
Rust Warranty	5 yr/unlim. mi	Better Than Average
Maintenance Warranty	N/A	
Roadside Assistance	1 yr/unlim. mi	

Resale Value

1993	1994	1995	1996	1997
$18,697	$18,081	$17,555	$16,336	$14,782

Ownership Costs (5yr)

Average	This Car
$28,057	$27,087
Cost/Mile 40¢	Cost/Mile 39¢

The 1993 MPV is available in 2WD or 4WD. New for 1993, the MPV features a remote keyless entry system, included in selected option packages, which allows drivers to lock and unlock the doors with a remote control transmitter. Other features include reclining bucket seats with three-point safety belts and headrests. The MPV offers several option packages including a Luxury Package and Towing Package. Options include power window and door locks, unique alloy wheels, leather interior and body-color side moldings.

Cumulative Costs

	1993	1994	1995	1996	1997
Annual	$5,367	$4,426	$5,045	$5,179	$7,070
Total	$5,367	$9,793	$14,838	$20,017	$27,087

Ownership Cost Rating

Excellent

* Includes shaded options

** Other purchase requirements apply

Poor  Worse Than Average  Average Better Than Average 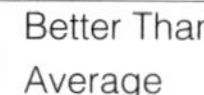 Excellent  Insufficient Information

Refer to *Section 3: Annotated Vehicle Charts* for an explanation of these charts.

Mazda MPV Wagon 4WD

3 Door Pass Van

3.0L 155 hp Gas Fuel Inject.

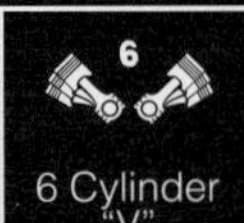
6 Cylinder "V"

Automatic 4 Speed

4 Wheel Full-Time

Manual Seatbelts Only

Mini Van

2WD Model Shown

Purchase Price

Car Item	Dealer Cost	List
Base Price	**$19,335**	**$21,700**
Anti-Lock Brakes	Std	Std
Manual Transmission	N/A	N/A
Optional Engine	N/A	N/A
Air Conditioning	$705	$860
Power Steering	Std	Std
Cruise Control	Pkg	Pkg
4 Wheel Full-Time Drive	Std	Std
AM/FM Stereo Cassette	Std	Std
Steering Wheel, Tilt	Std	Std
Power Windows	Pkg	Pkg
***Options Price**	$705	$860
***Total Price**	**$20,040**	**$22,560**
Target Price	$21,496	
Destination Charge	$400	
Avg. Tax & Fees	$1,325	
Total Target $	**$23,221**	
Average Dealer Option Cost:	***83%***	

Ownership Costs

Cost Area	5 Year Cost	Rate
Depreciation	$6,440	Excellent
Financing ($467/month)	$3,825	
Insurance (Rating 12)	$8,108	Better Than Average
State Fees	$920	
Fuel (Hwy 19 City 15)	$5,079	Poor
Maintenance	$4,785	Worse Than Average
Repairs	$650	Excellent

Ownership Cost By Year

$2,000 $4,000 $6,000 $8,000 $10,000

1993 1994 1995 1996 1997

Warranty/Maintenance Info

Item		Rate
Major Tune-Up	$297	Poor
Minor Tune-Up	$109	Better Than Average
Brake Service	$194	Excellent
Overall Warranty	3 yr/50k	Average
Drivetrain Warranty	3 yr/50k	Average
Rust Warranty	5 yr/unlim. mi	Better Than Average
Maintenance Warranty	N/A	
Roadside Assistance	1 yr/unlim. mi	

Resale Value

1993	1994	1995	1996	1997
$21,588	$20,515	$19,911	$18,534	$16,781

Ownership Costs (5yr)

Average	This Car
$30,485	$29,807
Cost/Mile 44¢	Cost/Mile 43¢

The 1993 MPV is available in 2WD or 4WD. New for 1993, the MPV 4WD features several option packages. The 4WD model offers Package C which includes a new keyless entry system which operates by a remote transmitter. Other options include unique alloy wheels, power window and door locks, two-tone paint and electronic heater mode control. The MPV also offers a Luxury Package which includes upgraded seating surfaces and a special Towing Package that permits a towing capacity of up to 4,500 pounds.

Cumulative Costs

	1993	1994	1995	1996	1997
Annual	$5,939	$5,232	$5,521	$5,606	$7,509
Total	$5,939	$11,171	$16,692	$22,298	$29,807

Ownership Cost Rating

Excellent

Mazda Navajo DX

2 Door Sport Utility

4.0L 160 hp Gas Fuel Inject.

6 Cylinder "V"

Manual 5 Speed

2 Wheel Rear

Manual Seatbelts Only

Utility

LX Model Shown

Purchase Price

Car Item	Dealer Cost	List
Base Price	**$14,618**	**$16,595**
Anti-Lock Brakes	Std	Std
Automatic 4 Speed	$757	$890
Optional Engine	N/A	N/A
Air Conditioning	Pkg	Pkg
Power Steering	Std	Std
Cruise Control	N/A	N/A
All Wheel Drive	N/A	N/A
AM/FM Stereo Cassette	Pkg	Pkg
Steering Wheel, Tilt	N/A	N/A
Power Windows	N/A	N/A
***Options Price**	$0	$0
***Total Price**	**$14,618**	**$16,595**
Target Price	$15,867	
Destination Charge	$490	
Avg. Tax & Fees	$989	
Total Target $	**$17,346**	
Average Dealer Option Cost:	***85%***	

Ownership Costs

Cost Area	5 Year Cost	Rate
Depreciation	$5,618	Better Than Average
Financing ($349/month)	$2,858	
Insurance (Rating 6)	$7,129	Excellent
State Fees	$685	
Fuel (Hwy 22 City 17)	$4,431	Average
Maintenance	$3,856	Better Than Average
Repairs	$580	Excellent

Ownership Cost By Year

$2,000 $4,000 $6,000 $8,000

1993 1994 1995 1996 1997

Warranty/Maintenance Info

Item		Rate
Major Tune-Up	$132	Excellent
Minor Tune-Up	$92	Better Than Average
Brake Service	$252	Average
Overall Warranty	3 yr/50k	Average
Drivetrain Warranty	3 yr/50k	Average
Rust Warranty	5 yr/unlim. mi	Better Than Average
Maintenance Warranty	N/A	
Roadside Assistance	1 yr/unlim. mi	

Resale Value

1993	1994	1995	1996	1997
$15,527	$14,603	$13,781	$12,756	$11,728

Ownership Costs (5yr)

Average	This Car
$27,260	$25,157
Cost/Mile 39¢	Cost/Mile 36¢

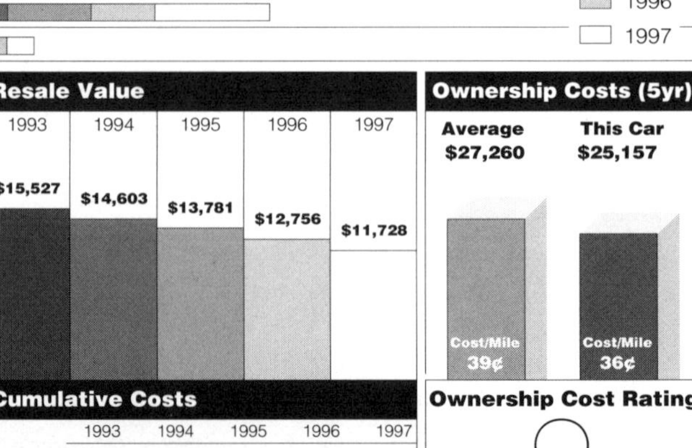

The 1993 Navajo is available in two models-DX and LX, and in either two- or four-wheel drive. New for 1993, the DX has increased horsepower from 155 to 160 horsepower. Powering the DX is a 4.0-liter V6 engine with multi-port electronic fuel injection. The DX with automatic transmission is available with a Towing Package, which gives the Navajo 2WD up to 5,400 pounds of towing capability. The Navajo is available in three new exterior colors and a new Mocha interior.

Cumulative Costs

	1993	1994	1995	1996	1997
Annual	$5,365	$4,408	$5,004	$4,895	$5,485
Total	$5,365	$9,773	$14,777	$19,672	$25,157

Ownership Cost Rating

Excellent

* Includes shaded options

** Other purchase requirements apply

 Poor  Worse Than Average  Average  Better Than Average 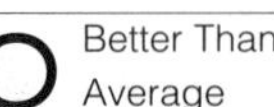 Excellent 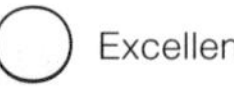 Insufficient Information

Refer to *Section 3: Annotated Vehicle Charts* for an explanation of these charts.

Mazda Navajo LX
2 Door Sport Utility

4.0L 160 hp Gas Fuel Inject.

6 Cylinder "V"

Manual 5 Speed

2 Wheel Rear

Manual Seatbelts Only

Utility

Purchase Price

Car Item	*Dealer Cost*	*List*
Base Price	**$16,028**	**$18,195**
Anti-Lock Brakes	Std	Std
Automatic 4 Speed	$757	$890
Optional Engine	N/A	N/A
Air Conditioning	Pkg	Pkg
Power Steering	Std	Std
Cruise Control	Pkg	Pkg
All Wheel Drive	N/A	N/A
AM/FM Stereo Cassette	Pkg	Pkg
Steering Wheel, Tilt	Pkg	Pkg
Power Windows	Std	Std
***Options Price**	$0	$0
***Total Price**	**$16,028**	**$18,195**
Target Price	$17,452	
Destination Charge	$490	
Avg. Tax & Fees	$1,084	
Total Target $	**$19,026**	
Average Dealer Option Cost:	***85%***	

Ownership Costs

Cost Area	*5 Year Cost*	*Rate*
Depreciation	$5,973	Better Than Average
Financing ($382/month)	$3,134	
Insurance (Rating 6)	$7,129	Excellent
State Fees	$747	
Fuel (Hwy 22 City 17)	$4,431	Average
Maintenance	$3,856	Better Than Average
Repairs	$580	Excellent

Ownership Cost By Year

$2,000 $4,000 $6,000 $8,000

1993 1994 1995 1996 1997

Warranty/Maintenance Info

Major Tune-Up	$132	Excellent
Minor Tune-Up	$92	Better Than Average
Brake Service	$252	Average
Overall Warranty	3 yr/50k	Average
Drivetrain Warranty	3 yr/50k	Average
Rust Warranty	5 yr/unlim. mi	Better Than Average
Maintenance Warranty	N/A	
Roadside Assistance	1 yr/unlim. mi	

Resale Value

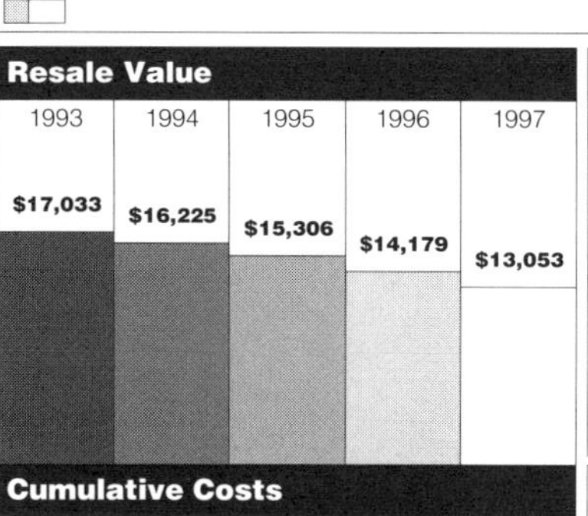

Ownership Costs (5yr)

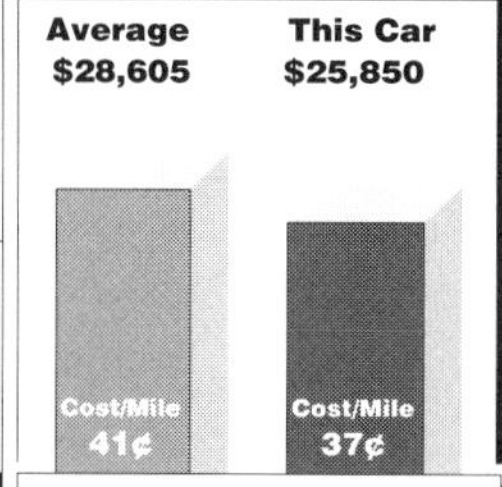

The 1993 Navajo is available in two models-DX and LX, and in either two- or four-wheel drive. New for 1993, the LX now comes standard with a four-wheel antilock braking system. Standard equipment for the LX includes power windows and locks, leather-wrapped steering wheel,a retractable cargo cover and optional CD player. There are two preferred equipment packages on the LX models: the Premium Package and the Leather Package. A Towing Package is available on models with automatic transmissions.

Cumulative Costs

	1993	1994	1995	1996	1997
Annual	$5,670	$4,393	$5,167	$5,028	$5,592
Total	$5,670	$10,063	$15,230	$20,258	$25,850

Ownership Cost Rating

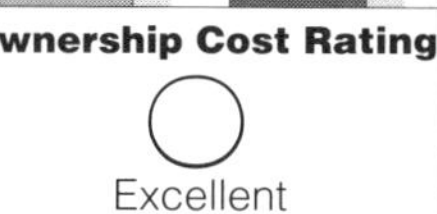

Excellent

Mazda Navajo DX 4WD
2 Door Sport Utility

4.0L 160 hp Gas Fuel Inject.

6 Cylinder "V"

Manual 5 Speed

4 Wheel On-Demand

Manual Seatbelts Only

Utility

LX Model Shown

Purchase Price

Car Item	*Dealer Cost*	*List*
Base Price	**$16,204**	**$18,395**
Anti-Lock Brakes	Std	Std
Automatic 4 Speed	$757	$890
Optional Engine	N/A	N/A
Air Conditioning	Pkg	Pkg
Power Steering	Std	Std
Cruise Control	N/A	N/A
4 Whl On-Demand Dr.	Std	Std
AM/FM Stereo Cassette	Pkg	Pkg
Steering Wheel, Tilt	N/A	N/A
Power Windows	N/A	N/A
***Options Price**	$0	$0
***Total Price**	**$16,204**	**$18,395**
Target Price	$17,651	
Destination Charge	$490	
Avg. Tax & Fees	$1,096	
Total Target $	**$19,237**	
Average Dealer Option Cost:	***85%***	

Ownership Costs

Cost Area	*5 Year Cost*	*Rate*
Depreciation	$6,193	Better Than Average
Financing ($387/month)	$3,168	
Insurance (Rating 8)	$7,432	Excellent
State Fees	$755	
Fuel (Hwy 21 City 17)	$4,543	Average
Maintenance	$3,856	Better Than Average
Repairs	$700	Excellent

Ownership Cost By Year

$2,000 $4,000 $6,000 $8,000

1993 1994 1995 1996 1997

Warranty/Maintenance Info

Major Tune-Up	$132	Excellent
Minor Tune-Up	$92	Better Than Average
Brake Service	$252	Average
Overall Warranty	3 yr/50k	Average
Drivetrain Warranty	3 yr/50k	Average
Rust Warranty	5 yr/unlim. mi	Better Than Average
Maintenance Warranty	N/A	
Roadside Assistance	1 yr/unlim. mi	

Resale Value

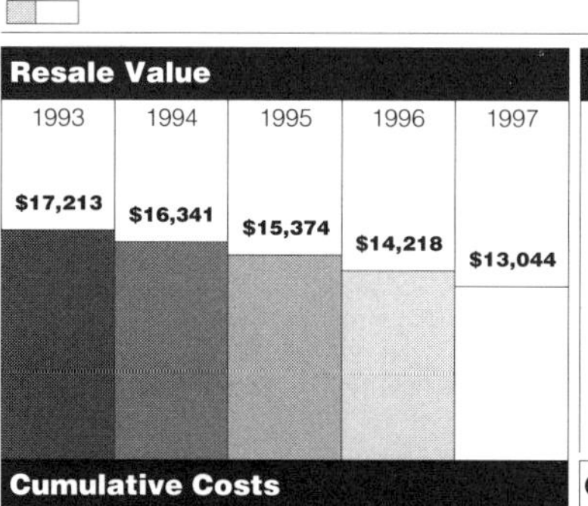

Ownership Costs (5yr)

Average
$28,774

This Car
$26,647

Cost/Mile 41¢

Cost/Mile 38¢

The 1993 Navajo is available in two models-DX and LX, and in either two- or four-wheel drive. New for 1993, horsepower in the DX 4WD's 4.0-liter V6 engine has increased fron 155 to 160. Standard equipment on the DX includes AM/FM stereo sound system with four speakers, cloth upholstery, intermittent wipers and bucket seats. Mazda's shift-on-the-fly Touch-Drive is also standard equipment. A Towing Package with up to 5,400 lbs of towing capability is available on models with automatic transmissions.

Cumulative Costs

	1993	1994	1995	1996	1997
Annual	$5,795	$4,548	$5,306	$5,201	$5,797
Total	$5,795	$10,343	$15,649	$20,850	$26,647

Ownership Cost Rating

Excellent

* Includes shaded options

** Other purchase requirements apply

 Poor  Worse Than Average  Average   Better Than Average  Excellent 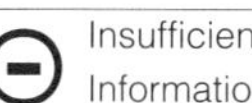 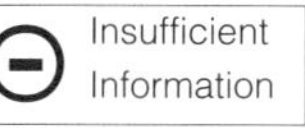 Insufficient Information

Refer to ***Section 3: Annotated Vehicle Charts*** for an explanation of these charts.

Mazda Navajo LX 4WD

2 Door Sport Utility

4.0L 160 hp Gas Fuel Inject.

6 Cylinder "V"

135 24R

Manual 5 Speed

4 Wheel On-Demand

Manual Seatbelts Only

Utility

Purchase Price

Car Item	Dealer Cost	List
Base Price	**$17,613**	**$19,995**
Anti-Lock Brakes	Std	Std
Automatic 4 Speed	$757	$890
Optional Engine	N/A	N/A
Air Conditioning	Pkg	Pkg
Power Steering	Std	Std
Cruise Control	Pkg	Pkg
4 Whl On-Demand Dr.	Std	Std
AM/FM Stereo Cassette	Pkg	Pkg
Steering Wheel, Tilt	Pkg	Pkg
Power Windows	Std	Std
***Options Price**	$0	$0
***Total Price**	**$17,613**	**$19,995**
Target Price	$19,246	
Destination Charge	$490	
Avg. Tax & Fees	$1,192	
Total Target $	**$20,928**	
Average Dealer Option Cost:	***85%***	

Ownership Costs

Cost Area	5 Year Cost	Rate
Depreciation	$6,943	Better Than Average
Financing ($421/month)	$3,448	
Insurance (Rating 8)	$7,432	Excellent
State Fees	$819	
Fuel (Hwy 21 City 17)	$4,543	Average
Maintenance	$3,856	Better Than Average
Repairs	$700	Excellent

Ownership Cost By Year

$2,000 $4,000 $6,000 $8,000

1993 1994 1995 1996 1997

Warranty/Maintenance Info

Major Tune-Up	$132	Excellent
Minor Tune-Up	$92	Better Than Average
Brake Service	$252	Average
Overall Warranty	3 yr/50k	Average
Drivetrain Warranty	3 yr/50k	Average
Rust Warranty	5 yr/unlim. mi	Better Than Average
Maintenance Warranty	N/A	
Roadside Assistance	1 yr/unlim. mi	

Resale Value

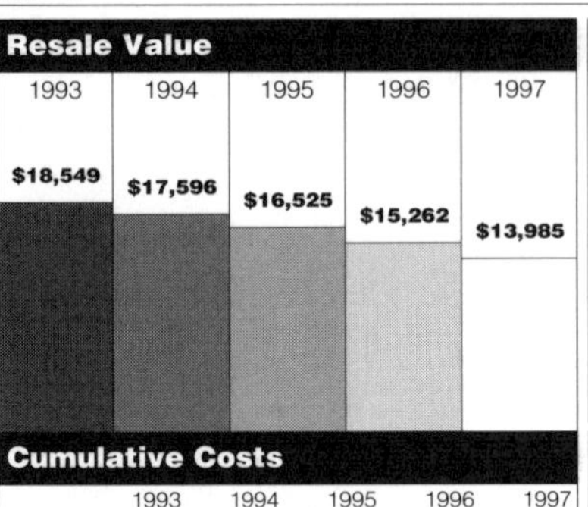

1993	1994	1995	1996	1997
$18,549	$17,596	$16,525	$15,262	$13,985

Ownership Costs (5yr)

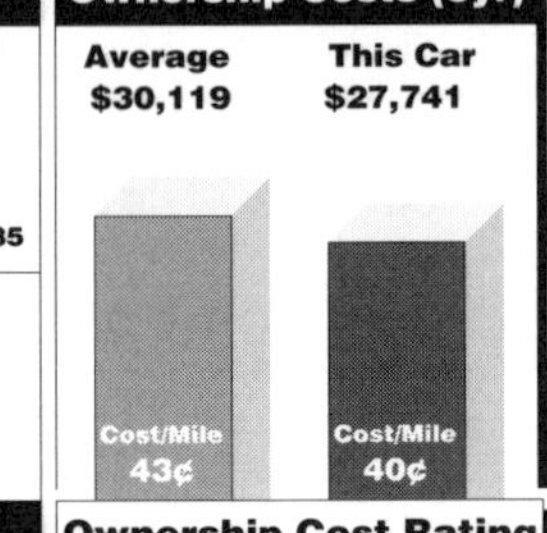

Average	This Car
$30,119	$27,741
Cost/Mile 43¢	Cost/Mile 40¢

Cumulative Costs

	1993	1994	1995	1996	1997
Annual	$6,282	$4,731	$5,479	$5,339	$5,910
Total	$6,282	$11,013	$16,492	$21,831	$27,741

Ownership Cost Rating

Excellent

The 1993 Navajo is available in two models-DX and LX, and in either two- or four-wheel drive. New for 1993, the LX 4WD comes standard with a four-wheel antilock braking system and Mazda's shift-on-the-fly Touch-Drive. There are two preferred packages on the LX models: the Premium Package and the Leather Package. The Leather Package includes the Premium Package plus leather seating surfaces, four-speed automatic transmission and the Towing Package. A CD player is also available as an option.

Mercedes Benz 300 TE

4 Door Wagon

3.2L 217 hp Gas Fuel Inject.

6 Cylinder In-Line

PRND321

Automatic 4 Speed

2 Wheel Rear

Driver/Psngr Airbags Std

Luxury

Purchase Price

Car Item	Dealer Cost	List
Base Price	**$45,150**	**$54,400**
Anti-Lock Brakes	Std	Std
Manual Transmission	N/A	N/A
Optional Engine	N/A	N/A
Auto Climate Control	Std	Std
Power Steering	Std	Std
Cruise Control	Std	Std
All Wheel Drive	N/A	N/A
AM/FM Stereo Cassette	Std	Std
Steering, Tilt w/Memory	Std	Std
Power Windows	Std	Std
***Options Price**	$0	$0
***Total Price**	**$45,150**	**$54,400**
Target Price	$50,342	
Destination Charge	$400	
Avg. Tax & Fees	$3,085	
Luxury Tax	$2,074	
Total Target $	**$55,901**	

Ownership Costs

Cost Area	5 Year Cost	Rate
Depreciation	$19,962	Excellent
Financing ($1,124/month)	$9,209	
Insurance (Rating 20)	$9,788	Excellent
State Fees	$2,192	
Fuel (Hwy 22 City 18 -Prem.)	$4,766	Worse Than Average
Maintenance	$5,623	Average
Repairs	$1,215	Average

Ownership Cost By Year

$5,000 $10,000 $15,000 $20,000

1993 1994 1995 1996 1997

Warranty/Maintenance Info

Major Tune-Up	$247	Average
Minor Tune-Up	$148	Worse Than Average
Brake Service	$205	Excellent
Overall Warranty	4 yr/50k	Better Than Average
Drivetrain Warranty	4 yr/50k	Better Than Average
Rust Warranty	4 yr/50k	Worse Than Average
Maintenance Warranty	N/A	
Roadside Assistance	4 yr/50k	

Resale Value

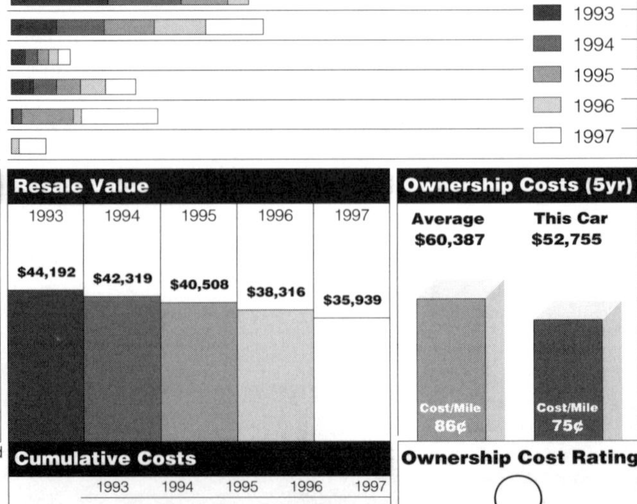

1993	1994	1995	1996	1997
$44,192	$42,319	$40,508	$38,316	$35,939

Ownership Costs (5yr)

Average	This Car
$60,387	$52,755
Cost/Mile 86¢	Cost/Mile 75¢

Cumulative Costs

	1993	1994	1995	1996	1997
Annual	$18,833	$8,386	$9,048	$6,889	$9,599
Total	$18,833	$27,219	$36,267	$43,156	$52,755

Ownership Cost Rating

Excellent

The 1993 300 Class is available in ten models - 300D 2.5 Turbo, 300E 2.6, 300E 2.8, 300E 4MATIC, 400E and 500E sedans; 300TE and 300TE 4MATIC wagons; and the 300CE coupe and convertible. For 1993, the 300TE wagon features an AM/FM/cellular antenna and integrated prewiring for a car phone. Other features include automatic climate control, anti-theft alarm system, power windows, 10-way power seats with two-position memory, electrically heated windshield washer system and special interior trim.

* Includes shaded options

** Other purchase requirements apply

 Poor  Worse Than Average  Average  Better Than Average ○ Excellent ⊖ Insufficient Information

Refer to *Section 3: Annotated Vehicle Charts* for an explanation of these charts.

Mercedes Benz 300 TE 4Matic

4 Door Wagon

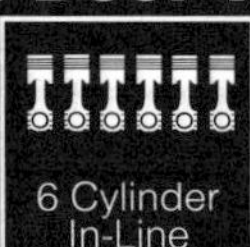

3.0L 177 hp Gas Fuel Inject. | 6 Cylinder In-Line | Automatic 4 Speed | 4 Wheel Full-Time | Driver/Psngr Airbags Std

Purchase Price

Car Item	Dealer Cost	List
Base Price	**$51,210**	**$61,700**
Anti-Lock Brakes	Std	Std
Manual Transmission	N/A	N/A
Optional Engine	N/A	N/A
Auto Climate Control	Std	Std
Power Steering	Std	Std
Cruise Control	Std	Std
4 Wheel Full-Time Drive	Std	Std
AM/FM Stereo Cassette	Std	Std
Steering, Tilt w/Memory	Std	Std
Power Windows	Std	Std
***Options Price**	$0	$0
***Total Price**	**$51,210**	**$61,700**
Target Price	$57,099	
Destination Charge	$400	
Avg. Tax & Fees	$3,496	
Luxury/Gas Guzzler Tax	$3,750	
Total Target $	**$64,745**	

Ownership Costs

Cost Area	5 Year Cost	Rate
Depreciation	$22,706	Excellent
Financing ($1,301/month)	$10,666	
Insurance (Rating 21)	$10,214	Excellent
State Fees	$2,485	
Fuel (Hwy 21 City 17 -Prem.)	$5,017	Worse Than Average
Maintenance	$5,646	Average
Repairs	$1,215	Average

Ownership Cost By Year

$5,000 $10,000 $15,000 $20,000 $25,000

1993 1994 1995 1996 1997

Warranty/Maintenance Info

Item		Rate
Major Tune-Up	$247	Average
Minor Tune-Up	$148	Worse Than Average
Brake Service	$205	Excellent
Overall Warranty	4 yr/50k	Better Than Average
Drivetrain Warranty	4 yr/50k	Better Than Average
Rust Warranty	4 yr/50k	Worse Than Average
Maintenance Warranty	N/A	
Roadside Assistance	4 yr/50k	

Resale Value

1993	1994	1995	1996	1997
$52,092	$49,799	$47,554	$44,889	$42,039

Ownership Costs (5yr)

Average	This Car
$66,870	$57,949
Cost/Mile 96¢	Cost/Mile 83¢

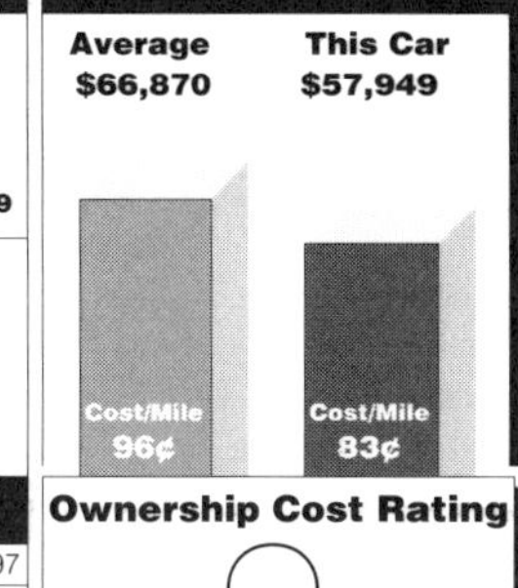

The 1993 300 Class is available in ten models - 300D 2.5 Turbo, 300E 2.6, 300E 2.8, 300E 4MATIC, 400E and 500E sedans; 300TE and 300TE 4MATIC wagons; and the 300CE coupe and convertible. For 1993, the 300TE 4MATIC features an AM/FM/cellular antenna and integrated prewiring for a car phone. Other features include automatic climate control, anti-theft alarm system, power windows, 10-way power seats with two-position memory, electrically heated windshield washer system and an active-bass sound system.

Cumulative Costs

	1993	1994	1995	1996	1997
Annual	$20,581	$9,458	$9,965	$7,659	$10,286
Total	$20,581	$30,039	$40,004	$47,663	$57,949

Ownership Cost Rating

Excellent

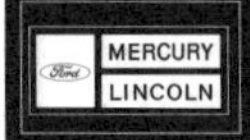

Mercury Sable GS

4 Door Wagon

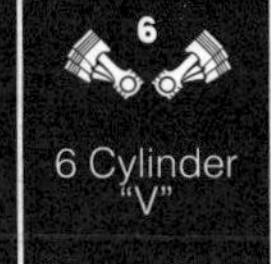

3.0L 140 hp Gas Fuel Inject. | 6 Cylinder "V" | Automatic 4 Speed | 2 Wheel Front | Driver/Psngr Airbags Std

Purchase Price

Car Item	Dealer Cost	List
Base Price	**$15,835**	**$18,459**
Anti-Lock Brakes	$506	$595
Manual Transmission	N/A	N/A
3.8L 140 hp Gas	$472	$555
Air Conditioning	Std	Std
Power Steering	Std	Std
Cruise Control	Pkg	Pkg
All Wheel Drive	N/A	N/A
AM/FM Stereo Cassette	$145	$171
Steering Wheel, Tilt	Std	Std
Power Windows	Pkg	** Pkg
***Options Price**	$145	$171
***Total Price**	**$15,980**	**$18,630**
Target Price	$17,334	
Destination Charge	$490	
Avg. Tax & Fees	$1,082	
Total Target $	**$18,906**	
Average Dealer Option Cost:	***85%***	

Ownership Costs

Cost Area	5 Year Cost	Rate
Depreciation	$8,565	Better Than Average
Financing ($380/month)	$3,113	
Insurance (Rating 5)	$6,786	Excellent
State Fees	$765	
Fuel (Hwy 30 City 21)	$3,405	Excellent
Maintenance	$4,369	Average
Repairs	$709	Better Than Average

Ownership Cost By Year

$2,000 $4,000 $6,000 $8,000 $10,000

1993 1994 1995 1996 1997

Warranty/Maintenance Info

Item		Rate
Major Tune-Up	$149	Excellent
Minor Tune-Up	$99	Better Than Average
Brake Service	$271	Worse Than Average
Overall Warranty	3 yr/36k	Average
Drivetrain Warranty	3 yr/36k	Average
Rust Warranty	6 yr/100k	Better Than Average
Maintenance Warranty	N/A	
Roadside Assistance	N/A	

Resale Value

1993	1994	1995	1996	1997
$15,455	$13,981	$12,849	$11,585	$10,341

Ownership Costs (5yr)

Average	This Car
$30,318	$27,712
Cost/Mile 43¢	Cost/Mile 40¢

Sable is offered as a four-door sedan and four-door wagon in GS and LS editions. The 1993 GS wagon features new body color bumpers and bodyside moldings, new integrated console, dual illuminated visor mirrors and new seat fabrics. Other standard features include a driver side air bag, rear heat ducts, backlighted instrument cluster with tachometer, temperature and fuel gauges, and luggage rack. A cargo cover and picnic tray are optional. The Sable is a sister to the Ford Taurus.

Cumulative Costs

	1993	1994	1995	1996	1997
Annual	$6,871	$4,803	$5,463	$4,813	$5,762
Total	$6,871	$11,674	$17,137	$21,950	$27,712

Ownership Cost Rating

Excellent

* Includes shaded options

** Other purchase requirements apply

 Poor  Worse Than Average  Average  Better Than Average  Excellent  Insufficient Information

Refer to *Section 3: Annotated Vehicle Charts* for an explanation of these charts.

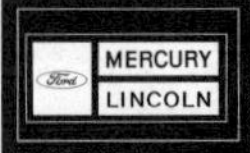

Mercury Sable LS
4 Door Wagon

3.8L 140 hp Gas Fuel Inject.

6 Cylinder "V"

Automatic 4 Speed

2 Wheel Front

Driver/Psngr Airbags Std

Midsize Wagon

Purchase Price

Car Item	Dealer Cost	List
Base Price	**$16,684**	**$19,457**
Anti-Lock Brakes	$506	$595
Manual Transmission	N/A	N/A
3.0L 140 hp Gas	($472)	($555)
Air Conditioning	Std	Std
Power Steering	Std	Std
Cruise Control	Pkg	Pkg
All Wheel Drive	N/A	N/A
AM/FM Stereo Cassette	$139	** $163
Steering Wheel, Tilt	Std	Std
Power Windows	Std	Std
***Options Price**	$0	$0
***Total Price**	**$16,684**	**$19,457**
Target Price	$18,130	
Destination Charge	$490	
Avg. Tax & Fees	$1,130	
Total Target $	**$19,750**	
Average Dealer Option Cost:	***85%***	

Ownership Costs

Cost Area	5 Year Cost	Rate
Depreciation	$8,692	Better Than Average
Financing ($397/month)	$3,253	
Insurance (Rating 6)	$6,919	Excellent
State Fees	$799	
Fuel (Hwy 27 City 19)	$3,775	Average
Maintenance	$4,436	Average
Repairs	$709	Better Than Average

Ownership Cost By Year

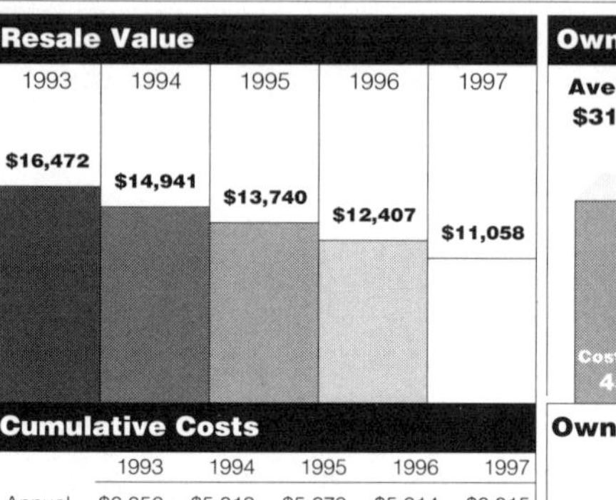

$2,000 $4,000 $6,000 $8,000 $10,000

1993 1994 1995 1996 1997

Warranty/Maintenance Info

Major Tune-Up	$159	Better Than Average
Minor Tune-Up	$109	Better Than Average
Brake Service	$271	Worse Than Average
Overall Warranty	3 yr/36k	Average
Drivetrain Warranty	3 yr/36k	Average
Rust Warranty	6 yr/100k	Better Than Average
Maintenance Warranty	N/A	
Roadside Assistance	N/A	

Resale Value

1993	1994	1995	1996	1997
$16,472	$14,941	$13,740	$12,407	$11,058

Ownership Costs (5yr)

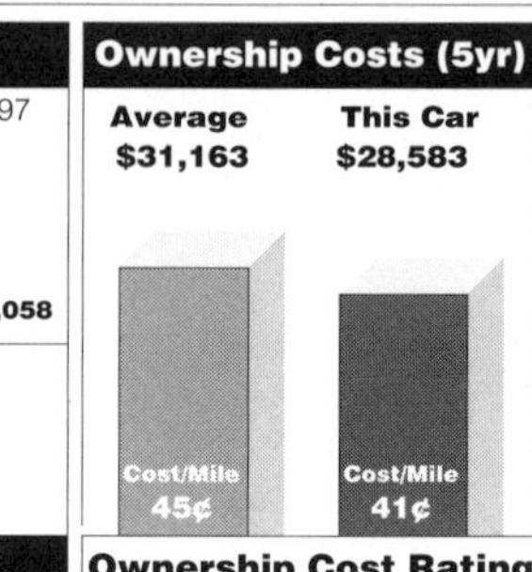

Sable is offered as a four-door sedan and four-door wagon in GS and LS editions. The 1993 LS wagon features new body color bumpers and bodyside moldings, new integrated console, dual illuminated visor mirrors and new seat fabrics. In addition to or in place of the base GS standard equipment, the LS wagon offers a larger standard engine, and a keyless remote entry system, power sun roof and electronic instrument cluster as optional. The Sable is a sister to the Ford Taurus.

Cumulative Costs

	1993	1994	1995	1996	1997
Annual	$6,856	$5,019	$5,679	$5,014	$6,015
Total	$6,856	$11,875	$17,554	$22,568	$28,583

Ownership Cost Rating

Excellent

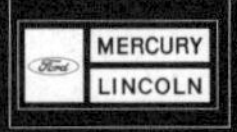

Mercury Tracer
4 Door Wagon

1.9L 88 hp Gas Fuel Inject.

4 Cylinder In-Line

Manual 5 Speed

2 Wheel Front

Automatic Seatbelts

Subcompact Wag

Purchase Price

Car Item	Dealer Cost	List
Base Price	**$9,903**	**$10,982**
Anti-Lock Brakes	N/A	N/A
Automatic 4 Speed	$622	$732
Optional Engine	N/A	N/A
Air Conditioning	$645	** $759
Power Steering	Std	Std
Cruise Control	$191	** $224
All Wheel Drive	N/A	N/A
AM/FM Stereo Cassette	$117	** $138
Steering Wheel, Tilt	$123	** $145
Power Windows	$281	** $330
***Options Price**	$0	$0
***Total Price**	**$9,903**	**$10,982**
Target Price	$10,422	
Destination Charge	$375	
Avg. Tax & Fees	$654	
Total Target $	**$11,451**	
Average Dealer Option Cost:	***85%***	

Ownership Costs

Cost Area	5 Year Cost	Rate
Depreciation	$6,658	Worse Than Average
Financing ($230/month)	$1,887	
Insurance (Rating 11)	$7,693	Worse Than Average
State Fees	$454	
Fuel (Hwy 36 City 29)	$2,656	Better Than Average
Maintenance	$4,374	Average
Repairs	$680	Average

Ownership Cost By Year

$2,000 $4,000 $6,000 $8,000

1993 1994 1995 1996 1997

Warranty/Maintenance Info

Major Tune-Up	$136	Better Than Average
Minor Tune-Up	$77	Better Than Average
Brake Service	$194	Average
Overall Warranty	3 yr/36k	Average
Drivetrain Warranty	3 yr/36k	Average
Rust Warranty	6 yr/100k	Better Than Average
Maintenance Warranty	N/A	
Roadside Assistance	N/A	

Resale Value

1993	1994	1995	1996	1997
$8,970	$7,582	$7,054	$6,443	$4,793

Ownership Costs (5yr)

Average	This Car
$23,934	$24,402
Cost/Mile 34¢	Cost/Mile 35¢

The 1993 Tracer is available in three models - (Base) sedan and wagon, and LTS sedan. Exterior styling enhancements for 1993 include a simulated light bar grille, several new colors, and wheel covers. The Base wagon model features a standard cargo cover, power steering, rear window wiper/washer, and dual power mirrors. Available options include power windows, premium sound system, luggage rack, and power moonroof.

Cumulative Costs

	1993	1994	1995	1996	1997
Annual	$5,338	$4,280	$4,356	$3,464	$6,964
Total	$5,338	$9,618	$13,974	$17,438	$24,402

Ownership Cost Rating

Average

* Includes shaded options

** Other purchase requirements apply

Poor  Worse Than Average  Average Better Than Average  Excellent Insufficient Information

Refer to *Section 3: Annotated Vehicle Charts* for an explanation of these charts.

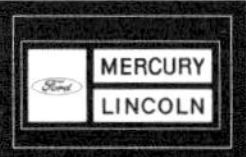

Mercury Villager GS
3 Door Pass Van

3.0L 151 hp Gas Fuel Inject.

6 Cylinder "V"

Automatic 4 Speed

2 Wheel Front

Automatic Seatbelts

Purchase Price

Car Item	Dealer Cost	List
Base Price	**$14,688**	**$16,504**
Anti-Lock Brakes	Std	Std
Manual Transmission	N/A	N/A
Optional Engine	N/A	N/A
Air Conditioning	$729	$857
Power Steering	Std	Std
Cruise Control	Grp	Grp
All Wheel Drive	N/A	N/A
AM/FM Stereo Cassette	$203	$239
Steering Wheel, Tilt	$316	$372
Power Windows	$451	$530
***Options Price**	$932	$1,096
***Total Price**	**$15,620**	**$17,600**
Target Price	$16,902	
Destination Charge	$540	
Avg. Tax & Fees	$1,053	
Total Target $	**$18,495**	
Average Dealer Option Cost:	***85%***	

Ownership Costs

Cost Area	5 Year Cost	Rate
Depreciation		Insufficient Information
Financing ($372/month)	$3,046	
Insurance (Rating 10)	$7,479	Average
State Fees	$725	
Fuel (Hwy 23 City 17)	$4,328	Better Than Average
Maintenance		Insufficient Information
Repairs	$740	Average

Ownership Cost By Year

$2,000 $4,000 $6,000 $8,000

Insufficient Depreciation Information

Insufficient Maintenance Information

1993 1994 1995 1996 1997

Warranty/Maintenance Info

Item		Rate
Major Tune-Up		Insufficient Information
Minor Tune-Up		Insufficient Information
Brake Service		Insufficient Information
Overall Warranty	3 yr/36k	Average
Drivetrain Warranty	3 yr/36k	Average
Rust Warranty	6 yr/100k	Better Than Average
Maintenance Warranty	N/A	
Roadside Assistance	N/A	

Resale Value

Insufficient Information

Ownership Costs (5yr)

Insufficient Information

The 1993 Mercury Villager is available in two models- GS and LS passenger vans. Brand new for 1993, the Villager GS comes standard with cloth-covered reclining seats, and the rear bench seat is mounted on a track allowing many possible seating and cargo configurations. For safety there are side guard beams, knee bolsters, rear headrests, a high mounted stop light, and motorized front shoulder belts with manual lap belts. The Villager was designed by Nissan and built by Ford.

Cumulative Costs

	1993	1994	1995	1996	1997
Annual	*Insufficient Information*				
Total	*Insufficient Information*				

Ownership Cost Rating

Insufficient Information

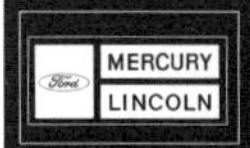

Mercury Villager LS
3 Door Pass Van

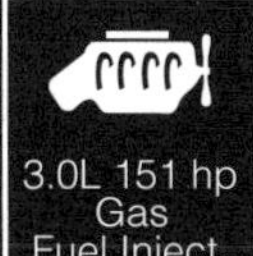
3.0L 151 hp Gas Fuel Inject.

6 Cylinder "V"

Automatic 4 Speed

2 Wheel Front

Automatic Seatbelts

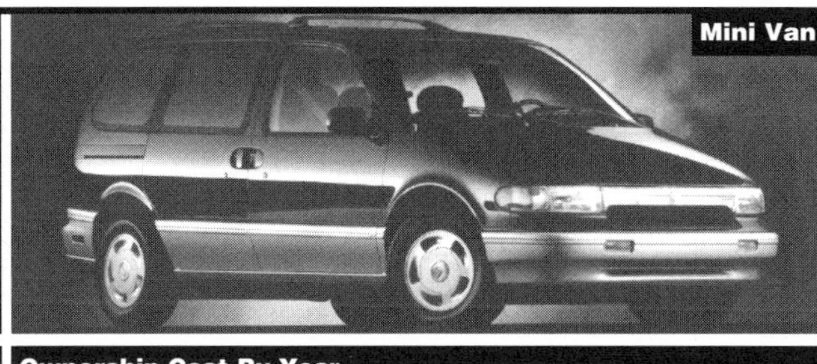

Purchase Price

Car Item	Dealer Cost	List
Base Price	**$19,347**	**$21,798**
Anti-Lock Brakes	Std	Std
Manual Transmission	N/A	N/A
Optional Engine	N/A	N/A
Air Conditioning	Std	Std
Power Steering	Std	Std
Cruise Control	Std	Std
All Wheel Drive	N/A	N/A
AM/FM Stereo Cassette	Std	Std
Steering Wheel, Tilt	Std	Std
Power Windows	Std	Std
***Options Price**	$0	$0
***Total Price**	**$19,347**	**$21,798**
Target Price	$21,143	
Destination Charge	$540	
Avg. Tax & Fees	$1,307	
Total Target $	**$22,990**	
Average Dealer Option Cost:	***85%***	

Ownership Costs

Cost Area	5 Year Cost	Rate
Depreciation		Insufficient Information
Financing ($462/month)	$3,787	
Insurance (Rating 10)	$7,479	Average
State Fees	$893	
Fuel (Hwy 23 City 17)	$4,328	Better Than Average
Maintenance		Insufficient Information
Repairs	$740	Average

Ownership Cost By Year

$2,000 $4,000 $6,000 $8,000

Insufficient Depreciation Information

Insufficient Maintenance Information

1993 1994 1995 1996 1997

Warranty/Maintenance Info

Item		Rate
Major Tune-Up		Insufficient Information
Minor Tune-Up		Insufficient Information
Brake Service		Insufficient Information
Overall Warranty	3 yr/36k	Average
Drivetrain Warranty	3 yr/36k	Average
Rust Warranty	6 yr/100k	Better Than Average
Maintenance Warranty	N/A	
Roadside Assistance	N/A	

Resale Value

Insufficient Information

Ownership Costs (5yr)

Insufficient Information

The 1993 Mercury Villager is available in two models- GS and LS passenger vans. Brand new for 1993, the Villager LS upgrades the GS making standard Bosch four-wheel anti-lock brakes. The Villager offers an optional towing package allowing a 3,500 pound towing capacity. Known for its safety features, the Villager includes side guard beams, knee bolsters, five-mph bumpers, rear headrests, and a high-mounted stop light. The Villager's sister van is the Nissan Quest.

Cumulative Costs

	1993	1994	1995	1996	1997
Annual	*Insufficient Information*				
Total	*Insufficient Information*				

Ownership Cost Rating

Insufficient Information

* Includes shaded options

** Other purchase requirements apply

 Poor  Worse Than Average  Average  Better Than Average   Excellent 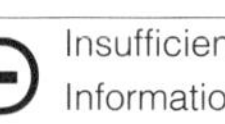 Insufficient Information

Refer to *Section 3: Annotated Vehicle Charts* for an explanation of these charts.

Mitsubishi Expo LRV

3 Door Wagon

1.8L 113 hp Gas Fuel Inject. | 4 Cylinder In-Line |  Manual 5 Speed |  2 Wheel Front | Automatic Seatbelts

Compact Wagon

Purchase Price

Car Item	Dealer Cost	List
Base Price	**$10,291**	**$11,429**
Anti-Lock Brakes	N/A	N/A
Automatic 4 Speed	$600	$670
Optional Engine	N/A	N/A
Air Conditioning	$640	$780
Power Steering	Std	Std
Cruise Control	$160	$200
All Wheel Drive	N/A	N/A
AM/FM Stereo Cassette	$312	$446
Steering Wheel, Tilt	Std	Std
Power Windows	Pkg	Pkg
***Options Price**	$1,552	$1,896
***Total Price**	**$11,843**	**$13,325**
Target Price	$12,509	
Destination Charge	$418	
Avg. Tax & Fees	$783	
Total Target $	**$13,710**	
Average Dealer Option Cost:	***79%***	

Ownership Costs

Cost Area	5 Year Cost	Rate
Depreciation	$7,010	Average
Financing ($276/month)	$2,259	
Insurance (Rating 6)	$6,919	Average
State Fees	$549	
Fuel (Hwy 28 City 23)	$3,385	Better Than Average
Maintenance	$5,041	Average
Repairs	$680	Average

Ownership Cost By Year

$2,000 | $4,000 | $6,000 | $8,000

1993 | 1994 | 1995 | 1996 | 1997

Warranty/Maintenance Info

Item		Rate
Major Tune-Up	$181	Average
Minor Tune-Up	$125	Worse Than Average
Brake Service	$243	Worse Than Average
Overall Warranty	3 yr/36k	Average
Drivetrain Warranty	5 yr/60k	Excellent
Rust Warranty	7 yr/100k	Excellent
Maintenance Warranty	N/A	
Roadside Assistance	3 yr/36k	

Resale Value

1993	1994	1995	1996	1997
$11,413	$10,069	$9,057	$7,652	$6,700

Ownership Costs (5yr)

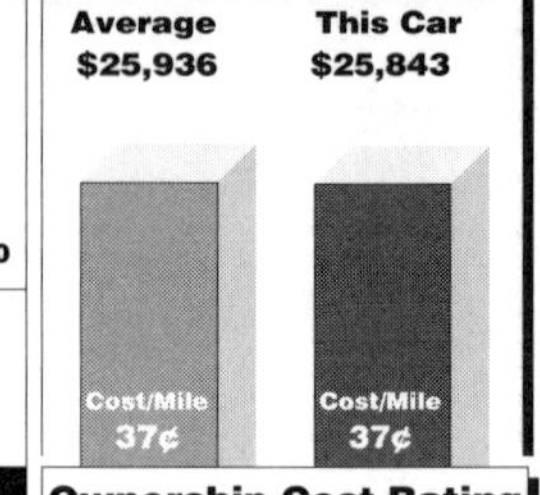

Average	This Car
$25,936	$25,843
Cost/Mile 37¢	Cost/Mile 37¢

Cumulative Costs

	1993	1994	1995	1996	1997
Annual	$5,323	$4,391	$5,152	$4,599	$6,378
Total	$5,323	$9,714	$14,866	$19,465	$25,843

Ownership Cost Rating

Average

The 1993 Expo LRV is available in three models-LRV, LRV Sport and LRV Sport AWD. New for 1993, the Expo LRV features full wheel covers and a new inner tailgate handle. Interior features an optional convenience package that includes center armrest and upgraded door trim with cloth insert. The exterior of Expo LRV has a functional aerodynamic design for good fuel economy and low wind noise. The LRV also features a sliding curbside rear passenger door that provides easy access to the back seat.

Mitsubishi Expo LRV Sport

3 Door Wagon

2.4L 136 hp Gas Fuel Inject. | 4 Cylinder In-Line |  Manual 5 Speed |  2 Wheel Front | Automatic Seatbelts

Compact Wagon

Purchase Price

Car Item	Dealer Cost	List
Base Price	**$12,413**	**$14,269**
Anti-Lock Brakes	$800	$976
Automatic 4 Speed	$600	$690
Optional Engine	N/A	N/A
Air Conditioning	$640	$780
Power Steering	Std	Std
Cruise Control	Std	Std
All Wheel Drive	N/A	N/A
AM/FM Stereo Cassette	Std	Std
Steering Wheel, Tilt	Std	Std
Power Windows	Std	Std
***Options Price**	$1,240	$1,470
***Total Price**	**$13,653**	**$15,739**
Target Price	$14,473	
Destination Charge	$418	
Avg. Tax & Fees	$907	
Total Target $	**$15,798**	
Average Dealer Option Cost:	***80%***	

Ownership Costs

Cost Area	5 Year Cost	Rate
Depreciation	$7,946	Average
Financing ($318/month)	$2,602	
Insurance (Rating 8)	$7,223	Average
State Fees	$646	
Fuel (Hwy 26 City 20)	$3,756	Worse Than Average
Maintenance	$5,173	Worse Than Average
Repairs	$680	Average

Ownership Cost By Year

$2,000 | $4,000 | $6,000 | $8,000

1993 | 1994 | 1995 | 1996 | 1997

Warranty/Maintenance Info

Item		Rate
Major Tune-Up	$181	Average
Minor Tune-Up	$125	Worse Than Average
Brake Service	$243	Worse Than Average
Overall Warranty	3 yr/36k	Average
Drivetrain Warranty	5 yr/60k	Excellent
Rust Warranty	7 yr/100k	Excellent
Maintenance Warranty	N/A	
Roadside Assistance	3 yr/36k	

Resale Value

1993	1994	1995	1996	1997
$13,341	$11,810	$10,603	$8,953	$7,852

Ownership Costs (5yr)

Average	This Car
$28,009	$28,026
Cost/Mile 40¢	Cost/Mile 40¢

Cumulative Costs

	1993	1994	1995	1996	1997
Annual	$5,777	$4,835	$5,623	$5,026	$6,765
Total	$5,777	$10,612	$16,235	$21,261	$28,026

Ownership Cost Rating

Average

The 1993 Expo LRV is available in three models-LRV, LRV Sport and LRV Sport AWD. New for 1993, the Expo LRV Sport features a power package that includes power windows and door locks, power remote door mirrors and the power tailgate lock/unlock mechanism as standard equipment. The exterior of Expo LRV has a functional aerodynamic design for good fuel economy and low wind noise. The LRV also features a sliding curbside rear passenger door that provides easy access to the back seat.

* Includes shaded options

** Other purchase requirements apply

 Poor | Worse Than Average |  Average | Better Than Average | Excellent | Insufficient Information

Refer to *Section 3: Annotated Vehicle Charts* for an explanation of these charts.

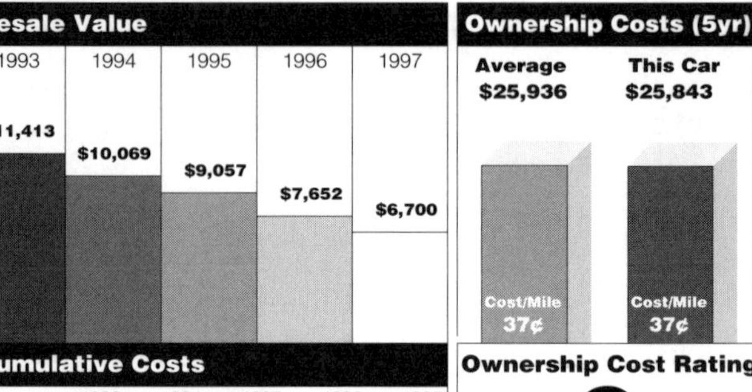

Mitsubishi Expo LRV AWD
3 Door Wagon

2.4L 136 hp Gas Fuel Inject.

4 Cylinder In-Line

Manual 5 Speed

4 Wheel Full-Time

Automatic Seatbelts

Compact Wagon

2WD Sport Shown

Purchase Price

Car Item	Dealer Cost	List
Base Price	**$11,857**	**$13,169**
Anti-Lock Brakes	N/A	N/A
Automatic 4 Speed	$600	$670
Optional Engine	N/A	N/A
Air Conditioning	$640	$780
Power Steering	Std	Std
Cruise Control	$160	$200
4 Wheel Full-Time Drive	Std	Std
AM/FM Stereo Cassette	$312	$446
Steering Wheel, Tilt	Std	Std
Power Windows	Pkg	Pkg
***Options Price**	$1,552	$1,896
***Total Price**	**$13,409**	**$15,065**
Target Price	$14,201	
Destination Charge	$418	
Avg. Tax & Fees	$886	
Total Target $	**$15,505**	
Average Dealer Option Cost:	***79%***	

Ownership Costs

Cost Area	5 Year Cost	Rate
Depreciation	$8,331	Average
Financing ($312/month)	$2,554	
Insurance (Rating 7)	$7,035	Average
State Fees	$619	
Fuel (Hwy 23 City 19)	$4,111	Poor
Maintenance	$5,196	Worse Than Average
Repairs	$680	Average

Ownership Cost By Year

$2,000 $4,000 $6,000 $8,000 $10,000

1993 1994 1995 1996 1997

Warranty/Maintenance Info

Major Tune-Up	$181	Average
Minor Tune-Up	$125	Worse Than Average
Brake Service	$243	Worse Than Average
Overall Warranty	3 yr/36k	Average
Drivetrain Warranty	5 yr/60k	Excellent
Rust Warranty	7 yr/100k	Excellent
Maintenance Warranty	N/A	
Roadside Assistance	3 yr/36k	

Resale Value

1993	1994	1995	1996	1997
$12,234	$10,824	$9,715	$8,206	$7,174

Ownership Costs (5yr)

	Average	This Car
Total	$27,430	$28,526
Cost/Mile	39¢	41¢

Cumulative Costs

	1993	1994	1995	1996	1997
Annual	$6,594	$4,725	$5,555	$4,912	$6,740
Total	$6,594	$11,319	$16,874	$21,786	$28,526

Ownership Cost Rating

Average

The 1993 Expo LRV is available in three models-LRV, LRV Sport and LRV Sport AWD. New for 1993, the Expo LRV AWD features a convenience package and a power package that includes power windows and door locks, power remote door mirrors and the power tailgate lock/unlock mechanism as standard equipment. The LRV AWD provides extra flexibility and cargo room with three rows of seating, four hinged doors and a rear liftgate for easy access and loading convenience.

Mitsubishi Expo
4 Door Wagon

2.4L 136 hp Gas Fuel Inject.

4 Cylinder In-Line

Manual 5 Speed

2 Wheel Front

Automatic Seatbelts

Midsize Wagon

SP Model Shown

Purchase Price

Car Item	Dealer Cost	List
Base Price	**$11,939**	**$13,569**
Anti-Lock Brakes	N/A	N/A
Automatic 4 Speed	$600	$680
Optional Engine	N/A	N/A
Air Conditioning	$640	$780
Power Steering	Std	Std
Cruise Control	$160	$200
All Wheel Drive	N/A	N/A
AM/FM Stereo Cassette	$312	$446
Steering Wheel, Tilt	Std	Std
Power Windows	Pkg	Pkg
***Options Price**	$1,712	$2,106
***Total Price**	**$13,651**	**$15,675**
Target Price	$14,459	
Destination Charge	$418	
Avg. Tax & Fees	$905	
Total Target $	**$15,782**	
Average Dealer Option Cost:	***79%***	

Ownership Costs

Cost Area	5 Year Cost	Rate
Depreciation		Insufficient Information
Financing ($317/month)	$2,600	
Insurance (Rating 7)	$7,035	Average
State Fees	$645	
Fuel (Hwy 26 City 20)	$3,756	Average
Maintenance	$5,176	Worse Than Average
Repairs	$680	Better Than Average

Ownership Cost By Year

$2,000 $4,000 $6,000 $8,000

Insufficient Depreciation Information

1993 1994 1995 1996 1997

Warranty/Maintenance Info

Major Tune-Up	$181	Average
Minor Tune-Up	$125	Average
Brake Service	$243	Average
Overall Warranty	3 yr/36k	Average
Drivetrain Warranty	5 yr/60k	Excellent
Rust Warranty	7 yr/100k	Excellent
Maintenance Warranty	N/A	
Roadside Assistance	3 yr/36k	

Resale Value

Insufficient Information

Ownership Costs (5yr)

Insufficient Information

Cumulative Costs

	1993	1994	1995	1996	1997
Annual	*Insufficient Information*				
Total	*Insufficient Information*				

Ownership Cost Rating

Insufficient Information

The 1993 Expo is available in four models- (Base) Expo and SP; Expo AWD and SP AWD. New for 1993, the Expo features remote keyless entry and Blue interior color availability. The interior features three rows of seats allowing a variety of different seating and cargo arrangements. The second and third rows feature 50/50 split bench seat backs for additional cargo storage. The option list includes a Convenience Package featuring cloth door trim, power tailgate, and dual power remote mirrors.

* Includes shaded options

** Other purchase requirements apply

 Poor  Worse Than Average  Average  Better Than Average  Excellent 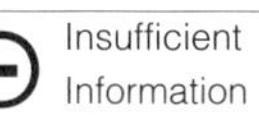 Insufficient Information

Refer to *Section 3: Annotated Vehicle Charts* for an explanation of these charts.

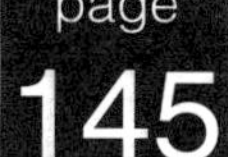

Mitsubishi Expo SP

4 Door Wagon

2.4L 136 hp Gas Fuel Inject.

4 Cylinder In-Line

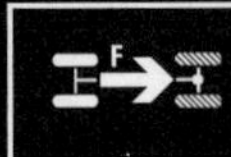
Manual 5 Speed

2 Wheel Front

Automatic Seatbelts

Midsize Wagon

Purchase Price

Car Item	Dealer Cost	List
Base Price	**$13,474**	**$15,669**
Anti-Lock Brakes	$800	$976
Automatic 4 Speed	$600	$680
Optional Engine	N/A	N/A
Air Conditioning	$640	$780
Power Steering	Std	Std
Cruise Control	Std	Std
All Wheel Drive	N/A	N/A
AM/FM Stereo Cassette	Std	Std
Steering Wheel, Tilt	Std	Std
Power Windows	Std	Std
***Options Price**	$1,240	$1,460
***Total Price**	**$14,714**	**$17,129**
Target Price	$15,626	
Destination Charge	$418	
Avg. Tax & Fees	$977	
Total Target $	**$17,021**	
Average Dealer Option Cost:	***81%***	

Ownership Costs

Cost Area	5 Year Cost	Rate
Depreciation		Insufficient Information
Financing ($342/month)	$2,804	
Insurance (Rating 10)	$7,479	Average
State Fees	$701	
Fuel (Hwy 26 City 20)	$3,756	Average
Maintenance	$5,173	Worse Than Average
Repairs	$680	Better Than Average

Warranty/Maintenance Info

Item		Rate
Major Tune-Up	$181	Average
Minor Tune-Up	$125	Average
Brake Service	$243	Average
Overall Warranty	3 yr/36k	Average
Drivetrain Warranty	5 yr/60k	Excellent
Rust Warranty	7 yr/100k	Excellent
Maintenance Warranty	N/A	
Roadside Assistance	3 yr/36k	

Ownership Cost By Year

$2,000 $4,000 $6,000 $8,000

Insufficient Depreciation Information

1993 1994 1995 1996 1997

Resale Value

Insufficient Information

Ownership Costs (5yr)

Insufficient Information

Cumulative Costs

	1993	1994	1995	1996	1997
Annual	*Insufficient Information*				
Total	*Insufficient Information*				

Ownership Cost Rating

Insufficient Information

The 1993 Expo is available in four models- (Base) Expo and SP; Expo AWD and SP AWD. New for 1993, the Expo SP features a remote keyless entry system, rear cargo cover and a Power Package that includes power windows and door locks. A Convenience Package featuring upgraded cloth door trim, power tailgate lock and front center armrest is standard on all Expo SP models. A new two-tone color scheme for 1993 is Norfolk Green with Silver Metallic and Oceanside Blue with Gray Metallic.

Mitsubishi Expo AWD

4 Door Wagon

2.4L 136 hp Gas Fuel Inject.

4 Cylinder In-Line

Manual 5 Speed

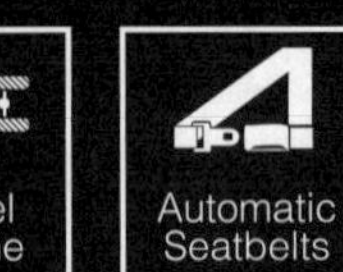
4 Wheel Full-Time

Automatic Seatbelts

Midsize Wagon

SP Model Shown

Purchase Price

Car Item	Dealer Cost	List
Base Price	**$13,105**	**$14,889**
Anti-Lock Brakes	N/A	N/A
Automatic 4 Speed	$600	$680
Optional Engine	N/A	N/A
Air Conditioning	$640	$780
Power Steering	Std	Std
Cruise Control	$160	$200
4 Wheel Full-Time Drive	Std	Std
AM/FM Stereo Cassette	$312	$446
Steering Wheel, Tilt	Std	Std
Power Windows	Pkg	Pkg
***Options Price**	$1,712	$2,106
***Total Price**	**$14,817**	**$16,995**
Target Price	$15,726	
Destination Charge	$418	
Avg. Tax & Fees	$981	
Total Target $	**$17,125**	
Average Dealer Option Cost:	***79%***	

Ownership Costs

Cost Area	5 Year Cost	Rate
Depreciation		Insufficient Information
Financing ($344/month)	$2,821	
Insurance (Rating 8)	$7,223	Average
State Fees	$696	
Fuel (Hwy 23 City 19)	$4,111	Poor
Maintenance	$5,196	Worse Than Average
Repairs	$680	Better Than Average

Warranty/Maintenance Info

Item		Rate
Major Tune-Up	$181	Average
Minor Tune-Up	$125	Average
Brake Service	$243	Average
Overall Warranty	3 yr/36k	Average
Drivetrain Warranty	5 yr/60k	Excellent
Rust Warranty	7 yr/100k	Excellent
Maintenance Warranty	N/A	
Roadside Assistance	3 yr/36k	

Ownership Cost By Year

$2,000 $4,000 $6,000 $8,000

Insufficient Depreciation Information

1993 1994 1995 1996 1997

Resale Value

Insufficient Information

Ownership Costs (5yr)

Insufficient Information

Cumulative Costs

	1993	1994	1995	1996	1997
Annual	*Insufficient Information*				
Total	*Insufficient Information*				

Ownership Cost Rating

Insufficient Information

The 1993 Expo is available in four models- (Base) Expo and SP; Expo AWD and SP AWD. New for 1993, the Expo AWD features remote keyless entry and Blue interior color availability. New options for the Expo AWD includes remote keyless entry and a power package that includes power windows and door locks. Standard features include protective bodyside moldings and dual manual remote door mirrors. Other features include three rows of seats allowing a variety of different seating and cargo arrangements.

* Includes shaded options

** Other purchase requirements apply

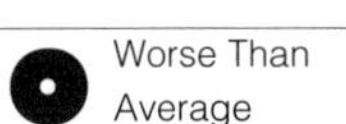
Poor

Worse Than Average

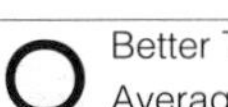
Average

Better Than Average

Excellent

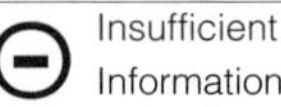
Insufficient Information

Refer to *Section 3: Annotated Vehicle Charts* for an explanation of these charts.

Mitsubishi Expo SP AWD
4 Door Wagon

2.4L 136 hp Gas Fuel Inject. | 4 Cylinder In-Line | Manual 5 Speed | 4 Wheel Full-Time | Automatic Seatbelts

Purchase Price

Car Item	Dealer Cost	List
Base Price	**$14,640**	**$17,019**
Anti-Lock Brakes	$800	$976
Automatic 4 Speed	$600	$680
Optional Engine	N/A	N/A
Air Conditioning	$640	$780
Power Steering	Std	Std
Cruise Control	Std	Std
4 Wheel Full-Time Drive	Std	Std
AM/FM Stereo Cassette	Std	Std
Steering Wheel, Tilt	Std	Std
Power Windows	Std	Std
***Options Price**	$1,240	$1,460
***Total Price**	**$15,880**	**$18,479**
Target Price	$16,898	
Destination Charge	$418	
Avg. Tax & Fees	$1,055	
Total Target $	**$18,371**	
Average Dealer Option Cost:	***81%***	

Ownership Costs

Cost Area	5 Year Cost	Rate
Depreciation		Insufficient Information
Financing ($369/month)	$3,027	
Insurance (Rating 11)	$7,693	Average
State Fees	$755	
Fuel (Hwy 23 City 19)	$4,111	Poor
Maintenance	$5,196	Worse Than Average
Repairs	$680	Better Than Average

Ownership Cost By Year

Insufficient Depreciation Information

$2,000 · $4,000 · $6,000 · $8,000 — 1993 · 1994 · 1995 · 1996 · 1997

Warranty/Maintenance Info

Item		Rate
Major Tune-Up	$181	Average
Minor Tune-Up	$125	Average
Brake Service	$243	Average
Overall Warranty	3 yr/36k	Average
Drivetrain Warranty	5 yr/60k	Excellent
Rust Warranty	7 yr/100k	Excellent
Maintenance Warranty	N/A	
Roadside Assistance	3 yr/36k	

Resale Value

Insufficient Information

Ownership Costs (5yr)

Insufficient Information

Cumulative Costs

	1993	1994	1995	1996	1997
Annual	Insufficient Information				
Total	Insufficient Information				

Ownership Cost Rating

Insufficient Information

The 1993 Expo is available in four models- (Base) Expo and SP; Expo AWD and SP AWD. New for 1993, the Expo SP AWD features a remote keyless entry system and a power package that includes power windows and door locks. The interior features three rows of seats allowing a variety of different seating and cargo arrangements. The second seat features a sliding mechanism that allows access tot he rear seat. The second and third rows feature special 50/50 split seat backs for additional cargo storage.

Mitsubishi Mighty Max
2 Door Regular Cab

2.4L 116 hp Gas Fuel Inject.

4 Cylinder In-Line

Manual 5 Speed

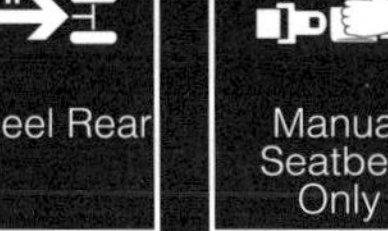

2 Wheel Rear | Manual Seatbelts Only

Purchase Price

Car Item	Dealer Cost	List
Base Price	**$7,712**	**$8,539**
Anti-Lock Brakes	N/A	N/A
Automatic 4 Speed	$597	$900
Optional Engine	N/A	N/A
Air Conditioning	$568	$693
Power Steering	$232	$290
Cruise Control	N/A	N/A
All Wheel Drive	N/A	N/A
AM/FM Stereo Cassette	Pkg	Pkg
Steering Wheel, Tilt	Std	Std
Power Windows	N/A	N/A
***Options Price**	$232	$290
***Total Price**	**$7,944**	**$8,829**
Target Price	$8,376	
Destination Charge	$393	
Avg. Tax & Fees	$530	
Total Target $	**$9,299**	
Average Dealer Option Cost:	***81%***	

Ownership Costs

Cost Area	5 Year Cost	Rate
Depreciation	$4,398	Average
Financing ($187/month)	$1,532	
Insurance (Rating 8)	$7,432	Worse Than Average
State Fees	$369	
Fuel (Hwy 23 City 19)	$4,111	Average
Maintenance	$4,077	Worse Than Average
Repairs	$580	Excellent

Ownership Cost By Year

$2,000 · $4,000 · $6,000 · $8,000 — 1993 · 1994 · 1995 · 1996 · 1997

Warranty/Maintenance Info

Item		Rate
Major Tune-Up	$197	Worse Than Average
Minor Tune-Up	$114	Poor
Brake Service	$201	Average
Overall Warranty	3 yr/36k	Average
Drivetrain Warranty	5 yr/60k	Excellent
Rust Warranty	5 yr/unlim. mi	Better Than Average
Maintenance Warranty	N/A	
Roadside Assistance	3 yr/36k	

Resale Value

1993	1994	1995	1996	1997
$7,812	$6,888	$6,275	$5,613	$4,901

Ownership Costs (5yr)

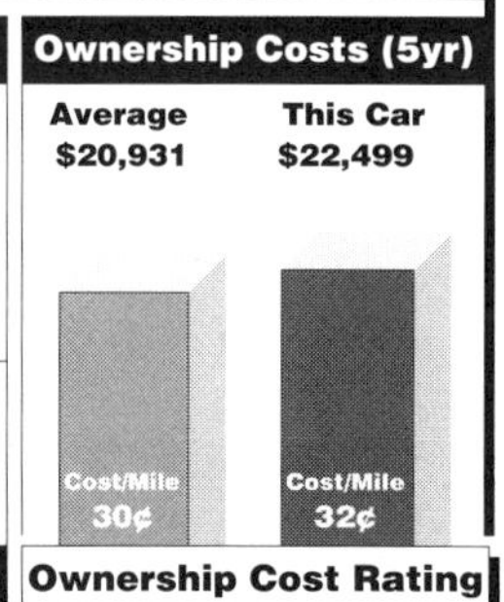

Cumulative Costs

	1993	1994	1995	1996	1997
Annual	$4,394	$3,958	$4,563	$4,216	$5,368
Total	$4,394	$8,352	$12,915	$17,131	$22,499

Ownership Cost Rating

Poor

The 1993 Mighty Max is available in three models-(Base) Mighty Max, Macrocab and Mighty Max 4WD. New for 1993, the Mighty Max features an upgraded interior that includes a new bench seat design that features full cloth seat trim for extra comfort. Additionally, the dashboard includes a new instrument cluster housing designed for easier visibility. The exterior features a new design chrome grille and turn signal bezels, a redesigned front bumper and integrated air dam.

* Includes shaded options

** Other purchase requirements apply

 Poor  Worse Than Average  Average 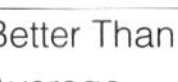 Better Than Average  Excellent 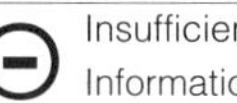 Insufficient Information

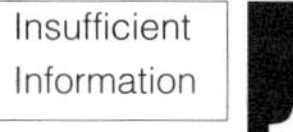

Refer to ***Section 3: Annotated Vehicle Charts*** for an explanation of these charts.

Mitsubishi Mighty Max Macrocab 2 Door Extended Cab

2.4L 116 hp Gas Fuel Inject. | 4 Cylinder In-Line | Manual 5 Speed | 2 Wheel Rear | Manual Seatbelts Only

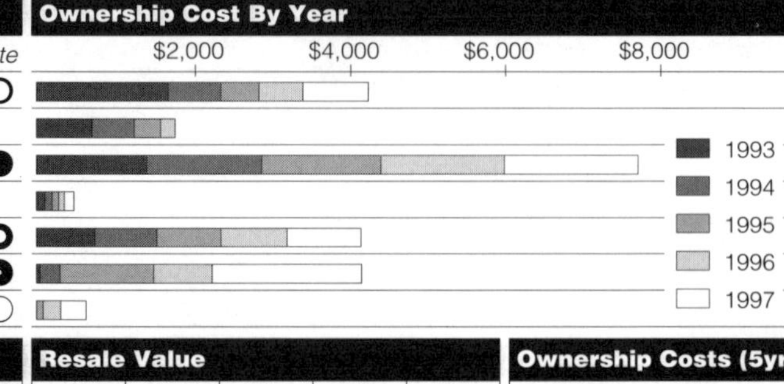

Small Pickup

Purchase Price

Car Item	Dealer Cost	List
Base Price	**$8,722**	**$9,909**
Anti-Lock Brakes	N/A	N/A
Automatic 4 Speed	$597	$680
Optional Engine	N/A	N/A
Air Conditioning	$568	$693
Power Steering	$232	$290
Cruise Control	N/A	N/A
All Wheel Drive	N/A	N/A
AM/FM Stereo Cassette	Pkg	Pkg
Steering Wheel, Tilt	Std	Std
Power Windows	N/A	N/A
***Options Price**	$232	$290
***Total Price**	**$8,954**	**$10,199**
Target Price	$9,459	
Destination Charge	$393	
Avg. Tax & Fees	$599	
Total Target $	**$10,451**	
Average Dealer Option Cost:	***87%***	

Ownership Costs

Cost Area	5 Year Cost	Rate
Depreciation	$4,206	Better Than Average
Financing ($210/month)	$1,721	
Insurance (Rating 10)	$7,689	Poor
State Fees	$424	
Fuel (Hwy 23 City 19)	$4,111	Average
Maintenance	$4,120	Worse Than Average
Repairs	$580	Excellent

Warranty/Maintenance Info

Major Tune-Up	$197	Worse Than Average
Minor Tune-Up	$114	Poor
Brake Service	$201	Average
Overall Warranty	3 yr/36k	Average
Drivetrain Warranty	5 yr/60k	Excellent
Rust Warranty	5 yr/unlim. mi	Better Than Average
Maintenance Warranty	N/A	
Roadside Assistance	3 yr/36k	

Ownership Cost By Year

$2,000 $4,000 $6,000 $8,000

1993 1994 1995 1996 1997

Resale Value

1993	1994	1995	1996	1997
$8,758	$8,082	$7,589	$7,024	$6,245

Ownership Costs (5yr)

Average	This Car
$22,324	$22,851
Cost/Mile 32¢	Cost/Mile 33¢

Cumulative Costs

	1993	1994	1995	1996	1997
Annual	$4,741	$3,830	$4,563	$4,195	$5,522
Total	$4,741	$8,571	$13,134	$17,329	$22,851

Ownership Cost Rating

Worse Than Average

The 1993 Mighty Max is available in three models-(Base) Mighty Max, Macrocab and Mighty Max 4WD. New for 1993, the Macrocab features an upgraded exterior with a new design chrome grille and a redesigned front bumper and integrated air dam. New interior upgrades includes a bench seat design that features full cloth seat trim for extra comfort. Additionally, the dashboard includes a new instrument cluster housing designed for easier visibility. Three new exterior color has been added for 1993.

Mitsubishi Mighty Max 4WD 2 Door Regular Cab

3.0L 151 hp Gas Fuel Inject. | 6 Cylinder "V" | Manual 5 Speed | 4 Wheel On-Demand | Manual Seatbelts Only

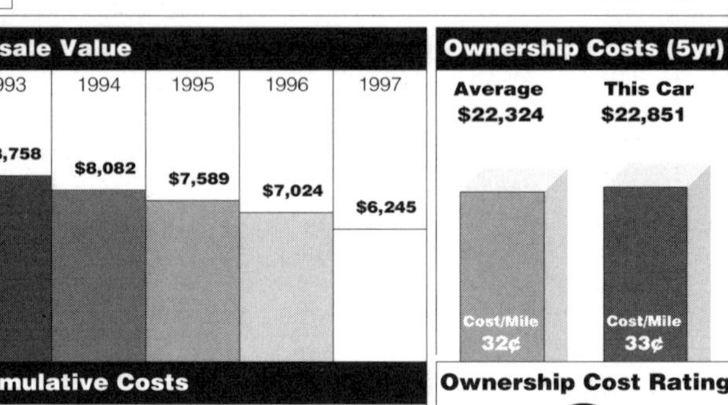

Small Pickup

Purchase Price

Car Item	Dealer Cost	List
Base Price	**$11,421**	**$12,979**
Anti-Lock Brakes	Std	Std
Automatic Transmission	N/A	N/A
Optional Engine	N/A	N/A
Air Conditioning	$568	$693
Power Steering	Std	Std
Cruise Control	N/A	N/A
4 Whl On-Demand Dr.	Std	Std
AM/FM Stereo Cassette	$320	$457
Steering Wheel, Tilt	Std	Std
Power Windows	N/A	N/A
***Options Price**	$320	$457
***Total Price**	**$11,741**	**$13,436**
Target Price	$12,463	
Destination Charge	$393	
Avg. Tax & Fees	$781	
Total Target $	**$13,637**	
Average Dealer Option Cost:	***77%***	

Ownership Costs

Cost Area	5 Year Cost	Rate
Depreciation	$6,521	Worse Than Average
Financing ($274/month)	$2,246	
Insurance (Rating 12)	$8,108	Poor
State Fees	$553	
Fuel (Hwy 22 City 17)	$4,431	Worse Than Average
Maintenance	$4,419	Worse Than Average
Repairs	$761	Better Than Average

Warranty/Maintenance Info

Major Tune-Up	$202	Worse Than Average
Minor Tune-Up	$119	Poor
Brake Service	$201	Average
Overall Warranty	3 yr/36k	Average
Drivetrain Warranty	5 yr/60k	Excellent
Rust Warranty	5 yr/unlim. mi	Better Than Average
Maintenance Warranty	N/A	
Roadside Assistance	3 yr/36k	

Ownership Cost By Year

$2,000 $4,000 $6,000 $8,000 $10,000

1993 1994 1995 1996 1997

Resale Value

1993	1994	1995	1996	1997
$10,183	$9,329	$8,657	$7,962	$7,116

Ownership Costs (5yr)

Average	This Car
$25,615	$27,039
Cost/Mile 37¢	Cost/Mile 39¢

Cumulative Costs

	1993	1994	1995	1996	1997
Annual	$6,892	$4,355	$4,982	$4,645	$6,165
Total	$6,892	$11,247	$16,229	$20,874	$27,039

Ownership Cost Rating

Worse Than Average

The 1993 Mighty Max is available in three models-(Base) Mighty Max, Macrocab and Mighty Max 4WD. New for 1993, the Mighty Max 4WD features an upgraded exterior with a chrome grille and front bumper with an integrated air dam. A color-key front bumper is optional. Interior features a new bench seat with full cloth seat trim for enhanced appearance and comfort. Additionally, the dashboard includes a new instrument cluster. New colors for 1993 are Alpine White, Reno Silver and Danube Blue Pearl.

* Includes shaded options

** Other purchase requirements apply

 Poor 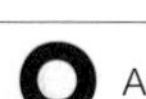 Worse Than Average  Average | Better Than Average | Excellent 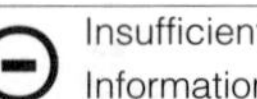 Insufficient Information

Refer to *Section 3: Annotated Vehicle Charts* for an explanation of these charts.

Mitsubishi Montero
4 Door Sport Utility

3.0L 151 hp Gas Fuel Inject.

6 Cylinder "V"

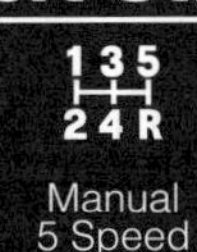
Manual 5 Speed

4 Wheel On-Demand

Manual Seatbelts Only

Purchase Price

Car Item	Dealer Cost	List
Base Price	**$16,376**	**$18,929**
Anti-Lock Brakes	N/A	N/A
Automatic 4 Speed	$714	$830
Optional Engine	N/A	N/A
Air Conditioning	$688	$860
Power Steering	Std	Std
Cruise Control	N/A	N/A
4 Whl On-Demand Dr.	Std	Std
AM/FM Stereo Cassette	$388	$555
Steering Wheel, Tilt	Std	Std
Power Windows	N/A	N/A
***Options Price**	$1,076	$1,415
***Total Price**	**$17,452**	**$20,344**
Target Price	$18,691	
Destination Charge	$418	
Avg. Tax & Fees	$1,163	
Total Target $	**$20,272**	
Average Dealer Option Cost:	***75%***	

Ownership Costs

Cost Area	5 Year Cost	Rate
Depreciation	$7,009	Average
Financing ($407/month)	$3,340	
Insurance (Rating 13)	$8,271	Average
State Fees	$831	
Fuel (Hwy 18 City 15)	$5,233	Worse Than Average
Maintenance	$4,576	Worse Than Average
Repairs	$740	Better Than Average

Ownership Cost By Year

$2,000 $4,000 $6,000 $8,000 $10,000

1993 1994 1995 1996 1997

Warranty/Maintenance Info

Item		Rate
Major Tune-Up	$163	Better Than Average
Minor Tune-Up	$102	Average
Brake Service	$208	Better Than Average
Overall Warranty	3 yr/36k	Average
Drivetrain Warranty	5 yr/60k	Excellent
Rust Warranty	5 yr/unlim. mi	Better Than Average
Maintenance Warranty	N/A	
Roadside Assistance	3 yr/36k	

Resale Value

1993	1994	1995	1996	1997
$17,198	$16,296	$15,356	$14,265	$13,263

Ownership Costs (5yr)

Average	This Car
$30,413	$30,000
Cost/Mile 43¢	Cost/Mile 43¢

The Montero is available in four models-Base, RS, LS and SR. New for 1993, the Montero features Mitsubishi's exclusive Active Trac 4WD and available Multi Mode ABS and argent wheels. Interior features include front reclining bucket seats with adjustable head restraints, fold-down rear bench center console with storage and electric rear window defroster. Exterior features include front end skid plates, side-opening rear door, halogen headlamps and 15-inch steel wheels.

Cumulative Costs

	1993	1994	1995	1996	1997
Annual	$7,217	$4,978	$5,932	$5,330	$6,543
Total	$7,217	$12,195	$18,127	$23,457	$30,000

Ownership Cost Rating

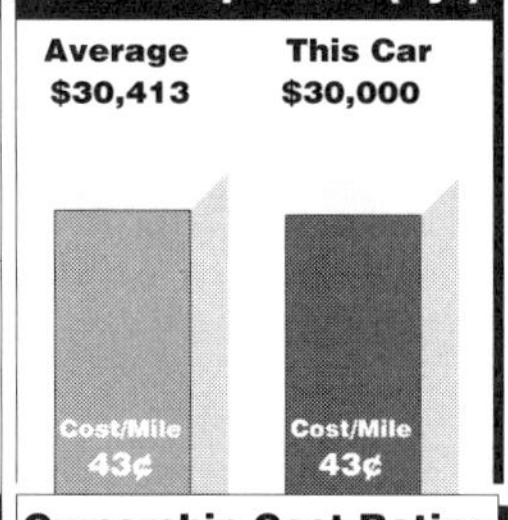

Better Than Average

Mitsubishi Montero RS
4 Door Sport Utility

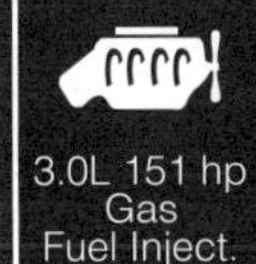
3.0L 151 hp Gas Fuel Inject.

6 Cylinder "V"

Manual 5 Speed

4 Wheel On-Demand

Manual Seatbelts Only

Utility

Purchase Price

Car Item	Dealer Cost	List
Base Price	**$17,759**	**$20,769**
Anti-Lock Brakes	$950	$1,188
Automatic 4 Speed	$714	$840
Optional Engine	N/A	N/A
Air Conditioning	$688	$860
Power Steering	Std	Std
Cruise Control	Pkg	Pkg
4 Whl On-Demand Dr.	Std	Std
AM/FM Stereo Cassette	Std	Std
Steering Wheel, Tilt	Std	Std
Power Windows	Pkg	Pkg
***Options Price**	$688	$860
***Total Price**	**$18,447**	**$21,629**
Target Price	$19,806	
Destination Charge	$418	
Avg. Tax & Fees	$1,231	
Total Target $	**$21,455**	
Average Dealer Option Cost:	***77%***	

Ownership Costs

Cost Area	5 Year Cost	Rate
Depreciation	$7,158	Average
Financing ($431/month)	$3,535	
Insurance (Rating 15)	$8,717	Average
State Fees	$880	
Fuel (Hwy 18 City 15)	$5,233	Worse Than Average
Maintenance	$4,576	Worse Than Average
Repairs	$740	Better Than Average

Ownership Cost By Year

$2,000 $4,000 $6,000 $8,000 $10,000

1993 1994 1995 1996 1997

Warranty/Maintenance Info

Item		Rate
Major Tune-Up	$163	Better Than Average
Minor Tune-Up	$102	Average
Brake Service	$208	Better Than Average
Overall Warranty	3 yr/36k	Average
Drivetrain Warranty	5 yr/60k	Excellent
Rust Warranty	5 yr/unlim. mi	Better Than Average
Maintenance Warranty	N/A	
Roadside Assistance	3 yr/36k	

Resale Value

1993	1994	1995	1996	1997
$17,895	$17,079	$16,279	$15,238	$14,297

Ownership Costs (5yr)

Average	This Car
$31,494	$30,839
Cost/Mile 45¢	Cost/Mile 44¢

The Montero is available in four models-Base, RS, LS and SR. New for 1993, the Montero RS has been completely redesigned and features expansive interior comfort and enhanced driving convenience. New features for the RS includes argent wheels with trim rings, Mitsubishi's exclusive Active Trac 4WD and two new optional packages; Multi-mode anti-lock braking and limited slip differential. Standard features include front bucket seats, fold-down rear seats, power package and lower body side cladding.

Cumulative Costs

	1993	1994	1995	1996	1997
Annual	$7,878	$5,050	$5,930	$5,395	$6,586
Total	$7,878	$12,928	$18,858	$24,253	$30,839

Ownership Cost Rating

Better Than Average

* Includes shaded options

** Other purchase requirements apply

Poor | Worse Than Average | Average | Better Than Average | Excellent |  Insufficient Information

Refer to ***Section 3: Annotated Vehicle Charts*** for an explanation of these charts.

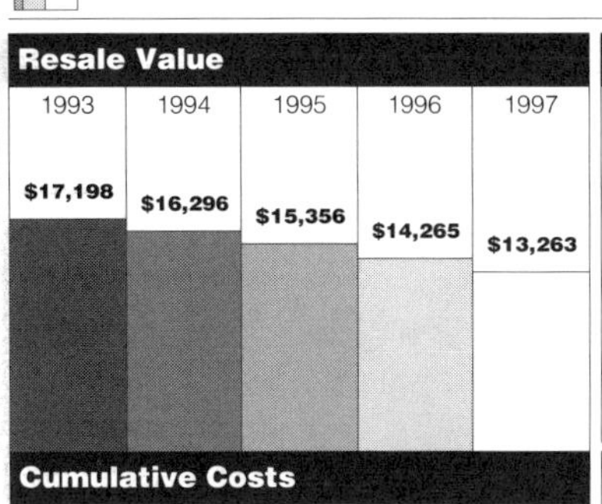

Mitsubishi Montero LS

4 Door Sport Utility

3.0L 151 hp Gas Fuel Inject.

6 Cylinder "V"

Automatic 4 Speed

4 Wheel On-Demand

Manual Seatbelts Only

Purchase Price

Car Item	Dealer Cost	List
Base Price	**$20,565**	**$24,650**
Anti-Lock Brakes	Std	Std
Manual Transmission	N/A	N/A
Optional Engine	N/A	N/A
Air Conditioning	$688	$860
Power Steering	Std	Std
Cruise Control	Std	Std
4 Whl On-Demand Dr.	Std	Std
AM/FM Stereo Cassette	Std	Std
Steering Wheel, Tilt	Std	Std
Power Windows	Std	Std
***Options Price**	$688	$860
***Total Price**	**$21,253**	**$25,510**
Target Price	$22,933	
Destination Charge	$418	
Avg. Tax & Fees	$1,427	
Total Target $	**$24,778**	
Average Dealer Option Cost:	***78%***	

Ownership Costs

Cost Area	5 Year Cost	Rate
Depreciation	$9,401	Average
Financing ($498/month)	$4,081	
Insurance (Rating 15)	$8,717	Average
State Fees	$1,036	
Fuel (Hwy 18 City 15)	$5,233	Worse Than Average
Maintenance	$4,765	Worse Than Average
Repairs	$740	Better Than Average

Warranty/Maintenance Info

Major Tune-Up	$163	Better Than Average
Minor Tune-Up	$102	Average
Brake Service	$208	Better Than Average
Overall Warranty	3 yr/36k	Average
Drivetrain Warranty	5 yr/60k	Excellent
Rust Warranty	5 yr/unlim. mi	Better Than Average
Maintenance Warranty	N/A	
Roadside Assistance	3 yr/36k	

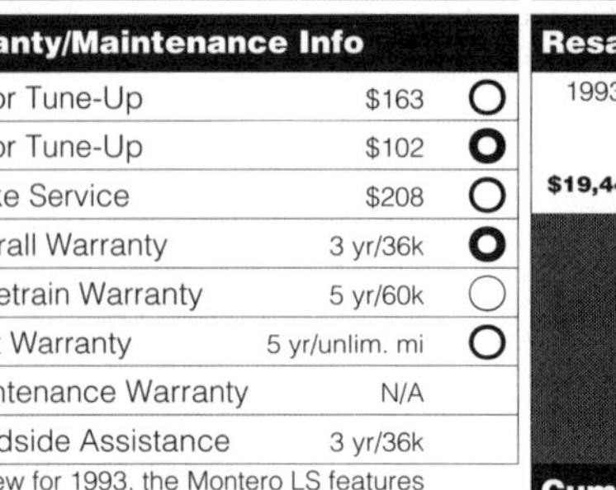

Ownership Cost By Year

Resale Value

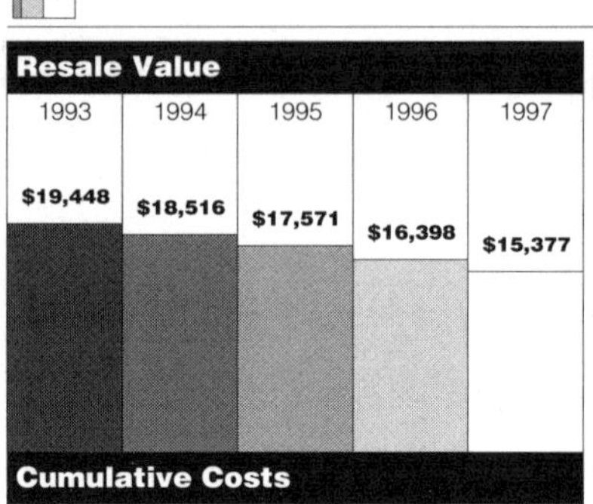

Ownership Costs (5yr)

The Montero is available in four models-Base, RS, LS and SR. New for 1993, the Montero LS features Multi-Mode ABS and Multi-Meter featuring electronic compass/thermometer, inclimeter and altimeter. Interior features includes front reclining bucket seats, premium knit fabric seating surfaces, lighted driver's-side visor vanity mirror and pre-wiring for cellular telephone. An optional leather and wood package includes leather seating surfaces, burled wood instrument panel trim and driver's and passenger's suspension seats.

Cumulative Costs

	1993	1994	1995	1996	1997
Annual	$9,915	$5,372	$6,305	$5,593	$6,788
Total	$9,915	$15,287	$21,592	$27,185	$33,973

Ownership Cost Rating

Better Than Average

Mitsubishi Montero SR

4 Door Sport Utility

3.0L 151 hp Gas Fuel Inject.

6 Cylinder "V"

Automatic 4 Speed

4 Wheel On-Demand

Manual Seatbelts Only

Purchase Price

Car Item	Dealer Cost	List
Base Price	**$21,063**	**$25,250**
Anti-Lock Brakes	Std	Std
Manual Transmission	N/A	N/A
Optional Engine	N/A	N/A
Air Conditioning	$688	$860
Power Steering	Std	Std
Cruise Control	Std	Std
4 Whl On-Demand Dr.	Std	Std
AM/FM Stereo Cassette	Std	Std
Steering Wheel, Tilt	Std	Std
Power Windows	Std	Std
***Options Price**	$688	$860
***Total Price**	**$21,751**	**$26,110**
Target Price	$23,491	
Destination Charge	$418	
Avg. Tax & Fees	$1,460	
Total Target $	**$25,369**	
Average Dealer Option Cost:	***78%***	

Ownership Costs

Cost Area	5 Year Cost	Rate
Depreciation	$8,650	Average
Financing ($510/month)	$4,180	
Insurance (Rating 16)	$8,995	Average
State Fees	$1,061	
Fuel (Hwy 18 City 15)	$5,233	Worse Than Average
Maintenance	$5,156	Poor
Repairs	$740	Better Than Average

Warranty/Maintenance Info

Major Tune-Up	$163	Better Than Average
Minor Tune-Up	$102	Average
Brake Service	$208	Better Than Average
Overall Warranty	3 yr/36k	Average
Drivetrain Warranty	5 yr/60k	Excellent
Rust Warranty	5 yr/unlim. mi	Better Than Average
Maintenance Warranty	N/A	
Roadside Assistance	3 yr/36k	

Ownership Cost By Year

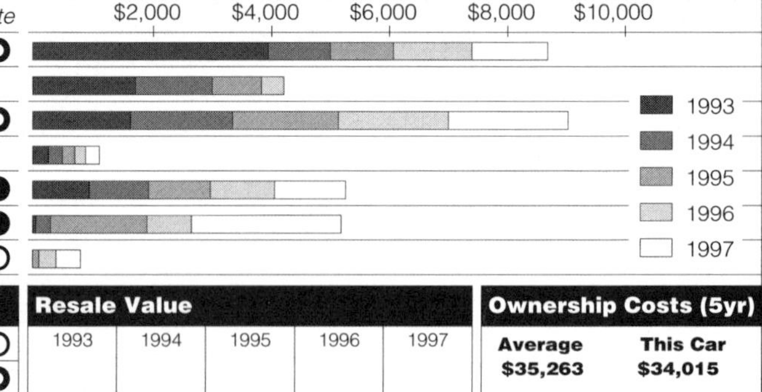

Resale Value

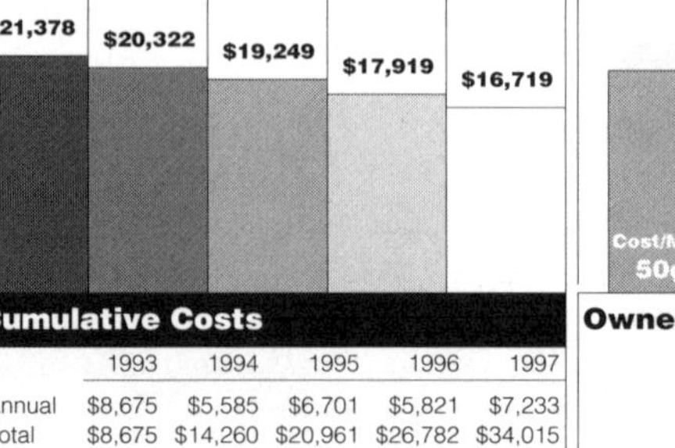

Ownership Costs (5yr)

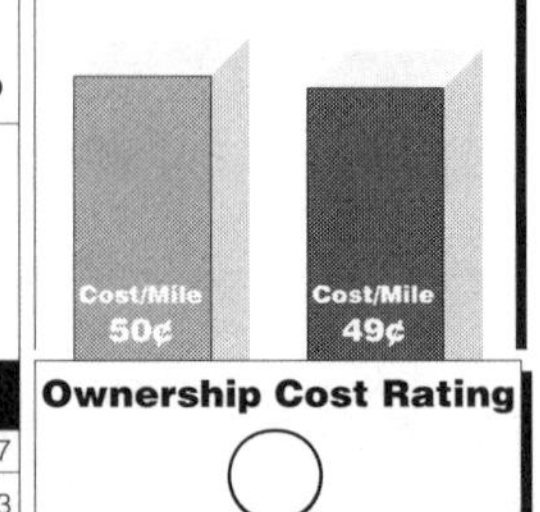

The 1993 Montero is available in four models -Base, RS, LS and SR compact sport utility trucks. New for 1993, the SR model features new exterior colors - Summit White, Sable Black, Morocco Red Pearl, Belize Green and Nairobi Beige. The Montero has been completely redesigned for 1992 with increased horsepower and aerodynamic styling. In 1990, the Montero was one of the top ten selling vehicles in the compact sport utility class.

Cumulative Costs

	1993	1994	1995	1996	1997
Annual	$8,675	$5,585	$6,701	$5,821	$7,233
Total	$8,675	$14,260	$20,961	$26,782	$34,015

Ownership Cost Rating

Excellent

* Includes shaded options

** Other purchase requirements apply

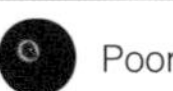 Poor 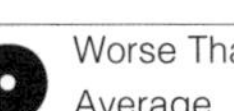 Worse Than Average  Average 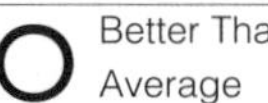 Better Than Average  Excellent 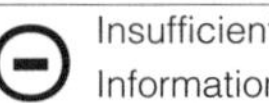 Insufficient Information

Refer to *Section 3: Annotated Vehicle Charts* for an explanation of these charts.

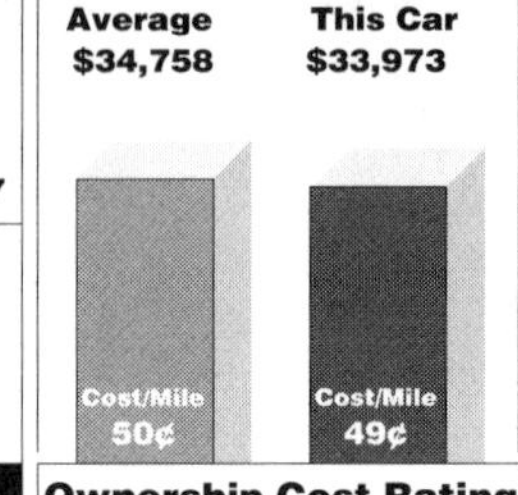

Nissan Pathfinder XE-V6
4 Door Sport Utility

Utility

3.0L 153 hp Gas Fuel Inject.

6 Cylinder "V"

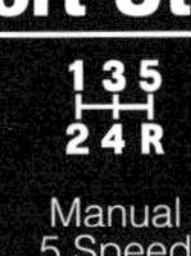
Manual 5 Speed

2 Wheel Rear

Manual Seatbelts Only

Purchase Price

Car Item	Dealer Cost	List
Base Price	**$15,868**	**$18,090**
Anti-Lock Brakes	Std	Std
Automatic 4 Speed	$1,115	$1,270
Optional Engine	N/A	N/A
Air Conditioning	$720	$850
Power Steering	Std	Std
Cruise Control	Grp	Grp
All Wheel Drive	N/A	N/A
AM/FM Stereo Cassette	Std	Std
Steering Wheel, Tilt	Std	Std
Power Windows	Pkg	Pkg
***Options Price**	$720	$850
***Total Price**	**$16,588**	**$18,940**
Target Price	$17,689	
Destination Charge	$350	
Avg. Tax & Fees	$1,095	
Total Target $	**$19,134**	
Average Dealer Option Cost:	***85%***	

Ownership Costs

Cost Area	5 Year Cost	Rate
Depreciation	$3,664	Excellent
Financing ($385/month)	$3,152	
Insurance (Rating 17)	$9,294	Worse Than Average
State Fees	$772	
Fuel (Hwy 19 City 15)	$5,079	Worse Than Average
Maintenance	$4,068	Average
Repairs	$670	Excellent

Ownership Cost By Year

$2,000 $4,000 $6,000 $8,000 $10,000

1993 1994 1995 1996 1997

Warranty/Maintenance Info

Item		Rate
Major Tune-Up	$183	Average
Minor Tune-Up	$79	Excellent
Brake Service	$195	Excellent
Overall Warranty	3 yr/36k	Average
Drivetrain Warranty	5 yr/60k	Excellent
Rust Warranty	5 yr/unlim. mi	Better Than Average
Maintenance Warranty	N/A	
Roadside Assistance	3 yr/36k	

Resale Value

1993	1994	1995	1996	1997
$18,082	$17,219	$16,656	$16,048	$15,470

Ownership Costs (5yr)

Average	This Car
$29,232	$26,699
Cost/Mile 42¢	Cost/Mile 38¢

Cumulative Costs

	1993	1994	1995	1996	1997
Annual	$5,261	$4,978	$5,515	$4,719	$6,226
Total	$5,261	$10,239	$15,754	$20,473	$26,699

Ownership Cost Rating

Excellent

The 1993 Nissan Pathfinder is available in three models - XE-V6, XE-V6 4WD and SE-V6 4WD utility wagons. New for 1993, the XE-V6 receives newly-designed front and rear bumpers, and integrated fender flares/mud guards. Interior features include side door beams for added passenger protection, an upgraded audio system, new seat materials and sew styles, and environmentally-friendly air conditioning refrigerant. Other features include reclining bucket seats in front and a reclining split rear bench seat.

Nissan Pathfinder XE-V6 4WD
4 Door Sport Utility

Utility

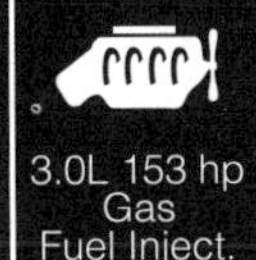
3.0L 153 hp Gas Fuel Inject.

6 Cylinder "V"

Manual 5 Speed

4 Wheel On-Demand

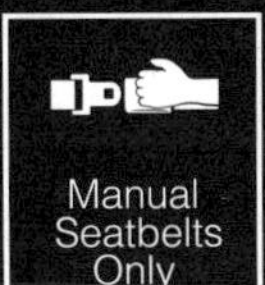
Manual Seatbelts Only

Purchase Price

Car Item	Dealer Cost	List
Base Price	**$17,378**	**$19,810**
Anti-Lock Brakes	Std	Std
Automatic 4 Speed	$1,201	$1,370
Optional Engine	N/A	N/A
Air Conditioning	$720	$850
Power Steering	Std	Std
Cruise Control	Grp	Grp
4 Whl On-Demand Dr.	Std	Std
AM/FM Stereo Cassette	Std	Std
Steering Wheel, Tilt	Std	Std
Power Windows	Pkg	Pkg
***Options Price**	$720	$850
***Total Price**	**$18,098**	**$20,660**
Target Price	$19,348	
Destination Charge	$350	
Avg. Tax & Fees	$1,195	
Total Target $	**$20,893**	
Average Dealer Option Cost:	***85%***	

Ownership Costs

Cost Area	5 Year Cost	Rate
Depreciation	$4,191	Excellent
Financing ($420/month)	$3,442	
Insurance (Rating 18)	$9,662	Worse Than Average
State Fees	$840	
Fuel (Hwy 18 City 15)	$5,233	Worse Than Average
Maintenance	$4,156	Average
Repairs	$720	Excellent

Ownership Cost By Year

$2,000 $4,000 $6,000 $8,000 $10,000

1993 1994 1995 1996 1997

Warranty/Maintenance Info

Item		Rate
Major Tune-Up	$183	Average
Minor Tune-Up	$79	Excellent
Brake Service	$195	Excellent
Overall Warranty	3 yr/36k	Average
Drivetrain Warranty	5 yr/60k	Excellent
Rust Warranty	5 yr/unlim. mi	Better Than Average
Maintenance Warranty	N/A	
Roadside Assistance	3 yr/36k	

Resale Value

1993	1994	1995	1996	1997
$19,208	$18,612	$18,081	$17,335	$16,702

Ownership Costs (5yr)

Average	This Car
$30,679	$28,244
Cost/Mile 44¢	Cost/Mile 40¢

Cumulative Costs

	1993	1994	1995	1996	1997
Annual	$6,128	$4,917	$5,708	$5,019	$6,472
Total	$6,128	$11,045	$16,753	$21,772	$28,244

Ownership Cost Rating

Excellent

The 1993 Pathfinder is available in three models - XE-V6, XE-V6 (4WD) and SE-V6 (4WD) utility wagons. New for 1993, the XE-V6 4WD receives newly-designed front and rear bumpers, and integrated fender flare/mud guards. Interior features include side door beams for added passenger protection, an upgraded audio system, new seat materials and sew styles, and environmentally-friendly air conditioning refrigerant. Other features include reclining bucket seats in front and auto-locking front hubs.

* Includes shaded options

** Other purchase requirements apply

 Poor  Worse Than Average  Average  Better Than Average  Excellent  Insufficient Information

Refer to *Section 3: Annotated Vehicle Charts* for an explanation of these charts.

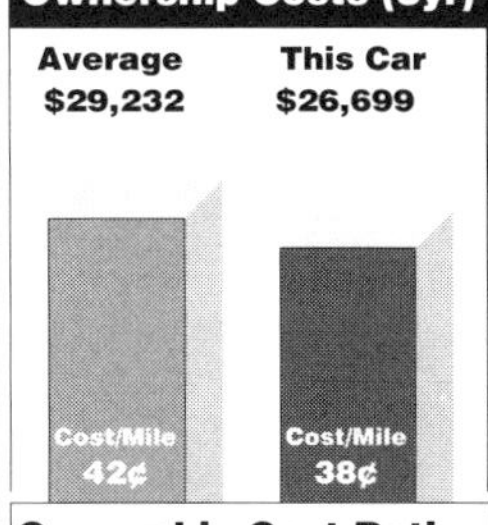

Nissan Pathfinder SE-V6 4WD

4 Door Sport Utility

Utility

3.0L 153 hp Gas Fuel Inject.

6 Cylinder "V"

135 24R Manual 5 Speed

4 Wheel On-Demand

Manual Seatbelts Only

XE Model Shown

Purchase Price

Car Item	Dealer Cost	List
Base Price	**$20,378**	**$23,230**
Anti-Lock Brakes	Std	Std
Automatic 4 Speed	$964	$1,100
Optional Engine	N/A	N/A
Air Conditioning	Std	Std
Power Steering	Std	Std
Cruise Control	Std	Std
4 Whl On-Demand Dr.	Std	Std
AM/FM Stereo Cassette	Std	Std
Steering Wheel, Tilt	Std	Std
Power Windows	Std	Std
***Options Price**	$0	$0
***Total Price**	**$20,378**	**$23,230**
Target Price	$21,897	
Destination Charge	$350	
Avg. Tax & Fees	$1,348	
Total Target $	**$23,595**	
Average Dealer Option Cost:	***85%***	

Ownership Costs

Cost Area	5 Year Cost	Rate
Depreciation	$5,034	Excellent
Financing ($474/month)	$3,887	
Insurance (Rating 18)	$9,269	Worse Than Average
State Fees	$943	
Fuel (Hwy 18 City 15)	$5,233	Worse Than Average
Maintenance	$4,156	Average
Repairs	$720	Excellent

Ownership Cost By Year

$2,000 $4,000 $6,000 $8,000 $10,000

1993 1994 1995 1996 1997

Warranty/Maintenance Info

Item		Rate
Major Tune-Up	$183	Average
Minor Tune-Up	$79	Excellent
Brake Service	$195	Excellent
Overall Warranty	3 yr/36k	Average
Drivetrain Warranty	5 yr/60k	Excellent
Rust Warranty	5 yr/unlim. mi	Better Than Average
Maintenance Warranty	N/A	
Roadside Assistance	3 yr/36k	

Resale Value

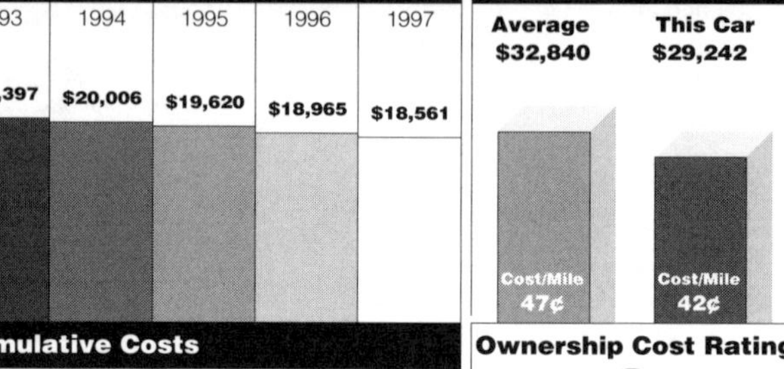

1993	1994	1995	1996	1997
$20,397	$20,006	$19,620	$18,965	$18,561

Ownership Costs (5yr)

Average	This Car
$32,840	$29,242
Cost/Mile 47¢	Cost/Mile 42¢

The 1993 Pathfinder is available in three models - XE-V6, XE-V6 (4WD) and SE-V6 (4WD) utility wagons. New for 1993, the SE-V6 4WD receives newly-designed front and rear bumpers, and integrated fender flare/mud guards. Interior features include side door beams for added passenger protection, an upgraded audio system, non-CFC air conditioner, and all new seat materials and sew styles.

Cumulative Costs

	1993	1994	1995	1996	1997
Annual	$7,779	$4,799	$5,595	$4,896	$6,173
Total	$7,779	$12,578	$18,173	$23,069	$29,242

Ownership Cost Rating

Excellent

Nissan Pickup

2 Door Regular Cab

Small Pickup

2.4L 134 hp Gas Fuel Inject.

4 Cylinder In-Line

135 24R Manual 5 Speed

2 Wheel Rear

Manual Seatbelts Only

Purchase Price

Car Item	Dealer Cost	List
Base Price	**$8,535**	**$9,195**
Anti-Lock Brakes	N/A	N/A
Automatic 4 Speed	$1,035	$1,115
Optional Engine	N/A	N/A
Air Conditioning	$720	$850
Power Steering	$266	$315
Cruise Control	N/A	N/A
All Wheel Drive	N/A	N/A
AM/FM Stereo Cassette	Dlr	Dlr
Steering Wheel, Tilt	N/A	N/A
Power Windows	N/A	N/A
***Options Price**	$266	$315
***Total Price**	**$8,801**	**$9,510**
Target Price	$9,268	
Destination Charge	$300	
Avg. Tax & Fees	$576	
Total Target $	**$10,144**	
Average Dealer Option Cost:	***88%***	

Ownership Costs

Cost Area	5 Year Cost	Rate
Depreciation	$4,249	Better Than Average
Financing ($204/month)	$1,670	
Insurance (Rating 7)	$7,244	Worse Than Average
State Fees	$392	
Fuel (Hwy 27 City 23)	$3,454	Excellent
Maintenance	$3,283	Better Than Average
Repairs	$580	Excellent

Ownership Cost By Year

$2,000 $4,000 $6,000 $8,000

1993 1994 1995 1996 1997

Warranty/Maintenance Info

Item		Rate
Major Tune-Up	$144	Better Than Average
Minor Tune-Up	$75	Excellent
Brake Service	$210	Average
Overall Warranty	3 yr/36k	Average
Drivetrain Warranty	5 yr/60k	Excellent
Rust Warranty	5 yr/unlim. mi	Better Than Average
Maintenance Warranty	N/A	
Roadside Assistance	3 yr/36k	

Resale Value

1993	1994	1995	1996	1997
$8,996	$8,118	$7,436	$6,660	$5,895

Ownership Costs (5yr)

Average	This Car
$21,623	$20,872
Cost/Mile 31¢	Cost/Mile 30¢

The 1993 Pickup is available in seven models - (Base), King Cab, V6 and SE-V6 two-wheel drive, and (Base), King Cab and SE-V6 four-wheel drive. New for 1993, the Base two-wheel drive model includes the new "green" air conditioning unit in an effort to decrease the use of CFCs. The base model makes standard a front stabilizer bar, a solid rear axle, towing hooks and tinted glass. The pickups also feature a revised instrument gauge appearance and bucket seats with new seat cloth.

Cumulative Costs

	1993	1994	1995	1996	1997
Annual	$3,963	$3,728	$4,391	$3,866	$4,924
Total	$3,963	$7,691	$12,082	$15,948	$20,872

Ownership Cost Rating

Excellent

* Includes shaded options

** Other purchase requirements apply

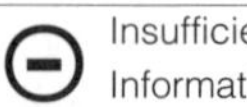

 Poor  Worse Than Average  Average  Better Than Average  Excellent Insufficient Information

Refer to *Section 3: Annotated Vehicle Charts* for an explanation of these charts.

Nissan Pickup V6
2 Door Regular Cab

Small Pickup

3.0L 153 hp Gas Fuel Inject.

6 Cylinder "V"

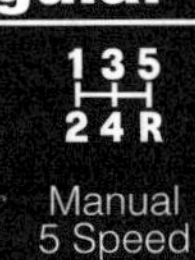
Manual 5 Speed

2 Wheel Rear

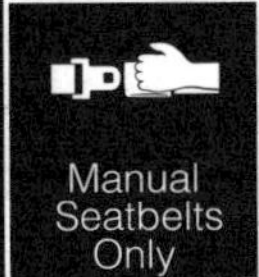
Manual Seatbelts Only

Purchase Price

Car Item	Dealer Cost	List
Base Price	**$9,790**	**$10,665**
Anti-Lock Brakes	N/A	N/A
Automatic 4 Speed	$827	$900
Optional Engine	N/A	N/A
Air Conditioning	$720	$850
Power Steering	Std	Std
Cruise Control	N/A	N/A
All Wheel Drive	N/A	N/A
AM/FM Stereo Cassette	Dlr	Dlr
Steering Wheel, Tilt	N/A	N/A
Power Windows	N/A	N/A
***Options Price**	$0	$0
***Total Price**	**$9,790**	**$10,665**
Target Price	$10,332	
Destination Charge	$300	
Avg. Tax & Fees	$642	
Total Target $	**$11,274**	
Average Dealer Option Cost:	***88%***	

Ownership Costs

Cost Area	5 Year Cost	Rate
Depreciation	$4,626	Better Than Average
Financing ($227/month)	$1,857	
Insurance (Rating 10)	$7,689	Poor
State Fees	$440	
Fuel (Hwy 23 City 19)	$4,111	Average
Maintenance	$3,583	Average
Repairs	$580	Excellent

Ownership Cost By Year

$2,000 $4,000 $6,000 $8,000

1993 1994 1995 1996 1997

Warranty/Maintenance Info

Item		Rate
Major Tune-Up	$157	Better Than Average
Minor Tune-Up	$79	Better Than Average
Brake Service	$210	Average
Overall Warranty	3 yr/36k	Average
Drivetrain Warranty	5 yr/60k	Excellent
Rust Warranty	5 yr/unlim. mi	Better Than Average
Maintenance Warranty	N/A	
Roadside Assistance	3 yr/36k	

Resale Value

1993	1994	1995	1996	1997
$9,423	$8,496	$8,117	$7,349	$6,648

Ownership Costs (5yr)

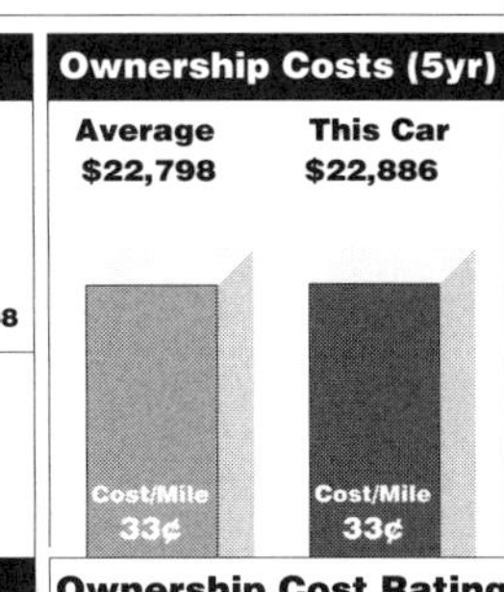

Average	This Car
$22,798	$22,886
Cost/Mile 33¢	Cost/Mile 33¢

The 1993 Pickup is available in seven models - (Base), King Cab, V6 and SE-V6 two-wheel drive, and (Base), King Cab and SE-V6 four-wheel drive. New for 1993, the Base V6 two-wheel drive model includes the "green" air conditioning unit in an effort to decrease the use of CFCs. The Base model makes standard a front stabilizer bar, a solid rear axle, towing hooks and tinted glass. The pickups also feature a revised instrument gauge appearance and bucket seats with new seat cloth.

Cumulative Costs

	1993	1994	1995	1996	1997
Annual	$4,964	$4,068	$4,315	$4,122	$5,417
Total	$4,964	$9,032	$13,347	$17,469	$22,886

Ownership Cost Rating

Average

Nissan King Cab
2 Door Extended Cab

Small Pickup

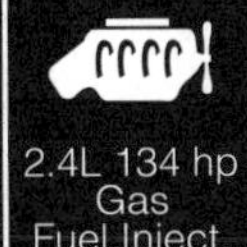
2.4L 134 hp Gas Fuel Inject.

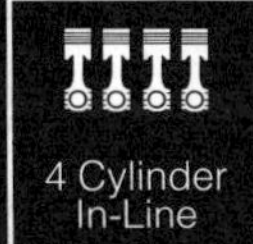
4 Cylinder In-Line

Manual 5 Speed

2 Wheel Rear

Manual Seatbelts Only

SE 4WD Model Shown

Purchase Price

Car Item	Dealer Cost	List
Base Price	**$10,435**	**$11,494**
Anti-Lock Brakes	N/A	N/A
Automatic 4 Speed	$726	$800
Optional Engine	N/A	N/A
Air Conditioning	$720	$850
Power Steering	Std	Std
Cruise Control	N/A	N/A
All Wheel Drive	N/A	N/A
AM/FM Stereo Cassette	Std	Std
Steering Wheel, Tilt	N/A	N/A
Power Windows	N/A	N/A
***Options Price**	$0	$0
***Total Price**	**$10,435**	**$11,494**
Target Price	$11,024	
Destination Charge	$300	
Avg. Tax & Fees	$684	
Total Target $	**$12,008**	
Average Dealer Option Cost:	***87%***	

Ownership Costs

Cost Area	5 Year Cost	Rate
Depreciation	$4,415	Excellent
Financing ($241/month)	$1,978	
Insurance (Rating 11)	$7,902	Poor
State Fees	$472	
Fuel (Hwy 27 City 23)	$3,454	Excellent
Maintenance	$3,283	Better Than Average
Repairs	$580	Excellent

Ownership Cost By Year

$2,000 $4,000 $6,000 $8,000

1993 1994 1995 1996 1997

Warranty/Maintenance Info

Item		Rate
Major Tune-Up	$144	Better Than Average
Minor Tune-Up	$75	Excellent
Brake Service	$210	Average
Overall Warranty	3 yr/36k	Average
Drivetrain Warranty	5 yr/60k	Excellent
Rust Warranty	5 yr/unlim. mi	Better Than Average
Maintenance Warranty	N/A	
Roadside Assistance	3 yr/36k	

Resale Value

1993	1994	1995	1996	1997
$10,359	$9,617	$9,044	$8,331	$7,593

Ownership Costs (5yr)

Average	This Car
$23,640	$22,084
Cost/Mile 34¢	Cost/Mile 32¢

The 1993 Pickup is available in seven models - (Base), King Cab, V6 and SE-V6 two-wheel drive, and (Base), King Cab and SE-V6 four-wheel drive. New for 1993, the King Cab two-wheel drive features the "green" air conditioning unit in an effort to decrease the use of CFCs. The King Cab offers an optional Chrome Package. Standard equipment include a front stabilizer bar, a double-wall construction on all cargo beds, and a revised instrument gauge appearance and layout.

Cumulative Costs

	1993	1994	1995	1996	1997
Annual	$4,734	$3,832	$4,490	$3,977	$5,051
Total	$4,734	$8,566	$13,056	$17,033	$22,084

Ownership Cost Rating

Excellent

* Includes shaded options

** Other purchase requirements apply

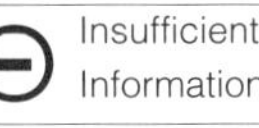

Poor |  Worse Than Average | Average | Better Than Average | Excellent | Insufficient Information

Refer to *Section 3: Annotated Vehicle Charts* for an explanation of these charts.

Nissan King Cab SEV6
2 Door Extended Cab

Small Pickup

3.0L 153 hp Gas Fuel Inject.

6 Cylinder "V"

Manual 5 Speed

2 Wheel Rear

Manual Seatbelts Only

4WD Model Shown

Purchase Price

Car Item	Dealer Cost	List
Base Price	**$12,472**	**$14,055**
Anti-Lock Brakes	N/A	N/A
Automatic 4 Speed	$799	$900
Optional Engine	N/A	N/A
Air Conditioning	$720	$850
Power Steering	Std	Std
Cruise Control	Std	Std
All Wheel Drive	N/A	N/A
AM/FM Stereo Cassette	Std	Std
Steering Wheel, Tilt	Std	Std
Power Windows	Pkg	Pkg
***Options Price**	$0	$0
***Total Price**	**$12,472**	**$14,055**
Target Price	$13,223	
Destination Charge	$300	
Avg. Tax & Fees	$820	
Total Target $	**$14,343**	
Average Dealer Option Cost:	***86%***	

Ownership Costs

Cost Area	5 Year Cost	Rate
Depreciation	$7,119	Worse Than Average
Financing ($288/month)	$2,362	
Insurance (Rating 13)	$8,271	Poor
State Fees	$574	
Fuel (Hwy 23 City 19)	$4,111	Average
Maintenance	$3,816	Average
Repairs	$580	Excellent

Ownership Cost By Year

$2,000 $4,000 $6,000 $8,000 $10,000

1993 1994 1995 1996 1997

Warranty/Maintenance Info

Item		Rate
Major Tune-Up	$157	Better Than Average
Minor Tune-Up	$79	Better Than Average
Brake Service	$210	Average
Overall Warranty	3 yr/36k	Average
Drivetrain Warranty	5 yr/60k	Excellent
Rust Warranty	5 yr/unlim. mi	Better Than Average
Maintenance Warranty	N/A	
Roadside Assistance	3 yr/36k	

Resale Value

1993	1994	1995	1996	1997
$10,249	$9,452	$8,811	$8,037	$7,224

Ownership Costs (5yr)

Average	This Car
$26,244	$26,833
Cost/Mile 37¢	Cost/Mile 38¢

Cumulative Costs

	1993	1994	1995	1996	1997
Annual	$7,558	$4,238	$4,933	$4,309	$5,795
Total	$7,558	$11,796	$16,729	$21,038	$26,833

Ownership Cost Rating

Worse Than Average

The 1993 Pickup is available in seven models - (Base), King Cab, V6 and SE-V6 two-wheel drive, and (Base), King Cab and SE-V6 four-wheel drive. New for 1993, the SE-V6 King Cab two-wheel drive features the "green" air conditioning unit in an effort to decrease the use of CFCs. The SE-V6 upgrades the Base with a Chrome package and offers a Sport/Power Package. Standard features include a solid rear axle, right hand mirror, front stabilizer bar and tinted glass.

Nissan Pickup 4WD
2 Door Regular Cab

Small Pickup

2.4L 134 hp Gas Fuel Inject.

4 Cylinder In-Line

Manual 5 Speed

4 Wheel On-Demand

Manual Seatbelts Only

2WD Model Shown

Purchase Price

Car Item	Dealer Cost	List
Base Price	**$11,393**	**$12,550**
Anti-Lock Brakes	Std	Std
Automatic Transmission	N/A	N/A
Optional Engine	N/A	N/A
Air Conditioning	$720	$850
Power Steering	Std	Std
Cruise Control	N/A	N/A
4 Whl On-Demand Dr.	Std	Std
AM/FM Stereo Cassette	Dlr	Dlr
Steering Wheel, Tilt	N/A	N/A
Power Windows	N/A	N/A
***Options Price**	$0	$0
***Total Price**	**$11,393**	**$12,550**
Target Price	$12,056	
Destination Charge	$300	
Avg. Tax & Fees	$747	
Total Target $	**$13,103**	
Average Dealer Option Cost:	***85%***	

Ownership Costs

Cost Area	5 Year Cost	Rate
Depreciation	$4,977	Excellent
Financing ($263/month)	$2,159	
Insurance (Rating 12)	$8,108	Poor
State Fees	$515	
Fuel (Hwy 22 City 18)	$4,316	Worse Than Average
Maintenance	$3,610	Average
Repairs	$720	Better Than Average

Ownership Cost By Year

$2,000 $4,000 $6,000 $8,000 $10,000

1993 1994 1995 1996 1997

Warranty/Maintenance Info

Item		Rate
Major Tune-Up	$144	Better Than Average
Minor Tune-Up	$75	Excellent
Brake Service	$202	Average
Overall Warranty	3 yr/36k	Average
Drivetrain Warranty	5 yr/60k	Excellent
Rust Warranty	5 yr/unlim. mi	Better Than Average
Maintenance Warranty	N/A	
Roadside Assistance	3 yr/36k	

Resale Value

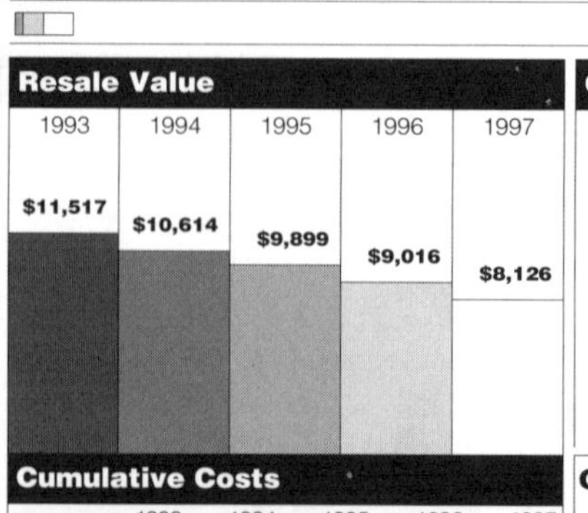

Ownership Costs (5yr)

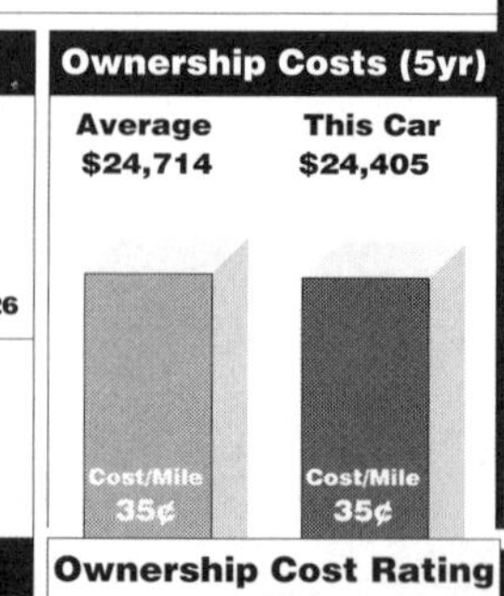

Cumulative Costs

	1993	1994	1995	1996	1997
Annual	$4,954	$4,266	$5,015	$4,462	$5,708
Total	$4,954	$9,220	$14,235	$18,697	$24,405

Ownership Cost Rating

Better Than Average

The 1993 Pickup is available in seven models - (Base), King Cab, V6 and SE-V6 two-wheel drive, and (Base), King Cab and SE-V6 four-wheel drive. New for 1993, the Base four-wheel drive model includes the new "green" air conditioning unit in an effort to decrease the use of CFCs. Also standard are triple skid plates, larger P235 tires, a solid rear axle, towing hooks, a revised instrument gauge appearance and layout, and bucket seats with new seat cloth.

* Includes shaded options

** Other purchase requirements apply

 Poor  Worse Than Average  Average — Better Than Average — Excellent — Insufficient Information

Refer to *Section 3: Annotated Vehicle Charts* for an explanation of these charts.

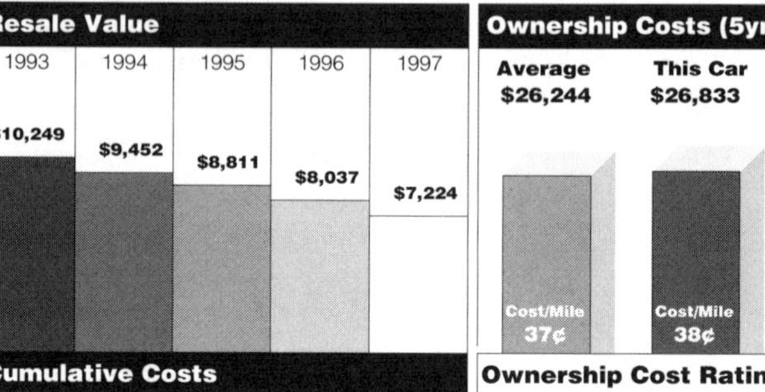

Nissan King Cab 4WD

2 Door Extended Cab

2.4L 134 hp Gas Fuel Inject.

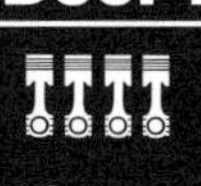

4 Cylinder In-Line

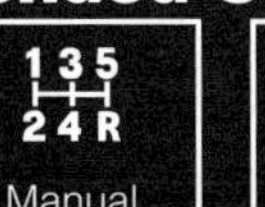

Manual 5 Speed

4 Wheel On-Demand

Manual Seatbelts Only

Small Pickup

SE Model Shown

Purchase Price

Car Item	Dealer Cost	List
Base Price	**$12,864**	**$14,665**
Anti-Lock Brakes	Std	Std
Automatic Transmission	N/A	N/A
Optional Engine	N/A	N/A
Air Conditioning	$720	$850
Power Steering	Std	Std
Cruise Control	N/A	N/A
4 Whl On-Demand Dr.	Std	Std
AM/FM Stereo Cassette	Std	Std
Steering Wheel, Tilt	N/A	N/A
Power Windows	N/A	N/A
***Options Price**	$0	$0
***Total Price**	**$12,864**	**$14,665**
Target Price	$13,647	
Destination Charge	$300	
Avg. Tax & Fees	$847	
Total Target $	**$14,794**	
Average Dealer Option Cost:	***85%***	

Ownership Costs

Cost Area	5 Year Cost	Rate
Depreciation	$5,308	Excellent
Financing ($297/month)	$2,437	
Insurance (Rating 14)	$8,446	Worse Than Average
State Fees	$600	
Fuel (Hwy 22 City 18)	$4,316	Worse Than Average
Maintenance	$3,600	Average
Repairs	$720	Better Than Average

Warranty/Maintenance Info

Item		Rate
Major Tune-Up	$144	Better Than Average
Minor Tune-Up	$75	Excellent
Brake Service	$202	Average
Overall Warranty	3 yr/36k	Average
Drivetrain Warranty	5 yr/60k	Excellent
Rust Warranty	5 yr/unlim. mi	Better Than Average
Maintenance Warranty	N/A	
Roadside Assistance	3 yr/36k	

Ownership Cost By Year

$2,000 $4,000 $6,000 $8,000 $10,000

1993 1994 1995 1996 1997

Resale Value

1993	1994	1995	1996	1997
$12,174	$11,452	$10,934	$10,235	$9,486

Ownership Costs (5yr)

Average	This Car
$26,864	$25,427
Cost/Mile 38¢	Cost/Mile 36¢

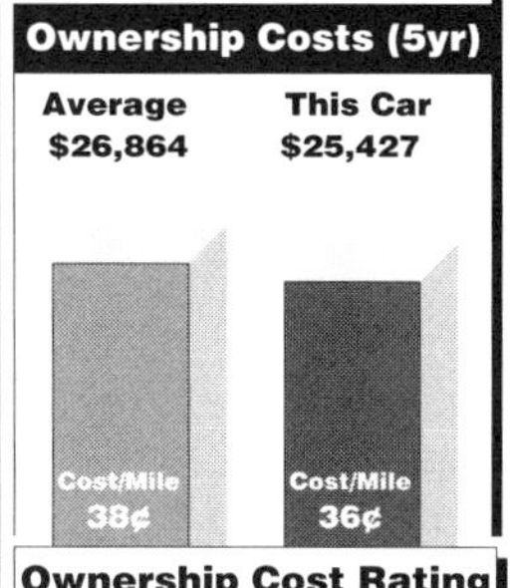

Cumulative Costs

	1993	1994	1995	1996	1997
Annual	$6,187	$4,256	$4,958	$4,373	$5,653
Total	$6,187	$10,443	$15,401	$19,774	$25,427

Ownership Cost Rating

Excellent

The 1993 Pickup is available in seven models - (Base), King Cab, V6 and SE-V6 two-wheel drive, and (Base), King Cab and SE-V6 four-wheel drive. New for 1993, the Base King Cab four-wheel drive features the new "green" air conditioning unit in an effort to decrease the use of CFCs. Standard features include larger P235 tires, triple skid plates, an upgraded audio system, double-wall construction on all cargo beds, a revised instrument gauge appearance, and Chrome Package.

Nissan King Cab SEV6 4WD

2 Door Extended Cab

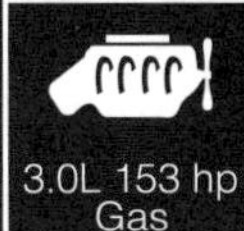

3.0L 153 hp Gas Fuel Inject.

6 Cylinder "V"

Manual 5 Speed

4 Wheel On-Demand

Manual Seatbelts Only

Small Pickup

Purchase Price

Car Item	Dealer Cost	List
Base Price	**$14,211**	**$16,200**
Anti-Lock Brakes	Std	Std
Automatic 4 Speed	$877	$1,000
Optional Engine	N/A	N/A
Air Conditioning	$720	$850
Power Steering	Std	Std
Cruise Control	Std	Std
4 Whl On-Demand Dr.	Std	Std
AM/FM Stereo Cassette	Std	Std
Steering Wheel, Tilt	Std	Std
Power Windows	Pkg	Pkg
***Options Price**	$0	$0
***Total Price**	**$14,211**	**$16,200**
Target Price	$15,111	
Destination Charge	$300	
Avg. Tax & Fees	$936	
Total Target $	**$16,347**	
Average Dealer Option Cost:	***85%***	

Ownership Costs

Cost Area	5 Year Cost	Rate
Depreciation	$6,855	Average
Financing ($329/month)	$2,694	
Insurance (Rating 15)	$8,717	Worse Than Average
State Fees	$661	
Fuel (Hwy 19 City 15)	$5,079	Poor
Maintenance	$4,131	Worse Than Average
Repairs	$720	Better Than Average

Warranty/Maintenance Info

Item		Rate
Major Tune-Up	$157	Better Than Average
Minor Tune-Up	$79	Better Than Average
Brake Service	$202	Average
Overall Warranty	3 yr/36k	Average
Drivetrain Warranty	5 yr/60k	Excellent
Rust Warranty	5 yr/unlim. mi	Better Than Average
Maintenance Warranty	N/A	
Roadside Assistance	3 yr/36k	

Ownership Cost By Year

$2,000 $4,000 $6,000 $8,000 $10,000

1993 1994 1995 1996 1997

Resale Value

1993	1994	1995	1996	1997
$12,153	$11,399	$10,827	$10,084	$9,492

Ownership Costs (5yr)

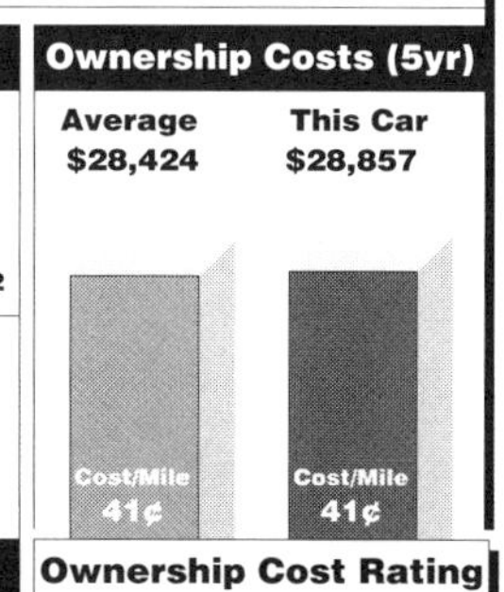

Average	This Car
$28,424	$28,857
Cost/Mile 41¢	Cost/Mile 41¢

Cumulative Costs

	1993	1994	1995	1996	1997
Annual	$8,078	$4,591	$5,353	$4,674	$6,161
Total	$8,078	$12,669	$18,022	$22,696	$28,857

Ownership Cost Rating

Average

The 1993 Pickup is available in seven models - (Base), King Cab, V6 and SE-V6 two-wheel drive, and (Base), King Cab and SE-V6 four-wheel drive. New for 1993, the SE-V6 King Cab four-wheel drive features the "green" air conditioning unit in an effort to decrease the use of CFCs. It upgrades the two-wheel drive with larger P235 tires and a Sport/Power Package which includes limited-slip differential. Other features include triple skid plates and an upgraded audio system.

* Includes shaded options

** Other purchase requirements apply

Poor | Worse Than Average | Average | Better Than Average | Excellent | Insufficient Information

Refer to *Section 3: Annotated Vehicle Charts* for an explanation of these charts.

Nissan Quest XE
3 Door Pass Van

Mini Van

3.0L 151 hp Gas Fuel Inject.

6 Cylinder "V"

Automatic 4 Speed

2 Wheel Front

Automatic Seatbelts

Purchase Price

Car Item	Dealer Cost	List
Base Price	**$15,212**	**$17,545**
Anti-Lock Brakes	$593	$700
Manual Transmission	N/A	N/A
Optional Engine	N/A	N/A
Air Conditioning	Std	Std
Power Steering	Std	Std
Cruise Control	Pkg	Pkg
All Wheel Drive	N/A	N/A
AM/FM Stereo Cassette	Std	Std
Steering Wheel, Tilt	Std	Std
Power Windows	Pkg	Pkg
***Options Price**	$0	$0
***Total Price**	**$15,212**	**$17,545**
Target Price	$16,313	
Destination Charge	$300	
Avg. Tax & Fees	$1,009	
Total Target $	**$17,622**	
Average Dealer Option Cost:	***85%***	

Ownership Costs

Cost Area	5 Year Cost	Rate
Depreciation		Insufficient Information
Financing ($354/month)	$2,903	
Insurance (Rating 10)	$7,479	Average
State Fees	$714	
Fuel (Hwy 23 City 17)	$4,328	Better Than Average
Maintenance	$4,124	Average
Repairs	$680	Better Than Average

Ownership Cost By Year

$2,000 $4,000 $6,000 $8,000

Insufficient Depreciation Information

1993 1994 1995 1996 1997

Warranty/Maintenance Info

Item		Rate
Major Tune-Up	$143	Excellent
Minor Tune-Up	$80	Excellent
Brake Service	$256	Average
Overall Warranty	3 yr/36k	Average
Drivetrain Warranty	5 yr/60k	Excellent
Rust Warranty	5 yr/unlim. mi	Better Than Average
Maintenance Warranty	N/A	
Roadside Assistance	3 yr/36k	

Resale Value

Insufficient Information

Ownership Costs (5yr)

Insufficient Information

The 1993 Nissan Quest is available in two models- XE and GXE. Brand new for 1993 the Quest XE features a full analog instrumentation, deluxe cloth reclining seats with head restraints, and color-keyed body side moldings. The Quest also comes standard with front cornering lamps, table-top surfaces on the back of second- and third-row seats, seven passenger flexible seating and full carpeting. The XE offers a Power Package, Convenience Package, and a Extra Performance Package.

Cumulative Costs

	1993	1994	1995	1996	1997
Annual	*Insufficient Information*				
Total	*Insufficient Information*				

Ownership Cost Rating

Insufficient Information

Nissan Quest GXE
3 Door Pass Van

Mini Van

3.0L 151 hp Gas Fuel Inject.

6 Cylinder "V"

Automatic 4 Speed

2 Wheel Front

Automatic Seatbelts

Purchase Price

Car Item	Dealer Cost	List
Base Price	**$18,597**	**$21,450**
Anti-Lock Brakes	$593	$700
Manual Transmission	N/A	N/A
Optional Engine	N/A	N/A
Air Cond., Front & Rear	Std	Std
Power Steering	Std	Std
Cruise Control	Std	Std
All Wheel Drive	N/A	N/A
AM/FM Stereo Cassette	Std	Std
Steering Wheel, Tilt	Std	Std
Power Windows	Std	Std
***Options Price**	$0	$0
***Total Price**	**$18,597**	**$21,450**
Target Price	$20,070	
Destination Charge	$300	
Avg. Tax & Fees	$1,237	
Total Target $	**$21,607**	
Average Dealer Option Cost:	***84%***	

Ownership Costs

Cost Area	5 Year Cost	Rate
Depreciation		Insufficient Information
Financing ($434/month)	$3,561	
Insurance (Rating 10)	$7,479	Average
State Fees	$871	
Fuel (Hwy 23 City 17)	$4,328	Better Than Average
Maintenance	$4,124	Average
Repairs	$680	Better Than Average

Ownership Cost By Year

$2,000 $4,000 $6,000 $8,000

Insufficient Depreciation Information

1993 1994 1995 1996 1997

Warranty/Maintenance Info

Item		Rate
Major Tune-Up	$143	Excellent
Minor Tune-Up	$80	Excellent
Brake Service	$256	Average
Overall Warranty	3 yr/36k	Average
Drivetrain Warranty	5 yr/60k	Excellent
Rust Warranty	5 yr/unlim. mi	Better Than Average
Maintenance Warranty	N/A	
Roadside Assistance	3 yr/36k	

Resale Value

Insufficient Information

Ownership Costs (5yr)

Insufficient Information

The 1993 Nissan Quest is available in two models- XE and GXE passenger vans. All new for 1993, the Quest GXE upgrades the XE, featuring an 8-way power driver's seat, rear seat air conditioning, power rear quarter windows, upgraded interior trim, and rear seat audio controls. The GXE offers a Power Package, Convenience Package, Leather Package, and a Luxury Package along with such options as a power sliding sunroof, leather seating surfaces.

Cumulative Costs

	1993	1994	1995	1996	1997
Annual	*Insufficient Information*				
Total	*Insufficient Information*				

Ownership Cost Rating

Insufficient Information

* Includes shaded options

** Other purchase requirements apply

 Poor  Worse Than Average  Average  Better Than Average  Excellent — Insufficient Information

Refer to *Section 3: Annotated Vehicle Charts* for an explanation of these charts.

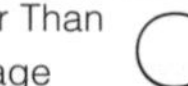

Nissan Quest Cargo Van
3 Door Cargo Van

3.0L 151 hp Gas Fuel Inject.

6 Cylinder "V"

Automatic 4 Speed

2 Wheel Front

Automatic Seatbelts

Mini Van

Passenger van Shown

Purchase Price

Car Item	*Dealer Cost*	*List*
Base Price	**$14,518**	**$16,745**
Anti-Lock Brakes	N/A	N/A
Manual Transmission	N/A	N/A
Optional Engine	N/A	N/A
Air Conditioning	Std	Std
Power Steering	Std	Std
Cruise Control	N/A	N/A
All Wheel Drive	N/A	N/A
AM/FM Stereo Cassette	Std	Std
Steering Wheel, Tilt	Std	Std
Power Windows	N/A	N/A
***Options Price**	$0	$0
***Total Price**	**$14,518**	**$16,745**
Target Price	$15,549	
Destination Charge	$300	
Avg. Tax & Fees	$962	
Total Target $	**$16,811**	
Average Dealer Option Cost:	***84%***	

Ownership Costs

Cost Area	*5 Year Cost*	*Rate*
Depreciation		Insufficient Information
Financing ($338/month)	$2,769	
Insurance (Rating 10)	$7,479	Average
State Fees	$680	
Fuel (Hwy 23 City 17)	$4,328	Better Than Average
Maintenance	$4,124	Average
Repairs	$680	Better Than Average

Ownership Cost By Year

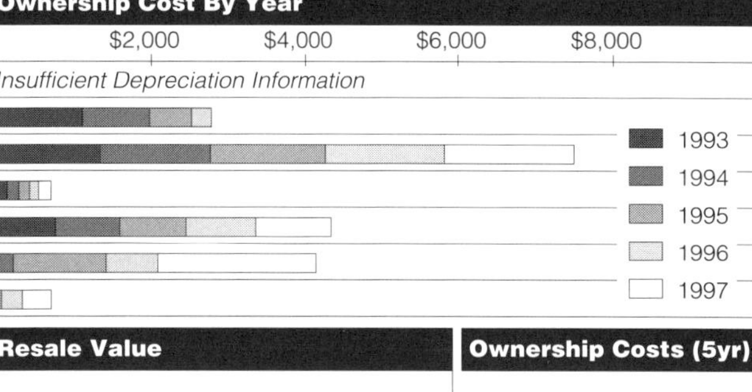

Warranty/Maintenance Info

		Rate
Major Tune-Up	$143	Excellent
Minor Tune-Up	$80	Excellent
Brake Service	$256	Average
Overall Warranty	3 yr/36k	Average
Drivetrain Warranty	5 yr/60k	Excellent
Rust Warranty	5 yr/unlim. mi	Better Than Average
Maintenance Warranty	N/A	
Roadside Assistance	3 yr/36k	

Resale Value

Insufficient Information

Ownership Costs (5yr)

Insufficient Information

Cumulative Costs

	1993	1994	1995	1996	1997
Annual	*Insufficient Information*				
Total	*Insufficient Information*				

Ownership Cost Rating

Insufficient Information

The 1993 Nissan Quest Cargo Van is a one model edition. All new for 1993, the Cargo Van comes equipped with tilt steering, electric rear window defroster, side window defoggers, cargo area rubber mat, remote hood and fuel-filler door releases, front door map pockets, digital quartz clock, two-passenger moquette cloth seating, steel belted radial tires, reclining seatbacks and color-keyed bodyside moldings. Other standard features include trip odometer, cornering lamps and privacy glass.

Oldsmobile Bravada
4 Door Sport Utility

4.3L 200 hp Gas Fuel Inject.

6 Cylinder "V"

Automatic 4 Speed

4 Wheel Full-Time

Manual Seatbelts Only

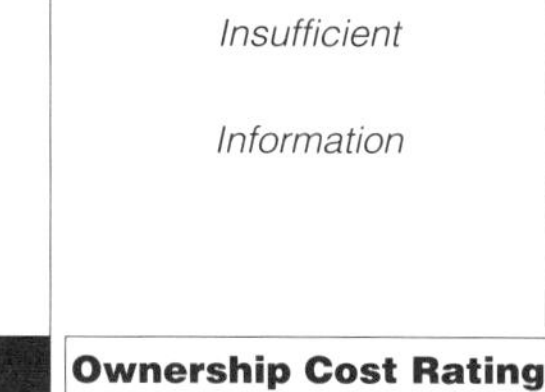

Utility

Purchase Price

Car Item	*Dealer Cost*	*List*
Base Price	**$22,941**	**$25,349**
Anti-Lock Brakes	Std	Std
Manual Transmission	N/A	N/A
Optional Engine	N/A	N/A
Air Conditioning	Std	Std
Power Steering	Std	Std
Cruise Control	Std	Std
4 Wheel Full-Time Drive	Std	Std
AM/FM Stereo Cassette	Std	Std
Steering Wheel, Tilt	Std	Std
Power Windows	Std	Std
***Options Price**	$0	$0
***Total Price**	**$22,941**	**$25,349**
Target Price	$24,960	
Destination Charge	$475	
Avg. Tax & Fees	$1,530	
Total Target $	**$26,965**	
Average Dealer Option Cost:	***86%***	

Ownership Costs

Cost Area	*5 Year Cost*	*Rate*
Depreciation	$13,639	Poor
Financing ($542/month)	$4,442	
Insurance (Rating 18)	$9,662	Worse Than Average
State Fees	$1,033	
Fuel (Hwy 20 City 15)	$4,941	Average
Maintenance	$5,156	Poor
Repairs	$945	Worse Than Average

Ownership Cost By Year

$2,000 $4,000 $6,000 $8,000 $10,000 $12,000 $14,000

1993 1994 1995 1996 1997

Warranty/Maintenance Info

		Rate
Major Tune-Up	$251	Poor
Minor Tune-Up	$138	Poor
Brake Service	$240	Average
Overall Warranty	3 yr/36k	Average
Drivetrain Warranty	3 yr/36k	Average
Rust Warranty	6 yr/100k	Better Than Average
Maintenance Warranty	N/A	
Roadside Assistance	3 yr/36k	

Resale Value

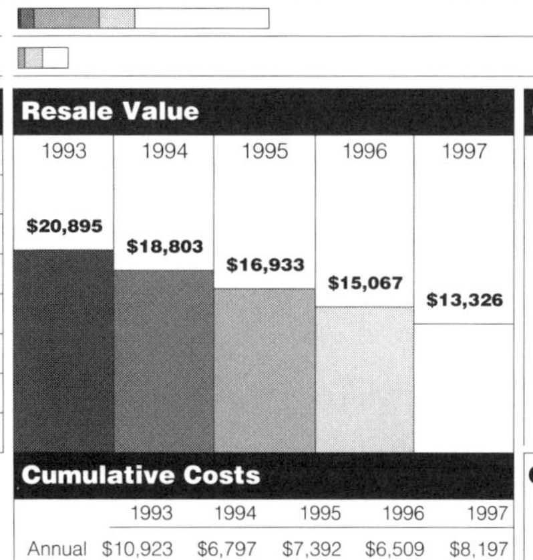

Ownership Costs (5yr)

Average	This Car
$34,623	$39,818
Cost/Mile 49¢	Cost/Mile 57¢

Cumulative Costs

	1993	1994	1995	1996	1997
Annual	$10,923	$6,797	$7,392	$6,509	$8,197
Total	$10,923	$17,720	$25,112	$31,621	$39,818

Ownership Cost Rating

Poor

The 1993 Bravada is available in a one model edition. New for 1993, the Bravada has a 4.3-liter Central Port Injection V-6 200 horsepower engine. It also features the Bravada's SmartTrak system. It offers the convenience of an overhead and center console with dual auxiliary outlets. With the optional Heavy-duty Towing Package, the Bravada can tow up to 5,250 pounds. Other optional features include leather seating surfaces, engine block heater and new for 1993 a blue color has been added.

* Includes shaded options

** Other purchase requirements apply

 Poor  Worse Than Average  Average  Better Than Average  Excellent  Insufficient Information

Refer to *Section 3: Annotated Vehicle Charts* for an explanation of these charts.

Oldsmobile Cutlass Ciera Cruiser S 4 Door Wagon

2.2L 110 hp Gas Fuel Inject.

4 Cylinder In-Line

Automatic 3 Speed

2 Wheel Front

Belts Std, Driv Air Opt

Midsize Wagon

Purchase Price

Car Item	Dealer Cost	List
Base Price	**$13,335**	**$14,899**
Anti-Lock Brakes	N/A	N/A
4 Spd Auto	$172	$200
3.3L 160 hp Gas	$568	$660
Air Conditioning	Std	Std
Power Steering	Std	Std
Cruise Control	$194	$225
All Wheel Drive	N/A	N/A
AM/FM Stereo Cassette	$142	$165
Steering Wheel, Tilt	$125	** $145
Power Windows	$292	$340
***Options Price**	$1,196	$1,390
***Total Price**	**$14,531**	**$16,289**
Target Price	$15,478	
Destination Charge	$500	
Avg. Tax & Fees	$967	
Total Target $	**$16,945**	
Average Dealer Option Cost:	***86%***	

Ownership Costs

Cost Area	5 Year Cost	Rate
Depreciation	$9,639	Worse Than Average
Financing ($341/month)	$2,791	
Insurance (Rating 5)	$6,786	Excellent
State Fees	$672	
Fuel (Hwy 29 City 19)	$3,640	Average
Maintenance	$4,171	Better Than Average
Repairs	$709	Better Than Average

Warranty/Maintenance Info

Item		Rate
Major Tune-Up	$181	Average
Minor Tune-Up	$127	Worse Than Average
Brake Service	$207	Better Than Average
Overall Warranty	3 yr/36k	Average
Drivetrain Warranty	3 yr/36k	Average
Rust Warranty	6 yr/100k	Better Than Average
Maintenance Warranty	N/A	
Roadside Assistance	3 yr/36k	

Ownership Cost By Year

$2,000 $4,000 $6,000 $8,000 $10,000

1993 1994 1995 1996 1997

Resale Value

1993	1994	1995	1996	1997
$11,535	$10,221	$9,296	$8,321	$7,306

Ownership Costs (5yr)

Average	This Car
$27,924	$28,408
Cost/Mile 40¢	Cost/Mile 41¢

Cumulative Costs

	1993	1994	1995	1996	1997
Annual	$8,716	$4,611	$4,903	$4,468	$5,710
Total	$8,716	$13,327	$18,230	$22,698	$28,408

Ownership Cost Rating

Average

The 1993 Ciera is available in four models- S and SL sedans and Cruiser Wagons. New for 1993, the S wagon now offers the option of a driver's-side air bag. It also features a 55/45 split-bench seat with power recliners and air conditioning as standard equipment. Other features include dual mirrors and bodyside molding. Options include aluminum wheels, leather seats, and woodgrain paneling. The S wagon also offers option packages which include power accessories and extra equipment.

Oldsmobile Cutlass Ciera Cruiser SL 4 Door Wagon

3.3L 160 hp Gas Fuel Inject.

6 Cylinder "V"

Automatic 4 Speed

2 Wheel Front

Driver Airbag Psngr Belts

Midsize Wagon

Purchase Price

Car Item	Dealer Cost	List
Base Price	**$16,099**	**$18,399**
Anti-Lock Brakes	N/A	N/A
Manual Transmission	N/A	N/A
Optional Engine	N/A	N/A
Air Conditioning	Std	Std
Power Steering	Std	Std
Cruise Control	$194	$225
All Wheel Drive	N/A	N/A
AM/FM Stereo Cassette	Std	Std
Steering Wheel, Tilt	Std	Std
Power Windows	$292	$340
***Options Price**	$486	$565
***Total Price**	**$16,585**	**$18,964**
Target Price	$17,754	
Destination Charge	$500	
Avg. Tax & Fees	$1,108	
Total Target $	**$19,362**	
Average Dealer Option Cost:	***86%***	

Ownership Costs

Cost Area	5 Year Cost	Rate
Depreciation	$10,991	Worse Than Average
Financing ($389/month)	$3,190	
Insurance (Rating 7)	$7,035	Excellent
State Fees	$779	
Fuel (Hwy 27 City 19)	$3,775	Average
Maintenance	$4,187	Average
Repairs	$709	Better Than Average

Warranty/Maintenance Info

Item		Rate
Major Tune-Up	$180	Average
Minor Tune-Up	$127	Worse Than Average
Brake Service	$207	Better Than Average
Overall Warranty	3 yr/36k	Average
Drivetrain Warranty	3 yr/36k	Average
Rust Warranty	6 yr/100k	Better Than Average
Maintenance Warranty	N/A	
Roadside Assistance	3 yr/36k	

Ownership Cost By Year

$2,000 $4,000 $6,000 $8,000 $10,000 $12,000

1993 1994 1995 1996 1997

Resale Value

1993	1994	1995	1996	1997
$13,160	$11,681	$10,587	$9,497	$8,371

Ownership Costs (5yr)

Average	This Car
$30,659	$30,666
Cost/Mile 44¢	Cost/Mile 44¢

Cumulative Costs

	1993	1994	1995	1996	1997
Annual	$9,772	$4,999	$5,258	$4,710	$5,927
Total	$9,772	$14,771	$20,029	$24,739	$30,666

Ownership Cost Rating

Average

The 1993 Ciera is available in four models- S and SL sedans and Cruiser Wagons. New for 1993, the SL wagon now offers as a standard feature a driver's-side air bag. It also has a new multiport-injected engine (instead of throttle-body injection) that produces 110 horsepower at 5200 rpm. In addition to the features of the S model, the SL offers a convenience group and split-bench front seat with power recline feature. Added options include leather seats and an upgraded sound system.

* Includes shaded options

** Other purchase requirements apply

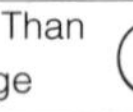

 Poor  Worse Than Average  Average  Better Than Average ○ Excellent ⊖ Insufficient Information

Refer to *Section 3: Annotated Vehicle Charts* for an explanation of these charts.

Oldsmobile Silhouette
3 Door Pass Van

3.1L 120 hp Gas Fuel Inject.

6 Cylinder "V"

Automatic 3 Speed

2 Wheel Front

Manual Seatbelts Only

Mini Van

Purchase Price

Car Item	Dealer Cost	List
Base Price	**$17,647**	**$19,499**
Anti-Lock Brakes	Std	Std
4 Spd Auto	Grp	Grp
3.8L 165 hp Gas	$688	$800
Air Conditioning	Std	Std
Power Steering	Std	Std
Cruise Control	$194	$225
All Wheel Drive	N/A	N/A
AM/FM Stereo Cassette	$120	$140
Steering Wheel, Tilt	Std	Std
Power Windows	$237	** $275
***Options Price**	$1,002	$1,165
***Total Price**	**$18,649**	**$20,664**
Target Price	$20,091	
Destination Charge	$530	
Avg. Tax & Fees	$1,243	
Total Target $	**$21,864**	
Average Dealer Option Cost:	***86%***	

Ownership Costs

Cost Area	5 Year Cost	Rate
Depreciation	$9,952	Worse Than Average
Financing ($439/month)	$3,602	
Insurance (Rating 10)	$7,689	Excellent
State Fees	$848	
Fuel (Hwy 25 City 17)	$4,145	Better Than Average
Maintenance	$4,341	Average
Repairs	$709	Better Than Average

Ownership Cost By Year

$2,000 $4,000 $6,000 $8,000 $10,000

1993 1994 1995 1996 1997

Warranty/Maintenance Info

Major Tune-Up	$212	Worse Than Average
Minor Tune-Up	$150	Poor
Brake Service	$207	Better Than Average
Overall Warranty	3 yr/36k	Average
Drivetrain Warranty	3 yr/36k	Average
Rust Warranty	6 yr/100k	Better Than Average
Maintenance Warranty	N/A	
Roadside Assistance	3 yr/36k	

Resale Value

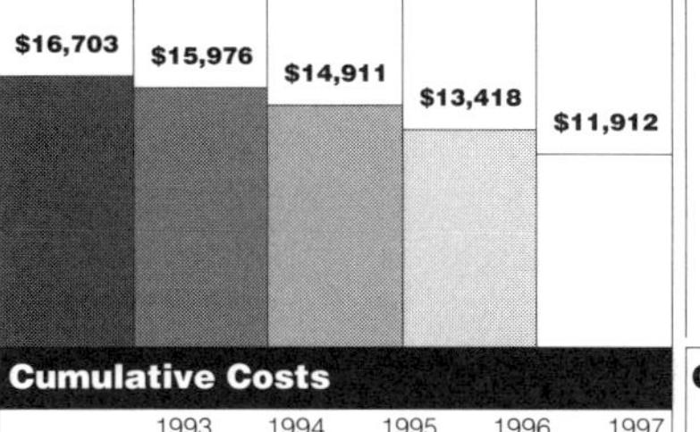

1993	1994	1995	1996	1997
$16,703	$15,976	$14,911	$13,418	$11,912

Ownership Costs (5yr)

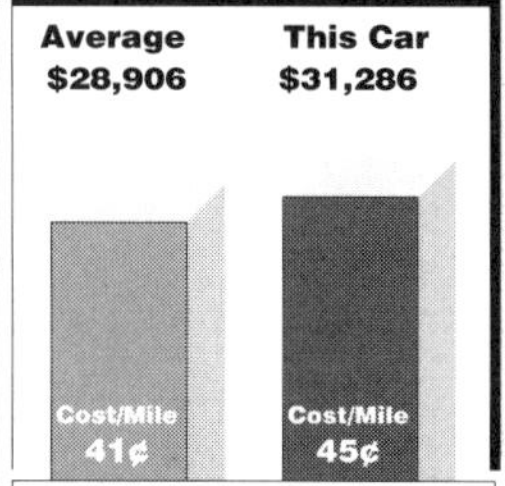

Average	This Car
$28,906	$31,286
Cost/Mile 41¢	Cost/Mile 45¢

The 1993 Silhouette is available in a one model edition. New for 1993, the Silhouette is powered by a 3800 V-6 engine and is equipped with four wheel ABS brakes. Standard features includes 15-inch aluminum wheels, a four-speed electronically controlled automatic transmission and floor and overhead consoles. In addition, a power-operated sliding side door that opens or closes at the touch of a button is standard. The options list includes engine block heater, custom leather seats and air conditioning.

Cumulative Costs

	1993	1994	1995	1996	1997
Annual	$9,107	$4,611	$5,581	$5,432	$6,555
Total	$9,107	$13,718	$19,299	$24,731	$31,286

Ownership Cost Rating

Worse Than Average

Plymouth Colt Vista
3 Door Wagon

1.8L 113 hp Gas Fuel Inject.

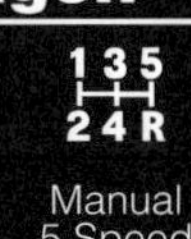
4 Cylinder In-Line

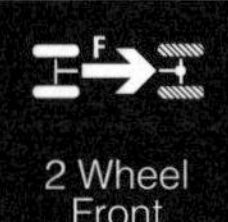
Manual 5 Speed

2 Wheel Front

Automatic Seatbelts

Compact Wagon

Purchase Price

Car Item	Dealer Cost	List
Base Price	**$10,660**	**$11,455**
Anti-Lock Brakes	$829	** $964
Automatic 4 Speed	$622	$723
2.4L 136 hp Gas	$156	$181
Air Conditioning	$673	$783
Power Steering	Std	Std
Cruise Control	Pkg	Pkg
All Wheel Drive	N/A	N/A
AM/FM Stereo Cassette	$156	** $181
Steering Wheel, Tilt	N/A	N/A
Power Windows	N/A	N/A
***Options Price**	$1,451	$1,687
***Total Price**	**$12,111**	**$13,142**
Target Price	$12,877	
Destination Charge	$400	
Avg. Tax & Fees	$799	
Total Target $	**$14,076**	
Average Dealer Option Cost:	***86%***	

Ownership Costs

Cost Area	5 Year Cost	Rate
Depreciation	$7,667	Average
Financing ($283/month)	$2,319	
Insurance (Rating 7)	$7,035	Average
State Fees	$541	
Fuel (Hwy 26 City 20)	$3,756	Worse Than Average
Maintenance		Insufficient Information
Repairs	$630	Better Than Average

Ownership Cost By Year

$2,000 $4,000 $6,000 $8,000

Insufficient Maintenance Information

1993 1994 1995 1996 1997

Warranty/Maintenance Info

Major Tune-Up		Insufficient Information
Minor Tune-Up		Insufficient Information
Brake Service	$165	Excellent
Overall Warranty	1 yr/12k	Poor
Drivetrain Warranty	7 yr/70k	Excellent
Rust Warranty	7 yr/100k	Excellent
Maintenance Warranty	N/A	
Roadside Assistance	N/A	

Resale Value

1993	1994	1995	1996	1997
$9,799	$8,825	$8,059	$7,201	$6,409

Ownership Costs (5yr)

Insufficient Information

The 1993 Plymouth Colt Vista wagon is available in three models - (Base), SE, and AWD. New for 1993, the Base model offers optional cargo security cover. Other options include anti-lock brakes, rear window defroster, tinted glass, luggage rack for the roof, dual electric mirrors, electronic speed control, tailgate power lock, and rear stabilizer bar. Standard features include child protection on rear sliding door lock, remote hood release, and vented side windows.

Cumulative Costs

	1993	1994	1995	1996	1997
Annual	*Insufficient Information*				
Total	*Insufficient Information*				

Ownership Cost Rating

Insufficient Information

* Includes shaded options

** Other purchase requirements apply

Poor  Worse Than Average 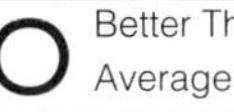 Average  Better Than Average — Excellent — Insufficient Information

Refer to *Section 3: Annotated Vehicle Charts* for an explanation of these charts.

Plymouth Colt Vista SE

3 Door Wagon

2.4L 136 hp Gas Fuel Inject.

4 Cylinder In-Line

Manual 5 Speed

2 Wheel Front

Automatic Seatbelts

Purchase Price

Car Item	Dealer Cost	List
Base Price	**$11,481**	**$12,368**
Anti-Lock Brakes	$829	** $964
Automatic 4 Speed	$622	$723
Optional Engine	N/A	N/A
Air Conditioning	Pkg	Pkg
Power Steering	Std	Std
Cruise Control	Pkg	Pkg
All Wheel Drive	N/A	N/A
AM/FM Stereo Cassette	Pkg	Pkg
Steering Wheel, Tilt	Std	Std
Power Windows	Pkg	Pkg
***Options Price**	$622	$723
***Total Price**	**$12,103**	**$13,091**
Target Price	$12,888	
Destination Charge	$400	
Avg. Tax & Fees	$799	
Total Target $	**$14,087**	
Average Dealer Option Cost:	***86%***	

Ownership Costs

Cost Area	5 Year Cost	Rate
Depreciation	$7,730	Average
Financing ($283/month)	$2,321	
Insurance (Rating 7)	$7,035	Average
State Fees	$539	
Fuel (Hwy 26 City 20)	$3,756	Worse Than Average
Maintenance		Insufficient Information
Repairs	$630	Better Than Average

Ownership Cost By Year

$2,000 $4,000 $6,000 $8,000

Legend: 1993, 1994, 1995, 1996, 1997

Insufficient Maintenance Information

Warranty/Maintenance Info

Item		Rate
Major Tune-Up		Insufficient Information
Minor Tune-Up		Insufficient Information
Brake Service	$165	Excellent
Overall Warranty	1 yr/12k	Poor
Drivetrain Warranty	7 yr/70k	Excellent
Rust Warranty	7 yr/100k	Excellent
Maintenance Warranty	N/A	
Roadside Assistance	N/A	

Resale Value

1993	1994	1995	1996	1997
$9,749	$8,765	$8,002	$7,147	$6,357

Ownership Costs (5yr)

Insufficient Information

Cumulative Costs

	1993	1994	1995	1996	1997
Annual	*Insufficient Information*				
Total	*Insufficient Information*				

Ownership Cost Rating

Insufficient Information

The 1993 Plymouth Colt Vista wagon is available in three models - (Base), SE, and AWD. The Colt Vista SE features standard power brakes, child protection on rear sliding door lock, a stainless steel exhaust system, power lock on tailgate, fixed intermittent wiper/washer in rear, tilt steering column, and dual electric mirrors. Options include keyless remote entry, electronic speed control, power windows and door locks, roof luggage rack, and two tone pain with accent colored bumpers.

Plymouth Colt Vista AWD

3 Door Wagon

1.8L 113 hp Gas Fuel Inject.

4 Cylinder In-Line

Manual 5 Speed

4 Wheel Full-Time

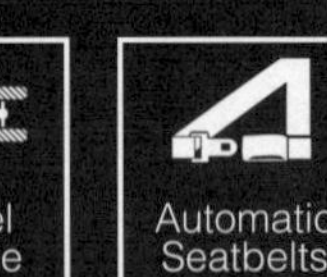
Automatic Seatbelts

Compact Wagon

2WD Base Shown

Purchase Price

Car Item	Dealer Cost	List
Base Price	**$12,535**	**$13,539**
Anti-Lock Brakes	$829	** $964
Automatic 4 Speed	$622	$723
2.4L 136 hp Gas	$156	$181
Air Conditioning	$673	$783
Power Steering	Std	Std
Cruise Control	Pkg	Pkg
4 Wheel Full-Time Drive	Std	Std
AM/FM Stereo Cassette	$156	** $181
Steering Wheel, Tilt	Std	Std
Power Windows	Pkg	Pkg
***Options Price**	$1,451	$1,687
***Total Price**	**$13,986**	**$15,226**
Target Price	$14,923	
Destination Charge	$400	
Avg. Tax & Fees	$922	
Total Target $	**$16,245**	
Average Dealer Option Cost:	***86%***	

Ownership Costs

Cost Area	5 Year Cost	Rate
Depreciation	$9,049	Average
Financing ($327/month)	$2,676	
Insurance (Rating 10)	$7,479	Average
State Fees	$625	
Fuel (Hwy 23 City 19)	$4,111	Poor
Maintenance		Insufficient Information
Repairs	$740	Worse Than Average

Ownership Cost By Year

$2,000 $4,000 $6,000 $8,000 $10,000

Legend: 1993, 1994, 1995, 1996, 1997

Insufficient Maintenance Information

Warranty/Maintenance Info

Item		Rate
Major Tune-Up		Insufficient Information
Minor Tune-Up		Insufficient Information
Brake Service	$165	Excellent
Overall Warranty	1 yr/12k	Poor
Drivetrain Warranty	7 yr/70k	Excellent
Rust Warranty	7 yr/100k	Excellent
Maintenance Warranty	N/A	
Roadside Assistance	N/A	

Resale Value

1993	1994	1995	1996	1997
$11,049	$9,939	$9,054	$8,095	$7,196

Ownership Costs (5yr)

Insufficient Information

Cumulative Costs

	1993	1994	1995	1996	1997
Annual	*Insufficient Information*				
Total	*Insufficient Information*				

Ownership Cost Rating

Insufficient Information

The 1993 Plymouth Colt Vista wagon is available in three models - (Base), SE, and AWD. New this year, the AWD model offers full cloth velour interior fabric with custom package. Exterior light blue and two-tone colors have been added to the choices. Other options include tachometer and low fuel warning light on the instrument cluster, keyless entry, power windows and locks, and electronic speed control. Standard features include mudguards and four speakers with radio, cassette, and clock.

* Includes shaded options

** Other purchase requirements apply

 Poor  Worse Than Average  Average  Better Than Average  Excellent  Insufficient Information

Refer to *Section 3: Annotated Vehicle Charts* for an explanation of these charts.

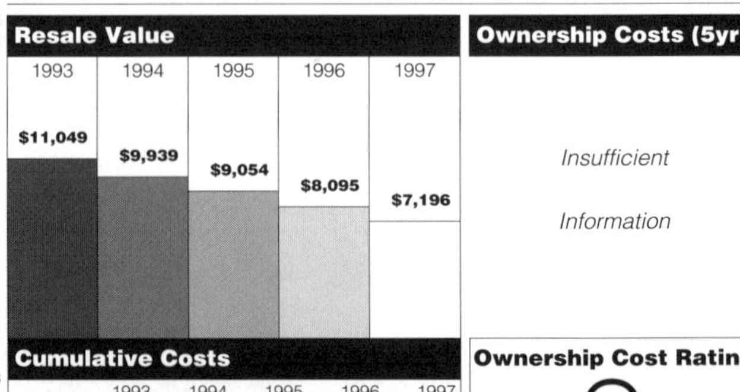

Plymouth Voyager
3 Door Pass Van

2.5L 100 hp Gas Fuel Inject.

4 Cylinder In-Line

1 3 5 / 2 4 R
Manual 5 Speed

2 Wheel Front

Driver Airbag Psngr Belts

Mini Van

Purchase Price

Car Item	Dealer Cost	List
Base Price	**$12,869**	**$14,073**
Anti-Lock Brakes	N/A	N/A
Automatic 3 Speed	$511	$601
3.0L 142 hp Gas	$590	** $694
Air Conditioning	$728	$857
Power Steering	Std	Std
Cruise Control	Pkg	Pkg
All Wheel Drive	N/A	N/A
AM/FM Stereo Cassette	$140	$165
Steering Wheel, Tilt	Pkg	Pkg
Power Windows	N/A	N/A
***Options Price**	$1,379	$1,623
***Total Price**	**$14,248**	**$15,696**
Target Price	$15,212	
Destination Charge	$540	
Avg. Tax & Fees	$950	
Total Target $	**$16,702**	
Average Dealer Option Cost:	***85%***	

Ownership Costs

Cost Area	5 Year Cost	Rate
Depreciation	$5,033	Better Than Average
Financing ($336/month)	$2,752	
Insurance (Rating 1)	$6,191	Better Than Average
State Fees	$649	
Fuel (Hwy 26 City 20)	$3,756	Better Than Average
Maintenance	$4,294	Average
Repairs	$731	Average

Warranty/Maintenance Info

Item		Rate
Major Tune-Up	$153	Better Than Average
Minor Tune-Up	$80	Excellent
Brake Service	$265	Worse Than Average
Overall Warranty	1 yr/12k	Poor
Drivetrain Warranty	7 yr/70k	Excellent
Rust Warranty	7 yr/100k	Excellent
Maintenance Warranty	N/A	
Roadside Assistance	N/A	

Ownership Cost By Year

Resale Value

1993	1994	1995	1996	1997
$15,416	$14,498	$13,718	$12,770	$11,669

Ownership Costs (5yr)

Average	This Car
$24,767	$23,406
Cost/Mile 35¢	Cost/Mile 33¢

The 1993 Voyager is available in five models -Base, SE, SE AWD, LE, and LE AWD. New for 1993, the Base Voyager offers a higher-performance torque converter and a modular clutch with 2.5L I-4 engines, a full stainless steel exhaust system, four new exterior colors, Wildberry, Light Driftwood, Sky Blue, and Flame Red, and new interior color choices, Slate Blue and Crimson Red. Other new features include air conditioning w/non-CFC refrigerant, and a quieter, higher capacity heater-air conditioner fan.

Cumulative Costs

	1993	1994	1995	1996	1997
Annual	$4,498	$4,233	$4,809	$4,116	$5,750
Total	$4,498	$8,731	$13,540	$17,656	$23,406

Ownership Cost Rating

Excellent

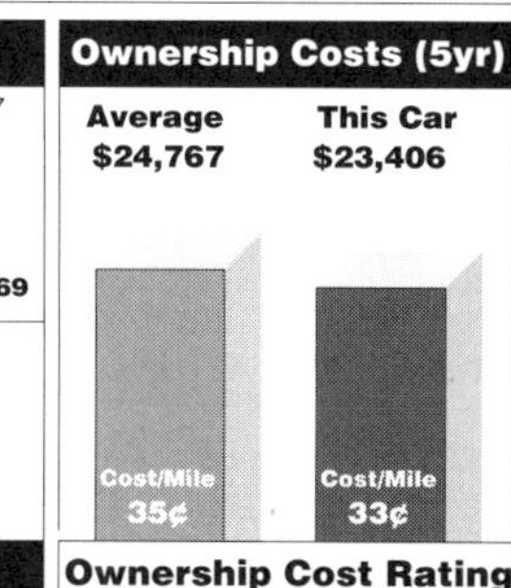

Plymouth Voyager SE
3 Door Pass Van

2.5L 100 hp Gas Fuel Inject.

4 Cylinder In-Line

Automatic 3 Speed

2 Wheel Front

Driver Airbag Psngr Belts

Mini Van

LX AWD Model Shown

Purchase Price

Car Item	Dealer Cost	List
Base Price	**$14,654**	**$16,101**
Anti-Lock Brakes	$584	** $687
4 Spd Auto Electronic	$168	** $198
3.3L 150 hp Gas	$677	$796
Air Conditioning	Pkg	Pkg
Power Steering	Std	Std
Cruise Control	Pkg	Pkg
All Wheel Drive	N/A	N/A
AM/FM Stereo Cassette	$140	$165
Steering Wheel, Tilt	Pkg	Pkg
Power Windows	Pkg	Pkg
***Options Price**	$817	$961
***Total Price**	**$15,471**	**$17,062**
Target Price	$16,574	
Destination Charge	$540	
Avg. Tax & Fees	$1,032	
Total Target $	**$18,146**	
Average Dealer Option Cost:	***85%***	

Ownership Costs

Cost Area	5 Year Cost	Rate
Depreciation	$5,969	Better Than Average
Financing ($365/month)	$2,989	
Insurance (Rating 2)	$6,333	Excellent
State Fees	$704	
Fuel (Hwy 23 City 18)	$4,213	Better Than Average
Maintenance	$4,153	Average
Repairs	$731	Average

Warranty/Maintenance Info

Item		Rate
Major Tune-Up	$160	Better Than Average
Minor Tune-Up	$100	Better Than Average
Brake Service	$265	Worse Than Average
Overall Warranty	1 yr/12k	Poor
Drivetrain Warranty	7 yr/70k	Excellent
Rust Warranty	7 yr/100k	Excellent
Maintenance Warranty	N/A	
Roadside Assistance	N/A	

Ownership Cost By Year

$2,000 · $4,000 · $6,000 · $8,000

1993 · 1994 · 1995 · 1996 · 1997

Resale Value

1993	1994	1995	1996	1997
$16,218	$15,219	$14,354	$13,337	$12,177

Ownership Costs (5yr)

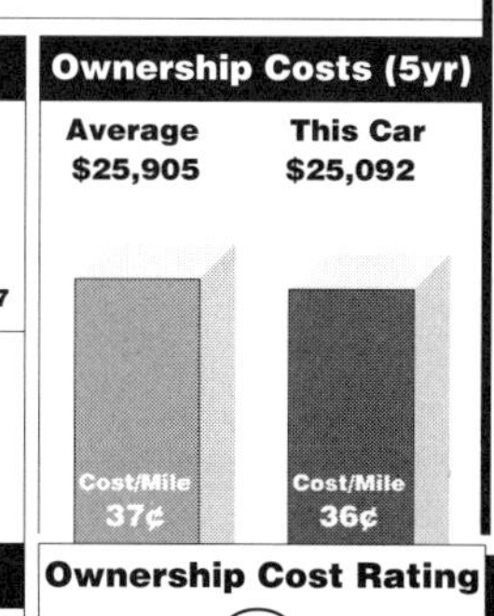

Average	This Car
$25,905	$25,092
Cost/Mile 37¢	Cost/Mile 36¢

The 1993 Voyager is available in five models -Base, SE, SE AWD, LE, and LE AWD. New for 1993, the SE provides a modular clutch and higher-performance torque converter with the 2.5L I-4 engine, a full stainless steel exhaust system, alloy wheels, air conditioning with non-CFC refrigerant, and a quieter, higher capacity heater-air conditioner fan. There are new exterior colors available--Wildberry, Light Driftwood, Sky Blue, and Flame Red Also new are two interior colors, Slate Blue and Crimson Red.

Cumulative Costs

	1993	1994	1995	1996	1997
Annual	$5,366	$4,541	$5,059	$4,363	$5,763
Total	$5,366	$9,907	$14,966	$19,329	$25,092

Ownership Cost Rating

Excellent

* Includes shaded options

** Other purchase requirements apply

Poor  Worse Than Average  Average  Better Than Average 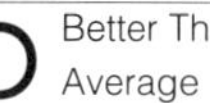 Excellent  Insufficient Information

Refer to *Section 3: Annotated Vehicle Charts* for an explanation of these charts.

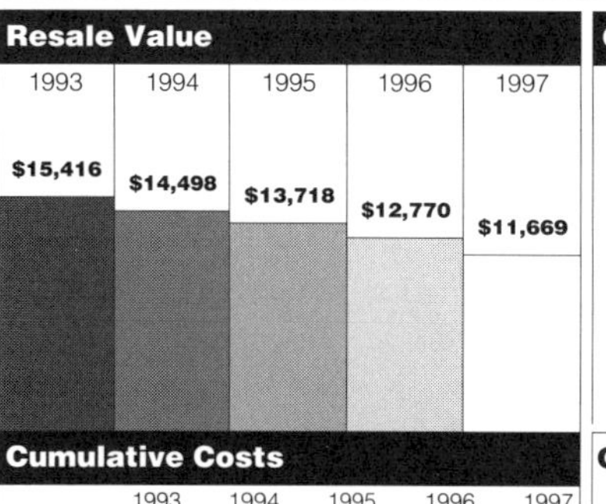

Plymouth Voyager LE
3 Door Pass Van

Mini Van

3.0L 142 hp Gas Fuel Inject.

6 Cylinder "V"

Automatic 3 Speed

2 Wheel Front

Driver Airbag Psngr Belts

AWD Model Shown

Purchase Price

Car Item	Dealer Cost	List
Base Price	**$18,704**	**$20,703**
Anti-Lock Brakes	$584	** $687
4 Spd Auto Electronic	$168	** $198
3.3L 150 hp Gas	$87	$102
Air Conditioning	Std	Std
Power Steering	Std	Std
Cruise Control	Std	Std
All Wheel Drive	N/A	N/A
AM/FM Stereo Cassette	$140	$165
Steering Wheel, Tilt	Std	Std
Power Windows	Pkg	Pkg
***Options Price**	$227	$267
***Total Price**	**$18,931**	**$20,970**
Target Price	$20,435	
Destination Charge	$540	
Avg. Tax & Fees	$1,264	
Total Target $	**$22,239**	
Average Dealer Option Cost:	***85%***	

Ownership Costs

Cost Area	5 Year Cost	Rate
Depreciation	$8,705	Average
Financing ($447/month)	$3,663	
Insurance (Rating 5)	$6,786	Excellent
State Fees	$861	
Fuel (Hwy 23 City 18)	$4,213	Better Than Average
Maintenance	$4,095	Average
Repairs	$731	Average

Ownership Cost By Year

$2,000 $4,000 $6,000 $8,000 $10,000

1993 1994 1995 1996 1997

Warranty/Maintenance Info

Item		Rate
Major Tune-Up	$160	Better Than Average
Minor Tune-Up	$100	Better Than Average
Brake Service	$265	Worse Than Average
Overall Warranty	1 yr/12k	Poor
Drivetrain Warranty	7 yr/70k	Excellent
Rust Warranty	7 yr/100k	Excellent
Maintenance Warranty	N/A	
Roadside Assistance	N/A	

Resale Value

1993	1994	1995	1996	1997
$17,852	$16,794	$15,884	$14,823	$13,534

Ownership Costs (5yr)

Average	This Car
$29,161	$29,054
Cost/Mile 42¢	Cost/Mile 42¢

The 1993 Voyager is available in five models -Base, SE, SE AWD, LE, and LE AWD. New for 1993, the LE provides a full stainless steel exhaust system, quad command seating w/tilt feature, air conditioning with non-CFC refrigerant, optional sport suspension package, and optional aluminum wheels. There are four new exterior colors to choose from--Wildberry, Light Driftwood, Sky Blue, and Flame Red. Also new are two interior colors, Slate Blue and Crimson Red, as well as new interior fabrics.

Cumulative Costs

	1993	1994	1995	1996	1997
Annual	$8,229	$4,934	$5,330	$4,578	$5,983
Total	$8,229	$13,163	$18,493	$23,071	$29,054

Ownership Cost Rating

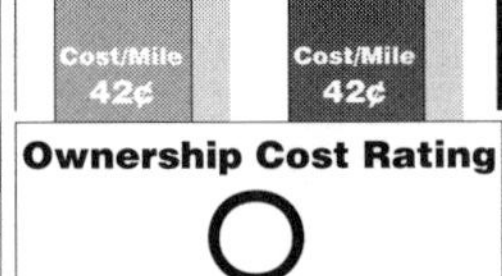

Better Than Average

Plymouth Grand Voyager
3 Door Pass Ext Van

Mini Van

3.0L 142 hp Gas Fuel Inject.

6 Cylinder "V"

Automatic 3 Speed

2 Wheel Front

Driver Airbag Psngr Belts

LE Model Shown

Purchase Price

Car Item	Dealer Cost	List
Base Price	**$15,958**	**$17,555**
Anti-Lock Brakes	N/A	N/A
Manual Transmission	N/A	N/A
Optional Engine	N/A	N/A
Air Conditioning	Pkg	Pkg
Power Steering	Std	Std
Cruise Control	Pkg	Pkg
All Wheel Drive	N/A	N/A
AM/FM Stereo Cassette	$140	$165
Steering Wheel, Tilt	Pkg	Pkg
Power Windows	N/A	N/A
***Options Price**	$140	$165
***Total Price**	**$16,098**	**$17,720**
Target Price	$17,288	
Destination Charge	$540	
Avg. Tax & Fees	$1,074	
Total Target $	**$18,902**	
Average Dealer Option Cost:	***85%***	

Ownership Costs

Cost Area	5 Year Cost	Rate
Depreciation	$5,421	Excellent
Financing ($380/month)	$3,113	
Insurance (Rating 3)	$6,520	Excellent
State Fees	$731	
Fuel (Hwy 24 City 19)	$4,015	Better Than Average
Maintenance	$4,565	Average
Repairs	$771	Average

Ownership Cost By Year

$2,000 $4,000 $6,000 $8,000

1993 1994 1995 1996 1997

Warranty/Maintenance Info

Item		Rate
Major Tune-Up	$172	Better Than Average
Minor Tune-Up	$103	Better Than Average
Brake Service	$265	Worse Than Average
Overall Warranty	1 yr/12k	Poor
Drivetrain Warranty	7 yr/70k	Excellent
Rust Warranty	7 yr/100k	Excellent
Maintenance Warranty	N/A	
Roadside Assistance	N/A	

Resale Value

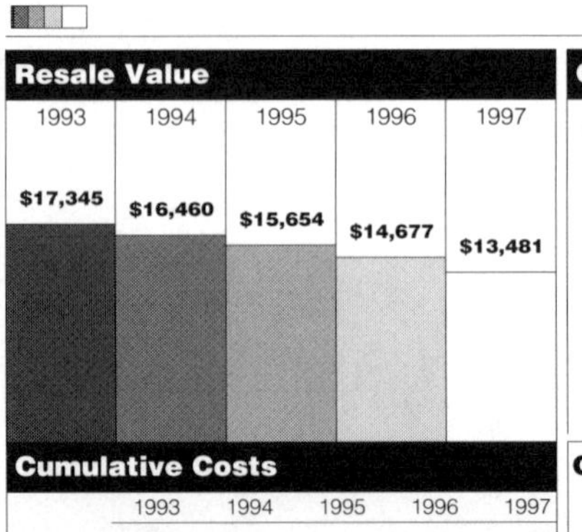

1993	1994	1995	1996	1997
$17,345	$16,460	$15,654	$14,677	$13,481

Ownership Costs (5yr)

Average	This Car
$26,453	$25,136
Cost/Mile 38¢	Cost/Mile 36¢

The 1993 Grand Voyager is available in five models - Base, SE, SE AWD, LE, and LE AWD passenger vans. New for 1993, the Grand Voyager is available in four new colors--Wildberry, Light Driftwood, Sky Blue, and Flame Red, and new interior colors, Slate Blue and Crimson Red. Other features include a full stainless steel exhaust system, new alloy wheels, quieter, higher capacity heater-air conditioner fan, alloy wheels, and air conditioning w/non-CFC refrigerant. Voyagers are built in Ontario, Canada.

Cumulative Costs

	1993	1994	1995	1996	1997
Annual	$5,054	$4,481	$5,114	$4,349	$6,138
Total	$5,054	$9,535	$14,649	$18,998	$25,136

Ownership Cost Rating

Excellent

* Includes shaded options

** Other purchase requirements apply

 Poor 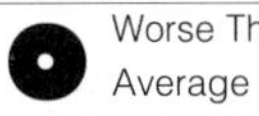 Worse Than Average  Average  Better Than Average  Excellent 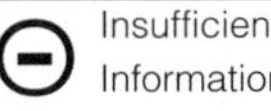 Insufficient Information

Refer to *Section 3: Annotated Vehicle Charts* for an explanation of these charts.

Plymouth Grand Voyager SE

3 Door Pass Ext Van

3.3L 150 hp Gas Fuel Inject.	6 Cylinder "V"	Automatic 4 Speed	2 Wheel Front	Driver Airbag Psngr Belts

Mini Van

Purchase Price

Car Item	Dealer Cost	List
Base Price	**$16,293**	**$17,935**
Anti-Lock Brakes	$509	** $599
Manual Transmission	N/A	N/A
Optional Engine	N/A	N/A
Air Conditioning	Pkg	Pkg
Power Steering	Std	Std
Cruise Control	Pkg	Pkg
All Wheel Drive	N/A	N/A
AM/FM Stereo Cassette	$140	$165
Steering Wheel, Tilt	Pkg	Pkg
Power Windows	Pkg	** Pkg
***Options Price**	$140	$165
***Total Price**	**$16,433**	**$18,100**
Target Price	$17,659	
Destination Charge	$540	
Avg. Tax & Fees	$1,096	
Total Target $	**$19,295**	
Average Dealer Option Cost:	***85%***	

Ownership Costs

Cost Area	5 Year Cost	Rate
Depreciation	$5,472	Excellent
Financing ($388/month)	$3,178	
Insurance (Rating 3)	$6,520	Excellent
State Fees	$745	
Fuel (Hwy 23 City 18)	$4,213	Better Than Average
Maintenance	$4,468	Average
Repairs	$771	Average

Ownership Cost By Year

$2,000 $4,000 $6,000 $8,000

1993 1994 1995 1996 1997

Warranty/Maintenance Info

Item		Rate
Major Tune-Up	$160	Better Than Average
Minor Tune-Up	$100	Better Than Average
Brake Service	$265	Worse Than Average
Overall Warranty	1 yr/12k	Poor
Drivetrain Warranty	7 yr/70k	Excellent
Rust Warranty	7 yr/100k	Excellent
Maintenance Warranty	N/A	
Roadside Assistance	N/A	

Resale Value

1993	1994	1995	1996	1997
$17,720	$16,820	$16,015	$15,021	$13,823

Ownership Costs (5yr)

	Average	This Car
Total	$26,770	$25,367
Cost/Mile	38¢	36¢

The 1993 Grand Voyager is available in five models -Base, SE, SE AWD, LE, and LE AWD. New for 1993, the Grand Voyager SE sports a full stainless steel exhaust system, sport suspension package, air conditioning with non-CFC refrigerant, and new alloy wheels. There are new exterior colors--Wildberry, Light Driftwood, Sky Blue, and Flame Red. New interior colors have been added as well, Slate Blue and Crimson Red. Other new features include quad command seating and more comfortable rear shoulder belts.

Cumulative Costs

	1993	1994	1995	1996	1997
Annual	$5,139	$4,555	$5,158	$4,410	$6,105
Total	$5,139	$9,694	$14,852	$19,262	$25,367

Ownership Cost Rating

Excellent

Plymouth Grand Voyager LE

3 Door Pass Ext Van

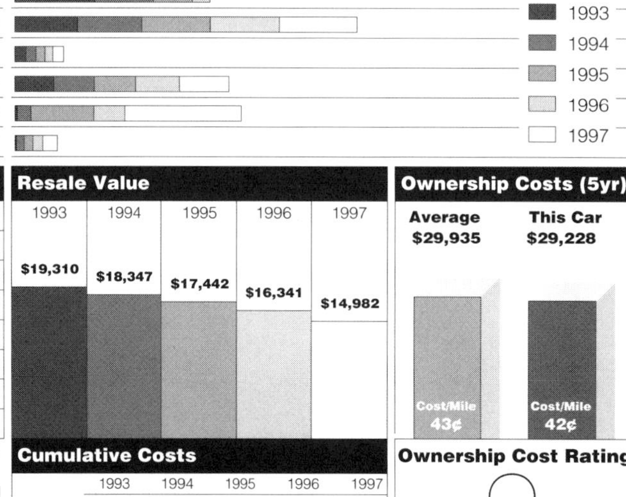

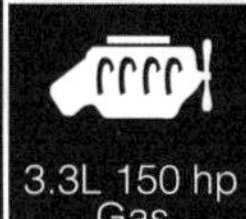	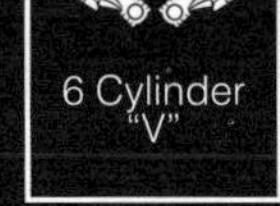	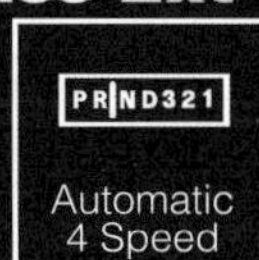		
3.3L 150 hp Gas Fuel Inject.	6 Cylinder "V"	Automatic 4 Speed	2 Wheel Front	Driver Airbag Psngr Belts

Mini Van

Purchase Price

Car Item	Dealer Cost	List
Base Price	**$19,637**	**$21,735**
Anti-Lock Brakes	$509	$599
Manual Transmission	N/A	N/A
Optional Engine	N/A	N/A
Air Conditioning	Std	Std
Power Steering	Std	Std
Cruise Control	Std	Std
All Wheel Drive	N/A	N/A
AM/FM Stereo Cassette	$140	$165
Steering Wheel, Tilt	Std	Std
Power Windows	Pkg	Pkg
***Options Price**	$140	$165
***Total Price**	**$19,777**	**$21,900**
Target Price	$21,385	
Destination Charge	$540	
Avg. Tax & Fees	$1,320	
Total Target $	**$23,245**	
Average Dealer Option Cost:	***85%***	

Ownership Costs

Cost Area	5 Year Cost	Rate
Depreciation	$8,263	Average
Financing ($467/month)	$3,829	
Insurance (Rating 5)	$6,786	Excellent
State Fees	$898	
Fuel (Hwy 23 City 18)	$4,213	Better Than Average
Maintenance	$4,468	Average
Repairs	$771	Average

Ownership Cost By Year

$2,000 $4,000 $6,000 $8,000 $10,000

1993 1994 1995 1996 1997

Warranty/Maintenance Info

Item		Rate
Major Tune-Up	$160	Better Than Average
Minor Tune-Up	$100	Better Than Average
Brake Service	$265	Worse Than Average
Overall Warranty	1 yr/12k	Poor
Drivetrain Warranty	7 yr/70k	Excellent
Rust Warranty	7 yr/100k	Excellent
Maintenance Warranty	N/A	
Roadside Assistance	N/A	

Resale Value

1993	1994	1995	1996	1997
$19,310	$18,347	$17,442	$16,341	$14,982

Ownership Costs (5yr)

	Average	This Car
Total	$29,935	$29,228
Cost/Mile	43¢	42¢

The 1993 Grand Voyager is available in five models -Base, SE, SE AWD, LE, and LE AWD. New for 1993, the LE is available in four new colors-- Wildberry, Light Driftwood, Sky Blue, and Flame Red. The LE is offering new interior fabrics and two new colors, Slate Blue and Crimson Red. Other features include a stainless steel exhaust system, an available sport suspension package, quad command seating , air conditioning with non-CFC refrigerant, a quieter , and higher capacity heater-air conditioning fan.

Cumulative Costs

	1993	1994	1995	1996	1997
Annual	$7,857	$4,907	$5,471	$4,646	$6,347
Total	$7,857	$12,764	$18,235	$22,881	$29,228

Ownership Cost Rating

Excellent

* Includes shaded options

** Other purchase requirements apply

 Poor  Worse Than Average  Average  Better Than Average 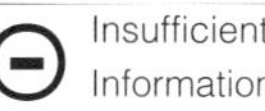 Excellent — Insufficient Information

Refer to *Section 3: Annotated Vehicle Charts* for an explanation of these charts.

Plymouth Voyager SE AWD
3 Door Pass Van

3.3L 150 hp Gas Fuel Inject.

6 Cylinder "V"

Automatic 4 Speed

4 Wheel Full-Time

Driver Airbag Psngr Belts

LX Model Shown

Purchase Price

Car Item	Dealer Cost	List
Base Price	**$17,481**	**$19,285**
Anti-Lock Brakes	$509	** $599
Manual Transmission	N/A	N/A
Optional Engine	N/A	N/A
Air Conditioning	Pkg	Pkg
Power Steering	Std	Std
Cruise Control	Pkg	Pkg
4 Wheel Full-Time Drive	Std	Std
AM/FM Stereo Cassette	$140	$165
Steering Wheel, Tilt	Pkg	Pkg
Power Windows	Pkg	Pkg
***Options Price**	$140	$165
***Total Price**	**$17,621**	**$19,450**
Target Price	$18,977	
Destination Charge	$540	
Avg. Tax & Fees	$1,176	
Total Target $	**$20,693**	
Average Dealer Option Cost:	***85%***	

Ownership Costs

Cost Area	5 Year Cost	Rate
Depreciation	$6,872	Better Than Average
Financing ($416/month)	$3,409	
Insurance (Rating 4)	$6,658	Excellent
State Fees	$800	
Fuel (Hwy 22 City 17)	$4,431	Average
Maintenance	$4,363	Average
Repairs	$731	Average

Ownership Cost By Year

$2,000 $4,000 $6,000 $8,000

1993 1994 1995 1996 1997

Warranty/Maintenance Info

Item		Rate
Major Tune-Up	$160	Better Than Average
Minor Tune-Up	$100	Better Than Average
Brake Service	$295	Poor
Overall Warranty	1 yr/12k	Poor
Drivetrain Warranty	7 yr/70k	Excellent
Rust Warranty	7 yr/100k	Excellent
Maintenance Warranty	N/A	
Roadside Assistance	N/A	

Resale Value

1993	1994	1995	1996	1997
$18,287	$17,192	$16,228	$15,112	$13,821

Ownership Costs (5yr)

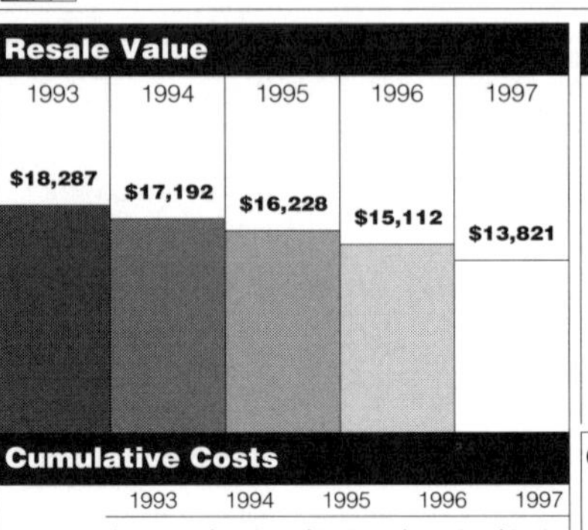

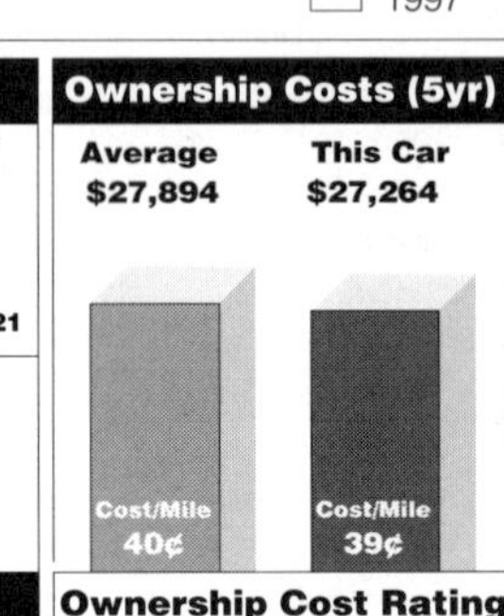

Average	This Car
$27,894	$27,264
Cost/Mile 40¢	Cost/Mile 39¢

The 1993 Voyager is available in five models -Base, SE, SE AWD, LE, and LE AWD. New for 1993, the SE AWD model presents a new decor package (with five-spoke wheels), a rear heater-air conditioner, and a stainless steel exhaust system. Also new are exterior colors--Wildberry, Light Driftwood, Sky Blue, and Flame Red, as well as added choices of interior color, Slate Blue and Crimson Red. Other new features include vertically-adjustable front shoulder belts, and more comfortable rear shoulder belts.

Cumulative Costs

	1993	1994	1995	1996	1997
Annual	$6,143	$4,894	$5,470	$4,623	$6,134
Total	$6,143	$11,037	$16,507	$21,130	$27,264

Ownership Cost Rating

Excellent

Plymouth Voyager LE AWD
3 Door Pass Van

3.3L 150 hp Gas Fuel Inject.

6 Cylinder "V"

Automatic 4 Speed

4 Wheel Full-Time

Driver Airbag Psngr Belts

Purchase Price

Car Item	Dealer Cost	List
Base Price	**$20,920**	**$23,193**
Anti-Lock Brakes	$509	$599
Manual Transmission	N/A	N/A
Optional Engine	N/A	N/A
Air Conditioning	Std	Std
Power Steering	Std	Std
Cruise Control	Std	Std
4 Wheel Full-Time Drive	Std	Std
AM/FM Stereo Cassette	$140	$165
Steering Wheel, Tilt	Std	Std
Power Windows	Pkg	Pkg
***Options Price**	$140	$165
***Total Price**	**$21,060**	**$23,358**
Target Price	$22,827	
Destination Charge	$540	
Avg. Tax & Fees	$1,407	
Total Target $	**$24,774**	
Average Dealer Option Cost:	***85%***	

Ownership Costs

Cost Area	5 Year Cost	Rate
Depreciation	$9,257	Average
Financing ($498/month)	$4,081	
Insurance (Rating 6)	$6,919	Excellent
State Fees	$955	
Fuel (Hwy 22 City 17)	$4,431	Average
Maintenance	$4,363	Average
Repairs	$731	Average

Ownership Cost By Year

$2,000 $4,000 $6,000 $8,000 $10,000

1993 1994 1995 1996 1997

Warranty/Maintenance Info

Item		Rate
Major Tune-Up	$160	Better Than Average
Minor Tune-Up	$100	Better Than Average
Brake Service	$295	Poor
Overall Warranty	1 yr/12k	Poor
Drivetrain Warranty	7 yr/70k	Excellent
Rust Warranty	7 yr/100k	Excellent
Maintenance Warranty	N/A	
Roadside Assistance	N/A	

Resale Value

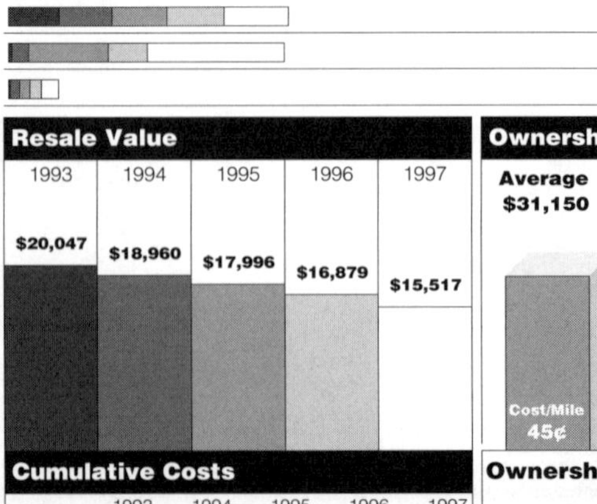

1993	1994	1995	1996	1997
$20,047	$18,960	$17,996	$16,879	$15,517

Ownership Costs (5yr)

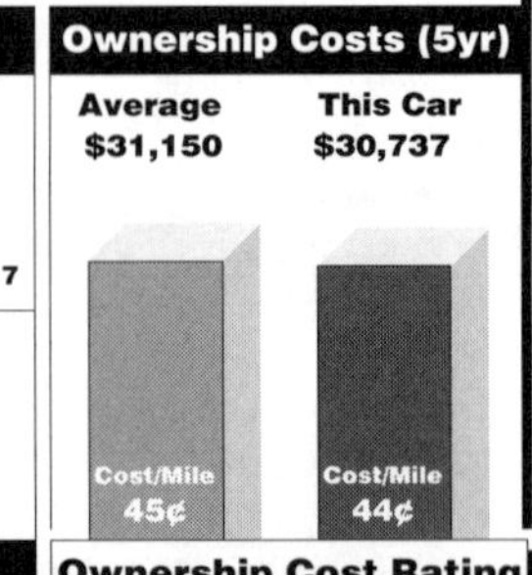

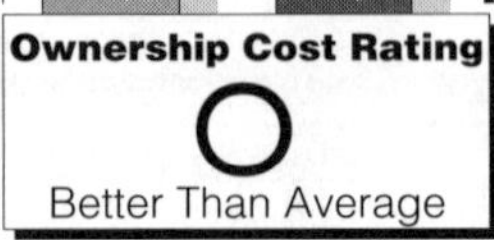

Average	This Car
$31,150	$30,737
Cost/Mile 45¢	Cost/Mile 44¢

The 1993 Voyager is available in five models -Base, SE, SE AWD, LE, and LE AWD. New for 1993, the LE AWD model presents four new exterior colors--Wildberry, Light Driftwood, Sky Blue, and Flame Red There are also two added interior colors, Slate Blue and Crimson Red, as well as new interior fabrics. Other new features include an added decor package (with five-spoke wheels), a rear heater-air conditioner, a full stainless steel exhaust system, and air conditioning with non-CFC refrigerant.

Cumulative Costs

	1993	1994	1995	1996	1997
Annual	$8,831	$5,183	$5,686	$4,753	$6,284
Total	$8,831	$14,014	$19,700	$24,453	$30,737

Ownership Cost Rating

Better Than Average

* Includes shaded options

** Other purchase requirements apply

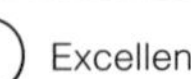

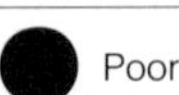 Poor  Worse Than Average 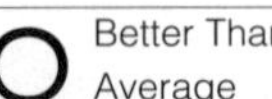 Average Better Than Average  Excellent Insufficient Information

Refer to *Section 3: Annotated Vehicle Charts* for an explanation of these charts.

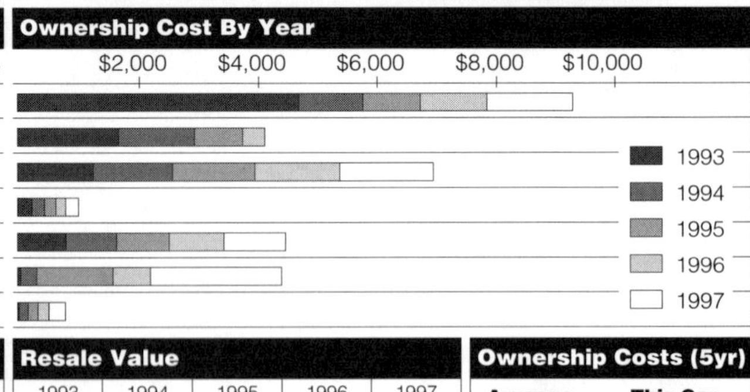

Plymouth Grand Voyager SE AWD 3 Door Pass Ext Van

Mini Van

3.3L 150 hp Gas Fuel Inject.

6 Cylinder "V"

Automatic 4 Speed

4 Wheel Full-Time

Driver Airbag Psngr Belts

2WD Model Shown

Purchase Price

Car Item	Dealer Cost	List
Base Price	**$18,141**	**$20,035**
Anti-Lock Brakes	$509	** $599
Manual Transmission	N/A	N/A
Optional Engine	N/A	N/A
Air Conditioning	Pkg	Pkg
Power Steering	Std	Std
Cruise Control	Pkg	Pkg
4 Wheel Full-Time Drive	Std	Std
AM/FM Stereo Cassette	$140	$165
Steering Wheel, Tilt	Pkg	Pkg
Power Windows	Pkg	** Pkg
***Options Price**	$140	$165
***Total Price**	**$18,281**	**$20,200**
Target Price	$19,713	
Destination Charge	$540	
Avg. Tax & Fees	$1,220	
Total Target $	**$21,473**	
Average Dealer Option Cost:	***85%***	

Ownership Costs

Cost Area	5 Year Cost	Rate
Depreciation	$5,341	Better Than Average
Financing ($432/month)	$3,537	
Insurance (Rating 5)	$6,786	Excellent
State Fees	$829	
Fuel (Hwy 22 City 17)	$4,431	Average
Maintenance	$4,402	Average
Repairs	$771	Average

Ownership Cost By Year

$2,000 $4,000 $6,000 $8,000

1993 1994 1995 1996 1997

Warranty/Maintenance Info

Item		Rate
Major Tune-Up	$160	Better Than Average
Minor Tune-Up	$100	Better Than Average
Brake Service	$295	Poor
Overall Warranty	1 yr/12k	Poor
Drivetrain Warranty	7 yr/70k	Excellent
Rust Warranty	7 yr/100k	Excellent
Maintenance Warranty	N/A	
Roadside Assistance	N/A	

Resale Value

1993	1994	1995	1996	1997
$20,125	$19,245	$18,430	$17,423	$16,132

Ownership Costs (5yr)

Average	This Car
$28,519	$26,097
Cost/Mile 41¢	Cost/Mile 37¢

Cumulative Costs

	1993	1994	1995	1996	1997
Annual	$5,171	$4,760	$5,386	$4,564	$6,216
Total	$5,171	$9,931	$15,317	$19,881	$26,097

Ownership Cost Rating

Excellent

The 1993 Grand Voyager is available in five models -Base, SE, SE AWD, LE, and LE AWD. New for 1993, the SE AWD adds a new decor package (with five-spoke aluminum wheels) and a rear heater-air conditioner. Other new features include a full stainless steel exhaust system, air conditioning with non-CFC refrigerant, a sport suspension package, and new interior colors (Wildberry, Light Driftwood, Sky Blue, and Flame Red). Two new interior colors have been added as well (Slate Blue and Crimson Red).

Plymouth

Plymouth Grand Voyager LE AWD 3 Door Pass Ext Van

Mini Van

3.3L 150 hp Gas Fuel Inject.

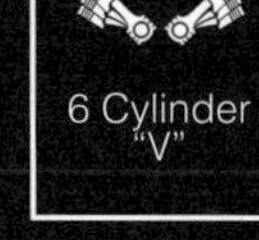
6 Cylinder "V"

Automatic 4 Speed

4 Wheel Full-Time

Driver Airbag Psngr Belts

2WD Model Shown

Purchase Price

Car Item	Dealer Cost	List
Base Price	**$21,485**	**$23,835**
Anti-Lock Brakes	$509	$599
Manual Transmission	N/A	N/A
Optional Engine	N/A	N/A
Air Conditioning	Std	Std
Power Steering	Std	Std
Cruise Control	Std	Std
4 Wheel Full-Time Drive	Std	Std
AM/FM Stereo Cassette	$140	$165
Steering Wheel, Tilt	Std	Std
Power Windows	Pkg	Pkg
***Options Price**	$140	$165
***Total Price**	**$21,625**	**$24,000**
Target Price	$23,464	
Destination Charge	$540	
Avg. Tax & Fees	$1,445	
Total Target $	**$25,449**	
Average Dealer Option Cost:	***87%***	

Ownership Costs

Cost Area	5 Year Cost	Rate
Depreciation	$8,331	Better Than Average
Financing ($511/month)	$4,192	
Insurance (Rating 6)	$6,919	Excellent
State Fees	$981	
Fuel (Hwy 22 City 17)	$4,431	Average
Maintenance	$4,536	Average
Repairs	$771	Average

Ownership Cost By Year

$2,000 $4,000 $6,000 $8,000 $10,000

1993 1994 1995 1996 1997

Warranty/Maintenance Info

Item		Rate
Major Tune-Up	$160	Better Than Average
Minor Tune-Up	$100	Better Than Average
Brake Service	$295	Poor
Overall Warranty	1 yr/12k	Poor
Drivetrain Warranty	7 yr/70k	Excellent
Rust Warranty	7 yr/100k	Excellent
Maintenance Warranty	N/A	
Roadside Assistance	N/A	

Resale Value

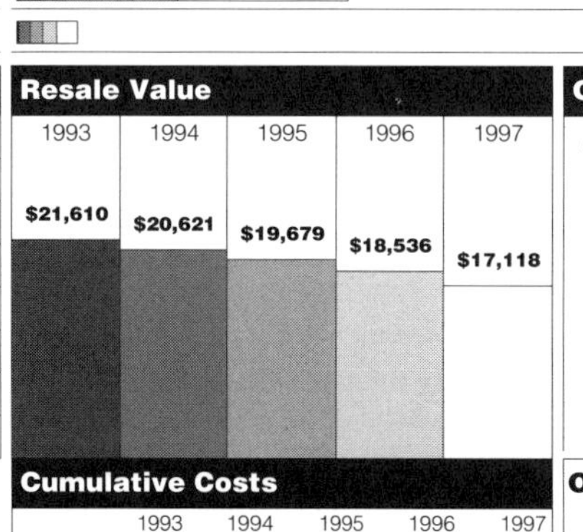

1993	1994	1995	1996	1997
$21,610	$20,621	$19,679	$18,536	$17,118

Ownership Costs (5yr)

Average	This Car
$31,685	$30,161
Cost/Mile 45¢	Cost/Mile 43¢

Cumulative Costs

	1993	1994	1995	1996	1997
Annual	$7,997	$5,133	$5,700	$4,803	$6,528
Total	$7,997	$13,130	$18,830	$23,633	$30,161

Ownership Cost Rating

Excellent

The 1993 Grand Voyager is available in five models -Base, SE, SE AWD, LE, and LE AWD. New for 1993, the LE AWD offers a new decor package (with five-spoke wheels), and a rear heater-air conditioner. Also added is a full stainless steel exhaust system, an optional sport suspension package, and air conditioning with non-CFC refrigerant. There are four new exterior colors added--Wildberry, Light Driftwood, Sky Blue, and Flame Red. Two new interior colors have also been added, Slate Blue and Crimson Red.

* Includes shaded options

** Other purchase requirements apply

Poor | Worse Than Average | Average | Better Than Average | Excellent | Insufficient Information

Refer to *Section 3: Annotated Vehicle Charts* for an explanation of these charts.

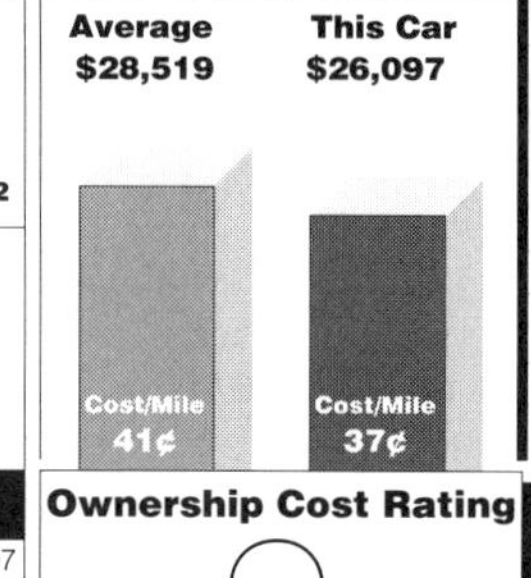

Pontiac Trans Sport SE
3 Door Pass Van

3.1L 120 hp Gas Fuel Inject.

6 Cylinder "V"

PR|ND21 Automatic 3 Speed

2 Wheel Front

Manual Seatbelts Only

Mini Van

Purchase Price

Car Item	Dealer Cost	List
Base Price	**$15,104**	**$16,689**
Anti-Lock Brakes	Std	Std
4 Spd Auto	N/C	N/C
3.8L 170 hp Gas	$704	$819
Air Conditioning	$714	$830
Power Steering	Std	Std
Cruise Control	$194	$225
All Wheel Drive	N/A	N/A
AM/FM Stereo Cassette	$120	$140
Steering Wheel, Tilt	$125	$145
Power Windows	$237	** $275
***Options Price**	$1,732	$2,014
***Total Price**	**$16,836**	**$18,703**
Target Price	$18,234	
Destination Charge	$530	
Avg. Tax & Fees	$1,130	
Total Target $	**$19,894**	
Average Dealer Option Cost:	***86%***	

Ownership Costs

Cost Area	5 Year Cost	Rate
Depreciation	$8,779	Worse Than Average
Financing ($400/month)	$3,277	
Insurance (Rating 8)	$7,432	Excellent
State Fees	$769	
Fuel (Hwy 25 City 17)	$4,145	Better Than Average
Maintenance	$4,675	Worse Than Average
Repairs	$709	Better Than Average

Ownership Cost By Year

$2,000 $4,000 $6,000 $8,000 $10,000

1993 1994 1995 1996 1997

Warranty/Maintenance Info

Item	Cost/Coverage	Rate
Major Tune-Up	$192	Average
Minor Tune-Up	$130	Worse Than Average
Brake Service	$209	Better Than Average
Overall Warranty	3 yr/36k	Average
Drivetrain Warranty	3 yr/36k	Average
Rust Warranty	6 yr/100k	Better Than Average
Maintenance Warranty	N/A	
Roadside Assistance	3 yr/36k	

Resale Value

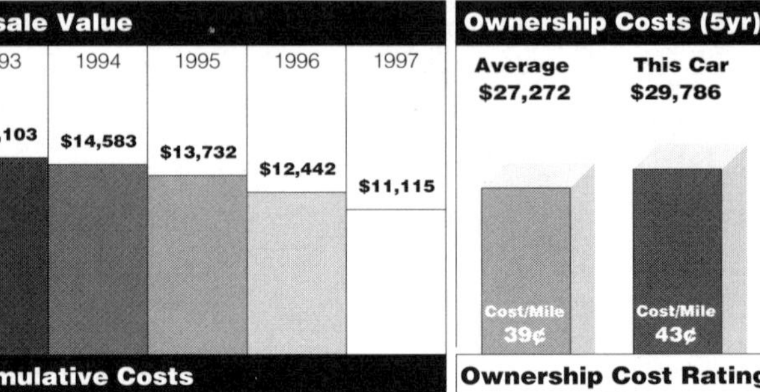

1993	1994	1995	1996	1997
$15,103	$14,583	$13,732	$12,442	$11,115

Ownership Costs (5yr)

Average	This Car
$27,272	$29,786
Cost/Mile 39¢	Cost/Mile 43¢

The 1993 Pontiac Trans Sport SE is a one model line-up. New for 1993, the Trans Sport SE adds a pop-up sunroof, steering wheel radio controls, rear storage saddlebags and a Quiet Package. Optional items include a solar glass windshield, driver's side four-way seat adjusters, deep tinted glass, luggage rack and power mirrors. A towing package is an option consisting of automatic level control, and a heavy-duty cooling system. The Trans Sport also offers leather seating areas, and modular seats.

Cumulative Costs

	1993	1994	1995	1996	1997
Annual	$8,545	$4,237	$5,265	$5,143	$6,596
Total	$8,545	$12,782	$18,047	$23,190	$29,786

Ownership Cost Rating

Poor

Saturn SW1
4 Door Wagon

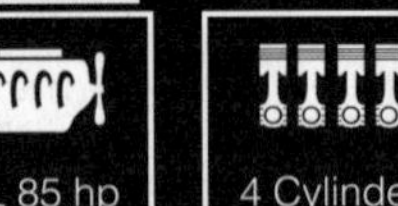

1.9L 85 hp Gas Fuel Inject.

4 Cylinder In-Line

Manual 5 Speed

2 Wheel Front

Driver Airbag Psngr Belts

Compact Wagon

Purchase Price

Car Item	Dealer Cost	List
Base Price	**$9,697**	**$10,895**
Anti-Lock Brakes	$530	$595
Automatic 4 Speed	$667	$750
Optional Engine	N/A	N/A
Air Conditioning	$739	$830
Power Steering	Std	Std
Cruise Control	$196	$220
All Wheel Drive	N/A	N/A
AM/FM Stereo Cassette	$160	$180
Steering Wheel, Tilt	Std	Std
Power Windows	Pkg	Pkg
***Options Price**	$1,566	$1,760
***Total Price**	**$11,263**	**$12,655**
Target Price	$12,355	
Destination Charge	$300	
Avg. Tax & Fees	$763	
Total Target $	**$13,418**	
Average Dealer Option Cost:	***89%***	

Ownership Costs

Cost Area	5 Year Cost	Rate
Depreciation		Insufficient Information
Financing ($270/month)	$2,211	
Insurance (Rating 4)	$6,658	Average
State Fees	$520	
Fuel (Hwy 35 City 25)	$2,890	Excellent
Maintenance	$3,617	Excellent
Repairs	$610	Excellent

Ownership Cost By Year

$2,000 $4,000 $6,000 $8,000

Insufficient Depreciation Information

1993 1994 1995 1996 1997

Warranty/Maintenance Info

Item	Cost/Coverage	Rate
Major Tune-Up	$116	Excellent
Minor Tune-Up	$86	Better Than Average
Brake Service	$178	Better Than Average
Overall Warranty	3 yr/36k	Average
Drivetrain Warranty	3 yr/36k	Average
Rust Warranty	6 yr/100k	Better Than Average
Maintenance Warranty	N/A	
Roadside Assistance	3 yr/36k	

Resale Value

Insufficient Information

Ownership Costs (5yr)

Insufficient Information

The all-new Saturn SW wagon is available in SW1 and SW2 editions. The Saturn wagon required a modification of the sedan's spaceframe to incorporate a cargo area which boasts a volume of 28.8 cubic feet. Standard features on the SW1 wagon include a 1.9L 4 Cylinder SOHC powertrain, power disc/drum brakes, rear seat heater ducts, intermittent windshield wipers, and remote tailgate release. Optional equipment includes an anti-lock braking system, air conditioning and cruise control.

Cumulative Costs

	1993	1994	1995	1996	1997
Annual	*Insufficient Information*				
Total	*Insufficient Information*				

Ownership Cost Rating

Insufficient Information

* Includes shaded options

** Other purchase requirements apply

Poor

Worse Than Average

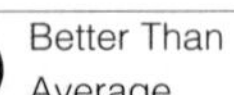

Average

Better Than Average

Excellent

Insufficient Information

Refer to *Section 3: Annotated Vehicle Charts* for an explanation of these charts.

Saturn SW2

4 Door Wagon

1.9L 124 hp Gas Fuel Inject. | 4 Cylinder In-Line | Manual 5 Speed | 2 Wheel Front | Driver Airbag Psngr Belts

Compact Wagon

Purchase Price

Car Item	Dealer Cost	List
Base Price	**$10,854**	**$12,195**
Anti-Lock Brakes	$530	$595
Automatic 4 Speed	$667	$750
Optional Engine	N/A	N/A
Air Conditioning	$739	$830
Power Steering	Std	Std
Cruise Control	$196	$220
All Wheel Drive	N/A	N/A
AM/FM Stereo Cassette	$160	$180
Steering Wheel, Tilt	Std	Std
Power Windows	Pkg	Pkg
***Options Price**	$1,566	$1,760
***Total Price**	**$12,420**	**$13,955**
Target Price	$13,655	
Destination Charge	$300	
Avg. Tax & Fees	$841	
Total Target $	**$14,796**	
Average Dealer Option Cost:	***89%***	

Ownership Costs

Cost Area	5 Year Cost	Rate
Depreciation		Insufficient Information
Financing ($297/month)	$2,437	
Insurance (Rating 5)	$6,786	Average
State Fees	$571	
Fuel (Hwy 33 City 24)	$3,039	Excellent
Maintenance	$4,436	Better Than Average
Repairs	$610	Excellent

Ownership Cost By Year

$2,000 $4,000 $6,000 $8,000

Insufficient Depreciation Information

1993 1994 1995 1996 1997

Warranty/Maintenance Info

Item		Rate
Major Tune-Up	$196	Worse Than Average
Minor Tune-Up	$166	Poor
Brake Service	$178	Better Than Average
Overall Warranty	3 yr/36k	Average
Drivetrain Warranty	3 yr/36k	Average
Rust Warranty	6 yr/100k	Better Than Average
Maintenance Warranty	N/A	
Roadside Assistance	3 yr/36k	

Resale Value

Insufficient Information

Ownership Costs (5yr)

Insufficient Information

The all-new Saturn SW wagon is available in SW1 and SW2 editions. In addition to or replacing all the standard features of the SW1 wagon, the SW2 comes with a 1.9L 4 Cylinder DOHC powertrain which provides considerably more perfomance and larger tires. The SW2 has numerous optional items such as front fog lamps, 15 inch alloy "geartooth" wheels and a variety of AM/FM cassette stereos. The SW wagons feature corrostion-resistant sheet molded compound (SMC) exterior roofs and tailgates.

Cumulative Costs

	1993	1994	1995	1996	1997
Annual	*Insufficient Information*				
Total	*Insufficient Information*				

Ownership Cost Rating

Insufficient Information

Subaru Legacy L

4 Door Wagon

2.2L 130 hp Gas Fuel Inject. | 4 Cylinder Opposing | Manual 5 Speed | 2 Wheel Front | Driver Airbag Psngr Belts

Compact Wagon

Purchase Price

Car Item	Dealer Cost	List
Base Price	**$15,025**	**$16,950**
Anti-Lock Brakes	N/A	N/A
Automatic 4 Speed	$721	$800
Optional Engine	N/A	N/A
Air Conditioning	Std	Std
Power Steering	Std	Std
Cruise Control	Std	Std
All Wheel Drive	N/A	N/A
AM/FM Stereo Cassette	Std	Std
Steering, Tilt w/Memory	Std	Std
Power Windows	Std	Std
***Options Price**	$721	$800
***Total Price**	**$15,746**	**$17,750**
Target Price	$16,200	
Destination Charge	$445	
Avg. Tax & Fees	$1,014	
Total Target $	**$17,659**	
Average Dealer Option Cost:	***90%***	

Ownership Costs

Cost Area	5 Year Cost	Rate
Depreciation	$8,279	Better Than Average
Financing ($355/month)	$2,909	
Insurance (Rating 7)	$7,035	Average
State Fees	$728	
Fuel (Hwy 29 City 22)	$3,390	Better Than Average
Maintenance	$5,279	Worse Than Average
Repairs	$560	Excellent

Ownership Cost By Year

$2,000 $4,000 $6,000 $8,000 $10,000

1993 1994 1995 1996 1997

Warranty/Maintenance Info

Item		Rate
Major Tune-Up	$145	Better Than Average
Minor Tune-Up	$89	Better Than Average
Brake Service	$239	Worse Than Average
Overall Warranty	3 yr/36k	Average
Drivetrain Warranty	5 yr/60k	Excellent
Rust Warranty	5 yr/unlim. mi	Better Than Average
Maintenance Warranty	N/A	
Roadside Assistance	3 yr/36k	

Resale Value

1993	1994	1995	1996	1997
$13,276	$12,236	$11,950	$10,632	$9,380

Ownership Costs (5yr)

Average	This Car
$29,735	$28,180
Cost/Mile 42¢	Cost/Mile 40¢

The 1993 Subaru Legacy is available in twelve models - L, LS, L 4WD, LS 4WD, LSi 4WD and Sport 4WD sedans; and L, LS, L 4WD, LS 4WD, LSi 4WD and Touring 4WD wagons. New for 1993, the L wagon receives a driver airbag, 60/40 rear split seats and one new color (Jasper Green). Features include power windows and door locks, rear-window defogger, 4-wheel independent suspension, intermittent windshield wipers and front bucket seats. Options include an automatic transmission and air conditioning.

Cumulative Costs

	1993	1994	1995	1996	1997
Annual	$7,746	$4,320	$4,195	$4,590	$7,329
Total	$7,746	$12,066	$16,261	$20,851	$28,180

Ownership Cost Rating

Better Than Average

* Includes shaded options

** Other purchase requirements apply

 Poor Worse Than Average  Average  Better Than Average 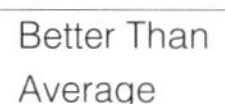 Excellent  Insufficient Information

Refer to *Section 3: Annotated Vehicle Charts* for an explanation of these charts.

Subaru Legacy LS

4 Door Wagon

2.2L 130 hp Gas Fuel Inject. | 4 Cylinder Opposing | Automatic 4 Speed

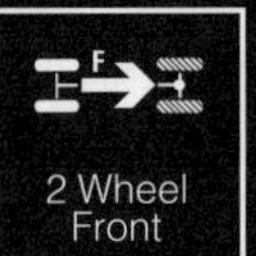

2 Wheel Front

Driver Airbag Psngr Belts

Compact Wagon

Purchase Price

Car Item	Dealer Cost	List
Base Price	**$17,444**	**$19,850**
Anti-Lock Brakes	Std	Std
Manual Transmission	N/A	N/A
Optional Engine	N/A	N/A
Air Conditioning	Std	Std
Power Steering	Std	Std
Cruise Control	Std	Std
All Wheel Drive	N/A	N/A
AM/FM Stereo Cassette	Std	Std
Steering, Tilt w/Memory	Std	Std
Power Windows	Std	Std
***Options Price**	$0	$0
***Total Price**	**$17,444**	**$19,850**
Target Price	$17,981	
Destination Charge	$445	
Avg. Tax & Fees	$1,124	
Total Target $	**$19,550**	
Average Dealer Option Cost:	***83%***	

Ownership Costs

Cost Area	5 Year Cost	Rate
Depreciation	$10,258	Average
Financing ($393/month)	$3,221	
Insurance (Rating 13)	$8,061	Average
State Fees	$812	
Fuel (Hwy 29 City 22)	$3,390	Better Than Average
Maintenance	$5,279	Worse Than Average
Repairs	$560	Excellent

Ownership Cost By Year

$2,000 $4,000 $6,000 $8,000 $10,000 $12,000

1993 1994 1995 1996 1997

Warranty/Maintenance Info

Item		Rate
Major Tune-Up	$145	Better Than Average
Minor Tune-Up	$89	Better Than Average
Brake Service	$239	Worse Than Average
Overall Warranty	3 yr/36k	Average
Drivetrain Warranty	5 yr/60k	Excellent
Rust Warranty	5 yr/unlim. mi	Better Than Average
Maintenance Warranty	N/A	
Roadside Assistance	3 yr/36k	

Resale Value

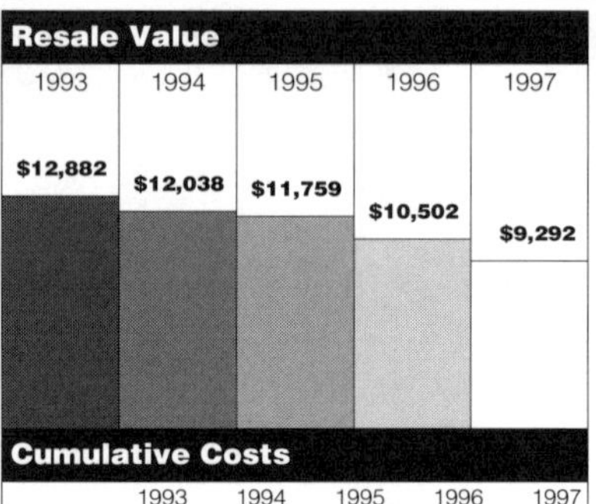

1993	1994	1995	1996	1997
$12,882	$12,038	$11,759	$10,502	$9,292

Ownership Costs (5yr)

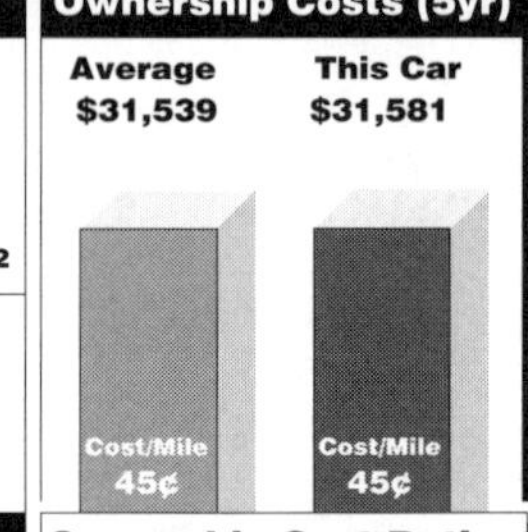

Average	This Car
$31,539	$31,581
Cost/Mile 45¢	Cost/Mile 45¢

Cumulative Costs

	1993	1994	1995	1996	1997
Annual	$10,370	$4,438	$4,471	$4,780	$7,522
Total	$10,370	$14,808	$19,279	$24,059	$31,581

Ownership Cost Rating

Average

The 1993 Subaru Legacy is available in twelve models - L, LS, L 4WD, LS 4WD, LSi 4WD and Sport 4WD sedans; and L, LS, L 4WD, LS 4WD, LSi 4WD and Touring 4WD wagons. New for 1993, the LS wagon receives a driver airbag, 60/40 rear split seats and one new exterior color (Jasper Green). Features include power windows and door locks, four-wheel independent suspension and front bucket seats. Other features include alloy wheels, power moon-roof with rear tilt feature and optional air conditioning.

Subaru Legacy L AWD

4 Door Wagon

2.2L 130 hp Gas Fuel Inject. | 4 Cylinder Opposing | Manual 5 Speed

4 Wheel Full-Time

Driver Airbag Psngr Belts

Compact Wagon

L 2WD Model Shown

Purchase Price

Car Item	Dealer Cost	List
Base Price	**$16,444**	**$18,550**
Anti-Lock Brakes	$873	$995
Automatic 4 Speed	$721	$800
Optional Engine	N/A	N/A
Air Conditioning	Std	Std
Power Steering	Std	Std
Cruise Control	Std	Std
4 Wheel Full-Time Drive	Std	Std
AM/FM Stereo Cassette	Std	Std
Steering, Tilt w/Memory	Std	Std
Power Windows	Std	Std
***Options Price**	$721	$800
***Total Price**	**$17,165**	**$19,350**
Target Price	$17,679	
Destination Charge	$445	
Avg. Tax & Fees	$1,104	
Total Target $	**$19,228**	
Average Dealer Option Cost:	***89%***	

Ownership Costs

Cost Area	5 Year Cost	Rate
Depreciation	$8,983	Better Than Average
Financing ($386/month)	$3,167	
Insurance (Rating 11)	$7,693	Average
State Fees	$792	
Fuel (Hwy 27 City 21)	$3,598	Average
Maintenance	$5,267	Worse Than Average
Repairs	$630	Better Than Average

Ownership Cost By Year

$2,000 $4,000 $6,000 $8,000 $10,000

1993 1994 1995 1996 1997

Warranty/Maintenance Info

Item		Rate
Major Tune-Up	$145	Better Than Average
Minor Tune-Up	$89	Better Than Average
Brake Service	$239	Worse Than Average
Overall Warranty	3 yr/36k	Average
Drivetrain Warranty	5 yr/60k	Excellent
Rust Warranty	5 yr/unlim. mi	Better Than Average
Maintenance Warranty	N/A	
Roadside Assistance	3 yr/36k	

Resale Value

1993	1994	1995	1996	1997
$14,429	$13,307	$12,995	$11,569	$10,245

Ownership Costs (5yr)

Average	This Car
$31,109	$30,130
Cost/Mile 44¢	Cost/Mile 43¢

Cumulative Costs

	1993	1994	1995	1996	1997
Annual	$8,444	$4,663	$4,467	$4,925	$7,631
Total	$8,444	$13,107	$17,574	$22,499	$30,130

Ownership Cost Rating

Better Than Average

The 1993 Subaru Legacy is available in twelve models - L, LS, L 4WD, LS 4WD, LSi 4WD and Sport 4WD sedans; and L, LS, L 4WD, LS 4WD, LSi 4WD and Touring 4WD wagons. New for 1993, the L 4WD wagon receives a driver airbag, 60/40 rear split seats and one new exterior color (Jasper Green). Features include power windows, power door locks, rear-window defogger, four-wheel independent suspension, intermittent windshield wipers, cloth upholstery and front bucket seats.

* Includes shaded options

** Other purchase requirements apply

 Poor  Worse Than Average  Average  Better Than Average 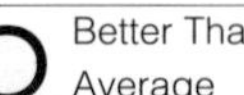 Excellent 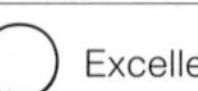 Insufficient Information

Refer to *Section 3: Annotated Vehicle Charts* for an explanation of these charts.

Subaru Legacy LS AWD

4 Door Wagon

2.2L 130 hp Gas Fuel Inject.

4 Cylinder Opposing

Automatic 4 Speed

4 Wheel Full-Time

Driver Airbag Psngr Belts

Purchase Price

Car Item	Dealer Cost	List
Base Price	**$18,850**	**$21,450**
Anti-Lock Brakes	Std	Std
Manual Transmission	N/A	N/A
Optional Engine	N/A	N/A
Air Conditioning	Std	Std
Power Steering	Std	Std
Cruise Control	Std	Std
4 Wheel Full-Time Drive	Std	Std
AM/FM Stereo Cassette	Std	Std
Steering, Tilt w/Memory	Std	Std
Power Windows	Std	Std
***Options Price**	$0	$0
***Total Price**	**$18,850**	**$21,450**
Target Price	$19,451	
Destination Charge	$445	
Avg. Tax & Fees	$1,214	
Total Target $	**$21,110**	
Average Dealer Option Cost:	***83%***	

Ownership Costs

Cost Area	5 Year Cost	Rate
Depreciation	$11,287	Average
Financing ($424/month)	$3,477	
Insurance (Rating 14)	$8,238	Average
State Fees	$875	
Fuel (Hwy 27 City 21)	$3,598	Average
Maintenance	$5,267	Worse Than Average
Repairs	$630	Better Than Average

Warranty/Maintenance Info

Major Tune-Up	$145	Better Than Average
Minor Tune-Up	$89	Better Than Average
Brake Service	$239	Worse Than Average
Overall Warranty	3 yr/36k	Average
Drivetrain Warranty	5 yr/60k	Excellent
Rust Warranty	5 yr/unlim. mi	Better Than Average
Maintenance Warranty	N/A	
Roadside Assistance	3 yr/36k	

Ownership Cost By Year

$2,000 $4,000 $6,000 $8,000 $10,000 $12,000

1993 1994 1995 1996 1997

Resale Value

1993	1994	1995	1996	1997
$13,842	$12,894	$12,549	$11,158	$9,823

Ownership Costs (5yr)

Average	This Car
$32,913	$33,372
Cost/Mile 47¢	Cost/Mile 48¢

Cumulative Costs

	1993	1994	1995	1996	1997
Annual	$11,164	$4,710	$4,687	$5,040	$7,771
Total	$11,164	$15,874	$20,561	$25,601	$33,372

Ownership Cost Rating

Average

The 1993 Subaru Legacy is available in twelve models - L, LS, L 4WD, LS 4WD, LSi 4WD and Sport 4WD sedans; and L, LS, L 4WD, LS 4WD, LSi 4WD and Touring 4WD wagons. New for 1993, the LS 4WD wagon receives a driver airbag, 60/40 rear split seats and one new exterior color (Jasper Green). Features include power windows and door locks, rear-window defogger, four-wheel independent suspension and front bucket seats. Other features include alloy wheels and power moon-roof with rear tilt feature.

Subaru Legacy LSi AWD

4 Door Wagon

2.2L 130 hp Gas Fuel Inject.

4 Cylinder Opposing

Automatic 4 Speed

4 Wheel Full-Time

Driver Airbag Psngr Belts

Purchase Price

Car Item	Dealer Cost	List
Base Price	**$19,904**	**$22,650**
Anti-Lock Brakes	Std	Std
Manual Transmission	N/A	N/A
Optional Engine	N/A	N/A
Air Conditioning	Std	Std
Power Steering	Std	Std
Cruise Control	Std	Std
4 Wheel Full-Time Drive	Std	Std
AM/FM Stereo Cassette	Std	Std
Steering, Tilt w/Memory	Std	Std
Power Windows	Std	Std
***Options Price**	$0	$0
***Total Price**	**$19,904**	**$22,650**
Target Price	$20,556	
Destination Charge	$445	
Avg. Tax & Fees	$1,281	
Total Target $	**$22,282**	
Average Dealer Option Cost:	***83%***	

Ownership Costs

Cost Area	5 Year Cost	Rate
Depreciation	$11,192	Average
Financing ($448/month)	$3,671	
Insurance (Rating 14)	$8,238	Average
State Fees	$925	
Fuel (Hwy 27 City 21)	$3,598	Average
Maintenance	$5,267	Worse Than Average
Repairs	$630	Better Than Average

Warranty/Maintenance Info

Major Tune-Up	$145	Better Than Average
Minor Tune-Up	$89	Better Than Average
Brake Service	$239	Worse Than Average
Overall Warranty	3 yr/36k	Average
Drivetrain Warranty	5 yr/60k	Excellent
Rust Warranty	5 yr/unlim. mi	Better Than Average
Maintenance Warranty	N/A	
Roadside Assistance	3 yr/36k	

Ownership Cost By Year

$2,000 $4,000 $6,000 $8,000 $10,000 $12,000

1993 1994 1995 1996 1997

Resale Value

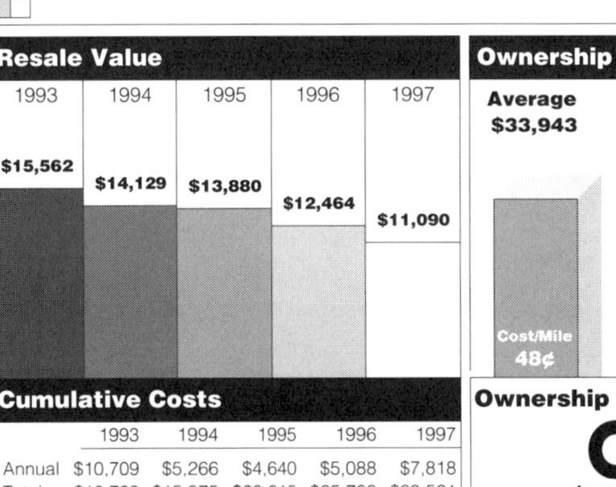

Ownership Costs (5yr)

Average	This Car
$33,943	$33,521
Cost/Mile 48¢	Cost/Mile 48¢

Cumulative Costs

	1993	1994	1995	1996	1997
Annual	$10,709	$5,266	$4,640	$5,088	$7,818
Total	$10,709	$15,975	$20,615	$25,703	$33,521

Ownership Cost Rating

Average

The 1993 Subaru Legacy is available in twelve models - L, LS, L 4WD, LS 4WD, LSi 4WD and Sport 4WD sedans; and L, LS, L 4WD, LS 4WD, LSi 4WD and Touring 4WD wagons. New for 1993, the LSi 4WD wagon receives a driver airbag, 60/40 rear split seats and one new exterior color (Jasper Green). Features include power windows and door locks, beige leather interior and four-wheel independent suspension. Other features include alloy wheels, power moon-roof with rear tilt feature and ABS brakes.

* Includes shaded options

** Other purchase requirements apply

 Poor   Worse Than Average  Average  Better Than Average 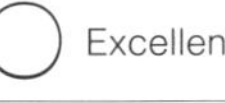 Excellent 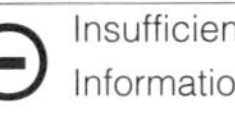 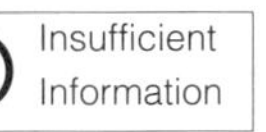 Insufficient Information

Refer to *Section 3: Annotated Vehicle Charts* for an explanation of these charts.

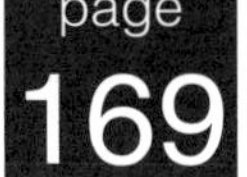

Subaru Legacy Touring Wagon AWD
4 Door Wagon

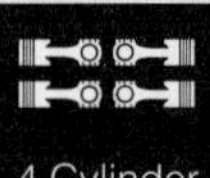

2.2L 160 hp Gas Fuel Inject. | 4 Cylinder Opposing | Automatic 4 Speed | 4 Wheel Full-Time | Driver Airbag Psngr Belts

Compact Wagon

Purchase Price

Car Item	Dealer Cost	List
Base Price	**$19,904**	**$22,650**
Anti-Lock Brakes	Std	Std
Manual Transmission	N/A	N/A
Optional Engine	N/A	N/A
Air Conditioning	Std	Std
Power Steering	Std	Std
Cruise Control	Std	Std
4 Wheel Full-Time Drive	Std	Std
AM/FM Stereo Cassette	Std	Std
Steering, Tilt w/Memory	Std	Std
Power Windows	Std	Std
***Options Price**	$0	$0
***Total Price**	**$19,904**	**$22,650**
Target Price	$20,556	
Destination Charge	$445	
Avg. Tax & Fees	$1,281	
Total Target $	**$22,282**	
Average Dealer Option Cost:	***83%***	

Ownership Costs

Cost Area	5 Year Cost	Rate
Depreciation		Insufficient Information
Financing ($448/month)	$3,671	
Insurance (Rating 14)	$8,238	Average
State Fees	$925	
Fuel (Hwy 23 City 18)	$4,213	Poor
Maintenance	$5,686	Poor
Repairs	$630	Better Than Average

Ownership Cost By Year

$2,000 $4,000 $6,000 $8,000 $10,000

Insufficient Depreciation Information

1993 1994 1995 1996 1997

Warranty/Maintenance Info

Item		Rate
Major Tune-Up	$145	Better Than Average
Minor Tune-Up	$89	Better Than Average
Brake Service	$239	Worse Than Average
Overall Warranty	3 yr/36k	Average
Drivetrain Warranty	5 yr/60k	Excellent
Rust Warranty	5 yr/unlim. mi	Better Than Average
Maintenance Warranty	N/A	
Roadside Assistance	3 yr/36k	

Resale Value

Insufficient Information

Ownership Costs (5yr)

Insufficient Information

Cumulative Costs

	1993	1994	1995	1996	1997
Annual	*Insufficient Information*				
Total	*Insufficient Information*				

Ownership Cost Rating

Insufficient Information

The 1993 Subaru Legacy is available in twelve models - L, LS, L 4WD, LS 4WD, LSi 4WD and Sport 4WD sedans; and L, LS, L 4WD, LS 4WD, LSi 4WD and Touring 4WD wagons. New for 1993, the Touring 4WD wagon receives a driver airbag, 60/40 rear split seats and one new exterior color (Jasper Green). Features include power moonroof with tilt feature, power windows and door locks, sport seats, an 80-watt stereo system with graphic equalizer, cruise control, alloy wheels and a functional hood scoop.

Subaru Loyale
4 Door Wagon

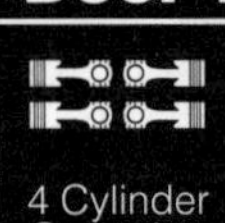

1.8L 90 hp Gas Fuel Inject. | 4 Cylinder Opposing | Manual 5 Speed | 2 Wheel Front | Automatic Seatbelts

Subcompact Wag

Purchase Price

Car Item	Dealer Cost	List
Base Price	**$10,068**	**$11,328**
Anti-Lock Brakes	N/A	N/A
Automatic 3 Speed	$488	$550
Optional Engine	N/A	N/A
Air Conditioning	Std	Std
Power Steering	Std	Std
Cruise Control	N/A	N/A
All Wheel Drive	N/A	N/A
AM/FM Stereo Cassette	N/A	N/A
Steering Wheel, Tilt	Std	Std
Power Windows	Std	Std
***Options Price**	$0	$0
***Total Price**	**$10,068**	**$11,328**
Target Price	$10,318	
Destination Charge	$445	
Avg. Tax & Fees	$656	
Total Target $	**$11,419**	
Average Dealer Option Cost:	***89%***	

Ownership Costs

Cost Area	5 Year Cost	Rate
Depreciation	$6,254	Average
Financing ($229/month)	$1,881	
Insurance (Rating 8)	$7,223	Worse Than Average
State Fees	$471	
Fuel (Hwy 30 City 25)	$3,140	Worse Than Average
Maintenance	$4,043	Average
Repairs	$560	Excellent

Ownership Cost By Year

$2,000 $4,000 $6,000 $8,000

1993 1994 1995 1996 1997

Warranty/Maintenance Info

Item		Rate
Major Tune-Up	$154	Average
Minor Tune-Up	$88	Average
Brake Service	$167	Better Than Average
Overall Warranty	3 yr/36k	Average
Drivetrain Warranty	5 yr/60k	Excellent
Rust Warranty	5 yr/unlim. mi	Better Than Average
Maintenance Warranty	N/A	
Roadside Assistance	3 yr/36k	

Resale Value

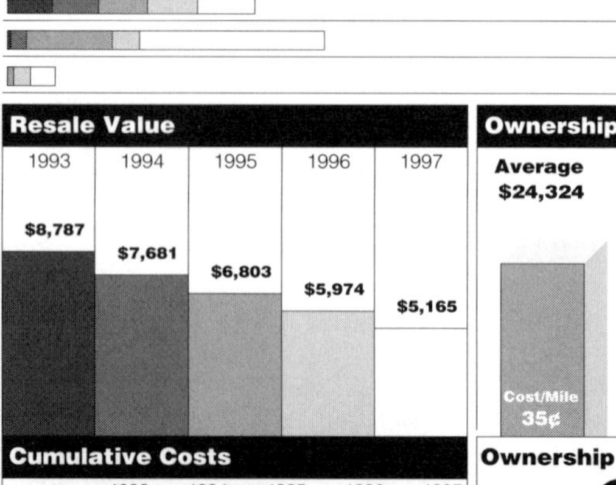

1993	1994	1995	1996	1997
$8,787	$7,681	$6,803	$5,974	$5,165

Ownership Costs (5yr)

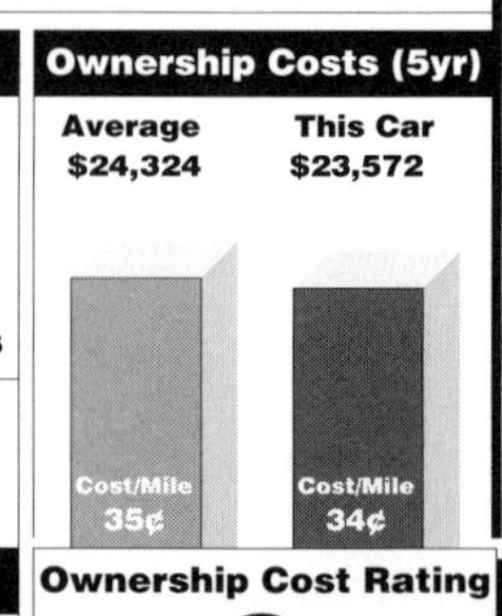

	Average	This Car
	$24,324	$23,572
Cost/Mile	35¢	34¢

Cumulative Costs

	1993	1994	1995	1996	1997
Annual	$5,490	$3,993	$4,609	$3,771	$5,709
Total	$5,490	$9,483	$14,092	$17,863	$23,572

Ownership Cost Rating

Better Than Average

The Subaru Loyale is available in two models - (Base) Loyale and 4WD wagons. For 1993, the Base Loyale wagon features air conditioning, power steering, power windows with driver-side automatic up and down, power mirrors, power locks, AM/FM cassette audio system, tilt steering wheel, 60/40 split rear seat, rear-window defogger, all-season radial tires and a digital clock. Three new exterior colors are offered (Teal, Misty Dawn and Freesia Red).

* Includes shaded options

** Other purchase requirements apply

Poor | Worse Than Average | Average | Better Than Average | Excellent | Insufficient Information

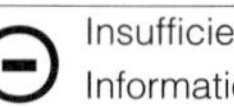

Refer to *Section 3: Annotated Vehicle Charts* for an explanation of these charts.

Subaru Loyale 4WD

4 Door Wagon

1.8L 90 hp Gas Fuel Inject.

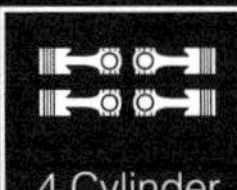
4 Cylinder Opposing

Manual 5 Speed

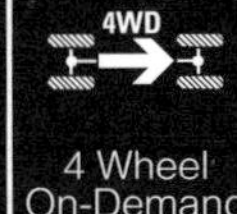
4 Wheel On-Demand

Automatic Seatbelts

Subcompact Wag

2WD Model Shown

Purchase Price

Car Item	Dealer Cost	List
Base Price	**$11,401**	**$12,828**
Anti-Lock Brakes	N/A	N/A
Automatic 3 Speed	$488	$550
Optional Engine	N/A	N/A
Air Conditioning	Std	Std
Power Steering	Std	Std
Cruise Control	N/A	N/A
4 Whl On-Demand Dr.	Std	Std
AM/FM Stereo Cassette	N/A	N/A
Steering Wheel, Tilt	Std	Std
Power Windows	Std	Std
***Options Price**	$0	$0
***Total Price**	**$11,401**	**$12,828**
Target Price	$11,696	
Destination Charge	$445	
Avg. Tax & Fees	$740	
Total Target $	**$12,881**	
Average Dealer Option Cost:	***89%***	

The Loyale is available in two models - (Base) Loyale and 4WD wagons. For 1993, the Base Loyale 4WD wagon features air conditioning, power steering, power windows with driver-side automatic up and down, power mirrors, power locks, stereo cassette audio system, tilt steering wheel, 60/40 split rear seat, rear-window defogger and all-season radial tires. Three new colors are offered (Teal, Misty Dawn and Freesia Red). Options include fog lamps, luggage rack, cruise control and a security system.

Ownership Costs

Cost Area	5 Year Cost	Rate
Depreciation	$7,042	Average
Financing ($259/month)	$2,122	
Insurance (Rating 10)	$7,479	Worse Than Average
State Fees	$531	
Fuel (Hwy 29 City 24)	$3,258	Worse Than Average
Maintenance	$4,028	Average
Repairs	$630	Better Than Average

Warranty/Maintenance Info

Major Tune-Up	$154	Average
Minor Tune-Up	$88	Average
Brake Service	$167	Better Than Average
Overall Warranty	3 yr/36k	Average
Drivetrain Warranty	5 yr/60k	Excellent
Rust Warranty	5 yr/unlim. mi	Better Than Average
Maintenance Warranty	N/A	
Roadside Assistance	3 yr/36k	

Ownership Cost By Year

$2,000 $4,000 $6,000 $8,000

1993 1994 1995 1996 1997

Resale Value

1993	1994	1995	1996	1997
$9,873	$8,638	$7,661	$6,725	$5,839

Ownership Costs (5yr)

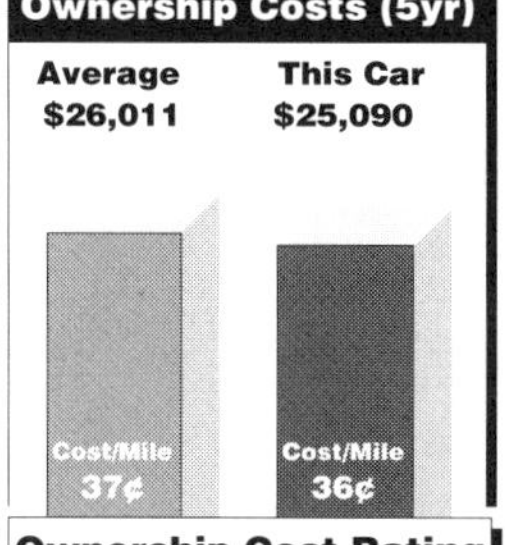

Average	This Car
$26,011	$25,090
Cost/Mile 37¢	Cost/Mile 36¢

Cumulative Costs

	1993	1994	1995	1996	1997
Annual	$6,050	$4,281	$4,760	$4,012	$5,987
Total	$6,050	$10,331	$15,091	$19,103	$25,090

Ownership Cost Rating

Better Than Average

Suzuki Samurai JA Soft Top

2 Door Sport Utility

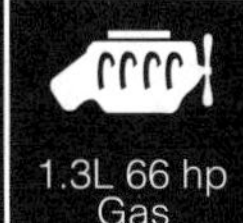
1.3L 66 hp Gas Fuel Inject.

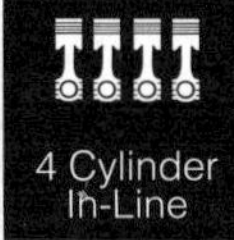
4 Cylinder In-Line

Manual 5 Speed

2 Wheel Rear

Manual Seatbelts Only

Utility

JL 4WD Shown

Purchase Price

Car Item	Dealer Cost	List
Base Price	**$6,498**	**$6,699**
Anti-Lock Brakes	N/A	N/A
Automatic Transmission	N/A	N/A
Optional Engine	N/A	N/A
Air Conditioning	Dlr	Dlr
Power Steering	N/A	N/A
Cruise Control	N/A	N/A
All Wheel Drive	N/A	N/A
AM/FM Stereo Cassette	Dlr	Dlr
Steering Wheel, Tilt	N/A	N/A
Power Windows	N/A	N/A
***Options Price**	$0	$0
***Total Price**	**$6,498**	**$6,699**
Target Price	$6,698	
Destination Charge	$320	
Avg. Tax & Fees	$421	
Total Target $	**$7,439**	
Average Dealer Option Cost:	***N/A***	

The Samurai two-door sport utility is offered in JA 2WD and JL 4WD Soft Top editions. Standard items on the JA 2WD Samurai include reclining bucket seats, trip odometer, halogen headlamps, passenger mirror, power brakes and styled steel wheels. Many dealer installed accessories are available such as an altimeter/inclinometer set, air conditioning, tailgate storage compartment, chrome bumpers, black or chrome side guards and mud guards.

Ownership Costs

Cost Area	5 Year Cost	Rate
Depreciation	$3,333	Average
Financing ($150/month)	$1,225	
Insurance (Rating 7)	$7,244	Poor
State Fees	$280	
Fuel (Hwy 29 City 28)	$3,050	Excellent
Maintenance	$4,450	Average
Repairs	$740	Better Than Average

Warranty/Maintenance Info

Major Tune-Up	$251	Poor
Minor Tune-Up	$80	Excellent
Brake Service	$252	Average
Overall Warranty	3 yr/36k	Average
Drivetrain Warranty	3 yr/36k	Average
Rust Warranty	3 yr/unlim. mi	Worse Than Average
Maintenance Warranty	N/A	
Roadside Assistance	3 yr/36k	

Ownership Cost By Year

$2,000 $4,000 $6,000 $8,000

1993 1994 1995 1996 1997

Resale Value

1993	1994	1995	1996	1997
$5,949	$5,359	$4,988	$4,564	$4,106

Ownership Costs (5yr)

Average	This Car
$18,936	$20,322
Cost/Mile 27¢	Cost/Mile 29¢

Cumulative Costs

	1993	1994	1995	1996	1997
Annual	$4,018	$3,206	$4,050	$3,752	$5,296
Total	$4,018	$7,224	$11,274	$15,026	$20,322

Ownership Cost Rating

Worse Than Average

* Includes shaded options

** Other purchase requirements apply

Poor | Worse Than Average |  Average | Better Than Average | Excellent | Insufficient Information

Refer to *Section 3: Annotated Vehicle Charts* for an explanation of these charts.

Suzuki Samurai JL Soft Top
2 Door Sport Utility

1.3L 66 hp Gas Fuel Inject.

4 Cylinder In-Line

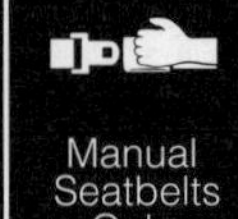
Manual 5 Speed

4 Wheel On-Demand

Manual Seatbelts Only

Purchase Price

Car Item	Dealer Cost	List
Base Price	**$7,739**	**$8,599**
Anti-Lock Brakes	N/A	N/A
Automatic Transmission	N/A	N/A
Optional Engine	N/A	N/A
Air Conditioning	Dlr	Dlr
Power Steering	N/A	N/A
Cruise Control	N/A	N/A
4 Whl On-Demand Dr.	Std	Std
AM/FM Stereo Cassette	Dlr	Dlr
Steering Wheel, Tilt	N/A	N/A
Power Windows	N/A	N/A
***Options Price**	$0	$0
***Total Price**	**$7,739**	**$8,599**
Target Price	$8,160	
Destination Charge	$320	
Avg. Tax & Fees	$513	
Total Target $	**$8,993**	
Average Dealer Option Cost:	***N/A***	

Ownership Costs

Cost Area	5 Year Cost	Rate
Depreciation	$4,257	Worse Than Average
Financing ($181/month)	$1,482	
Insurance (Rating 8)	$7,432	Poor
State Fees	$356	
Fuel (Hwy 29 City 28)	$3,050	Excellent
Maintenance	$4,639	Worse Than Average
Repairs	$770	Average

Ownership Cost By Year

Warranty/Maintenance Info

Major Tune-Up	$251	Poor
Minor Tune-Up	$80	Excellent
Brake Service	$252	Average
Overall Warranty	3 yr/36k	Average
Drivetrain Warranty	3 yr/36k	Average
Rust Warranty	3 yr/unlim. mi	Worse Than Average
Maintenance Warranty	N/A	
Roadside Assistance	3 yr/36k	

Resale Value

1993	1994	1995	1996	1997
$7,032	$6,315	$5,813	$5,284	$4,736

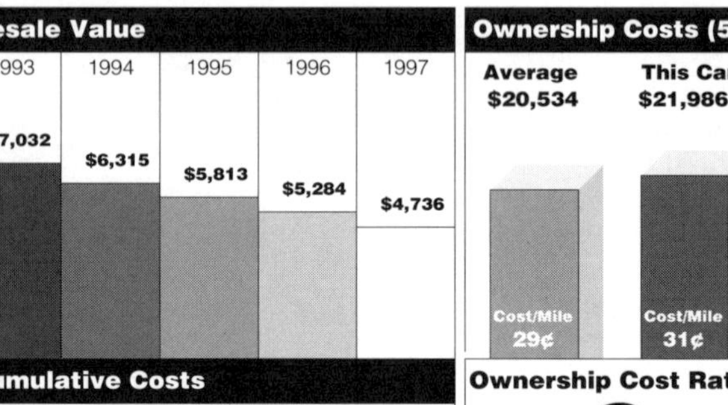

Ownership Costs (5yr)

Average	This Car
$20,534	$21,986
Cost/Mile 29¢	Cost/Mile 31¢

The Samurai two-door sport utility is offered in JA 2WD and JL 4WD Soft Top editions. In addition to the standard equipment of the JA 2WD, the JL 4WD adds 4-wheel on-demand drive, carpeting, mud guards, tinted window glass and larger tires. Many dealer installed accessories are available such as automatic locking hubs, altimeter/inclinometer set, air conditioning, tailgate storage compartment, chrome bumpers and black or chrome side guards.

Cumulative Costs

	1993	1994	1995	1996	1997
Annual	$4,650	$3,466	$4,379	$3,941	$5,550
Total	$4,650	$8,116	$12,495	$16,436	$21,986

Ownership Cost Rating

Worse Than Average

Suzuki Sidekick JS Soft Top
2 Door Sport Utility

1.6L 80 hp Gas Fuel Inject.

4 Cylinder In-Line

Manual 5 Speed

2 Wheel Rear

Manual Seatbelts Only

Purchase Price

Car Item	Dealer Cost	List
Base Price	**$10,119**	**$10,999**
Anti-Lock Brakes	Std	Std
Automatic Transmission	N/A	N/A
Optional Engine	N/A	N/A
Air Conditioning	Dlr	Dlr
Power Steering	N/A	N/A
Cruise Control	N/A	N/A
All Wheel Drive	N/A	N/A
AM/FM Stereo Cassette	N/A	N/A
Steering Wheel, Tilt	N/A	N/A
Power Windows	N/A	N/A
***Options Price**	$0	$0
***Total Price**	**$10,119**	**$10,999**
Target Price	$10,716	
Destination Charge	$320	
Avg. Tax & Fees	$665	
Total Target $	**$11,701**	
Average Dealer Option Cost:	***N/A***	

Ownership Costs

Cost Area	5 Year Cost	Rate
Depreciation	$4,225	Better Than Average
Financing ($235/month)	$1,927	
Insurance (Rating 11)	$7,902	Poor
State Fees	$453	
Fuel (Hwy 27 City 25)	$3,333	Excellent
Maintenance	$4,774	Worse Than Average
Repairs	$740	Better Than Average

Ownership Cost By Year

Warranty/Maintenance Info

Major Tune-Up	$253	Poor
Minor Tune-Up	$83	Better Than Average
Brake Service	$277	Worse Than Average
Overall Warranty	3 yr/36k	Average
Drivetrain Warranty	3 yr/36k	Average
Rust Warranty	3 yr/unlim. mi	Worse Than Average
Maintenance Warranty	N/A	
Roadside Assistance	3 yr/36k	

Resale Value

1993	1994	1995	1996	1997
$11,011	$9,860	$9,287	$8,506	$7,476

Ownership Costs (5yr)

Average	This Car
$22,553	$23,354
Cost/Mile 32¢	Cost/Mile 33¢

The Sidekick sport utilities are offered in JS 2WD and JX 4WD Soft Top two-door editions and JS 2WD and JX and JLX 4WD Hardtop four-door editions. The JS 2WD Soft Top two-door receives new exterior striping in 1993. Standard features include an anti-lock braking system, 1.6L 4 Cylinder engine with 80 horsepower and a separate body-on frame construction which reduces passenger cabin noise and dampens vibrations. Numerous Suzuki accessories may be added at the dealership.

Cumulative Costs

	1993	1994	1995	1996	1997
Annual	$3,728	$4,208	$4,562	$4,144	$6,712
Total	$3,728	$7,936	$12,498	$16,642	$23,354

Ownership Cost Rating

Average

* Includes shaded options

** Other purchase requirements apply

 Poor  Worse Than Average  Average Better Than Average  Excellent Insufficient Information

Refer to *Section 3: Annotated Vehicle Charts* for an explanation of these charts.

Suzuki Sidekick JS Hardtop
4 Door Sport Utility

1.6L 95 hp Gas Fuel Inject.

4 Cylinder In-Line

Manual 5 Speed

2 Wheel Rear

Manual Seatbelts Only

Purchase Price

Car Item	Dealer Cost	List
Base Price	**$10,590**	**$11,899**
Anti-Lock Brakes	Std	Std
Automatic Transmission	N/A	N/A
Optional Engine	N/A	N/A
Air Conditioning	Dlr	Dlr
Power Steering	Std	Std
Cruise Control	N/A	N/A
All Wheel Drive	N/A	N/A
AM/FM Stereo Cassette	Std	Std
Steering Wheel, Tilt	N/A	N/A
Power Windows	N/A	N/A
***Options Price**	$0	$0
***Total Price**	**$10,590**	**$11,899**
Target Price	$11,225	
Destination Charge	$330	
Avg. Tax & Fees	$700	
Total Target $	**$12,255**	
Average Dealer Option Cost:	***N/A***	

Ownership Costs

Cost Area	5 Year Cost	Rate
Depreciation	$5,443	
Financing ($246/month)	$2,019	
Insurance (Rating 12)	$8,108	
State Fees	$489	
Fuel (Hwy 26 City 24)	$3,466	
Maintenance	$4,876	
Repairs	$740	

Warranty/Maintenance Info

Item		Rate
Major Tune-Up	$253	
Minor Tune-Up	$83	
Brake Service	$287	
Overall Warranty	3 yr/36k	
Drivetrain Warranty	3 yr/36k	
Rust Warranty	3 yr/unlim. mi	
Maintenance Warranty	N/A	
Roadside Assistance	3 yr/36k	

The Sidekick sport utilities are offered in JS 2WD and JX 4WD Soft Top two-door editions and JS 2WD and JX and JLX 4WD Hardtop four-door editions. Standard features on the JS 2WD Hardtop four-door include an anti-lock braking system, 1.6L 4 Cylinder engine with 95 horsepower and a separate body-on frame construction which reduces passenger cabin noise and dampens vibrations. Numerous Suzuki accessories may be added at the dealership such as chrome bumpers, front mask/bra and rear defogger.

Ownership Cost By Year

$2,000 $4,000 $6,000 $8,000 $10,000

1993 1994 1995 1996 1997

Resale Value

1993	1994	1995	1996	1997
$9,554	$8,592	$8,057	$7,542	$6,812

Cumulative Costs

	1993	1994	1995	1996	1997
Annual	$5,849	$4,121	$4,627	$3,963	$6,581
Total	$5,849	$9,970	$14,597	$18,560	$25,141

Ownership Costs (5yr)

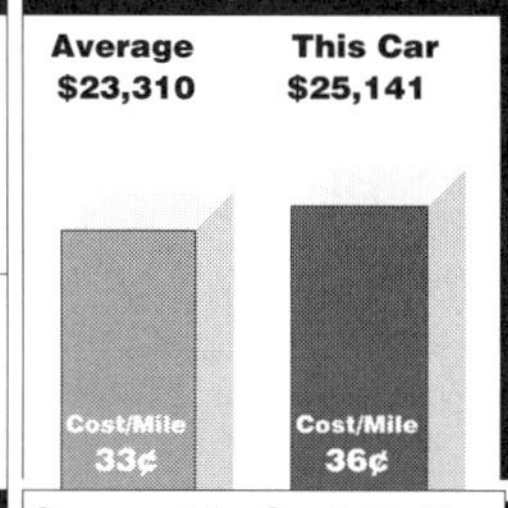

Ownership Cost Rating

Poor

Suzuki Sidekick JX Soft Top
2 Door Sport Utility

1.6L 80 hp Gas Fuel Inject.

4 Cylinder In-Line

Manual 5 Speed

4 Wheel On-Demand

Manual Seatbelts Only

Purchase Price

Car Item	Dealer Cost	List
Base Price	**$11,159**	**$12,399**
Anti-Lock Brakes	Std	Std
Automatic 3 Speed	$540	$600
Optional Engine	N/A	N/A
Air Conditioning	Dlr	Dlr
Power Steering	Std	Std
Cruise Control	N/A	N/A
4 Whl On-Demand Dr.	Std	Std
AM/FM Stereo Cassette	N/A	N/A
Steering Wheel, Tilt	N/A	N/A
Power Windows	N/A	N/A
***Options Price**	$0	$0
***Total Price**	**$11,159**	**$12,399**
Target Price	$11,840	
Destination Charge	$320	
Avg. Tax & Fees	$735	
Total Target $	**$12,895**	
Average Dealer Option Cost:	***90%***	

Ownership Costs

Cost Area	5 Year Cost	Rate
Depreciation	$5,470	
Financing ($259/month)	$2,124	
Insurance (Rating 12)	$8,108	
State Fees	$508	
Fuel (Hwy 27 City 25)	$3,333	
Maintenance	$4,873	
Repairs	$770	

Warranty/Maintenance Info

Item		Rate
Major Tune-Up	$253	
Minor Tune-Up	$83	
Brake Service	$277	
Overall Warranty	3 yr/36k	
Drivetrain Warranty	3 yr/36k	
Rust Warranty	3 yr/unlim. mi	
Maintenance Warranty	N/A	
Roadside Assistance	3 yr/36k	

The Sidekick sport utilities are offered in JS 2WD and JX 4WD Soft Top two-door editions and JS 2WD and JX and JLX 4WD Hardtop four-door editions. The JX 4WD Soft Top two-door receives new exterior striping in 1993. In addition to the standard features of the JS 2WD two-door Soft Top, the JX receives power steering, a tachometer, sculpted reclining front bucket seats, dual power mirrors and styled steel wheels. A detachable hardtop roof may be added as a dealer installed accessory.

Ownership Cost By Year

$2,000 $4,000 $6,000 $8,000 $10,000

1993 1994 1995 1996 1997

Resale Value

1993	1994	1995	1996	1997
$10,538	$9,633	$8,987	$8,316	$7,425

Cumulative Costs

	1993	1994	1995	1996	1997
Annual	$5,529	$4,076	$4,785	$4,115	$6,681
Total	$5,529	$9,605	$14,390	$18,505	$25,186

Ownership Costs (5yr)

Average $23,730 — This Car $25,186

Cost/Mile 34¢ — Cost/Mile 36¢

Ownership Cost Rating

Worse Than Average

* Includes shaded options

** Other purchase requirements apply

Poor

Worse Than Average

Average

Better Than Average
Excellent

Insufficient Information

Refer to *Section 3: Annotated Vehicle Charts* for an explanation of these charts.

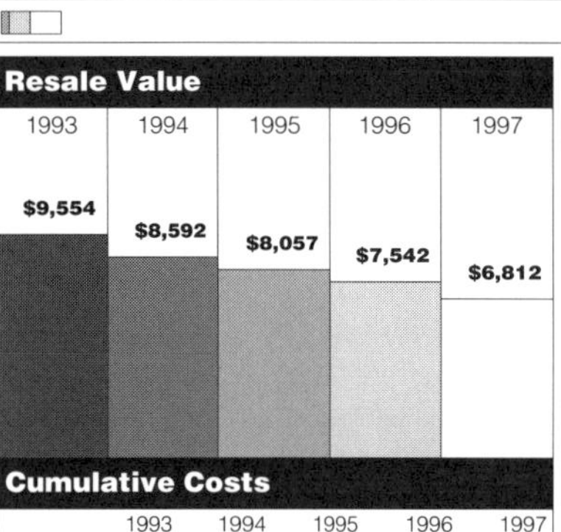

Suzuki Sidekick JX Hardtop

4 Door Sport Utility

1.6L 95 hp Gas Fuel Inject. | 4 Cylinder In-Line | Manual 5 Speed | 4 Wheel On-Demand | Manual Seatbelts Only

Purchase Price

Car Item	Dealer Cost	List
Base Price	**$11,309**	**$12,999**
Anti-Lock Brakes	Std	Std
Automatic 4 Speed	$783	$900
Optional Engine	N/A	N/A
Air Conditioning	Dlr	Dlr
Power Steering	Std	Std
Cruise Control	N/A	N/A
4 Whl On-Demand Dr.	Std	Std
AM/FM Stereo Cassette	Std	Std
Steering Wheel, Tilt	N/A	N/A
Power Windows	N/A	N/A
***Options Price**	$0	$0
***Total Price**	**$11,309**	**$12,999**
Target Price	$12,002	
Destination Charge	$330	
Avg. Tax & Fees	$750	
Total Target $	**$13,082**	
Average Dealer Option Cost:	***87%***	

Ownership Costs

Cost Area	5 Year Cost	Rate
Depreciation	$5,370	Average
Financing ($263/month)	$2,156	
Insurance (Rating 13)	$8,271	Poor
State Fees	$533	
Fuel (Hwy 27 City 25)	$3,333	Excellent
Maintenance	$5,025	Worse Than Average
Repairs	$770	Average

Ownership Cost By Year

$2,000 $4,000 $6,000 $8,000 $10,000

1993 1994 1995 1996 1997

Warranty/Maintenance Info

Item		Rate
Major Tune-Up	$253	Poor
Minor Tune-Up	$83	Better Than Average
Brake Service	$287	Poor
Overall Warranty	3 yr/36k	Average
Drivetrain Warranty	3 yr/36k	Average
Rust Warranty	3 yr/unlim. mi	Worse Than Average
Maintenance Warranty	N/A	
Roadside Assistance	3 yr/36k	

Resale Value

1993	1994	1995	1996	1997
$10,446	$9,464	$8,933	$8,437	$7,712

Ownership Costs (5yr)

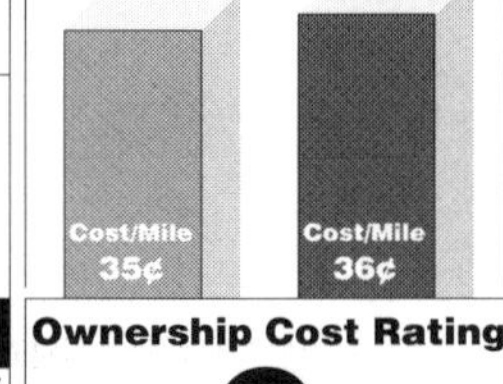

Average	This Car
$24,235	$25,458
Cost/Mile 35¢	Cost/Mile 36¢

Cumulative Costs

	1993	1994	1995	1996	1997
Annual	$5,857	$4,200	$4,725	$3,981	$6,695
Total	$5,857	$10,057	$14,782	$18,763	$25,458

Ownership Cost Rating

Average

The Sidekick sport utilities are offered in JS 2WD and JX 4WD Soft Top two-door editions and JS 2WD and JX and JLX 4WD Hardtop four-door editions. The JX 4WD Hardtop four-door comes standard with automatic locking hubs, mud & snow black sidewall tires and a Logic CD-ready AM/FM stereo with cassette. Dealer installed accessories include front center armrests, skid plates, spare tire case, cover and lock, floor mats and roof rack. Sidekicks are sisters to the Geo Tracker.

Suzuki Sidekick JLX Hardtop

4 Door Sport Utility

1.6L 95 hp Gas Fuel Inject. | 4 Cylinder In-Line | Manual 5 Speed | 4 Wheel On-Demand | Manual Seatbelts Only

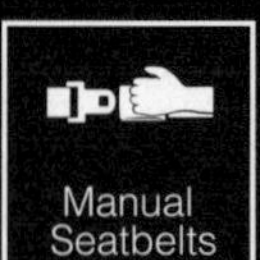

Purchase Price

Car Item	Dealer Cost	List
Base Price	**$12,353**	**$14,199**
Anti-Lock Brakes	Std	Std
Automatic 4 Speed	$783	$900
Optional Engine	N/A	N/A
Air Conditioning	Dlr	Dlr
Power Steering	Std	Std
Cruise Control	N/A	N/A
4 Whl On-Demand Dr.	Std	Std
AM/FM Stereo Cassette	Std	Std
Steering Wheel, Tilt	N/A	N/A
Power Windows	Std	Std
***Options Price**	$0	$0
***Total Price**	**$12,353**	**$14,199**
Target Price	$13,135	
Destination Charge	$330	
Avg. Tax & Fees	$818	
Total Target $	**$14,283**	
Average Dealer Option Cost:	***87%***	

Ownership Costs

Cost Area	5 Year Cost	Rate
Depreciation	$6,132	Worse Than Average
Financing ($287/month)	$2,352	
Insurance (Rating 13)	$8,271	Poor
State Fees	$581	
Fuel (Hwy 26 City 24)	$3,466	Excellent
Maintenance	$4,993	Worse Than Average
Repairs	$770	Average

Ownership Cost By Year

$2,000 $4,000 $6,000 $8,000 $10,000

1993 1994 1995 1996 1997

Warranty/Maintenance Info

Item		Rate
Major Tune-Up	$253	Poor
Minor Tune-Up	$83	Better Than Average
Brake Service	$287	Poor
Overall Warranty	3 yr/36k	Average
Drivetrain Warranty	3 yr/36k	Average
Rust Warranty	3 yr/unlim. mi	Worse Than Average
Maintenance Warranty	N/A	
Roadside Assistance	3 yr/36k	

Resale Value

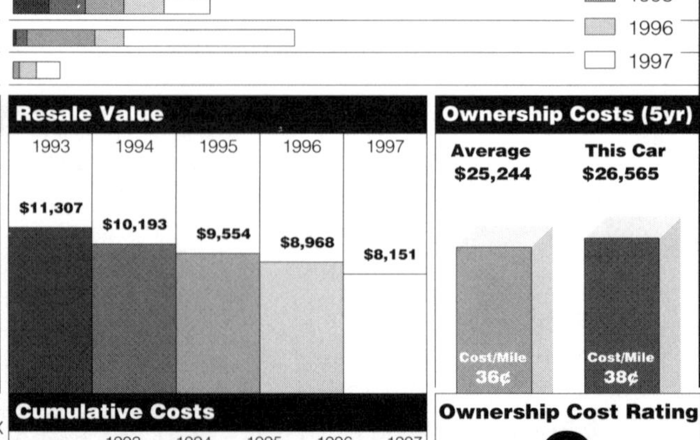

1993	1994	1995	1996	1997
$11,307	$10,193	$9,554	$8,968	$8,151

Ownership Costs (5yr)

Average	This Car
$25,244	$26,565
Cost/Mile 36¢	Cost/Mile 38¢

Cumulative Costs

	1993	1994	1995	1996	1997
Annual	$6,316	$4,429	$4,907	$4,122	$6,791
Total	$6,316	$10,745	$15,652	$19,774	$26,565

Ownership Cost Rating

Average

The Sidekick sport utilities are offered in JS 2WD and JX 4WD Soft Top two-door editions and JS 2WD and JX and JLX 4WD Hardtop four-door editions. In addition to or in place of the standard features of the JX, the JLX 4WD Hardtop four-door features chrome wheels, power windows and door locks, raised-outlined white letter steel-belted radial tires, and a hard case spare tire cover. Front and rear step plates and a rear defroster may be added as dealer installed accessories.

* Includes shaded options

** Other purchase requirements apply

 Poor  Worse Than Average  Average  Better Than Average Excellent 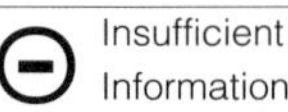 Insufficient Information

Refer to *Section 3: Annotated Vehicle Charts* for an explanation of these charts.

Toyota 4Runner SR5 V6

4 Door Sport Utility

Utility

3.0L 150 hp Gas Fuel Inject.

6 Cylinder "V"

Automatic 4 Speed

2 Wheel Rear

Manual Seatbelts Only

Purchase Price

Car Item	Dealer Cost	List
Base Price	**$16,831**	**$19,918**
Anti-Lock Brakes	Std	Std
Manual Transmission	N/A	N/A
Optional Engine	N/A	N/A
Air Conditioning	$704	$880
Power Steering	Std	Std
Cruise Control	$240	$300
All Wheel Drive	N/A	N/A
AM/FM Stereo Cassette	$209	$275
Steering Wheel, Tilt	Std	Std
Power Windows	Pkg	Pkg
***Options Price**	$913	$1,155
***Total Price**	**$17,744**	**$21,073**
Target Price	$19,557	
Destination Charge	$295	
Avg. Tax & Fees	$1,207	
Total Target $	**$21,059**	
Average Dealer Option Cost:	***83%***	

Ownership Costs

Cost Area	5 Year Cost	Rate
Depreciation	$3,577	
Financing ($423/month)	$3,469	
Insurance (Rating 18)	$9,662	
State Fees	$855	
Fuel (Hwy 21 City 17)	$4,543	
Maintenance	$5,011	
Repairs	$720	

Ownership Cost By Year

$2,000 $4,000 $6,000 $8,000 $10,000

1993 1994 1995 1996 1997

Warranty/Maintenance Info

Major Tune-Up	$189	
Minor Tune-Up	$117	
Brake Service	$221	
Overall Warranty	3 yr/36k	
Drivetrain Warranty	5 yr/60k	
Rust Warranty	5 yr/unlim. mi	
Maintenance Warranty	N/A	
Roadside Assistance	N/A	

Resale Value

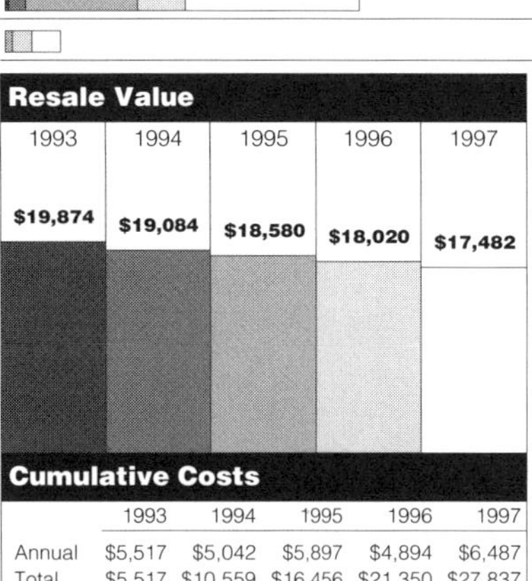

1993	1994	1995	1996	1997
$19,874	$19,084	$18,580	$18,020	$17,482

Ownership Costs (5yr)

Average	This Car
$31,026	$27,837
Cost/Mile 44¢	Cost/Mile 40¢

The 1993 4Runner is available in three models - 2WD SR5 V6, 4WD SR5 and 4WD SR5 V6 four-doors. New for 1993, the 2WD SR5 V6 is featured in one new color (Pewter Pearl). Functional exterior styling includes aerodynamic halogen headlights, front and rear mudgaurds, anti-chip rocker panels and silver styled-steel wheels with mud and snow radial tires. The 4Runner enters 1993 with an owner-driven six-year winning streak as the best compact sport utility vehicle in a customer satisfaction study.

Cumulative Costs

	1993	1994	1995	1996	1997
Annual	$5,517	$5,042	$5,897	$4,894	$6,487
Total	$5,517	$10,559	$16,456	$21,350	$27,837

Ownership Cost Rating

Excellent

Toyota 4Runner SR5 4WD

4 Door Sport Utility

Utility

2.4L 116 hp Gas Fuel Inject.

4 Cylinder In-Line

Manual 5 Speed

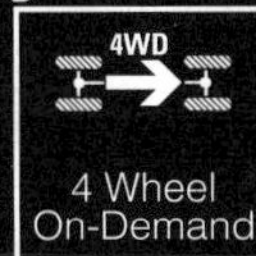
4 Wheel On-Demand

Manual Seatbelts Only

Purchase Price

Car Item	Dealer Cost	List
Base Price	**$16,097**	**$18,938**
Anti-Lock Brakes	$255	$300
Automatic 4 Speed	$935	$1,100
Optional Engine	N/A	N/A
Air Conditioning	$704	$880
Power Steering	Std	Std
Cruise Control	$240	$300
4 Whl On-Demand Dr.	Std	Std
AM/FM Stereo Cassette	$412	$550
Steering Wheel, Tilt	$153	$180
Power Windows	Pkg	Pkg
***Options Price**	$1,116	$1,430
***Total Price**	**$17,213**	**$20,368**
Target Price	$18,937	
Destination Charge	$295	
Avg. Tax & Fees	$1,169	
Total Target $	**$20,401**	
Average Dealer Option Cost:	***83%***	

Ownership Costs

Cost Area	5 Year Cost	Rate
Depreciation	$4,702	
Financing ($410/month)	$3,360	
Insurance (Rating 18)	$9,662	
State Fees	$827	
Fuel (Hwy 22 City 19)	$4,214	
Maintenance	$4,108	
Repairs	$720	

Ownership Cost By Year

$2,000 $4,000 $6,000 $8,000 $10,000

1993 1994 1995 1996 1997

Warranty/Maintenance Info

Major Tune-Up	$184	
Minor Tune-Up	$95	
Brake Service	$221	
Overall Warranty	3 yr/36k	
Drivetrain Warranty	5 yr/60k	
Rust Warranty	5 yr/unlim. mi	
Maintenance Warranty	N/A	
Roadside Assistance	N/A	

Resale Value

1993	1994	1995	1996	1997
$19,261	$18,085	$17,265	$16,448	$15,699

Ownership Costs (5yr)

Average	This Car
$30,433	$27,593
Cost/Mile 43¢	Cost/Mile 39¢

The 1993 4Runner is available in three models - 2WD SR5 V6, 4WD SR5 and 4WD SR5 V6 four-doors. New for 1993, the 4WD SR5 is featured in one new color (Pewter Pearl) and 4WDemand is standard. Exterior styling includes aerodynamic halogen headlights, front and rear mudgaurds, anti-chip rocker panels and silver styled-steel wheels with mud and snow tires. The 4Runner enters 1993 with an owner-driven six-year winning streak as the best compact sport utility vehicle in a customer satisfaction study.

Cumulative Costs

	1993	1994	1995	1996	1997
Annual	$5,356	$5,297	$5,863	$5,038	$6,039
Total	$5,356	$10,653	$16,516	$21,554	$27,593

Ownership Cost Rating

Excellent

* Includes shaded options

** Other purchase requirements apply

 Poor  Worse Than Average  Average  Better Than Average  Excellent  Insufficient Information

Refer to *Section 3: Annotated Vehicle Charts* for an explanation of these charts.

Toyota 4Runner SR5 V6 4WD

4 Door Sport Utility

3.0L 150 hp Gas Fuel Inject.

6 Cylinder "V"

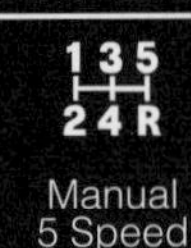
Manual 5 Speed

4 Wheel On-Demand

Manual Seatbelts Only

Utility

Purchase Price

Car Item	Dealer Cost	List
Base Price	**$17,557**	**$20,778**
Anti-Lock Brakes	Std	Std
Automatic 4 Speed	$888	$1,050
Optional Engine	N/A	N/A
Air Conditioning	$704	$880
Power Steering	Std	Std
Cruise Control	$240	$300
4 Whl On-Demand Dr.	Std	Std
AM/FM Stereo Cassette	$209	$275
Steering Wheel, Tilt	Std	Std
Power Windows	Pkg	Pkg
***Options Price**	$913	$1,155
***Total Price**	**$18,470**	**$21,933**
Target Price	$20,393	
Destination Charge	$295	
Avg. Tax & Fees	$1,256	
Total Target $	**$21,944**	
Average Dealer Option Cost: ***85%***		

Ownership Costs

Cost Area	5 Year Cost	Rate
Depreciation	$4,416	Excellent
Financing ($441/month)	$3,616	
Insurance (Rating 19)	$9,987	Worse Than Average
State Fees	$889	
Fuel (Hwy 18 City 15)	$5,233	Worse Than Average
Maintenance	$4,523	Average
Repairs	$720	Excellent

Warranty/Maintenance Info

Major Tune-Up	$189	Average
Minor Tune-Up	$117	Worse Than Average
Brake Service	$221	Average
Overall Warranty	3 yr/36k	Average
Drivetrain Warranty	5 yr/60k	Excellent
Rust Warranty	5 yr/unlim. mi	Better Than Average
Maintenance Warranty	N/A	
Roadside Assistance	N/A	

The 1993 4Runner is available in three models - 2WD SR5 V6, 4WD SR5 and 4WD SR5 V6 four-doors. New for 1993, the 4WD SR5 V6 is featured in one new color (Pewter Pearl) and 4WDemand is standard. Exterior styling includes aerodynamic halogen headlights, front and rear mud guards, anti-chip rocker panels and silver styled-steel wheels with mud and snow tires. The 4Runner enters 1993 with an owner-driven six-year winning streak as the best compact sport utility vehicle in a customer satisfaction study.

Ownership Cost By Year

$2,000 $4,000 $6,000 $8,000 $10,000

1993 1994 1995 1996 1997

Resale Value

1993	1994	1995	1996	1997
$20,701	$19,654	$18,938	$18,207	$17,528

Ownership Costs (5yr)

Average	This Car
$31,749	$29,384
Cost/Mile 45¢	Cost/Mile 42¢

Cumulative Costs

	1993	1994	1995	1996	1997
Annual	$5,831	$5,549	$6,124	$5,270	$6,610
Total	$5,831	$11,380	$17,504	$22,774	$29,384

Ownership Cost Rating

Excellent

Toyota Camry DX

4 Door Wagon

2.2L 130 hp Gas Fuel Inject.

4 Cylinder In-Line

Automatic 4 Speed

2 Wheel Front

Driver Airbag Psngr Belts

Compact Wagon

LE Model Shown

Purchase Price

Car Item	Dealer Cost	List
Base Price	**$14,608**	**$17,288**
Anti-Lock Brakes	$939	$1,145
Manual Transmission	N/A	N/A
Optional Engine	N/A	N/A
Air Conditioning	$732	$915
Power Steering	Std	Std
Cruise Control	$184	$230
All Wheel Drive	N/A	N/A
AM/FM Stereo Cassette	$112	$150
Steering Wheel, Tilt	Std	Std
Power Windows	N/A	N/A
***Options Price**	$844	$1,065
***Total Price**	**$15,452**	**$18,353**
Target Price	$16,937	
Destination Charge	$295	
Avg. Tax & Fees	$1,048	
Total Target $	**$18,280**	
Average Dealer Option Cost: ***81%***		

Ownership Costs

Cost Area	5 Year Cost	Rate
Depreciation	$6,740	Excellent
Financing ($367/month)	$3,011	
Insurance (Rating 6)	$6,919	Excellent
State Fees	$746	
Fuel (Hwy 28 City 21)	$3,530	Average
Maintenance	$5,404	Worse Than Average
Repairs	$550	Excellent

Warranty/Maintenance Info

Major Tune-Up	$185	Worse Than Average
Minor Tune-Up	$113	Average
Brake Service	$206	Average
Overall Warranty	3 yr/36k	Average
Drivetrain Warranty	5 yr/60k	Excellent
Rust Warranty	5 yr/unlim. mi	Better Than Average
Maintenance Warranty	N/A	
Roadside Assistance	N/A	

The 1993 Camry is available in ten models - DX, LE, and XLE sedans; DX, LE, XLE, and SE V6 sedans; and DX, LE and LE V6 wagons. New for 1993, the DX has a multi-cone synchromesh gearing in manual transmission models which provides an improved shift feel. Color-keyed bodyside molding has been added. Features include color-keyed bumpers, a 60/40 split back seat with over 40 cu. ft. of cargo room (with the rear seat up), and an optional third rear seat that comes with 3-point seatbelts.

Ownership Cost By Year

$2,000 $4,000 $6,000 $8,000

1993 1994 1995 1996 1997

Resale Value

1993	1994	1995	1996	1997
$15,728	$14,609	$13,552	$12,557	$11,540

Ownership Costs (5yr)

Average	This Car
$30,253	$26,900
Cost/Mile 43¢	Cost/Mile 38¢

Cumulative Costs

	1993	1994	1995	1996	1997
Annual	$5,968	$4,468	$5,477	$4,328	$6,659
Total	$5,968	$10,436	$15,913	$20,241	$26,900

Ownership Cost Rating

Excellent

* Includes shaded options

** Other purchase requirements apply

Poor  Worse Than Average  Average 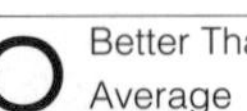 Better Than Average  Excellent 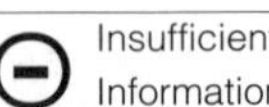 Insufficient Information

Refer to *Section 3: Annotated Vehicle Charts* for an explanation of these charts.

Toyota Camry LE

4 Door Wagon

2.2L 130 hp Gas Fuel Inject.

4 Cylinder In-Line

Automatic 4 Speed

2 Wheel Front

Driver Airbag Psngr Belts

Compact Wagon

Purchase Price

Car Item	Dealer Cost	List
Base Price	**$16,248**	**$19,228**
Anti-Lock Brakes	$939	$1,145
Manual Transmission	N/A	N/A
Optional Engine	N/A	N/A
Air Conditioning	Std	Std
Power Steering	Std	Std
Cruise Control	Std	Std
All Wheel Drive	N/A	N/A
AM/FM Stereo Cassette	Std	Std
Steering Wheel, Tilt	Std	Std
Power Windows	Std	Std
***Options Price**	$0	$0
***Total Price**	**$16,248**	**$19,228**
Target Price	$17,882	
Destination Charge	$295	
Avg. Tax & Fees	$1,104	
Total Target $	**$19,281**	
Average Dealer Option Cost:	***81%***	

Ownership Costs

Cost Area	5 Year Cost	Rate
Depreciation	$7,716	Excellent
Financing ($388/month)	$3,177	
Insurance (Rating 7)	$7,035	Excellent
State Fees	$781	
Fuel (Hwy 28 City 21)	$3,530	Average
Maintenance	$5,404	Worse Than Average
Repairs	$550	Excellent

Ownership Cost By Year

$2,000 $4,000 $6,000 $8,000

1993 1994 1995 1996 1997

Warranty/Maintenance Info

Major Tune-Up	$185	Worse Than Average
Minor Tune-Up	$113	Average
Brake Service	$206	Average
Overall Warranty	3 yr/36k	Average
Drivetrain Warranty	5 yr/60k	Excellent
Rust Warranty	5 yr/unlim. mi	Better Than Average
Maintenance Warranty	N/A	
Roadside Assistance	N/A	

Resale Value

1993	1994	1995	1996	1997
$15,619	$14,491	$13,462	$12,562	$11,565

Ownership Costs (5yr)

Average	This Car
$31,005	$28,193
Cost/Mile 44¢	Cost/Mile 40¢

The 1993 Camry is available in ten models - DX, LE, and XLE sedans; DX, LE, XLE, and SE V6 sedans; and DX, LE and LE V6 wagons. New for 1993, the LE has a new multi-cone synchromesh gearing added on manual transmission models for an improved shift feel. An oak colored interior has been introduced that includes standard bronze tinted glass. Features include a five-way adjustable driver's seat, color-keyed power outside mirrors, and an illuminated entry/exit fade-out system.

Cumulative Costs

	1993	1994	1995	1996	1997
Annual	$7,178	$4,559	$5,512	$4,275	$6,669
Total	$7,178	$11,737	$17,249	$21,524	$28,193

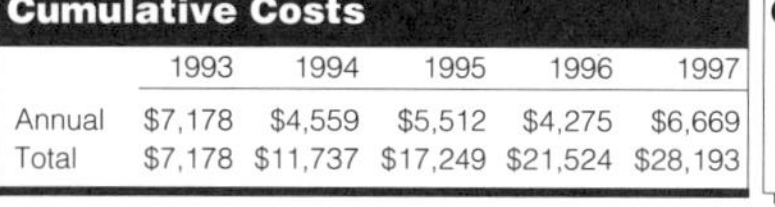

Ownership Cost Rating

Excellent

Toyota Camry LE V6

4 Door Wagon

3.0L 185 hp Gas Fuel Inject.

6 Cylinder "V"

Automatic 4 Speed

2 Wheel Front

Driver Airbag Psngr Belts

Compact Wagon

Base Model Shown

Purchase Price

Car Item	Dealer Cost	List
Base Price	**$17,921**	**$21,208**
Anti-Lock Brakes	$845	$1,030
Manual Transmission	N/A	N/A
Optional Engine	N/A	N/A
Air Conditioning	Std	Std
Power Steering	Std	Std
Cruise Control	Std	Std
All Wheel Drive	N/A	N/A
AM/FM Stereo Cassette	Std	Std
Steering Wheel, Tilt	Std	Std
Power Windows	Std	Std
***Options Price**	$0	$0
***Total Price**	**$17,921**	**$21,208**
Target Price	$19,805	
Destination Charge	$295	
Avg. Tax & Fees	$1,220	
Total Target $	**$21,320**	
Average Dealer Option Cost:	***82%***	

Ownership Costs

Cost Area	5 Year Cost	Rate
Depreciation	$8,774	Excellent
Financing ($429/month)	$3,512	
Insurance (Rating 8)	$7,223	Excellent
State Fees	$861	
Fuel (Hwy 24 City 18 -Prem.)	$4,547	Worse Than Average
Maintenance	$5,828	Poor
Repairs	$580	Excellent

Ownership Cost By Year

$2,000 $4,000 $6,000 $8,000 $10,000

1993 1994 1995 1996 1997

Warranty/Maintenance Info

Major Tune-Up	$211	Poor
Minor Tune-Up	$134	Poor
Brake Service	$191	Average
Overall Warranty	3 yr/36k	Average
Drivetrain Warranty	5 yr/60k	Excellent
Rust Warranty	5 yr/unlim. mi	Better Than Average
Maintenance Warranty	N/A	
Roadside Assistance	N/A	

Resale Value

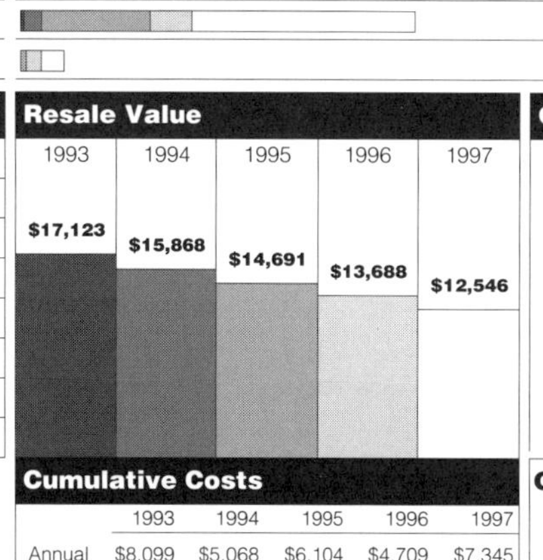

1993	1994	1995	1996	1997
$17,123	$15,868	$14,691	$13,688	$12,546

Ownership Costs (5yr)

Average	This Car
$32,705	$31,325
Cost/Mile 47¢	Cost/Mile 45¢

The 1993 Camry Wagon is available in three models - DX, LE, and LE V6. New for 1993, the LE V6 has two new exterior colors to choose from, a Red Pearl and a Blue Pearl. There is also a new oak interior color available that includes standard bronze tinted safety glass. Features include a five-way adjustable driver's seat, four-wheel disc brakes, color-keyed power outside mirrors, and an automatic illuminated entry/exit fade-out system, and an optional third rear seat with three-point seatbelts.

Cumulative Costs

	1993	1994	1995	1996	1997
Annual	$8,099	$5,068	$6,104	$4,709	$7,345
Total	$8,099	$13,167	$19,271	$23,980	$31,325

Ownership Cost Rating

Better Than Average

* Includes shaded options

** Other purchase requirements apply

Poor | Worse Than Average | Average | Better Than Average | Excellent | Insufficient Information

Refer to *Section 3: Annotated Vehicle Charts* for an explanation of these charts.

Toyota Corolla DX

4 Door Wagon

1.8L 115 hp Gas Fuel Inject. | 4 Cylinder In-Line | Manual 5 Speed | 2 Wheel Front | Driver Airbag Psngr Belts

Subcompact Wag

Purchase Price

Car Item	Dealer Cost	List
Base Price	**$11,160**	**$12,978**
Anti-Lock Brakes	$676	$825
Automatic 4 Speed	$689	$800
Optional Engine	N/A	N/A
Air Conditioning	$688	$860
Power Steering	Std	Std
Cruise Control	$184	$230
All Wheel Drive	N/A	N/A
AM/FM Stereo Cassette	$367	$490
Steering Wheel, Tilt	$124	$145
Power Windows	Pkg	Pkg
***Options Price**	$0	$0
***Total Price**	**$11,160**	**$12,978**
Target Price	$12,128	
Destination Charge	$295	
Avg. Tax & Fees	$754	
Total Target $	**$13,177**	
Average Dealer Option Cost:	***81%***	

Ownership Costs

Cost Area	5 Year Cost	Rate
Depreciation	$6,342	Better Than Average
Financing ($265/month)	$2,170	
Insurance (Rating 8 [Est.])	$7,223	Average
State Fees	$531	
Fuel (Hwy 34 City 28)	$2,784	Average
Maintenance	$5,463	Poor
Repairs	$540	Excellent

Ownership Cost By Year

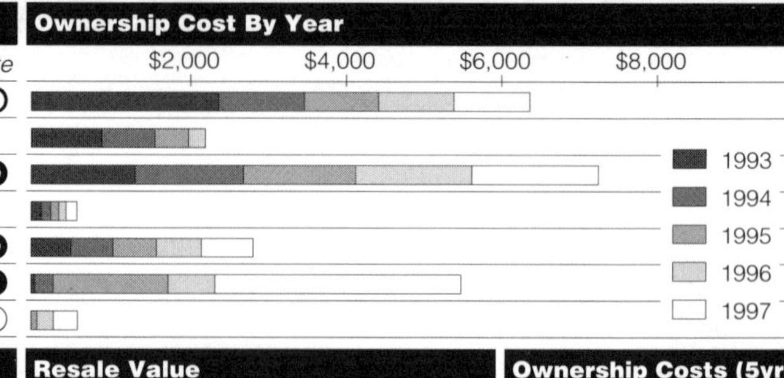

Warranty/Maintenance Info

Item		Rate
Major Tune-Up	$190	Poor
Minor Tune-Up	$118	Poor
Brake Service	$194	Average
Overall Warranty	3 yr/36k	Average
Drivetrain Warranty	5 yr/60k	Excellent
Rust Warranty	5 yr/unlim. mi	Better Than Average
Maintenance Warranty	N/A	
Roadside Assistance	N/A	

Resale Value

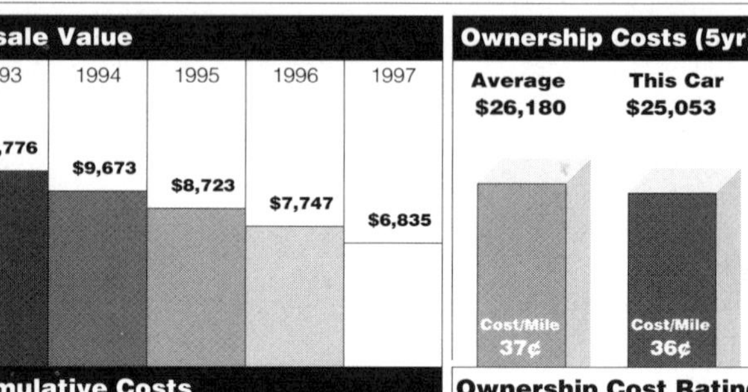

1993	1994	1995	1996	1997
$10,776	$9,673	$8,723	$7,747	$6,835

Ownership Costs (5yr)

Average	This Car
$26,180	$25,053
Cost/Mile 37¢	Cost/Mile 36¢

The 1993 Corolla is available in four models - (Base) Corolla, Deluxe and LE sedans; and Deluxe wagon. New for 1993, the Corolla Deluxe wagon has an all-new, larger, interior and exterior which moves it up one EPA size classification from subcompact to compact. The 1.8 liter engine increases performance with more horsepower and strong low-end torque and a reduction in noise, vibration and harshness. Features include black bodyside molding, remote-control outside mirrors and rear defroster.

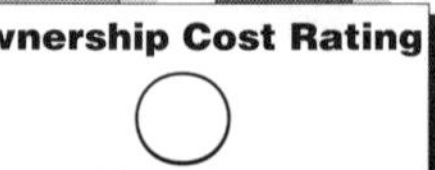

Cumulative Costs

	1993	1994	1995	1996	1997
Annual	$5,333	$4,060	$5,031	$4,120	$6,509
Total	$5,333	$9,393	$14,424	$18,544	$25,053

Ownership Cost Rating

Excellent

Toyota Land Cruiser

4 Door Sport Utility

4.0L 212 hp Gas Fuel Inject. | 6 Cylinder "V" | Automatic 4 Speed | 4 Wheel Full-Time | Manual Seatbelts Only

Utility

Purchase Price

Car Item	Dealer Cost	List
Base Price	**$26,034**	**$31,178**
Anti-Lock Brakes	$939	$1,145
Manual Transmission	N/A	N/A
Optional Engine	N/A	N/A
Air Conditioning	Std	Std
Power Steering	Std	Std
Cruise Control	Std	Std
4 Wheel Full-Time Drive	Std	Std
AM/FM Stereo Cassette	Std	Std
Steering Wheel, Tilt	Std	Std
Power Windows	Std	Std
***Options Price**	$0	$0
***Total Price**	**$26,034**	**$31,178**
Target Price	$29,346	
Destination Charge	$325	
Avg. Tax & Fees	$1,799	
Total Target $	**$31,470**	
Average Dealer Option Cost:	***81%***	

Ownership Costs

Cost Area	5 Year Cost	Rate
Depreciation	$10,752	Average
Financing ($633/month)	$5,184	
Insurance (Rating 19)	$9,987	Average
State Fees	$1,261	
Fuel (Hwy 15 City 12)	$6,395	Poor
Maintenance	$5,326	Poor
Repairs	$720	Excellent

Ownership Cost By Year

$2,000 | $4,000 | $6,000 | $8,000 | $10,000 | $12,000

1993 | 1994 | 1995 | 1996 | 1997

Warranty/Maintenance Info

Item		Rate
Major Tune-Up	$181	Average
Minor Tune-Up	$117	Worse Than Average
Brake Service	$208	Better Than Average
Overall Warranty	3 yr/36k	Average
Drivetrain Warranty	5 yr/60k	Excellent
Rust Warranty	5 yr/unlim. mi	Better Than Average
Maintenance Warranty	N/A	
Roadside Assistance	N/A	

Resale Value

1993	1994	1995	1996	1997
$23,863	$23,236	$22,558	$21,665	$20,718

Ownership Costs (5yr)

Average	This Car
$39,525	$39,625
Cost/Mile 56¢	Cost/Mile 57¢

The 1993 Toyota Land Cruiser is available in one model edition - Wagon. New for 1993, the Land Cruiser provides an all-new, 24-valve V-6 engine. Coupled to the new powerplant is an all-new, four-speed electronically controlled automatic transmission. A new leather interior package is now available. Standard equipment includes full instrumentation, air conditioning, deluxe stereo, larger fender flares, power windows/locks and cruise control. Options include 16-inch alloy wheels and privacy glass.

Cumulative Costs

	1993	1994	1995	1996	1997
Annual	$13,156	$5,909	$7,104	$5,900	$7,556
Total	$13,156	$19,065	$26,169	$32,069	$39,625

Ownership Cost Rating

Average

* Includes shaded options

** Other purchase requirements apply

Poor | Worse Than Average | Average | Better Than Average | Excellent | Insufficient Information

Refer to *Section 3: Annotated Vehicle Charts* for an explanation of these charts.

Toyota Pickup
2 Door Regular Cab

2.4L 116 hp Gas Fuel Inject.

4 Cylinder In-Line

Manual 5 Speed

2 Wheel Rear

Manual Seatbelts Only

Purchase Price

Car Item	Dealer Cost	List
Base Price	**$8,269**	**$9,188**
Anti-Lock Brakes	$255	** $300
Automatic Transmission	N/A	N/A
Optional Engine	N/A	N/A
Air Conditioning	Dlr	Dlr
Power Steering	$246	$290
Cruise Control	N/A	N/A
All Wheel Drive	N/A	N/A
AM/FM Stereo Cassette	$292	$390
Steering Wheel, Tilt	N/A	N/A
Power Windows	N/A	N/A
***Options Price**	$538	$680
***Total Price**	**$8,807**	**$9,868**
Target Price	$9,501	
Destination Charge	$295	
Avg. Tax & Fees	$592	
Total Target $	**$10,388**	
Average Dealer Option Cost:	***81%***	

Ownership Costs

Cost Area	5 Year Cost	Rate
Depreciation	$4,212	Better Than Average
Financing ($209/month)	$1,711	
Insurance (Rating 8)	$7,432	Worse Than Average
State Fees	$406	
Fuel (Hwy 26 City 22)	$3,597	Better Than Average
Maintenance	$3,984	Average
Repairs	$570	Excellent

Ownership Cost By Year

$2,000 $4,000 $6,000 $8,000

1993 1994 1995 1996 1997

Warranty/Maintenance Info

Item	Cost/Term	Rate
Major Tune-Up	$195	Worse Than Average
Minor Tune-Up	$107	Worse Than Average
Brake Service	$211	Average
Overall Warranty	3 yr/36k	Average
Drivetrain Warranty	5 yr/60k	Excellent
Rust Warranty	5 yr/unlim. mi	Better Than Average
Maintenance Warranty	N/A	
Roadside Assistance	N/A	

Resale Value

1993	1994	1995	1996	1997
$8,948	$8,184	$7,580	$6,900	$6,176

Ownership Costs (5yr)

Average	This Car
$21,987	$21,912
Cost/Mile 31¢	Cost/Mile 31¢

The 1993 Toyota Pickup is available in four models - (Base) Pickup, Deluxe, Deluxe 4WD and Deluxe 4WD V6. New for 1993, the Base pickup offers two new colors (Pewter Pearl and Bright Blue Metallic). Features include an analog speedometer, fuel gauge and coolant gauge, a tilt-forward bench seat with headrests, durable vinyl seats and trim, remote hood release and front brake pad warning indicator light. The double-wall bed features a one-touch release system and holds up to a 1,640-lb. payload.

Cumulative Costs

	1993	1994	1995	1996	1997
Annual	$4,338	$3,740	$4,585	$4,063	$5,186
Total	$4,338	$8,078	$12,663	$16,726	$21,912

Ownership Cost Rating

Average

Toyota Pickup DX
2 Door Regular Cab

2.4L 116 hp Gas Fuel Inject.

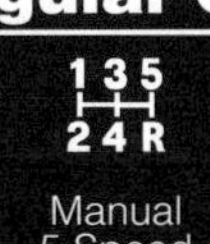

4 Cylinder In-Line

Manual 5 Speed

2 Wheel Rear

Manual Seatbelts Only

Purchase Price

Car Item	Dealer Cost	List
Base Price	**$9,034**	**$10,208**
Anti-Lock Brakes	$255	** $300
Automatic 4 Speed	$637	$720
Optional Engine	N/A	N/A
Air Conditioning	Dlr	Dlr
Power Steering	$246	$290
Cruise Control	N/A	N/A
All Wheel Drive	N/A	N/A
AM/FM Stereo Cassette	$292	$390
Steering Wheel, Tilt	$123	$145
Long Bed	$317	$540
***Options Price**	$538	$680
***Total Price**	**$9,572**	**$10,888**
Target Price	$10,347	
Destination Charge	$295	
Avg. Tax & Fees	$644	
Total Target $	**$11,286**	
Average Dealer Option Cost:	***84%***	

Ownership Costs

Cost Area	5 Year Cost	Rate
Depreciation	$4,568	Better Than Average
Financing ($227/month)	$1,859	
Insurance (Rating 10)	$7,689	Poor
State Fees	$447	
Fuel (Hwy 26 City 22)	$3,597	Better Than Average
Maintenance	$3,987	Average
Repairs	$570	Excellent

Ownership Cost By Year

$2,000 $4,000 $6,000 $8,000

1993 1994 1995 1996 1997

Warranty/Maintenance Info

Item	Cost/Term	Rate
Major Tune-Up	$195	Worse Than Average
Minor Tune-Up	$107	Worse Than Average
Brake Service	$221	Average
Overall Warranty	3 yr/36k	Average
Drivetrain Warranty	5 yr/60k	Excellent
Rust Warranty	5 yr/unlim. mi	Better Than Average
Maintenance Warranty	N/A	
Roadside Assistance	N/A	

Resale Value

1993	1994	1995	1996	1997
$9,529	$8,775	$8,166	$7,462	$6,718

Ownership Costs (5yr)

Average	This Car
$23,024	$22,717
Cost/Mile 33¢	Cost/Mile 32¢

The 1993 Toyota Pickup is available in four models - (Base) Pickup, Deluxe, Deluxe 4WD and Deluxe 4WD V6. New for 1993, the Deluxe pickup offers two new colors (Pewter Pearl and Bright Blue Metallic). Other features include dual outside mirrors, tilt-forward bench seat with headrests and analog gauges. Added options include cloth seats and trim, full carpeting, tilt steering wheel and a resettable tripmeter. The Toyota pickup ranked as the number one truckline in a customer satisfaction study.

Cumulative Costs

	1993	1994	1995	1996	1997
Annual	$4,774	$3,835	$4,690	$4,158	$5,260
Total	$4,774	$8,609	$13,299	$17,457	$22,717

Ownership Cost Rating

Better Than Average

* Includes shaded options

** Other purchase requirements apply

 Poor  Worse Than Average 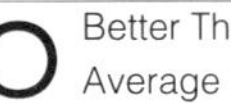 Average  Better Than Average — Excellent — Insufficient Information

Refer to *Section 3: Annotated Vehicle Charts* for an explanation of these charts.

Toyota Xtracab DX
2 Door Extended Cab

2.4L 116 hp Gas Fuel Inject.

4 Cylinder In-Line

Manual 5 Speed

2 Wheel Rear

Manual Seatbelts Only

Small Pickup

SR5 V6 Shown

Purchase Price

Car Item	Dealer Cost	List
Base Price	**$10,151**	**$11,668**
Anti-Lock Brakes	$255	** $300
Automatic 4 Speed	$627	$720
Optional Engine	N/A	N/A
Air Conditioning	Dlr	Dlr
Power Steering	$246	$290
Cruise Control	N/A	N/A
All Wheel Drive	N/A	N/A
AM/FM Stereo Cassette	$405	$540
Steering Wheel, Tilt	$123	$145
Power Windows	N/A	N/A
***Options Price**	$651	$830
***Total Price**	**$10,802**	**$12,498**
Target Price	$11,709	
Destination Charge	$325	
Avg. Tax & Fees	$730	
Total Target $	**$12,764**	
Average Dealer Option Cost:	***83%***	

Ownership Costs

Cost Area	5 Year Cost	Rate
Depreciation	$4,566	Excellent
Financing ($257/month)	$2,103	
Insurance (Rating 11)	$7,902	Poor
State Fees	$513	
Fuel (Hwy 26 City 22)	$3,597	Better Than Average
Maintenance	$4,029	Average
Repairs	$570	Excellent

Ownership Cost By Year

$2,000 $4,000 $6,000 $8,000

1993 1994 1995 1996 1997

Warranty/Maintenance Info

Item		Rate
Major Tune-Up	$195	Worse Than Average
Minor Tune-Up	$107	Worse Than Average
Brake Service	$221	Average
Overall Warranty	3 yr/36k	Average
Drivetrain Warranty	5 yr/60k	Excellent
Rust Warranty	5 yr/unlim. mi	Better Than Average
Maintenance Warranty	N/A	
Roadside Assistance	N/A	

Resale Value

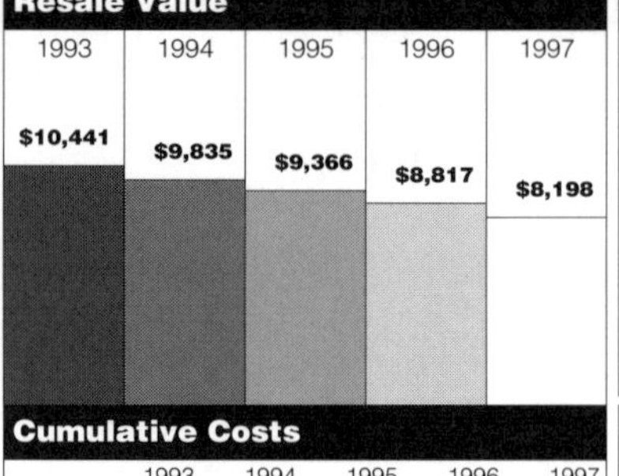

1993	1994	1995	1996	1997
$10,441	$9,835	$9,366	$8,817	$8,198

Ownership Costs (5yr)

Average	This Car
$24,661	$23,280
Cost/Mile 35¢	Cost/Mile 33¢

The 1993 Toyota Xtracab is available in six models - DX, DX V6 and SR5 V6 pickups with two- or four-wheel drive. New for 1993, the Deluxe Xtracab 2WD is offered in two new colors (Pewter Pearl and Bright Blue Metallic). Other features include dual outside mirrors, tilt-out rear quarter windows, full wheel covers, dual rear storage compartments, reclining bucket seats and optional jump-seats. Toyota trucks ranked as the number one truckline in a customer satisfaction product quality dealer service study.

Cumulative Costs

	1993	1994	1995	1996	1997
Annual	$5,497	$3,818	$4,675	$4,077	$5,213
Total	$5,497	$9,315	$13,990	$18,067	$23,280

Ownership Cost Rating

Excellent

Toyota Xtracab DX V6
2 Door Extended Cab

3.0L 150 hp Gas Fuel Inject.

6 Cylinder "V"

Manual 5 Speed

2 Wheel Rear

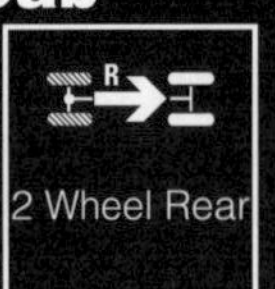

Manual Seatbelts Only

Small Pickup

SR5 Model Shown

Purchase Price

Car Item	Dealer Cost	List
Base Price	**$11,134**	**$12,798**
Anti-Lock Brakes	$255	$300
Automatic 4 Speed	$783	$900
Optional Engine	N/A	N/A
Air Conditioning	Dlr	Dlr
Power Steering	Std	Std
Cruise Control	N/A	N/A
All Wheel Drive	N/A	N/A
AM/FM Stereo Cassette	$405	$540
Steering Wheel, Tilt	$123	$145
Power Windows	N/A	N/A
***Options Price**	$405	$540
***Total Price**	**$11,539**	**$13,338**
Target Price	$12,539	
Destination Charge	$325	
Avg. Tax & Fees	$780	
Total Target $	**$13,644**	
Average Dealer Option Cost:	***83%***	

Ownership Costs

Cost Area	5 Year Cost	Rate
Depreciation	$5,509	Better Than Average
Financing ($274/month)	$2,247	
Insurance (Rating 12)	$8,108	Poor
State Fees	$547	
Fuel (Hwy 26 City 22)	$3,597	Better Than Average
Maintenance	$4,537	Poor
Repairs	$570	Excellent

Ownership Cost By Year

$2,000 $4,000 $6,000 $8,000 $10,000

1993 1994 1995 1996 1997

Warranty/Maintenance Info

Item		Rate
Major Tune-Up	$220	Poor
Minor Tune-Up	$133	Poor
Brake Service	$174	Excellent
Overall Warranty	3 yr/36k	Average
Drivetrain Warranty	5 yr/60k	Excellent
Rust Warranty	5 yr/unlim. mi	Better Than Average
Maintenance Warranty	N/A	
Roadside Assistance	N/A	

Resale Value

1993	1994	1995	1996	1997
$10,090	$9,600	$9,196	$8,686	$8,135

Ownership Costs (5yr)

Average	This Car
$25,515	$25,115
Cost/Mile 36¢	Cost/Mile 36¢

The 1993 Toyota Xtracab is available in six models - DX, DX V6 and SR5 V6 pickups with two- or four-wheel drive. New for 1993, the Deluxe Xtracab 2WD V6 is offered in two new colors (Pewter Pearl and Bright Blue Metallic). Other features include power-assist steering, tilt-out rear quarter windows, dual rear storage compartments, reclining bucket seats and optional jump-seats. Toyota trucks ranked as the number one truckline in a customer satisfaction product quality dealer service study.

Cumulative Costs

	1993	1994	1995	1996	1997
Annual	$6,838	$3,829	$4,721	$4,161	$5,566
Total	$6,838	$10,667	$15,388	$19,549	$25,115

Ownership Cost Rating

Better Than Average

* Includes shaded options

** Other purchase requirements apply

 Poor  Worse Than Average  Average  Better Than Average 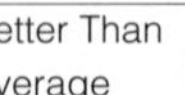 Excellent  Insufficient Information

Refer to *Section 3: Annotated Vehicle Charts* for an explanation of these charts.

Toyota Xtracab SR5 V6

2 Door Extended Cab

Small Pickup

3.0L 150 hp Gas Fuel Inject.

6 Cylinder "V"

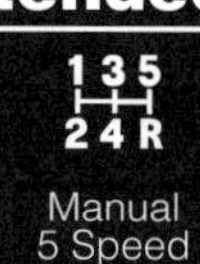

Manual 5 Speed

2 Wheel Rear

Manual Seatbelts Only

Purchase Price

Car Item	Dealer Cost	List
Base Price	**$12,515**	**$14,638**
Anti-Lock Brakes	Std	Std
Automatic 4 Speed	$770	$900
Optional Engine	N/A	N/A
Air Conditioning	Dlr	Dlr
Power Steering	Std	Std
Cruise Control	$248	$310
All Wheel Drive	N/A	N/A
AM/FM Stereo Cassette	$255	$340
Steering Wheel, Tilt	Std	Std
Power Windows	Pkg	Pkg
***Options Price**	$255	$340
***Total Price**	**$12,770**	**$14,978**
Target Price	$13,924	
Destination Charge	$325	
Avg. Tax & Fees	$865	
Total Target $	**$15,114**	
Average Dealer Option Cost:	***82%***	

Ownership Costs

Cost Area	5 Year Cost	Rate
Depreciation	$6,281	Average
Financing ($304/month)	$2,490	
Insurance (Rating 13)	$8,271	Poor
State Fees	$612	
Fuel (Hwy 23 City 18)	$4,213	Average
Maintenance	$4,486	Worse Than Average
Repairs	$570	Excellent

Ownership Cost By Year

$2,000 $4,000 $6,000 $8,000 $10,000

1993 1994 1995 1996 1997

Warranty/Maintenance Info

Major Tune-Up	$223	Poor
Minor Tune-Up	$134	Poor
Brake Service	$221	Average
Overall Warranty	3 yr/36k	Average
Drivetrain Warranty	5 yr/60k	Excellent
Rust Warranty	5 yr/unlim. mi	Better Than Average
Maintenance Warranty	N/A	
Roadside Assistance	N/A	

Resale Value

1993	1994	1995	1996	1997
$11,221	$10,623	$10,108	$9,488	$8,833

Ownership Costs (5yr)

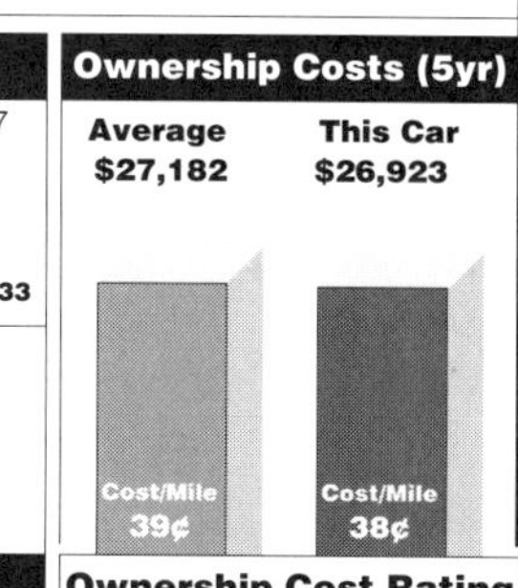

Average	This Car
$27,182	$26,923
Cost/Mile 39¢	Cost/Mile 38¢

Cumulative Costs

	1993	1994	1995	1996	1997
Annual	$7,438	$4,178	$5,050	$4,436	$5,821
Total	$7,438	$11,616	$16,666	$21,102	$26,923

Ownership Cost Rating

Average

The 1993 Toyota Xtracab is available in six models - DX, DX V6 and SR5 V6 pickups with two- or four-wheel drive. New for 1993, the SR5 Xtracab 2WD V6 is offered in two new colors (Pewter Pearl and Bright Blue Metallic) and has new graphics. Other features include power steering, tilt-out rear quarter windows, dual rear storage compartments, and an optional seven-way adjustable driver's seat. Toyota ranked as the number one truckline in a customer satisfaction product quality dealer service study.

Toyota Pickup DX 4WD

2 Door Regular Cab

Small Pickup

2.4L 116 hp Gas Fuel Inject.

4 Cylinder In-Line

Manual 5 Speed

4 Wheel On-Demand

Manual Seatbelts Only

2WD Model Shown

Purchase Price

Car Item	Dealer Cost	List
Base Price	**$11,828**	**$13,518**
Anti-Lock Brakes	$255	** $300
Automatic 4 Speed	$788	$900
Optional Engine	N/A	N/A
Air Conditioning	Dlr	Dlr
Power Steering	$238	$280
Cruise Control	$184	$230
4 Whl On-Demand Dr.	Std	Std
AM/FM Stereo Cassette	$292	$390
Steering Wheel, Tilt	$123	$145
Power Windows	N/A	N/A
***Options Price**	$530	$670
***Total Price**	**$12,358**	**$14,188**
Target Price	$13,452	
Destination Charge	$295	
Avg. Tax & Fees	$832	
Total Target $	**$14,579**	
Average Dealer Option Cost:	***84%***	

Ownership Costs

Cost Area	5 Year Cost	Rate
Depreciation	$5,667	Better Than Average
Financing ($293/month)	$2,401	
Insurance (Rating 12)	$8,108	Poor
State Fees	$579	
Fuel (Hwy 22 City 19)	$4,214	Worse Than Average
Maintenance	$4,158	Worse Than Average
Repairs	$680	Better Than Average

Ownership Cost By Year

$2,000 $4,000 $6,000 $8,000 $10,000

1993 1994 1995 1996 1997

Warranty/Maintenance Info

Major Tune-Up	$195	Worse Than Average
Minor Tune-Up	$107	Worse Than Average
Brake Service	$221	Average
Overall Warranty	3 yr/36k	Average
Drivetrain Warranty	5 yr/60k	Excellent
Rust Warranty	5 yr/unlim. mi	Better Than Average
Maintenance Warranty	N/A	
Roadside Assistance	N/A	

Resale Value

1993	1994	1995	1996	1997
$12,497	$11,520	$10,685	$9,774	$8,912

Ownership Costs (5yr)

Average	This Car
$26,379	$25,807
Cost/Mile 38¢	Cost/Mile 37¢

Cumulative Costs

	1993	1994	1995	1996	1997
Annual	$5,549	$4,456	$5,339	$4,685	$5,778
Total	$5,549	$10,005	$15,344	$20,029	$25,807

Ownership Cost Rating

Better Than Average

The 1993 Toyota Pickup is available in four models - (Base) Pickup, Deluxe, Deluxe 4WD and Deluxe 4WD V6. New for 1993, the Deluxe 4WD pickup offers two new colors (Pewter Pearl and Bright Blue Metallic) and features all-new graphics. Features include a push-button clutch-cancel control (5-speed manual transmissions), manual-locking front hubs or optional 4WDemand, skid plates to help protect the engine, fuel tank, front suspension and transfer case and an optional 31-inch wheel package.

* Includes shaded options

** Other purchase requirements apply

 Poor  Worse Than Average  Average  Better Than Average  Excellent  Insufficient Information

Refer to *Section 3: Annotated Vehicle Charts* for an explanation of these charts.

Toyota Pickup DX V6 4WD
2 Door Regular Cab

3.0L 150 hp Gas Fuel Inject. | 6 Cylinder "V" | Manual 5 Speed | 4 Wheel On-Demand | Manual Seatbelts Only

Small Pickup

Purchase Price

Car Item	Dealer Cost	List
Base Price	**$12,878**	**$14,718**
Anti-Lock Brakes	$255	$300
Automatic Transmission	N/A	N/A
Optional Engine	N/A	N/A
Air Conditioning	Dlr	Dlr
Power Steering	Std	Std
Cruise Control	$184	$230
4 Whl On-Demand Dr.	Std	Std
AM/FM Stereo Cassette	$292	$390
Steering Wheel, Tilt	$123	$145
Power Windows	N/A	N/A
***Options Price**	$292	$390
***Total Price**	**$13,170**	**$15,108**
Target Price	$14,374	
Destination Charge	$295	
Avg. Tax & Fees	$887	
Total Target $	**$15,556**	
Average Dealer Option Cost:	***81%***	

Ownership Costs

Cost Area	5 Year Cost	Rate
Depreciation	$6,063	Better Than Average
Financing ($313/month)	$2,562	
Insurance (Rating 14)	$8,446	Worse Than Average
State Fees	$616	
Fuel (Hwy 18 City 15)	$5,233	Poor
Maintenance	$4,504	Worse Than Average
Repairs	$680	Better Than Average

Warranty/Maintenance Info

Item		Rate
Major Tune-Up	$223	Poor
Minor Tune-Up	$134	Poor
Brake Service	$174	Excellent
Overall Warranty	3 yr/36k	Average
Drivetrain Warranty	5 yr/60k	Excellent
Rust Warranty	5 yr/unlim. mi	Better Than Average
Maintenance Warranty	N/A	
Roadside Assistance	N/A	

Ownership Cost By Year

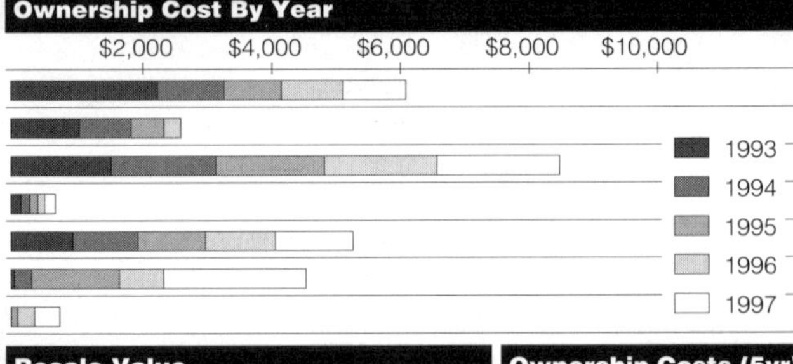

Resale Value

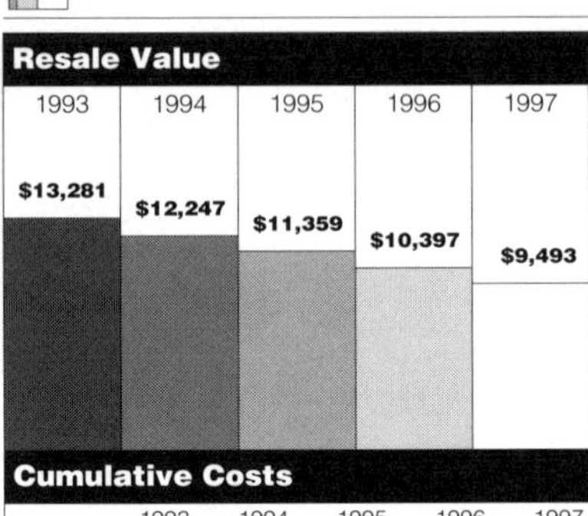

Ownership Costs (5yr)

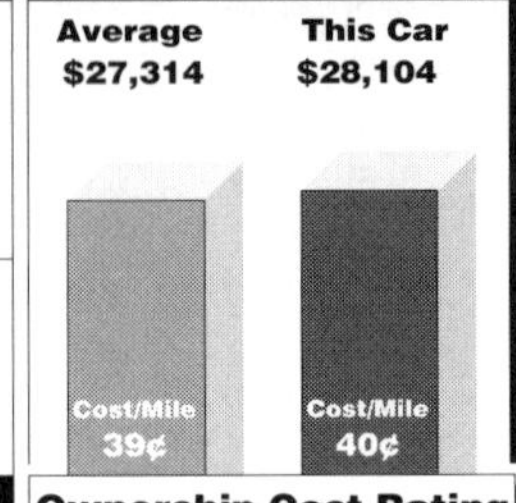

The 1993 Toyota Pickup is available in four models - (Base) Pickup, Deluxe, Deluxe 4WD and Deluxe 4WD V6. New for 1993, the Deluxe 4WD V6 pickup offers two new colors (Pewter Pearl and Bright Blue Metallic) and all-new graphics. Features include a push-button clutch-cancel control (5-speed manual transmissions), manual-locking front hubs or optional 4WDemand, power-assist steering, skid plates to protect the engine, fuel tank, front suspension and transfer case and an optional 31-inch wheel package.

Cumulative Costs

	1993	1994	1995	1996	1997
Annual	$6,071	$4,868	$5,713	$5,051	$6,401
Total	$6,071	$10,939	$16,652	$21,703	$28,104

Ownership Cost Rating

Worse Than Average

Toyota Xtracab DX 4WD
2 Door Extended Cab

2.4L 116 hp Gas Fuel Inject. | 4 Cylinder In-Line | Manual 5 Speed | 4 Wheel On-Demand | Manual Seatbelts Only

Small Pickup

SR5 V6 Shown

Purchase Price

Car Item	Dealer Cost	List
Base Price	**$12,898**	**$14,998**
Anti-Lock Brakes	$255	** $300
Automatic 4 Speed	$783	$910
Optional Engine	N/A	N/A
Air Conditioning	Dlr	Dlr
Power Steering	$246	$290
Cruise Control	$184	$230
4 Whl On-Demand Dr.	Std	Std
AM/FM Stereo Cassette	$405	$540
Steering Wheel, Tilt	$123	$145
Power Windows	N/A	N/A
***Options Price**	$651	$830
***Total Price**	**$13,549**	**$15,828**
Target Price	$14,788	
Destination Charge	$325	
Avg. Tax & Fees	$918	
Total Target $	**$16,031**	
Average Dealer Option Cost:	***83%***	

Ownership Costs

Cost Area	5 Year Cost	Rate
Depreciation	$5,468	Excellent
Financing ($322/month)	$2,641	
Insurance (Rating 12)	$8,108	Poor
State Fees	$646	
Fuel (Hwy 22 City 19)	$4,214	Worse Than Average
Maintenance	$4,177	Worse Than Average
Repairs	$680	Better Than Average

Warranty/Maintenance Info

Item		Rate
Major Tune-Up	$195	Worse Than Average
Minor Tune-Up	$107	Worse Than Average
Brake Service	$221	Average
Overall Warranty	3 yr/36k	Average
Drivetrain Warranty	5 yr/60k	Excellent
Rust Warranty	5 yr/unlim. mi	Better Than Average
Maintenance Warranty	N/A	
Roadside Assistance	N/A	

Ownership Cost By Year

$2,000 | $4,000 | $6,000 | $8,000 | $10,000

1993, 1994, 1995, 1996, 1997

Resale Value

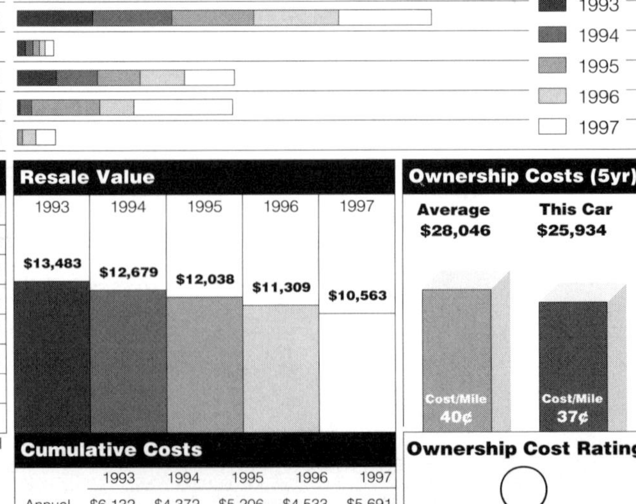

Ownership Costs (5yr)

Average $28,046 | This Car $25,934

Cost/Mile 40¢ | Cost/Mile 37¢

The 1993 Toyota Xtracab is available in six models - DX, DX V6 and SR5 V6 pickups with two- or four-wheel drive. New for 1993, the Deluxe Xtracab 4WD is offered in two new colors (Pewter Pearl and Bright Blue Metallic). Other features include dual outside mirrors, tilt-out rear quarter windows, dual rear storage compartments, reclining bucket seats and optional jump-seats. Toyota trucks ranked as the number one truckline in a customer satisfaction product quality dealer service study.

Cumulative Costs

	1993	1994	1995	1996	1997
Annual	$6,132	$4,372	$5,206	$4,533	$5,691
Total	$6,132	$10,504	$15,710	$20,243	$25,934

Ownership Cost Rating

Excellent

* Includes shaded options

** Other purchase requirements apply

 Poor  Worse Than Average  Average  Better Than Average  Excellent  Insufficient Information

Refer to *Section 3: Annotated Vehicle Charts* for an explanation of these charts.

Toyota Xtracab DX V6 4WD
2 Door Extended Cab

3.0L 150 hp Gas Fuel Inject.

6 Cylinder "V"

Manual 5 Speed

4 Wheel On-Demand

Manual Seatbelts Only

Purchase Price

Car Item	Dealer Cost	List
Base Price	**$13,896**	**$16,158**
Anti-Lock Brakes	$255	** $300
Automatic 4 Speed	$1,109	$1,290
Optional Engine	N/A	N/A
Air Conditioning	Dlr	Dlr
Power Steering	Std	Std
Cruise Control	$184	$230
4 Whl On-Demand Dr.	Std	Std
AM/FM Stereo Cassette	$405	$540
Steering Wheel, Tilt	$123	$145
Power Windows	N/A	N/A
***Options Price**	$405	$540
***Total Price**	**$14,301**	**$16,698**
Target Price	$15,648	
Destination Charge	$325	
Avg. Tax & Fees	$969	
Total Target $	**$16,942**	
Average Dealer Option Cost:	***83%***	

Ownership Costs

Cost Area	5 Year Cost	Rate
Depreciation	$6,240	Excellent
Financing ($341/month)	$2,791	
Insurance (Rating 14)	$8,446	Worse Than Average
State Fees	$680	
Fuel (Hwy 18 City 15)	$5,233	Poor
Maintenance	$4,751	Poor
Repairs	$680	Better Than Average

Ownership Cost By Year

$2,000 $4,000 $6,000 $8,000 $10,000

1993 1994 1995 1996 1997

Warranty/Maintenance Info

Item		Rate
Major Tune-Up	$223	Poor
Minor Tune-Up	$134	Poor
Brake Service	$174	Excellent
Overall Warranty	3 yr/36k	Average
Drivetrain Warranty	5 yr/60k	Excellent
Rust Warranty	5 yr/unlim. mi	Better Than Average
Maintenance Warranty	N/A	
Roadside Assistance	N/A	

Resale Value

1993	1994	1995	1996	1997
$13,214	$12,576	$12,019	$11,375	$10,702

Ownership Costs (5yr)

Average	This Car
$28,931	$28,821
Cost/Mile 41¢	Cost/Mile 41¢

Cumulative Costs

	1993	1994	1995	1996	1997
Annual	$7,636	$4,557	$5,515	$4,797	$6,316
Total	$7,636	$12,193	$17,708	$22,505	$28,821

Ownership Cost Rating

Average

The 1993 Toyota Xtracab is available in six models - DX, DX V6 and SR5 V6 pickups with two- or four-wheel drive. New for 1993, the Deluxe Xtracab 4WD V6 is offered in two new colors (Pewter Pearl and Bright Blue Metallic). Other features include optional power-assist steering, tilt-out rear quarter windows, dual rear storage compartments, reclining bucket seats and optional jump-seats. Toyota trucks ranked as the number one truckline in a customer satisfaction product quality dealer service study.

Toyota Xtracab SR5 V6 4WD
2 Door Extended Cab

3.0L 150 hp Gas Fuel Inject.

6 Cylinder "V"

Manual 5 Speed

4 Wheel On-Demand

Manual Seatbelts Only

Purchase Price

Car Item	Dealer Cost	List
Base Price	**$15,175**	**$17,958**
Anti-Lock Brakes	Std	Std
Automatic 4 Speed	$1,081	$1,280
Optional Engine	N/A	N/A
Air Conditioning	Dlr	Dlr
Power Steering	Std	Std
Cruise Control	$248	$310
4 Whl On-Demand Dr.	Std	Std
AM/FM Stereo Cassette	$255	$340
Steering Wheel, Tilt	Std	Std
Power Windows	Pkg	Pkg
***Options Price**	$255	$340
***Total Price**	**$15,430**	**$18,298**
Target Price	$16,937	
Destination Charge	$325	
Avg. Tax & Fees	$1,049	
Total Target $	**$18,311**	
Average Dealer Option Cost:	***82%***	

Ownership Costs

Cost Area	5 Year Cost	Rate
Depreciation	$6,917	Better Than Average
Financing ($368/month)	$3,016	
Insurance (Rating 16)	$8,995	Worse Than Average
State Fees	$745	
Fuel (Hwy 18 City 15)	$5,233	Poor
Maintenance	$4,615	Poor
Repairs	$680	Better Than Average

Ownership Cost By Year

$2,000 $4,000 $6,000 $8,000 $10,000

1993 1994 1995 1996 1997

Warranty/Maintenance Info

Item		Rate
Major Tune-Up	$223	Poor
Minor Tune-Up	$134	Poor
Brake Service	$221	Average
Overall Warranty	3 yr/36k	Average
Drivetrain Warranty	5 yr/60k	Excellent
Rust Warranty	5 yr/unlim. mi	Better Than Average
Maintenance Warranty	N/A	
Roadside Assistance	N/A	

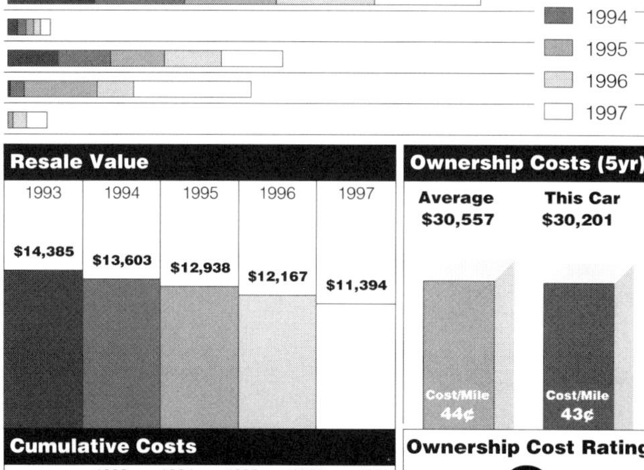

Resale Value

1993	1994	1995	1996	1997
$14,385	$13,603	$12,938	$12,167	$11,394

Ownership Costs (5yr)

Average	This Car
$30,557	$30,201
Cost/Mile 44¢	Cost/Mile 43¢

Cumulative Costs

	1993	1994	1995	1996	1997
Annual	$8,045	$4,892	$5,740	$5,053	$6,471
Total	$8,045	$12,937	$18,677	$23,730	$30,201

Ownership Cost Rating

Average

The 1993 Toyota Xtracab is available in six models - DX, DX V6 and SR5 V6 pickups with two- or four-wheel drive. New for 1993, the SR5 Xtracab 4WD V6 is offered in two new colors (Pewter Pearl and Bright Blue Metallic) and has all-new graphics. Other features include power-assist steering, tilt-out rear quarter windows, dual rear storage compartments and optional jump-seats. Toyota trucks ranked as the number one truckline in a customer satisfaction product quality dealer service study.

* Includes shaded options

** Other purchase requirements apply

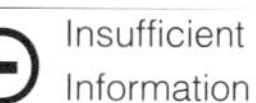

Poor 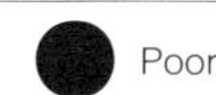 Worse Than Average  Average Better Than Average  Excellent Insufficient Information

Refer to *Section 3: Annotated Vehicle Charts* for an explanation of these charts.

Toyota Previa DX
3 Door Pass Van

2.4L 138 hp Gas Fuel Inject.

4 Cylinder In-Line

Manual 5 Speed

2 Wheel Rear

Driver Airbag Psngr Belts

Mini Van

Purchase Price

Car Item	Dealer Cost	List
Base Price	**$15,816**	**$18,498**
Anti-Lock Brakes	$1,065	** $1,305
Automatic 4 Speed	$684	$800
Optional Engine	N/A	N/A
Air Cond., Front & Rear	$1,260	$1,575
Power Steering	Std	Std
Cruise Control	$240	$300
All Wheel Drive	N/A	N/A
AM/FM Stereo Cassette	$397	$530
Steering Wheel, Tilt	Std	Std
Power Windows	Pkg	Pkg
***Options Price**	$2,581	$3,205
***Total Price**	**$18,397**	**$21,703**
Target Price	$20,225	
Destination Charge	$295	
Avg. Tax & Fees	$1,246	
Total Target $	**$21,766**	
Average Dealer Option Cost:	***81%***	

Ownership Costs

Cost Area	5 Year Cost	Rate
Depreciation	$6,775	Average
Financing ($437/month)	$3,585	
Insurance (Rating 13)	$8,061	Better Than Average
State Fees	$880	
Fuel (Hwy 22 City 17)	$4,431	Average
Maintenance	$5,842	Poor
Repairs	$580	Excellent

Ownership Cost By Year

$2,000 $4,000 $6,000 $8,000 $10,000

1993 1994 1995 1996 1997

Warranty/Maintenance Info

Major Tune-Up	$274	Poor
Minor Tune-Up	$185	Poor
Brake Service	$204	Better Than Average
Overall Warranty	3 yr/36k	Average
Drivetrain Warranty	5 yr/60k	Excellent
Rust Warranty	5 yr/unlim. mi	Better Than Average
Maintenance Warranty	N/A	
Roadside Assistance	N/A	

Resale Value

1993	1994	1995	1996	1997
$20,536	$18,705	$17,350	$16,096	$14,991

Ownership Costs (5yr)

Average	This Car
$29,771	$30,154
Cost/Mile 43¢	Cost/Mile 43¢

The 1993 Previa is available in four models - DX, All-Trac Deluxe, LE and All-Trac LE editions. New for 1993, the Previa DX features 7-passenger seating. Safety features include reinforced pillars, a crush-resistant roof and steel reinforcements in front doors. Materials used for the interior are selected to help cushion impact from a collision. The Previa is the only van to meet Passenger Car Federal Motor Vehicle Safety Standards. Previa ranked Best Compact Van in a '92 quality study.

Cumulative Costs

	1993	1994	1995	1996	1997
Annual	$5,296	$5,869	$6,645	$5,699	$6,645
Total	$5,296	$11,165	$17,810	$23,509	$30,154

Ownership Cost Rating

Average

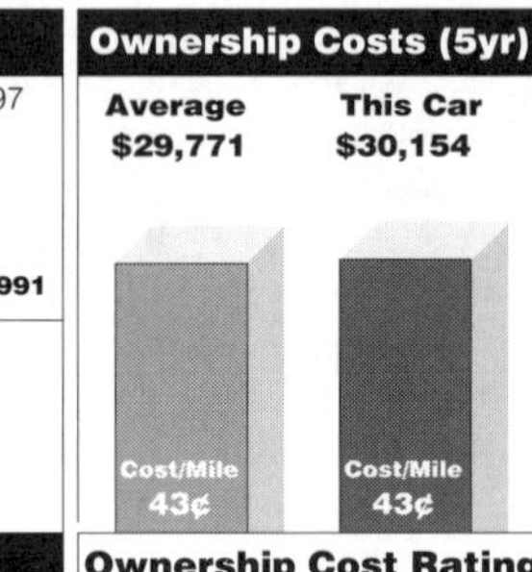

Toyota Previa LE
3 Door Pass Van

2.4L 138 hp Gas Fuel Inject.

4 Cylinder In-Line

Automatic 4 Speed

2 Wheel Rear

Driver Airbag Psngr Belts

Mini Van

Purchase Price

Car Item	Dealer Cost	List
Base Price	**$19,769**	**$23,258**
Anti-Lock Brakes	$845	$1,030
Manual Transmission	N/A	N/A
Optional Engine	N/A	N/A
Air Cond., Front & Rear	Std	Std
Power Steering	Std	Std
Cruise Control	Std	Std
All Wheel Drive	N/A	N/A
AM/FM Stereo Cassette	Std	Std
Steering Wheel, Tilt	Std	Std
Power Windows	Std	Std
***Options Price**	$0	$0
***Total Price**	**$19,769**	**$23,258**
Target Price	$21,947	
Destination Charge	$295	
Avg. Tax & Fees	$1,348	
Total Target $	**$23,590**	
Average Dealer Option Cost:	***81%***	

Ownership Costs

Cost Area	5 Year Cost	Rate
Depreciation	$8,607	Average
Financing ($474/month)	$3,886	
Insurance (Rating 13)	$8,061	Better Than Average
State Fees	$942	
Fuel (Hwy 22 City 17)	$4,431	Average
Maintenance	$6,031	Poor
Repairs	$580	Excellent

Ownership Cost By Year

$2,000 $4,000 $6,000 $8,000 $10,000

1993 1994 1995 1996 1997

Warranty/Maintenance Info

Major Tune-Up	$274	Poor
Minor Tune-Up	$185	Poor
Brake Service	$208	Better Than Average
Overall Warranty	3 yr/36k	Average
Drivetrain Warranty	5 yr/60k	Excellent
Rust Warranty	5 yr/unlim. mi	Better Than Average
Maintenance Warranty	N/A	
Roadside Assistance	N/A	

Resale Value

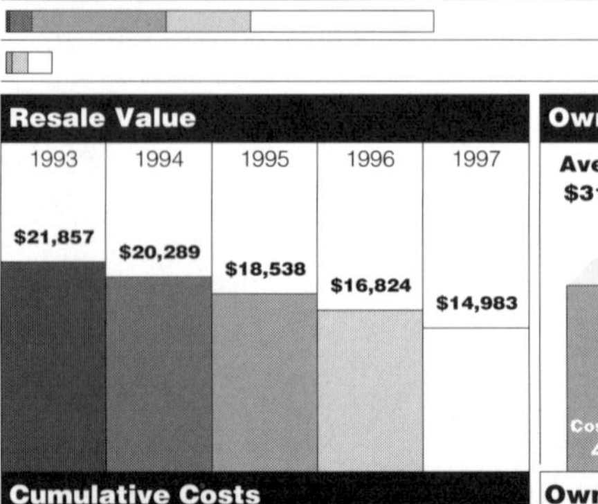

1993	1994	1995	1996	1997
$21,857	$20,289	$18,538	$16,824	$14,983

Ownership Costs (5yr)

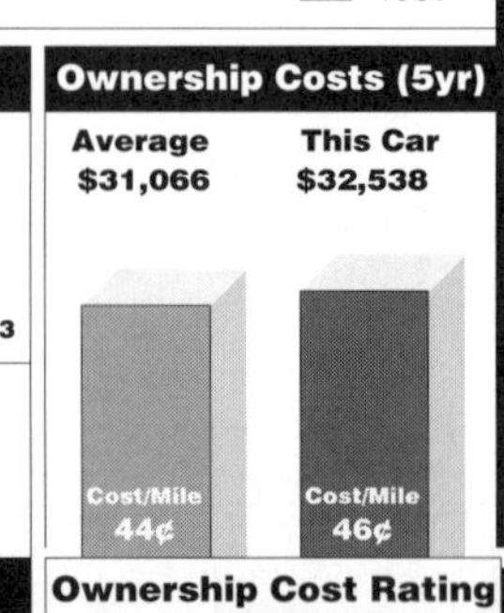

Average	This Car
$31,066	$32,538
Cost/Mile 44¢	Cost/Mile 46¢

The 1993 Previa is available in four models - DX, All-Trac Deluxe, LE and All-Trac LE editions. New for 1993, the Previa LE features seven-passenger seating and a full size spare. Features include dual air conditioners, power front windows, variable intermittent front windshield washers, cruise control, a rear wiper/washer with intermittent operation and dual-power outside mirrors. The LE also comes standard with a Toyota Deluxe electronically tuned radio (ETR)/Casstte with six speakers.

Cumulative Costs

	1993	1994	1995	1996	1997
Annual	$5,941	$5,714	$7,203	$6,192	$7,488
Total	$5,941	$11,655	$18,858	$25,050	$32,538

Ownership Cost Rating

Average

* Includes shaded options

** Other purchase requirements apply

 Poor  Worse Than Average  Average  Better Than Average  Excellent — Insufficient Information

Refer to *Section 3: Annotated Vehicle Charts* for an explanation of these charts.

Toyota Previa All-Trac DX
3 Door Pass Van

2.4L 138 hp Gas Fuel Inject.

4 Cylinder In-Line

Automatic 4 Speed

4 Wheel Full-Time

Driver Airbag Psngr Belts

Purchase Price

Car Item	Dealer Cost	List
Base Price	**$18,996**	**$22,348**
Anti-Lock Brakes	$1,065	** $1,305
Manual Transmission	N/A	N/A
Optional Engine	N/A	N/A
Air Cond., Front & Rear	$1,260	$1,575
Power Steering	Std	Std
Cruise Control	$192	$240
4 Wheel Full-Time Drive	Std	Std
AM/FM Stereo Cassette	$397	$530
Steering Wheel, Tilt	Std	Std
Power Windows	Pkg	Pkg
***Options Price**	$1,849	$2,345
***Total Price**	**$20,845**	**$24,693**
Target Price	$23,097	
Destination Charge	$295	
Avg. Tax & Fees	$1,420	
Total Target $	**$24,812**	
Average Dealer Option Cost:	***80%***	

Ownership Costs

Cost Area	5 Year Cost	Rate
Depreciation	$8,052	Average
Financing ($499/month)	$4,087	
Insurance (Rating 14)	$8,238	Better Than Average
State Fees	$1,000	
Fuel (Hwy 20 City 17)	$4,667	Worse Than Average
Maintenance	$5,882	Poor
Repairs	$680	Better Than Average

Warranty/Maintenance Info

Major Tune-Up	$274	Poor
Minor Tune-Up	$185	Poor
Brake Service	$204	Better Than Average
Overall Warranty	3 yr/36k	Average
Drivetrain Warranty	5 yr/60k	Excellent
Rust Warranty	5 yr/unlim. mi	Better Than Average
Maintenance Warranty	N/A	
Roadside Assistance	N/A	

Ownership Cost By Year

$2,000 $4,000 $6,000 $8,000 $10,000

1993 1994 1995 1996 1997

Resale Value

1993	1994	1995	1996	1997
$23,378	$21,193	$19,548	$18,059	$16,760

Ownership Costs (5yr)

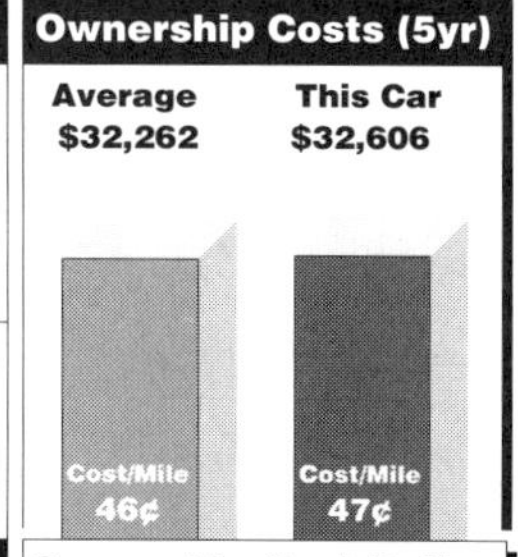

Average	This Car
$32,262	$32,606
Cost/Mile 46¢	Cost/Mile 47¢

The 1993 Previa is available in four models - DX, All-Trac Deluxe, LE and All-Trac LE editions. New for 1993, the Previa DX All-Trac features seven-passenger seating and a full size spare tire. Safety features include all-wheel drive, reinforced pillars, a crush-resistant roof and steel reinforcements in front doors. Materials used for the interior are selected to help cushion impact from a collision. The Previa is the only van to meet Passenger Car Federal Motor Vehicle Safety Standards.

Cumulative Costs

	1993	1994	1995	1996	1997
Annual	$5,816	$6,486	$7,154	$6,117	$7,033
Total	$5,816	$12,302	$19,456	$25,573	$32,606

Ownership Cost Rating

Average

Toyota Previa All-Trac LE
3 Door Pass Van

2.4L 138 hp Gas Fuel Inject.

4 Cylinder In-Line

Automatic 4 Speed

4 Wheel Full-Time

Driver Airbag Psngr Belts

Purchase Price

Car Item	Dealer Cost	List
Base Price	**$22,158**	**$26,068**
Anti-Lock Brakes	$845	$1,030
Manual Transmission	N/A	N/A
Optional Engine	N/A	N/A
Air Cond., Front & Rear	Std	Std
Power Steering	Std	Std
Cruise Control	Std	Std
4 Wheel Full-Time Drive	Std	Std
AM/FM Stereo Cassette	Std	Std
Steering Wheel, Tilt	Std	Std
Power Windows	Std	Std
***Options Price**	$0	$0
***Total Price**	**$22,158**	**$26,068**
Target Price	$24,743	
Destination Charge	$295	
Avg. Tax & Fees	$1,516	
Total Target $	**$26,554**	
Average Dealer Option Cost:	***81%***	

Ownership Costs

Cost Area	5 Year Cost	Rate
Depreciation	$9,940	Average
Financing ($534/month)	$4,374	
Insurance (Rating 15)	$8,507	Better Than Average
State Fees	$1,055	
Fuel (Hwy 20 City 17)	$4,667	Worse Than Average
Maintenance	$6,031	Poor
Repairs	$680	Better Than Average

Warranty/Maintenance Info

Major Tune-Up	$274	Poor
Minor Tune-Up	$185	Poor
Brake Service	$208	Better Than Average
Overall Warranty	3 yr/36k	Average
Drivetrain Warranty	5 yr/60k	Excellent
Rust Warranty	5 yr/unlim. mi	Better Than Average
Maintenance Warranty	N/A	
Roadside Assistance	N/A	

Ownership Cost By Year

$2,000 $4,000 $6,000 $8,000 $10,000

1993 1994 1995 1996 1997

Resale Value

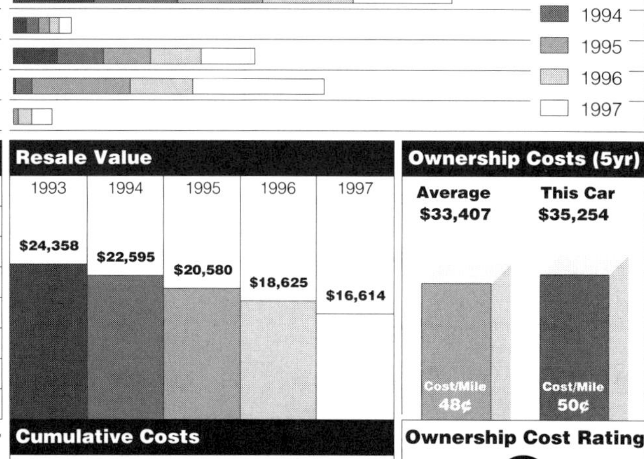

1993	1994	1995	1996	1997
$24,358	$22,595	$20,580	$18,625	$16,614

Ownership Costs (5yr)

Average	This Car
$33,407	$35,254
Cost/Mile 48¢	Cost/Mile 50¢

The 1993 Previa is available in four models - DX, All-Trac Deluxe, LE and All-Trac LE editions. New for 1993, the Previa LE All-Trac features seven-passenger seating and a full size spare. Features include dual air conditioners, power front windows, variable intermittent front windshield washers, cruise control, a rear wiper/washer with intermittent operation and dual-power outside mirrors. The LE also comes standard with a Toyota Deluxe electronically tuned radio casstte w/6 speakers.

Cumulative Costs

	1993	1994	1995	1996	1997
Annual	$6,762	$6,216	$7,737	$6,670	$7,869
Total	$6,762	$12,978	$20,715	$27,385	$35,254

Ownership Cost Rating

Average

* Includes shaded options

** Other purchase requirements apply

 Poor  Worse Than Average  Average  Better Than Average Excellent  Insufficient Information

Refer to *Section 3: Annotated Vehicle Charts* for an explanation of these charts.

Toyota T100
2 Door Regular Cab

3.0L 150 hp Gas Fuel Inject.

6 Cylinder "V"

Manual 5 Speed

2 Wheel Rear

Manual Seatbelts Only

Purchase Price

Car Item	Dealer Cost	List
Base Price	**$12,178**	**$13,998**
Anti-Lock Brakes	Std	Std
Automatic 4 Speed	$783	$900
Optional Engine	N/A	N/A
Air Conditioning	Dlr	Dlr
Power Steering	N/A	N/A
Cruise Control	$230	$285
All Wheel Drive	N/A	N/A
AM/FM Stereo Cassette	N/A	N/A
Steering Wheel, Tilt	Pkg	Pkg
Power Windows	N/A	N/A
***Options Price**	$0	$0
***Total Price**	**$12,178**	**$13,998**
Target Price	$13,268	
Destination Charge	$325	
Avg. Tax & Fees	$823	
Total Target $	**$14,416**	
Average Dealer Option Cost:	***83%***	

Ownership Costs

Cost Area	5 Year Cost	Rate
Depreciation		Insufficient Information
Financing ($290/month)	$2,374	
Insurance (Rating 7 [Est.])	$7,244	Average
State Fees	$573	
Fuel (Hwy 21 City 16)	$4,672	Excellent
Maintenance		Insufficient Information
Repairs	$519	Excellent

Ownership Cost By Year

$2,000 · $4,000 · $6,000 · $8,000

Insufficient Depreciation Information

Insufficient Maintenance Information

1993 · 1994 · 1995 · 1996 · 1997

Warranty/Maintenance Info

Major Tune-Up		Insufficient Information
Minor Tune-Up		Insufficient Information
Brake Service		Insufficient Information
Overall Warranty	3 yr/36k	Average
Drivetrain Warranty	5 yr/60k	Excellent
Rust Warranty	5 yr/unlim. mi	Better Than Average
Maintenance Warranty	N/A	
Roadside Assistance	N/A	

Resale Value

Insufficient Information

Ownership Costs (5yr)

Insufficient Information

Cumulative Costs

	1993	1994	1995	1996	1997
Annual	*Insufficient Information*				
Total	*Insufficient Information*				

Ownership Cost Rating

Insufficient Information

The all-new 1993 T100 is available in five models - (Base) T100, One Ton, T100 4WD; and (Base) SR5 and SR5 4WD. All T100 models feature standard rear wheel anti-lock brakes; flush body edges and exterior moldings; aerodynamic integrated mirrors and standard 1,550 lb. payload capacity. Base T100 standard equipment includes tinted glass, front/rear mudguards, one-touch tailgate release and double wall bed. Options include Chrome Package, five-speaker sound system, and sliding rear window.

Toyota T100 One Ton
2 Door Regular Cab

3.0L 150 hp Gas Fuel Inject.

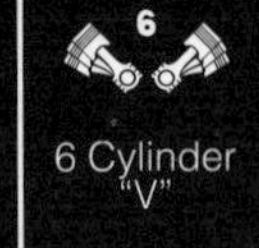
6 Cylinder "V"

Manual 5 Speed

2 Wheel Rear

Manual Seatbelts Only

Purchase Price

Car Item	Dealer Cost	List
Base Price	**$12,805**	**$14,718**
Anti-Lock Brakes	Std	Std
Automatic 4 Speed	$783	$900
Optional Engine	N/A	N/A
Air Conditioning	Dlr	Dlr
Power Steering	N/A	N/A
Cruise Control	$230	$285
All Wheel Drive	N/A	N/A
AM/FM Stereo Cassette	N/A	N/A
Steering Wheel, Tilt	Pkg	Pkg
Power Windows	N/A	N/A
***Options Price**	$0	$0
***Total Price**	**$12,805**	**$14,718**
Target Price	$13,973	
Destination Charge	$325	
Avg. Tax & Fees	$865	
Total Target $	**$15,163**	
Average Dealer Option Cost:	***83%***	

Ownership Costs

Cost Area	5 Year Cost	Rate
Depreciation		Insufficient Information
Financing ($305/month)	$2,497	
Insurance (Rating 7 [Est.])	$7,244	Average
State Fees	$600	
Fuel (Hwy 21 City 16)	$4,672	Excellent
Maintenance		Insufficient Information
Repairs	$519	Excellent

Ownership Cost By Year

$2,000 · $4,000 · $6,000 · $8,000

Insufficient Depreciation Information

Insufficient Maintenance Information

1993 · 1994 · 1995 · 1996 · 1997

Warranty/Maintenance Info

Major Tune-Up		Insufficient Information
Minor Tune-Up		Insufficient Information
Brake Service		Insufficient Information
Overall Warranty	3 yr/36k	Average
Drivetrain Warranty	5 yr/60k	Excellent
Rust Warranty	5 yr/unlim. mi	Better Than Average
Maintenance Warranty	N/A	
Roadside Assistance	N/A	

Resale Value

Insufficient Information

Ownership Costs (5yr)

Insufficient Information

Cumulative Costs

	1993	1994	1995	1996	1997
Annual	*Insufficient Information*				
Total	*Insufficient Information*				

Ownership Cost Rating

Insufficient Information

The all-new 1993 T100 is available in five models - (Base) T100, One Ton, T100 4WD; and (Base) SR5 and SR5 4WD. All T100 models feature standard rear wheel anti-lock brakes; flush body edges and exterior moldings; aerodynamic integrated mirrors and tinted glass. T100 One Ton comes equipped with full wheel covers, larger payload capacity, P235 Mud & Snow tires, front/rear mudguards, available compact disc changer and optional Chrome Package.

* Includes shaded options

** Other purchase requirements apply

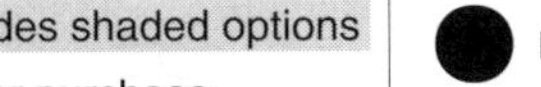

Poor

Worse Than Average

Average

Better Than Average

Excellent

Insufficient Information

Refer to *Section 3: Annotated Vehicle Charts* for an explanation of these charts.

Toyota T100 SR5
2 Door Regular Cab

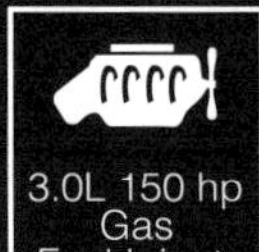
3.0L 150 hp Gas Fuel Inject.

6 Cylinder "V"

Manual 5 Speed

2 Wheel Rear

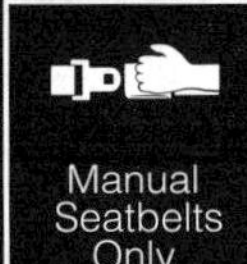
Manual Seatbelts Only

Large Pickup
4WD Model Shown

Purchase Price

Car Item	Dealer Cost	List
Base Price	**$13,596**	**$15,718**
Anti-Lock Brakes	Std	Std
Automatic 4 Speed	$779	$900
Optional Engine	N/A	N/A
Air Conditioning	Dlr	Dlr
Power Steering	N/A	N/A
Cruise Control	$228	$285
All Wheel Drive	N/A	N/A
AM/FM Stereo Cassette	$352	$470
Steering Wheel, Tilt	Std	Std
Power Windows	Pkg	Pkg
***Options Price**	$352	$470
***Total Price**	**$13,948**	**$16,188**
Target Price	$15,250	
Destination Charge	$325	
Avg. Tax & Fees	$944	
Total Target $	**$16,519**	
Average Dealer Option Cost:	***81%***	

Ownership Costs

Cost Area	5 Year Cost	Rate
Depreciation		Insufficient Information
Financing ($332/month)	$2,722	
Insurance (Rating 8 [Est.])	$7,432	Average
State Fees	$661	
Fuel (Hwy 21 City 16)	$4,672	Better Than Average
Maintenance		Insufficient Information
Repairs	$519	Better Than Average

Ownership Cost By Year

$2,000 $4,000 $6,000 $8,000

Insufficient Depreciation Information

Insufficient Maintenance Information

1993 1994 1995 1996 1997

Warranty/Maintenance Info

Item		Rate
Major Tune-Up		Insufficient Information
Minor Tune-Up		Insufficient Information
Brake Service		Insufficient Information
Overall Warranty	3 yr/36k	Average
Drivetrain Warranty	5 yr/60k	Better Than Average
Rust Warranty	5 yr/unlim. mi	Better Than Average
Maintenance Warranty	N/A	
Roadside Assistance	N/A	

Resale Value

Insufficient Information

Ownership Costs (5yr)

Insufficient Information

The all-new 1993 T100 is available in five models - (Base) T100, One Ton, T100 4WD; and (Base) SR5 and SR5 4WD. All T100 models feature standard rear wheel anti-lock brakes; flush body edges and exterior moldings; aerodynamic integrated mirrors and standard 1,550 lb. payload capacity. SR5 2WD comes equipped with 60/40 split folding seat, passenger vanity mirror, center armrest with storage compartment, five-speaker sound system, standard Chrome and Convenience Packages and optional Power Package.

Cumulative Costs

	1993	1994	1995	1996	1997
Annual	Insufficient Information				
Total	Insufficient Information				

Ownership Cost Rating

Insufficient Information

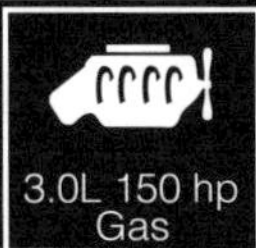

Toyota T100 4WD
2 Door Regular Cab

3.0L 150 hp Gas Fuel Inject.

6 Cylinder "V"

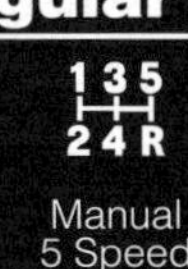
Manual 5 Speed

4 Wheel On-Demand

Manual Seatbelts Only

Large Pickup

Purchase Price

Car Item	Dealer Cost	List
Base Price	**$14,936**	**$17,368**
Anti-Lock Brakes	Std	Std
Automatic Transmission	N/A	N/A
Optional Engine	N/A	N/A
Air Conditioning	Dlr	Dlr
Power Steering	Std	Std
Cruise Control	$230	$285
4 Whl On-Demand Dr.	Std	Std
AM/FM Stereo Cassette	N/A	N/A
Steering Wheel, Tilt	Pkg	Pkg
Power Windows	N/A	N/A
***Options Price**	$0	$0
***Total Price**	**$14,936**	**$17,368**
Target Price	$16,385	
Destination Charge	$325	
Avg. Tax & Fees	$1,013	
Total Target $	**$17,723**	
Average Dealer Option Cost:	***81%***	

Ownership Costs

Cost Area	5 Year Cost	Rate
Depreciation		Insufficient Information
Financing ($356/month)	$2,919	
Insurance (Rating 10 [Est.])	$7,689	Average
State Fees	$708	
Fuel (Hwy 18 City 15)	$5,233	Average
Maintenance		Insufficient Information
Repairs	$621	Better Than Average

Ownership Cost By Year

$2,000 $4,000 $6,000 $8,000

Insufficient Depreciation Information

Insufficient Maintenance Information

1993 1994 1995 1996 1997

Warranty/Maintenance Info

Item		Rate
Major Tune-Up		Insufficient Information
Minor Tune-Up		Insufficient Information
Brake Service		Insufficient Information
Overall Warranty	3 yr/36k	Average
Drivetrain Warranty	5 yr/60k	Better Than Average
Rust Warranty	5 yr/unlim. mi	Better Than Average
Maintenance Warranty	N/A	
Roadside Assistance	N/A	

Resale Value

Insufficient Information

Ownership Costs (5yr)

Insufficient Information

The all-new 1993 T100 is available in five models - (Base) T100, One Ton, T100 4WD; and (Base) SR5 and SR5 4WD. All T100 models feature standard rear wheel anti-lock brakes; flush body edges and exterior moldings; aerodynamic integrated mirrors and standard 1,550 lb. payload capacity. T100 4WD features "shift-on-the-move" two-speed transfer case, standard P235 Mud & Snow tires, heavy duty power steering and styled steel wheels.

Cumulative Costs

	1993	1994	1995	1996	1997
Annual	Insufficient Information				
Total	Insufficient Information				

Ownership Cost Rating

Insufficient Information

* Includes shaded options

** Other purchase requirements apply

Poor | Worse Than Average | Average | Better Than Average | Excellent | Insufficient Information

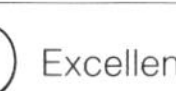

Refer to ***Section 3: Annotated Vehicle Charts*** for an explanation of these charts.

Toyota T100 SR5 4WD

2 Door Regular Cab

Large Pickup

3.0L 150 hp Gas Fuel Inject.

6 Cylinder "V"

Manual 5 Speed

4 Wheel On-Demand

Manual Seatbelts Only

Purchase Price

Car Item	Dealer Cost	List
Base Price	**$16,269**	**$19,028**
Anti-Lock Brakes	Std	Std
Automatic Transmission	N/A	N/A
Optional Engine	N/A	N/A
Air Conditioning	Dlr	Dlr
Power Steering	Std	Std
Cruise Control	$228	$285
4 Whl On-Demand Dr.	Std	Std
AM/FM Stereo Cassette	$352	$470
Steering Wheel, Tilt	Std	Std
Power Windows	Pkg	Pkg
***Options Price**	$352	$470
***Total Price**	**$16,621**	**$19,498**
Target Price	$18,293	
Destination Charge	$325	
Avg. Tax & Fees	$1,129	
Total Target $	**$19,747**	
Average Dealer Option Cost:	***79%***	

Ownership Costs

Cost Area	5 Year Cost	Rate
Depreciation		Insufficient Information
Financing ($397/month)	$3,253	
Insurance (Rating 11 [Est.])	$7,902	Average
State Fees	$793	
Fuel (Hwy 18 City 15)	$5,233	Average
Maintenance		Insufficient Information
Repairs	$621	Excellent

Ownership Cost By Year

$2,000 $4,000 $6,000 $8,000

Insufficient Depreciation Information

Insufficient Maintenance Information

1993 1994 1995 1996 1997

Warranty/Maintenance Info

Item		Rate
Major Tune-Up		Insufficient Information
Minor Tune-Up		Insufficient Information
Brake Service		Insufficient Information
Overall Warranty	3 yr/36k	Average
Drivetrain Warranty	5 yr/60k	Excellent
Rust Warranty	5 yr/unlim. mi	Better Than Average
Maintenance Warranty	N/A	
Roadside Assistance	N/A	

Resale Value

Insufficient Information

Ownership Costs (5yr)

Insufficient Information

Cumulative Costs

	1993	1994	1995	1996	1997
Annual	Insufficient Information				
Total	Insufficient Information				

Ownership Cost Rating

Insufficient Information

The all-new 1993 T100 is available in five models - (Base) T100, One Ton, T100 4WD; and (Base) SR5 and SR5 4WD. All T100 models feature standard rear wheel anti-lock brakes; flush body edges and exterior moldings; aerodynamic integrated mirrors and standard 1,550 lb. payload capacity. In addition to the equiment of the SR5 2WD, the SR5 4WD offers standard On-Demand "shift-on-the-move" two-speed transfer case and heavy duty power steering.

Volkswagen Eurovan CL

3 Door Pass Van

Mini Van

2.5L 109 hp Gas Fuel Inject.

5 Cylinder In-Line

Manual 5 Speed

2 Wheel Front

Automatic Seatbelts

Purchase Price

Car Item	Dealer Cost	List
Base Price	**$15,099**	**$16,640**
Anti-Lock Brakes	$835	$852
Automatic 4 Speed	$863	$895
Optional Engine	N/A	N/A
Air Cond., Front & Rear	Pkg	Pkg
Power Steering	Std	Std
Cruise Control	N/A	N/A
All Wheel Drive	N/A	N/A
AM/FM Stereo Cassette	Pkg	Pkg
Steering Wheel, Tilt	N/A	N/A
Power Windows	N/A	N/A
***Options Price**	$863	$895
***Total Price**	**$15,962**	**$17,535**
Target Price	$17,114	
Destination Charge	$490	
Avg. Tax & Fees	$1,060	
Total Target $	**$18,664**	
Average Dealer Option Cost:	***91%***	

Ownership Costs

Cost Area	5 Year Cost	Rate
Depreciation		Insufficient Information
Financing ($375/month)	$3,075	
Insurance (Rating 8)	$7,223	Excellent
State Fees	$720	
Fuel (Hwy 19 City 17)	$4,806	Worse Than Average
Maintenance	$5,021	Worse Than Average
Repairs	$925	Worse Than Average

Ownership Cost By Year

$2,000 $4,000 $6,000 $8,000

Insufficient Depreciation Information

1993 1994 1995 1996 1997

Warranty/Maintenance Info

Item		Rate
Major Tune-Up	$189	Average
Minor Tune-Up	$125	Worse Than Average
Brake Service	$340	Poor
Overall Warranty	2 yr/24k	Worse Than Average
Drivetrain Warranty	5 yr/50k	Better Than Average
Rust Warranty	6 yr/unlim. mi	Better Than Average
Maintenance Warranty	N/A	
Roadside Assistance	N/A	

Resale Value

Insufficient Information

Ownership Costs (5yr)

Insufficient Information

Cumulative Costs

	1993	1994	1995	1996	1997
Annual	Insufficient Information				
Total	Insufficient Information				

Ownership Cost Rating

Insufficient Information

The all-new 1993 Volkswagen Eurovan, which replaces Volkswagen's Vanagon, is available in three models - CL, GL and MV passenger van. The CL van features foldable, quick-release center seats and folding or removable rear seats that also tumble, allowing for more space for cargo. The Eurovan is covered by a 5-year/50K-mile powertrain warranty, a 6-year/unlimited mileage warranty against corrosion and rust perforation, and a 2-year/24K-mile bumper-to-bumper limited warranty.

* Includes shaded options

** Other purchase requirements apply

 Poor  Worse Than Average  Average  Better Than Average  Excellent ⊖ Insufficient Information

Refer to *Section 3: Annotated Vehicle Charts* for an explanation of these charts.

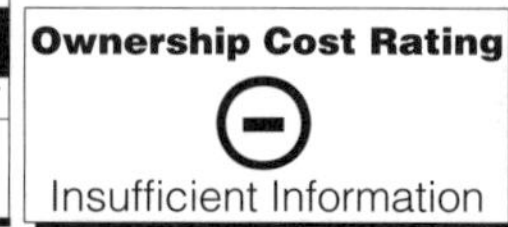

Volkswagen Eurovan GL
3 Door Pass Van

2.5L 109 hp Gas Fuel Inject.

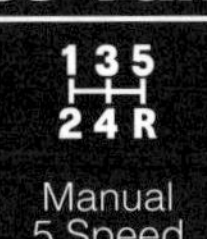

5 Cylinder In-Line

Manual 5 Speed

2 Wheel Front

Automatic Seatbelts

Purchase Price

Car Item	Dealer Cost	List
Base Price	**$18,009**	**$20,420**
Anti-Lock Brakes	$835	$852
Automatic 4 Speed	$863	$895
Optional Engine	N/A	N/A
Air Cond., Front & Rear	Std	Std
Power Steering	Std	Std
Cruise Control	Pkg	Pkg
All Wheel Drive	N/A	N/A
AM/FM Stereo Cassette	Std	Std
Steering Wheel, Tilt	N/A	N/A
Power Windows	Pkg	Pkg
***Options Price**	$863	$895
***Total Price**	**$18,872**	**$21,315**
Target Price	$20,345	
Destination Charge	$490	
Avg. Tax & Fees	$1,260	
Total Target $	**$22,095**	
Average Dealer Option Cost:	***94%***	

Ownership Costs

Cost Area	5 Year Cost	Rate
Depreciation		Insufficient Information
Financing ($444/month)	$3,640	
Insurance (Rating 11)	$7,693	Better Than Average
State Fees	$872	
Fuel (Hwy 19 City 17)	$4,806	Worse Than Average
Maintenance	$5,021	Worse Than Average
Repairs	$925	Worse Than Average

Ownership Cost By Year

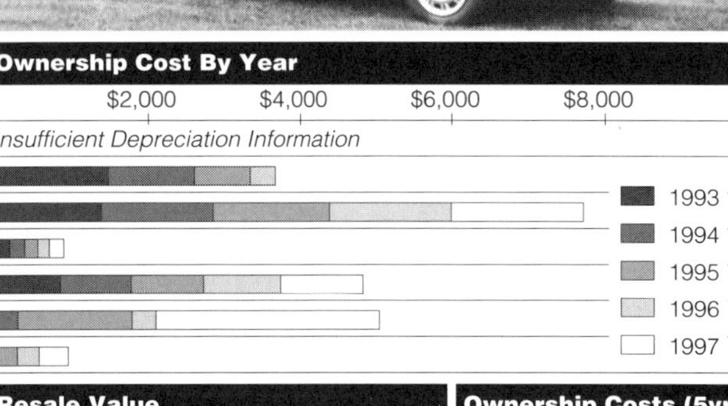

Warranty/Maintenance Info

Item		Rate
Major Tune-Up	$189	Average
Minor Tune-Up	$125	Worse Than Average
Brake Service	$340	Poor
Overall Warranty	2 yr/24k	Worse Than Average
Drivetrain Warranty	5 yr/50k	Better Than Average
Rust Warranty	6 yr/unlim. mi	Better Than Average
Maintenance Warranty	N/A	
Roadside Assistance	N/A	

Resale Value

Insufficient Information

Ownership Costs (5yr)

Insufficient Information

The 1993 Volkswagen Eurovan, which replaces Volkswagen's Vanagon, is available in three models - CL, GL and MV passenger van. The GL van features foldable, quick-release center seats and folding or removable rear seats that also tumble, which provides more space for cargo. An improved, non-CFC, front-and-rear dual air conditioning system is in place and uses vents mounted in the ceiling for improved ventilation. Standard equipment on all models includes improved front and rear dual heating.

Cumulative Costs

	1993	1994	1995	1996	1997
Annual	*Insufficient Information*				
Total	*Insufficient Information*				

Ownership Cost Rating

Insufficient Information

Volkswagen Eurovan MV
3 Door Pass Van

2.5L 109 hp Gas Fuel Inject.

5 Cylinder In-Line

Manual 5 Speed

2 Wheel Front

Automatic Seatbelts

Purchase Price

Car Item	Dealer Cost	List
Base Price	**$19,268**	**$21,850**
Anti-Lock Brakes	$835	$852
Automatic 4 Speed	$863	$895
Optional Engine	N/A	N/A
Air Cond., Front & Rear	Std	Std
Power Steering	Std	Std
Cruise Control	Pkg	Pkg
All Wheel Drive	N/A	N/A
AM/FM Stereo Cassette	Std	Std
Steering Wheel, Tilt	N/A	N/A
Power Windows	Pkg	Pkg
***Options Price**	$863	$895
***Total Price**	**$20,131**	**$22,745**
Target Price	$21,753	
Destination Charge	$490	
Avg. Tax & Fees	$1,344	
Total Target $	**$23,587**	
Average Dealer Option Cost:	***91%***	

Ownership Costs

Cost Area	5 Year Cost	Rate
Depreciation		Insufficient Information
Financing ($474/month)	$3,884	
Insurance (Rating 11)	$7,693	Better Than Average
State Fees	$929	
Fuel (Hwy 19 City 17)	$4,806	Worse Than Average
Maintenance	$5,021	Worse Than Average
Repairs	$925	Worse Than Average

Ownership Cost By Year

$2,000 $4,000 $6,000 $8,000

Insufficient Depreciation Information

1993 1994 1995 1996 1997

Warranty/Maintenance Info

Item		Rate
Major Tune-Up	$189	Average
Minor Tune-Up	$125	Worse Than Average
Brake Service	$340	Poor
Overall Warranty	2 yr/24k	Worse Than Average
Drivetrain Warranty	5 yr/50k	Better Than Average
Rust Warranty	6 yr/unlim. mi	Better Than Average
Maintenance Warranty	N/A	
Roadside Assistance	N/A	

Resale Value

Insufficient Information

Ownership Costs (5yr)

Insufficient Information

The 1993 Volkswagen Eurovan, which replaces Volkswagen's Vanagon, is available in three models - CL, GL and MV passenger van. The MV van features foldable, quick-release center seats and folding or removable rear seats that also tumble, which provides more space for cargo. An optional weekend package is offered which includes a pop-up roof, window and rear hatch screens, fixed left-hand rear facing seat with refrigerator, second battery, gathered/sliding window curtains and delete rear a/c unit.

Cumulative Costs

	1993	1994	1995	1996	1997
Annual	*Insufficient Information*				
Total	*Insufficient Information*				

Ownership Cost Rating

Insufficient Information

* Includes shaded options

** Other purchase requirements apply

Poor  Worse Than Average  Average 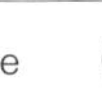 Better Than Average  Excellent  Insufficient Information

Refer to *Section 3: Annotated Vehicle Charts* for an explanation of these charts.

Volkswagen Passat GL

4 Door Wagon

2.0L 134 hp Gas Fuel Inject.

4 Cylinder In-Line

Manual 5 Speed

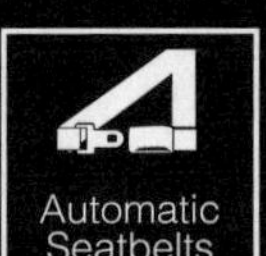
2 Wheel Front

Automatic Seatbelts

Compact Wagon

Purchase Price

Car Item	Dealer Cost	List
Base Price	**N/R**	**N/R**
Anti-Lock Brakes	N/R	N/R
Automatic 4 Speed	N/R	N/R
Optional Engine	N/A	N/A
Air Conditioning	Std	Std
Power Steering	Std	Std
Cruise Control	Std	Std
All Wheel Drive	N/A	N/A
AM/FM Stereo Cassette	Std	Std
Steering Wheel, Tilt	Std	Std
Power Windows	Std	Std
***Options Price**	$0	$0
***Total Price**	**N/R**	**N/R**
Target Price	N/R	
Destination Charge	N/R	
Avg. Tax & Fees	N/R	
Total Target $	**N/R**	
Average Dealer Option Cost:	***N/A***	

Ownership Costs

Cost Area	5 Year Cost	Rate
Depreciation		Insufficient Information
Financing ($0/month)		
Insurance (Rating 14 [Est.])	$8,238	Average
State Fees		
Fuel (Hwy 29 City 20)	$3,548	Better Than Average
Maintenance	$4,968	Average
Repairs	$800	Worse Than Average

Ownership Cost By Year

$2,000 $4,000 $6,000 $8,000 $10,000

Insufficient Depreciation Information

Insufficient Financing Information

Insufficient State Fee Information

1993 1994 1995 1996 1997

Warranty/Maintenance Info

Item		Rate
Major Tune-Up	$232	Poor
Minor Tune-Up	$97	Better Than Average
Brake Service	$238	Worse Than Average
Overall Warranty	2 yr/24k	Worse Than Average
Drivetrain Warranty	5 yr/50k	Better Than Average
Rust Warranty	6 yr/unlim. mi	Better Than Average
Maintenance Warranty	N/A	
Roadside Assistance	N/A	

Resale Value

Insufficient Information

Ownership Costs (5yr)

Insufficient Information

Cumulative Costs

	1993	1994	1995	1996	1997
Annual	*Insufficient Information*				
Total	*Insufficient Information*				

Ownership Cost Rating

Insufficient Information

The 1993 Passat is available in five models - GL sedan and wagon, GLS sedan and GLX sedan and wagon. New for 1993, the GL wagon includes an improved alarm system, deluxe cassette stereo with portable CD stereo input, a multi-function trip computer, lockable rear (split) folding seats, air conditioning, power windows, a front spoiler, power steering, cruise control, central locking with key-operated window closing and dual remote heated mirrors. Pricing was not available at time of printing.

Volkswagen Passat GLX

4 Door Wagon

2.8L 172 hp Gas Fuel Inject.

6 Cylinder "V"

Manual 5 Speed

2 Wheel Front

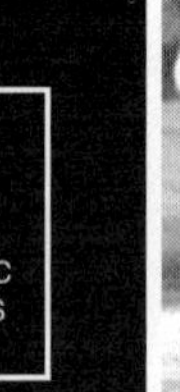
Automatic Seatbelts

Compact Wagon

Purchase Price

Car Item	Dealer Cost	List
Base Price	**$19,013**	**$21,560**
Anti-Lock Brakes	Std	Std
Automatic 4 Speed	$843	$875
Optional Engine	N/A	N/A
Air Conditioning	Std	Std
Power Steering	Std	Std
Cruise Control	Std	Std
All Wheel Drive	N/A	N/A
AM/FM Stereo Cassette	Std	Std
Steering Wheel, Tilt	Std	Std
Power Windows	Std	Std
***Options Price**	$843	$875
***Total Price**	**$19,856**	**$22,435**
Target Price	$21,207	
Destination Charge	$0	
Avg. Tax & Fees	$1,284	
Total Target $	**$22,491**	
Average Dealer Option Cost:	***94%***	

Ownership Costs

Cost Area	5 Year Cost	Rate
Depreciation	$9,930	Excellent
Financing ($452/month)	$3,705	
Insurance (Rating 15)	$8,507	Average
State Fees	$897	
Fuel (Hwy 24 City 17)	$4,232	Worse Than Average
Maintenance	$5,094	Average
Repairs	$965	Poor

Ownership Cost By Year

$2,000 $4,000 $6,000 $8,000 $10,000

1993 1994 1995 1996 1997

Warranty/Maintenance Info

Item		Rate
Major Tune-Up	$186	Worse Than Average
Minor Tune-Up	$115	Worse Than Average
Brake Service	$238	Worse Than Average
Overall Warranty	2 yr/24k	Worse Than Average
Drivetrain Warranty	5 yr/50k	Better Than Average
Rust Warranty	6 yr/unlim. mi	Better Than Average
Maintenance Warranty	N/A	
Roadside Assistance	N/A	

Resale Value

1993	1994	1995	1996	1997
$18,060	$15,925	$15,370	$13,946	$12,561

Ownership Costs (5yr)

Average	This Car
$33,758	$33,330
Cost/Mile 48¢	Cost/Mile 48¢

Cumulative Costs

	1993	1994	1995	1996	1997
Annual	$8,600	$6,236	$5,734	$5,080	$7,680
Total	$8,600	$14,836	$20,570	$25,650	$33,330

Ownership Cost Rating

Average

The 1993 Passat is available in five models - GL sedan and wagon, GLS sedan and GLX sedan and wagon. New for 1993, the GLX wagon offers the VR6 engine. Standard features include air conditioning, alloy wheels, a power glass sunroof, power windows, a front and rear spoiler, premium sound system with CD changer control capability, power steering, cruise control, central locking (doors, trunk lid and fuel filler) with key-operated window closing and dual remote heated mirrors.

* Includes shaded options

** Other purchase requirements apply

Poor

Worse Than Average

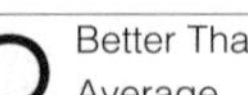
Average

Better Than Average

Excellent

Insufficient Information

Refer to *Section 3: Annotated Vehicle Charts* for an explanation of these charts.

Volvo 240
4 Door Wagon

2.3L 114 hp Gas Fuel Inject.

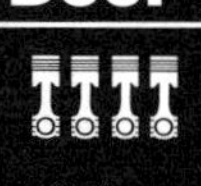
4 Cylinder In-Line

Manual 5 Speed

2 Wheel Rear

Driver Airbag Psngr Belts

Compact Wagon

Purchase Price

Car Item	Dealer Cost	List
Base Price	**$20,430**	**$22,820**
Anti-Lock Brakes	Std	Std
Automatic 4 Speed	$585	$675
Optional Engine	N/A	N/A
Air Conditioning	Std	Std
Power Steering	Std	Std
Cruise Control	N/A	N/A
All Wheel Drive	N/A	N/A
AM/FM Stereo Cassette	Std	Std
Steering Wheel, Tilt	N/A	N/A
Power Windows	Std	Std
***Options Price**	$585	$675
***Total Price**	**$21,015**	**$23,495**
Target Price	$23,019	
Destination Charge	$395	
Avg. Tax & Fees	$1,410	
Total Target $	**$24,824**	
Average Dealer Option Cost:	***87%***	

Ownership Costs

Cost Area	5 Year Cost	Rate
Depreciation	$9,713	Excellent
Financing ($499/month)	$4,089	
Insurance (Rating 7)	$7,035	Excellent
State Fees	$955	
Fuel (Hwy 25 City 20)	$3,837	Worse Than Average
Maintenance	$3,394	Excellent
Repairs	$760	Worse Than Average

Ownership Cost By Year

$2,000 $4,000 $6,000 $8,000 $10,000

1993 1994 1995 1996 1997

Warranty/Maintenance Info

Major Tune-Up	$237	Poor
Minor Tune-Up	$117	Worse Than Average
Brake Service	$141	Excellent
Overall Warranty	3 yr/50k	Average
Drivetrain Warranty	3 yr/50k	Average
Rust Warranty	8 yr/unlim. mi	Excellent
Maintenance Warranty	N/A	
Roadside Assistance	3 yr/unlim. mi	

Resale Value

1993	1994	1995	1996	1997
$21,372	$19,677	$18,225	$16,597	$15,111

Ownership Costs (5yr)

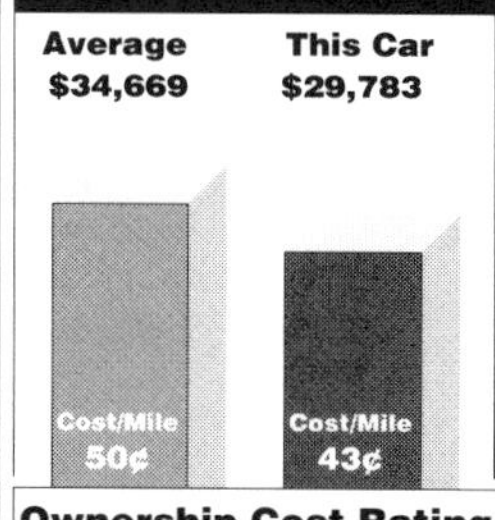

Average	This Car
$34,669	$29,783
Cost/Mile 50¢	Cost/Mile 43¢

Cumulative Costs

	1993	1994	1995	1996	1997
Annual	$7,447	$5,382	$5,560	$5,139	$6,255
Total	$7,447	$12,829	$18,389	$23,528	$29,783

Ownership Cost Rating

Excellent

The 1993 Volvo 240 is available in two bodystyles - sedan and wagon. New for 1993, the Volvo 240 wagon receives upgraded audio speakers, power operated and heated outside mirrors, metallic paint, a power antenna and a totally CFC-free air conditioning system which contains R134A, a refrigerant that has virtually no ozone depleting potential. The 240 wagon also features a matte black grille and trim package. Optional equipment includes leather seating and alloy wheels.

Volvo 940
4 Door Wagon

2.3L 114 hp Gas Fuel Inject.

4 Cylinder In-Line

Automatic 4 Speed

2 Wheel Rear

Driver Airbag Psngr Belts

Midsize Wagon

Purchase Price

Car Item	Dealer Cost	List
Base Price	**$22,920**	**$25,995**
Anti-Lock Brakes	Std	Std
Manual Transmission	N/A	N/A
Optional Engine	N/A	N/A
Auto Climate Control	Std	Std
Power Steering	Std	Std
Cruise Control	Std	Std
All Wheel Drive	N/A	N/A
AM/FM Stereo Cassette	Std	Std
Steering Wheel, Tilt	N/A	N/A
Power Windows	Std	Std
***Options Price**	$0	$0
***Total Price**	**$22,920**	**$25,995**
Target Price	$25,238	
Destination Charge	$395	
Avg. Tax & Fees	$1,546	
Total Target $	**$27,179**	
Average Dealer Option Cost:	***85%***	

Ownership Costs

Cost Area	5 Year Cost	Rate
Depreciation	$14,295	Average
Financing ($546/month)	$4,477	
Insurance (Rating 10)	$7,479	Excellent
State Fees	$1,056	
Fuel (Hwy 27 City 19)	$3,775	Average
Maintenance	$4,100	Better Than Average
Repairs	$760	Average

Ownership Cost By Year

$5,000 $10,000 $15,000

1993 1994 1995 1996 1997

Warranty/Maintenance Info

Major Tune-Up	$238	Poor
Minor Tune-Up	$122	Average
Brake Service	$147	Excellent
Overall Warranty	3 yr/50k	Average
Drivetrain Warranty	3 yr/50k	Average
Rust Warranty	8 yr/unlim. mi	Excellent
Maintenance Warranty	N/A	
Roadside Assistance	3 yr/unlim. mi	

Resale Value

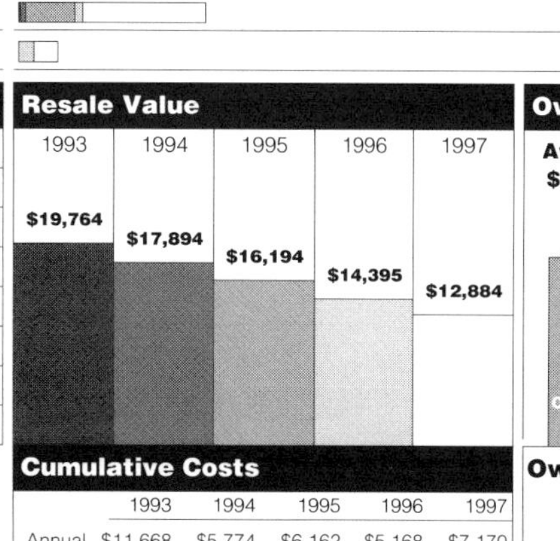

1993	1994	1995	1996	1997
$19,764	$17,894	$16,194	$14,395	$12,884

Ownership Costs (5yr)

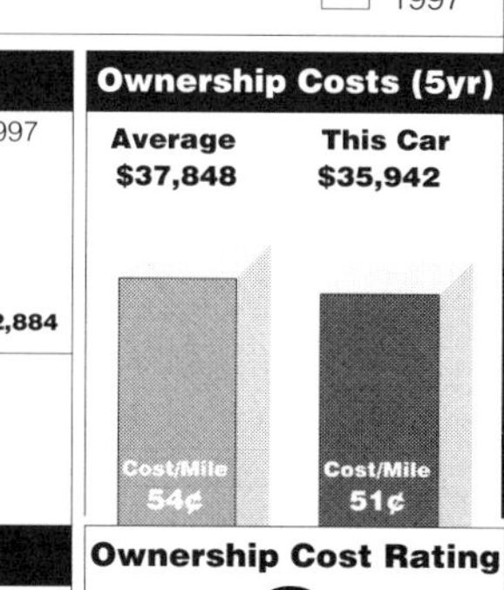

Average	This Car
$37,848	$35,942
Cost/Mile 54¢	Cost/Mile 51¢

Cumulative Costs

	1993	1994	1995	1996	1997
Annual	$11,668	$5,774	$6,162	$5,168	$7,170
Total	$11,668	$17,442	$23,604	$28,772	$35,942

Ownership Cost Rating

Better Than Average

The 1993 Volvo 940 is available with GL and Turbo trim levels in both sedan and wagon. New for 1993, the Volvo 940 wagon will be available in two distinctive equipment levels. One level includes an automatic transmission, SRS, ABS, SIPS, all-season tires, power windows, central locking, and a totally CFC-free air conditioner. The other level includes all of the above equipment plus twenty-spoke alloy wheels, power operated sunroof, leather upolstery and an upgraded full-logic audio system.

* Includes shaded options

** Other purchase requirements apply

 Poor  Worse Than Average  Average 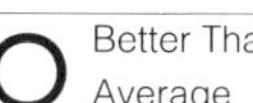 Better Than Average  Excellent ⊖ Insufficient Information

Refer to *Section 3: Annotated Vehicle Charts* for an explanation of these charts.

Volvo 940 Turbo
4 Door Wagon

2.3L 162 hp Turbo Gas Fuel Inject. | 4 Cylinder In-Line | Automatic 4 Speed

2 Wheel Rear

Driver Airbag Psngr Belts

Midsize Wagon

Purchase Price

Car Item	Dealer Cost	List
Base Price	**$25,885**	**$29,495**
Anti-Lock Brakes	Std	Std
Manual Transmission	N/A	N/A
Optional Engine	N/A	N/A
Auto Climate Control	Std	Std
Power Steering	Std	Std
Cruise Control	Std	Std
All Wheel Drive	N/A	N/A
AM/FM Stereo Cassette	Std	Std
Steering Wheel, Tilt	N/A	N/A
Power Windows	Std	Std
***Options Price**	$0	$0
***Total Price**	**$25,885**	**$29,495**
Target Price	$28,681	
Destination Charge	$395	
Avg. Tax & Fees	$1,753	
Total Target $	**$30,829**	
Average Dealer Option Cost:	***80%***	

Ownership Costs

Cost Area	5 Year Cost	Rate
Depreciation	$14,711	Better Than Average
Financing ($620/month)	$5,078	
Insurance (Rating 12)	$7,898	Excellent
State Fees	$1,195	
Fuel (Hwy 23 City 19)	$4,111	Poor
Maintenance	$3,850	Better Than Average
Repairs	$925	Worse Than Average

Ownership Cost By Year

$5,000 | $10,000 | $15,000

1993 | 1994 | 1995 | 1996 | 1997

Warranty/Maintenance Info

Item		Rate
Major Tune-Up	$241	Poor
Minor Tune-Up	$125	Average
Brake Service	$147	Excellent
Overall Warranty	3 yr/50k	Average
Drivetrain Warranty	3 yr/50k	Average
Rust Warranty	8 yr/unlim. mi	Excellent
Maintenance Warranty	N/A	
Roadside Assistance	3 yr/unlim. mi	

Resale Value

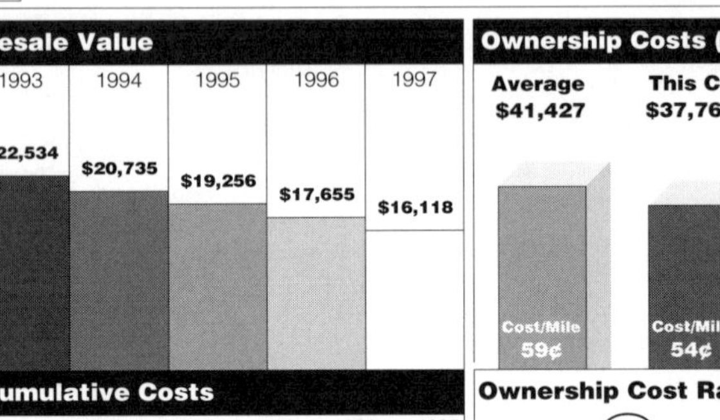

1993	1994	1995	1996	1997
$22,534	$20,735	$19,256	$17,655	$16,118

Ownership Costs (5yr)

Average	This Car
$41,427	$37,768
Cost/Mile 59¢	Cost/Mile 54¢

The 1993 Volvo 940 is available with GL and Turbo trim levels in either sedan or wagon. New for 1993, the Volvo 940 Turbo wagon includes a four-cylinder turbocharged engine, automatic transmission, SRS, ABS, SIPS, all-season tires, power windows, central locking, totally CFC-free air conditioning system, turbo grille, power sunroof, full leather interior (optional), alloy wheels, an upgraded audio system with a full logic cassette deck, a turbo tailgate emblem and front foglights.

Cumulative Costs

	1993	1994	1995	1996	1997
Annual	$12,972	$6,067	$6,097	$5,268	$7,364
Total	$12,972	$19,039	$25,136	$30,404	$37,768

Ownership Cost Rating

Excellent

Volvo 960
4 Door Wagon

2.9L 201 hp Gas Fuel Inject.

6 Cylinder In-Line

Automatic 4 Speed

2 Wheel Rear

Driver/Psngr Airbags Std

Luxury

Purchase Price

Car Item	Dealer Cost	List
Base Price	**$30,975**	**$36,675**
Anti-Lock Brakes	Std	Std
Manual Transmission	N/A	N/A
Optional Engine	N/A	N/A
Auto Climate Control	Std	Std
Power Steering	Std	Std
Cruise Control	Std	Std
All Wheel Drive	N/A	N/A
AM/FM Stereo Cassette	Std	Std
Steering Wheel, Tilt	Std	Std
Power Windows	Std	Std
***Options Price**	$0	$0
***Total Price**	**$30,975**	**$36,675**
Target Price	$34,537	
Destination Charge	$395	
Avg. Tax & Fees	$2,118	
Luxury Tax	$493	
Total Target $	**$37,543**	

Ownership Costs

Cost Area	5 Year Cost	Rate
Depreciation	$21,423	Average
Financing ($755/month)	$6,184	
Insurance (Rating 15)	$8,507	Excellent
State Fees	$1,483	
Fuel (Hwy 25 City 17)	$4,145	Average
Maintenance	$5,105	Better Than Average
Repairs	$740	Better Than Average

Ownership Cost By Year

$5,000 | $10,000 | $15,000 | $20,000 | $25,000

1993 | 1994 | 1995 | 1996 | 1997

Warranty/Maintenance Info

Item		Rate
Major Tune-Up	$161	Excellent
Minor Tune-Up	$71	Excellent
Brake Service	$173	Excellent
Overall Warranty	3 yr/50k	Average
Drivetrain Warranty	3 yr/50k	Average
Rust Warranty	8 yr/unlim. mi	Excellent
Maintenance Warranty	N/A	
Roadside Assistance	3 yr/unlim. mi	

Resale Value

1993	1994	1995	1996	1997
$23,757	$21,507	$19,767	$17,924	$16,120

Ownership Costs (5yr)

Average	This Car
$46,881	$47,587
Cost/Mile 67¢	Cost/Mile 68¢

The 1993 960 is available in two bodystyles - sedan and wagon. New for 1993, the 960 wagon receives a passenger side supplemental restraint system (SRS), which consists of an airbag and a knee bolster. The rear seat of the wagon features a 3-point safety belt and a head restraint for the center passenger. The new rear seat incorporates a higher backrest, along with repositioned seat controls for easier folding of the seat. The side impact protection system is standard.

Cumulative Costs

	1993	1994	1995	1996	1997
Annual	$19,118	$7,055	$7,052	$5,576	$8,786
Total	$19,118	$26,173	$33,225	$38,801	$47,587

Ownership Cost Rating

Average

* Includes shaded options

** Other purchase requirements apply

Poor

Worse Than Average | Average | Better Than Average

Excellent | Insufficient Information

Refer to *Section 3: Annotated Vehicle Charts* for an explanation of these charts.

Section Five
Appendices

Appendix A — *Best Overall Value*

Small Standard Pickup

2 Wheel Drive

Ford Ranger XLT
2 Door 2WD Regular Cab

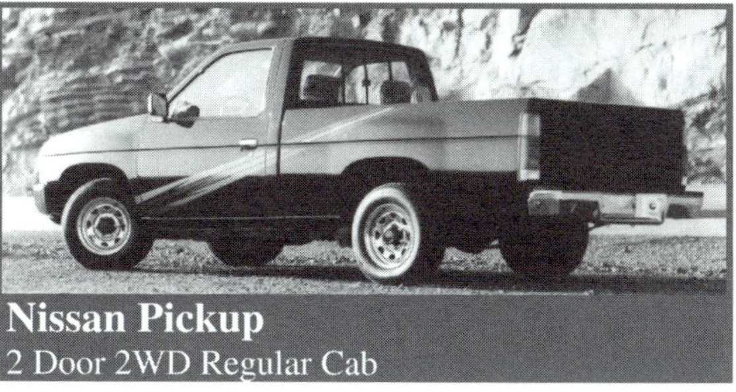
Nissan Pickup
2 Door 2WD Regular Cab

Mazda B2200
2 Door 2WD Regular Cab

4 Wheel Drive

2WD Model Shown
Toyota Pickup DX 4WD
2 Door 4WD Regular Cab

SuperCab Model Shown
Ford Ranger XLT 4WD
2 Door 4WD Regular Cab

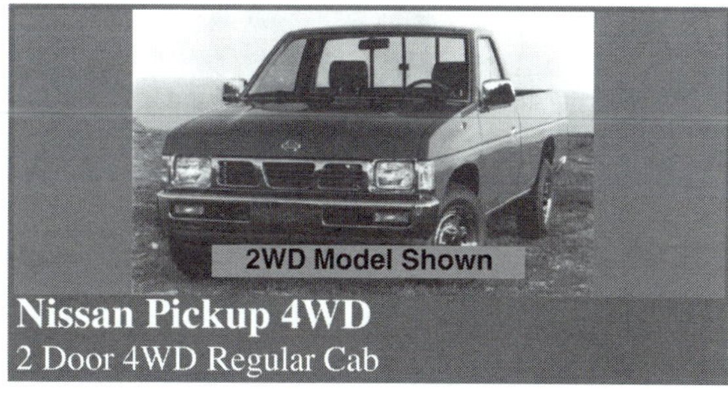
2WD Model Shown
Nissan Pickup 4WD
2 Door 4WD Regular Cab

This appendix lists the best economic values in vehicles in the above class and price ranges. The best value does not mean the lowest cost to own, but rather the best relationship between the cost to own and the price to buy.
Note that we've only shown one member of a model family, even when multiple members are excellent.

Appendix A — *Best Overall Value*

Large Standard Pickup

2 Wheel Drive

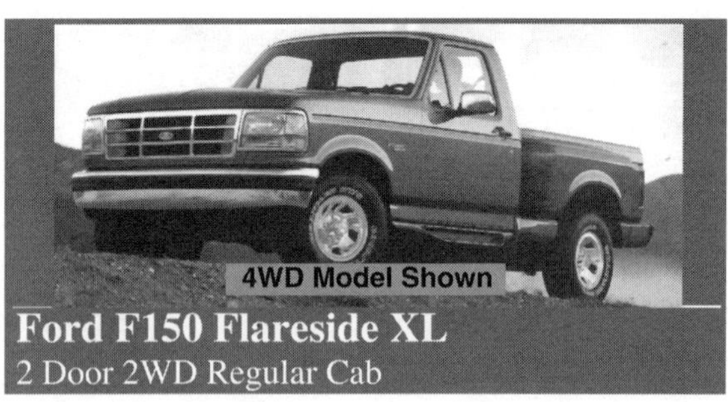

Ford F150 Flareside XL
2 Door 2WD Regular Cab

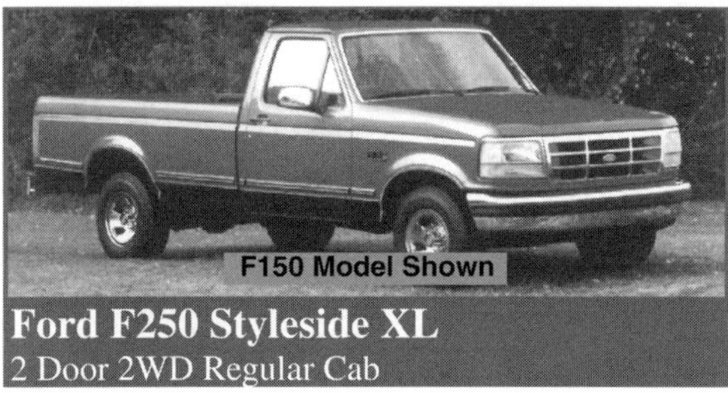

Ford F250 Styleside XL
2 Door 2WD Regular Cab

GMC Sierra C2500
2 Door 2WD Regular Cab

4 Wheel Drive

Ford F150 Flareside XL 4WD
2 Door 4WD Regular Cab

GMC Sierra K2500
2 Door 4WD Regular Cab

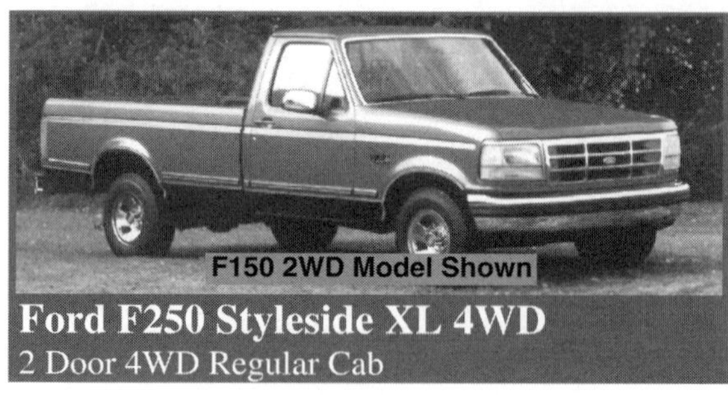

Ford F250 Styleside XL 4WD
2 Door 4WD Regular Cab

This appendix lists the best economic values in vehicles in the above class and price ranges. The best value does not mean the lowest cost to own, but rather the best relationship between the cost to own and the price to buy.
Note that we've only shown one member of a model family, even when multiple members are excellent.

Appendix A **Best Overall Value**

Utility

Under $20,000

Ford Explorer XL
4 Door 2WD

Mazda Navajo LX
2 Door 2WD

4WD Model Shown

Over $20,000

Nissan Pathfinder SE-V6 4WD
4 Door 4WD

Toyota 4Runner SR5 V6
4 Door 2WD

Chevrolet Suburban K1500
5 Door 4WD

This appendix lists the best economic values in vehicles in the above class and price ranges. The best value does not mean the lowest cost to own, but rather the best relationship between the cost to own and the price to buy.
Note that we've only shown one member of a model family, even when multiple members are excellent.

Appendix A — Best Overall Value

Mini - Vans

Under $17,000

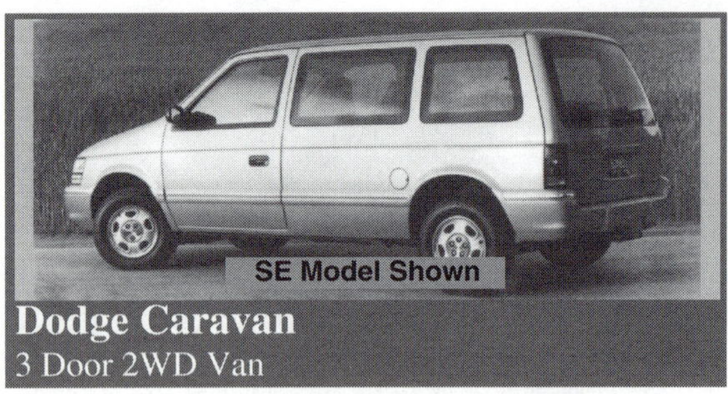

Dodge Caravan
3 Door 2WD Van

Plymouth Voyager
3 Door 2WD Van

Chevrolet Astro
3 Door 2WD Van

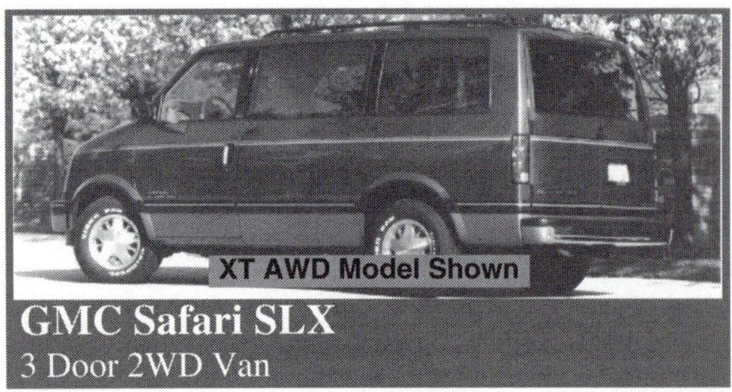

GMC Safari SLX
3 Door 2WD Van

Over $17,000

Dodge Grand Caravan SE AWD
3 Door 4WD Van

Plymouth Grand Voyager SE AWD
3 Door 4WD Van

Mazda MPV
3 Door 2WD Van

This appendix lists the best economic values in vehicles in the above class and price ranges. The best value does not mean the lowest cost to own, but rather the best relationship between the cost to own and the price to buy.
Note that we've only shown one member of a model family, even when multiple members are excellent.

Full-Size Vans

Ford Econoline E150
3 Door Cargo Van

Dodge Ram Van B350
3 Door Cargo Ext Van

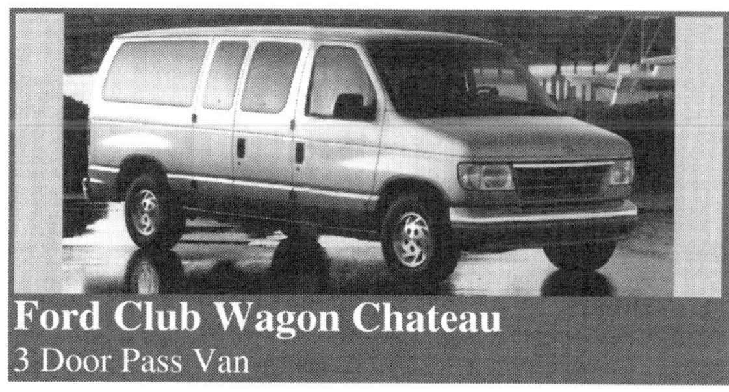
Ford Club Wagon Chateau
3 Door Pass Van

This appendix lists the best economic values in vehicles in the above class and price ranges. The best value does not mean the lowest cost to own, but rather the best relationship between the cost to own and the price to buy.
Note that we've only shown one member of a model family, even when multiple members are excellent.

Subcompact/Compact Wagon

Under $15,000

Toyota Corolla DX
4 Door 2WD Wagon

Ford Escort LX
4 Door 2WD Wagon

Over $15,000

Volvo 240
4 Door 2WD Wagon

Toyota Camry DX
4 Door 2WD Wagon

This appendix lists the best economic values in vehicles in the above class and price ranges. The best value does not mean the lowest cost to own, but rather the best relationship between the cost to own and the price to buy.
Note that we've only shown one member of a model family, even when multiple members are excellent.

Midsize Wagon

Under $20,000

Honda Accord LX
4 Door 2WD Wagon

Mercury Sable GS
4 Door 2WD Wagon

Over $20,000

Volvo 940 Turbo
4 Door 2WD Wagon

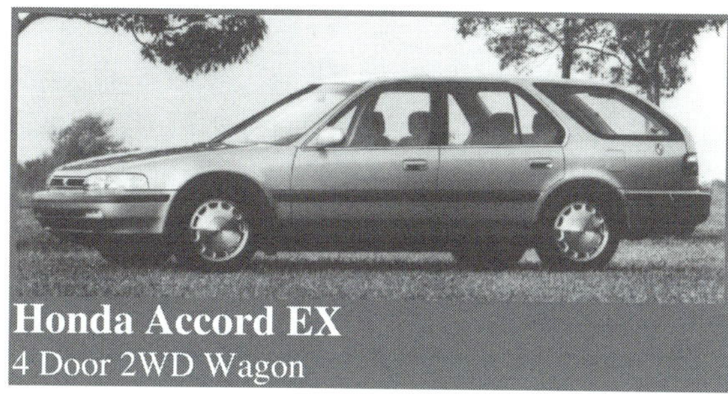

Honda Accord EX
4 Door 2WD Wagon

This appendix lists the best economic values in vehicles in the above class and price ranges. The best value does not mean the lowest cost to own, but rather the best relationship between the cost to own and the price to buy.
Note that we've only shown one member of a model family, even when multiple members are excellent.

Appendix A

Best Overall Value

* An American vehicle is one determined to be domestically produced by the U.S. Environmental Protection Agency, and whose parent company is headquartered in the United States.

** An Import vehicle is one determined to be imported by the U.S. Environmental Protection Agency, or whose parent company is headquartered outside of the United States.

Appendix A

Best Overall Value

Best American* Truck Value under $13,000

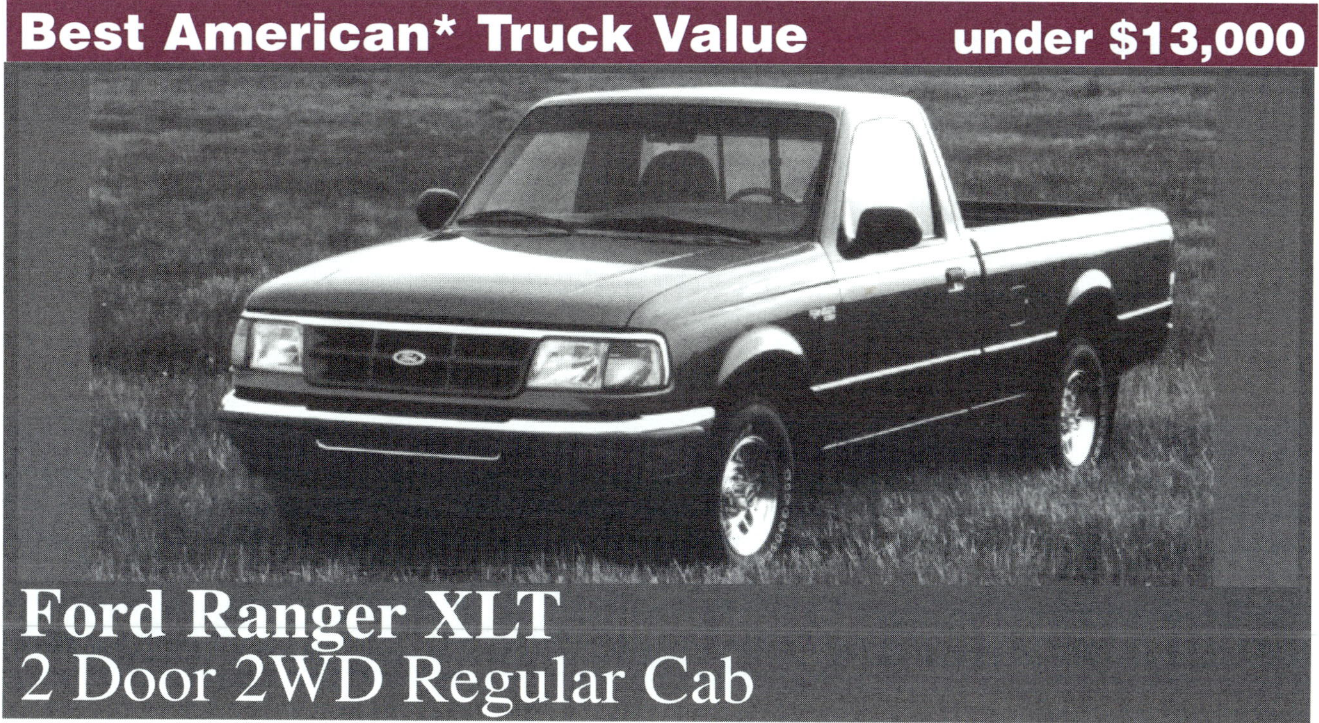

Ford Ranger XLT
2 Door 2WD Regular Cab

* An American vehicle is one determined to be domestically produced by the U.S. Environmental Protection Agency, and whose parent company is headquartered in the United States.

The best value does not mean the lowest cost to own, but rather the best relationship between the cost to own and the price to buy. All vehicles in this book are considered trucks for purposes of the "Best Overall Value" distinction.

Appendix A *Best Overall Value*

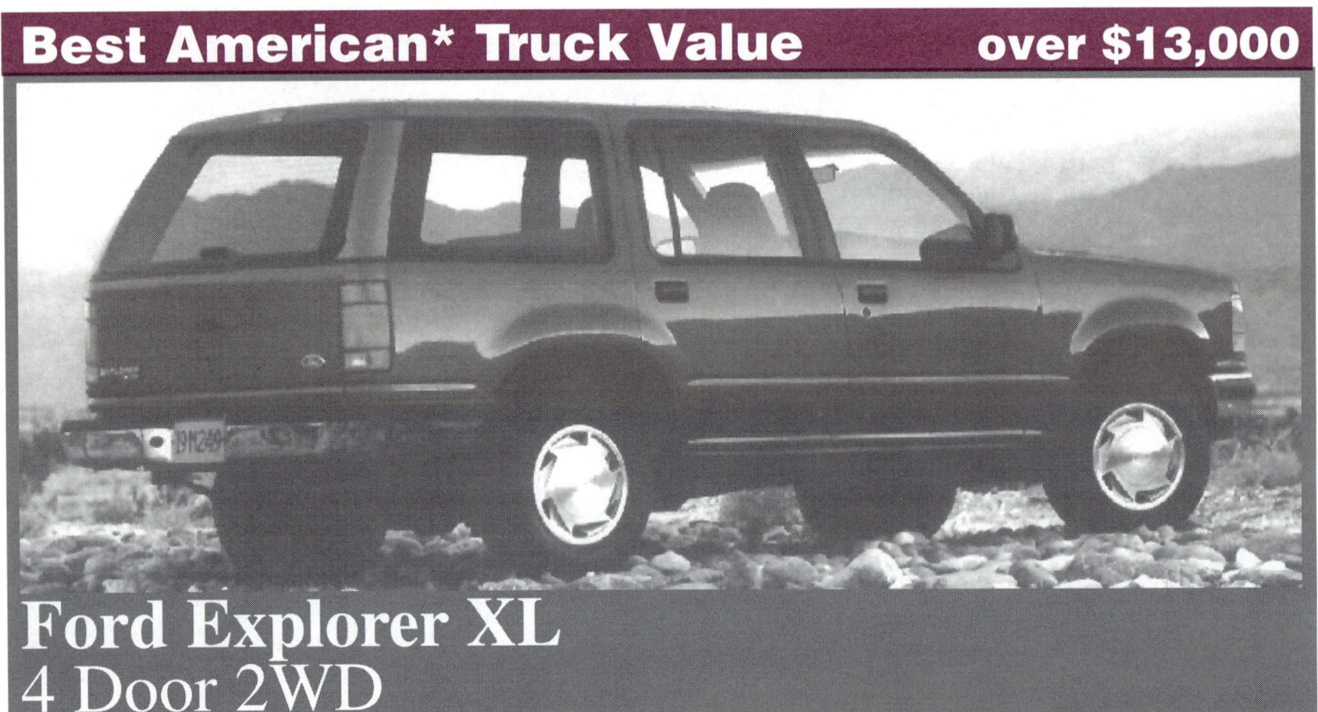

* An American vehicle is one determined to be domestically produced by the U.S. Environmental Protection Agency, and whose parent company is headquartered in the United States.

The best value does not mean the lowest cost to own, but rather the best relationship between the cost to own and the price to buy. All vehicles in this book are considered trucks for purposes of the "Best Overall Value" distinction.

* An Import vehicle is one determined to be imported by the U.S. Environmental Protection Agency, or whose parent company is headquartered outside of the United States.

The best value does not mean the lowest cost to own, but rather the best relationship between the cost to own and the price to buy. All vehicles in this book are considered trucks for purposes of the "Best Overall Value" distinction.

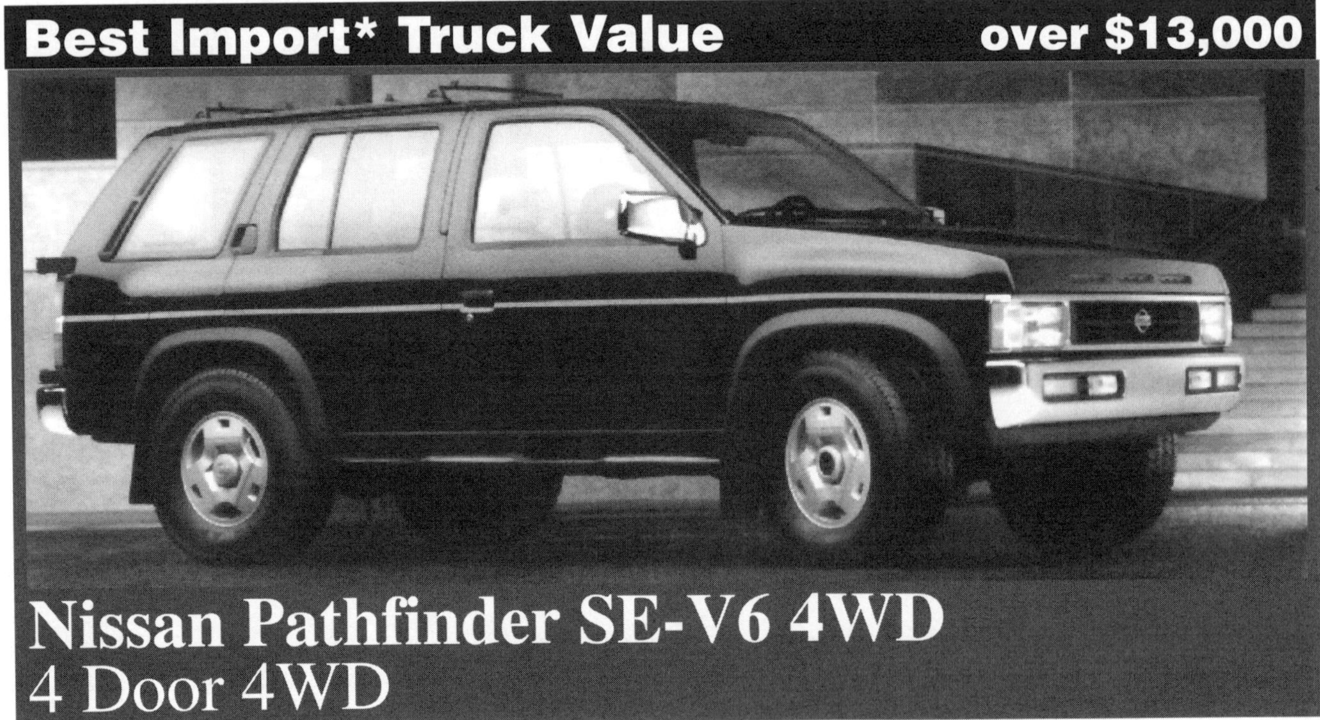

* An Import vehicle is one determined to be imported by the U.S. Environmental Protection Agency, or whose parent company is headquartered outside of the United States.

The best value does not mean the lowest cost to own, but rather the best relationship between the cost to own and the price to buy. All vehicles in this book are considered trucks for purposes of the "Best Overall Value" distinction.

Appendix B

Lowest/Highest Maintenance Cost

The vehicles listed below have the lowest and highest costs in the maintenance area. The dollar figure to the right of each vehicle represents the total expected maintenance cost over a five-year period.

Lowest			Highest	
Dodge Dakota	$3,221	Small Pickup	GMC Sonoma 4WD	$4,797
Nissan King Cab	$3,283		Toyota Xtracab DX V6 4WD	$4,751
Ford Ranger XL 4WD	$3,339		Chevrolet S-10 EL 4WD	$4,584
Dodge Ram D150	$3,452	Large Pickup	GMC Sierra K3500	$5,667
Ford F150 Styleside S	$3,647		Chevrolet K3500 extended cab	$5,296
Chevrolet C1500 Work Truck	$4,290		GMC Sierra K1500 extended cab	$5,210
Ford Explorer XL 2 door	$3,431	Utility	GMC Jimmy Typhoon 4WD	$7,092
Jeep Cherokee	$3,777		Land Rover Range Rover County	$6,894
Mazda Navajo series	$3,856		Toyota Land Cruiser	$5,326
Ford Aero. Eddie Bauer Ext Van 2WD	$3,703	Passenger Mini-Van	Toyota Previa LE	$6,031
Dodge Caravan SE 2WD	$3,835		GMC Safari SLX AWD	$5,109
Plymouth Voyager LE	$4,095		Chevrolet Astro AWD	$5,034
Dodge Ram Wagon B150	$3,592	Passenger Full-Size Van	GMC 3500 Rally Wagon Heavy Duty	$5,653
Ford Club Wagon Custom	$4,147		Chevrolet G30 Sportvan	$5,182
Ford Escort LX	$3,417	Subcompact Wagon	Toyota Corolla DX	$5,463
Subaru Loyale 4WD	$4,028			
Volvo 240 Wagon	$3,394	Compact Wagon	Toyota Camry LE V6	$5,828
Saturn SW1	$3,617		Subaru Legacy Touring Wagon AWD	$5,686
Chevrolet Cavalier VL	$4,060		Mitsubishi Expo LRV AWD	$5,169
Volvo 940 Turbo	$3,850	Midsize Wagon	Mitsubishi Expo SP AWD	$5,196
Oldsmobile Cutlass Ciera Cruiser S	$4,171		Honda Accord EX	$5,061
Ford Taurus GL	$4,173		Buick Century series	$4,611

Appendix B

Lowest/Highest Fuel Cost

The vehicles listed below have the lowest and highest costs in the fuel area. The number to the right of each vehicle represents the expected fuel costs over a five year period, based on highway and city fuel estimates reported by the Environmental Protection Agency, and the assumptions described in this book.

Lowest		Category	Highest	
Ford Ranger XL	$3,385	Small Pickup	Toyota Xtracab DX V6 4WD	$5,233
Nissan King Cab	$3,454		Dodge Dakota Sport 4WD	$5,079
GMC Sonoma	$3,454		Nissan King Cab SE 4WD	$5,079
Chevrolet S-10	$3,454			
Toyota T100	$4,672	Large Pickup	Dodge Ram W350 Club Cab	$9,311
GMC Sierra K1500 Special	$4,816		Chevrolet C1500 454 SS	$7,848
Chevrolet C1500 Work Truck	$4,816		Ford F250 Styleside XL Supercab 4WD	$7,613
Suzuki Samurai JA Soft Top	$3,050	Utility	Land Rover Defender 110	$8,667
Geo Tracker Soft Top	$3,333		Land Rover Range Rover County	$7,062
Suzuki Sidekick JS Soft Top	$3,333		Toyota Land Cruiser	$6,395
Ford Explorer XL	$4,213			
Dodge Caravan	$3,756	Passenger Mini-Van	GMC Safari SLX AWD	$5,458
Plymouth Voyager	$3,756		Chevrolet Astro AWD	$5,458
Mazda MPV Wagon Van	$4,117		Mazda MPV Wagon 4WD	$5,079
Chevrolet G10 Sportvan	$5,399	Passenger Full-Size Van	Ford Club Wagon Chateau Heavy Duty	$6,659
Dodge Ram Wagon B250 Maxiwagon	$5,403		Dodge Ram Wagon B350	$6,395
Ford Club Wagon Custom	$5,569			
Ford Escort LX	$2,656	Subcompact Wagon	Subaru Loyale 4WD	$3,258
Mercury Tracer	$2,656			
Saturn SW1	$2,890	Compact Wagon	Toyota Camry LE V6	$4,547
Chevrolet Cavalier VL	$3,152		Volkswagen Passat GLX	$4,232
Mitsubishi Expo LRV	$3,385		Subaru Legacy Tour. Wagon AWD	$4,213
Ford Taurus GL	$3,405	Midsize Wagon	Mitsubishi Expo SP AWD	$4,111
Mercury Sable GS	$3,405		Volvo 940 Turbo	$4,111
Honda Accord series	$3,598		Buick Century Special	$3,847

Appendix B

Lowest/Highest Insurance Cost

The vehicles listed below have the lowest and highest costs in the insurance area. The number to the right of each vehicle represents the expected insurance cost over a five-year period.

Lowest		Category	Highest	
Dodge Dakota S	$6,542	Small Pickup	Toyota Xtracab SR5 V6 4WD	$8,995
Chevrolet S-10	$6,867		Nissan King Cab SEV6 4WD	$8,717
GMC Sonoma Special	$6,867		Mitsubishi Mighty Max 4WD	$8,108
Ford F150 Styleside S	$6,542	Large Pickup	Dodge Ram W350 Club Cab	$8,717
GMC Sierra C1500 Special	$6,867		Chevrolet C1500 454 SS	$8,108
Chevrolet C1500 Work Truck	$6,996		GMC Sierra K3500	$8,108
Geo Tracker Soft Top	$7,129	Utility	Land Rover Range Rover County LWB	$13,194
Mazda Navajo LX 2 door	$7,129		GMC Jimmy Typhoon 4WD	$10,453
Suzuki Samurai JA Soft Top	$7,244		Toyota Land Cruiser	$9,987
Jeep Wrangler S	$7,244			
Plymouth Voyager	$6,191	Passenger Mini-Van	Toyota Previa All-Trac LE	$8,507
Dodge Caravan	$6,191		Mazda MPV Wagon 4WD	$8,108
Chevrolet Astro	$6,542		Volkswagen Eurovan series	$7,693
Dodge Ram Wagon B150	$6,867	Passenger Full-Size Van	Ford Club Wagon XLT Super	$7,689
Ford Club Wagon Chateau	$6,869		Chevrolet G30 Sportvan Heavy Duty	$7,432
Ford Escort LX	$7,223	Subcompact Wagon	Mercury Tracer	$7,693
Toyota Corolla DX	$7,223			
Subaru Loyale	$7,223			
Saturn SW1	$6,658	Compact Wagon	Volkswagen Passat GLX	$8,507
Chevrolet Cavalier VL	$6,658		Subaru Legacy LS AWD	$8,238
Mitsubishi Expo LRV/Toyota Camry DX	$6,919		Plymouth Colt Vista AWD	$7,479
Eagle Summit DL, LX	$6,919			
Ford Taurus GL	$6,658	Midsize Wagon	Volvo 940 Turbo	$7,898
Mercury Sable GS	$6,786		Honda Accord EX	$7,898
Oldsmobile Cutlass Ciera Cruiser S	$6,786		Mitsubishi Expo SP AWD	$7,693
Buick Century Special	$6,786			

Appendix B

Lowest/Highest Resale Value

The vehicles listed below have either the highest or lowest resale values after a five-year period. The percentage to the right of each vehicle represents how much of its original value the vehicle will retain at the end of five years. Resale value is based on the vehicles's rate of depreciation. Vehicles with better resale values have slower rates of depreciation.

Highest		Category	Lowest	
Mazda B2200 Cab Plus	74%	Small Pickup	Ford Ranger STX 4WD	49%
Toyota Xtracab DX 4WD	67%		Dodge Dakota Sport 4WD	49%
Nissan King Cab	66%		Nissan King Cab SE V6	51%
Dodge Power Ram 50	66%			
GMC Sierra K1500	81%	Large Pickup	Dodge Ram D350 Club Cab	49%
Chevrolet C1500 Work Truck	80%			
Ford F150 Styleside XL SuperCab 4WD	76%			
Toyota 4Runner SR5-V6	83%	Utility	Dodge Ramcharger AD 150	52%
Nissan Pathfinder XE-V6	82%		Oldsmobile Bravada	53%
Chevrolet Suburban K1500	81%		Suzuki Samurai JL Soft Top	55%
Plymouth Grand Voyager SE AWD	80%	Passenger Mini-Van	Oldsmobile Silhouette	58%
Dodge Grand Caravan SE AWD	79%		Pontiac Trans Sport SE	59%
GMC Safari SLX XT AWD	78%		Ford Aerostar Eddie Bauer	62%
Dodge Ram Wagon B250 Maxiwagon	57%	Passenger Full-Size Van	Ford Club Wagon Chateau Heavy Duty	43%
GMC G2500 Rally Wagon	55%			
Toyota Corolla DX	53%	Subcompact Wagon	Mercury Tracer	44%
Volvo 240	64%	Compact Wagon	Chevrolet Cavalier RS	42%
Toyota Camry DX	63%		Subaru Legacy LS AWD	46%
Volkswagen Passat GLX	56%		Mitsubishi Expo LRV AWD	48%
Honda Accord LX	64%	Midsize Wagon	Oldsmobile Cutlass Ciera SL	44%
Mercury Sable LS	57%		Buick Century Custom	46%
Ford Taurus GL	55%			
Volvo 940 Turbo	55%			

Appendix C

Financing Sources

When you consider a new auto loan, it really pays to shop around and compare rates. (The same is also true for leasing!) Commercial banks, savings banks, credit unions, and even auto manufacturers offer a variety of loan terms for new vehicles. You probably know of a dozen or more local institutions willing to loan you money — but do you know which one has the lowest rate?

The chart below lists for each major metropolitan area the bank that has at one time offered the lowest rate among competitive banks in that area. Keep in mind, however, that rates change frequently, so there is no guarantee that the institution shown below currently offers the lowest rate in your area. While it is wise to consider the institutions listed here, make sure you also get price quotes from other financial institutions.

A Sample of Competitive New Auto Loans in Major Markets Around the Country

Based on $10,000 loan

Region	Institution	Recent rate	Term (months)
Atlanta	Trust Company Bank	7.90	48
Baltimore	Mercantile Safe Deposit	8.00	60
Boston	Bank of Boston	8.90	60
Chicago	Cole Taylor Bank	7.50	48
Cleveland	Society National Bank	7.90	60
Dallas	NationsBank	7.69	36
Denver	Bank Western	7.90	48
Detroit	First of America Bank	7.25	60
Houston	Texas Commerce Bank	7.79	36
Los Angeles	Community Bank	8.25	60
Miami	United National Bank	8.50	48
Minneapolis	National City Bank	8.25	36
New York City	Marine Midland Bank	8.25	48
N. New Jersey	Columbia Federal Savings	8.75	36
Philadelphia	Meridian Bank	8.75	48
Phoenix	Republic National Bank	8.25	60
Pittsburgh	Three Rivers Bank	8.00	60
St. Louis	Pulaski Bank	8.25	48
San Diego	Escondido National Bank	8.90	48
San Francisco	Sumitomo Bank	7.75	48
Seattle	Seafirst Bank	8.25	60
S. W. Connecticut	Union Savings Bank	7.75	60
Tampa	Sun Bank of Tampa Bay	7.50	48
Washington, D. C.	Chevy Chase Federal Savings	7.50	48

Rates subject to change without notice.
Source: HSH Associates, 1200 Route 23, Butler NJ 07457. © 1993, HSH Associates

Appendix D

Insurance Companies

Insurance is one of the largest of the seven ownership cost areas discussed throughout this book. If you live in a non-competitive insurance state (Massachusetts or Texas) then the rates are controlled by an insurance commission or rating bureau, and all insurers are required to charge the same premium. However, in all other states the rates are determined by each insurance company and may vary dramatically from one company to the next. Therefore, if you live in a competitive insurance state, it really pays to shop for the lowest rates.

The ten insurance companies listed below are the largest private passenger car insurers in the United States. To ensure that you are getting the most competitive rate, obtain quotes from several of the companies listed here, and compare them to smaller companies or independent agents. You can find a listing of insurance agents in your area by looking in the yellow pages under "Insurance." To help you make a side-by-side evaluation of different insurers, use the Insurance Comparison Worksheet on page 11A.

Although there are many differences between insurance companies, one thing you should seriously evaluate is the company's reputation when it comes to processing claims. Before you buy, it makes sense to check with a few local repair or body shops to find out which insurers have the best and the worst reputation. Also, you may want to check with the Council of Better Business Bureaus (Appendix on page 88A).

The following is a listing of the top 10 auto insurers:

Aetna Life & Casualty Insurance
151 Farmington Avenue
Hartford, CT 06156
(203) 273-0123

Allstate Insurance
Allstate Plaza
Northbrook, IL 60062
(708) 402-5000

Farmers Insurance
4680 Wilshire Boulevard
Los Angeles, CA 90010
(213) 930-4019

Geico Corporation Insurance
One GEICO Plaza
Washington, D.C. 20076
(301) 986-3000

ITT Hartford
Hartford Plaza
Hartford, CT 06115
(203) 547-5000

Liberty Mutual Insurance
175 Berkeley Street
Boston, MA 02117
(800) 225-2390

Nationwide Insurance
One Nationwide Plaza
Columbus, OH 43216
(800) 882-2822

State Farm Insurance
One State Farm Plaza
Bloomington, IL 61701
(309) 766-2311

Travelers Insurance
One Tower Square
Hartford, CT 06183
(203) 277-0111

USAA Insurance
USAA Building
San Antonio, TX 78288
(800) 531-8100

Appendix E

Service Contract Locator

If you decide to purchase an Extended Service Contract, your choices may be limited. In most cases, the dealer will offer you a contract that is backed by the manufacturer. He may also offer a contract from an independent provider.

You probably won't choose a dealer based on the Extended Service Contract. However, if you are considering an Extended Service Contract that is offered by a provider other than the manufacturer, you may wish to learn more about that company's reputation. One source for this information is the Council of Better Business Bureaus (Appendix F). Also, you can directly contact the contract provider.

The following is a listing of the major independent Service Contract providers, and the insurance company that underwrites their policies:

GE Capital
Insurance Services Group
P.O. Box 14159
Denver, CO 80214-4159
(800) 445-4065

Backed by: Lexington Insurance
Other Info: In national service contract business approximately 5 years

General Insurance Administrators
16501 Ventura Blvd.
Suite 200
Encino, CA 91436
(818) 990-9590
(800) 242-9442

Backed by: Fireman's Fund/Western General Insurance Company
Other Info: In national service contract business approximately 4 years

JM&A Group
P.O. Box 1160
Deerfield Beach, FL 33443
(305) 429-2333

Backed by: Virginia Surety
Other Info: Available in 40 states

Ryan Warranty Services
123 N. Wacker Drive
Chicago, IL 60606
(312) 701-3700

Backed by: Virginia Surety
Other Info: In national service contract business approximately 14 years

Western National Warranty Corporation
4141 N. Scottsdale Road
Scottsdale, AZ 85252-2840
(800) 345-0191

Backed by: Continental Insurance Company
Other Info: In national service contract business approximately 11 years

Appendix F

Better Business Bureau Locations

Acquiring a new vehicle usually involves many more business transactions than just the deal for the truck. You will need insurance, financing, and you may deal with an extended service contract administrator. And after you've purchased your truck, you'll require the services of many more businesses — service stations, automobile clubs, car washes, and repair shops.

A key element to a satisfying overall purchase and ownership experience is ensuring that the related businesses you require service from are credible, honest, and deliver good value.

The Council of Better Business Bureaus (BBB) can help. While it is still up to you to choose your service provider, the BBB does keep a log of complaints registered against businesses in your community. You can consult this log to help determine which businesses you'd rather not associate with.

If the company you want information about is not headquartered in your community, your local BBB office may be able to refer you to the BBB Office in the community of the business you're inquiring about.

The following is a listing of BBB offices and phone numbers:

UNITED STATES BUREAUS

ALABAMA

BIRMINGHAM, AL 35205
1210 South 20th Street
P.O. Box 55268 (35255-5268) 205/558-2222
DOTHAN, AL 36301
118 Woodburn Street 205/792-3804
HUNTSVILLE, AL 35801
501 Church Street, N.W.
P.O. Box 383 (35804) .... (24 hrs.)205/533-1604
MOBILE, AL 36602-3221
707 Van Antwerp Building 205/433-5494, 95
So. AL 800/554-4174
MONTGOMERY, AL 36104-3559
Union Bank Building, Commerce St, Suite, 806 .... 205/262-5606

ALASKA

ANCHORAGE, AK 99503-5701
4011 Arctic Blvd.,#206 .... 907/562-0704

ARIZONA

PHOENIX, AZ 85014-4585
4428 North 12th Street 602/264-1721
TUCSON, AZ 85705-7353
50 W. Drachman St., Suite 103 .... Inq.602/622-7651
Comp. 622-7654
So. AZ only 800/696-2827

ARKANSAS

LITTLE ROCK, AR 72204-2605
1415 South University 501/664-7274

CALIFORNIA

BAKERSFIELD, CA 93301-4882
705 Eighteenth Street 805/322-2074
COLTON, CA 92324-0814
290 N. 10th St. Suite 206, P.O. Box 970 .... 714/825-7280
CYPRESS, CA 90630-3966
6101 Ball Road, Suite 309 .... Inq. & Comp. 714/527-0680
FRESNO, CA 93705-0341
1398 W. Indianapolis, #102 .... 209/222-8111
LOS ANGELES, CA 90020
3400 West 6th St., Suite 403 .... 213/251-9696
MONTEREY, CA 93940-2717
494 Alvarado St., Suite C 408/372-3149
OAKLAND, CA 94612-1564
510 16th St, Ste. 550 .... (24 hrs) 510/238-1000
SACRAMENTO, CA 95814-6997
400 S Street 916/443-6843
SAN DIEGO, CA 92108-1729
3111 Camino del Rio, N., Suite 600 .... (24 hrs) 619/521-5898
SAN FRANCISCO, CA 94105-4506
33 New Montgomery St. Tower, #290 .... 415/243-9999
SAN JOSE, CA 95125-5316
1505 Meridian Ave., Suite C 408/978-8700

CALIFORNIA *Continued*

SAN MATEO, CA 94402
400 S. El Camino Real, #450
P.O. Box 294 (94401-0294) 415/696-1240
SANTA BARBARA, CA 93101-0746
402 E. Carrillo St., Suite C, P.O. Box 746 ....805/963-8657
SANTA ROSA, CA 95401-8541
300 B Street 707/577-0300
STOCKTON, CA 95202-1383
1111 North Center Street 209/948-4880, 81

COLORADO

COLORADO SPRINGS, CO 80907-5454
3022 North El Paseo, P.O. Box 7970 (80933-7970) . 719/636-1155
DENVER, CO 80222-4350
1780 S. Bellaire, Suite 700 ....(24 hrs.) Inq. 303/758-2100
....Comp. 303/758-2212
FORT COLLINS, CO 80525-1073
1730 S. College Avenue, Suite 303 ....303/484-1348
S. WY only 800/878-3222
PUEBLO, CO 81003-3119
119 W. 6th St., Suite 203 ....719/542-6464

CONNECTICUT

FAIRFIELD, CT 06430-3267
Fairfield Woods Plaza, 2345 Black Rock Turnpike
P.O. Box 1410 (06430-1410) 203/374-6161
WALLINGFORD, CT 06492-4395
100 S. Turnpike Rd ....Inq. 203/269-2700
Comp. 269-4457

DELAWARE

WILMINGTON, DE 19808-5532
2055 Limestone Rd., Ste. 200 ....302/996-9200

DISTRICT OF COLUMBIA

1012 14th St, N.W, 14th Floor (20005-3410) 202/393-8000

FLORIDA

CLEARWATER, FL 34620
13770 - 58th St, North, #309
P.O BOX 7950 (34618-7950) 813/535-5522
FORT MYERS, FL 33901-6003
2976-E Cleveland Ave 813/334-7331
334-7152
JACKSONVILLE, FL 32216-2756
3100 University Blvd., South, Suite 239 ....904/721-2288
MAITLAND; FL 32751-7147 (Orlando)
2605 Maitland Center Parkway 407/660-9500
MIAMI, FL 33014-6709
16291 N.W. - 57th Avenue ....Inq. 305/625-0307
Comp. 625-1302
NEW PORT RICHEY, FL 34652
250 School Road Suite 11-W 813/842-5459
PENSACOLA, FL 32501
400 S. Alcaniz Street
P.O. Box 1511 (32597-1511) 904/433-6111
PORT ST. LUCIE, FL 34952
1950 Pt. St. Lucie Blvd., Suite 211 ....407/878-2010
TAMPA, FL 33607
1111 N. Westshore Blvd, Suite 207 ..... Inq. & Comp. 813/854-1154
WEST PALM BEACH, FL 33409-3408
2247 Palm Beach Lakes Blvd., Suite 211 ....407/686-2200

GEORGIA

ALBANY, GA 31707
611 N. Jefferson St, P.O. Box 3241 (31706-3241) 912/883-0744
ATLANTA, GA 30303-3075
100 Edgewood Avenue, Suite 1012 ....404/688-4910
AUGUSTA, GA 30901-1463
624 Ellis St., Suite 106
P.O. Box 2085 (30903-2085) 404/722-1574
COLUMBUS, GA 31901-2151
8 13th Street, P.O. Box 2587 (31902-2587) 404/324-0712, 13
MACON, GA 31211-2499
1765 Shurling Drive 912/742-7999
SAVANNAH, GA 31405
6606 Abercorn Street Suite 108-C
P.0. Box 13956 (31416-0956) 912/354-7521

HAWAII

HONOLULU, HI 96814-3801
1600 Kapiolani Blvd., Suite 714 ....808/942-2355

IDAHO

BOISE, ID 83702-5320
1333 West Jefferson 208/342-4649
T-F ID only 800/339-8737
IDAHO FALLS, ID 83402-5026
1547 So. Blvd 208/523-9754

ILLINOIS

CHICAGO, IL 60606
211 West Wacker Drive ....Inq. 312/444-1188
Comp. 346-3313
PEORIA, IL 61615-3770
3024 West Lake 309/688-3741
ROCKFORD, IL 61104
810 E. State St., 3rd Fl. 815/963-2222

Appendix F *continued* — *Better Business Bureau Locations*

INDIANA

ELKHART, IN 46514-2988
722 W. Bristol St., Suite H-2
P.O. Box 405 (46515-0405) 219/262-8996

EVANSVILLE, IN 47715-2265
4004 Morgan Ave., Suite 201 .... 812/473-0202

FORT WAYNE, IN 46802-3493
1203 Webster Street 219/423-4433
IN only 800-552-4631

GARY, IN 46408-2490
4231 Cleveland Street 219/980-1511
No. IN only 800/637-2118

INDIANAPOLIS, IN 46204-3584
Victoria Centre, 22 E. Washington Street,
Suite 200 .... 317/488-2222

SOUTH BEND, IN 46637-4200
52303 Emmons Road, Suite 9 .... 219/277-9121
.... No. IN only 800/439-5313

IOWA

BETTENDORF, IA 52722-4100
852 Middle Road., Suite 290 .... 319/355-6344

DES MOINES, IA 50309-2375
615 Insurance Exchange Building 515/243-8137

SIOUX CITY, IA 51101
318 Badgerow Building 712/252-4501

KANSAS

TOPEKA, KS 66607-1190
501 Jefferson, Suite 24 .... 913/232-0454

WICHITA, KS 67202-3857
212 S. Market St., #300 .... 316/263-3146

KENTUCKY

LEXINGTON, KY 40507-1203
311 W. Short Street 606/259-1008

LOUISVILLE, KY 40203-2186
844 S. Fourth Street 502/583-6546

LOUISIANA

ALEXANDRIA, LA 71301-6875
1605 Murray St., Suite 117 .... 318/473-4494

BATON ROUGE, LA 70806-1546
2055 Wooddale Blvd 504/926-3010

HOUMA, LA 70360-4455
501 E. Main St. 504/868-3456

LAFAYETTE, LA 70506
100 Huggins Rd., P.O. Box 30297 (70593-0297) 318/981-3497

LAKE CHARLES, LA 70605
3941-L Ryan St. P.O. Box 7314 (70606-7314) 318/478-6253

MONROE, LA 71201-7380
141 De Siard Street, Suite 808 .... 318/387-4600

NEW ORLEANS, LA 70130-5843
1539 Jackson Avenue, #400 .... (24 hrs) 504/581-6222

SHREVEPORT, LA 71105-2122
3612 Youree Dr. 318/861-6417

MAINE

PORTLAND, ME 04103-2648
812 Stevens Avenue 207/878-2715

MARYLAND

BALTIMORE, MD 21211-3215
2100 Huntingdon Avenue 301/347-3990

MASSACHUSETTS

BOSTON, MA 02116-4404
20 Park Plaza Suite 820 .... Inq. 617/426-9000
802 Area only 800/4BBB-811

SPRINGFIELD, MA 01103-1402
293 Bridge Street, Suite 320 .... 413/734-3114

WORCESTER, MA 01608
32 Franklin Street, P.O. Box 379 (01601-0379) 508/755-2548

MICHIGAN

GRAND RAPIDS, MI 49503-3001
620 Trust Building 616/774-8236

SOUTHFIELD, MI 48076-7751 (Detroit)
30555 Southfield Road, Suite 200 .... Inq. 313/644-1012
Comp. 644-9136

MINNESOTA

MINNEAPOLIS-ST. PAUL, MN 55116-2600
2706 Gannon Road 612/699-1111

MISSISSIPPI

JACKSON, MS 39206-3088
460 Briarwood Drive, Suite 340 .... 601/956-8282

MISSOURI

KANSAS CITY, MO 64106-2418
306 E. 12th Street, Suite 1024 .... 816/421-7800

ST. LOUIS, MO 63110-1400
5100 Oakland, Suite 200 .... Inq. 314/531-3300

SPRINGFIELD, MO 65806-1326
205 Park Central East, Suite 509 .... 417/862-9231

NEBRASKA

LINCOLN, NE 68504-3491
719 North 48th Street 402/467-5261
OMAHA, NE 68102-2158
1613 Farnam Street, #417 .... 402/346-3033

NEVADA

LAS VEGAS, NV 89104-1515
1022 E. Sahara Avenue 702/735-6900
702/735-1969
RENO, NV 89502
991 Bible Way, P.O. Box 21269 (89515-1269) 702/322-0657

NEW HAMPSHIRE

CONCORD, NH 03301-3459
410 South Main Street 603/224-1991

NEW JERSEY

NEWARK, NJ 07102-3294
494 Broad Street 201/642-INFO
PARAMUS, NJ 07652-5291
2 Forest Avenue 201/845-4044
PARSIPPANY, NJ 07054
1300A Route #46, West, #215 .... 201/334-5990
TOMS RIVER, NJ 08753-8239
1721 Route 37 East 908/270-5577
TRENTON, NJ 08690-3596
1700 Whitehorse, Hamilton Square, Suite D-5 .... 201/588-0808
WESTMONT, NJ 08108-0303
16 Maple Avenue, P.O. Box 303 .... 609/854-8467

NEW MEXICO

ALBUQUERQUE, NM 87109-1292
4600-A Montgomery N.E., Suite 200 .... 505/884-0500
NM only 800/873-2224
FARMINGTON, NM 87401-5855
308 North Locke 505/326-6501
LAS CRUCES, NM 88005
2407 W. Picacho, Ste B-2 .... 505/524-3130

NEW YORK

BUFFALO, NY 14202-1899
346 Delaware Avenue 716/856-7180
FARMINGDALE, NY (Long Island) 11735-9998
266 Main Street 900/463-6222
NEW YORK, NY 10010-7384
257 Park Avenue, South 212/533-7500, 6200
SYRACUSE, NY 13202-2552
847 James St., #200 .... 315/479-6635
WHITE PLAINS, NY 10603-3213
30 Glenn Street 914/428-1230, 31

NORTH CAROLINA

ASHEVILLE, NC 28801-3418
801 BB&T Building 704/253-2392
CHARLOTTE, NC 28204-2626
1130 East 3rd St., Suite 400 .... (24 hrs.) 704/332-7151
CONOVER, NC 28613-9608
3305-10 16th Avenue, SE #303 .... 704/464-0372
GREENSBORO, NC 27410-4895
3608 West Friendly Avenue 919/852-4240, 41, 42
RALEIGH, NC 27604-1080
3125 Poplarwood Ct., Suite 308 .... 919/872-9240
East NC only 800/222-0950
Durham 919/688-6143
Chapel Hill 919/967-0296
WINSTON-SALEM, NC 27103-2516
2110 Cloverdale Ave., Suite 2-B 919/725-8348

OHIO

AKRON, OH 44303-2111
222 W Market Street 216/253-4590
CANTON, OH 44703-3135
1434 Cleveland Avenue, N.W 216/454-9401
OH only 800/362-0494
CINCINNATI, OH 45202-2097
898 Walnut Street 513/421-3015
CLEVELAND, OH 44115-1299
2217 East 9th Street #200 .... 216/241-7678
COLUMBUS, OH 43215-1000
1335 Dublin Street, #30A 614/486-6336
DAYTON, OH 45402-1828
40 West Fourth St, Suite 1250 .... 513/222-5825
LIMA, OH 45802-0269
121 W. High St., #370, P O. Box 269 .... 419/223-7010
TOLEDO, OH 43604-1055
425 Jefferson Avenue, Suite 909 .... 419/241-6276
YOUNGSTOWN, OH 44501-1495
1102 Mahoning Bank Building, P O. Box 1495 .... 216/744-3111

OKLAHOMA

OKLAHOMA CITY, OK 73102
17 S. Dewey .... Inq. 405/239-6081
Inq. 239-6860
Comp. 239-6083
TULSA, OK 74136-3327
6711 South Yale, Suite 230 .... 918/492-1266

OREGON

PORTLAND, OR 97205
610 SW. Alder Street, Suite 615 .... 503/226-3981
(OR/WA) 800/488-4155

Appendix F *continued* — Better Business Bureau Locations

PENNSYLVANIA

BETHLEHEM, PA 18018-5789
528 North New Street 215/866-8780
LANCASTER, PA 17602-5205
6 Marion Court 717/291-1151
Toll Free, York Co. Resident 846-2700
PHILADELPHIA, PA 19103-0297
1930 Chestnut St., P.O. Box 2297 .... 215/448-6100
PITTSBURGH, PA 15222-2578
610 Smithfield Street 412/456-2700
SCRANTON, PA 18503-2204
407 Connell Building
P.O. Box 993 (18501-0993) 717/342-9129

PUERTO RICO

SAN JUAN, PR 00936-3488
P. O. Box 363488 .... 809/756-5400

RHODE ISLAND

WARWICK, RI 02887-1300 (Providence)
Bureau Park, Box 1300 .... Inq 401/785-1212
.... Comp. 785-1213

SOUTH CAROLINA

COLUMBIA, SC 29201
1830 Bull Street, P.O. Box 8326 (29202-8326) 803/254-2525
GREENVILLE, SC 29605
113 Mills Avenue 803/242-5052
MYRTLE BEACH, SC 29577-1601
1601 Oak St., #403 .... 803/626-6881

TENNESSEE

BLOUNTVILLE, TN 37616
P.O. Box 1178 TCAS 615/323-6311
CHATTANOOGA, TN 37402-2614
1010 Market Street, #200 .... 615/266-6144
KNOXVILLE, TN 37919
2633 Kingston Pike, #2
P.O. Box 10327 (37939-0327) 615/522-2552
MEMPHIS, TN 38115
3792 South Mendenhall
P.O. Box 750704 (38175-0704) 901/795-8771
NASHVILLE, TN 37219-1778
Nations Bank Plaza, 414 Union St., #1830 .... 615/254-5872

TEXAS

ABILENE, TX 79605-5052
3300 S. 14th Street, Suite 307 .... 915/691-1533
AMARILLO, TX 79101-3408
1000 South Polk, P.O. Box 1905 (79105-1905) 806/379-6222
AUSTIN, TX 78701-3403
221 W. 6 Street, #450 .... 512/476-1616
BEAUMONT, TX 77704-2988
476 Oakland Ave., P.O Box 2988 (77701-2011) 409/835-5348
BRYAN, TX 77802-4413
4346 Carter Creek Pkwy. 409/260-2222
CORPUS CHRISTI, TX 78411-4418
4535 S. Padre Island Drive, #28 .... 512/854-2892
DALLAS, TX 75201-3093
2001 Bryan Street, Suite 850 .... 214/220-2000
EL PASO, TX 79903-4904
5160 Montano Ave., Lower Level 915/772-2727
FORT WORTH, TX 76102-3968
512 Main Street, #807 .... 817/332-7585
HOUSTON, TX 77008-1085
2707 North Loop West, Suite 900 .... 713/868-9500
LUBBOCK, TX 97401
1015 15th Street, P.O. Box 1178 (79408-1178) 806/763-0459
MIDLAND, TX 79711-0206
10100 County Rd, 118 West, P.O. Box 60206 .... 915/563-1880
800/592-4433
SAN ANGELO, TX 76904
3121 Executive Dr., P.O. Box 3366 (76902-3366) 915/949-2989
SAN ANTONIO, TX 78217-5296
1800 Northeast Loop 410, Suite 400 .... 512/828-9441
TYLER, TX 75701
3600 Old Bullard Rd., #103-A
P.O. Box 6652 (75711-6652) 903/581-5704
WACO, TX 76710
6801 Sanger Avenue, Suite 125
P.O. Box 7203 (76714-7203) 817/772-7530
WESLACO, TX 78596-0069
609 Intl. Blvd., P.O Box 69 .... 512/968-3678
WICHITA FALLS, TX 76301-5079
1106 Brook Avenue 817/723-5526
TX only 800/388-1778

UTAH

SALT LAKE CITY, UT 84115-5382
1588 South Main Street 801/487-4656
UT only 800/388-1778

VIRGINIA

FREDERICKSBURG, VA 22407-4800
4022-B Plank Road 703/786-8397
NORFOLK, VA 23509-1499
3608 Tidewater Drive 804/627-5651
804/851-9101 (Peninsula Area)
RICHMOND, VA 23219-2332
701 East Franklin, Suite 712 .... 804/648-0016
ROANOKE, VA 24011-1301
31 West Campbell Avenue 703/342-3455

WASHINGTON

KENNEWICK, WA 99336-3819
127 W. Canal St. 509/582-0222
SEATTLE, WA 98121-1857
2200 Sixth Avenue, #828 .... 206/448-8888
(24 hrs.) 206-448-6222
SPOKANE, WA 99207-2356
E. 123 Indiana, #106 .... 509/328-2100
TACOMA, WA 98401-1274
1101 Fawcett Ave. #222 (98402), P.O. Box 1274 ..... 206/383-5561
YAKIMA, WA 98907-1584
424 Washington Mutual Bldg. (98901)
P.O. Box 1584 .... 509/248-1326

WISCONSIN

MILWAUKEE, WI 53203-2478
740 North Plankinton Avenue 414/273-1600

INTERNATIONAL BUREAUS

NATIONAL HEADQUARTERS FOR CANADIAN BUREAUS

CONCORD, ONTARIO L4K 2Z5
2180 Steeles Avenue West, Suite 219 .... 416/699-1248

ALBERTA

CALGARY, ALBERTA T2H 2H8
7330 Fisher Street, S.E., Suite 357 .... 403/258-2920
EDMONTON, ALBERTA T5K 2L9
9707 - 110th Street 403/482-2341
Red Deer, Alberta 403/343-3200

BRITISH COLUMBIA

VANCOUVER, BC V6B 2M1
788 Beatty Street, Suite 404 .... 604/682-2711
VICTORIA, BC V8W 1V7
201-1005 Langley Street 604/386-6348

MANITOBA

WINNIPEG, MANITOBA R3B 2K3
365 Hargrave Street, Room 204 .... 204/943-1486

NEWFOUNDLAND

ST. JOHN'S, NEWFOUNDLAND A1E 2B6
360 Topsail Road, P.O. Box 516 (A1C 5K4) 709/364-2222

NOVA SCOTIA

HALIFAX, NOVA SCOTIA B3J 2A4
1731 Barrington Street
P.O. Box 2124 B35 3B7 .... Inq.902/422-6581
Comp. 902/422-6582

ONTARIO

HAMILTON, ONTARIO L8P 4V9
50 Bay Street, South 416/526-1111
KITCHENER, ONTARIO N2G 4L5
354 Charles Street, East 519/579-3080
LONDON, ONTARIO N6A 5C7
700 Richmond St., #402
P.O. Box 2153 (N6A 4E3) 519/673-3222
OTTAWA, ONTARIO K1P 5N2
71 Bank Street, 6th Floor 613/237-4856
ST. CATHERINES, ONTARIO L2R 3H6
11-101 King St 416/687-6686
TORONTO, ONTARIO M6P 4C7
One St. John's Rd., Suite 501 .... 416/766-5744
WINDSOR, ONTARIO N9A 5K6
500 Riverside Drive West 519/258-7222

QUEBEC

MONTREAL, QUEBEC H3A 1V4
2055 Peel Street, Suite 460 .... 514/286-9281
QUEBEC CITY, PQ G1R 1K2
475 rue Richelieu 418/523-2555

SASKATCHEWAN

REGINA, SASKATCHEWAN, S4N 6H4
1601 McAra Street 306/352-7601

Appendix G

Automobile Manufacturers

Acura
100 W. Alondra Blvd., Gardena, CA 90247 213-327-8280

Alfa Romeo Distributors of North America
8259 Exchange Drive, P.O. Box 598026, Orlando, FL 32859-8026 407-856-5000

Audi of America, Inc.
888 West Big Beaver Rd., Troy, MI 48007-3951 313-362-6000

BMW of North America, Inc.
300 Chestnut Ridge Rd., Livonia, MI 48150 201-307-4000

Buick Motor Division
General Motor Corp., 902 E. Hamilton Ave., Flint, MI 48550 313-236-5000

Cadillac Motor Car Division
General Motors Corp., 2860 Clark Street, Detroit, MI 48232 313-554-5067

Chevrolet Motor Division
General Motors Corp., 30007 Van Dyke Ave., Warren, MI 48090 313-492-8846

Chrysler Corp.
12000 Chrysler Drive, Highland Park, MI 48288-1919 313-956-5741

Dodge Division
12000 Chrysler Drive, Highland Park, MI 48288-1919 313-956-5741

Eagle Division
12000 Chrysler Drive, Highland Park, MI 48288-1919 313-956-5741

Ford Division
P.O. Box 43301, 300 Renaissance Center, Detroit, MI 48243 313-446-3800

Geo
General Motors Corp., 30007 Van Dyke Ave., Warren, MI 48090 313-492-8846

Honda - American Honda Motor Co., Inc.
100 W. Alondra Blvd., Gardena, CA 90247 213-327-8280

Hyundai Motor America
10550 Talbert Ave., Fountain Valley, CA 92728 714-965-3508

Infiniti Division
18501 Figueroa St., Carson, CA 90248 213-532-3111

Isuzu - American Isuzu Motors Corp.
2300 Pellissier Place, Whittier, CA 90601 213-949-0611

Jaguar Cars, Inc.
555 MacArthur Blvd., Mahwah, NJ 07430 201-818-8500

Jeep Division
12000 Chrysler Drive, Highland Park, MI 48288-1919 313-956-5741

Land Rover of North America Inc.
4390 Parliament Place, P.O. Box 1503, Lanham, MD 20706 301-731-9040

Lexus
19001 S. Western Ave., Torrence, CA 90509 213-618-4000

Lincoln Division - Ford Motor Co.
300 Renaissance Center, P.O. Box 43322, Detroit, MI 48243 313-446-4450

Mazda Motor of America, Inc.
7755 Irvine Center Drive, Irvine, CA 92718 714-727-1990

Mercedes Benz of North America, Inc.
One Mercedes Drive, Montvale, NJ 07645-0350 201-573-0600

Mercury Division - Ford Motor Co.
300 Renaissance Center, P.O. Box 43322, Detroit, MI 48243 313-446-4450

Mitsubishi Motor Sales of America, Inc.
6400 West Katella Ave., Cypress, CA 90248 714-372-6000

Nissan Motor Corp. in U.S.A.
18501 Figueroa St., Carson, CA 90248 213-532-3111

Oldsmobile Division
General Motors Corp., 920 Townsend St., Lansing, MI 48921 517-377-5000

Plymouth Division
12000 Chrysler Drive, Highland Park, MI 48288-1919 313-956-5741

Pontiac Motor Division
General Motors Corp., 1 Pontiac Plaza, Pontiac, MI 48058-3484 313-857-5000

Porsche Cars North America, Inc.
100 W. Liberty St., Reno, NV 89501 702-348-3000

Saab-Scania of America, Inc.
P.O. Box 697, Saab Drive, Orange, CT 06477 203-795-5671

Saturn Corp. - General Motors Corp.
1400 Stephenson Hwy., Troy, MI 48007-7025 313-524-5721

Subaru of America, Inc.
P.O. Box 6000, Cherry Hill, NJ 08034-6000 609-488-8500

Suzuki - American Suzuki Motor Corp.
3251 E. Imperial Hwy., Brea, CA 92621-6722 714-996-7040

Toyota Motor Sales, USA, Inc.
19001 S. Western Ave., Torrance, CA 90509 213-618-4000

Volkswagen of America, Inc.
888 Big Beaver Rd., P.O. Box 3951, Troy, MI 48099 313-362-6000

Volvo of North America Corp.
Rockleigh, NJ 07647 201-768-7300

Appendix H

Lease Interest Rates

While there are a number of differences between a lease and a loan, they are both similar transactions to a financial analyst. Both involve the exchange of a major asset (in this case, a vehicle) between the "selling" party and the "using" party; both are for a fixed time period; both require periodic payments; and most importantly, both involve the use of an interest rate to set the periodic payment.

A loan's interest rate, or A.P.R. (Annual Percentage Rate) is the one and only true measure of the **cost** of a loan. With the APR, you can compare any number of loans on an apples-to-apples basis.

However, whereas lenders have strict disclosure requirements for automobile loans, lessors do not have the same stringent requirements to inform you of the interest rate being used to determine the monthly lease payments.

Same as with comparing APR between loans, the interest rate used to calculate the lease is the one true measure of the cost of a lease.

The following table will help you determine the interest rate in any lease transaction. You can use this table to help you compare different leases and/or compare a lease to a loan.

To use the tables, here are the things you need to know. The lessor should be able to provide you with this information.

- The acquisition price of the vehicle (Technically, since you're not purchasing the vehicle, the price is called the "capital cost" and is the price upon which the lease payments are based.)
- Any fees or "capital cost reduction" (down payment) required at the start of the lease
- The residual value percentage that is being used in the lease calculation
- The length of the lease
- The monthly lease payment

1. Find the table that corresponds to the length of your lease (24 months-pages 98-99, 36 months-pages 100-101, 48 months-pages 102-103, 60 months-pages 104-105).
2. There are eight tables for each lease term. Locate the table where the "Acquisition Price" is closest to the purchase price of the vehicle.
3. Read across the top row "Residual Value," and find the percent figure that is closest to the percent used to calculate your lease.
4. Trace down that column to the row corresponding to the monthly lease payment.
5. The figure at the intersection is an approximation of the interest rate of your lease.

You may find that the acquisition price of the vehicle you are considering is somewhere between the prices listed in these tables. (For example, the price of the vehicle is actually $22,500, which would be in between the $20,000 table and the $25,000 table.) If this is the case, ask the lessor to give you the lease payment as if the car cost $20,000 or $25,000, and then use the tables listed here.

Appendix H

Lease Interest Rates

See instructions on page 97A.

24 Month Lease

$10,000 – *Acquisition Price*

Capital Cost Reduction: $500

Monthly Payment	Residual Value													
	64%	62%	60%	58%	56%	54%	52%	50%	48%	46%	44%	42%	40%	38%
$200	10.80%	9.65%	8.47%	7.26%	6.02%	4.75%	3.44%	2.10%	0.71%	N.A.	N.A.	N.A.	N.A.	N.A.
$210	12.33%	11.20%	10.04%	8.85%	7.63%	6.38%	5.09%	3.77%	2.41%	1.01%	N.A.	N.A.	N.A.	N.A.
$220	13.86%	12.74%	11.60%	10.43%	9.24%	8.01%	6.74%	5.44%	4.11%	2.73%	1.31%	N.A.	N.A.	N.A.
$230	15.39%	14.29%	13.17%	12.02%	10.84%	9.63%	8.39%	7.12%	5.80%	4.46%	3.06%	1.63%	0.15%	N.A.
$240	16.92%	15.84%	14.74%	13.61%	12.45%	11.26%	10.04%	8.79%	7.50%	6.18%	4.81%	3.41%	1.96%	0.46%
$250	18.45%	17.39%	16.30%	15.19%	14.05%	12.89%	11.69%	10.46%	9.19%	7.90%	6.56%	5.18%	3.76%	2.29%
$260	19.98%	18.94%	17.87%	16.78%	15.66%	14.51%	13.33%	12.13%	10.89%	9.61%	8.30%	6.95%	5.56%	4.12%
$270	21.52%	20.49%	19.44%	18.36%	17.26%	16.14%	14.98%	13.80%	12.58%	11.33%	10.04%	8.72%	7.36%	5.95%
$280	23.05%	22.04%	21.01%	19.95%	18.87%	17.76%	16.63%	15.46%	14.27%	13.04%	11.78%	10.48%	9.15%	7.77%
$290	24.59%	23.59%	22.58%	21.54%	20.47%	19.39%	18.27%	17.13%	15.96%	14.75%	13.52%	12.25%	10.94%	9.59%
$300	26.12%	25.15%	24.15%	23.12%	22.08%	21.01%	19.92%	18.79%	17.64%	16.46%	15.25%	14.01%	12.72%	11.40%

$12,500 – *Acquisition Price*

Capital Cost Reduction: $500

Monthly Payment	Residual Value													
	64%	62%	60%	58%	56%	54%	52%	50%	48%	46%	44%	42%	40%	38%
$250	10.10%	8.95%	7.77%	6.56%	5.32%	4.05%	2.74%	1.39%	N.A.	N.A.	N.A.	N.A.	N.A.	N.A.
$260	11.32%	10.18%	9.01%	7.82%	6.60%	5.34%	4.05%	2.72%	1.35%	N.A.	N.A.	N.A.	N.A.	N.A.
$270	12.53%	11.41%	10.26%	9.08%	7.87%	6.63%	5.36%	4.05%	2.70%	1.31%	N.A.	N.A.	N.A.	N.A.
$280	13.75%	12.64%	11.50%	10.34%	9.15%	7.93%	6.67%	5.38%	4.05%	2.68%	1.28%	N.A.	N.A.	N.A.
$290	14.96%	13.87%	12.75%	11.60%	10.43%	9.22%	7.98%	6.71%	5.40%	4.05%	2.67%	1.24%	N.A.	N.A.
$300	16.18%	15.10%	13.99%	12.86%	11.70%	10.51%	9.29%	8.04%	6.75%	5.42%	4.06%	2.65%	1.20%	N.A.
$310	17.39%	16.33%	15.24%	14.12%	12.98%	11.80%	10.60%	9.36%	8.09%	6.79%	5.44%	4.06%	2.63%	1.15%
$320	18.61%	17.56%	16.48%	15.38%	14.25%	13.10%	11.91%	10.69%	9.44%	8.15%	6.83%	5.47%	4.06%	2.61%
$330	19.83%	18.79%	17.73%	16.64%	15.53%	14.39%	13.22%	12.02%	10.78%	9.52%	8.21%	6.87%	5.49%	4.06%
$340	21.05%	20.02%	18.97%	17.90%	16.80%	15.68%	14.53%	13.34%	12.13%	10.88%	9.60%	8.28%	6.92%	5.51%
$350	22.27%	21.26%	20.22%	19.16%	18.08%	16.97%	15.83%	14.67%	13.47%	12.24%	10.98%	9.68%	8.34%	6.96%

$15,000 – *Acquisition Price*

Capital Cost Reduction: $500

Monthly Payment	Residual Value													
	64%	62%	60%	58%	56%	54%	52%	50%	48%	46%	44%	42%	40%	38%
$300	9.64%	8.49%	7.31%	6.10%	4.86%	3.58%	2.27%	0.92%	N.A.	N.A.	N.A.	N.A.	N.A.	N.A.
$320	11.65%	10.53%	9.37%	8.19%	6.97%	5.73%	4.45%	3.13%	1.78%	0.38%	N.A.	N.A.	N.A.	N.A.
$340	13.67%	12.57%	11.44%	10.28%	9.09%	7.87%	6.62%	5.34%	4.01%	2.65%	1.25%	N.A.	N.A.	N.A.
$360	15.69%	14.61%	13.50%	12.37%	11.21%	10.02%	8.80%	7.54%	6.25%	4.92%	3.56%	2.15%	0.69%	N.A.
$380	17.71%	16.65%	15.57%	14.46%	13.33%	12.16%	10.97%	9.74%	8.49%	7.19%	5.86%	4.49%	3.07%	1.61%
$400	19.73%	18.69%	17.64%	16.55%	15.44%	14.31%	13.14%	11.94%	10.72%	9.45%	8.16%	6.82%	5.44%	4.02%
$420	21.75%	20.74%	19.70%	18.64%	17.56%	16.45%	15.31%	14.14%	12.94%	11.71%	10.45%	9.15%	7.81%	6.43%
$440	23.77%	22.78%	21.77%	20.73%	19.67%	18.59%	17.48%	16.34%	15.17%	13.97%	12.74%	11.47%	10.17%	8.82%
$460	25.80%	24.83%	23.84%	22.83%	21.79%	20.73%	19.64%	18.53%	17.39%	16.22%	15.02%	13.79%	12.52%	11.21%
$480	27.83%	26.88%	25.91%	24.92%	23.91%	22.87%	21.81%	20.73%	19.61%	18.47%	17.30%	16.10%	14.87%	13.60%
$500	29.85%	28.93%	27.98%	27.01%	26.02%	25.01%	23.97%	22.92%	21.83%	20.72%	19.58%	18.41%	17.21%	15.98%

$17,500 – *Acquisition Price*

Capital Cost Reduction: $500

Monthly Payment	Residual Value													
	64%	62%	60%	58%	56%	54%	52%	50%	48%	46%	44%	42%	40%	38%
$350	9.31%	8.16%	6.98%	5.77%	4.53%	3.25%	1.94%	0.59%	N.A.	N.A.	N.A.	N.A.	N.A.	N.A.
$370	11.03%	9.90%	8.74%	7.56%	6.34%	5.09%	3.80%	2.48%	1.12%	N.A.	N.A.	N.A.	N.A.	N.A.
$390	12.76%	11.65%	10.51%	9.34%	8.15%	6.92%	5.66%	4.36%	3.03%	1.66%	0.25%	N.A.	N.A.	N.A.
$410	14.48%	13.39%	12.27%	11.13%	9.96%	8.75%	7.52%	6.25%	4.94%	3.60%	2.22%	0.79%	N.A.	N.A.
$430	16.21%	15.13%	14.04%	12.92%	11.76%	10.58%	9.37%	8.13%	6.85%	5.54%	4.19%	2.79%	1.36%	N.A.
$450	17.93%	16.88%	15.80%	14.70%	13.57%	12.42%	11.23%	10.01%	8.76%	7.48%	6.15%	4.79%	3.39%	1.94%
$470	19.66%	18.63%	17.57%	16.49%	15.38%	14.25%	13.09%	11.89%	10.67%	9.41%	8.12%	6.78%	5.41%	4.00%
$490	21.39%	20.37%	19.33%	18.27%	17.19%	16.08%	14.94%	13.77%	12.57%	11.34%	10.07%	8.77%	7.43%	6.05%
$510	23.11%	22.12%	21.10%	20.06%	19.00%	17.91%	16.79%	15.65%	14.47%	13.27%	12.03%	10.76%	9.45%	8.10%
$530	24.84%	23.87%	22.87%	21.85%	20.80%	19.74%	18.64%	17.52%	16.37%	15.19%	13.98%	12.74%	11.46%	10.14%
$550	26.57%	25.62%	24.64%	23.63%	22.61%	21.56%	20.49%	19.40%	18.27%	17.12%	15.93%	14.72%	13.47%	12.18%

See instructions on page 97A.

24 Month Lease

$20,000 – *Acquisition Price*

Capital Cost Reduction: $500

Monthly Payment	Residual Value 64%	62%	60%	58%	56%	54%	52%	50%	48%	46%	44%	42%	40%	38%
$400	9.07%	7.92%	6.74%	5.52%	4.28%	3.01%	1.69%	0.34%	N.A.	N.A.	N.A.	N.A.	N.A.	N.A.
$420	10.57%	9.44%	8.28%	7.08%	5.86%	4.61%	3.32%	1.99%	0.63%	N.A.	N.A.	N.A.	N.A.	N.A.
$440	12.08%	10.96%	9.82%	8.64%	7.44%	6.21%	4.94%	3.64%	2.30%	0.92%	N.A.	N.A.	N.A.	N.A.
$460	13.58%	12.48%	11.36%	10.20%	9.02%	7.81%	6.56%	5.28%	3.97%	2.61%	1.22%	N.A.	N.A.	N.A.
$480	15.08%	14.00%	12.90%	11.76%	10.60%	9.41%	8.19%	6.93%	5.64%	4.31%	2.94%	1.53%	0.07%	N.A.
$500	16.59%	15.53%	14.44%	13.32%	12.18%	11.01%	9.81%	8.57%	7.30%	6.00%	4.66%	3.27%	1.85%	0.38%
$520	18.10%	17.05%	15.98%	14.88%	13.76%	12.61%	11.43%	10.21%	8.97%	7.69%	6.37%	5.02%	3.62%	2.18%
$540	19.60%	18.57%	17.52%	16.44%	15.34%	14.20%	13.04%	11.85%	10.63%	9.38%	8.09%	6.76%	5.39%	3.97%
$560	21.11%	20.10%	19.06%	18.00%	16.91%	15.80%	14.66%	13.49%	12.29%	11.06%	9.80%	8.49%	7.15%	5.77%
$580	22.62%	21.62%	20.60%	19.56%	18.49%	17.40%	16.28%	15.13%	13.95%	12.75%	11.50%	10.23%	8.91%	7.56%
$600	24.13%	23.15%	22.14%	21.12%	20.07%	19.00%	17.90%	16.77%	15.61%	14.43%	13.21%	11.96%	10.67%	9.34%

$25,000 – *Acquisition Price*

Capital Cost Reduction: $500

Monthly Payment	Residual Value 64%	62%	60%	58%	56%	54%	52%	50%	48%	46%	44%	42%	40%	38%
$500	8.73%	7.58%	6.39%	5.18%	3.94%	2.66%	1.35%	N.A.	N.A.	N.A.	N.A.	N.A.	N.A.	N.A.
$520	9.93%	8.79%	7.62%	6.43%	5.20%	3.94%	2.65%	1.31%	N.A.	N.A.	N.A.	N.A.	N.A.	N.A.
$540	11.13%	10.00%	8.85%	7.67%	6.46%	5.22%	3.94%	2.63%	1.28%	N.A.	N.A.	N.A.	N.A.	N.A.
$560	12.33%	11.22%	10.08%	8.91%	7.72%	6.49%	5.23%	3.94%	2.61%	1.24%	N.A.	N.A.	N.A.	N.A.
$580	13.52%	12.43%	11.31%	10.16%	8.98%	7.77%	6.53%	5.25%	3.94%	2.59%	1.20%	N.A.	N.A.	N.A.
$600	14.73%	13.64%	12.54%	11.40%	10.24%	9.05%	7.82%	6.56%	5.27%	3.94%	2.57%	1.16%	N.A.	N.A.
$620	15.93%	14.86%	13.76%	12.64%	11.50%	10.32%	9.11%	7.87%	6.60%	5.29%	3.94%	2.55%	1.12%	N.A.
$640	17.13%	16.07%	14.99%	13.89%	12.76%	11.60%	10.41%	9.18%	7.93%	6.64%	5.31%	3.94%	2.53%	1.08%
$660	18.33%	17.29%	16.22%	15.13%	14.01%	12.87%	11.70%	10.49%	9.26%	7.99%	6.68%	5.33%	3.94%	2.51%
$680	19.53%	18.50%	17.45%	16.37%	15.27%	14.14%	12.99%	11.80%	10.58%	9.33%	8.04%	6.72%	5.35%	3.94%
$700	20.73%	19.72%	18.68%	17.62%	16.53%	15.42%	14.28%	13.11%	11.91%	10.67%	9.41%	8.10%	6.76%	5.37%

$30,000 – *Acquisition Price*

Capital Cost Reduction: $500

Monthly Payment	Residual Value 64%	62%	60%	58%	56%	54%	52%	50%	48%	46%	44%	42%	40%	38%
$600	8.50%	7.35%	6.17%	4.96%	3.71%	2.44%	1.12%	N.A.	N.A.	N.A.	N.A.	N.A.	N.A.	N.A.
$625	9.75%	8.61%	7.44%	6.25%	5.02%	3.76%	2.47%	1.14%	N.A.	N.A.	N.A.	N.A.	N.A.	N.A.
$650	10.99%	9.87%	8.72%	7.54%	6.33%	5.09%	3.82%	2.50%	1.16%	N.A.	N.A.	N.A.	N.A.	N.A.
$675	12.24%	11.13%	10.00%	8.83%	7.64%	6.42%	5.16%	3.87%	2.54%	1.17%	N.A.	N.A.	N.A.	N.A.
$700	13.49%	12.39%	11.27%	10.13%	8.95%	7.74%	6.51%	5.23%	3.92%	2.58%	1.19%	N.A.	N.A.	N.A.
$725	14.74%	13.66%	12.55%	11.42%	10.26%	9.07%	7.85%	6.60%	5.31%	3.98%	2.61%	1.21%	N.A.	N.A.
$750	15.98%	14.92%	13.83%	12.71%	11.57%	10.40%	9.19%	7.96%	6.69%	5.38%	4.04%	2.65%	1.23%	N.A.
$775	17.23%	16.18%	15.11%	14.00%	12.88%	11.72%	10.53%	9.32%	8.07%	6.78%	5.46%	4.10%	2.69%	1.24%
$800	18.48%	17.44%	16.38%	15.30%	14.18%	13.05%	11.88%	10.68%	9.45%	8.18%	6.88%	5.54%	4.16%	2.74%
$825	19.73%	18.71%	17.66%	16.59%	15.49%	14.37%	13.22%	12.04%	10.82%	9.58%	8.30%	6.98%	5.62%	4.22%
$850	20.98%	19.97%	18.94%	17.88%	16.80%	15.69%	14.56%	13.40%	12.20%	10.98%	9.71%	8.42%	7.08%	5.71%

$40,000 – *Acquisition Price*

Capital Cost Reduction: $1,000

Monthly Payment	Residual Value 64%	62%	60%	58%	56%	54%	52%	50%	48%	46%	44%	42%	40%	38%
$800	9.07%	7.92%	6.74%	5.52%	4.28%	3.01%	1.69%	0.34%	N.A.	N.A.	N.A.	N.A.	N.A.	N.A.
$825	10.01%	8.87%	7.70%	6.50%	5.27%	4.01%	2.71%	1.37%	0.00%	N.A.	N.A.	N.A.	N.A.	N.A.
$850	10.95%	9.82%	8.66%	7.47%	6.26%	5.01%	3.72%	2.40%	1.05%	N.A.	N.A.	N.A.	N.A.	N.A.
$875	11.89%	10.77%	9.62%	8.45%	7.24%	6.01%	4.74%	3.43%	2.09%	0.71%	N.A.	N.A.	N.A.	N.A.
$900	12.83%	11.72%	10.59%	9.42%	8.23%	7.01%	5.75%	4.46%	3.13%	1.77%	0.36%	N.A.	N.A.	N.A.
$925	13.77%	12.67%	11.55%	10.40%	9.22%	8.01%	6.77%	5.49%	4.18%	2.83%	1.44%	N.A.	N.A.	N.A.
$950	14.71%	13.62%	12.51%	11.37%	10.21%	9.01%	7.78%	6.52%	5.22%	3.89%	2.51%	1.09%	N.A.	N.A.
$975	15.65%	14.57%	13.47%	12.35%	11.19%	10.01%	8.79%	7.54%	6.26%	4.94%	3.58%	2.18%	0.74%	N.A.
$1,000	16.59%	15.53%	14.44%	13.32%	12.18%	11.01%	9.81%	8.57%	7.30%	6.00%	4.66%	3.27%	1.85%	0.38%
$1,025	17.53%	16.48%	15.40%	14.30%	13.17%	12.01%	10.82%	9.60%	8.34%	7.06%	5.73%	4.36%	2.96%	1.50%
$1,050	18.47%	17.43%	16.36%	15.27%	14.15%	13.01%	11.83%	10.62%	9.38%	8.11%	6.80%	5.45%	4.06%	2.63%

Appendix H *continued* Lease Interest Rates

See instructions on page 97A.

36 Month Lease

$10,000 – *Acquisition Price*

Capital Cost Reduction: $500

Monthly Payment	Residual Value 58%	56%	54%	52%	50%	48%	46%	44%	42%	40%	38%	36%	34%	32%
$150	7.44%	6.65%	5.84%	5.01%	4.16%	3.28%	2.38%	1.45%	0.49%	N.A.	N.A.	N.A.	N.A.	N.A.
$160	9.01%	8.24%	7.45%	6.65%	5.82%	4.97%	4.09%	3.19%	2.26%	1.30%	0.30%	N.A.	N.A.	N.A.
$170	10.57%	9.83%	9.06%	8.28%	7.47%	6.65%	5.79%	4.92%	4.02%	3.09%	2.12%	1.13%	0.10%	N.A.
$180	12.14%	11.41%	10.67%	9.91%	9.12%	8.32%	7.49%	6.64%	5.77%	4.87%	3.94%	2.98%	1.98%	0.96%
$190	13.71%	13.00%	12.27%	11.53%	10.77%	9.99%	9.19%	8.36%	7.51%	6.64%	5.74%	4.81%	3.85%	2.86%
$200	15.27%	14.58%	13.87%	13.15%	12.41%	11.65%	10.87%	10.07%	9.25%	8.41%	7.53%	6.64%	5.71%	4.75%
$210	16.83%	16.16%	15.47%	14.77%	14.05%	13.31%	12.56%	11.78%	10.98%	10.16%	9.32%	8.45%	7.56%	6.63%
$220	18.39%	17.74%	17.07%	16.39%	15.69%	14.97%	14.24%	13.48%	12.71%	11.92%	11.10%	10.26%	9.40%	8.50%
$230	19.95%	19.31%	18.66%	18.00%	17.32%	16.62%	15.91%	15.18%	14.43%	13.66%	12.87%	12.06%	11.22%	10.36%
$240	21.51%	20.89%	20.25%	19.61%	18.95%	18.27%	17.58%	16.87%	16.15%	15.40%	14.64%	13.85%	13.04%	12.21%
$250	23.06%	22.46%	21.84%	21.22%	20.57%	19.92%	19.25%	18.56%	17.86%	17.13%	16.39%	15.63%	14.85%	14.05%

$12,500 – *Acquisition Price*

Capital Cost Reduction: $500

Monthly Payment	Residual Value 58%	56%	54%	52%	50%	48%	46%	44%	42%	40%	38%	36%	34%	32%
$200	8.51%	7.75%	6.96%	6.15%	5.32%	4.47%	3.59%	2.69%	1.75%	0.79%	N.A.	N.A.	N.A.	N.A.
$220	11.01%	10.27%	9.52%	8.74%	7.95%	7.13%	6.30%	5.44%	4.55%	3.63%	2.69%	1.71%	0.71%	N.A.
$240	13.49%	12.79%	12.07%	11.33%	10.57%	9.79%	8.99%	8.17%	7.32%	6.45%	5.56%	4.63%	3.68%	2.69%
$260	15.98%	15.30%	14.61%	13.90%	13.18%	12.43%	11.67%	10.89%	10.08%	9.26%	8.41%	7.53%	6.63%	5.69%
$280	18.45%	17.81%	17.15%	16.47%	15.78%	15.07%	14.34%	13.59%	12.83%	12.04%	11.23%	10.40%	9.55%	8.66%
$300	20.93%	20.31%	19.68%	19.03%	18.37%	17.69%	17.00%	16.28%	15.56%	14.81%	14.04%	13.25%	12.44%	11.61%
$320	23.40%	22.81%	22.20%	21.58%	20.95%	20.30%	19.64%	18.96%	18.27%	17.56%	16.83%	16.08%	15.31%	14.52%
$340	25.87%	25.30%	24.72%	24.13%	23.52%	22.91%	22.27%	21.63%	20.97%	20.29%	19.60%	18.89%	18.16%	17.42%
$360	28.33%	27.79%	27.23%	26.67%	26.09%	25.50%	24.90%	24.28%	23.66%	23.01%	22.36%	21.68%	20.99%	20.28%
$380	30.79%	30.27%	29.74%	29.20%	28.65%	28.09%	27.51%	26.93%	26.33%	25.72%	25.09%	24.45%	23.80%	23.13%
$400	33.25%	32.75%	32.24%	31.73%	31.20%	30.66%	30.12%	29.56%	28.99%	28.41%	27.82%	27.21%	26.59%	25.96%

$15,000 – *Acquisition Price*

Capital Cost Reduction: $500

Monthly Payment	Residual Value 58%	56%	54%	52%	50%	48%	46%	44%	42%	40%	38%	36%	34%	32%
$240	8.19%	7.42%	6.63%	5.83%	4.99%	4.14%	3.26%	2.36%	1.42%	0.46%	N.A.	N.A.	N.A.	N.A.
$260	10.26%	9.52%	8.76%	7.98%	7.18%	6.35%	5.51%	4.64%	3.74%	2.82%	1.87%	0.88%	N.A.	N.A.
$280	12.32%	11.61%	10.87%	10.12%	9.35%	8.56%	7.75%	6.91%	6.05%	5.16%	4.25%	3.31%	2.34%	1.33%
$300	14.38%	13.69%	12.99%	12.26%	11.52%	10.76%	9.97%	9.17%	8.35%	7.50%	6.62%	5.72%	4.79%	3.83%
$320	16.44%	15.78%	15.09%	14.39%	13.68%	12.95%	12.19%	11.42%	10.63%	9.82%	8.98%	8.12%	7.23%	6.31%
$340	18.50%	17.85%	17.20%	16.52%	15.83%	15.13%	14.41%	13.66%	12.90%	12.12%	11.32%	10.49%	9.64%	8.77%
$360	20.55%	19.93%	19.29%	18.65%	17.98%	17.30%	16.61%	15.90%	15.17%	14.42%	13.65%	12.86%	12.05%	11.21%
$380	22.60%	22.00%	21.39%	20.76%	20.13%	19.47%	18.80%	18.12%	17.42%	16.70%	15.96%	15.21%	14.43%	13.63%
$400	24.65%	24.07%	23.48%	22.88%	22.26%	21.63%	20.99%	20.33%	19.66%	18.97%	18.27%	17.54%	16.80%	16.04%
$420	26.69%	26.13%	25.57%	24.99%	24.39%	23.79%	23.17%	22.54%	21.89%	21.23%	20.56%	19.86%	19.15%	18.42%
$440	28.73%	28.20%	27.65%	27.09%	26.52%	25.94%	25.34%	24.74%	24.12%	23.49%	22.84%	22.17%	21.49%	20.80%

$17,500 – *Acquisition Price*

Capital Cost Reduction: $500

Monthly Payment	Residual Value 58%	56%	54%	52%	50%	48%	46%	44%	42%	40%	38%	36%	34%	32%
$280	7.96%	7.19%	6.40%	5.59%	4.76%	3.91%	3.03%	2.12%	1.19%	0.22%	N.A.	N.A.	N.A.	N.A.
$300	9.73%	8.98%	8.22%	7.43%	6.63%	5.80%	4.95%	4.07%	3.17%	2.24%	1.28%	0.29%	N.A.	N.A.
$320	11.49%	10.77%	10.03%	9.27%	8.49%	7.69%	6.86%	6.02%	5.15%	4.25%	3.32%	2.37%	1.38%	0.36%
$340	13.25%	12.55%	11.83%	11.10%	10.34%	9.57%	8.77%	7.95%	7.11%	6.25%	5.35%	4.43%	3.48%	2.50%
$360	15.01%	14.33%	13.64%	12.92%	12.19%	11.44%	10.67%	9.88%	9.07%	8.23%	7.37%	6.49%	5.57%	4.63%
$380	16.77%	16.11%	15.44%	14.74%	14.04%	13.31%	12.56%	11.80%	11.02%	10.21%	9.38%	8.53%	7.65%	6.74%
$400	18.53%	17.89%	17.23%	16.56%	15.87%	15.17%	14.45%	13.72%	12.96%	12.18%	11.38%	10.56%	9.71%	8.84%
$420	20.28%	19.66%	19.02%	18.37%	17.71%	17.03%	16.33%	15.62%	14.89%	14.14%	13.37%	12.58%	11.77%	10.93%
$440	22.03%	21.43%	20.81%	20.18%	19.54%	18.88%	18.21%	17.52%	16.82%	16.09%	15.35%	14.59%	13.80%	13.00%
$460	23.78%	23.20%	22.60%	21.99%	21.37%	20.73%	20.08%	19.42%	18.73%	18.04%	17.32%	16.59%	15.83%	15.06%
$480	25.53%	24.96%	24.38%	23.79%	23.19%	22.58%	21.95%	21.30%	20.64%	19.97%	19.28%	18.57%	17.85%	17.10%

See instructions on page 97A.

36 Month Lease

$20,000 – *Acquisition Price*

Capital Cost Reduction: $500

Monthly Payment	Residual Value													
	58%	56%	54%	52%	50%	48%	46%	44%	42%	40%	38%	36%	34%	32%
$320	7.79%	7.02%	6.23%	5.42%	4.59%	3.73%	2.85%	1.95%	1.01%	0.05%	N.A.	N.A.	N.A.	N.A.
$340	9.33%	8.58%	7.81%	7.03%	6.22%	5.39%	4.53%	3.65%	2.75%	1.81%	0.85%	N.A.	N.A.	N.A.
$360	10.87%	10.14%	9.40%	8.63%	7.84%	7.03%	6.20%	5.35%	4.47%	3.56%	2.63%	1.67%	0.67%	N.A.
$380	12.41%	11.70%	10.97%	10.23%	9.46%	8.68%	7.87%	7.04%	6.19%	5.31%	4.41%	3.47%	2.51%	1.51%
$400	13.95%	13.26%	12.55%	11.82%	11.08%	10.32%	9.53%	8.73%	7.90%	7.05%	6.17%	5.27%	4.34%	3.37%
$420	15.48%	14.81%	14.12%	13.41%	12.69%	11.95%	11.19%	10.41%	9.61%	8.78%	7.93%	7.06%	6.16%	5.23%
$440	17.02%	16.36%	15.69%	15.00%	14.30%	13.58%	12.84%	12.08%	11.31%	10.51%	9.68%	8.84%	7.97%	7.07%
$460	18.55%	17.91%	17.26%	16.59%	15.91%	15.21%	14.49%	13.75%	13.00%	12.22%	11.43%	10.61%	9.77%	8.90%
$480	20.08%	19.46%	18.82%	18.17%	17.51%	16.83%	16.13%	15.42%	14.69%	13.93%	13.16%	12.37%	11.56%	10.72%
$500	21.61%	21.00%	20.38%	19.75%	19.11%	18.45%	17.77%	17.08%	16.37%	15.64%	14.89%	14.13%	13.34%	12.53%
$520	23.14%	22.55%	21.94%	21.33%	20.70%	20.06%	19.40%	18.73%	18.04%	17.34%	16.61%	15.87%	15.11%	14.33%

$25,000 – *Acquisition Price*

Capital Cost Reduction: $500

Monthly Payment	Residual Value													
	58%	56%	54%	52%	50%	48%	46%	44%	42%	40%	38%	36%	34%	32%
$420	8.78%	8.03%	7.25%	6.46%	5.65%	4.81%	3.95%	3.06%	2.15%	1.21%	0.24%	N.A.	N.A.	N.A.
$440	10.01%	9.27%	8.52%	7.74%	6.94%	6.13%	5.29%	4.42%	3.53%	2.61%	1.66%	0.68%	N.A.	N.A.
$460	11.24%	10.52%	9.78%	9.02%	8.24%	7.44%	6.62%	5.77%	4.90%	4.01%	3.08%	2.13%	1.14%	0.12%
$480	12.46%	11.76%	11.03%	10.29%	9.53%	8.75%	7.94%	7.12%	6.27%	5.40%	4.50%	3.57%	2.61%	1.62%
$500	13.69%	13.00%	12.29%	11.56%	10.82%	10.05%	9.27%	8.46%	7.64%	6.78%	5.91%	5.00%	4.07%	3.10%
$520	14.92%	14.24%	13.54%	12.83%	12.10%	11.36%	10.59%	9.80%	9.00%	8.17%	7.31%	6.43%	5.52%	4.58%
$540	16.14%	15.47%	14.79%	14.10%	13.39%	12.66%	11.91%	11.14%	10.35%	9.54%	8.71%	7.85%	6.97%	6.05%
$560	17.36%	16.71%	16.05%	15.37%	14.67%	13.96%	13.23%	12.48%	11.71%	10.92%	10.10%	9.27%	8.41%	7.52%
$580	18.58%	17.95%	17.29%	16.63%	15.95%	15.25%	14.54%	13.81%	13.05%	12.28%	11.49%	10.68%	9.84%	8.98%
$600	19.80%	19.18%	18.54%	17.89%	17.23%	16.54%	15.85%	15.13%	14.40%	13.65%	12.88%	12.08%	11.27%	10.43%
$620	21.02%	20.41%	19.79%	19.15%	18.50%	17.83%	17.15%	16.46%	15.74%	15.01%	14.25%	13.48%	12.69%	11.87%

$30,000 – *Acquisition Price*

Capital Cost Reduction: $500

Monthly Payment	Residual Value													
	58%	56%	54%	52%	50%	48%	46%	44%	42%	40%	38%	36%	34%	32%
$500	8.41%	7.66%	6.88%	6.09%	5.27%	4.43%	3.56%	2.67%	1.76%	0.81%	N.A.	N.A.	N.A.	N.A.
$525	9.69%	8.95%	8.19%	7.42%	6.62%	5.80%	4.95%	4.08%	3.19%	2.27%	1.32%	0.34%	N.A.	N.A.
$550	10.97%	10.25%	9.50%	8.74%	7.96%	7.16%	6.34%	5.49%	4.62%	3.72%	2.79%	1.84%	0.85%	N.A.
$575	12.25%	11.54%	10.81%	10.07%	9.30%	8.52%	7.72%	6.89%	6.04%	5.17%	4.27%	3.33%	2.37%	1.38%
$600	13.52%	12.83%	12.12%	11.39%	10.64%	9.88%	9.10%	8.29%	7.46%	6.61%	5.73%	4.82%	3.89%	2.93%
$625	14.79%	14.11%	13.42%	12.71%	11.98%	11.23%	10.47%	9.68%	8.88%	8.04%	7.19%	6.31%	5.40%	4.46%
$650	16.06%	15.40%	14.72%	14.03%	13.32%	12.59%	11.84%	11.07%	10.28%	9.48%	8.64%	7.79%	6.90%	5.99%
$675	17.33%	16.68%	16.02%	15.34%	14.65%	13.94%	13.21%	12.46%	11.69%	10.90%	10.09%	9.26%	8.40%	7.51%
$700	18.60%	17.97%	17.32%	16.66%	15.98%	15.28%	14.57%	13.84%	13.09%	12.32%	11.53%	10.72%	9.89%	9.03%
$725	19.87%	19.25%	18.62%	17.97%	17.30%	16.63%	15.93%	15.22%	14.49%	13.74%	12.97%	12.18%	11.37%	10.53%
$750	21.14%	20.53%	19.91%	19.28%	18.63%	17.97%	17.29%	16.59%	15.88%	15.15%	14.40%	13.63%	12.84%	12.03%

$40,000 – *Acquisition Price*

Capital Cost Reduction: $1,000

Monthly Payment	Residual Value													
	58%	56%	54%	52%	50%	48%	46%	44%	42%	40%	38%	36%	34%	32%
$650	8.17%	7.41%	6.63%	5.82%	5.00%	4.15%	3.27%	2.37%	1.45%	0.49%	N.A.	N.A.	N.A.	N.A.
$675	9.14%	8.39%	7.62%	6.83%	6.01%	5.18%	4.32%	3.44%	2.53%	1.59%	0.62%	N.A.	N.A.	N.A.
$700	10.10%	9.36%	8.61%	7.83%	7.03%	6.21%	5.37%	4.50%	3.61%	2.69%	1.74%	0.76%	N.A.	N.A.
$725	11.07%	10.34%	9.59%	8.83%	8.04%	7.24%	6.41%	5.56%	4.69%	3.78%	2.85%	1.89%	0.90%	N.A.
$750	12.03%	11.31%	10.58%	9.83%	9.06%	8.27%	7.45%	6.62%	5.76%	4.88%	3.96%	3.02%	2.05%	1.04%
$775	12.99%	12.28%	11.56%	10.83%	10.07%	9.29%	8.49%	7.67%	6.83%	5.96%	5.07%	4.15%	3.20%	2.21%
$800	13.95%	13.26%	12.55%	11.82%	11.08%	10.32%	9.53%	8.73%	7.90%	7.05%	6.17%	5.27%	4.34%	3.37%
$825	14.91%	14.23%	13.53%	12.82%	12.09%	11.34%	10.57%	9.78%	8.97%	8.13%	7.27%	6.39%	5.48%	4.53%
$850	15.87%	15.20%	14.51%	13.81%	13.09%	12.36%	11.60%	10.83%	10.03%	9.21%	8.37%	7.50%	6.61%	5.69%
$875	16.83%	16.17%	15.49%	14.81%	14.10%	13.38%	12.63%	11.87%	11.09%	10.29%	9.47%	8.62%	7.74%	6.84%
$900	17.78%	17.14%	16.47%	15.80%	15.10%	14.39%	13.67%	12.92%	12.15%	11.37%	10.56%	9.72%	8.87%	7.98%

Appendix H *continued* Lease Interest Rates

See instructions on page 97A.

48 Month Lease

$10,000 – *Acquisition Price*

Capital Cost Reduction: $500

Monthly Payment	Residual Value 52%	50%	48%	46%	44%	42%	40%	38%	36%	34%	32%	30%	28%	26%
$140	8.21%	7.63%	7.04%	6.44%	5.82%	5.18%	4.52%	3.84%	3.14%	2.41%	1.66%	0.89%	0.08%	N.A.
$150	9.82%	9.27%	8.70%	8.12%	7.52%	6.91%	6.28%	5.63%	4.96%	4.26%	3.55%	2.81%	2.04%	1.25%
$160	11.42%	10.89%	10.35%	9.79%	9.22%	8.63%	8.02%	7.40%	6.76%	6.10%	5.42%	4.71%	3.98%	3.23%
$170	13.02%	12.51%	11.99%	11.45%	10.90%	10.34%	9.76%	9.16%	8.55%	7.92%	7.27%	6.60%	5.91%	5.19%
$180	14.62%	14.13%	13.62%	13.11%	12.58%	12.04%	11.48%	10.91%	10.33%	9.72%	9.10%	8.47%	7.81%	7.13%
$190	16.21%	15.74%	15.25%	14.76%	14.25%	13.73%	13.20%	12.65%	12.09%	11.52%	10.92%	10.32%	9.69%	9.04%
$200	17.80%	17.34%	16.87%	16.40%	15.91%	15.41%	14.90%	14.38%	13.85%	13.30%	12.73%	12.15%	11.55%	10.94%
$210	19.38%	18.94%	18.49%	18.03%	17.57%	17.09%	16.60%	16.10%	15.59%	15.06%	14.52%	13.97%	13.40%	12.82%
$220	20.95%	20.53%	20.10%	19.66%	19.21%	18.76%	18.29%	17.81%	17.32%	16.82%	16.30%	15.77%	15.23%	14.67%
$230	22.53%	22.12%	21.71%	21.29%	20.86%	20.42%	19.97%	19.51%	19.04%	18.56%	18.07%	17.56%	17.05%	16.52%
$240	24.09%	23.70%	23.31%	22.90%	22.49%	22.07%	21.64%	21.20%	20.75%	20.29%	19.82%	19.34%	18.85%	18.34%

$12,500 – *Acquisition Price*

Capital Cost Reduction: $500

Monthly Payment	Residual Value 52%	50%	48%	46%	44%	42%	40%	38%	36%	34%	32%	30%	28%	26%
$180	8.46%	7.89%	7.31%	6.71%	6.10%	5.47%	4.82%	4.15%	3.46%	2.75%	2.01%	1.25%	0.46%	N.A.
$200	11.01%	10.48%	9.93%	9.37%	8.80%	8.21%	7.60%	6.98%	6.34%	5.67%	4.99%	4.28%	3.55%	2.80%
$220	13.55%	13.05%	12.54%	12.01%	11.48%	10.92%	10.36%	9.78%	9.18%	8.56%	7.93%	7.27%	6.60%	5.90%
$240	16.08%	15.61%	15.13%	14.64%	14.13%	13.62%	13.09%	12.54%	11.99%	11.41%	10.82%	10.22%	9.60%	8.95%
$260	18.60%	18.16%	17.70%	17.24%	16.77%	16.28%	15.79%	15.28%	14.76%	14.23%	13.68%	13.12%	12.55%	11.95%
$280	21.10%	20.69%	20.26%	19.83%	19.39%	18.93%	18.47%	18.00%	17.51%	17.02%	16.51%	15.99%	15.46%	14.91%
$300	23.60%	23.20%	22.81%	22.40%	21.98%	21.56%	21.13%	20.69%	20.24%	19.78%	19.30%	18.82%	18.32%	17.82%
$320	26.08%	25.71%	25.34%	24.96%	24.57%	24.17%	23.77%	23.35%	22.93%	22.50%	22.07%	21.62%	21.16%	20.69%
$340	28.55%	28.21%	27.86%	27.50%	27.13%	26.76%	26.38%	26.00%	25.61%	25.21%	24.80%	24.38%	23.96%	23.52%
$360	31.02%	30.69%	30.36%	30.03%	29.68%	29.34%	28.98%	28.63%	28.26%	27.89%	27.51%	27.12%	26.72%	26.32%
$380	33.47%	33.17%	32.86%	32.54%	32.22%	31.90%	31.57%	31.23%	30.89%	30.54%	30.19%	29.83%	29.46%	29.09%

$15,000 – *Acquisition Price*

Capital Cost Reduction: $500

Monthly Payment	Residual Value 52%	50%	48%	46%	44%	42%	40%	38%	36%	34%	32%	30%	28%	26%
$220	8.62%	8.06%	7.49%	6.89%	6.29%	5.66%	5.02%	4.36%	3.67%	2.97%	2.24%	1.48%	0.70%	N.A.
$230	9.68%	9.14%	8.58%	8.00%	7.41%	6.80%	6.18%	5.53%	4.87%	4.18%	3.48%	2.75%	1.99%	1.21%
$240	10.74%	10.21%	9.66%	9.10%	8.53%	7.93%	7.33%	6.70%	6.06%	5.39%	4.71%	4.00%	3.27%	2.51%
$250	11.80%	11.28%	10.74%	10.20%	9.64%	9.06%	8.47%	7.87%	7.24%	6.60%	5.93%	5.25%	4.54%	3.81%
$260	12.85%	12.34%	11.83%	11.29%	10.75%	10.19%	9.61%	9.02%	8.42%	7.79%	7.15%	6.49%	5.80%	5.09%
$270	13.90%	13.41%	12.90%	12.38%	11.85%	11.31%	10.75%	10.18%	9.59%	8.98%	8.36%	7.72%	7.05%	6.37%
$280	14.95%	14.47%	13.98%	13.47%	12.96%	12.43%	11.88%	11.33%	10.75%	10.17%	9.56%	8.94%	8.30%	7.64%
$290	16.00%	15.53%	15.05%	14.56%	14.05%	13.54%	13.01%	12.47%	11.92%	11.34%	10.76%	10.16%	9.53%	8.89%
$300	17.04%	16.59%	16.12%	15.64%	15.15%	14.65%	14.14%	13.61%	13.07%	12.52%	11.95%	11.36%	10.76%	10.14%
$310	18.09%	17.64%	17.18%	16.72%	16.24%	15.75%	15.26%	14.74%	14.22%	13.68%	13.13%	12.57%	11.98%	11.38%
$320	19.13%	18.69%	18.25%	17.79%	17.33%	16.86%	16.37%	15.87%	15.37%	14.84%	14.31%	13.76%	13.20%	12.62%

$17,500 – *Acquisition Price*

Capital Cost Reduction: $500

Monthly Payment	Residual Value 52%	50%	48%	46%	44%	42%	40%	38%	36%	34%	32%	30%	28%	26%
$260	8.74%	8.18%	7.61%	7.02%	6.42%	5.80%	5.16%	4.50%	3.82%	3.12%	2.40%	1.65%	0.88%	0.07%
$280	10.55%	10.02%	9.47%	8.91%	8.33%	7.74%	7.13%	6.50%	5.86%	5.20%	4.51%	3.80%	3.07%	2.31%
$300	12.35%	11.84%	11.32%	10.78%	10.23%	9.67%	9.09%	8.49%	7.88%	7.25%	6.60%	5.93%	5.23%	4.52%
$320	14.15%	13.66%	13.16%	12.65%	12.12%	11.58%	11.03%	10.46%	9.88%	9.28%	8.66%	8.03%	7.37%	6.70%
$340	15.94%	15.47%	14.99%	14.50%	14.00%	13.49%	12.96%	12.42%	11.87%	11.30%	10.71%	10.11%	9.49%	8.85%
$360	17.72%	17.27%	16.82%	16.35%	15.87%	15.38%	14.88%	14.36%	13.84%	13.30%	12.74%	12.17%	11.58%	10.98%
$380	19.50%	19.07%	18.63%	18.18%	17.73%	17.26%	16.78%	16.29%	15.79%	15.28%	14.75%	14.21%	13.66%	13.09%
$400	21.27%	20.86%	20.44%	20.01%	19.58%	19.13%	18.67%	18.21%	17.73%	17.24%	16.74%	16.23%	15.71%	15.17%
$420	23.04%	22.64%	22.24%	21.83%	21.42%	20.99%	20.56%	20.11%	19.66%	19.20%	18.72%	18.24%	17.74%	17.23%
$440	24.80%	24.42%	24.04%	23.65%	23.25%	22.84%	22.43%	22.01%	21.57%	21.13%	20.68%	20.22%	19.75%	19.27%
$460	26.55%	26.19%	25.83%	25.45%	25.07%	24.68%	24.29%	23.89%	23.48%	23.06%	22.63%	22.19%	21.74%	21.29%

See instructions on page 97A.

48 Month Lease

$20,000 – *Acquisition Price*

Capital Cost Reduction: $500

Monthly Payment	Residual Value 52%	50%	48%	46%	44%	42%	40%	38%	36%	34%	32%	30%	28%	26%
$300	8.83%	8.27%	7.70%	7.12%	6.52%	5.90%	5.26%	4.61%	3.94%	3.24%	2.52%	1.78%	1.00%	0.20%
$320	10.41%	9.87%	9.32%	8.76%	8.19%	7.59%	6.98%	6.36%	5.71%	5.05%	4.36%	3.65%	2.92%	2.16%
$340	11.98%	11.47%	10.94%	10.40%	9.85%	9.28%	8.69%	8.09%	7.48%	6.84%	6.18%	5.51%	4.81%	4.09%
$360	13.55%	13.06%	12.55%	12.03%	11.50%	10.95%	10.39%	9.82%	9.23%	8.62%	7.99%	7.35%	6.68%	6.00%
$380	15.11%	14.64%	14.15%	13.65%	13.14%	12.62%	12.08%	11.53%	10.96%	10.38%	9.79%	9.17%	8.54%	7.88%
$400	16.67%	16.22%	15.75%	15.27%	14.78%	14.27%	13.76%	13.23%	12.69%	12.13%	11.56%	10.98%	10.37%	9.75%
$420	18.23%	17.79%	17.34%	16.87%	16.40%	15.92%	15.43%	14.92%	14.40%	13.87%	13.33%	12.77%	12.19%	11.60%
$440	19.78%	19.35%	18.92%	18.48%	18.02%	17.56%	17.09%	16.60%	16.11%	15.60%	15.08%	14.54%	14.00%	13.43%
$460	21.32%	20.91%	20.50%	20.07%	19.64%	19.19%	18.74%	18.27%	17.80%	17.31%	16.82%	16.31%	15.78%	15.25%
$480	22.86%	22.47%	22.07%	21.66%	21.24%	20.82%	20.38%	19.94%	19.48%	19.02%	18.54%	18.05%	17.56%	17.04%
$500	24.40%	24.02%	23.64%	23.24%	22.84%	22.43%	22.01%	21.59%	21.15%	20.71%	20.25%	19.79%	19.31%	18.83%

$25,000 – *Acquisition Price*

Capital Cost Reduction: $500

Monthly Payment	Residual Value 52%	50%	48%	46%	44%	42%	40%	38%	36%	34%	32%	30%	28%	26%
$375	8.63%	8.08%	7.51%	6.92%	6.32%	5.70%	5.07%	4.41%	3.74%	3.04%	2.32%	1.57%	0.80%	N.A.
$400	10.21%	9.67%	9.12%	8.56%	7.98%	7.39%	6.78%	6.15%	5.51%	4.84%	4.15%	3.44%	2.71%	1.95%
$425	11.78%	11.26%	10.73%	10.19%	9.64%	9.07%	8.48%	7.88%	7.27%	6.63%	5.97%	5.30%	4.60%	3.87%
$450	13.34%	12.85%	12.34%	11.82%	11.29%	10.74%	10.18%	9.60%	9.01%	8.40%	7.78%	7.13%	6.46%	5.78%
$475	14.90%	14.42%	13.93%	13.43%	12.92%	12.40%	11.86%	11.31%	10.74%	10.16%	9.56%	8.95%	8.31%	7.66%
$500	16.45%	15.99%	15.52%	15.04%	14.55%	14.05%	13.53%	13.01%	12.46%	11.91%	11.34%	10.75%	10.14%	9.52%
$525	18.00%	17.56%	17.11%	16.65%	16.18%	15.69%	15.20%	14.69%	14.17%	13.64%	13.09%	12.53%	11.96%	11.36%
$550	19.55%	19.12%	18.69%	18.24%	17.79%	17.33%	16.85%	16.37%	15.87%	15.36%	14.84%	14.30%	13.76%	13.19%
$575	21.09%	20.68%	20.26%	19.83%	19.40%	18.95%	18.50%	18.03%	17.56%	17.07%	16.57%	16.06%	15.54%	15.00%
$600	22.62%	22.23%	21.83%	21.42%	21.00%	20.57%	20.13%	19.69%	19.23%	18.77%	18.29%	17.80%	17.30%	16.79%
$625	24.15%	23.77%	23.39%	22.99%	22.59%	22.18%	21.76%	21.34%	20.90%	20.45%	20.00%	19.53%	19.06%	18.57%

$30,000 – *Acquisition Price*

Capital Cost Reduction: $500

Monthly Payment	Residual Value 52%	50%	48%	46%	44%	42%	40%	38%	36%	34%	32%	30%	28%	26%
$450	8.50%	7.95%	7.38%	6.79%	6.19%	5.57%	4.94%	4.28%	3.60%	2.91%	2.18%	1.44%	0.67%	N.A.
$475	9.81%	9.28%	8.72%	8.16%	7.57%	6.98%	6.36%	5.73%	5.08%	4.41%	3.71%	3.00%	2.25%	1.49%
$500	11.12%	10.60%	10.06%	9.51%	8.95%	8.37%	7.78%	7.17%	6.54%	5.90%	5.23%	4.54%	3.83%	3.09%
$525	12.42%	11.92%	11.40%	10.87%	10.32%	9.77%	9.19%	8.60%	8.00%	7.38%	6.73%	6.07%	5.39%	4.68%
$550	13.72%	13.23%	12.73%	12.22%	11.69%	11.15%	10.60%	10.03%	9.45%	8.85%	8.23%	7.59%	6.94%	6.26%
$575	15.02%	14.54%	14.06%	13.56%	13.05%	12.53%	11.99%	11.45%	10.88%	10.31%	9.71%	9.10%	8.47%	7.82%
$600	16.31%	15.85%	15.38%	14.90%	14.41%	13.90%	13.39%	12.86%	12.31%	11.76%	11.18%	10.60%	9.99%	9.37%
$625	17.60%	17.15%	16.70%	16.23%	15.75%	15.27%	14.77%	14.26%	13.74%	13.20%	12.65%	12.08%	11.50%	10.90%
$650	18.88%	18.45%	18.01%	17.56%	17.10%	16.63%	16.15%	15.65%	15.15%	14.63%	14.10%	13.56%	13.00%	12.42%
$675	20.16%	19.75%	19.32%	18.88%	18.44%	17.98%	17.52%	17.04%	16.56%	16.06%	15.55%	15.02%	14.49%	13.93%
$700	21.44%	21.04%	20.62%	20.20%	19.77%	19.33%	18.88%	18.42%	17.96%	17.47%	16.98%	16.48%	15.96%	15.43%

$40,000 – *Acquisition Price*

Capital Cost Reduction: $1,000

Monthly Payment	Residual Value 52%	50%	48%	46%	44%	42%	40%	38%	36%	34%	32%	30%	28%	26%
$600	8.83%	8.27%	7.70%	7.12%	6.52%	5.90%	5.26%	4.61%	3.94%	3.24%	2.52%	1.78%	1.00%	0.20%
$625	9.82%	9.27%	8.72%	8.15%	7.56%	6.96%	6.34%	5.70%	5.05%	4.37%	3.67%	2.95%	2.20%	1.43%
$650	10.80%	10.27%	9.73%	9.17%	8.60%	8.02%	7.41%	6.79%	6.15%	5.50%	4.82%	4.12%	3.39%	2.64%
$675	11.78%	11.27%	10.74%	10.20%	9.64%	9.07%	8.48%	7.88%	7.26%	6.62%	5.96%	5.28%	4.57%	3.85%
$700	12.77%	12.26%	11.74%	11.22%	10.67%	10.12%	9.54%	8.96%	8.35%	7.73%	7.09%	6.43%	5.75%	5.04%
$725	13.75%	13.25%	12.75%	12.23%	11.70%	11.16%	10.60%	10.03%	9.44%	8.84%	8.22%	7.58%	6.92%	6.23%
$750	14.72%	14.24%	13.75%	13.25%	12.73%	12.20%	11.66%	11.10%	10.53%	9.94%	9.34%	8.72%	8.08%	7.41%
$775	15.70%	15.23%	14.75%	14.26%	13.75%	13.24%	12.71%	12.17%	11.61%	11.04%	10.45%	9.85%	9.23%	8.59%
$800	16.67%	16.22%	15.75%	15.27%	14.78%	14.27%	13.76%	13.23%	12.69%	12.13%	11.56%	10.98%	10.37%	9.75%
$825	17.65%	17.20%	16.74%	16.27%	15.79%	15.30%	14.80%	14.29%	13.76%	13.22%	12.67%	12.10%	11.51%	10.91%
$850	18.62%	18.18%	17.73%	17.28%	16.81%	16.33%	15.84%	15.34%	14.83%	14.31%	13.77%	13.21%	12.65%	12.06%

Appendix H *continued* — Lease Interest Rates

See instructions on page 97A.

60 Month Lease

$10,000 – *Acquisition Price*

Capital Cost Reduction: $500

Monthly Payment	Residual Value													
	48%	46%	44%	42%	40%	38%	36%	34%	32%	30%	28%	26%	24%	22%
$120	6.94%	6.48%	6.00%	5.51%	5.01%	4.49%	3.95%	3.40%	2.83%	2.24%	1.63%	1.00%	0.34%	N.A.
$130	8.58%	8.14%	7.69%	7.22%	6.75%	6.25%	5.75%	5.23%	4.69%	4.14%	3.56%	2.97%	2.35%	1.71%
$140	10.21%	9.79%	9.36%	8.92%	8.47%	8.00%	7.53%	7.04%	6.53%	6.01%	5.47%	4.91%	4.34%	3.74%
$150	11.83%	11.43%	11.03%	10.61%	10.18%	9.74%	9.29%	8.82%	8.35%	7.85%	7.35%	6.83%	6.29%	5.73%
$160	13.44%	13.07%	12.68%	12.28%	11.88%	11.46%	11.03%	10.59%	10.14%	9.68%	9.21%	8.71%	8.21%	7.69%
$170	15.05%	14.69%	14.32%	13.94%	13.56%	13.17%	12.76%	12.35%	11.92%	11.49%	11.04%	10.58%	10.11%	9.62%
$180	16.65%	16.30%	15.95%	15.60%	15.23%	14.86%	14.48%	14.08%	13.68%	13.27%	12.85%	12.42%	11.98%	11.52%
$190	18.23%	17.91%	17.58%	17.24%	16.89%	16.54%	16.18%	15.81%	15.43%	15.04%	14.65%	14.24%	13.82%	13.39%
$200	19.82%	19.51%	19.19%	18.87%	18.54%	18.21%	17.86%	17.51%	17.16%	16.79%	16.42%	16.04%	15.64%	15.24%
$210	21.39%	21.10%	20.80%	20.49%	20.18%	19.86%	19.54%	19.21%	18.87%	18.53%	18.17%	17.81%	17.45%	17.07%
$220	22.96%	22.68%	22.39%	22.10%	21.81%	21.51%	21.20%	20.89%	20.57%	20.25%	19.91%	19.57%	19.23%	18.87%

$12,500 – *Acquisition Price*

Capital Cost Reduction: $500

Monthly Payment	Residual Value													
	48%	46%	44%	42%	40%	38%	36%	34%	32%	30%	28%	26%	24%	22%
$160	7.92%	7.48%	7.02%	6.55%	6.06%	5.57%	5.05%	4.53%	3.98%	3.42%	2.83%	2.23%	1.61%	0.96%
$170	9.22%	8.79%	8.35%	7.90%	7.44%	6.96%	6.47%	5.97%	5.45%	4.91%	4.36%	3.78%	3.19%	2.57%
$180	10.51%	10.10%	9.68%	9.25%	8.80%	8.35%	7.88%	7.40%	6.90%	6.39%	5.86%	5.32%	4.75%	4.17%
$190	11.80%	11.41%	11.00%	10.58%	10.16%	9.72%	9.27%	8.81%	8.34%	7.85%	7.35%	6.83%	6.30%	5.75%
$200	13.08%	12.70%	12.31%	11.91%	11.51%	11.09%	10.66%	10.22%	9.77%	9.30%	8.83%	8.33%	7.83%	7.30%
$210	14.36%	13.99%	13.62%	13.24%	12.85%	12.45%	12.04%	11.62%	11.18%	10.74%	10.29%	9.82%	9.34%	8.84%
$220	15.63%	15.28%	14.92%	14.55%	14.18%	13.79%	13.40%	13.00%	12.59%	12.17%	11.73%	11.29%	10.83%	10.36%
$230	16.89%	16.56%	16.21%	15.86%	15.50%	15.14%	14.76%	14.38%	13.98%	13.58%	13.17%	12.74%	12.31%	11.86%
$240	18.15%	17.83%	17.50%	17.16%	16.82%	16.47%	16.11%	15.74%	15.37%	14.98%	14.59%	14.18%	13.77%	13.34%
$250	19.41%	19.10%	18.78%	18.46%	18.13%	17.79%	17.45%	17.10%	16.74%	16.37%	15.99%	15.61%	15.22%	14.81%
$260	20.66%	20.36%	20.06%	19.75%	19.43%	19.11%	18.78%	18.44%	18.10%	17.75%	17.39%	17.03%	16.65%	16.27%

$15,000 – *Acquisition Price*

Capital Cost Reduction: $500

Monthly Payment	Residual Value													
	48%	46%	44%	42%	40%	38%	36%	34%	32%	30%	28%	26%	24%	22%
$200	8.57%	8.13%	7.69%	7.23%	6.76%	6.27%	5.77%	5.26%	4.73%	4.19%	3.62%	3.04%	2.43%	1.80%
$210	9.64%	9.22%	8.79%	8.35%	7.89%	7.43%	6.95%	6.45%	5.94%	5.42%	4.88%	4.32%	3.74%	3.14%
$220	10.71%	10.31%	9.89%	9.46%	9.02%	8.57%	8.11%	7.63%	7.14%	6.64%	6.12%	5.58%	5.03%	4.45%
$230	11.78%	11.39%	10.98%	10.57%	10.15%	9.71%	9.27%	8.81%	8.34%	7.85%	7.35%	6.84%	6.31%	5.76%
$240	12.84%	12.46%	12.07%	11.67%	11.26%	10.85%	10.42%	9.97%	9.52%	9.06%	8.58%	8.08%	7.57%	7.05%
$250	13.90%	13.53%	13.16%	12.77%	12.38%	11.97%	11.56%	11.13%	10.70%	10.25%	9.79%	9.32%	8.83%	8.32%
$260	14.96%	14.60%	14.24%	13.86%	13.48%	13.09%	12.69%	12.28%	11.87%	11.43%	10.99%	10.54%	10.07%	9.59%
$270	16.01%	15.66%	15.31%	14.95%	14.58%	14.21%	13.82%	13.43%	13.03%	12.61%	12.19%	11.75%	11.30%	10.84%
$280	17.06%	16.72%	16.38%	16.03%	15.68%	15.32%	14.95%	14.57%	14.18%	13.78%	13.37%	12.95%	12.52%	12.08%
$290	18.10%	17.78%	17.45%	17.11%	16.77%	16.42%	16.06%	15.70%	15.32%	14.94%	14.55%	14.15%	13.73%	13.31%
$300	19.14%	18.83%	18.51%	18.19%	17.86%	17.52%	17.17%	16.82%	16.46%	16.09%	15.72%	15.33%	14.93%	14.53%

$17,500 – *Acquisition Price*

Capital Cost Reduction: $500

Monthly Payment	Residual Value													
	48%	46%	44%	42%	40%	38%	36%	34%	32%	30%	28%	26%	24%	22%
$220	7.18%	6.73%	6.27%	5.79%	5.30%	4.79%	4.27%	3.73%	3.18%	2.61%	2.01%	1.40%	0.76%	0.10%
$240	9.03%	8.60%	8.16%	7.71%	7.25%	6.77%	6.28%	5.78%	5.26%	4.73%	4.17%	3.60%	3.01%	2.40%
$260	10.86%	10.45%	10.04%	9.61%	9.18%	8.73%	8.27%	7.80%	7.32%	6.82%	6.30%	5.77%	5.22%	4.65%
$280	12.67%	12.29%	11.90%	11.50%	11.09%	10.67%	10.24%	9.80%	9.35%	8.88%	8.40%	7.90%	7.39%	6.87%
$300	14.48%	14.12%	13.75%	13.37%	12.99%	12.59%	12.19%	11.78%	11.35%	10.91%	10.47%	10.01%	9.53%	9.04%
$320	16.28%	15.94%	15.59%	15.23%	14.87%	14.50%	14.12%	13.73%	13.33%	12.93%	12.51%	12.08%	11.64%	11.18%
$340	18.06%	17.74%	17.41%	17.08%	16.74%	16.39%	16.03%	15.67%	15.29%	14.91%	14.52%	14.12%	13.71%	13.29%
$360	19.84%	19.54%	19.23%	18.91%	18.59%	18.26%	17.92%	17.58%	17.23%	16.88%	16.51%	16.14%	15.75%	15.36%
$380	21.61%	21.32%	21.03%	20.73%	20.43%	20.12%	19.80%	19.48%	19.15%	18.82%	18.48%	18.13%	17.77%	17.40%
$400	23.36%	23.09%	22.82%	22.54%	22.25%	21.96%	21.66%	21.36%	21.06%	20.74%	20.42%	20.09%	19.76%	19.42%
$420	25.11%	24.86%	24.60%	24.33%	24.06%	23.79%	23.51%	23.23%	22.94%	22.65%	22.35%	22.04%	21.73%	21.41%

See instructions on page 97A.

60 Month Lease

$20,000 – *Acquisition Price*

Capital Cost Reduction: $500

Monthly Payment	Residual Value													
	48%	46%	44%	42%	40%	38%	36%	34%	32%	30%	28%	26%	24%	22%
$260	7.76%	7.32%	6.86%	6.39%	5.91%	5.42%	4.91%	4.38%	3.84%	3.28%	2.71%	2.11%	1.49%	0.84%
$280	9.36%	8.94%	8.51%	8.07%	7.61%	7.14%	6.66%	6.17%	5.65%	5.13%	4.58%	4.02%	3.44%	2.84%
$300	10.96%	10.56%	10.15%	9.73%	9.29%	8.85%	8.39%	7.93%	7.44%	6.95%	6.44%	5.91%	5.37%	4.80%
$320	12.55%	12.17%	11.77%	11.37%	10.96%	10.54%	10.11%	9.67%	9.22%	8.75%	8.27%	7.77%	7.26%	6.73%
$340	14.13%	13.76%	13.39%	13.01%	12.62%	12.22%	11.81%	11.40%	10.97%	10.53%	10.07%	9.61%	9.13%	8.64%
$360	15.70%	15.35%	15.00%	14.63%	14.27%	13.89%	13.50%	13.11%	12.70%	12.29%	11.86%	11.42%	10.97%	10.51%
$380	17.26%	16.93%	16.59%	16.25%	15.90%	15.54%	15.18%	14.80%	14.42%	14.03%	13.62%	13.21%	12.79%	12.36%
$400	18.81%	18.50%	18.18%	17.85%	17.52%	17.18%	16.84%	16.48%	16.12%	15.75%	15.37%	14.98%	14.59%	14.18%
$420	20.36%	20.06%	19.76%	19.45%	19.13%	18.81%	18.48%	18.15%	17.81%	17.46%	17.10%	16.73%	16.36%	15.98%
$440	21.90%	21.61%	21.33%	21.03%	20.73%	20.43%	20.12%	19.80%	19.48%	19.15%	18.81%	18.47%	18.11%	17.75%
$460	23.43%	23.16%	22.89%	22.61%	22.32%	22.03%	21.74%	21.44%	21.13%	20.82%	20.50%	20.18%	19.85%	19.51%

$25,000 – *Acquisition Price*

Capital Cost Reduction: $500

Monthly Payment	Residual Value													
	48%	46%	44%	42%	40%	38%	36%	34%	32%	30%	28%	26%	24%	22%
$325	7.60%	7.16%	6.70%	6.23%	5.75%	5.25%	4.75%	4.22%	3.68%	3.12%	2.54%	1.94%	1.32%	0.67%
$350	9.20%	8.78%	8.34%	7.90%	7.44%	6.97%	6.49%	5.99%	5.48%	4.96%	4.41%	3.85%	3.27%	2.66%
$375	10.79%	10.39%	9.98%	9.55%	9.12%	8.68%	8.22%	7.75%	7.27%	6.77%	6.26%	5.73%	5.19%	4.62%
$400	12.37%	11.99%	11.60%	11.20%	10.79%	10.36%	9.93%	9.49%	9.03%	8.57%	8.08%	7.59%	7.08%	6.55%
$425	13.94%	13.58%	13.21%	12.83%	12.44%	12.04%	11.63%	11.21%	10.78%	10.34%	9.89%	9.42%	8.94%	8.44%
$450	15.51%	15.16%	14.81%	14.45%	14.08%	13.70%	13.31%	12.92%	12.51%	12.09%	11.67%	11.23%	10.78%	10.31%
$475	17.07%	16.74%	16.40%	16.06%	15.70%	15.35%	14.98%	14.60%	14.22%	13.83%	13.43%	13.01%	12.59%	12.15%
$500	18.61%	18.30%	17.98%	17.65%	17.32%	16.98%	16.63%	16.28%	15.92%	15.55%	15.17%	14.78%	14.38%	13.97%
$525	20.16%	19.86%	19.55%	19.24%	18.93%	18.60%	18.28%	17.94%	17.60%	17.25%	16.89%	16.52%	16.15%	15.76%
$550	21.69%	21.41%	21.12%	20.82%	20.52%	20.22%	19.90%	19.59%	19.26%	18.93%	18.59%	18.25%	17.90%	17.53%
$575	23.22%	22.95%	22.67%	22.39%	22.11%	21.82%	21.52%	21.22%	20.91%	20.60%	20.28%	19.96%	19.62%	19.28%

$30,000 – *Acquisition Price*

Capital Cost Reduction: $500

Monthly Payment	Residual Value													
	48%	46%	44%	42%	40%	38%	36%	34%	32%	30%	28%	26%	24%	22%
$400	8.03%	7.59%	7.14%	6.68%	6.21%	5.72%	5.22%	4.70%	4.17%	3.62%	3.05%	2.47%	1.86%	1.23%
$425	9.35%	8.94%	8.50%	8.06%	7.61%	7.15%	6.67%	6.18%	5.67%	5.15%	4.61%	4.05%	3.47%	2.87%
$450	10.68%	10.27%	9.86%	9.44%	9.01%	8.56%	8.10%	7.63%	7.15%	6.65%	6.14%	5.61%	5.07%	4.50%
$475	11.99%	11.61%	11.21%	10.81%	10.39%	9.97%	9.53%	9.08%	8.62%	8.15%	7.66%	7.16%	6.64%	6.10%
$500	13.30%	12.93%	12.55%	12.16%	11.77%	11.36%	10.94%	10.52%	10.08%	9.63%	9.16%	8.69%	8.19%	7.69%
$525	14.61%	14.25%	13.89%	13.52%	13.14%	12.75%	12.35%	11.94%	11.52%	11.09%	10.65%	10.20%	9.73%	9.25%
$550	15.90%	15.56%	15.21%	14.86%	14.49%	14.12%	13.74%	13.35%	12.95%	12.54%	12.12%	11.69%	11.25%	10.80%
$575	17.20%	16.87%	16.54%	16.19%	15.85%	15.49%	15.13%	14.75%	14.37%	13.98%	13.58%	13.17%	12.75%	12.32%
$600	18.48%	18.17%	17.85%	17.52%	17.19%	16.85%	16.50%	16.15%	15.78%	15.41%	15.03%	14.64%	14.24%	13.83%
$625	19.77%	19.46%	19.16%	18.84%	18.53%	18.20%	17.87%	17.53%	17.18%	16.83%	16.46%	16.09%	15.71%	15.32%
$650	21.04%	20.75%	20.46%	20.16%	19.85%	19.54%	19.22%	18.90%	18.57%	18.23%	17.89%	17.53%	17.17%	16.80%

$40,000 – *Acquisition Price*

Capital Cost Reduction: $1,000

Monthly Payment	Residual Value													
	48%	46%	44%	42%	40%	38%	36%	34%	32%	30%	28%	26%	24%	22%
$550	8.96%	8.54%	8.10%	7.65%	7.19%	6.71%	6.22%	5.72%	5.20%	4.67%	4.12%	3.55%	2.96%	2.34%
$575	9.96%	9.55%	9.13%	8.69%	8.24%	7.78%	7.31%	6.83%	6.33%	5.81%	5.28%	4.73%	4.17%	3.58%
$600	10.96%	10.56%	10.15%	9.73%	9.29%	8.85%	8.39%	7.93%	7.44%	6.95%	6.44%	5.91%	5.37%	4.80%
$625	11.95%	11.56%	11.17%	10.76%	10.34%	9.91%	9.47%	9.02%	8.55%	8.08%	7.58%	7.08%	6.55%	6.01%
$650	12.94%	12.57%	12.18%	11.78%	11.38%	10.96%	10.54%	10.10%	9.66%	9.19%	8.72%	8.23%	7.73%	7.21%
$675	13.93%	13.56%	13.19%	12.81%	12.41%	12.01%	11.60%	11.18%	10.75%	10.31%	9.85%	9.38%	8.90%	8.40%
$700	14.91%	14.56%	14.19%	13.82%	13.45%	13.06%	12.66%	12.25%	11.84%	11.41%	10.97%	10.52%	10.05%	9.58%
$725	15.89%	15.55%	15.20%	14.84%	14.47%	14.10%	13.71%	13.32%	12.92%	12.50%	12.08%	11.65%	11.20%	10.74%
$750	16.87%	16.53%	16.19%	15.85%	15.49%	15.13%	14.76%	14.38%	13.99%	13.59%	13.19%	12.77%	12.34%	11.90%
$775	17.84%	17.52%	17.19%	16.85%	16.51%	16.16%	15.80%	15.43%	15.06%	14.67%	14.28%	13.88%	13.47%	13.04%
$800	18.81%	18.50%	18.18%	17.85%	17.52%	17.18%	16.84%	16.48%	16.12%	15.75%	15.37%	14.98%	14.59%	14.18%

Appendix I

Monthly Payments

If you know the amount you want to borrow, this appendix will allow you to calculate your monthly payment. It will also help you decide how much you can afford to spend on a new vehicle.

To use this table to determine monthly payments:

1. Choose one of the following payment terms (months).
2. Read across the top row, "Loan Amount," and find the dollar figure that is closest to the actual amount of your loan.
3. Read down the column to the row corresponding to the interest rate closest to your actual rate.
4. The figure at the intersection is your monthly payment.

To use this table to determine a price:

1. Choose one of the following payment terms (months).
2. Read down the column to find the interest rate closest to your expected rate.
3. Read across the row to the dollar figure which you can afford to pay each month.
4. Read up the column to the top row to find the dollar amount you can afford to pay for your new vehicle.

24 Months Loan Amount

Interest Rate	$5,000	$7,000	$9,000	$10,000	$11,000	$12,000	$13,000	$14,000	$15,000	$20,000	$25,000
5.00%	$219	$307	$395	$439	$483	$526	$570	$614	$658	$877	$1,097
7.00%	$224	$313	$403	$448	$492	$537	$582	$627	$672	$895	$1,119
9.00%	$228	$320	$411	$457	$503	$548	$594	$640	$685	$914	$1,142
9.50%	$230	$321	$413	$459	$505	$551	$597	$643	$689	$918	$1,148
9.75%	$230	$322	$414	$460	$506	$552	$598	$644	$690	$921	$1,151
10.00%	$231	$323	$415	$461	$508	$554	$600	$646	$692	$923	$1,154
10.25%	$231	$324	$416	$463	$509	$555	$601	$648	$694	$925	$1,157
10.50%	$232	$325	$417	$464	$510	$557	$603	$649	$696	$928	$1,159
10.75%	$232	$325	$418	$465	$511	$558	$604	$651	$697	$930	$1,162
11.00%	$233	$326	$419	$466	$513	$559	$606	$653	$699	$932	$1,165
12.00%	$235	$330	$424	$471	$518	$565	$612	$659	$706	$941	$1,177

36 Months Loan Amount

Interest Rate	$5,000	$7,000	$9,000	$10,000	$11,000	$12,000	$13,000	$14,000	$15,000	$20,000	$25,000
5.00%	$150	$210	$270	$300	$330	$360	$390	$420	$450	$599	$749
7.00%	$154	$216	$278	$309	$340	$371	$401	$432	$463	$618	$772
9.00%	$159	$223	$286	$318	$350	$382	$413	$445	$477	$636	$795
9.50%	$160	$224	$288	$320	$352	$384	$416	$448	$480	$641	$801
9.75%	$161	$225	$289	$321	$354	$386	$418	$450	$482	$643	$804
10.00%	$161	$226	$290	$323	$355	$387	$419	$452	$484	$645	$807
10.25%	$162	$227	$291	$324	$356	$389	$421	$453	$486	$648	$810
10.50%	$163	$228	$293	$325	$358	$390	$423	$455	$488	$650	$813
10.75%	$163	$228	$294	$326	$359	$391	$424	$457	$489	$652	$816
11.00%	$164	$229	$295	$327	$360	$393	$426	$458	$491	$655	$818
12.00%	$166	$233	$299	$332	$365	$399	$432	$465	$498	$664	$830

42 Months Loan Amount

Interest Rate	$5,000	$7,000	$9,000	$10,000	$11,000	$12,000	$13,000	$14,000	$15,000	$20,000	$25,000
5.00%	$130	$182	$234	$260	$286	$312	$338	$364	$390	$520	$650
7.00%	$135	$188	$242	$269	$296	$323	$350	$377	$404	$538	$673
9.00%	$139	$195	$251	$278	$306	$334	$362	$390	$418	$557	$696
9.50%	$140	$197	$253	$281	$309	$337	$365	$393	$421	$562	$702
9.75%	$141	$197	$254	$282	$310	$338	$367	$395	$423	$564	$705
10.00%	$142	$198	$255	$283	$311	$340	$368	$396	$425	$566	$708
10.25%	$142	$199	$256	$284	$313	$341	$370	$398	$427	$569	$711
10.50%	$143	$200	$257	$286	$314	$343	$371	$400	$428	$571	$714
10.75%	$143	$201	$258	$287	$315	$344	$373	$401	$430	$573	$717
11.00%	$144	$202	$259	$288	$317	$346	$374	$403	$432	$576	$720
12.00%	$146	$205	$263	$293	$322	$351	$381	$410	$439	$586	$732

48 Months Loan Amount

Interest Rate	$5,000	$7,000	$9,000	$10,000	$11,000	$12,000	$13,000	$14,000	$15,000	$20,000	$25,000
5.00%	$115	$161	$207	$230	$253	$276	$299	$322	$345	$461	$576
7.00%	$120	$168	$216	$239	$263	$287	$311	$335	$359	$479	$599
9.00%	$124	$174	$224	$249	$274	$299	$324	$348	$373	$498	$622
9.50%	$126	$176	$226	$251	$276	$301	$327	$352	$377	$502	$628
9.75%	$126	$177	$227	$252	$278	$303	$328	$353	$379	$505	$631
10.00%	$127	$178	$228	$254	$279	$304	$330	$355	$380	$507	$634
10.25%	$127	$178	$229	$255	$280	$306	$331	$357	$382	$510	$637
10.50%	$128	$179	$230	$256	$282	$307	$333	$358	$384	$512	$640
10.75%	$129	$180	$232	$257	$283	$309	$334	$360	$386	$514	$643
11.00%	$129	$181	$233	$258	$284	$310	$336	$362	$388	$517	$646
12.00%	$132	$184	$237	$263	$290	$316	$342	$369	$395	$527	$658

60 Months Loan Amount

Interest Rate	$5,000	$7,000	$9,000	$10,000	$11,000	$12,000	$13,000	$14,000	$15,000	$20,000	$25,000
5.00%	$94	$132	$170	$189	$208	$226	$245	$264	$283	$377	$472
7.00%	$99	$139	$178	$198	$218	$238	$257	$277	$297	$396	$495
9.00%	$104	$145	$187	$208	$228	$249	$270	$291	$311	$415	$519
9.50%	$105	$147	$189	$210	$231	$252	$273	$294	$315	$420	$525
9.75%	$106	$148	$190	$211	$232	$253	$275	$296	$317	$422	$528
10.00%	$106	$149	$191	$212	$234	$255	$276	$297	$319	$425	$531
10.25%	$107	$150	$192	$214	$235	$256	$278	$299	$321	$427	$534
10.50%	$107	$150	$193	$215	$236	$258	$279	$301	$322	$430	$537
10.75%	$108	$151	$195	$216	$238	$259	$281	$303	$324	$432	$540
11.00%	$109	$152	$196	$217	$239	$261	$283	$304	$326	$435	$544
12.00%	$111	$156	$200	$222	$245	$267	$289	$311	$334	$445	$556

Appendix J

Discount Financing

This appendix will show you the dollar value of a discount financing deal. To use this table, you need to know the "discounted" interest rate, the length and amount of the loan, and the interest rate you would normally pay. If need be, you can estimate any of the above.

To use the tables:

1. Choose the chart on this page or on the following pages to compare discount financing rates from 2.9% to 7.9%.
2. Choose one of the following payment terms.

2.90% "Discount" Interest Rate

24 Months Loan Amount

Normal rate	$5,000	$7,000	$9,000	$10,000	$11,000	$12,000	$13,000	$14,000	$15,000	$20,000	$25,000
8.00%	$253	$354	$456	$506	$557	$608	$658	$709	$760	$1,013	$1,266
9.00%	$301	$421	$541	$601	$662	$722	$782	$842	$902	$1,203	$1,504
9.25%	$313	$438	$563	$625	$688	$750	$813	$875	$938	$1,250	$1,563
9.50%	$324	$454	$584	$648	$713	$778	$843	$908	$973	$1,297	$1,621
9.75%	$336	$470	$605	$672	$739	$806	$873	$941	$1,008	$1,344	$1,680
10.00%	$348	$487	$626	$695	$765	$834	$904	$973	$1,043	$1,390	$1,738
10.25%	$359	$503	$647	$718	$790	$862	$934	$1,006	$1,078	$1,437	$1,796
10.50%	$371	$519	$667	$742	$816	$890	$964	$1,038	$1,112	$1,483	$1,854
10.75%	$382	$535	$688	$765	$841	$918	$994	$1,070	$1,147	$1,529	$1,912
11.00%	$394	$551	$709	$788	$866	$945	$1,024	$1,103	$1,181	$1,575	$1,969
11.50%	$417	$583	$750	$833	$917	$1,000	$1,083	$1,167	$1,250	$1,667	$2,083

36 Months Loan Amount

Normal rate	$5,000	$7,000	$9,000	$10,000	$11,000	$12,000	$13,000	$14,000	$15,000	$20,000	$25,000
8.00%	$367	$514	$660	$734	$807	$880	$954	$1,027	$1,101	$1,467	$1,834
9.00%	$434	$608	$782	$869	$956	$1,042	$1,129	$1,216	$1,303	$1,737	$2,172
9.25%	$451	$631	$812	$902	$992	$1,082	$1,173	$1,263	$1,353	$1,804	$2,255
9.50%	$468	$655	$842	$935	$1,029	$1,122	$1,216	$1,309	$1,403	$1,870	$2,338
9.75%	$484	$678	$871	$968	$1,065	$1,162	$1,259	$1,355	$1,452	$1,936	$2,421
10.00%	$501	$701	$901	$1,001	$1,101	$1,201	$1,301	$1,401	$1,502	$2,002	$2,503
10.25%	$517	$724	$930	$1,034	$1,137	$1,240	$1,344	$1,447	$1,551	$2,067	$2,584
10.50%	$533	$746	$960	$1,066	$1,173	$1,279	$1,386	$1,493	$1,599	$2,132	$2,665
10.75%	$549	$769	$989	$1,098	$1,208	$1,318	$1,428	$1,538	$1,648	$2,197	$2,746
11.00%	$565	$791	$1,018	$1,131	$1,244	$1,357	$1,470	$1,583	$1,696	$2,261	$2,827
11.50%	$597	$836	$1,075	$1,194	$1,314	$1,433	$1,553	$1,672	$1,792	$2,389	$2,986

48 Months Loan Amount

Normal rate	$5,000	$7,000	$9,000	$10,000	$11,000	$12,000	$13,000	$14,000	$15,000	$20,000	$25,000
8.00%	$476	$666	$856	$951	$1,047	$1,142	$1,237	$1,332	$1,427	$1,903	$2,379
9.00%	$562	$786	$1,011	$1,123	$1,235	$1,348	$1,460	$1,572	$1,685	$2,246	$2,808
9.25%	$583	$816	$1,049	$1,165	$1,282	$1,398	$1,515	$1,631	$1,748	$2,331	$2,913
9.50%	$604	$845	$1,087	$1,207	$1,328	$1,449	$1,569	$1,690	$1,811	$2,414	$3,018
9.75%	$624	$874	$1,124	$1,249	$1,374	$1,499	$1,624	$1,748	$1,873	$2,498	$3,122
10.00%	$645	$903	$1,161	$1,290	$1,419	$1,548	$1,677	$1,806	$1,935	$2,581	$3,226
10.25%	$666	$932	$1,198	$1,331	$1,464	$1,598	$1,731	$1,864	$1,997	$2,663	$3,328
10.50%	$686	$961	$1,235	$1,372	$1,509	$1,647	$1,784	$1,921	$2,058	$2,744	$3,430
10.75%	$706	$989	$1,271	$1,413	$1,554	$1,695	$1,837	$1,978	$2,119	$2,825	$3,532
11.00%	$727	$1,017	$1,308	$1,453	$1,598	$1,744	$1,889	$2,034	$2,180	$2,906	$3,633
11.50%	$766	$1,073	$1,379	$1,533	$1,686	$1,839	$1,993	$2,146	$2,299	$3,066	$3,832

3. Read across the top row, "Loan Amount," and find the dollar figure that is closest to the actual amount that you are financing.
4. Read down the column to the row corresponding to your normal, non-discounted interest rate.
5. The figure in the intersection is the dollar value of your discount financing arrangement. Compare this figure to any cash rebate offered. If the rebate amount is higher, choose the rebate. If the rebate amount is lower, choose the discount financing.

3.90% "Discount" Interest Rate

24 Months Loan Amount

Normal rate	$5,000	$7,000	$9,000	$10,000	$11,000	$12,000	$13,000	$14,000	$15,000	$20,000	$25,000
8.00%	$204	$286	$368	$408	$449	$490	$531	$572	$613	$817	$1,021
9.00%	$252	$353	$454	$504	$555	$605	$656	$706	$757	$1,009	$1,261
9.25%	$264	$370	$475	$528	$581	$634	$687	$739	$792	$1,056	$1,320
9.50%	$276	$386	$497	$552	$607	$662	$717	$773	$828	$1,104	$1,380
9.75%	$288	$403	$518	$576	$633	$691	$748	$806	$863	$1,151	$1,439
10.00%	$300	$419	$539	$599	$659	$719	$779	$839	$899	$1,198	$1,498
10.25%	$311	$436	$560	$623	$685	$747	$809	$872	$934	$1,245	$1,556
10.50%	$323	$452	$581	$646	$711	$775	$840	$904	$969	$1,292	$1,615
10.75%	$335	$468	$602	$669	$736	$803	$870	$937	$1,004	$1,338	$1,673
11.00%	$346	$485	$623	$692	$762	$831	$900	$969	$1,039	$1,385	$1,731
11.50%	$369	$517	$665	$739	$813	$886	$960	$1,034	$1,108	$1,477	$1,847

36 Months Loan Amount

Normal rate	$5,000	$7,000	$9,000	$10,000	$11,000	$12,000	$13,000	$14,000	$15,000	$20,000	$25,000
8.00%	$296	$415	$533	$593	$652	$711	$770	$830	$889	$1,185	$1,481
9.00%	$365	$511	$657	$730	$803	$876	$949	$1,021	$1,094	$1,459	$1,824
9.25%	$382	$534	$687	$763	$840	$916	$993	$1,069	$1,145	$1,527	$1,909
9.50%	$399	$558	$717	$797	$877	$957	$1,036	$1,116	$1,196	$1,594	$1,993
9.75%	$415	$581	$748	$831	$914	$997	$1,080	$1,163	$1,246	$1,661	$2,077
10.00%	$432	$605	$778	$864	$950	$1,037	$1,123	$1,210	$1,296	$1,728	$2,160
10.25%	$449	$628	$807	$897	$987	$1,076	$1,166	$1,256	$1,346	$1,794	$2,243
10.50%	$465	$651	$837	$930	$1,023	$1,116	$1,209	$1,302	$1,395	$1,860	$2,325
10.75%	$481	$674	$867	$963	$1,059	$1,155	$1,252	$1,348	$1,444	$1,926	$2,407
11.00%	$498	$697	$896	$996	$1,095	$1,195	$1,294	$1,394	$1,493	$1,991	$2,489
11.50%	$530	$742	$954	$1,060	$1,166	$1,272	$1,378	$1,484	$1,590	$2,121	$2,651

48 Months Loan Amount

Normal rate	$5,000	$7,000	$9,000	$10,000	$11,000	$12,000	$13,000	$14,000	$15,000	$20,000	$25,000
8.00%	$385	$539	$693	$770	$846	$923	$1,000	$1,077	$1,154	$1,539	$1,924
9.00%	$472	$661	$850	$945	$1,039	$1,134	$1,228	$1,322	$1,417	$1,889	$2,362
9.25%	$494	$691	$889	$988	$1,086	$1,185	$1,284	$1,383	$1,482	$1,975	$2,469
9.50%	$515	$721	$927	$1,030	$1,133	$1,237	$1,340	$1,443	$1,546	$2,061	$2,576
9.75%	$536	$751	$966	$1,073	$1,180	$1,288	$1,395	$1,502	$1,609	$2,146	$2,682
10.00%	$558	$781	$1,004	$1,115	$1,227	$1,338	$1,450	$1,561	$1,673	$2,230	$2,788
10.25%	$579	$810	$1,041	$1,157	$1,273	$1,388	$1,504	$1,620	$1,736	$2,314	$2,893
10.50%	$599	$839	$1,079	$1,199	$1,319	$1,438	$1,558	$1,678	$1,798	$2,397	$2,997
10.75%	$620	$868	$1,116	$1,240	$1,364	$1,488	$1,612	$1,736	$1,860	$2,480	$3,100
11.00%	$641	$897	$1,153	$1,281	$1,409	$1,537	$1,665	$1,794	$1,922	$2,562	$3,203
11.50%	$681	$954	$1,226	$1,363	$1,499	$1,635	$1,771	$1,908	$2,044	$2,725	$3,406

Appendix J *continued*

Discount Financing

This appendix will show you the dollar value of a discount financing deal. To use this table, you need to know the "discounted" interest rate, the length and amount of the loan, and the interest rate you would normally pay. If need be, you can estimate any of the above.

To use the tables:

1. Choose the chart on this page or on the pages preceding or following to compare discount financing rates from 2.9% to 7.9%.
2. Choose one of the following payment terms.

4.90% "Discount" Interest Rate

24 Months Loan Amount

Normal rate	$5,000	$7,000	$9,000	$10,000	$11,000	$12,000	$13,000	$14,000	$15,000	$20,000	$25,000
8.00%	$155	$217	$279	$310	$341	$372	$403	$434	$465	$619	$774
9.00%	$203	$285	$366	$407	$447	$488	$529	$569	$610	$813	$1,017
9.25%	$215	$302	$388	$431	$474	$517	$560	$603	$646	$862	$1,077
9.50%	$227	$318	$409	$455	$500	$546	$591	$637	$682	$909	$1,137
9.75%	$239	$335	$431	$479	$526	$574	$622	$670	$718	$957	$1,197
10.00%	$251	$352	$452	$502	$553	$603	$653	$703	$754	$1,005	$1,256
10.25%	$263	$368	$473	$526	$579	$631	$684	$737	$789	$1,052	$1,315
10.50%	$275	$385	$495	$550	$605	$660	$715	$770	$825	$1,099	$1,374
10.75%	$287	$401	$516	$573	$631	$688	$745	$803	$860	$1,147	$1,433
11.00%	$298	$418	$537	$597	$656	$716	$776	$835	$895	$1,193	$1,492
11.50%	$322	$450	$579	$643	$708	$772	$836	$901	$965	$1,287	$1,608

36 Months Loan Amount

Normal rate	$5,000	$7,000	$9,000	$10,000	$11,000	$12,000	$13,000	$14,000	$15,000	$20,000	$25,000
8.00%	$225	$315	$405	$450	$495	$540	$585	$630	$675	$900	$1,125
9.00%	$295	$412	$530	$589	$648	$707	$766	$825	$884	$1,178	$1,473
9.25%	$312	$436	$561	$624	$686	$748	$811	$873	$935	$1,247	$1,559
9.50%	$329	$460	$592	$658	$724	$789	$855	$921	$987	$1,315	$1,644
9.75%	$346	$484	$623	$692	$761	$830	$899	$968	$1,038	$1,383	$1,729
10.00%	$363	$508	$653	$726	$798	$871	$943	$1,016	$1,088	$1,451	$1,814
10.25%	$380	$531	$683	$759	$835	$911	$987	$1,063	$1,139	$1,518	$1,898
10.50%	$396	$555	$713	$793	$872	$951	$1,030	$1,110	$1,189	$1,585	$1,982
10.75%	$413	$578	$743	$826	$909	$991	$1,074	$1,156	$1,239	$1,652	$2,065
11.00%	$430	$601	$773	$859	$945	$1,031	$1,117	$1,203	$1,289	$1,718	$2,148
11.50%	$462	$647	$832	$925	$1,017	$1,110	$1,202	$1,295	$1,387	$1,850	$2,312

48 Months Loan Amount

Normal rate	$5,000	$7,000	$9,000	$10,000	$11,000	$12,000	$13,000	$14,000	$15,000	$20,000	$25,000
8.00%	$293	$410	$527	$585	$644	$702	$761	$819	$878	$1,171	$1,463
9.00%	$382	$535	$688	$764	$840	$917	$993	$1,069	$1,146	$1,528	$1,910
9.25%	$404	$565	$727	$808	$889	$969	$1,050	$1,131	$1,212	$1,616	$2,020
9.50%	$426	$596	$766	$851	$937	$1,022	$1,107	$1,192	$1,277	$1,703	$2,129
9.75%	$447	$626	$805	$895	$984	$1,074	$1,163	$1,253	$1,342	$1,790	$2,237
10.00%	$469	$656	$844	$938	$1,032	$1,125	$1,219	$1,313	$1,407	$1,876	$2,345
10.25%	$490	$686	$883	$981	$1,079	$1,177	$1,275	$1,373	$1,471	$1,961	$2,451
10.50%	$512	$716	$921	$1,023	$1,125	$1,228	$1,330	$1,432	$1,535	$2,046	$2,558
10.75%	$533	$746	$959	$1,065	$1,172	$1,278	$1,385	$1,491	$1,598	$2,130	$2,663
11.00%	$554	$775	$996	$1,107	$1,218	$1,329	$1,439	$1,550	$1,661	$2,214	$2,768
11.50%	$595	$833	$1,071	$1,190	$1,309	$1,428	$1,547	$1,666	$1,785	$2,380	$2,975

3. Read across the top row, "Loan Amount," and find the dollar figure that is closest to the actual amount that you are financing.
4. Read down the column to the row corresponding to your normal, non-discounted interest rate.
5. The figure in the intersection is the dollar value of your discount financing arrangement. Compare this figure to any cash rebate offered. If the rebate amount is higher, choose the rebate. If the rebate amount is lower, choose the discount financing.

5.90% "Discount" Interest Rate

24 Months Loan Amount

Normal rate	$5,000	$7,000	$9,000	$10,000	$11,000	$12,000	$13,000	$14,000	$15,000	$20,000	$25,000
8.00%	$105	$147	$189	$210	$231	$253	$274	$295	$316	$421	$526
9.00%	$154	$216	$278	$308	$339	$370	$401	$432	$463	$617	$771
9.25%	$166	$233	$299	$333	$366	$399	$433	$466	$499	$665	$832
9.50%	$178	$250	$321	$357	$393	$428	$464	$500	$535	$714	$892
9.75%	$191	$267	$343	$381	$419	$457	$495	$534	$572	$762	$953
10.00%	$203	$284	$365	$405	$446	$486	$527	$567	$608	$810	$1,013
10.25%	$215	$300	$386	$429	$472	$515	$558	$601	$644	$858	$1,073
10.50%	$226	$317	$408	$453	$498	$544	$589	$634	$679	$906	$1,132
10.75%	$238	$334	$429	$477	$524	$572	$620	$667	$715	$953	$1,192
11.00%	$250	$350	$450	$500	$550	$600	$651	$701	$751	$1,001	$1,251
11.50%	$274	$383	$493	$548	$602	$657	$712	$767	$821	$1,095	$1,369

36 Months Loan Amount

Normal rate	$5,000	$7,000	$9,000	$10,000	$11,000	$12,000	$13,000	$14,000	$15,000	$20,000	$25,000
8.00%	$153	$214	$276	$306	$337	$368	$398	$429	$459	$613	$766
9.00%	$224	$313	$403	$448	$492	$537	$582	$627	$671	$895	$1,119
9.25%	$241	$338	$434	$482	$531	$579	$627	$675	$724	$965	$1,206
9.50%	$259	$362	$465	$517	$569	$620	$672	$724	$776	$1,034	$1,293
9.75%	$276	$386	$496	$552	$607	$662	$717	$772	$827	$1,103	$1,379
10.00%	$293	$410	$527	$586	$644	$703	$762	$820	$879	$1,172	$1,465
10.25%	$310	$434	$558	$620	$682	$744	$806	$868	$930	$1,240	$1,550
10.50%	$327	$458	$589	$654	$719	$785	$850	$916	$981	$1,308	$1,635
10.75%	$344	$481	$619	$688	$757	$825	$894	$963	$1,032	$1,376	$1,720
11.00%	$361	$505	$649	$721	$794	$866	$938	$1,010	$1,082	$1,443	$1,804
11.50%	$394	$552	$709	$788	$867	$946	$1,025	$1,104	$1,182	$1,577	$1,971

48 Months Loan Amount

Normal rate	$5,000	$7,000	$9,000	$10,000	$11,000	$12,000	$13,000	$14,000	$15,000	$20,000	$25,000
8.00%	$199	$279	$359	$399	$439	$479	$519	$558	$598	$798	$997
9.00%	$291	$407	$523	$581	$639	$697	$755	$813	$872	$1,162	$1,453
9.25%	$313	$438	$563	$626	$688	$751	$814	$876	$939	$1,252	$1,564
9.50%	$335	$469	$603	$670	$737	$804	$871	$938	$1,005	$1,341	$1,676
9.75%	$357	$500	$643	$714	$786	$857	$929	$1,000	$1,072	$1,429	$1,786
10.00%	$379	$531	$683	$758	$834	$910	$986	$1,062	$1,138	$1,517	$1,896
10.25%	$401	$561	$722	$802	$882	$962	$1,043	$1,123	$1,203	$1,604	$2,005
10.50%	$423	$592	$761	$845	$930	$1,014	$1,099	$1,183	$1,268	$1,691	$2,113
10.75%	$444	$622	$799	$888	$977	$1,066	$1,155	$1,244	$1,332	$1,777	$2,221
11.00%	$466	$652	$838	$931	$1,024	$1,117	$1,210	$1,303	$1,397	$1,862	$2,328
11.50%	$508	$711	$914	$1,016	$1,117	$1,219	$1,320	$1,422	$1,524	$2,031	$2,539

Appendix J *continued*

Discount Financing

This appendix will show you the dollar value of a discount financing deal. To use this table, you need to know the "discounted" interest rate, the length and amount of the loan, and the interest rate you would normally pay. If need be, you can estimate any of the above.

To use the tables:

1. Choose the chart on this page or on the previous pages to compare discount financing rates from 4.9% to 7.9%.
2. Choose one of the following payment terms.

6.90% "Discount" Interest Rate

24 Months Loan Amount

Normal rate	$5,000	$7,000	$9,000	$10,000	$11,000	$12,000	$13,000	$14,000	$15,000	$20,000	$25,000
8.00%	$55	$77	$100	$111	$122	$133	$144	$155	$166	$221	$276
9.00%	$105	$147	$189	$210	$231	$252	$272	$293	$314	$419	$524
9.25%	$117	$164	$211	$234	$258	$281	$304	$328	$351	$468	$585
9.50%	$129	$181	$233	$259	$284	$310	$336	$362	$388	$517	$646
9.75%	$141	$198	$255	$283	$311	$340	$368	$396	$424	$566	$707
10.00%	$154	$215	$276	$307	$338	$369	$399	$430	$461	$614	$768
10.25%	$166	$232	$298	$331	$365	$398	$431	$464	$497	$663	$829
10.50%	$178	$249	$320	$356	$391	$427	$462	$498	$533	$711	$889
10.75%	$190	$266	$342	$380	$418	$455	$493	$531	$569	$759	$949
11.00%	$202	$282	$363	$403	$444	$484	$525	$565	$605	$807	$1,009
11.50%	$226	$316	$406	$451	$496	$541	$586	$632	$677	$902	$1,128

36 Months Loan Amount

Normal rate	$5,000	$7,000	$9,000	$10,000	$11,000	$12,000	$13,000	$14,000	$15,000	$20,000	$25,000
8.00%	$81	$113	$145	$161	$177	$193	$209	$226	$242	$322	$403
9.00%	$152	$213	$274	$305	$335	$365	$396	$426	$457	$609	$761
9.25%	$170	$238	$306	$340	$374	$408	$442	$476	$510	$680	$850
9.50%	$188	$263	$338	$375	$413	$450	$488	$525	$563	$750	$938
9.75%	$205	$287	$369	$410	$451	$492	$533	$574	$615	$820	$1,025
10.00%	$222	$311	$400	$445	$489	$534	$578	$623	$667	$890	$1,112
10.25%	$240	$336	$432	$480	$528	$576	$624	$671	$719	$959	$1,199
10.50%	$257	$360	$463	$514	$566	$617	$668	$720	$771	$1,028	$1,285
10.75%	$274	$384	$494	$548	$603	$658	$713	$768	$823	$1,097	$1,371
11.00%	$291	$408	$524	$583	$641	$699	$757	$816	$874	$1,165	$1,456
11.50%	$325	$455	$585	$650	$715	$780	$845	$910	$976	$1,301	$1,626

48 Months Loan Amount

Normal rate	$5,000	$7,000	$9,000	$10,000	$11,000	$12,000	$13,000	$14,000	$15,000	$20,000	$25,000
8.00%	$105	$147	$189	$210	$231	$252	$273	$294	$315	$420	$525
9.00%	$198	$277	$356	$396	$435	$475	$515	$554	$594	$792	$990
9.25%	$221	$309	$397	$442	$486	$530	$574	$618	$662	$883	$1,104
9.50%	$243	$341	$438	$487	$536	$584	$633	$682	$730	$974	$1,217
9.75%	$266	$372	$479	$532	$585	$638	$692	$745	$798	$1,064	$1,330
10.00%	$288	$404	$519	$577	$634	$692	$750	$807	$865	$1,153	$1,442
10.25%	$311	$435	$559	$621	$683	$745	$808	$870	$932	$1,242	$1,553
10.50%	$333	$466	$599	$665	$732	$798	$865	$931	$998	$1,331	$1,663
10.75%	$355	$496	$638	$709	$780	$851	$922	$993	$1,064	$1,418	$1,773
11.00%	$376	$527	$678	$753	$828	$903	$979	$1,054	$1,129	$1,506	$1,882
11.50%	$420	$587	$755	$839	$923	$1,007	$1,091	$1,175	$1,259	$1,678	$2,098

3. Read across the top row, "Loan Amount," and find the dollar figure that is closest to the actual amount that you are financing.
4. Read down the column to the row corresponding to your normal, non-discounted interest rate.
5. The figure in the intersection is the dollar value of your discount financing arrangement. Compare this figure to any cash rebate offered. If the rebate amount is higher, choose the rebate. If the rebate amount is lower, choose the discount financing.

7.90% "Discount" Interest Rate

24 Months Loan Amount

Normal rate	$5,000	$7,000	$9,000	$10,000	$11,000	$12,000	$13,000	$14,000	$15,000	$20,000	$25,000
8.00%	$5	$7	$9	$10	$11	$12	$13	$14	$15	$20	$25
9.00%	$55	$77	$99	$110	$121	$132	$143	$154	$165	$220	$275
9.25%	$67	$94	$121	$135	$148	$162	$175	$189	$202	$270	$337
9.50%	$80	$112	$144	$160	$176	$192	$207	$223	$239	$319	$399
9.75%	$92	$129	$166	$184	$203	$221	$239	$258	$276	$368	$461
10.00%	$104	$146	$188	$209	$230	$250	$271	$292	$313	$417	$522
10.25%	$117	$163	$210	$233	$256	$280	$303	$326	$350	$466	$583
10.50%	$129	$180	$232	$258	$283	$309	$335	$361	$386	$515	$644
10.75%	$141	$197	$254	$282	$310	$338	$366	$395	$423	$564	$705
11.00%	$153	$214	$275	$306	$337	$367	$398	$428	$459	$612	$765
11.50%	$177	$248	$319	$354	$390	$425	$460	$496	$531	$708	$885

36 Months Loan Amount

Normal rate	$5,000	$7,000	$9,000	$10,000	$11,000	$12,000	$13,000	$14,000	$15,000	$20,000	$25,000
8.00%	$7	$10	$13	$15	$16	$18	$19	$21	$22	$29	$37
9.00%	$80	$112	$144	$160	$176	$192	$208	$224	$240	$320	$401
9.25%	$98	$137	$177	$196	$216	$235	$255	$275	$294	$392	$490
9.50%	$116	$162	$209	$232	$255	$278	$301	$325	$348	$464	$580
9.75%	$134	$187	$241	$267	$294	$321	$348	$374	$401	$535	$668
10.00%	$151	$212	$272	$303	$333	$363	$394	$424	$454	$606	$757
10.25%	$169	$237	$304	$338	$372	$406	$439	$473	$507	$676	$845
10.50%	$186	$261	$336	$373	$410	$448	$485	$522	$559	$746	$932
10.75%	$204	$285	$367	$408	$449	$489	$530	$571	$612	$816	$1,019
11.00%	$221	$310	$398	$442	$487	$531	$575	$619	$664	$885	$1,106
11.50%	$256	$358	$460	$511	$562	$613	$665	$716	$767	$1,022	$1,278

48 Months Loan Amount

Normal rate	$5,000	$7,000	$9,000	$10,000	$11,000	$12,000	$13,000	$14,000	$15,000	$20,000	$25,000
8.00%	$10	$13	$17	$19	$21	$23	$25	$27	$29	$38	$48
9.00%	$104	$146	$188	$209	$229	$250	$271	$292	$313	$417	$521
9.25%	$128	$179	$230	$255	$281	$306	$332	$357	$383	$510	$638
9.50%	$151	$211	$271	$301	$332	$362	$392	$422	$452	$603	$753
9.75%	$174	$243	$313	$347	$382	$417	$451	$486	$521	$695	$868
10.00%	$196	$275	$354	$393	$432	$472	$511	$550	$589	$786	$982
10.25%	$219	$307	$394	$438	$482	$526	$570	$614	$657	$877	$1,096
10.50%	$242	$338	$435	$483	$532	$580	$628	$677	$725	$967	$1,208
10.75%	$264	$370	$475	$528	$581	$634	$686	$739	$792	$1,056	$1,320
11.00%	$286	$401	$515	$572	$630	$687	$744	$801	$859	$1,145	$1,431
11.50%	$330	$462	$594	$660	$726	$793	$859	$925	$991	$1,321	$1,651

Index

Index by Vehicle

P-Pickup V-Van EC-Extended Cab CN-Convertible 4WD-4-Wheel Drive W-Wagons

Index by Vehicle

P-Pickup V-Van EC-Extended Cab CN-Convertible 4WD-4-Wheel Drive W-Wagons

Index by Vehicle

P-Pickup V-Van EC-Extended Cab CN-Convertible 4WD-4-Wheel Drive W-Wagons

P-Pickup V-Van EC-Extended Cab CN-Convertible 4WD-4-Wheel Drive W-Wagons

For ArmChair Compare® *orders* – *Please complete information on other side of this form*

Customer Information

Name

Address

City **State** **Zip**

Home Phone ( ) _____ – ______

Charge Information:

☐ VISA ☐ Mastercard

Name on card ____________________

Account # ____________________

Expiration date ____________________

*Signature*____________________

Include order form with personal check or charge information for appropriate amount and mail to:

IntelliChoice, Inc.
1135 S. Saratoga-Sunnyvale Rd.
San Jose, CA 95129-3660
(408) 554-8711

Note: CA residents must add sales tax.

Just the Facts™

$14.95

Send following information for each model line report requested:

Year _____Make ____________________

Model ____________________

Number of Doors ____________________

Drive ☐ 2 WD ☐ 4 WD

BodyStyle ☐ Regular Cab ☐ Ext. Cab ☐ Wagon

☐ Pass. Van ☐ Ext. Pass. Van ☐ Utility ☐ Utility-Conv

For additional report:

Year _____Make ____________________

Model ____________________

Number of Doors ____________________

Drive ☐ 2 WD ☐ 4 WD

BodyStyle ☐ Regular Cab ☐ Ext. Cab ☐ Wagon

☐ Pass. Van ☐ Ext. Pass. Van ☐ Utility ☐ Utility-Conv

IntelliChoice Report Order Form

For ArmChair Compare® *orders* – *Please complete information on other side of this form*

Customer Information

Name

Address

City **State** **Zip**

Home Phone ( ) _____ – ______

Charge Information:

☐ VISA ☐ Mastercard

Name on card ____________________

Account # ____________________

Expiration date ____________________

*Signature*____________________

Include order form with personal check or charge information for appropriate amount and mail to:

IntelliChoice, Inc.
1135 S. Saratoga-Sunnyvale Rd.
San Jose, CA 95129-3660
(408) 554-8711

Note: CA residents must add sales tax.

Just the Facts™

$14.95

Send following information for each model line report requested:

Year _____Make ____________________

Model ____________________

Number of Doors ____________________

Drive ☐ 2 WD ☐ 4 WD

BodyStyle ☐ Regular Cab ☐ Ext. Cab ☐ Wagon

☐ Pass. Van ☐ Ext. Pass. Van ☐ Utility ☐ Utility-Conv

For additional report:

Year _____Make ____________________

Model ____________________

Number of Doors ____________________

Drive ☐ 2 WD ☐ 4 WD

BodyStyle ☐ Regular Cab ☐ Ext. Cab ☐ Wagon

☐ Pass. Van ☐ Ext. Pass. Van ☐ Utility ☐ Utility-Conv

IntelliChoice Report Order Form

IntelliChoice Report Order Form

Please complete information on both sides of this form

THE ARMCHAIR COMPARE® REPORT

$19.95

Your Annual Mileage __ __, __ __ __

Desired Down Payment: _____%, OR $_______, OR ☐ Trade-in value or minimum

Vehicle One

Describe the vehicle below:

Year _____ Make _______________________

Model _______________________________

Number of Doors _________________

Drive ☐ 2 WD ☐ 4 WD

BodyStyle ☐ Regular Cab ☐ Ext. Cab ☐ Wagon

☐ Pass. Van ☐ Ext. Pass. Van ☐ Utility ☐ Utility-Conv

Vehicle Two

Describe the vehicle below:

Year _____ Make _______________________

Model _______________________________

Number of Doors _________________

Drive ☐ 2 WD ☐ 4 WD

BodyStyle ☐ Regular Cab ☐ Ext. Cab ☐ Wagon

☐ Pass. Van ☐ Ext. Pass. Van ☐ Utility ☐ Utility-Conv

Complete this area if you have a 1981-1992 vehicle to trade-in.

Year _____ Make _______________________

Model _______________________________

Number of Doors _________________

Drive ☐ 2 WD ☐ 4 WD

BodyStyle ☐ Regular Cab ☐ Ext. Cab ☐ Wagon

☐ Pass. Van ☐ Ext. Pass. Van ☐ Utility ☐ Utility-Conv

Loan Balance (if known) $____________

If balance not known, complete the following:

Purchase Date: Month _____ Year _____

Months of loan _____ Monthly Pmt. $_______

Interest Rate (if known) _____%

IntelliChoice Report Order Form

Please complete information on both sides of this form

THE ARMCHAIR COMPARE® REPORT

$19.95

Your Annual Mileage __ __, __ __ __

Desired Down Payment: _____%, OR $_______, OR ☐ Trade-in value or minimum

Vehicle One

Describe the vehicle below:

Year _____ Make _______________________

Model _______________________________

Number of Doors _________________

Drive ☐ 2 WD ☐ 4 WD

BodyStyle ☐ Regular Cab ☐ Ext. Cab ☐ Wagon

☐ Pass. Van ☐ Ext. Pass. Van ☐ Utility ☐ Utility-Conv

Vehicle Two

Describe the vehicle below:

Year _____ Make _______________________

Model _______________________________

Number of Doors _________________

Drive ☐ 2 WD ☐ 4 WD

BodyStyle ☐ Regular Cab ☐ Ext. Cab ☐ Wagon

☐ Pass. Van ☐ Ext. Pass. Van ☐ Utility ☐ Utility-Conv

Complete this area if you have a 1981-1992 vehicle to trade-in.

Year _____ Make _______________________

Model _______________________________

Number of Doors _________________

Drive ☐ 2 WD ☐ 4 WD

BodyStyle ☐ Regular Cab ☐ Ext. Cab ☐ Wagon

☐ Pass. Van ☐ Ext. Pass. Van ☐ Utility ☐ Utility-Conv

Loan Balance (if known) $____________

If balance not known, complete the following:

Purchase Date: Month _____ Year _____

Months of loan _____ Monthly Pmt. $_______

Interest Rate (if known) _____%